Football
Yearbook
2001–2002

Acknowledgements

Compiling Editor: Rob Bateman
Style Editor: Gary Taphouse

Written by: Duncan Alexander, Paul Fowling,
Chris Green, Ian Hislam, Matt Pomroy,
William Rickson, Benji Romaner, Ed Shirbon,
Dominic Sutton, Rupert Webster, Tim Wheal
and Mark Willis

With contributions by: Mel Beckett, Jamie
Beckwith, Stuart Burchett and Iain Turner

Thanks are due to: Simon Fisher, Matt Ralphs,
Raffaella Valentino, Paul Townley for spreadsheet
wizardry, James Dennis, Russell Clarke, Joe
Endersby, Maree Lovell, Nina Long, Kris Bromley,
Olivia Tatton-Brown, Robin Hassan and Spencer
Field; Zoe Ward, Sarah Smith, Kelly Wright and
Philip Don at the FA Premier League; the clubs
for their assistance in verifying information;
the League Managers Association; our friends at
Planetfootball.com and the team at Carlton Books
for their hard work and patience.

THIS IS A CARLTON BOOK

First published in 2001 by Carlton Books

10 9 8 7 6 5 4 3 2 1

A CIP catalogue record for this book is available
from the British Library.

ISBN: 1 84222 312 7

Project Editor: Vanessa Daubney
Project Art Director: Mark Lloyd
Jacket design: Steve Lynn
Design and editorial team: Dave Sutton;
Lee Edwards; Phil Wisdom; Fehmi Comert.
Picture Research: Debora Fioravanti
Production: Sarah Corteel

Printed and bound in Italy

Carlton Books Limited
20 Mortimer Street
London W1T 3JW

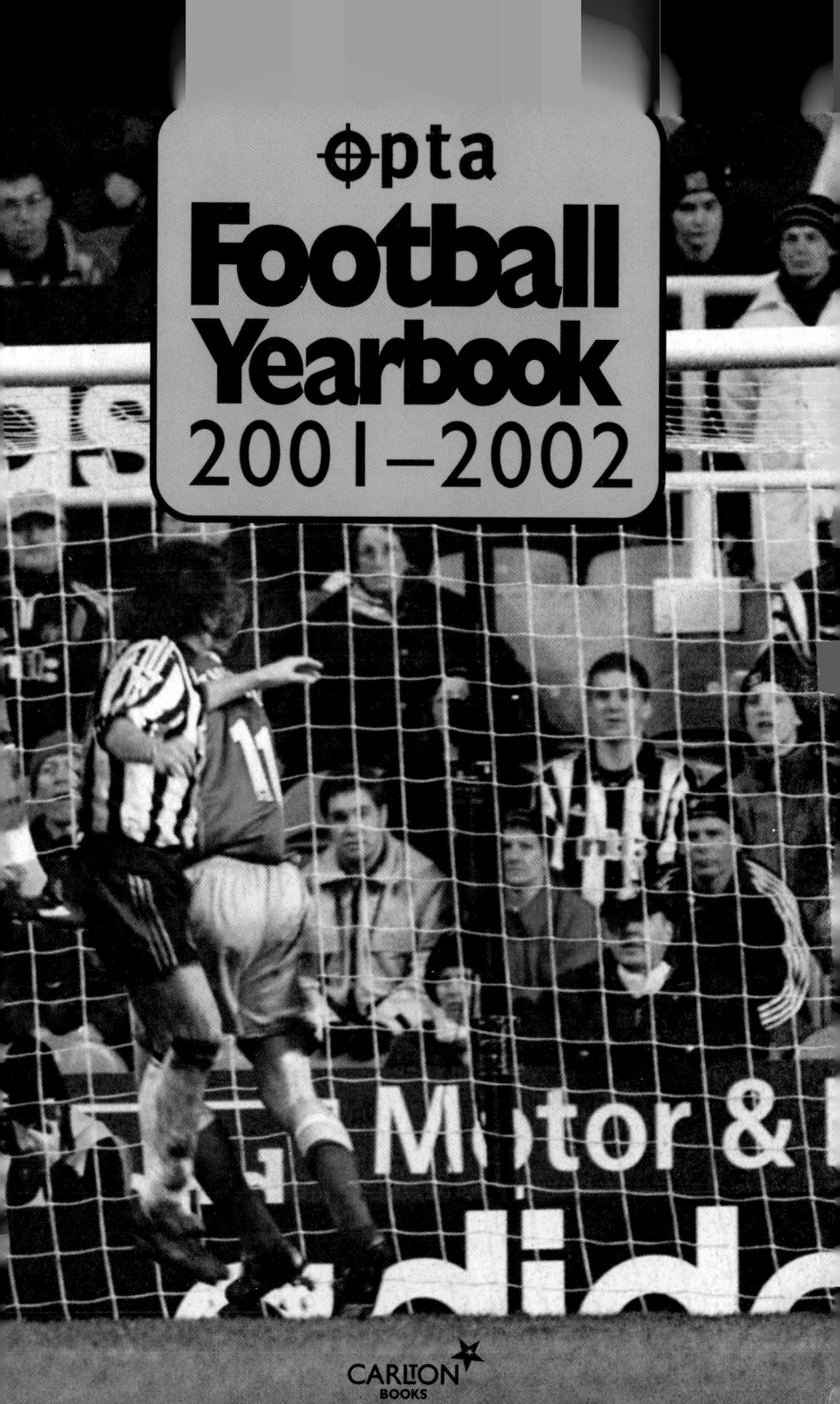

Өpta
Football
Yearbook
2001–2002

CARLTON BOOKS

CONTENTS

Foreword by Andy Gray

1 INTRODUCTION *9*

2 THE TEAMS *31*

3 THE PLAYERS *337*

Pen portraits and Opta statistics for every player who took to the pitch in a Premiership match in 2000–01.

4 COMPARATIVE TABLES *614*

FOREWORD BY ANDY GRAY

My good friend and Sky Sports co-presenter Richard Keys found himself on the Christmas "football bloopers" lists everywhere a few years back when he asked Liverpool's manager at the time Roy Evans: "Do you think that you'll have to finish above Manchester United to win the league?". Roy grinned and replied: "You have to finish above everyone to win the league, Richard."

It was a comical moment, but we all knew what Richard was trying to say – that United are the team to beat if you want to win the title. It's something I've said many times myself. And in the last few years nothing has changed.

United won the Premiership by a massive 18 points in 1999–2000 but despite that huge margin I was sure they wouldn't have it their own way when the season kicked off back in August 2000. I think back to Liverpool's domination in the 1970s and 1980s – that great side were toppled in the end. But Sir Alex Ferguson's team proved yet again what a phenomenal force they are to sweep to the Premiership title for an amazing seventh time in nine years.

RANK	TEAM	CHANCE CONVERSION
1	Chelsea	14.3%
2	Liverpool	14.0%
3	Man Utd	14.0%
10	Arsenal	11.7%

A quick look at United's Opta statistics for the season in this yearbook shows how they did it. They top so many of the team tables, in some cases by huge margins.

But more importantly, the figures reveal where the other teams expected to challenge United went wrong. For me, these are the most interesting stats in the book.

For example, look at the proportion of shots which hit the back of the net, the goals-to-shots ratios of the teams. It's no surprise to see the champions near the top of the list, but look at their nearest league challengers, Arsenal, who attempted a similar amount of shots at goal, but actually achieved a very disappointing strike rate – something that cost them in the FA Cup final too.

When I was playing in the English top flight in the late 1970s and 1980s, the idea of these "performance statistics" was unheard-of.

I must admit most footballers like to hear good things about themselves in the media. I can show players the speed of their shots these days, but I would love to have been able to check out my shooting accuracy and strike rates when I was a player and I'm sure Premiership players these days enjoy seeing they are the most accurate passer at their particular club or that they have made more tackles than any of their team-mates. It's great for the players to be able to see this information displayed as fact rather than comment by a football journalist.

But while it may be a bit of fun for the players, for their managers and those of us in the media, Opta offer a real insight into what happens in football matches, provided the stats are looked at in the context of what is actually happening on the pitch.

I only recently found out that managers receive a full Opta statistical report of how their team played after every Premiership match.

If I was a manager at a top-flight club I would definitely make full use of the stats to help show players areas in which there is room for improvement, both individually and as a team.

As a manager, you might note that your team's crossing accuracy is not particularly good. Perhaps this might be because your wide players' delivery is below par, so you could then encourage them to work on this aspect of their performance. But you also might want to look at who is in the middle getting on the end of their crosses – one of my favourite subjects.

Perhaps this is where the real problem lies. Here is another area in which Arsenal have struggled in the last few seasons, even with the likes of quality players such as Marc Overmars, Robert Pires and Ray Parlour on the wings at different times. The Opta stats show that

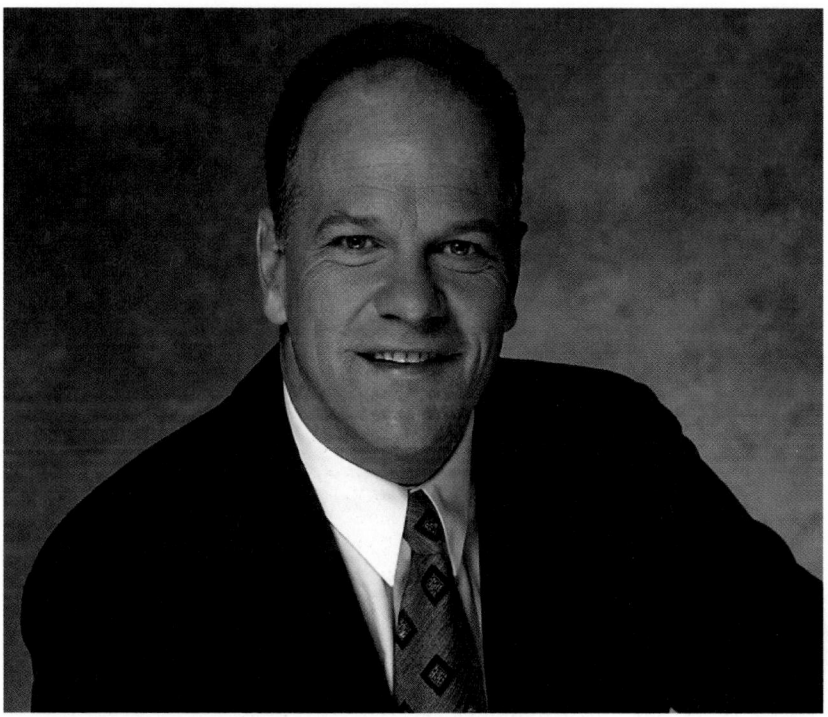

Arsenal have been the least accurate crossers of the ball in the Premiership in two of the last three seasons. But the Gunners also scored the lowest ratio of headed goals for the third season in a row. And when you look at the sort of strikers the Gunners have in their squad, who is likely to score lots of headed goals for them?

We started using Opta data on our review of the weekend's matches on *Monday Night Football* this year and I firmly believe having the figures in black and white for the viewers has enhanced our coverage of Premiership football.

I can't deny I've been sceptical of the real value of statistics in the past, but provided you look at them objectively and in the right context, there is no better way of assessing how players are progressing and pinpointing areas which need to be looked at.

Some people will invariably feel that the sort of technical wizardry we use at

Sky, as well as the sort of in-depth analysis compiled by Opta, is irrelevant to the game, but my eyes have been opened to the value of technology and statistics in football in recent years.

I'm not saying what Opta offer is a series of definitive answers. They would tell you themselves that's not what their work is about.

But if our office discussions are anything to go by, the stats certainly provide food for thought...and the odd heated debate!

Enjoy the book.

INTRODUCTION

This book is the definitive review of the 2000–01 Premiership campaign. In it you will discover the reasons why Manchester United became champions for the seventh time in nine seasons, what factors consigned Bradford City, Coventry City and Manchester City to relegation and who are the top-rated players in the division.

Every touch of the ball has been recorded, every foul registered and each goal analysed to provide a compelling insight into the performances of all 20 Premiership teams and every player who appeared during the nine months of passion and excitement that characterise the most exciting league in the world.

The first section covers the teams. You will find everything you need to know about each club that featured in the 2000–01 Premiership, plus the three teams which were promoted from the Nationwide League Division One, aiming to pit their wits against the élite in the 2001–02 season.

This is followed by a profile of every player who kicked a ball in anger, whether they were ever-present or made just one appearance as a substitute.

Finally, the section that is sure to cause debate and controversy in every bar, school and football-loving household in the country – the Comparative Tables. Here you will see how each team fared in relation to their adversaries and how the top players compared with each other across various categories. There are the teams of the season and you will also be able to see how the men in black performed in 2000–01 in our unique and exclusive insight into referees.

WHO ARE OPTA?

Opta are the official player performance statisticians to the Premier League. The company is five years old and has had a major impact on the way in which clubs monitor player performance and how the media offer their customers a revealing and unique insight into the game.

The idea was hatched prior to the 1996–97 season with support from the Premier League and the 20 clubs in the Premiership, who agreed Opta could have access to video footage of all Premiership matches to analyse.

The original system of analysis was developed in conjunction with former Arsenal and England coach Don Howe. He helped Opta create a ranking system to compare players' performances known as the Opta Index.

He worked with a software developer to create a unique database system that would fulfil all of his specifications. The Opta Index was first seen on Sky Sports' *Monday Night Football* with Andy Gray in August 1996.

Shortly after this debut media appearance, the statistics appeared in the *Observer* newspaper and interest among the national media and other parties snowballed.

At the end of the first year, the company – Opta Index Ltd – was given the title of Official Player Performance Statisticians To The Premier League and a sponsorship deal with the Premier League sponsors Carling was brokered.

At the end of the first season, Opta recruited its first journalist as the media began to demand an element of interpretation as well as the raw data. That demand has increased dramatically as the media seek to satisfy their customers' need for information and there are currently 18 journalists supplying statistics, stories and copy to a wide range of media. This meant Opta was able to offer the worldwide media a 24-hour press service during both World Cup 98 and Euro 2000.

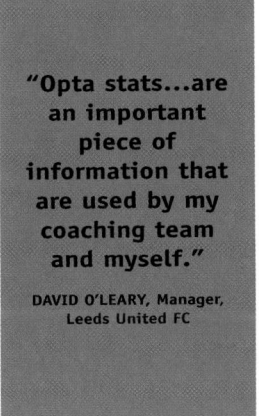

> "Opta stats...are an important piece of information that are used by my coaching team and myself."
>
> **DAVID O'LEARY, Manager, Leeds United FC**

In the summer of 1999, Opta Index Ltd was acquired by Sports Internet Group and expanded its coverage to include the Scottish Premier League and the three divisions of the Nationwide Football League.

A year later, Sports Internet Group was acquired by British Sky Broadcasting and Opta expanded into Europe and Asia, becoming the official player performance statisticians to the KPN-Eredivisie in Holland, La Liga in Spain and the Japanese "J" League, opening new offices and recruiting staff in all three countries. The company also covers the Italian Serie "A" and the Champions League from its central London headquarters.

Prior to the start of the 2000–01 season, Opta launched its new data collection tool OSCA (Opta Statistical Collection and Analysis), developed with assistance from FA technical director Howard Wilkinson, Charlton boss Alan Curbishley and referees officer Philip Don. This increased the number of categories monitored from 92 to more than 300 without increasing the time taken to analyse the game and has made for even more detailed comparisons of player and team performance for use by the clubs and the media alike.

During the season the company began monitoring Premiership matches live to offer the sports media a more immediate service. This dramatically increased the demand for Opta statistics: the data appeared in 85% of the national press titles in the UK. Such has been the success of the way the company educates its media partners on the value of such statistics that Opta has had a regular presence on both terrestrial and satellite TV. Opta has also started analysis of rugby union and rugby league.

Five years on from conception, Opta's values remain clearly defined in producing a service which is becoming a more accepted part of sport, not just by the media but by the professionals themselves.

HOW IS PLAYER PERFORMANCE MEASURED?

Opta originally developed the system of analysis in conjunction with former England coach Don Howe. The manual system has since been replaced by a custom-built, PC-based video analysis system called OSCA, which has cut the time required to analyse a game and dramatically increased the amount and type of data that is collected.

There are more than 300 distinct actions and outcomes for players which range from different kinds of shots and passes to tackles and blocks, and from different kinds of fouls and yellow cards to saves made by the goalkeeper. Every close season, the list of actions is discussed to determine the value of each element and then new categories may be added.

OSCA allows a specially-trained person to watch a match on video through a PC and, using the unique software, to click on icons to record each action performed by every single player on the ball, their fouls and discipline and also key decisions made by the officials. The new system was launched prior to the start of the 2000–01 Premiership season.

Opta receive a copy of the video after a game and then begin the analysis. An analyst takes several hours to complete a full match, depending on the flow of the game and the number of contentious decisions. Once the game is analysed, the data is downloaded into a database from which Opta are able to provide information in many diverse ways.

Managers' reports are created for each match and sent to a number of key personnel at the Premiership clubs involved, including managers, directors and coaching staff. In addition, some clubs request further details on player positions at set-pieces, moves leading to goalscoring opportunities, or where free-kicks are conceded or won, for both their own teams and forthcoming opposition.

Referees' reports are produced identifying key decisions (including commendable and controversial) made in

each match, details of goals and disciplinary issues. These are sent to referees officer Philip Don.

The data which is collected is then downloaded from the database into a spreadsheet, from which all the media requirements for player profiles, match reports and key data about the Premiership can be provided.

The analysis is checked by the operations manager and key information, such as cards issued, is checked with the official referees' reports.

Opta also produce a video tape highlighting disputed goals and the FA Premier League's goal committee rules on them within 48 hours. This system replaces the previous goal committee, which only convened every six months and attracted a measure of controversy. Any discrepancies or differences are checked and the database is updated if necessary.

The system of analysis is under constant review at Opta's central London headquarters. In the 2000-01 campaign, for the first time, Opta were able to provide information on whether shots were made with the left or right foot to make even more detailed comparisons between players.

Opta has worked with the League Managers Association to enhance the analysis and modify the data output from OSCA still further so that coaches were getting the information they wanted.

That, coupled with the company's detailed analysis of other leagues across Europe, also meant that the media were supplied with even more information with which to inform, provoke and entertain its football-hungry audience. Opta is a relatively young company but it has grown rapidly year-on-year since its inception and has stayed firmly at the forefront of sports analysis across Europe by constantly refining and expanding its analysis and output. That process will continue in the 2001-02 season as the company continues to develop and diversify.

"I am always interested to read the Opta statistics after each game and I find them both informative and useful. Congratulations to Opta for providing an excellent service."

GERARD HOULLIER, Manager, Liverpool FC

THE OPTA INDEX

The Opta Index is basically a form guide. When a match is analysed, each player's actions are recorded. For each of these actions, a player earns or loses points.

Over the course of a game, a player will accumulate a total number of points to give him a Game Score. This can be used to compare his performance with other players and the player with the most points is nominated as Opta's man-of-the-match.

The Index, which has featured in many newspapers and on television, uses these Game Scores to provide a form guide which is calculated over a period encompassing the previous six Premiership matches. You can see an example in the table below.

Each player's points from the last six games are added to give him a total, which is then divided by the number of minutes played and then multiplied by 90 (minutes), to give him an average score

per game played. This is his Index Score.

These Index Scores can then be used to compare players' performances over those six games, with the player who has the highest average being the most in-form player.

The players are then divided by the position in which they play – goalkeepers, defenders, midfielders, attacking midfielders and attackers – to create a series of tables providing an at-a-glance guide to current Premiership player form.

The following week, when Arsenal play again, Bergkamp's score will change as the Manchester United match drops out of the last six games recorded and is replaced with his score against the Gunners' next opponents.

Opta also produce a Season Index. This shows each player's average score across every game they have played during the 2000–01 season and this is the figure which is featured in tables throughout this book.

DENNIS BERGKAMP

OPPOSITION	MINS PLAYED	OPTA GAME SCORE
v Manchester United	90	1,112
v Everton	90	1,258
v Leeds United	90	1,473
v Southampton	0	0
v Sunderland	90	1,515
v West Ham United	71	1,611
Total	431	6,969

Opta Index Score	6,969/431 x 90(mins) = 1,455

WHO USES THIS INFORMATION?

The data gathered by Opta's team of highly-trained analysts is extremely valuable to a range of audiences. Over the past year in particular, Opta's multi-media coverage has expanded significantly. During Euro 2000, Opta's stats appeared in national papers across Europe, and continue to do so, while the data is now also available to WAP phone users.

● **THE PROFESSIONALS**

A report on each match is sent directly to the participating teams 24 hours after the game. Some clubs use the data to identify weaknesses in players' performances, others to set targets. Opta are currently working with the League Managers' Association to enhance the system of analysis and the data it yields to increase its value to people within the game.

● **THE BETTING INDUSTRY**

Spread-betting has become more common as the amount of data collected "live" has increased. Opta monitor live televised matches for a range of betting companies and supply "live" information so bookies can adjust the spread if necessary during the game. Opta also conduct post-match measurement and adjudication for several betting firms. Key incidents such as timing or distances from which goals are scored can be assessed – or Opta's analysts can be called upon to settle any disputes between the betting industry and its customers.

● **THE MEDIA**

Demand for football information and analysis has soared in recent years. There is huge coverage in Sunday newspapers and supplements in nearly all national titles on a Monday after the weekend's games, as well as several pages every day throughout the week. Not only are there TV channels dedicated to sport, but the first channel devoted to a single club has been introduced and is likely to be followed by others. There are also pages to fill in matchday programmes; regional newspapers seek in-depth information for readers on local clubs; and Internet sites meet the demand for Premiership football from a worldwide audience.

Football's profile has never been higher and Opta offer the media information to satisfy customer demand. Requests range from previews of forthcoming games, where opponents' key strengths can be identified, to match reviews from which it is possible to see just how and where a game was won or lost. In addition, Opta data can be used to back up stories or dispel media myths.

SAMPLE OF OPTA CLIENTS 2000–01 SEASON

NATIONAL NEWSPAPERS
The Sun, The Times, The Daily Telegraph
The Express, The Mirror, The Star
The Guardian, News of the World,
The Sunday Times, The Sunday Express
The Sunday Telegraph, The Sunday Mirror
The Sunday People, The Observer

REGIONAL NEWSPAPERS
London Evening Standard, Liverpool Echo
Manchester Evening News,
Birmingham Sunday Mercury,
North Eastern Evening Gazette, Coventry
Evening Telegraph, Leicester Evening Mercury

THE BETTING INDUSTRY
Surrey Sports, City Index, Sporting Index

MATCHDAY PROGRAMMES

TV STATIONS
Sky Sports – Soccer Extra,
Monday Night Football, Skysports.comTV
BBC – Football Focus, Match of the Day
TWI, MUTV, ITV – On the ball

MISCELLANEOUS
Virgin Net, BBC Online, ITV Teletext
Sports Interactive, AOL, Sky WAP,
Various club websites

MAGAZINES
Four Four Two, MOTD, Man Utd,
Leeds, Chelsea, Arsenal, Liverpool

GAMES
Opta's statistics are used by many clients
to run interactive fantasy games in their
publication or medium.

FANTASY FOOTBALL

The scene: an Everton fan sitting in a pub on a Monday night, watching an Ipswich Town v Manchester City match on the TV. His mate, an Aston Villa supporter, has gone to the little boys' room. Upon his return, he is told by the Everton fan that Ipswich have scored.

Villa fan: "Who got the goal?"

Everton fan: "Ipswich."

Villa fan: "No, who scored it?"

Everton fan: "Oh. Matt Holland."

Villa fan: "YES!"

It's a scene that many may recognise. A game in which most fans would ordinarily be neutral is nevertheless viewed eagerly and the performance of certain players scrutinised more carefully than others.

The reason? Fantasy football.

But have you ever wondered who runs the football games that give fans an extra dimension to their fixation with the game? No? That's probably for the best – because that's Opta's job. During the 2000–01 season, Opta have been the administrators of no fewer than 11 different fantasy football games, ranging from the simplistic to the downright obsessional.

The majority of fantasy football games in the past have been basic "goals and assists"-type affairs. Every weekend, a fantasy football player would check to see how many goals his strikers had scored and how many his 'keeper had let in at the other end. For the most part, it went little further.

The rise of the Internet has suddenly given new life to the format and Opta are at the forefront of interactive football game supply. Using the wealth of statistics available, it is now possible to develop a fantasy football game with more depth than ever before.

Shots on and off target, tackles won, clearances, successful passes – all these categories and more can now be used to make a fantasy football game both more enjoyable and more exciting.

Before, a striker may well have had a stinker of a match, hitting the corner flag with his attempts throughout the game, even that excellent chance on the stroke of half-time when the commentator yells: "Oh, my word, how on earth did he miss from there? It was easier to score!"

However, a stoppage-time goal, bundled in off his backside without the forward knowing a great deal about it, would ensure a healthy score in most fantasy games. At the same time, a Roy Keane-style midfielder who had made pass after pass and tackle after tackle in the centre for his team would be rewarded with a single point for an appearance and little else.

With Opta's depth of statistical data, the best and most consistent players suddenly become the highest scorers in a fantasy football environment. A quality player would achieve excellent scores week after week for his superb all-round performance.

Various clients across the world have taken the statistical data available for the

FANTASY FOOTBALL

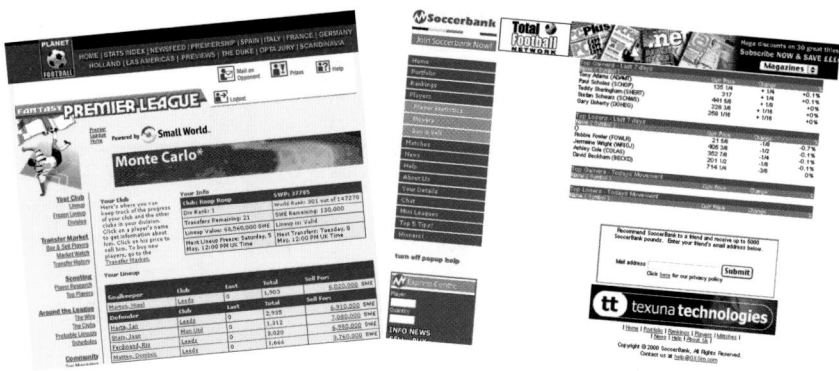

first time from Opta and have moulded their games into unique products which differ from each other in many ways. Opta maintain longstanding partnerships with top web-based companies such as Yahoo! and AOL, while developing new relationships with clients such as Hong Kong-based media company SuperFantasyGames and US interactive game giants Smallworld.

The type of game available differs greatly. While one will employ a unique system of player values which rise and fall by different amounts depending on the number of managers who buy and sell the player in question, another will use a system of "shares" whereby a manager can buy a stake in a player and make a profit or loss depending on the statistical performance of that player in Premiership matches.

The possibilities are virtually limitless for interactive football games, which have been given a new lease of life by Opta's statistical data.

The perfect companion to such fantasy football shenanigans is, of course, the Opta Yearbook. With every player individually analysed, each performance can be carefully scrutinised to see if this defender or that frontman can fit into the perfect team.

Each player's stats are available in the book and each can therefore be examined to see how well they would perform within the framework of certain fantasy game categories. You can see each player in the alphabetical section between pages 338

and 613. Or, if you know their team, there are even more stats in the individual club section. The figures are laid out in the perfect format to be able to compare like-for-like each player in their squad and others, to make sure that a better man is not available in the same position, or that a bargain alternative cannot be found.

Perhaps most useful of all are the comparative tables, listing the best performers in each of the most important areas of the game. Using the Opta Yearbook, it is therefore possible to avoid such disastrous decisions as selecting a player on reputation alone – a trap many have been known to fall into. As we have seen, a supposedly-average Bristol-born striker can easily outscore an expensive Colombian any day of the week...

One thing is for sure: it may not be such a great thing for those men in the pub:

Everton fan: "Hreidarsson's up for the corner."

Villa fan: "Who's taking it?"

Everton fan: "Reuser, I think."

Villa fan: "Damn. Well, at least Magilton won the corner in the first place – I'll get a load of points for him. Mind you, Scowcroft was booked."

Everton fan: "Anyway, who've you got this weekend?"

Villa fan: "Hasselbaink and Heskey up front, Barthez in goal..."

Everton fan: "Er, no. I meant who are Villa playing?"

Villa fan: "Eh? How should I know?"

THE OPTA PORTFOLIO

www.opta.co.uk

Soccer Extra
Sky Sports

Daily Express
23 December 2000

Opta's back catalogue of statistics is growing all the time and because of the inherent versatility of the database used to store and compile the statistics, the raw data can be presented in a variety of media-friendly ways.

Whether it is on a single match, season-long or season-on-season basis, Opta's system of analysis allows statistics to be tailored to clients' different needs. The full range can be found in the "Optimizer" section of www.planetfootball.com, Planet Football's comprehensive website. You can also type www.opta.co.uk into your web browser to access a range of player performance statistics on the Premiership, the Scottish Premier League, Italy's Serie "A", Spain's Primera Liga and Holland's Eredivisie, as well as Champions League and internationals.

There are team tables comparing key areas of performance such as shooting, discipline and tackling, statistical features, match reports and previews highlighting trends that may prove useful to those people who use the site's links to SurreySports' online betting service.

One of the most popular statistical services is Opta's Team of the Week. The company's system of analysis makes their Team of the Week the most objective around. Opta now compile similar teams

for each league they cover in Europe.

The Team of the Week is used in a host of regional newspapers. It can also be seen in the *Sunday Mirror*, while various "teams" can be seen in magazines and the *Times Monthly Handbook*.

As well as the Team of the Week, Opta produce a weekly Index of player form showing their top 50 players. The Index has certainly sparked many a debate and can be seen in regional newspapers, the *News of the World* and the *Sunday Mirror*.

Discipline, or the lack of it, is always a hot issue. While data on bookings and yellow cards is freely available, only Opta provide accurate data on fouls. Their discipline tables include teams, players and referees, with all rankings based on Opta's own disciplinary points system.

Of course, many clients require a more in-depth service. Opta cover every match played in the Premiership and also monitor European and international games. Opta's statistical match reports feature in many regional newspapers and for big games they can also be seen in the national and international press.

A host of top clubs including Arsenal, Chelsea, Leeds, Liverpool and Manchester United also use Opta's comprehensive statistics in the match report sections of their own official club magazines.

THE OPTA PORTFOLIO

News of the World
20 May 2001

Everton programme
19 May 2001

Daily Express
21 May 2001

For clients who do not have room for a full statistical match report, Opta provide a "Quick Stats" service. Featuring analysis of shots on and off target, fouls, offsides and cards, quick stats are used by a wide variety of clients including *The Mirror*, *The Sun* and Teletext.

Season 2000–01 saw the launch of Opta's new live service. Opta now has access to every match live and is therefore able to produce performance statistics on every team and every player. This has proved immensely popular with clients such as *The Observer*, the *News of the World* and Sky Sports, for whom the data was previously not available in time to meet their deadlines.

In 2001-02, Opta will enhance this service by developing an electronic version, which should allow dynamic updating of data; so, instead of having to wait until after games for statistics, websites and TV companies will be able to show and update the data on screen during the match as it happens.

Opta's statistical expertise is not limited to post-match analysis, though. One of their most popular services is their pre-match head-to-head material. Comparing rival players' statistics has proved a big hit and Opta's head-to-head profiles were featured in regional newspapers, matchday programmes and on websites during 2000–01.

Opta also provide clients such as Teletext and the *Daily Express* with comprehensive previews of the forthcoming weekend's fixtures.

Also popular are Opta's "splat stats". These are used by a variety of clients to highlight quirky aspects of player and team performance. You can see a selection of these statistics running along the bottom of many of the pages in this book.

The regional and national press often pick up Opta's own statistical features from Planet Football's website.

Opta are often asked for statistics to accompany breaking news on an *ad hoc* basis. If a big transfer story breaks, Opta will invariably be asked for statistics to prove the player's worth. If one player claims to be better than another, Opta will be asked to prove or disprove their claims and if a manager is appointed or sacked, Opta will usually be asked to provide statistics on his past achievements.

In fact, such is Opta's reputation that many clients now approach them for football-related information they might be able to find elsewhere. They come to Opta because of the company's growing reputation as THE authoritative voice of football statistics.

ENGLAND FAIL TO PASS EURO TEST

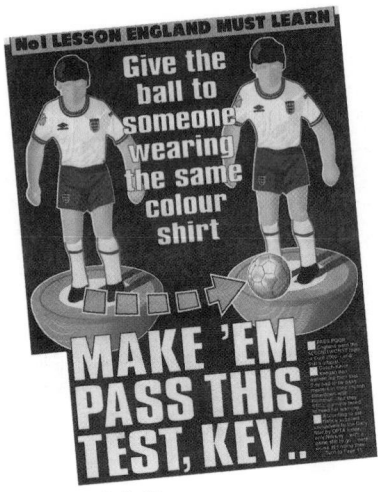

Daily Star
22 June 2000

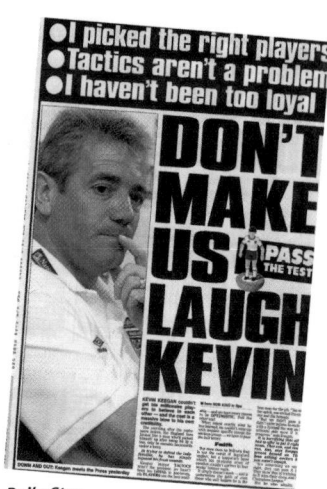

Daily Star
22 June 2000

"You can have all the tactics in the world but if you can't pass the ball they don't get a chance to kick in." (Kevin Keegan, June 2000).

England's performance at Euro 2000 was dismal. Kevin Keegan's men were beaten 3–2 by Portugal after taking a 2–0 lead and, although they laid a few old ghosts to rest with a 1–0 win over Germany several days later, the team still went into their last match against Romania needing at least a point to make sure of qualification for the second phase.

As everyone now knows, England lost against Romania and returned from the Low Countries with their tails between their legs. And as always when England go out of a big tournament, the media wanted to know why. Keegan's tactics had been criticised, but the general feeling among the supporters was that the team had just not been as good technically as their opponents.

Opta had been monitoring every kick of the Euro 2000 tournament and their statistical evidence backed up the view that England were simply not good enough at the basics of football to hold their own at the highest level.

Not only had England allowed the opposition more shots at goal than any other side in the tournament, but they had also managed an average of just three shots on target per game themselves.

But most damning of all was the revelation that only Norway – a team with a reputation for kick-and-rush football – had squandered possession more often than England in the group stages of the competition.

The Daily Star were particularly interested in this story, using it as their back-page lead two days after England's elimination and pinpointing their lack of passing accuracy as the prime reason for the national team's humiliation.

Asked to comment on his side's failure to put a decent passing game into practice, Keegan admitted it had been the main reason for their failure.

As he put it: "We didn't pass it; we didn't quite believe in each other with a football the way an international side must if it is to progress."

Opta had proved passing was England's Achilles heel and Keegan had been brave enough to admit that the statisticians were right.

Unfortunately for the England manager, he felt he could not resolve the problem himself. After England were defeated by Germany in a World Cup qualifier in October 2000, Keegan resigned as manager of the national side.

GROSS MISCONDUCT

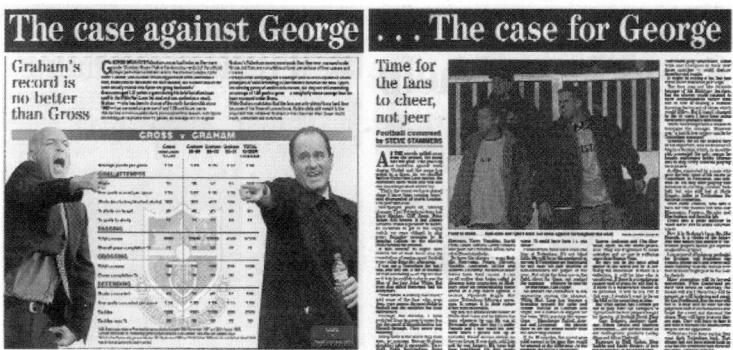

London Evening Standard
2 November 2000

George Graham's time at Tottenham will not be remembered as a golden era at White Hart Lane.

Graham's Arsenal connections made it hard for many Spurs supporters to accept him as their manager; and while Worthington Cup success in the 1998–99 season had temporarily silenced a few of the terrace wags, elimination from the same competition by Birmingham City at the third round stage in 2000–01 soon saw the locals revolting again.

Birmingham beat Spurs 3–1 at White Hart Lane, but in truth the seeds of discontent had been planted long before. Spurs' league form during Graham's reign at the Lane was less than impressive. At the time of the Birmingham defeat Spurs were lying in 12th place in the table with just four wins from 11 games and in the two previous seasons Graham had guided the club to 11th and 10th place respectively.

Opta were asked to look at Graham's record at Tottenham by the *London Evening Standard*, and the statisticians' findings did not make pleasant reading for the ex-Arsenal man.

Not only did Opta find that Tottenham were performing below the Premiership average in several key areas, but they also came to the worrying conclusion that Spurs were in fact a worse side under Graham than they had been during the disastrous reign of Christian Gross.

This conclusion was not based solely upon the fact that Graham's Tottenham were completing fewer passes and crosses than Gross's side, but also on the cold truths which the Premiership table revealed.

Under Gross, Spurs had averaged a paltry 1.31 points a game, but at the time of Opta's investigation Graham's team were actually faring even worse, averaging just 1.27 points a game.

The bad news did not stop there. Graham had always prided himself on his ability to organise his team's defence, but the statistics proved that Spurs had actually been leaking more goals since his arrival at White Hart Lane than they had been under Gross.

There was some comfort in the fact that Spurs were scoring more goals than under Gross's managership, but overall Opta's findings painted a bleak picture of Graham's time at Tottenham.

Sacked by new owners ENIC before the end of the 2000–01 season, Graham claimed he had not had time to put his plans into action at White Hart Lane. The statistics suggested that those plans had gone awry long before his dismissal.

GOONERS SPOONERS

The Mirror
21 September 2000

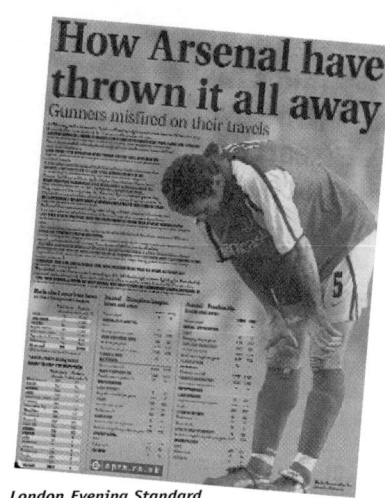

London Evening Standard
19 April 2001

Arsenal fans have become used to their team spurning chances to score goals, as it has become something of a trend for Arsène Wenger's team. This profligacy cost the Gunners dear in 2000–01 as they finished the campaign without any silverware for the third season in a row.

A team boasting the talents of Thierry Henry, Dennis Bergkamp, Sylvain Wiltord and Kanu should not have struggled but, despite a barrage of shots at goal, Arsenal consistently failed to turn pressure into results at crucial times.

While every player goes through a spell when scoring seems to be impossible, the situation at Highbury seemingly infected the whole club, becoming a serious restraint on the team.

Added to this was the growing concern about the Gunners' elderly defence and the inconsistent David Seaman in goal, leaving the supporters with a considerable amount to worry about.

Opta highlighted the problem as early as September after Arsenal's last-gasp victory against Shakhtar Donetsk in the Champions League.

The match stats were featured in *The Mirror,* showing how Arsenal had enjoyed 32 goal attempts in the game – and yet relied on defender Martin Keown to score a late brace. The corner count was just as dominant, with the Gunners racking up 17 to the Ukrainians' nil.

And when Arsenal did eventually get knocked out of the Champions League at the quarter-final stage, they were able to look back and identify chances that had been wasted – opportunities that cost them dear.

The *London Evening Standard* asked Opta to look at what went wrong and were provided with a detailed study of Arsenal's attacking play away from home.

It showed that by the end of April, Arsenal had the worst goals-to-shots ratio in the Premiership, with a measly seven per cent of their efforts on the road hitting the back of the net. Rivals such as Manchester United, Ipswich and Liverpool had rates of 13%, 15% and 14% respectively.

It was a similar story in the Champions League, where the Gunners had scored with just 6.78% of their shots, way behind surprise package Leeds, who had notched with almost 16% of their efforts away from Elland Road.

The team's goals-to-shots ratio at home in both competitions was a much more healthy 15% and this discrepancy must have infuriated players and fans alike.

With the Premiership and Champions

London Evening Standard
8 May 2001

The Times
15 May 2001

League out of their grasp, Arsenal could still focus on the FA Cup, though, and they reached their first final for three years with a 2–1 win against Tottenham in the semi-final.

Yet again they outplayed the opposition and made hard work of beating them. But for once a victory was secured and the club could prepare for a trip to the Millennium Stadium in Cardiff.

Opta produced an extensive preview of the final, which pointed out Liverpool's clinical finishing in all competitions and Arsenal's profligacy.

The preview noted: "They [Arsenal] normally need to create nine chances to score one goal. However, they do create lots of chances. They have fired in more shots than any team in the top flight. If the game goes to form, then Liverpool will score at least once and Arsenal will squander several chances."

The reality was almost identical, as the Gunners outplayed Liverpool for most of the game and yet failed to turn the pressure into goals.

A solitary strike from Fredrik Ljungberg looked like it was going to be enough, but Liverpool possess players who need only one chance and Michael Owen scored a late brace with his only two efforts of the game to give the Reds their second domestic cup of the season.

Thierry Henry was the main culprit, having five chances to score and forcing a save on just two occasions.

Opta examined this in the week after the final, and an article in *The Times* on 15 May showed how the Frenchman, despite being the third top scorer in the Premiership, wasted far more of his opportunities to score than any other leading striker.

The same piece also highlighted the fact that David Seaman had one of the lowest saves-to-shots ratios in the Premiership. In fact, only three regular 'keepers had been less reliable between the posts in 2000–01.

Fans have been urging the club to proceed with team rebuilding for some time and the problems that Opta helped highlight in 2000–01 seem to have been recognised by Arsène Wenger.

In the same article, the French manager said: "My only problem is finding the quality we need, but I will find it and pay the right price."

If he can achieve this aim then Arsenal should maintain a challenge for honours in the coming seasons. But whether or not the club scores goals or misses chances, Opta will once again be there to record the facts as they happen.

JUAN TO FORGET

Super Sunday
Sky Sports

News of the World
4 March 2001

Adjusting to life in a new country can be hard — adjusting to life in the Black Country can be harder still. Or at least that seemed to be the case for Aston Villa's £9.5 million Colombian striker Juan Pablo Angel.

Much was expected of Angel when John Gregory took him to Villa Park from River Plate in Argentina. Villa had been struggling for goals in the wake of Luc Nilis's career-ending injury and Angel was supposed to provide the solution to Villa's problems in the penalty area.

After a tough debut against Manchester United and a home game against Leeds, Angel featured against Bradford, setting up the opening goal for Darius Vassell in a 3–0 victory.

But the Colombian was looking less than lethal himself. In those first three appearances for Gregory's men, Angel rarely looked like scoring and never showed signs of improving on that in Villa's next game — a 2–1 defeat at Derby.

In fact Angel's performance at Pride Park was so bad that he was taken off at half-time, leaving John Gregory to comment: "I had to take him off at half-time for his own protection."

Gregory was quick to point out that Arsenal stars Dennis Bergkamp and Thierry Henry had also struggled to settle in when they first arrived in the Premiership.

But the News of the World asked Opta to take an in-depth look at Angel's contribution (or lack thereof) to the Villa cause.

Opta's stats were damning. In 349 minutes of competitive action, Angel had failed to hit a single shot on target, a statistic that led the News of the World to dub him "the worst striker in the Premiership".

Sky's Super Sunday programme also picked up on Opta's stats, running them across the screen before Villa's televised game with Arsenal — a match in which Angel once again failed to trouble the opposition 'keeper. Angel's stats also featured in The Times and The Observer.

And the Colombian's barren run continued until Villa's game against Everton when, after coming on as a substitute for the last 12 minutes, Angel finally managed a shot on target.

He had to wait a little longer for his first goal, though, finally hitting the back of the net in Villa's last home game of the season after 444 minutes of Premiership football.

That strike must have come as a huge relief to a player who has found Premiership football tough to come to terms with. Hopefully he will find it a little easier to hit the target in 2000–01.

Opta will be watching!

MY LEFT FOOT

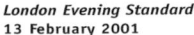

London Evening Standard
13 February 2001

Daily Express
19 February 2001

When Sven-Göran Eriksson was appointed as England manager in January 2001, there was much discussion about who he would choose to play in the problematic left-back position. The disappointing displays by Phil Neville in Euro 2000 and the long-term injuries affecting Chelsea's Graeme Le Saux led to calls for new talent to be given a try.

Peter Taylor had played Aston Villa's Gareth Barry in that role when he took temporary charge of the national side and many people expected Eriksson to continue with the youngster, given the level of performance Barry had shown in previous outings with England.

In February, with Eriksson's first match looming – a friendly with Spain – the London Evening Standard asked Opta to take a look at the various English left-backs in contention for a place in the team, after Arsenal manager Arsène Wenger had suggested that the Gunners' Ashley Cole was good enough to play for his country.

The results were good for Cole, as he came out with the most impressive statistics, even beating Silvinho, his Brazilian rival at Highbury. His average Opta points score was far better than players like Michael Ball, Wayne Bridge and Jon Harley. More importantly, his score was significantly better than Gareth Barry's total. Cole had also managed to score two goals in his short Arsenal career.

Less than a week later, Opta provided the Daily Express with more left-back-related information, this time noting that veteran Stuart Pearce had won more tackles than any other left-sided defender in the Premiership. It was pointed out, though, that his passing had been less than impressive and his age would certainly not count in his favour.

But the England manager surprised everyone with his shock decision to call up Charlton's Chris Powell. No one had predicted this elevation for the journeyman defender, but it showed that Eriksson was willing to give any player a chance if he admired his play.

Ashley Cole was also chosen, along with Michael Ball of Everton and, although Powell played in Eriksson's first two games as England manager, the Swede promoted Cole to the starting XI for the crucial game with Albania.

The youngster did not disappoint, either, playing well and helping England to a key win – and it looks likely that he will have a lengthy career with the national team.

THREE'S A CROWD

The Mirror
12 January 2001

Sunday Times
8 April 2001

Daily Express
22 May 2001

Hindsight is a useful ally and, while it is now easy to look at Liverpool's haul of trophies at the end of 2000–01 and imagine that Gérard Houllier had a masterplan all along, there were points during the season when the Reds were struggling and the Frenchman's rotation of his three England strikers seemed to be detrimental to the club.

The form of Michael Owen was a concern earlier in the campaign and the England star still seemed to be hampered by his recent hamstring injuries, both mentally and physically.

After defeat at the hands of Crystal Palace in the first leg of the Worthington Cup semi-final, *The Mirror* asked Opta to compare Owen with Robbie Fowler and Emile Heskey. The results showed that the youngster was still the most prolific scorer, notching every 126 minutes on average. Heskey was just behind on 151 minutes, but Fowler was considerably poorer on 378 minutes.

And while Owen and Heskey had goals-to-shots ratios of more than 22 per cent, Fowler was scoring with just seven per cent of his efforts on goal. Indeed, reports at the time suggested that Fowler was likely to leave Anfield and Houllier admitted that the club had recently turned down offers for the player.

But just five months later, the atmosphere at Anfield was far better. A haul of three cups and a place in the Champions League amounted to an exceptional season and, while Fowler still seemed to be the fall guy, a lengthy article in the *Daily Express* on 22 May examined the three strikers and what they had contributed to Liverpool in 2000–01.

Fittingly — given his remarkable return to form — Michael Owen finished as the most exemplary forward, with a shooting accuracy of 63% and a conversion rate of 23%. His accuracy was highest when he came on as a substitute and lowest when he played with Heskey. Fowler performed best as a lone striker, scoring five goals in five solo games. He was least impressive when alongside Heskey.

The ex-Leicester man was consistent with everyone, but scored most goals when playing alongside Owen, also recording his highest shooting accuracy with the diminutive hitman. But given that the three players scored 63 goals between them, and also had the support of former Barcelona striker Jari Litmanen, the decisions facing Gérard Houllier and his coaching staff are ones which many managers would be happy to have.

WHEN WE WERE KINGS

London Evening Standard
5 October 2000

The October meeting between England and Germany in a World Cup qualifying fixture was reason enough for excitement, but the fact that it was to be the last-ever game at Wembley Stadium gave it unparalleled significance. The whole country seemed to wallow in nostalgia for the stadium, and for the great battles between the two countries.

Unsurprisingly, the Wembley match which was most commented on was the 1966 World Cup Final, surely the stadium's finest hour.

Opta set to work and, using the unique OSCA analysis system, their experts examined that celebrated game kick by kick and shot by shot.

The results were published in the *London Evening Standard* on 5 October and they made fascinating reading.

The man of the match was Geoff Hurst. The hat-trick hero had a superb game, forcing two saves from Hans Tilkowski in the West German goal as well as scoring three times. The result was an Opta points total for Hurst of 2,679.

Shots at goal were something of a feature, with an incredible 46 attempts during the 120 minutes of action. This figure does not even include blocked shots, of which there were 22.

Football really was more exciting in those days, it seems. An average of just 2.6 minutes passed between shots, which certainly compares favourably with a current average in the Premiership of 4.1 minutes per attempt.

The best passer on the pitch was the England skipper, Bobby Moore. He ended the game with a completion rate of 91%, a great illustration of his superb distribution skills.

Moore also created two of England's four goals, a feat which netted him 2,261 Opta points, making him the second-best performer of the day.

Martin Peters, England's other goalscorer, was also the only player to be cautioned in the game, a far cry from World Cup finals in the 1990s, when flurries of cards became the norm.

The worst passer on the England side was defender Jack Charlton, who found a team-mate with just 52% of his passes. But "Big Jack" was never picked for his craft on the ball, rather for his uncompromising defensive nature.

Of course, the events of October 2000 were far less satisfying for England fans, as Germany ended the day singing in the rain after a 1-0 victory.

It was an ignominious end to the old stadium, but Opta had helped to remind the home support of better times.

WHERE ANGELS FEAR TO TREAD

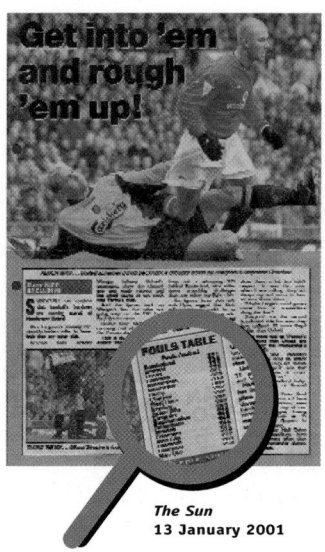

The Sun
13 January 2001

As Manchester United raced away to their third Premiership title in a row, the managers of other teams understandably became frustrated and looked for reasons to explain why their own clubs were lagging behind Sir Alex Ferguson's team.

Arsenal chief Arsène Wenger became increasingly convinced that teams were giving United an easy ride – an allegation which the Mancunian club quickly denounced.

The Frenchman commented: "Other teams need to attack United more.

"They are shown too much respect and that means they have it easier than the rest of us."

Opta got to work and examined this theory and, a few days later, *The Sun* published a table which backed up Wenger's claims and opened up a lengthy debate.

The Opta statistics showed that Manchester United players had been fouled fewer times than those at any other Premiership team – just 250 times.

Arsenal players, on the other hand, had been fouled on 336 occasions, the second-highest total in the top flight. Players at other leading clubs such as Sunderland and Leeds had also suffered a high number of fouls in their campaigns at this point.

The Sun showed the Opta stats to former Premiership referee Brian Hill and he said: "It doesn't surprise me at all. Manchester United's players get fouled less than any other team.

"Teams seem to show them a bit too much respect. It was the same when I was reffing. They are always top and seem to have an aura about them. Maybe Fergie's mind games come into it somewhere along the line."

The theory about the aura seemed to work, as the team just above Manchester United were Liverpool, another club who play at a ground where referees have been accused of respecting the past to the detriment of the present.

But the next team in the list was Bradford, a club which do not have the history of the two north-west giants.

By the end of the season, things had changed slightly. Sunderland were still the most-fouled team, but Manchester United had been replaced as the least-fouled team by Liverpool. In fact, the champions had started to suffer more illegal challenges, ending the campaign with 499. It seems that Arsène Wenger and the media attention could have affected the way teams approached the Red Devils in the second half of the season.

JEEPERS KEEPERS

The Observer
28 January 2001

Sports Centre
Sky Sports

Daily Express
15 February 2001

While the football world loves a prolific striker or a swashbuckling midfielder, goalkeepers often receive far less attention. But the performance of the men between the posts is vital and Opta's detailed analysis of the Premiership's shot-stoppers inspired a number of stories in the media during 2000–01.

Manchester United's Fabien Barthez is the most expensive goalkeeper in the top flight and also the most flamboyant. It was widely accepted that his arrival at Old Trafford added an extra dimension to the team and an article in *The Observer* on 28 January examined him in detail.

Opta stats accompanying the article showed how Barthez led the way in clean sheets – with 12 – and how he had only let in 10 league goals at that stage of the season.

But the Frenchman was not eulogised by everybody and, as his team prepared for their Champions League quarter-final against Bayern Munich, Liverpool defender Markus Babbel – formerly a player with the German side – claimed in the *Daily Express* that Barthez was the weak point of United's team.

Opta compared Barthez's European stats with the Munich goalkeeper Oliver Kahn's and, while there was very little difference between them, the German had performed slightly better. He had kept two more clean sheets and had a saves-to-shots ratio which was one percentage point superior, but this was hardly conclusive evidence.

While Kahn and Barthez were the leading German and French 'keepers respectively, there was no such dominant figure for England. Sven-Göran Eriksson was faced with a number of choices when he assumed control in January, from veterans like Seaman and Nigel Martyn to fledglings like Paul Robinson and Richard Wright.

On 15 February the *Daily Express* asked Opta to take a closer look at the form of those four men – plus Aston Villa's David James – and the results indicated that the main man was still Seaman. The Arsenal player was in excellent form at this point, having kept six consecutive clean sheets, and after a lot of criticism in 2000 was showing that he could still perform.

Ipswich star Wright also showed well, leading the way in clean sheets and being involved in more Premiership victories than any of the other candidates.

Eriksson plumped for the experience of Seaman in the World Cup qualifying matches, but the statistics showed that he has plenty of options available to him in the future when a change is needed.

CONTINENTAL DRIFT

UNITED SUFFERING FROM CONTINENTAL DRIFT

While it is a notable achievement for all three English sides to reach the European Cup quarter-finals, Manchester United will need to improve on their present form if they are to repeat their 1999 triumph.

Failure to win their group, despite taking six points from their first two games, was the result of an alarming slump – the type of which United rarely show domestically. Despite scoring 1.5 goals per game on average in this season's Champions League, their ratio in front of goal is still lower than in the Premiership.

Fewer chances are also being created than in the Premiership, meaning Sir Alex Ferguson's side need to be more clinical. Their passing is actually more accurate in Europe, but a drop of seven percentage points in United's crossing accuracy is perhaps a reflection of the dip in form of David Beckham, dropped to the bench against Sturm Graz.

Defensively, the English champions are also tighter in the Premiership; 76 per cent of tackles are won domestically, compared to 74 per cent in Europe, while more goals per game are conceded on average also on the Continent.

	Champions League	Premiership
Average goals per game	1.5	2.28
Average shots per game	9.58	13.9
Shots on target (%)	54	45
Shots scored (%)	16	16
Overall pass completion (%)	80	78
Cross completion (%)	20	27
Average goals conceded per game	0.83	0.66
Tackles won (%)	74	76
Average fouls per game	14.3	11.7

opta

The Times
17 March 2001

While Manchester United continued to dominate the English domestic scene in 2000–01, the Red Devils' European form was less impressive. United stumbled through the group stages of the Champions League, prompting many outside observers to suggest that Sir Alex Ferguson's side were just not good enough to compete with Europe's élite.

In the days leading up to United's quarter-final clash with Bayern Munich, Opta compared United's form at home with their form in Europe and highlighted several key areas of concern.

Opta discovered that United were finding it harder to create scoring chances and even harder to stop the opposition from creating opportunities.

In a feature in *The Times*, Opta warned that United would need to improve their performances in virtually every area if they were to stand a chance of beating Bayern.

The fact that the Red Devils were knocked out by the German champions came as no surprise to Opta, who had spotted the danger signs earlier in the competition.

But Roy Keane's assessment of United's shortcomings was more of a shock. The skipper was clearly upset by his side's failure to reach the semi-finals of the Champions League and was moved to speak out on the club's elimination, saying: "We have to face facts: when it comes to Europe we are an average team. The players gave their all against Bayern, but we are just not good enough."

Opta's statistics showed a decline in performance across the board and did seem to back up Keane's assessment. Ferguson was certainly concerned. The season had barely finished before the United boss submitted to his board a list of players he wanted to sign.

Ruud Van Nistelrooy was acquired soon after the end of the season and more high-profile names were widely expected to follow. While that can only be bad news for the rest of the Premiership, it is essential if United are to reclaim the European Cup.

But United's more established stars also need to up their efforts on the pitch. At times United can win matches in England without playing at the top of their game, but in Europe any slip in performance levels can be costly.

As Roy Keane said: "All you have to do is drop your standards by five or 10 per cent and it's obvious, especially in Europe."

Opta could not have put it any better themselves.

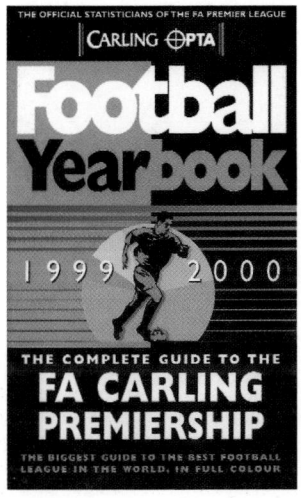 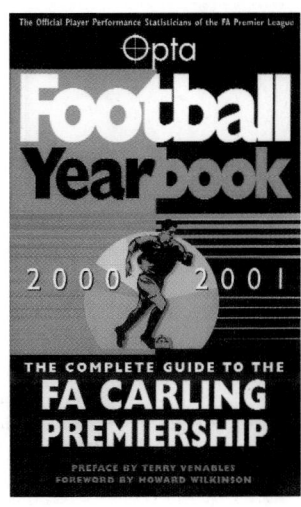

THE TEAMS

Each club that participated in the 2000-01 Premiership season has its own section within this part of the book. The sections are in alphabetical order with Arsenal at the beginning and West Ham at the end.

You will find:

- important details about each club, highlighting key personnel and contact details;
- a review of the season;
- a full breakdown of appearances, goalscorers and disciplinary issues;
- a profile of the manager;
- a graph charting the league position across the course of the season;
- charts that show how, when and where each team scored and conceded their goals as well as who netted for and against each side;
- a full breakdown of each player's performance;
- Index scores for the top players at each club and Opta's nomination for their player of the season;
- the top performers at each club across a series of key categories;
- a match report on one of the club's best performances during the season.

After this, you can find key details on the three sides who were promoted to the Premiership from the Nationwide League Division One and who will feature in the forthcoming 2001-02 season.

For Blackburn Rovers, Bolton Wanderers and Fulham

You will find:

- important details about each club, highlighting key personnel and contact details;
- a review of the season;
- a full breakdown of appearances and goalscorers;
- a profile of the manager;
- a graph charting the league position across the course of the season;
- charts that show how, when, who and where each team scored and conceded their goals.

ARSENAL

ADDRESS

Avenell Rd, Highbury, London N5 1BU

CONTACT NUMBERS

Telephone: 020 7704 4000
Fax: 020 7704 4001
Ticket Office: 020 7704 4040
Ticket Information: 020 7704 4242
GunnersLine: 09064 744000
(all calls charged at 60p per minute)
The Gunners Shop: 020 7704 4120
e-mail: enquiries@arsenal.co.uk
Website: www.arsenal.com

KEY PERSONNEL

Chairman: P D Hill-Wood
Vice-Chairman: D B Dein
Directors: Sir Roger Gibbs
C E B L Carr, D D Fiszman
K J Friar, R Carr
Managing Director: K Edelman
Club Secretary: D Miles
Manager: Arsène Wenger

SPONSORS

SEGA

FANZINES

The Gooner
Up The Arse
Highbury High

COLOURS

Home: Red shirts with white sleeves,
white shorts and white stockings
Away: Yellow shirts, navy shorts
and navy stockings

NICKNAME

The Gunners

HONOURS

League Champions:
1930-31, 1932-33, 1933-34,
1934-35, 1937-38, 1947-48,
1952-53, 1970-71, 1988-89,
1990-91, 1997-98
FA Cup Winners: 1930, 1936, 1950,
1971, 1979, 1993, 1998
League Cup Winners: 1987, 1993
European Cup Winners' Cup Winners:
1994
Fairs Cup Winners: 1970

RECORD GOALSCORER

Cliff Bastin – 150 league goals, 1930–47

BIGGEST WIN

12–0 v Loughborough Town –
Division Two, 12 March 1900

BIGGEST DEFEAT

0–8 v Loughborough Town –
Division Two, 12 December 1896

SEASON REVIEW

Arsenal were rarely off the back pages in 2000–01. They added two more runners-up positions to take their tally to five near-misses in three seasons as they finished second to Manchester United in the Premiership and lost the FA Cup final to Liverpool.

But they were making headlines even before the season began. Lauren joined from Mallorca and Robert Pires arrived from Marseille, while Davor Suker and legendary full-back Nigel Winterburn left for West Ham United.

But other deals created news for the wrong reasons. Firstly, Marc Overmars and Emmanuel Petit left for Barcelona in a £30 million package. Arsenal had been forced to sell after both demanded to leave. Following the Nicolas Anelka saga just the previous summer, the Gunners were on the wrong end of player power once again.

Then new signing Edu was stopped at Customs and denied entry to Great Britain when he was found to have a false passport.

Finally, Arsenal were the beneficiaries of player power when Bordeaux's Sylvain Wiltord refused to train with his club until they allowed him to join the Gunners for £13 million.

The Gunners began the season away to Sunderland and this game set the tone for their entire campaign. Despite outplaying the Mackems, Arsenal failed to convert a host of chances and lost 1–0.

Patrick Vieira was dismissed for retaliating against Darren Williams whom the Gunners claimed had been briefed to "wind him up" and Arsène Wenger was reported to the FA for a scuffle with fourth official Paul Taylor.

Vieira was sent off again just two days later when Graham Poll dismissed him along with Liverpool's Dietmar Hamann

> "It was a failure to win a trophy, but not a failure of overall performance. Many clubs would pay fortunes to be in our situation."
>
> Arsène Wenger

and Gary McAllister. The sense of injustice was heightened when video evidence seemed to show all three had been harshly dealt with, but Poll refused to change his decisions. Vieira served a five-match ban.

Home wins over Liverpool, Charlton and Coventry were undermined by draws at Chelsea, Bradford and Ipswich. The Gunners' home form was in fact the Premiership's best, but they won only three of their first 15 away matches, scoring just 10 goals – and this travel sickness cost them their title challenge.

Arsenal's Champions League campaign began with victories against Sparta Prague and Shakhtar Donetsk and the Gunners then defeated Lazio.

Just four days later, Arsenal beat Manchester United thanks to the brilliance of Thierry Henry. That result took the flying Gunners level on points with the champions and with four subsequent victories they matched United stride for stride as the two eased clear of the pack.

The only concern for Arsenal was the future of their manager. Wenger was linked with the vacant England coach's position and even after Sven-Göran Eriksson was appointed rumours continued to circulate of interest from major European clubs.

But what seemed more likely was that Wenger could quit club football altogether because of uncertainty over transfer rules. Happily, these fears receded as FIFA and UEFA reached an agreement with the European Union.

A draw with Lazio in Rome saw Arsenal qualify for the next stage of the Champions League, but the decision to rest players against Shakhtar broke the momentum.

A scoreless draw with Derby was followed by defeats at Everton and Leeds. The latter match was marred by eight

SEASON REVIEW

bookings, FA charges against Vieira and some unseemly verbal sparring between David O'Leary and Robert Pires.

The poor domestic results were compounded by a 4–1 drubbing by Spartak Moscow and the squandering of a two-goal lead against Bayern Munich.

A 5–0 win over Newcastle was the only good result leading up to Christmas; the worst, a 4–0 hammering at Anfield. Further poor results in January against Charlton, Chelsea and Leicester ended the title race as a contest.

Edu finally received his official passport and Dennis Bergkamp signed a new contract, but with United so far clear Arsenal's best chance of silverware seemed to rest in the FA Cup. Wins at Carlisle and QPR were followed by two home victories over Chelsea and Blackburn to book the Gunners a semi-final berth against Spurs.

Their league form proved variable, the worst result being a 6–1 annihilation by United at Old Trafford. The champions scored with virtually every shot and this highlighted the difference between the two teams. While United were the most clinical side in the top flight until they won the title, Arsenal were just 10th in terms of converting chances – and scored 16 fewer goals, despite having more shots on target than any Premiership side.

Arsenal made laboured progress in the Champions League. A 1–0 win in Lyon was followed by a 1–1 draw in the return and another 1–0 victory over Spartak. Defeat by Bayern Munich did not matter and the Gunners scraped into the quarter-finals.

Arsenal surged to a 2–1 win against Valencia at Highbury, but the away goal was to prove costly. Before the return, though, there was the little matter of the FA Cup semi-final against Spurs. Gunners fans had been left shocked by the death of

> **"I don't think we are cheating our supporters with the quality of our game, but I can understand their frustration."**
>
> **Arsène Wenger**

David Rocastle, aged just 33. This followed the loss of Niccolo Galli in a car crash and George Armstrong, one of Arsenal's greats and their reserve-team coach.

Rocky's name was continually chanted as the Gunners created a hatful of chances against Spurs. They took just two to ruin Glenn Hoddle's first game in charge.

The title was unexpectedly handed to United in a 3–0 defeat by Middlesbrough and just a few days later the Gunners were eliminated in the Champions League by Valencia, losing 1–0.

Wins over Everton, Derby and Leeds virtually secured second place in the Premiership and Arsenal travelled to Cardiff hopeful of winning the FA Cup.

Unfortunately, despite outplaying Liverpool for long periods, Fredrik Ljungberg's goal was the Gunners' only reward. With 10 minutes remaining, Arsenal fans were celebrating when Michael Owen stunned them with two late strikes to snatch the trophy. Arsenal finished the season empty-handed, but freed up a massive transfer kitty to help challenge United's domestic dominance.

The biggest problem could be replacing Tony Adams, who announced his retirement from international football in January and that he would retire from Arsenal at the end of 2001–02. New recruits have so far struggled to maintain Arsenal's traditional defensive strength.

One success story was Ashley Cole. The youngster stepped up to the first team and impressed so much that by the season end he was keeping Silvinho on the sidelines and had played for England.

Wenger claims 90% of the current squad will spearhead the challenge in 2001–02 and with one or two shrewd additions, Arsenal will be hoping to end three barren years in terms of silverware.

target than any other side

ARSENAL

DATE	OPPONENT	SCORE	ATT.	ADAMS	BERGKAMP	COLE	DANILEVICIUS	DIXON	EDU	GRIMANDI	HENRY	KANU	KEOWN	LAUREN
19.08.00	Sunderland A	0–1	47,121	90	s16	–	–	77	–	74	90□	90	90	s13
21.08.00	Liverpool H	2–0	38,014	90	76□	–	–	–	–	90	90¹	s14	90	90¹
26.08.00	Charlton H	5–3	38,025	90	s27	–	–	90	–	90	90²	90	90	63
06.09.00	Chelsea A	2–2	34,923	–	s20	–	–	70	–	90	90¹	90	90	90
09.09.00	Bradford A	1–1	17,160	–	–	90¹	–	90	–	90□	90	s23	90	–
16.09.00	Coventry H	2–1	37,794	90□	77	–	–	–	–	90	s23	s13	90	–
23.09.00	Ipswich A	1–1	22,030	–	90¹	–	–	–	–	70	90	s20	90□	–
01.10.00	Man Utd H	1–0	38,146	90□	78□	–	–	–	–	90	90¹	57	90	–
14.10.99	Aston Villa H	1–0	38,042	90	86	–	–	90	–	90	78¹□	s8	–	90
21.10.00	West Ham A	2–1*	26,034	–	88	–	–	–	–	90	s14	s2	90	90
28.10.00	Man City H	5–0	38,049	90	90¹	90¹	–	s21	–	90	90²	–	90	–
04.11.00	Middlesbro A	1–0	29,541	90	86	–	–	90	–	90□	90¹	–	90	s4
11.11.00	Derby Co H	0–0	37,679	–	90	–	–	s27	–	63	90	s24	90	–
18.11.00	Everton A	0–2	33,106	–	90	90	–	80□	–	–	–	90	90	–
26.11.00	Leeds Utd A	0–1	38,084	90□	–	–	–	–	–	–	90□	s15	90□	75□
02.12.00	Southampton H	1–0*	38,036	90	90	–	–	s45	–	90	s29	s24	90	–
09.12.00	Newcastle H	5–0	38,052	90	s24	–	–	90	–	57	90¹	66¹	90	s33
18.12.00	Tottenham A	1–1	36,062	90	s27	–	–	90	–	63	90	72	90	–
23.12.00	Liverpool A	0–4	44,144	–	73	–	–	90	–	90	90	s17	90	–
26.12.00	Leicester H	6–1	38,007	90¹	–	s5	–	90	–	77	90³	74	–	–
30.12.00	Sunderland H	2–2	38,026	90	–	–	s10	90¹	–	90	80	69	–	–
01.01.01	Charlton A	0–1	20,043	–	–	s26	s26	90	–	74	–	90	–	–
13.01.01	Chelsea H	1–1	38,071	–	–	–	–	90□	–	–	90	–	90	–
20.01.01	Leicester A	0–0	21,872	90	s28	–	–	90	s17	–	90	–	90□	–
30.01.01	Bradford H	2–0	37,318	90□	79	90	–	90	–	s26	90	s11	–	64¹
03.02.01	Coventry A	1–0	22,035	90□	90¹	90□	–	90	–	s26	–	–	–	64
10.02.01	Ipswich H	1–0	38,011	90	90	90	–	90	–	90□	s32¹	–	–	58
25.02.01	Man Utd A	1–6	67,535	–	–	45	–	–	–	90	90¹	–	–	–
03.03.01	West Ham H	3–0	38,071	90	90	56	–	90	s23	90	s30	–	–	90□
18.03.01	Aston Villa A	0–0	36,111	–	90	–	–	90	–	89■	s14	–	–	90
31.03.01	Tottenham H	2–0	38,121	90	–	90	–	83	–	–	90¹	s23	90	67
11.04.01	Man City A	4–0	33,444	–	–	90	–	–	70	–	s16	90¹	90	90
14.04.01	Middlesbro H	0–3	37,879	90	–	–	–	90	45	–	90□	90	90	–
21.04.01	Everton H	4–1	38,029	90	–	90	–	90	–	65¹	90¹	–	90	–
28.04.01	Derby Co A	2–1	29,567	90□	–	90	–	90	–	90	s23	89¹□	90	67□
05.05.01	Leeds Utd H	2–1	38,142	90□	–	90□	–	90	–	90□	90	–	90	–
15.05.01	Newcastle A	0–0	50,729	90	69	90	–	90	–	–	90	s21	90	90
19.05.01	Southampton A	2–3	15,252	90	34	90¹□	–	–	s16	90	90	s56	90	–

□ Yellow card, ■ Red card, s Substitute, 90² Goals scored

*including own goal

For more information visit our website:

2000–01 PREMIERSHIP APPEARANCES

LJUNGBERG	LUKIC	LUZHNY	MALZ	MANNINGER	PARLOUR	PIRES	SEAMAN	SILVINHO	STEPANOVS	UPSON	VERNAZZA	VIEIRA	VIVAS	WILTORD	TOTAL
66	–	–	–	–	90	s24	90	90	–	–	–	89□	–	–	989
–	–	90	–	–	–	90	90	90	–	–	–	74□	–	–	974
–	–	–	–	–	–	90	90	90¹	–	–	–	90²	–	–	990
s12	–	90	–	–	70	78	90	90¹□	–	–	–	–	–	s20	990
90□	–	90	–	–	90	90	90	–	–	–	–	–	–	67	990
90	–	90	–	–	67	90	90	90	–	–	s23¹	–	–	67¹	990
90	–	90	–	–	90□	–	90	90	–	–	s20	–	90	70	990
90	–	90	–	–	90	–	90	90	–	–	–	–	s33	s12	990
–	–	s4	–	–	90	82	90	90	–	–	–	90	–	s12	990
65	–	90	–	–	s25	90¹	90	90	–	–	–	90	–	76	990
s70	90	69	–	–	69	20	–	–	–	–	–	82	–	s21¹	982
90	90	–	–	–	90	–	–	90	–	–	–	90	–	–	990
66	90	90	–	–	90	–	–	90	–	–	–	90	–	90	990
90	–	90	–	90	90	90	–	–	–	s10	–	–	–	90	990
–	–	90□	–	90	90□	90	–	90□	–	–	–	90	–	90	990
90	–	90	–	90	–	66	–	45	–	–	–	90	–	61	990
81	–	s9	–	90	90³	90	–	–	–	–	–	–	90	–	990
90	–	–	–	90	90	63□	–	90	–	–	–	s27¹	–	s18	990
66	–	45	–	90	90	s45	–	90	–	–	–	90	–	s24	990
s16¹	–	–	–	90	90	85	–	90	90	–	–	90¹	s13	–	990
90	–	–	–	90	s21	90	–	90	90	–	–	90¹	–	–	990
90	–	–	s16	90	90□	64	–	64	90	–	–	90	90	–	990
87	–	–	–	–	90	90¹	90	90	90	–	–	90	s3	90	990
45	–	–	–	–	90	90	90	90□	–	–	–	90	–	90	990
–	–	–	–	–	90¹	90	90	–	90	–	–	90	–	–	990
–	–	–	–	–	90□	89	90	–	90	–	–	90□	s1	90	990
s20□	–	–	–	–	90	90	90	–	90	–	–	–	–	70	990
s45	–	90	–	–	69	90	90	90	90	–	–	90	s21	90	990
90	–	–	–	–	–	67	90	–	–	–	–	90□	s34	60³	990
76	–	90	–	90	84	s14	–	90	–	–	–	90□	s6	76	989
–	–	s7	–	–	90	90¹	90	–	–	–	–	90	–	90	990
90²	–	90	–	–	78	–	90	–	90	–	–	s20	s12	74¹	990
75	–	–	–	–	s15	90	90	90	–	–	–	90	–	s45	990
90¹	–	–	–	–	–	77	90	s13	–	–	–	90	s25	90¹	990
79□	–	–	–	–	s1	s11¹	90	–	–	–	–	90	–	90	990
90¹	–	–	–	–	s5	90	90	–	–	–	–	90□	–	85¹	990
–	–	–	–	–	90	90	90	–	–	–	–	90	–	–	990
74¹	–	–	–	90	90	86	–	–	–	s4	–	90□	–	–	990

THE MANAGER

ARSENE WENGER

Arsène Wenger was appointed Arsenal manager in 1997. Formerly in charge of Nancy Lorraine, Monaco (the club he guided to the French championship in 1988) and Japanese side Grampus Eight, Wenger's arrival was greeted with scepticism by many who questioned his credentials for the job. Five seasons later and Wenger is widely recognised as one of the brightest managerial talents in European football.

After guiding Arsenal to third place in 1996–97, Wenger led his side to the double in his first full season in charge. The Highbury trophy room has remained bare since then, but Arsenal have finished as runners-up to Manchester United in three successive seasons, reached a UEFA Cup and FA Cup final and, most importantly, established themselves as regulars in the Champions League.

Wenger said that he would quit club football altogether were the transfer law to be abolished. But the reforms to the current system agreed by UEFA and FIFA seem to have satisfied him. And despite interest from several high-profile foreign clubs – most notably Barcelona – Wenger ended the 2000–01 season by saying that he was keen to extend his contract at Arsenal.

LEAGUE POSITION

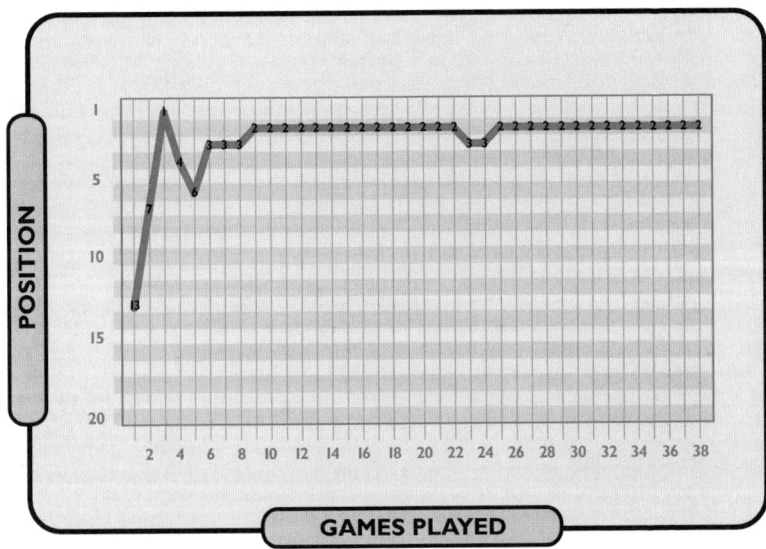

POSITION

GAMES PLAYED

9.5% of Arsenal's goals came from headers

THE GOALS

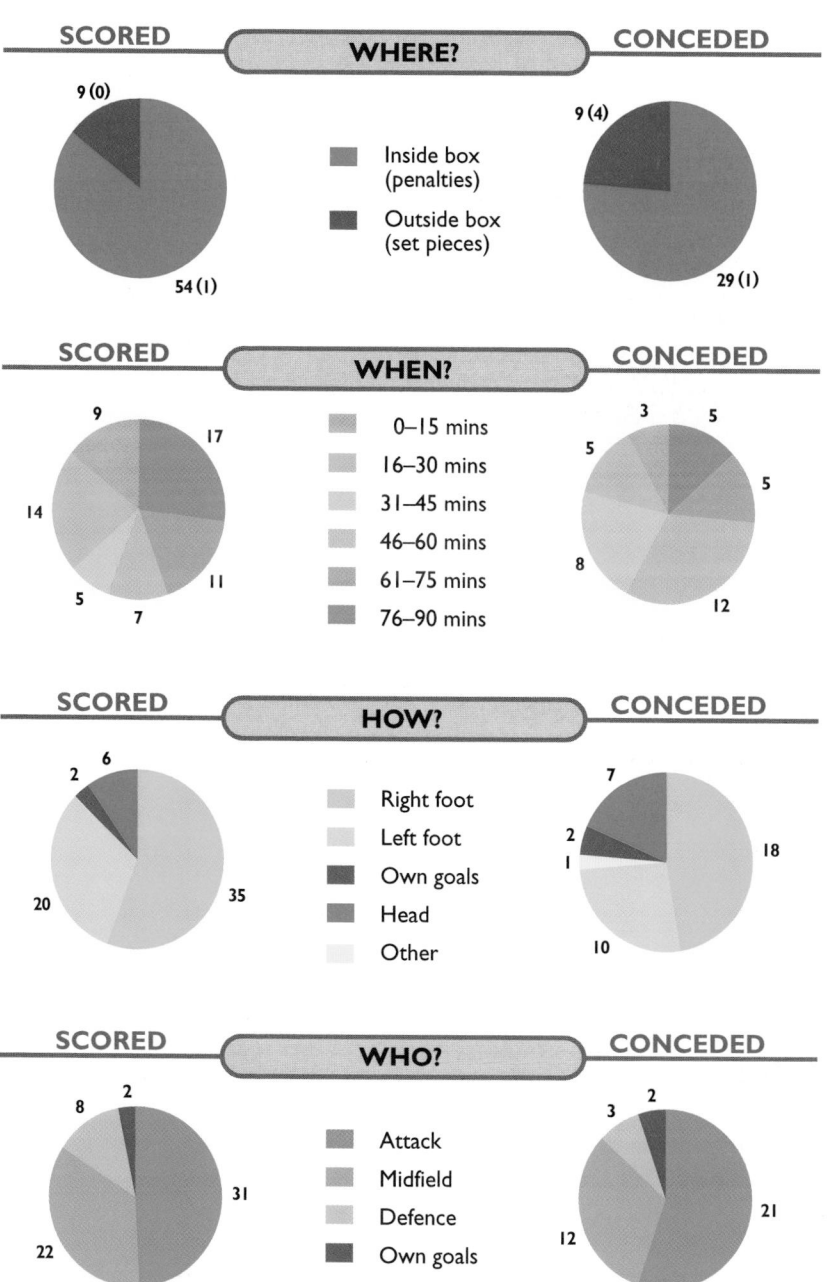

WHERE?
SCORED — CONCEDED

Inside box (penalties)
Outside box (set pieces)

Scored: 9 (0), 54 (1)
Conceded: 9 (4), 29 (1)

WHEN?
SCORED — CONCEDED

0–15 mins
16–30 mins
31–45 mins
46–60 mins
61–75 mins
76–90 mins

Scored: 9, 17, 14, 5, 7, 11
Conceded: 3, 5, 5, 5, 8, 12

HOW?
SCORED — CONCEDED

Right foot
Left foot
Own goals
Head
Other

Scored: 2, 6, 20, 35
Conceded: 7, 2, 1, 18, 10

WHO?
SCORED — CONCEDED

Attack
Midfield
Defence
Own goals

Scored: 8, 2, 31, 22
Conceded: 3, 2, 21, 12

– the lowest ratio in the Premiership

ARSENAL

	ADAMS	BERGKAMP	COLE	DANILEVICIUS	DIXON	EDU	GRIMANDI	HENRY	KANU	KEOWN	LAUREN
APPEARANCES											
Start	26	19	15	0	26	2	28	27	13	28	15
Sub	0	6	2	2	3	3	2	8	14	0	3
Minutes on pitch	2340	1698	1302	36	2383	171	2394	2589	1328	2520	1228
GOAL ATTEMPTS											
Goals	1	3	3	0	1	0	1	17	3	0	2
Shots on target	7	26	6	0	3	1	9	63	22	2	4
Shots off target	7	25	2	0	6	2	5	60	16	7	6
Shooting accuracy	50%	51%	75%	0%	33%	33%	64%	51%	58%	22%	40%
PASSING											
Goal assists	2	3	1	0	2	0	2	9	5	0	0
Long passes	423	169	133	0	441	34	371	141	119	342	104
Short passes	772	566	636	8	940	97	896	688	455	816	482
PASS COMPLETION											
Own half %	87%	78%	80%	100%	85%	86%	87%	77%	84%	86%	87%
Opposition half %	72%	65%	78%	86%	71%	76%	77%	57%	75%	66%	74%
CROSSING											
Total crosses	2	74	60	1	67	6	21	87	20	0	27
Cross completion %	0%	27%	25%	100%	30%	0%	19%	25%	40%	0%	19%
DRIBBLING											
Dribbles & runs	29	44	49	1	54	4	26	195	80	23	34
Dribble completion %	97%	66%	69%	100%	85%	50%	88%	56%	59%	100%	68%
DEFENDING											
Tackles made	68	25	67	0	49	14	81	21	27	58	42
Tackles won %	81%	88%	79%	0%	71%	57%	77%	71%	67%	69%	81%
Blocks	13	2	9	0	16	3	15	2	1	22	3
Clearances	225	3	50	0	60	3	70	8	1	229	11
Interceptions	15	0	10	0	6	1	17	3	0	6	6
DISCIPLINE											
Fouls	27	42	19	1	28	7	45	56	27	38	30
Offside	1	15	0	0	0	0	2	75	7	0	2
Yellow cards	7	2	3	0	2	0	4	4	1	3	3
Red cards	0	0	0	0	0	0	1	0	0	0	0

GOALKEEPER NAME	START/ (SUB)	TIME ON PITCH	GOALS CONCEDED	MINS/GOALS CONCEDED	SAVES MADE	SAVES/ SHOTS
LUKIC	3(0)	270	0	0	3	100%
MANNINGER	11(0)	990	15	66	26	63%
SEAMAN	24(0)	2160	23	94	49	68%

For more information visit our website:

PLAYERS' STATISTICS

	LJUNGBERG	LUZHNY	MALZ	PARLOUR	PIRES	SILVINHO	STEPANOVS	UPSON	VERNAZZA	VIEIRA	VIVAS	WILTORD	TOTAL	RANK
	25	16	0	28	29	23	9	0	0	28	3	20		
	5	3	1	5	4	1	0	2	2	2	9	7		
	2203	1394	16	2484	2491	2012	810	14	43	2542	418	1758		
	6	0	0	4	4	2	0	0	1	5	0	8	63*	5th
	32	3	0	14	23	8	1	0	1	11	1	30	267	1st
	26	2	0	20	16	10	4	0	0	16	1	23	254	3rd
	55%	60%	0%	41%	59%	44%	20%	0%	100%	41%	50%	57%	51%	1st
	3	2	0	1	7	2	0	0	0	4	1	5	49	3rd
	171	220	3	319	358	177	153	4	8	495	67	119	4675	3rd
	744	522	6	917	1025	731	235	3	15	1265	149	717	12804	2nd
	85%	87%	75%	80%	85%	80%	84%	100%	71%	86%	89%	84%	85%	2nd
	70%	75%	80%	74%	78%	73%	72%	75%	75%	79%	73%	69%	72%	2nd
	57	30	1	77	209	136	0	0	0	11	21	76	983	6th
	19%	27%	0%	19%	25%	15%	0%	0%	0%	27%	33%	25%	23%	20th
	127	33	0	114	224	89	2	0	0	100	8	126	1365	1st
	72%	76%	0%	72%	75%	55%	100%	0%	0%	66%	63%	62%	69%	9th
	92	47	1	99	61	78	18	0	7	122	15	18	1010	6th
	76%	68%	100%	76%	64%	72%	72%	0%	71%	62%	80%	78%	73%	9th
	3	1	0	3	6	10	8	0	0	9	5	1	132	20th
	15	83	0	23	14	60	86	0	1	68	8	1	1093	19th
	9	9	0	8	5	9	1	0	0	9	4	1	119	=7th
	31	8	0	45	17	32	9	0	1	67	5	11	547	14th
	4	0	0	1	4	3	0	0	0	3	0	49	166	=4th
	3	1	0	4	1	3	0	0	0	5	0	0	46	17th
	0	0	0	0	0	0	0	0	0	2	0	0	3	=7th

*Including two own goals

CROSSES CAUGHT	CROSSES PUNCHED	CROSSES DROPPED	CATCH SUCCESS	THROWS/ SHORT KICKS	% COMPLETION	LONG KICKS	% COMPLETION
0	2	0	0%	11	100%	35	66%
15	8	0	100%	40	98%	164	44%
31	8	0	100%	74	97%	356	55%

PLAYER OF THE SEASON

PLAYER	INDEX SCORE
PATRICK VIEIRA	1,088
Robert Pires	1,060
Fredrik Ljungberg	1,056
Tony Adams	1,046
Thierry Henry	1,025
Silvinho	881
Lee Dixon	842
Gilles Grimandi	819
Martin Keown	775
Ray Parlour	763

In what proved to be a testing campaign for the young Frenchman, Patrick Vieira emerged from the 2000–01 Premiership a more mature player.

The Gunners' midfielder was dismissed in successive matches at the start of the season, which led to a five-match absence from the league. But he subsequently went 16 games without a caution, and played with a determination which earned the respect of his fellow-professionals and helped fill the void left by Emmanuel Petit's departure.

Carling Player of the Year Vieira completed an outstanding 82% of passes, won more tackles than any other Gunner and scored five times to achieve an average Opta points score of 1,088 as Arsenal strived in vain to dethrone Manchester United. Consequently he was ranked by Opta as Arsenal's most effective player in 2000–01, after finishing third and fourth respectively in the previous two seasons.

Running him a close second was Robert Pires. The flying Frenchman proved an effective replacement for Barcelona-bound Marc Overmars and, after initially struggling to cope with the hectic pace of English football, Pires flourished in north London.

The Gallic marauder attempted more dribbles and runs than any other top-flight player and produced seven goal assists – the second-highest tally at Highbury – to record an average score of 1,060.

His wing partner Fredrik Ljungberg completes the top three. The Swede's energetic bursts into the box netted him six league goals, while he linked up to create a further three strikes for colleagues.

Old hand Tony Adams continued to make his presence felt, while 1999–2000 star performer Thierry Henry slumped down the Opta ratings after losing his way towards the end of 2000–01.

Ashley Cole burst on to the domestic and international scene and ranked highest of all Arsenal players, but unfortunately did not play enough to qualify for the Index.

75 Thierry Henry was caught offside more

FIVE OF THE BEST

Finishing second is almost becoming Arsenal's trademark and once again they had to settle for a place behind Manchester United in the Premiership. Arsène Wenger did manage to coax some great performances from his troops, but the lack of a consistent cutting edge cost the Gunners dear.

TOP GOALSCORERS

	GOALS	GOALS/SHOTS
THIERRY HENRY	17	14%
Sylvain Wiltord	8	15%
Fredrik Ljungberg	6	10%
Patrick Vieira	5	19%
Ray Parlour	4	12%

Thierry Henry matched his achievements of 1999–2000 and once again scored 17 Premiership goals in 2000–01, but his conversion rate fell to 14% as he missed a lot of chances for the Gunners. Fellow-Frenchman Sylvain Wiltord scored almost as many goals in the FA Cup as he did in the league, but was slightly more clinical than Henry, while Patrick Vieira managed a goal with almost one-fifth of his strikes.

Patrick Vieira stole the plaudits in 2000–01 with some awesome midfield displays. At times it seemed as if he alone was driving the Gunners' midfield forward. He made in excess of 300 passes more than any other Arsenal player and managed a superb completion rate of 82%. Newcomer Robert Pires was also slick on the ball as the team improved on their efforts in 1999–2000. Lee Dixon finished third, still a vital member of the side in his late 30s.

TOP PASSERS

	SUCC PASSES	COMPLETION
PATRICK VIEIRA	1,438	82%
Robert Pires	1,102	80%
Lee Dixon	1,063	77%
Gilles Grimandi	1,037	82%
Tony Adams	976	82%

TOP TACKLERS

	WON	SUCCESS
PATRICK VIEIRA	76	62%
Ray Parlour	75	76%
Fredrik Ljungberg	70	76%
Gilles Grimandi	62	77%
Silvinho	56	72%

Arsenal's midfield may be graceful but it is also tough-tackling, with Patrick Vieira, Ray Parlour and Fredrik Ljungberg all making more than 70 challenges. But Gilles Grimandi was the Gunners' most successful ball-winner, emerging with the ball in 77% of his tackles. Brazilian international Silvinho finished fifth but would have been higher if he could have displaced young Ashley Cole from the left-back berth.

Patrick Vieira's season started in disastrous fashion with red cards in successive games against Sunderland and Liverpool. It seemed likely to end his career in England at one point, but he battled back in style and accrued just five bookings in the rest of the season. Skipper Tony Adams collected seven yellow cards, but conceded just 27 fouls in the process. Gilles Grimandi was the only other Gunner to be sent off.

DISCIPLINE

	POINTS	FOULS & CARDS
PATRICK VIEIRA	94	67F, 5Y, 2R
Thierry Henry	68	56F, 4Y, 0R
Gilles Grimandi	63	45F, 4Y, 1R
Ray Parlour	57	45F, 4Y, 0R
Tony Adams	48	27F, 7Y, 0R

ACTION	ADAMS	COLE	DIXON	GRIMANDI	HENRY	KANU	LJUNGBERG	MANNINGER	PARLOUR	PIRES	SILVINHO	STEPANOVS	VIEIRA	VIVAS	TOTAL	LEICESTER CITY
Time on pitch	90	5	90	77	90	74	16	90	90	85	90	90	90	13	990	990
GOALS																
Goal	–	–	–	–	3	1	1	–	–	1	–	–	–	–	6	1
Shot on target (incl goals)	–	–	–	1	8	1	2	–	–	2	–	–	1	–	15	2
Shot off target	2	–	–	1	1	1	–	–	2	2	–	1	1	–	11	–
Blocked shot	–	–	–	–	–	–	–	–	–	–	–	–	–	–	4	–
Own goal	–	–	–	–	–	–	–	–	–	–	–	–	–	–	0	0
PASSES																
Pass to own player	48	–	50	54	23	39	3	10	41	51	48	39	73	7	486	206
Pass to opposition	5	–	10	5	7	12	2	3	13	11	9	6	8	1	92	110
Cross to own player	–	–	2	–	3	–	–	–	–	5	2	–	–	–	12	0
Cross to opposition player	–	–	1	–	2	2	–	–	1	8	6	–	–	1	21	1
Goal assist	–	–	1	–	2	1	–	–	–	1	–	–	–	–	5	0
Pass completion %	91%	0%	80%	92%	76%	75%	60%	77%	75%	75%	77%	87%	90%	89%	82%	65%
TACKLES & CLEARANCES																
Tackle	3	–	2	2	1	–	–	–	1	1	1	1	2	–	14	30
Clearances, blocks and interceptions	4	–	1	–	–	–	–	–	–	–	–	10	–	–	15	51
DRIBBLES & RUNS																
Dribbles ball retained	–	–	2	–	2	1	1	–	2	3	2	–	1	–	14	10
Dribbles ball lost	–	–	–	–	6	–	–	–	1	2	4	–	–	–	13	3
Dribble success %	0%	0%	100%	0%	25%	100%	100%	0%	67%	60%	33%	0%	100%	–	52%	77%
DISCIPLINE																
Fouls	–	–	–	3	2	1	1	–	1	–	–	1	5	–	14	10
Penalty conceded	–	–	–	–	–	–	–	–	–	–	–	–	–	–	0	0
Free kick – offside	–	–	–	–	4	1	–	–	–	1	–	–	1	–	7	3
Yellow cards	–	–	–	–	–	–	–	–	–	–	–	–	–	–	0	2
Red cards	–	–	–	–	–	–	–	–	–	–	–	–	–	–	0	0
GOALKEEPERS																
Distribution to own player	–	–	–	–	–	–	–	4	–	–	–	–	–	–	4	9
Distribution to opposition player	–	–	–	–	–	–	–	5	–	–	–	–	–	–	5	14
Goalkeeper distribution %	–	–	–	–	–	–	–	44%	–	–	–	–	–	–	44%	39%
Save	–	–	–	–	–	–	–	1	–	–	–	–	–	–	1	9
Ball caught	–	–	–	–	–	–	–	–	–	–	–	–	–	–	0	1
Ball dropped	–	–	–	–	–	–	–	–	–	–	–	–	–	–	0	0
Goal conceded	–	–	–	–	–	–	–	1	–	–	–	–	–	–	1	6

On Boxing Day 1997, Arsenal had kick-started their extraordinary romp to the title with a 2–1 win over Leicester at Highbury. Three years on and with a host of new faces in the side, the home fans wondered: could the Gunners repeat the feat?

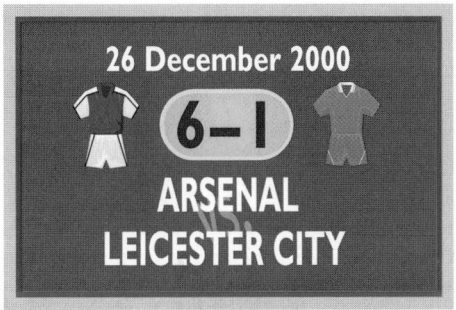

26 December 2000

6–1

ARSENAL
LEICESTER CITY

Tough-tackling Leicester were third in the table and had at the time the second-best defensive record in the Premiership, which made the eventual outcome all the more surprising.

Debutant Igors Stepanovs was among a whole host of players forced to don gloves on this bitterly cold afternoon, but thankfully Arsenal were full of enough running to ensure frostbite was kept at bay.

Despite dominating for the opening half-hour, the Gunners had to wait until the 34th minute for the breakthrough. The impressive Ray Parlour won a corner which Robert Pires sent across to the edge of the area. Thierry Henry was waiting in the 'D' and duly despatched a superb half-volley into the bottom right-hand corner of the net. One-nil to the Arsenal.

Three minutes later, Flowers flew brilliantly to his left to deny Patrick Vieira, who had been allowed space in the box by Gerry Taggart. The Foxes defender was clearly carrying a knock, and was duly taken off – resulting in yet more room to manoeuvre for Henry.

Five minutes after the break, the game's best move unfolded. An intricate collection of passes found Nwankwo Kanu in space. His ball to Henry was flipped up by the Frenchman to compatriot Vieira who surged into the box, controlling the ball on his knee, before lobbing it over Flowers and tapping into the unguarded net.

But any thoughts of the Gunners running away with the game were forgotten four minutes later when a Trevor Benjamin header was spilled by Alex Manninger and Ade Akinbiyi pounced to reduce the deficit.

Arsenal stepped up a gear. Another incredible Flowers save kept his side in the game, while a Tony Adams effort was bundled out by Andy Impey and the post.

Then the Gunners were denied a penalty when Impey brought down Pires in the box.

Arsenal extended their lead on 66 minutes. Matt Elliott was made to look foolish by Henry, who turned the big Scot just inside the box before slipping the ball under Flowers to restore the two-goal lead.

From then on, the Gunners ran riot. Substitute Fredrik Ljungberg scored with his first touch after Stepanovs had hit a post – and Henry, looking suspiciously offside, completed his hat-trick having rounded Flowers to make it five.

What better way to seal the win than with a goal from the skipper? Adams ran the length of the pitch in the closing stages to bury a Henry cross high into the net, to the delight of the Highbury faithful.

A fine afternoon's work from the Gunners was spearheaded by a remarkable performance from Henry. His three goals and two assists gave him the highest-ever Opta points score for a player in a single match – a splendid 3,931 points.

goals were scored by overseas players

ASTON VILLA

ADDRESS

Villa Park, Trinity Road,
Birmingham B6 6HE

CONTACT NUMBERS

Telephone: 0121 327 2299
Fax: 0121 322 2107
Commercial: 0121 327 5399
Ticket Office: 0121 327 5353
Club Call: 09068 121148
Villa Village Superstore:
0121 327 2800
e-mail: postmaster@astonvilla-fc.co.uk
Website: www.astonvilla-fc.co.uk

KEY PERSONNEL

Chairman: H D Ellis
President: J A Alderson
Executive Directors:
M J Ansell (Deputy Chief Executive),
S M Stride (Operations Director)
Non-Executive Directors: D M Owen,
A J Hales, P D Ellis, G Taylor
Manager: John Gregory

SPONSORS

NTL

FANZINES

Heroes and Villans
The Holy Trinity

COLOURS

Home: Claret shirts with
sky blue sleeves, sky blue
shorts and claret stockings
Away: black shirts,
black shorts and black stockings

NICKNAME

The Villans

HONOURS

League Champions: 1893-94,
1895-96, 1896-97, 1898-99,
1899-00, 1909-10, 1980-81
Division Two Champions:
1937-38, 1959-60
Division Three Champions: 1971-72
FA Cup Winners: 1887, 1895,
1897, 1905, 1913, 1920, 1957
League Cup Winners: 1961,
1975, 1977, 1994, 1996
European Cup Winners: 1982
European Super Cup Winners: 1983

RECORD GOALSCORER

Harry Hampton – 215 league goals,
1904–15

BIGGEST WIN

13–0 v Wednesbury Old Ath – FA Cup
1st round, 30 October 1886

BIGGEST DEFEAT

1–8 v Blackburn Rovers – FA Cup 3rd
round, 16 February 1889

SEASON REVIEW

Aston Villa have become known as one of English football's greatest underachievers over the past few years and their performances in the 2000–01 campaign did little to improve their faltering reputation.

Villa had narrowly lost out to Chelsea in the FA Cup final the previous season and therefore missed out on an automatic UEFA Cup place, scraping into Europe by qualifying for the Intertoto Cup. But the club was dealt a series of huge blows before it could begin to strengthen for the new campaign.

Club captain Gareth Southgate went on the transfer list after becoming disillusioned with the club's apparent lack of ambition, while defensive partner Ugo Ehiogu and striker Julian Joachim joined him there. Loan star Benito Carbone's decision to choose lowly Bradford City over Villa only served to heighten the frustration of manager John Gregory.

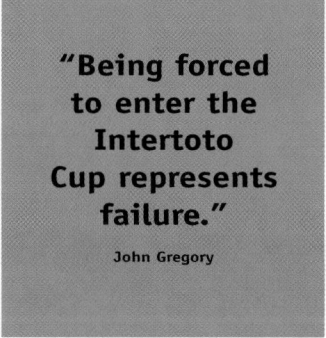

> "Being forced to enter the Intertoto Cup represents failure."
>
> John Gregory

The potential loss of both Southgate and Ehiogu was a crushing blow. Villa had prided themselves on their defensive abilities; indeed, they shipped just 35 goals in 1999–2000 – the third-lowest total in the Premiership.

Attempts to strengthen the squad saw numerous stars from across the continent linked with the club, but Gregory was unable to prise the player that he really wanted, Benni McCarthy, from his club Celta Vigo. Instead the Villa manager plumped for the solid presence of Turkish defender Alpay, while bolstering his attacking options with the signing of two ageing superstars, Tottenham's David Ginola and PSV Eindhoven's Luc Nilis.

The latter made an instant impact at Villa Park, scoring on his home debut in the 3–1 win over Dukla Pribram in the Intertoto Cup, a win that set up an intriguing tie with Celta in the next round. With predictable poignancy, Villa were dumped out 3–1 on aggregate, with McCarthy grabbing all of the Spanish side's goals to increase Gregory's disappointment at not getting his man.

Still, the club started their league campaign in relatively high spirits, with all three of their transfer rebels still on the payroll, admittedly because no club would meet Villa's asking prices. However, the first time that Ehiogu and Southgate were paired together in defence the club was trounced 3–1 by Liverpool, with Michael Owen grabbing a hat-trick. It was to be Ehiogu's last start for the club before an £8 million move to Middlesbrough.

The situation at Villa Park took a turn for the worse in the next game, when Ipswich 'keeper Richard Wright's tackle on Nilis broke the Belgian legend's leg in two places, ending his Villa career after just four starts.

Ironically, that match sparked what was arguably Villa's best run of the season, in which they won five of their next nine games, taking them from 19th place in the league to fifth spot.

However, the club's lack of firepower was beginning to take its toll. With Dion Dublin failing to find form or fitness Villa had no settled front line, so the fact that they managed to hit the target with just 39% of their shots all season – the worst rating in the Premiership – was no real surprise.

Ginola was a huge disappointment and Gregory seemed flummoxed as to where the Gallic genius would be deployed best. He often preferred the more workmanlike duo of George Boateng and Ian Taylor in midfield, while attempts to play Ginola at wing-back were inevitably unsuccessful.

Consequently, the former French international managed to complete 90 minutes on just five occasions all season.

SEASON REVIEW

For many pundits, this evoked memories of Ginola's strained relationship at Spurs with former manager George Graham and made a mockery of chairman Doug Ellis's earlier assertion that Ginola was "the most exciting player in Europe".

At least Gregory could still call on the services of the remarkably energetic Paul Merson. Going into his 34th year, the former Arsenal midfielder showed himself to be a model of consistency, starting every league game in 2000–01 and prompting speculation about a surprise England recall.

Merson grabbed the winning goal against Charlton in October and illuminated the following game when he scored the only goal of an otherwise drab affair at Everton with a superb last-minute chip, cementing the Villans' place in the top five.

But then the results tailed off dramatically. Villa won just one of their next 11 league fixtures – a disastrous run which culminated in five consecutive losses and left the club in the bottom half of the table. By this stage, the Villa Park faithful were baying not only for the manager's head, but also for the resignation of controversial chairman Ellis. The situation at last prompted the management to splash their cash, and Colombian forward Juan Pablo Angel was brought in to solve their goalscoring crisis for £9.5 million – five long months after Nilis's enforced retirement.

Angel had been one of the biggest superstars in Argentinean football at River Plate, where he had averaged better than a goal every other game.

However, his contribution to the Villa cause was brought into question almost immediately, as his repeatedly lacklustre performances brought scorn from fans and pundits alike.

> ## "Realistically, how high do you think Villa can get? Sixth would be a feat, I'd say. If we finish third, that would be as good as a championship."
>
> **Paul Merson**

Not only did Angel seem incapable of finding the back of the net, he could not even hit a shot on target. Indeed, by the time he forced a save from Paul Gerrard against Everton in April, the 25-year-old had gone through seven appearances, nine shots and 424 minutes of Premiership action before reeling off his first accurate effort on goal.

This period had also seen Villa crash out of the FA Cup to "bogey" team Leicester, a game in which Villa striker Darius Vassell was dismissed, much to Gregory's chagrin.

Fortunately, the club had at last turned around their league form, and midfielder Lee Hendrie was looking increasingly influential. The young England international scored four times in five games in March and April, forcing draws against West Ham and Charlton and sealing wins over Manchester City and (much to the joy of Villa fans) Leicester.

Hendrie finished the campaign as Villa's joint-third highest scorer with six goals and also set up five strikes for team-mates. Unfortunately, an FA fine for his over-exuberant goal celebrations tempered the youngster's end-of-season achievements.

Villa fans were at last given something to cheer about during their penultimate game of the season. The Villans came from 2–0 down to beat local rivals Coventry and relegate the Sky Blues to Division One. Even Angel got in on the act, coming off the bench to grab the equaliser – his first goal in English football.

But given their season, it seemed out of character for Villa to leave their fans with a sense of triumph during the summer months. The 3–0 last day defeat at Newcastle provided a more fitting conclusion to an uninspiring campaign which is probably best forgotten.

ASTON VILLA

DATE	OPPONENT	SCORE	ATT.	ALPAY	ANGEL	BARRY	BOATENG	DE BILDE	DELANEY	DUBLIN	EHIOGU	GINOLA
19.08.00	Leicester A	0–0	21,455	90	–	90	90	–	–	90	–	60□
27.08.00	Chelsea H	1–1	27,057	90	–	90	90	–	–	90	–	–
06.09.00	Liverpool A	1–3	43,360	69	–	90	65	–	–	90	90□	s21
09.09.00	Ipswich A	2–1	20,665	90	–	90	90□	–	–	90¹	s61	s29□
16.09.00	Bradford H	2–0	27,849	90	–	90	90	–	–	90¹	–	70
23.09.00	Middlesbro A	1–1	27,556	90	–	90	66	–	–	90	–	66
30.09.00	Derby Co H	4–1	26,534	90	–	90	s21	–	–	90	–	18
14.10.00	Arsenal A	0–1	38,042	90□	–	90	s19	–	–	71	–	–
22.10.00	Sunderland H	0–0	27,215	90□	–	90	s17	–	–	70	–	–
28.10.00	Charlton H	2–1	27,461	90□	–	90	90	–	–	90	–	–
05.11.00	Everton A	1–0	27,670	90	–	90	90□	76	s31	–	–	–
11.11.00	Tottenham H	2–0	33,608	90	–	90	90	–	s66	90	–	s12
18.11.00	Southampton A	0–2	14,979	90	–	62	90	–	s45	90	–	s28
25.11.00	Coventry A	1–1	21,464	90	–	90□	90□	–	s30	90¹	–	–
02.12.00	Newcastle H	1–1	34,225	90	–	90	90	–	–	90¹	–	79
09.12.00	West Ham A	1–1	25,888	90□	–	90□	90	–	–	90	–	90□
16.12.00	Man City H	2–2	29,281	90	–	62	90	–	s28	90¹	–	90¹□
23.12.00	Leeds Utd A	2–1	39,714	90□	–	90	90¹□	71	–	–	–	83
26.12.00	Man Utd H	0–1	40,889	37	–	86	90□	66	s53	s24	–	90
01.01.01	Chelsea A	0–1	33,159	–	–	–	90	90	90	76	–	–
13.01.01	Liverpool H	0–3	41,366	45□	–	90	–	–	–	90	–	45
20.01.01	Man Utd A	0–2	67,533	90	64	83	90□	–	–	90	–	s7
24.01.01	Leeds Utd H	1–2	29,335	90□	90	90□	90	–	s11	–	–	s21
03.02.01	Bradford A	3–0	19,591	90	75	44	90	–	90	–	–	–
10.02.01	Middlesbro H	1–1	28,912	90□	75	–	90	–	90	s15	–	–
24.02.01	Derby Co A	0–1	27,289	90	45	90	90□	–	–	90	–	s16
05.03.01	Sunderland A	1–1	47,196	90□	–	90	–	–	–	90	–	–
10.03.01	Ipswich H	2–1	28,216	90	–	s1	–	–	–	90	–	89□
18.03.01	Arsenal H	0–0	36,111	90	66	–	–	–	–	s13	–	90
31.03.01	Man City A	3–1	34,247	90	–	–	90□	–	90	89¹□	–	–
04.04.01	Leicester H	2–1	29,043	90□	–	–	71	–	90	90¹	–	s31
07.04.01	West Ham H	2–2	31,432	–	–	90	–	–	90	–	–	90¹□
14.04.01	Everton H	2–1	31,272	90	s12	–	90	–	90	78¹	–	s20
17.04.01	Charlton A	3–3	20,043	90□	–	–	45	–	90	90□	–	s45¹
21.04.01	Southampton H	0–0	29,336	–	–	90	90	–	90	90	–	s37
28.04.01	Tottenham A	0–0	36,096	–	–	90	90	–	90	90	–	s10
05.05.01	Coventry H	3–2	39,761	–	s26¹□	90	45	–	90	90	–	s49
19.05.01	Newcastle A	0–3	51,506	90□	63	–	s47□	–	90□	s45	–	43□

□ Yellow card, ■ Red card, s Substitute, 90² Goals scored
*including own goal

For more information visit our website:

2000–01 PREMIERSHIP APPEARANCES

HENDRIE	HITZLSPERGER	JAMES	JOACHIM	McGRATH	MERSON	NILIS	SAMUEL	SOUTHGATE	STAUNTON	STONE	TAYLOR	VASSELL	WRIGHT	TOTAL
90	–	90	–	–	90□	–	–	90	–	90	–	s30□	90	990
88	–	90	s20	–	90	70¹	–	90	–	90	s2	–	90	990
s25	–	90	–	–	90	90	–	90□	–	90¹	90□	–	–	990
90¹	–	90	–	–	90	8	–	29	–	90□	–	s53	90	990
58	–	90	s20	–	90	–	–	90¹	–	90	s32	–	90	990
s24	–	90	s24¹	–	90	–	–	90	–	90	90	–	90	990
69	–	90	s71²	–	90¹	–	–	90	–	90	90	s1	90¹	990
66□	–	90	90	–	90	–	–	90□	–	90□	90	s19	71	966
73	–	90	90	–	90	–	–	90	–	90	90	s20	90	990
–	–	90	74	–	90¹	–	–	90	–	90	90¹□	s16	90□	990
–	–	90	90	–	90¹	–	–	90	–	59	90	s14□	90	990
–	–	90	78	–	90	–	–	24	–	90	90²	–	90	990
s45	–	90	90	–	45	–	–	90	–	45	90	–	90	990
90	–	90	–	–	90	–	–	90	–	90	60	–	90	990
90□	–	90	–	–	90	–	s11	90	–	90	–	–	90□	990
90¹	–	90	–	–	90	–	–	90	–	90	–	–	90	990
77□	–	90	–	–	90	–	–	90	–	90□	–	–	90	977
90	–	90	–	–	90□	–	s7	90¹	–	90□	–	s19	90	990
90	–	90	–	–	90	–	–	90	–	90	–	s4	90	990
–	–	90	–	s8	90	–	–	90	82	90	90□	s14	90	990
–	s6	90	–	s45	90	–	84	90□	90	90	–	s45	90	990
90	–	90	–	–	90	–	–	–	90	90□	–	s26	90	990
90	–	90	–	–	90¹	–	–	–	90	79	54	s36	69	990
90	–	90	s15¹	s1	89	–	–	–	90	–	s46	90²	90	990
66	–	90	90	–	90	–	–	–	90	90¹	s24	–	90	990
s27	–	90	s45	–	90	–	–	–	90	90	74	–	63	990
90	–	90	90¹	–	90	–	–	–	90	90□	90	–	90	990
90	–	90	90²	–	90	–	–	90	90	90	90	–	–	990
90	–	90	77	–	90	–	–	90□	–	90□	90	s24	90	990
90¹	–	90	s15	–	75¹	–	–	90□	s32	90	58	s1	90□	990
90¹	–	90	s19	–	90	–	–	90	–	59□	90	–	90	990
90¹	–	90	90	–	90	–	–	90	62	61	90	s29	s28	990
70	–	90	–	–	90	–	–	90	–	62	90¹	s28	90	990
90¹	–	90	–	–	90	–	–	–	90	45	90	s45¹	90	990
90□	–	90	–	–	90	–	–	90	–	–	53	90	90	990
–	–	90	s10	–	90	–	–	90	80	–	90	80	90	990
s45□	–	90	–	–	90¹	–	–	90	41	–	90	64¹	90	990
90	–	90	–	–	90	–	–	90□	–	s27	84□	45	90	984

THE MANAGER

JOHN GREGORY

Few football fans have mixed feelings about John Gregory. His often controversial management style and forthright views have infuriated supporters of almost every top-flight team since he joined Aston Villa in February 1998 and yet he has become one of the most respected managers in the game for the very same modus operandi.

He is known to be able to bring the best out of young players such as Lee Hendrie and Darius Vassell, although Julian Joachim, Gareth Southgate and, most recently, David Ginola have certainly had their names crossed off the 47-year-old's Christmas card list.

Following his playing days with, among others, QPR, Derby and Villa themselves, Gregory's management career began at Portsmouth, but it was with Wycombe that he came to prominence, saving the club from relegation when the task was seemingly impossible before his arrival.

Gregory has stated that he wants the Aston Villa job for life, declaring: "I am a Villa man through and through, and I don't ever want to go anywhere else."

He may need to improve on eighth place in the Premiership in 2000–01, if the Villa fans are to keep the faith.

LEAGUE POSITION

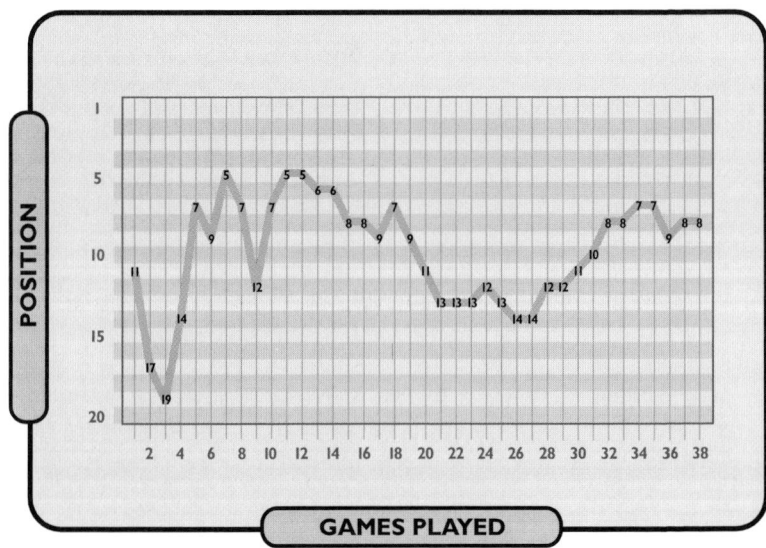

POSITION

GAMES PLAYED

4 goals for Julian Joachim when coming off the bench

THE GOALS

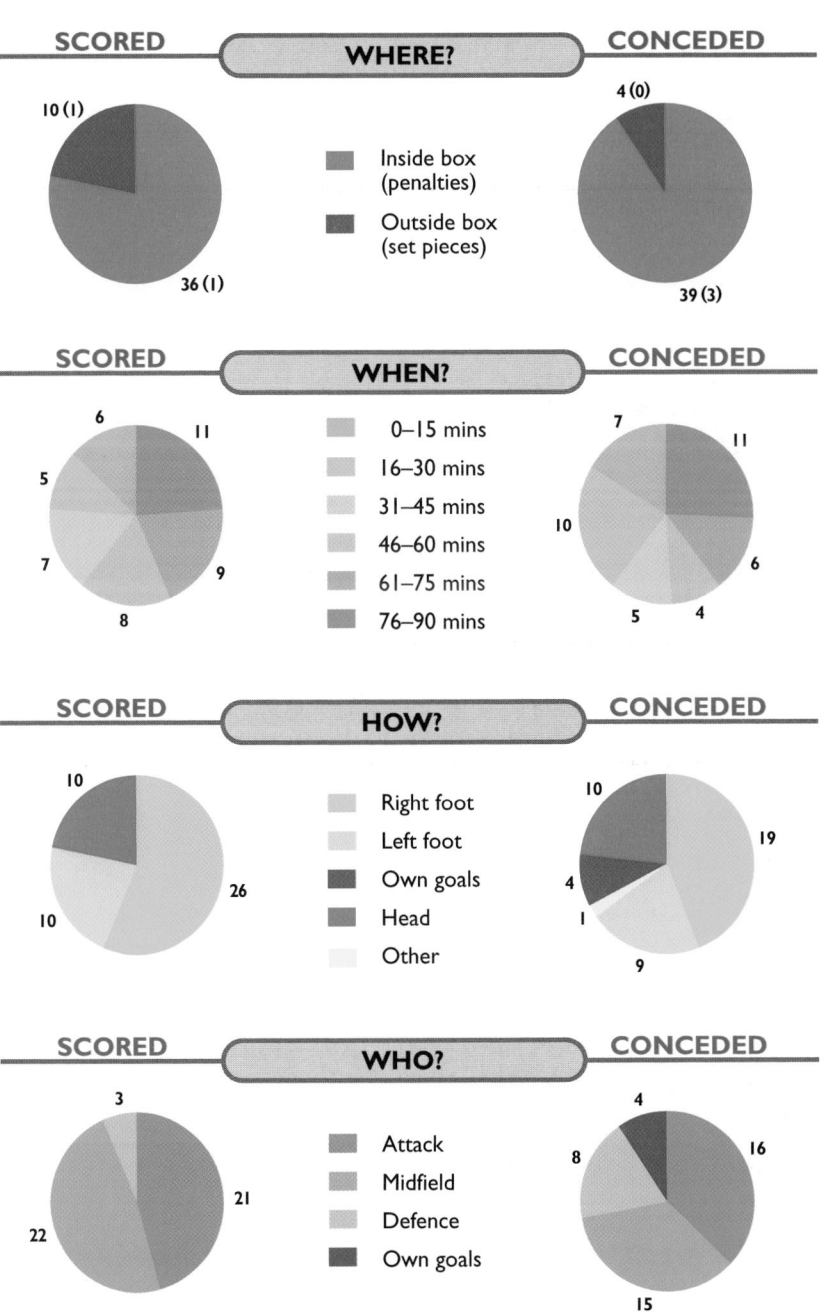

SCORED | **WHERE?** | CONCEDED

10 (1)

Inside box (penalties)

Outside box (set pieces)

36 (1)

4 (0)

39 (3)

SCORED | **WHEN?** | CONCEDED

6
11
5
7
9
8

0–15 mins
16–30 mins
31–45 mins
46–60 mins
61–75 mins
76–90 mins

7
11
10
6
5
4

SCORED | **HOW?** | CONCEDED

10
26
10

Right foot
Left foot
Own goals
Head
Other

10
19
4
1
9

SCORED | **WHO?** | CONCEDED

3
21
22

Attack
Midfield
Defence
Own goals

4
16
8
15

ASTON VILLA

	ALPAY	ANGEL	BARRY	BOATENG	DE BILDE	DELANEY	DUBLIN	EHIOGU	GINOLA
APPEARANCES									
Start	33	7	29	29	4	12	29	1	14
Sub	0	2	1	4	0	7	4	1	13
Minutes on pitch	2851	516	2498	2556	303	1344	2641	151	1329
GOAL ATTEMPTS									
Goals	0	1	0	1	0	0	8	0	3
Shots on target	4	2	3	6	2	0	33	0	12
Shots off target	15	12	7	12	3	0	48	1	11
Shooting accuracy	21%	14%	30%	33%	40%	0%	41%	0%	52%
PASSING									
Goal assists	0	1	0	0	0	0	4	0	4
Long passes	316	17	457	370	4	140	118	23	94
Short passes	745	155	750	1044	111	433	720	45	472
PASS COMPLETION									
Own half %	81%	83%	76%	87%	81%	80%	79%	78%	87%
Opposition half %	59%	64%	63%	75%	56%	66%	62%	58%	69%
CROSSING									
Total crosses	9	2	45	34	2	33	3	1	158
Cross completion %	0%	50%	22%	15%	0%	18%	33%	0%	21%
DRIBBLING									
Dribbles & runs	23	5	61	63	4	38	11	1	174
Dribble completion %	100%	40%	84%	76%	50%	82%	45%	100%	63%
DEFENDING									
Tackles made	121	9	70	123	3	67	22	7	10
Tackles won %	72%	44%	74%	72%	100%	76%	45%	100%	80%
Blocks	26	0	16	12	0	9	6	3	1
Clearances	292	1	194	31	0	69	53	16	1
Interceptions	23	0	7	7	0	10	2	3	3
DISCIPLINE									
Fouls	55	15	45	74	17	13	90	2	25
Offside	0	10	0	4	5	0	34	0	6
Yellow cards	12	1	3	9	0	1	2	1	7
Red cards	0	0	0	0	0	0	0	0	0

GOALKEEPER NAME	START/ (SUB)	TIME ON PITCH	GOALS CONCEDED	MINS/GOALS CONCEDED	SAVES MADE	SAVES/ SHOTS
JAMES	38(0)	3420	43	80	113	72%

For more information visit our website:

PLAYERS' STATISTICS

	HENDRIE	HITZLSPERGER	JOACHIM	McGRATH	MERSON	NILIS	SAMUEL	SOUTHGATE	STAUNTON	STONE	TAYLOR	VASSELL	WRIGHT	TOTAL	RANK
	27	0	11	0	38	3	1	31	13	33	25	5	35		
	5	1	9	3	0	0	2	0	1	1	4	18	1		
	2443	6	1188	54	3359	168	102	2663	1107	2777	2197	793	3111		
	6	0	7	0	6	1	0	2	0	2	4	4	1	46	=9th
	23	0	17	0	18	3	0	6	1	3	8	8	3	152	=18th
	31	1	7	0	44	1	0	8	4	9	11	12	4	241	10th
	43%	0%	71%	0%	29%	75%	0%	43%	20%	25%	42%	40%	43%	39%	20th
	5	0	1	0	6	0	0	1	2	2	2	1	4	33	=8th
	246	2	18	3	585	3	18	450	226	329	137	20	402	4446	7th
	1030	2	259	16	1500	50	40	612	390	1047	701	249	1176	11600	6th
	87%	100%	71%	50%	85%	77%	93%	84%	78%	80%	81%	81%	77%	81%	7th
	77%	33%	68%	60%	68%	70%	60%	58%	57%	72%	68%	62%	72%	66%	4th
	25	0	20	3	279	8	2	4	65	108	8	16	92	917	10th
	32%	0%	45%	33%	32%	25%	0%	50%	23%	29%	13%	19%	35%	27%	9th
	62	0	62	1	200	8	4	63	17	88	15	53	41	1001	6th
	69%	0%	44%	100%	73%	88%	50%	89%	65%	73%	67%	66%	88%	72%	2nd
	49	1	17	0	33	0	2	84	35	86	87	33	71	934	16th
	69%	0%	47%	0%	79%	0%	50%	73%	60%	76%	74%	70%	70%	71%	16th
	10	0	1	0	0	0	0	41	10	12	10	0	23	181	16th
	25	0	1	1	2	0	1	289	52	64	32	0	99	1303	14th
	7	0	2	0	1	0	0	15	6	9	10	0	14	119	=7th
	28	0	17	2	13	1	2	23	7	57	38	31	17	572	6th
	15	0	16	0	15	4	0	0	1	4	3	15	0	132	=12th
	3	0	0	0	2	0	0	6	0	8	3	2	3	63	10th
	2	0	0	0	0	0	0	0	0	0	1	0	0	3	=7th

CROSSES CAUGHT	CROSSES PUNCHED	CROSSES DROPPED	CATCH SUCCESS	THROWS/ SHORT KICKS	% COMPLETION	LONG KICKS	% COMPLETION
102	26	10	91%	61	66%	752	47%

PLAYER OF THE SEASON

PLAYER	INDEX SCORE
GARETH SOUTHGATE	905
Lee Hendrie	893
Paul Merson	817
Alan Wright	790
Alpay	774
George Boateng	758
Steve Stone	740
David James	731
Gareth Barry	694
Dion Dublin	665

Internal wrangling and player unrest characterised what was a disappointing 2000–01 season for Aston Villa. So it is perhaps fitting that Gareth Southgate was ranked as Villa's best player by Opta, with Lee Hendrie just behind him in second place with a score of 893.

Southgate repeatedly voiced his desire to move to a club with genuine European aspirations and quit as skipper at the end of the season, while Hendrie was in and out of the side after disciplinary problems saw him dismissed twice before Christmas as well as facing FA charges for over-enthusiastic celebrations.

But despite his misgivings, ex-Crystal Palace captain Southgate was solid in defence, with nearly 300 clearances and 84 tackles contested, helping him amass an average Opta score of 905 points. Indeed, Villa won just one and lost three of the seven matches he missed and his departure would leave a difficult gap to fill.

Gifted youngster Hendrie looked to force his way back into England contention by impressing new coach Sven-Göran Eriksson. He scored six for the Villans and created five strikes for colleagues, while maintaining an enviable 77% pass completion rate in the opposition half.

Paul Merson was arguably Villa's most consistently creative force. He was one of only four Premiership players to complete more than 1,500 passes, while he scored six goals and created the same number for colleagues to record a third-best average score of 817 points.

Ultimately Villa's lack of punch in front of goal cost them. Tellingly, only Dion Dublin from the attackers made it into the top 10, while not one player reached double figures for league goals.

Key big-name signings failed to impress either, as Villa's campaign petered out. Juan Pablo Angel did little to elevate spirits following his £9.5 million move from River Plate and he managed just two shots on target for Villa, while David Ginola never got going after arriving from Tottenham Hotspur.

FIVE OF THE BEST

John Gregory faced the prospect of the sack once again in 2000–01, but Aston Villa managed to pick up points when it mattered and ended the season in eighth place. The performances of such highly-paid stars as David Ginola and Juan Pablo Angel left a lot to be desired, though.

TOP GOALSCORERS

	GOALS	GOALS/SHOTS
DION DUBLIN	8	10%
Julian Joachim	7	29%
Lee Hendrie	6	11%
Paul Merson	6	10%
Ian Taylor	4	21%

Villa's main problem in 2000–01 was goalscoring – and the fact that top scorer Dion Dublin finished the campaign with only eight goals highlights that fact. Occasional strike partner Julian Joachim was not on speaking terms with his manager for much of the season, but still scored seven times, with a conversion rate of almost 30%. Midfielders Lee Hendrie and Paul Merson chipped in with six strikes apiece, but it simply was not enough.

After a wayward 1999–2000 season, the Villans improved their passing in 2000–01, with Paul Merson making the most successful deliveries. Tiny wing-back Alan Wright was also reliable on the left flank, while the team possessed a number of players who could be relied on to deliver accurate passes throughout a match. England prospect Lee Hendrie and Dutchman George Boateng both completed more than 80% of their distribution.

TOP PASSERS

	SUCC PASSES	COMPLETION
PAUL MERSON	1,513	73%
Alan Wright	1,163	74%
George Boateng	1,136	80%
Steve Stone	1,030	75%
Lee Hendrie	1,021	80%

TOP TACKLERS

	WON	SUCCESS
GEORGE BOATENG	88	72%
Alpay	87	72%
Steve Stone	65	76%
Ian Taylor	64	74%
Gareth Southgate	61	73%

George Boateng was Villa's busiest tackler for the second season in succession, winning 17 more tackles in 2000–01 than in 1999–2000. Turkish defender Alpay made just one successful challenge fewer than Boateng as he settled into the West Midlands with relative ease. Erstwhile skipper Gareth Southgate was only the fifth in this category, but much of his game is based on passing from the back. Steve Stone achieved a tackle success rate of 76%.

With his energetic style in midfield, George Boateng will occasionally fall foul of the referee and the 2000–01 season was no exception. The former Coventry City player racked up more than 100 Opta discipline points, thanks to nine yellow cards and 74 fouls. Dion Dublin was penalised on 90 occasions but accrued just two bookings. In contrast, Turk Alpay entered the referee's notebook 12 times despite committing just 55 fouls.

DISCIPLINE

	POINTS	FOULS & CARDS
GEORGE BOATENG	101	74F, 9Y, 0R
Dion Dublin	96	90F, 2Y, 0R
Alpay	91	55F, 12Y, 0R
Steve Stone	81	57F, 8Y, 0R
Gareth Barry	54	45F, 3Y, 0R

ACTION

ACTION	ANGEL	BARRY	BOATENG	DELANEY	DUBLIN	GINOLA	HENDRIE	JAMES	MERSON	SOUTHGATE	STAUNTON	TAYLOR	VASSELL	WRIGHT	TOTAL	COVENTRY CITY
Time on pitch	26	90	45	90	90	49	45	90	90	90	41	90	64	90	990	990
GOALS																
Goal	–	–	–	–	–	–	–	–	–	–	–	–	–	–	3	2
Shot on target (incl goals)	–	–	–	–	–	–	–	–	–	–	–	–	–	–	6	2
Shot off target	–	–	–	–	–	–	–	–	–	–	–	–	–	–	5	9
Blocked shot	–	–	–	–	–	–	–	–	–	–	–	–	–	–	7	0
Own goal	–	–	–	–	–	–	–	–	–	–	–	–	–	–	0	0
PASSES																
Pass to own player	4	28	13	30	18	15	21	3	35	22	8	28	14	38	277	166
Pass to opposition	–	10	5	9	19	6	2	6	16	8	3	4	7	8	103	109
Cross to own player	–	–	–	1	–	–	–	–	2	–	–	1	–	1	7	7
Cross to opposition player	–	–	–	–	–	10	–	–	3	2	2	3	3	1	22	20
Goal assist	–	–	–	–	–	–	–	–	–	–	–	–	–	–	0	2
Pass completion %	100%	74%	68%	75%	49%	50%	92%	33%	66%	72%	64%	88%	58%	81%	69%	58%
TACKLES & CLEARANCES																
Tackle	–	1	1	9	–	–	–	–	1	4	2	5	–	1	24	27
Clearances, blocks and interceptions	–	7	–	9	–	–	4	4	–	19	1	9	–	7	57	67
DRIBBLES & RUNS																
Dribbles ball retained	1	2	2	3	–	11	2	–	4	1	–	1	–	2	30	17
Dribbles ball lost	–	–	–	–	1	2	–	1	2	–	–	–	–	–	6	10
Dribbles success %	100%	100%	100%	100%	0%	85%	100%	0%	67%	100%	100%	100%	0%	100%	83%	63%
DISCIPLINE																
Fouls	2	–	1	1	2	2	–	–	1	–	–	2	3	1	15	25
Penalty conceded	–	–	–	–	–	–	–	–	–	–	–	–	–	–	0	0
Free kick – offside	–	–	–	–	–	–	–	–	–	–	–	–	2	–	2	1
Yellow cards	1	–	–	–	–	1	1	–	–	–	–	–	2	–	5	5
Red cards	–	–	–	–	–	–	–	–	–	–	–	–	–	–	0	0
GOALKEEPERS																
Distribution to own player	–	–	–	–	–	–	–	8	–	–	–	–	–	–	8	9
Distribution to opposition player	–	–	–	–	–	–	–	16	–	–	–	–	–	–	16	13
Goalkeeper distribution %	–	–	–	–	–	–	–	33%	–	–	–	–	–	–	33%	41%
Save	–	–	–	–	–	–	–	–	–	–	–	–	–	–	0	3
Ball caught	–	–	–	–	–	–	–	–	–	–	–	–	–	–	0	0
Ball dropped	–	–	–	–	–	–	–	–	–	–	–	–	–	–	0	1
Goal conceded	–	–	–	–	–	–	–	2	–	–	–	–	–	–	2	3

424 Number of minutes it took

Aston Villa ended Coventry City's 34-year reign in the top flight with a fantastic second-half comeback to break the hearts of their Midlands rivals. The game was also memorable for the only goal scored in 2000–01 by Villa's record signing, £9.5 million centre-forward Juan Pablo Angel.

5 May 2001

3–2

ASTON VILLA
COVENTRY CITY

Villa's final home match of the 2000–01 campaign was a rollercoaster ride of emotions for both sets of supporters. It was the visitors who had most to cheer in the first half as Gordon Strachan's side set about their task of win-or-bust with a purposeful and committed approach.

Moustapha Hadji fluffed a golden chance in the 13th minute when he failed to convert a free header from a John Hartson centre. But Villa appeared not to heed the warning as the Moroccan nodded the Sky Blues ahead five minutes later from Paul Telfer's pinpoint delivery.

The Coventry captain doubled his team's lead in stunning style in the 26th minute when he latched on to a Paul Williams clearance and crashed a sweetly-struck shot across David James and into the far corner of the net.

The majority of the crowd inside Villa Park were shell-shocked, but the Sky Blues failed to get another shot on target during the entire contest.

As expected, John Gregory made some substitutions, bringing on David Ginola and Lee Hendrie in an attempt to find a way back into the game. The pair helped Villa to dominate possession with Hendrie involved in some fine approach play. Despite only being on the pitch for 49 minutes, Ginola attempted 11 crosses, five more than any other player managed.

Villa were handed a lifeline just after the hour mark when Coventry goalkeeper Chris Kirkland spilled a cross from Mark Delaney and Darius Vassell duly punished the 'keeper's mistake to begin the fightback.

Despite this strike, Vassell was soon replaced by Angel. Many fans thought that Dion Dublin should have been substituted, as the striker had managed only a single shot against his former club.

But the home supporters were appeased when Angel netted his first goal for the club after 444 minutes of misfiring. The Colombian acrobatically half-volleyed the ball home despite the presence of several City defenders around him.

And with just six minutes remaining, Coventry's fate was sealed. Sky Blues defender Williams headed Ginola's free kick out to Paul Merson and the former Gunner curled an unstoppable effort into the corner of the net. Only 23% of long-range efforts from Merson had troubled goalkeepers throughout 2000–01 but, unfortunately for City, he certainly got it right on this occasion.

It capped a marvellous comeback by Villa in front of their home support – but their opponents were left crestfallen and contemplating life outside the top flight. As for Villa, the game summed up their season – poor on occasions and superb on others. However, this result did prove good enough to earn them a place in Europe, even if it was only in the Intertoto Cup.

Juan Pablo Angel to hit a shot on target

BRADFORD CITY

SEASON REVIEW

After the dramatic escape of the previous season, a tumultuous second Premiership campaign saw Bradford City relegated. However, whereas their survival in 1999–2000 came as a result of an unwillingness to accept their fate, their demise in season 2000–01 appeared to be an acceptance of the inevitable.

No top-flight club saw a greater turnaround in playing staff and it was clear from the time that Jim Jefferies was appointed in November that the Bantams were preparing for life outside the top flight the following term.

In fact, no sooner had the dust settled on the Bantams' magnificent last-day victory over Liverpool which secured their Premiership status in May 2000 than the problems set in.

Paul Jewell resigned in June to take over as boss at Sheffield Wednesday, with Chris Hutchings being promoted into the role of manager.

His first task was to prepare the squad for its first jaunt into European competition in the Intertoto Cup. The Bantams had qualified after applying to enter the tournament while teams which finished above them had chosen to give their players a summer rest.

Bradford knocked out FK Atlantas of Lithuania and then RKC Waalwijk of Holland before being eliminated by FC Zenit St Petersburg of Russia.

Meanwhile, the club was busy in the transfer market, bringing in Ian Nolan and Peter Atherton from Sheffield Wednesday, David Hopkin from Leeds and Dan Petrescu from Chelsea in July, with Benito Carbone and Ashley Ward joining in August.

With only a few departures, it seemed that Bradford were going to be stronger than in the previous campaign and that they might be able to consolidate their position in the top flight.

> **"The expectation level is to try and come straight back, but with the cuts that will have to be made it's going to be difficult."**
>
> **Jim Jefferies**

Despite an opening-day defeat at Liverpool, a midweek victory over Chelsea buoyed the Bantams faithful, and in the home match against Leicester the supporters celebrated their previous campaign's success as TV pundit Rodney Marsh had his hair shaved on the pitch as penance for writing off the Bantams in 1999–2000.

However, Bradford failed to score in the next two fixtures against Leicester and unsurprisingly at Old Trafford versus Manchester United. A 1–1 draw at home to Arsenal papered over the cracks as it was followed by two more scoreless outings and two more defeats, which also saw the Bantams drop into the relegation places, where they remained for the duration of the campaign.

A 1–1 draw at West Ham again raised hopes, but defeats by Ipswich Town and Manchester City meant that Bradford had scored only four goals in their opening 10 matches, accruing just six points.

Bradford were in a desperate situation and took a big gamble, deciding the answer lay with misfit striker Stan Collymore. After a colourful career, Cannock-born Collymore was struggling to make the first team at Leicester City under new boss Peter Taylor, who did not seem to have the same attitude towards his high-profile player as previous manager Martin O'Neill.

The risk seemed to pay off immediately, with Collymore scoring a spectacular scissor-kick goal to earn a 1–1 draw with Leeds. But he made just five league starts and two substitute appearances, scoring just one more goal – against Coventry City – before leaving for Real Oviedo in Spain.

The draw with Leeds was followed by defeat in the Worthington Cup by

SEASON REVIEW

Newcastle and a league defeat at Charlton, signalling the end of Chris Hutchings' tenure. Stuart McCall took temporary charge, but two more defeats without scoring heralded the arrival of Jim Jefferies from Hearts.

The impact was immediate, with Bradford taking a two-goal lead against Middlesbrough before being pegged back late in the game.

Billy McKinlay joined from Blackburn on a free transfer and Robert Molenaar arrived from Leeds soon after. Results picked up with a win over Coventry and a draw with Tottenham, but then Jefferies shocked the Bantams faithful by dropping 'keeper Matt Clarke in an alleged wage dispute, despite a general feeling that the former Sheffield Wednesday 'keeper had been one player who was exempt from criticism for the team's poor performances. Clarke was so disenchanted that he filed a transfer request and eventually left for Bolton on loan, where he helped the Trotters' push to the play-offs.

Two heavy defeats followed, but Bradford earned a surprise victory against high-flying Leicester thanks in part to the arrival of Eoin Jess on loan.

Bradford seemingly began to make plans for the following season by reducing the wage bill. Over the next two months Petrescu moved to Southampton, Isaiah Rankin to Barnsley, Collymore left on a free transfer, Peter Beagrie on a free to Wigan, Dean Windass to Middlesbrough, David Hopkin to Crystal Palace and Andy O'Brien to Newcastle. There were loan moves for Lee Sharpe to Portsmouth and Peter Atherton to Birmingham, while another permanent deal involving Benito Carbone and Middlesbrough fell through at the last minute. Gary Locke was the only player

> ## "We knew when I arrived here that there was going to be no quick fix."
>
> **Jim Jefferies**

heading in the other direction.

Bradford limped out of the FA Cup against Middlesbrough and went five games without netting in the league, making it 16 out of 26 fixtures without a goal.

Further defeats against West Ham and Ipswich were followed by home draws with Manchester City and Newcastle and a loss against Tottenham.

The final nail was waiting to be hammered in, but seemingly the pressure had also disappeared and suddenly Bradford found a new lease of life. Consecutive 2–0 victories over Charlton and Derby at least meant they would not be setting a new record for the lowest number of points in a Premiership season. But in their next fixture Bradford went down 2–1 at Everton, despite taking the lead, and their relegation was confirmed.

When assessing the reasons for Bradford's demise, Opta did not have to look too far. The major problems came in front of goal. No team scored fewer times in the top flight and the Bantams converted just eight per cent of the chances they created – the worst rate in the division.

But they also suffered at the other end of the pitch. No side conceded more goals and the wisdom of dropping Matt Clarke has to be questioned, given that Gary Walsh saved a lower percentage of shots than his rival for the number one slot.

The Bantams also struggled to keep the ball. Only Coventry City wasted possession more than Bradford, who found a team-mate with just 67% of their passes.

Unlike other teams who have dropped a division, Bradford have already made adjustments to their wage bill and will be hoping this early preparation will see them back among the élite in 2002–03.

BRADFORD CITY

DATE	OPPONENT	SCORE	ATT.	ATHERTON	BEAGRIE	BLAKE	CARBONE	CLARKE	COLLYMORE	DAVISON	GRANT	HALLE	HOPKIN	JACOBS	JESS	KERR
19.08.00	Liverpool A	0–1	44,183	90	s8	–	s15	90	–	–	–	–	75	–	–	–
22.08.00	Chelsea H	2–0	17,872	90	–	–	89¹	90	–	–	–	–	90	–	–	–
26.08.00	Leicester H	0–0	16,766	90	–	–	90	90	–	–	–	–	90	–	–	–
05.09.00	Man Utd A	0–6	66,447	90	–	–	90	90	–	–	–	90	90	–	–	–
09.09.00	Arsenal H	1–1	17,160	90	71	–	90	90	–	–	–	–	90	s9	–	–
16.09.00	Aston Villa A	0–2	27,849	90	s3	–	90	90	–	–	–	–	90	s30□	–	–
23.09.00	Southampton H	0–1	16,163	90	–	–	90	90	–	–	s8	90	–	90	–	–
30.09.00	West Ham A	1–1	25,407	90	s27	–	90	90	–	–	–	s27	–	63	–	–
14.10.00	Man City A	0–2	34,229	90	90	–	90	90	–	–	–	–	–	–	–	–
21.10.00	Ipswich H	0–2	17,045	90	90	–	90	90	–	–	–	–	–	–	–	–
29.10.00	Leeds Utd H	1–1	17,364	90	89□	–	72	90□	71¹	–	–	–	–	–	–	–
04.11.00	Charlton A	0–2	19,633	90	80	–	s13	90	–	–	s10	–	–	–	–	–
11.11.00	Everton H	0–1	17,276	90	s1	–	89	90□	90	–	–	–	–	–	–	–
18.11.00	Derby Co A	0–2	31,614	90	76	–	–	90	90	–	–	–	–	–	–	–
25.11.00	Middlesbro A	2–2	28,526	90	s9	–	81¹	90	s25	–	–	–	–	–	–	–
02.12.00	Coventry H	2–1	15,523	90	s25¹	–	90□	90□	90¹	–	–	–	–	–	–	–
09.12.00	Tottenham H	3–3*	17,225	90	82	s8	90¹□	90	90	–	–	–	–	–	–	–
16.12.00	Newcastle A	1–2	50,470	90	s20	70	88□	–	–	–	–	–	–	–	–	–
23.12.00	Chelsea A	0–3	33,377	90	s15	s15	75	–	–	–	–	–	–	–	–	–
26.12.00	Sunderland H	1–4	20,370	67□	90□	s35¹	55	–	–	–	–	–	90	–	–	–
01.01.01	Leicester A	2–1	19,278	74	–	85	–	–	s5	–	–	–	90¹□	90¹	–	–
13.01.01	Man Utd H	0–3	20,551	90	–	65	–	–	–	–	–	–	90	90	–	–
21.01.01	Sunderland A	0–0	47,812	90	s24	66	–	–	–	–	–	–	90	90	–	–
30.01.01	Arsenal A	0–2	37,318	90	–	s26	–	–	–	–	–	s26□	90	64	–	–
03.02.01	Aston Villa H	0–3	19,591	90	s34	90	–	–	–	–	–	70	56	90	–	–
10.02.01	Southampton A	0–2	14,651	–	79	s11	–	–	–	–	–	s18	–	90	–	–
24.02.01	West Ham H	1–2	20,469	–	–	s9	90	–	–	–	–	s25	81	90¹	–	–
04.03.01	Ipswich A	1–3	21,820	–	–	s10	90¹	–	–	–	–	s52	90	–	90	–
17.03.01	Man City H	2–2	19,117	–	–	90¹	90	–	–	–	–	–	–	90	90	–
31.03.01	Newcastle H	2–2	20,160	–	–	89¹	90	–	–	–	s1	s54	–	90	90	–
10.04.01	Tottenham A	1–2	28,306	–	–	90	90	–	–	–	–	90	–	90	90¹	–
13.04.01	Charlton H	2–0	17,511	–	–	81¹	90¹	–	–	–	–	90	–	90	90	–
21.04.01	Derby Co H	2–0	18,564	–	–	79	90	–	–	–	s11	90	–	90	90	–
28.04.01	Everton A	1–2	34,256	–	–	–	90	90	–	–	–	90	–	90	90	–
01.05.01	Liverpool H	0–2	22,057	–	–	–	90	90	–	–	–	90	–	90	90	–
05.05.01	Middlesbro H	1–1	20,921	–	–	–	90	90	–	–	–	90	–	90¹	90	–
13.05.01	Leeds Utd A	1–6	38,300	–	–	–	90	90	–	90	–	90	–	90	90	–
19.05.01	Coventry A	0–0	20,299	–	–	–	79	90	–	–	s11	90	–	90	–	s7

□ Yellow card, ■ Red card, S Substitute, 90² Goals scored

*including own goal

For more information visit our website:

2000–01 PREMIERSHIP APPEARANCES

LAWRENCE	LOCKE	McCALL	McKINLAY	MOLENAAR	MYERS	NOLAN	O'BRIEN	PETRESCU	RANKIN	SAUNDERS	SHARPE	WALSH	WARD	WETHERALL	WHALLEY	WINDASS	TOTAL
–	–	90	–	–	–	90	90	75	–	–	82	–	s15	90□	90	90	990
–	–	90	–	–	s1	90	90	76	–	–	79	–	s14	90	s11	90¹	990
–	–	90	–	–	s81	90	9	90	–	–	69	–	s10	90	s21	80□	990
–	–	90	–	–	–	90	–	–	–	–	64	–	s26	90	90	90□	990
–	–	90¹	–	–	81	90	–	90	–	–	s19	–	90	90	–	–	990
–	–	90	–	–	–	60	–	90	–	–	–	–	90□	90	87	90	990
s20	–	90	–	–	–	–	–	70□	–	–	82	–	90□	90	–	90□	990
90	–	90	–	–	–	–	–	90¹	–	–	s18	–	90	90□	45	90□	990
90□	–	90	–	–	–	90	–	90	–	–	–	–	90	90	–	90□	990
90	–	90□	–	–	–	90	–	75	s15	–	–	–	90	90	–	90	990
90□	–	90	–	–	–	90	–	90	s19	s1	–	–	s18	90	90	–	990
90	–	89□	–	–	–	90	–	63	77	–	–	–	90	90	90	s27	989
90	–	90	–	–	–	90	–	77	s9	–	–	–	81	90	90	s13	990
90	–	–	–	–	–	90	s51	90	–	s19	s14	–	90	39	90	71□	990
90□	–	90	90	–	s36	90	90	54	–	–	–	–	65□	–	–	90¹	990
–	–	90	90□	90	65	90	90	–	–	–	–	–	–	–	–	90	990
64	–	90	–	90	59	–	90	s26	–	–	s31	–	–	–	–	90¹□	990
–	–	90□	90	90¹	s2	90	90	74	–	s16	–	90	–	–	–	90	990
90	–	90□	90	90	–	s79	90	75	–	–	11	90	–	–	–	90	990
55	–	90	90	90	–	s23	90	–	–	–	–	90	s35	–	–	90	990
–	–	90	90□	90	s16	–	90	–	s3	87	–	90	–	–	–	90□	990
–	–	90	90	90□	–	–	90	–	–	s25	–	90	90	–	–	90	990
90	–	90	–	90	–	–	90	–	–	60	–	90□	s30	–	–	90	990
–	–	90	90	90	90	–	90	–	–	–	–	90	64□	–	–	90	990
–	–	90	90□	90	–	–	–	–	–	–	–	90	s20	–	–	90□	990
–	90	84	90	90	90	–	90	–	–	72	–	90	s6	–	–	90□	990
90	82□	s8	–	65	90	–	90	–	–	–	–	90	90	90	–	–	990
–	28□	90	–	90	90	–	90□	–	–	–	–	90□	90	90□	–	–	990
–	90	90	–	90□	–	–	–	–	–	–	–	90	90¹□	90	90	–	990
–	36	90	–	90	–	–	–	–	–	–	–	90	90	90¹	90	–	990
–	–	90	–	90□	90	–	–	–	–	–	–	90	90	–	90	–	990
–	–	90	s9	90	90	s1	–	–	–	–	–	90	90□	–	89	–	990
–	–	90	–	90	90	–	–	–	–	–	–	90	90²	–	90	–	990
90	–	90	–	90□	90¹	–	–	–	–	–	–	90	90□	–	–	–	990
–	–	90	–	90	90	–	–	–	–	–	–	90	90	–	90	–	990
s74□	–	90□	–	45	90□	s45	–	–	–	–	–	90	90□	–	16	–	990
90	s45	90	–	–	90	45	–	–	–	–	–	90	90¹□	–	90	–	990
–	90	90	–	–	90□	83	–	–	–	–	–	–	90	–	90	–	990

THE MANAGER

JIM JEFFERIES

Despite the distinct possibility of the club starting the 2001–02 season in the Nationwide League, Jim Jefferies felt it was the right move when he switched clubs from Hearts to Bradford in November 2000. The Bantams were indeed relegated and Jefferies must now set about ensuring they make a swift return to the top flight.

As a player, Jefferies made his mark as an uncompromising defender, able to play in a variety of positions and roles. His first club was Hearts, where he made his league debut in 1972. His finest hour with the Jam Tarts was when he took part in their famous Cup Winners' Cup triumph over Lokomotiv Leipzig in 1976.

Following his retirement, Jefferies left football altogether, but he could not stay away for long and success at a number of minor clubs led to his appointment as manager of Berwick in 1988. A move to Falkirk followed, before Hearts offered the Scot his dream job in 1995.

Unfortunately unable to break the dominance of the Glasgow giants, Jefferies eventually tired of his role and looked for a move to England, which he was duly offered by Bradford.

LEAGUE POSITION

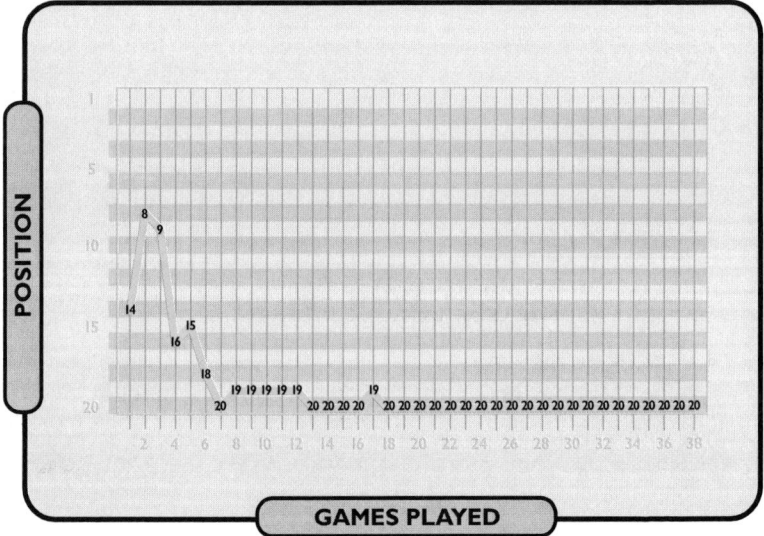

18 Bradford failed to score in 18 matches

THE GOALS

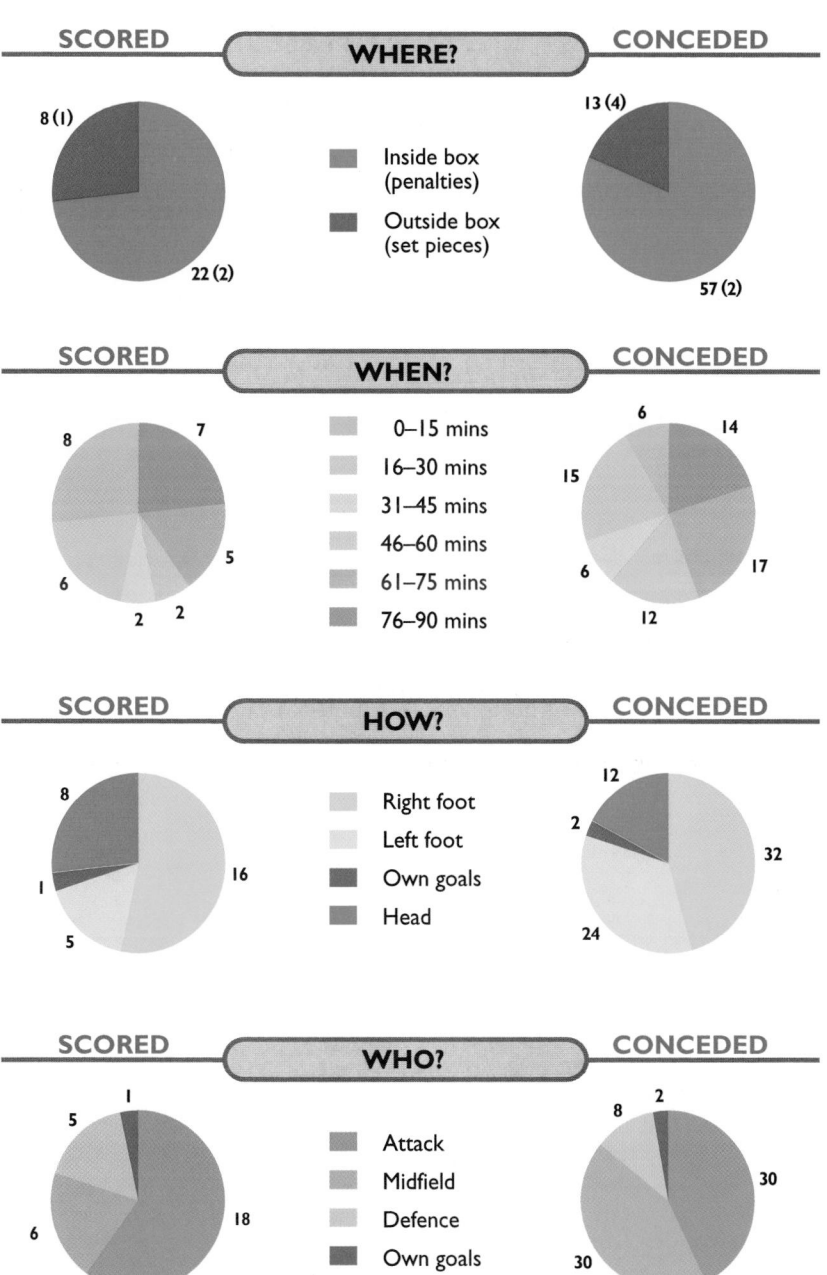

WHERE?

SCORED — CONCEDED

8 (1)
22 (2)

13 (4)
57 (2)

- Inside box (penalties)
- Outside box (set pieces)

WHEN?

SCORED — CONCEDED

8, 7, 5, 2, 2, 6

6, 14, 17, 12, 6, 15

- 0–15 mins
- 16–30 mins
- 31–45 mins
- 46–60 mins
- 61–75 mins
- 76–90 mins

HOW?

SCORED — CONCEDED

8, 1, 5, 16

12, 2, 32, 24

- Right foot
- Left foot
- Own goals
- Head

WHO?

SCORED — CONCEDED

1, 5, 6, 18

2, 8, 30, 30

- Attack
- Midfield
- Defence
- Own goals

– more than any other side

BRADFORD CITY

	ATHERTON	BEAGRIE	BLAKE	CARBONE	COLLYMORE	GRANT	HALLE	HOPKIN	JACOBS	JESS	KERR	LAWRENCE	LOCKE
APPEARANCES													
Start	25	9	14	29	5	0	10	8	19	17	0	15	6
Sub	0	10	7	2	2	5	3	3	2	0	1	2	1
Minutes on pitch	2211	913	1268	2557	461	41	1033	754	1679	1504	7	1383	461
GOAL ATTEMPTS													
Goals	0	1	4	5	2	0	0	0	2	3	0	0	0
Shots on target	1	3	19	27	9	1	0	3	6	14	0	2	0
Shots off target	1	6	13	53	5	0	3	8	8	15	0	7	0
Shooting accuracy	50%	33%	59%	34%	64%	100%	0%	27%	43%	48%	0%	22%	0%
PASSING													
Goal assists	2	1	0	4	0	0	0	0	0	4	0	1	0
Long passes	322	83	71	208	26	4	95	55	189	140	0	42	52
Short passes	525	242	386	866	125	13	244	180	476	475	4	289	103
PASS COMPLETION													
Own half %	74%	66%	78%	82%	73%	100%	72%	74%	70%	75%	100%	70%	74%
Opposition half %	53%	57%	66%	67%	67%	64%	65%	60%	64%	76%	50%	62%	69%
CROSSING													
Total crosses	20	93	42	152	5	3	30	4	63	77	0	23	17
Cross completion %	20%	32%	14%	26%	0%	67%	13%	0%	32%	26%	0%	13%	41%
DRIBBLING													
Dribbles & runs	5	43	69	142	11	5	14	17	12	62	0	66	5
Dribble completion %	100%	60%	55%	53%	82%	80%	79%	65%	67%	76%	0%	55%	20%
DEFENDING													
Tackles made	80	34	11	40	3	0	37	26	46	28	0	57	6
Tackles won %	78%	68%	73%	78%	67%	0%	81%	73%	74%	86%	0%	72%	67%
Blocks	21	0	0	1	1	0	11	2	16	4	0	4	2
Clearances	163	12	2	2	5	0	88	7	71	6	1	18	11
Interceptions	8	2	0	5	0	0	6	0	13	2	0	7	0
DISCIPLINE													
Fouls	32	17	15	37	10	0	24	7	18	10	0	28	8
Offside	0	1	23	52	15	0	1	2	3	2	0	0	1
Yellow cards	1	2	0	3	0	0	0	1	2	0	0	4	2
Red cards	0	0	0	0	0	0	0	0	0	0	0	0	0

GOALKEEPER NAME	START/ (SUB)	TIME ON PITCH	GOALS CONCEDED	MINS/GOALS CONCEDED	SAVES MADE	SAVES/ SHOTS
CLARKE	17(0)	1530	28	55	76	73%
DAVISON	2(0)	180	6	30	10	63%
WALSH	19(0)	1710	36	48	84	70%

For more information visit our website:

PLAYERS' STATISTICS

	McCALL	McKINLAY	MOLENAAR	MYERS	NOLAN	O'BRIEN	PETRESCU	RANKIN	SAUNDERS	SHARPE	WARD	WETHERALL	WHALLEY	WINDASS	TOTAL	RANK
	36	10	21	15	17	17	16	0	4	6	24	18	17	22		
	1	1	0	5	4	1	1	1	6	5	9	0	2	2		
	3241	909	1820	1421	1596	1500	1295	3	399	470	2274	1569	1439	1991		
	1	0	1	1	0	0	1	0	0	0	4	1	0	3	30*	20th
	2	1	4	2	1	1	7	0	1	0	30	5	3	16	158	14th
	8	4	4	2	0	2	2	0	6	3	26	8	5	30	219	15th
	20%	20%	50%	50%	100%	33%	78%	0%	14%	0%	54%	38%	38%	35%	42%	17th
	0	0	0	0	0	0	1	0	0	1	4	0	1	2	21	=19th
	516	128	202	134	231	142	115	0	20	37	70	139	186	210	3994	13th
	1030	348	374	294	407	287	399	1	105	141	719	342	515	575	9519	15th
	82%	83%	71%	69%	72%	66%	75%	0%	78%	80%	80%	74%	82%	86%	75%	19th
	64%	62%	43%	57%	63%	48%	65%	100%	69%	58%	64%	45%	73%	61%	61%	15th
	31	12	4	3	41	2	39	0	11	41	17	0	34	30	794	16th
	13%	25%	50%	0%	20%	50%	26%	0%	9%	32%	24%	0%	29%	33%	25%	14th
	45	1	10	7	28	8	21	0	9	8	96	7	24	37	754	20th
	84%	0%	90%	86%	79%	63%	62%	0%	44%	75%	43%	100%	83%	73%	62%	20th
	148	39	59	57	41	40	51	0	5	8	45	42	37	43	984	8th
	61%	62%	64%	81%	83%	70%	76%	0%	80%	75%	64%	74%	68%	70%	72%	14th
	22	5	31	19	13	21	5	0	0	2	5	22	5	7	219	=7th
	93	10	229	122	52	122	22	0	0	6	16	179	14	20	1347	11th
	14	0	6	10	4	7	7	0	0	0	1	8	7	1	108	12th
	47	28	33	16	14	8	15	0	3	3	95	31	8	52	560	11th
	0	0	0	3	3	0	2	0	6	0	30	0	0	22	166	=4th
	4	3	4	2	0	1	1	0	0	0	9	3	0	10	57	=11th
	1	0	0	0	0	0	0	0	0	0	0	0	0	0	1	=19th

*Including one own goal

CROSSES CAUGHT	CROSSES PUNCHED	CROSSES DROPPED	CATCH SUCCESS	THROWS/ SHORT KICKS	% COMPLETION	LONG KICKS	% COMPLETION
21	15	2	91%	32	66%	323	46%
8	4	0	100%	0	0%	39	46%
28	9	3	90%	18	78%	397	43%

PLAYER OF THE SEASON

PLAYER	INDEX SCORE
EOIN JESS	801
Benito Carbone	733
Matt Clarke	733
Wayne Jacobs	731
Gary Walsh	724
Robert Molenaar	687
Ashley Ward	675
Andy O'Brien	665
David Wetherall	664
Stuart McCall	643

After a dramatic escape from relegation the season before, Bantams fans had much to look forward to in 2000–01 – even after amiable gaffer Paul Jewell had surprisingly parted company with the club in the summer of 2000.

City swooped for Benito Carbone, Dan Petrescu and Stan Collymore as they looked to consolidate their top-flight status. But the move backfired and it was Eoin Jess, signed by Bradford's third manager of the season Jim Jefferies, who topped the Opta Index.

Jess arrived at the turn of the year with Bradford cemented to the bottom of the table, but for all his efforts there was little he could do to contrive another miraculous Houdini act.

The former Coventry player secured an average score of 801 points, winning 86% of his challenges and completing 76% of passes in opposition territory – both club-high ratios. Furthermore, only three players scored more goals than Jess, while he set up four more in his limited time at the Yorkshire club, who will hope to secure his services long-term.

Favoured by Chris Hutchings, Carbone was initially dropped by Jefferies but was reinstated to the side when City's top-flight status was threatened. He fired off more than 100 shots in total – nearly a quarter of all the Bantams' attempts – netting five times in the process and finishing as top scorer.

Matt Clarke lost his place to Gary Walsh, but was ranked third on the Index with a score of 733. Clarke recorded a goals-to-shots ratio superior to Walsh at 73%, but even so was loaned out to Bolton Wanderers as Walsh claimed a first-team spot.

Another favourite under Jefferies, Wayne Jacobs, registered the fourth-highest Index score at the club, with new signings Robert Molenaar and Ashley Ward also making the top 10. Molenaar made more than 200 clearances, while Ward rallied near the season's end, scoring four goals in his last 10 starts.

95 fouls committed by Ashley Ward –

FIVE OF THE BEST

Despite the heroics of 1999-2000, Bradford looked doomed almost from the start of 2000-01, collecting just five wins and having to dismantle their squad mid-season to stave off financial ruin. But the top-flight adventure came to an end a year later than most people had expected and there were some high points.

TOP GOALSCORERS

	GOALS	GOALS/SHOTS
BENITO CARBONE	5	6%
Robbie Blake	4	13%
Ashley Ward	4	7%
Eoin Jess	3	10%
Dean Windass	3	7%

Bradford almost broke the bank to sign Benito Carbone in summer 2000, and while the Italian ended the campaign as City's leading scorer, his total of just five goals was not a good return. His wayward shooting was illustrated by a goals-to-shots ratio of just six per cent. Ashley Ward and Dean Windass were almost as profligate, while latecomer Eoin Jess showed promise towards the end of the season, scoring three times from 29 attempts.

Veteran midfielder Stuart McCall topped the passing charts at Valley Parade for the second year in a row and was the only player at the club to make more than 1,000 successful passes. Former Crewe Alexandra player Gareth Whalley was very accurate when he played, while Benito Carbone and Dean Windass ended the campaign with completion rates of 70%. The quality of the Bantams' passing will not live in the memory for long, though.

TOP PASSERS

	SUCC PASSES	COMPLETION
STUART McCALL	1,089	70%
Benito Carbone	757	70%
Dean Windass	548	70%
Ashley Ward	537	68%
Gareth Whalley	534	76%

TOP TACKLERS

	WON	SUCCESS
STUART McCALL	91	61%
Peter Atherton	62	78%
Andy Myers	46	81%
Jamie Lawrence	41	72%
Dan Petrescu	39	76%

Ginger battler Stuart McCall was also the busiest tackler at Bradford City. The former Everton and Rangers man won 91 challenges in 2000-01, giving the fans something to cheer. He will not want to be reminded of his on-field fight with Andy Myers at the end of the season, despite the fact that Myers won an impressive 81% of his challenges. The two players would have been better concentrating on the opposition, as they were the men most likely to win the ball.

Ashley Ward racked up 122 Opta disciplinary points in 2000–01, conceding almost 100 fouls and being booked nine times. His flowing locks obviously did not do him any favours with the men in black. Fans were disappointed when Dean Windass was sold to rivals Middlesbrough as the forward always gave 100% to the Bantams' cause: so much so that he collected 10 yellow cards in his time at Valley Parade.

DISCIPLINE

	POINTS	FOULS & CARDS
ASHLEY WARD	122	95F, 9Y, 0R
Dean Windass	82	52F, 10Y, 0R
Stuart McCall	65	47F, 4Y, 1R
Benito Carbone	46	37F, 3Y, 0R
Robert Molenaar	45	33F, 4Y, 0R

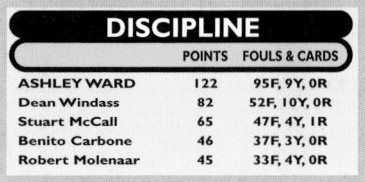

the most in the Premiership

ACTION	ATHERTON	CARBONE	CLARKE	HOPKIN	MCCALL	MYERS	NOLAN	O'BRIEN	PETRESCU	SHARPE	WARD	WETHERALL	WINDASS	WHALLEY	TOTAL	CHELSEA
Time on pitch	90	89	90	90	90	1	90	90	76	79	14	90	90	11	990	990
GOALS																
Goal	–	1	–	–	–	–	–	–	–	–	–	–	1	–	2	0
Shot on target (incl goals)	–	1	–	–	–	–	–	–	–	–	–	–	1	–	2	8
Shot off target	–	2	–	3	–	–	–	–	–	1	–	–	2	–	8	8
Blocked shot	–	–	–	–	–	–	–	–	–	–	–	–	–	–	0	–
Own goal	–	–	–	–	–	–	–	–	–	–	–	–	–	–	0	0
PASSES																
Pass to own player	17	29	6	14	21	–	26	14	19	26	5	19	20	4	220	338
Pass to opposition	9	17	11	9	12	–	14	9	6	10	1	9	15	3	125	117
Cross to own player	–	–	–	–	2	–	–	–	1	4	–	–	–	–	7	5
Cross to opposition player	5	4	–	2	–	–	–	–	1	6	–	–	1	–	19	27
Goal assist	–	–	–	–	–	–	–	–	–	–	–	–	–	–	2	0
Pass completion %	55%	59%	35%	61%	60%	0%	64%	61%	74%	66%	83%	68%	58%	57%	61%	70%
TACKLES & CLEARANCES																
Tackle	2	2	–	2	3	–	2	1	3	2	–	–	2	–	21	11
Clearances, blocks and interceptions	–	–	1	1	6	–	2	4	1	–	–	12	–	–	29	16
DRIBBLES & RUNS																
Dribbles ball retained	–	–	–	–	4	–	–	1	2	–	–	–	–	–	11	23
Dribbles ball lost	–	2	1	1	–	1	–	–	–	–	–	–	–	–	3	1
Dribble success %	0%	33%	0%	50%	100%	0%	0%	100%	100%	0%	0%	100%	100%	0%	79%	96%
DISCIPLINE																
Fouls	1	2	–	2	–	–	–	–	–	–	–	–	3	1	15	17
Penalty conceded	–	–	–	–	–	–	–	–	–	–	–	–	–	–	0	0
Free kick – offside	–	2	–	–	–	1	–	–	–	–	–	–	–	–	5	5
Yellow cards	–	–	–	–	–	–	–	–	–	–	–	–	–	–	0	1
Red cards	–	–	–	–	–	–	–	–	–	–	–	–	–	–	0	0
GOALKEEPERS																
Distribution to own player	–	–	11	–	–	–	–	–	–	–	–	–	–	–	11	13
Distribution to opposition player	–	–	15	–	–	–	–	–	–	–	–	–	–	–	15	7
Goalkeeper distribution %	–	–	42%	–	–	–	–	–	–	–	–	–	–	–	42%	65%
Save	–	–	6	–	–	–	–	–	–	–	–	–	–	–	6	6
Ball caught	–	–	3	–	–	–	–	–	–	–	–	–	–	–	3	5
Ball dropped	–	–	–	–	–	–	–	–	–	–	–	–	–	–	0	0
Goal conceded	–	–	–	–	–	–	–	–	–	–	–	–	–	–	0	2

9 Bradford cleared more shots off

Bradford had survived relegation by a hair's breadth at the end of the previous campaign and with a host of new signings, they were looking to consolidate their position in the top flight. Chelsea were Valley Parade's first visitors during 2000—01, looking for their second win in a row.

22 August 2000

2–0

BRADFORD CITY
CHELSEA

Chris Hutchings made one change from the side defeated at Anfield on the opening day, with Gareth Whalley dropping out for Italian midfielder Benito Carbone, making his first start for the Bantams.

The opening exchanges gave an indication of the game to follow, as both sides looked to attack from the outset. Chelsea had an early chance which Gustavo Poyet headed wide, while at the other end a Lee Sharpe cross was struck narrowly off target by David Hopkin, running into the box from midfield.

As if demonstrating a newfound desire to win every challenge, Bradford's tackling was already starting to cause the Blues problems. With the ball ricocheting around the area, Bradford closed quickly on every Chelsea player to prevent a shot from being struck at Matt Clarke's goal.

Chelsea demonstrated their ability to counter-attack at pace, but Bradford refused to succumb to their supposedly superior opponents. The Bantams began to exert serious pressure of their own on the Chelsea goal, clearly believing that attack was the best form of defence, and with Carbone at the centre of almost every forward move.

With 25 minutes on the clock, the deadlock was broken. An excellent cross from Sharpe found Dean Windass rising highest on the edge of the six-yard area to head across the goal and inside the far post for the Bantams' first goal of the campaign.

Three minutes later the Chelsea defence was once more exposed. A superb ball forward from Carbone sent Hopkin clear, but although he managed to beat Chelsea 'keeper Ed De Goey with his flick, there was not enough power in the effort to beat the two defenders tracking back.

Carbone was continuing to pull the strings for the Bantams in almost every area of the park. Clearly Dennis Wise thought so, as the Chelsea skipper was booked for flooring the little Italian five minutes after the break.

It somehow seemed inevitable that the former Torino forward would have a further impact on the result, and so it proved. Picking up on a sloppy pass from Christian Panucci, Windass raced forward and spread the ball wide to Carbone.

Taking the ball in his stride, the Italian playmaker let fly from 25 yards and his superb swerving effort beat the despairing Chelsea 'keeper to double Bradford's lead.

Chelsea never looked likely to recover, although more than once Bradford were grateful for the heroics of Clarke between the sticks. The Bantams' stopper made six saves during the match, including crucial blocks to deny Zola and Tore Andre Flo.

But it was Carbone who stole the show with his almost endless reserves of energy, and the crowd responded with rapturous applause for the Italian when he was taken off as the game drew to a close.

the line than any other team

CHARLTON ATHLETIC

ADDRESS

The Valley, Floyd Road,
Charlton, London SE7 8BL

CONTACT NUMBERS

Telephone: 020 8333 4000
Fax: 020 8333 4001
Box Office: 020 8333 4010
Club Call: 09068 121146
Club Shop: 020 8333 4010
e-mail: info@cafc.co.uk
Website: www.cafc.co.uk

KEY PERSONNEL

Chairman: M Simons
Deputy Chairman: R Murray
Chief Executive: P Varney
Directors: R Alwen, D G Bone
R Collins, G Franklin
D Hughes, M Stevens
D Sumners, D Ufton
D White, R Whitehand
Club Secretary: C Parkes
Manager: Alan Curbishley

SPONSORS

Redbus

FANZINES

The Voice of the Valley
Goodbye Horse

COLOURS

Home: Red shirts, white
shorts and red stockings
Away: White shirts, red shorts
and white stockings

NICKNAME

The Addicks

HONOURS

Division One Champions: 1999–2000
Division Three (South) Champions:
1928–29, 1934–35
FA Cup Winners: 1947

RECORD GOALSCORER

Stuart Leary – 153 league goals,
1953–62

BIGGEST WIN

8–1 v Middlesbrough – Division One,
12 September 1953

BIGGEST DEFEAT

1–11 v Aston Villa – Division Two,
14 November 1959

SEASON REVIEW

When Charlton won promotion to the 2000–01 Premiership, manager Alan Curbishley was keen to avoid the struggle his team endured on their last stay in the top flight, which culminated in relegation.

That meant strengthening the squad, and while pre-season moves for Gary Rowett and Don Hutchison bore no fruit, additions were made to the Addicks' roster.

Claus Jensen was a £4 million signing from Bolton, while Finnish striker Jonatan Johansson arrived for £3.75 million from Rangers. Bulgarian international defender Radostin Kishishev also joined the Addicks before the start of the campaign, and all three were to prove to be successful signings.

Charlton fans could not have wished for a better start to the season, with a packed Valley seeing the vibrant home side comprehensively beat fellow-promoted team Manchester City 4–0 on a hot summer's day.

But the Addicks were brought back down to earth a few days later, suffering a 3–0 defeat at Goodison Park. The following Saturday saw the highest-scoring game of the Premiership season at Highbury, where Charlton were defeated 5–3.

Andy Hunt, Charlton's top scorer in 1999–2000, scored once on the opening day and twice at Highbury, but was forced to retire at the end of the 2000–01 campaign due to illness. Curbishley lamented: "We would have to spend four or five million pounds to sign a player of Andy's quality."

The Arsenal result saw Curbishley's side drop to 14th in the Premiership, but they would go no lower throughout the rest of the campaign.

More disappointment was to come in the Worthington Cup in late September when, despite having beaten Stoke 4–3 at The Valley, Charlton could only draw 5–5 on aggregate after a first-leg defeat and the team from the Potteries progressed via the away goals rule.

While Charlton were by no means struggling in the top flight, Curbishley clearly felt more strengthening of the squad was needed.

An interest in signing John Hartson dwindled because of doubts over the Welshman's fitness, but South African international pair Mark Fish and Shaun Bartlett were brought in, the latter on loan until the end of the 2000–01 season.

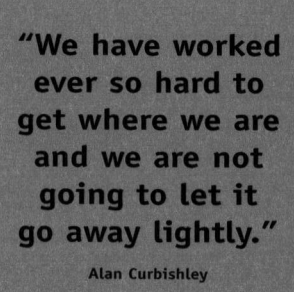

> "We have worked ever so hard to get where we are and we are not going to let it go away lightly."
>
> **Alan Curbishley**

Both signings were big hits. Bartlett, who had been set to sign for south London rivals Crystal Palace before Charlton's intervention, went on to score seven goals in just 16 starts, while former Bolton man Fish became a fans' favourite with consistently sound displays at the back.

Arguably Charlton's game of the season came in December when Manchester United were the visitors. The two sides shared six goals in a pulsating match that was both open and entertaining.

Many may remember the match for Ryan Giggs's volley from the half-way line which rebounded off the bar, but Charlton fans will prefer to recall their side battling back from 3–1 down with 10 minutes to go.

The Addicks were now glancing eagerly up the table at a possible European place, as opposed to looking precariously down at the teams beneath them.

Curbishley's reputation continued to soar and when Kevin Keegan's resignation as England manager resulted in a headache for the FA, the Charlton boss was continually linked with a coaching role within the national set-up.

However, that would have been the furthest thing from his mind on Boxing Day, when Charlton were thrashed 5–0 by West Ham at Upton Park.

86% of Shaun Bartlett's goals were

SEASON REVIEW

Christmas may well have been a nervy time for Charlton fans, but the West Ham game was followed by a run of nine Premiership matches without defeat, which took the Addicks from 13th to as high as seventh at one stage.

This was to steer them permanently away from the bottom three.

The FA Cup gave Charlton a chance to take a break from league action, although it nearly embarrassed them completely.

Non-league Dagenham & Redbridge found themselves a goal up against the Premiership side at The Valley with just a few minutes remaining, but John Salako equalised right at the death to give Charlton a rather fortunate replay, in which they scraped a 1–0 win after extra time.

After such a narrow escape, the fourth round was to prove much more painful. Two-nil up after 50 minutes against Spurs at The Valley, the Addicks were looking at a place in the last 16, but the away side blitzed them with four second-half goals and Charlton's FA Cup dream was over.

With league points still being won, however, Charlton were proving themselves worthy members of the Premiership and could even boast their own England international after Addicks full-back Chris Powell was named in Sven-Göran Eriksson's first England squad.

There were a few surprised looks at Powell's call-up, but when Curbishley was again touted as a manager elsewhere – this time at Tottenham, who had parted company with George Graham – no one was surprised.

But the Charlton boss stayed, and in April there were renewed talks about a role in the England set-up at the end of the 2000–01 season, possibly with the Under-21s.

April Fools' Day saw Charlton entertain Leicester, and Shaun Bartlett's stunning goal in a 2–0 victory was subsequently named Goal of the Season on BBC1's *Match Of The Day* programme.

More disruption was to follow, however, when Harry Redknapp left West Ham "by mutual consent". Curbishley's strong links with the club – he was brought through the Hammers' youth scheme and played for them – inevitably led to speculation he would be the next boss at Upton Park.

It was even reported that Curbishley had a clause written into his contract allowing him to talk to West Ham if they made an approach. Charlton fans knew that this was the closest they had come to losing their manager.

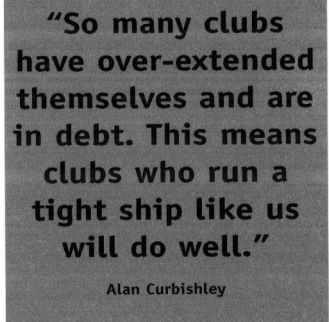

> "So many clubs have over-extended themselves and are in debt. This means clubs who run a tight ship like us will do well."
>
> Alan Curbishley

The Premiership season ended as it had started, with a 4–0 result at The Valley. Sadly for the Addicks, their visitors Liverpool were the winning team, but despite this heavy home defeat, the season was a huge success, with Charlton rarely looking in any trouble and playing good football too.

After the final game, Curbishley announced to the fans that he would be staying at The Valley next season – and judging by the cheers, you would have thought he had just guided his team to the Premiership title.

A finish of ninth place, with money to spend and a sound youth system, all bode well for the future; but hanging on to Curbishley will no doubt be top of the board's list.

Charlton – and Curbishley – showed in 2000–01 that in a sport of quick fixes, continuity can often bring its rewards.

While a UEFA Cup place was just out of its reach, the club will be hoping that a few additions to the squad will result in Charlton Athletic becoming a permanent fixture in the Premiership.

CHARLTON ATHLETIC

DATE	OPPONENT	SCORE	ATT.	BAGHERI	BARTLETT	BROWN	CAIG	FISH	HUNT	ILIC	JENSEN	JOHANSSON	KIELY	KINSELLA
19.08.00	Man City H	4–0	20,043	–	–	s15	–	–	90¹	–	75	–	90	90¹
23.08.00	Everton A	0–3	36,300	–	–	s49	–	–	90	–	72	–	90	90
26.08.00	Arsenal A	3–5	38,025	–	–	–	–	–	90²	–	66	s17	90	78□
06.09.00	Southampton H	1–1	20,043	–	–	60■	–	–	90	–	73	s17¹	90	90
10.09.00	Derby Co A	2–2	22,310	–	–	s8	–	–	82	–	90¹	90¹	90	90
16.09.00	Tottenham H	1–0	20,043	–	–	90	–	–	88	–	73	90¹	90	90
23.09.00	Newcastle A	1–0	50,866	–	–	90	–	–	89	–	90	73	90	90
30.09.00	Coventry H	2–2		–	–	90	–	–	61¹	–	90	90¹	90	90
14.10.00	Leeds Utd A	1–3	38,837	–	–	90	–	–	–	–	90¹	90	90	90
21.10.00	Middlesbro H	1–0	20,043	–	–	90	–	–	–	–	90	85	90	90□
28.10.00	Aston Villa A	1–2*	27,461	–	–	90	–	–	–	–	90	90	90	90□
04.11.00	Bradford H	2–0	19,633	–	–	90	–	–	–	–	72	85¹	90	90
11.11.00	Ipswich A	0–2	22,263	s17	–	90	–	90	–	–	90	90	90	90
18.11.00	Chelsea H	2–0	20,043	–	–	–	–	90	–	–	84	90¹	90	90
25.11.00	Sunderland H	0–1	20,043	–	–	–	–	90	–	–	90	90	90	90
02.12.00	Liverpool A	0–3	43,515	–	s24	s3	–	90	–	–	90	90	90	90
09.12.00	Man Utd H	3–3	20,043	–	87²	–	–	90	–	–	90	90	90	90
16.12.00	Leicester A	1–3	19,371	–	–	90	–	90	–	–	90	90¹□	90	90
23.12.00	Everton H	1–0	20,043	–	–	s58	–	32	–	–	90	89	90	90
26.12.00	West Ham A	0–5	26,046	–	–	90	–	–	–	–	90	90	90	90
30.12.00	Man City A	4–1	33,280	–	72	s7	–	90	–	–	90¹	83²	90	–
01.01.01	Arsenal H	1–0	20,043	–	80	–	–	90	–	–	90	90¹	90	–
13.01.01	Southampton A	0–0	15,220	–	83	s6	–	90	–	–	89	–	90	–
22.01.01	West Ham H	1–1	20,043	–	90¹	–	–	90	–	–	75	–	90	–
30.01.01	Derby Co H	2–1*	20,043	–	90	s6	s45	90	–	–	90	–	45□	–
03.02.01	Tottenham A	0–0	35,368	–	90	90	–	–	–	90	82	–	–	–
11.02.01	Newcastle H	2–0	20,043	–	77¹	–	–	90	–	90	90	s13	–	s1
24.02.01	Coventry A	2–2	19,480	–	–	–	–	90	–	90	87	89¹	–	80
03.03.01	Middlesbro A	0–0	28,177	–	89	90	–	90	–	90	89	90	–	s1
17.03.01	Leeds Utd H	1–2	20,043	–	90¹	–	–	63	–	90	90	90□	–	s27
01.04.01	Leicester H	2–0	20,043	–	90¹	–	–	90	–	90	90	84	–	s24
10.04.01	Man Utd A	1–2	67,505	–	90	–	–	90¹	–	90	59	90	–	s31
13.04.01	Bradford A	0–2	17,511	–	s21	–	–	90	–	90	s21	90	–	90
17.04.01	Aston Villa H	3–3*	20,043	–	90	s8	–	90	–	90	90¹	82	–	90¹□
21.04.01	Chelsea A	1–0	34,983	–	90¹	s45	–	45	–	90	90	90	–	90
30.04.01	Ipswich H	2–1	20,043	–	90	–	–	90	–	90	87	–	–	90
05.05.01	Sunderland A	2–3	47,671	–	–	90	–	90	–	90	90¹	77	–	90
19.05.01	Liverpool H	0–4	20,043	–	90	90	–	90	–	90□	90	s31	–	90

□ Yellow card, ■ Red card, s Substitute, 90² Goals scored

*including own goal

For more information visit our website:

2000–01 PREMIERSHIP APPEARANCES

KISHISHEV	KONCHESKY	LISBIE	MACDONALD	NEWTON	PARKER	POWELL	PRINGLE	ROBINSON	RUFUS	SALAKO	SHIELDS	STUART	SVENSSON	TILER	TODD	TOTAL
90	s4	81	–	s9	–	90	–	86[1]	90	–	–	90[1]□	–	90	–	990
90	–	41	–	s18	s25	90	–	65	90□	–	–	90	–	38□	–	938
90	–	73	–	s24	s12	90	–	90	90	–	–	90[1]	–	90	–	990
90□	–	72	–	s18	–	90	–	63	90□	–	–	90	–	–	s27	960
45	s45	s45	–	–	–	90	–	45	90□	–	–	90	–	90	–	990
–	90	s2	–	s17	–	90	–	90	90	–	–	90	–	–	–	990
–	90	–	s1	s17	–	90	–	90□	90	–	–	87[1]	–	–	s3	990
–	78	s29	–	–	–	90	–	48	90□	s42	s12	90	–	–	–	990
–	77	77	s21	–	–	90□	–	69	90	s13	s13	90	–	–	–	990
–	–	–	66	–	–	90	–	90	–	s5	–	90	s24[1]	90	90	990
–	s25□	s25	–	–	–	65	–	65	–	s16	–	90□	74	90	90	990
–	–	s13	–	–	–	90	–	90	90	s5	90	90[1]	77	–	s18	990
–	–	–	–	–	–	90	–	67□	–	s23	90	90□	73	–	–	990
90□	s6	–	–	–	–	90	s19[1]	–	90	79□	–	90	71	–	s11	990
90	s13	s25	–	–	–	77	s24	–	90	65	–	90	66	–	–	990
87	–	–	–	s16	–	90	66	90□	74	–	–	90	–	–	–	990
88	s2	–	–	–	–	90	–	s21[1]□	90	69	–	90	s3	–	–	990
90	–	–	–	–	–	90	s6	s57	–	s6	–	33	84□	84	–	990
85	s5	–	–	–	–	90	s1	90	90	–	–	90□	90[1]	–	–	990
70	s8	–	–	s20	–	90	s64	82	90	–	–	90	26	–	–	990
90	90	–	–	–	–	72	–	s18	s18	90□	–	90[1]□	–	–	90	990
90	90	–	–	–	–	79	s2	s10	s11	90	–	88□	–	–	90	990
90	90	s7	–	–	–	84	–	–	90	s1	–	90	90	–	90	990
90	75	s24	–	–	–	90	s15	–	90	s15	–	90	66	–	90	990
90	–	s2	–	84[1]□	–	90	–	–	90	–	–	90	88	–	90	990
90	–	–	–	–	–	90	–	90	–	s8	–	90	90	–	90	990
84	–	–	–	89□	–	90	–	s6	90	–	–	90	90[1]□	–	90	990
90	s3	s1	–	s10	–	90	–	90[1]	–	90	–	90	90	–	90	990
84□	–	s1	–	–	–	90	90	–	s6	90	–	90	–	–	90	990
80	–	–	–	73□	–	90	–	90	90	s10	–	–	s17	–	90□	990
66	–	–	–	66□	–	90	–	s24	90	–	–	90	s6	–	90[1]□	990
72	s18□	–	–	90	–	90	–	s31	90	–	–	59	–	–	90	990
69□	90	–	–	74□	–	90	–	90□	s16	–	–	69	–	–	90	990
–	70□	–	–	s20	–	70	–	90□	37□	s20	–	–	–	–	90	937
s12	90	–	–	–	–	80	–	78	90	–	–	s10	–	–	90	990
–	s3	s13	–	–	–	38	90	–	90	90[1]	–	s52	77[1]	–	90	990
s5	–	s13	s21	–	–	90	–	69	–	–	–	90	90[1]	–	85	990
–	s16	–	–	66	s24	90	–	–	–	–	–	90	59	–	74	990

THE MANAGER

ALAN CURBISHLEY

The fact that Alan Curbishley has been courted by the FA for a role within the England set-up, as well as being linked to the manager's post at West Ham, is testament to his superb management ability. He has even been linked with the soon-to-be-vacant Manchester United job – high praise for a man who has coached just a single club in his career.

Curbishley's days with the Addicks began in 1991 and his managerial talents have won him a legion of admirers in the world of football. He is a great believer in maintaining consistency in his team selection, while at the same time introducing new faces to the squad to ensure strong competition for first-team places.

Curbishley has pledged his immediate future to the club, although without the conviction Addicks fans may have been hoping for. "I said that I'd envisage being back here next season and I don't see anything different from that," he said. "I've not been offered anything and I'm contracted here at Charlton."

Charlton were keen to ensure they kept their manager happy at The Valley by offering him a new long-term contract.

LEAGUE POSITION

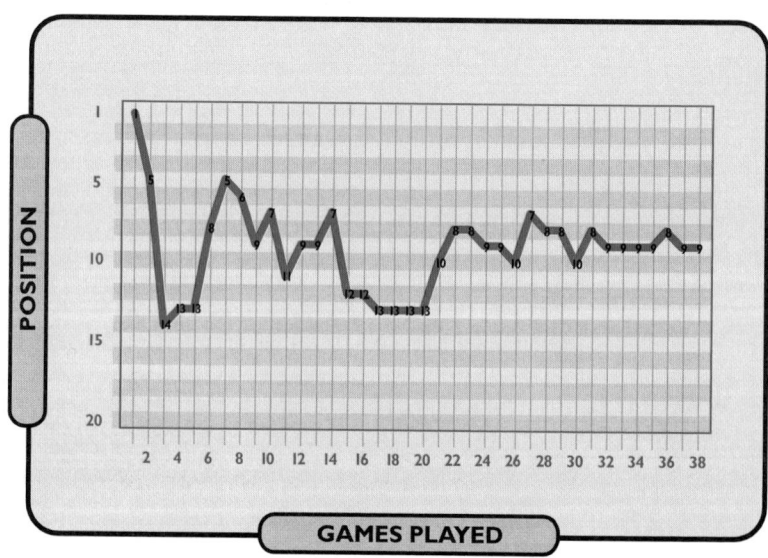

POSITION

GAMES PLAYED

55% Charlton were more accurate

THE GOALS

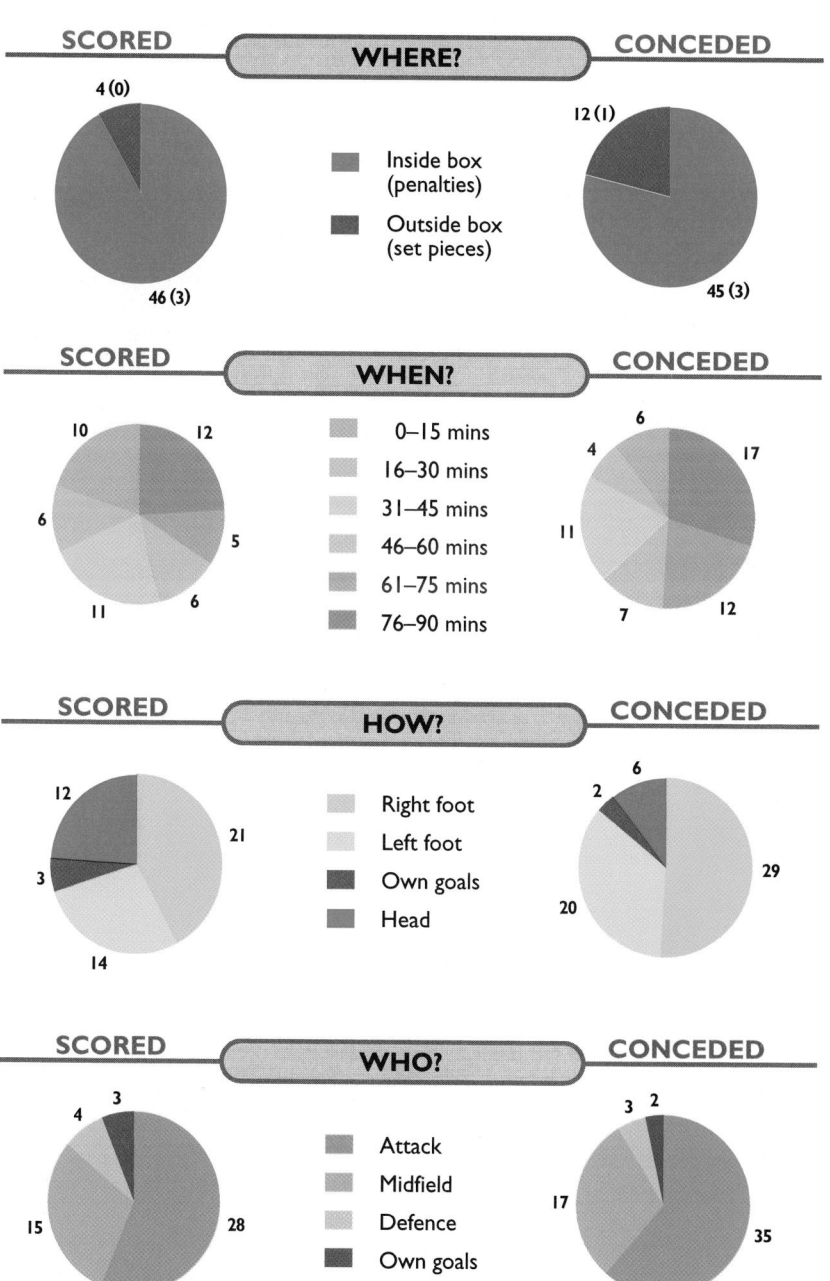

from set-pieces than any other side

CHARLTON ATHLETIC

	BAGHERI	BARTLETT	BROWN	FISH	HUNT	JENSEN	JOHANSSON	KINSELLA	KISHISHEV	KONCHESKY	LISBIE
APPEARANCES											
Start	0	16	15	24	8	37	27	27	25	11	5
Sub	1	2	10	0	0	1	4	5	2	12	13
Minutes on pitch	17	1433	1525	2030	680	3174	2445	2492	2107	1078	544
GOAL ATTEMPTS											
Goals	0	7	0	1	4	5	11	2	0	0	0
Shots on target	0	18	1	2	6	31	42	20	3	0	4
Shots off target	0	9	1	4	3	30	31	14	8	0	6
Shooting accuracy	0%	67%	50%	33%	67%	51%	58%	59%	27%	0%	40%
PASSING											
Goal assists	0	1	0	0	1	3	3	2	3	2	2
Long passes	2	53	149	174	20	295	66	478	240	161	10
Short passes	4	392	320	502	171	1218	506	1031	688	312	147
PASS COMPLETION											
Own half %	100%	74%	81%	82%	82%	81%	76%	86%	72%	72%	64%
Opposition half %	50%	65%	53%	63%	72%	77%	59%	71%	59%	59%	59%
CROSSING											
Total crosses	0	14	3	4	8	266	81	29	43	20	14
Cross completion %	0%	14%	67%	25%	25%	34%	21%	31%	28%	35%	21%
DRIBBLING											
Dribbles & runs	0	22	2	28	9	125	95	26	50	16	29
Dribble completion %	0%	55%	100%	93%	89%	76%	37%	81%	78%	88%	62%
DEFENDING											
Tackles made	2	28	33	78	4	57	33	103	81	27	6
Tackles won %	100%	71%	70%	74%	25%	77%	73%	79%	83%	89%	100%
Blocks	1	2	25	45	1	8	6	25	9	15	1
Clearances	0	19	175	232	3	16	6	48	73	65	0
Interceptions	0	4	9	8	0	5	1	17	12	5	0
DISCIPLINE											
Fouls	0	31	20	21	21	10	37	26	38	14	13
Offside	0	5	0	0	12	2	65	0	3	1	17
Yellow cards	0	0	0	0	0	0	2	4	4	3	0
Red cards	0	0	1	0	0	0	0	0	0	0	0

GOALKEEPER NAME	START/ (SUB)	TIME ON PITCH	GOALS CONCEDED	MINS/GOALS CONCEDED	SAVES MADE	SAVES/ SHOTS
CAIG	0(1)	45	0	0	1	100%
ILIC	13(0)	1170	19	62	47	71%
KIELY	25(0)	2205	38	58	84	69%

For more information visit our website:

PLAYERS' STATISTICS

	MACDONALD	NEWTON	PARKER	POWELL	PRINGLE	ROBINSON	RUFUS	SALAKO	SHIELDS	STUART	SVENSSON	TILER	TODD	TOTAL	RANK
	1	1	15	31	1	21	32	4	2	33	18	7	19		
	2	9	5	2	7	8	0	13	2	2	4	0	4		
	88	220	1266	2769	208	1811	2827	467	205	2939	1420	572	1748		
	0	0	1	0	1	2	2	0	0	5	5	0	1	50*	7th
	1	0	11	2	2	18	8	1	0	14	13	1	3	201	8th
	1	1	12	4	2	12	12	2	0	23	14	5	3	197	17th
	50%	0%	48%	33%	50%	60%	40%	33%	0%	38%	48%	17%	50%	51%	2nd
	0	1	0	2	0	2	1	1	0	9	0	0	0	33	=8th
	1	18	152	362	11	133	177	41	25	262	66	60	198	3621	19th
	13	77	508	750	72	593	496	157	49	1138	482	121	446	10251	10th
	17%	76%	83%	71%	87%	71%	73%	81%	62%	81%	77%	76%	78%	78%	14th
	75%	66%	59%	62%	65%	66%	53%	70%	68%	66%	59%	57%	68%	63%	10th
	1	6	9	76	0	85	7	44	4	47	20	2	4	787	18th
	0%	33%	33%	28%	0%	27%	14%	11%	0%	21%	20%	0%	0%	27%	8th
	1	10	48	86	5	71	18	24	0	103	15	0	14	799	16th
	0%	50%	79%	81%	40%	56%	89%	71%	0%	74%	33%	0%	93%	69%	7th
	0	8	96	61	3	56	85	9	4	97	29	10	48	962	12th
	0%	38%	79%	77%	67%	79%	69%	78%	75%	68%	72%	80%	71%	75%	2nd
	0	2	14	33	2	10	27	3	1	15	2	12	19	278	2nd
	1	5	12	94	2	11	296	3	5	51	18	67	127	1374	9th
	0	2	3	8	0	3	18	1	0	8	2	1	7	114	9th
	0	1	26	16	4	26	57	3	1	30	51	12	22	483	18th
	3	1	1	3	2	6	0	3	2	4	9	0	0	139	=10th
	0	0	5	1	0	4	7	1	0	7	3	0	2	45	18th
	0	0	0	0	0	0	1	0	0	0	0	1	0	3	=7th

*Including three own goals

CROSSES CAUGHT	CROSSES PUNCHED	CROSSES DROPPED	CATCH SUCCESS	THROWS/SHORT KICKS	% COMPLETION	LONG KICKS	% COMPLETION
1	0	1	50%	0	0%	2	50%
32	15	5	86%	15	93%	284	42%
45	13	3	94%	44	75%	512	44%

PLAYER OF THE SEASON

PLAYER	INDEX SCORE
MARK KINSELLA	999
Claus Jensen	912
Mark Fish	901
Graham Stuart	779
Andy Todd	711
Richard Rufus	707
Dean Kiely	686
Jonatan Johansson	680
Chris Powell	631
Radostin Kishishev	622

Mark Kinsella, Charlton's player of the year last time round in the Premiership in 1998–99, was again the highest-ranked Addick on the Opta Index in 2000–01.

The Charlton skipper was the driving force behind his side's excellent campaign and led by example as Alan Curbishley's men claimed a top-10 finish.

Kinsella made more successful challenges than any of his colleagues and was one of only two players to complete more than 1,000 passes. His probing from deep allowed Charlton's attackers to create space further forward, while he also showed an eye for goal, maintaining a shooting accuracy of 69% from outside the area – easily the best at the club.

The Republic of Ireland international was ably supported by record signing Claus Jensen. His average Opta score of 912 points for the season was 87 short of his skipper's and made the Dane Charlton's second-highest rated player.

Jensen was Charlton's most prolific and accurate passer, while his tally of 90 successful crosses was bettered by just two top-flight players. The former Bolton star also weighed in with five goals and was a threat at set-pieces, with the league's third-highest tally of free-kick efforts on target.

Another ex-Trotter, Mark Fish, made 147 headed clearances in his debut season at The Valley, while Graham Stuart's tigerish contributions landed him a top-four spot on the Addicks' Index.

Meanwhile, Jonatan Johansson started the 2000-01 season in emphatic style, but struggled to maintain the momentum of his first 20 matches, which saw him score on average every other game – netting 11 by the season's end.

Chris Powell's shock inclusion in the England set-up was a huge boost to the club, but in truth his Opta stats were not especially impressive at Charlton, while skilful youngster Scott Parker is only absent from the top 10 through lack of playing time.

10 Claus Jensen committed just 10 fouls,

FIVE OF THE BEST

Charlton Athletic were tipped for relegation by many, but finished in the top half of the Premiership with ease. Alan Curbishley's team showed that they had learned their lesson from 1998–99 and they enjoyed some excellent results, especially at The Valley. The club can be proud of their achievement.

TOP GOALSCORERS

	GOALS	GOALS/SHOTS
JONATAN JOHANSSON	11	15%
Shaun Bartlett	7	26%
Matthias Svensson	5	19%
Graham Stuart	5	14%
Claus Jensen	5	8%

The signing of Jonatan Johansson proved to be one of the transfers of the 2000–01 season, the Finn scoring 11 times in the Premiership. He was joined in the spring by South African striker Shaun Bartlett who settled in well, too, bagging seven goals. He notched with more than a quarter of his strikes, a highly-impressive ratio. Midfielders Graham Stuart and Claus Jensen chipped in with five goals each.

Balding midfielder Claus Jensen turned down Ipswich to join Charlton in summer 2000 and immediately became a hero with the fans. His passing was exceptional and he formed a good partnership with Republic of Ireland international Mark Kinsella. The former Colchester man made just 16 fewer successful passes than Jensen. Chris Powell's passing was good, too – one of the reasons why he was elevated into the full England squad.

TOP PASSERS

	SUCC PASSES	COMPLETION
CLAUS JENSEN	1,182	78%
Mark Kinsella	1,166	77%
Graham Stuart	996	71%
Chris Powell	723	65%
Radostin Kishishev	592	64%

TOP TACKLERS

	WON	SUCCESS
MARK KINSELLA	81	79%
Scott Parker	76	79%
Radostin Kishishev	67	83%
Graham Stuart	66	68%
Richard Rufus	59	69%

Mark Kinsella relished a second chance to pit himself against some of the best midfielders in the world in 2000–01 and again he did very well. The Irishman won 81 tackles and finished with a success rate of 79%. Scott Parker showed that he could do more than advertise hamburgers by making 76 successful challenges, while Bulgarian international Radostin Kishishev won an impressive 83% of his tackles.

Bustling defender Richard Rufus topped the Charlton indiscipline table. He committed only 57 fouls but was booked seven times and sent off once. Charlton were a relatively clean team, though, and only two teams were booked less than the Addicks. Swedish striker Matthias Svensson was the second-worst offender, and he was booked just three times. Crime does not pay in the Premiership.

DISCIPLINE

	POINTS	FOULS & CARDS
RICHARD RUFUS	84	57F, 7Y, 1R
Matthias Svensson	60	51F, 3Y, 0R
Graham Stuart	51	30F, 7Y, 0R
Radostin Kishishev	50	38F, 4Y, 0R
Jonatan Johansson	43	37F, 2Y, 0R

ACTION	BARTLETT	FISH	JENSEN	JOHANSSON	KIELY	KINSELLA	MISHKREY	KONCHESKY	POWELL	ROBINSON	RUFUS	SALAKO	STUART	SVENSSON	TOTAL	MAN UTD
Time on pitch	87	90	90	90	90	90	88	2	90	21	90	69	90	3	990	990
GOALS																
Goal	2	–	–	–	–	–	–	–	–	–	–	–	–	–	3	3
Shot on target (incl goals)	2	–	2	–	–	–	–	–	–	–	–	–	–	–	7	7
Shot off target	1	–	1	2	–	–	1	–	1	–	–	1	1	–	7	13
Blocked shot	–	–	1	–	–	–	–	–	–	–	–	–	–	–	2	5
Own goal	–	–	–	–	–	–	–	–	–	–	–	–	–	–	0	0
PASSES																
Pass to own player	19	27	42	17	6	59	34	–	33	7	20	20	32	1	317	318
Pass to opposition	14	9	13	14	12	9	11	–	12	2	8	7	12	–	123	109
Cross to own player	–	–	4	3	–	–	2	–	1	–	–	–	–	–	10	4
Cross to opposition player	1	–	6	2	–	–	1	–	–	–	–	1	1	–	13	15
Goal assist	–	–	–	–	–	–	1	–	–	–	–	–	–	–	3	2
Pass completion %	56%	75%	71%	56%	33%	87%	77%	0%	72%	70%	71%	71%	72%	100%	71%	72%
TACKLES & CLEARANCES																
Tackle	1	2	4	–	–	1	3	–	1	–	–	2	4	–	18	19
Clearances, blocks and interceptions	1	16	3	–	1	3	5	2	2	6	6	3	2	–	45	46
DRIBBLES & RUNS																
Dribbles ball retained	–	–	1	1	–	1	4	–	–	1	–	–	3	–	12	23
Dribbles ball lost	–	–	3	4	–	–	–	–	–	–	–	–	2	–	9	10
Dribble success %	100%	0%	25%	20%	0%	100%	100%	0%	0%	100%	0%	0%	60%	0%	57%	70%
DISCIPLINE																
Fouls	–	–	–	–	–	1	1	–	–	1	1	–	–	–	4	11
Penalty conceded	–	–	–	–	–	–	–	–	–	–	–	–	–	–	0	0
Free kick – offside	–	–	1	3	–	–	–	–	–	–	–	–	–	–	6	0
Yellow cards	–	–	–	–	–	–	–	–	–	1	–	–	–	–	0	1
Red cards	–	–	–	–	–	–	–	–	–	–	–	–	–	–	0	0
GOALKEEPERS																
Distribution to own player	–	–	–	–	17	–	–	–	–	–	–	–	–	–	17	14
Distribution to opposition player	–	–	–	–	13	–	–	–	–	–	–	–	–	–	13	12
Goalkeeper distribution %	–	–	–	–	57%	–	–	–	–	–	–	–	–	–	57%	54%
Save	–	–	–	–	4	–	–	–	–	–	–	–	–	–	4	4
Ball caught	–	–	–	–	1	–	–	–	–	–	–	–	–	–	–	7
Ball dropped	–	–	–	–	–	–	–	–	–	–	–	–	–	–	0	0
Goal conceded	–	–	–	–	3	–	–	–	–	–	–	–	–	–	3	3

11% Charlton conceded the lowest

In December, Arsène Wenger lamented that many teams were beaten before a ball was kicked against Manchester United. But the following week, newly-promoted Charlton certainly gave the champions a run for their money in one of the most thrilling games of the 2000–01 season.

9 December 2000
3–3
CHARLTON ATHLETIC
MANCHESTER UNITED

The Addicks named a few surprises in their starting XI, with loan-signing Shaun Bartlett thrown in at the deep end against the champions for his first start of the campaign.

The South African international almost made an instant impact when he connected with Jonatan Johansson's cross in the sixth minute. But Bartlett saw his powerful header bounce back off the inside of the post, much to his obvious disappointment.

However, Bartlett did not have to wait long before he grabbed his first goal in English football. Graham Stuart whipped in a dangerous cross which Bartlett nodded past Raimond van der Gouw and into the back of the net after just 10 minutes.

At this stage, the Premiership newcomers were dominating the match and it was some surprise that they failed to extend their advantage.

Over the 90 minutes, Alan Curbishley's side were accurate with 71% of their passes – the best proportion that they managed in any game in the 2000–01 season – and this helped create a host of chances.

So the fact that the Addicks went in at half-time a goal down must have been demoralising indeed. Ryan Giggs grabbed United's equaliser in the 42nd minute with a swerving shot from the edge of the box, and moments later the Red Devils led 2–1 after the Welshman's incredible 45-yard chip had cannoned off the crossbar and

into the path of Ole Gunnar Solskjaer, who rifled the ball past a disorientated Dean Kiely.

United even managed to extend their advantage after the break. Roy Keane was allowed too much time on the edge of the box and drilled the ball home powerfully to give the champions a 3–1 lead.

Curbishley seemed anxious for his players to get more physical, and the fact that they conceded only four fouls all afternoon – the fewest that Charlton recorded in any match all season – seemed to back up the Arsenal boss's opinion that teams tended to afford United rather too much respect.

However, Bartlett gave the Addicks a lifeline with 11 minutes remaining when he headed Radostin Kishishev's cross through van der Gouw's legs to make the score 3–2.

And with Mark Kinsella driving Charlton on from the centre of the park, they were still creating chances. Over the 90 minutes the Republic of Ireland international made 59 accurate passes – more than any other player on the pitch – and it was his header in the 84th minute that set up the Addicks' deserved equaliser.

John Robinson collected Kinsella's flick-on and quickly swivelled before drilling the ball into the far corner of the net to seal a fantastic comeback and complete one of the most entertaining matches that The Valley has seen in recent seasons.

proportion of goals from headers

CHELSEA

Stamford Bridge, Fulham Road,
London SW6 1HS

CONTACT NUMBERS

Telephone: 020 7385 5545
Fax: 020 7381 4831
Ticket Office: 020 7386 7799
Club Call: 09068 121159
Chelsea Megastore: 020 7565 1490
Website: www.chelseafc.co.uk

KEY PERSONNEL

Chairman: K W Bates
Directors: C Hutchinson
Ms Y S Todd, M Russell
Assistant Club Secretary: C Lait
Head Coach: Claudio Ranieri

SPONSORS

2000–01: Autoglass
2001–02: Emirates Airlines

FANZINES

The Chelsea Independent
Cockney Rebel
Curious Blue
Matthew Harding's Blue & White Army

COLOURS

Home: Royal blue shirts with
white trim, royal blue shorts
with white trim and white stockings
Away: Light gold shirts with deep
royal trim, deep royal shorts with
light gold trim, light gold stockings
with deep royal trim

NICKNAME

The Blues

HONOURS

League Champions: 1954–55
Division Two Champions:
1983–84, 1988–89
FA Cup Winners: 1970, 1997, 2000
League Cup Winners: 1965, 1998
European Cup Winners' Cup Winners:
1971, 1998
UEFA Super Cup Winners: 1998

RECORD GOALSCORER

Bobby Tambling –
164 league goals, 1958–70

BIGGEST WIN

13–0 v Jeunesse Hautcharage –
European Cup Winners' Cup, 1st round
2nd leg, 29 September 1971

BIGGEST DEFEAT

1–8 v Wolverhampton Wanderers –
Division One, 26 September 1953

SEASON REVIEW

Much was expected from Chelsea at the start of the 2000–01 campaign. Silverware to follow up the previous season's FA Cup triumph was the priority, preferably the Premiership, but failing that the UEFA Cup. At the very least, a top-three finish was essential.

The close season saw a number of changes in personnel, with the much-maligned Chris Sutton departing for Celtic, to be replaced by Eidur Gudjohnsen, a £4 million signing from Bolton. World Cup winner Didier Deschamps also made tracks, but in Croatian Mario Stanic the club appeared to have found the ideal replacement, so all seemed well at the Bridge.

In addition, Chelsea had splashed out a club record £15 million on Dutch striker Jimmy Floyd Hasselbaink, who returned to England following a season in Spain's Primera Liga with Atletico Madrid.

An excellent Charity Shield triumph over Manchester United was followed by a 4–2 win over West Ham in the Premiership. Confidence was on the up among the Blues faithful, before a 2–0 away defeat by lowly Bradford City brought them back down to earth. It was the beginning of an appalling away record that would ultimately wreck the club's season.

Three crucial Premiership matches followed, but the Blues could only manage three draws, against Aston Villa, Arsenal and Newcastle. The Newcastle result – a dour, goalless affair – proved too much for chairman Ken Bates, and an announcement was made by the club three days later.

The statement read: "Chelsea have great admiration for the achievements of Gianluca Vialli in his two-and-a-half years in charge of team affairs. However, the Club feels that in a wider context it is in our best interests to seek a change of direction." With that, Vialli was gone, much to the astonishment of the fans and backroom staff.

Perhaps more surprising still was the man announced as Vialli's replacement a few days later – former Valencia and Atletico Madrid coach Claudio Ranieri. Having come to managing director Colin Hutchinson's attention some years before, Chelsea snapped up the 48-year-old Italian, who was at the time without a club. Cue raised eyebrows everywhere.

> "I know that Chelsea and all their fans are dreaming of the championship. In football you can't promise anything, especially in England where there is a certain Manchester United."
>
> Claudio Ranieri

Ranieri played no part in Chelsea's next Premiership match – a disappointing 2–0 home defeat by Leicester – but was in full charge for their away match at Old Trafford. One of the season's most exciting games ensued, with Chelsea demonstrating hitherto-unseen spirit and determination to hold the champions to a 3–3 draw.

However, any heart gained from the result was soon lost as the Blues bowed out of Europe at the first hurdle. Having beaten St Gallen 1–0 at Stamford Bridge shortly after Vialli's dismissal, Chelsea were expected to better the result in the away leg. The Swiss champions had other ideas - and two first-half goals were enough to win the tie 2–1 on aggregate.

Chelsea simply could not win away from home, as three victories at Stamford Bridge in October were tempered by a 1–0 defeat at Sunderland. Not only did Southampton, Charlton and Everton all take three points against Chelsea on their own patches in November, but the Blues also bowed out of the Worthington Cup, again away, at eventual winners Liverpool.

November also saw the departure of one of the more popular members of the squad – Tore Andre Flo. The Norwegian supersub

SEASON REVIEW

had grown tired of warming the bench and was sold to Glasgow Rangers for a club record £12 million.

Despite the club's immaculate home form – three more wins followed at the Bridge in December – the tension was mounting in the changing room amid stories of player unrest and continued anger at the change of management. Rumours emerged of a training ground punch-up between on-loan defender Christian Panucci and another Chelsea star.

Ranieri's poor grasp of English was allegedly making it difficult for him to communicate his tactics to the players. Add to this bizarre stories of Dennis Wise winding up the various translators posted around the players and staff with bogus translations of his own and the whole situation seemed very muddled.

Comedy turned to drama at the turn of the year as Wise, one of the most popular players at the club in recent years, announced his desire to leave, having been left out of the side that beat Aston Villa 1–0 on New Year's Day. However, having been convinced by everyone from the manager to the tea lady that he was still wanted at Chelsea, Wise recanted his transfer request.

At the time the Blues were lying in ninth place in the table, with all thoughts of the Premiership title gone. The only remaining route to a trophy was the FA Cup, which the club put the bulk of their efforts into retaining. And having bolstered the squad with the signings of Jesper Gronkjaer and Slavisa Jokanovic for a combined fee of £9.5 million – as well as the surprise acquisition of Mark Bosnich on a free – it certainly seemed a possibility.

However, following victories over Peterborough and Gillingham, the Blues

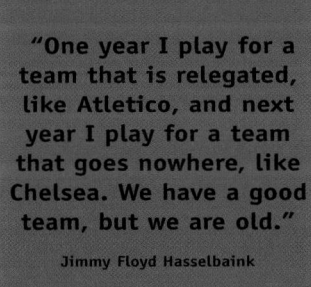

"One year I play for a team that is relegated, like Atletico, and next year I play for a team that goes nowhere, like Chelsea. We have a good team, but we are old."

Jimmy Floyd Hasselbaink

were given a tough away tie at Arsenal. Despite Hasselbaink's superb equalising strike – a contender for goal of the season – Chelsea succumbed to two late goals to go down 3–1, consigning the club to a trophy-less campaign.

Having again failed away, this time at Leicester, Chelsea were rapidly heading towards the end of the season yet to win on their travels. However, they finally capitalised on a long West Ham casualty list by taking all three points at Upton Park in a 2–0 triumph in March.

Incredibly, of their five remaining away fixtures, Chelsea managed to secure three wins and a draw, only failing to register at least a point at Elland Road. This end-of-season blitz saw Chelsea finish with the ninth-best away record in the top flight – a target that had seemed impossible two months into the year.

Most crucial of all was that the last away win – a 2–1 victory at Manchester City on the final day of the season – guaranteed that the Blues snatched the final UEFA Cup spot from the grasp of Sunderland and they will be able at least to attempt to do better than their dreadful showing in Europe in 2000–01.

The season was therefore a very troubled one for the Blues, although it did have its positive points. Ranieri's reliance on younger players – such as John Terry and Sam Dalla Bona – is a positive move, while the signing of 23-year-old French defender William Gallas shows that the coach is willing to spend to secure a better campaign.

The future may well be brighter, but unless the Blues can do something about the dreadful away form that plagued their season they may well be in for an equally rough ride in 2001–02.

CHELSEA

DATE	OPPONENT	SCORE	ATT.	ALEKSIDZE	BABAYARO	BOGARDE	CUDICINI	DALLA BONA	DE GOEY	DESAILLY	DI MATTEO	FERRER	FLO	GRONKJA...
19.08.00	West Ham H	4–2	34,914	–	70	–	–	–	90	90	90	–	s20	–
22.08.00	Bradford A	0–2	17,872	–	45	–	–	–	90	90	90	–	s34	–
27.08.00	Aston Villa A	1–1	27,057	–	90	–	90	–	–	90¹	90	–	90	–
06.09.00	Arsenal H	2–2	34,923	–	90	–	90	–	–	90	90	–	s12	–
09.09.00	Newcastle A	0–0	51,687	–	–	–	90	s7	–	90□	90	–	82□	–
17.09.00	Leicester H	0–2	33,697	–	–	90	90	–	–	90	90	–	90	–
23.09.00	Man Utd A	3–3	67,568	–	–	s3	90	s6	–	90	90	–	90²	–
01.10.00	Liverpool H	3–0*	34,966	–	s19	–	–	75	90	90	–	71	s11	–
14.10.00	Sunderland A	0–1	45,078	–	s17	s59	–	90	90	90	–	90	s45	–
21.10.00	Coventry H	6–1	34,646	–	70	s20	–	65	90	90	–	33	s57¹	–
28.10.00	Tottenham H	3–0	34,966	–	90□	–	–	90□	90	90	–	90	s26	–
04.11.00	Southampton A	2–3	15,236	–	90	–	–	90	90	–	–	–	89	–
12.11.00	Leeds Utd H	1–1	35,121	–	90□	–	–	76□	90	90□	–	76	s14	–
18.11.00	Charlton A	0–2	20,043	–	90	–	–	45	90	90□	–	–	s45	–
25.11.00	Everton H	1–2	33,515	–	–	81	–	90¹	90	90□	–	–	–	–
03.12.00	Man City H	2–1	34,971	–	75	s11	–	90	90	90	–	–	–	–
09.12.00	Derby Co H	4–1	34,317	s6	90	s14	s45	90	45	76	–	–	–	–
16.12.00	Middlesbro A	0–1	29,442	s11	–	–	–	90	90	90□	–	–	–	–
23.12.00	Bradford H	3–0	33,377	–	–	s7	–	90¹	90	90	–	–	–	–
26.12.00	Ipswich A	2–2	22,237	–	–	s30	–	90□	90	90□	–	–	–	–
01.01.01	Aston Villa H	1–0	33,159	–	–	–	90	90	–	–	s3	–	–	–
13.01.01	Arsenal A	1–1	38,071	–	–	–	90	90□	–	90□	–	s45	–	s45
20.01.01	Ipswich H	4–1	34,948	–	90	–	90	83□	–	90	–	78□	–	s12
31.01.01	Newcastle H	3–1	35,108	–	90	–	90	90	–	–	–	90	–	s60¹
03.02.01	Leicester A	1–2	21,502	–	90	–	90	90□	–	–	–	90	–	65
10.02.01	Man Utd H	1–1	34,960	–	90	–	90	90	–	90	–	88	–	70
03.03.01	Coventry A	0–0	21,609	–	–	–	90	–	–	45	–	90	–	90
07.03.01	West Ham A	2–0	26,016	–	–	–	90	s6	–	90	–	90□	–	90□
17.03.01	Sunderland H	2–4	34,981	–	–	–	90	–	–	90¹	–	73	–	71
31.03.01	Middlesbro H	2–1	34,933	–	90	–	90	90□	–	90	–	–	–	45
07.04.01	Derby Co A	4–0	29,320	–	s10	–	90	90	–	90	–	–	–	s1
14.04.01	Southampton H	1–0	35,136	–	–	–	90	90	–	90	–	–	–	–
17.04.01	Tottenham A	3–0	36,074	–	90□	–	90	90	–	90□	–	–	–	s23
21.04.01	Charlton H	0–1	34,983	–	–	–	90	90	–	90	–	–	–	s45
28.04.01	Leeds Utd A	0–2	39,253	–	90□	–	90	90□	–	90□	–	–	–	s13
05.05.01	Everton H	2–1	35,196	–	s14	–	90	–	–	90	–	–	–	s27
08.05.01	Liverpool H	2–2	43,588	–	s6	–	90□	90	–	90□	–	–	–	–
19.05.01	Man City A	2–1	34,479	–	65	–	90	–	–	90	–	–	–	–

□ Yellow card, ■ Red card, s Substitute, 90² Goals scored

*including own goal

For more information visit our website:

2000–01 PREMIERSHIP APPEARANCES

GUDJOHNSEN	HARLEY	HASSELBAINK	JOKANOVIC	LAMBOURDE	LE SAUX	LEBOEUF	MELCHIOT	MORRIS	PANUCCI	POYET	STANIC	TERRY	THOME	WISE	ZOLA	TOTAL
–	–	90¹	–	–	s20	–	90	s8	90□	82	90²	–	–	90	70¹	990
–	s45	56	–	–	–	–	63	90	s27	90	–	–	90	90□	90	990
s13	–	77□	–	–	–	90	–	s64	90	90	26	–	–	90	–	990
–	–	90¹	–	–	80□	90□	s18	s10	90□	72	–	–	–	90	78¹	990
–	83	90	–	–	90	90	78	s12	90□	–	–	–	–	90	s8	990
s11	–	79□	–	–	90	–	s1	90□	89	–	–	–	–	90□	90	990
–	45	87¹	–	–	90	90	s45	90□	90□	–	–	–	–	–	84	990
90¹	–	79¹	–	–	90	90	90	s15	–	–	–	–	–	90□	90	990
73	–	45	–	–	66■	31	90	–	–	–	–	–	–	90	90	966
–	–	90⁴	s25	–	–	90	90	–	–	90	–	–	–	90	90¹	990
–	–	90²	s22	–	–	90□	90	–	–	64	–	–	–	90	68¹	990
s1	–	90	s1	–	–	90□	–	–	90	90¹	–	90	–	90¹□	89	990
s14	–	90	–	–	–	90	90	s14	–	90¹	–	–	–	90□	76	990
s45	–	74	s16□	–	–	90□	90	90	–	45	–	–	–	90	90	990
90	s15	70■	45	–	–	90□	90	s45	–	s9□	–	–	–	90	75	970
59	s15	90¹	–	–	–	90	90	90	–	s31□	–	79□	–	–	90¹	990
84²	–	–	–	–	–	–	90	90	–	90¹	–	90	–	90	90¹	990
90	45	–	–	–	–	s45□	90	90□	–	90	–	90	–	90	79	990
90¹	90	–	s12	–	–	66	83	s24	–	78¹	–	90	–	90	90	990
90²	s8	68	s22□	–	–	90	60	90□	–	–	–	90	–	90	82	990
87	89	80¹	90	–	–	90	90	90	–	90	–	90	–	s1	s10	990
76	90□	90	45□	–	–	45	–	–	–	90	–	90¹	–	90	s14	990
45	–	90¹	s7	–	–	–	s45	–	–	90²	–	90	–	90¹□	90	990
s5	–	90	–	–	30	90	90	–	–	87¹	s3	–	–	90	85¹	990
s45	–	90¹	s49	–	–	90	90	–	–	41	s25	–	–	90	45	990
s1	–	90¹	s20	s2	–	90	–	–	–	–	–	90	–	90	89	990
82	–	90	90□	–	90	90	–	–	–	82	s8□	s45	–	90	s8	990
90¹	–	90¹	84	–	87	90	–	–	–	s67	23	s3	–	90	–	990
90¹	–	90	90	–	90	90	–	–	–	s32	58	s17	–	90	s19	990
s45¹	–	90	–	–	s23	–	67	–	–	–	90	90	–	90	90¹□	990
45	–	90¹	–	–	89	–	90	–	–	s45²	90	90	–	90□	80¹	990
–	–	90	s44□	–	90	–	90□	–	–	90¹	46	90□	–	90	90	990
s12¹	–	90¹	–	–	67	–	90	–	–	76¹	s14	90	–	90	78	990
s45	–	45□	–	–	90	–	90	–	–	90□	90	90	–	90□	45	990
s2	–	90□	–	–	88	–	90	64□	–	s26	–	90	–	90	77	990
63	–	90²	s5	–	90	–	90	90	–	76	–	90□	–	90	85	990
84	–	90²	s3	–	90□	–	90□	87	–	s1	–	90	–	90	89	990
s3	–	90¹□	90	–	90	s9	81	87	–	s25	–	90	–	90¹□	90	990

THE MANAGER

CLAUDIO RANIERI

There could have been few Chelsea supporters that were not amazed by the appointment of Claudio Ranieri in September 2000, following the sacking of fans' favourite Gianluca Vialli earlier in the month.

Ranieri certainly came with impressive credentials. Having begun his coaching career at Cagliari, where he took the club to Serie A with successive promotions, he became coach of Napoli in 1991 where he managed Gianfranco Zola among others.

The following season Ranieri moved to Fiorentina and set about turning them into one of the country's most entertaining sides with Italian Cup and Super Cup successes. In 1996 he moved to Spain to coach Valencia, continuing his run of elevating smaller sides to grander stature.

His next challenge was with Atletico Madrid, but not even Ranieri could save the cash-strapped club from relegation. He left the club in March 2000 and six months later joined the Blues, managing director Colin Hutchinson having closely followed the Italian's progress with his various clubs.

If Ranieri can mould Chelsea from giants-in-waiting to a side consistently challenging for the title, then his appointment may be viewed as one of the greatest coups in recent seasons.

LEAGUE POSITION

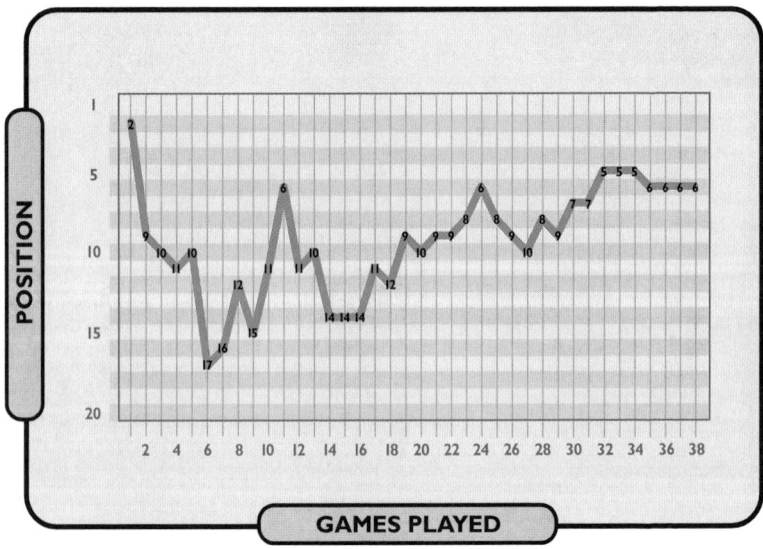

GAMES PLAYED

16 The Blues scored more headed goals

THE GOALS

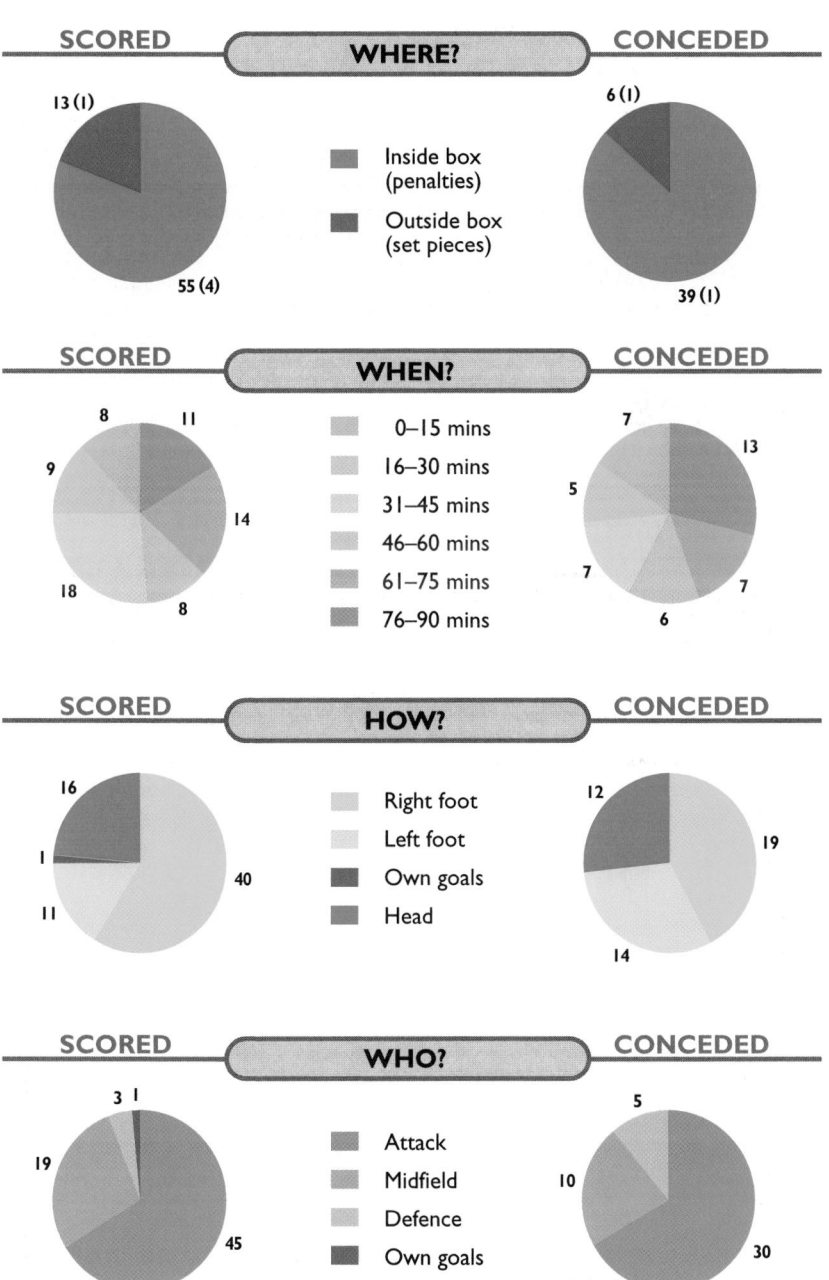

SCORED | **WHERE?** | **CONCEDED**

Inside box (penalties)
Outside box (set pieces)

Scored: 13 (1), 55 (4)
Conceded: 6 (1), 39 (1)

SCORED | **WHEN?** | **CONCEDED**

0–15 mins
16–30 mins
31–45 mins
46–60 mins
61–75 mins
76–90 mins

Scored: 8, 11, 9, 14, 18, 8
Conceded: 7, 13, 5, 7, 7, 6

SCORED | **HOW?** | **CONCEDED**

Right foot
Left foot
Own goals
Head

Scored: 16, 1, 11, 40
Conceded: 12, 19, 14

SCORED | **WHO?** | **CONCEDED**

Attack
Midfield
Defence
Own goals

Scored: 3, 1, 19, 45
Conceded: 5, 10, 30

than any other Premiership team

CHELSEA

	ALEKSIDZE	BABAYARO	BOGARDE	DALLA BONA	DESAILLY	DI MATTEO	FERRER	FLO	GRONKJAER	GUDJOHNSEN	HARLEY
APPEARANCES											
Start	0	19	2	26	34	7	12	5	6	17	6
Sub	2	5	7	3	0	0	2	9	8	13	4
Minutes on pitch	17	1651	315	2253	3001	630	1007	705	657	1570	525
GOAL ATTEMPTS											
Goals	0	0	0	2	2	0	0	3	1	10	0
Shots on target	1	0	0	9	5	6	1	12	8	27	2
Shots off target	0	4	1	27	4	7	2	8	8	17	3
Shooting accuracy	100%	0%	0%	25%	56%	46%	33%	60%	50%	61%	40%
PASSING											
Goal assists	0	5	0	3	1	1	0	3	1	6	0
Long passes	0	188	40	364	524	89	128	20	39	106	46
Short passes	10	728	119	886	1007	227	347	219	179	488	141
PASS COMPLETION											
Own half %	0%	85%	89%	86%	87%	87%	78%	88%	60%	79%	71%
Opposition half %	29%	73%	80%	66%	75%	72%	70%	69%	67%	68%	62%
CROSSING											
Total crosses	0	61	4	15	0	15	26	26	44	30	15
Cross completion %	0%	30%	50%	20%	0%	20%	19%	31%	25%	47%	27%
DRIBBLING											
Dribbles & runs	0	61	5	40	45	16	14	28	80	72	17
Dribble completion %	0%	62%	100%	68%	93%	81%	57%	68%	69%	54%	59%
DEFENDING											
Tackles made	0	48	8	100	125	22	36	17	14	13	20
Tackles won %	0%	75%	38%	69%	79%	68%	78%	65%	64%	54%	85%
Blocks	0	12	1	5	54	0	6	0	1	1	5
Clearances	0	63	26	23	290	6	29	4	10	10	8
Interceptions	0	7	0	4	18	0	4	0	4	3	0
DISCIPLINE											
Fouls	0	27	4	41	39	14	19	24	10	21	8
Offside	0	1	0	0	1	1	2	3	4	20	3
Yellow cards	0	4	0	8	10	0	2	1	2	0	1
Red cards	0	0	0	0	0	0	0	0	0	0	0

GOALKEEPER NAME	START/ (SUB)	TIME ON PITCH	GOALS CONCEDED	MINS/GOALS CONCEDED	SAVES MADE	SAVES/ SHOTS
CUDICINI	23(1)	2115	27	78	57	68%
DE GOEY	15(0)	1305	18	73	37	67%

For more information visit our website:

PLAYERS' STATISTICS

	HASSELBAINK	JOKANOVIC	LAMBOURDE	LE SAUX	LEBOEUF	MELCHIOT	MORRIS	PANUCCI	POYET	STANIC	TERRY	THOME	WISE	ZOLA	TOTAL	RANK
	35	7	0	18	23	27	13	7	22	8	19	1	35	31		
	0	12	1	2	2	4	8	1	8	4	3	0	1	5		
	2920	760	2	1540	1996	2431	1330	656	2019	563	1764	90	3151	2603		
	23	0	0	0	0	0	0	0	11	2	1	0	3	9	68*	3rd
	55	1	0	4	1	1	3	2	26	5	5	1	16	24	215	4th
	58	4	0	6	6	8	7	1	34	7	4	0	8	29	253	=4th
	49%	20%	0%	40%	14%	11%	30%	67%	43%	42%	56%	100%	67%	45%	46%	5th
	9	1	0	2	0	4	0	0	7	0	0	0	3	4	50	2nd
	106	183	0	172	512	245	161	123	226	48	360	14	566	296	4938	2nd
	821	351	1	525	664	939	506	175	740	162	630	37	1248	1016	12319	3rd
	86%	86%	0%	78%	85%	84%	85%	77%	80%	75%	87%	82%	86%	83%	84%	3rd
	70%	76%	100%	69%	61%	75%	77%	58%	70%	62%	64%	53%	73%	73%	69%	3rd
	88	8	0	70	15	47	11	34	31	23	4	0	185	189	941	9th
	31%	13%	0%	26%	20%	23%	27%	12%	23%	9%	25%	0%	34%	30%	28%	5th
	106	15	1	83	26	78	20	20	39	26	12	5	59	124	995	7th
	69%	80%	100%	64%	92%	71%	75%	85%	72%	77%	100%	100%	68%	70%	70%	4th
	14	50	0	72	81	75	38	20	37	15	52	1	77	28	964	11th
	43%	72%	0%	71%	78%	77%	55%	85%	78%	87%	73%	100%	65%	79%	73%	10th
	6	1	0	9	21	13	5	2	7	4	29	0	22	2	206	10th
	6	22	0	59	184	92	13	44	28	10	205	0	25	4	1245	15th
	1	2	0	2	22	7	6	3	2	0	11	1	11	1	109	11th
	51	22	0	29	30	35	33	10	32	20	24	3	54	20	571	=7th
	42	0	1	1	0	3	0	0	8	0	0	0	3	19	112	19th
	6	5	0	2	6	2	5	4	3	1	3	0	9	1	76	=3rd
	1	0	0	1	0	0	0	0	0	0	0	0	0	0	2	=15th

*Including one own goal

CROSSES CAUGHT	CROSSES PUNCHED	CROSSES DROPPED	CATCH SUCCESS	THROWS/ SHORT KICKS	% COMPLETION	LONG KICKS	% COMPLETION
42	11	1	98%	62	89%	373	53%
26	15	0	100%	58	95%	219	58%

PLAYER OF THE SEASON

PLAYER	INDEX SCORE
GUSTAVO POYET	1,052
Marcel Desailly	1,039
John Terry	1,037
Jimmy Floyd Hasselbaink	984
Eidur Gudjohnsen	967
Gianfranco Zola	891
Frank Leboeuf	886
Mario Melchiot	820
Dennis Wise	798
Sam Dalla Bona	753

News that fans' favourite Gustavo Poyet would be allowed to leave Stamford Bridge after handing in a transfer request will have come as a big blow to the Blues' faithful.

The disappointment would have been compounded by the fact that for the third season in succession, Poyet was ranked as the club's best player in 2000–01 on the Opta Index with an average score of 1,052 points.

The Uruguayan star was the league's highest-scoring midfielder with 11 goals to his credit, despite the fact that he started just 22 league matches. This makes his tally of seven assists – bettered by only seven players in the division – all the more impressive.

Central defensive duo Marcel Desailly and John Terry came out second and third respectively on Opta's system, after playing a vital part in Chelsea's late push for a Champions League place.

"The Rock" won more tackles in the Premiership than any other player barring compatriot Olivier Dacourt and made almost 300 clearances for Claudio Ranieri's men.

But it was Terry who really caught the eye at the back. The young England hopeful contributed more than 200 clearances and 52 crunching tackles, despite playing roughly half as much time as the experienced Frenchman.

Even the Premiership's top scorer took a back seat to this trio. Jimmy Floyd Hasselbaink smashed 23 goals and set up a fifth of Chelsea's other strikes, but Opta's system of all-round analysis ranked him below his team-mates. Although a practically permanent feature in the side, nine other Chelsea players completed more passes than Hasselbaink, while his poor disciplinary record further damaged his rating.

Eidur Gudjohnsen showed promise, while the evergreen Gianfranco Zola extended his Chelsea contract following a nine-goal haul in the 2000–01 Premiership.

Ranieri will look for all-round improvement throughout the side, though, after a largely disappointing campaign.

FIVE OF THE BEST

Chelsea defeated Manchester United with apparent ease in the Charity Shield, but when the Premiership started they found themselves lacking. Gianluca Vialli was sacked and Claudio Ranieri introduced, but the Pensioners took an age to hit form. A late surge saw the Blues qualify for the UEFA Cup.

TOP GOALSCORERS

	GOALS	GOALS/SHOTS
JIMMY HASSELBAINK	23	20%
Gustavo Poyet	11	18%
Eidur Gudjohnsen	10	23%
Gianfranco Zola	9	17%
Tore Andre Flo	3	15%

Chelsea paid £15 million in the hope that Jimmy Floyd Hasselbaink would be their first 20-goals-a-season striker since Kerry Dixon and the Dutchman did not disappoint. He won the Golden Boot with 23 goals of high quality. His conversion rate of 20% was a testament to his ability. Their 1999–2000 top scorer Gus Poyet went one better in 2000–01 and scored 11 times, while Eidur Gudjohnsen also reached double figures.

Dennis Wise topped the passing charts at Chelsea for the second season in succession, making 1,412 successful passes with a completion rate of 78%. French defender Marcel Desailly was exceedingly accurate on the ball, finding a team-mate with 83% of his distribution. Newcomer Sam Dalla Bona makes the top five too and the success of the young Italian will cheer those Chelsea fans who worry about the average age of the west London team.

TOP PASSERS

	SUCC PASSES	COMPLETION
DENNIS WISE	1,412	78%
Marcel Desailly	1,270	83%
Gianfranco Zola	1,002	76%
Mario Melchiot	948	80%
Sam Dalla Bona	933	75%

TOP TACKLERS

	WON	SUCCESS
MARCEL DESAILLY	99	79%
Sam Dalla Bona	69	69%
Frank Leboeuf	63	78%
Mario Melchiot	58	77%
Graeme Le Saux	51	71%

Hulking defender Marcel Desailly was the rock in Chelsea's defence in 2000–01 and ended the campaign just one successful tackle short of 100. His emerging partnership with John Terry was one of the success stories of the season at Stamford Bridge. Sam Dalla Bona proved he could mix it in the middle of the park, while Frank Leboeuf – so often criticised – still managed to win 78% of his challenges.

Dennis Wise accrued nine yellow cards in 2000–01 and the diminutive schemer topped the Chelsea indiscipline charts. Fiery Jimmy Floyd Hasselbaink was second after being one of just two Pensioners to be sent off. Marcel Desailly was the only player to reach 10 yellow cards, but he committed only 39 fouls. Sam Dalla Bona and Frank Leboeuf were the other players in the top five.

DISCIPLINE

	POINTS	FOULS & CARDS
DENNIS WISE	81	54F, 9Y, 0R
Jimmy Hasselbaink	75	51F, 6Y, 1R
Marcel Desailly	69	39F, 10Y, 0R
Sam Dalla Bona	65	41F, 8Y, 0R
Frank Leboeuf	48	30F, 6Y, 0R

ACTION	BOGARDE	CUDICINI	DALLA BONA	DESAILLY	DI MATTEO	FLO	HARLEY	HASSELBAINK	LE SAUX	LEBOEUF	MELCHIOT	MORRIS	PANUCCI	ZOLA	TOTAL	MAN UTD
Time on pitch	3	90	6	90	90	90	45	87	90	45	90	90	90	84	990	990
GOALS																
Goal	–	–	–	–	–	2	–	1	–	–	–	–	–	–	3	3
Shot on target (incl goals)	–	–	–	–	2	2	–	1	–	–	–	–	–	–	5	6
Shot off target	–	–	–	2	–	–	2	3	–	1	–	–	–	1	9	7
Blocked shot	–	–	–	–	–	–	–	–	–	–	–	–	–	–	0	3
Own goal	–	–	–	–	–	–	–	–	–	–	–	–	–	–	0	0
PASSES																
Pass to own player	1	8	3	42	39	35	8	15	33	6	43	26	16	27	318	281
Pass to opposition	–	9	2	2	21	11	4	4	6	2	2	16	8	8	99	102
Cross to own player	–	–	–	–	–	–	1	–	2	–	–	–	1	1	8	5
Cross to opposition player	–	–	–	–	3	3	–	3	1	–	–	2	6	–	17	12
Goal assist	–	–	–	–	–	1	–	–	–	–	–	–	1	1	3	2
Pass completion %	100%	47%	60%	95%	66%	73%	69%	76%	80%	71%	96%	60%	67%	67%	74%	72%
TACKLES & CLEARANCES																
Tackle	–	–	–	3	4	2	1	2	3	–	2	5	–	–	21	19
Clearances, blocks and interceptions	1	–	–	10	1	1	–	6	8	–	–	9	–	–	37	51
DRIBBLES & RUNS																
Dribbles ball retained	–	–	–	2	2	2	–	5	1	–	–	3	3	–	18	17
Dribbles ball lost	–	–	–	–	–	1	1	–	–	–	–	1	–	–	3	5
Dribble success %	0%	0%	0%	100%	100%	67%	0%	100%	100%	0%	0%	75%	100%	100%	86%	77%
DISCIPLINE																
Fouls	–	–	1	–	3	3	4	4	–	–	4	1	–	–	20	18
Penalty conceded	–	–	–	–	–	–	–	–	–	–	–	–	–	–	0	0
Free kick – offside	–	–	–	–	1	1	–	1	–	–	–	–	–	3	6	3
Yellow cards	–	–	–	–	–	–	–	1	1	–	–	–	–	–	2	3
Red cards	–	–	–	–	–	–	–	–	–	–	–	–	–	–	0	0
GOALKEEPERS																
Distribution to own player	–	18	–	–	–	–	–	–	–	–	–	–	–	–	20	18
Distribution to opposition player	–	7	–	–	–	–	–	–	–	–	–	–	–	–	7	3
Goalkeeper distribution %	–	72%	–	–	–	–	–	–	–	–	–	–	–	–	72%	73%
Save	–	2	–	–	–	–	–	–	–	–	–	–	–	–	2	2
Ball caught	–	1	–	–	–	–	–	–	–	–	–	–	–	–	1	–
Ball dropped	–	–	–	–	–	–	–	–	–	–	–	–	–	–	–	0
Goal conceded	–	3	–	–	–	–	–	–	–	–	–	–	–	–	3	3

21 The number of overseas players used

A trip to Old Trafford is a daunting propect at the best of times. Claudio Ranieri's first game in charge of Chelsea produced a thrilling comeback, as the Blues became the first team in six months to take a point from the Theatre of Dreams.

23 September 2000

3–3

MANCHESTER UNITED
CHELSEA

Manchester United had yet to concede a single goal at home when Chelsea visited in late September. But eventual Golden Boot winner Jimmy Floyd Hasselbaink obliterated that record as early as the eighth minute. Tore Andre Flo got on the end of Graeme Le Saux's deep cross and knocked the ball down to the Dutchman, whose rasping drive flew into the top corner of the net.

However, the Red Devils were determined not to lose their proud unbeaten home run, which dated back to December 1998. A gritty display from Sir Alex Ferguson's team saw them win 84% of their challenges in a passionate encounter.

Paul Scholes grabbed a spectacular equaliser in the 14th minute when he fired home from the edge of the box after Teddy Sheringham had flicked back David Beckham's corner.

A bad-tempered spell followed in which cautions were issued to Christian Panucci, Gary Neville and Roy Keane, who had only just returned from a suspension for getting dismissed in the Charity Shield.

United then hit a purple patch with two quick goals. First Sheringham converted at the back post after Denis Irwin's hopeful pass eluded several players in the penalty area.

Then Beckham scored his fourth goal of the season when he poked the ball into an empty net after Andy Cole's effort had rebounded off the post.

But Chelsea grabbed a lifeline on the stroke of half-time when Le Saux stormed down the left. Flo met the Channel Islander's cross with a stooping header which Raimond van der Gouw could only spill into the net.

It had been a breathless first half for the 67,000 capacity crowd, as well as the millions of armchair viewers watching on television.

Ranieri replaced Jon Harley with Mario Melchiot in midfield at the start of the second half and the tactic seemed to pay off, with the Blues playing much the better football. They were successful with 74% of their passing attempts – two percentage points better than United – and created a host of goal-scoring opportunities.

Nevertheless United could have finished off the game in the 65th minute, but were thwarted when Le Saux expertly cleared Cole's shot off the line.

Then four minutes later another great burst from Le Saux ended with a telling cross which Gianfranco Zola laid into the path of Flo for the Norwegian to slot coolly home.

Ryan Giggs blazed narrowly over the bar after substitute Ole Gunnar Solskjaer crossed from the right. But another United goal would have been harsh on a Chelsea team who deservedly took a share of the spoils after showing their mettle to come back from a two-goal deficit at the home of the champions.

by Chelsea in the 2000–01 campaign

COVENTRY CITY

ADDRESS

**Highfield Road Stadium,
King Richard Street, Coventry CV2 4FW**

CONTACT NUMBERS

**Telephone: 024 7623 4000
Fax: 024 7623 4099
Ticket Office: 024 7623 4020
Club Call: 09068 121166
Superstore: 024 7623 4030
e-mail: info@ccfc.co.uk
Website: www.ccfc.co.uk**

KEY PERSONNEL

**President: Geoffrey Robinson MP
Chairman: B A Richardson
Deputy Chairman: M C McGinnity
Directors: A M Jepson
J F W Reason, D A Higgs
Miss B Price, G P Hover
Club Secretary: G P Hover
Manager: Gordon Strachan**

SPONSORS

Subaru/Isuzu

FANZINES

**Peeping Tom
Gary Mabbutt's Knee
Twist And Shout**

COLOURS

**Home: Sky blue and white
striped shirts, white shorts
and white stockings
Away: Black shirts, black shorts
and black stockings**

NICKNAME

The Sky Blues

HONOURS

**Division Two Champions: 1966–67
Division Three Champions: 1963–64
Division Three (South)
Champions: 1935–36
FA Cup Winners: 1987**

RECORD GOALSCORER

**Clarrie Bourton –
171 league goals, 1931–37**

BIGGEST WIN

**9–0 v Bristol City – Division Three
(South), 28 April 1934**

BIGGEST DEFEAT

**2–10 v Norwich City – Division Three
(South), 15 March 1930**

SEASON REVIEW

One of the oldest football-related jokes was that if the Titanic had been painted sky-blue, there was no way it would have sunk. This, of course, related to the fact that Coventry City were the only club to reach the top flight of English football and never get relegated from it, despite a number of close-calls.

But season 2000–01 saw an end to this fine record, and Coventry were relegated with one game to spare in the match against Midlands rivals Aston Villa. It ended a 34-season sojourn in the top division for the Sky Blues – only Everton, Liverpool and Arsenal had a longer current run.

Every team below the élite suffers from the same problems – bigger clubs come looking for their best players. City had somehow survived over the years by finding cheaper replacements for players who had moved for big money. In the summer of 2000 the Honduran Ivan Guerrero was recruited, along with David Thompson and Jay Bothroyd, while Gary McAllister left on a free and Noel Whelan departed for Middlesbrough.

However, possibly the most crucial factor in Coventry's ultimately-catastrophic season was when Inter Milan agreed to pay £13 million for striking starlet Robbie Keane. The young Irishman bagged 12 Premiership goals in his first top-flight campaign for the Sky Blues and when he returned on loan to Leeds at the turn of the year he managed to score nine in half a season for David O'Leary's men. City's top scorer managed just six.

To replace Keane, Coventry turned to Welshman Craig Bellamy, but the signing from Norwich had played very few games in the previous year due to a serious injury and took time to settle. And both John Aloisi and Cedric Roussel failed to strike up a prolific partnership with the new front-man.

Indeed, for much of the season Moustapha Hadji, the newly-appointed captain, was deployed as a striker, and towards the end of the campaign the Moroccan partnered John Hartson up front while Bellamy attacked from a left-wing position.

This chronic lack of firepower saw City rack up the second-lowest tally of goals, behind bottom club Bradford. It was an even worse scenario at Highfield Road, where they scored just 14 goals – the lowest total of home strikes in Premiership history.

There was nothing to suggest such a bleak outlook at the start of the season, though. Despite an opening-day home defeat by Middlesbrough, away victories at Southampton and Manchester City saw Coventry in the dizzy position of fourth in the table. But a run of three home matches without a goal, plus a defeat at Arsenal, gleaned just one more point and saw them plummet to 17th. A brief rally of four points from two matches was short-lived and a 6–1 defeat by Chelsea heralded a run of six losses in seven outings.

Gordon Strachan's side had slipped into the bottom three and, although a 1–0 win over Leicester saw them briefly escape the drop zone, defeat in their next match left them back in the relegation places.

This was the period in which City were effectively relegated. They won just two matches out of 21 between 14 October and 31 March. The boss tried to freshen things up by signing Lee Carsley and allowing Carlton Palmer and Colin Hendry to go out on loan, but it was ultimately all in vain.

The situation was exacerbated by international calls on City's players.

> "I would like to start next season immediately. There are ideas bouncing around in my head and I want to get on with it."
>
> **Gordon Strachan**

76% The Sky Blues were the most

SEASON REVIEW

Youssef Chippo and Moustapha Hadji in particular were sorely missed on their frequent trips to play for Morocco. On one infamous occasion, John Aloisi was called up to play for Australia while Paul Okon and Mark Schwarzer of Middlesbrough – one of City's main rivals in the battle to beat the drop – were excused duty. Strachan was incensed, claiming Boro coach Terry Venables had pulled strings thanks to his relationship with the Australian FA after previously having been their national coach.

The situation looked so bad that some fans attempted to confront Strachan at the end of a 3–1 defeat by Everton and had to be restrained by stewards. Chairman Bryan Richardson backed his manager, but this did not stop the regular calls for a change at the top from City's fans.

Popular former Sky Blue Roland Nilsson joined the coaching staff and it was hoped that his influence would have a positive effect on the team. But the Swede was not able to help arrest the decline.

Strachan tried to solve the goalscoring problems by bidding for John Hartson, but issues over the price and Cedric Roussel being offered in part-exchange delayed the transfer until finally a pay-as-you-play deal was arranged in early March.

Hartson scored six goals in the run-in, but it was too little, too late. Coventry seemed doomed – then won back-to-back matches against Derby and Leicester to raise hopes of a miraculous escape.

Even defeat by Manchester United did not dampen spirits, as City had matched the champions in a pulsating first half and were only beaten by two late goals. The growing belief in the side, and a newfound resilience, saw City win an Easter Monday encounter with Sunderland to put them in sight of safety.

> "In order to escape relegation trouble, I always feel it is necessary for a team to average slightly more than a point a game over the season."
>
> **Gordon Strachan**

But high-flying Ipswich and Liverpool both eased past Coventry and that set up a win-or-bust scenario, in which nothing less than two victories would see City stay up. It was ironic that Gary McAllister scored for the Reds against his former club, adding to the goal he bagged in the earlier encounter at Anfield.

Away at Aston Villa, the Sky Blues stormed into a two-goal lead by half-time courtesy of Moroccan Moustapha Hadji. With Bradford at home on the final day, City fans must have thought they would pull off a great escape once again. But the introduction of David Ginola turned the match. After Villa pulled one back early in the second half, two late goals earned them a 3–2 win and saw Coventry relegated.

Conceding late goals was a constant problem for Strachan's side. No team conceded more in the last 15 minutes of matches and these 17 strikes cost a total of 16 points – more than enough to have survived.

Former Sky Blue George Boateng laid the blame at the feet of Bryan Richardson, whom he claimed forced Strachan to sell all his best players. The Dutchman immodestly included himself in that category.

Another area in which City struggled was retaining possession. Coventry players found a team-mate with just 62% of their passes – the worst rating of any team in the division and some six percentage points worse than their accuracy for the previous campaign.

While obviously sad at the fact they have finally succumbed to relegation, the Sky Blues are confident that they can bounce back. One consolation, of course, is that they will never have to hear that Titanic joke again.

successful tacklers in the Premiership

COVENTRY CITY

DATE	OPPONENT	SCORE	ATT.	ALOISI	BELLAMY	BETTS	BOTHROYD	BREEN	CARSLEY	CHIPPO	DAVENPORT	EDWORTHY	EUSTACE	GUERRERO	HADJI
19.08.00	Middlesbro H	1–3	20,624	s10	90	–	–	80□	–	90	–	–	69^1□	–	–
23.08.00	Southampton A	2–1	14,801	–	84^1□	–	–	–	–	90	–	90	90	–	–
26.08.00	Man City A	2–1*	34,140	–	90^1	–	–	–	–	45	–	90□	90	–	–
06.09.00	Newcastle H	0–2	22,109	s20	70	–	–	–	–	90□	–	90	61	–	s29
09.09.00	Leeds Utd A	0–0	20,377	–	65	–	–	–	–	90□	–	90	s19	–	90
16.09.00	Arsenal A	1–2	37,794	–	63	–	–	s9	–	90	–	81	s33□	–	90^1
23.09.00	West Ham H	0–3	21,020	s25	90	–	–	s15	–	90	–	90	s45	–	90
30.09.00	Charlton A	2–2	20,043	76^1	90^1□	–	–	–	–	90□	–	90	90	–	–
14.10.00	Tottenham H	2–1	21,435	73^1	82	–	–	90	–	90	–	90	90^1	–	90
21.10.00	Chelsea A	1–6	34,646	23	59	–	–	90	–	90□	–	90	45	–	90
28.10.00	Sunderland A	0–1	44,526	51	90	–	–	90	–	90□	–	–	s17	80	90
04.11.00	Man Utd H	1–2	21,079	–	–	–	45	90	–	90	–	90	s33□	90	90
12.11.00	Liverpool A	1–4	43,701	–	90	–	–	90	–	58	–	s34	s8	56	90
20.11.00	Ipswich A	0–1	19,324	s22	90	–	–	90	–	90□	–	90	–	–	90
25.11.00	Aston Villa H	1–1	21,464	s45	–	–	–	90	–	45	–	90	s45	–	90^1
02.12.00	Bradford A	1–2	15,523	90^1	s7	–	–	90	–	s10	–	–	90□	–	–
10.12.00	Leicester H	1–0	17,283	77	90^1	–	–	90	90	–	–	–	–	–	90
16.12.00	Derby Co A	0–1	27,869	60	90	–	–	90	90□	s11	–	–	s6	–	90
22.12.00	Southampton H	1–1	18,090	–	69	–	–	90	90	s45	–	–	s14	–	90
26.12.00	Everton A	2–1	35,704	s12	85	–	–	90^1□	90	s5	–	s67	–	–	90^1
30.12.00	Middlesbro A	1–1*	30,499	s25	78□	–	–	90	90	s12	–	90	–	–	90
01.01.01	Man City H	1–1	21,999	s33	73	–	–	90	90	s17	–	90^1	s24	–	90
13.01.01	Newcastle A	1–3	50,159	73	90□	–	s17	90	90□	–	–	90	90	–	–
20.01.01	Everton H	1–3	19,174	s31	–	–	–	90	90^1	s45	–	90	90	–	90
31.01.01	Leeds Utd A	0–1	36,555	–	90□	–	s14	90	76	s14	–	–	90□	–	90□
03.02.01	Arsenal H	0–1	22,035	–	90	–	s6	–	90□	–	–	–	90□	–	90
12.02.01	West Ham A	1–1*	22,586	–	89	–	s2	90□	77	s13	–	s1	90□	–	90
24.02.01	Charlton H	2–2	19,480	s31	90^1	–	–	90	90	59	–	90	–	–	–
03.03.01	Chelsea H	0–0	21,609	s14	90	–	–	90□	60	s30	–	–	90□	–	76
17.03.01	Tottenham A	0–3	35,606	–	90	–	–	90□	90□	s14	–	s12	90	–	90
31.03.01	Derby Co H	2–0	19,654	–	84	–	–	90	90	s6	–	–	90	–	73^1□
07.04.01	Leicester A	3–1	19,545	–	90^1□	–	–	90	90^1□	s8	–	–	82	–	88
14.04.01	Man Utd A	2–4	67,637	–	90	–	–	90□	90	s27	–	–	78	–	–
16.04.01	Sunderland H	1–0	20,946	–	–	–	90	90□	90	–	–	–	89□	–	–
21.04.01	Ipswich A	0–2	24,612	–	90	–	57	90	62	–	–	s28	90□	–	–
28.04.01	Liverpool H	0–2	23,063	–	64	–	–	90□	–	90	–	–	90	–	90
05.05.01	Aston Villa A	2–3	39,761	–	90□	–	–	90	90□	–	–	s52	90□	–	90^2
19.05.01	Bradford H	0–0	20,299	–	–	s1	s11	–	90	79□	s45	90	–	–	90

□ Yellow card, ■ Red card, s Substitute, 90^2 Goals scored

*including own goal

2000–01 PREMIERSHIP APPEARANCES

HALL	HARTSON	HEDMAN	HENDRY	KIRKLAND	KONJIC	MILLER	PALMER	QUINN	ROUSSEL	SHAW	STRACHAN	TELFER	THOMPSON	WILLIAMS	ZUNIGA	TOTAL
90	–	90	90	–	–	–	90□	–	90	–	–	s21	71□	90□	–	971
90	–	90	–	–	–	–	90□	–	90[1]	90	–	90	–	90□	s6	990
90	–	90	–	–	–	–	90□	–	90	90	–	90	s45	90□	–	990
90	–	90	–	–	–	–	90	–	90	90	–	90	–	90	–	990
90	–	90	–	–	–	–	90	–	90	90□	–	71	–	90	s25	990
90	–	90	–	–	–	–	90	–	90	90	–	57	–	90	s27□	990
75	–	90	–	–	–	–	90	–	–	90	–	–	45	90	65	990
90	–	90	–	–	–	–	90	–	s14	90	–	90	–	90	–	990
–	–	–	s8	90	–	–	72□	–	s17	90	–	90	–	–	–	972
–	–	–	–	22□	–	s67	90	–	s31[1]	s45	–	90	–	90	–	922
–	–	–	–	90□	–	–	73	s39	90	–	90	s10	90	–	–	990
–	–	–	–	90	–	–	–	57	–	90	–	s33	57	90	s45[1]	990
–	–	–	–	90	–	–	90	–	s32	90	82	–	90[1]□	90	–	990
–	–	–	–	90	90	–	–	–	68	–	–	90	90	90	–	990
–	–	–	–	90	90	–	s18	–	45	–	–	90	90□	90	72	990
–	–	–	–	90	80	–	90□	90	–	–	–	90	83	90	–	990
–	–	90	–	–	90	–	s10	90	s13	–	–	80	90	90	–	990
–	–	90	–	–	90	–	–	90□	s30	–	–	90	84	79□	–	990
–	–	–	–	90	90	–	–	90	45	–	–	90	76[1]□	90	s21	990
–	–	–	–	90	23	–	–	90	–	–	–	90	90	90	78	990
–	–	–	–	90	–	–	–	90	–	–	–	90□	90□	90	65	990
–	–	–	–	90	–	–	–	66□	–	–	–	90	90	90	57	990
–	–	90	–	–	–	–	–	90	–	–	–	90	90[1]□	90	–	990
–	–	–	–	90	27	–	s63	90	–	–	–	45	90	–	59	990
90	–	90	–	–	–	–	–	52	–	90	–	s38	76□	90□	–	990
90	–	90	–	–	–	–	–	90	90	90	–	–	84□	90	–	990
90	90□	90	–	–	–	–	–	88□	–	90	–	–	90□	–	–	990
90	90[1]	90	–	–	–	–	–	90	–	90	–	–	90	–	–	990
90	90	–	–	90	–	–	–	90	–	90	–	–	90	–	–	990
90	64	–	–	90	–	–	–	90	–	90	–	s26	64	–	–	990
90	90[1]	–	–	90	–	–	–	90	–	90	–	90	–	–	–	973
90	90[1]	–	–	90	–	–	–	90	–	90	–	90	–	s2	–	990
90	90[2]□	–	–	90	–	–	–	90	–	90	–	63	90□	s12□	–	990
90	90[1]	–	–	90	–	–	–	90	–	90	–	90	s1	–	–	990
90□	90□	–	–	90	–	–	–	77	–	90	–	90	–	s13	s33□	990
90	90	–	–	90	–	–	–	90□	–	90	–	90	–	90□	s26	990
86□	90□	–	–	90	–	–	–	90	–	–	–	38	–	90	s4	990
–	90	–	–	90	–	–	–	90	–	90	89	–	–	45	90	990

THE MANAGER

GORDON STRACHAN

The scowl on the face of Gordon Strachan was more pronounced than ever during 2000–01, as Coventry finally succumbed to the relegation with which they had flirted for five of the previous six campaigns.

The energetic and determined demeanour for which Strachan had become well known often seemed a distant memory during a difficult season. More than once he questioned his own position, contemplating ending his six-year association with the club as player and manager.

Although others at the club are convinced it will be an immediate return to the big time for the Sky Blues, the 44-year-old Scot is typically cautious, stating: "I'm making no predictions. Relegation has obviously been a bad experience for us and we will soon learn how it has affected us."

The former Leeds and Manchester United star still has the backing of his chairman, and it seems likely that some time out of the limelight will be good for Strachan. Relegation has often been an important part of a successful manager's learning of the trade – but Strachan knows that it is vital to get off to a good start in 2001–02 if Coventry are to bounce back immediately.

LEAGUE POSITION

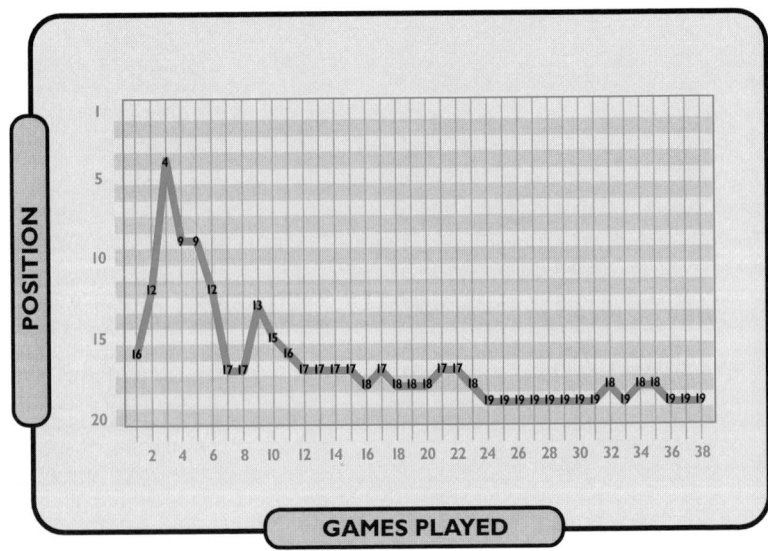

GAMES PLAYED

17 No side conceded more goals

THE GOALS

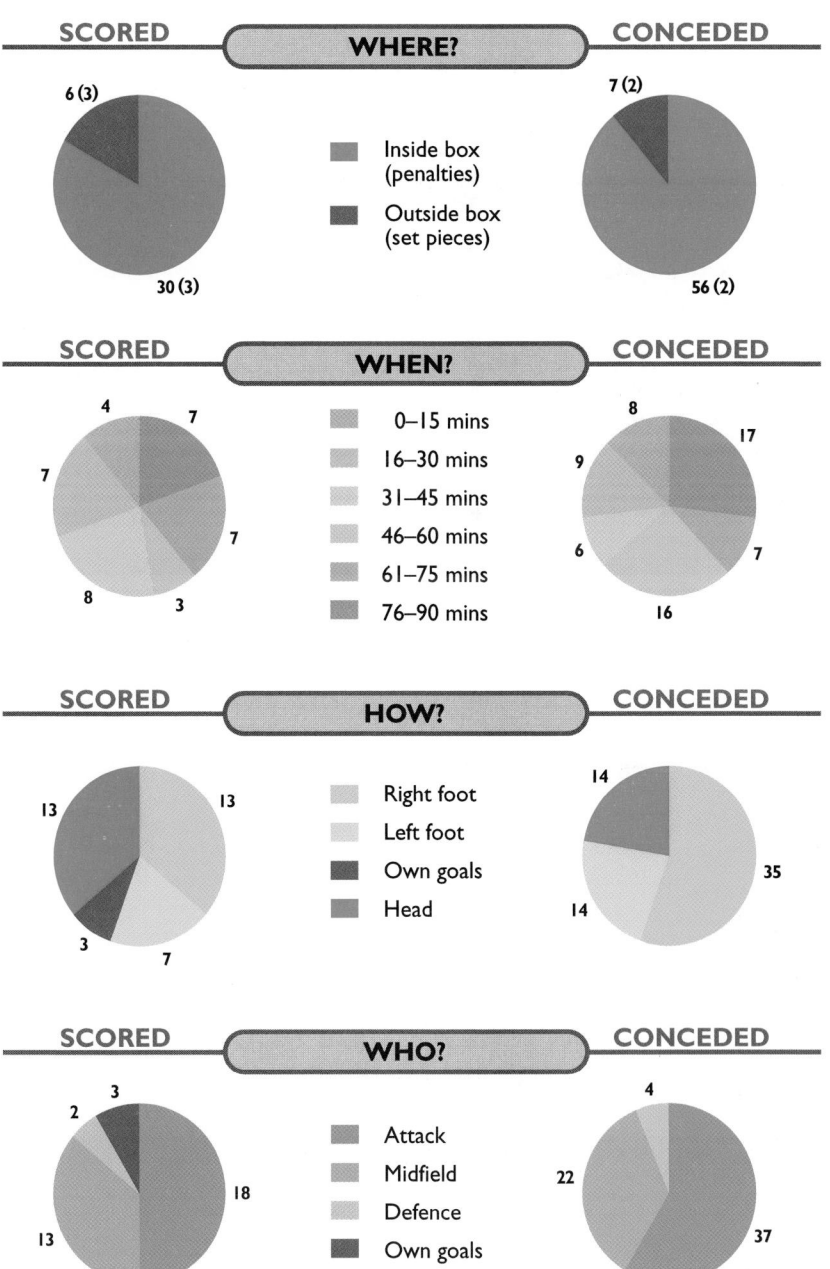

WHERE?

SCORED

CONCEDED

6 (3)
30 (3)

7 (2)
56 (2)

- Inside box (penalties)
- Outside box (set pieces)

WHEN?

SCORED

CONCEDED

4
7
7
7
8
3

8
17
9
6
7
16

- 0–15 mins
- 16–30 mins
- 31–45 mins
- 46–60 mins
- 61–75 mins
- 76–90 mins

HOW?

SCORED

CONCEDED

13
13
3
7

14
35
14

- Right foot
- Left foot
- Own goals
- Head

WHO?

SCORED

CONCEDED

3
2
18
13

4
22
37

- Attack
- Midfield
- Defence
- Own goals

in the last 15 minutes of games than Coventry

COVENTRY CITY

	ALOISI	BELLAMY	BETTS	BOTHROYD	BREEN	CARSLEY	CHIPPO	DAVENPORT	EDWORTHY	EUSTACE	GUERRERO
APPEARANCES											
Start	8	33	0	3	29	21	18	0	18	22	3
Sub	11	1	1	5	2	0	14	1	6	10	0
Minutes on pitch	791	2772	1	242	2624	1805	1713	45	1805	2108	226
GOAL ATTEMPTS											
Goals	3	6	0	0	1	2	0	0	1	2	0
Shots on target	6	28	0	2	4	9	4	1	1	13	0
Shots off target	6	17	0	1	7	9	8	0	4	24	1
Shooting accuracy	50%	62%	0%	67%	36%	50%	33%	100%	20%	35%	0%
PASSING											
Goal assists	2	1	0	0	2	1	0	0	0	1	0
Long passes	18	92	1	13	305	204	143	4	205	187	25
Short passes	184	674	0	57	545	515	558	7	483	525	45
PASS COMPLETION											
Own half %	74%	78%	0%	70%	74%	76%	82%	50%	74%	75%	65%
Opposition half %	48%	70%	0%	53%	45%	60%	59%	60%	64%	53%	56%
CROSSING											
Total crosses	1	66	0	6	28	18	27	0	45	23	5
Cross completion %	0%	23%	0%	33%	14%	50%	11%	0%	11%	22%	0%
DRIBBLING											
Dribbles & runs	9	161	0	5	44	11	76	2	54	36	6
Dribble completion %	33%	57%	0%	80%	84%	73%	68%	50%	85%	64%	100%
DEFENDING											
Tackles made	7	34	0	5	48	69	89	0	44	94	5
Tackles won %	86%	74%	0%	60%	75%	74%	74%	0%	84%	72%	80%
Blocks	0	3	0	0	43	10	11	1	15	7	1
Clearances	3	3	0	0	334	56	18	6	66	27	6
Interceptions	2	6	0	0	12	4	12	1	7	5	0
DISCIPLINE											
Fouls	21	42	0	9	40	26	48	1	27	56	2
Offside	12	40	0	8	1	0	1	0	1	2	1
Yellow cards	0	7	0	0	8	6	7	0	1	11	0
Red cards	0	0	0	0	0	0	0	0	0	0	0

GOALKEEPER NAME	START/ (SUB)	TIME ON PITCH	GOALS CONCEDED	MINS/GOALS CONCEDED	SAVES MADE	SAVES/ SHOTS
HEDMAN	15(0)	1350	23	59	61	73%
KIRKLAND	23(0)	2002	34	59	88	72%
MILLER	0(1)	67	6	11	8	57%

For more information visit our website:

PLAYERS' STATISTICS

	HADJI	HALL	HARTSON	HENDRY	KONJIC	PALMER	QUINN	ROUSSEL	SHAW	STRACHAN	TELFER	THOMPSON	WILLIAMS	ZUNIGA	TOTAL	RANK
	28	21	12	1	8	12	25	10	23	2	27	22	27	7		
	1	0	0	1	0	3	0	7	1	0	4	3	3	8		
	2516	1871	1054	98	580	1153	2123	964	2115	171	2362	1866	2401	673		
	6	0	6	0	0	0	0	2	0	0	0	3	0	1	36*	19th
	26	2	16	1	1	2	1	11	0	0	5	11	2	8	154	16th
	53	9	20	1	5	3	1	9	0	1	12	35	8	9	243	=8th
	33%	18%	44%	50%	17%	40%	50%	55%	0%	0%	29%	24%	20%	47%	39%	19th
	3	0	0	0	0	0	1	0	0	0	6	3	1	0	21	=19th
	191	189	47	10	50	110	267	21	169	14	267	144	438	18	3566	20th
	680	362	254	17	111	357	537	213	330	65	742	517	461	175	8458	20th
	73%	66%	85%	79%	66%	78%	69%	70%	76%	95%	78%	74%	74%	77%	75%	20th
	52%	52%	55%	54%	41%	63%	53%	63%	51%	75%	57%	57%	41%	67%	55%	20th
	91	65	8	0	1	12	66	12	3	10	185	212	12	8	904	11th
	24%	15%	38%	0%	0%	25%	21%	0%	67%	50%	29%	27%	58%	50%	25%	18th
	119	35	18	0	1	8	31	11	2	0	22	100	21	4	780	19th
	54%	86%	28%	0%	100%	88%	81%	82%	100%	0%	77%	53%	86%	75%	65%	19th
	36	49	2	0	18	43	62	10	50	4	50	64	78	23	889	19th
	78%	82%	50%	0%	83%	74%	76%	70%	70%	100%	64%	84%	76%	96%	76%	1st
	4	17	1	1	4	10	22	2	28	0	5	5	43	1	234	6th
	19	96	14	7	101	16	116	2	192	2	48	12	257	3	1500	4th
	1	4	0	2	1	2	9	1	10	0	4	4	16	0	104	14th
	39	15	47	0	7	9	16	8	29	0	18	47	35	17	561	10th
	14	1	18	0	0	0	1	27	0	0	0	6	0	11	144	8th
	1	2	4	0	0	4	4	0	1	0	1	9	7	2	76	=3rd
	1	0	0	0	0	1	0	0	0	0	0	1	0	0	4	=5th

*Including three own goals

CROSSES CAUGHT	CROSSES PUNCHED	CROSSES DROPPED	CATCH SUCCESS	THROWS/SHORT KICKS	% COMPLETION	LONG KICKS	% COMPLETION
46	9	2	96%	26	54%	307	47%
33	10	4	89%	18	61%	481	44%
0	1	0	0%	2	100%	15	60%

PLAYER OF THE SEASON

PLAYER	INDEX SCORE
CHRIS KIRKLAND	689
David Thompson	656
Lee Carsley	647
Paul Williams	642
Gary Breen	640
Moustapha Hadji	599
Marc Edworthy	579
Barry Quinn	576
Paul Telfer	550
Richard Shaw	520

The 34-year adventure is over for the time being for Coventry City, but there are plenty of plus points to be taken from the 2000–01 season.

One was the emergence of rookie 'keeper Chris Kirkland, who emerged as the Sky Blues' player of the season according to the Opta Index, with an average points score of 689.

The youngster – who signed an extended contract during the campaign – pulled off 88 saves during his 33 hours on pitch, which made him the fifth-busiest regular 'keeper in the league in terms of average minutes per save made.

Kirkland saved 72% of all strikes at his goal – the best ratio of any first-choice shot-stopper at the bottom six clubs – and this kind of form attracted interest from the likes of Liverpool.

Midfield dynamos David Thompson and Lee Carsley made up the top three thanks to their tireless efforts. Thompson mustered three goals and three assists for City, while his 84% tackle success rate – the best at the club – clearly showed his combative prowess. Carsley, who particularly impressed in the run-in, scored twice and maintained a decent 66% pass completion rate.

But City sorely missed their top-ranked player of 1999–2000, Gary McAllister, and fourth-placed Robbie Keane. Moustapha Hadji attempted 79 shots: the most by a Premiership midfielder, although he played several times in attack.

Defensive stalwarts Paul Williams and Gary Breen were two of the busiest men, completing 591 clearances between them.

John Hartson grabbed six goals from 36 shots and, had he arrived earlier, City might well have stayed in the Premiership. He will be vital to the club's bid to return to the top flight.

Hartson bettered Kirkland's average score of 689 points, but did not play enough to qualify for the Index. He also helped fellow-Welshman Craig Bellamy find his cutting edge, although the £6.5 million signing still did not make the top 10.

54.7% Coventry were the least accurate

FIVE OF THE BEST

Coventry City's proud stay in the top flight finally ended in 2000–01 and the lack of a regular goalscorer was the main reason for their demise. The decision to sell Robbie Keane in pre-season backfired and only when John Hartson arrived at the club in February did the Sky Blues really threaten the goal.

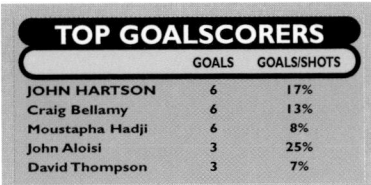

TOP GOALSCORERS	GOALS	GOALS/SHOTS
JOHN HARTSON	6	17%
Craig Bellamy	6	13%
Moustapha Hadji	6	8%
John Aloisi	3	25%
David Thompson	3	7%

John Hartson only joined Coventry in February, but still ended the season as the leading scorer at Highfield Road. He scored six times but to no avail. His Welsh team-mate Craig Bellamy also bagged six goals but that still worked out at more than a million pounds a goal for the former Norwich player. Moustapha Hadji was the third City player to score six, but it is unlikely he will be with the club in the Nationwide League.

Coventry were the worst passers in the Premiership, a fact starkly illustrated by their top five. Paul Telfer made just 657 successful passes but this was enough to make him the top man at City. Craig Bellamy managed to find a team-mate with more than 70% of his distribution, but he was the exception to the rule. Paul Williams, Moustapha Hadji and Gary Breen did not even achieve 60%, yet they finished third, fourth and fifth respectively.

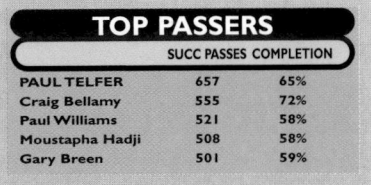

TOP PASSERS	SUCC PASSES	COMPLETION
PAUL TELFER	657	65%
Craig Bellamy	555	72%
Paul Williams	521	58%
Moustapha Hadji	508	58%
Gary Breen	501	59%

TOP TACKLERS	WON	SUCCESS
JOHN EUSTACE	68	72%
Youssef Chippo	66	74%
Paul Williams	59	76%
David Thompson	54	84%
Lee Carsley	51	74%

His surname may sound similar to "useless" but John Eustace proved that he was anything but in 2000–01. Coventry were reasonably good at tackling – they were given plenty of practice – and the midfielder won 68 challenges. David Thompson, a summer signing from Liverpool, won an excellent 84% of his tackles, while Lee Carsley, bought from Blackburn mid-season, added some real bite to the Sky Blues' midfield.

He may have been strong in the tackle but John Eustace was occasionally too fiery, picking up 11 bookings during 2000–01. David Thompson was not far behind on nine, and the youngster also saw red on his debut against Middlesbrough in August. Youssef Chippo was third, having racked up 69 disciplinary points, while Gary Breen and Craig Bellamy completed the top five.

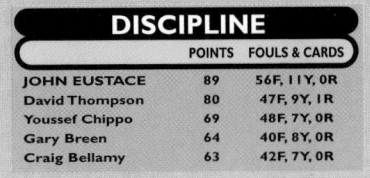

DISCIPLINE	POINTS	FOULS & CARDS
JOHN EUSTACE	89	56F, 11Y, 0R
David Thompson	80	47F, 9Y, 1R
Youssef Chippo	69	48F, 7Y, 0R
Gary Breen	64	40F, 8Y, 0R
Craig Bellamy	63	42F, 7Y, 0R

ACTION	ALOISI	BELLAMY	BREEN	CHIPPO	CARSLEY	EDWORTHY	HADJI	KIRKLAND	KONJIC	QUINN	TELFER	THOMPSON	WILLIAMS	ZICGA	TOTAL	EVERTON
Time on pitch	12	85	90	5	90	67	90	90	23	90	90	90	90	78	990	990
GOALS																
Goal	–	–	–	–	–	–	–	–	–	–	–	–	–	–	2	1
Shot on target (incl goals)	–	1	1	–	–	–	3	–	–	–	–	–	–	1	6	6
Shot off target	–	1	–	–	–	–	2	–	–	–	–	1	–	–	6	8
Blocked shot	–	–	–	–	1	–	–	–	–	–	–	–	–	–	2	2
Own goal	–	–	–	–	–	–	–	–	–	–	–	–	–	–	0	0
PASSES																
Pass to own player	3	9	22	2	16	12	12	2	2	15	23	18	16	14	166	200
Pass to opposition	2	9	9	2	15	12	19	4	5	13	17	10	17	8	142	140
Cross to own player	–	–	–	–	–	–	1	–	–	–	–	2	–	–	3	–
Cross to opposition player	–	–	–	–	–	–	–	–	–	2	–	4	–	–	10	9
Goal assist	–	–	–	–	–	–	–	–	–	–	–	2	–	1	10	14
Pass completion %	60%	50%	71%	50%	52%	48%	38%	33%	29%	50%	57%	61%	48%	61%	53%	58%
TACKLES & CLEARANCES																
Tackle	–	1	3	–	6	1	1	–	–	4	–	9	2	4	33	17
Clearances, blocks and interceptions	–	1	19	1	9	1	1	–	5	4	–	2	11	–	55	37
DRIBBLES & RUNS																
Dribbles ball retained	–	2	–	–	–	–	3	–	–	–	–	3	–	–	8	7
Dribbles ball lost	–	1	–	–	–	–	–	–	–	–	–	2	–	–	3	4
Dribble success %	0%	67%	0%	0%	0%	0%	100%	0%	0%	0%	0%	60%	0%	0%	73%	64%
DISCIPLINE																
Fouls	1	1	2	1	–	1	1	–	1	–	1	3	2	–	14	20
Penalty conceded	–	–	–	–	–	–	–	–	–	–	–	–	–	–	0	0
Free kick – offside	–	–	1	–	–	–	3	–	–	–	–	–	2	–	6	3
Yellow cards	–	–	1	–	–	–	–	–	–	–	–	–	–	–	1	2
Red cards	–	–	–	–	–	–	–	–	–	–	–	–	–	–	0	0
GOALKEEPERS																
Distribution to own player	–	–	–	–	–	–	–	13	–	–	–	–	–	–	13	15
Distribution to opposition player	–	–	–	–	–	–	–	12	–	–	–	–	–	–	12	11
Goalkeeper distribution %	–	–	–	–	–	–	–	52%	–	–	–	–	–	–	52%	58%
Save	–	–	–	–	–	–	–	4	–	–	–	–	–	–	4	4
Ball caught	–	–	–	–	–	–	–	2	–	–	–	–	–	–	2	2
Ball dropped	–	–	–	–	–	–	–	–	–	–	–	–	–	–	0	0
Goal conceded	–	–	–	–	–	–	–	1	–	–	–	–	–	–	1	2

14 Coventry scored the fewest home

Although Coventry's 34-year tenure in the top flight came crashing to an end in 2000–01, there were performances during the season in which the players showed a real fighting spirit — not least the Boxing Day win at Goodison Park.

26 December 2000

1–2

EVERTON
COVENTRY CITY

Everton started predictably with a number of long balls being launched towards target man Duncan Ferguson – in his first start since returning from Newcastle – and in the third minute he reached a Gary Naysmith cross to force Chris Kirkland into a save under his bar. The talented young 'keeper proved to be a big plus for Gordon Strachan during the season and kept Magnus Hedman on the sidelines for much of the campaign.

Both sides managed six attempts on target in the encounter, but it was two second-half headers from Coventry which proved crucial. Both came from set-piece deliveries by the ever-industrious David Thompson, who was proving to be a good buy for Strachan.

Coventry had a great chance to take the lead when Ysrael Zuniga got away from David Weir on the right and crossed for Thompson, only to see the former Liverpool star's effort saved by Thomas Myhre. And so the first half finished scoreless, despite the effort from both sides which was more than enough to warm up the chilly December afternoon.

The two teams continued to battle it out in the second half and City's resilience paid dividends. It was no more than they deserved after a gritty performance which saw them make almost twice as many tackles as Walter Smith's side. Thompson alone went in for nine challenges – more than any other player on the pitch.

Moustapha Hadji was particularly impressive in his support striker role. He hit the target three times and had two more efforts which went wide, the Moroccan posing the greatest threat to the Everton back-line. With 20 minutes remaining, the Sky Blues took the lead. Thompson's long free-kick found Hadji charging into the box unmarked to head past the helpless Myhre. Events appeared to be going Coventry's way for once.

But with five minutes left, Duncan Ferguson set up Scot Gemmill, who buried his shot into the corner to equalise and seemingly deny Strachan's men their just reward. It was to be a common theme in City's season: no team conceded as many late goals as the Sky Blues.

However, with the manager urging his battlers on, the players refused to settle for a point and struck a late winner. Another Thompson cross was met and buried by Irish defender Gary Breen, an unlikely scorer but a solid performer who epitomised their spirit. Besides grabbing the winner, he contributed 18 clearances to ward off Everton's increasingly desperate attacks.

Throughout 2000–01 Coventry recorded the best tackle success rate in the top flight, having won 76% of all their challenges. In the end they suffered relegation but, as both that statistic and this super away victory illustrated, they did not go down without a fight.

goals in any Premiership season

DERBY COUNTY

ADDRESS

Pride Park Stadium, Pride Park,
Derby DE24 8XL

CONTACT NUMBERS

Telephone: 01332 202 202
Fax: 01332 667 540
Ticket Office: 01332 209 209
Ticket Line: 09068 332 213
Club Call: 09068 121187
Superstore: 01332 209 000
e-mail: pressoffice@dcfc.co.uk
Website: www.dcfc.co.uk

KEY PERSONNEL

Chairman: L Pickering
Vice-Chairman: P J Gadsby
Chief Executive: K Loring
Directors: J N Kirkland OBE
R Clarke
Club Secretary: K Pearson ACIS
Manager: Jim Smith

SPONSORS

2000–01: EDS

FANZINES

Official Magazine:
Rampage

COLOURS

Home: White shirts, black
shorts and white stockings
Away: Dark navy shirts, dark navy
shorts and dark navy stockings

NICKNAME

The Rams

HONOURS

League Champions: 1971–72, 1974–75
Division Two Champions: 1911–12,
1914–15, 1968–69, 1986–87
Division Three (North) Champions:
1956–57
FA Cup Winners: 1946

RECORD GOALSCORER

Steve Bloomer – 292 league goals,
1892–1906, 1910–14

BIGGEST WIN

12–0 v Finn Harps – UEFA Cup 1st
round 1st leg, 15 September 1976

BIGGEST DEFEAT

2–11 v Everton – FA Cup 1st Round,
1889–90

SEASON REVIEW

Derby County will enjoy a sixth consecutive season in the top flight thanks to a battling campaign by Jim Smith and his players.

After finishing 16th in 1999–2000 with just 38 points, the summertime comings-and-goings did not inspire many people outside Pride Park into thinking 2000–01 would be anything other than a season of struggle.

Plenty of new blood was injected into the squad, but few of the latest recruits were household names.

The young Danny Higginbotham was the Rams' major investment at £2 million, despite having played just four times for Manchester United. Joining him at Pride Park were Simo Valakari, Bjorn Otto Bragstad, Youl Mawene and Con Blatsis.

With the departures of various players including Francesco Baiano and Tony Dorigo, much seemed to depend on keeping key men such as Craig Burley, Georgi Kinkladze and Branko Strupar fit.

> "I always say clean sheets will win us games. People reply they will only guarantee draws but, provided the attitude is positive, they will do more."
>
> Colin Todd

Unfortunately Kinkladze was forced to have surgery even before the season started and, after scoring in each of the four opening games, Strupar also succumbed to injury.

Those opening weeks of the campaign were a rollercoaster ride for the fans. The Rams gave Southampton a two-goal lead before pegging them back for a draw. They then lost 3–2 at St James' Park to Newcastle before coming back to 2–2 from two-down against Everton. As if they had not been making life hard enough, they gave Middlesbrough a three-goal start before forcing a draw with three strikes in the last 25 minutes, and even when they reversed roles and took a two-goal lead against Charlton, they let the Addicks leave Pride Park with a point.

On top of all the goals being conceded, Derby were once again running into disciplinary problems, running up 13 yellow cards – the second-highest tally – in just five games. The Rams had already been warned as to their conduct after racking up 93 yellows and four reds in 1999–2000.

To remedy matters, Derby invited former referee Kevin Lynch in to advise the club on how they could reduce the number of cards being incurred. One piece of advice was that certain players might grow their hair so they did not look quite so "aggressive".

Derby had the second-highest number of cards, but only five teams had committed fewer fouls.

By season's end, though, Derby had earned more yellow cards than any other team and a £100,000 suspended fine hanging over their heads may well be levied.

Another unwanted record arrived in October when defeat by Tottenham meant Derby had gone 10 league games without a win from the start of the season, setting a new club record. Jim Smith's side had also slipped to the bottom of the Premiership table. They extended this unwanted accolade to 13 matches, but at least managed to keep clean sheets in matches 12 and 13, the latter a hard-fought draw at Highbury against Arsenal.

Much of this new parsimony in defence was attributed to Colin Todd, who arrived as assistant manager at the end of October along with defensive players such as Lilian Martin and the enigmatic Taribo West.

Finally, on 18 November, Derby recorded their first Premiership win over fellow-strugglers Bradford City and, although defeat followed against Manchester United, the Rams won three of the next four games without conceding a goal – the only blip being a 4–1 drubbing by Chelsea.

This healthy run of league form unfortunately coincided with the end of

81 yellow cards for the Rams – more

SEASON REVIEW

their Worthington Cup aspirations. Having already beaten West Brom over two legs and Norwich in the third round, Fulham edged a five-goal thriller to knock the Rams out.

Better news came with Seth Johnson's call-up to the full England squad by caretaker boss Peter Taylor. The feisty midfielder was delighted to make his debut as a second-half substitute against Italy and will hope to feature in England's future.

The player merry-go-round continued with Brian O'Neil joining from Wolfsburg and Dean Sturridge, Lars Bohinen and Deon Burton all being transfer-listed. Sturridge was snapped up by Leicester while Bohinen eventually had his contract cancelled. This came as no great surprise after the Norwegian burned his bridges by criticising the club and the manager on his personal website in 1999–2000.

The Rams continued to be tough to break down, but now also seemed to be struggling to score in the Premiership. It was a different story in the FA Cup, though, with a 3–2 win ensuring a cup double over West Brom.

Derby seemed to have done the hard work by earning a 0–0 draw at Ewood Park against Blackburn in the fourth round, but the floodgates opened in the replay as Rovers ran out 5–2 winners.

Thankfully Derby's defence continued their good form in the Premiership and two home wins, plus draws at Elland Road and Anfield, edged them away from the bottom of the table. Unfortunately three subsequent defeats closed the gap again.

A victory over Leicester brought some respite, but with Coventry and Manchester City both finding form, the worries returned after a 2–0 defeat by bottom club Bradford.

With games against the top three sides to come, Derby were suddenly under intense pressure. Defeat by Arsenal at Pride Park did nothing to ease the nerves with a visit to Old Trafford next on the agenda.

But, with Manchester United having already won the title and looking forward to receiving the trophy at the end of the match, Derby grabbed a first-half goal through Malcolm Christie and held on to record a brilliant 1–0 win and secure their Premiership status.

"Confirming our safety at Old Trafford makes it extra special – it's days like this that remind me why I still love football."

Jim Smith

After a couple of close calls, Derby will be looking to bolster their squad to avoid a struggle in 2001–02. Chairman Lionel Pickering said: "Jim will have to wheel and deal to get new players in." But at least the future looks bright.

Derby's reserves and Under-17 side both won their respective divisions while the Under-19 team finished as runners-up in their league and the management team will be hoping to bring one or two more players like Chris Riggott through the ranks. The impressive young defender was voted Derby's player of the season in his first full campaign.

Otherwise, Smith will be looking once more in the overseas bargain basement, which has proved variable in terms of success in the past.

With Stefano Eranio heading back to Italy, no doubt there will be more changes to the Derby squad. Taribo West made a big difference to Derby's defensive solidity, but will not be at Pride Park in 2001–02 after missing several training sessions, while Lilian Martin left by mutual consent.

Jim Smith is also in the final year of his contract and may retire in June 2002, leaving the way clear for Colin Todd. But if it is to be his final fling, Rams fans should see another season of nail-biting drama.

DERBY COUNTY

DATE	OPPONENT	SCORE	ATT.	BLATSIS	BOERTIEN	BOHINEN	BOLDER	BRAGSTAD	BURLEY	BURTON	CARBONARI	CHRISTIE	DELAP	ELLIOTT	ERANIO	EVATT	GUDJ
19.08.00	Southampton H	2–2	27,223	90□	–	–	–	90	–	$s45^1$	–	–	83	s7	90	–	–
23.08.00	Newcastle A	2–3	51,327	85	–	–	–	90	–	90	–	–	–	90	66	–	–
26.08.00	Everton A	2–2	34,840	–	–	–	–	90	–	90□	–	–	–	90	89□	–	–
06.09.00	Middlesbro H	3–3	24,290	–	–	–	–	90	–	90	–	$s25^2$	90	90	65	–	–
10.09.00	Charlton H	2–2	22,310	–	–	–	–	90	–	90	–	90^1□	90	–	88□	–	–
16.09.00	Sunderland A	1–2	45,343	–	–	–	–	90	–	90	90	90^1□	–	76	64	–	–
23.09.00	Leeds Utd H	1–1	26,248	–	–	–	–	73	90	90□	36□	73	–	–	73□	–	–
30.09.00	Aston Villa A	1–4	26,534	–	–	–	–	90	90□	45	–	45	s45	–	90	–	–
15.10.00	Liverpool H	0–4	30,532	–	–	–	–	90	90□	–	–	90	90	–	68	–	–
21.10.00	Tottenham A	1–3	34,483	–	–	s10	–	90	90	90	–	58	90	–	–	–	–
28.10.00	Leicester A	1–2	20,525	–	–	–	–	90	90	–	s45□	90^1	90□	45	–	–	–
06.11.00	West Ham H	0–0	24,621	–	–	–	–	90	s9	90	81	90	–	–	–	–	–
11.11.00	Arsenal A	0–0	37,679	–	–	–	–	90	–	90	52	90	–	–	–	–	–
18.11.00	Bradford H	2–0	31,614	–	–	–	–	–	–	90□	89^1	90^1	–	65	–	–	–
25.11.00	Man Utd H	0–3	32,910	–	–	–	–	–	–	68	90	90	–	s22	–	–	–
02.12.00	Ipswich A	1–0	22,003	–	–	–	–	90	s12	90	78	90^1□	–	56	–	–	–
09.12.00	Chelsea A	1–4	34,317	–	–	76	–	90	s45	45	90	90	–	–	–	–	–
16.12.00	Coventry H	1–0	27,869	–	–	–	–	90	s30	90	89^1□	90	–	78	–	–	–
23.12.00	Newcastle H	2–0	29,978	–	–	–	–	90	87^1	90^1	90	90	–	71□	–	–	–
26.12.00	Man City A	0–0	34,321	–	–	–	–	90	90	90	90	90□	–	–	–	–	–
30.12.00	Southampton A	0–1	15,075	–	–	–	–	90□	90	–	64	90	–	64	–	–	–
01.01.01	Everton H	1–0	27,358	–	–	–	–	42	90^1	90□	90	90	–	68	–	–	–
13.01.01	Middlesbro A	0–4	29,041	–	–	–	–	90□	90	90□	57	90	–	63	–	–	–
20.01.01	Man City H	1–1	31,174	–	–	–	–	90	90	90	90	90	–	–	–	–	–
30.01.01	Charlton A	1–2	20,043	–	–	–	–	s53	90^1	90	90	90	90	–	s17	–	–
03.02.01	Sunderland H	1–0	29,129	–	90	–	–	–	90^1□	90	90□	45□	57	–	90□	–	–
10.02.01	Leeds Utd A	0–0	38,789	–	–	–	–	s45	90	90□	90□	89	–	–	45□	–	–
24.02.01	Aston Villa H	1–0	27,289	–	s21	–	–	–	90	90^1	–	–	90	–	–	–	–
03.03.01	Tottenham H	2–1	29,410	–	–	–	–	–	90	s33□	90	77	90	–	–	–	s13
18.03.01	Liverpool A	1–1	43,362	–	–	–	–	–	90	90^1	90	81	90	–	s4	–	s9
31.03.01	Coventry A	0–2	19,654	–	–	–	–	–	75	90	90	90	90	–	–	–	59
07.04.01	Chelsea H	0–4	29,320	–	90	–	–	–	–	90	83	90	90	–	–	–	s7
14.04.01	West Ham A	1–3	25,319	–	–	–	–	–	–	90	90	s45	90	–	45□	–	$s10^1$
16.04.01	Leicester H	2–0	28,387	–	90^1□	–	–	–	–	89□	90□	s15	90□	–	90^1	–	s59
21.04.01	Bradford A	0–2	18,564	–	90□	–	–	–	–	90	90	s29	90	–	76	–	s14□
28.04.01	Arsenal H	1–2	29,567	–	90□	–	–	–	66	s11	90	79	90	–	90^1	–	s3
05.05.01	Man Utd A	1–0	67,526	–	90	–	s1	–	–	–	90	89^1	90	–	90	–	s14
19.05.01	Ipswich H	1–1	33,239	–	90	–	s4	–	–	–	90	90^1	90	–	86	s12	78

□ Yellow card, ■ Red card, s Substitute, 90^2 Goals scored

*including own goal

For more information visit our website:

2000–01 PREMIERSHIP APPEARANCES

HIGGINBOTHAM	JACKSON	JOHNSON	KINKLADZE	MARTIN	MAWENE	MORRIS	MURRAY	OAKES	O'NEIL	POOM	POWELL	RIGGOTT	SCHNOOR	STRUPAR	STURRIDGE	VALAKARI	WEST	TOTAL
90	–	90	–	–	–	45	–	–	–	90	90	–	–	83[1]	s7	90	–	990
90	–	90[1]□	–	–	–	s5	–	–	–	90	90	–	–	90[1]	s24□	90□	–	990
45	45	90	–	–	–	–	90	–	–	90	–	s1	s45	90[1]	s45[1]	90	–	990
–	–	90□	s25	–	–	–	s1	–	–	90	–	–	90□	89[1]	90	65□	–	990
90	–	90	s29	–	–	–	s2	–	–	90	–	–	90□	–	61	90[1]	–	990
90	–	90□	64	–	–	s14	s26	–	–	90	–	–	–	–	s26□	90	–	990
90	–	90	s17[1]	–	–	–	–	–	–	90	–	s17	90	–	s17	90	–	936
90	–	90	s45	–	–	–	–	–	–	90	90	90[1]	45	–	s45	–	–	990
–	–	90	90	–	–	–	–	–	–	90	90	43	–	s47	s22	90	–	990
58	–	80□	–	–	–	s32	–	–	–	90	90	90[1]□	s32	–	90	–	–	990
–	–	90	s8	–	–	–	–	–	–	90	90	90	82	–	–	90□	–	990
–	–	90	90	87□	–	s3	–	–	–	90	45	90	90	–	–	s45	–	990
90	–	90	83	69□	–	s38□	–	–	–	90	90	90	–	–	s7	s21	–	990
–	–	90	90□	90	–	s25□	–	–	–	90	90	90	–	–	s1	–	90	990
–	–	90□	90	68□	–	s45	–	45	–	90	90	90	–	–	s22	–	90	990
s8	–	90	–	82	–	s34	–	–	–	90	90	90	–	–	–	–	90	990
90	–	–	–	62	–	s28	s14□	–	–	90	90	90[1]	–	–	–	–	90	990
–	–	90	–	60	–	s1	s12	–	–	90	90	90	–	–	–	–	90	990
–	–	90	s19	–	–	s3	–	–	–	90	90	90	–	–	–	–	90	990
s33	–	90	78	s12	–	–	–	–	–	90	57	90□	–	–	–	–	90	990
90	–	90□	s26	–	90	–	–	–	–	90	–	90	–	–	s26	–	90	990
90	–	90	s22	–	–	–	s48	–	–	90	–	90	–	–	–	–	90□	990
75	–	–	s27	–	90□	s15	–	–	–	90	90	90□	–	s33	–	–	–	990
87	–	–	–	s20	90□	s3	70	–	–	90	90[1]	–	–	–	–	90□	–	990
73	–	–	–	–	37	–	–	90□	90	90	90	–	–	–	–	–	–	990
–	–	–	–	–	–	s45□	s56	90	s33	–	34□	90□	–	–	–	90	–	990
s78	–	–	–	–	–	s1	–	90	12	–	90□	90□	–	90	–	–	90	990
90	–	90□	–	–	–	88	s2	90	–	–	90	90	–	69	–	–	90	990
90	–	90	–	–	–	–	–	90	–	–	90	90□	–	57[2]	–	–	90	990
86	–	90□	–	–	–	–	–	90	–	90□	90	–	–	–	–	–	90	990
90□	–	90	s31	–	90	–	s15	10	–	s80	90	–	–	–	–	–	–	990
–	–	90□	s34	–	–	–	56	–	–	90	90	90	–	–	–	–	90	990
74	–	90	80	–	–	s16	–	–	–	90	90	90	–	–	–	90□	–	990
–	–	90	75□	–	s1	–	–	–	–	90	30	90	–	–	–	–	90	989
–	–	57□	90	–	–	61	90	–	–	90	–	90	–	–	–	–	–	957
90	–	90□	87	–	–	–	s24	–	–	90	–	90	–	–	–	–	90	990
90	–	76	–	–	90	90	–	–	–	90	–	90	–	–	–	–	–	990
90□	s45	–	90	–	90	–	–	–	–	90	–	45	–	–	–	–	–	990

THE MANAGER

JIM SMITH

For the second year in a row, the worry lines on Jim Smith's brow were deepened by his side's continued flirtation with relegation. The look of sheer relief on the Derby manager's face when the club secured their Premiership safety with a win at Old Trafford showed the 60-year-old's passion for the game has not diminished.

Smith has certainly done the rounds in English football: he has managed as far north as Newcastle and as far south as Portsmouth, the club which he guided to within a single goal of the Premiership in 1993.

Smith joined Derby in 1995, and took the Rams to the Premiership in his first campaign. He will certainly be hoping for a top-half finish to round his career off in style, as 2000–01 is likely to be Smith's last season in charge at Pride Park.

Assistant manager Colin Todd is being groomed as Smith's successor for when he decides to hang up his tracksuit, but any thoughts of Smith finishing sooner were banished when he recently declared: "I have one year left on my contract and I intend to see it through. I love Derby."

LEAGUE POSITION

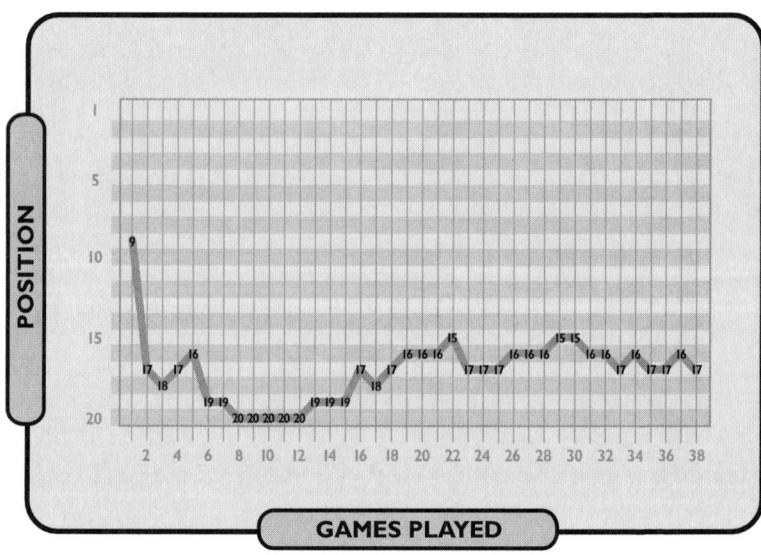

GAMES PLAYED

57 Mart Poom conceded more goals

THE GOALS

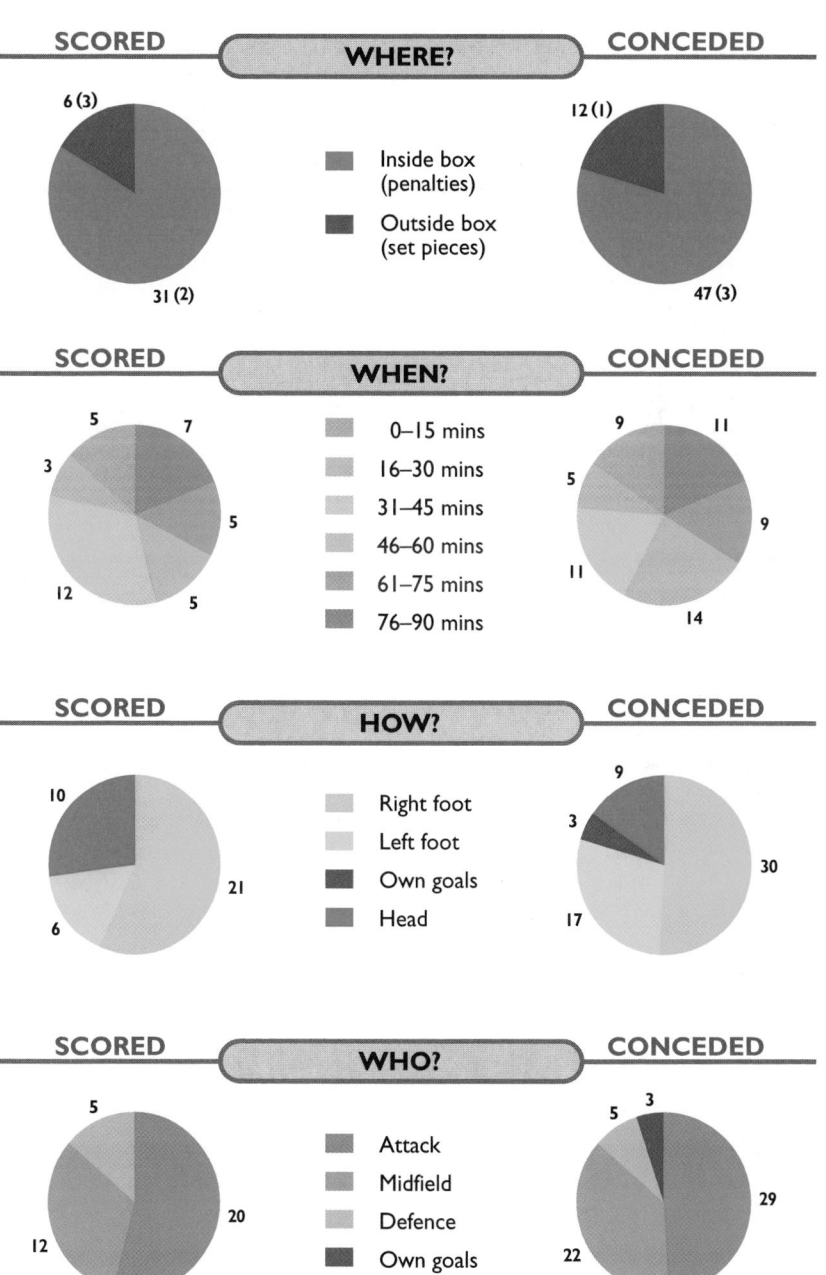

SCORED **WHERE?** CONCEDED

6 (3)   12 (1)

- Inside box (penalties)
- Outside box (set pieces)

31 (2)   47 (3)

SCORED **WHEN?** CONCEDED

SCORED: 5, 7, 3, 5, 12, 5
CONCEDED: 9, 11, 5, 9, 11, 14

- 0–15 mins
- 16–30 mins
- 31–45 mins
- 46–60 mins
- 61–75 mins
- 76–90 mins

SCORED **HOW?** CONCEDED

SCORED: 10, 21, 6
CONCEDED: 9, 3, 30, 17

- Right foot
- Left foot
- Own goals
- Head

SCORED **WHO?** CONCEDED

SCORED: 5, 20, 12
CONCEDED: 5, 3, 29, 22

- Attack
- Midfield
- Defence
- Own goals

than any other Premiership goalkeeper

DERBY COUNTY

	BLATSIS	BOERTIEN	BOHINEN	BOLDER	BRAGSTAD	BURLEY	BURTON	CARBONARI	CHRISTIE	DELAP	ELLIOTT	ERANIO	EVATT	GUDJO...
APPEARANCES														
Start	2	7	1	0	10	24	25	27	29	32	5	25	0	2
Sub	0	1	1	2	2	0	7	0	5	1	1	3	1	8
Minutes on pitch	175	651	86	5	981	2073	2386	2302	2475	2885	443	1858	12	266
GOAL ATTEMPTS														
Goals	0	1	0	0	0	2	5	1	8	3	0	2	0	1
Shots on target	0	1	0	0	0	9	23	5	26	15	1	3	0	4
Shots off target	0	0	0	0	2	21	23	10	19	22	1	6	0	4
Shooting accuracy	0%	100%	0%	0%	0%	30%	50%	33%	58%	41%	50%	33%	0%	50%
PASSING														
Goal assists	0	1	0	0	1	2	2	0	1	0	0	6	0	0
Long passes	25	47	10	2	112	309	108	301	85	252	62	150	1	20
Short passes	46	160	39	1	171	645	662	410	559	775	71	828	7	76
PASS COMPLETION														
Own half %	85%	74%	82%	100%	80%	81%	81%	73%	74%	68%	73%	83%	100%	75%
Opposition half %	52%	52%	63%	50%	46%	59%	63%	49%	64%	56%	44%	74%	67%	67%
CROSSING														
Total crosses	1	13	1	0	2	126	31	4	36	61	3	50	1	8
Cross completion %	0%	23%	0%	0%	0%	26%	23%	0%	25%	23%	0%	36%	0%	38%
DRIBBLING														
Dribbles & runs	1	11	2	0	0	52	36	28	90	104	2	84	0	16
Dribble completion %	0%	91%	100%	0%	0%	69%	67%	79%	58%	72%	100%	71%	0%	63%
DEFENDING														
Tackles made	5	38	3	0	37	90	32	71	47	93	11	32	1	4
Tackles won %	100%	71%	67%	0%	78%	66%	66%	70%	70%	71%	73%	63%	0%	75%
Blocks	4	11	0	0	15	11	4	43	3	22	7	7	0	0
Clearances	15	28	1	0	105	41	22	283	3	130	47	6	0	1
Interceptions	0	1	1	0	6	5	1	16	1	10	1	5	0	1
DISCIPLINE														
Fouls	3	8	1	0	12	24	88	27	53	39	8	40	0	3
Offside	0	2	0	0	0	4	35	0	40	9	0	14	0	2
Yellow cards	1	3	0	0	0	5	4	6	5	3	1	7	0	1
Red cards	0	0	0	0	0	0	1	1	0	0	0	0	0	0

GOALKEEPER NAME	START/ (SUB)	TIME ON PITCH	GOALS CONCEDED	MINS/GOALS CONCEDED	SAVES MADE	SAVES/ SHOTS
OAKES	6(0)	460	2	230	20	91%
POOM	32(1)	2960	57	52	140	71%

For more information visit our website:

PLAYERS' STATISTICS

	HIGGINBOTHAM	JACKSON	JOHNSON	KINKLADZE	MARTIN	MAWENE	MORRIS	MURRAY	O'NEIL	POWELL	RIGGOTT	SCHNOOR	STRUPAR	STURRIDGE	VALAKARI	WEST	TOTAL	RANK
	23	1	30	13	7	7	4	4	3	27	29	6	7	3	9	18		
	3	1	0	11	2	1	16	10	1	0	2	2	2	11	2	0		
	2057	90	2657	1366	550	578	592	506	180	2236	2536	564	648	483	851	1620		
	0	0	1	1	0	0	0	0	0	1	3	0	6	1	1	0	37	18th
	2	0	6	3	1	0	0	0	0	11	3	1	9	4	2	1	130	20th
	5	1	15	7	2	0	2	3	0	12	4	1	5	7	3	2	177	19th
	29%	0%	29%	30%	33%	0%	0%	0%	0%	48%	43%	50%	64%	36%	40%	33%	42%	16th
	1	0	5	3	1	0	0	0	0	0	2	1	0	1	1	0	28	12th
	226	12	385	158	49	57	17	70	27	187	258	71	43	12	110	211	3691	17th
	417	23	688	533	155	154	119	139	52	712	499	100	210	139	327	346	9128	19th
	67%	90%	76%	90%	71%	76%	63%	67%	77%	77%	75%	82%	73%	83%	83%	73%	76%	18th
	51%	56%	61%	82%	58%	60%	51%	57%	53%	68%	46%	52%	54%	63%	74%	56%	61%	19th
	65	2	124	49	24	3	10	5	1	22	3	6	1	17	7	3	679	19th
	29%	0%	27%	51%	42%	33%	20%	40%	0%	14%	0%	17%	0%	6%	14%	0%	27%	7th
	32	3	57	103	16	15	30	12	1	33	9	3	7	43	7	53	850	13th
	88%	100%	75%	82%	69%	87%	60%	58%	100%	58%	78%	100%	43%	51%	100%	79%	71%	3rd
	50	3	94	23	14	35	11	29	7	71	90	21	10	10	30	61	1023	5th
	72%	67%	70%	78%	93%	66%	64%	72%	100%	69%	69%	76%	80%	30%	77%	74%	71%	19th
	27	3	8	0	3	12	2	7	2	10	36	9	1	1	3	34	285	1st
	158	5	68	1	13	47	7	10	6	39	311	38	5	0	10	131	1563	1st
	13	0	11	1	2	2	1	2	1	8	13	2	1	0	1	19	125	4th
	21	0	38	18	7	12	9	12	3	46	37	6	15	14	21	28	593	5th
	3	0	1	1	2	0	3	0	0	2	0	0	6	3	0	0	127	16th
	3	0	10	2	3	2	3	1	1	3	6	2	1	2	3	3	81	1st
	0	0	1	0	0	0	0	0	0	0	0	0	0	0	0	0	3	=7th

CROSSES CAUGHT	CROSSES PUNCHED	CROSSES DROPPED	CATCH SUCCESS	THROWS/ SHORT KICKS	% COMPLETION	LONG KICKS	% COMPLETION
18	5	2	90%	3	100%	124	35%
105	26	7	94%	53	83%	673	42%

PLAYER OF THE SEASON

PLAYER	INDEX SCORE
MART POOM	890
Horacio Carbonari	792
Chris Riggott	742
Taribo West	730
Craig Burley	676
Rory Delap	672
Danny Higginbotham	591
Seth Johnson	582
Darryl Powell	564
Malcolm Christie	559

Voted Player of the Year by Derby fans for the 1999–2000 campaign, goalkeeper Mart Poom was ranked by Opta as the Rams' most effective player in 2000–01 with an average score of 890 points, thanks to some superb displays.

At one stage, demotion to Division One seemed a distinct possibility, but Poom and his rearguard dug in and eked out the necessary points to keep Derby afloat.

Poom was one of only six 'keepers to reach double figures for clean sheets and made 140 saves in total – second only to Tottenham's Neil Sullivan. Poom's athleticism was remarkable at times, and he caught the eye of several rival Premiership managers during the season, including Sir Alex Ferguson.

Not surprisingly, given Derby's season, three defenders ranked just below Poom on the Index.

Argentinean centre-back Horacio Carbonari made his third consecutive appearance in the Opta top three for Derby. For his average Index score of 792 points, Carbonari won 50 tackles, made 16 interceptions and 283 clearances – a total bettered only by third-ranked Chris Riggott.

Impressive newcomer Riggott cleared the ball 311 times and was one of a select band of players to head the danger clear on more than 200 occasions, arguably having the biggest impact of all Derby youngsters.

Taribo West came "on a mission from God" to save Derby and immediately helped turn things around, as the Rams kept nine clean sheets in West's first 13 appearances. The belated arrival intercepted more opposition passes than any of his colleagues on his way to an average of 730 points.

The top-rated player of 1999–2000, Rory Delap, again showed his versatility, pitching in with three goals, 1,027 passes, nearly 100 tackles and more than a century of clearances.

Malcolm Christie made the top 10 with eight goals, and will want to continue his steady progress in 2001–02.

FIVE OF THE BEST

Derby County flirted with relegation all season, but secured their Premiership status with an excellent 1–0 win at Old Trafford. The Rams struggled to score throughout 2000–01 and know that unless they rectify the situation with strategic signings in the summer they will face another difficult campaign in 2001–02.

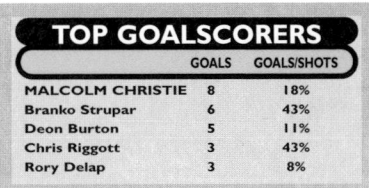

TOP GOALSCORERS	GOALS	GOALS/SHOTS
MALCOLM CHRISTIE	8	18%
Branko Strupar	6	43%
Deon Burton	5	11%
Chris Riggott	3	43%
Rory Delap	3	8%

England Under-21 international Malcolm Christie finished the 2000–01 campaign as the Rams' leading scorer. The man plucked from the non-league scene bagged eight goals for County, but the club missed Belgian international Branko Strupar, who started the season in fine form. Whenever he was fit, Strupar looked likely to score, but injury made this a rare occurrence. Nevertheless, he did end with a magnificent conversion rate of 43%, which was equalled by defender Chris Riggott.

Jim Smith has nurtured the talents of many individuals over the years, but has described Stefano Eranio as one of the most technically-gifted players he has ever worked with. The former AC Milan star calmed the relegation-threatened Rams with his composure on the ball and found a white shirt with an unrivalled 78% of his distribution. Nearest challenger Seth Johnson was 11 percentage points adrift of this impressive ratio, as the Rams strung together the second-fewest number of passes in the division.

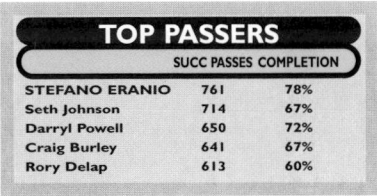

TOP PASSERS	SUCC PASSES	COMPLETION
STEFANO ERANIO	761	78%
Seth Johnson	714	67%
Darryl Powell	650	72%
Craig Burley	641	67%
Rory Delap	613	60%

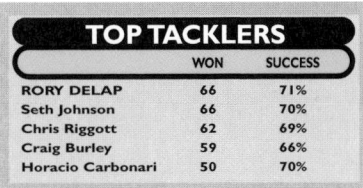

TOP TACKLERS	WON	SUCCESS
RORY DELAP	66	71%
Seth Johnson	66	70%
Chris Riggott	62	69%
Craig Burley	59	66%
Horacio Carbonari	50	70%

Derby's ball-winning skills deserted them as they hovered perilously close to the danger zone for most of the 2000–01 season. The Rams won just 71% of their tackles and only West Ham registered a poorer success rate. Fortunately for the Midlands outfit, midfield duo Rory Delap and Seth Johnson displayed a determined nature and emerged triumphant from 66 challenges apiece, adding a necessary element of steel to an otherwise war-weary team which lost more than 300 tackles.

Devilish Deon Burton finished the season as the sixth-dirtiest player in the Premiership and tested Jim Smith's already-stretched patience to the limit with his gung-ho style in attack. Often a victim of his own over-enthusiasm, the Jamaican international was the only Derby player to amass more than a century of Opta disciplinary points over the course of the season. He was also one of three Rams red-carded, along with Seth Johnson and Horacio Carbonari.

DISCIPLINE	POINTS	FOULS & CARDS
DEON BURTON	106	88F, 4Y, 1R
Seth Johnson	74	38F, 10Y, 1R
Malcolm Christie	68	53F, 5Y, 0R
Stefano Eranio	61	40F, 7Y, 0R
Chris Riggott	55	37F, 6Y, 0R

the most committed by a player in a single game

ACTION	BOERTIEN	BOLDER	CARBONARI	CHRISTIE	DELAP	ERANIO	GUDJONSSON	HIGGINBOTHAM	KINKLADZE	MAWENE	MORRIS	POOM	RIGGOTT	TOTAL	MAN UTD
Time on pitch	90	1	90	89	90	90	14	90	76	90	90	90	90	990	990
GOALS															
Goal	–	–	–	–	–	–	–	–	–	–	–	–	–	1	0
Shot on target (incl goals)	–	–	1	3	–	–	–	–	–	–	–	–	–	4	6
Shot off target	–	–	2	–	–	–	–	–	2	–	1	–	–	6	9
Blocked shot	–	–	–	–	–	–	–	–	–	–	–	–	–	–	8
Own goal	–	–	–	–	–	–	–	–	–	–	–	–	–	0	0
PASSES															
Pass to own player	20	1	18	14	18	49	2	5	47	27	11	2	14	228	464
Pass to opposition	16	–	10	9	11	10	6	4	5	11	8	9	4	104	121
Cross to own player	–	–	–	–	–	–	–	–	2	–	–	–	–	2	9
Cross to opposition player	–	–	–	–	1	1	–	–	1	1	2	–	–	6	0
Goal assist	–	–	–	–	–	–	–	–	–	–	–	–	–	1	0
Pass completion %	56%	50%	64%	61%	60%	82%	25%	56%	89%	69%	52%	18%	78%	68%	75%
TACKLES & CLEARANCES															
Tackle	3	–	3	1	2	1	1	–	1	6	1	–	4	23	12
Clearances, blocks and interceptions	5	–	20	–	5	3	–	19	–	10	2	–	24	88	21
DRIBBLES & RUNS															
Dribbles ball retained	6	–	1	6	3	6	–	2	7	5	4	–	2	42	59
Dribbles ball lost	–	–	–	–	–	–	–	–	–	1	–	–	–	1	4
Dribble success %	100%	0%	100%	100%	100%	100%	0%	100%	100%	83%	100%	0%	100%	98%	94%
DISCIPLINE															
Fouls	3	–	–	2	–	3	1	–	–	4	–	–	1	14	14
Penalty conceded	–	–	–	–	–	–	–	–	–	–	–	–	–	0	0
Free kick – offside	–	–	–	–	–	–	–	–	–	–	1	–	–	3	2
Yellow cards	–	–	–	–	–	–	–	–	–	–	–	–	–	0	–
Red cards	–	–	–	–	–	–	–	–	–	–	–	–	–	0	0
GOALKEEPERS															
Distribution to own player	–	–	–	–	–	–	–	–	–	–	–	12	–	14	14
Distribution to opposition player	–	–	–	–	–	–	–	–	–	–	–	15	–	15	3
Goalkeeper distribution %	–	–	–	–	–	–	–	–	–	–	–	44%	–	44%	82%
Save	–	–	–	–	–	–	–	–	–	–	–	4	–	4	3
Ball caught	–	–	–	–	–	–	–	–	–	–	–	4	–	4	–
Ball dropped	–	–	–	–	–	–	–	–	–	–	–	–	–	–	–
Goal conceded	–	–	–	–	–	–	–	–	–	–	–	0	–	0	1

Derby whipped in fewer successful

On the day that Manchester United picked up their seventh Premiership trophy, Derby County spoiled the Old Trafford party with a fantastic win which preserved the Rams' status in the top division. They became only the second team to triumph at the Theatre of Dreams in 47 league matches.

5 May 2001

0–1

MANCHESTER UNITED
DERBY COUNTY

To the majority of the 67,000-plus crowd, the Rams were meant to be put to the slaughter by the champions. But the sober reality for United fans was very different, as Derby battled their way to a crucial three points. The East Midlanders attempted 11 more tackles than United and their determination was evident in all areas of the pitch.

Mart Poom was alert to all that came his way, defender Chris Riggott was inspirational at the back, making 22 clearances and Malcolm Christie ploughed a lone furrow in attack as he gave United's defensive pairing of the two Ronnies, Wallwork and Johnsen, a challenging afternoon.

And it was Christie who had Derby's first sight of goal in the 28th minute when Fabien Barthez gathered the striker's right-footed shot. United retaliated, with Luke Chadwick firing over the bar after a one-two with Andy Cole.

Sir Alex Ferguson used this match to give some of his youngsters some valuable first-team experience – a fact which no doubt disappointed Derby's relegation rivals. But the youngsters certainly did not look out of place. Michael Stewart worked hard in his first appearance on home soil, attempting 41 passes in the opposition half – 11 more than any other Derby player, even though he was only on the pitch for three-quarters of the contest.

But despite such perseverance from the

youngsters, it was Derby who forged ahead in the 34th minute when lifelong United fan Malcolm Christie scored a stunning goal. He collected a ball from Stefano Eranio and spun away from a couple of defenders before sending an unstoppable left-footed strike past Fabien Barthez.

Wallwork attempted to level matters, but saw his header blocked by some valiant Derby defending.

The Rams' defence was resolute in shutting out United's attacking play and made a total of eight blocks from the champions' shots – more than any other Premiership team made on this penultimate Saturday of the 2000–01 campaign.

And Jim Smith's team were again on their toes when former United youngster Danny Higginbotham blocked Nicky Butt's powerful drive. Christie then spurned a great chance when Lee Morris set him up on a plate, the striker blazing the ball wide of a gaping goal to leave the Rams biting their nails until the bitter end.

United threw on Ryan Giggs for the last quarter but the Welsh wonder was unable to create an equaliser, coming closest with a shot which was cleared off the line by defender Youl Mawene. And although the champions forced a total of 13 corners compared to the Rams' one, it was the visitors' day, as their mammoth 88 clearances, blocks and interceptions helped secure a win which ensured Premiership football for Derby in 2000–01.

crosses than any other team

EVERTON

Goodison Park, Liverpool L4 4EL

Telephone: 0151 330 2200
Fax: 0151 286 9112
Ticket Office: 0151 330 2300
Ticket Line: 09068 121599
Clubcall: 09068 121199
Everton FC Megastore: 0151 330 2030
e-mail: everton@evertonfc.com
Website: www.evertonfc.com

Chairman: Sir Phillip Carter CBE
Deputy Chairman: Bill Kenwright CBE
Directors: Keith Tamlin,
Arthur Abercromby,
Paul Gregg, Jon Woods
Chief Executive: Michael Dunford
Manager: Walter Smith OBE

One2One

When Skies Are Grey
Speke From The Harbour
Satis?

Home: Blue shirts, white
shorts and blue stockings
Away: Yellow shirts, blue shorts
and yellow stockings

The Toffees

League Champions:
1890–91, 1914–15 1927–28,
1931–32, 1938–39, 1962–63,
1969–70, 1984–85, 1986–87
Division Two Champions: 1930–31
FA Cup Winners: 1906, 1933,
1966, 1984, 1995
European Cup Winners' Cup Winners:
1985

William Ralph 'Dixie' Dean –
349 league goals, 1925–37

11–2 v Derby County – FA Cup 1st
round, 18 January 1890

4–10 v Tottenham Hotspur – Division
One, 11 October 1958

SEASON REVIEW

Everton's last Championship back in 1986–87 must seem a very long time ago now to the Toffees' supporters. And following another flirtation with relegation for the blue half of Merseyside in 2000–01, Everton fans were left looking across Stanley Park with envy at their rejuvenated neighbours, Liverpool.

Walter Smith secured a few impressive signings during the summer, such as Alessandro Pistone, Alex Nyarko, Paul Gascoigne, Thomas Gravesen and Steve Watson – and most notably Duncan Ferguson, who returned to his spiritual home after a troubled spell at Newcastle.

There were, however, three highly significant exits. Don Hutchison left for Sunderland, John Collins surprisingly dropped a division to play at Fulham, but most galling of all for the supporters was the sale of Nick Barmby to arch-rivals Liverpool for the sum of £6 million.

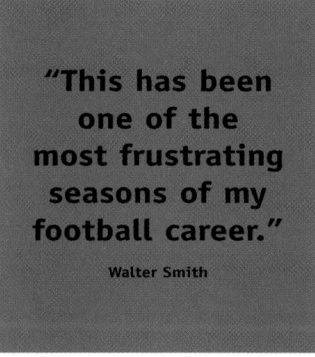

"This has been one of the most frustrating seasons of my football career."

Walter Smith

Following a disappointing defeat on the opening day of the season away to Leeds, Everton opened their home campaign with an emphatic 3–0 win over newly-promoted Charlton. The re-signing of Ferguson seemed an instant success, as the Scot came off the bench to score two goals in the last 10 minutes to seal the win.

However, a problem which would eventually have a massive impact on the Toffeemen's season had already begun to emerge. Every season a clutch of managers use a long injury list to attempt to explain away their side's poor form, but rarely can such an excuse have been more justified than when espoused by Walter Smith. At the height of the crisis during November, Smith had no fewer than 11 regular first-team players unavailable for selection.

The second major problem faced by Everton during 2000–01 was inconsistency.

The Merseysiders let a two-goal lead slip to Derby in a 2–2 draw, but worse was to follow. Two-nil up through Francis Jeffers and Nyarko in the first half against Spurs, the Toffeemen allowed their opponents to nick a goal just before the break and ended up losing the match 3–2.

Smith reflected on two consecutive lapses in concentration, saying: "We must find more resilience, particularly in our midfield area. That is going to have to come from the players we already have here, but we must find it from somewhere."

Such a comment seemed to imply that Everton were not in the market for new players, but this was proved to be incorrect during October, when Smith raided Hearts for highly-rated Scottish international defender Gary Naysmith. Israeli Idan Tal also signed for the Toffeemen, although overall the club made a profit thanks to unsettled centre-back Richard Dunne's sale to Manchester City.

However, neither new arrival was to get the opportunity to play in the Worthington Cup, due to Everton's embarrassing exit at the hands of second division Bristol Rovers. A late equaliser gifted Rovers a 1–1 draw in the first leg at Goodison, and despite an early goal from Jeffers Ian Holloway's side again managed to draw level at the Memorial Ground a week later, eventually winning 4–2 on penalties.

Everton fans hoping that Smith would bang some heads together appeared thwarted, as the manager was in a more reflective mood. He said: "We're obviously disappointed. We had enough opportunities to do better over the two games, but you have to give credit to Rovers. They worked very hard."

A 3–0 defeat at home to Ipswich

SEASON REVIEW

followed, suggesting that Everton were going through something of a crisis of confidence. However, a draw with Southampton was followed by an excellent 1–0 win away to Newcastle, Campbell scoring the winner in the absence of former Magpie Ferguson.

The inconsistency continued in the run-up to Christmas: great wins over Arsenal and Chelsea were balanced out by defeats to Sunderland and Bradford. Most disappointing of all was a 5–0 spanking at the hands of Manchester City – prompting Smith to cancel the team's Christmas party.

Having returned the fancy-dress costumes and disco lights to the party shop, Smith forced his players to sit through a video of the match instead, grumbling: "We are too soft. We need to be stronger."

The new year started badly for the Toffeemen, with a 1–0 defeat at Derby adding to the winter gloom. With another league campaign already looking to be over, and all thoughts of Europe replaced by yet another battle to avoid the drop, the fans' dreams turned instead to the FA Cup, especially after negotiating a potential banana skin with a 2–1 win at Watford.

However, the draw was unkind to Everton, as neighbours Tranmere Rovers were paired with the Goodison side. At least it is at home, thought the fans. We should have stayed at home, they later thought, following their humiliating 3–0 defeat.

The club's unpredictability was to continue. A well-earned draw at home to Leeds was followed by a 2–1 win over Leicester, as players gradually began to emerge from the treatment room.

One of the most exciting Premiership games of the season was the visit of Liverpool to Goodison Park in April. Everton came back twice, and had the post to thank for denying Robbie Fowler from the penalty spot, but ultimately fell to a Gary McAllister free-kick in the dying seconds. One of Everton's scorers, David Unsworth, summed up the mood in the dressing room. He said: "It's unbelievable; it's like a morgue. I've never known anything like it and it's a very bitter pill to swallow at the moment."

A bizarre incident was to follow five days later at Highbury, during Everton's 4–1 defeat to Arsenal. An irate Everton fan ran on to the pitch to offer to swap shirts with Ghanaian Nyarko, in apparent disgust at his lack of effort. Nyarko immediately stormed to the touchline and demanded to be substituted and following his departure from the field duly announced to stunned journalists his intention to quit football for good.

> **"You can't keep saying to the manager: 'By the way, you have to sell millions of pounds-worth of players and then get on with it'."**
>
> **Richard Gough**

The defeat left Everton desperate for a win to move them clear of the drop zone, and they duly got one with a good fightback at home to Bradford. The side showed resilience to come back from a goal down to win 2–1 and secure their Premiership future through goals from Ferguson and Niclas Alexandersson.

For Everton to stand any chance of avoiding a similarly-disappointing season in 2001–02, Walter Smith may have to make some astute purchases during the summer – particularly in defence. Perhaps more important still, he will need to hang on to the key members of his squad. There was some doubt at the end of 2000–01 that players such as Francis Jeffers and Michael Ball would remain at Goodison.

It may well be a long, hard season ahead for the Toffeemen, as the memories of that last Championship fade further still.

EVERTON

DATE	OPPONENT	SCORE	ATT.	ALEXANDERSSON	BALL	CADAMARTERI	CAMPBELL	CLARKE	CLELAND	DUNNE	FERGUSON	GASCOIGNE	GEMMILL	GERRARD	GOUGH	GRAVESEN*
19.08.00	Leeds Utd A	0–2	40,010	–	90	–	–	–	–	–	s33	s16	74	90	–	–
23.08.00	Charlton H	3–0	36,300	–	–	–	–	–	–	–	$s23^2$	78	–	90	90	90
26.08.00	Derby Co H	2–2	34,840	90	–	s9	–	–	–	–	–	s30□	–	90	60	90^1
05.09.00	Tottenham A	2–3	35,316	90□	–	s8	–	–	s14	–	–	82	–	90	–	90
09.09.00	Middlesbro A	2–1	30,885	90	–	–	s8	–	s2	–	–	90	–	90	–	90
16.09.00	Man Utd H	1–3	38,541	90	–	–	s21	–	–	90□	–	69	s21□	90	–	90^1
24.09.00	Leicester A	1–1	18,084	90	–	–	85	–	–	90	–	90	–	90	–	90
30.09.00	Ipswich H	0–3	32,597	76	–	–	90	–	–	–	–	90	90	90	–	90
14.10.00	Southampton H	1–1	29,491	–	90^1	–	90	–	–	90	–	90□	–	90	–	90
21.10.00	Newcastle A	1–0	51,625	–	90□	–	90^1	–	–	–	–	90	–	90	–	90□
29.10.00	Liverpool A	1–3	44,718	–	54	–	90^1	–	–	–	–	90	–	90	–	76□
05.11.00	Aston Villa H	0–1	27,670	–	–	s53	90	–	–	–	–	37	s28	90	–	90
11.11.00	Bradford A	1–0	17,276	–	–	s7	90	–	–	–	–	–	s26	90	–	90
18.11.00	Arsenal H	2–0	33,106	–	90	90^1	90^1	90	–	–	–	–	90□	90	–	–
25.11.00	Chelsea H	2–1	33,515	–	90	89^1	90^1	–	–	–	–	–	90	90	–	–
04.12.00	Sunderland A	0–2	46,372	–	90	71	90□	–	–	–	–	–	71	90	–	s45
09.12.00	Man City A	0–5	34,516	–	90	s44	–	–	–	–	–	–	90	90	–	90
16.12.00	West Ham A	1–1	31,260	s5	90	90^1□	90	–	–	–	–	–	90	89	–	85
23.12.00	Charlton A	0–1	20,043	90	90	61	–	–	–	–	s29	–	90	–	–	90□
26.12.00	Coventry H	1–2	35,704	–	90	67□	–	–	–	–	90□	–	90^1	–	–	90
01.01.01	Derby Co A	0–1	27,358	79	90	–	–	–	–	–	90	–	90	–	–	45□
13.01.01	Tottenham H	0–0	32,290	77	90	s13	90	–	s80	–	–	–	–	–	–	90
20.01.01	Coventry A	3–1	19,174	27	90	90^1	90^1	s58	32	–	–	–	90^1□	–	–	–
31.01.01	Middlesbro H	2–2	34,244	–	90	–	90	–	–	–	–	–	90	–	90	77
03.02.01	Man Utd A	0–1	67,528	–	90	s13	90	–	–	–	–	–	90□	90	90	90□
07.02.01	Leeds Utd H	2–2	34,224	–	90	–	90^1	–	–	–	35^1	–	90□	90	90	90□
10.02.01	Leicester H	2–1	30,409	–	90	s7	90^1	–	–	–	–	–	90□	90	36	90
24.02.01	Ipswich A	0–2	22,220	–	90	–	90	–	–	–	–	–	–	90	–	90
03.03.01	Newcastle H	1–1	35,779	–	90	–	90	–	–	–	–	s18	90	90	–	90
17.03.01	Southampton A	0–1	15,251	72	90	–	–	–	–	–	90	s18	86	90	90	90
31.03.01	West Ham A	2–0	26,044	90^1	90□	–	–	–	–	–	90	–	90	90	–	79
08.04.01	Man City H	3–1	36,561	77	90^1	–	90	–	–	–	45^1	–	90	90	–	90
14.04.01	Aston Villa A	1–2	31,272	69	90□	–	90	–	–	–	–	–	90	90	–	59□
16.04.01	Liverpool H	2–3	40,260	s17□	90□	–	90	–	–	–	90^1□	–	90	90□	73□	–
21.04.01	Arsenal A	1–4	38,029	73	90	–	90^1	–	–	–	–	–	90	90	–	90
28.04.01	Bradford H	2–1	34,256	90^1	90	–	90	–	–	–	90^1	–	90	90	45	s45
05.05.01	Chelsea A	1–2	35,196	45	90	–	90^1	–	–	–	–	–	90□	90	–	–
19.05.01	Sunderland H	2–2	37,444	s10	90^1□	s10	90	–	–	–	–	–	90	90□	–	80□

□ Yellow card, ■ Red card, s Substitute, 90^2 Goals scored

*including own goal

2000–01 PREMIERSHIP APPEARANCES

HIBBERT	M HUGHES	S HUGHES	JEFFERS	JEVONS	McLEOD	MOORE	MYHRE	NAYSMITH	NYARKO	PEMBRIDGE	PISTONE	SIMONSEN	TAL	UNSWORTH	WATSON	WEIR	XAVIER	TOTAL
–	64	57	90□	–	–	s26	–	–	90□	–	90	–	–	90	90□	90	–	990
–	67□	90	90[1]□	–	–	s12	–	–	90	–	39	–	–	s51	90	90	–	990
–	s15	90	75[1]	–	–	81□	–	–	90	–	–	–	–	90	90	90	–	990
–	82	76	90[1]	–	–	s8	–	–	90[1]	–	–	–	–	90□	90	90	–	990
–	82	90	90[2]	–	–	–	–	–	88	–	–	–	–	–	90	90	90	990
–	69	45	90□	–	–	–	–	–	90□	–	–	–	–	s45□	90	90	–	990
–	s5	–	85	–	–	s5	–	–	90	–	–	–	–	90[1]	90□	90	–	990
–	s23	s23	–	–	s14	67	–	–	90□	–	–	–	–	67	90	90	–	990
–	46	s27	–	–	–	s44	–	–	90	63	–	–	–	–	90	90	–	990
–	–	–	–	–	–	–	s21	90	69□	–	–	69	s21	90	90	90	–	990
–	–	–	–	–	–	s22	–	s36	90	90□	–	–	68	–	90	90	90	976
–	–	90	–	–	–	–	90□	–	90	–	–	s15	75□	62	90	90□	–	990
–	–	83□	–	–	–	s45	–	90[1]	90	64□	–	–	45	90	–	90	90	990
–	–	90	–	–	s18□	–	–	90	–	90	–	–	72□	–	–	90	–	990
–	–	90	–	–	s1	–	–	90	–	90	–	–	87	s3	90	90	–	990
–	–	90□	–	–	–	s19	–	90	s19□	90	–	–	45	–	90	90	–	990
–	–	–	–	–	–	–	–	90	90□	90	–	–	46	90	90	–	–	990
–	–	90	–	–	–	–	–	90	–	90	–	s1	–	–	90	90	–	990
–	–	61	–	–	–	45	90	90	–	–	–	–	s45□	s29	90□	90□	–	990
–	–	–	–	–	–	s23	90	90	s15	75	–	–	67	s23	90	90	–	990
–	–	–	–	–	–	s45	90	90	45□	90	–	–	s11	s45	90	90□	–	990
–	–	90□	–	–	–	77	90	–	–	90	–	–	s13	90	90	10	–	990
–	–	–	–	s63	–	–	90	–	–	90	–	–	90	90	90	–	–	990
–	–	–	–	–	–	88	90	90[1]	–	–	–	–	s13[1]	–	90□	90	s2	990
–	–	–	–	s6	–	77	–	72	–	–	–	–	84	s18	90	90	–	990
–	–	–	–	–	–	67	–	90□	–	–	–	–	s55	s23	90	90	–	990
–	–	80	83[1]	–	–	s10□	–	90	–	–	–	–	–	s54□	90	90	–	990
–	–	90	74	s16	s16	–	–	90	72□	–	–	–	74	–	–	90	90□	972
–	–	–	90	–	–	–	–	29□	44	–	–	–	s46	s61[1]	90	90	72	990
–	–	–	–	–	–	–	–	–	79	s11□	–	–	s4	90	90	90	–	990
90	–	–	s11	–	–	–	–	90	–	–	–	–	–	90[1]□	90	90	–	990
–	–	–	s25	–	–	–	–	–	–	s20	89□	–	s13	90	90	90[1]	–	989
–	–	–	–	–	–	s5	–	–	s31	90	90□	–	s21	85[1]	90	90□	–	990
–	–	–	–	–	–	–	–	90	–	–	s28	–	90[1]□	62	90	90	–	990
s8	–	–	–	–	–	s17	–	73	82	90	–	–	s17□	–	–	90	81□	981
s45	–	–	–	–	–	–	–	90	–	–	–	–	45□	90	90	–	–	990
–	–	–	s20	s6	70	–	s45	–	84	–	–	–	90	90	90	90	–	990
–	–	–	–	–	–	–	90	–	90	–	–	–	80[1]□	90	90□	90□	–	990

THE MANAGER

WALTER SMITH

One of the most difficult problems for a manager to overcome is underachievement – an affliction Everton Football Club have suffered from for some time now. It is a mark of the determination of Walter Smith that he has not already decided to give up on the Merseysiders, given his past success.

Smith began his managerial career with the Scotland youth team, before enjoying his first title success as assistant boss to Jim McLean at Dundee United in 1982. He continued his success as number two at Rangers from 1986, before being made manager in his own right five years later.

Having tasted great success at Ibrox – picking up no fewer than twelve major trophies during his time there – Smith has yet to pick up his first piece of silverware with the Goodison club. With little money available to spend, he has had to use his wheeler-dealing skills to introduce new faces to the squad.

Everton may need those skills more than ever in 2000–01 and if injuries continue to hamper their progress, Smith's ability to get the best out of the younger players will also be essential.

LEAGUE POSITION

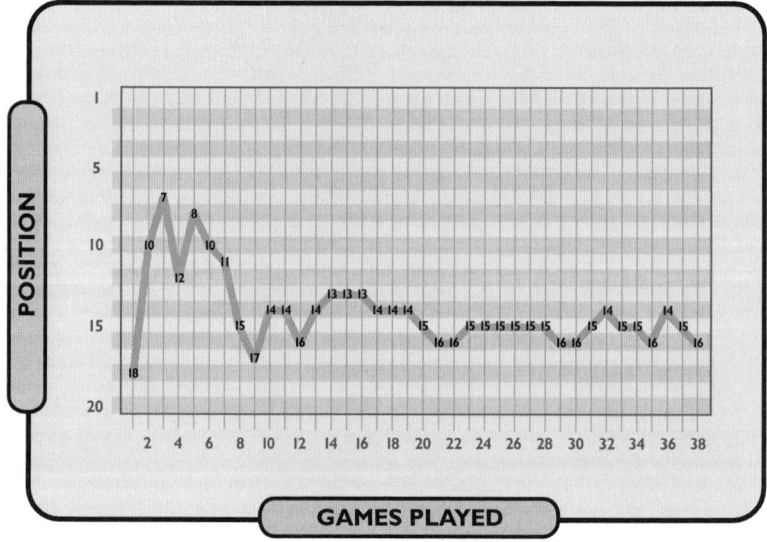

16 Everton conceded more headed goals

THE GOALS

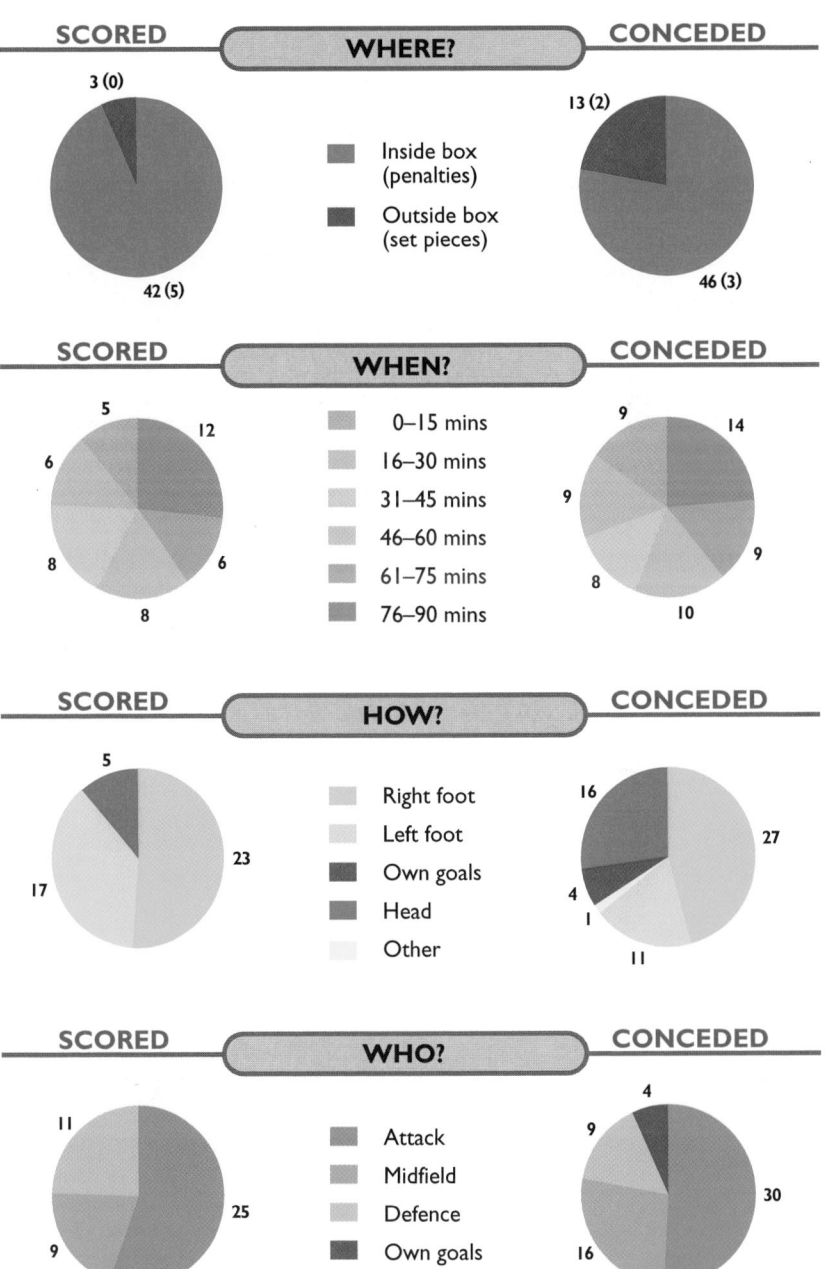

SCORED | WHERE? | CONCEDED

3 (0)
42 (5)

- Inside box (penalties)
- Outside box (set pieces)

13 (2)
46 (3)

SCORED | WHEN? | CONCEDED

5
12
6
8
6
8

- 0–15 mins
- 16–30 mins
- 31–45 mins
- 46–60 mins
- 61–75 mins
- 76–90 mins

9
14
9
9
8
10

SCORED | HOW? | CONCEDED

5
23
17

- Right foot
- Left foot
- Own goals
- Head
- Other

16
27
4
1
11

SCORED | WHO? | CONCEDED

11
25
9

- Attack
- Midfield
- Defence
- Own goals

4
9
30
16

EVERTON

	ALEXANDERSSON	BALL	CADAMARTERI	CAMPBELL	CLARKE	CLELAND	DUNNE	FERGUSON	GASCOIGNE	GEMMILL	GOUGH	GRAVESEN	HIBBERT
APPEARANCES													
Start	17	29	7	27	0	2	3	9	10	25	9	30	1
Sub	3	0	9	2	1	3	0	3	4	3	0	2	2
Minutes on pitch	1347	2574	722	2454	58	218	270	795	888	2286	664	2661	143
GOAL ATTEMPTS													
Goals	2	3	4	9	0	0	0	6	0	2	0	2	0
Shots on target	5	4	7	23	0	0	0	22	5	7	0	16	0
Shots off target	9	2	9	23	0	0	0	12	4	10	5	26	0
Shooting accuracy	36%	67%	44%	50%	0%	0%	0%	65%	56%	41%	0%	38%	0%
PASSING													
Goal assists	1	0	2	1	0	0	0	2	1	1	0	2	0
Long passes	76	337	25	111	7	29	35	48	152	292	106	393	13
Short passes	362	491	198	733	10	63	93	284	341	835	201	859	25
PASS COMPLETION													
Own half %	73%	76%	79%	77%	75%	68%	82%	68%	87%	79%	82%	81%	75%
Opposition half %	60%	53%	64%	68%	22%	57%	62%	64%	72%	71%	55%	62%	50%
CROSSING													
Total crosses	103	17	31	11	0	5	1	6	61	34	1	149	8
Cross completion %	21%	29%	19%	18%	0%	60%	100%	33%	33%	15%	0%	28%	25%
DRIBBLING													
Dribbles & runs	59	42	43	35	0	2	4	10	32	36	8	99	3
Dribble completion %	63%	79%	56%	40%	0%	100%	100%	50%	81%	81%	88%	71%	67%
DEFENDING													
Tackles made	37	107	17	33	3	2	9	9	47	70	15	110	10
Tackles won %	68%	74%	94%	91%	67%	100%	78%	44%	72%	61%	87%	75%	100%
Blocks	8	31	0	5	1	1	1	2	2	16	9	7	0
Clearances	11	177	0	15	8	6	16	18	5	31	68	38	7
Interceptions	4	11	0	2	0	1	1	1	3	18	4	6	1
DISCIPLINE													
Fouls	12	33	24	40	0	3	6	41	19	46	11	69	1
Offside	3	0	14	51	0	0	0	6	3	1	0	5	0
Yellow cards	2	5	2	1	0	0	1	2	2	7	1	7	0
Red cards	0	0	0	0	0	0	0	0	0	0	0	1	0

GOALKEEPER NAME	START/ (SUB)	TIME ON PITCH	GOALS CONCEDED	MINS/GOALS CONCEDED	SAVES MADE	SAVES/ SHOTS
GERRARD	32(0)	2879	52	55	99	66%
MYHRE	6(0)	540	7	77	15	68%
SIMONSEN	0(1)	1	0	0	0	0%

For more information visit our website:

PLAYERS' STATISTICS

	HUGHES M	HUGHES S	JEFFERS	JEVONS	McLEOD	MOORE	NAYSMITH	NYARKO	PEMBRIDGE	PISTONE	TAL	UNSWORTH	WATSON	WEIR	XAVIER	TOTAL	RANK
	6	16	10	0	0	8	17	19	20	5	12	17	34	37	10		
	3	2	2	4	5	13	3	3	1	2	10	12	0	0	1		
	453	1352	893	105	55	853	1553	1647	1706	437	1120	1775	3004	3250	875		
	0	0	6	0	0	0	2	1	0	0	2	5	0	1	0	45	=11th
	6	4	21	1	0	8	4	8	8	0	9	9	9	6	2	184	10th
	1	8	10	1	1	5	6	11	19	0	16	14	14	14	3	223	14th
	86%	33%	68%	50%	0%	62%	40%	42%	30%	0%	36%	39%	39%	30%	40%	45%	10th
	0	1	1	0	0	1	1	0	0	0	0	3	3	2	0	22	18th
	25	140	31	11	6	48	176	143	197	50	67	260	407	370	77	4081	11th
	151	527	207	39	15	313	489	579	612	136	357	506	785	750	231	10236	11th
	83%	77%	80%	67%	100%	82%	78%	82%	78%	85%	63%	73%	75%	75%	86%	78%	13th
	68%	66%	71%	50%	45%	69%	60%	75%	66%	66%	58%	57%	62%	57%	58%	62%	12th
	1	58	15	2	5	30	38	3	41	14	72	82	97	6	4	895	13th
	100%	24%	13%	50%	40%	13%	29%	0%	24%	36%	21%	29%	25%	33%	25%	25%	15th
	7	27	23	6	8	24	54	55	43	12	57	21	157	32	14	913	10th
	86%	70%	65%	67%	25%	50%	67%	62%	63%	92%	61%	76%	68%	91%	79%	68%	15th
	7	62	8	8	1	22	60	49	84	15	53	68	78	86	25	1096	2nd
	43%	65%	88%	50%	0%	77%	77%	63%	74%	67%	64%	76%	71%	73%	76%	72%	11th
	0	2	1	1	1	1	13	5	8	4	2	6	38	36	6	207	9th
	1	22	1	1	1	1	58	25	20	30	8	150	157	363	58	1342	12th
	0	6	1	1	0	2	8	6	6	1	3	5	5	9	2	107	13th
	18	30	17	4	1	15	21	29	29	4	35	50	50	36	12	658	2nd
	16	0	24	0	0	6	1	1	0	0	18	3	1	1	1	155	6th
	1	3	3	0	1	2	3	6	3	2	4	7	5	4	2	78	2nd
	0	0	0	0	0	0	0	1	0	1	0	0	0	0	1	4	=5th

CROSSES CAUGHT	CROSSES PUNCHED	CROSSES DROPPED	CATCH SUCCESS	THROWS/ SHORT KICKS	% COMPLETION	LONG KICKS	% COMPLETION
45	24	5	90%	42	81%	573	49%
12	7	0	100%	4	25%	110	46%
0	0	0	0%	0	0%	0	0%

PLAYER OF THE SEASON

PLAYER	INDEX SCORE
DAVID WEIR	744
Gary Naysmith	734*
Thomas Gravesen	712
Michael Ball	682
Mark Pembridge	675
Kevin Campbell	659
Steve Watson	650
Scot Gemmill	614
Alex Nyarko	576*
Paul Gerrard	503

All players played 75 minutes in at least 16 matches except those marked* who played in 15 games.

Three out of the top five rated players from 1999–2000 were missing from the Everton squad for 2000–01 while a fourth, Richard Gough, managed a mere smattering of appearances.

Small wonder, then, that Everton endured a less-than-satisfactory season under Walter Smith, and were only sure of safety after Bradford City squandered two penalties in the penultimate home match of the campaign.

The other player in that top five from 1999–2000 was David Weir, and the former Hearts man ranked as Everton's best player in 2000–01 with an average of 744 points.

David was a veritable Goliath in defence and his tally of 383 clearances was the third-highest of any Premiership player. Furthermore, Weir won a commendable 63 challenges, while he caused problems in attack with 15 headers at goal and two assists.

Another ex-Jam Tart, Gary Naysmith, ranked second with 734 points. The left-sided defender won an above-average 77% of tackles and showed a willingness to surge forward. He completed the fourth-largest number of dribbles and runs in the side despite missing the majority of the campaign and scored twice.

New signing Thomas Gravesen was Everton's most industrious player. The Dane won 82 tackles and completed 855 passes – both club bests – to help him accumulate an average 712 points in third position, faring significantly better than fellow-newcomer Alex Nyarko.

Newly-capped England star Michael Ball's switch to centre-back saw his form improve dramatically. He nearly matched Gravesen in tackling terms, made close to 200 clearances and netted three times in arguably his best season yet for Everton.

Everton's biggest problem was injuries, with 28 outfield players used – only West Ham fielded more. Paul Gascoigne, Duncan Ferguson and Francis Jeffers all recorded higher Index scores than Weir, but their impact was severely hampered by their regular absences.

FIVE OF THE BEST

The Goodison Park treatment room witnessed an endless stream of traffic throughout 2000–01 as Everton suffered a season-long injury crisis. Consequently, honours were never within reach – and while relegation was avoided, survival was always the key objective. It will take shrewd transfer business and a fully-fit squad to avoid a similar fate in 2001–02.

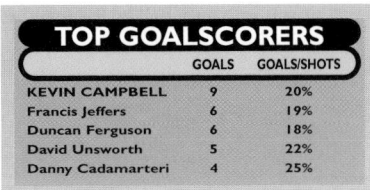

TOP GOALSCORERS

	GOALS	GOALS/SHOTS
KEVIN CAMPBELL	9	20%
Francis Jeffers	6	19%
Duncan Ferguson	6	18%
David Unsworth	5	22%
Danny Cadamarteri	4	25%

For the third successive season Kevin Campbell topped the Everton goal charts, and almost single-handedly preserved the club's top-flight status. The former Gunner smashed home nine league goals and looked to have formed a formidable partnership with Francis Jeffers, who weighed in with half-a-dozen strikes before injury wrecked both his season and Walter Smith's promising attack. Meanwhile, Danny Cadamarteri was always a danger when selected and scored with 25% of his shots.

Everton's disappointing 1999–2000 season ended with a summer exodus which forced Walter Smith to delve into the transfer market and totally rebuild the Toffees' midfield. The finesse of John Collins and Nick Barmby was replaced with the fire of Thomas Gravesen and the Danish international responded with more successful passes than any of his colleagues, while bushy-haired Scot Gemmill was afforded an opportunity to shine in the first team and was the chief architect, with a 73% success rate.

TOP PASSERS

	SUCC PASSES	COMPLETION
THOMAS GRAVESEN	855	68%
Scot Gemmill	828	73%
Steve Watson	789	66%
David Weir	752	67%
Kevin Campbell	591	70%

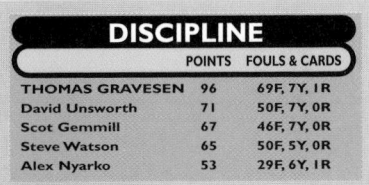

TOP TACKLERS

	WON	SUCCESS
THOMAS GRAVESEN	82	75%
Michael Ball	79	74%
David Weir	63	73%
Mark Pembridge	62	74%
Steve Watson	55	71%

Since the "Dogs of War" era of the mid-1990s Everton teams have been founded upon true grit and Thomas Gravesen upheld this tradition with a series of combative performances. The balding Dane emerged triumphant from 75% of his 110 challenges in the Blues' engine room, alongside a myriad of partners including Paul Gascoigne. Not surprisingly, lifelong Evertonian Michael Ball demonstrated equal devotion to the cause, winning 79 tackles for his team.

Lack of success has resulted in a sense of frustration at Goodison Park. Thomas Gravesen's wholly-committed approach did not go unpunished by top-flight officials and he was the primary reason for Everton's second-place ranking in the disciplinary chart. The former Hamburg star allowed his passion to spill over in the Merseyside derby, seeing red for a foul on Liverpool's Vladimir Smicer. Fellow-Premiership debutant Alex Nyarko also received his marching orders on one occasion, in the 2–0 defeat at Ipswich.

DISCIPLINE

	POINTS	FOULS & CARDS
THOMAS GRAVESEN	96	69F, 7Y, 1R
David Unsworth	71	50F, 7Y, 0R
Scot Gemmill	67	46F, 7Y, 0R
Steve Watson	65	50F, 5Y, 0R
Alex Nyarko	53	29F, 6Y, 1R

but none with his head

ACTION	BALL	CADAMARTERI	CAMPBELL	CLELAND	GEMMILL	GERRARD	S HUGHES	McLEOD	NAYSMITH	PEMBRIDGE	TAL	WEIR	TOTAL	ARSENAL
Time on pitch	90	90	90	90	90	90	90	18	90	90	72	90	990	990
GOALS														
Goal	–	1	1	–	–	–	–	–	–	–	–	–	2	0
Shot on target (incl goals)	–	1	1	–	–	–	–	–	–	–	–	–	2	5
Shot off target	–	1	1	–	–	–	–	–	–	–	2	–	4	5
Blocked shot	–	–	–	–	–	–	–	–	–	–	–	–	0	2
Own goal	–	–	–	–	–	–	–	–	–	–	–	–	0	0
PASSES														
Pass to own player	7	17	18	20	17	8	27	6	14	25	9	18	186	428
Pass to opposition	7	6	17	10	11	7	10	1	14	15	14	12	124	126
Cross to own player	–	3	–	1	–	–	–	–	–	–	1	–	5	6
Cross to opposition player	–	4	–	–	1	–	1	1	1	–	2	–	10	18
Goal assist	–	–	–	–	–	–	–	–	1	–	–	–	1	0
Pass completion %	50%	68%	51%	68%	59%	53%	71%	75%	48%	63%	38%	60%	59%	75%
TACKLES & CLEARANCES														
Tackle	4	1	5	1	3	–	10	–	4	5	2	2	37	31
Clearances, blocks and interceptions	6	–	1	3	–	1	2	–	2	2	–	5	22	20
DRIBBLES & RUNS														
Dribbles ball retained	–	2	1	1	–	–	2	1	4	–	2	–	13	19
Dribbles ball lost	–	4	–	–	–	–	–	3	–	1	–	–	8	20
Dribble success %	0%	33%	100%	100%	0%	0%	100%	25%	100%	0%	100%	0%	62%	49%
DISCIPLINE														
Fouls	4	6	3	1	4	–	2	1	1	1	1	3	26	11
Penalty conceded	–	–	–	–	–	–	–	–	–	–	–	–	0	0
Free kick – offside	–	–	–	–	–	–	–	–	–	–	–	–	2	5
Yellow cards	–	–	–	–	1	–	–	–	–	–	–	–	3	1
Red cards	–	–	–	–	–	–	–	–	–	–	–	–	0	0
GOALKEEPERS														
Distribution to own player	–	–	–	–	–	10	–	–	–	–	–	–	10	6
Distribution to opposition player	–	–	–	–	–	14	–	–	–	–	–	–	14	6
Goalkeeper distribution %	–	–	–	–	–	42%	–	–	–	–	–	–	42%	50%
Save	–	–	–	–	–	3	–	–	–	–	–	–	3	0
Ball caught	–	–	–	–	–	1	–	–	–	–	–	–	1	0
Ball dropped	–	–	–	–	–	–	–	–	–	–	–	–	0	0
Goal conceded	–	–	–	–	–	–	–	–	–	–	–	–	0	2

11 Everton had more goals scored by

Decimated by injury and with just a solitary victory over Arsenal since the inauguration of the Premiership, few would have anticipated a home win from this fixture. However, a two-goal Everton blast left the Gunners both shell-shocked and empty-handed.

18 November 2000
2–0
EVERTON
ARSENAL

Arsène Wenger's side had not lost since the opening day of 2000–01 and settled into an assertive stride at Goodison Park. The battling Blues had nine players sidelined through injury and suspension and the high-flying Gunners racked up 250 more passes than their opponents, who in turn amassed 26 fouls in their pursuit of possession.

Sylvain Wiltord's seventh-minute shot was blocked by 'keeper Paul Gerrard and the astutely-positioned Gary Naysmith headed Fredrik Ljungberg's follow-up strike off the line seconds later.

The central defensive pairing of Michael Ball and David Weir stood firm in the face of Arsenal's attacking verve and the duo contributed half of the team's 22 clearances, blocks and interceptions.

The visitors constantly sought to unhinge the Everton rearguard with a series of forward forays, but with the hosts defending in numbers clear-cut chances were minimal. Wiltord's wayward strike from range after 26 minutes was to prove his final effort of the game and illustrated the shrewdness of Walter Smith's tactics.

Yet for all their hard work at the back, Everton rarely threatened the Arsenal goal during the opening period. A curling free-kick from Israeli winger Idan Tal was the closest of three first-half efforts, all of which sailed harmlessly wide of the target.

After the break, the hosts increased the tempo and should have taken the lead.

Mark Pembridge was the architect of a penetrating move which culminated in former Gunner Kevin Campbell wastefully volleying over the bar.

However, the Everton faithful did not have to wait long to rejoice. Oleg Luzhny failed to intercept Naysmith's searching pass successfully, which found Danny Cadamarteri lurking with intent inside the box. The pacy striker chested the ball down and rifled his only shot of the game beyond a previously-redundant Alex Manninger.

Arsenal continued to enjoy the greater possession but did not prove accurate enough in the final third, as two Kanu efforts finished in the Gwladys Street End.

Without the assured presence of Tony Adams in the back four, Arsenal looked increasingly vulnerable and Everton doubled their lead with 17 minutes remaining. Cadamarteri turned provider when he fed Campbell inside the area and the journeyman duly smashed a right-footed drive high into the net.

Dennis Bergkamp fired a volley into the welcoming arms of Gerrard with Arsenal's final flourish, but the Toffees' clean sheet remained intact and they ultimately secured the points by converting their only two shots on target of the day.

The Arsenal fans who had endured a nightmare train journey to Merseyside thanks to emergency speed restrictions must have wished they had not bothered. But nothing could derail Everton's joy.

IPSWICH TOWN

ADDRESS

Portman Road, Ipswich,
Suffolk IP1 2DA

CONTACT NUMBERS

Telephone: 01473 400 500
Fax: 01473 400 040
Ticket Office:
0845 605 0129 (local rate)
Club Call: 09068 121068
Superstore: 01473 400 563
e-mail: enquiries@itfc.co.uk
Website: www.itfc.co.uk

KEY PERSONNEL

Chairman and Chief Executive:
D Sheepshanks
Directors: R Finbow, P Hope-Cobbold,
J Kerr MBE, R Moore,
Rt Hon Lord Ryder OBE
Club Secretary: D Rose
Manager: George Burley

SPONSORS

2000–01: Greene King
2001–02: TXU Energi

FANZINES

Those Were The Days

COLOURS

Home: Royal blue shirts, white shorts
and royal blue stockings
Away: White shirts, black shorts
and white stockings

NICKNAMES

The Blues
Town

HONOURS

Division One Champions: 1961–62
Division Two Champions: 1960–61,
1967–68, 1991–92
Division Three (South) Champions:
1953–54, 1956–57
FA Cup Winners: 1978
UEFA Cup Winners: 1981
Texaco Cup Winners: 1973

RECORD GOALSCORER

Ray Crawford – 203 league goals
1958–63, 1966–69

BIGGEST WIN

Biggest Win: 10–0 v Floriana –
European Cup preliminary round,
25 September 1962

BIGGEST DEFEAT

1–10 v Fulham – Division One,
26 December 1963

SEASON REVIEW

After three failed attempts to gain promotion through the Division One play-offs, Ipswich finally regained top-flight status in the summer of 2000 after a five-year absence. In that period outside the Premiership, the club's amiable Scottish manager George Burley had gradually put together a hungry, exciting and well-organised side. But even so, those who expected the Suffolk club to struggle in the 2000–01 campaign far outnumbered the optimists.

In fact, it was generally accepted that a 17th-placed finish would be an excellent achievement for Ipswich who had spent very little in the close-season transfer market, leaving their side bereft of many, if any, household names.

And 2000–01 began as many expected it to go on, with a disappointing defeat against Tottenham, who exploited some sloppy defending to record a 3–1 win on the opening day at White Hart Lane.

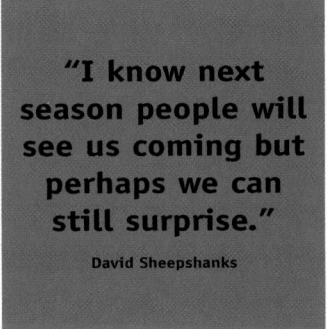

> "I know next season people will see us coming but perhaps we can still surprise."
>
> David Sheepshanks

As they were to do throughout the campaign, though, Ipswich swiftly turned things round, earning creditable 1–1 draws against Manchester United and Arsenal and beating Sunderland and Leeds before September was out.

Despite that run of form, the Blues had scored more than once in a game on just one occasion in their first seven matches and the management team moved quickly to sort out the profligacy in front of goal. By dropping David Johnson – their top scorer in 1999–2000 with 22 league goals – before eventually selling him to Nottingham Forest for £3.5 million, Burley spurred his attack into life. The strikers shot the side into the top six by November – a position they never relinquished after the season's 13th game.

It was during this run that striker Marcus Stewart – a £2.5 million capture from Huddersfield towards the end of 1999–2000 – began to start making headlines in the national press. The likeable Bristol-born forward went through a mid-season spell of 14 goals in 19 league games and was understandably linked with a call-up to the full England squad. His intelligent running and link-up play was becoming a major feature of Ipswich's style, while his left-footed finishing skills were peerless.

Arguably his best goal of the term came in the outstanding 1–0 win at Liverpool, when he coolly cut in from the goal line and rounded two defenders before slotting home.

Stewart was also given some welcome goalscoring support by bargain buy Alun Armstrong, who swapped life in Middlesbrough's reserves for a move to Portman Road, where he scored on his debut in a win over Southampton.

By the start of 2001, Ipswich were rapidly approaching the 40-point mark widely regarded as ensuring top-flight safety. It seemed their priorities were changing when they lost four games out of five in the Premiership, but embarked upon good runs in the FA and Worthington Cups. However, they quickly regained their league feet with wins over Everton and Bradford, while the cup runs came to an end at Sunderland in the FA Cup fourth round and Birmingham in the Worthington Cup semi-finals.

The Tractor Boys' best chance of success swung back to being the possibility of qualification for Europe from a high finishing position. It was being whispered very quietly, but Ipswich could well be competing in the UEFA Cup or even the Champions League in 2001–02 if they maintained their winning form –

SEASON REVIEW

and that, it seemed, was no sweat at all.

In March and April, they won three consecutive away games, including a stunning, Stewart-inspired 3–0 victory at Southampton in a televised Monday night match. That win, and those at West Ham and Middlesbrough, took the Blues' total of away-day triumphs to nine – a total that no side could better and one that only Leeds and Manchester United could match.

But defeat at Charlton in April proved crucial as neither of their challengers for the third spot in the division, Liverpool and Leeds, were dropping points on anything like a regular basis. Despite that, Ipswich still went into their match at Derby on the final day of 2000–01 knowing that a win and the right results in other matches would take them into Europe's major club competition.

Having won five times after going behind, Ipswich were not too concerned at going a goal down to the Rams, especially as Liverpool were struggling in their key match at Charlton. Following a deflected equaliser, hopes were raised further, but a four-goal blast by the Anfield men and a win for Leeds over Leicester meant Town had to settle for finishing in fifth place.

After the initial disappointment of missing out on the Champions League was overcome, Ipswich reflected proudly on an amazing season that ended with them being just the fourth promoted side in the history of the Premiership (after Blackburn, Newcastle and Nottingham Forest) to attain a top-five placing in their first campaign up.

Their recipe for success was no secret. Burley stuck with one of the most consistent line-ups in the top flight – 11 members of his squad featured in 25 Premiership games or more – and every man knew his job and worked hard in an effective system. No side worked more crossing positions in 2000–01 than Ipswich, whose wide men delivered 1,110 balls into the box. Jermaine Wright and Jamie Clapham were responsible for more than a hundred crosses each, while record £4 million signing Hermann Hreidarsson surprised everyone by adapting to the attacking left-back role with aplomb.

A fresh face would be introduced or an existing squad member would raise his game when they did suffer the occasional dip in form – for example Chris Makin, Ipswich's £1.4 million signing from Sunderland, and Martijn Reuser, a fringe player until the closing stages, contributed much during the run-in to 2000–01.

In May, Burley was awarded the League Managers' Association Manager of the Year award – the first time in 26 years it had been given to a boss who had not led his side to a title win.

> "We began the season thinking finishing 17th would be fantastic, so to qualify for Europe has been nothing short of phenomenal."
>
> George Burley

That fact is testament not only to how high Ipswich finished in relation to how much money they had to spend, but also to the level of attractive and attacking football they attempted to play. While Liverpool's Gérard Houllier would argue that winning three cups and a Champions League place was a greater achievement, nobody disputed that Burley had come close to working miracles on a relatively low budget.

Inevitably, the Scotsman's name will be linked with managerial roles at "bigger" clubs in the coming seasons. But with the capacity at Portman Road growing, a new five-year contract under his belt, a fine young squad at his disposal and European competition to look forward to, there seems no reason for Burley to move on in the immediate future.

IPSWICH TOWN

DATE	OPPONENT	SCORE	ATT.	ABIDALLAH	ARMSTRONG	BRAMBLE	BRANAGAN	BROWN	BURCHILL	CLAPHAM	CROFT	HOLLAND	HREIDAR
19.08.00	Tottenham A	1–3	36,148	–	–	90	–	s15	–	90	90	90	90
22.08.00	Man Utd H	1–1	22,007	–	–	90	–	–	–	90	–	49	90
26.08.00	Sunderland H	1–0	21,830	–	–	90¹	–	–	–	90	–	90	90
06.09.00	Leicester A	1–2	19,598	–	–	90□	–	–	–	90	–	90	90
09.09.00	Aston Villa H	1–2	20,665	–	–	90□	–	–	–	90	–	90	90
16.09.00	Leeds Utd A	2–1	35,552	–	–	90	–	–	–	90	–	90	90□
23.09.00	Arsenal H	1–1	22,030	–	–	90	–	–	–	90	–	90	90
30.09.00	Everton A	3–0	32,597	–	–	90	–	–	–	90	–	90	90
14.10.00	West Ham A	1–1	22,243	–	–	–	–	–	–	90	–	90	90
21.10.00	Bradford A	2–0*	17,045	–	–	–	–	–	–	90¹	–	90	90
28.10.00	Middlesbro H	2–1	21,771	–	–	–	–	–	–	90	–	90	90
04.11.00	Newcastle A	1–2	50,922	–	–	–	–	–	–	90	–	90	73
11.11.00	Charlton H	2–0	22,263	–	–	s26	–	–	–	90	–	90¹	90
20.11.00	Coventry A	1–0	19,324	–	–	s20	–	–	–	90	–	90	90
25.11.00	Man City A	3–2	33,741	–	–	–	–	–	–	90	–	90	90¹
02.12.00	Derby Co H	0–1	22,003	–	–	s45	90	–	–	90	–	90	90
10.12.00	Liverpool A	1–0	43,509	–	s1	–	–	–	–	90□	s10□	90	90
16.12.00	Southampton H	3–1*	22,228	–	s45¹	–	–	–	–	90	90	90	90
23.12.00	Man Utd A	0–2	67,597	–	s45	–	–	–	–	90	90	90	s15
26.12.00	Chelsea H	2–2	22,237	–	90	90	–	–	–	63	s16	90	90
30.12.00	Tottenham H	3–0	22,234	–	80¹	90	–	–	–	s5¹	–	90	90
01.01.01	Sunderland A	1–4	46,053	–	90	90□	–	–	–	58	–	90	90□
14.01.01	Leicester H	2–0	22,002	–	82	90□	–	–	–	89	–	90	90
20.01.01	Chelsea A	1–4	34,948	–	74	–	–	s16	–	90	70	90	90
03.02.01	Leeds Utd H	1–2	22,015	–	66	90□	–	s1	–	90	79	90	89
10.02.01	Arsenal A	0–1	38,011	–	–	90□	–	s52	–	90	38	90	–
24.02.01	Everton H	2–0	22,220	s9	s45¹	90□	–	–	90	90	–	90¹	–
04.03.01	Bradford H	3–1	21,820	s5	s45	90	–	–	90¹	s13	–	90	77
10.03.01	Aston Villa A	1–2	28,216	–	90¹	–	–	–	s4	53	–	90	90□
17.03.01	West Ham A	1–0	26,046	–	90	–	–	–	s1	s14	–	90	90
02.04.01	Southampton A	3–0	15,244	–	s23	90	–	–	s5	90	–	90	90
10.04.01	Liverpool H	1–1	23,504	–	90¹	63	–	–	–	–	–	90	90
14.04.01	Newcastle H	1–0	24,028	–	90	–	–	–	–	s14	–	90	90
16.04.01	Middlesbro A	2–1	34,294	–	81²	90	–	–	s1	s45	–	90	90
21.04.01	Coventry H	2–0	24,612	–	90	90	90	–	–	s28□	–	90	90
30.04.01	Charlton A	1–2	20,043	–	90	90	–	–	s24	–	–	90	90
07.05.01	Man City H	2–1	25,004	–	90	90	–	–	–	s27	–	90¹	63
19.05.01	Derby Co A	1–1*	33,239	–	90	90	–	–	–	–	–	90	90

□ Yellow card, ■ Red card, s Substitute, 90^2 Goals scored
*including own goal

For more information visit our website:

2000–01 PREMIERSHIP APPEARANCES

JOHNSON	MAKIN	MAGILTON	McGREAL	NAYLOR	REUSER	SCALES	SCOWCROFT	STEWART	VENUS	WILNIS	J WRIGHT	R WRIGHT	TOTAL
90	–	90	–	–	s20	–	90	70	75¹	–	–	90	990
90	–	90	–	–	s41	–	s5	85	90	90¹□	90	90	990
90	–	90	–	–	–	–	s34	56	90	90	90□	90	990
90	–	90¹	–	–	–	90	s24	90	–	90	66	90	990
73	–	90	s30	–	s30	–	90	s17¹	60	90	60	90	990
–	–	90	90□	–	–	–	90¹	90	–	90□	90¹	90	990
–	–	90	–	s32	–	–	58□	90¹	90	90	90	90	990
s13	–	90	90¹	62	–	–	s28	77²	–	90	90	90	990
s7	–	90	90	83	–	–	s18	72¹	90	90	90	90	990
s25	–	80	90	90	–	–	s10	65	90	90	90	90	990
s17	–	89	90	90¹	–	–	s1	73	90¹	90	90	90	990
s30	–	90	90	60	s17	–	s30	60¹	90	90	90	90	990
s1	–	90	90	s13	–	–	77	89¹	90	64	90	90	990
–	–	90	70	–	s22	–	90	90	90	90¹□	68	90	990
s23	–	90	–	–	–	90□	67	90²	90	90□	90	90	990
49	–	90	90	–	s13	–	s41	90²	90	45□	77	–	990
–	–	90	90	–	–	–	89	80¹	90□	90	90	90	990
–	–	90	90	–	s1	–	89¹	90	90□	–	45	90	990
–	–	89	90	–	s1	–	90	90	90	75□	45	90	990
–	–	–	–	–	s27	–	90¹	90¹	90	74	90	90	990
s10	–	–	s8	–	90	–	90	85¹	90	82	90	90	990
–	–	–	s7	–	s32	–	90	90¹□	90□	83□	90	90	990
–	–	90	90	–	s1	–	90¹	90¹	–	90	s8	90	990
–	–	90	72□	–	–	–	90	90¹	–	90	s20	90	972
–	–	–	–	s24	s11	–	90	74□	90¹	–	90	90	974
–	–	90	–	s12	78	–	90	90□	90	–	90	90	990
–	–	81	90	–	s16	–	90	–	74	45	90	90	990
–	–	45	90	–	90²	–	90	–	–	90	85	90	990
–	90	s37	90	–	90	–	90	–	–	90	86	90	990
–	90	90	90	–	76¹	–	–	89	–	90	90	90	990
–	90	–	90	–	76□	–	67	85³	s14	–	90	90	990
–	90	90	90	–	90	–	s32	90	–	s27	58	90	990
–	90	67	90	–	76	–	s23	90¹	s37	53	90	90	990
–	90	90	–	s9	45	–	–	89	90□	–	90	90	990
–	90	90	90	s1	62¹	–	–	89	–	–	90¹	–	990
–	90□	90	90	–	90¹	–	–	66	–	–	90	90	990
–	90	90	90	s19	90¹	–	90	–	–	–	71	90	990
–	74	90□	90	s48	90	–	s63	42	–	s16	27	90	990

THE MANAGER

GEORGE BURLEY

Since being appointed Ipswich manager in December 1994 – and experiencing the disappointment of relegation from the top flight just five months later – the name George Burley has become synonymous with perseverance.

After narrowly missing out on a Division One play-off spot at the end of 1995–96, the Tractor Boys then lost in the top six lottery three seasons in a row, before finally succeeding at Wembley in 2000. And the mild-mannered Ipswich boss has gone from strength to strength ever since.

Burley has exceeded all expectations by guiding the Blues back into Europe and almost snatching a Champions League spot at the first attempt. Rarely out of the top five, the Premiership newcomers held Manchester United and Arsenal to draws at Portman Road and defeated both Leeds and Liverpool on their travels before Christmas had even passed.

As a result of Ipswich's outstanding achievements throughout 2000–01, the Scotsman was named the League Managers Association's Manager of the Year and also collected the Carling equivalent. That haul represents a stunning achievement for a man whose team were among the bookmakers' favourites to return to Division One with immediate effect.

LEAGUE POSITION

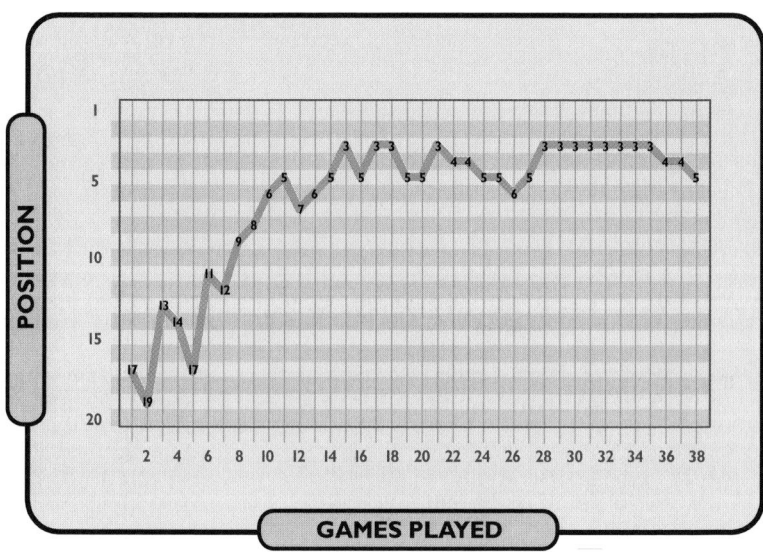

POSITION

GAMES PLAYED

11 Marcus Stewart scored more goals

THE GOALS

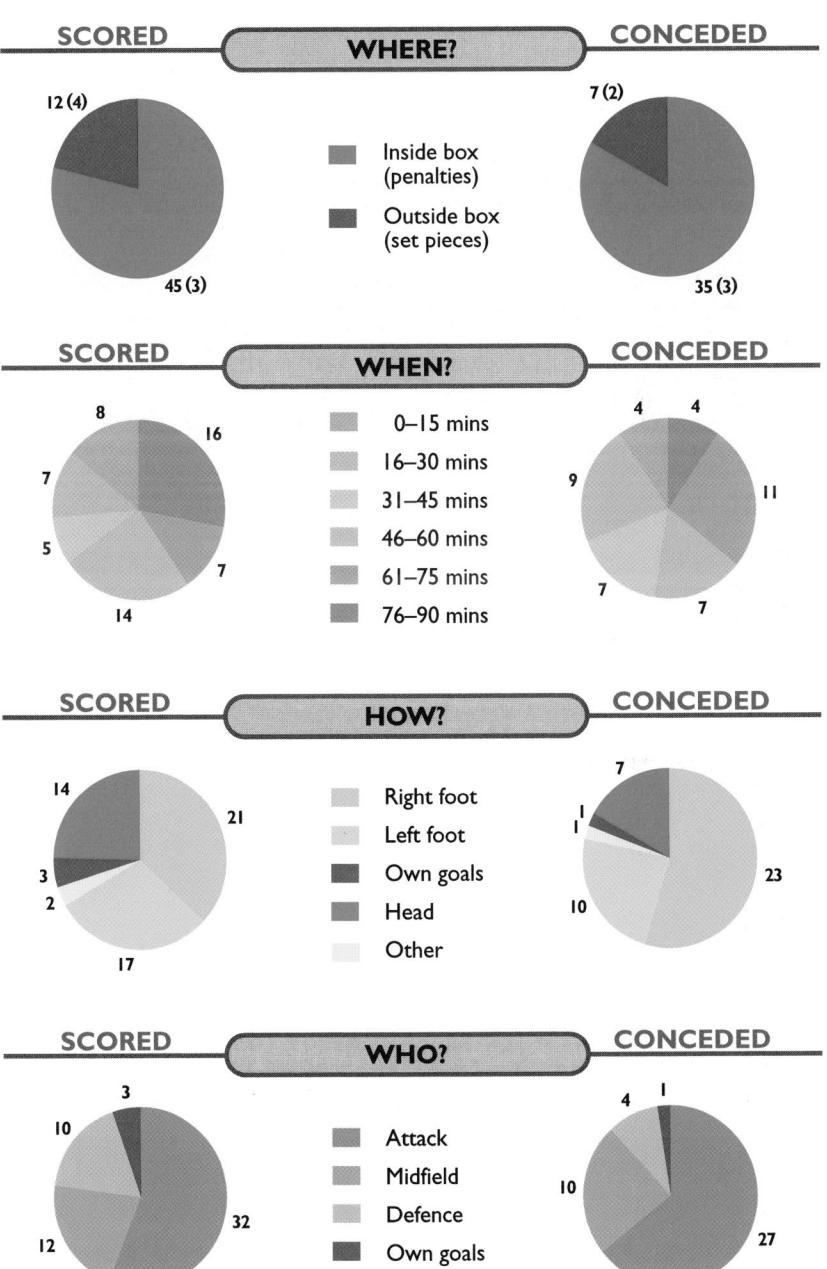

SCORED · **WHERE?** · **CONCEDED**

12 (4)
45 (3)

7 (2)
35 (3)

- Inside box (penalties)
- Outside box (set pieces)

SCORED · **WHEN?** · **CONCEDED**

8
16
7
5
7
14

4   4
9
11
7   7

- 0–15 mins
- 16–30 mins
- 31–45 mins
- 46–60 mins
- 61–75 mins
- 76–90 mins

SCORED · **HOW?** · **CONCEDED**

14
21
3
2
17

7
1
1
23
10

- Right foot
- Left foot
- Own goals
- Head
- Other

SCORED · **WHO?** · **CONCEDED**

3
10
32
12

4   1
10
27

- Attack
- Midfield
- Defence
- Own goals

away from home than any other player

IPSWICH TOWN

	ABIDALLAH	ARMSTRONG	BRAMBLE	BROWN	BURCHILL	CLAPHAM	CROFT	HOLLAND	HREIDARSSON	JOHNSON
APPEARANCES										
Start	0	15	23	0	2	28	6	38	35	6
Sub	2	6	3	4	5	7	2	0	1	8
Minutes on pitch	14	1487	2134	84	215	2569	483	3379	3107	608
GOAL ATTEMPTS										
Goals	0	7	1	0	1	2	0	3	1	0
Shots on target	0	23	7	0	3	14	1	14	8	5
Shots off target	0	20	15	0	2	14	0	27	16	16
Shooting accuracy	0%	53%	32%	0%	60%	50%	100%	34%	33%	24%
PASSING										
Goal assists	0	2	0	0	1	3	0	5	4	1
Long passes	2	68	368	12	4	216	56	310	389	17
Short passes	9	527	496	17	62	893	147	1211	916	162
PASS COMPLETION										
Own half %	100%	85%	74%	90%	64%	82%	72%	89%	74%	82%
Opposition half %	43%	65%	49%	50%	56%	68%	62%	76%	61%	67%
CROSSING										
Total crosses	0	25	24	1	9	153	20	20	89	7
Cross completion %	0%	16%	21%	0%	11%	29%	25%	30%	25%	43%
DRIBBLING										
Dribbles & runs	2	28	66	1	7	99	14	37	141	17
Dribble completion %	50%	57%	70%	100%	43%	71%	71%	76%	65%	65%
DEFENDING										
Tackles made	1	18	116	1	2	62	13	111	89	9
Tackles won %	0%	78%	76%	100%	100%	66%	77%	68%	72%	56%
Blocks	0	0	8	3	0	18	6	18	38	1
Clearances	0	4	214	6	0	36	16	46	214	0
Interceptions	0	2	11	0	1	8	1	15	12	0
DISCIPLINE										
Fouls	1	22	33	0	4	13	5	20	63	22
Offside	0	17	0	0	1	1	0	1	2	17
Yellow cards	0	0	7	0	0	2	1	0	3	0
Red cards	0	0	0	0	0	0	0	0	0	0

GOALKEEPER NAME	START/ (SUB)	TIME ON PITCH	GOALS CONCEDED	MINS/GOALS CONCEDED	SAVES MADE	SAVES/ SHOTS
BRANAGAN	2(0)	180	1	180	4	80%
WRIGHT R	36(0)	3240	41	79	103	72%

For more information visit our website:

PLAYERS' STATISTICS

	MAGILTON	MAKIN	McGREAL	NAYLOR	REUSER	SCALES	SCOWCROFT	STEWART	VENUS	WILNIS	WRIGHT J	TOTAL	RANK
	32	10	25	5	13	2	22	33	23	27	35		
	1	0	3	8	13	0	12	1	2	2	2		
	2828	884	2257	543	1275	180	2196	2713	2060	2274	2876		
	1	0	1	1	6	0	4	19	3	2	2	57*	6th
	7	0	4	5	25	0	13	48	12	2	14	205	6th
	21	2	7	6	13	2	27	33	3	9	20	253	=4th
	25%	0%	36%	45%	66%	0%	33%	59%	80%	18%	41%	45%	11th
	5	1	0	2	2	0	3	4	0	3	3	39	6th
	632	118	410	21	86	23	112	147	442	295	403	4526	6th
	1490	345	612	157	418	37	757	1026	622	821	1187	11985	5th
	91%	81%	84%	76%	84%	79%	75%	81%	85%	82%	82%	83%	4th
	73%	74%	59%	66%	64%	65%	64%	74%	63%	63%	71%	66%	5th
	102	24	36	6	174	0	31	55	132	98	104	1110	1st
	37%	25%	25%	17%	34%	0%	13%	24%	31%	28%	32%	29%	2nd
	41	21	16	16	50	1	41	49	24	61	51	785	18th
	80%	76%	69%	38%	60%	100%	68%	73%	83%	74%	80%	70%	5th
	65	41	67	18	30	4	35	43	53	85	67	931	17th
	72%	88%	70%	72%	80%	50%	80%	70%	60%	85%	75%	73%	8th
	7	7	18	1	1	3	4	4	16	16	9	178	17th
	27	34	198	3	10	17	12	4	181	57	22	1184	18th
	3	4	11	0	2	1	4	2	6	10	3	96	=18th
	28	13	24	16	19	0	56	42	30	28	22	462	19th
	6	0	1	2	10	0	7	36	0	0	3	104	20th
	1	1	1	0	1	1	1	2	4	7	1	33	20th
	0	0	1	0	0	0	0	1	0	0	0	2	=15th

*Including three own goals

CROSSES CAUGHT	CROSSES PUNCHED	CROSSES DROPPED	CATCH SUCCESS	THROWS/SHORT KICKS	% COMPLETION	LONG KICKS	% COMPLETION
2	2	0	100%	7	100%	24	67%
76	20	7	92%	91	86%	691	51%

PLAYER OF THE SEASON

PLAYER	INDEX SCORE
MARCUS STEWART	1,001
Mark Venus	941
Jim Magilton	931
John McGreal	858
Matt Holland	814
Titus Bramble	801
Hermann Hreidarsson	776
Jamie Clapham	765
Richard Wright	753
Fabian Wilnis	741

In an exhilarating 2000–01 Premiership campaign, Ipswich took the top flight by storm as they clinched a UEFA Cup spot, courtesy of some attractive and neatly-crafted football which won plaudits from every quarter.

If one man epitomised the surprise package that was the side from East Anglia, it was surely Marcus Stewart.

Stewart came within a whisker of claiming the Golden Boot and was touted for the England squad, in a season which saw him grab 19 goals. The former Huddersfield striker converted an exemplary 23% of shots – all from inside the area – and set up four strikes for his colleagues as he recorded an average of 1,001 Opta Index points. He bagged a league-high 11 away from home and was "first goalscorer" on 11 occasions too.

If Stewart provided the goals, the spine of the team contained the likes of Mark Venus and Jim Magilton. Venus, whose average Opta score of 941 points placed him second in the Ipswich Index, made more than 1,000 passes and more than 100 headed clearances along with his three goals.

So much of Town's play went through the prolific Magilton. The former Saint was the only player anywhere near Roy Keane in terms of passes, completing 1,701 and creating five goals in the process.

Matt Holland ran Magilton close, however, recording a superb pass completion rate of 81%, also setting up five strikes and scoring three himself as he averaged 814 points on Opta's Index.

Hermann Hreidarsson went on 141 marauding runs, largely down the left flank, to provide the ammunition, while the stoic Titus Bramble won the eighth-highest tally of tackles in the Premiership.

Richard Wright also did enough to make the Ipswich top 10 with 103 saves and a dozen clean sheets, while Martijn Reuser won plenty of admirers on the strength of his sparkling displays on the left wing and might have ousted Stewart from top spot had he played more often.

3 Ipswich failed to score on fewer

FIVE OF THE BEST

Ipswich defied the bookmakers, the pundits and even their own expectations by securing a top five spot in the Premiership in 2000–01. Manager George Burley effortlessly reproduced the Suffolk team's slick passing style and organisation, for which they were famed in Division One, on the bigger stage and established Town as a bona fide force.

TOP GOALSCORERS

	GOALS	GOALS/SHOTS
MARCUS STEWART	19	23%
Alun Armstrong	7	16%
Martijn Reuser	6	16%
James Scowcroft	4	10%
Mark Venus	3	20%

Despite never having kicked a ball in the Premiership prior to August 2001, striker Marcus Stewart played like a veteran of the top flight, consistently finding the back of the net and running opposition defences ragged with his constant movement. The former Huddersfield hitman netted with 23% of his shots on target and only Chelsea's Jimmy Floyd Hasselbaink scored with greater frequency. Alun Armstrong bagged seven strikes in six months after arriving from Middlesbrough to help maintain the European assault.

The combined stamina and accuracy of Jim Magilton and Matt Holland provided Ipswich with a solid midfield nucleus from which they were able to launch endless assaults. Only Roy Keane amassed more successful passes than Magilton, who found a fellow-blue shirt with more than 80% of his distribution. Skipper Matt Holland proved just as industrious in possession as his Irish team-mate and played a pivotal role in Ipswich becoming the fourth-most accurate passing outfit.

TOP PASSERS

	SUCC PASSES	COMPLETION
JIM MAGILTON	1,701	80%
Matt Holland	1,238	81%
Jermaine Wright	1,183	74%
Marcus Stewart	891	76%
Hermann Hreidarsson	866	66%

TOP TACKLERS

	WON	SUCCESS
TITUS BRAMBLE	88	76%
Matt Holland	76	68%
Fabian Wilnis	72	85%
Hermann Hreidarsson	64	72%
Jermaine Wright	50	75%

Defender Titus Bramble rose to prominence during Ipswich's successful march to the Premiership and a year later has proved that he can contend with the best strikers in the country. He was the only Tractor Boy to win in excess of 80 challenges as the newcomers sought to protect their pride and place in the top flight. Captain Matt Holland was hot on Bramble's heels, though, winning 76 tackles as the Blues held their own.

Adding to an already glowing array of statistics, Ipswich were the cleanest team in the Premiership throughout 2000–01. But every team has a chief sinner and Hermann Hreidarsson laid claim to the unfortunate title at Portman Road. The Icelandic international hardly disgraced himself by committing little more than 60 fouls and collecting a paltry tally of three yellow cards. Still, he was some way ahead of his well-behaved team-mates, with James Scowcroft a distant runner-up with 59 disciplinary points.

DISCIPLINE

	POINTS	FOULS & CARDS
HERMANN HREIDARSSON	72	63F, 3Y, 0R
James Scowcroft	59	56F, 1Y, 0R
Marcus Stewart	54	42F, 2Y, 1R
Titus Bramble	54	33F, 7Y, 0R
Fabian Wilnis	49	28F, 7Y, 0R

ACTION	ARMSTRONG	CLAPHAM	CROFT	HOLLAND	HREIDARSSON	MAGILTON	McGREAL	SCOWCROFT	STEWART	VENUS	J WRIGHT	R WRIGHT	WILNIS	TOTAL	LIVERPOOL
Time on pitch	1	90	10	90	90	90	90	89	80	90	90	90	90	990	990
GOALS															
Goal	–	–	–	–	–	–	–	–	1	–	–	–	–	1	0
Shot on target (incl goals)	–	1	–	1	–	–	1	–	2	–	–	–	–	5	4
Shot off target	–	–	–	1	–	1	–	2	–	–	–	–	–	4	11
Blocked shot	–	–	–	–	–	–	–	–	–	–	–	–	–	0	6
Own goal	–	–	–	–	–	–	–	–	–	–	–	–	–	0	0
PASSES															
Pass to own player	2	23	2	32	27	58	21	26	29	25	33	5	28	311	314
Pass to opposition	–	10	3	6	5	17	11	6	6	11	12	2	10	103	119
Cross to own player	–	1	–	–	–	1	–	–	1	1	1	–	1	6	11
Cross to opposition player	–	3	–	–	2	–	–	1	–	3	3	–	1	13	26
Goal assist	–	–	–	–	–	–	–	–	–	–	–	–	–	0	0
Pass completion %	100%	66%	40%	84%	80%	77%	66%	72%	81%	64%	69%	71%	74%	73%	69%
TACKLES & CLEARANCES															
Tackle	–	1	1	3	2	6	4	1	1	2	2	2	2	24	36
Clearances, blocks and interceptions	–	–	–	1	15	1	16	–	1	16	2	3	6	61	37
DRIBBLES & RUNS															
Dribbles ball retained	–	5	–	–	3	1	2	1	2	–	2	–	–	16	16
Dribbles ball lost	–	4	–	1	5	–	3	2	1	–	1	1	–	18	12
Dribble success %	–	56%	–	0%	38%	100%	40%	33%	67%	–	67%	0%	–	47%	57%
DISCIPLINE															
Fouls	–	2	–	1	3	2	3	–	–	1	1	–	–	13	13
Penalty conceded	–	–	–	–	–	–	–	–	–	–	–	–	–	0	0
Free kick – offside	–	–	–	–	–	–	–	–	3	–	–	–	–	3	3
Yellow cards	–	1	–	–	1	–	1	–	–	–	–	–	–	3	1
Red cards	–	–	–	–	–	–	–	–	–	–	–	–	–	0	0
GOALKEEPERS															
Distribution to own player	–	–	–	–	–	–	–	–	–	–	–	11	–	11	12
Distribution to opposition player	–	–	–	–	–	–	–	–	–	–	–	16	–	16	8
Goalkeeper distribution %	–	–	–	–	–	–	–	–	–	–	–	41%	–	41%	60%
Save	–	–	–	–	–	–	–	–	–	–	–	3	–	3	4
Ball caught	–	–	–	–	–	–	–	–	–	–	–	2	–	2	2
Ball dropped	–	–	–	–	–	–	–	–	–	–	–	–	–	–	0
Goal conceded	–	–	–	–	–	–	–	–	–	–	–	–	–	–	1

5 Ipswich lost more games, despite having

Back in December, Ipswich were seen as a surprise package whose league position was a fluke and Liverpool were viewed as a side rebuilding and unlikely to win anything. Hindsight illustrates that this was not a one-off, but a true declaration of intent from George Burley's newly-promoted team.

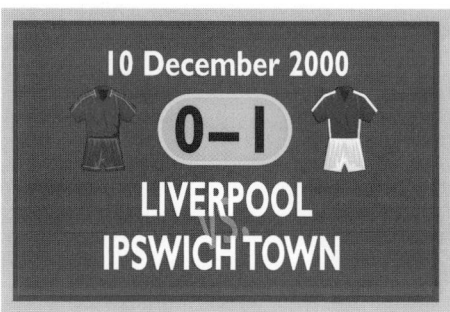

10 December 2000

0 – 1

LIVERPOOL
IPSWICH TOWN

After their shock defeat against lowly Derby the previous week – the first occasion Ipswich had failed to score in the Premiership – the pundits were already predicting a slide down the table.

But Burley's men showed no signs of repeating that performance as they returned to their fluent passing game. The visitors pinged the ball around with confidence, finding a blue shirt with 73% of their distribution – four percentage points better than the home side – on what was a very poor playing surface.

Jim Magilton was the driving force behind the Town midfield and he made 58 successful passes – more than any other player on the pitch – as he bridged defence with attack time and again.

Gérard Houllier's gamble to leave top scorer Emile Heskey on the bench backfired as Michael Owen and Robbie Fowler failed to pierce a solid Town rearguard, which made 61 clearances, blocks and interceptions. Not for the first time, Liverpool were being outplayed on their own pitch, but there was always the threat of a breakaway goal from the home side.

However, the persistent Blues got their reward on the stroke of half-time when Jamie Clapham fed Marcus Stewart. The former Huddersfield hitman skipped past Stephane Henchoz, rounded Sander Westerveld and planted a shot beyond Jamie Carragher on the goal line to put Town in front. Few would argue it was undeserved.

In the second period, Clapham attempted to double the lead with a stinging drive, which forced Westerveld to make his fourth and final save of the afternoon. Liverpool responded with a barrage of shots, but the visiting defence was on top of its game, defending with as much perspiration as inspiration.

The Reds battled hard to win possession, winning 83% of their 36 challenges – 16 percentage points better than Ipswich – as they stepped up the search for a crucial equaliser. But commitment alone does not win games and Liverpool's failure to find the back of the net during their brief moments of dominance ultimately led to their downfall.

The newly-promoted "relegation certainties" had proved they could play with the big sides and even beat them.

Much of the credit for the victory went to Town goalkeeper Richard Wright, who kept his sixth clean sheet of the season. The Ipswich shot-stopper pulled off three vital saves from strike-duo Fowler and Owen to help the Tractor Boys gain their ninth win of the campaign and plough on to third in the Premiership.

The Ipswich bubble never burst. They qualified for the UEFA Cup and Burley was named Manager of the Year, but this was the result which epitomised the fact that his side were not just there to make up the numbers.

taken the lead, than any other team

LEEDS UNITED

ADDRESS

Elland Road, Leeds,
West Yorkshire LS11 0ES

CONTACT NUMBERS

Telephone: 0113 226 6000
Fax: 0113 226 6050
Ticket Office: 0113 292 1000
Club Call: 09068 121180
Club shop: 0113 225 1144
E-mail: football@lufc.co.uk
Website: www.lufc.co.uk

KEY PERSONNEL

President: The Right Honourable
Earl of Harewood KBE LLD
Chairman: P Ridsdale
Leeds United Directors: S Harrison,
A Hudson, D Spencer, D Walker
Club Secretary: I Silvester
Manager: David O'Leary

SPONSORS

Strongbow

FANZINES

The Square Ball
Till the World Stops
We Are Leeds
To Ell And Back

COLOURS

Home: White shirts, white
shorts and white stockings
Away: Yellow shirts, yellow
shorts and yellow stockings

NICKNAMES

United
The Whites

HONOURS

League Champions:
1968–69, 1973–74, 1991–92
Division Two Champions:
1923–24, 1963–64, 1989–90
FA Cup Winners: 1972
League Cup Winners: 1968
Fairs Cup Winners: 1968, 1971

RECORD GOALSCORER

Peter Lorimer – 168 league goals
1965–79, 1983–86

BIGGEST WIN

10–0 v Lyn (Oslo), European Cup 1st
round 1st leg, 17 September 1969

BIGGEST DEFEAT

1–8 v Stoke City –
Division One, 27 August 1934

SEASON REVIEW

Fourth place in the league and a UEFA Cup spot could be seen as under-achievement for big-spending Leeds, who finished third in 1999–2000. But as any Whites fan will tell you, the 2000–01 season was a great adventure – and a wonderful time to be a Leeds supporter.

Having qualified for the Champions League, Leeds spent the summer shopping and were one of the biggest spenders in the transfer market, bringing in Olivier Dacourt from Lens and Celtic striker Mark Viduka to strengthen their young squad. Injury problems were already appearing before a ball had been kicked, though, with David Batty and Harry Kewell falling foul of long-term problems, and David O'Leary made it clear that the big spending was not yet over.

The season got off to an early start with a preliminary tie in the Champions League against 1860 Munich. Despite being reduced to nine men in the first leg, United came through 3–1 on aggregate with two-goal Alan Smith the hero. Smith's impressive early-season form was not confined to Europe, as he also bagged the winning goals in both Leeds' opening Premiership encounters.

Transfer talk remained very much alive at Elland Road as Leeds were linked with a £15 million bid for West Ham defender Rio Ferdinand – a player known to be much admired by manager David O'Leary. The Hammers turned this bid for their prized asset down, but one player who did arrive in West Yorkshire was the versatile Dominic Matteo from Liverpool for £4.25 million.

The draw for the first round proper of the Champions League did the Whites no favours, putting them in a group with Barcelona, AC Milan and Turkish side Besiktas. Many pundits immediately began to write off Leeds' Euro hopes. A 4–0 hammering in the Nou Camp did nothing to change the pundits' opinions, while things were equally uncomfortable at home. Defeats by recently-promoted Manchester City and Ipswich at Elland Road brought out the boo-boys and had Leeds already way behind in the title reckoning at an early stage.

The club's European adventure, though, was looking a lot healthier thanks to a 1–0 win over a star-studded AC Milan side at Elland Road. Besiktas were then hammered 6–0 to give Leeds a great chance of progression to the next stage.

The return leg against Besiktas was an emotional moment for all those connected with Leeds as they returned to Istanbul just six months after the murder of two supporters in the city. Thankfully there was no repeat of the violence this time and a 0–0 draw maintained Leeds' hopes of qualifying for the next round.

Despite the big spending, O'Leary was still struggling to cope with the squad that he had and further injuries to Nigel Martyn and the previous season's top scorer Michael Bridges contrived to make the situation worse. A weakened team was swept aside 3–0 at Old Trafford by Manchester United, and this served as a wake-up call pinpointing how far they still had to progress.

The injury to Martyn brought young 'keeper Paul Robinson into the spotlight and, following some fearless performances from the 21-year-old – most notably in a 1–1 draw with Barcelona – he found himself in the England squad to face Italy in Turin. This was just the latest in a long line of

> **"There was a time in January when we'd have thrown a party on the strength of qualifying for the Intertoto Cup."**
>
> David O'Leary

SEASON REVIEW

successes produced by the Leeds youth system.

Progression to the next stage of the Champions League was assured, but once again O'Leary's side had no luck in the draw and were paired with big guns Real Madrid, Lazio and Anderlecht. The board at Leeds were ready to show their ambition, though, and backed O'Leary to go after Rio Ferdinand again. This time the manager got his man – but at a price. The British transfer record was shattered when the Hammers accepted an £18 million bid and Rio was heading north.

The drama of the Champions League continued with a sensational 1–0 win against Sven-Göran Eriksson's Lazio in Rome, but United were still struggling to show any kind of form in the Premiership. Defeats by West Ham, Leicester, Southampton, Aston Villa and Newcastle in the run-up to New Year meant Leeds went into 2001 languishing in the bottom half of the table. O'Leary continued to ring the changes as he tried to build the squad he wanted and in came striker Robbie Keane on loan from Inter Milan until the end of the season.

Little excitement was provided in the FA Cup as United were knocked out by eventual winners Liverpool in the fourth round. But as the injury list shortened, results in the Premiership began to pick up. David Batty returned to first-team action, Harry Kewell was on his way back, Ian Harte rediscovered his form and Robbie Keane was scoring plenty of goals. A 2–1 win over Aston Villa set the Whites off on a run of 13 games unbeaten in the league, which lifted them out of the bottom half and left them fighting for a place in Europe once again.

But on the negative side, three Leeds players provided the media with one of the hottest stories of the season. Lee Bowyer, Jonathon Woodgate and Michael Duberry all faced several weeks on trial at Hull Crown Court following an alleged incident outside a nightclub in Leeds city centre. The injured Woodgate and Duberry were able to remain out of the limelight, but Bowyer was enjoying probably his best-ever season as a player. He was forced into making many a mad dash along the M62 to feature in games after a day in court but, thankfully for Leeds, his inspired form was not affected.

A fantastic 4–1 win over Anderlecht in Brussels put Leeds through to the quarter-finals of the Champions League where they would meet Deportivo La Coruña, while impressive league form continued to help push Leeds towards the European places. Deportivo were swept aside 3–0 in the first leg at Elland Road and, with Leeds surviving in the second leg and other English teams failing, the supporters were able proudly to claim that there was only one United in Europe.

Sadly it all came to an end in a semi-final against Valencia, who comfortably won the second leg 3–0 after a goalless first leg at Elland Road. A 2–1 defeat at Arsenal in the league ultimately cost Leeds another shot at the Champions League, but the 2000–01 campaign really should not be remembered as a season of disappointment. The squad grew stronger and gained valuable experience and people will be looking to Leeds to make a serious title challenge in 2001–02.

O'Leary's side might not have any silverware to display just yet, but they have already had one hell of an adventure.

> "We've come a long way in three-and-a-half years. It's a sign of that when people say they're disappointed."
>
> David O'Leary

LEEDS UNITED

DATE	OPPONENT	SCORE	ATT.	BAKKE	BATTY	BOWYER	BRIDGES	BURNS	DACOURT	DUBERRY	EVANS	FERDINAND	HARTE	HAY
19.08.00	Everton H	2–0	40,010	79	–	90	79	–	90	–	–	–	90	–
26.08.00	Middlesbro A	2–1	31,626	18	–	90¹	90	–	90	90	–	–	90	–
05.09.00	Man City H	1–2	40,055	–	–	90¹	90	–	90□	90	s33	–	90	–
09.09.00	Coventry A	0–0	20,377	–	–	90□	90	–	90	90	–	–	90	–
16.09.00	Ipswich H	1–2	35,552	–	–	90¹	90	–	90	90	–	–	90	–
23.09.00	Derby Co A	1–1	26,248	88	–	90□	90	–	90□	45	–	–	90¹	–
30.09.00	Tottenham H	4–3	37,562	90	–	90	s9	–	35	–	–	–	90	s45
14.10.00	Charlton H	3–1	38,837	90	–	90	–	90	–	–	–	–	90	–
21.10.00	Man Utd A	0–3	67,525	–	–	90□	–	90	–	–	–	–	–	90
29.10.00	Bradford A	1–1	17,364	90□	–	63	–	s27	90□	–	–	–	90□	90
04.11.00	Liverpool H	4–3	40,055	90	–	90□	–	90	90	–	–	–	90	s74
12.11.00	Chelsea A	1–1	35,121	90□	–	90	–	–	90	–	–	–	90	–
18.11.00	West Ham H	0–1	40,005	45	–	90	–	–	90	–	–	–	90	–
26.11.00	Arsenal H	1–0	38,084	90	–	90	–	–	90¹□	–	–	–	90	–
02.12.00	Leicester A	1–3	21,486	–	–	90	–	–	90	–	–	90	–	–
09.12.00	Southampton A	0–1	15,225	90□	–	90	–	–	90□	–	–	90	–	–
16.12.00	Sunderland H	2–0	40,053	90□	s10	90¹	–	–	80	–	–	90	–	–
23.12.00	Aston Villa H	1–2	39,714	90	–	90□	–	–	–	–	–	90	–	–
26.12.00	Newcastle A	1–2	52,118	75	s15	90	–	–	90¹□	–	–	90	–	–
01.01.01	Middlesbro H	1–1	39,251	–	90	90□	–	–	90□	–	–	90	–	–
13.01.01	Man City A	4–0	34,288	90¹□	–	90¹	–	–	90□	–	–	90	–	–
20.01.01	Newcastle H	1–3	40,005	90	–	90	–	–	90	–	–	–	–	–
24.01.01	Aston Villa A	2–1	29,335	90	s13	90¹	–	–	77	–	–	90	90¹	–
31.01.01	Coventry H	1–0	36,555	90□	90	90□	–	–	–	–	–	90	90	–
03.02.01	Ipswich A	2–1*	22,015	s3	90□	90	–	–	87	–	–	90	90	–
07.02.01	Everton A	2–2	34,224	s11	90	79	–	–	90¹	–	–	90	90¹	–
10.02.01	Derby Co H	0–0	38,789	s21□	90	69	–	–	90	–	–	90	90	–
24.02.01	Tottenham A	2–1	36,070	45	90	90¹	–	–	90	–	–	90	90¹	–
03.03.01	Man Utd H	1–1	40,055	–	90	90□	–	–	90	–	–	90	90	–
17.03.01	Charlton A	2–1	20,043	–	90□	90	–	–	90	–	–	90	90	–
31.03.01	Sunderland A	2–0	48,285	s81	90	90	–	–	9	–	–	90	90	–
07.04.01	Southampton H	2–0	39,267	90	90	90	–	–	–	–	–	90	90	–
13.04.01	Liverpool A	2–1	44,116	–	90	90¹	–	–	90	–	–	90¹	90	–
21.04.01	West Ham A	2–0	26,041	90	50□	90	–	–	90□	–	–	90¹	90	–
28.04.01	Chelsea H	2–0	39,253	s16□	90	74	–	–	90□	–	–	90	90	–
05.05.01	Arsenal A	1–2	38,142	75	–	90	–	–	90□	–	–	90	90¹	–
13.05.01	Bradford H	6–1	38,300	90¹	–	90¹	–	–	76□	–	–	90	90¹	–
19.05.01	Leicester H	3–1	39,105	90□	–	90□	–	–	69□	–	–	90	90¹	–

□ Yellow card, ■ Red card, s Substitute, 90² Goals scored
*including own goal

For more information visit our website:

2000–01 PREMIERSHIP APPEARANCES

HUCKERBY	JONES	KEANE	KELLY	KEWELL	MARTYN	MATTEO	McPHAIL	MILLS	RADEBE	ROBINSON	SMITH	VIDUKA	WILCOX	WOODGATE	TOTAL
s11	–	–	90	–	90	–	–	s11	90	–	90²	90	–	90□	990
–	s68	–	90	–	90	–	–	s4	s67	–	90¹	90	–	23	990
–	57	–	90	–	90	–	–	–	90□	–	90	90	–	–	990
73	–	–	90	–	90	–	90	–	90	–	90□	–	s17	–	990
90	–	–	90	–	90	–	90	90□	–	–	90	–	–	–	990
–	–	–	90	–	90	90	s2	s45	90	–	90	–	–	–	990
–	–	–	90	–	90	90	s55	90	45	–	90²	81²	–	–	990
–	–	–	90	–	71	90	–	90	–	s19	90¹	90²	–	90	990
s12	90	–	90	–	–	90	90	–	–	90	78□	90	–	90	990
–	–	–	90	–	–	90	–	–	–	90	90	90¹□	–	90	990
–	–	–	90	–	–	90	–	–	–	90	90	90⁴	–	16	990
s13	–	–	90□	–	–	90□	–	90	90□	90	90	77¹	–	–	990
s45	–	–	90	–	–	90	–	90□	90	90	90	90	–	–	990
–	–	–	90	–	–	–	–	–	90	90	90	90	90	90	990
–	62	–	90	s28	–	90	–	–	67□	90	90□	90¹	s52	38	967
–	–	–	90	s33	–	90	–	–	–	90	90□	90	57	90□	990
s3	–	–	90	90	–	90	–	–	–	90	90	87¹□	–	90□	990
–	–	s23	90	90	–	90	–	–	67	90	90	90	–	90¹	990
–	–	s34	90	56	–	90	–	–	–	90	90□	90	–	90	990
–	–	75¹	90	–	–	90	–	–	90	90	s15	90	90	–	990
–	–	s19²	–	–	–	90	–	90□	90	90	71	90	90	–	990
–	–	90¹	–	–	–	90	–	90	90□	90	s11	90	79	90□	990
–	–	77	90	–	–	45	–	–	–	90	s13	90	s45	90	990
–	–	90¹	–	90	–	–	90□	90	–	–	90□	90	–	–	990
–	–	87¹	–	–	90	90	–	90	90□	–	s3	90	–	–	990
–	–	74	–	–	90	77	–	90	90□	–	s16	90	s13	–	990
–	–	90	–	s27	90	90	–	–	90	–	s21□	69	63	–	990
–	–	90□	–	s45	90	90	–	90	–	–	–	90	–	–	990
–	–	45	–	s45	90	45	–	90□	90□	–	s45	90¹	–	–	990
–	–	–	–	81□	90	90	–	90□	–	–	90¹	90¹	s9	–	990
–	–	s7	s45	83	90	–	–	90	45□	–	71¹■	90¹	–	–	971
–	–	90¹	–	70¹	90	90	–	90	–	–	–	90	s20	–	990
–	–	s3	–	84	90	90	–	90□	–	–	87	90	s6	–	990
–	–	90¹	–	82	90	90	–	90□	–	–	–	90	s8	–	950
–	–	s9¹	–	81	90	90	–	90□	–	–	90	90¹	–	–	990
–	–	44	90	90□	90	90	s15	–	–	–	–	90□	s46	–	990
–	–	–	–	90¹	90	90	s14	90	–	–	90¹	90¹	–	–	990
–	–	–	–	90	90	90	–	90	–	–	90²	90	s21	–	990

THE MANAGER

DAVID O'LEARY

The wisdom in appointing David O'Leary, an untried and untested manager, at the helm of a club of the size and stature of Leeds United, is rapidly becoming apparent. O'Leary has all the qualities of a fantastic coach and has quickly developed his side into a force to be reckoned with.

Having taken over from George Graham in October 1998, O'Leary soon set about moulding the side into his own, introducing a number of players other managers would have considered too young for the rigours of Premiership football. The gamble paid off, as Leeds arguably now have the most close-knit first XI in the Premiership, based around O'Leary's youngsters.

His playing days were spent almost solely at Arsenal, whose appearance record he still retains. His 20-year spell with the Gunners ended in 1993 and he saw out his playing career at Elland Road.

Leeds' Champions League semi-final appearance is testament to O'Leary's management skills and, although he will not get the opportunity to better the feat in that tournament during 2001–02, it is certain that he will be looking for a top-three Premiership finish at the very least.

LEAGUE POSITION

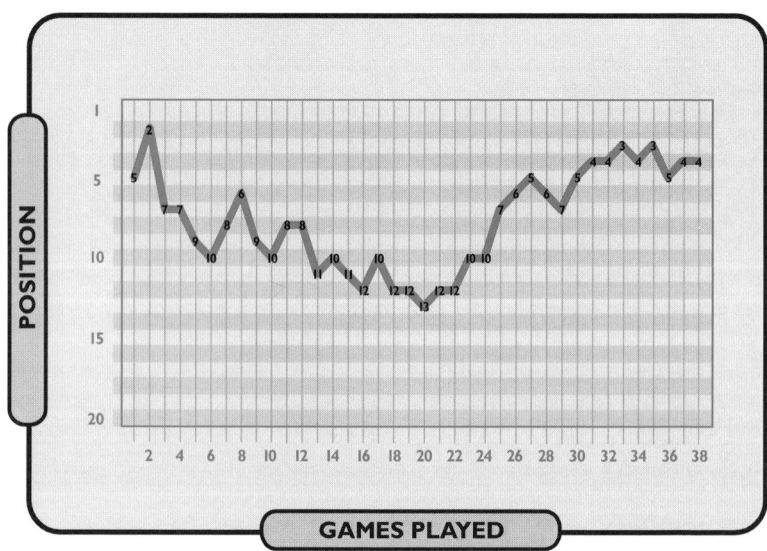

POSITION

GAMES PLAYED

6 Mark Viduka scored more headed goals

THE GOALS

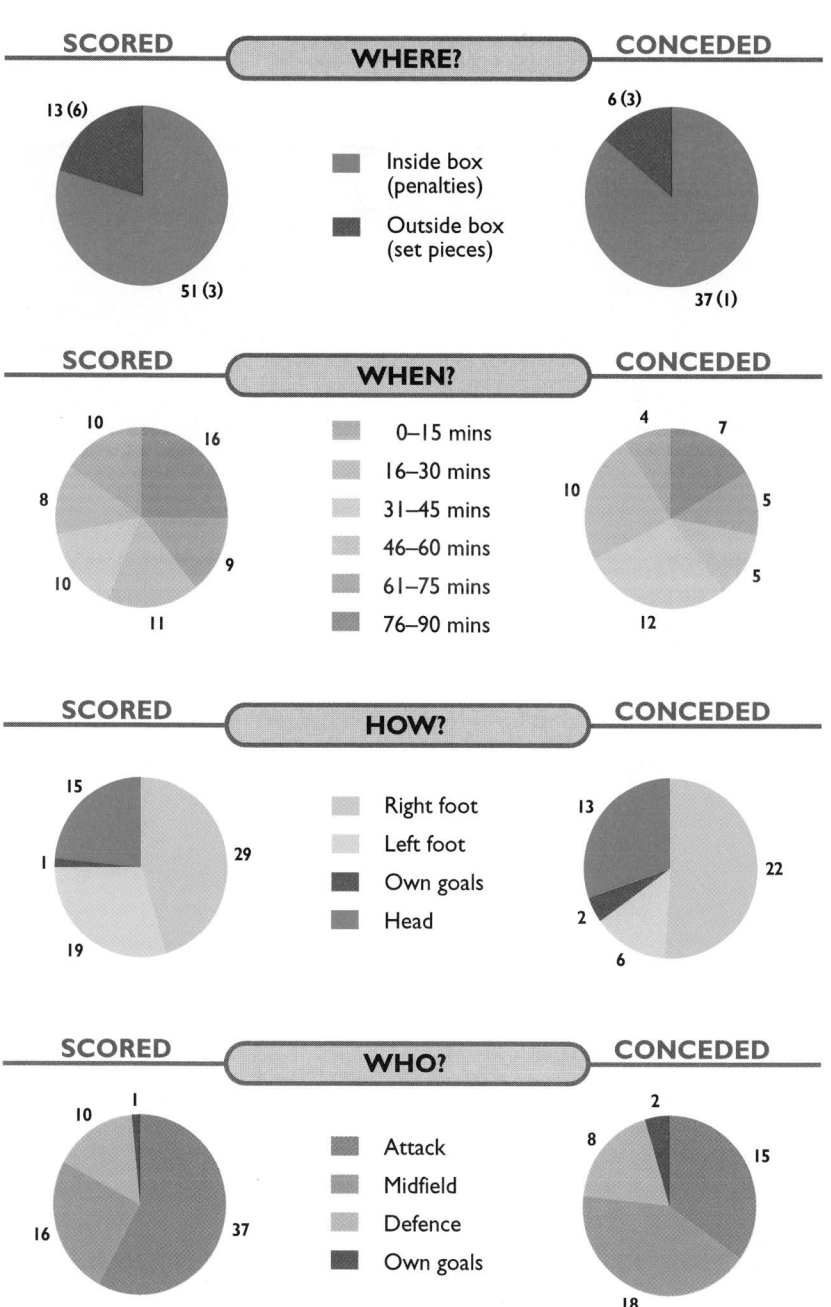

WHERE?

SCORED — CONCEDED

- Inside box (penalties)
- Outside box (set pieces)

SCORED: 13 (6), 51 (3)
CONCEDED: 6 (3), 37 (1)

WHEN?

- 0–15 mins
- 16–30 mins
- 31–45 mins
- 46–60 mins
- 61–75 mins
- 76–90 mins

SCORED: 10, 16, 8, 9, 10, 11
CONCEDED: 4, 7, 10, 5, 5, 12

HOW?

- Right foot
- Left foot
- Own goals
- Head

SCORED: 15, 29, 1, 19
CONCEDED: 13, 22, 2, 6

WHO?

- Attack
- Midfield
- Defence
- Own goals

SCORED: 10, 1, 16, 37
CONCEDED: 2, 8, 15, 18

than any other player in the Premiership

LEEDS UNITED

	BAKKE	BATTY	BOWYER	BRIDGES	BURNS	DACOURT	DUBERRY	EVANS	FERDINAND	HARTE	HAY
APPEARANCES											
Start	24	13	38	6	3	33	5	0	23	29	2
Sub	5	3	0	1	1	0	0	1	0	0	2
Minutes on pitch	2087	1168	3345	538	297	2773	405	33	2070	2610	299
GOAL ATTEMPTS											
Goals	2	0	9	0	0	3	0	0	2	7	0
Shots on target	7	1	38	10	0	18	0	0	8	21	3
Shots off target	19	1	39	6	0	32	1	0	6	32	2
Shooting accuracy	27%	50%	49%	63%	0%	36%	0%	0%	57%	40%	60%
PASSING											
Goal assists	1	0	5	3	0	3	0	0	0	6	0
Long passes	229	172	319	28	15	357	48	2	319	543	15
Short passes	727	567	965	146	82	944	83	9	553	762	63
PASS COMPLETION											
Own half %	74%	86%	78%	81%	54%	75%	67%	60%	74%	76%	85%
Opposition half %	69%	75%	62%	65%	48%	70%	53%	83%	55%	59%	63%
CROSSING											
Total crosses	34	6	259	8	1	31	1	1	3	186	0
Cross completion %	18%	17%	27%	25%	0%	35%	100%	0%	33%	30%	0%
DRIBBLING											
Dribbles & runs	70	21	129	21	10	126	2	0	49	73	5
Dribble completion %	76%	100%	64%	57%	50%	75%	100%	0%	94%	92%	80%
DEFENDING											
Tackles made	104	63	115	4	12	173	6	0	49	73	7
Tackles won %	74%	70%	72%	100%	67%	71%	100%	0%	76%	78%	71%
Blocks	16	4	10	2	3	9	1	0	19	23	6
Clearances	31	13	23	1	2	12	30	0	251	93	39
Interceptions	3	12	12	0	2	16	3	0	15	4	1
DISCIPLINE											
Fouls	51	26	58	10	8	94	12	1	21	23	1
Offside	2	0	16	13	1	1	0	0	0	5	0
Yellow cards	9	2	9	0	0	13	0	0	0	1	0
Red cards	0	1	0	0	0	0	0	0	0	0	0

GOALKEEPER NAME	START/ (SUB)	TIME ON PITCH	GOALS CONCEDED	MINS/GOALS CONCEDED	SAVES MADE	SAVES/ SHOTS
MARTYN	23(0)	2051	20	103	69	78%
ROBINSON	15(1)	1369	23	60	46	67%

For more information visit our website:

PLAYERS' STATISTICS

	HUCKERBY	JONES	KEANE	KELLY	KEWELL	MATTEO	McPHAIL	MILLS	RADEBE	SMITH	VIDUKA	WILCOX	WOODGATE	TOTAL	RANK
	2	3	12	22	12	30	3	20	19	26	34	7	14		
	5	1	6	1	5	0	4	3	1	7	0	10	0		
	247	277	1037	2025	1165	2597	356	1860	1641	2411	3014	796	1067		
	0	0	9	0	2	0	0	0	0	11	17	0	1	64*	4th
	3	3	20	1	10	4	0	1	1	28	31	4	2	214	5th
	0	2	7	1	20	2	1	9	1	31	33	3	2	250	7th
	100%	60%	74%	50%	33%	67%	0%	10%	50%	47%	48%	57%	50%	46%	4th
	0	0	3	3	4	1	0	1	0	6	4	1	0	42	5th
	4	30	33	269	62	291	40	255	192	91	92	48	105	3957	14th
	42	92	258	622	354	900	158	525	519	661	877	248	234	10497	8th
	71%	82%	85%	76%	76%	81%	81%	71%	83%	81%	80%	70%	81%	78%	11th
	59%	65%	62%	63%	70%	65%	77%	57%	68%	65%	61%	66%	54%	63%	11th
	13	2	24	77	73	31	5	44	2	65	25	73	0	964	7th
	15%	0%	17%	29%	25%	16%	20%	27%	0%	12%	12%	21%	0%	25%	17th
	21	5	65	64	125	45	4	88	6	77	154	36	10	1210	3rd
	29%	40%	51%	89%	57%	87%	100%	80%	100%	47%	43%	83%	90%	68%	12th
	0	6	11	40	22	86	10	54	101	56	33	18	65	1109	1st
	0%	67%	73%	68%	77%	77%	90%	83%	71%	79%	67%	78%	72%	74%	5th
	0	0	0	12	2	27	2	21	15	6	3	0	17	198	13th
	0	4	1	63	5	118	3	113	142	14	11	4	124	1189	16th
	0	0	0	8	7	11	2	7	21	2	2	1	8	137	1st
	7	8	13	16	18	34	1	30	26	90	65	8	20	641	4th
	7	0	24	0	8	2	1	1	0	42	58	4	0	185	1st
	0	0	1	1	2	1	0	8	7	7	5	0	4	70	7th
	0	0	0	0	0	0	0	0	1	1	0	0	0	3	=7th

*Including one own goal

CROSSES CAUGHT	CROSSES PUNCHED	CROSSES DROPPED	CATCH SUCCESS	THROWS/ SHORT KICKS	% COMPLETION	LONG KICKS	% COMPLETION
35	16	2	95%	42	81%	407	56%
19	9	2	90%	35	74%	276	53%

PLAYER OF THE SEASON

PLAYER	INDEX SCORE
IAN HARTE	1,046
Lucas Radebe	936
Lee Bowyer	876
Rio Ferdinand	869
Olivier Dacourt	847
Nigel Martyn	811
Mark Viduka	719
Alan Smith	712
Dominic Matteo	705
Eirik Bakke	699

David O'Leary's brave youngsters performed heroics in the European Cup, but despite a late surge missed out on another chance to shine in the 2001–02 Champions League.

Their ultimately disappointing fourth-placed finish in the Premiership can be largely put down to inconsistent early-season form, at a time when eventual Opta Player of the Season for 2000–01 Ian Harte could not even make the starting line-up.

But Harte recovered from his personal slump to bag seven goals and set up a further six for fellow-Leeds players – both best figures for a Premiership defender.

He was also strong in the challenge, winning possession with nearly 80% of tackles, while a steady stream of more than 100 crosses helped him record an average Opta score of 1,046 points.

Top man for 1999–2000 Lucas Radebe was significantly missing throughout much of Leeds' sticky patch, but the skipper was always heavily involved when playing, making more interceptions than any other Leeds player and contesting a challenge every 16 minutes on average – a frequency matched by very few players in the English top flight.

Lee Bowyer provided a shining example of triumph through adversity during 2000–01. Bowyer did not let off-field distractions affect his game as he won 83 tackles, set up five goals and notched nine for his average Index score of 876 points.

Rio Ferdinand coped admirably with his £18 million move and was joined in the top five by Olivier Dacourt – the player with the most winning tackles in the Premiership – while Nigel Martyn, Alan Smith and Mark Viduka all thoroughly merited their top 10 rankings.

Notable absences Robbie Keane and Jonathon Woodgate both recorded impressive Index scores, but missed out through lack of time on the pitch. Indeed, Leeds might have secured third place had Keane, who netted nine goals from 12 starts, joined them sooner from Italian giants Inter Milan.

123 Olivier Dacourt was the player who

FIVE OF THE BEST

After a torrid start to a season brimming with expectancy, Leeds redeemed themselves with a post-Christmas charge up the table which earned a UEFA Cup spot. Manager David O'Leary can be proud of building a squad which took Europe by storm and, when primed and fully-fit, it should be capable of challenging for the Premiership crown.

TOP GOALSCORERS

	GOALS	GOALS/SHOTS
MARK VIDUKA	17	27%
Alan Smith	11	19%
Robbie Keane	9	33%
Lee Bowyer	9	12%
Ian Harte	7	13%

Many questioned whether Mark Viduka could replicate the scoring exploits he achieved with Celtic south of the border. But the Antipodean goal machine lived up to his star billing and crashed home 17 league strikes, including a four-goal haul against Liverpool. Fellow-frontrunner Alan Smith rattled home seven more goals than he managed during 1999–2000, while the skilful Robbie Keane posed a greater threat by scoring with a third of his shots.

When he plied his trade at Everton, Olivier Dacourt was predominantly perceived as a ball-winner, but at Leeds he has been instrumental in providing link-up play between the back four and the frontrunners. The Frenchman was the only player to complete more than 900 passes for the Yorkshire club. Fellow-newcomer Dominic Matteo hailed from the Anfield school of 'pass and move' and was ready-primed, subsequently finding a white shirt with a superior 73% of his distribution.

TOP PASSERS

	SUCC PASSES	COMPLETION
OLIVIER DACOURT	931	72%
Dominic Matteo	865	73%
Lee Bowyer	856	67%
Ian Harte	846	65%
Eirik Bakke	679	71%

TOP TACKLERS

	WON	SUCCESS
OLIVIER DACOURT	123	71%
Lee Bowyer	83	72%
Eirik Bakke	77	74%
Lucas Radebe	72	71%
Dominic Matteo	66	77%

The Leeds midfield was packed full of competitiveness and commitment, but Olivier Dacourt led the way in the realm of tenacious tackling. The former Lens man attempted a staggering total of 173 challenges and was the only player in the Premiership to come away with the ball more than 100 times. Lee Bowyer is similarly renowned for his desire to win possession and the Londoner was the next best ankle-biter at the club with 83 victorious challenges.

For a man who appears to revel in the physical nature of the game, it comes as no great surprise that Olivier Dacourt was the main offender in the Premiership. The bustling midfielder collected more yellow cards than any other player in the top flight and reclaimed his place in Opta's dirty dozen. Youngster Alan Smith courted controversy on more than one occasion with his fiery brand of play, which culminated in a red card at the Stadium of Light.

DISCIPLINE

	POINTS	FOULS & CARDS
OLIVIER DACOURT	133	94F, 13Y, 0R
Alan Smith	117	90F, 7Y, 1R
Lee Bowyer	85	58F, 9Y, 0R
Mark Viduka	80	65F, 5Y, 0R
Eirik Bakke	78	51F, 9Y, 0R

won the most tackles in the league

ACTION	BAKKE	BOWYER	BURNS	DACOURT	HARTE	HAY	KELLY	MATTEO	ROBINSON	SMITH	VIDUKA	WOODGATE	TOTAL	LIVERPOOL
Time on pitch	90	90	90	90	90	74	90	90	90	90	90	16	990	990
GOALS														
Goal	–	–	–	–	–	–	–	–	–	–	4	–	4	3
Shot on target (incl goals)	–	–	–	1	–	–	–	–	–	1	4	–	6	6
Shot off target	–	1	–	–	–	–	–	–	–	–	–	–	2	5
Blocked shot	–	–	2	1	3	–	–	–	–	–	–	–	6	5
Own goal	–	–	–	–	–	–	–	–	–	–	–	–	0	0
PASSES														
Pass to own player	27	8	13	21	31	17	28	40	5	15	17	1	223	225
Pass to opposition	13	13	15	8	13	5	16	6	11	7	12	3	122	139
Cross to own player	–	3	1	1	2	–	1	–	–	–	–	–	6	8
Cross to opposition player	–	14	–	1	1	–	–	–	–	–	–	–	18	14
Goal assist	–	–	–	2	–	–	1	–	–	1	–	–	4	3
Pass completion %	68%	29%	45%	72%	70%	77%	65%	87%	31%	70%	57%	25%	62%	61%
TACKLES & CLEARANCES														
Tackle	1	1	5	5	2	3	3	–	–	1	1	1	23	33
Clearances, blocks and interceptions	2	–	–	2	3	12	5	13	3	3	–	2	45	46
DRIBBLES & RUNS														
Dribbles ball retained	1	4	–	–	3	–	2	–	–	1	2	–	13	13
Dribbles ball lost	1	–	2	–	–	–	–	–	–	2	2	–	6	9
Dribble success %	50%	100%	0%	0%	100%	0%	100%	0%	0%	33%	67%	0%	68%	59%
DISCIPLINE														
Fouls	5	2	1	2	1	–	2	1	–	1	1	1	17	20
Penalty conceded	–	–	–	–	–	–	–	–	–	–	–	–	0	0
Free kick – offside	–	1	–	1	1	–	–	–	–	5	3	–	10	3
Yellow cards	–	–	–	–	–	–	–	–	–	–	–	–	1	4
Red cards	–	–	–	–	–	–	–	–	–	–	–	–	0	0
GOALKEEPERS														
Distribution to own player	–	–	–	–	–	–	–	–	13	–	–	–	13	6
Distribution to opposition player	–	–	–	–	–	–	–	–	12	–	–	–	12	7
Goalkeeper distribution %	–	–	–	–	–	–	–	–	52%	–	–	–	52%	46%
Save	–	–	–	–	–	–	–	–	2	–	–	–	2	1
Ball caught	–	–	–	–	–	–	–	–	2	–	–	–	2	3
Ball dropped	–	–	–	–	–	–	–	–	–	–	–	–	0	0
Goal conceded	–	–	–	–	–	–	–	–	3	–	–	–	3	4

7 Ian Harte was the Premiership's

An outstanding performance by Mark Viduka guided Leeds to a pulsating win over Liverpool at Elland Road. The Australian international had been in tremendous form prior to this game, scoring five goals in the previous four Premiership matches, but nothing in the opening clashes suggested that this was to be his day.

4 November 2000

4–3

**LEEDS UNITED
LIVERPOOL**

Some fans were still taking their seats when the visitors took the lead in front of the live Sky TV cameras. Only 100 seconds had elapsed when Liverpool's Patrik Berger floated a free-kick into United's penalty area, which captain Sami Hyypia nodded into the net.

Then, after just 18 minutes, the Reds were 2–0 up. Gary McAllister drifted in a carbon-copy centre and Christian Ziege reacted quickest to power his header past Paul Robinson.

Against the Premiership's best defence of 1999–2000 there should have been no way back for David O'Leary's side. But Leeds fought hard, winning 83% of their tackles – seven percentage points better than Gérard Houllier's team – and were rewarded for their fighting spirit in the 24th minute.

Combative striker Alan Smith challenged Ziege for the ball deep in the Liverpool half and was fortunate when the ball ricocheted to Viduka, who chipped delicately past Sander Westerveld and into the net.

Encouraged by the goal, United continued to press the Reds, rarely allowing them any time on the ball and effectively stifling their patient build-up play. The result was that Liverpool found a team-mate with just 61% of their passes – 10 percentage points worse than their seasonal average – and created little up-front from then on.

The Reds did manage to hold out until half-time. But just a minute after the restart the scores were level, when Gary Kelly's cross was firmly headed home by Viduka. Houllier's men did manage to restore their advantage briefly with a well-taken goal by Vladimir Smicer in the 61st minute, but did not look like hanging on to it.

Leeds' French midfielder Olivier Dacourt was a constant menace to the Reds. The former Evertonian went in for five tackles – more than any other United player – and showed his creative side by setting up the game's last two goals in quick succession.

A delicate through-ball from Dacourt found Viduka in the Liverpool penalty area in the 73rd minute and the Australian wriggled out of a couple of challenges before hammering the ball home. And just two minutes later, the same two players combined to create a chance which Viduka gleefully chipped over Westerveld for the winning goal, and his fourth.

The Australian had scored his brilliant quartet against Liverpool from just four attempts on goal – an amazing exhibition of top-quality finishing.

It was a rousing display by O'Leary's youthful side in front of the ecstatic Leeds supporters and proved to be the first half of a league double over their rivals. Unfortunately, however, it did not prove to be enough to help them finish above the Reds, who clinched the all-important third place.

highest-scoring defender

LEICESTER CITY

ADDRESS

City Stadium, Filbert Street,
Leicester LE2 7FL

CONTACT NUMBERS

Telephone: 0116 291 5000
Fax: 0116 247 0585
Ticket Office: 0116 291 5232
Club Call: 09068 121185
Fox Leisure: 0116 291 5253
Website: www.lcfc.com

KEY PERSONNEL

Chairman: J M Elsom
Directors: Martin George,
Steve Kind FCCA
Club Secretary: Andrew Neville
Manager: Peter Taylor

SPONSORS

2000–01: Walkers Crisps
2001–02: LG Electronics

FANZINES

The Fox
When You're Smiling
Foxed Off
O'Neill And Pray

COLOURS

Home: Blue shirts, white shorts
and blue stockings
Away: White shirts, blue shorts
and white stockings

NICKNAME

The Foxes

HONOURS

Division Two Champions:
1924–25, 1936–37, 1953–54,
1956–57, 1970–71, 1979–80
League Cup Winners: 1964, 1997, 2000

RECORD GOALSCORER

Arthur Chandler –
259 league goals, 1923–35

BIGGEST WIN

10–0 v Portsmouth – Division One,
20 October 1928

BIGGEST DEFEAT

0–12 (as Leicester Fosse) v
Nottingham Forest – Division One,
21 April 1909

SEASON REVIEW

It was ultimately a disappointing season for Leicester City supporters. The club were grateful for their early good form, as a slump in the second half of the campaign saw the team slide from the top of the Premiership in October to the bottom half of the table by the end of the season.

The 2000–01 campaign was one of great upheaval at Filbert Street. The changes began in the summer, with Martin O'Neill leaving to become Celtic manager.

The Leicester board moved quickly to appoint Peter Taylor. The former England Under-21 coach had a good reputation from his time with the national set-up and had enhanced it by taking Gillingham to promotion from Nationwide Division Two.

Taylor set about adding to the squad, but was concerned about interest in Neil Lennon, Matt Elliott and Gerry Taggart, who were all linked with moves to join their former boss at Celtic.

Trevor Benjamin and Ade Akinbiyi were brought in to bolster Leicester's attacking options, while Gary Rowett arrived to shore up the defence. And there was further good news when Lennon signed a new four-year deal.

Leicester's league campaign got off to a good start with five clean sheets in six matches and 14 points. The one concern was that the Foxes had scored just six times.

Taylor led his side into UEFA Cup action against Red Star Belgrade, but conceding a first-minute goal was a big setback and, despite grabbing an equaliser, the Foxes would travel to the away leg needing to score at least once.

Exactly where they would travel was not clear. Due to the ongoing problems in the Balkans, Leicester were unable to get insurance for their players and lobbied UEFA to move the tie to a neutral venue. Eventually, the match was played in Vienna

and the Yugoslavs secured a 3–1 win and passage to the next round.

More changes to playing staff saw Steve Walsh and Tony Cottee leave, while Richard Cresswell arrived from Sheffield Wednesday.

Two league draws either side of the UEFA Cup tie with Red Star, combined with Manchester United slipping up against Arsenal, saw the Foxes briefly edge to the top of the table.

Unfortunately defeats by United and Liverpool saw them slip off the Premiership summit as quickly as they had arrived.

Leicester then made headlines for the wrong reasons as a dressing-room altercation between Stan Collymore and another Leicester player saw the controversial striker offloaded to Bradford City.

The Foxes got back on track with wins over strugglers Derby and Manchester City, but sandwiched between these results was an embarrassing 3–0 home defeat by first division Crystal Palace in the Worthington Cup.

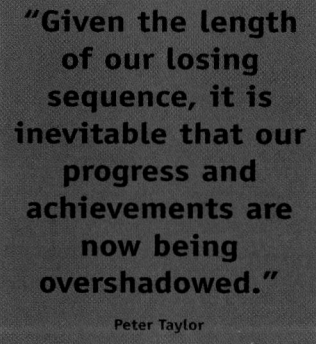

"Given the length of our losing sequence, it is inevitable that our progress and achievements are now being overshadowed."

Peter Taylor

Better news was around the corner. Kevin Keegan resigned from the England manager's job and Leicester's excellent start, combined with Taylor's national team connections, saw the Foxes boss put forward as a coach to work with a more senior figure on a part-time basis.

Eventually, the FA appointed Sven-Göran Eriksson, but Taylor was in charge along with Manchester United's Steve McClaren for the friendly international with Italy. The proud Taylor selected a youthful squad and his team performed well in a narrow 1–0 defeat by the Italians.

The entire club seemed buoyed by this honour, and wins over Middlesbrough and Leeds were only dampened by a defeat at Spurs.

However, the event which many saw as

SEASON REVIEW

the turning point in Leicester's season – the sale of Neil Lennon to Celtic – finally happened. O'Neill claimed that Taylor had called him up and offered Lennon because the Irish midfielder was not playing particularly well. After lengthy negotiations over the fee, a deal was finally agreed and Lennon left for Parkhead.

Taylor moved swiftly to replace Lennon with Matthew Jones from Leeds, but having gained 29 points in their first 16 fixtures, Leicester took a mere 19 from their next 22 games in the absence of the popular Lennon.

Negative headlines were generated in the first fixture without Lennon, when Matt Elliott appeared to elbow Craig Bellamy. The incident was highlighted even more by some unseemly verbal sparring after the event between David Thompson and an irate Taylor.

A couple of victories leading up to the festive period brought Christmas cheer and, sitting in third place, many Foxes fans could be forgiven for dreaming of a Champions League place.

By Boxing Day they were punch-drunk, having been hit for six by a rampant Arsenal. Suddenly the momentum was lost and a disastrous 2–1 defeat at home to struggling Bradford was followed by no goals and just one point in their next three league fixtures.

Taylor attempted to remedy the problems by snapping up Dean Sturridge from Derby, Junior Lewis from Gillingham and former Italian international Roberto Mancini, who had been on Eriksson's coaching staff at Lazio. But the erstwhile Sampdoria striker stayed only briefly. After just a month he left to take up the vacant Fiorentina coaching post.

Meanwhile, there was some respite in the FA Cup. York City were trounced 3–0 and then the Foxes delighted their travelling support with a 2–1 win against Aston Villa.

> "Of course, no one ever gets it 100% right. I'm confident that the players still here are good signings. All I'm saying is 'Trust me'."
>
> Peter Taylor

Some indifferent league form did not affect them as they breezed past Bristol City and earned a home quarter-final against second division Wycombe Wanderers.

Thoughts were probably turning to a final in Cardiff and the confidence imbued in the players was illustrated by back-to-back 2–0 victories over Sunderland and Liverpool.

There seemed little doubt that Leicester would progress, but somehow Wycombe upset the formbook to snatch a 2–1 victory in one of the biggest FA Cup upsets for many years.

While the country's faith in the FA Cup as the greatest cup competition in the world seemed to have been restored, Leicester City and their supporters were not rejoicing.

The team tried to put the result behind them, but it clearly affected their confidence. With injuries to key players, the Foxes embarked on a run of eight consecutive defeats which saw them plummet from a UEFA Cup spot to 13th position.

This disastrous run prompted criticism from all quarters. Many blamed the job-share with England, but former Fox Steve Walsh was in no doubt who was to blame. Walsh claimed: "In eight months, he [Taylor] has systematically dismantled the team. We've spent a lot on players who are yet to convince the fans of their Premiership quality. I feel they've just wasted money."

This damning assessment angered Taylor, who is determined to get things right at Filbert Street. Many of his signings are young players whom he hopes will come good.

After a dream start to his Leicester career and the accolades he received when being appointed to England's coaching squad, Taylor is now under intense pressure to deliver and season 2001–02 is sure to be a testing time for one of the brightest young coaches in the game.

LEICESTER CITY

DATE	OPPONENT	SCORE	ATT.	AKINBIYI	BENJAMIN	COLLYMORE	COTTEE	CRESSWELL	DAVIDSON	DELANEY	EADIE	ELLIOTT	ELLISON	FLOWERS	GILCHRIST
19.08.00	Aston Villa H	0–0	21,455	90	–	90	–	–	60	–	s30	90	–	90	–
23.08.00	West Ham A	1–0	25,195	90	–	–	s8	–	–	82^1□	90	–	90	–	–
26.08.00	Bradford A	0–0	16,766	90	–	–	s15	–	–	–	90	90	–	90	s1
06.09.00	Ipswich H	2–1	19,598	90^1	–	s45	–	–	–	–	90	90^1	–	90	–
09.09.00	Southampton H	1–0	18,366	90	–	s45	–	–	–	–	90	90	–	90	s19
17.09.00	Chelsea A	2–0	33,697	70	–	$s20^1$	–	s20	s5	–	70	90	–	90	90
24.09.00	Everton H	1–1	18,084	67^1	–	s37	–	s23	–	–	67□	90	–	90	s23
01.10.00	Sunderland A	0–0	45,338	75	s15	–	–	79	90	–	89	90	–	90	–
14.10.00	Man Utd H	0–3	22,132	59	–	–	–	s31	90	–	90	90	–	90	90
21.10.00	Liverpool A	0–1	44,395	s28	–	–	–	62	90□	–	78	90□	–	90	90□
28.10.00	Derby Co H	2–1	20,525	90	–	–	–	69	90	–	s21	90	–	90	–
04.11.00	Man City A	1–0	34,279	90	82	–	–	–	90□	–	–	90	–	45	–
11.11.00	Newcastle H	1–1	21,406	90	55	–	–	–	90	–	–	90	–	90	–
18.11.00	Middlesbro A	3–0	27,965	90	81^1	–	–	–	54	–	$s36^1$	90	–	76	s9
25.11.00	Tottenham A	0–3	35,636	68	78	–	–	s12	90	–	s22	90	–	–	–
02.12.00	Leeds Utd H	3–1	21,486	89^1	–	–	–	–	90	–	90	90	–	–	–
10.12.00	Coventry A	0–1	17,283	90	s45□	–	–	–	90	–	72	90	–	–	90
16.12.00	Charlton H	3–1	19,371	68^1	s27	–	–	–	75	–	90□	90^1	–	90	–
23.12.00	West Ham H	2–1	21,524	82	s16	–	–	–	–	–	s8	45	–	90	–
26.12.00	Arsenal A	1–6	38,007	90^1	s39	–	–	–	–	–	–	90	–	90	–
01.01.01	Bradford H	1–2	19,278	90	s30	–	–	–	–	–	45	90	–	45	90
14.01.01	Ipswich A	0–2	22,002	62	75	–	–	s28□	90	–	–	90	–	–	s15
20.01.01	Arsenal H	0–0	21,872	s17	–	–	–	–	90	–	–	90	–	–	s22
31.01.01	Southampton A	0–1	14,909	87	–	–	–	–	90	–	–	90□	–	–	–
03.02.01	Chelsea H	2–1	21,502	s29	–	–	–	–	90	–	s12	90	–	–	–
10.02.01	Everton A	1–2	30,409	–	–	–	–	–	–	–	s45	90	–	–	–
24.02.01	Sunderland H	2–0	21,086	88^1	–	–	–	–	45	–	–	90	–	–	–
03.03.01	Liverpool H	2–0	21,924	73^1	s9	–	–	–	90	–	–	90	–	–	–
17.03.01	Man Utd A	0–2	67,516	70	s20	–	–	–	–	90□	90	90	s6	–	90
01.04.01	Charlton A	0–2	20,043	s19	90	–	–	–	71	–	40	90	–	–	–
04.04.01	Aston Villa H	1–2	29,043	76	s14	–	–	–	76^1	–	–	90	–	–	–
07.04.01	Coventry H	1–3	19,545	90^1□	s8	–	–	–	45	–	–	45	–	–	–
14.04.01	Man City H	1–2	20,224	88^1	s2	–	–	–	s21	–	s21	90	–	90	–
16.04.01	Derby Co A	0–2	28,387	90	45	–	–	–	71	–	90□	90□	–	–	–
21.04.01	Middlesbro H	0–3	18,162	90	–	–	–	–	s18	90	–	–	–	–	–
28.04.01	Newcastle A	0–1	50,501	84	s6	–	–	–	90	90	–	–	–	90	–
05.05.01	Tottenham H	4–2	21,056	79	s11	–	–	–	90	s9	–	–	–	90	–
19.05.01	Leeds Utd A	1–3*	39,105	90	s24□	–	–	–	90□	s11	–	–	–	90	–

□ Yellow card, ■ Red card, s Substitute, 90^2 Goals scored
*including own goal

For more information visit our website:

2000–01 PREMIERSHIP APPEARANCES

GUNNLAUGSSON	GUPPY	IMPEY	IZZET	JONES	LENNON	LEWIS	MANCINI	MARSHALL	OAKES	ROWETT	ROYCE	SAVAGE	SINCLAIR	STURRIDGE	TAGGART	WALSH	TOTAL
–	–	90	90	–	90□	–	–	–	–	85	–	90□	–	–	90	s5	990
–	90	90	90□	–	90	–	–	–	–	90	–	90	–	–	90□	–	990
–	90	90	75	–	89	–	–	–	–	90□	–	90	–	–	90□	–	990
–	90	90	45	–	–	–	–	–	90	90	–	90	–	–	90□	–	990
–	90	90	71	–	45	–	–	–	–	90	–	90	–	–	90¹	–	990
–	85	90	90¹□	–	90	–	–	–	–	90	–	90	–	–	–	–	990
–	90	53	90	–	90	–	–	–	–	90	–	90□	–	–	90□	–	990
–	s1	90	–	–	90	–	–	–	s11	90	–	90	–	–	90□	–	990
–	s31	59	72	–	90	–	–	–	–	90	–	90	s18	–	–	–	990
–	s20	70	90	–	90	–	–	–	–	90	–	90	s12	–	–	–	990
s16¹	74	–	90¹	–	90	–	–	–	–	90	–	90	90	–	–	–	990
s8	–	–	90	–	90	–	–	–	–	90	s45	90¹	90□	–	90	–	990
s35¹	–	–	90	–	90	–	–	–	–	90	–	90□	90	–	90	–	990
–	–	–	90¹	–	90□	–	–	–	–	90	s14	90	90	–	90	–	990
–	–	s22	90	–	90□	–	–	–	–	90	90	68□	90	–	64■	–	964
–	–	s18	90	–	90□	–	–	–	s1	90	90	90¹	72	–	90¹	–	990
–	s18	s27	45	–	–	–	–	–	90	90	90	90	63	–	–	–	990
s22¹	63	90	–	90	–	–	–	–	s15	90	–	90	–	–	90	–	990
–	s45	90	74¹	90	–	–	–	–	–	90	–	90¹	90	–	90□	–	990
–	s51	90	90	90	–	–	–	–	51	90	–	90	90	–	39	–	990
90	s45	90	90¹	60	–	–	–	–	–	90	s45	90	–	–	–	–	990
s5	90	90	90	85	–	–	–	–	–	90	90	90	–	–	–	–	990
s9	–	90	68	37■	–	–	73	–	–	90	90	90	–	81□	90	–	937
s3	90□	90	90□	–	–	90	64	–	–	90	90	90	–	s26	–	–	990
–	90	90	90¹	–	–	90	61	–	–	90¹	90	90	–	78	–	–	990
–	45	90□	90	45	–	90	s45	–	–	90□	90	90	s45	90¹	45	–	990
s2	s45	–	90	s6	–	90	–	–	–	90	90	84	90	90¹	90	–	990
s17	–	s56	90¹□	–	–	90	–	–	–	90	90	90	34	81	90	–	990
–	s1	90	–	89	–	90	–	–	–	90	90	–	84	–	–	–	990
s29	–	90□	–	–	–	90	–	90	s50	90	–	90	–	–	61□	90	990
s56	s14	90	–	–	–	90□	–	90	90	90	90	–	–	34	90□	–	990
90	s45	90	82	–	–	90	–	90	s45	90□	90	–	–	–	90□	–	990
69	90	90	–	–	–	90	–	69	–	90□	–	90	–	–	90□	–	990
s45	45	90	–	–	–	90	–	s45	s19	90	90	90	–	–	–	–	990
s45	90	90	–	–	–	90	–	s35	–	90	90	90□	55□	45	72□	–	990
s28	90	90	–	50	–	90	–	90	s40	90	–	–	–	62□	–	–	990
–	90¹	90	–	–	–	90	–	90	–	81¹	–	90¹□	90□	90¹□	–	–	990
–	–	51	–	79	–	90	–	90	s39	90	–	90□	90□	66	–	–	990

THE MANAGER

PETER TAYLOR

Having plied his managerial trade at non-league Dartford and then Southend, Peter Taylor became the first full-time boss of the England Under-21 squad in 1996. But he cast himself into the managerial limelight by gaining promotion to Division One with Gillingham at the first time of asking in 1999–2000.

After serving his apprenticeship at both domestic and international level, it was inevitable that Taylor would eventually grace the Premiership. And when Martin O'Neill ventured north of the border to manage Celtic, the Leicester board headhunted the former Spurs player as the popular Ulsterman's successor.

A summer spending spree brought a handful of new signings to Filbert Street, including striker Ade Akinbiyi and full-back Gary Rowett, who proved a shrewd investment and featured in every single league game for the Foxes.

Taylor's inaugural term in the top flight was a learning curve and he will doubtless be looking to strengthen his squad during the close season. While he is currently a member of the full national team coaching staff under Sven-Göran Eriksson, Leicester remain his priority as the club go in search of European football in 2001–02.

LEAGUE POSITION

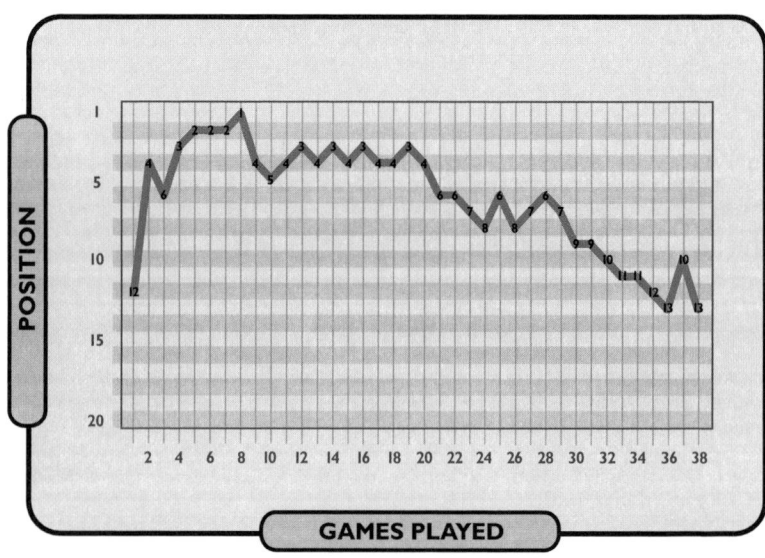

POSITION

GAMES PLAYED

8 Leicester's eight-game losing streak

THE GOALS

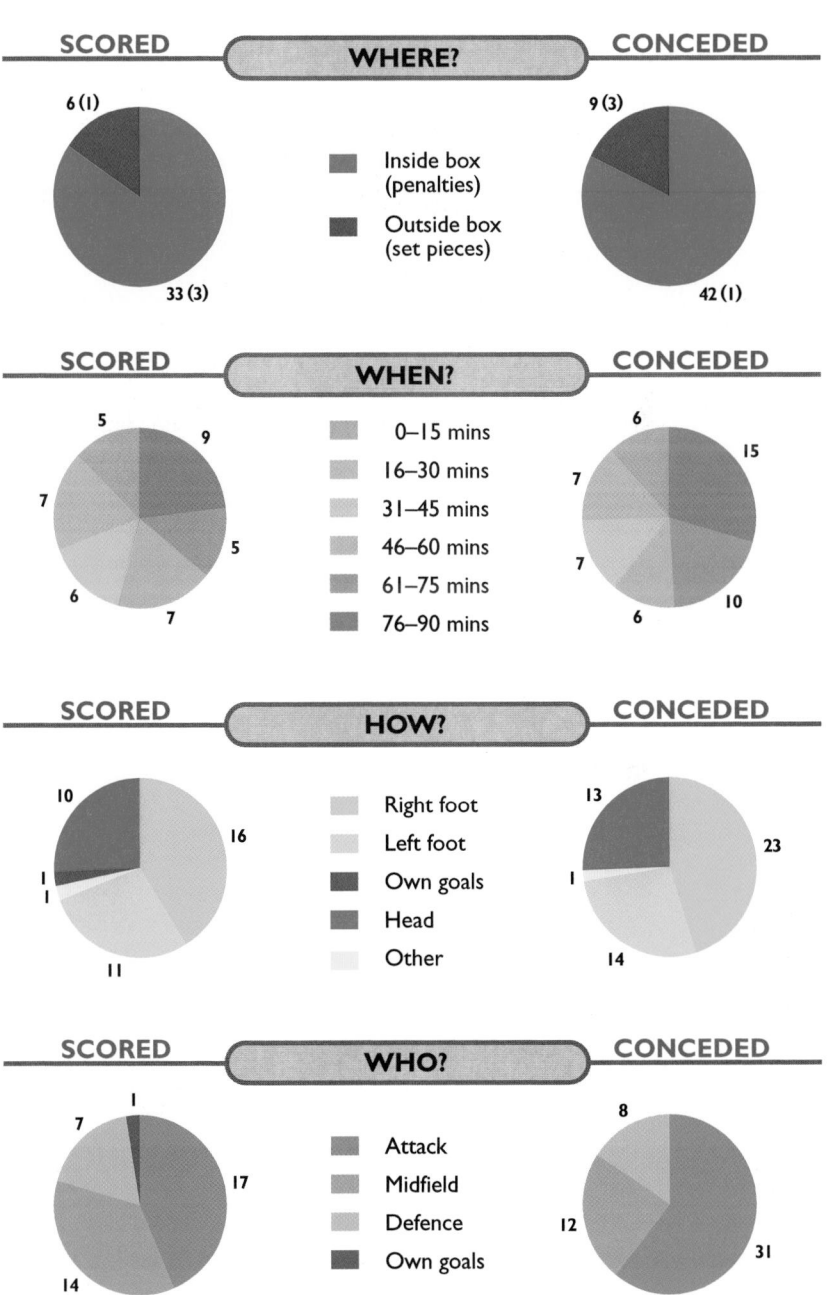

WHERE?

SCORED — CONCEDED

- Inside box (penalties)
- Outside box (set pieces)

Scored: 6 (1), 33 (3)
Conceded: 9 (3), 42 (1)

WHEN?

SCORED — CONCEDED

- 0–15 mins
- 16–30 mins
- 31–45 mins
- 46–60 mins
- 61–75 mins
- 76–90 mins

Scored: 9, 5, 5, 7, 6, 7
Conceded: 15, 10, 6, 7, 7, 6

HOW?

SCORED — CONCEDED

- Right foot
- Left foot
- Own goals
- Head
- Other

Scored: 16, 11, 1, 1, 10
Conceded: 23, 14, 1, 13

WHO?

SCORED — CONCEDED

- Attack
- Midfield
- Defence
- Own goals

Scored: 17, 14, 7, 1
Conceded: 31, 12, 8

was the worst of the season

LEICESTER CITY

	AKINBIYI	BENJAMIN	COLLYMORE	COTTEE	CRESSWELL	DAVIDSON	DELANEY	EADIE	ELLIOTT	ELLISON	GILCHRIST	GUNNLAUGSSON	GUPPY
APPEARANCES													
Start	33	7	1	0	3	25	3	16	34	0	6	3	17
Sub	4	14	4	2	5	3	2	8	0	1	6	14	11
Minutes on pitch	2818	772	237	23	324	2071	290	1458	2970	6	629	569	1708
GOAL ATTEMPTS													
Goals	9	1	1	0	0	1	0	2	2	0	0	3	1
Shots on target	38	8	3	0	4	4	2	12	9	0	1	9	4
Shots off target	27	8	5	0	4	4	1	9	9	0	0	7	10
Shooting accuracy	58%	50%	38%	0%	50%	50%	67%	57%	50%	0%	100%	56%	29%
PASSING													
Goal assists	2	0	0	0	0	1	0	1	1	0	0	1	3
Long passes	64	19	20	0	8	240	33	64	451	0	78	40	245
Short passes	621	176	70	6	60	504	68	320	785	0	118	158	465
PASS COMPLETION													
Own half %	79%	81%	91%	100%	79%	76%	76%	69%	86%	0%	67%	89%	78%
Opposition half %	63%	52%	58%	100%	68%	57%	60%	69%	65%	0%	46%	72%	65%
CROSSING													
Total crosses	35	11	7	2	4	67	6	46	7	0	3	14	225
Cross completion %	14%	27%	0%	50%	0%	31%	50%	17%	29%	0%	0%	0%	28%
DRIBBLING													
Dribbles & runs	67	26	5	0	9	36	7	76	39	0	4	37	73
Dribble completion %	54%	23%	60%	0%	56%	78%	71%	66%	92%	0%	50%	78%	74%
DEFENDING													
Tackles made	27	20	3	0	11	79	15	44	52	0	18	11	26
Tackles won %	78%	60%	67%	0%	55%	67%	87%	73%	63%	0%	67%	64%	81%
Blocks	3	5	1	0	0	16	7	3	54	0	18	1	7
Clearances	9	8	4	0	1	92	27	16	366	0	87	2	26
Interceptions	0	0	0	0	0	12	0	2	9	0	3	2	3
DISCIPLINE													
Fouls	72	23	6	0	13	24	9	24	39	1	8	7	14
Offside	59	19	2	0	6	2	1	3	3	0	0	0	3
Yellow cards	1	2	0	0	1	3	1	4	3	0	1	0	1
Red cards	0	0	0	0	0	0	0	0	0	0	0	0	0

GOALKEEPER NAME	START/ (SUB)	TIME ON PITCH	GOALS CONCEDED	MINS/GOALS CONCEDED	SAVES MADE	SAVES/ SHOTS
FLOWERS	22(0)	1876	26	72	94	78%
ROYCE	16(3)	1544	25	62	63	72%

PLAYERS' STATISTICS

	IMPEY	IZZET	JONES	LENNON	LEWIS	MANCINI	MARSHALL	OAKES	ROWETT	SAVAGE	SINCLAIR	STURRIDGE	TAGGART	WALSH	TOTAL	RANK
	29	27	10	15	15	3	7	5	38	33	14	12	24	0		
	4	0	1	0	0	1	2	8	0	0	3	1	0	1		
	2606	2242	721	1304	1350	243	689	631	3406	2942	1199	888	2020	5		
	0	7	0	0	0	0	0	0	2	4	0	3	2	0	39*	17th
	1	17	1	1	2	2	0	0	7	8	1	8	10	0	152	=18th
	7	12	3	0	7	1	3	5	9	16	2	12	8	0	169	20th
	13%	59%	25%	100%	22%	67%	0%	0%	44%	33%	33%	40%	56%	0%	47%	3rd
	1	1	0	3	0	0	1	2	1	0	2	3	1	0	24	=16th
	153	227	92	149	162	10	67	132	564	376	189	38	388	2	4115	10th
	624	939	208	687	486	73	194	204	891	842	287	201	557	2	9647	14th
	77%	85%	80%	87%	85%	65%	79%	78%	83%	79%	78%	70%	82%	50%	81%	8th
	72%	71%	59%	77%	68%	62%	66%	52%	54%	64%	52%	54%	52%	50%	62%	13th
	106	82	4	32	10	4	27	42	41	78	32	6	12	0	903	12th
	25%	23%	50%	38%	10%	75%	15%	26%	24%	21%	25%	33%	25%	0%	25%	16th
	101	70	9	15	26	6	21	16	41	35	30	39	62	0	852	12th
	66%	56%	89%	87%	77%	50%	71%	63%	95%	69%	73%	31%	87%	0%	68%	10th
	66	90	16	35	45	0	23	21	92	125	58	7	54	0	940	14th
	76%	71%	81%	69%	67%	0%	65%	71%	75%	66%	86%	71%	80%	0%	72%	13th
	21	11	4	18	9	0	10	5	32	10	11	0	24	0	270	3rd
	71	20	23	17	51	0	21	8	286	71	71	1	215	1	1538	3rd
	8	12	1	3	4	0	5	5	21	10	7	2	11	0	120	6th
	22	25	13	13	14	6	4	5	28	45	12	44	26	0	497	17th
	2	10	0	0	1	2	0	0	0	2	1	12	3	0	131	14th
	2	4	0	4	1	0	0	0	4	7	4	4	10	0	57	=11th
	0	0	1	0	0	0	0	0	0	0	0	0	1	0	2	=15th

*Including one own goal

CROSSES CAUGHT	CROSSES PUNCHED	CROSSES DROPPED	CATCH SUCCESS	THROWS/ SHORT KICKS	% COMPLETION	LONG KICKS	% COMPLETION
39	17	2	95%	60	82%	430	46%
26	19	5	84%	85	88%	313	50%

PLAYER OF THE SEASON

PLAYER	INDEX SCORE
TIM FLOWERS	983
Muzzy Izzet	974
Gerry Taggart	903
Matt Elliott	874
Gary Rowett	792
Simon Royce	717
Callum Davidson	661
Robbie Savage	656
Andy Impey	575
Ade Akinbiyi	550

For two-thirds of the 2000–01 season, Peter Taylor appeared to have stepped comfortably into the shoes of Martin O'Neill as Leicester held their place among the Premiership's elite.

But a spectacular collapse – precipitated to some extent by the loss of Neil Lennon (Opta's highest-rated Fox of 1998–99 and 1999–2000) – left City with no place in European competition in 2001–02.

It meant Tim Flowers, who missed the majority of that lacklustre run-in, was City's top-rated player on Opta's system with 983 points – and he was rated second overall in goalkeeping rankings behind Fabien Barthez.

Flowers made nearly 100 stops and kept out a hefty 78% of all efforts on his goal. Only Barthez could better that proportion out of all top-flight regulars.

But, when Flowers was absent, Simon Royce stepped into the breach superbly.

Muzzy Izzet carried on the fine form of 1999–2000 in the absence of Lennon, running Flowers close on Opta's scoring system. The Turkish international scored seven times, maintaining an excellent 59% shooting accuracy and netting with roughly one in four efforts. He also completed more passes in the opposition half than any of his colleagues as he achieved an average of 974 Opta points.

Leicester's central defensive trio make up third, fourth and fifth places on the Foxes' 2000–01 Index. The three were responsible for 867 clearances between them, with Scottish international Matt Elliott racking up 255 clearing headers – the third-highest tally in the league.

But Gerry Taggart beat Elliott into third place, thanks in part to a far superior rate of success in the tackle, while Gary Rowett achieved his average of 874 points with 1,027 accurate passes – more than any fellow-Fox.

Emile Heskey was sorely missed and Ade Akinbiyi just scraped into the top 10 after his nine Premiership goals. Lack of punch up-front held Leicester back, and Akinbiyi will look to improve in 2001–02.

FIVE OF THE BEST

Leicester entered a new era following the departure of Martin O'Neill and appeared to have unearthed a worthy successor in Peter Taylor. However, as the season progressed the Foxes found it increasingly difficult to find the back of the net and endured a club record run of eight straight defeats which left them in the lower reaches of the Premiership.

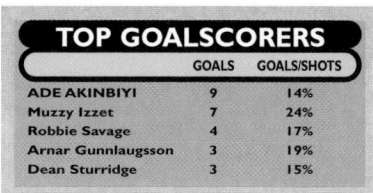

TOP GOALSCORERS

	GOALS	GOALS/SHOTS
ADE AKINBIYI	9	14%
Muzzy Izzet	7	24%
Robbie Savage	4	17%
Arnar Gunnlaugsson	3	19%
Dean Sturridge	3	15%

Peter Taylor broke the existing club record when he acquired the services of Ade Akinbiyi to spearhead the Leicester attack, yet results were far from instantaneous. The former Wolves forward scored just twice in the opening 15 games, but finally notched nine goals to earn the accolade of top scorer at the club. However, his poor goals-to-shots ratio highlights the Foxes' lack of firepower, and midfielder Muzzy Izzet played a crucial role by scoring seven times.

Like most teams, Leicester had to contend with missing key players at various stages of the campaign, yet they were fortunate to have a player of Gary Rowett's stature in the side. The former Birmingham full-back was the only Fox to start every single game and he was also the most competent in possession, racking up more than 1,000 passes. Fellow-defender Matt Elliott displayed comparable composure, but delivered the ball with greater accuracy than his colleague.

TOP PASSERS

	SUCC PASSES	COMPLETION
GARY ROWETT	1,027	71%
Matt Elliott	958	78%
Muzzy Izzet	895	77%
Robbie Savage	850	70%
Neil Lennon	686	82%

TOP TACKLERS

	WON	SUCCESS
ROBBIE SAVAGE	83	66%
Gary Rowett	69	75%
Muzzy Izzet	64	71%
Callum Davidson	53	67%
Frank Sinclair	50	86%

Love him or loathe him, Robbie Savage cannot be faulted for his commitment to the Leicester cause, as he proved with a season of full-blooded tackling. The footballer with the surf boy mentality won 14 more tackles than his nearest challenger as he marauded up and down the pitch with obvious intent. The ever-reliable Gary Rowett complemented his own astute passing ability with decisiveness in the challenge, winning three-quarters of his lunges.

While attempting to make a nuisance of himself in the opposition half, Ade Akinbiyi gave as good as he got against the Premiership's hardened defenders. Although Leicester were the fourth-cleanest team in the division, the imposing striker committed more than 70 misdemeanours as he fought to win the ball and put himself in a goalscoring position. Robbie Savage's collection of seven bookings ensured that he was firmly established in second place, with Gerry Taggart following closely in third.

DISCIPLINE

	POINTS	FOULS & CARDS
ADE AKINBIYI	75	72F, 1Y, 0R
Robbie Savage	66	45F, 7Y, 0R
Gerry Taggart	62	26F, 10Y, 1R
Dean Sturridge	56	44F, 4Y, 0R
Matt Elliott	48	39F, 3Y, 0R

ACTION	AXINBIYI	COLLYMORE	CRESSWELL	DAVIDSON	EADIE	ELLIOTT	FLOWERS	GILCHRIST	GUPPY	IMPEY	IZZET	LENNON	ROWETT	SAVAGE	TOTAL	CHELSEA
Time on pitch	70	20	20	5	70	90	90	90	85	90	90	90	90	90	990	990
GOALS																
Goal	–	1	–	–	–	–	–	–	–	–	–	–	–	–	2	0
Shot on target (incl goals)	1	1	1	–	–	–	–	–	–	–	1	–	–	–	3	7
Shot off target	–	–	–	–	–	1	–	–	–	–	–	–	1	–	2	7
Blocked shot	1	1	–	–	–	–	–	–	–	–	–	–	–	–	1	15
Own goal	–	–	–	–	–	–	–	–	–	–	–	–	–	–	0	0
PASSES																
Pass to own player	6	5	6	1	13	12	3	6	18	28	31	37	19	20	205	351
Pass to opposition	7	4	1	–	8	10	5	3	5	8	10	11	6	8	86	86
Cross to own player	–	–	–	–	–	–	–	3	3	–	–	2	–	–	5	9
Cross to opposition player	–	1	–	2	2	–	–	6	6	–	4	2	–	1	16	36
Goal assist	–	–	–	–	–	–	–	–	–	–	–	1	–	–	2	0
Pass completion %	46%	50%	86%	100%	57%	55%	38%	67%	67%	78%	69%	75%	76%	69%	68%	75%
TACKLES & CLEARANCES																
Tackle	2	–	4	–	4	3	–	2	–	1	1	3	2	7	29	18
Clearances, blocks and interceptions	2	1	2	2	–	21	–	15	2	2	6	8	8	7	74	43
DRIBBLES & RUNS																
Dribbles ball retained	–	1	1	–	4	–	–	4	4	2	–	3	2	–	18	26
Dribbles ball lost	2	–	–	–	2	–	–	–	1	2	–	–	–	–	8	5
Dribble success %	0%	50%	100%	0%	67%	0%	0%	0%	80%	50%	100%	100%	100%	0%	69%	84%
DISCIPLINE																
Fouls	2	1	1	–	–	5	–	–	1	1	–	2	2	1	17	14
Penalty conceded	–	–	–	–	–	–	–	–	–	–	–	–	–	–	0	0
Free kick – offside	1	2	–	–	1	–	–	–	–	–	–	–	–	–	4	1
Yellow cards	–	–	–	–	–	–	–	–	–	–	–	–	–	1	1	3
Red cards	–	–	–	–	–	–	–	–	–	–	–	–	–	–	0	0
GOALKEEPERS																
Distribution to own player	–	–	–	–	–	–	17	–	–	–	–	–	–	–	17	9
Distribution to opposition player	–	–	–	–	–	–	16	–	–	–	–	–	–	–	16	9
Goalkeeper distribution %	–	–	–	–	–	–	52%	–	–	–	–	–	–	–	52%	50%
Save	–	–	–	–	–	–	6	–	–	–	–	–	–	–	6	0
Ball caught	–	–	–	–	–	–	10	–	–	–	–	–	–	–	10	4
Ball dropped	–	–	–	–	–	–	–	–	–	–	–	–	–	–	0	0
Goal conceded	–	–	–	–	–	–	–	–	–	–	–	–	–	–	0	2

Having conceded just one goal in six games, Leicester were flying high during the early part of the season and taking on all-comers under new manager Peter Taylor. They had conceded just one goal and were confident of getting a result against Chelsea, who had just parted company with Gianluca Vialli.

17 September 2000

0-2

CHELSEA
LEICESTER CITY

A trip to Stamford Bridge is never easy but Chelsea's new coach Claudio Ranieri watched on from the directors' box as his players lost their heads in full view of 30,000 home fans, who greeted Leicester's second goal with mutinous chants of "Vialli". The Foxes were again upsetting the big sides and the odds.

It took only eight minutes for the visitors to open the scoring. Neil Lennon – City's most industrious player, who made more than 50 passes – picked out Muzzy Izzet, who glanced the ball past Carlo Cudicini in the Chelsea goal; a sweet return for the former Chelsea player.

It was not until the 18th minute that Chelsea registered a shot on target when their man of the match Roberto Di Matteo tested Tim Flowers from distance. The Italian looked the most likely source for a Chelsea goal as he attempted seven shots – three on target – but he could not find a way past the former Blackburn stopper.

Flowers made six saves to keep Chelsea at bay. The former England 'keeper displayed his confidence by also making 10 successful catches and the side were to miss him later in the campaign when his injury forced a lengthy absence.

The home team were subdued by the Foxes for long periods of the match and credit should be given to the Leicester back-line who defended stoutly despite the absence of the injured Gerry Taggart. Phil Gilchrist slotted in alongside Matt Elliott

and the centre-backs made a combined 36 blocks, clearances and interceptions throughout the 90 minutes.

That defensive solidity put paid to the ambition of Chelsea's most dangerous attacker. Jimmy Floyd Hasselbaink had a frustrating day, managing just one fluffed shot on target and an effort which hit the woodwork before he was withdrawn from the action on 79 minutes. It was a rare occasion during the season when Hasselbaink was unable to get into the game.

It was left to another big-name striker to seal an historic victory for the battling visitors. Substitute Stan Collymore emphatically volleyed home a Steve Guppy cross on 82 minutes to give Leicester their first league win at Stamford Bridge for 35 years. The strike was Collymore's last goal in Leicester colours.

Taylor's men blocked an incredible 15 of Chelsea's shots and the Londoners also failed to score with 14 other efforts – half of which were on target – as Flowers and Co repelled attack after attack.

The Foxes failed to come out after their winter hibernation and lost nine out of their last 10 league games. In the end it was arguably their excellent early-season form which saved them being later sucked into a relegation fight, but in the autumnal glow of September the defence was solid and their tails were bushy as the Blues were brushed aside.

corners than Leicester City

LIVERPOOL

ADDRESS

Anfield Road, Anfield, Liverpool L4 0TH

CONTACT NUMBERS

Telephone: 0151 263 2361
Fax: 0151 260 8813
Ticket Office: 0151 260 8680
Club Call: 09068 121184
Superstore: 0151 263 1760
Website: www.liverpoolfc.tv

KEY PERSONNEL

Chairman: D R Moores
Chief Executive: R N Parry BSC, FCA
Directors: N White FSCA, T D Smith,
K E B Clayton FCA, J Burns
Vice-Presidents: T W Saunders,
J T Cross, H E Roberts
Club Secretary: W B Morrison
Manager: Gérard Houllier

SPONSORS

Carlsberg

FANZINES

All Day and All of the Night
Red All Over the Land
Another Vintage Liverpool Performance

COLOURS

Home: Red shirts, red shorts
and red stockings
Away: Gold shirts, navy shorts
and navy stockings

NICKNAME

The Reds

HONOURS

League Champions:
1900–01, 1905–06, 1921–22,
1922–23, 1946–47, 1963–64,
1965–66, 1972–73, 1975–76,
1976–77, 1978–79, 1979–80,
1981–82, 1982–83, 1983–84,
1985–86, 1987–88, 1989–90.
Division Two Champions: 1893–94,
1895–96, 1904–05, 1961–62.
FA Cup Winners: 1965, 1974,
1986, 1989, 1992, 2001.
League Cup Winners: 1981, 1982,
1983, 1984, 1995, 2001
European Cup Winners:
1977, 1978, 1981, 1984
UEFA Cup Winners: 1973, 1976, 2001
European Super Cup Winners: 1977

RECORD GOALSCORER

Roger Hunt – 245 league goals,
1959–69

BIGGEST WIN

11–0 v Stromsgodset Drammen –
European Cup Winners' Cup 1st round
1st leg, 17 September 1974

BIGGEST DEFEAT

1–9 v Birmingham City – Division Two,
11 December 1954

SEASON REVIEW

Liverpool's aims at the start of the season were clear: Champions League qualification, a wholehearted commitment to the Worthington Cup and progression as far as possible in both FA and UEFA Cup competitions.

The fact that they won all three cups as well as finishing third in the Premiership is quite a remarkable feat, and unprecedented.

Prior to the campaign, Dominic Matteo was sold to Leeds, but Gérard Houllier strengthened the squad by purchasing Christian Ziege from Middlesbrough, Nick Barmby from Everton and veteran Gary McAllister from Coventry City.

After an opening day 1–0 win over Bradford Liverpool travelled to Highbury, where they had two men sent off in a 2–0 defeat.

Meanwhile Rapid Bucharest and Slovan Liberec were dismissed in the UEFA Cup and Chelsea were beaten 2–1 after extra time in the Worthington Cup, a tournament which Houllier had made clear he would be setting out to win, despite other teams' apparent non-interest.

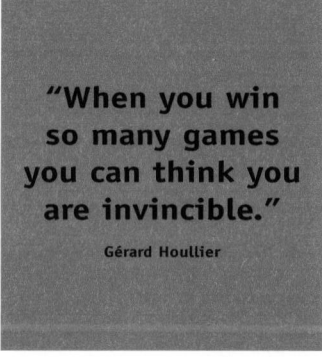

"When you win so many games you can think you are invincible."

Gérard Houllier

While Liverpool's league form was good enough to keep them in the top six, their fixture list was getting congested, although this did little to stop them in the cups. By early December Stoke had been humiliated 8–0 at home to the Reds in the Worthington Cup, while Olympiakos were Liverpool's next victims in Europe.

Not content with that, Houllier then strengthened the squad further. Highly-rated Croatian midfielder Igor Biscan was signed from Croatia Zagreb and experienced Finnish international Jari Litmanen joined from Barcelona.

December was Liverpool's finest month in the Premiership. A 1–0 win at Old Trafford against bitter rivals Manchester United was followed a week later with a 4–0 win against Arsenal, showing that on their day they could compete with and beat the top sides in the country.

The Reds started 2001 with a Worthington Cup semi-final against Crystal Palace. The Eagles managed to beat Liverpool 2–1 at Selhurst Park, one of only two defeats in 25 cup matches all season for Gérard Houllier's side. But the return leg at Anfield was a classic Liverpool performance, as they ran out 5–0 winners.

In mid-February, within the space of a week, Manchester City were defeated in the FA Cup and Italian champions-elect Roma were beaten over two legs which were reminiscent of the classic European nights etched in Liverpool folklore.

Suddenly there was talk that a cup treble could really be on the cards. The FA Cup draw was being as kind as it could possibly have been, while Nationwide League opposition awaited them in the League Cup final.

Those opponents were Birmingham City, who were largely outplayed for 89 minutes, yet scored a last-minute penalty to take the game to extra time. However, Liverpool won a penalty shoot-out to claim their first trophy under Gérard Houllier. Liverpool's first game after the final was a Premiership trip to Leicester. The Foxes won 2–0, highlighting Houllier's worry that the bread and butter of the league was being forsaken in the pursuit of cup glory.

That said, Liverpool continued to sparkle in knockout tournaments. Porto were eliminated in the UEFA Cup quarter-finals, while domestically Tranmere Rovers were beaten as the Reds progressed to the last four of the FA Cup.

Liverpool's remarkable achievement in 2000–01 obviously reflects a season-long effort, but it was the hard work put in

SEASON REVIEW

during April that set up the success of May.

Wycombe Wanderers enjoyed the greatest day in their history as they met Liverpool for a place in the FA Cup final. The second division side were narrowly beaten 2–1, however and the Reds were returning to Cardiff's Millennium Stadium.

That game was sandwiched between two legs against Barcelona for a place in the UEFA Cup final.

Liverpool hung on grimly for a goalless draw in the Nou Camp. Houllier's side came in for criticism from some quarters, who felt that Liverpool's style was too defensive and that they preferred to hit teams on the break rather than play like traditional, attacking Liverpool teams. Nevertheless, the scene was set for another European full house at Anfield.

Step forward Gary McAllister, who three days earlier had scored a 45-yard last-minute free-kick against Everton to seal a 3–2 win. He slotted home the penalty that would send Liverpool to their first European final in 16 years.

Liverpool continued to maintain their league form. While April did see a 2–1 home defeat by Leeds, the Reds were to drop just two points in their last seven Premiership fixtures, a great effort from a squad of players involved in a total of 63 matches all season.

Before knowing whether or not they would be playing in the Champions League in 2001–02, Liverpool had to address the small matter of the FA and UEFA Cup finals.

On a hot day in Cardiff Arsenal peppered the Liverpool defence and took the lead with 20 minutes to go. Sami Hyypia made three goal-line clearances in a final which was fast slipping away from the Reds. That was when Michael Owen came to life. He scored two fantastic goals to break Arsenal's hearts and steer Liverpool to

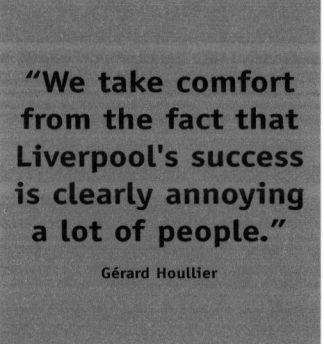

"We take comfort from the fact that Liverpool's success is clearly annoying a lot of people."

Gérard Houllier

their second trophy in 11 weeks.

Four days later Houllier's men made their way to Dortmund, where they and Alaves contested one of the most memorable European finals of all time.

Leads of 2–0, 3–1 and 4–3 in the last minute led Liverpool fans to believe that they were about to achieve their "treble" in fantastic and dramatic style.

But few who watched the game will ever forget the performance of Alaves, who yet again came back, this time in injury time, to force a 4–4 draw and take the UEFA Cup final to extra time.

Eventually, three minutes from the end of a gripping two hours, an Alaves own-goal provided Liverpool with a Golden Goal winner, a dramatic end to a breathtaking game.

Liverpool had been judged fortunate in all three finals by some, but the Reds made their own luck, with Roma, Barcelona, Chelsea and Arsenal all beaten on the way to the "treble".

A league double over rivals Manchester United only added to the wonderful memories every Liverpool fan will have of the 2000–01 season, with a final-day 4–0 win over Charlton confirming third place and a guaranteed slot in the 2001–02 Champions League.

Liverpool's failure to challenge Manchester United for the title was a result of their inconsistent away form. Houllier's side lost seven matches away from Anfield and this will need to be addressed for 2001–02 if the Merseysiders are to go on to the next level.

As for 2000–01, Liverpool scored 127 goals in 63 games. Both domestic cups were won, along with the UEFA Cup and the Premiership table confirmed Gérard Houllier's men as being back among the best teams in the country.

LIVERPOOL

DATE	OPPONENT	SCORE	ATT.	BABBEL	BARMBY	BERGER	BISCAN	CARRAGHER	DIOMEDE	FOWLER	GERRARD	HAMANN	HEGGEM	HENCH
19.08.00	Bradford H	1–0	44,183	90	90	s8	–	s14	–	–	68	90	–	90
21.08.00	Arsenal A	0–2	38,014	90	77□	–	–	90□	–	–	–	78□	–	90□
26.08.00	Southampton A	3–3	15,202	90	81	–	–	90	–	–	90	90	–	90
06.09.00	Aston Villa H	3–1	43,360	90	s73	–	–	90	–	–	90□	90	–	90
09.09.00	Man City H	3–2	44,692	90	90	–	–	90□	–	–	70	90²□	–	90
17.09.00	West Ham A	1–1	25,998	90	90	–	–	90	–	–	72¹	90	s18	90
23.09.00	Sunderland H	1–1	44,713	90	90	–	–	90	72□	s18	s28	62	–	90
01.10.00	Chelsea A	0–3	34,966	90	66	–	–	66	–	s24	90□	90	s24	90
15.10.00	Derby Co A	4–0	30,532	90	81□	90¹	–	90	–	s68	–	–	6	–
21.10.00	Leicester H	1–0	44,395	90	90	90	–	–	–	78	90	90	–	90
29.10.00	Everton H	3–1	44,718	90	90¹	90¹	–	s3	–	70	87	90	–	90
04.11.00	Leeds Utd A	3–4	40,055	90□	s18	72□	–	90	–	s23	s22□	90	–	–
12.11.00	Coventry H	4–1	43,701	90	90	–	–	s13	–	–	77¹	–	–	90
19.11.00	Tottenham A	1–2	36,036	90□	s29	–	–	s11	–	90¹	s25	90	–	90
26.11.00	Newcastle A	1–2	51,949	90□	90	–	–	90	–	90	74	90	–	90□
02.12.00	Charlton H	3–0*	43,515	90¹	90	–	–	90	–	69	90	s7	–	90
10.12.00	Ipswich H	0–1	43,509	90	45	–	s19	90	–	90	–	–	–	90
17.12.00	Man Utd A	1–0	67,533	90	90	–	90	90	–	–	90	–	–	90
23.12.00	Arsenal H	4–0	44,144	90□	90¹	–	90	90□	–	s10¹	77¹	–	–	90
26.12.00	Middlesbro A	0–1	34,696	81	90□	–	54	90□	–	s36	90	–	–	90
01.01.01	Southampton H	2–1	38,474	90¹	52	–	s12	90	–	90	90¹	–	–	90
13.01.01	Aston Villa A	3–0	41,366	90	–	–	s20	90	–	–	87¹	90	–	90
20.01.01	Middlesbro H	0–0	43,042	90	62	–	–	90	–	s28	90	90□	–	90
31.01.01	Man City A	1–1	34,629	90	–	–	s13	–	s36□	s29	90	90	–	90
03.02.01	West Ham H	3–0	44,045	34	s17	–	45	–	–	90²	90	90	–	90
10.02.01	Sunderland A	1–1	47,553	90	–	–	87□	–	–	90	56	90	–	90
03.03.01	Leicester A	0–2	21,924	90	81	–	–	90	–	90	90	s15	–	61
18.03.01	Derby Co H	1–1	43,362	90□	–	–	55	90	–	s11	s35	90□	–	90
31.03.01	Man Utd H	2–0	44,806	90	s21	69	–	90	–	69¹	87¹	90	–	90
10.04.01	Ipswich H	1–1	23,504	90	–	90	82	90	–	–	90	s17	–	–
13.04.01	Leeds Utd H	1–2	44,116	90	–	45	–	90	–	90	70¹	66□	–	90
16.04.01	Everton A	3–2	40,260	90¹	–	–	77□	90□	–	84	–	90□	–	90□
22.04.01	Tottenham H	3–1	43,547	90	–	90	–	64	–	s50¹	90	s36	–	90
28.04.01	Coventry A	2–0	23,063	90	–	74	s4	90	–	63	–	90	–	90
01.05.01	Bradford A	2–0	22,057	90	–	s9	–	90□	–	–	90	90	–	90
05.05.01	Newcastle H	3–0	44,363	90	–	s21	–	90	–	s14	64	90	–	90
08.05.01	Chelsea H	2–2	43,588	90□	–	58	–	90	–	s9	90	72	–	90
19.05.01	Charlton A	4–0	20,043	90	55	89	–	90	–	90²	90□	–	–	–

□ Yellow card, ■ Red card, s Substitute, 90² Goals scored

*including own goal

For more information visit our website:

2000–01 PREMIERSHIP APPEARANCES

HESKEY	HYYPIA	LITMANEN	McALLISTER	MEIJER	MURPHY	OWEN	SMICER	SONG	STAUNTON	TRAORE	VIGNAL	WESTERVELD	WRIGHT	ZIEGE	TOTAL
82¹	90	–	s22	–	–	76	90	–	–	90□	–	90	–	–	990
80	90	–	39■	s10	s13	s20	70	–	–	90	–	90	–	–	927
–	90¹	–	–	–	s16	90²	74	–	s9	90	–	90	–	–	990
62	90	–	–	s28	–	90³	17	–	–	90	–	90	–	–	990
90□	–	–	–	s3	–	87¹	–	90	–	90	–	90	–	s20	990
90	–	–	–	–	70□	–	–	90□	–	90	–	90	–	s20	990
10	–	–	–	–	s80	90¹	–	90□	–	–	–	90	–	90	990
90	90	–	–	–	–	90	–	–	–	–	–	90	–	90	990
90³	90	–	90	–	s84	22	s9	–	–	–	–	90	–	90	990
90¹	90	–	90	–	s12	–	–	–	–	–	–	90	–	90□	990
90¹	90	–	90	–	–	–	s20	–	–	–	–	90	–	90	990
90	90¹	–	67	–	68	–	90¹	–	–	–	–	90	–	90¹□	990
90²	90	–	90¹	–	s23	67	86	–	–	90	–	90	–	s4	990
–	90	–	90	–	79	90	61□	–	–	65	–	90	–	–	990
90¹	90	–	s16	–	58	–	s32	–	–	–	–	90	–	–	990
90¹□	90	–	83	–	s21	–	s21	–	–	–	–	90	–	69	990
s30	90	–	90	–	90	60	s45	–	–	–	–	90	–	71□	990
90	90	–	s1	–	89¹	76	s14	–	–	–	–	90	–	–	990
90	90	–	s13	–	61	80¹	s29	–	–	–	–	90	–	–	990
90	90	–	s36	–	s9	54	90	–	–	–	–	90	–	–	990
78	90	–	90	–	s38	s18	72	–	–	–	–	90	–	–	990
81	90	70	s3	–	90²	s9	90	–	–	–	–	90	–	–	990
45	90	75	–	–	s15	s45	90	–	–	–	–	90	–	–	990
90¹	90	61	77	–	–	–	90	–	–	–	–	90	–	54	990
90	90	–	–	–	–	–	90¹	–	–	–	90	90	s56	s28	990
28	90	s62¹□	90	–	–	s34	–	–	–	–	90□	90	s3	–	990
90□	90	–	75	–	s9	s29	–	–	–	–	–	90	–	90	990
90	90	66	79	–	–	90¹	s24	–	–	–	–	90	–	–	990
90	90	–	s21	–	68■	s3	–	–	–	–	–	90	–	–	968
90¹	90	–	s8	–	90	–	–	–	–	–	90	90	–	73	990
s24	90	–	s45	–	45	90	s45□	–	–	–	–	90	–	–	970
90¹	90	–	90¹□	–	–	–	90	–	–	–	s6	90	–	–	977
40¹	90	–	90¹	–	–	90	54	–	–	–	s26□	90	–	–	990
86□	90¹	–	90¹	–	90	s27	–	–	–	–	–	90	–	s16	990
90	90	–	81¹	–	81	90¹	s9	–	–	–	–	90□	–	–	990
76	90	–	90	–	s26	90³	69	–	–	–	–	90	–	–	990
81	90	–	90	–	s18	90²	s32	–	–	–	–	90	–	–	990
s1	90	–	90	–	s35¹	90¹	–	–	–	–	90	90	–	–	990

THE MANAGER

GERARD HOULLIER

Gérard Houllier came to Anfield to work alongside Roy Evans as joint manager in 1998. But the partnership lasted just four months before Houllier was given sole charge.

His previous managerial experience came in his home country with Nöeux Les Mines between 1976 and 1982. He then managed Lens for three years and helped them qualify for the UEFA Cup before moving to Paris St Germain in 1985, leading them to the French title the following year.

Houllier worked as Platini's number two in the French national side from 1988 to 1992 and took over when Platini stepped down. But France failed to qualify for the 1994 World Cup and Houllier left the post, returning to the national set-up to manage the Under-18 side that won the 1996 European Under-18 Championship.

He also became head coach of the French Under-20 team and was the national technical director of the French Football Association from 1990 to 1998.

The studious Frenchman and long-time Liverpool fan led his club to their most successful season for many years and appears to be well on the way to making the famous club a potent force once again.

LEAGUE POSITION

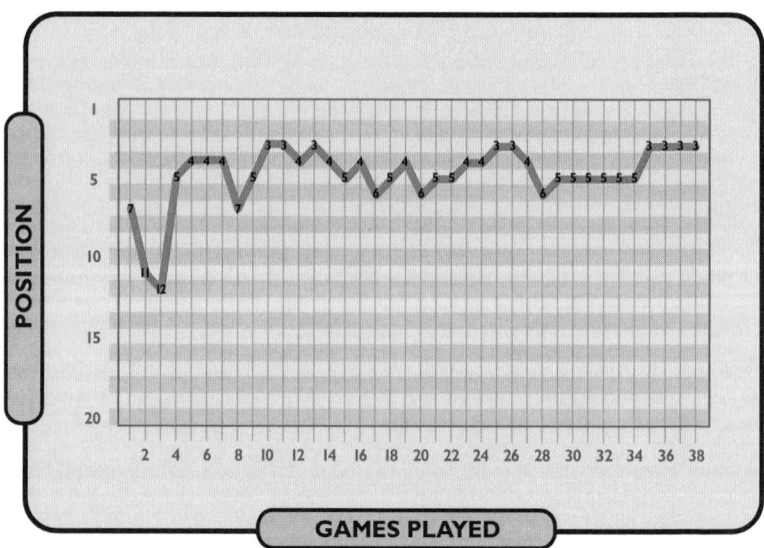

POSITION

GAMES PLAYED

13 Liverpool scored the most goals

THE GOALS

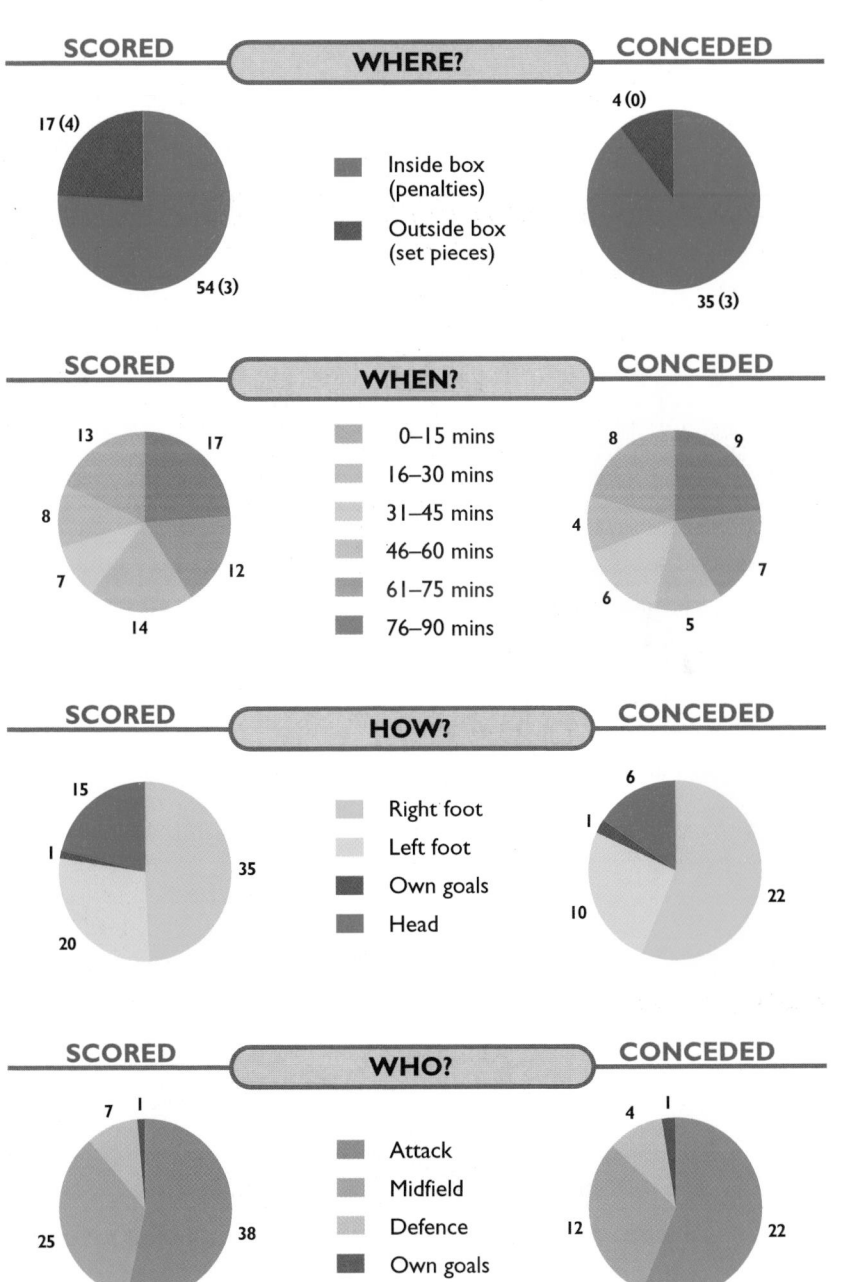

in the opening 15 minutes of matches

LIVERPOOL

	BABBEL	BARMBY	BERGER	BISCAN	CARRAGHER	DIOMEDE	FOWLER	GERRARD	HAMANN	HEGGEM	HENCHO
APPEARANCES											
Start	38	21	11	8	30	1	15	29	26	1	32
Sub	0	5	3	5	4	1	12	4	4	2	0
Minutes on pitch	3355	1838	895	648	2691	108	1563	2529	2333	48	2851
GOAL ATTEMPTS											
Goals	3	2	2	0	0	0	8	7	2	0	0
Shots on target	6	8	8	4	3	1	25	23	10	0	0
Shots off target	13	15	14	6	4	0	26	27	26	0	1
Shooting accuracy	32%	35%	36%	40%	43%	100%	49%	46%	28%	0%	0%
PASSING											
Goal assists	3	3	5	0	0	0	3	2	3	0	0
Long passes	406	133	95	67	393	9	115	540	425	4	325
Short passes	1004	628	215	208	819	14	419	936	936	25	628
PASS COMPLETION											
Own half %	80%	81%	77%	72%	82%	86%	81%	86%	85%	100%	88%
Opposition half %	66%	69%	61%	63%	65%	75%	60%	65%	74%	67%	63%
CROSSING											
Total crosses	93	56	21	3	40	11	28	91	29	6	0
Cross completion %	24%	21%	24%	0%	23%	36%	11%	21%	14%	17%	0%
DRIBBLING											
Dribbles & runs	89	61	17	35	34	4	52	76	55	4	11
Dribble completion %	81%	80%	76%	54%	85%	50%	62%	78%	84%	50%	100%
DEFENDING											
Tackles made	87	58	24	21	95	2	19	128	114	3	91
Tackles won %	67%	62%	88%	67%	81%	50%	74%	69%	76%	67%	80%
Blocks	9	1	3	2	13	0	0	10	10	0	41
Clearances	218	11	4	4	188	0	3	63	37	1	275
Interceptions	9	5	1	4	16	0	2	18	13	0	13
DISCIPLINE											
Fouls	48	19	14	18	36	6	16	49	49	0	42
Offside	1	13	5	0	1	1	22	5	1	0	0
Yellow cards	6	3	1	1	6	2	0	4	5	0	3
Red cards	0	0	0	1	0	0	0	1	1	0	0

GOALKEEPER NAME	START/ (SUB)	TIME ON PITCH	GOALS CONCEDED	MINS/GOALS CONCEDED	SAVES MADE	SAVES/ SHOTS
WESTERVELD	38(0)	3420	39	88	122	76%

For more information visit our website:

PLAYERS' STATISTICS

	HESKEY	HYYPIA	LITMANEN	McALLISTER	MEIJER	MURPHY	OWEN	SMICER	SONG	STAUNTON	TRAORE	VIGNAL	WRIGHT	ZIEGE	TOTAL	RANK
	33	35	4	21	0	13	20	16	3	0	8	4	0	11		
	3	0	1	9	3	14	8	11	0	1	0	2	2	5		
	2694	3150	334	1926	41	1378	1787	1503	270	9	695	392	59	985		
	14	3	1	5	0	4	16	2	0	0	0	0	0	1	71*	2nd
	43	12	5	13	1	10	42	11	0	0	0	0	0	4	229	3rd
	39	10	2	11	0	13	28	21	0	2	0	1	0	12	271	2nd
	52%	55%	71%	54%	100%	43%	60%	34%	0%	0%	0%	0%	0%	25%	46%	7th
	4	1	0	5	0	4	3	9	0	0	0	0	1	2	48	4th
	117	548	37	253	3	182	59	144	25	0	80	50	6	134	4585	5th
	733	810	149	760	9	487	345	523	45	4	176	128	26	263	10386	9th
	82%	85%	84%	85%	83%	76%	78%	79%	63%	50%	70%	69%	91%	80%	82%	5th
	65%	59%	70%	71%	67%	66%	70%	65%	46%	100%	54%	55%	62%	58%	64%	8th
	45	3	14	184	0	45	23	102	8	1	9	8	0	64	884	14th
	16%	67%	29%	38%	0%	33%	39%	27%	38%	0%	11%	0%	0%	20%	26%	12th
	90	22	7	48	0	46	103	101	5	0	11	9	2	31	920	9th
	61%	86%	57%	69%	0%	63%	48%	68%	60%	0%	73%	89%	100%	68%	70%	6th
	51	93	6	48	3	58	28	48	13	0	27	21	1	30	1071	4th
	80%	69%	83%	75%	33%	81%	71%	60%	85%	0%	67%	76%	100%	87%	74%	7th
	5	28	0	9	0	2	1	1	1	0	7	1	1	7	153	18th
	44	466	0	34	0	15	3	9	14	0	40	23	1	35	1556	2nd
	3	16	0	5	0	4	1	3	1	0	3	6	0	9	132	2nd
	76	29	3	25	2	16	21	29	6	0	9	10	1	16	542	15th
	44	0	3	2	0	3	34	9	0	0	0	0	0	1	145	7th
	4	0	1	1	0	1	0	2	2	0	1	2	0	3	49	=14th
	0	0	0	1	0	1	0	0	0	0	0	0	0	0	5	=3rd

*Including one own goal

CROSSES CAUGHT	CROSSES PUNCHED	CROSSES DROPPED	CATCH SUCCESS	THROWS/ SHORT KICKS	% COMPLETION	LONG KICKS	% COMPLETION
71	29	3	96%	74	84%	601	56%

PLAYER OF THE SEASON

PLAYER	INDEX SCORE
SAMI HYYPIA	1,086
Michael Owen	1,083
Steven Gerrard	1,034
Gary McAllister	960
Emile Heskey	919
Dietmar Hamann	912
Jamie Carragher	821
Sander Westerveld	803
Stephane Henchoz	770
Markus Babbel	732

Picking out an individual from Liverpool's incredible 2000–01 campaign is a difficult task, but one man remained consistently pivotal to the club's aspirations throughout the campaign – Sami Hyypia.

For the second year running, the stand-in skipper was Liverpool's highest-ranked player and the Premiership's top defender on Opta's system, with a whopping average of 1,086 points.

The Finnish man-mountain made an incredible 466 clearances, with 345 of these coming via the head and no Premiership player was anywhere near matching Hyypia's massive total.

Hyypia also won 64 tackles and used his aerial strength to head home three league goals as the Reds clinched third place in the league.

Michael Owen, Opta's top-rated striker in 2000–01, finished just three points shy of Hyypia in second place. Owen's blistering form in the month of May – including his match-winning brace in the FA Cup final – saw him take his tally to 16 Premiership goals, with the England man netting 23% of efforts, and hitting the target with 60% of his shots.

While Owen's late burst helped secure cup success and a Champions League place, Steven Gerrard kept Liverpool chugging along nicely throughout 2000–01. The tough-tackling midfielder made 88 successful challenges, nearly 1,500 passes, and scored seven goals – including one cracker against Manchester United – leading to him being widely touted as the future of the England midfield.

Two new signings, Gary McAllister and Emile Heskey, also made their mark. McAllister's experience proved crucial as he found his second wind in the season's climax, while Heskey's 14 goals and four assists earned him an average of 919 points.

Dietmar Hamann ranked highly with Opta thanks to his proficient passing and 87 successful tackles, while Jamie Carragher and Markus Babbel also featured after consistently solid performances in the league.

466 Sami Hyypia made more clearances

FIVE OF THE BEST

Liverpool's unrelenting finish to the 2000–01 season proved that Gérard Houllier has finally brought a sense of self-belief back to Anfield. Key signings and the implementation of a successful rotation system combined to yield historic cup success and a top three league finish which ensured Champions League football for the first time in 2001–02.

TOP GOALSCORERS

	GOALS	GOALS/SHOTS
MICHAEL OWEN	16	23%
Emile Heskey	14	17%
Robbie Fowler	8	16%
Steven Gerrard	7	14%
Gary McAllister	5	21%

Michael Owen made a mockery of the early-season criticism which was thrown his way by notching seven goals in the final four games to take his league tally to a respectable 16. Emile Heskey and Robbie Fowler managed to notch 14 and eight goals respectively, but neither striker could compete with the youngster's impressive 23% goals-to-shots ratio. Hapless Newcastle felt the full might of Owen's wrath when the diminutive hitman struck a hat-trick to bury the Magpies.

As a unit, the Reds may not have been the Premiership's pass masters during 2000–01, but individually, accuracy was evident in abundance. Four players completed more than 1,000 passes – including two defenders – as Liverpool pinged the ball around with ease and patiently built their attacks from the back. Dietmar Hamann may have only narrowly edged Steven Gerrard into second place, but the German international's pinpoint precision was better by a full seven percentage points.

TOP PASSERS

	SUCC PASSES	COMPLETION
DIETMAR HAMANN	1,073	79%
Steven Gerrard	1,066	72%
Markus Babbel	1,020	72%
Sami Hyypia	1,006	74%
Jamie Carragher	871	72%

TOP TACKLERS

	WON	SUCCESS
STEVEN GERRARD	88	69%
Dietmar Hamann	87	76%
Jamie Carragher	77	81%
Stephane Henchoz	73	80%
Sami Hyypia	64	69%

Liverpool were one of only seven clubs to attempt more than 1,000 tackles, and visits to the dentist and growing pains were not enough to prevent Steven Gerrard from contributing his share. The midfield maestro won more challenges than any of his colleagues, as the Reds fought for every ball in their successful bid for a place in Europe's premier club competition. Dietmar Hamann was the only other Anfield player to win more than 80 tackles at the club.

While he may have been criticised for his own inability to remain vertical at times, Emile Heskey was not afraid to knock others into a horizontal position with his all-action displays in attack. The former Fox committed more than 70 fouls and sneaked into the Opta top 20 offenders' list for his trouble. Five Liverpool players, including Dietmar Hamann and Steven Gerrard, saw red for their moments of indiscipline, but the Reds still finished in the lower reaches of the Premiership table of crime.

DISCIPLINE

	POINTS	FOULS & CARDS
EMILE HESKEY	88	76F, 4Y, 0R
Dietmar Hamann	70	49F, 5Y, 1R
Steven Gerrard	67	49F, 4Y, 1R
Markus Babbel	66	48F, 6Y, 0R
Jamie Carragher	54	36F, 6Y, 0R

than any other Premiership player

ACTION	BABBEL	BARMBY	BISCAN	CARRAGHER	GERRARD	HENCHOZ	HESKEY	HYYPIA	MCALLISTER	MURPHY	OWEN	SMICER	WESTERVELD	TOTAL	MAN UTD
Time on pitch	90	90	90	90	90	90	90	90	1	89	76	14	90	990	989
GOALS															
Goal	–	–	–	–	–	–	–	–	–	1	–	–	–	1	0
Shot on target (incl goals)	–	–	–	–	–	–	2	–	–	2	2	–	–	6	4
Shot off target	–	2	–	–	–	–	2	–	–	1	1	–	–	6	3
Blocked shot	–	–	–	–	–	–	–	–	–	–	1	–	–	1	1
Own goal	–	–	–	–	–	–	–	–	–	–	–	–	–	0	0
PASSES															
Pass to own player	20	30	29	20	43	11	29	14	1	27	14	6	4	248	522
Pass to opposition	9	8	6	12	16	5	17	6	–	13	7	1	6	106	131
Cross to own player	1	3	–	–	–	–	–	–	–	1	–	–	–	5	10
Cross to opposition player	2	1	–	1	1	–	–	–	–	–	–	–	–	5	28
Goal assist	–	–	–	–	–	–	–	–	–	–	–	–	0	0	0
Pass completion %	66%	79%	83%	63%	72%	69%	63%	70%	100%	67%	67%	86%	40%	70%	77%
TACKLES & CLEARANCES															
Tackle	4	6	2	3	7	3	2	5	–	2	2	2	–	38	31
Clearances, blocks and interceptions	10	3	3	13	6	11	2	16	–	1	2	–	6	73	29
DRIBBLES & RUNS															
Dribbles ball retained	2	3	2	–	2	–	1	–	–	2	2	1	–	15	13
Dribbles ball lost	1	1	2	2	2	–	2	–	–	2	2	–	–	12	18
Dribble success %	67%	75%	50%	0%	50%	0%	33%	0%	0%	50%	50%	100%	0%	56%	42%
DISCIPLINE															
Fouls	1	–	–	3	2	–	1	–	–	1	2	–	–	10	12
Penalty conceded	–	–	–	–	–	–	–	–	–	–	–	–	–	0	0
Free kick – offside	–	–	–	–	–	–	2	–	–	–	2	–	–	4	1
Yellow cards	–	–	–	–	–	–	–	–	–	–	–	–	–	0	1
Red cards	–	–	–	–	–	–	–	–	–	–	–	–	–	0	1
GOALKEEPERS															
Distribution to own player	–	–	–	–	–	–	–	–	–	–	–	–	9	9	15
Distribution to opposition player	–	–	–	–	–	–	–	–	–	–	–	–	14	14	7
Goalkeeper distribution %	–	–	–	–	–	–	–	–	–	–	–	–	39%	39%	68%
Save	–	–	–	–	–	–	–	–	–	–	–	–	4	4	3
Ball caught	–	–	–	–	–	–	–	–	–	–	–	–	4	4	1
Ball dropped	–	–	–	–	–	–	–	–	–	–	–	–	–	0	0
Goal conceded	–	–	–	–	–	–	–	–	–	–	–	–	–	0	1

Liverpool had not won at Old Trafford for a decade. Manchester United had not lost at home in the league for more than two years. It was to be a match which would make people believe that Liverpool were making serious progress under Gérard Houllier.

17 December 2000

0–1

MANCHESTER UNITED
LIVERPOOL

The Reds were without a clean sheet in eight games and United had the most miserly defence in the Premiership. However, Michael Owen should have scored two goals in the opening exchanges. Twice he was given a clear run on goal, yet Fabien Barthez was able to claim the ball at his feet on both occasions. The visitors looked the stronger of the two sides, with Steven Gerrard going in for seven tackles – more than any other player – as he started to get the better of Roy Keane.

After 43 minutes Gary Neville, unchallenged on the edge of his box, handled Steven Gerrard's through ball and gave away a free-kick. Danny Murphy stepped up and curled the ball perfectly beyond Barthez and into the far corner to give his side a precious lead.

Liverpool fired in 12 shots throughout the game – five more than the home side – belying the notion that they were totally defensive throughout. And Owen came desperately close to making it two just 40 seconds into the second half.

Markus Babbel surged down the right and found Owen with a clever pull-back. The young English forward was unlucky to see his first-time shot crash off the crossbar.

Ole Gunnar Solskjaer had the only two clear chances for United, but Sander Westerveld pulled off two smart saves, both at his near post.

Houllier stood wide-eyed on the touchline with the look of an athlete waiting for a starter's pistol as Sir Alex Ferguson made changes in search of the equaliser, but the Liverpool defence stood firm, making 56 clearances, blocks and interceptions between them. In the final seconds, United's desperation saw young winger Luke Chadwick sent off for hauling back Vladimir Smicer when the Czech midfielder was clean through on goal.

The final whistle eventually did arrive and the French tactician had overcome the only side he had previously been unable to beat. It was his 50th win, coming in his 100th game in charge. As anniversary presents go, it was a sweet one.

This performance was a barometer for the progress being made by the club and an example of how Liverpool were able to dig out results through resilient defending which would later serve them well in Rome, Barcelona and Cardiff.

The Reds followed it up with a 4–0 thrashing of Arsenal, though defeat away at Middlesbrough in the next game showed the problems Liverpool still have against lesser opposition.

United still wrapped up the title with ease, but Liverpool went on to beat Ferguson's side at Anfield as well. And although the gap in points between the two sides was 11 at the end of the season, the gap in class appears to be shrinking at last.

MANCHESTER CITY

ADDRESS

Maine Road, Moss Side,
Manchester M14 7WN

CONTACT NUMBERS

Telephone: 0161 232 3000
Fax: 0161 232 8999
Ticket Office: 0161 226 2224
Dial-A-Seat: 0161 828 1200
Clubcall: 09068 121 191
Superstore: 0161 232 1111
Mail Order: 0161 828 1201
e-mail: mcfc@mcfc.co.uk
Website: www.mcfc.co.uk

KEY PERSONNEL

Chairman: D Bernstein
Directors: C Bird, B Bodek,
A Lewis, A Mackintosh,
A Thomas, D Tueart, J Wardle
Club Secretary: B Halford
Manager: Kevin Keegan

SPONSORS

Eidos

FANZINES

Bert Trautmann's Helmet
King of the Kippax
This Charming Fan
Chips 'n' Gravy
City Til I Cry

COLOURS

Home: Sky blue shirts, white
shorts and navy stockings.
Away: Silver shirts, black shorts
and luminous yellow stockings

NICKNAMES

The Blues
The Citizens

HONOURS

Division One Champions:
1936–37, 1967-68
Division Two Champions:
1898–99, 1902–03, 1909–10,
1927–28, 1946–47, 1965–66
FA Cup Winners:
1904, 1934, 1956, 1969
League Cup Winners: 1970, 1976
European Cup Winners' Cup Winners:
1970

RECORD GOALSCORER

Tommy Johnson – 158 league goals,
1919–30

BIGGEST WINS

10–1 v Huddersfield Town –
Division Two, 7 November 1987
10–1 v Swindon Town – FA Cup
4th round, 29 January 1930

BIGGEST DEFEAT

1–9 v Everton – Division One,
3 September 1906

SEASON REVIEW

Coming on the back of two consecutive emotionally-charged promotion campaigns, there was always the chance that Manchester City's first season back in the top flight was going to be something of a disappointment. But the way that Joe Royle's side capitulated in the second half of the 2000–01 campaign left even the most loyal City fans questioning the direction their club was going in.

City had surprised many by finishing second in Division One in the 1999–2000 campaign, thereby regaining the top-flight status that they had relinquished four years previously. And after a summer spent recruiting exciting new players, many of the Maine Road faithful felt that they would have a side capable of making a serious impact at Premiership level.

Skilful Costa Rican forward Paulo Wanchope was signed for £3.65 million and paired in attack with former World Player of the Year George Weah. Former England centre-back Steve Howey was brought in to strengthen the back line, while early-season signings Paul Ritchie, Laurent Charvet and Richard Dunne gave Royle further defensive options.

And although City suffered an instant blip when losing their opening game 4–0 to Charlton, the opening months of the season seemed to bode well. City's first home fixture saw the visit of Sunderland and the Black Cats were despatched in emphatic fashion.

Wanchope led the rout, scoring a hat-trick in his first match at Maine Road, helping to seal a morale-boosting 4–2 win. Royle's side followed this up with a fantastic win over Leeds in their next away fixture and also beat Southampton and Bradford before the end of October.

> "I'm proud of my record; I don't feel I've anything to prove. The chairman said they wanted a change of direction; now they can have it."
>
> Joe Royle

Those last two wins were inspired by a resurgent Paul Dickov, who was clearly trying to make up for lost time after being sold by Arsenal earlier in his career. The Scot opened the scoring in both games, winning rave reviews for his all-action displays. He even gained his first call-up to Craig Brown's Scotland squad, coming on as a substitute in the 2–0 win over San Marino in October.

After 10 Premiership matches, the Citizens were looking in good shape in 10th place, having won four and drawn two of their games. Unfortunately, the momentum that the players had gained until that point seemed to fade away rapidly.

The dismissal of Danny Tiatto at Highbury in the next league match precipitated a 5–0 drubbing by the Gunners from which City never truly recovered. It was the first of six consecutive defeats from October to December in which the Citizens conceded a total of 16 goals – a run which left them only two points clear of the relegation zone.

Royle's men rallied to win their last home fixture before Christmas, trouncing the manager's former side Everton 5–0 in their best performance of the season. And further respite from their Premiership woes was provided shortly after, when Wanchope was officially declared the 22nd best footballer on the planet by a FIFA poll.

The fact that the Costa Rican's only nomination for the World Player of the Year award was given to him by his national team coach Gilson Nuñez Siqueira seemed to matter little to the gangly forward. He celebrated being ranked above the likes of Roy Keane, Ryan Giggs and Michael Owen by firing a crucial goal in the next league match, helping City claim a 2–2 draw at Villa Park.

SEASON REVIEW

However, by that stage of the 2000–01 campaign Weah had been sent back to France, where he joined Marseille on a free transfer. And even Wanchope was unsure of his place in the side, having clashed several times with Royle since joining the club.

The Worthington Cup did provide the club with an interesting interlude to their struggles in the Premiership, and good wins over Aston Villa and Wimbledon set up a clash against the Premiership's surprise package, Ipswich Town, in the quarter-finals. City led going into the final 30 minutes, but they were pegged back and then beaten by a goal 11 minutes from the end of extra time.

In the league the gulf in class between Royle's men and the top sides was displayed in the statistics. They struggled to maintain possession in most matches. Indeed, over the course of the 2000–01 season they were accurate with just 67% of their passes, which was the fifth-worst ratio in the Premiership.

It must have been a worrying sign for City fans that their most intelligent passer of the ball, Ian Bishop, was 35 and well past his best. Still, it may have been even more galling when he was offloaded to the MLS in the States in March, just when the Citizens most needed an experienced hand to steady their sinking ship.

As a result of their poor distribution, the Citizens struggled to create sufficient goal-scoring chances for their forwards. Indeed, they fired in just 366 shots in 2000–01 – the fourth-lowest total in the division – and scored only 41 goals.

Defeat by Liverpool in the FA Cup fifth round meant that Premiership survival was all that the Citizens had left to battle for. But the fighting spirit

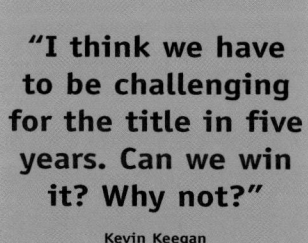

> "I think we have to be challenging for the title in five years. Can we win it? Why not?"
>
> **Kevin Keegan**

that had been a feature of their back-to-back promotion campaigns seemed to have left them.

Royle's side embarked on a run of 16 league matches with only one win to show for their efforts and by the end of that period, they were five points from safety and staring relegation in the face.

The manager seemed unable to motivate his troops, illustrated by the fact that they failed to win a single game in which they had trailed their opponents. Moreover, City conceded four or more goals on six separate occasions in the league alone – more than any other side – and shipped a staggering total of 65 goals over the course of the 2000–01 campaign.

The Citizens' fate was sealed when they were again beaten by Ipswich in their penultimate game. Again they led against Town after Shaun Goater's 74th-minute opener, but two late strikes from Matt Holland and Martijn Reuser confirmed City's relegation back to the Nationwide.

City reacted to their demotion by sacking Royle. The fact that he had steered the club to successive promotions before the disappointment of this term had been expected to ensure his job at Maine Road for another campaign and many in the game felt that chairman David Bernstein was acting rashly.

Royle had certainly enjoyed plenty of support from the fans since his appointment in 1998. But during the rocky Premiership campaign even the City faithful had begun to question his decisions in what was a disastrous season for the Citizens. With their incredible record of bouncing back and forth between divisions, however, who would bet against Kevin Keegan inspiring a return to the top flight in 2001–02?

MANCHESTER CITY

DATE	OPPONENT	SCORE	ATT.	ALLSOPP	BISHOP	CHARVET	CROOKS	DICKOV	DUNNE	DUNFIELD	EDGHILL	GOATER	GRANT	GRANVILLE	HAALAND	HORLO
19.08.00	Charlton A	0–4	20,043	–	–	–	–	–	–	–	90	–	–	–	90□	45
23.08.00	Sunderland H	4–2	34,410	–	–	–	–	–	–	–	90	–	–	–	90^1□	90
26.08.00	Coventry H	1–2	34,140	–	–	–	s34□	–	–	–	45	–	s45	–	90	90^1
05.09.00	Leeds Utd A	2–1	40,055	–	–	–	–	–	–	–	–	–	–	s12	90□	90
09.09.00	Liverpool A	2–3	44,692	–	–	–	–	90□	–	–	–	–	–	–	90	90^1
17.09.00	Middlesbro H	1–1	32,053	–	s32	–	–	s17	–	–	–	–	–	–	90	58
23.09.00	Tottenham A	0–0	36,069	–	–	–	s70□	62	–	–	–	–	–	–	90	90□
30.09.00	Newcastle H	0–1	34,497	–	s20	–	s13	90	–	–	–	–	–	–	77	45
14.10.00	Bradford H	2–0	34,229	–	s24	–	–	90^1	–	–	–	–	–	–	90^1	–
23.10.00	Southampton A	2–0	15,056	–	–	–	–	90^1□	90	–	–	s22	–	–	90	–
28.10.00	Arsenal A	0–5	38,049	–	–	90	–	90□	–	–	–	69□	–	–	90	–
04.11.00	Leicester H	0–1	34,279	–	s31	90	–	90	–	–	–	–	–	–	90	–
11.11.00	West Ham A	1–4	26,022	s15	–	90	–	–	s22	–	–	–	–	–	90	–
18.11.00	Man Utd H	0–1	34,429	–	s45	90	–	90□	–	–	–	s45	–	–	90	–
25.11.00	Ipswich H	2–3	33,741	–	90	–	–	56	45	–	–	56	–	–	90	–
03.12.00	Chelsea A	1–2	34,971	–	–	90	–	s45¹	–	–	–	90	–	–	90	90
09.12.00	Everton H	5–0*	34,516	–	–	90	–	s46¹	90	–	–	44¹	–	–	46	90
16.12.00	Aston Villa A	2–2	29,281	–	–	90	–	–	90	–	–	60	–	–	90^1	72
23.12.00	Sunderland A	0–1	47,475	–	s53	90	–	s74	90	–	–	90	–	–	90	90
26.12.00	Derby Co H	0–0	34,321	–	90	90	–	–	90	–	–	90	–	–	90	57
30.12.00	Charlton H	1–4	33,280	–	s62	41	–	56□	90	–	–	90	–	s34	90	28
01.01.01	Coventry A	1–1	21,999	–	82	–	–	–	90	–	90	s11	–	90	90	–
13.01.01	Leeds Utd H	0–4	34,288	–	–	–	–	s20	90	–	90□	70	s44	46	90□	–
20.01.01	Derby Co A	1–1	31,174	–	–	–	–	–	90	–	–	s23	–	s11	90	–
31.01.01	Liverpool H	1–1	34,629	–	–	–	–	–	90	–	–	90	–	90	90	–
03.02.01	Middlesbro A	1–1*	31,794	–	–	–	–	–	90	–	–	90	s20	89	90	–
10.02.01	Tottenham H	0–1	34,399	–	–	–	–	–	90	–	–	90	s5	90	90	–
24.02.01	Newcastle A	1–0	51,981	–	–	s28	–	–	90	–	–	90^1	90	90	62	–
03.03.01	Southampton H	0–1	33,990	–	–	s31	–	–	90	–	–	90	90	59	90	–
17.03.01	Bradford A	2–2	19,117	–	–	90	–	–	90□	–	–	90^1	59	72	–	–
31.03.01	Aston Villa H	1–3	34,247	–	–	90□	–	–	90	–	–	90^1	–	45	90□	–
08.04.01	Everton A	1–3	36,561	–	–	–	–	89□	90	–	–	–	–	45	90	–
11.04.01	Arsenal H	0–4	33,444	–	–	s17	–	–	90	–	–	90	–	90□	90	–
14.04.01	Leicester A	2–1	20,224	–	–	45	–	–	90□	–	–	72¹	s29□	90	90	–
21.04.01	Man Utd A	1–1	67,535	–	–	90	–	90	90	–	–	s5	45	90	90	–
28.04.01	West Ham H	1–0*	33,737	–	s22	–	–	71	90	–	–	74	–	90	68□	–
07.05.01	Ipswich A	1–2	25,004	–	–	90	–	57	90	–	–	s31¹	45	90	–	–
19.05.01	Chelsea H	1–2	34,479	–	–	–	–	90□	90□	s58	90	90	–	90□	–	–

□ Yellow card, ■ Red card, s Substitute, 90^2 Goals scored
*including own goal

For more information visit our website:

2000–01 PREMIERSHIP APPEARANCES

HOWEY	HUCKERBY	KANCHELSKIS	KENNEDY	MORRISON	NASH	OSTENSTAD	PRIOR	RITCHIE	TIATTO	WANCHOPE	WEAH	WEAVER	WHITLEY	WIEKENS	WRIGHT	WRIGHT-PHILLIPS	TOTAL
90	–	–	90	–	–	–	90	–	90	90□	90	90□	–	90	–	s45	990
90	–	–	90	–	–	90□	–	90	90^3	90	90	–	90	–	–	–	990
90	–	–	56	–	–	90	–	90	90	90	90	–	90□	–	–	–	990
90^1□	–	–	67	–	–	–	90	90	90	90	–	90	90	78^1	–	s23	990
90□	–	–	57	–	–	90	90	–	90□	s33¹	90	90□	90	–	–	–	990
90	–	–	90	–	–	90	90	s57□	90^1□	73	90	90	33	–	–	–	990
20	–	–	s41	–	–	90	90	49	90	s28	90	90	90	–	–	–	990
–	–	–	s45	–	–	90	90	90	90	70	–	90	90	90	–	–	990
66	–	–	90	–	–	90	90	90	90	–	90	90	90	–	–	–	990
90□	–	–	–	–	–	90	90	90^1	68	–	90	90	90	–	–	–	990
90	–	–	s21	–	–	90	90	43□	–	–	90	90	90	–	–	–	943
90	–	–	s31	–	–	90	59□	90	90	–	90	90	59	–	–	–	990
90	–	–	90	–	–	90^1	68	–	75	–	90	90□	90	–	90	–	990
90	–	–	45	–	–	90□	–	90□	–	–	90	90	45	–	90	–	990
90^1	–	–	90	–	–	90	–	s45	s34¹	–	90	s34	–	–	90	–	990
90	–	–	–	–	–	90	–	68	45	–	90	90	s22	–	90	–	990
90^1	–	–	s29	–	–	–	–	90	90^1	–	90	90	s44	–	61	–	990
90	–	–	s30	–	–	–	–	90	90^1□	–	90	90	s18	–	90	–	990
90□	–	–	16	–	–	–	–	90	–	–	90	37□	–	–	90	–	990
90	–	–	–	–	–	–	–	90□	90	–	90	–	s33□	–	90	–	990
90	s49¹	–	–	–	–	–	–	90	–	–	90	–	90	–	90	–	990
90	79□	–	–	90	–	–	–	90□	90^1	–	90	–	–	–	s8	–	990
90□	–	–	–	81□	–	–	–	90□	90	–	90	90	–	–	s9	–	990
90^1	67	–	–	–	–	90	79	51□	90□	–	90	90	90	–	s39	–	990
90	77	s45	–	45	–	–	s13	90^1	–	–	90	90□	90	–	–	–	990
90	70□	90	–	–	–	–	–	90	–	–	90	90□	90	–	s1	–	990
90	90	60	–	–	–	s30	–	–	90□	–	–	90	90	85	–	–	990
90	78	90	–	–	–	–	–	90	–	–	90	s12	90	–	–	–	990
90□	59	90	–	–	–	s31	–	–	90	–	–	90	–	90	–	–	990
90	51	90	s18	–	–	s31	–	–	90	–	–	90	s39	90^1	–	–	990
–	s35	55	s45□	–	–	83	90□	–	81□	–	–	90	90□	s7	–	–	981
90	s16	74	s45	–	–	–	–	–	90□	90□	–	90□	90^1□	90	–	–	989
90	s17	–	90□	–	90	–	–	–	90	73	–	–	73	90	–	–	990
90	–	s45	90	–	90	–	–	s18	–	90^1□	–	–	90	61	–	–	990
90^1	–	s40	–	–	90	–	–	s21	–	–	90	–	90	69	–	–	990
90□	s16	–	–	90	–	–	–	90□	s19	–	–	90	90	–	–	–	990
90	–	–	s33	–	90	–	–	s14	–	90	90	–	–	90	90	–	990
90^1	–	–	90	–	90	–	–	–	90□	–	–	32	90	–	–	–	990

THE MANAGER

KEVIN KEEGAN

It was never likely to be an easy task to keep Manchester City in the top flight on such a meagre budget. So Joe Royle will undoubtedly regard his sacking in May 2001 following relegation as extremely harsh.

It was a clear indication that the success-starved Citizens were determined to regain their Premiership status as soon as possible. City swiftly moved to appoint Kevin Keegan, who had resigned from the England manager's position seven months earlier.

Keegan had been widely tipped to move to Southampton. He made 68 appearances for the Saints, scoring 37 goals in the process, but clearly felt the potential at Maine Road outweighed the benefits of returning to the south coast.

He is best remembered for his days at Newcastle, firstly as a player and later for his first senior management role. Having narrowly missed out on the 1995–96 Premiership title, Keegan quit in 1997–98 before later joining Fulham, where his success led to a knock on his door from the FA.

The pressures at Maine Road are likely to be on a similar scale to those he faced with the national job, but he has told the fans he is relishing the challenge.

LEAGUE POSITION

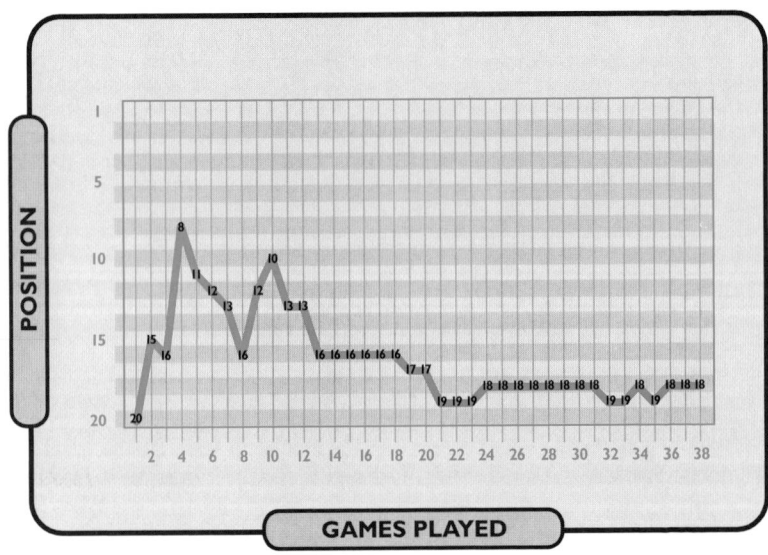

3 No team scored fewer goals than City

THE GOALS

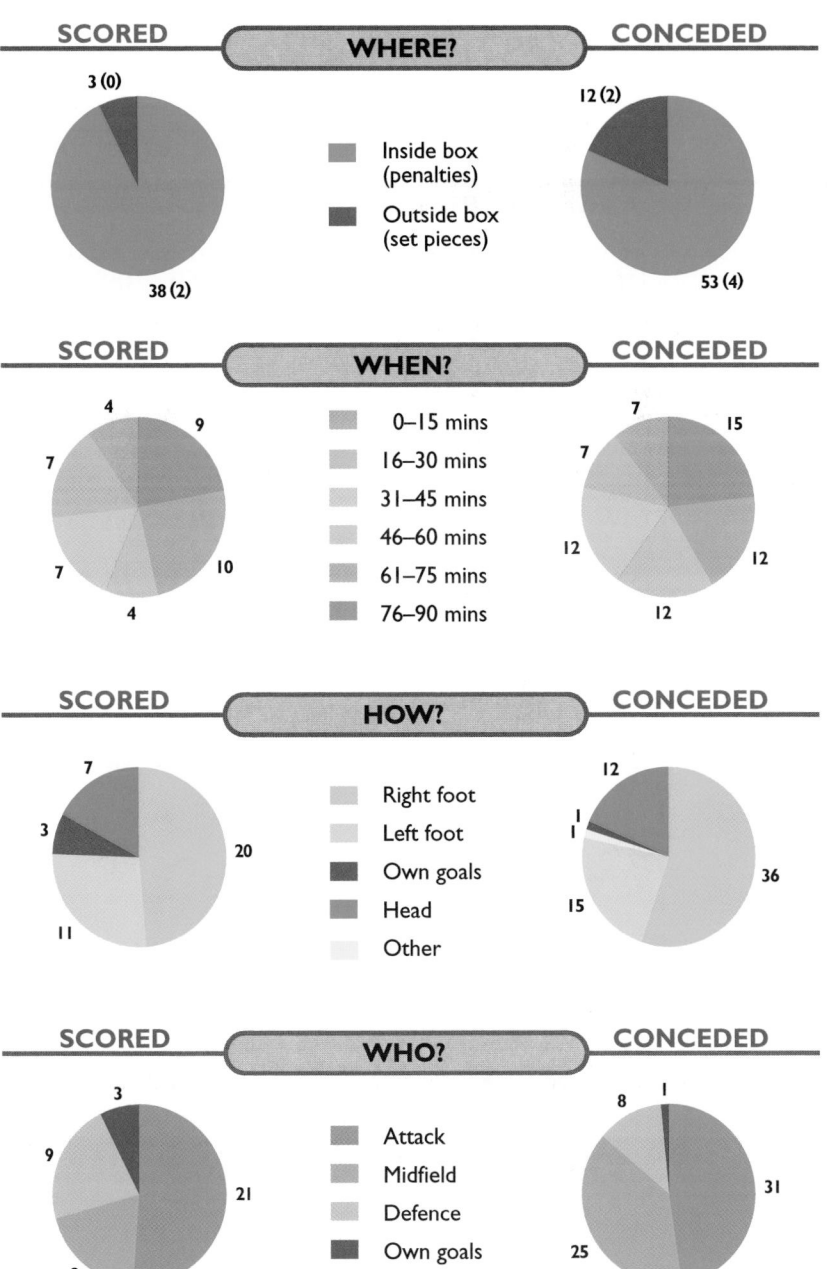

SCORED | WHERE? | CONCEDED

3 (0)
38 (2)

12 (2)
53 (4)

Inside box (penalties)
Outside box (set pieces)

SCORED | WHEN? | CONCEDED

4
9
7
7
10
4

7
15
7
12
12
12

0–15 mins
16–30 mins
31–45 mins
46–60 mins
61–75 mins
76–90 mins

SCORED | HOW? | CONCEDED

7
3
20
11

12
1
1
36
15

Right foot
Left foot
Own goals
Head
Other

SCORED | WHO? | CONCEDED

3
9
21
8

8
1
31
25

Attack
Midfield
Defence
Own goals

from outside the area in 2000–01

MANCHESTER CITY

	ALLSOPP	BISHOP	CHARVET	CROOKS	DICKOV	DUNFIELD	DUNNE	EDGHILL	GOATER	GRANT	GRANVILLE	HAALAND	HORLOC
APPEARANCES													
Start	0	3	16	0	15	0	24	6	20	5	16	35	14
Sub	1	7	4	2	6	1	1	0	6	5	3	0	0
Minutes on pitch	15	529	1444	83	1437	58	2137	495	1752	472	1313	3043	1025
GOAL ATTEMPTS													
Goals	0	0	0	0	4	0	0	0	6	0	0	3	2
Shots on target	0	1	2	0	12	0	1	0	15	1	3	13	8
Shots off target	0	4	4	0	13	0	2	1	17	3	2	18	9
Shooting accuracy	0%	20%	33%	0%	48%	0%	33%	0%	47%	25%	60%	42%	47%
PASSING													
Goal assists	0	0	1	0	2	0	0	0	0	0	1	1	1
Long passes	0	122	156	10	78	18	346	82	52	62	140	268	121
Short passes	6	271	484	11	377	21	491	140	458	200	314	836	278
PASS COMPLETION													
Own half %	100%	90%	75%	22%	75%	100%	75%	80%	74%	84%	66%	76%	75%
Opposition half %	40%	75%	66%	67%	66%	77%	51%	59%	65%	63%	61%	58%	62%
CROSSING													
Total crosses	0	35	51	3	78	0	8	13	9	4	43	41	81
Cross completion %	0%	29%	18%	67%	19%	0%	38%	15%	0%	50%	19%	17%	28%
DRIBBLING													
Dribbles & runs	1	2	42	0	22	0	30	5	16	7	36	37	6
Dribble completion %	100%	100%	67%	0%	59%	0%	83%	100%	75%	86%	83%	73%	83%
DEFENDING													
Tackles made	1	15	30	1	34	3	71	13	22	18	35	83	33
Tackles won %	100%	33%	87%	100%	62%	33%	76%	85%	73%	50%	77%	72%	76%
Blocks	0	1	11	0	3	1	41	3	1	0	15	14	12
Clearances	0	6	61	4	6	0	200	18	27	1	88	76	26
Interceptions	0	3	9	0	0	0	8	1	0	4	3	10	3
DISCIPLINE													
Fouls	0	3	9	1	47	0	37	10	45	9	19	57	19
Offside	0	0	0	1	16	0	0	0	19	1	2	6	4
Yellow cards	0	0	1	1	7	0	3	1	1	1	2	6	1
Red cards	0	0	0	0	1	0	0	0	0	0	0	0	0

GOALKEEPER NAME	START/ (SUB)	TIME ON PITCH	GOALS CONCEDED	MINS/GOALS CONCEDED	SAVES MADE	SAVES/ SHOTS
NASH	6(0)	540	10	54	29	74%
WEAVER	31(0)	2790	54	52	96	64%
WRIGHT	1(0)	90	1	90	7	88%

For more information visit our website:

PLAYERS' STATISTICS

	HOWEY	HUCKERBY	KANCHELSKIS	KENNEDY	MORRISON	OSTENSTAD	PRIOR	RITCHIE	TIATTO	WANCHOPE	WEAH	WHITLEY	WIEKENS	WRIGHT-PHILLIPS	TOTAL	RANK
	36	8	7	15	3	1	18	11	31	25	5	28	29	9		
	0	5	3	10	0	3	3	1	2	2	2	3	5	6		
	3146	704	679	1479	216	175	1673	939	2734	2204	474	2477	2534	906		
	6	1	0	0	0	0	1	0	2	9	1	1	2	0	41*	15th
	11	3	2	6	0	2	1	0	11	35	7	10	8	4	156	15th
	11	10	9	12	0	2	2	1	19	29	4	17	5	16	210	16th
	50%	23%	18%	33%	0%	50%	33%	0%	37%	55%	64%	37%	62%	20%	43%	15th
	1	1	1	4	0	0	0	0	3	3	1	4	0	0	24	=16th
	430	10	30	111	28	5	215	120	435	89	25	237	323	68	4224	8th
	672	102	211	373	37	38	409	234	802	591	109	877	819	246	9500	16th
	79%	76%	66%	80%	71%	67%	80%	72%	73%	76%	77%	77%	82%	80%	77%	16th
	56%	54%	69%	59%	57%	73%	64%	57%	57%	61%	66%	69%	69%	59%	61%	18th
	2	24	43	248	1	4	8	9	142	20	9	22	15	33	946	8th
	50%	17%	19%	27%	100%	50%	25%	22%	25%	20%	33%	18%	13%	21%	24%	19th
	11	75	52	87	0	7	13	5	156	123	11	46	9	68	869	11th
	100%	35%	62%	77%	0%	86%	100%	80%	78%	40%	64%	54%	89%	65%	66%	18th
	97	5	2	27	7	1	42	42	111	40	1	96	80	23	935	15th
	77%	40%	100%	59%	71%	100%	67%	83%	70%	78%	0%	79%	78%	87%	74%	6th
	42	0	0	3	2	0	13	11	13	2	0	10	18	3	219	=7th
	333	1	3	7	27	0	191	70	61	31	0	37	80	5	1452	8th
	14	0	1	1	1	0	7	2	15	3	0	7	3	3	98	=16th
	64	12	6	11	4	7	22	17	53	85	9	46	39	10	643	3rd
	0	20	1	10	0	6	0	0	2	43	5	2	0	1	139	=10th
	7	2	0	2	1	0	3	1	9	9	0	7	2	0	69	=8th
	0	0	0	0	0	0	0	0	2	0	0	0	0	0	3	=7th

*Including three own goals

CROSSES CAUGHT	CROSSES PUNCHED	CROSSES DROPPED	CATCH SUCCESS	THROWS/ SHORT KICKS	% COMPLETION	LONG KICKS	% COMPLETION
10	5	0	100%	3	100%	126	38%
34	21	4	89%	61	80%	615	49%
3	0	0	100%	0	0%	24	38%

PLAYER OF THE SEASON

PLAYER	INDEX SCORE
STEVE HOWEY	802
Spencer Prior	743
Paulo Wanchope	662
Danny Tiatto	661
Gerard Wiekens	660
Richard Dunne	647
Jeff Whitley	624
Alfie Haaland	539
Nicky Weaver	514
Shaun Goater	490

Joe Royle's shock departure brought an end to his eventful three-year association with the club.

With two successive promotions achieved and restricted time to consolidate, City were always likely to struggle, but they kept fighting until the penultimate match of the season.

One reason their campaign stayed alive was the battling spirit of the rearguard, and in particular City's highest-ranked player in the Opta Index, Steve Howey. Signed from Newcastle in August 2000, Howey was an influential figure at the heart of City's defence.

With 333 clearances and nearly 100 tackles, Howey systematically staved off opposition assaults, but also found time to get forward himself. Indeed, only one City player scored more goals than Howey's six, which helped him to an average Opta score of 802 points.

Perhaps surprisingly to some City fans, transfer-listed Spencer Prior came in second on Opta's system, with Paulo Wanchope third. Prior racked up points thanks largely to his 149 headed clearances. Only four Premiership players were busier in terms of clearing headers per 90 minutes, while he was comfortably the tidiest passer of all City defenders.

Wanchope, with an average of 662 points, was City's top scorer with nine goals, and only seventh-placed Jeff Whitley and Mark Kennedy assisted more goals than the Costa Rican's three.

The 2000–01 Supporters' Player of the Year Danny Tiatto came in fourth with Opta. The industrious Australian wing-back was the only Citizen with more than 100 crosses, dribbles and runs and tackles to his name. He also scored twice from 30 efforts and set up three goals. Were it not for his poor disciplinary record, he would have ranked much higher.

Richard Dunne impressed alongside Howey after his arrival from Everton, but Nicky Weaver's woeful 64% saves-to-shots ratio and tally of 54 goals conceded is reflected in his lowly score.

27% Steve Howey scored with more

FIVE OF THE BEST

After two successive promotions, Manchester City returned to losing ways in 2000–01, dropping out of the Premiership after just one season back in the top flight. Joe Royle's side rarely looked good enough to survive and Royle paid for their failure with his job, opening the door for Kevin Keegan to be appointed as City's new boss.

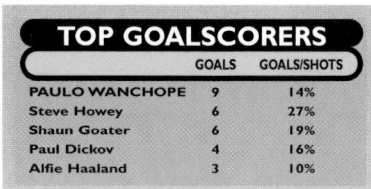

TOP GOALSCORERS	GOALS	GOALS/SHOTS
PAULO WANCHOPE	9	14%
Steve Howey	6	27%
Shaun Goater	6	19%
Paul Dickov	4	16%
Alfie Haaland	3	10%

Paulo Wanchope and George Weah were supposed to be the Dream Team for Manchester City, but although Wanchope scored nine goals and proved a big hit with City's fans, Weah's brief stay with the club was a disaster. Shaun Goater and Paul Dickov chipped in with 10 goals between them in Weah's absence, but defender Steve Howey was the only other City player to make a significant contribution in front of goal.

Dutch midfielder Gerard Wiekens was Manchester City's top passer in 2000–01, but that in itself is hardly a claim to fame. City struggled to keep possession in many of their matches, and only Coventry made fewer passes during the course of the season. At least Wiekens recorded a half-decent pass completion rate, which is more than can be said for some of his team-mates, many of whom struggled to complete more than 60% of their attempted passes.

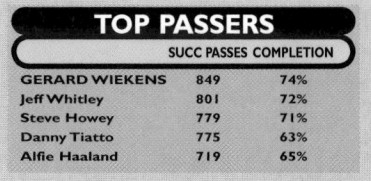

TOP PASSERS	SUCC PASSES	COMPLETION
GERARD WIEKENS	849	74%
Jeff Whitley	801	72%
Steve Howey	779	71%
Danny Tiatto	775	63%
Alfie Haaland	719	65%

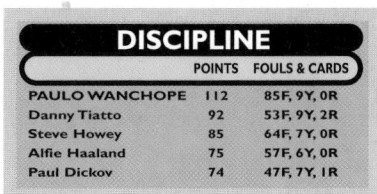

TOP TACKLERS	WON	SUCCESS
DANNY TIATTO	78	70%
Jeff Whitley	76	79%
Steve Howey	75	77%
Gerard Wiekens	62	78%
Alfie Haaland	60	72%

Hard-working midfielder Danny Tiatto won City's Player of the Year award, and there is no doubt that he worked himself into the ground for Joe Royle's team in 2000–01. Tiatto topped City's tackling chart with 78 successful challenges – just ahead of Jeff Whitley, who made two fewer tackles but enjoyed a higher success rate than Tiatto. In general, City won a fair proportion of the challenges they made, but hard work alone was not enough to keep them up.

Paulo Wanchope's ungainly style often worked against him. The Costa Rican beanpole committed 85 fouls in 2000–01, picking up nine yellow cards along the way. Volatile Danny Tiatto was not far behind Wanchope. The Aussie firebrand committed fewer fouls, but picked up the same number of yellow cards and was also one of just four Premiership players to receive his marching orders twice in the season. Steve Howey, Paul Dickov and Alfie Haaland were the other City stars in trouble most often.

DISCIPLINE	POINTS	FOULS & CARDS
PAULO WANCHOPE	112	85F, 9Y, 0R
Danny Tiatto	92	53F, 9Y, 2R
Steve Howey	85	64F, 7Y, 0R
Alfie Haaland	75	57F, 6Y, 0R
Paul Dickov	74	47F, 7Y, 1R

ACTION	CHARNET	DICKOV	DUNNE	GOATER	HAALAND	HORLOCK	HOWEY	KENNEDY	TIATTO	WANCHOPE	WEAVER	WHITLEY	WIEKENS	WRIGHT-PHILLIPS	TOTAL	EVERTON
Time on pitch	90	46	90	44	46	90	90	29	90	90	90	90	44	61	990	990
GOALS																
Goal	–	–	–	–	–	–	–	–	–	–	–	–	–	–	4	0
Shot on target (incl goals)	–	1	–	–	–	–	–	–	–	–	–	–	–	1	8	4
Shot off target	–	–	–	1	–	1	1	–	–	–	–	1	–	–	3	11
Blocked shot	–	–	–	–	–	–	–	–	–	–	–	–	–	1	4	4
Own goal	–	–	–	–	–	–	–	–	–	–	–	–	–	–	0	1
PASSES																
Pass to own player	23	10	22	8	15	29	18	6	28	15	2	32	13	14	235	318
Pass to opposition	18	9	11	4	3	14	9	2	21	10	11	8	3	15	138	143
Cross to own player	2	–	–	–	–	–	–	2	–	–	–	–	–	–	3	8
Cross to opposition player	–	–	–	–	–	9	–	–	–	1	–	–	–	2	17	22
Goal assist	–	–	–	–	–	–	–	–	1	–	–	–	–	–	2	0
Pass completion %	53%	53%	67%	62%	83%	57%	67%	73%	56%	59%	15%	80%	81%	45%	61%	66%
TACKLES & CLEARANCES																
Tackle	2	1	5	1	–	3	3	–	2	2	–	4	3	1	26	27
Clearances, blocks and interceptions	10	1	11	–	–	3	6	–	3	3	5	–	2	–	42	41
DRIBBLES & RUNS																
Dribbles ball retained	1	–	1	–	–	–	–	1	2	2	1	1	–	3	12	15
Dribbles ball lost	–	2	–	–	–	–	–	–	–	4	–	–	–	1	8	5
Dribble success %	100%	0%	100%	0%	0%	0%	0%	100%	100%	33%	100%	100%	0%	75%	60%	75%
DISCIPLINE																
Fouls	–	1	1	–	–	1	1	1	2	6	3	3	1	1	17	15
Penalty conceded	–	–	–	–	–	–	–	–	–	–	–	–	–	–	0	0
Free kick – offside	–	–	–	–	–	–	–	–	–	3	–	–	–	–	4	2
Yellow cards	–	–	–	–	–	–	–	–	–	–	–	–	–	–	0	1
Red cards	–	–	–	–	–	–	–	–	–	–	–	–	–	–	0	0
GOALKEEPERS																
Distribution to own player	–	–	–	–	–	–	–	–	–	–	12	–	–	–	12	13
Distribution to opposition player	–	–	–	–	–	–	–	–	–	–	15	–	–	–	15	6
Goalkeeper distribution %	–	–	–	–	–	–	–	–	–	–	44%	–	–	–	44%	68%
Save	–	–	–	–	–	–	–	–	–	–	4	–	–	–	4	4
Ball caught	–	–	–	–	–	–	–	–	–	–	2	–	–	–	2	3
Ball dropped	–	–	–	–	–	–	–	–	–	–	–	–	–	–	0	0
Goal conceded	–	–	–	–	–	–	–	–	–	–	–	–	–	–	0	5

6 Manchester City conceded four goals

Although City's return to the Premiership ended in relegation, there were some great memories from the season for the supporters. And when Everton went to Maine Road, the Citizens showed just what they were capable of doing. In fact, they achieved their biggest ever win over Everton.

9 December 2000

5–0

MANCHESTER CITY
EVERTON

Paulo Wanchope was the first to get into the goalmouth action after 13 minutes, when the tall Costa Rican reacted quickest to Paul Gerrard's fumble from a Kevin Horlock free-kick. Then, 10 minutes later, it was two. Central defender Steve Howey profited this time from some slack marking as he rose to power in a header direct from a Horlock corner.

Horlock had found himself back in the Citizens' line-up after a run of bad losses for Joe Royle's men, and was rapidly repaying his manager's faith with an assist as well as hitting the target with all three of his efforts at goal.

City virtually ended any hopes that Everton might have been entertaining of a comeback when Shaun Goater collected the mercurial Wanchope's flick-on and calmly slid the ball past Gerrard three minutes before the break. Royle's men were firing on all cylinders by this stage, and Gerrard did well to save from the talented Shaun Wright-Phillips with the last kick of an awesome first half.

After six successive Premiership defeats, a three-goal cushion going into the second half meant that Manchester City could play the ball around but, despite this fact, the Merseysiders actually ended the game with the superior passing accuracy. However, it did not make any difference to the embarrassing scoreline for Everton, as City continued to finish clinically after the break.

Overall, the Citizens managed to strike 73% of their efforts on target in front of a packed Maine Road – compared to Everton's total of 27% – and it was this superior shooting accuracy which was to see the Toffeemen get hammered.

First Paul Dickov got into the action by firing into the Everton goal following an error by 'keeper Gerrard on 53 minutes. And then, just 13 minutes later, City found themselves five goals to the good when the hapless Gary Naysmith put into his own net to complete Everton's misery and send the home fans delirious.

Ironically enough, Smith's beleaguered men won the corner count by 14 to five as they went in search of a consolation goal, but despite shots on target from Thomas Gravesen and Naysmith they were thwarted by Nicky Weaver.

It was an afternoon in which every ball was falling to Manchester City, and their extra hunger for the result was evident to all as Royle's battlers won an amazing 92% of their challenges. It stopped the Citizens' slide down the Premiership table and instilled some belief into the ailing Manchester side.

Although City consider themselves a massive club, ultimately they were not ready for the overall demands of the top flight. This match, though, gave them at least a taste of the champagne lifestyle back among the élite – something they will be keen to experience again soon.

in a game on the most occasions

MANCHESTER UNITED

ADDRESS

Sir Matt Busby Way, Old Trafford,
Manchester M16 0RA

CONTACT NUMBERS

Telephone: 0161 868 8000
Fax: 0161 868 8668
Ticket and Match Information:
0161 868 8020
Clubcall: 09068 121 161
Megastore: 0161 868 8567
Museum and Tour Centre:
0161 868 8631
e-mail: webmaster@office.manutd.com
Website: www.manutd.com

KEY PERSONNEL

Chairman: C M Edwards
Chief Executive: P F Kenyon
Deputy Chief Executive: D A Gill
Directors: Sir Bobby Charlton CBE,
J M Edelson, R L Olive
E M Watkins LI.M
Club Secretary: K R Merrett
Manager: Sir Alex Ferguson CBE

SPONSORS

Vodafone

FANZINES

Red News
United We Stand
Red Attitude
Red Army

NICKNAME

The Red Devils

COLOURS

Home: Red shirts, white shorts
and black stockings
Away: White shirts, navy shorts
and white stockings

HONOURS

League Champions: 1907–08,
1910–11, 1951–52, 1955–56, 1956–57,
1964–65, 1966–67, 1992–93, 1993–94,
1995–96, 1996–97, 1998–99,
1999–2000, 2000–01
Division Two Champions:
1935–36, 1974–75
FA Cup Winners: 1909, 1948, 1963, 1977,
1983, 1985, 1990, 1994, 1996, 1999
League Cup Winners: 1992
European Cup Winners: 1968, 1999
European Cup Winners' Cup Winners: 1991
World Club Championship
Inter-Continental Cup Winners: 1999
European Super Cup Winners: 1991

RECORD GOALSCORER

Bobby Charlton –
199 league goals, 1956–73

BIGGEST WIN

10-0 v RSC Anderlecht, European Cup
preliminary round 2nd leg,
26 September 1956

BIGGEST DEFEATS

0–7 v Blackburn Rovers –
Division One, 10 April, 1926
0–7 v Aston Villa – Division One,
27 December 1930
0–7 v Wolverhampton Wanderers –
Division Two, 26 December 1931

SEASON REVIEW

Nineteen teams in the Premiership would have been delighted to have endured as "disappointing" a season as Manchester United felt they had.

The Championship was almost over as a contest by Christmas and was finally sealed with five games to spare – a record in Premiership history – to clinch a hat-trick of titles. But it was failure in Europe that upset United's followers.

Sir Alex Ferguson made just one major investment in the close season, securing the services of flamboyant French goalkeeper Fabien Barthez. Massimo Taibi moved back to Italy and, despite vowing to fight for his place, Mark Bosnich eventually moved to Chelsea.

It was a disappointing opening to the season. United were beaten 2–0 by Chelsea in the Charity Shield and Roy Keane picked up a red card that was to earn him a three-match ban.

The league campaign started well, though, with a 2–0 victory over Newcastle, but United were surprisingly held by Ipswich at Portman Road and gave away a two-goal lead at West Ham.

Normal service resumed at Old Trafford with a 6–0 win over Bradford and a three-goal victory against Sunderland. This was followed by an away win at Everton, which propelled United to the top of the table.

The Champions League campaign began with an impressive 5–1 home win over Anderlecht and a valuable draw against Dynamo Kiev away.

But United played an understrength side against PSV, choosing to rest several players for a key Premiership match against Arsenal the following weekend. A somewhat peeved Dutch side overcame the hurdle of going a goal down to win 3–1.

To compound matters, Arsenal inflicted United's first league defeat with a spectacular Thierry Henry goal. However, the Red Devils started a run of eight consecutive wins which blitzed the rest of the field and left United eight points clear by December.

There was more good news as David Beckham was made captain of England and Steve McClaren was appointed to the national squad's coaching team.

Revenge was earned over PSV at Old Trafford, but United's poor away form haunted them as Anderlecht won 2–1 in Belgium. Despite this, the formality of qualifying seemed assured as United took a lead against Dynamo Kiev, but they were grateful for a glaring late miss by George Demetradze.

Roy Keane was incensed at the impatience of the fans disappointed at the lacklustre performance. He said: "I don't think some of the people can spell football, never mind understand it. They have a few drinks and probably the prawn sandwiches and they don't realise what's going on out on the pitch."

In the second group stage, wins over Panathinaikos at home and Sturm Graz away allowed United to concentrate on winning the Premiership before European hostilities resumed in the spring.

A minor blip at Charlton, where United drew 3–3, was followed by their first home Premiership defeat for two years as Liverpool dug out a 1–0 win. But United then embarked on another eight consecutive victories, while their rivals faltered.

With the Premiership and the Champions League bubbling along, United started contemplating another "treble", but a 2–1 win against Fulham in the third round of the FA Cup was followed by a home defeat by West Ham. A late goal by Paolo Di Canio ended the dream.

> "I might go into painting or something like that. There are a lot of things I can do, I'm such a talented guy."
>
> **Sir Alex Ferguson**

SEASON REVIEW

The delight from the rest of the nation was tangible. United consoled themselves by concluding a deal with the New York Yankees which would see the two massive sports organisations working together to enhance their interests across the globe.

The Champions League campaign resumed with back-to-back fixtures against Valencia, and two draws edged United towards qualification.

A disappointing 1–1 draw with Panathinaikos, earned with a late equaliser, again raised questions about United's away form, but at least the 3–0 victory over Sturm Graz meant they made the quarter-finals of the competition for the fifth year in a row.

Despite the stuttering European form, United eased towards the Premiership title. An astonishing 6–1 victory over Arsenal at Old Trafford was particularly satisfying. After this, the only blip before the title was won was a 2–0 defeat by Liverpool at Anfield.

United beat Coventry with two late goals in an early kick-off and were looking forward to winning the title against Manchester City in the following week's fixture. Later that day, though, Arsenal unexpectedly contrived to lose 3–0 at home to Middlesbrough and the title was United's for the seventh time in nine seasons.

However, more problems followed. United's fans had repeatedly ignored warnings from the city council to remain seated in certain areas of the ground and United were now threatened with having parts of Old Trafford closed.

When these warnings were ignored in the 1–0 defeat by Bayern Munich, the council announced that they would implement their threat if United reached the semi-final. It was irrelevant, as United were beaten 2–1 in the second leg and limped out of the competition.

Some blamed the poor European form on a lack of competition in the Premiership. The absence of a consistent challenge meant the champions struggled to reach the levels of performance required to succeed in Europe's premier club competition. Roy Keane had other views. The United skipper claimed: "When it comes to Europe, we are an average team...we are just not good enough. Maybe it's the end of the road for this team."

> ### "Maybe it's the end of the road for this team."
>
> **Roy Keane**

United, however, signalled their intentions for 2001–02, immediately breaking the British transfer record by spending £19 million to buy Ruud van Nistelrooy, and more new faces were expected to arrive to bolster Ferguson's last season in charge.

United collected the Premiership trophy against Derby, but surprisingly lost 1–0.

Teddy Sheringham picked up both the Football Writers' and PFA Player of the Year awards, and statistically United were the best team in virtually every category.

Amazingly, some critics and even some supporters claimed that 2000–01 was a disappointing season. Ferguson's side have obviously spoiled their supporters with all their recent success, and particularly the massive highs of the treble-winning season of 1999. Winning what the manager calls "the hardest league in the world" does not sate the ravenous appetite of the new breed of fans, who voted Eric Cantona the best player in Manchester United's history.

Perhaps they should remember the 26-year gap between league titles and celebrate the final season of arguably the greatest manager British football has ever seen who rocked the football world by announcing he will sever all ties with the club when his contract expires.

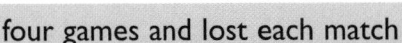

four games and lost each match

MANCHESTER UNITED

DATE	OPPONENT	SCORE	ATT.	BARTHEZ	BECKHAM	BERG	BROWN	BUTT	CHADWICK	COLE	DJORDJIC	FORTUNE	GIGGS	GORAM	GREENING	HEALY
20.08.00	Newcastle H	2–0	67,477	90	90	–	–	–	–	76¹	–	–	90	–	–	–
22.08.00	Ipswich H	1–1	22,007	90	90¹□	–	–	–	–	s27	–	–	90	–	–	–
26.08.00	West Ham A	2–2	25,998	90	90¹	s45	–	–	–	90¹	–	–	90	–	–	–
05.09.00	Bradford H	6–0	66,447	90	90¹	–	–	71	–	63¹	90²	–	–	–	90	–
09.09.00	Sunderland H	3–0	67,503	90	90	–	–	90□	–	79	–	–	90	–	–	–
16.09.00	Everton A	3–1	38,541	78	90	–	90	90¹	–	–	–	–	45¹	–	–	–
23.09.00	Chelsea H	3–3	67,568	–	90¹	–	s9	s13	–	81	–	–	90	–	–	–
01.10.00	Arsenal A	0–1	38,146	90	90□	–	–	–	–	90	–	–	85	–	–	–
14.10.00	Leicester A	3–0	22,132	90	–	–	90	90	–	–	–	90	s19	–	–	–
21.10.00	Leeds Utd H	3–0*	67,525	90	s59¹	–	s45	90	–	–	–	90	–	–	–	–
28.10.00	Southampton H	5–0	67,581	90	–	–	90	90	–	75²	–	–	90	–	–	–
04.11.00	Coventry A	2–1	21,079	90	90¹	–	90	–	–	90¹	–	–	90	–	–	–
11.11.00	Middlesbro H	2–1	67,576	90	90	–	45	90¹	s1	–	–	–	–	–	–	–
18.11.00	Man City A	1–0	34,429	90	90¹	–	90	90□	–	–	–	–	s14	–	–	–
25.11.00	Derby Co A	3–0	32,910	81	–	–	90	90¹□	74	–	s16	–	–	–	–	–
02.12.00	Tottenham H	2–0	67,583	90	90	–	90	74	–	–	–	–	s16	–	–	–
09.12.00	Charlton A	3–3	20,043	–	75	–	90□	90	59	–	–	–	90¹	–	s21	–
17.12.00	Liverpool H	0–1	67,533	90	90	–	90	71	s9□	–	–	–	90	–	s19	–
23.12.00	Ipswich H	2–0	67,597	–	83	–	90	–	–	–	90	60	–	–	s7	s30
26.12.00	Aston Villa A	1–0	40,889	90	90	–	90□	90□	–	–	–	–	90	–	–	–
30.12.00	Newcastle A	1–1	52,134	90	90¹	–	90□	89	s1	–	–	–	90□	–	–	–
01.01.01	West Ham H	3–1*	67,603	90	90	–	90□	s10	–	–	–	–	62	–	s28	–
13.01.01	Bradford A	3–0	20,551	90	90	–	s25	–	s25¹	s15	–	–	90¹	–	–	–
20.01.01	Aston Villa H	2–0	67,533	90	–	–	–	90□	s27	s27	–	–	90	–	63	–
31.01.01	Sunderland A	1–0	48,260	90	90	–	90	s13	–	56¹□	–	–	90	–	–	–
03.02.01	Everton H	1–0*	67,528	90	72	–	90	–	80	90	–	–	s45	–	–	–
10.02.01	Chelsea A	1–1	34,960	–	90	–	90	–	–	90¹□	–	–	90	–	–	–
25.02.01	Arsenal H	6–1	67,535	90	90	–	90	90	s15	–	–	–	–	–	–	–
03.03.01	Leeds Utd A	1–1	40,055	90□	90	–	90	45□	s45¹	–	–	–	–	–	–	–
17.03.01	Leicester H	2–0	67,516	–	–	–	–	68	s22	–	–	–	–	–	45□	–
31.03.01	Liverpool A	0–2	44,806	90	–	–	90	75	s19	–	–	–	90	–	–	–
10.04.01	Charlton H	2–1	67,505	90	–	–	90	76□	–	90¹	–	–	90	–	–	–
14.04.01	Coventry H	4–2	67,637	–	s21	–	90□	69	–	82	–	–	90¹	67	–	–
21.04.01	Man City H	1–1	67,535	90	90	–	69	s14	61	–	–	–	s29	–	–	–
28.04.01	Middlesbro A	2–0	34,417	–	90¹□	–	90	90	s5	s15	–	72	s18	–	–	–
05.05.01	Derby Co H	0–1	67,528	87	90	–	–	90	90	90	–	–	s26	–	–	–
13.05.01	Southampton A	1–2	15,246	–	–	–	90	–	90	–	–	90	90¹	58	–	–
19.05.01	Tottenham A	1–3	36,072	–	–	–	90	90□	–	90	s15	–	90	–	–	–

□ Yellow card, ▪ Red card, s Substitute, 90² Goals scored
*including own goal

For more information visit our website:

2000–01 PREMIERSHIP APPEARANCES

IRWIN	JOHNSEN	KEANE	MAY	G NEVILLE	P NEVILLE	RACHUBKA	SCHOLES	SHERINGHAM	SILVESTRE	SOLSKJAER	STAM	STEWART	VAN DER GOUW	WALLWORK	YORKE	TOTAL
–	63¹	90	–	90	90	–	90	76	–	s14	90	–	–	s27	s14	990
–	–	90	–	90□	76	–	90	s11	s14	63	90□	–	–	90	79□	990
–	–	90	–	90	90	–	90	90	90	–	45	–	–	–	–	990
–	65	–	–	90	s25	–	s19	90²	90	s27	–	–	–	90	–	990
s45	90	–	–	90	–	–	90²	90¹	90	s11	45	–	–	–	–	990
90	–	–	–	90	s16	–	74□	90	90	90¹	–	–	s12	–	s45	990
81	90	90□	–	90□	–	–	90¹	77¹□	90	s9	–	–	90	–	–	990
90□	90	90	–	90□	–	–	90	68	90	s5	–	–	–	–	s22	990
90	90	90	–	–	–	–	–	71²	90	90¹	–	–	–	–	90	990
–	45	31	–	90	90	–	90	–	90	90	–	–	–	–	90¹	990
90	–	–	–	59	90	–	90	75³	–	s15	–	–	–	s31	s15	990
90	–	90□	–	90	90	–	51	71	–	s39	–	–	–	–	s19	990
–	–	90	–	90	90	–	90	s50¹	90	40	–	–	–	s45	89	990
90	–	90	–	90	90	–	90	76	–	–	–	–	–	–	90	990
90	–	90	–	90	–	–	74	90¹	90	s16	–	–	s9	–	90¹	990
–	–	90	–	90□	90	–	90¹	90	90	s16¹	–	–	–	–	74□	990
–	–	69¹	–	90	90	–	s31	s15	90	90¹	–	–	90	–	–	990
80	–	90	–	90	–	–	90	–	90□	90	–	–	–	–	–	989
–	–	83	–	90	90	–	90	–	90	90²	–	–	–	s7	–	990
59	–	90	–	90	s45	–	90	–	45	90¹	–	–	–	s31	–	990
–	–	90	–	90	90	–	s19	–	62□	71	–	–	–	s28	90	990
–	–	62	–	90	90	–	80	–	90	90¹	–	–	–	s28	90¹	990
90	–	90	–	90	65	–	–	90¹	90	75	65	–	–	–	–	990
90	–	90	–	90¹	90	–	–	90¹	–	63	90	–	–	–	–	990
–	–	90	–	90	s4	–	77	67	86	s23	90	–	–	–	–	956
90	–	–	–	–	90	–	45	s10	90	–	90	–	–	s18	90	990
–	–	90	–	90	–	–	90□	–	90	90	–	–	90	–	–	990
–	–	75¹	–	90	–	–	90	s15¹	90	90¹	90	–	–	–	75³	990
90	–	–	–	90	90□	–	90□	69	–	90□	90	–	–	–	s21	990
90	–	90	–	90	80	90	90	90	s10¹	90	90	–	–	–	s45¹	990
71	–	90	–	90	90□	–	s15	71	s19	–	–	–	–	–	90	990
89	–	90	–	90	s1	–	90	s14	90	s14¹	–	–	–	–	76	990
–	–	90	–	90	–	–	90¹	–	90	s8	90	–	s23	–	90²	990
–	–	86□	–	90	90	–	76	90¹	s21	90	90	–	–	–	–	986
–	90	–	–	90¹□	–	–	90	–	75	90	85□	90	–	–	–	990
90	90	–	–	76□	–	–	90	s14	–	–	64	s3	90	–	–	990
90	90□	–	s18	–	90	–	–	–	–	–	–	90	s32	72	90	990
75□	90	–	90	–	90	–	90¹	90	90	–	–	–	90	–	–	990

THE MANAGER

SIR ALEX FERGUSON

Sir Alex Ferguson succeeded Ron Atkinson as manager of Manchester United in November 1986 and in his first full season guided United to a league runners-up position. This was nothing compared to the success he was to enjoy at Old Trafford later on as he built a squad capable of beating the best.

He cut his managerial teeth in Scotland and accepted the manager's job at Aberdeen in 1978. At Pittodrie he broke the dominance of the Old Firm winning three league titles and in 1983 he led Aberdeen to victory over Real Madrid in the European Cup Winners' Cup.

In 1990, there were calls from some Manchester United fans for him to be sacked, but he won the FA Cup that year – and that started an avalanche of trophies, including seven titles in nine years and the Champions League.

Ferguson plans to retire as manager of United after the 2001–02 season, but will be looking for one last hurrah before he bows out. It will be a difficult job to replace him although the foundations he has laid should stand his successor in good stead for many years.

LEAGUE POSITION

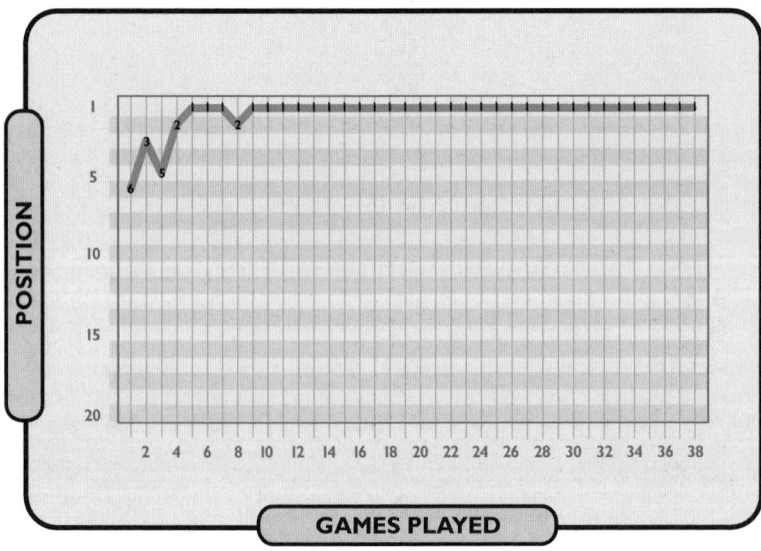

POSITION

GAMES PLAYED

5 David Beckham scored the most

THE GOALS

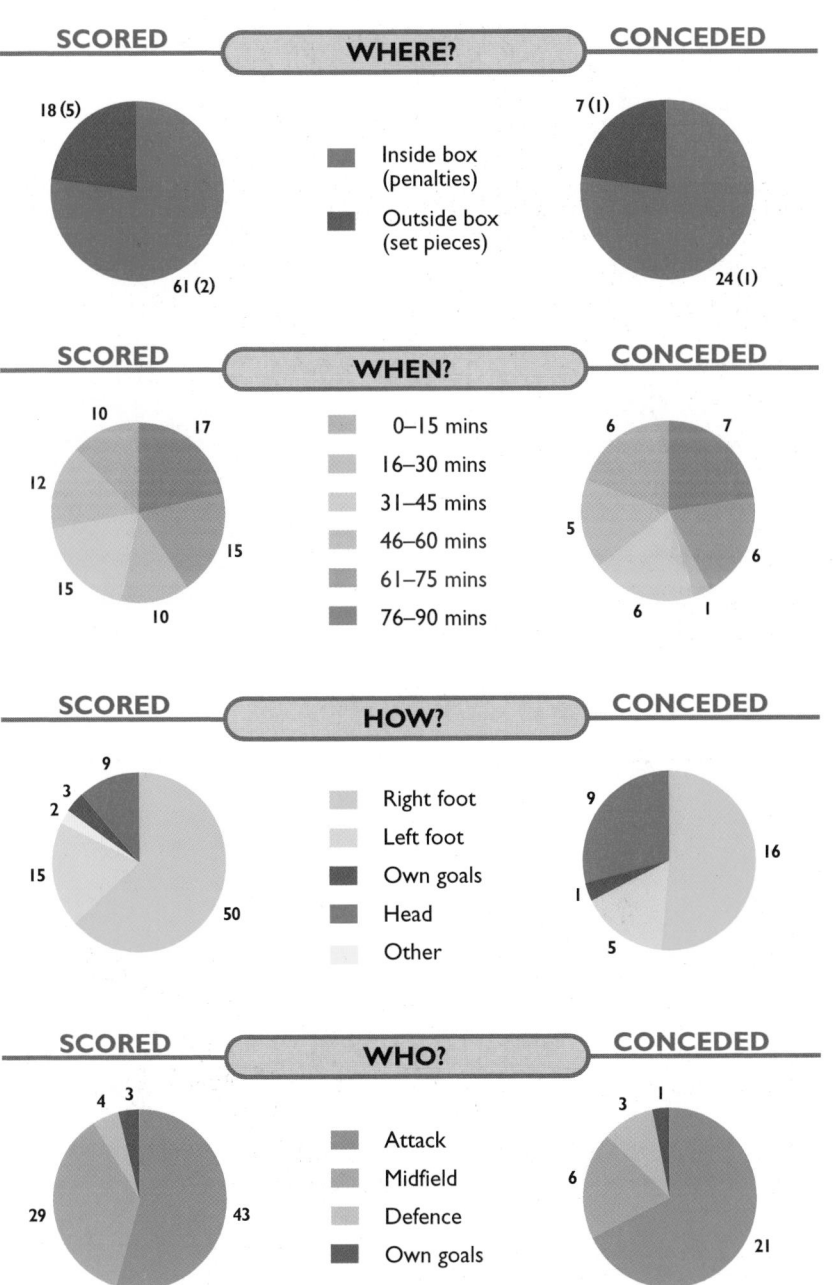

WHERE?

SCORED | CONCEDED

18 (5) / 61 (2)

7 (1) / 24 (1)

- Inside box (penalties)
- Outside box (set pieces)

WHEN?

SCORED: 10, 17, 12, 15, 15, 10

CONCEDED: 6, 7, 5, 6, 6, 1

- 0–15 mins
- 16–30 mins
- 31–45 mins
- 46–60 mins
- 61–75 mins
- 76–90 mins

HOW?

SCORED: 9, 3, 2, 15, 50

CONCEDED: 9, 16, 1, 5

- Right foot
- Left foot
- Own goals
- Head
- Other

WHO?

SCORED: 4, 3, 29, 43

CONCEDED: 3, 1, 6, 21

- Attack
- Midfield
- Defence
- Own goals

set-piece goals in 2000–01

MANCHESTER UNITED

	BECKHAM	BERG	BROWN	BUTT	CHADWICK	COLE	DJORDJIC	FORTUNE	GIGGS	GREENING	HEALY	IRWIN	JOHNSE
APPEARANCES													
Start	29	0	25	24	6	15	0	6	24	3	0	20	11
Sub	2	1	3	4	10	4	1	1	7	4	1	1	0
Minutes on pitch	2650	45	2263	2038	623	1316	15	538	2219	273	30	1760	893
GOAL ATTEMPTS													
Goals	9	0	0	3	2	9	0	2	5	0	0	0	1
Shots on target	32	0	0	11	4	17	0	5	25	0	0	2	2
Shots off target	26	0	5	24	9	26	0	6	20	1	1	2	2
Shooting accuracy	55%	0%	0%	31%	31%	40%	0%	45%	56%	0%	0%	50%	50%
PASSING													
Goal assists	12	0	0	2	0	3	0	0	8	1	0	2	0
Long passes	718	7	297	332	38	53	3	39	179	41	3	260	77
Short passes	1363	8	734	962	226	341	10	186	662	133	10	820	274
PASS COMPLETION													
Own half %	89%	67%	87%	89%	87%	85%	100%	88%	76%	85%	100%	90%	94%
Opposition half %	73%	33%	71%	76%	68%	68%	70%	75%	63%	85%	89%	73%	78%
CROSSING													
Total crosses	353	0	3	17	28	14	1	25	165	16	0	77	0
Cross completion %	30%	0%	0%	35%	14%	21%	0%	28%	27%	19%	0%	31%	0%
DRIBBLING													
Dribbles & runs	104	1	30	50	97	42	3	33	234	21	2	36	12
Dribble completion %	86%	100%	93%	82%	62%	69%	67%	61%	66%	62%	50%	86%	92%
DEFENDING													
Tackles made	31	2	79	107	20	8	0	14	54	6	0	40	13
Tackles won %	68%	100%	76%	75%	60%	50%	0%	86%	76%	100%	0%	78%	69%
Blocks	8	0	20	2	1	0	0	0	3	2	0	14	4
Clearances	19	1	216	26	0	0	0	1	4	2	0	73	58
Interceptions	5	2	9	6	1	0	0	2	8	0	0	3	3
DISCIPLINE													
Fouls	31	2	40	58	2	19	1	6	20	5	0	14	24
Offside	8	0	0	3	0	28	0	1	10	0	0	1	1
Yellow cards	3	0	5	8	0	1	0	0	1	1	0	2	1
Red cards	0	0	0	0	1	1	0	0	0	0	0	0	0

GOALKEEPER NAME	START/ (SUB)	TIME ON PITCH	GOALS CONCEDED	MINS/GOALS CONCEDED	SAVES MADE	SAVES/ SHOTS
BARTHEZ	30(0)	2676	17	157	79	82%
GORAM	2(0)	125	4	31	2	33%
RACHUBKA	1(0)	90	0	0	0	0%
VAN DER GOUW	5(5)	529	10	53	13	57%

For more information visit our website:

PLAYERS' STATISTICS

	KEANE	MAY	NEVILLE G	NEVILLE P	SCHOLES	SHERINGHAM	SILVESTRE	SOLSKJAER	STAM	STEWART	WALLWORK	YORKE	TOTAL	RANK
	28	1	32	24	28	23	25	19	15	3	4	15		
	0	1	0	5	4	6	5	12	0	0	8	7		
	2386	108	2849	2188	2451	2006	2251	1754	1235	239	557	1474		
	2	0	1	1	6	15	1	10	0	0	0	9	79*	1st
	15	0	5	5	21	28	1	42	1	1	0	29	246	2nd
	32	1	6	3	35	28	13	27	2	3	1	24	298	1st
	32%	0%	45%	63%	38%	50%	7%	61%	33%	25%	0%	55%	45%	9th
	7	0	1	0	5	5	2	4	0	0	0	4	56	1st
	561	25	542	310	383	167	403	62	183	52	89	79	5511	1st
	1623	33	1149	1055	1069	778	887	506	423	95	188	591	14297	1st
	93%	86%	89%	87%	90%	88%	81%	86%	93%	81%	89%	89%	88%	1st
	82%	61%	69%	76%	79%	70%	66%	73%	78%	69%	71%	78%	72%	1st
	54	0	44	86	24	26	73	46	0	1	2	14	1069	3rd
	19%	0%	36%	29%	21%	15%	19%	15%	0%	0%	0%	36%	27%	11th
	109	0	40	52	44	18	123	63	16	8	10	71	1223	2nd
	80%	0%	93%	81%	89%	89%	81%	57%	100%	38%	90%	63%	75%	1st
	77	4	50	57	78	27	83	21	38	13	15	16	856	20th
	75%	75%	68%	79%	73%	70%	86%	76%	74%	69%	73%	69%	75%	3rd
	6	2	17	18	12	5	13	2	9	2	3	1	145	19th
	32	8	194	63	12	8	118	1	71	0	25	2	1049	20th
	8	1	15	3	10	2	10	1	18	2	2	1	112	10th
	26	3	23	26	53	15	27	25	10	8	1	20	461	20th
	5	0	1	7	4	16	0	21	0	0	0	35	141	9th
	2	0	4	4	3	1	2	1	1	1	0	2	44	19th
	1	0	0	0	0	0	0	0	0	0	0	0	3	=7th

*Including three own goals

CROSSES CAUGHT	CROSSES PUNCHED	CROSSES DROPPED	CATCH SUCCESS	THROWS/ SHORT KICKS	% COMPLETION	LONG KICKS	% COMPLETION
63	15	6	91%	116	95%	479	58%
0	1	0	0%	6	83%	22	50%
1	0	1	50%	4	100%	9	89%
19	5	0	100%	34	91%	104	60%

PLAYER OF THE SEASON

PLAYER	INDEX SCORE
ROY KEANE	1,377
David Beckham	1,347
Paul Scholes	1,088
Teddy Sheringham	1,057
Fabien Barthez	990
Nicky Butt	980
Denis Irwin	968
Gary Neville	948
Ryan Giggs	939
Mikael Silvestre	938

Runaway champions Manchester United boasted no fewer than four of the players ranked in the top eight by Opta in 2000–01, including overall player of the season Roy Keane.

Rated United's second-best player in 1998–99 and 1999–2000, Keane finally went one better, averaging 1,377 points – the highest-ever Opta Index score over a season.

For the third consecutive season United's skipper completed more passes than any other top-flight player, with an astonishing 1,893 finding a colleague – equating to 87% of all attempts. His efforts directly led to seven goals for team-mates and two for himself in the league, with his strong tackling wresting possession from opponents on 58 occasions.

England captain David Beckham continued to exert his authority on the Premiership, if not in Europe. Beckham's missiles from the right flank produced 12 goals for colleagues – the most assists by any Premiership player. He also notched an impressive nine strikes, with five direct from free-kicks, as he averaged 1,347 Opta points.

Fellow-England international Paul Scholes made the top three for the second season running with six goals from 56 attempts, five assists and in excess of 1,200 completed passes.

A resurgent Teddy Sheringham was United's top striker on Opta's system in his last season at Old Trafford. The PFA and Football Writers' Player of the Year notched the majority of his 15 league goals before December, with 27% of strikes overall finding the net, while his intelligent link-up play created five goals for team-mates. Fellow-forwards Dwight Yorke and Ole Gunnar Solskjaer ranked highly, but did not meet the time requirements to qualify for the Index.

Fabien Barthez, meanwhile, looked an ideal replacement for Peter Schmeichel. The flamboyant Frenchman saved an unrivalled 82% of shots, kept 14 clean sheets and conceded just 17 league goals all season, to finish as Opta's top 'keeper for 2000–01.

87% Roy Keane was the most

FIVE OF THE BEST

United made it three in a row with a runaway championship victory in 2000–01. Sir Alex Ferguson's men fell short in Europe, but on the home front they were simply in a class of their own. Eventually triumphing by 10 points, United's victory was in truth even more comfortable than that margin suggests.

TOP GOALSCORERS

	GOALS	GOALS/SHOTS
TEDDY SHERINGHAM	15	27%
Ole Solskjaer	10	14%
Andy Cole	9	21%
Dwight Yorke	9	17%
David Beckham	9	16%

Double Player of the Year Teddy Sheringham signed off at Manchester United in style, scoring 15 Premiership goals for the champions and recording a superb goals-to-shots-ratio of 27%. Ole Gunnar Solskjaer was United's second-most effective striker, scoring 10 goals. Andy Cole and Dwight Yorke both had disappointing seasons by their own high standards, but still netted nine goals apiece. David Beckham was United's leading goalscorer in midfield, equalling Cole and Yorke's final tally.

Opta Player of the Season Roy Keane made more passes than any other Premiership player, recording a superb 87% pass completion rate in the process. But Keane was not the only United player to feature in Opta's list of the Premiership's pass masters. United saw more of the ball than any other team in 2000–01. Not only did the champions finish the season with more passes than anyone else, but six of their players made more than 1,000 successful passes.

TOP PASSERS

	SUCC PASSES	COMPLETION
ROY KEANE	1,893	87%
David Beckham	1,605	77%
Gary Neville	1,373	81%
Paul Scholes	1,202	83%
Philip Neville	1,098	80%

TOP TACKLERS

	WON	SUCCESS
NICKY BUTT	80	75%
Mikael Silvestre	71	86%
Wes Brown	60	76%
Roy Keane	58	75%
Paul Scholes	57	73%

United's midfield quartet of Beckham, Keane, Scholes and Giggs has rightly been hailed as the best in Britain. But the contribution of Nicky Butt to United's success should not be underestimated. Butt enjoyed his best season in a United shirt to date, finishing top of United's tackling chart in the process. Mikael Silvestre and Wes Brown both won plenty of ball at the back, while Roy Keane and Paul Scholes continued to make a high number of successful challenges in midfield.

Although they picked up three red cards, United finished 2000–01 with one of the best disciplinary records in the Premiership. Nicky Butt was the Red Devils' worst offender – hardly surprising given the number of tackles that he attempted. Roy Keane was in the headlines for his disciplinary record after high-profile dismissals against Chelsea in the Charity Shield and Manchester City in the Premiership, but in general the United skipper kept himself out of trouble, committing just 26 fouls all season.

DISCIPLINE

	POINTS	FOULS & CARDS
NICKY BUTT	82	58F, 8Y, 0R
Paul Scholes	62	53F, 3Y, 0R
Wes Brown	55	40F, 5Y, 0R
David Beckham	40	31F, 3Y, 0R
Roy Keane	38	26F, 2Y, 1R

ACTION	BARTHEZ	BECKHAM	BROWN	BUTT	CHADWICK	KEANE	G NEVILLE	SCHOLES	SHERINGHAM	SILVESTRE	SOLSKJAER	STAM	YORKE	TOTAL	ARSENAL
Time on pitch	90	90	90	90	15	75	90	90	15	90	90	90	75	990	990
GOALS															
Goal	–	–	–	–	–	–	–	–	–	–	–	–	3	6	–
Shot on target (incl goals)	–	1	–	–	–	–	–	–	–	–	–	–	4	9	–
Shot off target	–	–	–	–	–	–	–	–	–	–	–	–	6	6	4
Blocked shot	–	–	–	–	–	–	–	–	–	–	–	–	2	2	4
Own goal	–	–	–	–	–	–	–	–	–	–	–	–	0	0	0
PASSES															
Pass to own player	10	50	28	47	7	56	41	47	5	44	17	50	23	425	362
Pass to opposition	12	10	5	17	2	14	13	16	1	27	5	4	9	135	118
Cross to own player	–	2	–	–	1	–	–	2	–	–	–	–	1	8	2
Cross to opposition player	–	3	–	–	–	–	–	–	–	1	2	–	–	8	12
Goal assist	–	1	–	–	–	–	–	–	–	–	–	–	1	6	–
Pass completion %	45%	80%	85%	74%	80%	79%	76%	75%	83%	61%	72%	93%	74%	75%	74%
TACKLES & CLEARANCES															
Tackle	–	4	2	9	2	2	2	3	–	3	4	4	3	30	21
Clearances, blocks and interceptions	6	1	15	2	–	3	6	1	1	10	8	8	–	53	47
DRIBBLES & RUNS															
Dribbles ball retained	–	2	1	2	3	2	–	2	4	–	1	–	3	20	14
Dribbles ball lost	–	1	–	–	2	2	–	–	–	–	–	–	1	8	8
Dribble success %	0%	67%	100%	100%	60%	50%	0%	100%	0%	80%	0%	100%	75%	71%	64%
DISCIPLINE															
Fouls	–	2	2	6	1	–	2	3	–	4	1	–	1	18	17
Penalty conceded	–	–	–	–	–	–	–	–	–	–	–	–	–	0	0
Free kick – offside	–	–	–	–	–	–	–	–	–	–	–	–	3	5	8
Yellow cards	–	–	–	–	–	–	–	–	–	–	–	–	–	0	0
Red cards	–	–	–	–	–	–	–	–	–	–	–	–	–	0	0
GOALKEEPERS															
Distribution to own player	10	–	–	–	–	–	–	–	–	–	–	–	–	10	8
Distribution to opposition player	6	–	–	–	–	–	–	–	–	–	–	–	–	6	12
Goalkeeper distribution %	63%	–	–	–	–	–	–	–	–	–	–	–	–	63%	40%
Save	1	–	–	–	–	–	–	–	–	–	–	–	–	0	3
Ball caught	–	–	–	–	–	–	–	–	–	–	–	–	–	1	2
Ball dropped	–	–	–	–	–	–	–	–	–	–	–	–	–	0	0
Goal conceded	1	–	–	–	–	–	–	–	–	–	–	–	–	1	6

71.8% Manchester United were the most

The Sky cameras were in place at Old Trafford anticipating a tight contest between the existing champions and the main challengers to their crown. However, what they and the viewers witnessed was an astonishingly one-sided affair as the Red Devils swept Arsenal aside.

25 February 2001
6 - 1
MANCHESTER UNITED
ARSENAL

Manchester United tore a makeshift Gunners defence apart with a devastating first-half performance. Frenchman Gilles Grimandi partnered Latvian Igors Stepanovs in the centre while the full-backs, Englishman Ashley Cole and Ukrainian Oleg Luzhny, completed a backline who were clearly not speaking the same language.

The hosts, and Dwight Yorke in particular, were at their clinical best and had scored five times from just seven shots on target before the break as they scythed through the disorganised Arsenal defence seemingly at will. The Trinidad and Tobago star single-handedly accounted for five efforts and had beaten David Seaman three times within 22 minutes of the kick-off.

And by the time Roy Keane had added United's fourth goal, with just 25 minutes on the clock, the match was effectively over as a contest.

But only 10 minutes before that, Arsenal had looked far from out of it. Following good work down the right by Sylvain Wiltord and Robert Pires, Thierry Henry provided the perfect finish to a well-crafted move, cancelling out Yorke's simple opener.

However, that was the Gunners' only shot on target of the entire match and it was the only time during the 2000–01 season that they had been restricted to a solitary accurate strike on goal by any Premiership side.

Yorke made it 2–1 just two minutes later when he slotted home a pass from skipper

Keane and completed his hat-trick in the 22nd minute, getting on the end of a pinpoint David Beckham through-ball before beating Seaman.

The United frontrunner capped a man-of-the-match performance by picking out Keane with a ball from the left which the Irishman slotted deftly into the net.

By now, United's midfield had a firm grip on the game. The quartet of Nicky Butt, Keane, Beckham and Scholes completed exactly 200 passes between them and finished the first half with a goal assist apiece. Butt's came in the 37th minute when his low cross found Ole Gunnar Solskjaer, who swept home the fifth to stun a shell-shocked Gunners defence.

Arsenal's resistance was broken, and after such a highly-charged opening 45 minutes the second half was always going to be anti-climactic.

England captain Beckham almost caught out Seaman with an effort just after the hour mark and then found Jaap Stam with a free-kick which the Dutchman headed into the side netting.

Fredrik Ljungberg almost grabbed a consolation goal for the visitors with a chip, before Teddy Sheringham rounded off a spectacular afternoon's work for the champions with United's sixth goal. The double Player of the Year scored following good work from Solskjaer after the Norwegian had hit the woodwork with his third effort of an action-packed game.

MIDDLESBROUGH

ADDRESS

BT Cellnet Riverside Stadium,
Middlesbrough TS3 6RS

CONTACT NUMBERS

Telephone: 01642 877 700
Fax: 01642 877 840
Ticket Office: 01642 877 745
Club Call: 09068 121 181
Stadium Store: 01642 877 720
e-mail: user@mfc.co.uk
Website: www.mfc.co.uk

KEY PERSONNEL

Chairman: Steve Gibson
Chief Executive: Keith Lamb
Club Secretary: Karen Nelson
Manager: Bryan Robson

SPONSORS

BT Cellnet

FANZINES

Fly Me To The Moon

COLOURS

Home: Red shirts, red shorts and red
stockings, all with white and black trim
Away: Black shirts with red and white
stripe, black shorts and black stockings

NICKNAME

Boro

HONOURS

Division One Champions: 1994–95
Division Two Champions:
1926–27, 1928–29, 1973–74
Anglo-Scottish Cup: 1976

RECORD GOALSCORER

George Camsell –
326 league goals, 1925–39

BIGGEST WIN

9–0 v Brighton & Hove Albion –
Division Two, 23 August 1958

BIGGEST DEFEAT

0–9 v Blackburn Rovers – Division Two,
6 November 1954

SEASON REVIEW

Following a mid-table finish in the 1999–2000 campaign, The Riverside was a hive of transfer activity in the summer as chairman Steve Gibson once again gave manager Bryan Robson free rein with his chequebook in order to bring footballing success to Teesside. As in previous summers, Robson made full use of the cash on offer in an attempt to get his team into the top six.

All did not go to plan, though – and the Boro faithful experienced a nervous season watching their side cling to Premiership survival.

There appears to be no such thing as a quiet summer in Middlesbrough and the 2000-01 close season was no different, with plenty of new arrivals. Paul Okon, Christian Karembeu, Joseph-Desiré Job, Mark Crossley and Noel Whelan all arrived, but most attention – possibly with the exception of Karembeu's supermodel wife – was focussed on the signing of Croatian hitman Alen Boksic, who was rumoured to be earning a salary of around £60,000 per week. Boksic quickly endeared himself to the Boro supporters by stating his intention to win a trophy while at the club.

Notable departures from The Riverside included the much-maligned Paul Gascoigne, who transported himself on to the Everton wage bill, and Brazilian Juninho, whose loan period ended with the previous campaign. There was also much talk of German Christian Ziege – the 1999–2000 Supporters' Player of the Year – moving to Liverpool. Naturally Boro were determined not to lose one of their most influential players from the previous campaign and attempted to stand in the way of Ziege's move.

But the German made it clear that he wanted to swap the Tees for the Mersey and even threatened to sue the north-east club if they prevented his transfer taking place. Eventually the deal went through for £5.5 million, but Boro fans could not resist a wry smile as Ziege struggled to hold down a first-team place at his new club.

Amid this background of strife, Middlesbrough got off to the best possible start on the pitch with a 3–1 win at Coventry on the opening day. New signings Alen Boksic and Joseph-Desiré Job were both on target. Boro even led the Premiership – albeit temporarily – after the second game of the season, but such good times were soon a distant memory as results began to go against them.

A three-goal lead against Derby was thrown away and, following a home defeat by Everton, the murmurings of discontent with manager Robson – which had plagued the club in the previous season – began to surface once again. Robson, however, stood firm and stated his aim of getting Middlesbrough into Europe. Injury problems were mounting, with Boksic, Job and Schwarzer struggling and Robson was forced to bring in former team-mate Gary Walsh on loan from Bradford. Further transfer talk focused on Aston Villa centre-back Ugo Ehiogu, with Boro rumoured to be interested in the unsettled star.

Despite the unrest at The Riverside, Robson's name was one of those bandied around in connection with the England job following Kevin Keegan's shock resignation, but his popularity on Teesside slipped to an all-time low following a 3–1 home defeat to north-east rivals Newcastle in mid-October. Robson finally got his man when Villa agreed an £8 million fee for Ehiogu, but such were

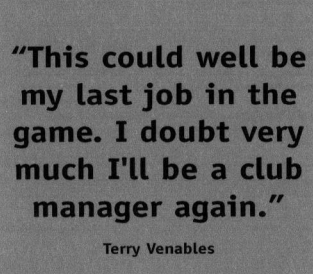

> **"This could well be my last job in the game. I doubt very much I'll be a club manager again."**
>
> **Terry Venables**

SEASON REVIEW

Boro's fortunes at the time that the defender lasted just five minutes into his debut at Charlton before going off injured.

Defeat in the Worthington Cup by first division Wimbledon was sandwiched between a run of six consecutive league defeats and Boro, far from chasing a place in Europe, slipped towards the Premiership's relegation zone. Following a 3–0 home defeat at the hands of Leicester, the players and management were called in for an emergency meeting and there was a genuine belief that Bryan Robson could be on his way out of an ailing Middlesbrough. Initially Hibernian boss Alex McLeish was linked with the position, but as the days went on, the name of Terry Venables was being mentioned with increasing frequency.

With all this speculation in the background, it was hard for the team to concentrate on the football, but there was

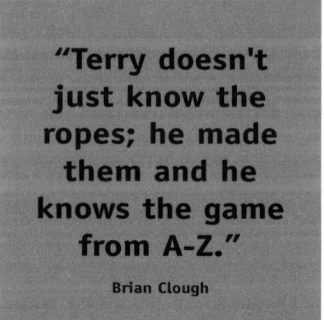

"Terry doesn't just know the ropes; he made them and he knows the game from A-Z."

Brian Clough

relief all round when a last-minute Paul Ince strike rescued a point in a relegation head-to-head with Bradford. In early December it was eventually announced that Terry Venables would be coming to The Riverside to work with Bryan Robson, although it was stressed that Robson was in no way being asked to step down as manager and Venables would be there in the role of "head coach". However, it was noticeable from the moment he walked through the door that it was the former England boss who appeared to be in charge.

Venables watched from the stands as a now bottom-of-the-table Boro went down 1–0 to rivals Sunderland. But when he took charge for the home game against Chelsea, a turnabout in Boro's fortunes was about to take place.

The team became more organised, their defence became meaner and they embarked on a 10-game unbeaten run – a sequence of results which was crucial in maintaining their Premiership status. This included notable victories over Chelsea and Liverpool and a 4–0 thumping of Derby County at The Riverside.

The El Tel revolution could not quite transfer itself to the FA Cup as once again Wimbledon were the scourge of Middlesbrough, this time winning 3–1 in a fourth-round replay. Ehiogu was red-carded for a second time in the cup exit and his consequent four-match ban left him missing crucial survival games. There was better news for the former Villa man, though, when he earned his second England cap against Spain and even managed to get himself on the scoresheet.

With cup interest over, the season was all about survival and Dean Windass arrived on Teesside from Bradford to join in the fight. Despite their efforts, Boro just could not pull themselves too far away from the drop zone, but vital 3–0 away wins at both Arsenal and Leicester left them looking one of the stronger candidates to survive.

There were just 12 days of the season left when Ipswich consigned Manchester City to relegation and the whole of Teesside breathed a huge sigh of relief. Despite big-money signings and hopes of Europe, Boro were forced into a season-long relegation battle – a situation they would have hoped to have left way behind them.

With the departures of Venables and Robson at the end of the season, there is a great deal of work to be done as Steve Gibson tries to ensure that sooner or later he can see some sort of return on his investment.

MIDDLESBROUGH

DATE	OPPONENT	SCORE	ATT.	BERESFORD	BOKSIC	CAMPBELL	COOPER	CROSSLEY	DEANE	EHIOGU	FESTA	FLEMING	GAVIN	GORDON	HUDSON	INCE
19.08.00	Coventry A	3–1	20,624	–	76^2□	–	90□	–	90	–	–	90	s10	–	–	90□
22.08.00	Tottenham H	1–1	31,254	–	–	s8	–	–	90	–	–	90	–	–	–	–
26.08.00	Leeds Utd H	1–2	31,626	–	–	–	90□	–	90	–	–	90	–	–	–	90□
06.09.00	Derby Co A	3–3	24,290	–	60^1	–	–	–	90^1	–	90□	90	s32	–	–	90
09.09.00	Everton H	1–2*	30,885	–	90	–	–	–	s14	–	90	90□	s65	90	–	76
17.09.00	Man City A	1–1	32,053	–	–	84	90□	–	90	–	90^1	90	90□	–	–	90□
23.09.00	Aston Villa H	1–1*	27,556	–	90□	–	90	–	–	–	–	90□	–	–	–	90
30.09.00	Southampton A	3–1	14,903	–	90^2	–	90	s8	–	–	90^1	90	–	–	–	90
16.10.00	Newcastle H	1–3	31,436	–	90	–	90□	90	$s15^1$	–	90	45	–	90	–	90
21.10.00	Charlton A	0–1	20,043	–	–	90	90	90	90	5	s85□	–	–	90	–	90□
28.10.00	Ipswich A	1–2	21,771	–	–	–	79	90	90	76	–	90	90	–	–	90
04.11.00	Arsenal H	0–1	29,541	s67	–	73	90□	22□	90	–	s17	90	–	–	–	–
11.11.00	Man Utd A	1–2	67,576	–	s26	64	45	–	90	–	–	90	–	s45	–	–
18.11.00	Leicester H	3–0	27,965	–	90	–	–	–	90	90	s14	90□	–	90	–	–
25.11.00	Bradford H	2–2	28,526	–	45	–	90	–	s45	90^1	90□	90	–	–	–	90^1
02.12.00	West Ham A	0–1	25,459	–	–	–	63	–	76	87□	90	90□	–	–	–	90□
09.12.00	Sunderland A	0–1	47,742	–	–	–	90□	–	90	90	–	90	–	–	–	90
16.12.00	Chelsea H	1–0	29,442	–	–	–	90	–	90	–	90	–	–	$s23^1$	–	90
23.12.00	Tottenham A	0–0	35,638	–	76	–	90	–	s14□	90	–	s4	–	s1	–	90
26.12.00	Liverpool H	1–0	34,696	–	75	–	90□	–	s15	90	90	90	–	–	s21	90
30.12.00	Coventry H	1–1	30,499	–	$s45^1$	–	45□	–	s23	90	90	90	–	–	–	90
01.01.01	Leeds Utd A	1–1	39,251	–	89^1	–	–	–	s1	90	90	90	–	90□	–	–
13.01.01	Derby Co H	4–0	29,041	–	82^2	–	–	–	s8	90^1	90	90	–	s27	–	90
20.01.01	Liverpool A	0–0	43,042	–	90	–	s67□	–	–	90	23	90	–	90	–	90
31.01.01	Everton A	2–2	34,244	–	90	–	90^1□	–	–	90□	s32	90	–	58□	–	90□
03.02.01	Man City H	1–1	31,794	–	89	s1	90^1	–	–	90	–	90	–	–	–	90
10.02.01	Aston Villa A	1–1	28,912	–	66	–	90	–	s24	90^1	90	90	–	s17	–	90
24.02.01	Southampton H	0–1	28,725	–	90	–	–	–	–	90	90	45	s45	s45	–	90□
03.03.01	Charlton H	0–0	28,177	–	90	–	–	–	–	90	90	90	76	s24	–	–
17.03.01	Newcastle A	2–1	51,751	–	88^2	–	90	–	–	–	90	90	–	–	–	90□
31.03.01	Chelsea A	1–2	34,933	–	90	–	6	–	–	–	90	–	90	–	–	–
09.04.01	Sunderland H	0–0	31,284	–	90□	–	–	–	s19□	–	19	71	90□	s71	–	–
14.04.01	Arsenal A	3–0**	37,879	–	89	–	–	–	–	90	–	90	90	–	–	90
16.04.01	Ipswich H	1–2	34,294	–	90	–	–	–	–	90	–	90□	90	–	–	90
21.04.01	Leicester A	3–0	18,162	–	80^1	–	90	–	–	90	–	90	90	–	–	90^1
28.04.01	Man Utd H	0–2	34,417	–	90	–	85	–	–	90	–	90□	s5	–	–	90
05.05.01	Bradford A	1–1	20,921	–	23	–	90	–	s67	90	–	73	–	–	–	90
19.05.01	West Ham H	2–1	33,057	–	–	–	90	–	s52	90	–	90	–	s1	–	90

□ Yellow card, ▪ Red card, s Substitute, 90^2 Goals scored
*including own goal, ** including two own goals

For more information visit our website:

2000–01 PREMIERSHIP APPEARANCES

JOB	KAREMBEU	MARINELLI	MUSTOE	O'NEILL	OKON	PALLISTER	RICARD	SCHWARZER	STAMP	SUMMERBELL	VICKERS	WALSH	WHELAN	WINDASS	TOTAL
83[1]	90	–	–	90	s7	80	–	90	–	–	90	–	s14	–	990
86	90	–	–	90	90□	90	82	90	–	90[1]□	90	–	s4	–	990
s52	90	–	–	38	75	90	63	90	s15[1]	–	90	–	s27	–	990
71[1]	90	–	–	–	–	58	–	90	90	s19□	90	–	s30	–	990
76	90	–	–	–	–	–	s14	90	90□	–	25	–	90□	–	990
45	–	–	90	90□	–	–	s45□	–	–	–	–	90	s6	–	990
66	–	s13	90	90	–	–	–	–	77□	90	–	90	s24	–	990
–	76□	–	90	90□	–	–	87	–	–	s14	90	82	s3	–	990
–	90□	s32	75	–	–	90	90	–	s13	–	–	–	–	–	990
–	85	s12	–	–	–	90	78	–	–	–	–	–	s5	–	990
s11	90	s14	–	–	–	–	33	–	–	90□	90□	–	s57[1]	–	990
–	–	–	–	–	–	90	23	–	90	90□	90	–	90	–	922
–	90[1]	s12	–	–	–	90	78	90	90	90	90	–	–	–	990
67	76	s23□	s23	–	–	–	–	90	67□	–	90	–	90	–	990
s18	–	68□	90	–	–	–	–	90	90	–	–	–	72	–	968
s14	s27	–	90□	–	–	–	–	90	90	–	90	–	90	–	987
–	s76	–	90	90□	–	90□	90	14	–	90	–	–	–	–	990
–	90	–	90	90	67	–	–	90	–	–	90	–	90	–	990
–	90	–	90	89□	90□	–	–	90	–	–	90	–	86	–	990
–	69[1]	–	–	90	90	–	–	90	–	–	–	–	90□	–	990
–	45	–	–	90	90	–	90	90	–	–	s45	–	67	–	990
–	66	–	90	–	90□	–	81□	90	s24	–	90	–	s9	–	990
–	90	–	s15	63	75	–	90[1]	90	–	–	90	–	–	–	990
–	63	–	s27	–	63□	–	–	90	s27	–	90	–	90	–	990
–	69	–	s21	–	90	–	56[1]	90□	–	–	90□	–	s34	–	990
–	90	–	s1	85□	89	–	79	90	–	–	90	–	s11	–	985
–	45	–	–	73	90	–	90	90	s45□	–	–	–	–	–	990
–	90	s20	90	–	90	–	70	90	–	–	45	–	–	–	990
–	90	–	s14	–	66	–	66□	90	–	–	90	–	s24	–	990
–	65	–	s25	–	90	–	s2	90	45□	–	90	–	90□	–	945
–	69	s21	90□	s84	90	–	s21	90	–	–	90	–	90	69[1]	990
–	84□	–	90	–	90	–	s45	90	–	–	90	–	45	90□	984
–	90	–	s1	–	90□	–	79[1]	90	s11	–	90	–	–	90	990
–	58	s13	s32	–	90	–	90	90	s32	–	58	–	–	77[1]	990
–	74	–	s16	–	90	–	70[1]	90	s20	–	–	s10	90□	–	990
–	–	s22	s5	–	90□	–	85	90	68	–	90	–	–	90	990
–	90[1]□	s17	s5	–	90	–	85□	90	–	–	90	–	–	90	990
90[1]	89[1]	38	–	–	90	–	–	90	–	–	90	–	–	90	990

THE MANAGER

BRYAN ROBSON

Bryan Robson took his first managerial post with Middlesbrough in 1994, beginning as player-manager before hanging up his boots in January 1998. He last played for Boro at Arsenal on New Year's Day 1997, becoming the oldest ever player to appear for the first team.

Robson took the club to Wembley three times, first in the League Cup and FA Cup finals in 1997 and in the League Cup again in 1998. They all ended in defeat and Boro were also relegated in 1997 before bouncing back the following season.

He began his playing career with West Brom before a move to Manchester United in 1981. As one of the game's greatest competitors throughout the 1980s, Robson won 90 England caps, 65 as captain.

Boro chairman Steve Gibson brought in the help of Terry Venables in December 2000 after a poor start to the season had left the side struggling in the relegation zone and without a win at The Riverside in the first four months.

Together Robson and Venables turned it around and avoided the drop, but Robson decided to end his seven-year affiliation with the club at the end of the campaign and Boro went in search of a new boss.

LEAGUE POSITION

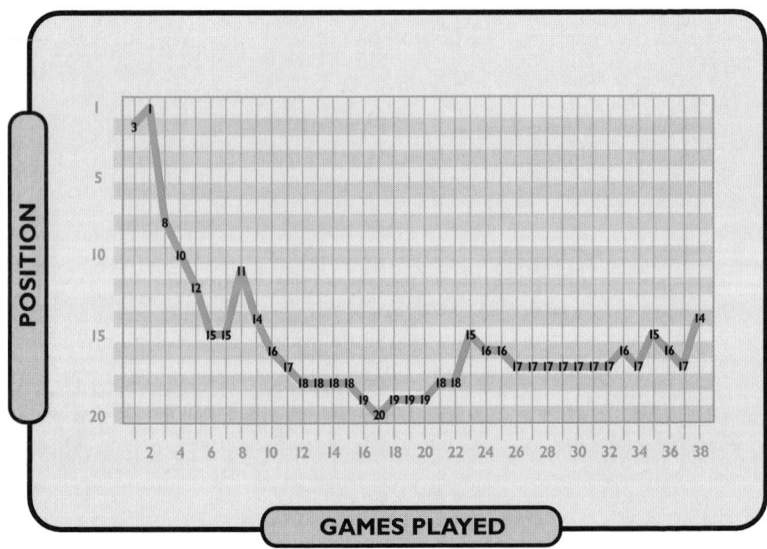

POSITION

GAMES PLAYED

4 Boro benefited from more own goals

THE GOALS

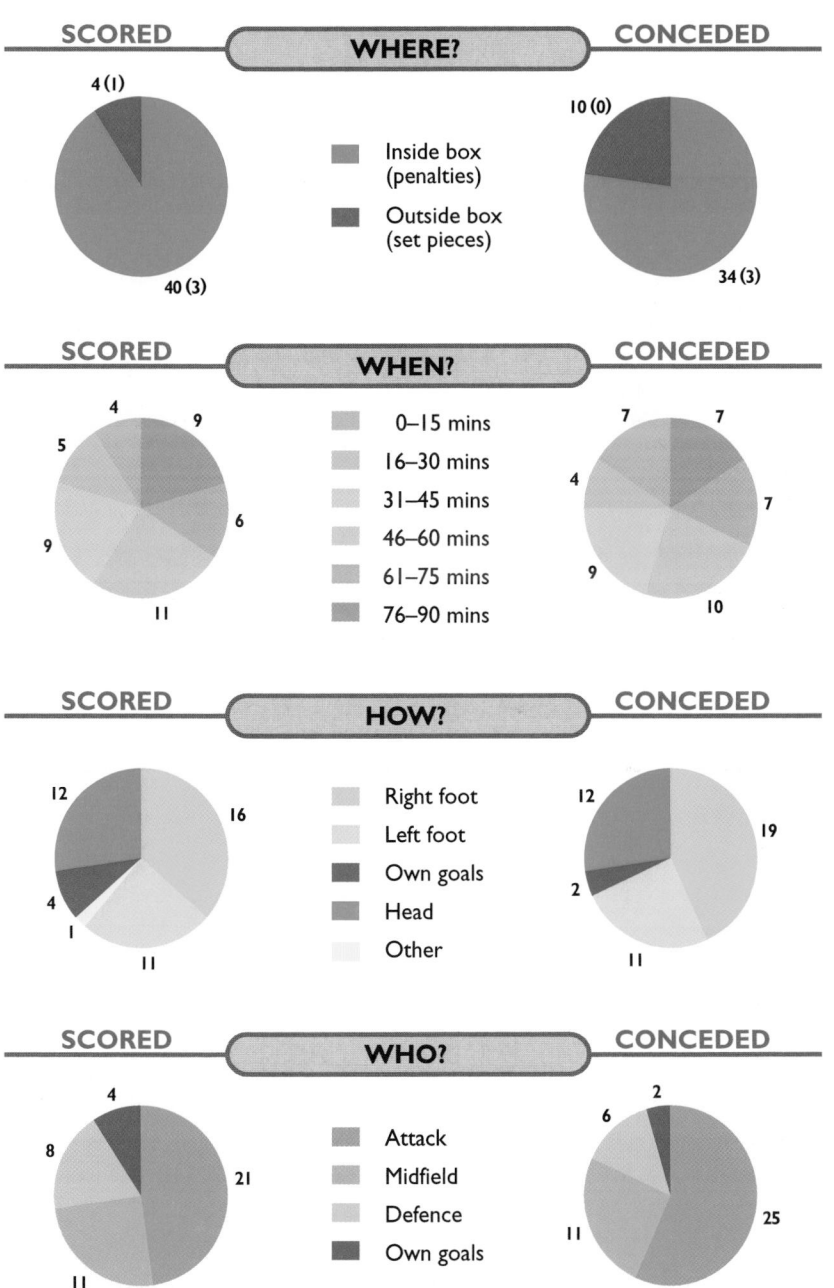

SCORED | **WHERE?** | **CONCEDED**

Inside box (penalties)
Outside box (set pieces)

Scored: 4 (1), 40 (3)
Conceded: 10 (0), 34 (3)

SCORED | **WHEN?** | **CONCEDED**

0–15 mins
16–30 mins
31–45 mins
46–60 mins
61–75 mins
76–90 mins

Scored: 4, 9, 5, 6, 9, 11
Conceded: 7, 7, 4, 7, 9, 10

SCORED | **HOW?** | **CONCEDED**

Right foot
Left foot
Own goals
Head
Other

Scored: 12, 16, 4, 1, 11
Conceded: 12, 19, 2, 11

SCORED | **WHO?** | **CONCEDED**

Attack
Midfield
Defence
Own goals

Scored: 4, 8, 21, 11
Conceded: 2, 6, 11, 25

than any other team in the Premiership

MIDDLESBROUGH

	BOKSIC	CAMPBELL	COOPER	DEANE	EHIOGU	FESTA	FLEMING	GAVIN	GORDON	HUDSON	INCE
APPEARANCES											
Start	26	5	26	13	21	21	29	10	12	0	30
Sub	2	2	1	12	0	4	1	4	8	3	0
Minutes on pitch	2179	399	2201	1439	1802	1900	2505	1035	1268	46	2686
GOAL ATTEMPTS											
Goals	12	0	2	2	3	2	0	0	1	0	2
Shots on target	30	0	5	7	6	3	1	0	2	0	21
Shots off target	36	3	5	12	5	7	4	0	10	0	13
Shooting accuracy	45%	0%	50%	37%	55%	30%	20%	0%	17%	0%	62%
PASSING											
Goal assists	3	1	0	1	1	0	1	0	2	0	1
Long passes	81	16	302	49	209	214	229	118	139	2	329
Short passes	510	75	648	367	418	486	761	256	330	21	967
PASS COMPLETION											
Own half %	77%	79%	78%	78%	82%	80%	80%	81%	66%	100%	84%
Opposition half %	57%	62%	62%	58%	56%	58%	68%	57%	54%	60%	66%
CROSSING											
Total crosses	49	6	21	11	2	9	44	17	65	0	39
Cross completion %	24%	33%	24%	27%	0%	22%	30%	53%	25%	0%	26%
DRIBBLING											
Dribbles & runs	115	16	18	24	14	31	46	8	34	0	73
Dribble completion %	53%	81%	72%	75%	93%	81%	80%	100%	76%	0%	81%
DEFENDING											
Tackles made	12	4	54	17	46	65	84	24	43	1	108
Tackles won %	75%	50%	65%	59%	74%	85%	77%	63%	74%	0%	69%
Blocks	1	1	32	3	27	17	20	11	20	0	16
Clearances	4	3	145	20	212	171	75	80	39	0	54
Interceptions	0	1	11	1	6	11	5	3	4	0	12
DISCIPLINE											
Fouls	30	2	29	33	25	27	32	16	15	0	33
Offside	56	4	0	5	1	0	3	0	0	0	3
Yellow cards	3	0	10	2	1	3	4	4	2	0	8
Red cards	0	0	0	0	1	0	0	0	0	0	0

GOALKEEPER NAME	START/ (SUB)	TIME ON PITCH	GOALS CONCEDED	MINS/GOALS CONCEDED	SAVES MADE	SAVES/ SHOTS
BERESFORD	0(1)	67	1	67	7	88%
CROSSLEY	4(1)	300	6	50	15	71%
SCHWARZER	31(0)	2790	34	82	117	77%
WALSH	3(0)	262	3	87	15	83%

For more information visit our website:

PLAYERS' STATISTICS

	JOB	KAREMBEU	MARINELLI	MUSTOE	O'NEILL	OKON	PALLISTER	RICARD	STAMP	SUMMERBELL	VICKERS	WHELAN	WINDASS	TOTAL	RANK
	8	31	2	13	14	23	8	22	11	5	29	13	8		
	4	2	11	12	1	1	0	5	8	2	1	14	0		
	679	2576	305	1340	1242	1972	678	1782	998	483	2513	1338	686		
	3	4	0	0	0	0	0	4	1	1	0	1	2	44*	=13th
	13	9	3	2	4	1	1	20	4	3	3	8	7	153	17th
	9	8	2	4	10	5	0	21	9	0	2	10	15	190	18th
	59%	53%	60%	33%	29%	17%	100%	49%	31%	100%	60%	44%	32%	45%	12th
	1	4	0	1	1	1	2	3	1	0	0	1	0	25	=14th
	26	296	38	108	136	306	71	99	73	23	194	127	69	3744	16th
	214	914	127	415	319	896	157	442	258	123	510	446	202	9927	13th
	85%	79%	88%	83%	70%	87%	85%	76%	80%	84%	85%	78%	86%	80%	9th
	64%	60%	77%	70%	53%	74%	64%	55%	62%	60%	57%	63%	60%	61%	17th
	7	92	34	7	64	16	2	48	38	1	3	61	4	640	20th
	29%	37%	32%	14%	39%	31%	100%	23%	16%	0%	33%	38%	25%	30%	1st
	28	87	31	12	55	48	2	66	35	1	4	40	11	801	15th
	68%	62%	52%	92%	65%	90%	100%	50%	57%	100%	50%	58%	55%	68%	16th
	16	83	2	52	49	56	27	26	35	31	55	18	11	920	18th
	56%	73%	100%	77%	69%	68%	63%	73%	49%	71%	76%	78%	64%	71%	17th
	1	6	0	7	9	11	7	5	4	10	34	7	3	252	4th
	1	25	0	17	58	49	76	6	11	7	246	10	6	1372	10th
	1	3	0	5	2	5	8	2	3	3	12	0	0	98	=16th
	8	43	8	24	29	26	6	75	15	11	38	22	4	552	13th
	11	11	1	0	0	0	0	19	3	0	0	9	4	130	15th
	0	3	1	2	4	6	0	5	4	4	2	3	2	74	6th
	0	1	1	0	1	0	0	0	0	1	0	0	0	6	=1st

*Including four own goals

CROSSES CAUGHT	CROSSES PUNCHED	CROSSES DROPPED	CATCH SUCCESS	THROWS/ SHORT KICKS	% COMPLETION	LONG KICKS	% COMPLETION
0	0	0	0%	2	100%	18	33%
4	2	0	100%	4	75%	58	36%
82	20	5	94%	65	77%	650	48%
7	0	0	100%	4	50%	67	45%

PLAYER OF THE SEASON

PLAYER	INDEX SCORE
MARK SCHWARZER	892
Ugo Ehiogu	870
Paul Ince	850
Gianluca Festa	773
Paul Okon	772
Colin Cooper	668
Steve Vickers	634
Curtis Fleming	611
Alen Boksic	608
Christian Karembeu	578

Middlesbrough were kept largely on the back foot throughout the majority of the 2000–01 Premiership, a fact well-illustrated in the club's Opta rankings for the season.

Five of Boro's top 10 protagonists played in defence, while goalkeeper Mark Schwarzer headed the list for the second year on the trot.

The Australian giant was having a mediocre season before Terry Venables arrived at The Riverside. But Schwarzer responded magnificently under the former England coach, saving a massive 84% of shots – to boost his season's ratio to 77% – and keeping nine clean sheets as Boro secured top-flight status. Only three 'keepers could better his tally of 117 saves for 2000–01, which helped him to average 892 points on Opta's scale.

Ugo Ehiogu's high-profile switch from Aston Villa got off to the worst possible start when he was injured on his debut and dismissed in his fourth match, but he bounced back to inspire the revival.

Ehiogu thumped the ball clear more than 200 times for his new club, won three-quarters of his tackles and drove forward to net three crucial goals for his average score of 870 points.

Paul Ince came in third behind Ehiogu, with an Opta average of 850 points. Ince was the driving force in the midfield, winning more tackles and making more passes than any Boro colleague, and adding another two goals to his Premiership tally.

Gianluca Festa's dependable displays attracted Chelsea's attention for a period, while Steve Vickers and Colin Cooper were quietly efficient, the former making a club-high 246 clearances in 2000-01.

Newcomers Paul Okon, Alen Boksic and Christian Karembeu all made their mark and will provide a nucleus to build from in 2001–02, although Boksic and Karembeu sometimes played below expectations. Boksic started well and ultimately claimed 12 strikes, while Karembeu both scored and assisted four goals.

94' 52" Hamilton Ricard scored the

FIVE OF THE BEST

Middlesbrough looked relegation certainties until the arrival of Terry Venables. The ex-England manager sorted the Riversiders out at the back, eventually guiding them to safety with one game to spare. Survival cannot disguise the fact that Boro's season was a disappointing one, though, particularly given the large outlay the club invested in the transfer market.

TOP GOALSCORERS

	GOALS	GOALS/SHOTS
ALEN BOKSIC	12	18%
Christian Karembeu	4	24%
Hamilton Ricard	4	10%
Ugo Ehiogu	3	27%
Joseph-Desiré Job	3	14%

Alen Boksic was the Premiership's highest-paid player in 2000–01, but with 12 vital goals for the Teessiders he was probably worth every penny of the £60,000 he was reputed to be picking up every week. Apart from Boksic, Boro struggled to find the net. Hamilton Ricard scored just four goals in the Premiership, while Brian Deane managed just two strikes, a disappointing total that did not even earn him a place in the top five.

Paul Okon was one of Middlesbrough's better performers in 2000–01. The no-nonsense Aussie international played the occasional game at the back but spent most of the season in midfield, where he managed to outshine his more established team-mates Paul Ince and Christian Karembeu. Okon completed 80% of all his attempted passes, a figure which put him clear at the top of Boro's passing chart, although Paul Ince actually attempted more passes overall.

TOP PASSERS

	SUCC PASSES	COMPLETION
PAUL OKON	963	80%
Paul Ince	952	73%
Christian Karembeu	807	67%
Curtis Fleming	725	73%
Colin Cooper	668	70%

TOP TACKLERS

	WON	SUCCESS
PAUL INCE	75	69%
Curtis Fleming	65	77%
Christian Karembeu	61	73%
Gianluca Festa	55	85%
Steve Vickers	42	76%

Paul Ince is in the twilight of his career, but he remains one of the Premiership's most competitive players. Ince finished just above long-serving defender Curtis Fleming in the list of Boro's top tacklers. Gianluca Festa was the club's most accurate tackler, winning possession with an impressive 85% of his challenges, but it is fair to say that everyone at The Riverside won more tackles after the arrival of Terry Venables on Teesside.

Middlesbrough finished the season with six red cards, the joint-highest total in the Premiership, but only one of their players – Hamilton Ricard – makes Opta's league of indiscipline. Ricard could hardly be described as one of the Premiership's dirtiest players, but he did make some clumsy challenges in 2000–01, conceding 75 fouls and picking up five yellow cards. Paul Ince finished with the same number of bookings he picked up in 1999–2000, but once again avoided any red cards.

DISCIPLINE

	POINTS	FOULS & CARDS
HAMILTON RICARD	90	75F, 5Y, 0R
Colin Cooper	59	29F, 10Y, 0R
Christian Karembeu	58	43F, 3Y, 1R
Paul Ince	57	33F, 8Y, 0R
Keith O'Neill	47	29F, 4Y, 1R

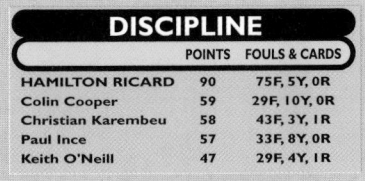

latest goal in the Premiership

ACTION	BOKSIC	EHIOGU	GAVIN	GORDON	INCE	KAREMBEU	MUSTOE	OKON	RICARD	SCHWARZER	STAMP	VICKERS	WINDASS	TOTAL	ARSENAL
Time on pitch	89	90	90	90	90	90	1	90	79	90	11	90	90	990	990
GOALS															
Goal	–	–	–	–	–	–	–	–	–	–	–	–	–	1	0
Shot on target (incl goals)	–	–	–	–	–	–	–	–	–	–	–	–	1	2	8
Shot off target	–	–	–	–	1	–	–	–	–	–	–	–	2	4	10
Blocked shot	2	–	–	–	–	–	–	–	–	–	–	–	–	3	8
Own goal	–	–	–	–	–	–	–	–	–	–	–	–	–	0	2
PASSES															
Pass to own player	18	10	15	15	26	19	2	38	16	9	2	13	25	208	451
Pass to opposition	8	4	8	7	14	14	–	7	8	6	–	6	11	93	92
Cross to own player	–	–	–	–	–	–	–	1	1	–	–	–	1	1	11
Cross to opposition player	–	–	2	2	1	–	–	–	–	–	–	–	–	6	45
Goal assist	1	–	–	–	–	–	–	–	–	–	–	–	–	1	0
Pass completion %	68%	71%	60%	63%	63%	58%	100%	84%	68%	60%	100%	68%	69%	68%	77%
TACKLES & CLEARANCES															
Tackle	1	4	1	3	8	6	–	1	1	–	–	3	3	31	36
Clearances, blocks and interceptions	–	17	8	6	5	2	–	9	4	3	1	10	1	66	20
DRIBBLES & RUNS															
Dribbles ball retained	5	–	–	2	3	2	–	2	–	–	1	–	2	17	34
Dribbles ball lost	7	–	–	2	1	7	–	1	4	–	–	–	–	22	28
Dribble success %	42%	0%	0%	50%	75%	22%	0%	67%	0%	0%	100%	0%	100%	44%	55%
DISCIPLINE															
Fouls	–	1	1	1	–	1	–	1	5	–	–	4	–	13	17
Penalty conceded	–	–	–	–	–	–	–	–	–	–	–	–	–	0	0
Free kick – offside	1	–	–	–	–	1	–	–	–	–	–	–	–	2	2
Yellow cards	–	–	–	–	–	–	–	1	–	–	–	–	–	1	1
Red cards	–	–	–	–	–	–	–	–	–	–	–	–	–	0	0
GOALKEEPERS															
Distribution to own player	–	–	–	–	–	–	–	–	–	14	–	–	–	14	14
Distribution to opposition player	–	–	–	–	–	–	–	–	–	21	–	–	–	21	4
Goalkeeper distribution %	–	–	–	–	–	–	–	–	–	40%	–	–	–	40%	78%
Save	–	–	–	–	–	–	–	–	–	8	–	–	–	8	1
Ball caught	–	–	–	–	–	–	–	–	–	5	–	–	–	5	1
Ball dropped	–	–	–	–	–	–	–	–	–	–	–	–	–	0	0
Goal conceded	–	–	–	–	–	–	–	–	–	–	–	–	–	0	3

30% Boro were the most accurate

Middlesbrough produced one of the shock results of the 2000–01 season by becoming the first and only team in the Premiership to win at Highbury for almost 15 months, since Liverpool had taken all three points during the previous campaign in January 1999.

14 April 2001

0–3

ARSENAL
MIDDLESBROUGH

Not many people outside Teesside had given Middlesbrough much chance of taking anything from this contest. After all, Arsenal had just reached their 14th FA Cup final and had received a standing ovation at Manchester City three days earlier after blitzing the home side with four goals in the opening period.

But while the Gunners had one eye on their Champions League quarter-final second leg against Valencia, Terry Venables' team proved to be real party-poopers.

Boro were by no means in awe of the Gunners' lightning-quick attackers, who sought to gain the early advantage. Nwankwo Kanu was the first to be denied when Mark Schwarzer blocked his right-footed effort. Schwarzer went on to make a further seven saves during the game – the most he made in a single match during the 2000–01 campaign.

Boro were not really much of an attacking threat, their only opportunity in the opening half-hour a long-range Dean Windass effort on David Seaman's goal which flew harmlessly over the bar.

Then came two moments of madness in a five-minute spell that stunned the home fans. First Brazilian midfielder Edu, on his first start at Highbury, deflected a weak-looking shot from Windass past a stranded Seaman.

Then good approach play involving Hamilton Ricard and Paul Ince found Dean Gordon on the left. The former Crystal Palace wing-back's cross was converted not by one of his team-mates but by Arsenal defender Silvinho, whose attempted clearance flew past a bemused Seaman.

The Boro supporters housed in the corner of the Clock End were ecstatic that their team were two goals up despite no Boro player having managed a shot on target.

Arsène Wenger threw on an extra striker in Sylvain Wiltord at half-time, but it was Boro who extended their lead in the 58th minute. A neat move ended when Alen Boksic's back-heel wrong-footed the Gunners defence and Ricard ran on to stroke the ball home to put the Teessiders into an unassailable lead.

Although the home team forced 12 corners without reply, the Boro defence stood firm. Ugo Ehiogu was magnificent on his return after a four-match ban. The former Aston Villa stopper re-established his England credentials with 17 blocks, clearances and interceptions.

But when Arsenal managed to get behind Ehiogu, Schwarzer was equal to headers from Thierry Henry and Kanu. Although Wenger's team dominated the second-half possession, Windass had a chance to make the scoreline more emphatic, but the former Bradford dynamo could only blaze the ball over the bar.

That miss was ultimately academic, as Boro won at Highbury for the first time since 1939 and inflicted the Gunners' heaviest home defeat in seven years.

crossers in the Premiership

NEWCASTLE UNITED

ADDRESS

St James' Park,
Newcastle-upon-Tyne NE1 4ST

CONTACT NUMBERS

Telephone: 0191 201 8400
Fax: 0191 201 8600
Ticket Office: 0191 261 1571
Club Call: 09068 121190
St James' Park Shop: 0191 201 8426
Website: www.nufc.com

KEY PERSONNEL

President: Sir John Hall
Patron: T Bennett
Honorary President: B Young
Chairman: W F Shepherd
Deputy Chairman: D S Hall
Chief Executive: D Stonehouse
Directors: W F Shepherd, D S Hall,
R Jones, D Stonehouse
Director of Football Administration
& Secretary: R Cushing
Manager: R Robson CBE

SPONSORS

NTL

FANZINES

The Mag
True Faith

COLOURS

Home: Black and white striped shirts,
black shorts and white stockings
Away: Black shirts, black shorts and
black stockings

NICKNAME

The Magpies

HONOURS

League Champions: 1904–05, 1906–07,
1908–09, 1926–27
Division One Champions: 1992–93
Division Two Champions: 1964–65
FA Cup Winners: 1910, 1924, 1932,
1951, 1952, 1955
Fairs Cup Winners: 1969

RECORD GOALSCORER

Jackie Milburn –
178 league goals, 1946–57

BIGGEST WIN

13–0 v Newport County – Division Two,
5 October 1946

BIGGEST DEFEAT

0–9 v Burton Wanderers – Division Two,
15 April 1895

SEASON REVIEW

The 2000–01 campaign was a largely forgettable affair for Newcastle United and their supporters.

The club was suffering from financial problems at the start of the season and manager Bobby Robson was briefed to reduce the wage bill as a legacy of the Ruud Gullit and Kenny Dalglish eras.

Big earners such as Duncan Ferguson and surplus squad members such as Temuri Ketsbaia, Steve Howey, Laurent Charvet, Didier Domi and latterly Alain Goma moved on, while Carl Cort proved to be the Magpies' only major investment.

Worse still, rumours of overtures by other clubs towards Kieron Dyer continued throughout the season. The young midfielder was the jewel in Newcastle's crown and it was feared that the club would not rebuff an offer of £20 million from one of Dyer's many suitors.

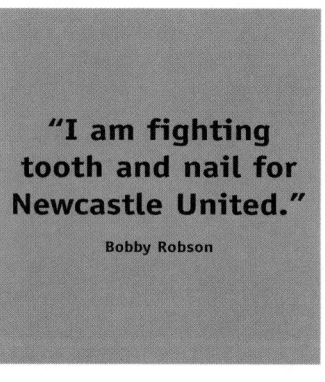

"I am fighting tooth and nail for Newcastle United."

Bobby Robson

But the major problem for Newcastle was the overcrowding of the treatment room at St James' Park. Alan Shearer featured in just half of the Magpies' Premiership matches and just four times from November; Carl Cort played just three games before March; Nikos Dabizas missed the majority of the campaign and Kieron Dyer's season ended in February thanks to a shin injury.

Things were so bad that Bobby Robson was only able to name the same team for consecutive Premiership matches on three occasions during the campaign.

A creditable performance on the opening weekend against Manchester United at Old Trafford did not bring any points, but was followed up by three victories in a row to take Robson's side top of the table and earn the erstwhile England boss the Manager of the Month award for August.

Daniel Cordone – the Magpies' new £2 million signing – looked a snip. Two goals in August, however, were very much a case of flattering to deceive and the Argentinean really struggled to make an impact as winter settled over the north east.

Shearer celebrated a milestone in the 2–0 win over Coventry City, scoring his 200th league goal. Unfortunately, Newcastle then embarked upon a run of three games without scoring.

Away victories against Manchester City and Middlesbrough were well-received, but their problems resurfaced in defeats by Everton and West Ham.

Their inconsistent form saw two wins, two draws and two defeats follow, including a win over Liverpool and a 5–0 thumping at Arsenal. This sequence was also the opening of a 25-game run without a clean sheet – the longest by any side in the top flight in 2000–01.

More worrying for Newcastle fans was the resignation of Kevin Keegan from the England manager's job. With a dearth of suitable replacements, Robson's name leapt to the top of the list of potential candidates, even if it was only on a temporary basis or in an advisory role with an up-and-coming young coach such as Peter Taylor or Steve McClaren. In the end, Newcastle refused to countenance any job-sharing arrangement and England turned their attentions elsewhere.

Newcastle were knocked out of the Worthington Cup by Birmingham at St Andrews. The Magpies had eliminated Leyton Orient over two legs and edged Bradford in the previous round in a seven-goal thriller but, despite taking the lead against the Blues, Michael Johnson grabbed a last-minute winner.

Newcastle's inconsistency was summed up perfectly over the festive period. Defeat by struggling Derby County was followed by

SEASON REVIEW

the news that Shearer needed a knee operation and was likely to miss a significant chunk of the season. So it was amazing that this result was followed by a 2–1 win against Leeds on Boxing Day and a 1–1 draw against Manchester United. But Newcastle were the architects of their own downfall in the next fixture, as Dyer and Nolberto Solano were sent off in a controversial encounter with Spurs which ended 4–2 in favour of the Londoners.

This was followed up by an FA Cup exit in a third round replay. After drawing 1–1 at St James' Park, Aston Villa grabbed the only goal of the game to end Newcastle's chances of silverware.

Shay Given stunned the club with a transfer request after losing his place to Steve Harper following an injury to the Irishman against Derby, but Harper himself succumbed to an ankle knock to let Given back between the sticks and harmony returned.

Injuries were also exacerbated by international calls, with regulars such as Solano and Acuna being joined by fringe players such as Diego Gavilan on long trips back to South America to play several fixtures.

This period gave an opportunity to other players who would not have featured but for the strains being placed on the squad. The club signed young defenders Wayne Quinn and Andy O'Brien and introduced front-man Shola Ameobi to the first team.

The striker immediately warmed to the challenge. Back-to-back 3–1 victories against Coventry and Leeds saw Ameobi bagging a goal in each match and Newcastle surged into the top six.

But then Robson's side embarked on a run of seven matches without a win, despite four of their fixtures being against sides in the bottom six of the table, as the lack of

experience and depth in the squad began to take its toll.

The start of this run saw two more defeats in London and by season's end the Magpies' run of bad form in the capital stretched back some three years and 24 matches without a victory.

With games in hand, the fact that Newcastle slipped to 14th at one stage was not enough to generate concern about relegation, but Robson was determined to end the season well and the return of Carl Cort to action certainly boosted the Magpies. The former Wimbledon striker will certainly hope to play more than the four games alongside Shearer that he managed in 2000–01.

Gary Speed set a new record for Premiership appearances when he racked up his 318th outing, as Newcastle beat Leicester 1–0.

Robson was also able to give youngsters such as Lomana Tresor Lua Lua, Ameobi, Aaron Hughes and Stephen Caldwell experience which will stand them in good stead.

Issues which will have to be addressed are the club's disciplinary record and the contribution of their strikers. Newcastle earned five red cards in the Premiership and only north east rivals Middlesbrough and Sunderland incurred more dismissals during the campaign.

But more worrying was the fact that no team's strikers made a smaller contribution to the "goals scored" column than the Magpies' front men. Robson's strikers bagged just 15 of Newcastle's 44 goals – just 34%, compared to the league average contribution of 53%.

However, the club looks to be on firmer foundations now and with significant transfer activity planned for the close season, the Toon Army can look forward to a more profitable campaign in 2001–02.

> "I said that last season was Phase One, and this season was meant to be Phase Two. Phase Two has been stalled."
>
> **Bobby Robson**

NEWCASTLE UNITED

DATE	OPPONENT	SCORE	ATT.	ACUNA	AMEOBI	BARTON	BASSEDAS	CALDWELL	CHARVET	COPPINGER	CORDONE	CORT	DABIZAS	DOMI	DYER	GALLA
20.08.00	Man Utd A	0–2	67,477	–	–	90	–	–	–	–	90	90	90	–	s45	–
23.08.00	Derby Co H	3–2	51,327	–	–	78■	–	–	s10	–	90¹	31¹	44	90	90	–
26.08.00	Tottenham H	2–0	51,573	–	–	90	–	–	–	s11	79¹	–	–	90	90	–
06.09.00	Coventry A	2–0	22,109	–	–	–	–	–	90	–	89	–	–	21	90	s45¹
09.09.00	Chelsea H	0–0	51,687	–	s20	90	–	–	90	–	90	–	–	–	90	70
16.09.00	Southampton A	0–2	15,221	–	s17	–	–	–	90	–	90	–	–	83	90	73
23.09.00	Charlton H	0–1	50,866	–	–	–	–	–	63	–	63	90	–	s27	90	–
30.09.00	Man City A	1–0	34,497	–	–	–	–	s45	90	–	63	–	–	90	73	90
16.10.00	Middlesbro A	3–1	31,436	–	–	–	–	–	90	–	76	–	–	90	90¹	–
21.10.00	Everton H	0–1	51,625	–	–	23	–	–	–	–	61	–	–	90□	90	s67
28.10.00	West Ham A	0–1	26,044	90	–	–	–	–	–	–	s10	–	–	–	90	–
04.11.00	Ipswich A	2–1	50,922	88□	–	–	s2	s46	–	–	60	–	–	90	90	–
11.11.00	Leicester A	1–1	21,406	90□	–	–	–	90	–	–	s22	–	–	90	90	–
18.11.00	Sunderland H	1–2	52,030	78	–	s12	57	90	–	–	–	–	–	90	90	–
26.11.00	Liverpool H	2–1	51,949	s10	–	90□	80	–	–	–	–	–	–	90	90¹	–
02.12.00	Aston Villa A	1–1	34,255	90	–	90	–	s70	–	–	90	–	–	s54□	90	–
09.12.00	Arsenal A	0–5	38,052	90	–	90□	–	90□	–	–	s12	–	–	s24	78	–
16.12.00	Bradford H	2–1	50,470	s9	–	90	81	–	–	–	–	–	–	–	90¹	–
23.12.00	Derby Co A	0–2	29,978	90	–	90	90	66	–	–	s11	–	–	–	90	–
26.12.00	Leeds Utd H	2–1	52,118	90¹□	90	90□	90□	–	–	–	–	–	–	–	90	–
30.12.00	Man Utd H	1–1	52,134	75	75	90	75□	–	–	–	s15	–	–	–	90	–
02.01.01	Tottenham A	2–4	34,324	90	70	90	90□	–	–	–	–	–	–	52¹■	–	–
13.01.01	Coventry H	3–1	50,159	90	90¹	90	77	–	–	–	–	–	–	90¹	–	–
20.01.01	Leeds Utd A	3–1	40,005	90¹	89¹	90	s16	–	–	–	–	–	–	–	–	74
31.01.01	Chelsea A	1–3	35,108	90	78	90□	90¹□	–	–	–	s12	–	–	–	78	–
11.02.01	Charlton A	0–2	20,043	59	90	90□	s17	–	–	–	–	–	–	–	90	s31
24.02.01	Man City H	0–1	51,981	69	69	s21	–	–	–	–	–	–	–	–	90	69
03.03.01	Everton A	1–1*	35,779	90	72	–	89	90	–	–	s1	–	–	–	–	s18
17.03.01	Middlesbro H	1–2	51,751	83	83	83	–	90	–	–	s7	90¹	–	–	–	s7
31.03.01	Bradford A	2–2	20,160	84¹	90	90	s6	–	–	–	–	90¹	–	–	–	s8
14.04.01	Ipswich A	0–1	24,028	90	81	90	–	–	–	–	–	90	–	–	–	s9
16.04.01	West Ham H	2–1	51,107	s13	–	9	90	s81	–	–	–	90¹	90	–	–	89
21.04.01	Sunderland A	1–1	48,277	77□	s14	90□	90□	–	–	–	s13	90	90	–	–	76
28.04.01	Leicester H	1–0	50,501	90	s23	90	77	–	–	–	–	90¹□	90	–	–	67
01.05.01	Southampton H	1–1	50,439	90	s3	90	86	–	–	–	–	90	90	–	–	87¹
05.05.01	Liverpool A	0–3	44,363	73□	s13	90	s17	–	–	–	–	77	90□	–	–	73
15.05.01	Arsenal A	0–0	50,729	–	s10	90	90	–	–	–	–	90	90	–	–	80
19.05.01	Aston Villa A	3–0*	51,506	–	s19	90	90	–	–	–	–	90¹	90	–	–	71

□ Yellow card, ■ Red card, S Substitute, 90² Goals scored

*including own goal

For more information visit our website:

2000–01 PREMIERSHIP APPEARANCES

GAVILAN	GIVEN	GLASS	GOMA	GRIFFIN	HARPER	HUGHES	KERR	LEE	LUA-LUA	MARCELINO	O'BRIEN	QUINN	SHEARER	SOLANO	SPEED	TOTAL
–	90	–	45□	–	–	90	–	59	–	90	–	–	90	s31	90	990
–	90	s59[1]	s46	–	–	90	–	–	–	–	–	–	90	80	90	978
–	90	74	90	s16	–	90	–	–	–	–	–	–	90	90	90[1]	990
–	90	45□	90	s69	–	90	s1	90	–	–	–	–	90[1]	–	90	990
s5	90	–	90	–	–	90	–	–	–	–	–	–	90	85	90	990
–	90	–	90	s7	–	90	–	–	–	–	–	–	90	90	90	990
–	90	–	90	90	–	90	–	s27	s27	–	–	–	90	63	90□	990
–	90	–	–	45□	–	90	–	90	s27	–	–	–	90[1]	s17	90	990
–	90	–	90[1]	–	–	90□	–	90	s14	–	–	–	90[1]	90	90	990
–	90	–	90	–	–	90	–	90	s29	–	–	–	90	90	90	990
–	90	s9	90	90	–	90	–	81	80□	–	–	–	90	90□	90	990
–	90	–	90	–	–	90	–	90	s30	–	–	–	90[2]	44	90	990
–	90	–	90	90	–	90	–	68	–	–	–	–	90	–	90[1]	990
–	90	–	–	–	–	90	–	90□	s33	–	–	–	90	90	90[1]	990
–	90	–	–	90□	–	90	–	90	–	–	–	–	90	90[1]	90□	990
–	90	–	36	90	–	20	–	75	s15	–	–	–	–	90[1]	90□	990
–	90	s25	–	66	–	90	–	65	90	–	–	–	–	90	90□	990
–	90	–	–	90	–	90	–	90	–	90	–	–	90	90	90[1]	990
–	45	s24	–	90	s45	90	–	79□	–	90□	–	–	90	–	–	990
–	–	–	–	90	90	90	–	–	–	90	–	–	–	90[1]	90□	990
–	–	s15[1]	90□	90	90	90	–	–	s15	–	–	–	–	90	90	990
–	–	s20	90□	70	90	90	–	–	s20	–	–	–	32[1]■	–	90	894
–	–	s13	90	–	90	90	–	–	–	–	–	90	–	90	90[1]	990
–	90	–	90	–	–	90	–	74	s16	s1	–	90	–	90[1]■	90	990
–	90	–	90□	–	–	90	–	–	s12	–	–	90	–	90	90	990
–	90	–	–	–	–	90	–	73	s17	90	–	90	–	73	90	990
–	90	s21□	90	90	–	90	–	–	s21	–	–	90	90	90	–	990
–	90	s1	–	90	–	90	–	90□	–	–	–	90	90□	89	–	990
–	90	–	–	s7	–	90□	–	90	–	–	–	90	–	90	90	990
–	90	–	–	–	–	90	–	90	–	–	90	90	–	82	90□	990
–	90□	–	–	–	–	90	–	81	s9	–	90	90	–	75■	90	975
–	90	–	–	–	–	–	–	77	s1	–	90	90	–	90[1]	90	990
–	90	–	–	s13	–	–	–	–	–	–	90[1]	90	–	77	90□	990
–	90	90	–	–	–	–	–	–	s13	–	90	90	–	–	90	990
–	90	–	–	–	–	s4	–	–	90□	–	90	90	–	–	90□	990
–	90	–	–	–	–	90	–	–	s17	–	90	90	–	90	90	990
–	90	90	–	–	–	90	–	–	–	–	90	–	–	90□	90	990
–	90	77[1]	–	–	–	90	–	–	s6	–	90	s13	–	84	84■	984

THE MANAGER

BOBBY ROBSON

The gran daddy of Premiership management has been rebuilding at St James' Park after saving Newcastle from the threat of relegation during 1999–2000.

Robson's impressive CV is not one to dismiss lightly. Although he won 20 caps for England it was as a manager that he made his name, starting by leading Ipswich to glory in the FA and UEFA Cups.

In his eight-year spell as national manager, Robson guided England to the quarter-finals in the 1986 World Cup and then went one better four years later, before announcing that he was resigning from the top management job in the country.

He returned to club management and brought two league titles apiece to PSV Eindhoven and Porto as well as the cup at Sporting Lisbon. His time at the Nou Camp saw Barcelona win the Spanish Cup and the Cup Winners' Cup and his reputation as one of the top managers in the game grew.

Robson went back to his native north east in 1999 and is slowly building the Magpies into a side capable of competing again, despite limited budgets. He was linked with a caretaker role for England when Kevin Keegan resigned, but the Newcastle board blocked the move.

LEAGUE POSITION

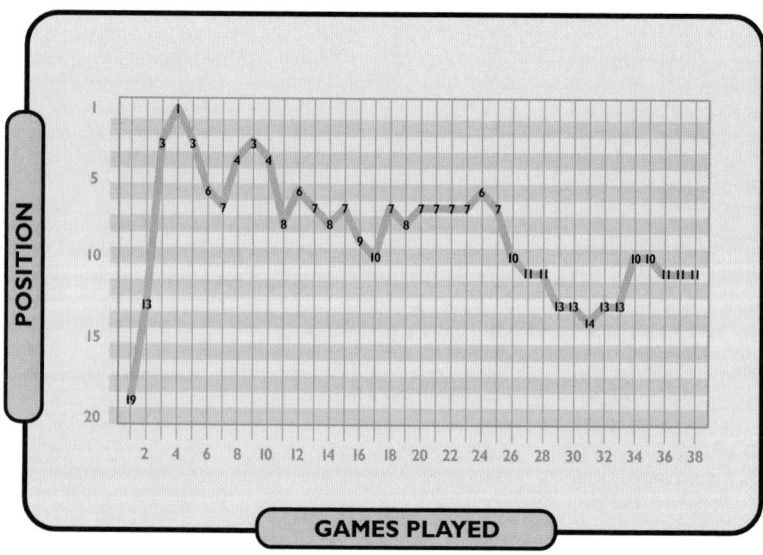

POSITION

GAMES PLAYED

25 The number of Premiership games

THE GOALS

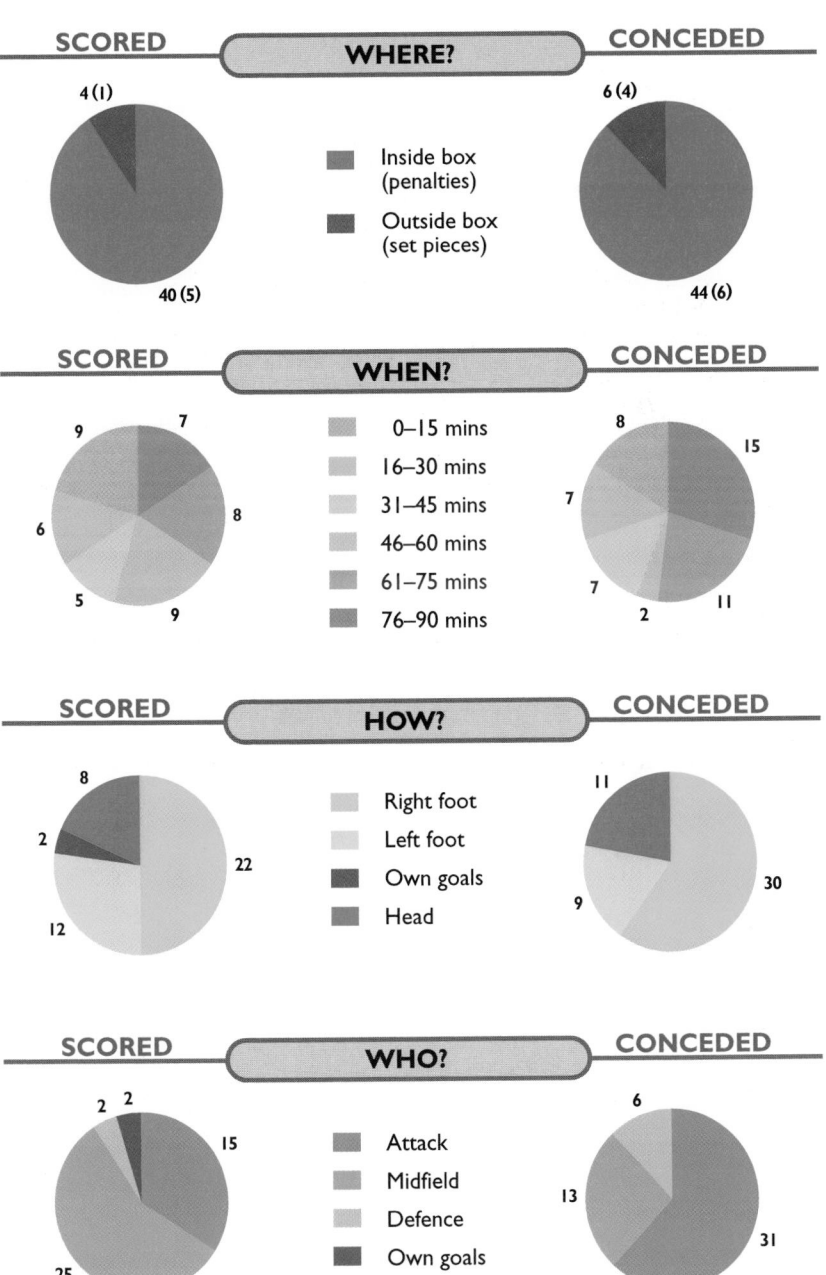

WHERE?

SCORED — CONCEDED

4 (1) — 6 (4)

40 (5) — 44 (6)

- Inside box (penalties)
- Outside box (set pieces)

WHEN?

SCORED — CONCEDED

Scored: 7, 8, 9, 5, 6, 9

Conceded: 8, 15, 11, 2, 7, 7

- 0–15 mins
- 16–30 mins
- 31–45 mins
- 46–60 mins
- 61–75 mins
- 76–90 mins

HOW?

SCORED — CONCEDED

Scored: 8, 2, 22, 12

Conceded: 11, 30, 9

- Right foot
- Left foot
- Own goals
- Head

WHO?

SCORED — CONCEDED

Scored: 2, 2, 15, 25

Conceded: 6, 13, 31

- Attack
- Midfield
- Defence
- Own goals

Newcastle went without keeping a clean sheet

NEWCASTLE UNITED

	ACUNA	AMEOBI	BARTON	BASSEDAS	CALDWELL	CHARVET	COPPINGER	CORDONE	CORT	DABIZAS	DOMI	DYER	GALLAC
APPEARANCES													
Start	23	12	27	17	5	6	0	12	13	9	11	25	12
Sub	3	8	2	5	4	1	1	9	0	0	3	1	7
Minutes on pitch	1978	1096	2296	1490	668	523	11	1044	1098	764	1019	2216	1104
GOAL ATTEMPTS													
Goals	3	2	0	1	0	0	0	2	6	0	0	5	2
Shots on target	5	8	4	5	1	1	0	9	22	3	3	15	15
Shots off target	10	13	6	3	1	6	0	7	16	4	3	20	16
Shooting accuracy	33%	38%	40%	63%	50%	14%	0%	56%	58%	43%	50%	43%	48%
PASSING													
Goal assists	0	2	0	0	0	0	0	1	2	0	0	5	0
Long passes	123	31	480	118	101	86	3	48	30	91	104	156	66
Short passes	554	337	977	606	199	212	1	267	366	278	314	867	327
PASS COMPLETION													
Own half %	79%	73%	84%	79%	83%	84%	100%	87%	80%	83%	77%	88%	78%
Opposition half %	70%	57%	59%	73%	62%	72%	67%	73%	65%	60%	63%	78%	65%
CROSSING													
Total crosses	8	21	57	25	7	17	0	96	9	2	22	65	43
Cross completion %	13%	14%	28%	20%	0%	12%	0%	35%	33%	50%	14%	28%	21%
DRIBBLING													
Dribbles & runs	20	55	80	60	11	13	0	63	25	19	36	149	45
Dribble completion %	60%	49%	79%	62%	100%	92%	0%	56%	44%	100%	67%	70%	47%
DEFENDING													
Tackles made	80	23	67	62	19	7	0	3	12	34	36	21	21
Tackles won %	61%	65%	76%	73%	68%	86%	0%	33%	83%	71%	72%	90%	67%
Blocks	11	2	32	6	8	7	0	0	1	7	7	7	3
Clearances	32	10	139	13	55	38	0	0	13	51	29	1	3
Interceptions	4	1	11	4	0	3	0	0	0	12	0	0	1
DISCIPLINE													
Fouls	22	38	36	37	9	4	1	11	19	10	10	28	21
Offside	6	19	6	0	1	0	0	33	19	0	1	30	5
Yellow cards	5	0	6	5	1	0	0	0	1	1	2	0	0
Red cards	0	0	1	0	0	0	0	0	0	0	0	1	0

GOALKEEPER NAME	START/ (SUB)	TIME ON PITCH	GOALS CONCEDED	MINS/GOALS CONCEDED	SAVES MADE	SAVES/ SHOTS
GIVEN	34(0)	3015	42	72	101	71%
HARPER	4(1)	405	8	51	16	67%

For more information visit our website:

PLAYERS' STATISTICS

	GAVILAN	GLASS	GOMA	GRIFFIN	HUGHES	KERR	LEE	LUA LUA	MARCELINO	O'BRIEN	QUINN	SHEARER	SOLANO	SPEED	TOTAL	RANK
	0	5	18	14	34	0	21	3	5	9	14	19	31	35		
	1	9	1	5	1	1	1	18	1	0	1	0	2	0		
	5	563	1567	1283	2994	1	1749	582	451	810	1273	1710	2632	3144		
	0	3	1	0	0	0	0	0	0	1	0	5	6	5	44*	=13th
	0	3	3	0	2	0	4	10	0	3	2	26	18	20	182	11th
	0	5	3	2	3	0	9	10	0	2	6	15	21	53	234	11th
	0%	38%	50%	0%	40%	0%	31%	50%	0%	60%	25%	63%	46%	27%	44%	13th
	0	0	1	0	1	0	0	2	0	0	1	2	10	3	30	=10th
	1	52	155	217	378	0	334	33	79	79	228	90	373	517	4619	4th
	3	175	412	454	861	3	806	194	149	193	393	467	1174	1298	12065	4th
	100%	82%	75%	77%	84%	100%	85%	85%	75%	85%	77%	82%	77%	82%	81%	6th
	33%	61%	59%	63%	64%	100%	75%	64%	59%	60%	56%	61%	67%	67%	65%	7th
	0	66	3	36	16	0	19	27	3	3	86	23	327	26	1007	5th
	0%	39%	0%	22%	13%	0%	37%	19%	33%	0%	24%	0%	34%	23%	28%	6th
	0	27	19	31	27	0	45	62	6	8	32	26	87	78	1026	5th
	0%	59%	79%	74%	89%	0%	87%	56%	83%	75%	59%	73%	69%	74%	68%	11th
	1	17	54	46	75	0	84	20	20	36	34	13	55	113	955	13th
	0%	82%	78%	78%	76%	0%	68%	75%	70%	75%	82%	77%	67%	68%	72%	12th
	0	0	11	8	29	0	14	0	5	12	15	2	8	10	205	=11th
	0	3	139	50	216	0	45	1	43	58	39	23	24	51	1186	17th
	0	0	10	4	6	0	7	2	1	4	4	1	4	10	89	20th
	0	11	32	13	13	0	47	10	8	6	15	51	42	74	568	9th
	0	0	0	2	1	0	0	7	0	0	0	25	13	6	174	=2nd
	0	2	4	2	2	0	3	2	1	0	0	1	3	8	50	13th
	0	0	0	0	0	0	0	0	0	0	0	0	2	1	5	=3rd

*Including two own goals

CROSSES CAUGHT	CROSSES PUNCHED	CROSSES DROPPED	CATCH SUCCESS	THROWS/ SHORT KICKS	% COMPLETION	LONG KICKS	% COMPLETION
61	23	3	95%	115	96%	608	60%
2	3	0	100%	14	100%	71	44%

PLAYER OF THE SEASON

PLAYER	INDEX SCORE
NOLBERTO SOLANO	851
Warren Barton	850
Shay Given	836
Robert Lee	809
Gary Speed	778
Alan Shearer	740
Kieron Dyer	738
Aaron Hughes	681
Alain Goma	674
Christian Bassedas	625

Injuries severely hampered Newcastle's season and, with several players forced to operate in unaccustomed roles, their mid-table finish was realistically all they could have hoped for.

The onus was on the more senior members of the squad to increase their efforts and 1999–2000 player of the season Nolberto Solano was well up to the task.

Solano clinched the 2000–01 Opta top spot for Newcastle, having quit the captaincy of Peru during the season to concentrate on the job in hand at St James' Park. The move paid dividends, as he netted six times and connected with a Premiership-best 110 crosses for 10 assists – meaning that he had a direct hand in 36% of Newcastle's league goals.

Three vastly-experienced campaigners made the top five along with Solano, with Warren Barton ranked second on 850 points, Rob Lee fourth on 809 and Gary Speed one place behind with 778.

Barton's second spot may surprise some, but he was one of only three Magpies to connect with more than 1,000 passes and also won 76% of his tackles to score well with Opta. Lee made 84 challenges in his limited time on the pitch, while Speed completed a mammoth 1,313 passes and weighed in with five goals and three assists.

Ahead of even these old hands was Shay Given, who averaged 836 points. Given showed fine reactions to make 65 saves from shots struck inside the area and kept seven clean sheets as he established his number one status at the club.

Alan Shearer's five goals landed him a sixth-best 740 points, while the versatile Kieron Dyer was an effective makeshift striker, also netting five times and recording an outstanding 81% passing accuracy.

The unfortunate Carl Cort looked a handful, but injury curtailed his involvement. Nonetheless he was still joint-top scorer with six goals, and will be itching for an extended run in 2001–02.

FIVE OF THE BEST

After a bright start to 2000–01, Newcastle's season was ruined by injury, and the Magpies eventually finished a disappointing 11th in the Premiership table. Bobby Robson could not have asked for much more effort from his players, but ultimately his squad was just not good enough to cope with a debilitating casualty list.

TOP GOALSCORERS

	GOALS	GOALS/SHOTS
CARL CORT	6	16%
Nolberto Solano	6	15%
Kieron Dyer	5	14%
Alan Shearer	5	12%
Gary Speed	5	7%

No Newcastle player managed to reach double figures in the Premiership goalscoring charts. Carl Cort did make an impressive return from injury at the end of the season, finishing up with six goals and recording a useful goals-to-shots ratio of 16%. Peruvian international Nolberto Solano joined Cort on six goals. But Alan Shearer managed just five goals, the same total as Gary Speed and Kieron Dyer, who was also a regular on the treatment table.

For the third season in succession, Newcastle were among the Premiership's most prolific passers. Three Magpies completed more than 1,000 passes as Bobby Robson encouraged his team to play possession rather than percentage football. Gary Speed made the most successful passes and was followed by Nolberto Solano and Warren Barton. Aaron Hughes earned comparisons with the late Bobby Moore for his composure on the ball, while Rob Lee proved he is still a class act, recording a 79% pass completion rate.

TOP PASSERS

	SUCC PASSES	COMPLETION
GARY SPEED	1,313	72%
Nolberto Solano	1,079	70%
Warren Barton	1,019	70%
Aaron Hughes	941	76%
Robert Lee	906	79%

TOP TACKLERS

	WON	SUCCESS
GARY SPEED	77	68%
Aaron Hughes	57	76%
Robert Lee	57	68%
Warren Barton	51	76%
Clarence Acuna	49	61%

Top passer Gary Speed was also Newcastle's ball-winner-in-chief. The Welsh international has a reputation for being one of the most competitive players in the Premiership and proved it by winning more challenges than any of his team-mates. Defenders Aaron Hughes and Warren Barton both won plenty of ball at the back, while veteran Rob Lee and Chilean star Clarence Acuna battled hard for possession in the midfield, winning 106 tackles between them.

Although Gary Speed was not sent off until the last day of the season, only six other players finished higher in Opta's league of indiscipline. Speed accrued 41 more disciplinary points than second-placed Nolberto Solano in Newcastle's own indiscipline chart, although the Peruvian was one of just four Premiership players to see red twice in 2000–01. Alan Shearer missed plenty of games through injury, but the former England skipper certainly made his presence felt when fit, conceding 51 fouls.

DISCIPLINE

	POINTS	FOULS & CARDS
GARY SPEED	104	74F, 8Y, 1R
Nolberto Solano	63	42F, 3Y, 2R
Warren Barton	60	36F, 6Y, 1R
Robert Lee	56	47F, 3Y, 0R
Alan Shearer	54	51F, 1Y, 0R

crosses than any other Premiership player

ACTION	ACUNA	AMOOBI	BARTON	BASSEDAS	GALLACHER	GIVEN	GOMA	HUGHES	LEE	LUA LUA	MARCELINO	QUINN	SPEED	SOLANO	TOTAL	LEEDS UNITED
Time on pitch	90	89	90	16	74	90	90	90	74	16	1	90	90	90	990	990
GOALS																
Goal	1	1	–	–	–	–	–	–	–	–	–	–	–	–	3	–
Shot on target (incl goals)	2	1	–	–	2	–	–	–	–	–	–	–	–	1	6	4
Shot off target	2	–	–	–	–	–	–	–	–	–	–	–	–	2	5	7
Blocked shot	–	–	–	–	–	–	–	–	–	–	–	–	1	–	2	5
Own goal	–	–	–	–	–	–	–	–	–	–	–	–	–	–	0	0
PASSES																
Pass to own player	21	14	34	4	19	8	16	16	45	6	1	16	23	25	248	297
Pass to opposition	9	15	16	1	6	6	10	5	11	1	2	26	15	26	149	160
Cross to own player	–	–	1	–	–	–	–	–	–	–	–	2	–	2	5	8
Cross to opposition player	–	–	–	–	–	–	–	–	–	–	–	1	–	2	4	26
Goal assist	–	–	–	–	–	–	–	–	–	–	–	–	–	2	2	1
Pass completion %	70%	48%	69%	67%	76%	57%	62%	76%	80%	86%	33%	40%	62%	50%	63%	62%
TACKLES & CLEARANCES																
Tackle	4	–	4	1	1	–	6	4	6	–	–	3	2	1	32	26
Clearances, blocks and interceptions	3	2	6	1	1	3	9	9	3	–	1	9	5	–	51	19
DRIBBLES & RUNS																
Dribbles ball retained	–	2	4	–	–	–	1	–	–	1	–	–	–	–	9	14
Dribbles ball lost	–	1	–	3	3	–	–	–	–	–	–	–	–	1	5	3
Dribble success %	0%	67%	100%	0%	0%	0%	100%	0%	100%	100%	0%	0%	0%	0%	64%	82%
DISCIPLINE																
Fouls	–	2	1	1	3	–	3	1	2	2	–	–	1	2	18	10
Penalty conceded	–	–	–	–	–	–	–	–	–	–	–	–	–	–	0	1
Free kick – offside	–	2	–	–	1	–	–	–	1	1	–	–	–	4	4	2
Yellow cards	–	–	–	–	–	–	–	–	–	–	–	–	–	–	2	2
Red cards	–	–	–	–	–	–	–	–	–	–	–	–	–	–	0	0
GOALKEEPERS																
Distribution to own player	–	–	–	–	–	13	–	–	–	–	–	–	–	–	13	17
Distribution to opposition player	–	–	–	–	–	16	–	–	–	–	–	–	–	–	16	5
Goalkeeper distribution %	–	–	–	–	–	45%	–	–	–	–	–	–	–	–	45%	77%
Save	–	–	–	–	–	3	–	–	–	–	–	–	–	–	3	3
Ball caught	–	–	–	–	–	3	–	–	–	–	–	–	–	–	3	3
Ball dropped	–	–	–	–	–	1	–	–	–	–	–	–	–	–	1	0
Goal conceded	–	–	–	–	–	–	–	–	–	–	–	–	–	–	1	3

65% Shay Given was the most accurate goalkeeper

For the Newcastle side under Bobby Robson, 2000–01 was a season of consolidation and rebuilding, but there were still performances to inspire the Toon Army – and the away win at Leeds was as accomplished as any from the Magpies.

20 January 2001

1–3

LEEDS UNITED
NEWCASTLE UNITED

Not only was it Newcastle's biggest-ever win at Elland Road, but it also showed that the north-east side can attack and win without the talismanic Alan Shearer. The visitors imposed themselves well as Leeds were out-passed in midfield, and Newcastle's central pairing of Robert Lee and Clarence Acuna found a team-mate with 80% and 70% of their distribution respectively.

However, it was the home side who took the lead after just three minutes. Eirik Bakke had already headed off-target before the Norwegian fortuitously set up Robbie Keane in the area and the on-loan Inter Milan striker smashed the ball home.

Unfortunately for the Leeds faithful, their one-goal advantage lasted just 60 seconds. Whites defender Danny Mills was adjudged to have handled in the box, and Nolberto Solano converted the resulting penalty.

It was the first of the Magpies' six shots on target – two more than their hosts were able to manage.

Both teams continued to create chances in a frenetic opening, with Mark Viduka and Lee Bowyer hitting efforts on target for Leeds, while Acuna and Kevin Gallagher tested Paul Robinson at the other end.

One minute before the half-time whistle, Newcastle grabbed what proved to be a vital second goal. Man of the match Acuna sped through a statuesque Leeds defence

and chipped over the advancing Robinson, despite a despairing challenge.

The second half saw profligacy from both sides as Leeds fought to haul themselves back into the contest.

Viduka and Keane both wasted good chances and Bakke was thwarted by Shay Given before Newcastle revelation Shola Ameobi wrapped up the points in the final five minutes, finishing coolly past the Leeds 'keeper.

Newcastle demonstrated their attacking credentials with aplomb. Six of the Magpies' 11 shots were on target and three of them were good enough to beat Robinson.

Leeds ended the game having racked up a corner count of 16 to nil in their favour, but found the recalled Newcastle 'keeper Shay Given in top form as the Republic of Ireland international pulled off three saves to deny David O'Leary's attacking line-up time and time again.

It was a battling victory for Newcastle and, although Leeds were to go on and have a good season, Bobby Robson and his players demonstrated that they had the ability to compete with the top sides. Consistency may have let them down overall throughout 2000–01, but in terms of the rebuilding job Robson started at St James' Park, this was a solid brick in the foundations and a result to delight the faithful Toon Army.

with his distribution in the top flight

SOUTHAMPTON

ADDRESS

The Friends Provident St Mary's
Stadium, Britannia Road,
Southampton SO14 5FP

CONTACT NUMBERS

Telephone: 0870 2200 000
Ticket Office: 0870 2200 150
Club Shop: 0870 2200 185
Club Call: 09068 121178
e-mail: sfc@saintsfc.co.uk
Website: www.saintsfc.co.uk

KEY PERSONNEL

President: E T Bates MBE
Chairman: R J G Lowe
Vice-Chairman: B H D Hunt
Directors: A E Cowen, I L Gordon
M R Richards FCA, K St J Wiseman
R M Withers
Company Secretary: Brian Truscott
Manager: TBA

SPONSORS

Friends Provident

FANZINES

The Ugly Inside
The Beautiful South

COLOURS

Home: Red and white shirts, black
shorts and black stockings
Away: Navy shirts, navy shorts
and yellow stockings

NICKNAME

The Saints

HONOURS

Division Three (South) Champions:
1921–22
Division Three Champions: 1959–60
FA Cup Winners: 1976

RECORD GOALSCORER

Mike Channon – 185 league goals,
1966–77, 1979–82

BIGGEST WIN

9–3 v Wolverhampton Wanderers –
Division Two, 18 September 1965

BIGGEST DEFEATS

0–8 v Tottenham Hotspur – Division
Two, 28 March 1936
0–8 v Everton – Division One,
20 November 1971

SEASON REVIEW

Having had a relatively happy 1999–2000 season by their standards, Southampton fans were hoping for more of the same in 2000–01, especially as it was to be the last season at The Dell before the move to their new stadium.

Even the most ardent of supporters realised that it would not be easy in such a competitive league and, despite having master tactician Glenn Hoddle in charge, everyone knew it would be another hard-fought campaign.

Never a club with huge budgets, Hoddle's most expensive signing before the start of the campaign was Mark Draper, who cost £1.5 million from Aston Villa.

Hoddle picked Draper when England boss and clearly felt that the midfielder would be a vital addition to his Saints squad.

Former Manchester City striker Uwe Rosler was also drafted in, while ex-Arsenal forward Luis Boa Morte joined Fulham on a season's loan, where he played a vital part in the Londoners' promotion to the top flight, scoring 18 league goals.

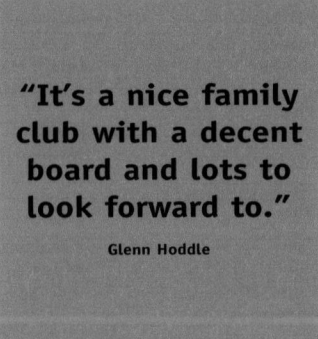

"It's a nice family club with a decent board and lots to look forward to."

Glenn Hoddle

The season started in worrying fashion for Hoddle's side. Just three points were earned in the opening five games of the campaign and Saints were 19th in the Premiership.

Then, in September, striker James Beattie rejected a move to Crystal Palace after the two clubs had reportedly agreed a fee. It was to prove a pivotal point in the Saints' season.

Two consecutive wins against Newcastle and Bradford briefly saw Southampton in the top half of the table, but just as quickly they then lost to both Manchester clubs and ended October back in the bottom three.

Enter Beattie. The man who two months earlier had been set to drop a division suddenly hit a patch of form more purple than the blushing Southampton board who were willing to sell him.

From 1 November to the turn of the year Beattie scored 10 goals in as many Premiership matches, a run which saw Southampton collect 17 points and end 2000 in a healthy 12th position.

By then Southampton's Worthington Cup dream had ended. A two-legged victory over Mansfield in the second round was followed by a 1–0 home defeat to Coventry City, also struggling in the league.

The new calendar year began with a narrow defeat at Anfield, but better news was to follow. Dan Petrescu was signed from Bradford City, linking up with the manager who signed him to Chelsea, while the FA Cup brought more cheer, albeit short-lived.

A third-round win over Sheffield United in January was followed three weeks later by a fourth-round win against United's city rivals, Sheffield Wednesday.

In the league the Saints went on a superb run, keeping seven consecutive clean sheets, with just four points dropped out of a possible 21.

That terrific form meant that the Saints were eighth in the table, and the perennial strugglers were suddenly looking towards Europe. Southampton fans had not had it so good for years. Surely it could not last?

Sadly, it could not. Their FA Cup run was halted in dramatic fashion at Prenton Park. Southampton were 3–0 up at half-time to a Tranmere side renowned for knocking out Premiership opposition.

What followed after the break will haunt Southampton fans for many years to come. Tranmere amazingly fought back with four

SEASON REVIEW

goals in the second half and it was they who progressed to a quarter-final against Liverpool, not the Saints.

While life at The Dell was rosy, things were not so great at the other end of the M27 and beyond in north London.

The news that all Southampton fans had feared – the sacking of George Graham as Tottenham manager – became reality in March, with Glenn Hoddle the firm favourite to take over.

While Hoddle himself gave no immediate assurances that he would go, many felt it was only a matter of time before the former White Hart Lane idol returned to his footballing roots. The manager refused even to discuss the speculation, with many seeing this as a clear sign he wanted the job.

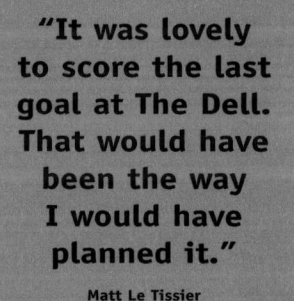

"It was lovely to score the last goal at The Dell. That would have been the way I would have planned it."

Matt Le Tissier

By the end of March, Hoddle had flown the nest and joined his former club. On the day of his departure, Southampton were one point from a UEFA Cup place and five away from a Champions League spot. Saints chairman Rupert Lowe was unimpressed by the way Hoddle's switch had come about, but there was nothing he could do to stop it.

Many names were bandied about as a replacement for the former England boss, most noticeably Kevin Keegan, who had enjoyed a successful spell with the club as a player.

But it was Stuart Gray who took one step up to become caretaker manager, at least until the end of the season.

Hoddle was clearly going to be a hard act to follow. And so it proved, with Southampton failing to score in their next five league matches. Just one point gained from those matches saw the Saints drop back into mid-table.

The south coast side's chances of European football had now all but vanished, but thanks to the good work of Hoddle, there would be no nail-biting finish to this particular campaign.

Instead, fans were looking towards the end of The Dell. Almost as if fate played a part, the club's last two matches of the season were both at home and to Manchester United and Arsenal.

The Saints would win both matches, to give the old stadium the perfect send-off, though no one could have predicted exactly how 103 years of football at The Dell would come to an end.

With the score at 2–2 against Arsenal on the final day of the season, Stuart Gray brought on Southampton legend Matt Le Tissier, who that week had been voted the best Saints player of all time by the fans.

As the final minute of competitive football at The Dell approached, the Channel Islander picked up the ball on the edge of the penalty area with his back to goal.

In one movement, Le Tissier showed just why he was given such an accolade by the fans, turning and firing a blistering left-footed shot into the top corner, to give Southampton a 3–2 win against Arsenal.

A better script could not have been written and with the Le Tissier goal came a noise from the crowd so loud they almost saved the demolition workers a job by virtually bringing the place down.

It was a wonderful dénouement to the season. The loss of Hoddle was clearly a huge blow but, if the new manager can keep the current squad and add to it and the new stadium also has a positive effect on the players, there is no reason why Southampton cannot build on the 2000–01 season and cement themselves as a mid-table Premiership side.

outfield player to play every minute of every game

SOUTHAMPTON

DATE	OPPONENT	SCORE	ATT.	BEATTIE	BENALI	BLEIDELIS	BRIDGE	DAVIES	DODD	DRAPER	EL-KHALEJ	GIBBENS	JONES	KACHL
19.08.00	Derby Co A	2–2	27,223	s7	–	–	90	90	90	90	90□	–	90	90²
23.08.00	Coventry H	1–2	14,801	s7	–	–	90	25□	90	90	90□	–	90	83□
26.08.00	Liverpool H	3–3	15,202	s9	–	–	90	–	61	90	s29¹	–	–	61
06.09.00	Charlton A	1–1	20,043	s26	–	–	90	–	–	90□	90	–	–	s26
09.09.00	Leicester A	0–1	18,366	s19	–	–	90	–	–	75	90	–	–	90
16.09.00	Newcastle H	2–0	15,221	82	–	–	90	–	90	–	90	–	90	88
23.09.00	Bradford A	1–0*	16,163	67	–	–	90	–	90□	–	90	–	90	87
30.09.00	Middlesbro H	1–3	14,903	s18□	–	–	90	–	90	–	90	–	90	81□
14.10.00	Everton A	1–1	29,491	–	–	–	90	90□	90¹	–	90	–	90	90□
23.10.00	Man City H	0–2	15,056	s18	–	–	90	s45	90	–	90□	–	90	90
28.10.00	Man Utd A	0–5	67,581	s24	s8	–	90	90	90	90	82	–	90	90
04.11.00	Chelsea H	3–2	15,236	90²□	–	–	90	s29	90	–	90□	–	90	–
11.11.00	Sunderland A	2–2	45,064	90¹	–	–	90	–	90	–	87	–	90	s3
18.11.00	Aston Villa H	2–0	14,979	90²	–	–	90	73	90	s17	–	s1	90	90
25.11.00	West Ham H	2–3	15,232	90¹	–	–	90	–	90	s55	90□	–	90	90
02.12.00	Arsenal A	0–1	38,036	78	–	–	90	90□	90	87	90	s3	90	90□
09.12.00	Leeds Utd H	1–0	15,225	90¹	–	–	90	90	90	s15□	90	–	90	85□
16.12.00	Ipswich A	1–3	22,228	90¹	–	–	90	70□	80□	s60	90	–	90	s20
22.12.00	Coventry A	1–1	18,090	90	–	–	90	s21	–	90□	90	69	90	90
27.12.00	Tottenham H	2–0	15,237	88¹	–	–	90	90¹	90	64	s45□	–	90	–
30.12.00	Derby Co H	1–0	15,075	90¹	–	–	90	90	90	–	90	–	90	90
01.01.01	Liverpool A	1–2	38,474	90	–	–	90	90	90	–	90	–	90	s7
13.01.01	Charlton H	0–0	15,220	90	–	–	90	76	90	s23	–	–	90	90
20.01.01	Tottenham A	0–0	36,095	90	–	–	90	90	90	90	90	–	90	83
31.01.01	Leicester H	1–0	14,909	90	–	–	90	45	90	–	s14	–	90	s6
10.02.01	Bradford H	2–0	14,651	90¹	–	s6	90	–	79	s31	s11	–	90	–
24.02.01	Middlesbro A	1–0	28,725	90	–	–	90	s10	–	90¹	–	–	90	80
03.03.01	Man City A	1–0	33,990	30	–	–	90	s1	–	90	90□	–	90	89
17.03.01	Everton H	1–0	15,251	90□	–	–	90□	–	s3	90	87	–	90	–
02.04.01	Ipswich H	0–3	15,244	90□	–	–	90	–	s31	–	90	–	90	–
07.04.01	Leeds Utd A	0–2	39,267	90	–	–	90	90	90	73	–	–	90	–
14.04.01	Chelsea A	0–1	35,136	90□	–	–	90	79	90	69□	s11	–	90	s21
21.04.01	Aston Villa A	0–0	29,336	90	–	–	90	89□	90	90□	s4	–	90	90
28.04.01	Sunderland H	0–1	15,249	84	–	–	90	s6□	84	–	90	–	90	90□
01.05.01	Newcastle A	1–1	50,439	79	s36	–	90	90□	90	–	54	–	90	90
05.05.01	West Ham A	0–3	26,041	90	–	–	90	90□	90	–	–	–	90	69
13.05.01	Man Utd H	2–1*	15,246	90	s6	–	90	90	–	–	–	–	90	76
19.05.01	Arsenal H	3–2	15,252	90	s8	–	90	75□	–	–	s15	–	90	82²

□ Yellow card, ▪ Red card, S Substitute, 90² Goals scored

*including own goal

For more information visit our website:

2000–01 PREMIERSHIP APPEARANCES

LE TISSIER	LUNDEKVAM	MARSDEN	MONK	MOSS	OAKLEY	PAHARS	PETRESCU	RICHARDS	RIPLEY	ROSLER	SOLTVEDT	TESSEM	TOTAL
–	90	90	–	–	72	–	–	–	–	83	–	s18	990
–	90□	45	–	–	90	s65	–	–	–	90□	–	s45¹	990
s29	90	–	–	90	90	90²	–	90	–	81	–	90	990
–	90	64□	–	90	90	90¹	–	90	–	64□	–	90□	990
–	90	s15	–	90	90	90	–	90	–	71	–	90	990
s2	90	–	–	–	90	65²	–	90	s25	s8	–	90	990
–	90	s3	–	–	90	90	–	90	–	s23	s45	45	990
90	90	–	–	–	90	90¹	–	64	s9	72	s26	–	990
–	90	90□	–	–	90	90	–	–	–	–	90	–	990
45	90	s45	–	–	45	90	–	–	72	–	90	–	990
–	90	s18	–	–	72	90	–	–	–	–	–	66	990
–	90	90□	–	–	61	90□	–	90	–	–	–	90¹	990
–	90□	90	–	–	90	80	–	90¹	–	s10	–	90	990
–	90	–	–	–	90	89	–	90	–	–	–	90	990
–	35	–	–	–	90¹	90	–	90	–	s15	–	75	990
–	90	–	–	–	90	–	–	–	–	s12	–	90	990
–	90	–	–	–	90□	75	–	–	–	–	–	90	985
–	90	–	–	–	30	90	–	90	–	s10	–	90	990
–	90	90	–	–	–	–	–	90	–	–	–	90¹	990
–	90	45	–	–	90	–	90	–	–	s2	s26	90	990
–	90	–	–	–	90	90	–	–	–	–	–	90	990
–	90	–	–	–	90	83	–	–	–	s1□	90¹	89	990
–	90	67	–	–	90	–	s14	90	–	–	–	90	990
–	90	–	–	–	90	s7	–	90□	–	–	–	–	990
–	76	90	–	–	90	90	84¹	90	–	–	–	s45	990
–	90	59	–	–	90	90¹	84	90	–	–	–	90	990
–	90	90	–	–	90	–	90	90	–	–	–	90	990
–	90	90	–	–	90	–	81¹	90	–	s60	–	s9	990
–	90	–	–	–	90	90	90	90	–	–	–	90¹	990
s15□	90	75	–	–	90	75	59	90	–	s15	–	90	990
–	90	90	–	–	90	s17	90	90	–	–	–	–	990
–	90	–	–	–	79	–	90	90	–	s11	–	90	990
–	90	–	–	–	86	s1	–	90	–	–	–	90	990
s25	90	–	–	–	90	65	–	90	–	s6	–	90	990
–	90	90	–	–	90	s19¹	–	–	–	s11	–	71	990
s11	90□	90	–	–	90	79	–	90	–	s16	–	s5	990
–	90	90□	84	–	90	90¹	–	90	–	–	–	s14	990
s15¹	90	90	75	–	–	90	–	90	–	–	–	90	990

THE MANAGER

STUART GRAY

For the second successive season there were managerial changes at The Dell. Glenn Hoddle began the season in the Southampton hot seat, but the lure of his beloved Tottenham proved too tempting and the former England coach swapped the south coast for north London at the end of March.

Hoddle had led the Saints into the top 10 and left them when the club was dreaming of Europe, after a run of seven consecutive clean sheets immediately before his departure.

Chairman Rupert Lowe was not pressured into making an immediate appointment and confirmed first-team coach Stuart Gray as caretaker manager until the end of the 2000–01 season.

The former Nottingham Forest and Aston Villa defender had nine games to make an impact, but the transition period clearly took its toll on the club. Gray's reign began with three straight defeats, which evolved into a seven-game stretch without a win.

But ending the campaign with back-to-back home wins over Manchester United and Arsenal respectively should serve to keep Gray in the running for the permanent position at the new St Mary's stadium.

LEAGUE POSITION

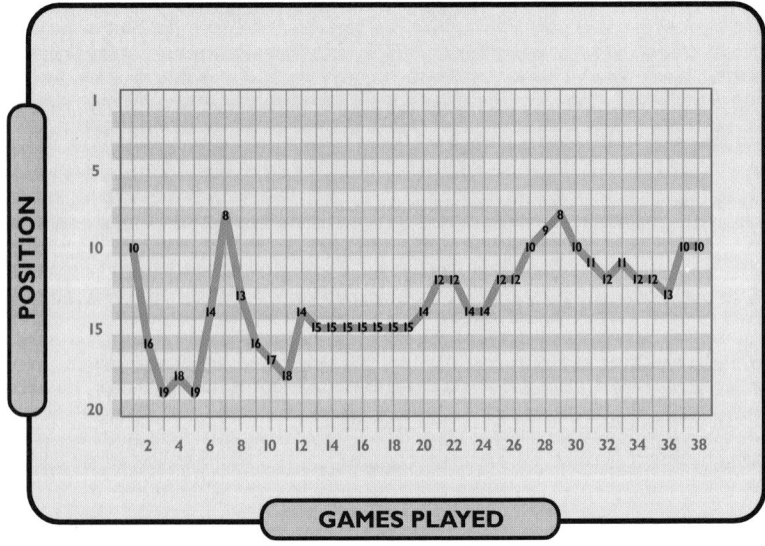

14 Paul Jones was one of the three Premiership

THE GOALS

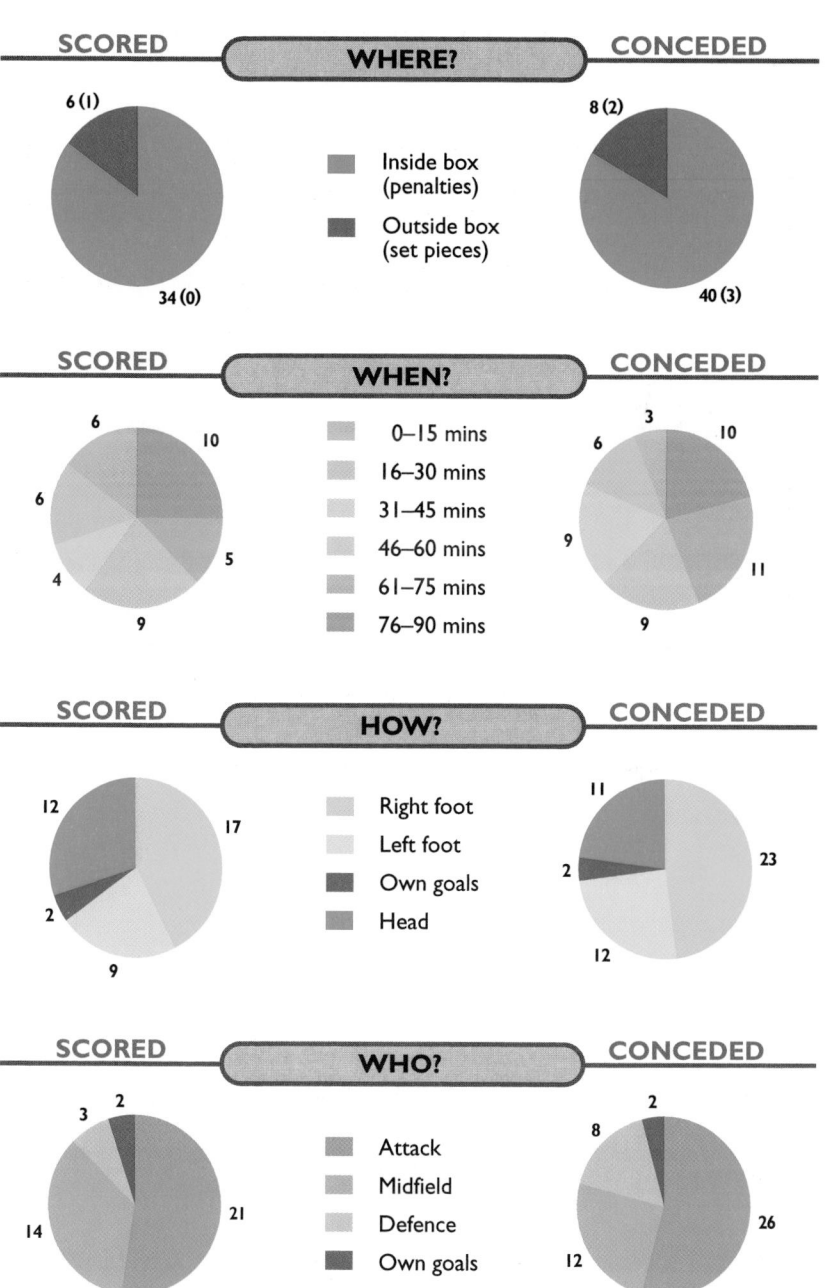

WHERE?

SCORED | CONCEDED

6 (1)
34 (0)

8 (2)
40 (3)

- Inside box (penalties)
- Outside box (set pieces)

WHEN?

SCORED | CONCEDED

6, 10, 6, 4, 9, 5

3, 10, 6, 9, 9, 11

- 0–15 mins
- 16–30 mins
- 31–45 mins
- 46–60 mins
- 61–75 mins
- 76–90 mins

HOW?

SCORED | CONCEDED

12, 17, 2, 9

11, 2, 23, 12

- Right foot
- Left foot
- Own goals
- Head

WHO?

SCORED | CONCEDED

3, 2, 14, 21

2, 8, 12, 26

- Attack
- Midfield
- Defence
- Own goals

goalkeepers to keep 14 clean sheets

SOUTHAMPTON

	BEATTIE	BENALI	BLEIDELIS	BRIDGE	DAVIES	DODD	DRAPER	EL KHALEJ	GIBBENS	KACHLOUL	LE TISSIER
APPEARANCES											
Start	29	0	0	38	21	29	16	25	1	26	2
Sub	8	4	1	0	6	2	6	7	2	6	6
Minutes on pitch	2616	58	6	3420	1814	2588	1559	2329	73	2307	232
GOAL ATTEMPTS											
Goals	11	0	0	0	1	1	1	1	0	4	1
Shots on target	33	0	0	7	12	2	4	12	0	16	3
Shots off target	43	0	0	2	22	1	13	16	0	28	1
Shooting accuracy	43%	0%	0%	78%	35%	67%	24%	43%	0%	36%	75%
PASSING											
Goal assists	3	0	0	2	3	1	1	0	0	7	0
Long passes	108	5	0	528	149	465	181	217	2	187	24
Short passes	583	11	1	911	536	828	536	456	20	686	74
PASS COMPLETION											
Own half %	74%	78%	0%	71%	71%	77%	86%	77%	57%	76%	76%
Opposition half %	51%	57%	0%	61%	53%	65%	71%	63%	47%	58%	73%
CROSSING											
Total crosses	51	0	1	125	45	54	43	33	1	272	36
Cross completion %	18%	0%	0%	31%	20%	28%	30%	15%	0%	29%	39%
DRIBBLING											
Dribbles & runs	73	0	1	159	83	30	33	60	0	109	4
Dribble completion %	51%	0%	100%	82%	65%	87%	67%	63%	0%	58%	75%
DEFENDING											
Tackles made	42	1	1	94	84	75	53	57	1	91	2
Tackles won %	79%	100%	100%	73%	70%	79%	85%	75%	100%	79%	100%
Blocks	9	0	0	27	3	34	8	16	0	5	0
Clearances	29	3	0	135	22	142	37	163	0	12	0
Interceptions	0	1	0	20	1	3	3	5	0	2	0
DISCIPLINE											
Fouls	75	2	0	25	48	26	26	58	1	39	4
Offside	31	0	0	0	4	0	2	7	0	14	1
Yellow cards	5	0	0	1	9	2	5	7	0	5	1
Red cards	0	0	0	0	0	0	0	0	0	1	0

GOALKEEPER NAME	START/ (SUB)	TIME ON PITCH	GOALS CONCEDED	MINS/GOALS CONCEDED	SAVES MADE	SAVES/ SHOTS
JONES	35(0)	3150	43	73	117	73%
MOSS	3(0)	270	5	54	8	62%

For more information visit our website:

PLAYERS' STATISTICS

	LUNDEKVAM	MARSDEN	MONK	OAKLEY	PAHARS	PETRESCU	RICHARDS	RIPLEY	ROSLER	SOLTVEDT	TESSEM	TOTAL	RANK
	38	19	2	35	26	8	28	1	6	3	27		
	0	4	0	0	5	1	0	2	14	3	6		
	3351	1606	159	2965	2340	682	2494	106	661	367	2462		
	0	0	0	1	9	2	1	0	0	1	4	40*	16th
	0	2	0	11	24	5	6	0	9	1	21	168	12th
	4	12	0	17	33	3	18	0	14	2	23	252	6th
	0%	14%	0%	39%	42%	63%	25%	0%	39%	33%	48%	40%	18th
	0	1	0	0	6	1	0	0	0	0	2	27	13th
	411	222	24	483	147	51	291	12	27	31	123	4053	12th
	677	578	36	1082	605	224	541	42	121	97	664	9371	18th
	79%	81%	65%	81%	80%	87%	75%	100%	76%	73%	74%	77%	15th
	49%	70%	53%	70%	68%	71%	52%	38%	66%	61%	64%	61%	16th
	16	29	4	43	169	26	5	15	12	0	101	1081	2nd
	25%	34%	50%	35%	30%	35%	20%	40%	17%	0%	22%	28%	4th
	34	17	5	47	140	10	26	9	7	3	81	936	8th
	91%	88%	80%	66%	58%	60%	81%	67%	57%	100%	65%	68%	13th
	59	82	4	110	27	15	69	3	11	11	73	965	10th
	69%	67%	100%	75%	89%	73%	75%	67%	45%	64%	71%	75%	4th
	65	11	1	17	3	2	30	0	1	2	10	245	5th
	393	28	6	42	9	6	315	2	0	8	47	1453	7th
	17	7	0	19	4	4	32	0	0	0	6	124	5th
	23	44	3	43	19	6	32	2	27	2	48	553	12th
	0	2	0	1	21	3	1	0	12	0	19	118	18th
	3	4	0	1	1	0	1	0	3	0	1	49	=14th
	0	0	0	0	0	0	0	0	0	0	0	1	=19th

*Including two own goals

CROSSES CAUGHT	CROSSES PUNCHED	CROSSES DROPPED	CATCH SUCCESS	THROWS/ SHORT KICKS	% COMPLETION	LONG KICKS	% COMPLETION
64	28	7	90%	64	84%	756	48%
3	3	0	100%	11	82%	54	56%

PLAYER OF THE SEASON

PLAYER	INDEX SCORE
DEAN RICHARDS	898
Paul Jones	808
Jason Dodd	792
Hassan Kachloul	741
Marian Pahars	731
Matt Oakley	725
Claus Lundekvam	697
James Beattie	679
Wayne Bridge	655
Jo Tessem	651

Southampton were progressing well, just outside the top six in the 2000–01 Premiership, until Glenn Hoddle left for White Hart Lane a week before the FA Cup semi-final.

The main reason Southampton had flourished for much of the campaign was their resolute defence – led by their 1999–2000 and 2000–01 Opta Saints player of the season Dean Richards.

Indeed, just two out of the Saints' 14 clean sheets came in the absence of Richards, and with 315 clearances to his name he was instrumental in keeping the opposition at bay.

His anticipation was also immaculate. Richards made 32 interceptions, which was more than any other top-flight player – despite missing nearly 1,000 minutes of league action.

Richards, well-supported by Claus Lundekvam with nearly 400 clearances, provided excellent protection for Paul Jones, who responded in kind. Jones made 117 saves and maintained a joint-highest total by any Premiership 'keeper of 14 shut-outs, including a club record seven on the trot, as he accumulated an average Opta score of 808 points.

Skipper Jason Dodd completed the top three in his testimonial season at Southampton. The captain's fair-but-committed approach saw him win nearly 80% of his tackles while accumulating just two bookings throughout the season, with only two Saints supplying more passes.

Wayne Bridge may have been the Supporters' Player of the Year, but he did not rank as highly on Opta's system. While he burst forward to connect with a commendable 31% of crosses, Bridge's passing was sloppier than most and he created just two goals for colleagues – five fewer than fourth-ranked Hassan Kachloul, for instance.

Kachloul scored four himself to boost his average score to 741 points, while James Beattie rattled in 11 goals in a 15-game burst and would have ranked much higher had he kept this up all season.

FIVE OF THE BEST

The departure of Glenn Hoddle came as a big blow to everyone at Southampton, particularly as the south coast club was making real progress under the former England manager. But Southampton are on a firmer footing than they were before Hoddle's arrival and can take pride in a top-10 finish at the end of the 2000–01 season.

TOP GOALSCORERS

	GOALS	GOALS/SHOTS
JAMES BEATTIE	11	14%
Marian Pahars	9	16%
Hassan Kachloul	4	9%
Jo Tessem	4	9%
Dan Petrescu	2	25%

Between 11 November and 30 December, James Beattie hit the hottest scoring streak of his career, netting 10 goals in 10 games, but thereafter found the net just once more. That amazing 10-match streak proved good enough to put Beattie at the top of Saints' goalscoring chart. Beattie was followed by Marian Pahars, who started the season in terrific style, but faded at around the same time as Beattie found his form.

Underrated midfielder Matt Oakley was Saints' top passer in 2000–01. But Southampton did not see as much of the ball in midfield as some other Premiership teams and three of their top five passers were defenders. Wayne Bridge impressed everyone with his composure on the ball and took the second spot in the list, while reliable defenders Jason Dodd and Claus Lundekvam also made an appearance. Chris Marsden could not compete with Oakley's workrate, but he was slightly more accurate.

TOP PASSERS

	SUCC PASSES	COMPLETION
MATT OAKLEY	1,165	74%
Wayne Bridge	933	65%
Jason Dodd	901	70%
Claus Lundekvam	728	67%
Chris Marsden	599	75%

TOP TACKLERS

	WON	SUCCESS
MATT OAKLEY	83	75%
Hassan Kachloul	72	79%
Wayne Bridge	69	73%
Jason Dodd	59	79%
Kevin Davies	59	70%

Matt Oakley's status as Southampton's busiest midfielder is underlined by his presence at the top of Saints' tackling chart. Oakley made more challenges than anyone else at The Dell, but was not the club's most successful tackler. That honour went to Moroccan international Hassan Kachloul, who proved that he is more than just a flair player by winning 79% of all his challenges. Kevin Davies also deserves a mention for attempting and winning more challenges than any other Premiership striker.

James Beattie's game is all about power, so it was no real surprise to see him concede more fouls than anyone else at Southampton. Beattie was not Saints' most booked player, though. That distinction went to Kevin Davies, who was yellow-carded nine times. Overall, though, Southampton lived up to their nickname, finishing the season as one of only two clubs with just one red card to their name – a dismissal received by Hassan Kachloul in a fractious game against Leeds.

DISCIPLINE

	POINTS	FOULS & CARDS
JAMES BEATTIE	90	75F, 5Y, 0R
Tahar El Khalej	79	58F, 7Y, 0R
Kevin Davies	75	48F, 9Y, 0R
Hassan Kachloul	60	39F, 5Y, 1R
Chris Marsden	56	44F, 4Y, 0R

ACTION	BEATTIE	BENALI	BRIDGE	DAVIES	EL KHALEJ	JONES	KACHLOUL	LE TISSIER	LUNDEKVAM	MARSDEN	MONK	PAHARS	RICHARDS	TESSEM	TOTAL	ARSENAL
Time on pitch	90	8	90	75	15	90	82	15	90	90	75	90	90	90	990	990
GOALS																
Goal	–	–	–	–	–	–	–	–	–	–	–	–	–	–	3	2
Shot on target (incl goals)	2	–	1	1	–	–	2	1	–	1	–	2	–	–	10	6
Shot off target	2	–	–	–	–	–	2	–	–	–	–	3	–	2	8	5
Blocked shot	–	–	–	–	–	–	1	–	1	–	–	–	–	1	5	4
Own goal	–	–	–	–	–	–	–	–	–	–	–	–	–	–	0	0
PASSES																
Pass to own player	11	–	27	23	2	6	27	8	22	42	19	15	15	27	244	361
Pass to opposition	8	1	8	5	2	7	7	6	9	13	12	13	2	10	103	112
Cross to own player	–	–	1	–	–	–	3	–	–	–	1	–	–	–	5	4
Cross to opposition player	2	–	4	1	–	–	9	–	–	1	2	–	–	–	19	14
Goal assist	–	–	–	–	–	–	–	–	–	–	–	–	–	–	–	1
Pass completion %	52%	0%	70%	79%	50%	46%	65%	57%	71%	75%	59%	54%	88%	73%	67%	74%
TACKLES & CLEARANCES																
Tackle	1	1	3	9	2	–	3	–	5	5	–	1	–	4	34	28
Clearances, blocks and interceptions	–	–	3	1	–	2	–	–	9	–	2	–	5	3	25	41
DRIBBLES & RUNS																
Dribbles ball retained	1	–	5	–	1	1	4	1	–	1	2	3	3	3	25	27
Dribbles ball lost	–	–	–	2	–	–	–	–	–	–	–	2	–	–	4	2
Dribble success %	100%	0%	100%	0%	100%	100%	100%	100%	0%	100%	100%	60%	100%	100%	86%	93%
DISCIPLINE																
Fouls	2	–	2	5	1	–	1	–	2	2	1	–	1	2	17	12
Penalty conceded	–	–	–	–	–	–	–	–	–	–	–	–	–	–	0	0
Free kick – offside	–	–	–	–	–	–	–	1	–	–	–	1	–	–	2	2
Yellow cards	–	–	–	–	–	–	–	–	–	–	–	–	–	–	1	2
Red cards	–	–	–	–	–	–	–	–	–	–	–	–	–	–	0	0
GOALKEEPERS																
Distribution to own player	–	–	–	–	–	18	–	–	–	–	–	–	–	–	18	18
Distribution to opposition player	–	–	–	–	–	11	–	–	–	–	–	–	–	–	11	8
Goalkeeper distribution %	–	–	–	–	–	62%	–	–	–	–	–	–	–	–	62%	69%
Save	–	–	–	–	–	4	–	–	–	–	–	–	–	–	4	6
Ball caught	–	–	–	–	–	2	–	–	–	–	–	–	–	–	2	4
Ball dropped	–	–	–	–	–	1	–	–	–	–	–	–	–	–	–	0
Goal conceded	–	–	–	–	–	2	–	–	–	–	–	–	–	–	2	3

Southampton's prodigal son Matt Le Tissier brought the curtain down on 103 years of competitive football at The Dell in fairytale fashion with a stunning last-gasp winner. Having defeated champions Manchester United a week earlier, it was a fitting end to one of the most charismatic venues in English football.

19 May 2001
3–2
SOUTHAMPTON
ARSENAL

There was a carnival atmosphere inside The Dell for this last match of the 2000–01 season and Southampton's ever-present full-back Wayne Bridge picked up the Saints' Player of the Year trophy before the game.

But it was the Gunners who forged ahead in the 28th minute when Robert Pires produced a brilliant dummy, leaving Ashley Cole a clear run down the left. Paul Jones parried the full-back's initial shot, but the Welshman could do little to stop Cole converting the rebound for his first right-footed goal of the season.

Opta's Index scoring system ranked Cole as Arsenal's best performer on the day. He won four challenges – a higher tally than most of his experienced colleagues – and illustrated his attacking threat with three successful crosses, a figure only matched by overall man of the match Hassan Kachloul.

And it was the Moroccan who dragged the Saints back on to level terms a few seconds into the second half. Chris Marsden charged down an attempted clearance from Gilles Grimandi and the ball fell kindly for Kachloul to loft the ball expertly over Alex Manninger for his first Premiership goal since the opening day of the season.

But the Gunners restored their lead with the next effort of the game. Thierry Henry broke down the right and, rather than adding to his total of 123 shots this season – the highest figure by an individual player – he unselfishly laid the ball off into the path of Fredrik Ljungberg and the Swede slotted the ball past a rather exposed Jones.

But just as in the FA Cup final a week earlier when the Arsenal midfielder had also scored, the opposition struck twice in reply. The first of these came when Manninger failed to claim a teasing ball from James Beattie and the ball dropped for Kachloul to fire his second into an empty net.

The Gunners, frustrated at having twice surrendered their lead, looked to regain their advantage and were only denied another goal when Patrick Vieira's volley hit the base of Jones's left-hand upright in the 83rd minute.

And then, with just a minute remaining, substitute Matt Le Tissier provided a fairy-tale ending to life at The Dell by scoring a stunning strike to send Saints supporters into an absolute state of frenzy. Arsenal failed to clear a long kick from Jones and Le Tissier swivelled and hit an unstoppable left-footed shot into the top corner to register his only Premiership goal of the season.

It was a golden moment for Saints supporters which must have left the hairs on the back of their necks standing up and ensured Le Tissier's place as one of the true legends in the history of Southampton Football Club.

SUNDERLAND

ADDRESS

The Stadium of Light, Stadium Park,
Sunderland SR5 1SU

CONTACT NUMBERS

Telephone: 0191 551 5000
Fax: 0191 551 5123
Ticket Office: 0191 551 5151
Ticket Office Fax: 0191 551 5150
Club Call: 09068 121 140
Club Shop: 0191 551 5050
Club Shop Fax: 0191 551 5123
e-mail: communications@safc.com
Website: www.safc.com

KEY PERSONNEL

Chairman: R S Murray
Vice-Chairman: J M Fickling
Chief Executive: H Roberts
Commercial Director: G M McDonnell
Marketing Director: J Slater
Company Secretary: M Blackbourne
Manager: Peter Reid

SPONSORS

Reg Vardy

FANZINES

The Wearside Roar
A Love Supreme
Sex and Chocolate

COLOURS

Home: Red and white striped shirts,
black shorts and black stockings
Away: White shirts, white shorts
and white stockings

NICKNAMES

The Black Cats
The Mackems

HONOURS

League Champions: 1891–92, 1892–93
1894–95, 1901–02, 1912–13, 1935–36
Division One Champions:
1995–96, 1998–99
Division Two Champions: 1975–76
Division Three Champions: 1987–88
FA Cup Winners: 1937, 1973

RECORD GOALSCORER

Charlie Buchan –
209 league goals, 1911–25

BIGGEST WIN

11–1 v Fairfield – FA Cup 1st round,
2 February 1895

BIGGEST DEFEATS

0–8 v West Ham United –
Division One, 19 October 1968
0–8 v Watford – Division One,
25 September, 1982
0–8 v Sheffield Wednesday –
Division One, 26 December 1911

SEASON REVIEW

A season which had promised so much ultimately delivered nothing for Sunderland, as Chelsea pipped them to the last automatic European place on the final day of the campaign.

For much of the season the Black Cats had looked clear favourites for at least a UEFA Cup spot, but a dreadful run of results, beginning with defeat by Manchester United in January, wrecked the club's hopes.

A handful of new faces arrived during the summer, including midfielder Don Hutchison, signed from Everton for £2.5 million. Manager Peter Reid also gambled on two less well-known players: Stanislav Varga, a Slovakian centre-back, and Julio Arca, a promising Argentinean Under-21 international who could play in defence or midfield.

The Black Cats' opening game of the season was a stormy affair – a 1–0 win over Arsenal, with Niall Quinn grabbing the goal against his former club. It was the beginning of an excellent unbeaten run at the Stadium of Light, which Sunderland maintained until their January defeat to the champions, Manchester United.

But it was the other Manchester side which began Sunderland's away record with a defeat. A Paulo Wanchope hat-trick for City ensured a 4–2 beating for the Wearsiders, whose performance before the break did not impress their manager. "I just wish we had turned up in the first half and competed," grumbled Reid afterwards.

Competing in either half would have been useful in their next match – a 1–0 loss to Ipswich at Portman Road. A home draw with West Ham followed, as did a defeat at Old Trafford, before the Black Cats finally began to claw their way up the table with a hard-fought 2–1 win over Derby, having

> **"Crucial decisions have gone against us...I see players from other clubs doing the same as my players and nothing happens and I just find that galling".**
>
> Peter Reid

previously slumped to 17th in the table.

Reid had snapped up Emerson Thome to bolster his defensive options in September, as the Mackems began their assault on the Worthington Cup with a comfortable win over Luton Town over two legs.

They then embarked upon a five-game unbeaten run in October, including a win over their next opponents in the Worthington Cup, Bristol Rovers.

Next followed an unfortunate 2–1 defeat at White Hart Lane. Kevin Phillips set the tone for the performance by blazing a penalty over the bar with the score at 0–0. Reid blasted his side's "naïve" defending as they conceded a 79th-minute Spurs winner, but he refused to hold Phillips responsible. "He didn't miss it on purpose," he informed reporters afterwards.

Following the great disappointment of conceding an 89th-minute equaliser to Southampton in a 2–2 draw at the Stadium of Light, Sunderland embarked on an excellent run of five straight victories, of which two matches were particularly notable. A 2–1 extra-time win over a decidedly under-strength Manchester United in the Worthington Cup was well-received, although far more important – at least as far as the fans were concerned – was a superb away win over fierce rivals Newcastle United.

Two successive defeats brought the good run to an end, firstly at Elland Road in the league, but more crucially at Selhurst Park, where struggling Crystal Palace snatched a remarkable 2–1 win to knock the Premiership side out of the Worthington Cup.

Sunderland refused to allow the disappointment of the Palace result to affect their subsequent league form and a run of four wins and a draw in their next

SEASON REVIEW

five league matches saw the club climb to a lofty second place in the Premiership.

The Wearsiders' FA Cup campaign had also begun and which club should they face first in the competition but Crystal Palace. Revenge was duly gained, although it took a replay to secure their 4–2 triumph over the battling Eagles. A single strike from Danny Dichio was also enough to see off Ipswich at the Stadium of Light in the fourth round.

But the situation soon started to deteriorate for Sunderland. The defeat by Manchester United was notable for an 11-minute spell of bad language and violent conduct which saw three players – including Michael Gray and Alex Rae – receive their marching orders. Sunderland ultimately ended the season with the worst disciplinary record for fouls and cards in the Premiership.

An away loss to Derby by the same 1–0 scoreline followed. Despite a creditable 1–1 draw at home to Liverpool, it was clear that the bubble had burst as the Mackems slumped to four defeats and just a single victory in their next nine league games.

Perhaps the most disappointing result of the season came at home to Tottenham. Having been 2–0 up at the break, Sunderland allowed the north London side to get right back into it with two second-half strikes before some comical defending allowed Gary Doherty to claim his second, Spurs' third and all three points.

Furthermore, any thoughts of a trip to Cardiff were banished by Frederic Kanouté, as West Ham knocked Sunderland out of the FA Cup at the Stadium of Light with a 1–0 win.

The only hope left of salvaging something from a barren season was a place in Europe. Although Reid allowed

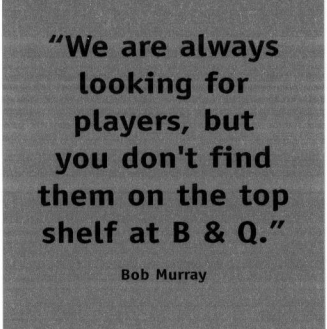

"We are always looking for players, but you don't find them on the top shelf at B & Q."

Bob Murray

Chris Makin to leave for Ipswich, the side was bolstered by the arrival of French full-back Patrice Carteron and the Black Cats' single win in March against their main rivals for sixth spot – Chelsea – suggested that there might yet be hope. Victories over Southampton and Charlton as the season neared its end also gave the Sunderland fans cause for optimism.

But the London club's good form towards the end of the campaign left the Black Cats needing a win over Everton in the final game of the season to stand any chance of playing on the continent during 2001–02. Sadly Sunderland had to battle to earn a single point in a 2–2 draw, which was not enough, although Chelsea's 2–1 win at Manchester City had made it all academic.

So Sunderland had failed to live up to their early-season promise for the second campaign in a row, matching their seventh-placed position in the table from 1999–2000. Their season appeared to be epitomised by the failure of Phillips to equal or better his Golden Boot-winning haul of 30 Premiership goals from the previous campaign – in 2000–01 he managed just 14.

Nonetheless, they will wish to ensure that transfer speculation linking the striker with a move away from the north east comes to nothing, as a host of clubs look to strengthen their front lines.

Danish shot-stopper Thomas Sorensen summed up the side's lack of success by saying: "We can't afford again to have eight or nine games in a crucial part of the season when we only get one or two wins."

Clearly Reid will need to find the missing element of consistency during 2001–02 if Sunderland are to make their dream of qualifying for the UEFA Cup, or better still the Champions League, a reality.

SUNDERLAND

DATE	OPPONENT	SCORE	ATT.	ARCA	BOULD	BUTLER P	BUTLER T	CARTERON	CRADDOCK	DICHIO	GRAY	HOLLOWAY	HUTCHISON	KILBANE	KYLE	MACH
19.08.00	Arsenal H	1–0	47,121	–	–	90	–	–	–	–	90	90□	–	90	–	s45
23.08.00	Man City A	2–4	34,410	–	s43	90	–	–	–	–	90	85□	90□	90	–	90
26.08.00	Ipswich A	0–1	21,830	–	–	90	–	–	90	–	90	90□	90	90	–	90
05.09.00	West Ham H	1–1	46,605	90¹	–	–	–	–	90	–	90	90	90□	90	–	90
09.09.00	Man Utd A	0–3	67,503	69	–	–	–	–	90	–	90	45□	90□	90	–	90
16.09.00	Derby Co H	2–1	45,343	90	–	–	–	–	90	–	90□	–	90	90¹	–	–
23.09.00	Liverpool A	1–1	44,713	90	–	–	–	–	90	–	90	–	90□	90	–	–
01.10.00	Leicester H	0–0	45,338	70	–	–	–	–	90	–	90□	–	90	90	–	–
14.10.00	Chelsea H	1–0	45,078	90	–	–	–	–	90	s10	90	–	–	66□	–	–
22.10.00	Aston Villa A	0–0	27,215	90□	–	–	–	–	90	–	90	–	s1	90	–	–
28.10.00	Coventry H	1–0	44,526	90	–	–	–	–	90	s5	90	–	90	–	–	–
04.11.00	Tottenham A	1–2	36,016	77	–	–	–	–	90□	–	90	–	90¹	–	–	–
11.11.00	Southampton H	2–2	45,064	–	–	–	–	–	90	–	90	–	90¹	90	–	–
18.11.00	Newcastle A	2–1	52,030	s23	–	–	–	–	90	s5	90□	–	90¹□	90	–	–
25.11.00	Charlton A	1–0	20,043	–	–	–	–	–	90	s8	90	–	90	90	–	–
04.12.00	Everton H	2–0	46,372	90	–	–	–	–	90	–	90	–	–	90	–	–
09.12.00	Middlesbro H	1–0	47,742	90	–	–	–	–	90	–	90¹	–	–	90	–	–
16.12.00	Leeds Utd A	0–2	40,053	90	–	–	–	–	90□	s8	90	–	–	90	–	–
23.12.00	Man City H	1–0	47,475	90□	–	–	–	–	90	s7	90	–	83¹	81	–	–
26.12.00	Bradford A	4–1	20,370	90	–	–	–	–	90	s22	90	–	90	–	–	–
30.12.00	Arsenal A	2–2	38,026	–	–	–	–	–	90	s33□	90	–	90	–	–	–
01.01.01	Ipswich H	4–1	46,053	74¹	–	–	–	–	71¹	90¹	90	–	90	–	–	–
13.01.01	West Ham A	2–0	26,014	–	–	–	–	–	–	–	90	–	90¹	s9	–	–
21.01.01	Bradford H	0–0	47,812	–	–	–	–	–	90	s16	90	–	90	s16	–	–
31.01.01	Man Utd H	0–1	48,260	–	–	–	–	–	90	–	46□	–	90□	s62	–	–
03.02.01	Derby Co A	0–1	29,129	–	–	–	–	–	90	90□	90	–	90□	–	–	–
10.02.01	Liverpool H	1–1	47,553	70	–	–	–	–	–	–	90□	–	90¹□	s20	–	–
24.02.01	Leicester A	0–2	21,086	75	–	–	–	–	90	s15	–	–	–	75□	–	–
05.03.01	Aston Villa H	1–1	47,196	90□	–	–	s11	–	90	s54	90	–	90	–	–	–
17.03.01	Chelsea A	4–2	34,981	73	–	–	–	90	90	s1	90	–	90²	90	–	–
31.03.01	Leeds Utd H	0–2	48,285	90	–	–	s23	90	76	s23	90	–	67	67	–	–
09.04.01	Middlesbro A	0–0	31,284	81	–	–	s9	90	90	–	90	–	90	65	–	–
14.04.01	Tottenham H	2–3	48,029	90□	–	–	–	90	90	–	90	–	90	90¹	–	–
16.04.01	Coventry A	0–1	20,946	52□	–	–	–	–	–	s38	–	–	70	90	–	–
21.04.01	Newcastle H	1–1	48,277	90	–	–	–	90¹	90	–	90□	–	90□	–	–	–
28.04.01	Southampton A	1–0	15,249	87	–	–	s3	90	90	–	90	–	90□	90¹	s15	–
05.05.01	Charlton H	3–2	47,671	–	–	–	–	90	90	–	90	–	90	90¹	s20	–
19.05.01	Everton A	2–2	37,444	44	–	–	–	90	90□	–	69	–	s20□	90□	s21	–

□ Yellow card, ■ Red card, s Substitute, 90² Goals scored

*including own goal

For more information visit our website:

2000–01 PREMIERSHIP APPEARANCES

MAKIN	McCANN	McCARTNEY	OSTER	PHILLIPS	QUINN	RAE	REDDY	ROY	SCHWARZ	SORENSEN	THIRLWELL	THOME	VARGA	WILLIAMS	TOTAL
90	–	–	–	90	79[1]□	–	s11	59	–	45	90	–	90	s31□	990
90	–	–	–	90[1]	90[1]	–	s5	s45	–	–	45□	–	47	–	990
90	–	–	s31	90	90	–	–	–	–	–	59	–	–	–	990
90	–	–	–	90□	90	–	–	–	–	–	–	90	–	–	990
90	–	–	s21	90	90	–	–	s45	–	–	–	90□	–	–	990
90	–	–	–	90[1]	90	–	–	–	–	90	–	90	–	90	990
90	–	–	–	90[1]□	90	–	–	–	–	90	–	90	–	90	990
90	–	–	s20	90	90	–	–	–	–	90	–	90□	–	90	990
90	–	–	–	90[1]	80	78	–	–	–	90	s12	90	–	90	966
90	–	–	–	89□	90	90□	–	–	–	90	–	90	–	90	990
90□	–	–	–	90	85	90	–	–	–	90	–	90[1]	–	90□	990
90	–	–	s13	90	90	90	–	–	–	90	–	–	90	90	990
90	–	–	–	90	90[1]	90	–	–	–	90	–	90□	–	90	990
67	–	–	–	90	85[1]	90	–	–	–	90	–	90□	–	90	990
90	–	–	–	90	82	90[1]	–	–	–	90	–	90	–	90□	990
–	90	–	s1	89[1]	82	87[1]	–	–	s3	90	–	90	s8	90	990
–	90	–	–	90□	90	90	–	–	–	90	–	90	–	90	990
–	90□	–	–	90□	82	90	–	–	–	90	–	90□	–	90	990
s9	90□	–	–	–	90	90	–	–	–	90	–	90	–	90	990
90	75	–	–	90[3]	68[1]	90	–	–	s15	90	–	90	–	–	990
90	90[1]□	–	–	90[1]	57	90□	–	–	90	90	–	–	90	–	990
90	69	–	–	90[1]	–	90	–	–	s16[1]	90	–	90	s19	s21	990
–	90	–	–	90□	81□	90	–	–	90	90	–	90	90[1]	90	990
–	90	–	–	90	74	90	–	–	74	90	–	90	–	90	990
s33	90	–	–	90	28	56□	–	–	51	90	–	s6	90	90	912
–	90	–	s8	90□	–	90	–	–	82	90	–	–	90	90	990
90	90	–	–	90□	90	–	–	–	90	90	–	–	90□	90□	990
90	90	s15	55□	–	90□	–	–	–	90	90	–	90	–	90□	955
90	90[1]	–	79	–	36	–	–	–	90	90	–	90	–	–	990
–	90[1]	–	–	89[1]	–	–	–	–	90	90	–	90	–	s17	990
–	90	–	–	90□	–	–	–	–	90	90	–	90	s14□	–	990
–	78□	–	–	90	s25	–	–	–	90□	90	–	90	–	s12□	990
–	–	–	–	90	67[1]	–	–	–	90	90	–	90	–	s23	990
–	90	90	–	90	s20	–	–	–	70□	90	s20	90□	49□	90□	949
–	90	–	–	90□	90□	–	–	–	90□	90	–	90	–	–	990
–	90	–	–	–	75	–	–	–	90	90	–	90	–	–	990
–	90	–	–	90[1]	70[1]	–	–	–	77□	90	–	90	–	s13	990
–	90	–	–	90[2]	69	–	–	–	90□	90	–	90	–	s21	964

THE MANAGER

PETER REID

Sunderland may have narrowly missed out on qualification for the UEFA Cup, but manager Peter Reid is responsible for achieving a level of consistency between 1999–2000 and 2000–01 which has previously been lacking at the club.

When the former Everton midfielder took the helm back in 1995, the Wearsiders were languishing in Division One. And despite suffering relegation from the top flight during his six-year tenure, Reid has persevered and guided the Black Cats to seventh in the Premiership for the past two seasons.

Consequently, he has been handsomely rewarded with a new contract which will keep him at the Stadium of Light until 2005, yielding bonuses in tune with the club's progress. Where previous incentive schemes were based on survival and winning the title, chairman Bob Murray has upped the ante and the targets are now silverware and Champions League success.

Having established Sunderland as a strong Premiership force, Reid will be hoping to inspire his team to qualify for European competition by the end of 2001–02. Consecutive near-misses have set expectation levels on Wearside and Reid will now want to deliver.

LEAGUE POSITION

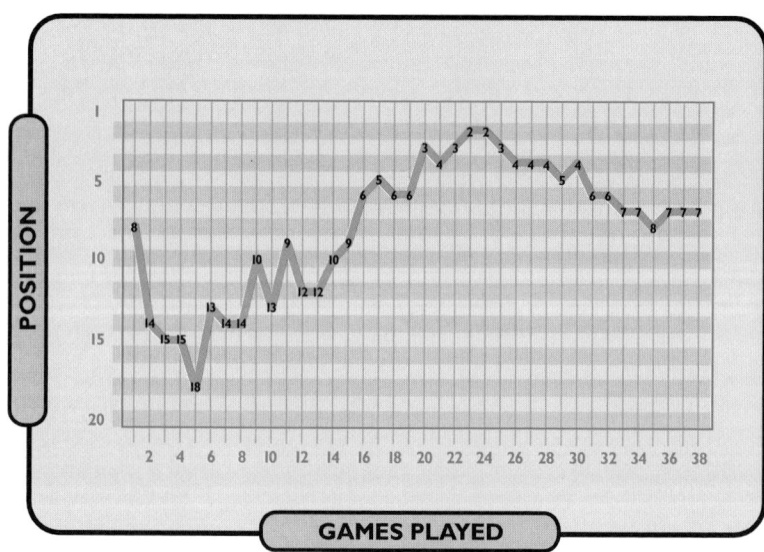

6 Sunderland were one of two teams

THE GOALS

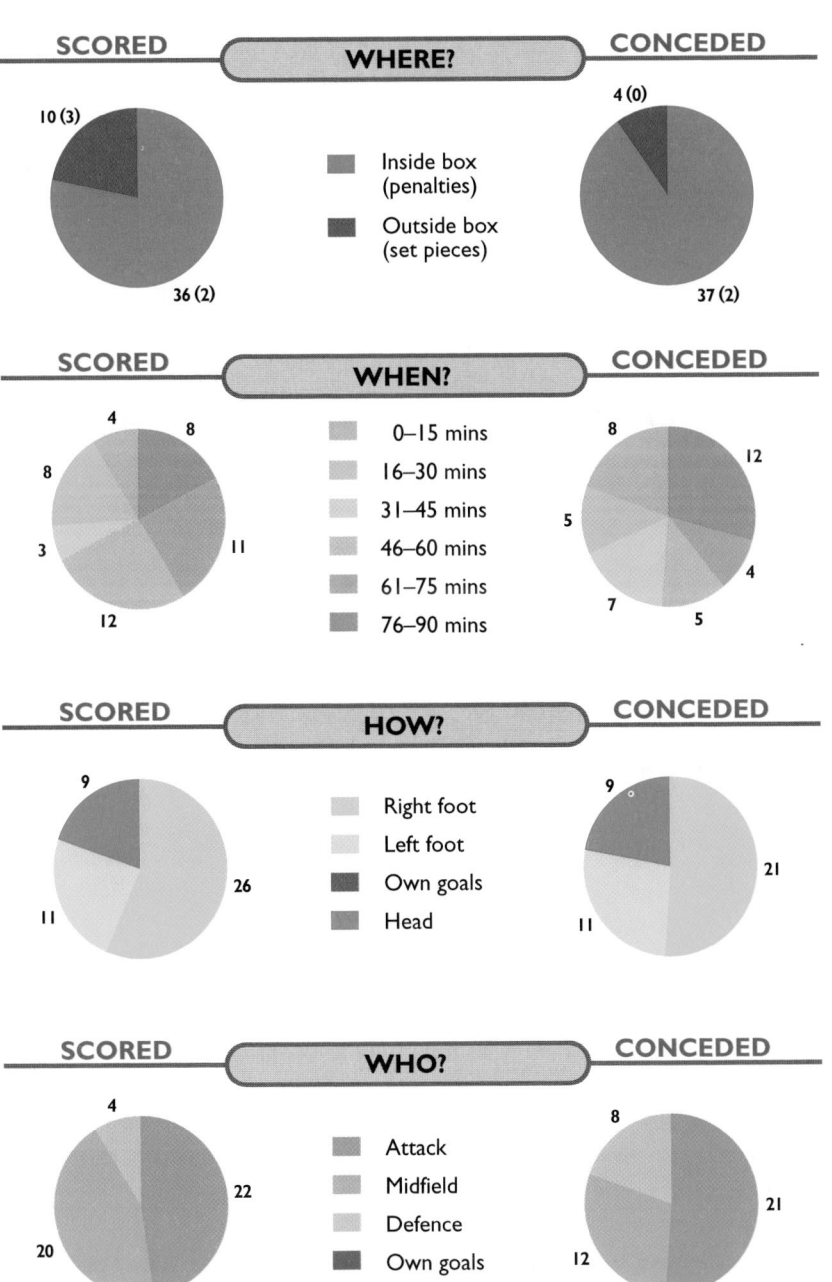

SCORED · WHERE? · CONCEDED

Inside box (penalties)
Outside box (set pieces)

SCORED: 10 (3), 36 (2)
CONCEDED: 4 (0), 37 (2)

SCORED · WHEN? · CONCEDED

0–15 mins
16–30 mins
31–45 mins
46–60 mins
61–75 mins
76–90 mins

SCORED: 4, 8, 8, 3, 11, 12
CONCEDED: 8, 12, 5, 4, 7, 5

SCORED · HOW? · CONCEDED

Right foot
Left foot
Own goals
Head

SCORED: 9, 26, 11
CONCEDED: 9, 21, 11

SCORED · WHO? · CONCEDED

Attack
Midfield
Defence
Own goals

SCORED: 4, 22, 20
CONCEDED: 8, 21, 12

to be shown six red cards

SUNDERLAND

	ARCA	BOULD	BUTLER P	BUTLER T	CARTERON	CRADDOCK	DICHIO	GRAY	HOLLOWAY	HUTCHISON	KILBANE	KYLE	MAKIN
APPEARANCES													
Start	26	0	3	0	8	33	2	36	5	30	26	0	21
Sub	1	1	0	4	0	1	13	0	0	2	4	3	2
Minutes on pitch	2145	43	270	46	720	2975	387	3175	400	2671	2351	56	1909
GOAL ATTEMPTS													
Goals	2	0	0	0	1	0	1	1	0	8	4	0	0
Shots on target	10	0	0	0	2	4	6	2	0	24	19	1	1
Shots off target	13	0	0	1	7	9	4	3	1	22	18	1	9
Shooting accuracy	43%	0%	0%	0%	22%	31%	60%	40%	0%	52%	51%	50%	10%
PASSING													
Goal assists	4	0	0	0	1	1	1	2	0	6	2	1	2
Long passes	163	3	33	3	85	407	13	589	35	271	137	5	235
Short passes	694	14	40	11	144	499	135	1022	88	845	595	7	589
PASS COMPLETION													
Own half %	65%	64%	93%	50%	60%	72%	83%	73%	86%	77%	75%	100%	77%
Opposition half %	71%	33%	37%	58%	57%	52%	65%	63%	69%	61%	62%	40%	65%
CROSSING													
Total crosses	124	0	1	8	17	4	2	206	4	105	163	0	38
Cross completion %	21%	0%	100%	13%	41%	25%	50%	31%	25%	30%	16%	0%	37%
DRIBBLING													
Dribbles & runs	81	0	1	4	23	14	1	167	2	92	123	0	47
Dribble completion %	69%	0%	100%	50%	91%	86%	100%	79%	100%	58%	55%	0%	85%
DEFENDING													
Tackles made	55	1	9	1	26	105	10	96	10	68	51	0	69
Tackles won %	65%	100%	89%	100%	65%	75%	80%	70%	40%	66%	82%	0%	68%
Blocks	5	0	6	0	6	36	0	19	1	13	16	0	5
Clearances	9	2	35	3	21	383	8	94	10	31	26	3	53
Interceptions	4	1	1	0	2	9	0	22	4	6	2	0	6
DISCIPLINE													
Fouls	21	0	1	0	11	41	22	31	9	80	33	4	26
Offside	4	0	0	0	0	0	4	0	0	21	5	2	0
Yellow cards	5	0	0	0	0	4	2	5	4	11	2	0	1
Red cards	0	0	0	0	0	0	0	1	0	1	1	0	0

GOALKEEPER NAME	START/ (SUB)	TIME ON PITCH	GOALS CONCEDED	MINS/GOALS CONCEDED	SAVES MADE	SAVES/ SHOTS
MACHO	4(1)	405	9	45	20	69%
SORENSEN	34(0)	3015	32	94	95	75%

For more information visit our website:

PLAYERS' STATISTICS

	McCANN	McCARTNEY	OSTER	PHILLIPS	QUINN	RAE	REDDY	ROY	SCHWARZ	THIRLWELL	THOME	VARGA	WILLIAMS	TOTAL	RANK
	22	1	2	34	32	18	0	1	17	3	30	9	21		
	0	1	6	0	2	0	2	2	3	2	1	3	7		
	1932	105	228	3057	2595	1571	16	149	1468	226	2706	767	2028		
	3	0	0	14	7	2	0	0	1	0	1	1	0	46	=9th
	9	0	2	52	34	9	0	0	8	0	4	3	4	194	9th
	12	0	1	60	27	15	0	1	12	0	3	5	5	229	12th
	43%	0%	67%	46%	56%	38%	0%	0%	40%	0%	57%	38%	44%	46%	6th
	3	0	0	4	2	3	0	0	3	0	0	0	0	35	7th
	235	16	15	176	76	217	0	7	121	21	481	94	197	4158	9th
	678	25	69	808	729	558	2	51	399	69	605	174	567	9498	17th
	73%	46%	86%	86%	72%	81%	0%	67%	81%	87%	78%	83%	76%	76%	17th
	65%	57%	54%	71%	55%	68%	50%	50%	64%	77%	49%	55%	66%	62%	14th
	67	4	19	53	17	96	0	1	35	4	13	2	30	1014	4th
	30%	25%	16%	25%	18%	25%	0%	100%	29%	50%	46%	0%	17%	26%	13th
	33	2	13	89	21	20	0	2	19	3	25	9	22	816	14th
	48%	0%	77%	65%	43%	70%	0%	100%	95%	33%	96%	78%	50%	69%	8th
	105	3	3	11	17	75	0	4	58	7	96	42	78	1000	7th
	65%	100%	100%	73%	82%	63%	0%	75%	64%	29%	79%	86%	73%	71%	18th
	11	2	0	1	5	8	0	2	8	1	31	9	20	205	=11th
	23	2	0	4	37	23	0	0	16	4	310	73	61	1310	13th
	7	0	2	2	0	3	0	0	7	0	9	7	7	101	15th
	59	0	7	46	84	31	0	4	27	3	68	20	33	662	1st
	0	0	3	27	48	2	0	0	1	0	0	1	3	121	17th
	4	0	0	10	5	2	0	0	5	1	6	2	7	76	=3rd
	0	0	1	0	0	1	0	0	0	0	0	1	0	6	=1st

CROSSES CAUGHT	CROSSES PUNCHED	CROSSES DROPPED	CATCH SUCCESS	THROWS/SHORT KICKS	% COMPLETION	LONG KICKS	% COMPLETION
3	8	1	75%	16	75%	88	53%
68	17	7	91%	57	86%	597	54%

PLAYER OF THE SEASON

PLAYER	INDEX SCORE
THOMAS SORENSEN	836
Alex Rae	824
Don Hutchison	800
Kevin Phillips	788
Michael Gray	752
Jody Craddock	732
Emerson Thome	708
Gavin McCann	673
Niall Quinn	672
Kevin Kilbane	653

The late-season jitters yet again robbed Sunderland of a European place, as they ran out of steam in the climax to the 2000–01 season.

But there were several outstanding individuals who helped the Mackems consolidate after their outstanding 1999–2000 campaign, led on Opta's points system by Thomas Sorensen.

The Danish shot-stopper saved 75% of all strikes at his goal and was particularly adept at dealing with close-range efforts, beating away 67% of shots struck inside his area – the fourth-best ratio of any first-choice 'keeper.

He kept 12 clean sheets and was one of a handful of goalkeepers to concede less than a goal a game on average, amassing a total of 836 Opta points.

Midfield general Alex Rae and Supporters' Player of the Season Don Hutchison made up the Opta top three.

Rae featured heavily in Sunderland's mid-season push and his industry garnered 824 points. Despite a lack of appearances,

only three colleagues created more goals than Rae all season, while his tally of 96 crosses, 75 tackles and two strikes highlighted his willingness to get involved.

Meanwhile, had it not been for his poor disciplinary record Hutchison would have topped Opta's Sunderland rankings. The Scottish international was a revelation for Peter Reid's men, scoring eight times and setting up a further six – the most at the club.

Kevin Phillips, top Black Cat according to Opta in 1999–2000, may have disappointed somewhat in 2000–01, but his 14 goals and four assists still put him fourth in the Opta Season Index.

Jody Craddock and Emerson Thome provided stability at the back, while Michael Gray's club-high 1,611 passes and 206 crosses provided vital ammunition for the forwards.

Argentinean starlet Julio Arca impressed with his verve on the left, but dropped points with a poor cross completion rate of 21% – the fourth-worst of any player attempting at least 100 centres.

113 Don Hutchison was fouled more times

FIVE OF THE BEST

Sunderland finished in exactly the same position and with exactly the same number of points that they had accrued in 1999–2000. But while they made a solid start to the 2000–01 season, a shaky finish left fans feeling that the club's season had been one of underachievement as Peter Reid's men failed to achieve their target of European football.

TOP GOALSCORERS

	GOALS	GOALS/SHOTS
KEVIN PHILLIPS	14	13%
Don Hutchison	8	17%
Niall Quinn	7	11%
Kevin Kilbane	4	11%
Gavin McCann	3	14%

Kevin Phillips struggled to match the standards that he set himself in 1999–2000, but still finished the 2000–01 campaign with 14 Premiership goals. Niall Quinn also found it hard to match his achievements of the previous season, eventually finishing with seven goals. Summer signing Don Hutchison did his best to cover the shortfall, notching eight strikes and recording a fine goals-to-shots ratio of 17%. The rest of Peter Reid's squad found it hard to find the net, though.

Midfielders Gavin McCann and Stefan Schwarz were forced to miss large chunks of the 2000–01 season through injury, and in their absence it fell to wing-back Michael Gray to take on the mantle of pass master. Gray was the only Sunderland player to complete more than 1,000 passes although, in common with most of his team-mates, his pass completion rate was not particularly impressive. Kevin Phillips was an honourable exception to this rule, completing 75% of all his distribution.

TOP PASSERS

	SUCC PASSES	COMPLETION
MICHAEL GRAY	1,074	67%
Don Hutchison	736	66%
Kevin Phillips	734	75%
Emerson Thome	695	64%
Gavin McCann	617	68%

TOP TACKLERS

	WON	SUCCESS
JODY CRADDOCK	79	75%
Emerson Thome	76	79%
Gavin McCann	68	65%
Michael Gray	67	70%
Darren Williams	57	73%

The emergence of Jody Craddock pleased everyone at the Stadium of Light, and the defender capped an impressive season by finishing as Sunderland's top tackler. Craddock won 79 of his attempted challenges, just ahead of Brazilian star Emerson Thome. Gavin McCann, who only played his first game in December, did well to record the joint-highest number of attempted tackles at the club, although his success rate was not as high as the likes of Craddock or Thome.

Sunderland finished the season with more Opta disciplinary points than any other side and their most persistent offender, Don Hutchison, finished at number three in Opta's league of indiscipline. Only two other Premiership players were shown more yellow cards than Hutchison, although in his defence he was also fouled more often than anyone else in the top flight. Niall Quinn also committed a surprisingly high number of fouls, while his strike partner Kevin Phillips was one of the Premiership's two most-booked strikers.

DISCIPLINE

	POINTS	FOULS & CARDS
DON HUTCHISON	119	80F, 11Y, 1R
Niall Quinn	99	84F, 5Y, 0R
Emerson Thome	86	68F, 6Y, 0R
Kevin Phillips	76	46F, 10Y, 0R
Gavin McCann	71	59F, 4Y, 0R

ACTION	ARCA	CRADDOCK	DICHIO	GRAY	HUTCHISON	KILBANE	MAHON	PHILLIPS	QUINN	RAE	SORENSEN	THOME	WILLIAMS	TOTAL	NEWCASTLE
Time on pitch	23	90	5	90	90	90	67	90	85	90	90	90	90	990	990
GOALS															
Goal	–	–	–	–	1	–	–	–	–	–	–	–	–	2	1
Shot on target (incl goals)	–	1	–	–	–	–	–	–	3	–	–	–	1	6	6
Shot off target	–	–	–	–	1	1	1	–	1	–	–	–	–	3	11
Blocked shot	–	–	–	–	–	–	–	–	–	–	–	–	–	0	3
Own goal	–	–	–	–	–	–	–	–	–	–	–	–	–	0	0
PASSES															
Pass to own player	6	10	3	23	8	17	19	16	22	28	16	15	14	197	262
Pass to opposition	4	12	2	15	12	4	10	9	20	6	5	9	8	116	104
Cross to own player	1	–	–	5	–	–	1	1	–	2	–	1	1	12	7
Cross to opposition player	–	–	–	5	–	5	2	2	–	4	–	–	1	19	18
Goal assist	–	–	–	–	–	–	–	–	–	–	–	–	–	2	0
Pass completion %	64%	45%	60%	59%	40%	67%	63%	62%	52%	75%	76%	64%	61%	61%	69%
TACKLES & CLEARANCES															
Tackle	–	5	–	2	3	2	2	–	–	2	–	2	3	21	18
Clearances, blocks and interceptions	–	19	–	3	2	4	–	–	2	3	1	14	–	49	33
DRIBBLES & RUNS															
Dribbles ball retained	–	–	–	4	1	–	1	1	–	1	–	–	–	9	14
Dribbles ball lost	–	–	–	2	–	3	–	–	–	–	–	–	1	6	2
Dribble success %	0%	0%	0%	67%	100%	25%	50%	100%	0%	100%	0%	0%	0%	60%	88%
DISCIPLINE															
Fouls	–	4	–	2	5	1	1	1	3	5	–	5	1	28	22
Penalty conceded	–	–	–	–	–	–	–	–	1	–	–	–	–	1	0
Free kick – offside	–	–	–	–	1	–	–	2	1	–	–	–	–	4	9
Yellow cards	–	–	–	1	–	–	–	–	–	–	–	1	1	3	1
Red cards	–	–	–	–	–	–	–	–	–	–	–	–	–	0	0
GOALKEEPERS															
Distribution to own player	–	–	–	–	–	–	–	–	–	–	13	–	–	13	11
Distribution to opposition player	–	–	–	–	–	–	–	–	–	–	9	–	–	9	9
Goalkeeper distribution %	–	–	–	–	–	–	–	–	–	–	59%	–	–	59%	55%
Save	–	–	–	–	–	–	–	–	–	–	5	–	–	5	4
Ball caught	–	–	–	–	–	–	–	–	–	–	1	–	–	1	4
Ball dropped	–	–	–	–	–	–	–	–	–	–	–	–	–	0	0
Goal conceded	–	–	–	–	–	–	–	–	–	–	1	–	–	1	2

Sunderland entered the Tyne-Wear derby at St James' Park hoping to emulate their morale-boosting 2–1 victory in the 1999–2000 campaign, which had precipitated Ruud Gullit's departure from Newcastle, and continue a good run of form in this fixture against their bitter rivals.

18 November 2000

1–2

NEWCASTLE UNITED vs. SUNDERLAND

Sunderland were on the back foot from the start and almost conceded a first-minute goal when Gary Speed fired wide after finding space in the Black Cats' penalty area. The Welsh international was not to be denied for long, though, and he opened the scoring after just four minutes to silence the 3,000 travelling fans, and a further 20,000 supporters watching back on Wearside.

Reid recognised that his team were being outmanoeuvered and made a telling substitution, with Sunderland reverting to three centre-backs, Chris Makin making way for Argentinean wonder kid Julio Arca.

The tactical switch improved the Black Cats' attacking options immensely, and they seemed much more confident going forward. Over the 90 minutes Sunderland hit the target with 67% of their shots, while the Magpies were accurate with just 40%, and it seemed only a matter of time before Shay Given's goal would be breached.

However, the equaliser did not come until the 68th minute, when Kevin Phillips's trickery got Reid's side back in the game. The England international, who was booed mercilessly throughout the game, jinked down the left wing before crossing expertly for Don Hutchison to slam the ball in at the back post.

However, for a few anxious moments Hutchison feared the goal wouldn't stand, as referee Graham Poll looked as if he had signalled for an earlier foul. The goal, the Scottish international's fifth in four matches, stood – and it sparked wild scenes of celebrations both on and off the pitch.

The scores would remain tied for just eight minutes before a moment of genius from substitute Arca set up the winner. The former Argentinos Juniors midfielder executed an exquisite dummy to send Michael Gray clear down the left wing. The local-born hero crossed superbly for Niall Quinn, who powered the ball emphatically past former Sunderland keeper Given.

Quinn, with his winning goal, two shots on target and one shot wide, was the Opta man of the match.

However, there was more drama still to come. In a passionate and full-blooded affair, referee Graham Poll awarded more than 50 free-kicks, and late in the game he pointed to the penalty spot for a foul by Quinn on Robert Lee.

That gave Alan Shearer the chance to equalise for the Magpies, but Thomas Sorensen saved and the points were Sunderland's. The Mackem fans were in raptures.

Needless to say the journey home was an enjoyable one. Once again the Black Cats had come from behind to beat their rivals and delight their hordes of travelling fans, and their joy was made all the sweeter by the penalty miss from their arch-rivals' skipper.

TOTTENHAM HOTSPUR

ADDRESS

Bill Nicholson Way, 748 High Road,
Tottenham, London N17 0AP

CONTACT NUMBERS

Telephone: 020 8365 5000
Fax: 020 8365 5005
Spurs Ticketline: 08700 112222
Spurs Line: 09068 100 500
(all calls charged at 60p a minute)
Spurs Megastore: 020 8365 5042
e-mail: mail@tottenhamhotspur.co.uk
Website: www.spurs.co.uk

KEY PERSONNEL

Executive Directors:
D Buchler (Vice-Chairman),
J Sedgwick (Finance Director),
D J Pleat (Football Director)
Non-Executive Directors:
D Levy (Chairman), M S Peters MBE,
C T Sandy, I Yawetz
Club Secretary: John Alexander
Manager: Glenn Hoddle

SPONSORS

Holsten

FANZINES

Cock A Doodle Doo
My Eyes Have Seen The Glory

COLOURS

Home: White shirts, navy shorts
and navy stockings
Away: Navy shirts, white shorts
and white stockings

NICKNAMES

Spurs
The Lilywhites

HONOURS

League Champions: 1950–51, 1960–61
Division Two Champions:
1919–20, 1949–50
FA Cup Winners: 1901, 1921, 1961,
1962, 1967, 1981, 1982, 1991
League Cup Winners: 1971, 1973, 1999
European Cup Winners' Cup Winners:
1963
UEFA Cup Winners: 1972, 1984

RECORD GOALSCORER

Jimmy Greaves –
220 league goals, 1961–70

BIGGEST WIN

13–2 v Crewe Alexandra – FA Cup 4th
round replay, 3 February 1960

BIGGEST DEFEAT

0–8 v Cologne – UEFA Intertoto Cup,
22 July 1995

SEASON REVIEW

Season 2000–01 at White Hart Lane provided the usual blend of controversy, drama and tales from the treatment room which has become synonymous with the Lilywhites in recent years.

Manager George Graham was under great pressure to start adding success to the Worthington Cup triumph of 1999.

Neil Sullivan joined on a free transfer from relegated Wimbledon and was joined by Ben Thatcher. But the biggest coup of the summer was the capture of Sergei Rebrov for £11 million.

Despite these signings, it was the sale of David Ginola to Aston Villa which generated most headlines. The Frenchman's sporadic levels of contribution did not seem to sit well with the more pragmatic approach adopted by Graham, and the only surprise was that it took almost two seasons under Graham for Ginola to be sold.

The season began indifferently and Graham and chairman Alan Sugar started to endure severe criticism from sections of the crowd, with each poor performance being greeted with calls for one or both to be ousted.

The team's major problem was their away form. While the season began with three home victories, there were two defeats and a draw on the club's travels.

Injuries exacerbated the situation. Sol Campbell, Darren Anderton, Steffen Iversen and Oyvind Leonhardsen were all kept on the sidelines for various amounts of time in the early months of the campaign and this miserable state of affairs was not to improve all season.

And there was also unrest in the camp. Ian Walker was unhappy at being replaced by Neil Sullivan and put in a transfer request. According to the club, Campbell was refusing to sit down and discuss a new contract, while the player was adamant that

> **"George Graham is the manager, he has a contract until the end of next season and I'm looking forward to him being successful for the club."**
>
> David Buchler

Spurs had not made him an offer. With big clubs around Europe queuing up to secure the Spurs skipper's services on a free transfer, this was a particular worry for the supporters. And Anderton and Les Ferdinand were also out of contract at the end of the season and seemingly could not agree new deals with the club.

On the field, the early period set the tone and four more home victories, including a 2–1 win against Liverpool, were offset by five consecutive away defeats. The rot was stopped in the next away fixture, but drawing 3–3 at bottom club Bradford was still a disappointment for the supporters.

The voices of dissent grew louder, especially as Spurs' fine home record had been blemished by a 3–1 home defeat in the Worthington Cup at the hands of eventual finalists Birmingham.

The result of all these negative feelings towards the chairman resulted in Sugar announcing the club was up for sale, the day after Spurs drew the north London derby with Arsenal.

Two days later, it was revealed that investment group ENIC would take over the club – news that was greeted with delight by the supporters. While ENIC publicly stated that they had no intention of changing the manager, most people assumed that it was only a matter of time before Graham's uneasy tenure would soon be over.

In the league, the club equalled a Premiership record set by Graham's Arsenal of four consecutive 0–0 draws, but beat Leyton Orient and Charlton in the FA Cup. The latter win was earned in fine style as the team came back from two-down, eventually winning 4–2.

Of course, with the year ending in a '1' talk was rife of a Spurs FA Cup win and the

SEASON REVIEW

side used this impetus to record their first away league win of the season against Manchester City. They followed this with a comprehensive 4–0 home win over Stockport in the cup and momentum seemed to be with Graham's side.

ENIC officially took over at the end of February and, despite rumours that Graham would be axed, West Ham were the next victims of Tottenham's seemingly-inexorable drive to the FA Cup final. On a sodden pitch and in teeming rain, Spurs won 3-2 and booked a semi-final place against Arsenal.

The manager then masterminded a 3–0 win over Coventry and was building up to the FA Cup semi-final when suddenly he was relieved of his duties.

In an interview with the media, Graham revealed a discussion with the newly-appointed David Buchler in which the Scot had expressed the need to secure Campbell, Ferdinand and Anderton on new contracts, while also being informed of his "limited" budget for new transfers.

Buchler asked Graham to explain why he had revealed these details and claimed Graham was trying to portray the club as having a lack of ambition at a delicate time when negotiations with Sol Campbell's agent had just started. The Scot allegedly reacted in an "aggressive" and "defensive" manner to these allegations.

Buchler claimed Graham was not a "team player" and that Spurs needed a "cohesive unit" to take the club forward, with everyone pulling together. Graham ridiculed the claims made by the Spurs board and said he would sue for wrongful dismissal.

Despite Buchler claiming they had no replacement in mind, Glenn Hoddle duly resigned from Southampton just two weeks later and, after compensation was finally

> **"If we haven't qualified for the Champions League by the end of five years then I'd say that I would have failed."**
>
> Glenn Hoddle

agreed, the erstwhile England boss joined his former club claiming he felt like he was "coming home".

Hoddle's first game in charge was therefore the FA Cup semi-final, but his most difficult problem was getting a team on the pitch. Sol Campbell was doubtful after picking up an injury on international duty and players such as Tim Sherwood, Stephen Carr, Sergei Rebrov and Steffen Iversen were not fully fit.

Spurs had little to lose and the supporters headed to Old Trafford full of confidence. With the year ending in '1' an early goal by Gary Doherty buoyed Spurs' hopes. But Arsenal were simply too good on the day. A series of attacks overwhelmed Spurs, and when Campbell conceded a free-kick and injured himself at the same time, the Gunners scored their equaliser. Campbell had to limp off and only some outstanding goalkeeping by Sullivan and poor finishing by Arsenal kept the score down. Robert Pires finally grabbed the winning goal.

Spurs returned to league action, with Hoddle claiming a UEFA Cup spot was within the team's reach. This seemed somewhat optimistic and, despite early success against Bradford and Sunderland, Spurs played out the season in mid-table.

Hoddle has claimed that if Spurs are not in the Champions League within five years (the duration of his contract) then he will have failed. While this sounded familiar to those who had heard Alan Sugar claim that Spurs would win the Premiership within three seasons, Hoddle's status as a Spurs hero should give him some more breathing space than Graham enjoyed.

But with Campbell turning down a reputed £130k a week to stay at Spurs, Hoddle's objective is already looking like an uphill task.

TOTTENHAM HOTSPUR

DATE	OPPONENT	SCORE	ATT.	ANDERTON	ARMSTRONG	BOOTH	CAMPBELL	CARR	CLEMENCE	DAVIES	DOHERTY	DOMINGUEZ	ETHERINGTON	FERDINAND	FREUND	GARDN...
19.08.00	Ipswich H	3–1	36,148	90^1	–	–	90	90^1□	–	–	–	–	–	s15^1	90	–
22.08.00	Middlesbro A	1–1	31,254	90	–	–	90	90	–	–	–	–	–	s14	90	–
26.08.00	Newcastle A	0–2	51,573	90	–	–	90	90	–	–	–	–	–	s50	90	–
05.09.00	Everton H	3–2	35,316	18	–	–	90	90	s72	–	–	–	–	89^1	90	–
11.09.00	West Ham H	1–0	33,282	–	–	–	90^1	90	–	–	–	–	–	90	90□	–
16.09.00	Charlton A	0–1	20,043	–	–	–	90	90□	s16	–	–	–	–	90	90	–
23.09.00	Man City H	0–0	36,069	–	–	–	–	90	–	–	s8	–	–	82	90	–
30.09.00	Leeds Utd A	3–4	37,562	s60	–	–	–	90	–	–	–	–	–	30	90	–
14.10.00	Coventry A	1–2	21,435	90□	–	–	–	90□	–	–	–	s6	–	90	77	–
21.10.00	Derby Co H	3–1	34,483	90□	–	–	–	90^1	90	s3	–	s23	–	87	–	–
28.10.00	Chelsea A	0–3	34,966	90□	–	–	–	90□	90	s10	s10	–	–	90	80	–
04.11.00	Sunderland H	2–1	36,016	90	s18^1	–	–	90	90	–	–	–	–	90	–	–
11.11.00	Aston Villa A	0–2	33,608	90□	s45	–	–	90	90	–	s7	–	–	45	–	–
19.11.00	Liverpool H	2–1	36,036	90□	s6	–	–	90	90	–	–	–	–	90^1	s6	–
25.11.00	Leicester H	3–0	35,636	90	s9	–	90	81	90□	–	–	–	–	90^3	s9	–
02.12.00	Man Utd A	0–2	67,583	90	62	–	90	90	90	–	–	–	–	90□	–	–
09.12.00	Bradford A	3–3	17,225	–	87^1	–	90^1	90	90	–	–	–	–	90	90	–
18.12.00	Arsenal H	1–1	36,062	90	s8	–	90	90	90	–	–	–	–	90□	–	–
23.12.00	Middlesbro H	0–0	35,638	90	s45	–	90	90	90	–	–	–	–	45	–	–
27.12.00	Southampton A	0–2	15,237	90□	81	–	90□	45	90□	–	s30	–	–	–	–	–
30.12.00	Ipswich A	0–3	22,234	90	–	–	90	–	90	s10	90	–	–	–	–	–
02.01.01	Newcastle H	4–2	34,324	83^1	–	–	90	–	90	–	90^1	–	–	90^1	–	–
13.01.01	Everton A	0–0	32,290	90	–	–	–	–	90	s27	90	–	–	–	–	–
20.01.01	Southampton H	0–0	36,095	90	–	–	90	–	90	–	90	–	–	21	77	–
31.01.01	West Ham A	0–0	26,048	90	–	90	90	–	84	–	90	–	–	–	90	–
03.02.01	Charlton H	0–0	35,368	90□	–	90	90	–	66	–	90	–	s24□	–	90	–
10.02.01	Man City A	1–0	34,399	60	–	s45	90	s30	–	–	90	–	–	–	90	–
24.02.01	Leeds Utd H	1–2	36,070	–	–	–	90	–	79	45	90	–	s11	79^1	90□	–
03.03.01	Derby Co A	1–2*	29,410	–	–	90	90	–	76□	–	90	–	–	90□	90□	s45
17.03.01	Coventry H	3–0	35,606	–	–	–	90	–	90	–	90	–	–	90^1	90	–
31.03.01	Arsenal A	0–2	38,121	–	–	–	–	–	–	79	90	–	s11	90	90□	90
10.04.01	Bradford H	2–1	28,306	–	–	–	–	90	90	90^1	90□	–	–	–	–	–
14.04.01	Sunderland A	3–2	48,029	–	–	–	–	90	90^1	86	90^2□	–	–	–	–	s70
17.04.01	Chelsea H	0–3	36,074	–	–	–	–	90	83	75	90□	–	s7	–	–	s53
22.04.01	Liverpool A	1–3	43,547	–	–	–	–	90	90□	78	90	–	–	–	–	90
28.04.01	Aston Villa H	0–0	36,096	–	–	–	–	90	90	76	90	–	s14	76	–	90
05.05.01	Leicester A	2–4	21,056	–	–	–	90^1□	90	90^1	90	–	–	90□	–	90
19.05.01	Man Utd H	3–1	36,072	–	–	–	–	90	90	90	90	–	83	90^1	–	16

□ Yellow card, ■ Red card, s Substitute, 90^2 Goals scored
*including own goal

2000–01 PREMIERSHIP APPEARANCES

IVERSEN	KING	KORSTEN	LEONHARDSEN	McEWEN	PERRY	PIERCY	REBROV	SHERWOOD	SULLIVAN	TARICCO	THATCHER	THELWELL	VEGA	WALKER	YOUNG	TOTAL
75	–	–	90	–	90	–	90	90	90	s1	89	–	–	–	–	990
90□	–	–	90^1	–	90	–	76	90	90	–	90	–	–	–	–	990
40	–	–	71	–	90	–	90	90	90	s19	71	–	–	–	s19	990
s1	–	–	90	–	90	–	90^2□	90	90	s52	38	–	–	–	–	990
90	–	–	90	–	–	–	90	90	90	73	s17	–	s40	–	50	990
90	–	–	74	–	s16	–	90	74	90□	90□	–	–	90	–	–	990
90	–	–	90	–	90	–	90	90	90	–	88	–	90	–	s2	990
90□	–	–	90	–	90^1	–	90^2	90	90	–	90	–	90□	–	–	990
s13	–	–	84	–	90□	–	90^1	90	–	–	90□	–	90□	90	–	990
–	–	s3	67^2	–	90	–	87	90	90	–	90□	–	90	–	–	990
–	–	80	–	–	90	–	–	90□	90	–	–	–	90	–	90	990
–	–	–	–	–	90	–	72	90^1	90	–	89■	–	90	–	90	989
–	–	–	–	–	90	–	83	90□	90	–	90	–	90□	–	90	990
–	90	–	–	–	90	–	84	84^1	90	–	–	90	–	–	90	990
–	90	–	–	–	31	–	81	90	90	–	s59	90	–	–	–	990
–	90	s28	–	–	90	–	–	90	90	–	–	90	–	–	–	990
–	90^1	s3	–	–	90	–	–	89	90	–	–	90	s1	–	–	990
–	90	–	–	–	90	–	82^1	90□	90	–	–	90	–	–	–	990
–	90	–	s5	–	90□	–	90	85□	90	–	–	90	–	–	–	990
–	90	s9	90	–	90	–	60	s45	90	–	–	90	–	–	–	990
–	90	80	90	–	90	–	s10	80	90	–	–	90	–	–	–	990
–	90	–	48	–	90^1	–	90^1	90	48■	–	–	–	–	s42	s7	948
–	90	63	63	s27	90	–	90	90	90	–	–	–	–	–	90	990
–	90	–	s13	s69	90	–	90	–	–	–	–	–	–	90	90	990
–	90	–	90	s6	90□	–	84	–	–	–	–	–	–	90	s6	990
–	66	–	90	–	90	–	90	s24	90	–	–	–	–	–	–	990
–	90	–	90	–	45	–	90^1	90	90	–	–	–	–	–	90	990
s11	90	–	–	–	–	–	90	90	90□	–	s45	–	–	–	90	990
s14	90	–	–	–	–	–	–	90	90	–	45	–	–	–	90	990
90^1	90	–	–	–	90	–	90^1	–	90	–	–	–	–	–	90	990
90	–	66	–	–	90	s24	–	–	90	–	–	90	–	–	90	990
74^1	–	s7	83	–	90	–	90	90	90	–	s16	–	–	–	90	990
–	20	s45	45	–	90	s4	90	90	90	–	–	–	–	–	90□	990
–	–	43■	–	–	37	s15	90	90	90	–	90	–	–	–	90	943
–	–	90^1	90	–	–	s12	–	90	90	–	90	–	–	–	90	990
–	–	90	90	–	–	–	–	90	90	–	s14	–	–	90□	90	990
–	–	–	90	–	–	–	–	90	90	–	90	–	–	–	90	990
–	–	90^2	90	–	s74	s7	–	–	90	–	–	–	–	–	90	990

THE MANAGER

GLENN HODDLE

The Messiah might have returned to White Hart Lane, but his managerial career to date has been varied. Glenn Hoddle's first assignment in management arrived when he became player-manager at Swindon, leading them to the Premiership for the first time in their history.

He left Swindon for Chelsea and laid down foundations that would see silverware follow in seasons after his departure. For Hoddle, England was calling.

As national coach he endured mixed fortunes, but it was his off-the-field comments which led to his resignation. Before too long, the born-again Christian became a Saint and took charge at The Dell. As manager at Southampton he won 42.3% of his matches – the best win percentage since Bill Dodgin Snr in 1949.

But once again the lure of another job was too great, this time that of his former team Tottenham and Hoddle took over at White Hart Lane in April 2001 following protracted negotiations. Spurs fans firmly believe he will be the man to take the club back to their glory days following the sacking of George Graham and the 2001–02 season is one of the supporters' most eagerly-awaited campaigns for many years.

LEAGUE POSITION

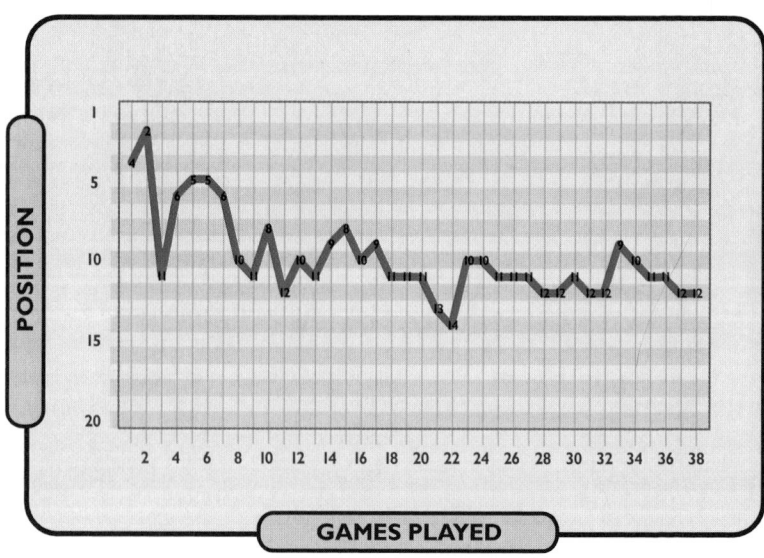

POSITION

GAMES PLAYED

THE GOALS

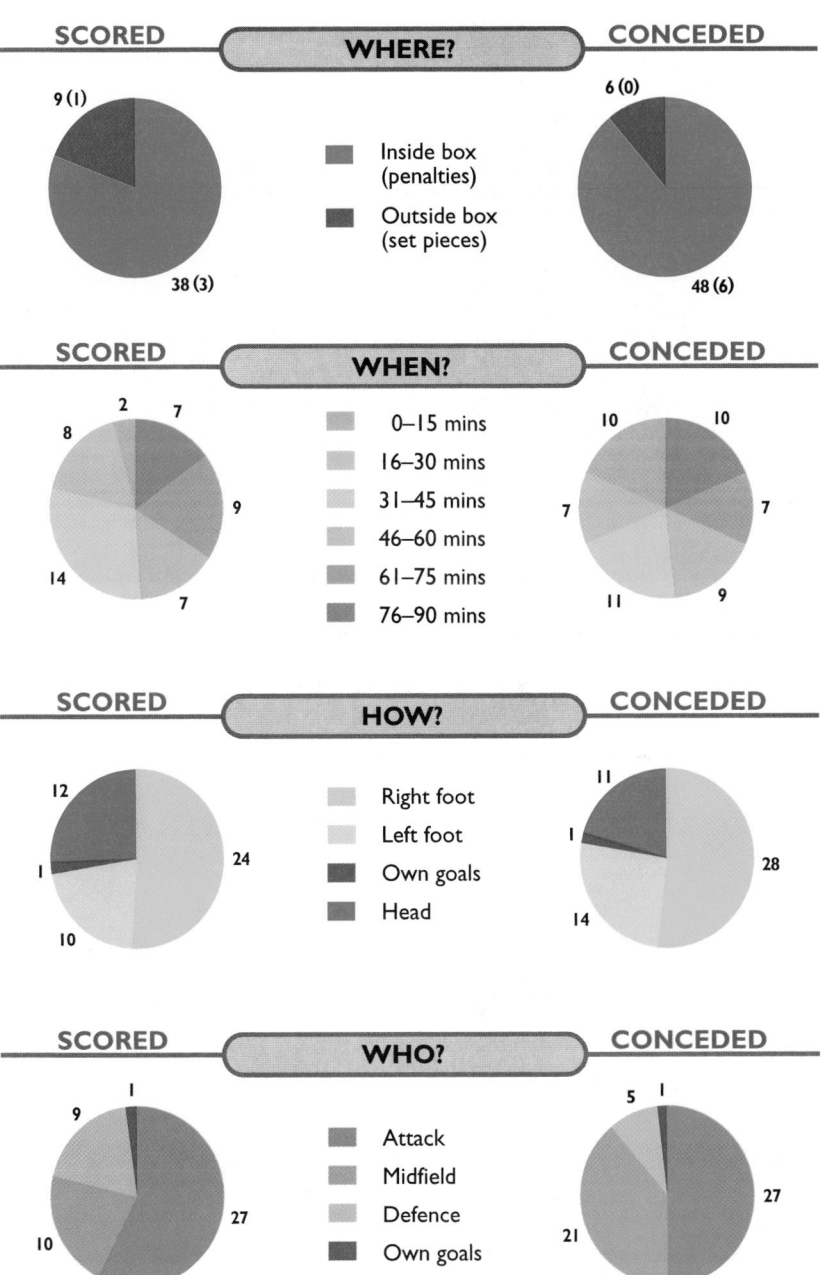

SCORED | **WHERE?** | **CONCEDED**

Inside box (penalties)
Outside box (set pieces)

Scored: 9 (1), 38 (3)
Conceded: 6 (0), 48 (6)

SCORED | **WHEN?** | **CONCEDED**

0–15 mins
16–30 mins
31–45 mins
46–60 mins
61–75 mins
76–90 mins

Scored: 2, 7, 8, 9, 14, 7
Conceded: 10, 10, 7, 7, 11, 9

SCORED | **HOW?** | **CONCEDED**

Right foot
Left foot
Own goals
Head

Scored: 12, 1, 24, 10
Conceded: 11, 1, 28, 14

SCORED | **WHO?** | **CONCEDED**

Attack
Midfield
Defence
Own goals

Scored: 1, 9, 27, 10
Conceded: 5, 1, 27, 21

of the 2000–01 season after just 10 seconds

TOTTENHAM HOTSPUR

	ANDERTON	ARMSTRONG	BOOTH	CAMPBELL	CARR	CLEMENCE	DAVIES	DOHERTY	DOMINGUEZ	ETHERINGTON	FERDINAND	FREUND	GARDNER
APPEARANCES													
Start	22	3	3	21	27	27	9	18	0	1	25	19	5
Sub	1	6	1	0	1	2	4	4	2	5	3	2	3
Minutes on pitch	1931	361	315	1890	2406	2456	759	1675	29	150	2073	1689	544
GOAL ATTEMPTS													
Goals	2	2	0	2	3	1	2	3	0	0	10	0	0
Shots on target	16	3	1	4	8	10	5	10	0	0	21	4	1
Shots off target	19	3	8	8	16	13	6	3	0	0	21	17	0
Shooting accuracy	46%	50%	11%	33%	33%	43%	45%	77%	0%	0%	50%	19%	100%
PASSING													
Goal assists	3	0	0	0	2	7	3	1	0	0	1	0	0
Long passes	290	12	13	226	293	269	56	151	2	7	114	121	58
Short passes	797	91	115	433	803	832	236	438	3	31	710	604	130
PASS COMPLETION													
Own half %	74%	86%	79%	80%	78%	75%	79%	78%	0%	91%	85%	77%	82%
Opposition half %	63%	62%	57%	57%	71%	68%	69%	58%	100%	74%	65%	75%	55%
CROSSING													
Total crosses	154	2	2	7	102	162	26	21	1	9	19	28	1
Cross completion %	29%	0%	0%	29%	26%	27%	27%	10%	0%	11%	26%	25%	0%
DRIBBLING													
Dribbles & runs	45	7	3	30	129	54	36	60	7	13	60	17	11
Dribble completion %	73%	57%	67%	73%	80%	56%	56%	67%	43%	31%	67%	53%	100%
DEFENDING													
Tackles made	53	4	5	73	54	67	25	56	0	3	25	61	29
Tackles won %	60%	50%	80%	73%	81%	70%	76%	75%	0%	0%	80%	70%	66%
Blocks	8	0	0	23	12	5	2	13	0	0	3	9	4
Clearances	26	0	1	214	79	87	7	124	0	0	23	20	54
Interceptions	6	0	0	7	11	7	4	4	0	0	4	5	2
DISCIPLINE													
Fouls	24	13	6	36	29	32	7	48	0	1	53	31	12
Offside	3	13	2	0	10	7	2	13	0	0	33	0	0
Yellow cards	7	0	0	1	5	4	0	3	0	1	4	4	0
Red cards	0	0	0	0	0	0	0	0	0	0	0	0	0

GOALKEEPER NAME	START/ (SUB)	TIME ON PITCH	GOALS CONCEDED	MINS/GOALS CONCEDED	SAVES MADE	SAVES/ SHOTS
SULLIVAN	35(0)	3108	51	61	142	74%
WALKER	3(1)	312	3	104	14	82%

For more information visit our website:

PLAYERS' STATISTICS

	IVERSEN	KING	KORSTEN	LEONHARDSEN	McEWEN	PERRY	PIERCY	REBROV	SHERWOOD	TARICCO	THATCHER	THELWELL	VEGA	YOUNG	TOTAL	RANK
	10	18	8	23	0	30	0	28	31	2	10	13	8	19		
	4	0	6	2	3	2	5	1	2	3	2	3	2	4		
	858	1526	697	1903	102	2633	62	2429	2821	235	901	1200	761	1704		
	2	1	3	3	0	1	0	9	2	0	0	0	0	0	47*	8th
	12	3	11	11	1	3	0	28	10	1	0	1	3	0	167	13th
	17	7	3	14	0	1	0	29	26	2	3	1	1	6	224	13th
	41%	30%	79%	44%	100%	75%	0%	49%	28%	33%	0%	50%	75%	0%	43%	14th
	1	1	0	4	0	0	0	4	3	0	0	0	0	0	30	=10th
	51	151	37	103	2	253	10	155	471	29	94	136	81	191	3915	15th
	313	481	160	573	35	592	22	813	1250	86	197	306	164	438	10715	7th
	77%	78%	73%	76%	90%	78%	86%	78%	84%	73%	69%	75%	80%	72%	78%	12th
	67%	70%	56%	70%	59%	59%	60%	65%	73%	73%	52%	54%	52%	58%	65%	6th
	22	9	21	37	1	19	0	54	58	7	27	4	3	32	828	15th
	36%	33%	19%	30%	0%	16%	0%	35%	31%	43%	30%	0%	0%	13%	27%	10th
	18	23	25	32	3	15	0	51	25	6	28	16	10	67	792	17th
	78%	61%	48%	72%	33%	100%	0%	65%	80%	100%	71%	88%	100%	48%	68%	14th
	14	52	16	50	1	124	3	15	77	9	36	46	23	56	979	9th
	79%	83%	69%	68%	100%	72%	67%	67%	62%	78%	61%	67%	78%	82%	72%	15th
	3	14	1	5	1	30	0	1	10	0	2	17	9	19	191	=14th
	19	52	6	12	0	296	1	1	71	9	40	93	87	103	1482	5th
	1	0	1	1	0	12	0	0	7	2	1	6	7	8	96	=18th
	11	9	14	37	1	35	1	33	61	1	21	16	27	10	571	=7th
	3	0	5	9	0	0	0	26	3	0	0	0	3	0	132	=12th
	2	0	0	0	0	3	0	1	4	1	2	0	3	2	48	16th
	0	0	1	0	0	0	0	0	0	0	1	0	0	0	3	=7th

*Including one own goal

CROSSES CAUGHT	CROSSES PUNCHED	CROSSES DROPPED	CATCH SUCCESS	THROWS/ SHORT KICKS	% COMPLETION	LONG KICKS	% COMPLETION
84	5	2	98%	55	89%	746	51%
10	1	0	100%	12	75%	68	51%

PLAYER OF THE SEASON

PLAYER	INDEX SCORE
NEIL SULLIVAN	974
Sol Campbell	866
Chris Perry	805
Stephen Carr	804
Darren Anderton	787
Tim Sherwood	774
Stephen Clemence	741
Gary Doherty	739
Les Ferdinand	712
Ledley King	699

Upheaval and wholesale change characterised the season at White Hart Lane in 2000–01 and Spurs fans will enter 2001–02 in good spirits, with their Messiah Glenn Hoddle at the helm.

Hoddle is sure to tinker with the team, but one player who appears assured of a place in 2001–02 is Opta player of the season Neil Sullivan.

Tottenham's last man standing made more saves than any other Premiership 'keeper, and his 142 stops often earned Spurs points they perhaps were not entitled to. Overall, 74% of efforts on target were not good enough to beat him, as he accrued an average of 974 Opta points.

Meanwhile 1999–2000 player of the season Sol Campbell had another excellent campaign. He won 53 tackles and made more than 200 clearances at the back in an injury-shortened campaign, while chipping in with two goals. He picked up just one booking in the process after receiving six in the 1999–2000 Premiership – a clear indication of his magnificent self-discipline.

Defensive partner Chris Perry is the second ex-Don in the top three, having made nearly 300 clearances and won 89 tackles – the sixth-highest tally in the top flight.

Several promising youngsters came to prominence in 2000–01, with Gary Doherty, Stephen Clemence and Ledley King making their mark in the top 10. Centre-back-cum-striker Doherty impressed in both positions, with a phenomenal 77% shooting accuracy, three goals in attack and more than 100 clearances and nearly 50 successful tackles at the back.

Left-footer Clemence mustered a club-high seven assists with his dangerous deliveries to register 741 points, while King's occasionally majestic displays clinched him a top-10 spot.

Elsewhere, Darren Anderton's 154 crosses and three assists boosted his score and Tim Sherwood, with 1,080 passes in the opposition half, also tallied well on Opta's system.

FIVE OF THE BEST

Tottenham endured a traumatic season, which saw changes at both managerial and boardroom level. Supporters had been unhappy with a 10th-placed finish in 1999–2000, but 2000–01 saw them drop even further to finish a disappointing 12th. The team won plenty of games at White Hart Lane, but their poor away form proved costly.

TOP GOALSCORERS

	GOALS	GOALS/SHOTS
LES FERDINAND	10	24%
Sergei Rebrov	9	16%
Gary Doherty	3	23%
Willem Korsten	3	21%
Stephen Carr	3	13%

The lack of a settled strike partnership did not help Tottenham's cause. Les Ferdinand finished as the club's leading Premiership goalscorer with 10 goals, but despite a promising start to his career in England £11 million signing Sergei Rebrov could only manage nine goals in the league. Steffen Iversen missed most of the season through injury, scoring just twice. And while utility man Gary Doherty filled in up-front at times, he only scored three goals in the Premiership.

George Graham built a hard-working team, but Spurs still lacked a creative influence in midfield. Tim Sherwood finished as the club's top distributor of the ball in 2000–01, but of his 1,321 passes just three led directly to a goal. Stephen Clemence was the team's top goal-provider, with seven assists from 808 passes. Stephen Carr also ranked highly in the list of Tottenham's top passers. Darren Anderton and Sergei Rebrov completed the top five.

TOP PASSERS

	SUCC PASSES	COMPLETION
TIM SHERWOOD	1,321	77%
Stephen Carr	808	74%
Stephen Clemence	775	70%
Darren Anderton	719	66%
Sergei Rebrov	662	68%

TOP TACKLERS

	WON	SUCCESS
CHRIS PERRY	89	72%
Sol Campbell	53	73%
Tim Sherwood	48	62%
Stephen Clemence	47	70%
Luke Young	46	82%

The loss of Sol Campbell is a bitter blow to Spurs' hopes of a successful 2001–02 campaign. Campbell missed 17 of Tottenham's 38 games in 2000–01, but still finished second in the list of Tottenham's top tacklers, a fact that proves how important he was to the club. Chris Perry topped the list, although he was not the club's most consistent ball-winner. That honour went to Luke Young, who won the ball with 82% of all his challenges.

Tottenham's disciplinary record in 2000–01 was good. Opta's league of player indiscipline did not feature anyone from White Hart Lane and the club's worst offender, Tim Sherwood, picked up only 73 points on Opta's system. Surprisingly, given his lack of a reputation for indiscipline, Darren Anderton was Tottenham's most-booked player with seven yellow cards, while German hardman Steffen Freund was booked just four times and does not even make the list.

DISCIPLINE

	POINTS	FOULS & CARDS
TIM SHERWOOD	73	61F, 4Y, 0R
Les Ferdinand	65	53F, 4Y, 0R
Gary Doherty	57	48F, 3Y, 0R
Darren Anderton	45	24F, 7Y, 0R
Stephen Carr	44	29F, 5Y, 0R

Neil Sullivan – the most in the Premiership

ACTION	ARMSTRONG	ANDERSON	CARR	CLEMENCE	FERDINAND	FREUND	KING	PERRY	REBROV	SHERWOOD	SULLIVAN	THELWELL	YOUNG	TOTAL	LIVERPOOL
Time on pitch	6	90	90	90	90	6	90	90	84	84	90	90	90	990	990
GOALS															
Goal	–	–	–	–	–	–	–	–	–	–	–	–	–	2	1
Shot on target (incl goals)	–	1	1	–	1	–	–	–	–	–	–	–	–	5	4
Shot off target	–	–	1	–	2	–	–	1	–	–	–	–	–	2	8
Blocked shot	–	–	–	–	–	–	–	–	–	–	–	–	–	2	5
Own goal	–	–	–	–	–	–	–	–	–	–	–	–	–	0	0
PASSES															
Pass to own player	3	53	27	32	14	1	39	21	23	30	4	27	25	299	262
Pass to opposition	3	16	12	12	13	2	6	15	14	11	4	6	10	124	149
Cross to own player	–	2	5	3	–	–	–	–	2	–	–	–	–	6	8
Cross to opposition player	–	2	5	3	–	–	–	–	2	–	–	–	–	12	18
Goal assist	–	–	–	2	–	–	–	–	–	–	–	–	2	2	1
Pass completion %	50%	75%	62%	71%	52%	33%	87%	58%	59%	73%	50%	82%	71%	69%	62%
TACKLES & CLEARANCES															
Tackle	–	–	–	2	3	–	3	2	–	–	–	2	3	16	35
Clearances, blocks and interceptions	–	2	10	7	2	–	1	18	–	2	1	7	19	69	44
DRIBBLES & RUNS															
Dribbles ball retained	–	–	3	–	–	–	1	–	–	–	–	3	–	11	13
Dribbles ball lost	–	2	2	1	1	–	–	3	1	1	–	–	–	7	3
Dribble success %	0%	33%	60%	0%	50%	0%	100%	0%	100%	50%	0%	100%	0%	61%	81%
DISCIPLINE															
Fouls	–	1	–	2	3	–	2	3	1	–	–	–	–	13	12
Penalty conceded	–	–	–	–	–	–	–	–	–	–	–	–	–	0	0
Free kick – offside	–	1	–	–	1	–	–	–	–	–	–	–	–	1	3
Yellow cards	–	1	–	–	–	–	–	–	–	–	–	–	–	0	2
Red cards	–	–	–	–	–	–	–	–	–	–	–	–	–	0	0
GOALKEEPERS															
Distribution to own player	–	–	–	–	–	–	–	–	–	–	14	–	–	14	5
Distribution to opposition player	–	–	–	–	–	–	–	–	–	–	11	–	–	11	11
Goalkeeper distribution %	–	–	–	–	–	–	–	–	–	–	56%	–	–	56%	31%
Save	–	–	–	–	–	–	–	–	–	–	2	–	–	2	2
Ball caught	–	–	–	–	–	–	–	–	–	–	1	–	–	1	1
Ball dropped	–	–	–	–	–	–	–	–	–	–	–	–	–	0	0
Goal conceded	–	–	–	–	–	–	–	–	–	–	1	–	–	1	2

With the Sky television cameras focusing on Liverpool's visit to White Hart Lane, Tottenham supporters were planning a demonstration against chairman Alan Sugar. But George Graham's youthful-looking outfit produced a spirited display to defeat their more experienced opponents and temporarily placate their demanding fans.

19 November 2000

2 – 1

TOTTENHAM HOTSPUR
LIVERPOOL

Following his side's lacklustre display at Aston Villa a week earlier, Graham surprised a few people by dropping £5million signing Ben Thatcher and Ramon Vega for youngsters Alton Thelwell and Ledley King. These were to be their first appearances of a campaign in which they and many other young players were blooded as Spurs' perennial injury crisis bit deep into the squad.

And both players were excellent in their distribution, giving the ball away only six times each during the contest. Of all the players on the pitch, only Reds striker Michael Owen was more thrifty in possession – and he saw much less of the ball.

It was Owen's strike partner Robbie Fowler who stamped his mark early in the game. After Danny Murphy had hooked a long ball from Sami Hyypia into his path, the Liverpool forward confidently drove his shot into the bottom right-hand corner of the net for his first Premiership goal in 11 months.

Fowler was the Reds' most dangerous player on the day, firing in a total of five shots – three more than his nearest rival Les Ferdinand – and he was unfortunate not to earn a penalty when Chris Perry appeared to halt his progress with a clumsy challenge.

However, just as in their previous away game at Leeds, the Merseysiders were to return home empty-handed as Tottenham clawed their way back into the contest thanks to some poor defending.

Stephane Henchoz and Markus Babbel were too intricate in clearing the ball. The German international was easily dispossessed and a neat back-heel by Sergei Rebrov gave Stephen Clemence the chance to whip in a delightful low cross which Les Ferdinand connected with at the near post to record his first goal in two months.

It was Spurs' first shot on target of the afternoon and, with the supporters fully behind them, they soon scored another with their next effort. Defender Luke Young hit a lofted pass to the left flank and with the Reds defence confused by Ferdinand running back from an offside position, Clemence had plenty of time to weigh up his options. His lofted cross was met by a towering header from Tim Sherwood which flew into the top corner.

Despite Liverpool having the majority of second-half possession, they rarely threatened Neil Sullivan's goal and fell to one of seven league defeats on the road.

Spurs held out to record their most impressive win of the campaign and display what they are capable of without skipper Sol Campbell.

The same youth teams from which he graduated also produced another five of the players on display including man of the match Stephen Carr, who made more dribbles and runs than any other player.

WEST HAM UNITED

SEASON REVIEW

There was an air of excitement around Upton Park at the start of the season, with fans believing that the likes of Paolo Di Canio, Joe Cole and the now permanently-signed Frederic Kanouté could make it a successful campaign.

Early additions to the Hammers squad were Arsenal pair Nigel Winterburn and Davor Suker, while Neil Ruddock and Paulo Wanchope were sold to Crystal Palace and Manchester City respectively.

With Rio Ferdinand at the back and Cole, Michael Carrick and Frank Lampard in midfield, manager Harry Redknapp seemed rightfully optimistic.

Until, that is, mid-September, when the team found themselves bottom of the Premiership without a win in six games.

"I'm very confident we will still finish in the top half," said Redknapp – and while the Hammers remained in the bottom three after 10 games, they then embarked on an eight-game unbeaten run and had propelled themselves into the top six by the start of December.

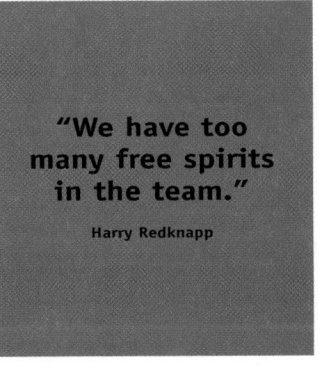

"We have too many free spirits in the team."

Harry Redknapp

During this fine run, however, Rio Ferdinand was sold to Leeds United for £18 million – a world record fee for a defender. Hammers fans had mixed feelings about the sale, but it was obvious that Redknapp would have to strengthen the squad with quality, not only to appease the supporters, but also to continue the club's good form.

After a shock 1–0 defeat at home to Sheffield Wednesday in the Worthington Cup, West Ham signed Rigobert Song and Titi Camara from Liverpool.

Camara arrived confidently, declaring: "I have come to play, play, play and score, score, score!" In fact he ended up playing just 392 minutes without scoring and was transfer-listed at the end of the season.

West Ham started 2001 in eighth place in the Premiership, and with more new boys – Christian Dailly and impressive loan signing Hannu Tihinen – at the back, it looked as though the sale of Ferdinand might not prove too much of a burden.

The end of January saw the highlight of the Hammers' season – a shock 1–0 win at Old Trafford against Manchester United in the fourth round of the FA Cup.

Paolo Di Canio got the only goal of the game 15 minutes from time, despite Fabien Barthez's attempt to trick the Italian into thinking he was offside.

West Ham's reward for such a fantastic result was an away trip to Sunderland in the fifth round and, when this was followed by another 1–0 win, many felt that the East Enders' name was on the trophy.

But this dream was to end at the quarter-final stage. The Hammers lost 3–2 at home to Tottenham in a game which the supporters must even now be wondering how they managed to lose.

Redknapp's team were just one down during the final 20 minutes and did just about everything to find the vital equaliser – but it was Spurs who progressed to the semi-finals.

West Ham's FA Cup run lasted from 6 January to 11 March. During this time they collected just six league points from the 24 that were on offer, and with the hangover of FA Cup elimination came the realisation that much hard work was needed to turn things around.

Di Canio remained West Ham's key player, but by the maverick Italian's usual standards this was not his best year and there were comments from many quarters that having Di Canio and Cole in the same

SEASON REVIEW

team was simply too much flair for a team which needed on occasions to grind out results.

Signings made earlier in the season were now being frowned upon and the fact that no other side fielded more players throughout the Premiership season shows why there was no real consistency, not just in the line-ups, but also in the team's general performances.

West Ham were certainly not short of experience, with veteran Stuart Pearce earning the Hammer of the Year award and the likes of Winterburn, Steve Lomas and John Moncur still very much involved.

But the Hammers could still boast a midfield of Frank Lampard, Michael Carrick and Joe Cole and, despite an average age of just 20, all three were included in Sven-Göran Eriksson's first England squad.

Meanwhile, 117 miles away in Bournemouth, West Ham's Jermain Defoe more than made the most of his loan spell with the Cherries by scoring in 10 consecutive league matches, breaking the post-war record.

While all this is a testament to the way in which West Ham handle and develop young players, on the pitch things were never really "cushty" for the London side during 2000–01.

With the Premiership campaign just weeks from ending, West Ham were still by no means assured of their top-flight status and it needed a 3–0 home win against Southampton in the penultimate week of the season to put an end to any fears of relegation.

While many breathed a huge sigh of relief, most people connected with the club were wondering where it had all gone so badly wrong.

When Redknapp turned up to work on the morning of 9 May, he clearly had no idea that just hours later he and West Ham would have parted company "by mutual consent".

The wheeler-dealer's reign at Upton Park had come to an end after seven happy seasons.

"The last eight weeks or so of the season haven't been particularly enjoyable and I feel maybe it's time for a change," said Redknapp, who could not even have imagined the threat of relegation just four months earlier.

Many believed that Redknapp was not given enough money from the Ferdinand sale to buy players, or that the players he did buy were not up to scratch, but there is no doubt that the team did miss the England centre-back.

They conceded 1.07 goals per game on average while he was at the club, but 1.43 after he left, and West Ham's frequent changes of formation and personnel were clearly having an unsettling effect.

> "The club has been a major part of my life, both as a player and as a manager. I would like to think the club is in a better position now than seven years ago when I took over."
>
> **Harry Redknapp**

While the new manager clearly has much to work with at the club, he also has many issues to resolve.

A large squad and a huge wage bill, not matched by results or the league position, would mean problems at any football club whatever their size.

Add to that having to convince international and future international players of a young age to stay at West Ham and it could well be that next season will simply be one of transition.

West Ham remains a great club with tradition and pedigree and, although the 2000–01 season will be remembered by Hammers fans as the end of an era, those supporters will be hoping that 2001–02 marks the beginning of a new and successful one.

WEST HAM UNITED

DATE	OPPONENT	SCORE	ATT.	BASSILA	BYWATER	CAMARA	CARRICK	CHARLES	COLE	DAILLY	DEFOE	DIAWARA	DI CANIO	FERDINAND	FORREST	FOXE	HISLOP	KANOUTE
19.08.00	Chelsea A	2–4	34,914	–	–	–	85	–	s5	–	–	–	90¹	–	–	–	90□	90¹
23.08.00	Leicester H	0–1	25,195	–	–	–	90□	s45	s29	–	–	–	90□	90	–	–	90	59
26.08.00	Man Utd H	2–2	25,998	s22	–	–	90	–	90	–	–	–	90¹	68	–	–	90	–
05.09.00	Sunderland A	1–1	46,605	–	–	–	90	–	90	–	–	–	90	–	–	–	90	–
11.09.00	Tottenham A	0–1	33,282	–	–	–	90	–	90	–	–	–	90	90	–	–	90	90
17.09.00	Liverpool H	1–1	25,998	–	–	–	90	–	90	–	–	–	90¹	90	–	–	90	90
23.09.00	Coventry A	3–0	21,020	–	–	–	s77	–	90¹	–	–	s5	90¹	13	–	–	90	85
30.09.00	Bradford H	1–1	25,407	–	–	–	90	–	90¹	–	–	–	90□	90	–	–	90	90
14.10.00	Ipswich A	1–1	22,243	–	–	–	–	–	90□	–	–	–	90¹	90	–	–	90	90□
21.10.00	Arsenal H	1–2	26,034	–	–	–	–	–	90	–	–	–	90	90	–	–	90	90
28.10.00	Newcastle H	1–0	26,044	–	–	–	90	–	68	–	–	–	90	90	–	–	90	87¹
06.11.00	Derby Co A	0–0	24,621	–	–	–	90	–	–	–	–	s25	90	90	–	–	90	75□
11.11.00	Man City H	4–1	26,022	–	–	–	90	–	–	–	–	–	89¹	90	–	–	90	90
18.11.00	Leeds Utd A	1–0	40,005	–	–	–	90	–	–	–	90	–	90	–	–	–	90	90
25.11.00	Southampton A	3–2	15,232	–	–	–	90	–	–	–	–	–	90	90	–	–	90	90¹
02.12.00	Middlesbro H	1–0	25,459	–	–	–	90	–	–	–	–	–	90	90¹	–	–	90	90
09.12.00	Aston Villa H	1–1	25,888	–	–	–	90¹	–	–	–	–	73	90	–	–	–	90	90
16.12.00	Everton A	1–1	31,260	–	–	–	90	–	–	–	–	–	90	–	–	–	90	90¹□
23.12.00	Leicester A	1–2	21,524	–	–	90	90	–	s21	–	–	–	–	–	–	–	90	90¹
26.12.00	Charlton H	5–0*	26,046	–	–	80	90	–	s10	–	–	–	86	–	–	–	90	90²
01.01.01	Man Utd A	1–3	67,603	–	–	45□	90	–	s45	–	–	–	–	–	–	–	90	90¹
13.01.01	Sunderland H	0–2	26,014	–	s16	–	–	90	–	–	–	–	90	–	s45	–	45	90
22.01.01	Charlton A	1–1	20,043	–	–	–	90	89	90	–	–	–	90¹□	90	–	–	–	90
31.01.01	Tottenham H	0–0	26,048	–	–	–	90	90	90	–	–	–	90	–	–	–	90	90
03.02.01	Liverpool A	0–3	44,045	–	–	90	90	82	90	–	–	–	–	–	–	90	–	74□
12.02.01	Coventry H	1–1	22,586	–	–	–	90	–	90¹□	90	–	–	90□	–	90	–	–	90
24.02.01	Bradford A	2–1	20,469	–	90	71	90	–	90	90□	–	–	90□	–	–	–	–	–
03.03.01	Arsenal A	0–3	38,071	–	–	–	–	–	–	90□	–	76	–	–	–	–	90	–
07.03.01	Chelsea H	0–2	26,016	s18	–	–	–	–	90	90	–	s45	90	–	–	–	90	–
17.03.01	Ipswich H	0–1	26,046	–	–	–	90	–	45	–	–	–	90	–	–	–	90	90
31.03.01	Everton H	0–2	26,044	–	–	–	90	–	90	–	–	–	90□	–	–	90	90	90□
07.04.01	Aston Villa A	2–2	31,432	–	–	–	90	–	s11□	–	–	–	89	–	–	–	90	90¹
14.04.01	Derby Co H	3–1	25,319	–	–	–	90	–	90¹	–	–	–	90	–	–	–	90	90¹
16.04.01	Newcastle A	1–2	51,107	–	–	–	90	–	90	s45□	–	s20	–	–	–	–	90	22
21.04.01	Leeds Utd H	0–2	26,041	–	–	–	90	–	90□	60	–	s30	90	–	–	s53□	90	10
28.04.01	Man City A	0–1	33,737	–	–	–	90□	–	90□	90□	–	76	90	–	–	s4	90	–
05.05.01	Southampton H	3–0	26,041	s39	–	–	90	–	90¹	90	–	–	90¹	–	–	90□	90	90¹
19.05.01	Middlesbro A	1–2	33,057	–	–	–	90	–	90	90	s22	–	90	–	–	90	90	90

□ Yellow card, ■ Red card, s Substitute, 90² Goals scored
*including own goal

For more information visit our website:

2000–01 PREMIERSHIP APPEARANCES

KITSON	LAMPARD	LOMAS	MARGAS	McCANN	MINTO	MONCUR	I PEARCE	S PEARCE	POTTS	SCHEMMEL	SINCLAIR	SOMA	SONG	STIMAC	SUKER	TIHINEN	TODOROV	WINTERBURN	TOTAL
–	90□	90	90□	–	–	–	–	90	–	–	–	–	–	90	90	–	–	90	990
s31	–	90	61	–	–	–	–	90	–	–	–	–	–	45□	45	–	–	90	945
s3	–	90	87	–	–	–	–	90	–	–	–	–	–	90	90¹□	–	–	90	990
–	90	90	–	–	–	s23	–	90	–	–	90□	–	–	90	67¹□	–	–	90□	990
–	90□	90	–	–	–	–	–	90□	–	–	90	–	–	–	–	–	–	90	990
–	–	90	–	–	–	–	–	90	–	–	90	–	–	90	–	–	–	90	990
–	90¹	90	–	–	–	–	–	90	s12	–	78	–	–	90	–	–	–	90□	990
–	–	90	–	–	–	–	–	90□	–	–	90	–	–	90□	–	–	–	90	990
–	90	90	–	–	–	s34□	–	90□	s1	–	90	–	–	89	–	–	–	56	990
–	90	90	–	–	–	75□	–	90¹	–	–	90	–	–	–	s15	–	–	90	990
–	90	–	–	–	–	s3□	90	90	s25	–	90	–	–	–	s22□	–	65□	–	990
–	90	90	–	–	–	s15	90	90	–	–	90	–	–	–	65	–	–	–	990
–	90	90¹	–	–	–	–	90¹	90	s1	–	90¹	–	–	–	–	–	–	90□	990
–	90	90□	–	–	–	–	73	90	s17	–	90	–	–	–	–	–	–	90¹	990
–	81	90	–	–	–	s9	–	90¹	–	–	90¹	–	–	90□	–	–	–	90□	990
–	45	–	–	–	–	s45□	–	90	s45	–	90	–	90	45	–	–	–	90	990
–	–	90	–	–	–	s17	90	90□	90	–	90	–	90	–	–	–	–	–	990
–	90	90□	–	–	–	–	–	90	–	–	90	–	90	–	–	–	–	90	990
–	90	90	–	–	–	–	69	90	–	–	90	–	90	–	–	–	–	90	990
–	90¹	90□	–	–	–	s10	–	90	–	–	80¹	–	90	–	–	s4	–	90	990
–	90	90	–	–	–	45	–	90□	–	–	90	–	90	–	–	s45	–	90	990
–	90	90□	–	–	–	–	–	90□	–	–	90	–	90□	–	74	–	90□	–	990
–	90	–	–	–	–	s1	–	–	90	–	90	–	–	90	–	90	–	90	990
–	90	–	–	–	–	–	–	90	–	90	–	–	–	–	90□	–	90	–	990
–	90	–	–	–	–	–	–	90	–	55	–	s8	s35	–	90	s16	90	–	990
–	90	–	–	–	–	–	–	90	–	90	–	–	–	–	90	–	90	–	990
–	90²	–	–	–	–	s7	90	–	83	–	–	–	90	s19	–	–	90	–	990
–	90	–	–	–	–	s14	83□	–	90	–	90	90	76	90	s7	s14□	90	–	990
–	90□	–	–	–	–	90	11	90	s34	–	90	90	–	72□	–	–	–	–	990
–	90	–	–	–	s45	90	90	–	45	–	–	90	–	–	s45	90	–	–	990
–	90	–	–	–	–	–	45□	–	–	–	–	90	90	–	–	–	90	–	945
–	90¹	–	–	–	90□	–	90	–	79	–	s1	90□	90	–	–	–	90	–	990
–	90¹	–	–	–	90	90	–	–	–	–	90	90	–	–	–	90	–	990
–	90¹	–	–	–	70	90	–	45	–	–	90	90	–	–	s68	90	–	990
–	90	–	–	–	37□	90	–	–	–	–	–	90□	–	s80	90□	–	990
–	–	–	–	86	90□	–	–	90	90	s14□	–	s49	41	–	990
–	–	–	–	90□	–	s18	–	90	51	–	72	–	990
–	–	s1	89	–	90	–	90	–	90	–	–	68¹	990

THE MANAGER

HARRY REDKNAPP

The jacket may not be sheepskin, but there is no doubt that Harry Redknapp is cut from an older managerial cloth. He proved his worth with just under 10 years in charge at Bournemouth, leading the Cherries through their most successful spell.

In 1992 he joined West Ham as assistant manager and eventually replaced Billy Bonds at the helm in August 1994.

Redknapp assembled arguably the best squad at Upton Park since he was a player at West Ham himself, but that was not enough to ensure a successful season.

Rio Ferdinand was sold to Leeds for a record £18 million, but the money recouped from the sale was not spent too wisely and, although there is still quality in the side, the Hammers slipped down the table and there was even a brief flirtation with relegation. Redknapp and West Ham eventually parted company when the 54-year-old left by mutual consent.

After three successive finishes in the top 10, 2000–01 was a disappointment and one of the Premiership's most quotable bosses left the East End club he so clearly loves, leaving his replacement excellent foundations on which to build.

LEAGUE POSITION

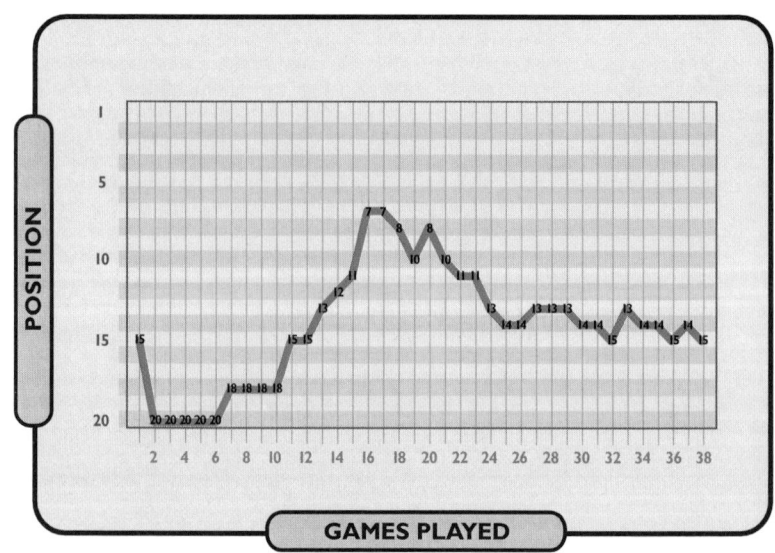

5 West Ham conceded more goals

THE GOALS

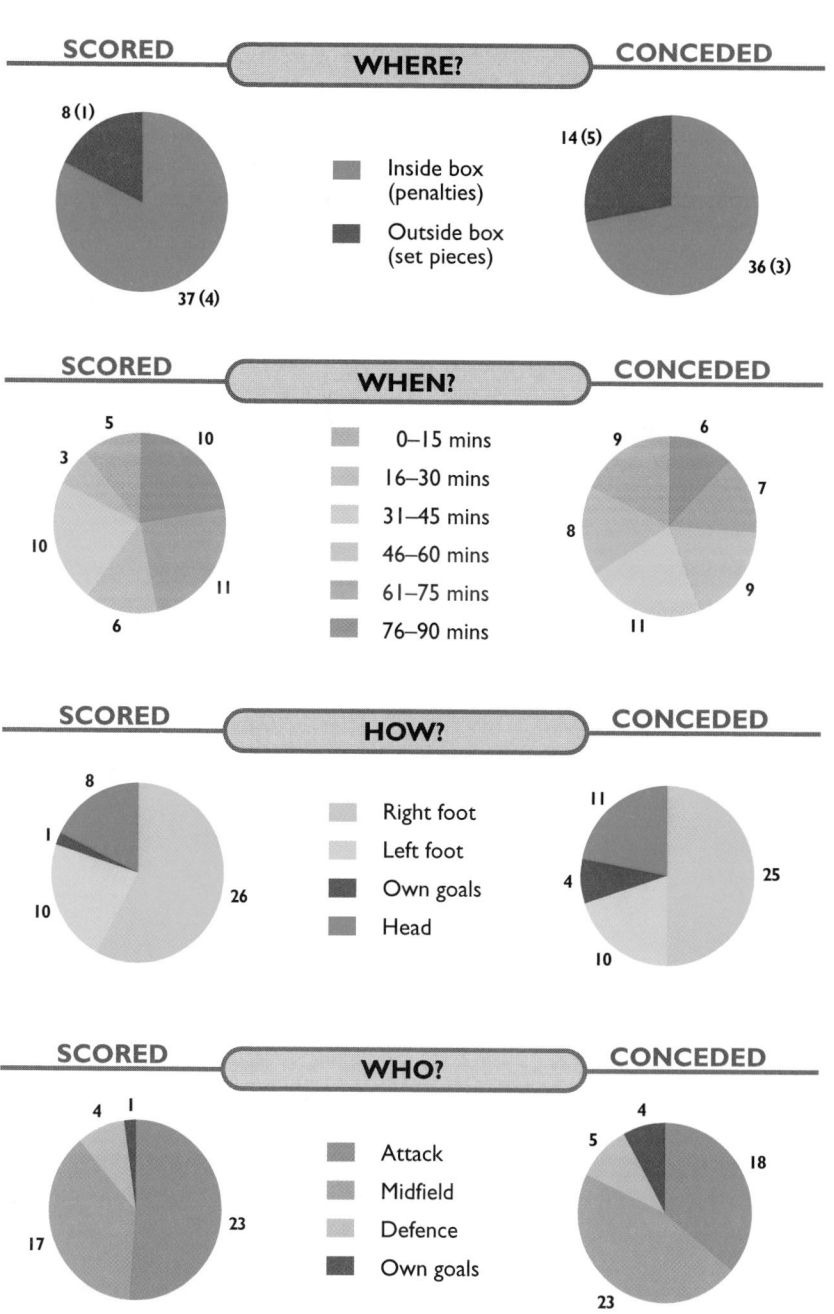

SCORED — **WHERE?** — **CONCEDED**

Scored: 8 (1), 37 (4)
Conceded: 14 (5), 36 (3)

- Inside box (penalties)
- Outside box (set pieces)

SCORED — **WHEN?** — **CONCEDED**

Scored: 5, 10, 3, 11, 10, 6
Conceded: 6, 9, 7, 9, 8, 11

- 0–15 mins
- 16–30 mins
- 31–45 mins
- 46–60 mins
- 61–75 mins
- 76–90 mins

SCORED — **HOW?** — **CONCEDED**

Scored: 8, 1, 26, 10
Conceded: 11, 25, 4, 10

- Right foot
- Left foot
- Own goals
- Head

SCORED — **WHO?** — **CONCEDED**

Scored: 4, 1, 23, 17
Conceded: 4, 5, 18, 23

- Attack
- Midfield
- Defence
- Own goals

direct from set-pieces than any other team

WEST HAM UNITED

	BASSILA	CAMARA	CARRICK	CHARLES	COLE	DAILLY	DEFOE	DI CANIO	DIAWARA	FERDINAND	FOXE	KANOUTE	KITSON	LAMPARD	LOMAS
APPEARANCES															
Start	0	5	32	0	24	11	0	31	6	12	3	32	0	30	20
Sub	3	1	1	1	6	1	1	0	5	0	2	0	2	0	0
Minutes on pitch	79	392	2952	45	2205	1005	22	2784	620	981	327	2662	34	2646	1800
GOAL ATTEMPTS															
Goals	0	0	1	0	5	0	0	9	0	0	0	11	0	7	1
Shots on target	0	4	20	0	22	0	0	26	4	3	0	46	0	26	4
Shots off target	0	9	22	0	33	1	0	23	11	6	0	34	0	34	7
Shooting accuracy	0%	31%	48%	0%	40%	0%	0%	53%	27%	33%	0%	58%	0%	43%	36%
PASSING															
Goal assists	0	0	3	0	2	0	0	7	0	0	0	4	0	3	0
Long passes	8	30	365	10	181	129	0	228	41	128	50	85	1	297	224
Short passes	32	92	917	16	814	276	3	1065	162	210	80	753	10	845	546
PASS COMPLETION															
Own half %	72%	79%	85%	83%	79%	78%	0%	79%	68%	76%	82%	69%	100%	81%	81%
Opposition half %	73%	65%	67%	29%	74%	54%	67%	66%	58%	59%	63%	60%	56%	67%	66%
CROSSING															
Total crosses	1	5	21	2	41	5	0	265	13	5	5	60	2	39	43
Cross completion %	100%	40%	43%	50%	27%	40%	0%	29%	15%	40%	20%	30%	0%	41%	21%
DRIBBLING															
Dribbles & runs	0	23	50	0	168	10	0	203	15	14	6	199	0	55	39
Dribble completion %	0%	39%	70%	0%	69%	100%	0%	67%	40%	93%	100%	55%	0%	69%	79%
DEFENDING															
Tackles made	5	5	143	1	65	36	0	58	11	32	7	23	0	104	51
Tackles won %	80%	100%	66%	100%	71%	58%	0%	72%	64%	72%	57%	61%	0%	76%	71%
Blocks	0	1	11	3	9	7	0	6	1	11	6	3	0	7	10
Clearances	2	0	63	2	11	85	0	4	11	114	37	16	0	28	54
Interceptions	1	0	18	0	4	2	0	3	1	7	2	1	0	5	2
DISCIPLINE															
Fouls	2	5	23	0	38	16	0	26	9	6	10	63	0	26	27
Offside	0	3	0	0	6	0	1	33	16	0	0	65	0	3	2
Yellow cards	0	1	2	0	5	4	0	6	0	0	2	5	0	3	4
Red cards	0	0	0	0	0	0	0	0	0	0	0	0	0	0	0

GOALKEEPER NAME	START/ (SUB)	TIME ON PITCH	GOALS CONCEDED	MINS/GOALS CONCEDED	SAVES MADE	SAVES/ SHOTS
BYWATER	1(0)	90	1	90	6	86%
FORREST	3(1)	315	6	53	15	71%
HISLOP	34(0)	3015	43	70	109	72%

For more information visit our website:

PLAYERS' STATISTICS

	MARGAS	McCANN	MINTO	MONCUR	PEARCE I	PEARCE S	POTTS	SCHEMMEL	SINCLAIR	SOMA	SONG	STIMAC	SUKER	TIHINEN	TODOROV	WINTERBURN	TOTAL	RANK
	3	0	1	6	13	34	2	10	19	2	18	19	7	5	2	33		
	0	1	0	10	2	0	6	2	0	2	1	0	4	3	6	0		
	238	1	89	609	1149	2929	281	809	1688	189	1655	1566	589	490	412	2862		
	0	0	0	0	1	2	0	0	3	0	0	0	2	0	1	1	45*	=11th
	0	0	1	3	3	10	0	0	7	0	3	2	6	2	8	2	202	7th
	0	0	0	2	0	13	0	7	9	1	7	6	6	2	5	5	243	=8th
	0%	0%	100%	60%	100%	43%	0%	0%	44%	0%	30%	25%	50%	50%	62%	29%	45%	8th
	0	0	0	0	0	1	0	0	3	0	0	0	0	0	1	1	25	=14th
	23	0	2	79	83	422	15	52	109	20	176	275	45	40	12	231	3624	18th
	56	0	24	227	179	689	64	339	489	72	367	362	168	158	116	891	10072	12th
	76%	0%	90%	87%	74%	74%	73%	73%	78%	84%	69%	82%	70%	75%	71%	81%	78%	10th
	61%	0%	75%	71%	52%	53%	64%	72%	66%	61%	51%	56%	61%	53%	60%	72%	63%	9th
	1	0	0	6	2	90	2	41	54	2	19	3	14	1	4	45	791	17th
	100%	0%	0%	33%	0%	21%	50%	29%	30%	50%	26%	0%	29%	0%	0%	29%	28%	3rd
	2	0	3	6	5	14	1	22	63	4	29	19	31	4	18	30	1037	4th
	100%	0%	33%	83%	100%	86%	100%	64%	51%	50%	86%	100%	71%	100%	50%	73%	66%	17th
	8	0	1	22	14	105	8	38	33	15	72	61	8	16	10	131	1084	3rd
	75%	0%	0%	59%	71%	72%	50%	68%	67%	80%	69%	67%	100%	69%	50%	69%	69%	20th
	2	0	0	1	12	42	1	2	2	1	15	13	0	6	0	19	191	=14th
	16	0	3	8	140	345	14	4	28	5	166	171	0	45	2	58	1478	6th
	3	0	0	1	2	17	0	5	2	3	14	17	2	2	0	13	127	3rd
	3	0	0	25	19	47	4	13	9	0	35	27	13	6	14	41	509	16th
	0	0	0	0	0	0	0	9	16	0	3	1	10	0	4	2	174	=2nd
	1	0	0	6	0	9	0	0	1	0	2	3	5	1	1	7	69	=8th
	0	0	0	0	0	1	0	0	0	0	0	1	0	0	0	0	2	=15th

*Including one own goal

CROSSES CAUGHT	CROSSES PUNCHED	CROSSES DROPPED	CATCH SUCCESS	THROWS/ SHORT KICKS	% COMPLETION	LONG KICKS	% COMPLETION
2	3	0	100%	0	0%	25	24%
7	2	1	88%	7	86%	65	55%
37	12	2	95%	77	84%	614	46%

PLAYER OF THE SEASON

PLAYER	INDEX SCORE
PAOLO DI CANIO	883
Joe Cole	881
Frank Lampard	870
Stuart Pearce	870
Michael Carrick	809
Frederic Kanouté	746
Igor Stimac	746
Rigobert Song	690
Nigel Winterburn	637
Steve Lomas	624

Harry Redknapp's surprise departure rocked the Hammers immensely, after Tottenham had initially knocked the stuffing out of West Ham's season by beating them in the FA Cup quarter-final and a lowly 15th-placed finish in the 2000–01 Premiership rounded off a largely miserable campaign.

Even 1999–2000 Opta Premiership player of the season Paolo Di Canio's form suffered, although he still did enough to rank as the hottest Iron in 2000–01.

The Italian superstar netted nine times, set up seven goals, fired over 265 crosses and was West Ham's chief creative force. But he could not quite match up to his epic efforts in 1999–2000, when he either scored or set up 56% of the Hammers' league goals.

West Ham's hugely-talented youngsters in midfield also rated highly on Opta's system in 2000–01.

The effervescent Joe Cole ran Di Canio very close for top spot and was only two points shy of his skipper's total with 881 points. Cole's skill and pace took him on 116 successful dribbles and runs, while he bagged five goals and assisted two more during the season.

Frank Lampard secured a second successive top-three spot in the Hammers' rankings thanks in part to an impressive goal haul. He struck seven times from midfield and set up three more, while Michael Carrick made more successful passes than any Hammer and won an outstanding 95 tackles to make the top five ball-winners.

Veteran Stuart Pearce is still performing admirably in his twilight years, while fellow-old campaigner Nigel Winterburn's seven yellow cards counted against him on Opta's analysis in what was a good season for him.

Top scorer Frederic Kanouté was a massive hit in 2000–01. He grabbed 11 goals and strived tirelessly, often alone up-front, but his 65 offsides – the league's second-highest tally – and 63 fouls saw him penalised on Opta's scoring system.

69.4% The Hammers were the least

FIVE OF THE BEST

West Ham included some of the most exciting players in the Premiership on their squad list in 2000–01, but Harry Redknapp found it impossible to find a winning blend on the pitch. And despite an exciting FA Cup run, the season must go down as one of failure for the Hammers.

TOP GOALSCORERS

	GOALS	GOALS/SHOTS
FREDERIC KANOUTE	11	14%
Paolo Di Canio	9	18%
Frank Lampard	7	12%
Joe Cole	5	9%
Trevor Sinclair	3	19%

Frederic Kanouté finished as West Ham's top scorer, but the talented Frenchman should probably have notched up more than the 11 goals with which he finished. Kanouté's goals-to-shots ratio was four percentage points lower than that of Paolo Di Canio, but the Italian will still be unhappy with his contribution to the Hammers' cause after scoring seven fewer goals than he had managed in the 1999–2000 season. Frank Lampard and Joe Cole both chipped in with some important strikes.

Michael Carrick capped an impressive season with an appearance for England against Mexico, and Opta's statistics proved that the young Geordie was the most influential of West Ham's highly-rated midfield trio. Carrick saw more of the ball than any other player at Upton Park, completing 962 passes. Paolo Di Canio continued to exert an influence up-front, although his pass completion rate was down on 1999–2000. Nigel Winterburn adjusted well to the wing-back role, finishing with more passes than Frank Lampard and Joe Cole.

TOP PASSERS

	SUCC PASSES	COMPLETION
MICHAEL CARRICK	962	75%
Paolo Di Canio	890	69%
Nigel Winterburn	853	76%
Frank Lampard	831	73%
Joe Cole	752	76%

TOP TACKLERS

	WON	SUCCESS
MICHAEL CARRICK	95	66%
Nigel Winterburn	90	69%
Frank Lampard	79	76%
Stuart Pearce	76	72%
Rigobert Song	50	69%

While Michael Carrick is a good passer, it was the youngster's desire to win the ball that really marked him out as a top talent in 2000–01. Only two other Premiership players – Olivier Dacourt and Marcel Desailly – won more challenges than Carrick. Nigel Winterburn was not far behind the youngster, while wantaway midfielder Frank Lampard also made his fair share of ball-winning challenges. Ex-England star Stuart Pearce also made his usual high number of full-blooded tackles.

Stuart Pearce's competitive streak shows no sign of waning, and it was hardly a shock to see the veteran at the top of the Hammers' indiscipline charts. The other names in the list were more of a surprise, though. Bustling frontman Frederic Kanouté conceded plenty of fouls and came in at number two, while Joe Cole and Paolo Di Canio also made appearances. Nigel Winterburn completed the list, proving that his feisty style of play is undiminished.

DISCIPLINE

	POINTS	FOULS & CARDS
STUART PEARCE	80	47F, 9Y, 1R
Frederic Kanouté	78	63F, 5Y, 0R
Nigel Winterburn	62	41F, 7Y, 0R
Joe Cole	53	38F, 5Y, 0R
Paolo Di Canio	44	26F, 6Y, 0R

ACTION	CAMARA	CARRICK	COLE	DI CANIO	HISLOP	KANOUTE	LAMPARD	LOMAS	MONCUR	S PEARCE	SINCLAIR	SONG	THININEN	WINTERBURN	TOTAL	CHARLTON
Time on pitch	80	90	10	86	90	90	90	90	10	90	80	90	4	90	990	990
GOALS																
Goal	–	–	–	–	–	2	1	–	–	–	–	–	–	–	4	0
Shot on target (incl goals)	1	–	–	–	–	3	2	–	–	–	–	–	–	–	8	7
Shot off target	2	2	–	1	–	–	–	–	–	–	1	–	–	–	7	5
Blocked shot	–	–	–	1	–	2	–	–	–	–	–	–	–	–	4	2
Own goal	–	–	–	–	–	–	–	–	–	–	–	–	–	–	0	1
PASSES																
Pass to own player	18	24	2	25	6	16	23	23	2	11	25	9	2	20	206	320
Pass to opposition	16	15	2	8	4	14	9	16	1	8	14	13	–	6	126	139
Cross to own player	–	1	–	2	–	2	–	1	–	–	–	1	–	2	9	7
Cross to opposition player	–	–	–	6	–	2	–	–	3	3	–	–	–	–	16	19
Goal assist	–	–	–	–	–	–	–	–	–	–	–	–	–	2	2	0
Pass completion %	51%	62%	40%	67%	60%	53%	71%	60%	67%	52%	65%	41%	100%	74%	60%	67%
TACKLES & CLEARANCES																
Tackle	2	6	–	3	–	1	8	3	–	3	3	2	–	3	35	32
Clearances, blocks and interceptions	–	3	–	1	1	–	–	5	–	20	1	17	1	1	49	41
DRIBBLES & RUNS																
Dribbles ball retained	2	2	–	6	–	–	1	1	–	–	–	–	–	2	16	13
Dribbles ball lost	6	–	–	1	–	2	–	–	–	–	1	–	–	–	12	4
Dribble success %	25%	100%	50%	86%	0%	33%	0%	100%	0%	0%	50%	0%	0%	100%	57%	76%
DISCIPLINE																
Fouls	–	4	1	2	–	1	2	3	2	1	–	6	–	1	23	13
Penalty conceded	–	–	–	–	–	–	–	–	–	–	–	–	–	–	0	0
Free kick – offside	–	–	–	–	–	2	–	–	–	1	–	–	–	–	3	1
Yellow cards	–	–	–	–	–	–	–	1	–	–	–	–	–	–	1	0
Red cards	–	–	–	–	–	–	–	–	–	–	–	–	–	–	0	0
GOALKEEPERS																
Distribution to own player	–	–	–	–	11	–	–	–	–	–	–	–	–	–	11	9
Distribution to opposition player	–	–	–	–	9	–	–	–	–	–	–	–	–	–	9	10
Goalkeeper distribution %	–	–	–	–	55%	–	–	–	–	–	–	–	–	–	55%	47%
Save	–	–	–	–	7	–	–	–	–	–	–	–	–	–	7	4
Ball caught	–	–	–	–	2	–	–	–	–	–	–	–	–	–	2	0
Ball dropped	–	–	–	–	–	–	–	–	–	–	–	–	–	–	0	0
Goal conceded	–	–	–	–	–	–	–	–	–	–	–	–	–	–	0	5

46% of all goals West Ham conceded were netted

West Ham went into their Boxing Day clash with Charlton looking to end a run of three games without a win. The Addicks themselves had lost five away games on the spin, but if they were expecting any seasonal goodwill from their local rivals, they were to be sorely disappointed.

26 December 2000

5–0

WEST HAM UNITED
CHARLTON ATHLETIC

Alan Curbishley's side looked sluggish from the start. The Hammers, conversely, were clearly ready to do battle and duly took control of the game with some bruising encounters in the middle of the park.

West Ham's midfield duo of Frank Lampard and Michael Carrick were in particularly combative mood, going in for 14 tackles between them over the 90 minutes – double the amount that their Charlton counterparts Claus Jensen and Mark Kinsella managed.

It was not long before the Hammers' committed approach reaped dividends. Stuart Pearce sent forward a hopeful chip into the area on 13 minutes and Paolo Di Canio beat three Addicks defenders to the ball to control with a deft touch. He then produced an impudent back-heel chip which deflected off Richard Rufus and into the back of the net.

To their credit, Charlton endeavoured to get back into the match and created a few chances. The best of these was a cracking drive from Mark Kinsella which Shaka Hislop did well to hold on to – one of seven saves the 'keeper would make during the afternoon.

But the Addicks were instantly caught by a West Ham sucker punch. A three-man move involving Frederic Kanouté, Di Canio and Trevor Sinclair ended with the latter back-heeling a through ball to the French forward. Kanouté then skipped past the challenge of Steve Brown and slotted home confidently.

The Hammers were clearly keen on providing some festive entertainment. Sinclair repeated his earlier back-heel on 45 minutes to put Lampard through against Kiely, but the Irish 'keeper made a great stop.

However, the England midfielder was not to be denied, and within a minute he had put the Hammers 3–0 up after half-volleying Di Canio's cross into the back of the net. The Italian was a constant source of chances for his colleagues, whipping in eight centres – more than any other player on the pitch.

The second half saw Harry Redknapp's side produce even more fantasy football, with Sinclair again the principal exponent. He scored the fourth of the game with a crashing volley from outside the area that had even Di Canio singing his praises.

A beautifully-weighted pass from Carrick then put Kanouté in the clear in the 84th minute, and the Frenchman rounded Kiely to complete the scoring. The goal sealed a 5–0 win which was undoubtedly the Hammers' finest moment during the 2000–01 campaign and took them to eighth place in the Premiership – their highest position of the season.

It was to prove a high point in the league for West Ham, who managed just three wins in their next 18 Premiership games – a run which, arguably, was to ultimately cost Harry Redknapp his job.

by midfielders – the highest proportion in the Premiership

BLACKBURN ROVERS

ADDRESS

Ewood Park, Blackburn,
Lancashire BB2 4JF

CONTACT NUMBERS

Telephone: 01254 698 888
Fax: 01254 671 042
Ticket Office: 01254 671 666
Clubcall: 09068 121 179
The Roverstore: 01254 665 606
e-mail: enquiries@rovers.co.uk
Website: www.rovers.co.uk

KEY PERSONNEL

Club President: W H Bancroft
Chairman: R D Coar BSc
Vice-Chairman: R L Matthewman
Chief Executive: J O Williams BSc
Directors: D M Brown, T M Finn,
K C Lee, G R Root FCMA, I R Stanners
Club Secretary: T M Finn
Manager: Graeme Souness

SPONSORS

Time Computers

FANZINES

Loadsamoney

COLOURS

Home: Blue and white halved shirts,
white shorts and white stockings
Away: Red and black striped shirts,
black shorts and red stockings

NICKNAME

Rovers

HONOURS

League Champions 1911–12,
1913–14, 1994–95
Division Two Champions 1938–39
Division Three Champions 1974–75
FA Cup: 1884, 1885, 1886, 1890,
1891, 1928

RECORD GOALSCORER

Simon Garner 168 league goals,
1978–1992

BIGGEST WIN

11–0 v Rossendale – FA Cup 1st Round,
13 October 1884

BIGGEST DEFEAT

0–8 v Arsenal – Division 1,
25 February 1933

SEASON REVIEW

Graeme Souness was in charge of Blackburn for the final 10 matches of the 1999–2000 season and used these fixtures to assess the strength of his squad in preparation for the 2000–01 campaign.

Blackburn's failure to bounce straight back after their relegation from the Premiership meant that there was a great deal of pressure on the Scotsman's shoulders to deliver this time around. He was all too aware that the longer they spent in Division One, the harder it would be to attract the calibre of players required to mount a successful promotion bid.

So Souness spent his summer bringing new talent into the club – namely Craig Hignett from Barnsley, John Curtis from Manchester United and left-back Stig Bjornebye from Liverpool.

To balance the books, a number of players were moved on. The major deals saw Callum Davidson move to Leicester, Per Frandsen rejoin Bolton and, on the eve of the Premiership season, Bradford swoop for Ashley Ward.

Crystal Palace were defeated at Ewood Park in Blackburn's first match of the season, but the following week was a devastating one for everyone concerned at the club as Jack Walker, the man whose millions helped Blackburn establish themselves as one of the biggest clubs in England, lost his battle with cancer.

Seven days after the Palace match, Blackburn travelled to Crewe. Unfortunately Rovers could not claim all three points, but it became clear that success on the pitch would be the most fitting tribute for the club's most famous fan.

League progress was steady in the following weeks, as home victories against Norwich and Nottingham Forest established Rovers as one of the likely contenders for a top six place come May.

Keen to strengthen his squad with proven talent, Souness signed Henning Berg from Manchester United, initially on loan before capturing his permanent signature in December, and he made his bow in the Forest game.

Rovers' first defeat in the league came in controversial circumstances against Watford. An enthralling encounter ended 4–3 in the Hornets' favour, but Souness was not happy with the officiating and could not contain his rage in a post-match interview.

Referee Mike Jones was lambasted by the furious Rovers manager, who claimed that he felt "mugged" and that the Chester official's performance was "very poor". Jones ruled out a Matt Jansen goal for a foul on Watford 'keeper Espen Baardsen and Rovers felt two of the Hertfordshire club's goals should not have stood because of indiscretions in the build-up.

> **"There has been a lot of pressure on us to perform this season but that was for Jack Walker and his family."**
>
> **Matt Jansen**

This defeat took a while to get over and it was not until mid-October that another league win was recorded. Victory against Wimbledon, though, was the catalyst for a string of good results which included wins over Grimsby, Tranmere, Huddersfield, Stockport and Barnsley. During this period veteran striker Mark Hughes was signed from Everton to add experience to the attack and made an immediate impact, netting twice on his debut in a 3–2 victory over Tranmere.

In November, another new squad number was found for American international goalkeeper Brad Friedel.

On the way out of Ewood was Lee Carsley. The former Rovers skipper struggled to hold down a place during 2000–01 and jumped at the chance to play Premiership football again at Coventry.

Following defeat at home to Gillingham and draws against Tranmere and QPR,

SEASON REVIEW

Rovers finished the year off in style, winning four matches in a row – including the derby against Burnley. A draw with Norwich on New Year's Day – which featured Christian Dailly in his last appearance before his switch to West Ham – and then a win against Preston moved them back into third place in the table.

Blackburn's participation in the Worthington Cup came to an end in round three at the hands of West Ham, but their FA Cup run was more impressive.

Having overcome Chester, Rovers drew 0–0 at home with Derby in round four. It appeared that they had blown their chance, but they produced one of their best performances of the season in the replay to defeat Jim Smith's men 5–2 at Pride Park.

Once Division One adversaries Bolton were eliminated a round later, Rovers travelled to Arsenal but were unable to repeat their giant-killing act. The Gunners showed the difference in standard between the Premiership and Division One, winning by three goals to nil – all of which were scored in the first half.

With just the league to concentrate on, Rovers went on a fantastic run in which they lost just one more match all season – against leaders Fulham – following defeat at Nottingham Forest in February. This included a vitally-important 4–1 win over second-placed Bolton at the Reebok Stadium.

One of the reasons for their consistency over this period was the exceptional array of quality midfielders at the manager's disposal. David Dunn, Craig Hignett, Jason McAteer, Garry Flitcroft, Keith Gillespie, Damien Duff and Damien Johnson were already at the club, but Souness made further reinforcements by bringing in Alan Mahon in mid-December from Sporting Lisbon and Eyal Berkovic from Celtic two months later, both on loan deals.

The forward line, too, was in great shape. Matt Jansen finished the campaign on 23 league goals, assisted by former Sheffield United striker Marcus Bent, another mid-season signing, along with the evergreen Mark Hughes.

The most memorable result of the campaign came on April Fools' Day, when Burnley were beaten 5–0 at Ewood.

In an ordinary season, Rovers fans would arguably have settled for a lack of success in exchange for two wins in their fixtures with the Clarets, so for it to happen in such emphatic style in a promotion-winning campaign was an achievement which will be remembered for years to come.

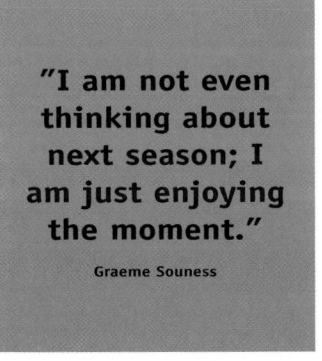

"I am not even thinking about next season; I am just enjoying the moment."

Graeme Souness

Promotion was finally assured at play-off candidates Preston in Rovers' penultimate game of the campaign. Although they could not finish with a win – the final match at Gillingham was drawn 1–1 – the club had, more importantly, shown over the course of the season that they were not the sort of side which would give up easily, a fact that Bolton discovered to their cost once they had been ousted from second place.

Despite the celebrations at Deepdale, Souness was quick to dedicate the club's triumph to one man and went so far as to suggest that nobody could ever emulate Walker's achievements. "He is unique; he will never, ever be repeated; as long as a ball is kicked there will never, ever be another Jack Walker," said Souness.

With the club's finances secure thanks to provisions Walker made before his death, and with such a strong squad already in place, Souness has a great opportunity in the coming years to establish Blackburn as a Premiership force once again.

BLACKBURN ROVERS

DATE	OPPONENT	SCORE	ATT.	BENT	BERG	BERKOVIC	BJORNEBYE	BLAKE	BROOMES	CARSLEY	CURTIS	DAILLY	DIAWARA	DUFF	DUNN
12.08.00	C Palace H	2–0	18,733	–	–	–	90	90¹	–	–	90	90	–	90□	76
19.08.00	Crewe A A	0–0	8,059	–	–	–	90	90□	–	–	90	90	–	90	90
26.08.00	Norwich H	3–2	19,542	–	–	–	90	90¹□	–	s4	90	90□	s18	72□	90¹□
28.08.00	Sheff Wed A	1–1	15,646	–	–	–	90□	90	90	–	90	–	s22	68	90
09.09.00	Nottm Forest H	3–0	18,471	–	90	–	90	70¹	–	s13	90	–	s20	90	90¹
12.09.00	Watford H	3–4	17,258	–	90	–	90	90²	–	s29	90□	–	s51	90	90¹
15.09.00	Sheff Utd A	0–2	10,816	–	90	–	90	90	–	–	90	s41	79	90	90
23.09.00	Bolton W H	1–1	23,660	–	90	–	90	90	90	90□	–	–	–	90□	s33
30.09.00	West Brom A	0–1	16,791	–	90	–	90	90□	–	–	90	–	–	80	90
15.10.00	Fulham A	1–2	15,247	–	90□	–	90	90	–	45	90	–	–	s37	90
18.10.00	Wimbledon A	2–0*	6,019	–	90	–	90	–	–	–	90	–	–	48	90
21.10.00	Grimsby H	2–0	16,397	–	90	–	90	–	–	s4	90	–	–	–	90
25.10.00	Tranmere H	3–2	17,010	–	90	–	90	–	–	s37	90	–	–	–	90
28.10.00	Huddersfield A	1–0	12,837	–	90□	–	–	–	–	–	90	–	–	–	90
04.11.00	Stockport H	2–1	17,404	–	90	–	90	–	–	–	90	s12	–	–	90
08.11.00	Barnsley A	2–1	13,622	–	90	–	90□	–	–	–	90	s20	–	–	90¹□
11.11.00	Portsmouth A	2–2	14,141	–	90	–	90¹	–	–	–	90	s24	–	–	90□
18.11.00	Wolves H	1–0	20,380	–	90	–	82	–	–	90	90	s45	–	–	90¹
25.11.00	Gillingham H	1–2	18,061	s33	90	–	12	–	–	–	90	s45	–	90	68□
02.12.00	Tranmere A	1–1	10,063	90	90	–	–	–	–	–	90	–	–	90	90¹
09.12.00	QPR H	0–0	16,886	90	90□	–	–	–	–	–	90	–	–	90	–
17.12.00	Burnley H	2–0	21,369	90¹	90	–	90	–	–	–	90	–	–	89	90
22.12.00	C Palace A	3–2	15,010	90	90	–	90	–	–	–	90	–	–	64	90²
26.12.00	Birmingham H	2–1	24,899	61	90□	–	90	–	–	–	90□	–	–	90	90
30.12.00	Crewe A H	1–0	18,554	64	90	–	90	–	–	–	90	–	–	90	90□
01.01.01	Norwich A	1–1	16,695	90¹	90	–	56	–	–	–	90	s10	–	90	90
10.01.01	Preston H	3–2	23,983	s24	90□	–	90□	–	–	–	90	–	–	82	90
13.01.01	Sheff Wed H	2–0	19,308	90¹	90	–	90	–	–	–	90	–	–	90□	–
03.02.01	Barnsley H	0–0	18,573	s34	90	–	–	s13	–	–	90	–	–	90	90
10.02.01	Nottm Forest A	1–2	24,455	90	90	s34	–	–	–	–	90	–	–	90	90
20.02.01	Watford A	1–0	15,970	90¹	90	s37	–	–	–	–	90	–	–	90□	90
23.02.01	Bolton W A	4–1	20,017	90¹	90	–	–	–	–	–	90	–	–	90	90¹
03.03.01	West Brom H	1–0	23,926	90¹	90	90	–	–	–	–	90	–	–	90	90
14.03.01	Birmingham A	2–0	29,150	74¹	90	–	90	–	–	–	90	–	–	90	90¹
17.03.01	Wimbledon H	1–1	19,000	60	90	s60	30	–	–	–	90	–	–	90□	–
01.04.01	Burnley H	5–0*	23,515	90	73	–	s60	–	–	–	90	–	–	30	90
04.04.01	Sheff Utd H	1–1	26,276	90	90¹	52	s38	–	–	–	90	–	–	–	90
07.04.01	QPR A	3–1	12,449	90	90	s15¹	–	–	–	–	90	–	–	90	90¹
11.04.01	Fulham H	1–2	21,578	90	90	s26	s78	–	–	–	90	–	–	12	90
14.04.01	Stockport A	0–0	9,705	s23	90	–	90	–	–	–	90	–	–	–	90
16.04.01	Huddersfield H	2–0	29,406	71	90	s31	59□	–	–	–	90	–	–	–	90
21.04.01	Wolves A	0–0	20,018	74	90	s45□	45	–	–	–	90	–	–	90□	–
24.04.01	Grimsby A	4–1	6,507	s28	90	90¹	–	–	–	–	90	–	–	–	90¹□
29.04.01	Portsmouth H	3–1*	24,257	s36¹	90	89	–	–	–	–	90	–	–	–	90¹
02.05.01	Preston A	1–0	16,975	s32	90	–	–	–	–	–	90	–	–	90	90□
06.05.01	Gillingham A	1–1	10,319	90	–	–	–	59¹	–	–	90	–	–	–	–

□ Yellow card, ■ Red card, s Substitute, 90² Goals scored, *including own goal

For more information visit our website:

2000–01 DIVISION ONE APPEARANCES

DUNNING	FILAN	FLITCROFT	FRIEDEL	GILLESPIE	HIGNETT	HUGHES	JANSEN	JOHNSON	KELLER	KELLY	KENNA	MAHON	McATEER	OSTENSTAD	SHORT	TAYLOR	THOMAS	TOTAL
–	–	90	–	–	–	90^1	s14	–	90	–	–	90	–	–	90	–	–	990
–	–	90	–	s14	–	–	90	–	90	–	–	76	–	–	90	–	–	990
–	–	86	–	–	–	–	90^1	–	90	–	–	90	–	–	90	–	–	990
–	–	90□	–	–	–	–	90	s3	90	–	–	87	–	–	42	$s48^1$	–	990
–	–	77	–	–	–	–	82^1	–	90	–	–	90	–	s8	90	–	–	990
–	–	90	–	–	–	–	23	–	90	–	–	61	–	s16	90	–	–	990
–	–	90	–	–	–	–	–	–	90	–	–	90	–	–	–	49	s11	990
–	90	57□	–	–	–	–	–	s33	–	–	–	57	–	s8	90	–	82^1	990
–	90	–	–	s27	–	–	90	–	–	–	–	90	63	–	–	90	s10	990
–	90	90	–	–	s45□	–	53^1	–	–	–	90	–	–	–	40□	s50	–	990
–	90	90^1	–	–	90	–	–	90	–	–	–	s42	66	–	90	s24	–	990
–	90	90^1	–	–	86	–	$s29^1$	90	–	–	–	61	90	–	90	–	–	990
–	90	90	–	–	90□	90^2□	–	76	–	–	–	s14	53^1	–	90	–	–	990
–	90	90	–	–	61	90□	–	90	–	–	90	–	s29□	90^1	–	–	–	990
–	90	90□	–	–	90^1	90^1	–	72	–	–	–	s18	78	–	90□	–	–	990
–	90	90	–	–	90	90	$s26^1$	70	–	–	–	–	–	64	90	–	–	990
–	90	90	–	–	90	90	$s28^1$	66	–	–	–	–	–	62	90	–	–	990
–	–	–	90	–	70	90□	90□	45□	–	–	–	–	s20	–	90	–	s8	990
–	–	90	90	–	57	90^1	90	–	–	s33	–	–	–	–	90	–	–	968
–	–	90□	90	–	67□	62	s28	–	–	–	90	–	s23	–	90	–	–	990
–	–	90□	90	–	s18	90	90	–	–	72	–	85	s5	–	90	–	–	990
–	–	90□	90	–	–	66	s24	–	–	–	–	s1	90^1	–	–	90	–	990
–	–	90	90	–	–	64	s26	–	–	–	–	s26	90	–	–	90^1	–	990
–	s45	90	45	–	–	84	$s29^2$	–	–	–	–	–	90	s6	–	90	–	990
–	90	–	–	–	s26	90□	90^1	–	–	–	–	–	90	–	–	90	–	990
–	90	–	–	–	s34	45□	74	–	–	–	–	–	80□	s16	–	90	–	945
–	–	90	90	–	90	66^1	90^2	–	–	–	–	s8	–	–	–	90	–	990
–	–	90	90	–	62	–	90	–	s28	–	–	90	–	–	–	90^1	–	990
–	–	90	90	–	–	56	90	–	s26	–	–	77	64	–	–	90	–	990
–	–	90	90	s20	–	56	$s34^1$	–	–	–	–	56	70	–	–	90	–	990
–	–	53	90	70	s20	s12	78	–	–	–	–	90	–	–	90	–	–	990
–	–	90	90	63	$s27^1$	s2	88^1	–	–	–	–	90	–	–	90□	–	–	990
–	–	–	90	79	s11	s7	83	–	–	–	–	90	–	–	90	–	–	990
–	–	90	90	90	–	–	90	–	–	–	–	s16	–	–	90□	–	–	990
–	–	90	90	90	s30	s30	90^1	–	–	–	–	60	–	–	90	–	–	990
–	–	90	90	–	$s23^1$	s17	90^2	–	–	–	–	90	67	–	90^1	–	–	990
–	–	90	90	24	s13	–	90	s53	–	–	–	90□	–	–	90	–	–	990
–	–	90	90	69	s21	s4	86^1	–	–	–	–	75	–	–	90	–	–	990
–	–	90	90	73	s17	–	90^1	–	–	–	–	90	–	–	64	–	–	990
–	–	90	90	–	67□	90	–	–	–	–	–	90	–	–	90	–	–	990
–	90^1	90	45	s45	s19	90^1	–	–	–	–	–	90	–	–	90	–	–	990
–	–	90	90	s47	90	s16	90	–	–	–	–	43	–	–	90□	–	–	990
–	–	90	90	s16	74	62	90^2	90	–	–	–	–	–	–	78□	s12	–	990
–	–	90	90	s21	54	69	90	90	–	–	–	–	s1	–	90	–	–	990
–	–	90□	90	90	s28	58	90^1□	62	–	–	–	–	–	–	90	–	–	990
90	–	90	90	90	s31	–	s14	76	–	–	–	–	90	–	90	90	–	990

THE MANAGER

GRAEME SOUNESS

Once Brian Kidd was relieved of the Blackburn manager's job in November 1999 it became clear that his permanent successor had to be someone with the necessary managerial experience to take the club back into the Premiership.

The club's choice to replace caretaker boss Tony Parkes was Graeme Souness, who met this criterion having enjoyed a vastly successful career both as a player and manager. He worked wonders at Rangers, winning trophies galore before moving on to Liverpool in 1991.

The only silverware he won at Anfield was the 1992 FA Cup, but it was a difficult time for the Scot as he underwent a heart by-pass operation following the semi-final tie against Portsmouth.

His last experience as a Premiership boss came at Southampton, where he was in charge for the 1996–97 campaign. Away from the British game, he has had spells as manager of Galatasaray, Benfica and Torino.

On appointing Souness, the Blackburn board must have hoped that he would repeat his Ibrox success at Ewood Park. By winning promotion to the Premiership in his first full season he has taken the first steps in returning the club to greatness.

LEAGUE POSITION

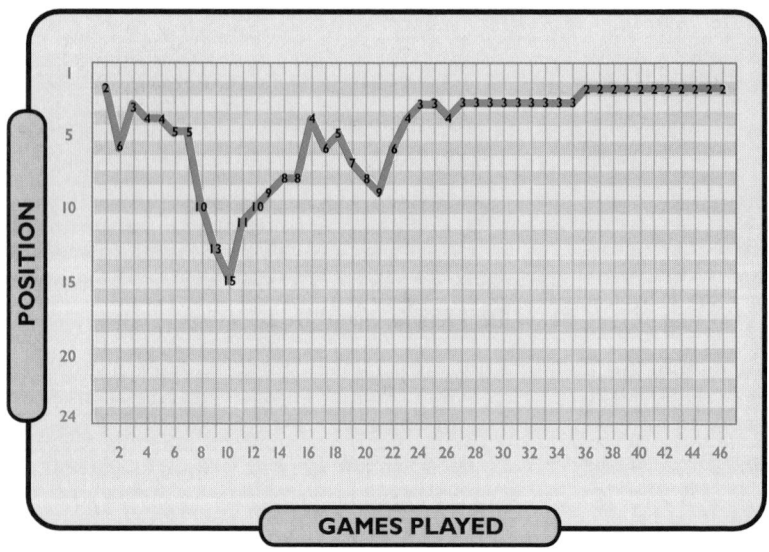

GAMES PLAYED

24 The number of goals scored by Matt Jansen and

THE GOALS

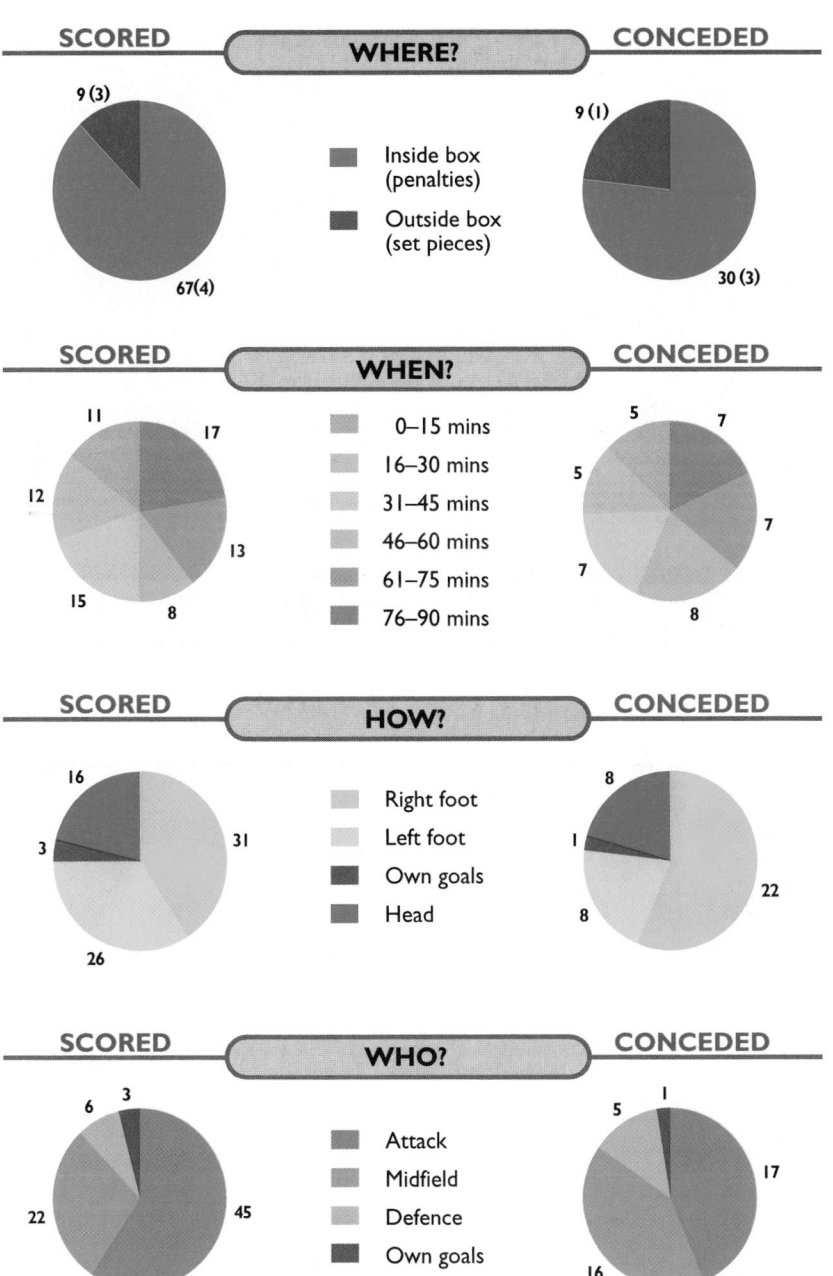

WHERE?

SCORED — CONCEDED

Inside box (penalties)
Outside box (set pieces)

SCORED: 9 (3), 67 (4)
CONCEDED: 9 (1), 30 (3)

WHEN?

SCORED — CONCEDED

0–15 mins
16–30 mins
31–45 mins
46–60 mins
61–75 mins
76–90 mins

SCORED: 11, 17, 12, 13, 15, 8
CONCEDED: 5, 7, 5, 7, 7, 8

HOW?

SCORED — CONCEDED

Right foot
Left foot
Own goals
Head

SCORED: 16, 31, 3, 26
CONCEDED: 8, 22, 1, 8

WHO?

SCORED — CONCEDED

Attack
Midfield
Defence
Own goals

SCORED: 6, 3, 22, 45
CONCEDED: 1, 5, 17, 16

Marcus Bent in the 28 games they played together

BOLTON WANDERERS

COLOURS

Home: White shirts, navy shorts
and white stockings.
Away: Sky blue shirts, sky blue
shorts and sky blue stockings.

NICKNAME

The Trotters

HONOURS

Division One Champions: 1996–97
Division Two Champions:
1908–09, 1977–78
Division Three Champions: 1972–73
FA Cup Winners: 1923, 1926,
1929, 1958

RECORD GOALSCORER

Nat Lofthouse – 255 league goals,
1946-61

BIGGEST WIN

13–0 v Sheffield United –
FA Cup 2nd round, 1 February 1890

BIGGEST DEFEAT

1–9 v Preston – FA Cup 2nd round,
10 December 1887

SEASON REVIEW

The play-offs system does not always reward the team that finishes in third place, but justice was done at the end of the 2000–01 season when Bolton, who had been in either second or third spot for more than half of their Division One campaign, beat Preston 3–0 at Cardiff's Millennium Stadium.

Following their loss to Ipswich at the semi-final stage the year before, manager Sam Allardyce was forced to sell some of his best players in the summer of 2000 as the Trotters prepared for their first full season under the former Notts County manager's leadership.

Claus Jensen and Eidur Gudjohnsen completed multi-million pound moves to Charlton and Chelsea respectively – and some of that cash financed Allardyce's more modest purchases.

The popular Per Frandsen re-signed from Blackburn, but he was the only purchase to rise above the £1 million mark. A fee of £400,000 was splashed out on Michael Ricketts from Walsall, while other deals of note saw Anthony Barness, Simon Charlton and Ian Marshall arrive on free transfers.

Apart from a shock exit at the first round stage of the Worthington Cup to Macclesfield, the Trotters started the season brightly, going eight league matches without defeat before their loss at home to Fulham in late September.

Mid-October's goalless draw with Nottingham Forest was notable for the return to fitness of Ricardo Gardner, who had been out since the previous February with a knee ligament injury sustained against Barnsley.

The next match at Stockport ended in a frustrating defeat for Wanderers. Andy Kilner's spirited Hatters side - who had not won since the first day of the season - raced into a three-goal lead by half-time.

Two second-half efforts from Marshall and one from Ricketts made the scores level as the final whistle drew near, but unfortunately for Bolton, County striker Aaron Wilbraham struck a last-gasp winner to end the Trotters' unbeaten away record.

Defeat at Watford quickly followed, but Bolton put this blip behind them and went on to lose just two more fixtures before the New Year.

One man who would not see out the season at Bolton was Mark Fish. Wanderers'

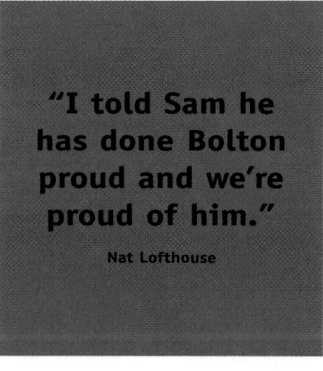

"I told Sam he has done Bolton proud and we're proud of him."

Nat Lofthouse

South African defender had expressed a desire for Premiership football, so when Charlton, who had chased his signature before, made an offer in the region of £750,000 for him in November, Fish departed for The Valley.

He was replaced a month later by Colin Hendry, who joined, initially on a loan basis, from Coventry City. The Scottish international did well enough in the following months for the deal to be made permanent in February. Another new face arrived in the shape of Nicky Summerbee, who moved to Bolton from Sunderland for an undisclosed fee at the beginning of January.

One early casualty in 2001 was Jussi Jaaskelainen, who had been in such fine form in the Bolton goal. The Finnish international injured a knee against Tranmere and played no further part in the remainder of his side's season.

Steve Banks was given the opportunity to take over as first choice, but following his dismissal against QPR, the Trotters were faced with a goalkeeping crisis ahead of their FA Cup fifth round tie with Blackburn.

With Banks suspended and his back-up (the on-loan Tommy Wright) denied permission to play by Manchester City, American Jurgen Sommer, formerly of QPR and Luton, was signed on a short-term

SEASON REVIEW

contract and filled the void against Graeme Souness's men.

The goalkeeping situation was finally solved when Bradford's Matt Clarke, out of favour at Valley Parade following Jim Jefferies' appointment as manager, joined on loan at the end of March.

With Fulham running away with the title, it became clear that only one of Bolton and Blackburn would be promoted automatically. Rovers' response was to win seven of their last 13 league fixtures – including the all-important clash between the two clubs at the Reebok Stadium by an emphatic margin of four goals to one.

The loss to Rovers knocked the stuffing out of Bolton. Although they were not losing, drawing five of their next six matches was not good enough to keep up with a Blackburn side which had games in hand. Wanderers' draw with Stockport put them into second spot for the last time – Rovers' point at Sheffield United the following evening put them back above the Trotters, where they stayed for the remainder of the season.

This meant that, for the third successive year, if Bolton were to go up it would have to be via the play-offs.

They were paired with Gary Megson's experienced West Brom side. The first leg at The Hawthorns started dreadfully for the Trotters, as they were two goals down by the hour mark. Jason Roberts opened the scoring for the Baggies before strike partner Lee Hughes made it 2–0 from the penalty spot.

But Bolton fought back, scoring twice in the last 10 minutes of the match to make things level. After Gudni Bergsson had halved the deficit, Frandsen beat Russell Hoult with a penalty two minutes from time. The second leg was much more clear-cut.

> **"Let's worry about what's to come in a couple of weeks, in the meantime I'm going to every presentation and party I can find."**
>
> Sam Allardyce

Bergsson broke the deadlock early on, Gardner doubled the lead mid-way through the second half and Ricketts sealed matters in the final moments of the game, just minutes after coming off the bench.

The reward for Bolton was a trip to Cardiff to face Preston, who were looking to become the third side in as many years to go from the second division to the Premiership in successive seasons. On the day, though, Bolton's class shone through. Gareth Farrelly, whose goal for Everton against Coventry three years previously played a part in saving the Toffees from relegation at Bolton's expense, put Wanderers into the lead.

Although Matt Clarke was required to pull off one or two good saves to keep Preston out, the Bolton forwards always looked the more threatening in front of goal. It was left to Ricketts – arguably Division One's bargain of the season – to give them a deserved two-goal cushion, following his introduction as a substitute with 20 minutes to go. In the final moments, the livewire Gardner sealed the victory with a superb solo effort which saw him receive the ball in his own half and then charge past Preston's weary defence before unleashing his shot past David Lucas.

Charlton and Ipswich have shown that Premiership survival – and more – can be achieved without making sweeping changes. But Allardyce will want his side to start the campaign off brightly, as their last two spells in the top flight ended in relegation after just one season.

After the final, Allardyce commented: "The important thing now is to stay in the Premiership, because if you can do that, you just start growing bigger and better".

Quite how he will achieve this, though, is another matter.

than any other Division One side

BOLTON WANDERERS

DATE	OPPONENT	SCORE	ATT.	BANKS	BARNESS	BERGSSON	CAMPBELL	CHARLTON	CLARKE	DOWNEY	ELLIOTT	FARRELLY	FISH	FRANDSEN	FREDGAARD	GARDNER	GOPE
12.08.00	Burnley H	1-1	20,662		90	90		90			90□	90	90¹□				
19.08.00	West Brom A	2-0	17,316		90	90		11			90¹	90	90				
26.08.00	Preston H	2-0	19,954		90	90					90	90	90				
28.08.00	Tranmere A	1-0	9,350		90	90					90	90	90				
09.09.00	Huddersfield A	3-2	12,248		90	90					90		90				
12.09.00	Grimsby A	1-0	3,732		90	90							90				
16.09.00	Portsmouth H	2-0	14,113		90	90					90	61	90				
23.09.00	Blackburn A	1-1	23,660		90	90					90	90	90				
30.09.00	Fulham A	0-2	19,924		67□	90		s23			90	90	90□				
06.10.00	Gillingham A	2-2	9,311	90		90		90		s12	86		90				
14.10.00	Wolves H	2-1	15,585			83¹		90		s7	90□	s45	90□				
17.10.00	Nottm Forest H	0-0	13,017					90		70	90	90	90			s33	
21.10.00	Stockport A	3-4	8,266		s35	90		90		90	61	90	90			s58□	
24.10.00	Watford A	0-1	11,799		90	90		90		71	s27	90	90			90	
28.10.00	C Palace H	3-3	12,879		79	90¹		42		90	s48□	90	90¹			90	
31.10.00	QPR H	3-1	10,180			90¹				90¹	90	90	90			90	
04.11.00	Birmingham A	1-1	20,043			90				90□	90	56	90□			90	
11.11.00	Barnsley H	2-0	13,406			90				90	90		90			90¹	
18.11.00	Norwich A	2-0	15,224		90	90¹				90			90□	s26		86	s4
25.11.00	Sheff Utd A	0-1	14,962			90□				90			90	s6		90	
03.12.00	Watford H	2-1	13,904			90□				90	90					90¹	s2
09.12.00	Crewe A H	4-1	12,836			90¹				90	56		90¹	s4		90	
16.12.00	Wimbledon A	1-0	6,076			90				90	90			29		90	
23.12.00	Burnley A	2-0	19,552			90				90□	90			s1		90	
26.12.00	Sheff Wed H	2-0	21,316			90			s20	90□	90					90	
30.12.00	West Brom H	0-1	18,985			90			s26	90	90		s45			90	
01.01.01	Preston A	2-0	15,863			90				90	90¹		90□			90	
13.01.01	Tranmere H	2-0*	15,493	s37		90				90	90		90			90	
20.01.01	Sheff Wed A	3-0	17,638	90	s49	90				90			90			90¹	
03.02.01	QPR A	1-1	10,293	18■		90				90	64		90¹			s26	
10.02.01	Huddersfield H	2-2	14,866	90		90¹				90	90		90¹			s52	
13.02.01	Portsmouth A	2-1	11,377	90□	s12	90				90	90		90			90	
20.02.01	Grimsby H	2-2	24,249	90		90¹				90	90		90			90	
23.02.01	Blackburn H	1-4	20,017	90		90□		s20		90□	90□		90			90	
04.03.01	Fulham A	1-1	16,468			90		90		90□	51		90¹				
10.03.01	Gillingham A	3-3*	13,161			90□	s38	90		90	90		70¹				
17.03.01	Nottm Forest A	2-0	22,162			90	81	90		90	s2¹					90	
31.03.01	Wimbledon H	2-2	14,562			90□	58	90	90	90¹□	s23					90	
03.04.01	Stockport H	1-1	12,492			90	71	90	90	90	s28					90	
13.04.01	Birmingham H	2-2	15,025			90¹	s8	90	90				90□			90	
16.04.01	C Palace A	2-0	16,268		90	90		90	90		90		s5			90	
18.04.01	Crewe A A	1-2	8,054		90	90	s11	90	90		90□		s12			79	
21.04.01	Norwich H	1-0	17,967		90	90			90	90	90		90			90	
28.04.01	Barnsley A	1-0	13,979		90	90		90□	90□	90	90		62			s28	
01.05.01	Wolves A	2-0	16,242		90	90		90	90	90	90		s4			90	
06.05.01	Sheff Utd H	1-1	14,836	90						s25			90□				

□ Yellow card, ■ Red card, s Substitute, 90² Goals scored, *including one own goal

For more information visit our website:

2000–01 DIVISION ONE APPEARANCES

HANSEN	HENDRY	HOLDEN	HOLDSWORTH	HUNT	JAASKELAINEN	MARSHALL	MORINI	NOLAN	O'KANE	PASSI	RANKIN	RICHARDSON	RICKETTS	SMITH	SUMMERBEE	WARHURST	WHITLOW	WRIGHT	TOTAL
62					90	s28		83	90	90	s7								990
90□		s36			90	s23		67	90□	54[1]	s79								990
84		58			90	s32		90	67[1]		s6	s23[1]			90				990
90		s45□			90	45			90	s25		65				90[1]			990
84		73[1]			90	s17		90	90	53	s6	s37[2]				90			990
84		54			90	90	s6	90	90	90	s51	s36[1]				39			990
90		85[1]			90	s29	s5	90	90	45		s45[1]							990
90[1]□		58□			90	s32	s24	90	66	s13		77							990
73		60□			90	s30		90	90	s17		90							990
90[1]		90□			90□			78	90[1]□	s4	71	s19							990
90		45[1]			90	90		90	90	55		s35							990
90					90	90		s20	90	57		90							990
32					90	90[2]		s29	55			90[1]							990
78					90			90□	s19	s12		63□							990
90					90	90		56		s11		s34[1]							990
90					90			90	90	s11		79[1]□							990
51					90			90	90	s39		90[1]			s34				990
89		s16			90	s1		90	90□			74[1]			90				990
83		90□						64	90□	s7		90[1]□			90□				990
65					90	s25		90	84			90			90				990
88					90	s45[1]		90	90			45			90				990
86		s34			90	68[1]		90[1]	90			s22			90				990
	90	s45[1]			90	45		90	90			s6[1]			90				990
89	90	53			90			90	90	90		s37[2]							990
76	90[1]	61[1]			90	s29		90	69□	s14		70							969
76	90	90			90	s14		90□	64			45□							990
83□	90□	62			90	s28		61	s29			s7[1]			90				990
87[1]	90		53			s25		90				65			90	s3			990
78	90		s16[1]			90						74[1]□	s12	90	41				990
90	90	90			s11	90							19	79	s71				918
81	90		s61			38□	s9					90	90	29					990
90[1]	90□		s21			90		78□	s1□			68[1]□							990
90[1]	90	s45				s4		90				86□	45						990
58	90	90				79		70□	s11			s32[1]							990
88	90□	76	s14			90						s39	s2		90□	90			990
90	90□	63[1]	s27			s20						52□				90	90		990
	90	88[1]				58					90	s9	s32	90			90		990
s32	90[1]	76	s14			90□						67				90			990
s19	90[1]	90	s13			90						77				62			990
45	90	s45[1]	s5			85					90	82□							990
	90	73	85[1]								s17	90[1]				90			990
	90	s45[1]	45								90□	90				78			990
s45	90	90[1]	45			s5									85				990
82		s38				s8						90[1]	52			90			990
90		86[1]	s3									87[1]					90		990
	83	90[1]□	s7		90	65		90	s14	86□	76□		90			90			986

THE MANAGER

SAM ALLARDYCE

Some managers are given the chance to start their careers at established top-flight clubs. But Sam Allardyce earned the right to join football's elite through many years of hard work in the Football League.

After a caretaker spell at Preston, Allardyce took over as manager of Blackpool in 1994. He spent two seasons at Bloomfield Road, but was sacked in 1996, even though the Tangerines had finished in third place.

Allardyce returned to management at Notts County in January 1997 and, although he could not prevent their relegation from Division Two, the following season the Magpies won the Division Three title with a 99 points tally.

He remained at County until October 1999, when the opportunity to replace Colin Todd at Bolton – where Allardyce spent the majority of his playing career – proved to be too tempting an offer to turn down.

In less than a season, he led the Trotters to semi-final fixtures in both domestic cup competitions and the play-offs, but all three ties ended in defeat.

But Allardyce, who has a 10-year contract at the Reebok Stadium, was more successful in 2000–01, taking Bolton back to the Premiership via the play-offs.

LEAGUE POSITION

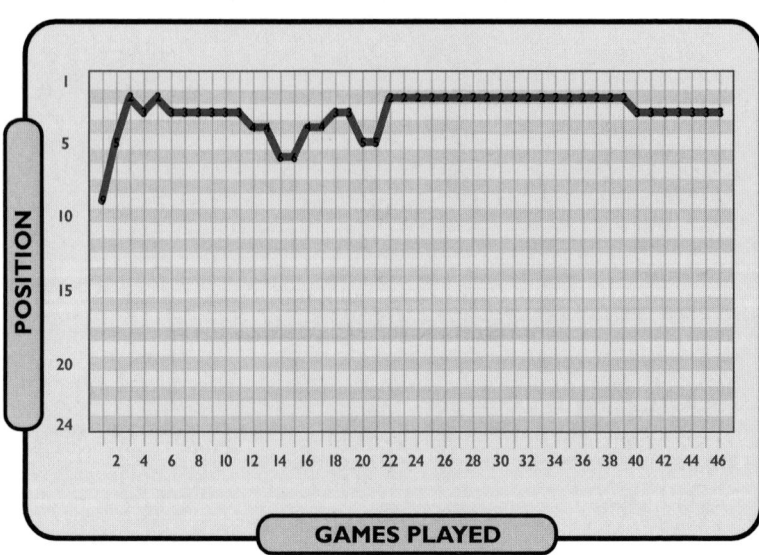

POSITION

GAMES PLAYED

21 Bolton were the most prolific Division One

THE GOALS

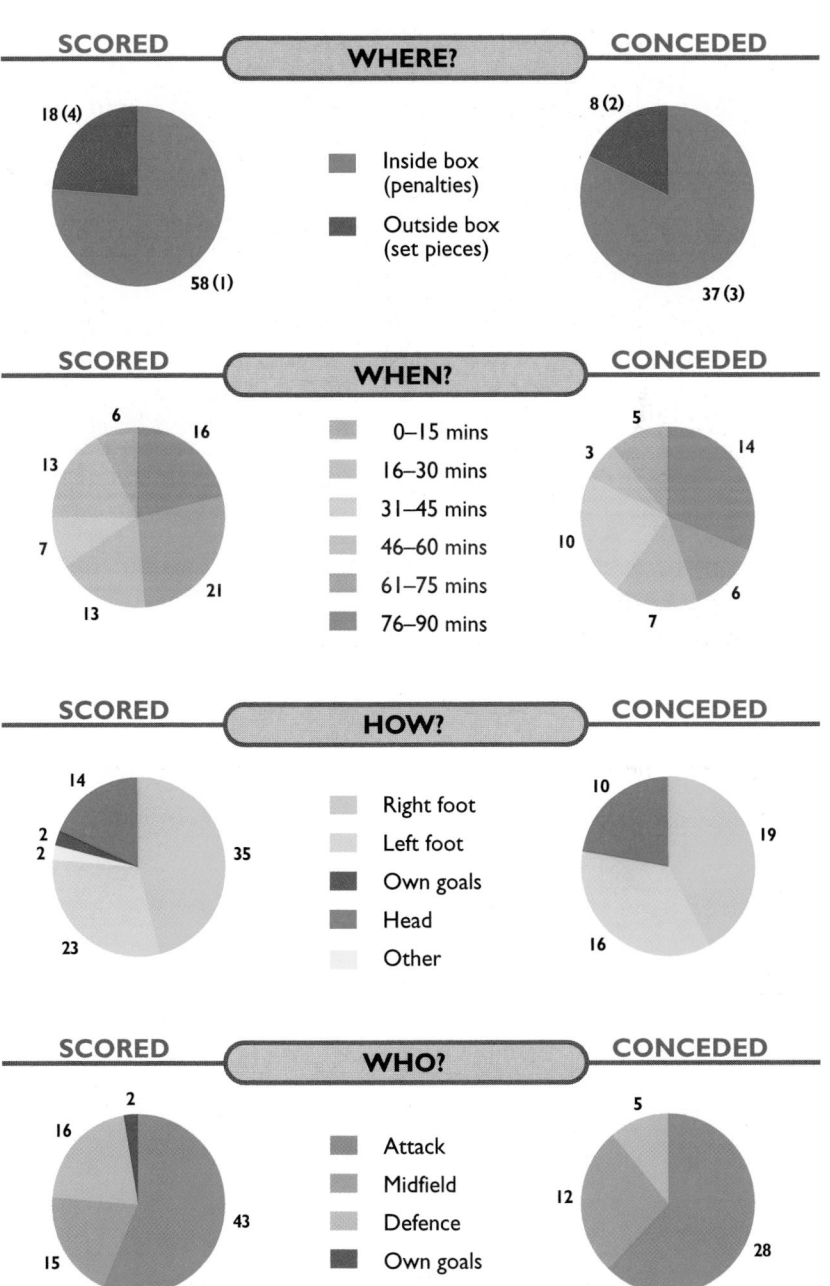

WHERE?

SCORED | CONCEDED

18 (4) | 58 (1) | 8 (2) | 37 (3)

- Inside box (penalties)
- Outside box (set pieces)

WHEN?

SCORED | CONCEDED

6, 16, 13, 7, 21, 13 | 5, 3, 14, 10, 6, 7

- 0–15 mins
- 16–30 mins
- 31–45 mins
- 46–60 mins
- 61–75 mins
- 76–90 mins

HOW?

SCORED | CONCEDED

14, 2, 2, 35, 23 | 10, 19, 16

- Right foot
- Left foot
- Own goals
- Head
- Other

WHO?

SCORED | CONCEDED

2, 16, 43, 15 | 5, 12, 28

- Attack
- Midfield
- Defence
- Own goals

team between the 61st and 75th minutes

FULHAM

ADDRESS

Craven Cottage, Stevenage Road,
Fulham, London SW6 6HH

CONTACT NUMBERS

Telephone: 020 7893 8383
Fax: 020 7384 4715
Ticket Office: 020 7384 4710
Club Call: 09068 440 044
Club Shop: 020 7384 4807
e-mail:
enquiries@fulham-fc.demon.co.uk
Website: www.fulhamfc.co.uk

KEY PERSONNEL

Key Personnel
Chairman: M Al Fayed
Vice-Chairman: B Muddyman
Directors: S Benson
T Delaney, M Griffiths, A Muddyman
Managing Director: M Fiddy
Deputy Managing Director: L Hoos
Manager: Jean Tigana

SPONSORS

2000–01: Demon Internet

FANZINES

There's Only One F In Fulham

COLOURS

Home: White shirts, black shorts
and white stockings
Away: Red shirts, white shorts
and black stockings

NICKNAME

The Cottagers

HONOURS

Division One Champions: 2000–01
Division Two Champions:
1948–49, 1998–99
Division Three (South) Champions
1931–32

RECORD GOALSCORER

Gordon Davies – 159 league goals,
1978–84, 1986–91

BIGGEST WIN

10–1 v Ipswich Town, Division 1,
26 December 1963

BIGGEST DEFEAT

0–10 v Liverpool –
League Cup 2nd Round 1st leg,
23 September 1986

SEASON REVIEW

Fulham's rapid rise to the Premiership is a remarkable achievement considering they were promoted from Division Three as recently as 1997.

Much of the credit for their progress must go to chairman Mohamed Al Fayed, whose financial support has enabled the club to enter the transfer market at will and also attract one of the biggest names in European football as manager.

Although the formations for their 2000–01 success were laid by Kevin Keegan and Paul Bracewell, Jean Tigana brought out the best in his players with his revolutionary training methods, which had reaped rewards earlier in his managerial career at Monaco, where he won the French Championship in 1997.

Before Fulham's opening match at home to Crewe, a number of new players were brought into the squad. Tigana's first signing was Louis Saha, who joined for a fee of £2.1 million from Metz. He already had experience of the English game thanks to a loan spell with Newcastle in 1999.

Saha was his largest purchase, with John Collins arriving from Everton to become player-coach for an undisclosed fee, believed to be in the region of £2 million. French youngster Fabrice Fernandes and Luis Boa Morte were secured on season-long loan deals from Rennes and Southampton respectively.

As expected, Dario Gradi's men were seen off in professional if unspectacular fashion by two goals to nil, but this result was the first of 11 straight wins which put the club seven points clear of third place by the time the Cottagers were held to a 0–0 draw by Wolves at Molineux. Fulham's performances in this period stood out because the winning margins were so great. Only one victory in the sequence

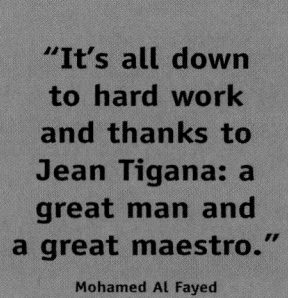

"It's all down to hard work and thanks to Jean Tigana: a great man and a great maestro."

Mohamed Al Fayed

was by a 1–0 scoreline – the defeat of Norwich at Carrow Road.

In their opening seven home games, Fulham scored 22 goals. Barnsley and Stockport were severely punished, the Tykes conceding five times and County four.

Three days after the 100 per cent record had gone at Wolves, Preston put paid to the unbeaten league run, too, winning 1–0 at the Cottage. The Fulham fans argued that the defeat was a relief, as it meant the players could now go into games under slightly less pressure. As long as they maintained a respectable level of form for the remainder of the season, they would be sure to claim one of the two automatic promotion places.

Although they failed to win their next game – a 3–3 draw at Sheffield Wednesday – most managers would have settled for a record of 11 wins, two draws and a defeat going into November. But Tigana evidently felt that his team was going off the boil a little, so in the following weeks new players were given a chance to impress. He gave Nicolas Sahnoun, signed in October on loan from Bordeaux, a debut as substitute against Portsmouth and splashed out £2 million on Latvian Andrejs Stolcers.

Stolcers became the second Fulham player to score on his debut during the season when he netted in the 3–1 win against West Brom, repeating the feat achieved by Louis Saha in his first game on the opening day of the campaign.

With league form now on an even keel going into the festive season, Fulham's exploits in the Worthington Cup came to the fore. Fielding weakened teams had meant defeats in the first leg of earlier rounds against Northampton and Chesterfield, but following these scares stronger sides were selected to win the

SEASON REVIEW

return fixtures. Further wins against Wolves and Derby meant a quarter-final tie with Liverpool at Anfield.

The Reds won 3–0 after extra-time – but Fulham did not let this setback alter their league form. Their next three matches were all won, the most emphatic of these seeing Watford, who looked for the first half of the season like the only side capable of beating them to the title, annihilated 5–0 on Boxing Day.

Defeat at Stockport was followed by the most-anticipated tie of the FA Cup third round – a home draw against Manchester United. The Red Devils won 2–1, but it was only a late Teddy Sheringham strike which denied Fulham a replay at Old Trafford.

Preparations for this match were disrupted when captain Chris Coleman was involved in a car accident the evening after defeat at Stockport. The leg injuries he sustained ruled him out for the season, but the team did not suffer greatly as the experienced Kit Symons was able to fill the breach alongside Andy Melville for much of the rest of the campaign.

With Barry Hayles struggling with injury and Boa Morte suspended, Tigana recruited Danish striker Peter Moller on loan from Real Oviedo. He got his first goal in Fulham colours in the 2–0 win over local rivals QPR, but did not hold down a place once Boa Morte returned from his ban.

With matters on the pitch continuing to run smoothly – defeat at Burnley aside – the highlight of February came when Hammersmith Council gave permission for the multi-million-pound redevelopment of Craven Cottage. And the multi-million-pound development of the team continued in March when Alain Goma was snapped up in a record £4 million package from Newcastle United.

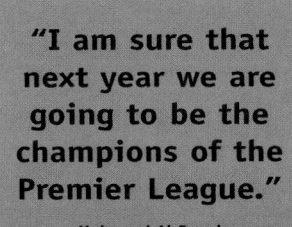

"I am sure that next year we are going to be the champions of the Premier League."

Mohamed Al Fayed

The form of Sean Davis meant that he was regularly involved with the England Under-21 squad during the season, and his classy displays became even more important once Fabrice Fernandes had his loan spell terminated in mid-March.

Davis netted an injury-time winner against Blackburn at Ewood Park in the televised clash between the top two in April and also scored the last-gasp equaliser at home to Sheffield Wednesday which finally secured the title. Promotion had been assured the week before at Huddersfield, when Boa Morte's 85th-minute strike ensured Fulham a 2–1 victory over Lou Macari's relegation-threatened Terriers.

Although they managed to register just one win in their last five matches, Fulham still finished on 101 points, 10 clear of second-placed Blackburn. In all, six members of Tigana's side – Maik Taylor, Steve Finnan, Chris Coleman, Lee Clark, Sean Davis and Louis Saha – the division's leading scorer with 27 goals – were selected in the PFA's Division One Team of the Season.

Tigana said shortly after gaining promotion that Fulham was likely to be his last job before he retired. "I love being on the field but at home my family are starting to repeat to me that there's more to life than football," he said.

Chairman Mohamed Al Fayed will hope that the Frenchman's tenure comes to an end with Fulham established as the biggest club in the country. After the win at Huddersfield the Harrods owner proclaimed: "We already have all the ammunition for next season and we hope to be the Champions of the Premier League."

Manchester United, you have been warned.

FULHAM

DATE	OPPONENT	SCORE	ATT.	BETSY	BOA MORTE	BREVETT	CLARK	COLEMAN	COLLINS J	COLLINS W	DAVIS	FERNANDES	FINNAN	GOLDBAEK	GOMA	HAHNEMANN
12.08.00	Crewe A H	2–0	11,157	s13	60	90	84	90	90			s6	90	90		
18.08.00	Birmingham A	3–1	21,659		s24□	90	90	90□	90^1		90^1		90	90		
26.08.00	Stockport H	4–1	11,009		$s13^1$	90□	90	90	90^1		90□	s12	90	77		
28.08.00	Norwich A	1–0	16,678		$s28^1$	90	75	90□	90		90□	s15	90□	81		
10.09.00	Barnsley H	5–1	10,437		$s26^1$	90	79	90□			90	90	90	71		
12.09.00	Burnley H	3–1	11,863		s16	90	90	90		s15	75	90	90	90^1		
16.09.00	Nottm Forest A	3–0	18,737		s19	24	90	90		90		90^1	90	90		
23.09.00	Gillingham H	3–0	13,032		s27		90^1	90	90	90		90	90	90		
30.09.00	Bolton W A	2–0	19,924		90^2□		90	90	90□			90	90□	90		
15.10.00	Blackburn H	2–1	15,247		54		90	90	90			90^1	90	89		
18.10.00	C Palace H	3–1	16,040		55		80^2	90	90		s23	90	90	67		
21.10.00	Wolves A	0–0	21,080		s31□	90	90	90	90			90	90	90		
24.10.00	Preston A	0–1	14,354		s18	90	90	90	s38		89	72	90	52		
28.10.00	Sheff Wed A	3–3	17,559		s13	76	90	90□	90		90	77	90□	s13		
04.11.00	Huddersfield H	3–0	13,108			90	90	90	90		45	s45□	90^1	90^1		
11.11.00	Wimbledon A	3–0	14,071		67	90□	90	90	90		90	s33	90	57		
18.11.00	Portsmouth H	3–1	19,005		s32	90	90^1	90			83□	90□	90	58		
21.11.00	Sheff Utd A	1–1	16,041		s29	90	71	90			90	90	90^1	71		
25.11.00	Grimsby H	2–1	12,107		90^1	90	90	90			90	90	90	56		
02.12.00	Preston A	1–1	16,047		67□	90□	90	90			90^1	90	90			
09.12.00	West Brom A	3–1	22,301		s15	90	90□	90	s29		90^2	62□	90	61□		
16.12.00	Tranmere H	3–1	13,157		90^2	90	90^1	90			s45	72□	90	s18		
23.12.00	Crewe A A	2–1	6,935		90^1	90	90	90	s20		70□		90	90		
26.12.00	Watford H	5–0	19,373		s18	90	90	77			90□	63□	90	90		
01.01.01	Stockport A	0–2	6,100		s47□	90□	90	90			56	55	90	90		
13.01.00	Norwich H	2–0	16,052	72	90^1	90					90		90	90		
20.01.01	Watford A	3–1	18,333		90^2□	90	90				90□	90	90	90		
27.01.01	Birmingham H	0–1	17,077			90□	75				90□	90□	90	90		
31.01.01	QPR A	2–0	16,403			90		90			90□	90	90	90		
04.02.01	Sheff Utd H	1–1	12,480			90^1	90□	90			90	90	90	61□		
10.02.01	Barnsley A	0–0	14,654			90		90			90	63	90□	90		
17.02.01	Nottm Forest H	1–0	17,425			90□	90□	90		80	90		90	64		
20.02.01	Burnley A	1–2	15,737			80	90	90		67	90	s23	90	90		
24.02.01	Gillingham A	2–0	9,931		$s26^1$	90	90			90^1	68		90	64		
04.03.01	Bolton W H	1–1	16,468		s23□	90	90			90	90		90	58		
10.03.01	QPR H	2–0	16,021		s26	90	90^1			90	90		90	69		
17.03.01	C Palace A	2–0	21,133		90^2	90	90			87	90		90	90		
30.03.01	Tranmere A	4–1	12,362				90	90^1		90	90		90			
07.04.01	West Brom H	0–0	17,795				90	90		66	90		90	s34		
11.04.01	Blackburn A	2–1	21,578				41□	90		90	90^1		90	90		
14.04.01	Huddersfield A	2–1	15,882		90^1	90	90				s10		90	71		
16.04.01	Sheff Wed H	1–1	17,500		90□	90	76			68□	90^1□		90□	45		90
21.04.01	Portsmouth A	1–1	17,651	s8	82□	90□	90			90	90□		90	67	44	
24.04.01	Wolves H	2–0	15,375	90			90	90		67	77		90			
28.04.01	Wimbledon H	1–1	18,576		90^1		90				90		90	77	62	
06.05.01	Grimsby A	0–1	8,706	s25	90□		90				90		90	65	90	90

□ Yellow card, ■ Red card, s Substitute, 90^2 Goals scored, *including one own goal

2000–01 DIVISION ONE APPEARANCES

HAYLES	HAYWARD	LEWIS	MELVILLE	MOLLER	MORGAN	NEILSON	PHELAN	RIEDLE	SAHA	SAHNOUN	STOLCERS	SYMONS	TAYLOR	TROLLOPE	WILLOCK	TOTAL
s30¹		90	90					77¹				90				990
90		90						66¹				90				990
90²		90						78				90				990
62□	s9	90						90				90				990
64¹	s19	s11	90					90³				90				990
74	s4	90						86²				90				990
90¹		90						71¹□				90	s66			990
90²		90						63□				90				990
90		90										90	90□			990
90	s1	90□						s36¹				90	90			990
s35	s10							90¹			90□	90	90			990
90□		90						59				90				990
90		90						90				90	s1			990
77¹□		90¹						90¹				90	s14			990
90								89¹□			90	90			s1	990
s23¹		90						88²				90	s2			990
90²		90						90	s7			90				990
90		90						61	s19			90	s19□			990
90								s34¹			90	90				990
s23		90						90□				90				990
90		90						75	s28¹□			90				990
s34		90						56	45□	90		90				990
90¹		90						s45	45□			90				990
90³		90						72¹	s27¹	s13		90				990
43		90						90	s35□	s34		90				990
		90				s33		90¹□	s18	57	90□	90				990
		90						90¹			90	90				990
	s15	90□	90				s34				56	90	90			990
90				70¹			s20¹		90			90	90			990
90							s29		90			90	90			990
90							s27		90			90	90	90		990
90				s6			s26		84¹		s10	90	90			990
90¹		90					s10					90	90			990
90		90				s22	s6		84		90□	90				990
90¹		90							90			90				981
64		90					s21		80¹		s10	90	90			990
62		90□			s3			s28				90	90			990
90¹		90							90²		90	90	90			990
90		90					s24		90		56	90	90			990
42		90			s48				90¹			90	90			941
90			s1				s19		89¹	80	90	90	90			990
s45		90					s14				s22	90				990
90							s23		90¹		s46	90				990
90			s11	s13				79	90²	s23		90	90			990
			s28				s28		62		s13	90	90□	90		990
s34		90						90	90		56					990

THE MANAGER

JEAN TIGANA

When it was announced in April 2000 that Jean Tigana was to be Fulham's new manager, supporters hoped that the Frenchman would lead their club to the Premiership in emphatic style – and he did just that.

Although the financial support on hand from chairman Mohamed Al Fayed helped Tigana sign the likes of Louis Saha, John Collins, Andrejs Stolcers and latterly Alain Goma, not all arrivals in SW6 were as costly. Luis Boa Morte, Fabrice Fernandes and Nicolas Sahnoun all came to the club on a loan basis.

Experienced squad members, signed by previous managers Kevin Keegan and Paul Bracewell, benefited from Tigana's coaching methods, with the former Monaco chief improving the play of senior players such as Andy Melville and Rufus Brevett in a similar fashion to the way in which fellow countryman Arsène Wenger extended the careers of his vintage back four at Highbury.

As a player, Tigana represented France 52 times, while his managerial career began at Lyon before he replaced Wenger at Monaco in 1995, winning the French Championship in 1997 – the club's first title for 10 seasons.

LEAGUE POSITION

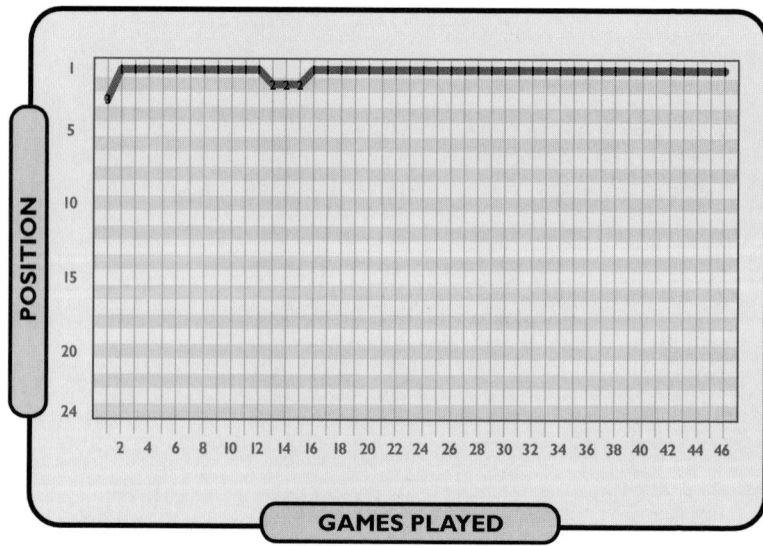

GAMES PLAYED

32 Fulham conceded fewer goals

THE GOALS

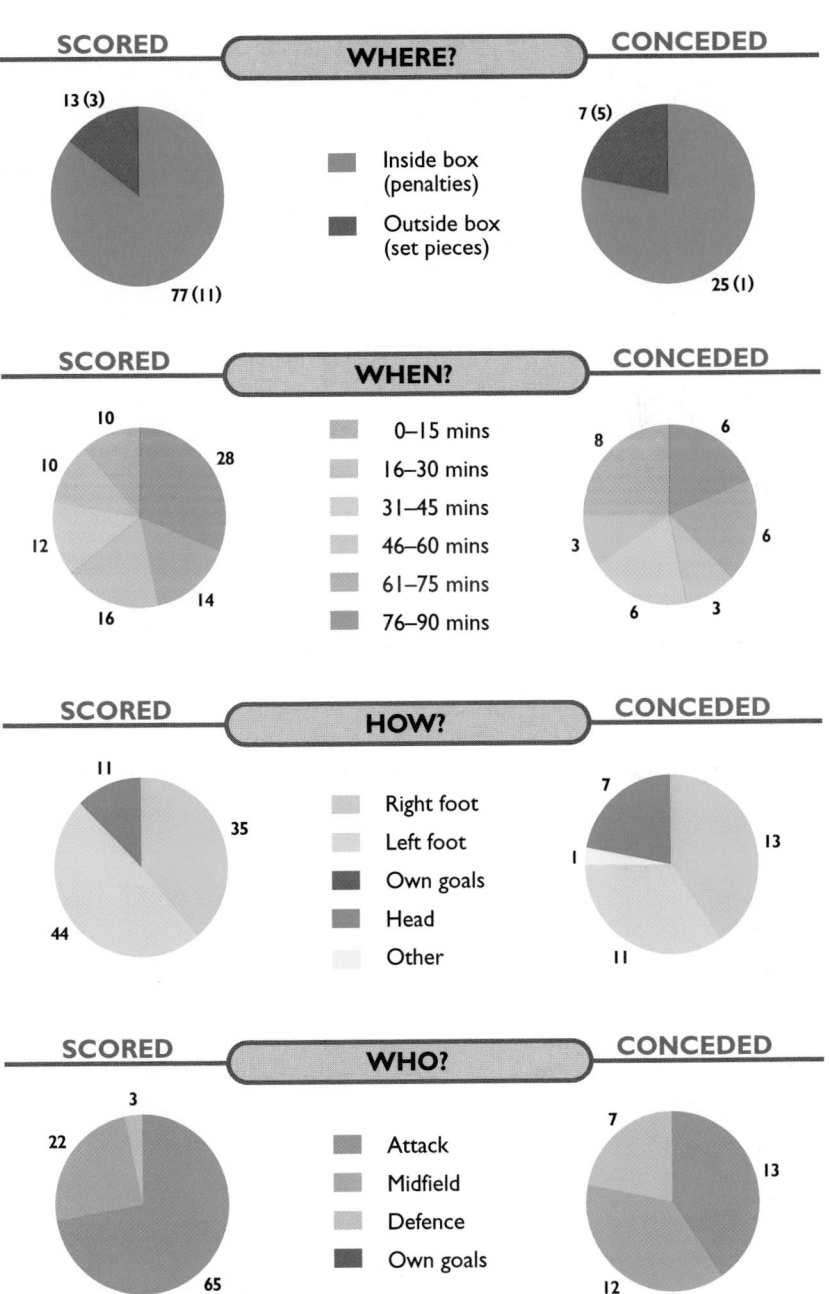

WHERE?

SCORED — CONCEDED

13 (3)
77 (11)

7 (5)
25 (1)

- Inside box (penalties)
- Outside box (set pieces)

WHEN?

SCORED — CONCEDED

10, 28, 14, 16, 12, 10

6, 6, 3, 6, 3, 8

- 0–15 mins
- 16–30 mins
- 31–45 mins
- 46–60 mins
- 61–75 mins
- 76–90 mins

HOW?

SCORED — CONCEDED

11, 35, 44

7, 13, 11, 1

- Right foot
- Left foot
- Own goals
- Head
- Other

WHO?

SCORED — CONCEDED

3, 22, 65

7, 13, 12

- Attack
- Midfield
- Defence
- Own goals

than any other team in Division One

THE PLAYERS

During the 2000–01 season, 543 players made an appearance on the pitch – just one more than in 1999–2000 but two short of 1998–99's tally. Each player is featured in the following section, whether he was ever-present or played just one match as a substitute.

The players are featured in alphabetical order and the statistics that are shown are an individual's total contribution from 2000–01, even if he played for more than one club. If you would like to see a player's contribution to a particular club, all you have to do is turn to the relevant page in the club section showing all players' performances for that particular team. The page references for these more detailed statistics are highlighted at the bottom of each player profile.

The club colours shown are the club with whom the player finished the season or for whom he made his last appearance in the 2000–01 Premiership.

The small lozenge alongside each player's name indicates his usual position.

G = Goalkeeper   **FB** = Full-back   **CB** = Centre-back

M = Midfielder   **AM** = Attacking Midfielder   **S** = Striker

You will find that the categories of statistics vary according to the players' positions. More emphasis has been placed on goal attempts for strikers, whereas defenders will have tackling and defensive clearances featured. All players feature discipline figures for the season.

PLAYERS' AVERAGES

CATEGORY	STRIKER	ATTACKING MIDFIELDER	MIDFIELDER	DEFENDER
Goals-to-shots ratio	15%	11%	7%	9%
Shooting accuracy	51%	43%	39%	38%
Passing accuracy	68%	71%	74%	70%
Short passing accuracy	69%	73%	77%	76%
Long passing accuracy	66%	64%	67%	58%
Crossing accuracy	25%	27%	28%	26%
Dribble completion rate	56%	66%	73%	79%
Tackle success	72%	73%	70%	74%

GOALKEEPER	
Saves-to-shots ratio 72%	Catch success 93%

Nabil ABIDALLAH • 28
IPSWICH TOWN • BORN: 5.8.82

Brought to Suffolk from just across the North Sea in Amsterdam in the summer of 2000, Nabil Abidallah did not play a significant part in Ipswich's 2000–01 campaign.

In fact, the tiny midfielder played just 14 minutes in the Premiership; nine as a late substitute in the 2–0 win against Everton and five minutes in the 3–1 triumph over Bradford a week later.

At just nine stone, Abidallah looked like a schoolboy sent out to play with grown men, but the home crowd had heard of his abilities and were suitably excited by his brief appearances.

He made 11 passes – completing seven of them – but will hope that he is given a lengthier chance to impress in 2001–02. Hailed by some in time-honoured fashion as "the new Kieron Dyer", Abidallah may have a chance to play in Europe as Town embark on their UEFA Cup adventure. He may even get the chance to play against former club Ajax.

SEE PAGE 152 FOR FULL STATS

 Clarence ACUNA • 6
NEWCASTLE UNITED • BORN: 8.2.75

Bargain: Clarence Acuna

Signed for a bargain fee of £1 million in September 2000, Clarence Acuna added bite to the Newcastle midfield and ended the 2000–01 season with three goals. A seasoned Chilean international with more than 50 caps for his country, Acuna is widely regarded as one of the better South American imports at St James' Park.

He started his footballing career with the memorably-named Chilean club O'Higgins, something that may have helped him settle in Britain. His first goal for the Magpies came on Boxing Day with the winning strike against Leeds United. Yorkshire teams seem to bring out the best in him, as he scored in the return game at Elland Road and also at Bradford City in March.

While Acuna's tackling was admirable – he went in for 80 challenges – Bobby Robson will hope his midfielder can add a creative element to his game. He ended the campaign without an assist and, despite the reputation of South American players' technique, recorded an average pass completion rate.

APPEARANCES	
Start (sub)	23(3)
Minutes on pitch	1978
GOAL ATTEMPTS	
Goals	3
Shots on target	5
Shooting accuracy	33%
PASSING & CROSSING	
Goal assists	0
Passes in opp half	373
Passing accuracy in opp half	70%
Successful crosses	1
Cross completion	13%
DEFENDING	
Interceptions	4
Clearances	32
Tackles	80
Tackles won %	61%
DISCIPLINE	
Fouls	22
Yellow cards	5
Red cards	0

SEE PAGE 250 FOR FULL STATS

For more information visit our website:

Tony ADAMS • 6
ARSENAL • BORN: 10.10.66

Arsenal skipper Tony Adams is often portrayed as being as delicate as an antique chair, but he managed to play more than 2,300 minutes of Premiership football in 2000–01. And while he again ended the season without a medal to prop on his mantelpiece, he can look back on appearances in the FA Cup final and a Champions League quarter-final clash with Valencia.

Notable statistics included a tackle success rate of 81% and a pass completion rate of 82%, sure-fire evidence that he is still one of the league's top defenders. Indeed, Arsenal's defence kept just three of their 17 clean sheets in Adams's absence.

Adams retired from international football in January 2001, saying: "I want to give the benefit of the time I have left in the game to Arsenal", an admirable stance to take. Even so, 2001–02 will be his swansong as a player. The back injury that has plagued him finally persuaded Adams to draw the curtain on his illustrious career after one more crack at the Champions League.

APPEARANCES	
Start (sub)	26(0)
Minutes on pitch	2340
GOAL ATTEMPTS	
Goals	1
DEFENDING	
Blocks	13
Shots cleared off line	0
Headed clearances	154
Other clearances	71
Interceptions	15
Last man saving tackles	0
Tackles won	55
Tackles won %	81%
PASSING	
Passing accuracy own half	87%
Passing accuracy opp half	72%
DISCIPLINE	
Fouls	27
Fouls in danger area	8
Yellow cards	7
Red cards	0
SEE PAGE 40 FOR FULL STATS	

Ade AKINBIYI • 22
LEICESTER CITY • BORN: 10.10.74

APPEARANCES	
Start (sub)	33(4)
Minutes on pitch	2818
GOAL ATTEMPTS	
Goals inside box	9
Goals outside box	0
Minutes per goal scored	313
Goals/shots ratio	14%
SHOOTING	
Shots on target inside box	35
Shots on target outside box	3
Shooting accuracy	58%
PASSING	
Goal assists	2
Key passes	11
Passing accuracy in opp half	63%
DISCIPLINE	
Fouls committed	72
Fouls won	36
Offside	59
Yellow cards	1
Red cards	0
SEE PAGE 180 FOR FULL STATS	

Peter Taylor made a quick impression on the transfer market when he became Leicester manager in summer 2000 and his most expensive indulgence was striker Ade Akinbiyi, ostensibly brought in to replace the recently-departed Emile Heskey.

A fee of £5 million was paid to Wolves for Akinbiyi and, after a steady pre-season, hopes were high. Nine months later and the Foxes faithful were less enamoured with their record signing, despite nine goals in his first attempt at top-flight football. Opta stats, though, showed that the burly striker had actually performed better than Heskey had for Leicester in 1999–2000.

Akinbiyi scored more league goals than any other Leicester player, but often looked clumsy in possession. He also missed some good chances at vital moments. But he featured in all bar one of City's league games and, after three big-money summer moves in as many years, Akinbiyi should stay out of the transfer headlines in 2001–02 and hope for better things to come.

Rati ALEKSIDZE • 27
CHELSEA • BORN: 6.8.78

Signed for £200,000 in February 2000, Rati Aleksidze broke into the Chelsea team in 2000–01, firstly in the UEFA Cup, before making his league debut in the 4–1 thrashing of Derby County at Stamford Bridge in December.

He played six minutes that day and followed it up with an 11-minute appearance a week later at Middlesbrough. This spell saw him complete just two of his 10 passes, which could be the reason he was despatched back into the reserve team very quickly.

But as captain of the Georgian Under-21 team, Aleksidze has the ability to make a name for himself at Chelsea. The example of Sam Dalla Bona, another young import who has battled into the first-team picture, should give him heart. And with rumours of a cull of many of the older heads in the Pensioners' midfield, his youth could be a major asset as Chelsea continue to rebuild under new boss Claudio Ranieri.

SEE PAGE 96 FOR FULL STATS

Danny ALLSOP • 12
MANCHESTER CITY • BORN: 10.8.78

After loan spells with Notts County and Wrexham in 1999–2000, many people were surprised that Danny Allsopp was retained by Manchester City as they returned to the Premiership – and his subsequent career at Maine Road is unlikely to live long in the memory.

Having returned to the club after spending a month at Bristol Rovers, he experienced just one substitute appearance for City in the 4–1 rout at West Ham before joining Notts County permanently. He enjoyed success at Meadow Lane but, while he is effective in Division Two, he does not seem to have the ability required at the highest level.

Indeed, his appearance was only notable because he replaced gangly Costa Rican forward Paulo Wanchope, a former Hammer who was suffering an extremely bad day back at Upton Park. Still, in years to come, Allsopp will be able to tell people he had 15 minutes of fame in the top flight.

SEE PAGE 208 FOR FULL STATS

Niclas ALEXANDERSSON • 7
EVERTON • BORN: 29.12.71

Walter Smith drafted Niclas Alexandersson into the Everton midfield in July 2000 and he would have hoped for more from the Swedish international.

The former IFK Gothenburg and Halmstads player had been linked with a move to Aston Villa, before eventually plumping for a £2.5 million move to Merseyside.

After parading around the lower reaches of the Premiership with Sheffield Wednesday, Alexandersson did the same for Everton, with injury disrupting his first season at Goodison Park.

A goal in March and one in April represented the Swede's impression on the goalscoring charts, while a cross completion rate of 21% was six percentage points down on the previous season.

But Alexandersson can point to calf and knee injuries which sidelined him for most of the winter and he showed a definite return to form in the last few weeks of the season.

The whole Everton squad underachieved yet again and, while Alexandersson has not come under the sort of scrutiny afforded to players like Alex Nyarko, his hefty fee is hefty enough to demand a better return in 2001–02.

APPEARANCES	
Start (sub)	17(3)
Minutes on pitch	1347
GOAL ATTEMPTS	
Goals	2
Shots on target	5
Shooting accuracy	36%
Goals/shots ratio	14%
PASSING	
Goal assists	1
Passes in opp half	331
Passing accuracy in opp half	60%
Crosses	103
Crossing accuracy	21%
DRIBBLING	
Dribbles & runs	59
Dribble completion	63%
Corners forced	13
DISCIPLINE	
Fouls	12
Yellow cards	2
Red cards	0

SEE PAGE 138 FOR FULL STATS

12 Alpay was the Premiership's most-booked

A

John ALOISI • 16
COVENTRY CITY • BORN: 5.2.76

Australian striker John Aloisi has struggled with injuries since moving from Portsmouth to Coventry in 1998 and the 2000–01 campaign was no different.

He enjoyed a productive spell in the autumn, scoring in consecutive games against Charlton and Spurs, but even this could not persuade manager Gordon Strachan to give him a long run in the first team.

A goal in the defeat at Bradford proved to be Aloisi's last strike of the campaign. He only managed 12 shots all season, as he seemed to be affected by the goalscoring malaise that gripped Highfield Road. And once John Hartson had been purchased, Aloisi rarely figured, especially after injuring his hamstring on international duty.

He did, however, enjoy success on the international stage, smashing home six goals in one game as Australia eased past Tonga 22–0. But such frivolities will be of no comfort to him as he looks to his future, whether that is with Coventry in the Nationwide League or elsewhere.

APPEARANCES	
Start (sub)	8(11)
Minutes on pitch	791
GOAL ATTEMPTS	
Goals inside box	2
Goals outside box	1
Minutes per goal scored	264
Goals/shots ratio	25%
SHOOTING	
Shots on target inside box	4
Shots on target outside box	2
Shooting accuracy	50%
PASSING	
Goal assists	2
Key passes	7
Passing accuracy in opp half	48%
DISCIPLINE	
Fouls committed	21
Fouls won	21
Offside	12
Yellow cards	0
Red cards	0

SEE PAGE 110 FOR FULL STATS

ALPAY • 16
ASTON VILLA • BORN: 29.5.73

CB

APPEARANCES	
Start (sub)	33(0)
Minutes on pitch	2851
GOAL ATTEMPTS	
Goals	0
DEFENDING	
Blocks	26
Shots cleared off line	1
Headed clearances	192
Other clearances	100
Interceptions	23
Last man saving tackles	1
Tackles won	87
Tackles won %	72%
PASSING	
Passing accuracy own half	81%
Passing accuracy opp half	59%
DISCIPLINE	
Fouls	55
Fouls in danger area	17
Yellow cards	12
Red cards	0

SEE PAGE 54 FOR FULL STATS

Turkish defender Alpay Fehmi Ozalan signed for Aston Villa from Fenerbahce in a £5.6 million deal in July 2000.

He came with a reputation for arguing with officials and one of his most infamous spats saw him sent off for punching Portugal's Fernando Couto. Two days later he also came to blows with an Istanbul taxi driver.

So it was no surprise that Alpay's volatile nature frothed to the surface. He appeared to slap David James after making a mistake, which gifted Liverpool a goal in a 3–0 defeat. Alpay later claimed that he thought James had sworn at him.

Twelve yellow cards illustrated his uncompromising style, but Alpay proved to be a solid signing, allowing Villa to part with Ugo Ehiogu in the knowledge they had a decent replacement.

The feisty Turk won a creditable 72% of his tackles and made almost 300 clearances for a Villa defence which conceded just 43 goals – the joint-sixth lowest tally in the league during the 2000–01 campaign.

defender, picking up 12 yellow cards

Shola AMEOBI • 23
NEWCASTLE UNITED • BORN: 12.10.81

Newcastle United's injury crisis saw the club give certain players the opportunity of making the long journey from youth team to first-team recognition. One of the players in question was Shola Ameobi, a striker who took advantage of injuries to players such as Alan Shearer and Carl Cort.

The Nigerian-born player made his debut in the 0–0 draw with Chelsea in September 2000, but it was not until Boxing Day that he was fully unleashed by Bobby Robson.

From that moment onwards he either started or came on in all but one of United's games, scoring two goals and making a couple for team-mates as well.

He also made a splash on the international scene, making his debut for the England Under-21s and scoring a superb brace in a 4–0 win against Finland. Unfortunately he was racially-abused by fans when playing Albania, which prompted an official complaint to UEFA.

His chances at Newcastle next season could be diminished with the return of senior players but he is a star in the making.

APPEARANCES	
Start (sub)	12(8)
Minutes on pitch	1096
GOAL ATTEMPTS	
Goals inside box	1
Goals outside box	1
Minutes per goal scored	548
Goals/shots ratio	10%
SHOOTING	
Shots on target inside box	6
Shots on target outside box	2
Shooting accuracy	38%
PASSING	
Goal assists	2
Key passes	9
Passing accuracy in opp half	57%
DISCIPLINE	
Fouls committed	38
Fouls won	25
Offside	19
Yellow cards	0
Red cards	0
SEE PAGE 250 FOR FULL STATS	

Darren ANDERTON • 7
TOTTENHAM HOTSPUR • BORN: 3.3.72

APPEARANCES	
Start (sub)	22(1)
Minutes on pitch	1931
GOAL ATTEMPTS	
Goals	2
Shots on target	16
Shooting accuracy	46%
Goals/shots ratio	6%
PASSING	
Goal assists	3
Passes in opp half	798
Passing accuracy in opp half	63%
Crosses	154
Crossing accuracy	29%
DRIBBLING	
Dribbles & runs	45
Dribble completion	73%
Corners forced	15
DISCIPLINE	
Fouls	24
Yellow cards	7
Red cards	0
SEE PAGE 292 FOR FULL STATS	

Another season at White Hart Lane, another season in which Darren Anderton made his weary way to the treatment room. Some things never change.

The England midfielder did play for almost 2,000 minutes, though, and despite often featuring in the unorthodox position of right wing-back, Anderton once again performed adequately under George Graham.

He scored twice and created a further three goals, as well as whipping in 154 crosses with an accuracy of 29%.

But in a season of disappointment at Tottenham, Anderton succumbed to an Achilles injury in February which prematurely ended his season and saw him miss the FA Cup semi-final with Arsenal.

It means that he has not yet been able to show new Spurs chief Glenn Hoddle what he can do, but the former England manager must be confident that he can tease Anderton's best form out of him if he signs a new contract, providing – as always – that "Dazza" can stay injury-free.

For more information visit our website:

Juan Pablo ANGEL • 8
ASTON VILLA • BORN: 21.10.75

Reeling from the career-ending injury suffered by Luc Nilis, John Gregory finally persuaded Villa chairman Doug Ellis to open the war-chest and splash out on a new striker in the form of Colombian international Juan Pablo Angel. The Villans paid a club record £9.5 million for the River Plate forward to add much-needed firepower to their ailing, goal-shy front-line.

Angel commented at the time: "Sure, it's another country, another culture, another system of playing, but I want to adapt as soon as possible".

Sadly his actions did not mirror his brave words. Indeed, only a goal in Villa's last home game of the season rescued Angel from the depths of despair.

He played more than 500 minutes for the club but managed just two shots on target, a poor tally for a supposed "hotshot". While he can explain his under-achievement by pointing to personal problems and the difficulty of adapting to a new culture, he will have to do much better in 2001–02.

APPEARANCES	
Start (sub)	7(2)
Minutes on pitch	516
GOAL ATTEMPTS	
Goals inside box	1
Goals outside box	0
Minutes per goal scored	516
Goals/shots ratio	7%
SHOOTING	
Shots on target inside box	2
Shots on target outside box	0
Shooting accuracy	14%
PASSING	
Goal assists	1
Key passes	4
Passing accuracy in opp half	64%
DISCIPLINE	
Fouls committed	15
Fouls won	3
Offside	10
Yellow cards	1
Red cards	0
SEE PAGE 54 FOR FULL STATS	

Julio ARCA • 33
SUNDERLAND • BORN: 31.1.81

APPEARANCES	
Start (sub)	26(1)
Minutes on pitch	2145
GOAL ATTEMPTS	
Goals	2
Shots on target	10
Shooting accuracy	43%
Goals/shots ratio	9%
PASSING	
Goal assists	4
Passes in opp half	590
Passing accuracy in opp half	71%
Crosses	124
Crossing accuracy	21%
DRIBBLING	
Dribbles & runs	81
Dribble completion	69%
Corners forced	14
DISCIPLINE	
Fouls	21
Yellow cards	5
Red cards	0
SEE PAGE 278 FOR FULL STATS	

Newcastle and Leeds were interested in signing Julio Arca – captain of the Argentinean Under-21 team – but Peter Reid nipped in and paid £3.5 million for the midfielder and he proved to be one of the best young imports to arrive in the Premiership in 2000–01.

Arca made an instant impact, scoring on his debut against West Ham in September. It was to be one of only two goals he scored all season, but his creativity and speed of thought saw him create four goals for the Black Cats.

His second strike came when he scored the Sunderland opener in the 4–1 thrashing of Ipswich on New Year's Day.

He also delivered a large number of crosses, a vital element of Sunderland's game, although he will hope to improve on his completion rate of 21% in 2001–02. The fans quickly became enamoured with the young South American and, after a season of acclimatisation, the best is yet to come from the talented youngster.

Alun ARMSTRONG • 34
IPSWICH TOWN • BORN: 22.2.75

Alun Armstrong found his route to the first team at Middlesbrough increasingly blocked as the Teesside club collected strikers seemingly by the dozen. He therefore jumped at the chance to move to Ipswich Town and joined the Suffolk club in December for the bargain fee of £500,000.

After making a brief debut in the 1–0 win at Anfield, Armstrong opened his account on 16 December with a goal against Southampton and cheekily tried to claim a second which was a clear own goal by unfortunate Saints defender Wayne Bridge.

He went on to score six more goals for the Tractor Boys, complementing the prolific Marcus Stewart. He managed to get the majority of his shots on target and also chipped in with a couple of assists as well.

Town manager George Burley knows he has to hunt for bargains and Armstrong was a shrewd purchase. After delays caused by injuries, his top-flight career now looks set to prosper. Middlesbrough must be kicking themselves.

APPEARANCES	
Start (sub)	15(6)
Minutes on pitch	1487
GOAL ATTEMPTS	
Goals inside box	6
Goals outside box	1
Minutes per goal scored	212
Goals/shots ratio	16%
SHOOTING	
Shots on target inside box	14
Shots on target outside box	9
Shooting accuracy	53%
PASSING	
Goal assists	2
Key passes	10
Passing accuracy in opp half	65%
DISCIPLINE	
Fouls committed	22
Fouls won	32
Offside	17
Yellow cards	0
Red cards	0
SEE PAGE 152 FOR FULL STATS	

Chris ARMSTRONG • 16
TOTTENHAM HOTSPUR • BORN: 19.6.70

APPEARANCES	
Start (sub)	3(6)
Minutes on pitch	361
GOAL ATTEMPTS	
Goals inside box	2
Goals outside box	0
Minutes per goal scored	181
Goals/shots ratio	33%
SHOOTING	
Shots on target inside box	2
Shots on target outside box	1
Shooting accuracy	50%
PASSING	
Goal assists	0
Key passes	3
Passing accuracy in opp half	62%
DISCIPLINE	
Fouls committed	13
Fouls won	5
Offside	13
Yellow cards	0
Red cards	0
SEE PAGE 292 FOR FULL STATS	

Chris Armstrong's 2000–01 season was decimated by a series of groin injuries which reduced him to just 361 minutes of football. He did manage to score two goals in the autumn, but he will be keen to forget the whole campaign and prepare for a fresh start in 2001–02.

The highlight of his season was the winner he bagged as Spurs defeated Sunderland at White Hart Lane in November. He also managed to score in Tottenham's 3–3 draw at Bradford, but this game was notable for the number of times he was caught offside. He was flagged on eight occasions, one of the highest totals in a single Premiership game.

Armstrong's last appearance came in the Christmas defeat at Southampton, an ignominious end to a forgettable season. He will be praying for an end to his injury woe and a chance to regain his place in the first team, but will now have Teddy Sheringham to contend with again.

Good in the air and fleet of foot, he could be an asset to new boss Glenn Hoddle.

Peter ATHERTON • 20
BRADFORD CITY • BORN: 6.4.70

Bradford's ultimately-doomed manager Chris Hutchings persuaded Peter Atherton to leave relegated Sheffield Wednesday and join the Bantams in July 2000, something that gave the player the chance to maintain his position as the man with the most Premiership appearances.

But Atherton's season – like his club's – did not go to plan and he ended the campaign on loan to Birmingham. At least he had the chance to do plenty of defending while at Valley Parade, something he took advantage of, making 80 tackles and winning 78% of them. He also made 163 clearances while only picking up one booking.

Nevertheless, his proud Premiership appearance record was eclipsed by Gary Speed in April, when the Newcastle midfielder made his 318th outing in the competition, while Atherton was performing in the Nationwide League. It is unlikely to have bothered him unduly, but it was a sign that his time in the upper echelon of English football has probably come to an end.

APPEARANCES	
Start (sub)	25(0)
Minutes on pitch	2211
GOAL ATTEMPTS	
Goals	0
PASSING & CROSSING	
Goal assists	2
Passing	847
Passing accuracy	63%
Crosses	20
Crossing accuracy	20%
DEFENDING	
Tackles	80
Tackles won %	78%
Blocks	21
Interceptions	8
Clearances	163
Shots cleared off line	2
DISCIPLINE	
Fouls	32
Yellow cards	1
Red cards	0
SEE PAGE 68 FOR FULL STATS	

Celestine BABAYARO • 3
CHELSEA • BORN: 29.8.78

APPEARANCES	
Start (sub)	19(5)
Minutes on pitch	1651
GOAL ATTEMPTS	
Goals	0
PASSING & CROSSING	
Goal assists	5
Passing	916
Passing accuracy	79%
Crosses	61
Crossing accuracy	30%
DEFENDING	
Tackles	48
Tackles won %	75%
Blocks	12
Interceptions	7
Clearances	63
Shots cleared off line	0
DISCIPLINE	
Fouls	27
Yellow cards	4
Red cards	0
SEE PAGE 96 FOR FULL STATS	

Chelsea left-back Celestine Babayaro was once again at the centre of the ongoing club-versus-country debate, eventually representing his country, Nigeria, at the Sydney Olympics.

But in only his second game of the finals – against host nation Australia – he received his marching orders in the 56th minute after a bust-up with opposition captain Brett Emerton. Having salvaged a 3–3 draw with Honduras, the defending champions bowed out in emphatic fashion, going down 4–1 to Chile in the quarter-finals, but the suspended Babayaro was already Stamford Bridge-bound.

Babayaro figured in around half of Chelsea's Premiership matches, as Claudio Ranieri rotated his defenders in the Blues' push towards sixth spot in the Premiership and a UEFA Cup place. Despite not having scored a first-team goal since his strike against Feyenoord in the 1999–2000 Champions League, Babayaro created five goals and completed 79% of his passes in 2000–01, in a largely forgettable campaign for Chelsea.

than any other Bradford defender

Markus BABBEL • 6
LIVERPOOL • BORN: 8.9.72

German international Markus Babbel left the security of hometown giants Bayern Munich in summer 2000 to seek a new challenge on Merseyside and in his first season his own form and Liverpool's promise to deliver success did not disappoint.

A centre-back by trade, the superb partnership between Messrs Henchoz and Hyypia saw Babbel commanding the Liverpool right flank as a marauding full-back.

Always looking to get forward, Babbel was one of the most consistent performers in Liverpool's historic treble-winning side. The German weighed in with a total of 89 dribbles and runs, being successful on 81% of occasions and swung in more than 90 crosses. Defensively, he also fashioned 200 clearances.

Babbel also contributed with three Premiership goals, including a late winner against Southampton at Anfield and the goal which took Liverpool into a 2–1 lead in the Merseyside derby at Goodison. He also bagged the opener in the amazing 5–4 UEFA Cup final win over Alaves.

APPEARANCES	
Start (sub)	38(0)
Minutes on pitch	3355
GOAL ATTEMPTS	
Goals	3
PASSING & CROSSING	
Goal assists	3
Passing	1410
Passing accuracy	72%
Crosses	93
Crossing accuracy	24%
DEFENDING	
Tackles	87
Tackles won %	67%
Blocks	9
Interceptions	9
Clearances	218
Shots cleared off line	0
DISCIPLINE	
Fouls	48
Yellow cards	6
Red cards	0

SEE PAGE 194 FOR FULL STATS

Karim BAGHERI • 31
CHARLTON ATHLETIC • BORN: 20.2.74

After his £400,000 move from Iranian club side Piroozi in the summer, Karim Bagheri failed to impress at The Valley. Indeed, he played only 18 minutes as a substitute for Matthias Svensson in Charlton's 2–0 defeat at Portman Road by Ipswich.

Bagheri has won more than 70 caps for his country and once scored seven goals in a 17–0 drubbing of the Maldives in a World Cup qualifier.

Also, in 1998, he was selected in the best all-time team of players from Asia and played in the finals in France.

Poor form, constant injury problems and the pressure that must come with being described as "the Iranian Zidane" by the press did not help Bagheri's first-team opportunities at Charlton, though.

All of these aspects, coupled with the good form of Charlton's other strikers, meant the the Premiership's first Iranian import was released by the club at the end of the season.

SEE PAGE 82 FOR FULL STATS

Marauding: Markus Babbel

For more information visit our website:

Eirik BAKKE • 19
LEEDS UNITED • BORN: 13.9.77

Eirik Bakke endured a rollercoaster season with Leeds. He featured in the Whites' run to the Champions League quarter-final and also the surge up the Premiership to the UEFA Cup places by the end of 2000–01.

Injury hampered Bakke's progress and he claimed his rehabilitation was not helped by the autumn fuel crisis. The Norwegian opined on his website: "I've been driving on my reserve tank for the last two days, so I have to fill up today. If I can't, then I'm afraid I won't be able to go in for treatment — the petrol stations have nothing at all."

Whether boss David O'Leary swallowed that excuse is unknown, but when fit and selected the combative Bakke made 104 tackles, with a 74% success rate. But in keeping with Leeds' disciplinary problems, he did pick up nine bookings.

Goals against Manchester City and Bradford were a poor return and Bakke has a hard task to break up the impressive partnership of Olivier Dacourt and David Batty if he is to become more than a fringe player.

APPEARANCES	
Start (sub)	24(5)
Minutes on pitch	2087
GOAL ATTEMPTS	
Goals	2
Shots on target	7
Shooting accuracy	27%
Goals/shots ratio	8%
PASSING	
Goal assists	I
Passes in opp half	635
Passing accuracy in opp half	69%
Crosses	34
Crossing accuracy	18%
DRIBBLING	
Dribbles & runs	70
Dribble completion	76%
Corners forced	17
DISCIPLINE	
Fouls	51
Yellow cards	9
Red cards	0
SEE PAGE 166 FOR FULL STATS	

Michael BALL • 12
EVERTON • BORN: 2.10.79

APPEARANCES	
Start (sub)	29(0)
Minutes on pitch	2574
GOAL ATTEMPTS	
Goals	3
DEFENDING	
Blocks	31
Shots cleared off line	1
Headed clearances	99
Other clearances	78
Interceptions	11
Last man saving tackles	4
Tackles won	79
Tackles won %	74%
PASSING	
Passing accuracy own half	76%
Passing accuracy opp half	53%
DISCIPLINE	
Fouls	33
Fouls in danger area	9
Yellow cards	5
Red cards	0
SEE PAGE 138 FOR FULL STATS	

Michael Ball's pace, agility and quick thinking at the back helped him shackle together an occasionally fragile Everton back line in yet another disappointing season on Merseyside.

Comfortable at either centre-half or left-back, Ball's consistent form led to him being awarded his first full international cap by Sven-Göran Eriksson. He replaced Chris Powell at half-time in the friendly victory against Spain at Villa Park. The step up from under-21 to full international level is never an easy one, but Ball performed admirably and, as a left-footed defender, his international future looks increasingly bright.

Unafraid to take a penalty, Ball netted twice from the spot, as well as scoring against Manchester City at Goodison Park from open play. Ball also made an impressive 31 blocks and launched into 107 tackles, winning 74% of them.

As the youngster in the Toffees' veteran defence, Everton will be desperate to hang on to Ball, who has been linked with a move to city rivals Liverpool.

Nick BARMBY • 20
LIVERPOOL • BORN: 11.2.74

Nick Barmby enjoyed a successful campaign with the Reds, his appearances only limited by the strict squad rotation policy enforced by Gérard Houllier and an ankle ligament injury.

Following his controversial £6 million move from city rivals Everton in the summer, Barmby became the first player in more than 40 years to swap blue for red across Stanley Park. This did not seem to daunt him and, perhaps predictably, he scored the opener in the 3–1 victory over Everton at Anfield.

He completed 72% of the 775 passes he attempted and a respectable 80% of his dribbles and runs down the Liverpool flanks.

Such is the current competition for midfield places on Merseyside, Barmby is never assured of a place in the starting line-up, but his performances were good enough to get him a start at international level.

The effervescent midfielder scored the opener at Villa Park against Spain for England and will no doubt be in contention for the left midfield berth in future as England look to qualify for World Cup 2002.

APPEARANCES	
Start (sub)	21(5)
Minutes on pitch	1838
GOAL ATTEMPTS	
Goals	2
Shots on target	8
Shooting accuracy	35%
Goals/shots ratio	9%
PASSING	
Goal assists	3
Passes in opp half	529
Passing accuracy in opp half	69%
Crosses	56
Crossing accuracy	21%
DRIBBLING	
Dribbles & runs	61
Dribble completion	80%
Corners forced	14
DISCIPLINE	
Fouls	19
Yellow cards	3
Red cards	0
SEE PAGE 194 FOR FULL STATS	

Gareth BARRY • 15
ASTON VILLA • BORN: 23.2.81

APPEARANCES	
Start (sub)	29(1)
Minutes on pitch	2498
GOAL ATTEMPTS	
Goals	0
DEFENDING	
Blocks	16
Shots cleared off line	0
Headed clearances	110
Other clearances	84
Interceptions	7
Last man saving tackles	2
Tackles won	52
Tackles won %	74%
PASSING	
Passing accuracy own half	76%
Passing accuracy opp hal	63%
DISCIPLINE	
Fouls	45
Fouls in danger area	16
Yellow cards	3
Red cards	0
SEE PAGE 54 FOR FULL STATS	

Gareth Barry was a regular in Villa's defence, playing most often on the left-hand side of a back three. Despite such a season of under-achievement, Villa were again solid at the back, with Barry providing pace, guile and a strong tackle. These qualities enabled him to form an excellent unit with fellow-centre-backs Gareth Southgate and Alpay.

Barry won 74% of the tackles he attempted and launched 194 clearances to avert danger to the Villa goal, helping his defence concede the joint-sixth lowest tally of goals in the Premiership.

John Gregory slapped a £20 million price tag on the youngster, but Barry appears to be one player who is happy at Villa, reflected by the fact he has signed a new long-term contract with the club.

Despite impressive performances at left-back at international level, he has not played at all under new England manager Sven-Göran Eriksson, with the Swede instead deciding the youngster needs more experience at under-21 level.

G — Fabien BARTHEZ • 1
MANCHESTER UNITED • BORN: 28.6.71

The eccentric Fabien Barthez has finally laid to rest the ghost of Peter Schmeichel, establishing himself between the Old Trafford sticks and succeeding where Massimo Taibi and Mark Bosnich had failed.

Despite being hampered throughout the 2000–01 season by back problems, Barthez showed just why Alex Ferguson paid £7.8 million for his services. The smoking Frenchman's resistance to shots fired at him was awesome. He saved 82% of the efforts he faced – eight percentage points better than his Danish predecessor managed in the treble-winning season!

Although the World Cup and Euro 2000 winner is under six feet tall, the shaven-headed shot-stopper makes up for that with great athleticism and commands his area as well as any 'keeper in the game.

Having dropped six crosses, it is clear that he is still prone to the occasional lapse, but it seems that Manchester United have found the 'keeper with presence as well as ability whom they were looking for.

APPEARANCES	
Start (sub)	30(0)
Minutes on pitch	2676
SHOT STOPPING	
Goals conceded (inside box)	14
Goals conceded (outside box)	3
Minutes per goal conceded	157
Clean sheets	14
Saves (shots inside box)	33
Saves (shots outside box)	46
Saves/shots	82%
DISTRIBUTION	
Long kick %	58%
Throws/short passes %	95%
CATCHING	
Crosses caught	63
Crosses punched	15
Crosses dropped	6
Catch success %	91%
DISCIPLINE	
Yellow cards	1
Red cards	0
SEE PAGE 222 FOR FULL STATS	

S — Shaun BARTLETT • 37
CHARLTON ATHLETIC • BORN: 31.10.72

APPEARANCES	
Start (sub)	16(2)
Minutes on pitch	1433
GOAL ATTEMPTS	
Goals inside box	7
Goals outside box	0
Minutes per goal scored	205
Goals/shots ratio	26%
SHOOTING	
Shots on target inside box	17
Shots on target outside box	1
Shooting accuracy	67%
PASSING	
Goal assists	1
Key passes	19
Passing accuracy in opp half	65%
DISCIPLINE	
Fouls committed	31
Fouls won	11
Offside	5
Yellow cards	0
Red cards	0
SEE PAGE 82 FOR FULL STATS	

Charlton nabbed striker Shaun Bartlett on loan from FC Zurich from under the noses of Division One rivals Crystal Palace, and he impressed the club enough for them to splash out £2 million for his services full-time.

Bartlett hit seven goals in 18 Premiership appearances, including a brace on his home debut in the 3–3 draw against Manchester United. He looked impressive throughout and, with a goals-to-shots ratio of 26%, he was a threat to even the meanest defences.

The South Africa captain was also effective down the wings, finding a team-mate with 33% of his crosses – the best proportion at the club.

Although he is likely to miss key Premiership fixtures during the Bafana Bafana's World Cup qualification campaign, in today's market £2 million hardly represents an enormous gamble for a top-flight club.

To cap 2000–01 off, he won the BBC *Match Of The Day* Goal of the Season award for his stunning volley against Leicester – a worthy reward for a promising first campaign.

were scored at The Valley

Warren BARTON • 2
NEWCASTLE UNITED • BORN: 19.3.69

When Warren Barton joined Newcastle United in 1995, it was for a British defensive transfer record £4 million.

However, after Kevin Keegan's departure he struggled to find his best form under successors Kenny Dalglish and Ruud Gullit. But with Bobby Robson now in control, his true form appears to be returning.

Barton was one of only three players at Newcastle to make more than 1,000 passes – and he completed 70% of those, as well as pushing forward to support the Magpies' attacks and whip in 57 crosses.

During his defensive duties, the Londoner won 76% of his tackles and that solidity has allowed Nolberto Solano in front of him to concentrate on his attacking game.

Now in his early thirties, the rumour mill linked him with a player-coach position at Crystal Palace in the summer, but with Newcastle going through a period of rebuilding, it will be older heads like Barton who will play a key part in the Magpies' development.

APPEARANCES	
Start (sub)	27(2)
Minutes on pitch	2296
GOAL ATTEMPTS	
Goals	0
PASSING & CROSSING	
Goal assists	0
Passing	1457
Passing accuracy	70%
Crosses	57
Crossing accuracy	28%
DEFENDING	
Tackles	67
Tackles won %	76%
Blocks	32
Interceptions	11
Clearances	139
Shots cleared off line	1
DISCIPLINE	
Fouls	36
Yellow cards	6
Red cards	1

SEE PAGE 250 FOR FULL STATS

 ## Christian BASSILA • 24
WEST HAM UNITED • BORN: 5.10.77

Christian Bassila joined West Ham in August 2000 on a season-long loan deal from French side Rennes.

The defensive midfielder made only three substitute appearances during the 2000–01 Premiership with a total playing time of just 79 minutes, but won four of his five tackles and completed 73% of his passes.

The young schemer injured his knee after making his debut in the battling 2–2 draw with Manchester United in August. He endeared himself to the Upton Park faithful by clattering Roy Keane and David Beckham within minutes of coming on, but the Hammers' fans did not see him in action again until the new year.

Bassila is a former French Under-21 midfielder and plays in a similar style to his fellow-countryman Patrick Vieira – something West Ham could really do with in their talented but occasionally fragile midfield, if he remains at Upton Park.

SEE PAGE 306 FOR FULL STATS

Solid: Warren Barton

For more information visit our website:

Christian BASSEDAS • 10
NEWCASTLE UNITED • BORN: 16.2.73

Christian Bassedas signed for Newcastle in the summer of 2000 for a fee of £3.5 million, ending a six-month hunt by Bobby Robson for his services. An Italian grandparent negated the need for a work permit and the South American was able to put on the coveted number 10 of Newcastle United.

It did not start too well for the Argentinean, who broke his foot just weeks after signing, but he recovered and made an impact during the second half of the season. He hit the target with five of his eight shots – scoring once – as well as also getting stuck into 62 tackles to illustrate his defensive capabilities.

With 71% of his 118 long passes reaching their target, it is clear he also has a good range. At his former club, Velez Sarsfield, he made more than 300 appearances and won four league championships and that kind of experience will make Bassedas a valuable asset to Robson as the rebuilding in 2001–02 continues.

SEE PAGE 250 FOR FULL STATS

Sprightly: David Batty

David BATTY • 23
LEEDS UNITED • BORN: 2.12.68

APPEARANCES	
Start (sub)	13(3)
Minutes on pitch	1168
GOAL ATTEMPTS	
Goals	0
Shots on target	1
Shooting accuracy	50%
PASSING & CROSSING	
Goal assists	0
Passes in opp half	461
Passing accuracy in opp half	75%
Successful crosses	1
Cross completion	17%
DEFENDING	
Interceptions	12
Clearances	13
Tackles	63
Tackles won %	70%
DISCIPLINE	
Fouls	26
Yellow cards	2
Red cards	1

SEE PAGE 166 FOR FULL STATS

David Batty started the season in the treatment room and ended it in the sin-bin after a controversial dismissal against West Ham. But for the former England midfielder, the middle part of 2000–01 was excellent as he helped his side to a fourth consecutive top-five placing and the semi-finals of the Champions League.

The fact that David O'Leary's young team won nine games and drew the others in the 13 Premiership matches Batty started is a testament to just how important his experience was.

And considering he had almost a year out of the game due to a calf injury and a heart problem, Batty looked surprisingly sprightly on his return to action. He formed an effective partnership with Olivier Dacourt in the heart of Leeds' midfield, snapping into 63 trademark tackles and completing 79% of his passes.

However, his campaign ended in controversy when he was sent off for elbowing West Ham's Joe Cole at Upton Park.

Peter BEAGRIE • 11
BRADFORD CITY • BORN: 28.11.65

Somersaulting wing-king Peter Beagrie finally waved goodbye to the top flight in 2001 when he signed for second division promotion hopefuls Wigan Athletic.

A major figure in Bradford's successful battle against the drop in 1999–2000, Beagrie had signed a new deal with the Bantams which should have kept him at Valley Parade until the end of the 2000–01 season.

But the former Everton and Manchester City star quickly found himself surplus to new manager Jim Jefferies' plans and played his last game for Bradford in early February.

A skilful wideman, Beagrie's delivery from the flanks continued to be of high quality. Although he only set up one goal for his struggling team-mates, Beagrie still managed to find a claret-and-amber shirt with 32% of his attempted crosses – a figure some way above the Premiership average.

Now in his mid-30s, Beagrie has almost certainly done his last back-flip in Premiership football. But he obviously still has plenty to offer in the lower leagues.

APPEARANCES	
Start (sub)	9(10)
Minutes on pitch	913
GOAL ATTEMPTS	
Goals	1
Shots on target	3
Shooting accuracy	33%
Goals/shots ratio	11%
PASSING	
Goal assists	1
Passes in opp half	234
Passing accuracy in opp half	57%
Crosses	93
Crossing accuracy	32%
DRIBBLING	
Dribbles & runs	43
Dribble completion	60%
Corners forced	8
DISCIPLINE	
Fouls	17
Yellow cards	2
Red cards	0

SEE PAGE 68 FOR FULL STATS

James BEATTIE • 16
SOUTHAMPTON • BORN: 27.2.78

APPEARANCES	
Start (sub)	29(8)
Minutes on pitch	2616
GOAL ATTEMPTS	
Goals inside box	9
Goals outside box	2
Minutes per goal scored	238
Goals/shots ratio	14%
SHOOTING	
Shots on target inside box	27
Shots on target outside box	6
Shooting accuracy	43%
PASSING	
Goal assists	3
Key passes	26
Passing accuracy in opp half	51%
DISCIPLINE	
Fouls committed	75
Fouls won	69
Offside	31
Yellow cards	5
Red cards	0

SEE PAGE 264 FOR FULL STATS

As the Saints' top goalscorer during the 2000–01 Premiership, James Beattie was one of the revelations of the season. Seemingly coming into his own under the tutelage of Glenn Hoddle, Beattie first saw a move to Crystal Palace collapse and then won the December Carling Player of the Month award after scoring 10 goals in 10 games.

He was rewarded for this fine form with an extension to his contract.

But there was more to the former Blackburn striker's game than just his goals. He won a very impressive 79% of the 42 tackles that he went in for as well as setting up three strikes for team-mates.

Only 43% of his 76 shots hit the target, but his physical presence means he will always create chances for himself.

The best years are still to come from Beattie, but the real test for him will be how he adapts under new management at Southampton after such a promising year with Hoddle. He will be hoping to be knocking on the door of the England squad soon.

David BECKHAM • 7
MANCHESTER UNITED • BORN: 2.5.75

B

Season 2000–01 saw David Beckham fly out of the traps with seven goals in his first 13 Premiership games to counter criticism that he does not score regularly enough.

His five free-kick goals during the campaign were taken from a top drawer so full of high-quality strikes that there can be no room for his underpants — which perhaps explains why he wears his wife's at times.

But what he continued to do better than anyone was provide ammunition for strikers. He sent over 107 successful crosses — a tally only Nolberto Solano bettered — and the tabloids' favourite star also set up more goals than any other player for the third season running.

A dip in form caused headlines, but the season was mainly positive, with Beckham being appointed England captain and netting his first international goal from open play.

He may now look like the last of the Mohicans but he will always be one of the first on the team-sheet for both Manchester United and England.

APPEARANCES	
Start (sub)	29(2)
Minutes on pitch	2650

GOAL ATTEMPTS	
Goals	9
Shots on target	32
Shooting accuracy	55%
Goals/shots ratio	16%

PASSING	
Goal assists	12
Passes in opp half	1493
Passing accuracy in opp half	73%
Crosses	353
Crossing accuracy	30%

DRIBBLING	
Dribbles & runs	104
Dribble completion	86%
Corners forced	49

DISCIPLINE	
Fouls	31
Yellow cards	3
Red cards	0

SEE PAGE 222 FOR FULL STATS

A cut above: David Beckham

corners than any other player

Craig BELLAMY • 18
COVENTRY CITY • BORN: 13.1.79

Craig Bellamy was signed from Norwich for £6.5 million just before the start of 2000–01 as a big-money replacement for Robbie Keane.

He may have struggled to fill the boots of the Inter-bound Irishman, but Bellamy did offer glimpses of what he can do. Although he was often deployed out on the wing, the Welsh international hit the target with an excellent 62% of his efforts, yet only 13% found the net.

The pacy frontman's passing was crisp and prolific too. Only Paul Telfer recorded more successful passes at Coventry, but Bellamy's 555 accurate passes represented a solid 72% of all that he attempted — 10 percentage points better than the team as a whole managed for the season.

However, his scoring record and dribbling skills clearly left room for improvement, as the Opta stats show. But with Coventry dropping down a division, Bellamy should have more joy against defenders in Division One as he fights to try and ensure a swift return to the Premiership for the Sky Blues.

APPEARANCES	
Start (sub)	33(1)
Minutes on pitch	2772
GOAL ATTEMPTS	
Goals	6
Shots on target	28
Shooting accuracy	62%
Goals/shots ratio	13%
PASSING	
Goal assists	1
Passes in opp half	523
Passing accuracy in opp half	70%
Crosses	66
Crossing accuracy	23%
DRIBBLING	
Dribbles & runs	161
Dribble completion	57%
Corners forced	35
DISCIPLINE	
Fouls	42
Yellow cards	7
Red cards	0

SEE PAGE 110 FOR FULL STATS

Francis BENALI • 15
SOUTHAMPTON • BORN: 30.12.68

It was a frustrating season for curry-house owner and Saints stalwart Francis Benali, as impressive performances from Wayne Bridge in Benali's accustomed left-back position meant the veteran defender spent much of Saints' campaign watching from the sidelines.

Southampton's longest-serving player made just four appearances as a substitute for his home-town side and if it is regular first-team action he is after then he may have to move elsewhere, although it will be a wrench to leave the club he has been with for 14 years.

In January, Nottingham Forest took the defender on loan to add some much-needed experience to their young side. Benali started 15 games for the Reds in his three-month loan spell but, with Forest not willing to make the move permanent, Benali had to return to watching the action from the sidelines, although he and Matt Le Tissier did feature as sentimental substitutes in The Dell's farewell Premiership fixture.

SEE PAGE 264 FOR FULL STATS

Crisp: Craig Bellamy

For more information visit our website:

Trevor BENJAMIN • 20
LEICESTER CITY • BORN: 8.2.79

Trevor Benjamin struggled to win a place in the Leicester first team after his £1.5 million transfer from Cambridge United, but hit the headlines following an alleged clash with wantaway striker Stan Collymore during a reserve match.

Benjamin eventually made his Foxes debut in a 0–0 draw at Sunderland and his first goal came in November 2000 as he contributed to a 3–0 win at Middlesbrough – sadly, it was to be his only Premiership goal of the season.

The Fox made 14 substitute appearances – twice the number of times he was in the starting line-up – and struggled to make a real impact at Filbert Street.

During his time on the pitch Benjamin attempted 16 shots, with half of them hitting the target, but he never really looked as dangerous as other options that Peter Taylor had at his disposal.

The 2001–02 campaign might have more in store for Benjamin, but he will have to work very hard to fulfil his potential and repay the faith shown in him by Taylor.

APPEARANCES	
Start (sub)	7(14)
Minutes on pitch	772
GOAL ATTEMPTS	
Goals inside box	1
Goals outside box	0
Minutes per goal scored	772
Goals/shots ratio	6%
SHOOTING	
Shots on target inside box	5
Shots on target outside box	3
Shooting accuracy	50%
PASSING	
Goal assists	0
Key passes	4
Passing accuracy in opp half	52%
DISCIPLINE	
Fouls committed	23
Fouls won	24
Offside	19
Yellow cards	2
Red cards	0

SEE PAGE 180 FOR FULL STATS

Marlon BERESFORD • 13
MIDDLESBROUGH • BORN: 2.6.69

When Middlesbrough signed Welsh international Mark Crossley on a free transfer in summer 2000, reserve team goalkeeper Marlon Beresford justifiably feared for his future on Teesside.

His suspicion that first-team chances would be at a premium was proved correct, as he was used just once in 2000–01 as a substitute following Crossley's dismissal for a professional foul against Arsenal. The penalty awarded in that incident was the only goal the former Burnley man conceded in the 67 minutes that formed his Premiership campaign.

In January, the 6'1" 'keeper was loaned out to Sheffield Wednesday – the club with whom he had started his career as a trainee. But after conceding 12 goals in four starts for the Owls, Beresford was packed off back to The Riverside and the reserves.

And it seems more than likely that Beresford will have to look elsewhere for his regular football in 2001–02.

SEE PAGE 236 FOR FULL STATS

Henning BERG • 21
MANCHESTER UNITED • BORN: 1.9.69

Norwegian international Henning Berg ended a three-year association with Manchester United when he returned to Blackburn Rovers in September 2000.

Berg, who played just 45 minutes of football for United at the start of the 2000–01 season, initially joined Graeme Souness's promotion-chasing side on loan, but a permanent £1.75 million move was finally agreed in December.

A key member of Rovers' 1995 Championship-winning side, Berg's move to Old Trafford was not a popular one at Ewood Park, but he endeared himself to United's fans with some solid performances.

The emergence of Wes Brown meant that Berg was surplus to United's requirements, though – and a return to Ewood Park seemed to have revived his career.

With Blackburn promoted, Berg will be back on the big stage in 2001–02. His experience will be vital to the club as they bid to make a successful return to the Premiership.

SEE PAGE 222 FOR FULL STATS

Patrik BERGER • 15
LIVERPOOL • BORN: 10.11.73

After a suffering a knee injury in the seven-goal thriller at Elland Road, Patrik Berger feared he might never play football again, but after visiting the same specialist in the USA as Ronaldo and his club-mate Jamie Redknapp he ended the treble-winning season in decent form.

Berger's out-and-out wing play provides Liverpool with much-needed natural width and balance and with his fast-paced running he achieved a dribble completion rate of 76%, only letting his side down with a below-par 24% cross completion rate.

Berger helped his side to victories with no fewer than five assists and two goals; a long-range left-footed drive to see off Derby County and a penalty to seal the 3–1 win over Merseyside rivals Everton.

After nearly leaving the club when Roma were interested in buying the Czech in 1998, Berger will have been delighted to end the season with FA and UEFA cup medals and the memory of setting up the winning FA Cup goal in Cardiff for Michael Owen.

APPEARANCES	
Start (sub)	11(3)
Minutes on pitch	895
GOAL ATTEMPTS	
Goals	2
Shots on target	8
Shooting accuracy	36%
Goals/shots ratio	9%
PASSING	
Goal assists	5
Passes in opp half	219
Passing accuracy in opp half	61%
Crosses	21
Crossing accuracy	24%
DRIBBLING	
Dribbles & runs	17
Dribble completion	76%
Corners forced	5
DISCIPLINE	
Fouls	14
Yellow cards	1
Red cards	0
SEE PAGE 194 FOR FULL STATS	

Dennis BERGKAMP • 10
ARSENAL • BORN: 18.5.69

APPEARANCES	
Start (sub)	19(6)
Minutes on pitch	1698
GOAL ATTEMPTS	
Goals inside box	3
Goals outside box	0
Minutes per goal scored	566
Goals/shots ratio	6%
SHOOTING	
Shots on target inside box	18
Shots on target outside box	8
Shooting accuracy	51%
PASSING	
Goal assists	3
Key passes	34
Passing accuracy in opp half	65%
DISCIPLINE	
Fouls committed	42
Fouls won	27
Offside	15
Yellow cards	2
Red cards	0
SEE PAGE 40 FOR FULL STATS	

Dennis Bergkamp's discontent at not commanding a regular place in the starting line-up at Highbury spilled over into threats to quit the club due to their "lack of respect". The matter was resolved and he signed a new two-year deal.

But the Dutchman's season was hampered by persistent injuries which frustrated both Bergkamp and Arsène Wenger. The number of occasions on which Bergkamp has been able to start games has been falling for the last three seasons, from 28 in 1998–99 to 23 in 1999–2000 and just 19 games in 2000–01 – and questions continue to be raised about his durability.

When playing, Bergkamp hit the target with more than half of his shots, although his shooting accuracy actually fell by 10 percentage points compared with 1999–2000. He only scored three times in the Premiership and set up three others. And with four world-class strikers on the books, fitness and form are crucial if he is to fit into Wenger's plans to bring silverware to Highbury.

9 Dennis Bergkamp played the full

 **Robert BETTS • 35**
COVENTRY CITY • BORN: 21.12.81

Robert Betts played a grand total of one minute during the 2000–01 season and that was in the final game of the campaign once Coventry were already relegated.

But the fact he only had time to make one inaccurate pass should not worry him unduly. Gordon Strachan sees a bright future for Betts and said: "He has got mental strength and he will be fine."

Betts, the grandson of Eire legend Maurice Setters, is a former captain of the Coventry youth team and highly-regarded at Highfield Road. He joined third division Plymouth Argyle on loan in January, where he made four appearances which will have given him valuable first-team experience as he seeks to break through at Highfield Road.

With the Sky Blues playing their football in Division One in 2001–02, there could well be more opportunities for this youngster to make an impact at the Midlands club, and time is certainly on his side.

SEE PAGE 110 FOR FULL STATS

Versatile: Igor Biscan

 Igor BISCAN • 25
LIVERPOOL • BORN: 4.5.78

A Christmas signing from Croatia Zagreb, Igor Biscan is young enough and talented enough to become a regular for seasons to come at Anfield. Gérard Houllier showed great confidence in his new signing by playing Biscan against Ipswich just two days after the Croatian's arrival at Liverpool.

Biscan's versatility was quickly noted by his manager, who played him wide on the right and occasionally even at right-back. But this versatility limited his appearances; he managed only two full 90-minute league games.

He played in the Worthington Cup final but his form dipped, as did his confidence. He missed the FA Cup and UEFA Cup finals and did not feature in the last four games of the 2000–01 Premiership season.

Season 2001–02 will see Biscan trying to earn a regular berth in the Liverpool midfield, although he will be vying with returning skipper Jamie Redknapp among others. He will have to show the form that saw him captain his former club at 21.

APPEARANCES	
Start (sub)	8(5)
Minutes on pitch	648
GOAL ATTEMPTS	
Goals	0
Shots on target	4
Shooting accuracy	40%
PASSING & CROSSING	
Goal assists	0
Passes in opp half	174
Passing accuracy in opp half	63%
Successful crosses	0
Cross completion	0%
DEFENDING	
Interceptions	4
Clearances	4
Tackles	21
Tackles won %	67%
DISCIPLINE	
Fouls	18
Yellow cards	1
Red cards	1

SEE PAGE 194 FOR FULL STATS

90 minutes just nine times for Arsenal

Ian BISHOP • 8
MANCHESTER CITY • BORN: 29.5.65

Stylish veteran Ian Bishop played only a minor role in Manchester City's 2000–01 season. The former West Ham man made 10 appearances but only three from the start, as boss Joe Royle preferred the more caustic skills of Alfie Haaland and Gerard Wiekens in central midfield.

During the 529 minutes of action in which he did feature, Bishop completed an impressive 81% of his passes, but was unable to run from box to box as he had done in the earlier years of his career.

Still, that did not put a selection of Division One clubs off trying to sign the veteran and he looked set to join newly-promoted Gillingham before the deal collapsed in its final stages.

In March, he finally left Maine Road to play in America for Miami Fusion, whose league season was just beginning. The early months of Bishop's career Stateside were certainly a success, as the Fusion romped to the top of the MLS's Eastern division. Check out his performances for the Fusion on www.miamifusion.com.

APPEARANCES	
Start (sub)	3(7)
Minutes on pitch	529
GOAL ATTEMPTS	
Goals	0
Shots on target	1
Shooting accuracy	20%
PASSING & CROSSING	
Goal assists	0
Passes in opp half	257
Passing accuracy in opp half	75%
Successful crosses	10
Cross completion	29%
DEFENDING	
Interceptions	3
Clearances	6
Tackles	15
Tackles won %	33%
DISCIPLINE	
Fouls	3
Yellow cards	0
Red cards	0
SEE PAGE 208 FOR FULL STATS	

Robbie BLAKE • 8
BRADFORD CITY • BORN: 4.3.76

APPEARANCES	
Start (sub)	14(7)
Minutes on pitch	1268
GOAL ATTEMPTS	
Goals inside box	3
Goals outside box	1
Minutes per goal scored	317
Goals/shots ratio	13%
SHOOTING	
Shots on target inside box	13
Shots on target outside box	6
Shooting accuracy	59%
PASSING	
Goal assists	0
Key passes	18
Passing accuracy in opp half	66%
DISCIPLINE	
Fouls committed	15
Fouls won	19
Offside	23
Yellow cards	0
Red cards	0
SEE PAGE 68 FOR FULL STATS	

Robbie Blake began the season by playing for the Bantams in the Intertoto Cup, but he found himself out of shape and out of favour and was shipped off to Nottingham Forest on loan at the end of August.

Blake claimed: "Everyone should know that Geoffrey Richmond virtually picks the team. That's why I've found myself out of the reckoning."

Both sides appeared keen to make the move permanent, but a lack of funds at the City Ground saw Blake heading back to Yorkshire at the end of his loan spell.

This time at Bradford, though, the former Darlington man had regained his sharpness and was playing under a new manager, so the chance was there to regain his first-team place. This he managed to do, and he hit four goals in the Bantams' forlorn bid for survival.

Blake's impressive shooting accuracy of 59% and strike rate of 13% showed that he still has a great deal to offer and he could be a key figure in the Bantams' search for promotion back to the top flight.

For more information visit our website:

Con BLATSIS • 27
DERBY COUNTY • BORN: 6.7.77

After letting the likes of Spencer Prior, Vas Borbokis, Tony Dorigo and Jacob Laursen leave Pride Park in 1999–2000, Derby boss Jim Smith swooped for several defensive reinforcements in the summer.

Powerful Australian defender Con Blatsis was one of them when he signed for £150,000 from South Melbourne. But after the first week of 2000–01, when he started the games against Southampton and Newcastle, Blatsis was not used at all in the Premiership.

Instead, he spent September down under playing for the Socceroos in the Olympic games before returning to the East Midlands for reserve-team football.

In January he was signed on loan by Sheffield Wednesday, where he spent more than a month playing eight matches in either the right- or centre-back positions. Blatsis was recalled by the Rams in the midst of an injury crisis in February, but was not afforded any more first-team action.

SEE PAGE 124 FOR FULL STATS

 Imants BLEIDELIS • 26
SOUTHAMPTON • BORN: 16.7.75

After signing for Southampton just before Christmas 1999, Latvian midfielder Imants Bleidelis had to wait more than a year for his Premiership debut.

It finally came in February 2001, when the £600,000 capture came on for Dan Petrescu for the final six minutes of the match against Bradford City at The Dell. His only previous appearances had been in the Worthington Cup ties against Mansfield Town and Coventry City.

Recommended to the club by former Skonto Riga team-mate Marian Pahars, Bleidelis was unlucky to see Dave Jones, the manager who had signed him, leave soon after he had arrived. But he knuckled down in the reserves, producing some impressive performances to earn his brief first-team chance.

A regular in Latvia's campaign to qualify for the 2002 World Cup finals, Bleidelis will be hoping that more opportunities at club level come his way under new management in the 2001–02 season.

SEE PAGE 264 FOR FULL STATS

 George BOATENG • 6
ASTON VILLA • BORN: 5.9.75

George Boateng had to endure a season of mixed fortunes at Villa Park. The former Coventry man was a regular fixture in the Aston Villa starting line-up, but the club were again seen as under-achievers.

Playing the holding role in midfield, Boateng allowed his team-mates more freedom when going forward. His general play was good, 80% of his passes were accurate and he won 72% of his tackles.

Boateng scored only one goal in 2000–01, a late strike in Villa's impressive 2–1 victory at Leeds, and failed to get an assist for the second season running. His disciplinary record was poor; with nine bookings he was Villa's second-worst offender, and crucially he was forced to miss their 3–0 loss to Liverpool.

If Villa want to improve in 2001–02, they need to be more potent in front of goal and need players such as Boateng to help out their ailing attack.

With Gareth Southgate giving up the captaincy, Boateng has stated that he would "love to be captain".

APPEARANCES	
Start (sub)	29(4)
Minutes on pitch	2556
GOAL ATTEMPTS	
Goals	1
Shots on target	6
Shooting accuracy	33%
PASSING & CROSSING	
Goal assists	0
Passes in opp half	787
Passing accuracy in opp half	75%
Successful crosses	5
Cross completion	15%
DEFENDING	
Interceptions	7
Clearances	31
Tackles	123
Tackles won %	72%
DISCIPLINE	
Fouls	74
Yellow cards	9
Red cards	0

SEE PAGE 54 FOR FULL STATS

Paul BOERTIEN • 23
DERBY COUNTY • BORN: 20.1.79

Paul Boertien played a fuller part in the Derby first team in 2000–01 than previously. He broke into the side towards the end of the season playing at wing-back as Jim Smith piloted Derby's successful course to avoid relegation.

The gangly youngster started seven games for the Rams and managed to get on the scoresheet in the match against local rivals Leicester at Pride Park on Easter Monday.

His right-footed strike was the opener in a 2–0 victory and was his first goal for the club, coming from his only attempt all season. He also set up Stefano Eranio for County's second goal of the game in a performance which earned him a place in Opta's coveted team of the week.

He was not the best passer of the ball at Derby, completing only 63% of his attempts, but showed himself to be a capable defender. Boertien is competing with the likes of Seth Johnson and Danny Higginbotham for his place, so has got his work cut out if he is to make his mark at Pride Park.

APPEARANCES	
Start (sub)	7(1)
Minutes on pitch	651
GOAL ATTEMPTS	
Goals	1
PASSING & CROSSING	
Goal assists	1
Passing	207
Passing accuracy	63%
Crosses	13
Crossing accuracy	23%
DEFENDING	
Tackles	38
Tackles won %	71%
Blocks	11
Interceptions	1
Clearances	28
Shots cleared off line	1
DISCIPLINE	
Fouls	8
Yellow cards	3
Red cards	0

SEE PAGE 124 FOR FULL STATS

Winston BOGARDE • 7
CHELSEA • BORN: 22.10.70

APPEARANCES	
Start (sub)	2(7)
Minutes on pitch	315
GOAL ATTEMPTS	
Goals	0
DEFENDING	
Blocks	1
Shots cleared off line	0
Headed clearances	18
Other clearances	8
Interceptions	0
Last man saving tackles	0
Tackles won	3
Tackles won %	38%
PASSING	
Passing accuracy own half	89%
Passing accuracy opp half	80%
DISCIPLINE	
Fouls	4
Fouls in danger area	2
Yellow cards	0
Red cards	0

SEE PAGE 96 FOR FULL STATS

Winston Bogarde endured an unhappy season. His move from the sunny shores of Spain to the King's Road seemed to be one that was mutually beneficial for both club and player.

But Gianluca Vialli, the manager who signed Bogarde from Barcelona, was sacked soon after the Dutch international joined the Blues and the former Ajax player was left to flounder in the reserves or at best on the substitutes' bench.

Bogarde started just two league games for Chelsea and made a handful of appearances from the bench, but injury did not help his cause. Indeed, he missed the last four months of the season with a knee injury.

Despite these setbacks, Bogarde seems intent on sticking with the Pensioners and is hoping to be fighting fit and ready to fight for his place in 2001–02. With Claudio Ranieri signalling his intention to build a British backbone to the team, Bogarde's future may lie elsewhere, although he claimed: "My aim is to be in peak condition for pre-season training in July."

75% of Alen Boksic's goals for

B

Lars BOHINEN • 14
DERBY COUNTY • BORN: 8.9.69

Fans of Lars Bohinen's website are still waiting for the surreal Scandinavian to update his infamous diary column. But since leaving Derby for Danish outfit Lyngby, loopy Lars has been mysteriously quiet.

Bohinen played just 86 minutes of first-team football for Derby in 2000–01, but he continued to entertain his fans with regular updates on the internet.

Plagued by injuries, Bohinen used his website to rail against "the Gods" whom he claimed must be punishing him for "awful things in a previous life" and philosophised on such weighty matters as the *Sunday Sport* and the state of his teeth, which he revealed had "no cavities".

On departing the Premiership, Bohinen wrote: "I'm not sorry to be leaving England. I'll be back later with a list of what I'll miss and what I'll be glad to see the back of." But unfortunately concerned fans have heard nothing from him since.

SEE PAGE 124 FOR FULL STATS

Alen BOKSIC • 11
MIDDLESBROUGH • BORN: 31.1.70

Success: Alen Boksic

Despite getting his fingers burned with previous big-money foreign imports Branco, Fabrizio Ravanelli and Emerson, Middlesbrough boss Bryan Robson re-entered the overseas market in the summer of 2000 to bring Croatian star Alen Boksic to Teesside.

There were concerns that the former Lazio man only moved for the money – a reported £60,000 a week – and doubts about his fitness. But Boksic was a big success, ending 2000–01 as Boro's top scorer and leading them away from relegation trouble.

Without his 12 goals, the Riverside club would have finished up 10 points worse off and consigned to the Nationwide League, so it was no surprise when the former European Cup-winner clinched the team's Player of the Year award in May.

Still regarded within the game as one of the best strikers in the world, Boksic scored stunning goals against Newcastle and Leicester among others and also created three strikes for team-mates, while attempting a club-best 115 dribbles.

APPEARANCES	
Start (sub)	26(2)
Minutes on pitch	2179
GOAL ATTEMPTS	
Goals inside box	10
Goals outside box	2
Minutes per goal scored	182
Goals/shots ratio	18%
SHOOTING	
Shots on target inside box	22
Shots on target outside box	8
Shooting accuracy	45%
PASSING	
Goal assists	3
Key passes	21
Passing accuracy in opp half	57%
DISCIPLINE	
Fouls committed	30
Fouls won	32
Offside	56
Yellow cards	3
Red cards	0

SEE PAGE 236 FOR FULL STATS

Middlesbrough came away from home

Adam BOLDER • 31
DERBY COUNTY • BORN: 25.10.80

A £90,000 signing from Hull City at the end of the 1999–2000 season, young midfielder Adam Bolder was handed his Premiership debut by Derby County in the penultimate game of 2000–01 as a substitute against Manchester United at Old Trafford.

Coming on in the last minute for Malcolm Christie, Bolder was given the briefest taste of top-flight action before showing promise in a slightly longer chance to impress on the final day, when he replaced Italian Stefano Eranio against Ipswich.

But 2000–01 was mainly about reserve-team football for the Hull-born schemer, who helped the Rams' second string win the FA Premier Reserve League South title for a second consecutive year with some fine displays.

Alongside other youngsters like Richard Jackson, Lee Grant and Lewis Hunt, Bolder played a significant role in the championship campaign, which only bodes well for Derby's long-term future at first-team level.

SEE PAGE 124 FOR FULL STATS

Andy BOOTH • 19
TOTTENHAM HOTSPUR • BORN: 6.12.73

Signed on a short-term loan deal at the back end of George Graham's reign at White Hart Lane, hulking target man Andy Booth was hardly the big name Spurs fans had been clamouring for.

The Sheffield Wednesday star had never been a prolific scorer for the Owls and, although an injury crisis made a move for a striker imperative, the loan deal for Booth was still something of a shock solution.

Denied a debut goal against West Ham by the offside flag, Booth rarely threatened in his brief spell at the club, failing to score and managing just one shot on target.

He returned to Sheffield after just four appearances for Tottenham, but ended the season back at his hometown club Huddersfield on transfer deadline day.

The Terriers were subsequently relegated, leaving Booth to wonder what might have been as he contemplates starting the 2001–02 season in Division Two.

SEE PAGE 292 FOR FULL STATS

Jay BOTHROYD • 28
COVENTRY CITY • BORN: 5.5.82

Jay Bothroyd was earmarked for great things when he starred in Arsenal's FA Youth Cup triumph in 1999–2000. But the temperamental striker wore out the Gunners' patience when he threw his shirt at former England coach Don Howe after being substituted in an Academy match against West Ham.

Bothroyd was immediately placed on the transfer list, but his antics did not deter Coventry, who snapped up the youngster for £1 million. In November 2000 he was handed his Premiership debut against Manchester United and went on to feature in seven more games, mainly as a substitute.

Without scoring, Bothroyd showed glimpses of his skill and was rewarded with an England Under-21 debut against Mexico, which he marked with an amazing overhead kick goal.

A tall yet exceptionally gifted frontman, Bothroyd could prove an ideal foil for John Hartson as Coventry bid to get back into the Premiership at the first time of asking.

SEE PAGE 110 FOR FULL STATS

Steve BOULD • 5
SUNDERLAND • BORN: 16.11.62

Steve Bould brought his distinguished career to an end when he announced his decision to retire from football at the age of 37.

The former Stoke and Arsenal defender found himself limited to just 43 minutes of football for Sunderland at the very start of 2000–01 and finally admitted defeat in his bid to overcome a persistent toe injury in September.

One of the most underrated players of his generation, Bould moved to Sunderland just before the 1999–2000 season and enjoyed a commanding first year at the Stadium of Light.

But it is his time at Arsenal for which Bould will be best remembered. In 11 years with the Gunners he made more than 300 appearances, forming an integral part of one of the meanest defences in English football history – the only surprise being that he failed to win more than the two international caps he earned with England; outings against Greece and Norway at Wembley.

SEE PAGE 278 FOR FULL STATS

Lee BOWYER • 11
AM
LEEDS UNITED • BORN: 3.1.77

Few players commanded more newspaper column inches in 2000–01 than Leeds midfielder Lee Bowyer. Unfortunately, because of his highly-publicised court case, the majority of them were away from the sports pages.

That is not to say that Bowyer did not enjoy an excellent season on the pitch; in fact, few players impressed quite as much as the former Charlton star, who was superb in the Premiership, tremendous in the Champions League and was subsequently voted Leeds' Player of the Season.

Domestically, he netted nine goals and created five others in an ever-present term, while in Europe only Real Madrid's Raul managed to outscore Bowyer's tally of six.

His court case dramatically collapsed just before a verdict was expected, so Bowyer will have to face a retrial scheduled for October. But with an abundance of talent and a much-improved attitude, Bowyer's name should be in the papers for the right reasons for years to come if he is acquitted of the charges facing him.

APPEARANCES	
Start (sub)	38(0)
Minutes on pitch	3345
GOAL ATTEMPTS	
Goals	9
Shots on target	38
Shooting accuracy	49%
Goals/shots ratio	12%
PASSING	
Goal assists	5
Passes in opp half	910
Passing accuracy in opp half	62%
Crosses	259
Crossing accuracy	27%
DRIBBLING	
Dribbles & runs	129
Dribble completion	64%
Corners forced	33
DISCIPLINE	
Fouls	58
Yellow cards	9
Red cards	0

SEE PAGE 166 FOR FULL STATS

 Bjorn Otto BRAGSTAD • 22
CB
DERBY COUNTY • BORN: 5.1.71

APPEARANCES	
Start (sub)	10(2)
Minutes on pitch	981
GOAL ATTEMPTS	
Goals	0
DEFENDING	
Blocks	15
Shots cleared off line	0
Headed clearances	71
Other clearances	34
Interceptions	6
Last man saving tackles	1
Tackles won	29
Tackles won %	78%
PASSING	
Passing accuracy own half	80%
Passing accuracy opp half	46%
DISCIPLINE	
Fouls	12
Fouls in danger area	7
Yellow cards	0
Red cards	0

SEE PAGE 124 FOR FULL STATS

Derby beat several other European clubs to the signature of Bjorn Otto Bragstad after the Norwegian defender had enjoyed an impressive Euro 2000 campaign.

An imposing 6'5'' centre-back, Bragstad immediately won over the Pride Park faithful with his hard-but-fair brand of defending. He quickly notched up more than 100 clearances while managing to navigate the entire season without a booking.

But after that promising start, a hamstring injury ruled out the former Rosenborg man for almost three months and his path back into the first team was blocked by the in-form trio of Chris Riggott, Horacio Carbonari and Taribo West. In the final 14 games of 2000–01, Bragstad featured just twice as a substitute, although he did help the club's young reserve side to a title win.

But the absence of Bragstad from the Rams' line-up came as a big blow to the local hacks, who had grown fond of the witty Scandinavian's one-liners in post-match press conferences.

Titus BRAMBLE • 19
CB — IPSWICH TOWN • BORN: 21.7.81

Despite being one of the country's most promising young defenders, teenager Titus Bramble was still a bit star-struck when he came up against the Premiership's biggest names.

After facing the likes of Tony Adams, Andy Cole, Sol Campbell and Marcel Desailly in 2000-01, Bramble plucked up the courage to ask for their shirts as mementos.

When he added to his collection with the jersey of Kevin Campbell after a game against Everton in February, Bramble was surprised to be asked for his own top in return. But as Campbell said: "I think he's a good player. Ipswich have a good system and he is coming through and excelling."

The stats support Campbell's sentiments, as Bramble won 76% of his tackles and completed 214 clearances, a tally no player at Portman Road could better.

Very comfortable on the ball and deceptively quick, Bramble has established himself in the England Under-21 set-up and is likely to earn a senior cap before too long.

APPEARANCES	
Start (sub)	23(3)
Minutes on pitch	2134

GOAL ATTEMPTS	
Goals	1

DEFENDING	
Blocks	8
Shots cleared off line	0
Headed clearances	139
Other clearances	75
Interceptions	11
Last man saving tackles	0
Tackles won	88
Tackles won %	76%

PASSING	
Passing accuracy own half	74%
Passing accuracy opp half	49%

DISCIPLINE	
Fouls	33
Fouls in danger area	10
Yellow cards	7
Red cards	0

SEE PAGE 152 FOR FULL STATS

Keith BRANAGAN • 21
G — IPSWICH TOWN • BORN: 10.7.66

APPEARANCES	
Start (sub)	2(0)
Minutes on pitch	180

SHOT STOPPING	
Goals conceded (inside box)	1
Goals conceded (outside box)	0
Minutes per goal conceded	180
Clean sheets	1
Saves (shots inside box)	3
Saves (shots outside box)	1
Saves/shots	80%

DISTRIBUTION	
Long kick %	67%
Throws/short passes %	100%

CATCHING	
Crosses caught	2
Crosses punched	2
Crosses dropped	0
Catch success %	100%

DISCIPLINE	
Yellow cards	0
Red cards	0

SEE PAGE 152 FOR FULL STATS

Ipswich's back-up goalkeeper Keith Branagan sat on the sidelines for the majority of 2000-01 as first-choice custodian Richard Wright got a first season of Premiership experience under his belt.

But Branagan — a man with international caps and almost 400 football league appearances to his name — is more than capable in a crisis and filled in for Wright on two occasions, giving the Irishman the chance to play at least a small part in Town's excellent campaign.

His first opportunity came in December 2000, when Wright missed out on the visit of Derby to Portman Road because of a cracked bone in his wrist. Unfortunately, Ipswich failed to score for the first time in season 2000-01. Branagan made two saves against the Rams, but was helpless to stop Rory Delap's winner.

He enjoyed greater fortune in his other outing against Coventry, this time when Wright was suffering from back spasms. The ex-Bolton man made two stops in a 2–0 win.

76% Gary Breen helped Coventry to the

Gary BREEN • 17
COVENTRY CITY • BORN: 12.12.73

To the theme of the Beatles' *Yellow Submarine*, "We all dream of a team of Gary Breens" was one of the most popular chants at Highfield Road during the 2000–01 season.

In reality, a side comprising 11 skinny centre-backs with records of five goals in more than 300 league games would probably struggle for success, but you could see where the Coventry fans were coming from.

Breen, who finally established himself as first-choice defender for the Sky Blues in 2000–01 after three seasons in and out of the team, is one of the Premiership's most committed players. He made a massive 334 clearances, comfortably the best record at the club and a total that only six other top-flight defenders could better.

Like many of his team-mates, though, his distribution was poor.

The campaign also saw Breen skipper the Republic of Ireland for the first time in a friendly against South Africa and he capped a season of personal achievements by winning Coventry's Player of the Year award.

APPEARANCES	
Start (sub)	29(2)
Minutes on pitch	2624
GOAL ATTEMPTS	
Goals	1
DEFENDING	
Blocks	43
Shots cleared off line	0
Headed clearances	225
Other clearances	109
Interceptions	12
Last man saving tackles	1
Tackles won	36
Tackles won %	75%
PASSING	
Passing accuracy own half	74%
Passing accuracy opp half	45%
DISCIPLINE	
Fouls	40
Fouls in danger area	10
Yellow cards	8
Red cards	0

SEE PAGE 110 FOR FULL STATS

Wayne BRIDGE • 18
SOUTHAMPTON • BORN: 5.8.80

APPEARANCES	
Start (sub)	38(0)
Minutes on pitch	3420
GOAL ATTEMPTS	
Goals	0
PASSING & CROSSING	
Goal assists	2
Passing	1439
Passing accuracy	65%
Crosses	125
Crossing accuracy	31%
DEFENDING	
Tackles	94
Tackles won %	73%
Blocks	27
Interceptions	20
Clearances	135
Shots cleared off line	0
DISCIPLINE	
Fouls	25
Yellow cards	1
Red cards	0

SEE PAGE 264 FOR FULL STATS

Of the 495 outfield players to appear in the 2000–01 Premiership season, only one featured in every minute of all 38 games for his team: Southampton's Wayne Bridge.

The consistent England Under-21 international was entrusted with the left-back berth by Glenn Hoddle and caretaker-manager Stuart Gray saw no reason to change the situation during his time in charge.

Hence Bridge's impressive and unrivalled total of 3,420 minutes of action in 2000–01, during which time he delivered 125 crosses into the area and embarked on 159 dribbles.

But the local-born youngster will have been disappointed not to score during the campaign, having displayed his excellent shooting skills by netting a stunning free-kick on the final day of 1999–2000 against Wimbledon.

A lack of goals was perhaps the only black mark on Bridge's card. He wound up 2000–01 by helping his side beat Arsenal in the last-ever league match at The Dell, having received the club's Player of the Year award before kick-off.

best tackle success rate in the Premiership

Michael BRIDGES • 8
LEEDS UNITED • BORN: 5.8.78

Michael Bridges endured a frustrating season on the sidelines for Leeds and now faces an uncertain future at Elland Road.

After netting 19 league goals in 1999–2000 – his first season at the club – Bridges sustained a serious Achilles injury in Leeds' Champions League game against Besiktas in October and was forced to miss the remainder of 2000–01.

With the likes of Robbie Keane, Alan Smith and Mark Viduka now ahead of him in the pecking order for striking places, Bridges faces a tough fight to regain his place in David O'Leary's team.

Before his injury, Bridges had been struggling for goals in 2000–01 – playing his way through 538 minutes of Premiership football without scoring.

Bridges did manage a comeback for Leeds' reserves against his old club at the tail-end of the campaign, but he will know that his road back to Premiership stardom has only just begun; and with interest being shown by Newcastle, it may not occur in Yorkshire.

APPEARANCES	
Start (sub)	6(1)
Minutes on pitch	538
GOAL ATTEMPTS	
Goals inside box	0
Goals outside box	0
Minutes per goal scored	n/a
Goals/shots ratio	0%
SHOOTING	
Shots on target inside box	7
Shots on target outside box	3
Shooting accuracy	63%
PASSING	
Goal assists	3
Key passes	4
Passing accuracy in opp half	65%
DISCIPLINE	
Fouls committed	10
Fouls won	19
Offside	13
Yellow cards	0
Red cards	0
SEE PAGE 166 FOR FULL STATS	

Steve BROWN • 12
CHARLTON ATHLETIC • BORN: 13.5.72

APPEARANCES	
Start (sub)	15(10)
Minutes on pitch	1525
GOAL ATTEMPTS	
Goals	0
DEFENDING	
Blocks	25
Shots cleared off line	0
Headed clearances	124
Other clearances	51
Interceptions	9
Last man saving tackles	0
Tackles won	23
Tackles won %	70%
PASSING	
Passing accuracy own half	81%
Passing accuracy opp half	53%
DISCIPLINE	
Fouls	20
Fouls in danger area	3
Yellow cards	0
Red cards	1
SEE PAGE 82 FOR FULL STATS	

Compared to several other periods of Steve Brown's career, the 2000–01 season was a fairly uneventful one for the Charlton Athletic defender.

In the past, he has fought back from a career-threatening cruciate ligament injury and played as a goalkeeper in several emergencies. He is also the only member of the current Charlton squad to have played a home match for the Addicks while ground-sharing at Selhurst Park.

There was no such drama in 2000–01, with Brown being a fairly regular squad member, making 33 tackles and 469 passes as the team finished comfortably in mid-table on their top-flight return.

In August 2000, Brown was rewarded for his loyalty to the south London club with a testimonial match against Vicenza. He was also handed a new two-year contract to end talk of a move to Crystal Palace. As Brown said: "I am part of the furniture around here. I have seen the bad times and now I want to carry on enjoying the good ones."

For more information visit our website:

CB **Wayne BROWN • 17**
IPSWICH TOWN • BORN: 20.8.77

Young centre-back Wayne Brown featured prominently in Ipswich's promotion season, but injury curtailed his appearances during 2000–01.

Brown came on as a substitute on the opening day of the season, but after that he featured similarly on just three further occasions.

A product of Ipswich's very successful youth system, Brown is a strong, powerful defender and, with age on his side, is set to continue as a regular member of the first-team squad.

Brown went out on loan to QPR in March, but this was seen as George Burley giving the youngster experience of first-team football to recover from his injury problems, as opposed to wanting to release him from Ipswich.

Having surpassed all expectations in 2000–01, it remains to be seen whether or not Brown plays more frequently for Ipswich, but he clearly has a talent that will not go unnoticed.

SEE PAGE 152 FOR FULL STATS

 CB **Wes BROWN • 24**
MANCHESTER UNITED • BORN: 13.10.79

Wes Brown grew up in the Longsight district of Manchester, but nobody needs glasses to see how accomplished the young defender is. After a 1999–2000 campaign which was decimated by injury, he returned in 2000–01 and made the considerable progress which was expected of him.

The start of the season saw him partnering Gary Neville in the centre of defence, but when Jaap Stam recovered from injury Brown and the Dutchman formed what seems likely to be Alex Ferguson's first-choice defensive partnership. His tackling and passing were excellent, though he will be looking to add an attacking element to his game in 2001–02.

England manager Sven-Göran Eriksson was impressed by Brown and, when fit, the player has been involved with the England squad. His season was crowned when he came on to replace the injured Sol Campbell during England's World Cup qualifier in Albania. He immediately looked at ease and is likely to earn a number of international caps in the coming years.

Progress: Wes Brown

APPEARANCES	
Start (sub)	25(3)
Minutes on pitch	2263
GOAL ATTEMPTS	
Goals	0
DEFENDING	
Blocks	20
Shots cleared off line	2
Headed clearances	158
Other clearances	58
Interceptions	9
Last man saving tackles	1
Tackles won	60
Tackles won %	76%
PASSING	
Passing accuracy own half	87%
Passing accuracy opp half	71%
DISCIPLINE	
Fouls	40
Fouls in danger area	17
Yellow cards	5
Red cards	0

SEE PAGE 222 FOR FULL STATS

Mark BURCHILL • 35
IPSWICH TOWN • BORN: 18.8.80

Once dubbed "the Scottish Michael Owen", Mark Burchill's career at Celtic seemed to falter in 2000–01. New manager Martin O'Neill preferred the partnership of Chris Sutton and Henrik Larsson and so Burchill was forced to look elsewhere for first-team football.

Birmingham were the first club to sign him on loan and his spell at St Andrew's in the autumn was successful. But the financial details of a permanent move became too prohibitive and so the Scot returned to Parkhead.

George Burley moved to bring him to Ipswich in February, when a combination of injury and suspension meant that he needed more firepower up front.

Burchill made his Premiership debut against Everton and produced a lively performance, creating a goal in a 2–0 win.

He scored a week later and looked to be a fine addition to Town's roster, but rarely hit the heights again, failing to add to his tally. He returned to Celtic once again – his future still uncertain.

APPEARANCES	
Start (sub)	2(5)
Minutes on pitch	215
GOAL ATTEMPTS	
Goals inside box	1
Goals outside box	0
Minutes per goal scored	215
Goals/shots ratio	20%
SHOOTING	
Shots on target inside box	3
Shots on target outside box	0
Shooting accuracy	60%
PASSING	
Goal assists	1
Key passes	2
Passing accuracy in opp half	56%
DISCIPLINE	
Fouls committed	4
Fouls won	3
Offside	1
Yellow cards	0
Red cards	0

SEE PAGE 152 FOR FULL STATS

Craig BURLEY • 6
DERBY COUNTY • BORN: 24.9.71

APPEARANCES	
Start (sub)	24(0)
Minutes on pitch	2073
GOAL ATTEMPTS	
Goals	2
Shots on target	9
Shooting accuracy	30%
PASSING & CROSSING	
Goal assists	2
Passes in opp half	606
Passing accuracy in opp half	59%
Successful crosses	33
Cross completion	26%
DEFENDING	
Interceptions	5
Clearances	41
Tackles	90
Tackles won %	66%
DISCIPLINE	
Fouls	24
Yellow cards	5
Red cards	0

SEE PAGE 124 FOR FULL STATS

Having inspired Derby County to safety in 1999–2000, Craig Burley again played solidly, anchoring the Rams' midfield and helping some of the younger players settle in.

The former Chelsea and Celtic man scored two league goals, one of which was the winner in the important 1–0 victory against Sunderland in February. That game was memorable for the sight of Derby players – one of them being Burley – continually berating a linesman over some questionable offside decisions. The Scot collected one of six yellow cards for his protests.

He made 90 tackles in 2000–01, with a success rate of 66%, but Burley must have been slightly disappointed with his passing. A completion rate of 67% is not a fair reflection of his abilities.

He can look back on two assists, though, and hope that Derby shake off their malaise of the last few years and enjoy a successful 2001–02. Rams fans will be keen that interest from Uncle George at Ipswich does not come to fruition.

II fouls committed by Deon Burton in Derby's game

Jacob BURNS • 25
LEEDS UNITED • BORN: 1.1.78

Jacob Burns took the not-so-well-trodden road from Parramatta Power to Leeds United in August 2000, joining the Australian contingent at Elland Road. He was bought as a squad player and, even with Leeds' horrendous injury problems, he ended up playing just 297 minutes of Premiership football.

The midfielder showed himself to be a tenacious tackler and he did not seem to be fazed by his rapid elevation to first-team football. His second league game for Leeds was at the home of bitter rivals Manchester United and he seemed to relish the chance to pit himself against the champions. He did give away the foul that allowed David Beckham to score, but otherwise showed his manager that he could be relied on.

His finest moments came in non-Premiership games, though. He played for Australia in their 2–0 win against Scotland in November 2000, while his final two appearances for Leeds in 2000–01 were in the Champions League against Real Madrid and Lazio.

APPEARANCES	
Start (sub)	3(1)
Minutes on pitch	297
GOAL ATTEMPTS	
Goals	0
Shots on target	0
Shooting accuracy	0%
PASSING & CROSSING	
Goal assists	0
Passes in opp half	62
Passing accuracy in opp half	48%
Successful crosses	0
Cross completion	0%
DEFENDING	
Interceptions	2
Clearances	2
Tackles	12
Tackles won %	67%
DISCIPLINE	
Fouls	8
Yellow cards	0
Red cards	0

SEE PAGE 166 FOR FULL STATS

Deon BURTON • 9
DERBY COUNTY • BORN: 25.10.76

APPEARANCES	
Start (sub)	25(7)
Minutes on pitch	2386
GOAL ATTEMPTS	
Goals inside box	5
Goals outside box	0
Minutes per goal scored	477
Goals/shots ratio	11%
SHOOTING	
Shots on target inside box	16
Shots on target outside box	7
Shooting accuracy	50%
PASSING	
Goal assists	2
Key passes	19
Passing accuracy in opp half	63%
DISCIPLINE	
Fouls committed	88
Fouls won	46
Offside	35
Yellow cards	4
Red cards	1

SEE PAGE 124 FOR FULL STATS

Jamaican international Deon Burton started the 2000–01 season strongly, netting in County's 2–2 draw with Southampton, but he managed to score just four more goals in the Premiership as the goalscoring problems at Pride Park affected him acutely.

He played a lot of football – almost 40 hours, in fact – but rarely found his way to goal. At least he can say that his strikes were important ones, as he secured a point for Derby at Anfield against Liverpool and wins over Newcastle United, Everton and Aston Villa.

Sadly for Burton, his season ended on a low note as he was sent off after an ugly confrontation with Leicester's feisty midfielder Robbie Savage.

There is no love lost between the two East Midlands clubs and both Burton and his manager Jim Smith felt that the City schemer made the most of the clash.

The striker was repentant, though, commenting: "I just lost my head and I really regret what I did."

against Everton, the most by a player in a single match

CB Paul BUTLER • 6
SUNDERLAND • BORN: 2.11.72

Paul Butler started 2000—01 in the Sunderland first team, but soon found himself sidelined when the Black Cats imported Stanislav Varga and Emerson Thome.

He played just 270 minutes of football in the Premiership before Wolves decided that he would boost the Molineux defence and completed a loan deal.

Butler became a crowd favourite at Wolves very quickly and was eager to make the move permanent, but just as he was about to sign, Colin Lee was sacked as manager and the deal was put on ice. Luckily for Butler, new boss Dave Jones was equally keen to bring the defender to the West Midlands and paid £1 million for his services.

Sunderland were more than happy with this arrangement, as it meant that they recouped the fee they paid to Bury in 1998. Butler will be hoping that he will get his chance to play in the top flight again as Wolves make another bid for promotion.

SEE PAGE 278 FOR FULL STATS

M Thomas BUTLER • 26
SUNDERLAND • BORN: 25.4.81

Young midfielder Thomas Butler was pursued by a number of top-flight clubs before he chose to join Sunderland. The former Republic of Ireland under-15 Player of the Season is highly-rated and 2000—01 saw him add another 46 minutes of top-flight action to his record.

He spent a spell at Darlington on loan in the autumn and was well-received at the Division Three club. He did not manage to score any goals, but his link play was exceptional and helped the Quakers out of a slump in league form.

He will probably look back on his nine-minute appearance for Sunderland at Middlesbrough with most fondness. This fixture is always a memorable experience and though this match ended goalless, at least he was involved in the hurly-burly of a local derby. He will need to progress in 2001—02, though, or risk his long-term future at the Stadium of Light.

SEE PAGE 278 FOR FULL STATS

M Nicky BUTT • 8
MANCHESTER UNITED • BORN: 21.1.75

Nicky Butt occupies a strange position at Manchester United; never a first-choice midfielder, but always a reliable option for Sir Alex Ferguson should Paul Scholes, Roy Keane or David Beckham be unavailable.

Despite playing less often than any of United's other regular midfielders in 2000—01, the campaign was arguably Butt's finest to date. He showed his usual tenacity in midfield, making 107 tackles — more than any other player at the club — and also got forward regularly, bagging three Premiership goals, as well as a stunning strike against Sturm Graz in the Champions League.

Butt's consistent performances in 2000—01 caught the eye of Sven-Göran Eriksson and he has consequently re-established himself in the England set-up after being a peripheral figure for the national team over the last few years. However, he seems destined to occupy a similar position to the one he fills at United, being second choice for the holding role in England's midfield behind Liverpool's new star Steven Gerrard.

APPEARANCES	
Start (sub)	24(4)
Minutes on pitch	2038
GOAL ATTEMPTS	
Goals	3
Shots on target	11
Shooting accuracy	31%
PASSING & CROSSING	
Goal assists	2
Passes in opp half	809
Passing accuracy in opp half	76%
Successful crosses	6
Cross completion	35%
DEFENDING	
Interceptions	6
Clearances	26
Tackles	107
Tackles won %	75%
DISCIPLINE	
Fouls	58
Yellow cards	8
Red cards	0

SEE PAGE 222 FOR FULL STATS

For more information visit our website:

 Stephen BYWATER • 32
WEST HAM UNITED • BORN: 7.6.81

Promising young 'keeper Stephen Bywater again found himself unable to claim a regular place at West Ham during 2000–01.

Bywater featured in just one game – a win at relegation-bound Bradford – and although he impressed with his quick reflexes, the England Under-21 international was quickly relegated to the reserves once Shaka Hislop and Craig Forrest regained full fitness.

During the match at Valley Parade, Bywater made six stops and conceded one goal, thereby saving 86% of the shots which he faced, and dealt with five of the six crosses he came for.

Bywater was even called up to train with the England squad and has consistently earned rave reviews for his displays for West Ham's second string. However, Bywater is unlikely to be the Hammers' first-choice 'keeper in 2001–02 and may well be sent on loan to the Nationwide League to gain some valuable experience.

SEE PAGE 306 FOR FULL STATS

 Tony CAIG • 35
CHARLTON ATHLETIC • BORN: 11.4.74

Tony Caig began the season at "Vegas of the North" side Blackpool but, after just nine appearances for Steve McMahon's Tangerines, he found himself heading for the Premiership as goalkeeping cover at Charlton.

He initially arrived on loan in November as back-up for Dean Kiely and Sasa Ilic, but the move was made permanent in January. Caig was thrust into the spotlight at the end of that month when he made his only Premiership appearance to date by replacing the injured Kiely in a 2–1 win over Derby County at The Valley.

Caig came on for the second half and enjoyed a relatively easy debut, being forced into only one save. Nerves got the better of him as he dropped one cross, but he remained unbeaten by Derby's shot-shy attack.

The return of Ilic, however, meant he was unable to retain his place in the side and Caig was released by the Addicks at the end of the season.

SEE PAGE 82 FOR FULL STATS

 Danny CADAMARTERI • 21
EVERTON • BORN: 12.10.79

It was a frustrating season for Everton youth team product Danny Cadamarteri, who struggled to hold down a first-team place despite his versatility. Cadamarteri can play up front or wide on the right, but only managed to make seven starts for the Toffees in 2000–01 due to injuries and stiff competition for places when other strikers were available.

The Bradford-born player hit the back of the net on four occasions – most notably in the victories against Arsenal and Chelsea – these goals coming from just seven shots on target. Cadamarteri linked well when playing up front alongside Kevin Campbell and also managed to claim two assists.

But he was mainly used from the bench and, despite these reasonable stats, Walter Smith clearly had Cadamarteri some way down the pecking-order behind the likes of Campbell, Duncan Ferguson and Francis Jeffers. It remains to be seen whether he can force his way back into the first-team picture in 2001–02.

Cadamarteri's only other claim to fame in 2000–01 was that he appeared in a matchday programme advert from Carling, informing people that Everton fans eat more pies than any other group of supporters.

APPEARANCES	
Start (sub)	7(9)
Minutes on pitch	722
GOAL ATTEMPTS	
Goals inside box	4
Goals outside box	0
Minutes per goal scored	181
Goals/shots ratio	25%
SHOOTING	
Shots on target inside box	6
Shots on target outside box	1
Shooting accuracy	44%
PASSING	
Goal assists	2
Key passes	3
Passing accuracy in opp half	64%
DISCIPLINE	
Fouls committed	24
Fouls won	16
Offside	14
Yellow cards	2
Red cards	0

SEE PAGE 138 FOR FULL STATS

CB — **Steve CALDWELL • 30**
NEWCASTLE UNITED • BORN: 12.9.80

It was quite a season for former Newcastle United trainee Steve Caldwell. The youngster not only made his Premiership debut, but also found himself taking his international bow for Scotland against Poland in a friendly in April.

The Stirling-born defender made his debut as a substitute at Manchester City in September and scored in his first start for the club – November's Worthington Cup win over Bradford City.

Although by no means a regular in the first team, he clearly did enough to catch the eye of Bobby Robson – not bad for a player who was transfer-listed back in February 2000. In his nine Premiership appearances, he made 55 clearances and demonstrated good ability on the ball, making 300 passes with an accuracy of 75%.

Having had a taste of Premiership and international action he will no doubt be looking for more first-team outings and Magpies fans may see more of Steve Caldwell in 2001–02.

APPEARANCES	
Start (sub)	5(4)
Minutes on pitch	668
GOAL ATTEMPTS	
Goals	0
DEFENDING	
Blocks	8
Shots cleared off line	0
Headed clearances	36
Other clearances	19
Interceptions	0
Last man saving tackles	0
Tackles won	13
Tackles won %	68%
PASSING	
Passing accuracy own half	83%
Passing accuracy opp half	62%
DISCIPLINE	
Fouls	9
Fouls in danger area	4
Yellow cards	1
Red cards	0
SEE PAGE 250 FOR FULL STATS	

S — **Titi CAMARA • 29**
WEST HAM UNITED • BORN: 7.11.72

APPEARANCES	
Start (sub)	5(1)
Minutes on pitch	392
GOAL ATTEMPTS	
Goals inside box	0
Goals outside box	0
Minutes per goal scored	n/a
Goals/shots ratio	0%
SHOOTING	
Shots on target inside box	1
Shots on target outside box	3
Shooting accuracy	31%
PASSING	
Goal assists	0
Key passes	5
Passing accuracy in opp half	65%
DISCIPLINE	
Fouls committed	5
Fouls won	3
Offside	3
Yellow cards	1
Red cards	0
SEE PAGE 306 FOR FULL STATS	

Very little was seen of Guinean forward Titi Camara during 2000–01, despite his £2.2 million move from Liverpool to West Ham in December.

Clearly way down the pecking order at Liverpool, Camara had been linked with several clubs before West Ham decided to bring him to the capital. After promising he had come to "score, score, score!" he made his debut in a 2–1 defeat at Leicester just before Christmas and featured in the next three games.

But he failed to set Upton Park alight and only featured in two further games. When he did appear, it tended to be on the left wing rather than up front and he managed just 13 shots at goal, with only four of them hitting the target.

For the price they paid the Hammers must have expected a better return, but with a new manager in place it is unclear whether Camara will feature in east London in 2001–02. The former St Etienne, Marseille and Lens forward may return to France.

7 Middlesbrough failed to win any of the

Andy CAMPBELL • 18
MIDDLESBROUGH • BORN: 18.4.76

C

Former Boro youth protégé Andy Campbell found himself unable to make much of an impact at The Riverside in 2000–01 and ended up contributing to Bolton Wanderers' successful chase for promotion instead.

With Alen Boksic and Noel Whelan arriving on Teeside in the summer, Campbell found himself forced down the pecking order and consequently was able to start only five Premiership games for Boro in the 2000–01 campaign. He failed to manage a single shot on target during 399 minutes of first-team football – 398 of which came before Terry Venables arrived at the club.

After being linked to several clubs he eventually made a loan move to the Reebok Stadium in March.

Campbell made six appearances for Sam Allardyce's team in the run-in to the season, but again failed to score and was unable to help them clinch automatic promotion. The Trotters eventually triumphed in the play-offs, but Campbell was left with an uncertain future.

APPEARANCES	
Start (sub)	5(2)
Minutes on pitch	399
GOAL ATTEMPTS	
Goals inside box	0
Goals outside box	0
Minutes per goal scored	n/a
Goals/shots ratio	0%
SHOOTING	
Shots on target inside box	0
Shots on target outside box	0
Shooting accuracy	0%
PASSING	
Goal assists	1
Key passes	1
Passing accuracy in opp half	62%
DISCIPLINE	
Fouls committed	2
Fouls won	7
Offside	4
Yellow cards	0
Red cards	0
SEE PAGE 236 FOR FULL STATS	

Kevin CAMPBELL • 9
EVERTON • BORN: 4.2.70

APPEARANCES	
Start (sub)	27(2)
Minutes on pitch	2454
GOAL ATTEMPTS	
Goals inside box	9
Goals outside box	0
Minutes per goal scored	273
Goals/shots ratio	20%
SHOOTING	
Shots on target inside box	22
Shots on target outside box	1
Shooting accuracy	50%
PASSING	
Goal assists	1
Key passes	35
Passing accuracy in opp half	68%
DISCIPLINE	
Fouls committed	40
Fouls won	27
Offside	51
Yellow cards	1
Red cards	0
SEE PAGE 138 FOR FULL STATS	

"Super" Kevin Campbell is proving to be one of Walter Smith's best signings as Everton manager, having topped the Toffees' goalscoring charts for the third season running.

The former Arsenal and Nottingham Forest marksman hit nine goals in an otherwise dismal campaign for the Goodison Park side, but these strikes allowed the Toffees to keep their heads just above water and without them they would have been in serious danger of dropping out of the Premiership.

Injured at the start of the season, Campbell came back into the side in September and notched vital winning goals against Newcastle, Chelsea and Leicester. He also scored in both games against Arsenal and demonstrated some accurate shooting, with exactly half of all his shots ending up on target and 20% finding the net.

He was unable to play with a regular strike partner for long because of injuries, but by consistently producing the goals he has made himself one of Everton's most valuable assets.

seven games in which Andy Campbell played

CB Sol CAMPBELL • 5
TOTTENHAM HOTSPUR • BORN: 18.9.74

The furore surrounding Sol Campbell's contract negotiations commanded more back-page headlines in 2000–01 than his performances could ever hope to match.

Spurs failed to persuade the defender to remain at the club despite an offer to make him the highest-paid player in Britain after his dominating displays at the heart of the Lilywhites' defence.

Campbell led the way for Tottenham in terms of blocking shots and also won a healthy total of 53 tackles. And as usual, he proved to be a powerful presence at set-pieces, scoring headed goals in the draw at Bradford and the win against West Ham.

Campbell expressed a surprising affinity for the Hammers when he stated that he would like to have his ashes scattered at Upton Park. This perhaps indicated that leaving Spurs would not be the emotional wrench some claimed it would be. And with Barcelona and a host of domestic clubs vying for his services, a move away from N17 became inevitable.

APPEARANCES	
Start (sub)	21(0)
Minutes on pitch	1890

GOAL ATTEMPTS	
Goals	2

DEFENDING	
Blocks	23
Shots cleared off line	1
Headed clearances	132
Other clearances	82
Interceptions	7
Last man saving tackles	1
Tackles won	53
Tackles won %	73%

PASSING	
Passing accuracy own half	80%
Passing accuracy opp half	57%

DISCIPLINE	
Fouls	36
Fouls in danger area	12
Yellow cards	1
Red cards	0

SEE PAGE 292 FOR FULL STATS

Headlines: Sol Campbell

For more information visit our website:

Horacio CARBONARI • 2
DERBY COUNTY • BORN: 2.5.74

During his time at Rosario Central in Argentina, Horacio Carbonari earned the nickname "Petaco", meaning Bazooka, for his rocket-propelled set-pieces.

But despite taking five direct free-kicks in 2000–01, Carbonari was unable to score a single goal from a dead-ball situation all season.

This did not curb Carbonari's natural attacking instinct, though. He ventured forward to fire in a total of 15 shots over the course of the 2000–01 season, which was more than striking team-mates Branko Strupar or Georgi Kinkladze managed. And the defender was finally rewarded for his efforts when he rammed home the opening goal in the 2–0 win over Newcastle in December.

Carbonari also performed admirably in an ever-changing Rams back line, making club-high totals of 283 clearances and 43 blocks over the course of the campaign to help steer Jim Smith's side to Premiership safety. He can also be proud that, despite their lowly position, only five teams kept more clean sheets than Derby.

APPEARANCES	
Start (sub)	27(0)
Minutes on pitch	2302
GOAL ATTEMPTS	
Goals	1
DEFENDING	
Blocks	43
Shots cleared off line	0
Headed clearances	135
Other clearances	148
Interceptions	16
Last man saving tackles	2
Tackles won	50
Tackles won %	70%
PASSING	
Passing accuracy own half	73%
Passing accuracy opp half	49%
DISCIPLINE	
Fouls	27
Fouls in danger area	12
Yellow cards	6
Red cards	1
SEE PAGE 124 FOR FULL STATS	

 Benito CARBONE • 10
BRADFORD CITY • BORN: 14.8.71

APPEARANCES	
Start (sub)	29(2)
Minutes on pitch	2557
GOAL ATTEMPTS	
Goals inside box	1
Goals outside box	4
Minutes per goal scored	511
Goals/shots ratio	6%
SHOOTING	
Shots on target inside box	6
Shots on target outside box	21
Shooting accuracy	34%
PASSING	
Goal assists	4
Key passes	49
Passing accuracy in opp half	67%
DISCIPLINE	
Fouls committed	37
Fouls won	58
Offside	52
Yellow cards	3
Red cards	0
SEE PAGE 68 FOR FULL STATS	

Benito Carbone was unveiled at Bradford before the start of the 2000–01 campaign as the club looked to build upon the previous season's successful fight against relegation.

Carbone had attracted plenty of interest from across the continent, but he was enticed by then-manager Chris Hutchings' offer and surprised many by moving to Valley Parade.

Over the course of 2000–01, Carbone fired in 80 shots, but only six per cent of the Italian's efforts found their way into the net. The fact that he finished the season as the Bantams' top scorer with five league goals illustrates perfectly why the team finished bottom of the Premiership.

Carbone pledged to stay at Bradford, but this may be beyond his control. He was almost sold for nothing to Middlesbrough before transfer deadline day and he could be off-loaded if the right offer is made, in order to reduce the burden of his reported £2 million-per-season salary from the wage bill.

Wherever he plays in 2001–02 his skills are sure to be appreciated.

FB — Stephen CARR • 2
TOTTENHAM HOTSPUR • BORN: 29.8.76

After landing the Supporters' Player of the Year award in 1999-2000, Stephen Carr further enhanced his popularity at White Hart Lane on the opening day of the 2000–01 campaign by scoring against Ipswich.

The Irish full-back continued to show his attacking instincts throughout the season, embarking on 129 dribbles and runs – more than any other player at the club. He also distributed the ball with confidence and was accurate with 74% of his passes – a better completion rate than any other Spurs defender.

A fixture in the side since breaking into the starting XI in 1996, Carr found life on the sidelines extremely frustrating after undergoing a hernia operation at the turn of the year which kept him out of action for more than three months.

But the athletic full-back bounced back from the first major injury of his career to score a stunning free-kick against Leicester and will undoubtedly be a key player in Glenn Hoddle's plans.

APPEARANCES	
Start (sub)	27(1)
Minutes on pitch	2406
GOAL ATTEMPTS	
Goals	3
PASSING & CROSSING	
Goal assists	2
Passing	1096
Passing accuracy	74%
Crosses	102
Crossing accuracy	26%
DEFENDING	
Tackles	54
Tackles won %	81%
Blocks	12
Interceptions	11
Clearances	79
Shots cleared off line	0
DISCIPLINE	
Fouls	29
Yellow cards	5
Red cards	0

SEE PAGE 292 FOR FULL STATS

FB — Jamie CARRAGHER • 23
LIVERPOOL • BORN: 28.1.78

APPEARANCES	
Start (sub)	30(4)
Minutes on pitch	2691
GOAL ATTEMPTS	
Goals	0
PASSING & CROSSING	
Goal assists	0
Passing	1212
Passing accuracy	72%
Crosses	39
Crossing accuracy	23%
DEFENDING	
Tackles	95
Tackles won %	81%
Blocks	13
Interceptions	16
Clearances	188
Shots cleared off line	1
DISCIPLINE	
Fouls	36
Yellow cards	6
Red cards	0

SEE PAGE 194 FOR FULL STATS

Jamie Carragher has been in Liverpool's first-team squad since the arrival of Gérard Houllier in 1998. But until the 2000-01 campaign, his great versatility had perhaps worked against him and he had been unable to claim a permanent place in any of his favourite positions, namely right-back, central defence or the anchor role in midfield.

With the Reds bolstering their defensive options with the signings of German pair Markus Babbel and Christian Ziege, Carragher's chances of regular action seemed even bleaker at the start of the 2000-01 season. But his tremendous work ethic saw him emerge as the club's surprise choice at left-back, as he helped Liverpool complete their historic cup treble.

Carragher clearly deserved his place in the starting XI. He won 77 tackles in 2000–01 – more than any other Liverpool defender – and earned a deserved recall to the England squad from a highly-impressed Sven-Göran Eriksson, who rewarded Carragher with a cap against Mexico.

Michael CARRICK • 21
WEST HAM UNITED • BORN: 28.7.81

The fanfare surrounding Joe Cole's development at West Ham ensured that Michael Carrick was able to mature out of the limelight. Cole emerged as a first-team regular in 1999–2000, while Carrick spent time on loan at Swindon and Birmingham.

But Carrick started the 2000–01 campaign very much at the forefront of Harry Redknapp's plans. Although renowned for his vision and distribution, Carrick's pass completion rate in the opposition half still showed room for improvement. The young Geordie did show tenacity, though, by making 143 tackles – more than any other Englishman in the Premiership. He also has a fierce shot from distance.

The departure of Redknapp seemed to cast doubt over the futures of many of the Hammers' players. Carrick is known to favour a move to his boyhood idols Newcastle, but if he became available there would surely be many suitors.

It was no great surprise when he was given his first cap against Mexico at the end of May.

APPEARANCES	
Start (sub)	32(1)
Minutes on pitch	2952
GOAL ATTEMPTS	
Goals	1
Shots on target	20
Shooting accuracy	48%
PASSING & CROSSING	
Goal assists	3
Passes in opp half	714
Passing accuracy in opp half	67%
Successful crosses	6
Cross completion	43%
DEFENDING	
Interceptions	18
Clearances	63
Tackles	143
Tackles won %	66%
DISCIPLINE	
Fouls	23
Yellow cards	2
Red cards	0

SEE PAGE 306 FOR FULL STATS

Tenacity: Michael Carrick

more times than any other defender

Lee CARSLEY • 32
COVENTRY CITY • BORN: 28.2.74

Republic of Ireland international Lee Carsley started the 2000–01 campaign in Blackburn's reserve side. But Gordon Strachan brought him to Coventry for £2 million to rescue him from his Ewood Park nightmare.

Carsley's fighting spirit was acquired to add more steel to the Sky Blues midfield. And his infectious enthusiasm, which saw him make a challenge every 26 minutes on average, certainly seemed to pay off at first.

Coventry lost just one of the tenacious tackler's first six games back in the top flight and the club consequently pulled clear of the relegation zone.

The former Derby player even went so far as to say that he had learned more in his first three weeks under Strachan than he had done in three months under Graeme Souness.

But Carsley's new-found fountain of knowledge was not enough to prevent Coventry's mid-season slump that resulted in their slide towards relegation, ironically enough while Blackburn were bouncing back to the top flight in style.

APPEARANCES	
Start (sub)	21(0)
Minutes on pitch	1805
GOAL ATTEMPTS	
Goals	2
Shots on target	9
Shooting accuracy	50%
PASSING & CROSSING	
Goal assists	1
Passes in opp half	441
Passing accuracy in opp half	60%
Successful crosses	9
Cross completion	50%
DEFENDING	
Interceptions	4
Clearances	56
Tackles	69
Tackles won %	74%
DISCIPLINE	
Fouls	26
Yellow cards	6
Red cards	0

SEE PAGE 110 FOR FULL STATS

Patrice CARTERON • 2
SUNDERLAND • BORN: 30.7.70

APPEARANCES	
Start (sub)	8(0)
Minutes on pitch	720
GOAL ATTEMPTS	
Goals	1
PASSING & CROSSING	
Goal assists	1
Passing	229
Passing accuracy	59%
Crosses	17
Crossing accuracy	41%
DEFENDING	
Tackles	26
Tackles won %	65%
Blocks	6
Interceptions	2
Clearances	21
Shots cleared off line	1
DISCIPLINE	
Fouls	11
Yellow cards	0
Red cards	0

SEE PAGE 278 FOR FULL STATS

After signing for ambitious Lyon in 1998, Patrice Carteron established himself as a solid performer. Indeed, he was selected at right-back in Le Championnat team of the season at the end of the 1998–99 campaign, fuelling much interest from across the continent.

So it was some surprise that the attack-minded full-back was offloaded to St Etienne before the start of 2000–01.

A visibly-unhappy Carteron never really settled and he went to Sunderland on loan in March in a bid to relaunch his career in England.

Carteron clearly enjoyed his time with the Black Cats. He got forward to find a colleague with an excellent 41% of his crosses and won a special place in the hearts of the fans at the Stadium of Light when he scored in the 1–1 draw with fierce rivals Newcastle.

It is now up to Peter Reid to make a decision on whether to sign the Frenchman on a permanent basis.

One thing is for sure – he will never have to buy a drink on Wearside again.

For more information visit our website:

Luke CHADWICK • 36
MANCHESTER UNITED • BORN: 18.11.80

Manchester United's youth academy seems to supply a never-ending stream of top-quality talent. The latest graduate to make a name for himself is Luke Chadwick, who broke into the first-team picture in 2000–01.

Chadwick spent much of 1999–2000 at United's feeder club, Royal Antwerp in Belgium. And it was his performances there, particularly when firing a hat-trick against Kortrijk, which persuaded Sir Alex Ferguson that the youngster was worth blooding in the Premiership.

It was November before Chadwick finally made the first team, though, when he came on as a substitute in the 2–1 win over Middlesbrough. He was a regular in the first-team squad from that point, making a total of 16 appearances and scoring twice.

Indeed, Chadwick's finishing was one of his strongest points. He scored with 15% of his shots, recording a better ratio than Ryan Giggs, Paul Scholes or Roy Keane managed in 2000–01 and this seems to indicate a bright future for the young winger.

APPEARANCES	
Start (sub)	6(10)
Minutes on pitch	623
GOAL ATTEMPTS	
Goals	2
Shots on target	4
Shooting accuracy	31%
Goals/shots ratio	15%
PASSING	
Goal assists	0
Passes in opp half	195
Passing accuracy in opp half	68%
Crosses	28
Crossing accuracy	14%
DRIBBLING	
Dribbles & runs	97
Dribble completion	62%
Corners forced	10
DISCIPLINE	
Fouls	2
Yellow cards	0
Red cards	1

SEE PAGE 222 FOR FULL STATS

 Gary CHARLES • 2
WEST HAM UNITED • BORN: 13.4.70

Gary Charles is probably best-remembered as the player Paul Gascoigne was attempting to tackle when he infamously damaged his cruciate ligaments in the 1991 FA Cup final.

However, in recent years Charles has been just as unfortunate with his fitness as the injury-prone Gazza. Ankle problems effectively ended his spell at Aston Villa and fitness woes have dogged subsequent spells at Benfica and West Ham.

Charles did make one fleeting appearance for the Hammers in the 2000–01 season, coming on as a substitute in the defeat to Leicester in August. But he failed to impress, finding a colleague with just 54% of his passes and subsequently found himself offloaded to Birmingham on loan.

Charles's problems mounted in January when his Mercedes was found abandoned with a bottle of whisky on the front seat. Charles later went to Scotland Yard voluntarily to help police with their enquiries.

SEE PAGE 306 FOR FULL STATS

Bright future: Luke Chadwick

FB Laurent CHARVET • 31
MANCHESTER CITY • BORN: 8.5.73

Laurent Charvet arrived at Manchester City in late October, but failed to make a decent impression at the club. His first game was the 5–0 defeat at Highbury and the team were triumphant in only one of his 14 full Premiership appearances.

The £1 million capture from Newcastle did not have the best of fortunes down the right flank, as he could produce only nine successful crosses. And he was not much of an attacking threat, firing in just two shots on target for City.

Consequently the fans on the Kippax began to voice their discontent at Charvet's performances and started to make unfair comparisons between his more energetic team-mate Danny Tiatto employed in a similar position on the opposite side of the pitch.

Following the club's relegation from the Premiership, Charvet demanded a transfer and has been linked with a move back to his native France. Nevertheless, the arrival of Kevin Keegan could possibly revitalise his Maine Road career.

APPEARANCES	
Start (sub)	22(5)
Minutes on pitch	1967
GOAL ATTEMPTS	
Goals	0
PASSING & CROSSING	
Goal assists	1
Passing	938
Passing accuracy	72%
Crosses	68
Crossing accuracy	16%
DEFENDING	
Tackles	37
Tackles won %	86%
Blocks	18
Interceptions	12
Clearances	99
Shots cleared off line	0
DISCIPLINE	
Fouls	13
Yellow cards	1
Red cards	0

SEE PAGES 208 & 250 FOR FULL STATS

M Youssef CHIPPO • 8
COVENTRY CITY • BORN: 10.5.73

APPEARANCES	
Start (sub)	18(14)
Minutes on pitch	1713
GOAL ATTEMPTS	
Goals	0
Shots on target	4
Shooting accuracy	33%
PASSING & CROSSING	
Goal assists	0
Passes in opp half	381
Passing accuracy in opp half	59%
Successful crosses	3
Cross completion	11%
DEFENDING	
Interceptions	12
Clearances	18
Tackles	89
Tackles won %	74%
DISCIPLINE	
Fouls	48
Yellow cards	7
Red cards	0

SEE PAGE 110 FOR FULL STATS

Youssef Chippo failed to match the high standards that he set in 1999–2000, as the edge was often missing from his game. He attempted 89 challenges – 58 down on the tally he managed in his inaugural campaign in the top flight.

It should be taken into account that Chippo's frequent trips back to represent Morocco may have affected his overall sharpness. Indeed, John Eustace was the only Coventry player to win more than Chippo's 66 successful tackles.

Chippo was unable to claim a single assist in 2000–01 and his shooting accuracy was 22 percentage points lower than in his debut season in English football.

The ex-FC Porto schemer also found his distribution powers had waned as his pass completion rate in the opposition half was 10 percentage points down on his 1999–2000 rate. Sky Blues supporters will hope he can improve when they begin their quest for an instant return to the Premiership in the 2001–02 campaign.

Malcolm CHRISTIE • 12
DERBY COUNTY • BORN: 11.4.79

Malcolm Christie's antics during Derby's winter break in Marbella resulted in some scathing criticism from manager Jim Smith. Like so many English tourists who travel to the Costa Del Sol, the young forward returned complaining of "stomach problems". And along with several members of the first team squad, he was unsurprisingly disappointing in the next game, an FA Cup tie against first division Blackburn.

However, this was a small hiccup in what was otherwise an immensely promising campaign for Christie. The former supermarket shelf-stacker finished as the Rams' top scorer with eight goals, having found the back of the net with 18% of his shots – a better proportion than Emile Heskey, Robbie Fowler or Thierry Henry managed.

And after a season of struggling at the foot of the table, Christie had the pleasure of scoring at Old Trafford in May, clinching a 1–0 win over Manchester United which ensured Derby's Premiership status and spoiled the Red Devils' championship party.

APPEARANCES	
Start (sub)	29(5)
Minutes on pitch	2475
GOAL ATTEMPTS	
Goals inside box	7
Goals outside box	1
Minutes per goal scored	309
Goals/shots ratio	18%
SHOOTING	
Shots on target inside box	20
Shots on target outside box	6
Shooting accuracy	58%
PASSING	
Goal assists	1
Key passes	20
Passing accuracy in opp half	64%
DISCIPLINE	
Fouls committed	53
Fouls won	58
Offside	40
Yellow cards	5
Red cards	0
SEE PAGE 124 FOR FULL STATS	

 Jamie CLAPHAM • 3
IPSWICH TOWN • BORN: 7.12.75

APPEARANCES	
Start (sub)	28(7)
Minutes on pitch	2569
GOAL ATTEMPTS	
Goals	2
Shots on target	14
Shooting accuracy	50%
Goals/shots ratio	7%
PASSING	
Goal assists	3
Passes in opp half	717
Passing accuracy in opp half	68%
Crosses	153
Crossing accuracy	29%
DRIBBLING	
Dribbles & runs	99
Dribble completion	71%
Corners forced	14
DISCIPLINE	
Fouls	13
Yellow cards	2
Red cards	0
SEE PAGE 152 FOR FULL STATS	

Like many of his Ipswich team-mates, Jamie Clapham gave a great account of himself in his first full season of Premiership football. The left-sided player was ranked as Town's eighth-best player in the Opta Index.

His tally of crosses from open play was the highest by any Ipswich player and his deliveries were often gratefully received by the likes of James Scowcroft and Marcus Stewart, lurking menacingly in the opposition penalty area.

Clapham may not have received as much attention from the media as several of his team-mates, but his consistency was recognised by those within the club when he was offered a new contract to tie him to Portman Road until 2004.

Another personal high for Clapham would have been when he scored within three minutes of coming on as a substitute in Ipswich's 3–0 win over Spurs. Clapham was never given a chance to prove himself at White Hart Lane after four years as a professional at the club.

Malcolm Christie between December and May

Matt CLARKE • 13
BRADFORD CITY • BORN: 3.11.73

It all went wrong at Bradford for Matt Clarke in 2000–01. Signed on a free transfer from Sheffield Wednesday in July 1999, Clarke had played a starring role in City's successful fight against relegation, seeing off Gary Walsh in the battle to be the Bantams' undisputed number one.

He started the 2000–01 campaign where he had left off the previous season and was playing so well that that there were even calls for his inclusion in the England squad.

Linked with a move to Arsenal, he fell out with new Bantams boss Jim Jefferies after demanding a better contract with the club and was dropped from the team before being eventually farmed out on loan to Bolton.

While Walsh performed well between the sticks, Clarke's superior saves-to-shots ratio suggests he was the better shot-stopper and that Jefferies did himself no favours by dropping the former Owl. But given their obvious defensive deficiencies, it is unlikely that Bradford would have survived whoever was in goal.

APPEARANCES	
Start (sub)	17(0)
Minutes on pitch	1530
SHOT STOPPING	
Goals conceded (inside box)	22
Goals conceded (outside box)	6
Minutes per goal conceded	55
Clean sheets	2
Saves (shots inside box)	52
Saves (shots outside box)	24
Saves/shots	73%
DISTRIBUTION	
Long kick %	46%
Throws/short passes %	66%
CATCHING	
Crosses caught	21
Crosses punched	15
Crosses dropped	2
Catch success %	91%
DISCIPLINE	
Yellow cards	3
Red cards	0

SEE PAGE 68 FOR FULL STATS

Peter CLARKE • 30
EVERTON • BORN: 3.1.82

If ever there is a time to make your first team debut, it has got to be when your team is 3–0 up after just half an hour of the game gone. That is what happened to Everton's Peter Clarke when he made his senior bow just a few weeks after his 19th birthday in the 3–1 win at Coventry.

After replacing the unfortunate Alec Cleland, Clarke performed well alongside David Unsworth and Michael Ball as he made eight clearances and won two challenges to prevent the Sky Blues getting back into the game.

He displayed good composure in not committing a foul during his 58 minutes on the pitch and, as a former England youth captain, he looks to have a bright future within the higher echelons of the game.

Unfortunately for Clarke, Everton boss Walter Smith plumped for the experience of fit-again Richard Gough for the team's next fixture against Middlesbrough.

SEE PAGE 138 FOR FULL STATS

Demanding: Matt Clarke

For more information visit our website:

C

 FB

Alec CLELAND • 20
EVERTON • BORN: 10.12.70

Once again injuries ruined Alec Cleland's season, as he was only able to make two starts for the club and, in the latter of these against Coventry in January, he sustained a torn thigh muscle which kept him out for the rest of the campaign.

It was frustrating for the versatile defender after being sidelined for much of his previous two seasons on Merseyside, and dashed his hopes of making a greater contribution to Walter Smith's team. In fact, Cleland has made just 28 starts since joining Everton in 1998.

In his only full game of the season Cleland helped the Toffees to their most memorable result, a 2–0 win over Arsenal. He helped cut off the supply line from Robert Pires with several clearances and timely tackles.

The season did end on a positive note when he was named in the squad for the last couple of matches.

Once regarded as Scotland's best uncapped defender, Cleland will be aiming to regain full fitness and challenge Steve Watson for the right-sided slot.

APPEARANCES	
Start (sub)	2(3)
Minutes on pitch	218
GOAL ATTEMPTS	
Goals	0
PASSING & CROSSING	
Goal assists	0
Passing	92
Passing accuracy	61%
Crosses	5
Crossing accuracy	60%
DEFENDING	
Tackles	2
Tackles won %	100%
Blocks	1
Interceptions	1
Clearances	6
Shots cleared off line	0
DISCIPLINE	
Fouls	3
Yellow cards	0
Red cards	0
SEE PAGE 138 FOR FULL STATS	

 AM

Stephen CLEMENCE • 25
TOTTENHAM HOTSPUR • BORN: 31.3.78

APPEARANCES	
Start (sub)	27(2)
Minutes on pitch	2456
GOAL ATTEMPTS	
Goals	1
Shots on target	10
Shooting accuracy	43%
Goals/shots ratio	4%
PASSING	
Goal assists	7
Passes in opp half	719
Passing accuracy in opp half	68%
Crosses	162
Crossing accuracy	27%
DRIBBLING	
Dribbles & runs	54
Dribble completion	56%
Corners forced	21
DISCIPLINE	
Fouls	32
Yellow cards	4
Red cards	0
SEE PAGE 292 FOR FULL STATS	

After promising to make a breakthrough at Spurs over the last couple of seasons, Stephen Clemence finally cemented a regular place in the first team in 2000–01 with some excellent individual performances.

Because of the club's ongoing injury crisis throughout the campaign, Clemence was forced to perform in a number of roles for the Lilywhites. He spent most of his time operating on the left side of midfield and filled in admirably at wing-back, where his tenacity was a huge asset.

But by the end of the 2000–01 season, Clemence had settled into his favoured central midfield role and his incisive distribution proved to be one of the club's most potent attacking weapons.

Indeed, Clemence was arguably Tottenham's most effective passer over the course of the 2000–01 season. He connected with a colleague with 27% of his crosses and set up seven goals for team-mates – more than any other player at Spurs and the joint-seventh highest total in the Premiership.

Andy COLE • 9
MANCHESTER UNITED • BORN: 15.10.71

The highlight of Andy Cole's season was undoubtedly when he finally netted his first international goal in England's 3–1 win over Albania. Having suffered much criticism for his performances for the national side it was a huge weight off his shoulders following 12 previously barren appearances, especially after missing a sitter just a few days earlier against Finland at Anfield.

Domestically Cole weighed in with nine goals as he collected his fifth Championship medal with the club and notched four in the Champions League to overhaul Denis Law's long-standing club record.

However, he will have been disappointed with his shooting accuracy of 40%, considerably lower than his ratio in 1999–2000.

He will certainly have competition for his place with the arrival of Ruud van Nistelrooy, but he has been at United long enough to know that no one is guaranteed a starting slot. One thing is for sure: he is likely to be spending even less time talking to his now ex-team-mate Teddy Sheringham.

APPEARANCES	
Start (sub)	15(4)
Minutes on pitch	1316
GOAL ATTEMPTS	
Goals inside box	7
Goals outside box	2
Minutes per goal scored	146
Goals/shots ratio	21%
SHOOTING	
Shots on target inside box	13
Shots on target outside box	4
Shooting accuracy	40%
PASSING	
Goal assists	3
Key passes	19
Passing accuracy in opp half	68%
DISCIPLINE	
Fouls committed	19
Fouls won	15
Offside	28
Yellow cards	1
Red cards	1
SEE PAGE 222 FOR FULL STATS	

Ashley COLE • 29
ARSENAL • BORN: 20.12.80

APPEARANCES	
Start (sub)	15(2)
Minutes on pitch	1302
GOAL ATTEMPTS	
Goals	3
PASSING & CROSSING	
Goal assists	1
Passing	769
Passing accuracy	79%
Crosses	60
Crossing accuracy	25%
DEFENDING	
Tackles	67
Tackles won %	79%
Blocks	9
Interceptions	10
Clearances	50
Shots cleared off line	0
DISCIPLINE	
Fouls	19
Yellow cards	3
Red cards	0
SEE PAGE 40 FOR FULL STATS	

Ashley Cole has been like a breath of fresh air to the English game as his meteoric rise from Arsenal reserves to the national first team has been nothing short of remarkable.

Arsène Wenger gave him his first start of the season against Bradford in September. Cole was on target to net a vital equaliser for the Gunners and the east Londoner went on to register a further two Premiership goals during the campaign.

But goalscoring is just a small part of Cole's game as his lightning bursts down the flanks caused great excitement for Arsenal fans and struck terror into opposing defenders. He accurately delivered a quarter of his crosses and successfully found a team-mate with 79% of his distribution.

Still living at home with his mum, there are no airs or graces from Cole, who displayed great maturity throughout the season. The youngster looks like being a key figure in the Gunners' assault on the major honours in 2001–02 after they rebuffed a reported £20 million offer from Barcelona.

2 Ashley Cole scored with his

Joe COLE • 26
WEST HAM UNITED • BORN: 8.11.81

Joe Cole capped a brilliant individual season when he made his international debut alongside team-mate Michael Carrick in England's resounding win over Mexico in May.

While 2000–01 may not have been a particularly memorable campaign for the Hammers, Joe Cole was one of the few shining lights for the Upton Park faithful. Cole's close control and awesome dribbling skills were a joy to behold and his 58 successful dribbles were the highest tally by an Englishman in the Premiership.

Despite reservations about Cole playing in the same team as Opta's 1999–2000 player of the season Paolo Di Canio, the pair often combined to tear opposition defences apart, as illustrated in the Hammers' wins late in the season against Southampton and Derby County.

The new West Ham boss will know that in Joe Cole he has arguably the most exciting prospect in football at his disposal and would do well to base the team around the youngster's priceless talents.

APPEARANCES	
Start (sub)	24(6)
Minutes on pitch	2205

GOAL ATTEMPTS	
Goals	5
Shots on target	22
Shooting accuracy	40%
Goals/shots ratio	9%

PASSING	
Goal assists	2
Passes in opp half	658
Passing accuracy in opp half	74%
Crosses	41
Crossing accuracy	27%

DRIBBLING	
Dribbles & runs	168
Dribble completion	69%
Corners forced	14

DISCIPLINE	
Fouls	38
Yellow cards	5
Red cards	0

SEE PAGE 306 FOR FULL STATS

Priceless: Joe Cole

first two shots of the season

Stan COLLYMORE • 28
BRADFORD CITY • BORN: 22.1.71

Stan Collymore started the season at Leicester City, but quickly fell out with new manager Peter Taylor following a bust-up with a team-mate in a Foxes reserve match. Bradford City snapped up the controversial forward in October, but after scoring a stunning goal on his debut against Leeds United, things once again turned sour for the Cannock-born striker.

Chris Hutchings' replacement Jim Jefferies was no fan of Collymore and by January the striker was on the move again – this time to Real Oviedo in Spain.

Collymore announced that this was his last chance to prove himself. But after just a handful of disappointing substitute appearances he declared that his heart was no longer in football and he retired from the game. He announced that he might follow Vinnie Jones into the movies and claimed he fancied playing James Bond, although the villainous Ernst Stavro Blofeld would surely find a sulk and a strop far less of a threat than a Walther PPK.

APPEARANCES	
Start (sub)	6(6)
Minutes on pitch	698
GOAL ATTEMPTS	
Goals inside box	3
Goals outside box	0
Minutes per goal scored	233
Goals/shots ratio	14%
SHOOTING	
Shots on target inside box	7
Shots on target outside box	5
Shooting accuracy	55%
PASSING	
Goal assists	0
Key passes	6
Passing accuracy in opp half	64%
DISCIPLINE	
Fouls committed	16
Fouls won	5
Offside	17
Yellow cards	0
Red cards	0

SEE PAGES 68 & 180 FOR FULL STATS

Colin COOPER • 28
MIDDLESBROUGH • BORN: 28.2.67

APPEARANCES	
Start (sub)	26(1)
Minutes on pitch	2201
GOAL ATTEMPTS	
Goals	2
DEFENDING	
Blocks	32
Shots cleared off line	0
Headed clearances	91
Other clearances	54
Interceptions	11
Last man saving tackles	0
Tackles won	35
Tackles won %	65%
PASSING	
Passing accuracy own half	78%
Passing accuracy opp half	62%
DISCIPLINE	
Fouls	29
Fouls in danger area	5
Yellow cards	10
Red cards	0

SEE PAGE 236 FOR FULL STATS

Colin Cooper played a key role in helping Middlesbrough to avoid relegation with some impressive displays which made the Boro defence harder to break down in the latter stages of the season.

His performances saw him ranked as the sixth-most effective player in the Opta Riverside rankings as his 145 clearances and 32 blocks snuffed out many strikers.

Cooper was also the fifth-most prolific distributor of the ball at Boro, playing 668 successful passes. And the former England international was a menace in the opposition box, scoring equalisers in consecutive matches against fellow-strugglers Everton and Manchester City.

The Durham-born defender will hope to play a significant role in Boro's Premiership campaign in 2001–02, and in his spare time help improve literacy among children by continuing his sterling work with the National Reading Association.

Any youngsters pursuing a career in football would do well to study Cooper's example.

For more information visit our website:

C

 James COPPINGER • 26
NEWCASTLE UNITED • BORN: 10.1.81

James Coppinger made his solitary Premiership appearance as a late substitute for goalscorer Daniel Cordone in the Magpies' 2–0 win over Tottenham in August.

He was signed by Kenny Dalglish from Darlington in March 1998 and that late outing against Spurs was his first in a Newcastle shirt. Despite signing a new three-year contract in September, the young striker, who has drawn comparisons with ex-Toon star Peter Beardsley, failed to make an impact on the first team and was loaned to QPR at the tail-end of 2000–01.

Although the former England Under-16 international found himself down the pecking order at St James' Park behind the likes of Shola Ameobi and Kevin Gallacher, he showed some clever touches and subtle skills against Tottenham.

With Hearts and Hartlepool both showing an interest in the past, it may be to the Teessider's benefit to move on if he fails to make an impression with the club.

SEE PAGE 250 FOR FULL STATS

 Daniel CORDONE • 17
NEWCASTLE UNITED • BORN: 6.1.74

Earful: Daniel Cordone

Daniel Cordone joined Newcastle on loan at the start of the 2000–01 season and initially impressed the Toon Army.

The Racing Club player's dazzling performances behind frontman Alan Shearer were vital to Bobby Robson's side as the club made a solid start to the campaign. Cordone scored twice in his first three games in English football, prompting talk of a more permanent move to Tyneside.

Unfortunately, Cordone was then given an earful by the footballing authorities after the FA deemed the soldered jewellery he wore "dangerous". And although the Argentinean removed his earrings before each subsequent game, the incident seemed to take the shine off his performances during the remainder of the 2000–01 campaign.

Indeed, Cordone failed to find the back of the net after August and at the end of his one-year loan spell the former Velez Sarsfield player was looking for a new club, having been told that his services were no longer required at Newcastle.

APPEARANCES	
Start (sub)	12(9)
Minutes on pitch	1044

GOAL ATTEMPTS	
Goals inside box	2
Goals outside box	0
Minutes per goal scored	522
Goals/shots ratio	13%

SHOOTING	
Shots on target inside box	6
Shots on target outside box	3
Shooting accuracy	56%

PASSING	
Goal assists	1
Key passes	21
Passing accuracy in opp half	73%

DISCIPLINE	
Fouls committed	11
Fouls won	10
Offside	33
Yellow cards	0
Red cards	0

SEE PAGE 250 FOR FULL STATS

Carl CORT • 16
NEWCASTLE UNITED • BORN: 1.11.77

Newcastle surprised many when they splashed out £7 million on 6'5" Wimbledon striker Carl Cort, adding him to a growing number of target men at St James' Park, including Alan Shearer and Duncan Ferguson.

Bobby Robson's outlay seemed a sound enough investment at the start of 2000–01, though, when Ferguson was offloaded to Everton and Cort scored just five minutes into his home debut against Derby.

But an injury sustained later in that game kept Cort out of action apart from a brief return until March and, with Shearer failing to reach full fitness, the Magpies were left struggling without a recognised forward for much of 2000–01.

Cort returned in triumphant fashion in March, netting against Middlesbrough. The towering striker followed that up with four further goals and finished as the club's joint-top scorer with six. The fact that five of Cort's strikes came in just eight appearances at St James' Park has already made him a firm fans' favourite.

APPEARANCES	
Start (sub)	13(0)
Minutes on pitch	1098
GOAL ATTEMPTS	
Goals inside box	6
Goals outside box	0
Minutes per goal scored	183
Goals/shots ratio	16%
SHOOTING	
Shots on target inside box	17
Shots on target outside box	5
Shooting accuracy	58%
PASSING	
Goal assists	2
Key passes	7
Passing accuracy in opp half	65%
DISCIPLINE	
Fouls committed	19
Fouls won	18
Offside	19
Yellow cards	1
Red cards	0
SEE PAGE 250 FOR FULL STATS	

Tony COTTEE • 27
LEICESTER CITY • BORN: 11.7.65

The 2000–01 season will not go down as a happy one for Tony Cottee. Released by Leicester City after just 23 minutes of action Cottee moved on to Norwich, but made just five starting appearances for the Canaries before being tempted into management by Division Three Barnet.

Cottee's managerial career got off to a sensational start as he scored in a 7–0 rout of Blackpool. But that result was to prove a false dawn as the Bees rapidly lost their buzz.

By March, Barnet had slipped to within five points of bottom-placed Halifax. This decline in form prompted Cottee's exit from Underhill.

Cottee was given another chance to prove he still had something to offer as a player. But after joining Millwall, he managed just two appearances before being released. This fleeting stay meant Cottee played in all four divisions in one season – a fact which will be exciting trivia buffs for years to come.

SEE PAGE 180 FOR FULL STATS

Triumphant: Carl Cort

| Tony Cottee was the only player to play in each

CB — **Jody CRADDOCK • 17**
SUNDERLAND • BORN: 25.7.75

Despite pre-season interest from Division One strugglers Portsmouth, Jody Craddock had his best season for Sunderland since his arrival on Wearside in 1997. The former Cambridge United stopper won 79 tackles — more than any other Black Cat.

He saw off the challenge of Slovakia skipper Stanislav Varga to link up with Emerson Thome at the heart of the Sunderland defence. The pair gave the team much-needed stability at the back as they pushed for a European place.

Craddock's total of 383 clearances was the third-highest by a Premiership defender and the most by an Englishman. While the likes of Don Hutchison and Kevin Phillips may have grabbed most of the headlines, it was Craddock's trusty displays which helped further Sunderland's standing as an established Premiership outfit.

It will be intriguing to see if Craddock can sustain such a high level of performance as the Black Cats look to step up their challenge for a place in Europe.

APPEARANCES	
Start (sub)	33(1)
Minutes on pitch	2975
GOAL ATTEMPTS	
Goals	0
DEFENDING	
Blocks	36
Shots cleared off line	0
Headed clearances	253
Other clearances	130
Interceptions	9
Last man saving tackles	2
Tackles won	79
Tackles won %	75%
PASSING	
Passing accuracy own half	72%
Passing accuracy opp half	52%
DISCIPLINE	
Fouls	41
Fouls in danger area	7
Yellow cards	4
Red cards	0

SEE PAGE 278 FOR FULL STATS

 S — **Richard CRESSWELL • 23**
LEICESTER CITY • BORN: 20.9.77

APPEARANCES	
Start (sub)	3(5)
Minutes on pitch	324
GOAL ATTEMPTS	
Goals inside box	0
Goals outside box	0
Minutes per goal scored	n/a
Goals/shots ratio	0%
SHOOTING	
Shots on target inside box	3
Shots on target outside box	1
Shooting accuracy	50%
PASSING	
Goal assists	0
Key passes	1
Passing accuracy in opp half	68%
DISCIPLINE	
Fouls committed	13
Fouls won	16
Offside	6
Yellow cards	1
Red cards	0

SEE PAGE 180 FOR FULL STATS

Richard Cresswell failed to make an impact at Filbert Street following his £750,000 move from Sheffield Wednesday in September 2000 and was farmed out on loan to First Division Preston North End with a view to a permanent transfer.

The Lilywhites had originally tried to sign him before the start of the 1999–2000 season, but the Owls did not want to sell to their Division One rivals. But when Peter Taylor offered him the prospect of European football it was too good for the former England Under-21 striker to turn down.

Cresswell's first appearance for the Foxes was in the UEFA Cup tie against Red Star Belgrade, and just as the Midlanders' European adventure never got going, nor did the striker's career at Filbert Street.

Making just three Premiership starts for the club, Cresswell could manage only four shots on target. The arrival of Dean Sturridge meant that the former York City talisman had to look elsewhere for first-team football.

Gary CROFT • 16
IPSWICH TOWN • BORN: 17.2.74

Back in the 1999–2000 season, Gary Croft became the first professional footballer to be electronically-tagged by the police, after he was caught driving without a valid licence.

But while the local constabulary were then able to monitor Croft's every move, Opta have been limited in their analysis of the player by the full-back's inability to make Ipswich Town's starting XI.

Over the course of the club's fantastic 2000–01 campaign, Croft managed to complete 90 minutes on just three occasions, during which time his passing accuracy of 66% was well below Ipswich's average. Moreover, George Burley's side lost five of the six games that Croft started and his boss consequently slammed the defender for his lacklustre performances.

However, Croft is a versatile performer who can pass the ball effectively with both feet and should still have a role to play for Burley's side in the future if he can oust Jamie Clapham, Fabian Wilnis or Chris Makin from the starting line-up.

APPEARANCES	
Start (sub)	6(2)
Minutes on pitch	483
GOAL ATTEMPTS	
Goals	0
PASSING & CROSSING	
Goal assists	0
Passing	203
Passing accuracy	66%
Crosses	20
Crossing accuracy	25%
DEFENDING	
Tackles	13
Tackles won %	77%
Blocks	6
Interceptions	1
Clearances	16
Shots cleared off line	1
DISCIPLINE	
Fouls	5
Yellow cards	1
Red cards	0
SEE PAGE 152 FOR FULL STATS	

Lee CROOKS • 2
MANCHESTER CITY • BORN: 14.1.78

APPEARANCES	
Start (sub)	0(2)
Minutes on pitch	83
GOAL ATTEMPTS	
Goals	0
PASSING & CROSSING	
Goal assists	0
Passing	21
Passing accuracy	48%
Crosses	3
Crossing accuracy	67%
DEFENDING	
Tackles	1
Tackles won %	100%
Blocks	0
Interceptions	0
Clearances	4
Shots cleared off line	0
DISCIPLINE	
Fouls	1
Yellow cards	1
Red cards	0
SEE PAGE 208 FOR FULL STATS	

After playing only a peripheral role in Manchester City's promotion from Division One in 1999–2000, versatile defender Lee Crooks was only going to be used as a squad player upon the Citizens' return to the big time.

He made two substitute appearances in September, replacing Steve Howey and Alfie Haaland in the matches against Tottenham and Newcastle respectively.

Crooks helped City to become the first team to leave White Hart Lane with a point after making four clearances and one timely tackle.

But he could not force his way into Joe Royle's plans and was subsequently loaned out to Northampton Town in Nationwide Division Two, where he impressed before injury curtailed his loan spell.

With both Bolton and Barnsley expressing an interest in Crooks, it would be surprising if the Yorkshire-born defender was still at Maine Road in 2001–02, but a move to his beloved Leeds can only be a distant dream.

C

G   Mark CROSSLEY • 25
MIDDLESBROUGH • BORN: 16.6.69

Mark Crossley made a surprise return to the Premiership when he left Nottingham Forest after 13 years of service to link up with Middlesbrough in the top flight.

Originally signed as cover for Mark Schwarzer, he was at first unable to replace the Aussie when he found himself suffering from a hamstring strain ahead of the trip to Manchester City in September.

But he recovered in time to appear in Boro's second win of the season, a 3–2 victory at Southampton, and played in the subsequent four matches.

Fifteen stops proved he was still a 'keeper capable of playing in the top flight and he did his best in Schwarzer's absence. But Crossley's final appearance was to end on a disappointing note when he was dismissed by referee Andy D'Urso for bringing down Fredrik Ljungberg in Arsenal's visit.

The rest of the season was spent on the substitutes' bench impressing his fellow-reserves with an uncanny impression of Norman Wisdom.

APPEARANCES	
Start (sub)	4(1)
Minutes on pitch	300
SHOT STOPPING	
Goals conceded (inside box)	4
Goals conceded (outside box)	2
Minutes per goal conceded	50
Clean sheets	0
Saves (shots inside box)	8
Saves (shots outside box)	7
Saves/shots	71%
DISTRIBUTION	
Long kick %	36%
Throws/short passes %	75%
CATCHING	
Crosses caught	4
Crosses punched	2
Crosses dropped	0
Catch success %	100%
DISCIPLINE	
Yellow cards	0
Red cards	1

SEE PAGE 236 FOR FULL STATS

G   Carlo CUDICINI • 23
CHELSEA • BORN: 6.9.73

APPEARANCES	
Start (sub)	23(1)
Minutes on pitch	2115
SHOT STOPPING	
Goals conceded (inside box)	24
Goals conceded (outside box)	3
Minutes per goal conceded	78
Clean sheets	7
Saves (shots inside box)	35
Saves (shots outside box)	22
Saves/shots	68%
DISTRIBUTION	
Long kick %	53%
Throws/short passes %	89%
CATCHING	
Crosses caught	42
Crosses punched	11
Crosses dropped	1
Catch success %	98%
DISCIPLINE	
Yellow cards	1
Red cards	0

SEE PAGE 96 FOR FULL STATS

The arrival of Claudio Ranieri in the Chelsea hot-seat in September helped progress the Stamford Bridge career of shot-stopper Carlo Cudicini during 2000–01.

Shrugging off the challenge of Ed De Goey, the former AC Milan and Lazio goalkeeper became the undisputed first choice under Ranieri as his excellent agility and anticipation skills became evident. He made more smothers than De Goey and his saves-to-shots ratio of 68% was marginally better than the Dutchman's.

Cudicini originates from a fine footballing pedigree, as his father Fabio was widely regarded as one of Italy's best post-war goalkeepers, representing Milan and his country with distinction.

One of the Italian's best games for the club was the dramatic final-day win at Manchester City which secured a UEFA Cup slot for the Blues, in which he made a string of fine saves. It remains to be seen whether he can follow in the footsteps of his famous father and achieve European glory.

Nikos DABIZAS • 34
NEWCASTLE UNITED • BORN: 3.8.73

CB

Towering defender Nikos Dabizas had a less eventful time in 2000–01 than he experienced in the previous campaign.

After being left out by Ruud Gullit at the start of 1999–2000, Dabizas was hoping for a continuation of the long run in the first XI he enjoyed under Bobby Robson. But his bubble burst in the first home game of the season against Derby when he was carried off with a knee injury.

It was the first major injury for the Greek international and put him on the sidelines for seven months while surgery was carried out to repair the ligament damage.

He was sorely missed at the heart of the Newcastle defence as they went on a run of 25 league games without a clean sheet after his injury.

On his return, Dabizas inspired the Magpies to a 2–1 win over West Ham and a run of seven games with only one defeat, illustrating how his presence tightened up the Newcastle defence. They also kept three clean sheets in the last seven games.

APPEARANCES	
Start (sub)	9(0)
Minutes on pitch	764
GOAL ATTEMPTS	
Goals	0
DEFENDING	
Blocks	7
Shots cleared off line	0
Headed clearances	39
Other clearances	12
Interceptions	12
Last man saving tackles	2
Tackles won	24
Tackles won %	71%
PASSING	
Passing accuracy own half	83%
Passing accuracy opp half	60%
DISCIPLINE	
Fouls	10
Fouls in danger area	1
Yellow cards	1
Red cards	0
SEE PAGE 250 FOR FULL STATS	

Olivier DACOURT • 4
LEEDS UNITED • BORN: 25.9.74

M

APPEARANCES	
Start (sub)	33(0)
Minutes on pitch	2773
GOAL ATTEMPTS	
Goals	3
Shots on target	18
Shooting accuracy	36%
PASSING & CROSSING	
Goal assists	3
Passes in opp half	839
Passing accuracy in opp half	70%
Successful crosses	11
Cross completion	35%
DEFENDING	
Interceptions	16
Clearances	12
Tackles	173
Tackles won %	71%
DISCIPLINE	
Fouls	94
Yellow cards	13
Red cards	0
SEE PAGE 166 FOR FULL STATS	

The 2000–01 season must have surpassed all of Olivier Dacourt's expectations. Joining from Lens in the close season, the French midfielder was pivotal to Leeds' success both at home and in Europe.

Dacourt was one of the top performers in the Premiership, leading the division in tackles attempted and far exceeding renowned stoppers such as Marcel Desailly and Patrick Vieira in the process.

Dacourt came to his friend Vieira's aid when the Arsenal man was hauled up in front of the FA for an apparent kick to Dacourt's throat in the teams' feisty encounter at Elland Road in November.

As a permanent fixture for the Peacocks, Dacourt scored three goals and created another three, showing the strength in his all-round game.

To cap an impressive return to English football, the former Everton man was called up to the French squad by manager Roger Lemerre for the Confederations Cup tournament in the summer.

19 Olivier Dacourt was subjected to more

Christian DAILLY • 7
WEST HAM UNITED • BORN: 23.10.73

Scottish international Christian Dailly moved to West Ham from Blackburn in January 2001 for £1.7 million and quickly established himself in the first team. Purchased in an attempt to shore up a stuttering defence, he did little to reverse the Hammers' fortunes as they continued their alarming slide towards the relegation zone.

Often partnered in defence by the accident-prone Rigobert Song and the ever-dependable Stuart Pearce, Dailly put in performances below the standard set by the departing Rio Ferdinand.

Dailly's tackling was below average and his passing and discipline were in need of improvement too, though his performances were not helped by the fact he was asked to play in midfield on many an occasion.

His status among Hammers fans was further undermined by a last-gasp own goal at home to Coventry in only his fourth appearance in a claret-and-blue shirt. Everyone at the Boleyn Ground will be looking for a big improvement from the Scot in 2001–02.

APPEARANCES	
Start (sub)	11(1)
Minutes on pitch	1005
GOAL ATTEMPTS	
Goals	0
DEFENDING	
Blocks	7
Shots cleared off line	0
Headed clearances	49
Other clearances	36
Interceptions	2
Last man saving tackles	0
Tackles won	21
Tackles won %	58%
PASSING	
Passing accuracy own half	78%
Passing accuracy opp half	54%
DISCIPLINE	
Fouls	16
Fouls in danger area	2
Yellow cards	4
Red cards	0
SEE PAGE 306 FOR FULL STATS	

Sam DALLA BONA • 24
CHELSEA • BORN: 6.2.81

APPEARANCES	
Start (sub)	26(3)
Minutes on pitch	2253
GOAL ATTEMPTS	
Goals	2
Shots on target	9
Shooting accuracy	25%
PASSING & CROSSING	
Goal assists	3
Passes in opp half	717
Passing accuracy in opp half	66%
Successful crosses	3
Cross completion	20%
DEFENDING	
Interceptions	4
Clearances	23
Tackles	100
Tackles won %	69%
DISCIPLINE	
Fouls	41
Yellow cards	8
Red cards	0
SEE PAGE 96 FOR FULL STATS	

Flaxen-haired Italian Sam Dalla Bona was made a regular in the Chelsea line-up in 2000–01 and established himself as a class performer in midfield.

Dalla Bona was limited to a handful of substitute appearances under ex-manager Gianluca Vialli, but when Claudio Ranieri took over at Stamford Bridge, Dalla Bona was quickly thrust into regular first-team action.

After coming off the bench in Chelsea's battling draw at Old Trafford, the ex-Atalanta player started his first match in Chelsea's whipping of Liverpool. In subsequent matches he showed how potent he can be in the opposition half with two quality goals against Everton and Bradford; he also set up three goals before Christmas.

The future looks rosy for the Chelsea youngster. The former Italian Under-18 captain generated interest from several Serie A giants during the course of the campaign. For the time being, though, he says he is more than happy with west London life and his role under Ranieri.

cautionable fouls against him than anyone else

 **Tomas DANILEVICIUS • 21**
ARSENAL • BORN: 18.7.78

  Calum DAVENPORT • 36
COVENTRY CITY • BORN: 1.1.83

Footballing ability was not the reason why Tomas Danilevicius hit the headlines during 2000–01. After scoring for the Gunners in a trial match in a summer tournament against Barcelona, the Lithuanian international came to England in a £1 million move from Swiss club FC Lausanne. But after a couple of substitute appearances at the turn of the year, questions were raised over the validity of his Greek passport.

The Greek government initially claimed it had never heard of Tomas, but the doubts over the validity of his documents eventually proved to be without foundation. Arsène Wenger imposed a playing ban on Tomas until the matter was resolved and, in order to provide some first-team experience, sent him off to Dunfermline Athletic. While there Tomas teamed up with national captain Andrius Skerla, but manager Jimmy Calderwood quickly shipped him back to London, saying overseas forwards took time to settle in the SPL.

SEE PAGE 40 FOR FULL STATS

The final day of the season may have been a non-event as far as Coventry City were concerned, as they played fellow-relegated side Bradford City, but it is a day which will live long in the memory of teenage defender Calum Davenport.

The 6'4" defender, who was a part of Coventry's successful youth side which made the final of the FA Youth Cup in 1999–2000, made his first-team debut against the Bantams. The player only turned 18 at the start of 2001, but clearly Gordon Strachan sees him having an important role to play as the Sky Blues try to fight their way out of Nationwide Division One.

Davenport was a second-half substitute for the experienced Paul Williams in the Bradford match. The youngster used his height to good effect, making five headed clearances in that game and will be looking forward to many more opportunities for the first team in the 2001–02 campaign.

SEE PAGE 110 FOR FULL STATS

 Callum DAVIDSON • 14
LEICESTER CITY • BORN: 25.6.76

Callum Davidson joined the Foxes from Blackburn Rovers in the summer of 2000 after being pursued by a number of Premiership clubs and at £1.7 million was Peter Taylor's second signing.

The pacy and tenacious Scottish defender settled into the first team in October and enjoyed Leicester's early-season rise to the top of the Premiership. However, a knee ligament injury in December put him out of action for several weeks.

By the time he returned, Leicester's fortunes had already turned and Davidson was moved to centre-back as cover for the injured Gerry Taggart. He scored his only goal of the season in the 2–1 defeat at Villa Park, the same place where he had been sent off in an FA Cup match earlier in the campaign for a late challenge.

Davidson has continued to play regularly for the Scottish national team with fellow-Fox Matt Elliott and should play a major part at Filbert Street as Peter Taylor tries to reverse the 2000–01 end-of-season slump.

APPEARANCES	
Start (sub)	25(3)
Minutes on pitch	2071
GOAL ATTEMPTS	
Goals	1
PASSING & CROSSING	
Goal assists	1
Passing	744
Passing accuracy	66%
Crosses	67
Crossing accuracy	31%
DEFENDING	
Tackles	79
Tackles won %	67%
Blocks	16
Interceptions	12
Clearances	92
Shots cleared off line	0
DISCIPLINE	
Fouls	24
Yellow cards	3
Red cards	0

SEE PAGE 180 FOR FULL STATS

For more information visit our website:

Kevin DAVIES • 10
SOUTHAMPTON • BORN: 26.3.77

Yorkshire-born striker Kevin Davies endured a less successful campaign than in 1999–2000. Playing on the right side of a three-pronged attack, Davies struggled to convert the chances presented to him. A woeful goals-to-shots ratio of just three per cent illustrated his poor finishing.

His only league goal of the season arrived in Saints' 2–0 victory over Tottenham. His finish was the culmination of a slick move which was reputed to be the first-ever goal scored by a player being featured on Sky Digital's PlayerCam. His distribution was also below par, with only 58% of his passes and 20% of his crosses finding their target.

Davies did, however, set up three goals; he assisted both of Hassan Kachloul's strikes at Derby and also Marian Pahars's goal at Newcastle United.

One possible reason for his struggle in 2000–01 was that he was often played out of position on the wing. Davies will hope that Saints' new boss will give him a run in his more natural role as a striker.

APPEARANCES	
Start (sub)	21(6)
Minutes on pitch	1814
GOAL ATTEMPTS	
Goals inside box	1
Goals outside box	0
Minutes per goal scored	1814
Goals/shots ratio	3%
SHOOTING	
Shots on target inside box	9
Shots on target outside box	3
Shooting accuracy	35%
PASSING	
Goal assists	3
Key passes	24
Passing accuracy in opp half	53%
DISCIPLINE	
Fouls committed	48
Fouls won	46
Offside	4
Yellow cards	9
Red cards	0

SEE PAGE 264 FOR FULL STATS

Simon DAVIES • 29
TOTTENHAM HOTSPUR • BORN: 23.10.79

APPEARANCES	
Start (sub)	9(4)
Minutes on pitch	759
GOAL ATTEMPTS	
Goals	2
Shots on target	5
Shooting accuracy	45%
Goals/shots ratio	18%
PASSING	
Goal assists	3
Passes in opp half	180
Passing accuracy in opp half	69%
Crosses	26
Crossing accuracy	27%
DRIBBLING	
Dribbles & runs	36
Dribble completion	56%
Corners forced	1
DISCIPLINE	
Fouls	7
Yellow cards	0
Red cards	0

SEE PAGE 292 FOR FULL STATS

Midfielder Simon Davies was a George Graham signing for Spurs when he moved down from Peterborough with Matthew Etherington in December 1999.

He wasted little time in impressing new boss Glenn Hoddle, though, and we can expect to see much more of the Welshman for Tottenham in 2001–02.

Davies started every game for Spurs under Hoddle compared to just one start and four appearances as a substitute for Graham in 2000–01.

The tricky midfielder also scored twice and claimed three assists during his run in the first team as he grew stronger with each game he played.

On top of his performances in the Premiership, he also had cause to celebrate as Mark Hughes awarded the youngster his first cap for Wales against the Ukraine at the end of March.

With Hoddle having shown his faith in the player, Davies seems likely to have a key role to play in future campaigns for Tottenham.

G Aidan DAVISON • 17
BRADFORD CITY • BORN: 11.5.68

Bradford shot-stopper Aidan Davison began the season as third-choice 'keeper at Valley Parade and when he did finally make it into the first team, it was too late to have any effect on the Bantams' final fate.

The Ulsterman appeared early on in the Intertoto and Worthington Cup competitions, but had to wait until the final two games of the season to play in the Premiership. His first game is one he will want to forget, conceding six at local rivals Leeds, but at least he managed a clean sheet the following week against Coventry.

He was busy in both games, making a total of 10 saves and dealing with 12 crosses into his box.

At least he was used to playing in a struggling side, with Bradford's second string finishing in the bottom two of the Reserve League North.

With Bradford now having to reduce their wage bill, there may be more opportunities for Davison as the likes of Matt Clarke look set to move on.

APPEARANCES

Start (sub)	2(0)
Minutes on pitch	180

SHOT STOPPING

Goals conceded (inside box)	5
Goals conceded (outside box)	1
Minutes per goal conceded	30
Clean sheets	1
Saves (shots inside box)	8
Saves (shots outside box)	2
Saves/shots	63%

DISTRIBUTION

Long kick %	46%
Throws/short passes %	0%

CATCHING

Crosses caught	8
Crosses punched	4
Crosses dropped	0
Catch success %	100%

DISCIPLINE

Yellow cards	0
Red cards	0

SEE PAGE 68 FOR FULL STATS

S Gilles DE BILDE • 11
ASTON VILLA • BORN: 9.6.71

APPEARANCES

Start (sub)	4(0)
Minutes on pitch	303

GOAL ATTEMPTS

Goals inside box	0
Goals outside box	0
Minutes per goal scored	n/a
Goals/shots ratio	0%

SHOOTING

Shots on target inside box	2
Shots on target outside box	0
Shooting accuracy	40%

PASSING

Goal assists	0
Key passes	3
Passing accuracy in opp half	56%

DISCIPLINE

Fouls committed	17
Fouls won	8
Offside	5
Yellow cards	0
Red cards	0

SEE PAGE 54 FOR FULL STATS

With Aston Villa struggling in front of goal, they took the opportunity to get Belgian international Gilles 'Bob' De Bilde in on loan from Sheffield Wednesday to help solve the problem. Could he fix it? No – he couldn't.

De Bilde had been out of favour at Hillsborough and the temporary move to Villa in October gave him the chance to resurrect a career in the Premiership. It failed to work out, though, and De Bilde ended up making just four appearances for John Gregory's men without scoring, before heading back to Sheffield.

One of the main factors was that he managed just two shots on target.

Following the departure of Paul Jewell, De Bilde found himself back in the Wednesday side on a regular basis under the guidance of Peter Shreeves. The Belgian ending up scoring four goals for the Owls as they eased away from the relegation trap door, but it remains to be seen whether the striker will stick around at Wednesday for another season in the Nationwide.

1.2 The average number of goals

G Ed DE GOEY • 1
CHELSEA • BORN: 20.12.66

Chelsea 'keeper Ed De Goey looks to have played his last game for the club after losing his first-team place to Italian star Carlo Cudicini during the 2000–01 campaign and the Dutchman appears ready to leave the Premiership and return to playing on the continent.

De Goey – who at 6'6" is the tallest player ever to have played for Chelsea – began the season as Gianluca Vialli's number one. An injury after just two games kept him out of the first-team picture for a while, but when Claudio Ranieri took over he initially kept the Dutchman on as his first choice.

But by the start of 2001, De Goey had only kept three clean sheets and Ranieri turned to Cudicini to go between the sticks. With the capture of Mark Bosnich from Manchester United, it was clear that De Goey's days were numbered and the Dutch international spent the remainder of the season looking for a move away from Stamford Bridge.

The former Feyenoord 'keeper will be a great loss should he depart.

APPEARANCES	
Start (sub)	15(0)
Minutes on pitch	1305
SHOT STOPPING	
Goals conceded (inside box)	15
Goals conceded (outside box)	3
Minutes per goal conceded	73
Clean sheets	3
Saves (shots inside box)	17
Saves (shots outside box)	20
Saves/shots	67%
DISTRIBUTION	
Long kick %	58%
Throws/short passes %	95%
CATCHING	
Crosses caught	26
Crosses punched	15
Crosses dropped	0
Catch success %	100%
DISCIPLINE	
Yellow cards	0
Red cards	0

SEE PAGE 96 FOR FULL STATS

S Brian DEANE • 10
MIDDLESBROUGH • BORN: 7.2.68

APPEARANCES	
Start (sub)	13(12)
Minutes on pitch	1439
GOAL ATTEMPTS	
Goals inside box	2
Goals outside box	0
Minutes per goal scored	720
Goals/shots ratio	11%
SHOOTING	
Shots on target inside box	6
Shots on target outside box	1
Shooting accuracy	37%
PASSING	
Goal assists	1
Key passes	14
Passing accuracy in opp half	58%
DISCIPLINE	
Fouls committed	33
Fouls won	16
Offside	5
Yellow cards	2
Red cards	0

SEE PAGE 236 FOR FULL STATS

Veteran striker Brian Deane is still knocking about in the Premiership, but after getting on the scoresheet just twice in 2000–01 – and often being relegated to the bench – his days of top-flight football seem numbered.

"Deano" began the season as first-choice striker at Boro alongside Alen Boksic but, hampered by injuries, he struggled for a regular place in the Teessiders' starting line-up. By the end of the campaign, rumours were linking him with a return to former side Sheffield United.

The big target man found the net against Derby and Newcastle, but attempted just 19 shots all season. He also claimed an assist, but the former Leeds player was not involved enough to make a lasting impression for Boro.

It seems like a long time ago that Deane won his three England caps, but of course his place in Premiership history is assured – he scored the first-ever goal on the opening day of the newly-formed Premier League in 1992–93 against eventual champions Manchester United.

Jermain DEFOE • 35
WEST HAM UNITED • BORN: 7.10.82

Jermain Defoe had to wait until the final game of the season for his Premiership debut, but the youngster had already hit the headlines thanks to his sensational scoring record during a loan period at Bournemouth in Division Two.

The prolific teenager broke a post-war league record by scoring in 10 consecutive games for the Cherries and it is no wonder that West Ham issued a stern "hands off" warning when other clubs began sniffing around.

Defoe made his Hammers debut in the Worthington Cup at Walsall, where he scored the only goal of the game. He played in the final 22 minutes of the league season, but there is no doubt that he will feature more prominently before too long.

His growing reputation also earned him a call-up to the England Under-21s at the end of the season and he scored once again in a 3–0 win over Mexico.

SEE PAGE 306 FOR FULL STATS

Damien DELANEY • 29
LEICESTER CITY • BORN: 29.7.81

Midfielder-cum-defender Damien Delaney caused a stir when he joined Leicester from Cork City for just £50,000 in October. Fans of the Irish club were incensed, and when the Foxes went back for one of Delaney's team-mates there were mass pitch invasions and protests at Cork's games.

Delaney made his first appearances for Leicester in the FA Cup, but his Premiership bow was in the rather daunting trip to Old Trafford.

Delaney acquitted himself well against the Premiership champions and went on to make two more starts for Peter Taylor's men against Middlesbrough and Newcastle United.

The Irishman has a job on his hands if he is to earn himself a regular spot in the first team at Leicester.

But having won 13 out of the 15 tackles he has attempted so far and with further changes likely to occur at Filbert Street, Delaney will be pushing for a place in the starting line-up come the recommencement of Premiership hostilities.

Stir: Damien Delaney

APPEARANCES	
Start (sub)	3(2)
Minutes on pitch	290
GOAL ATTEMPTS	
Goals	0
Shots on target	2
Shooting accuracy	67%
PASSING & CROSSING	
Goal assists	0
Passes in opp half	50
Passing accuracy in opp half	60%
Successful crosses	3
Cross completion	50%
DEFENDING	
Interceptions	0
Clearances	27
Tackles	15
Tackles won %	87%
DISCIPLINE	
Fouls	9
Yellow cards	1
Red cards	0
SEE PAGE 180 FOR FULL STATS	

For more information visit our website:

Mark DELANEY • 2
ASTON VILLA • BORN: 13.5.76

The 2000–01 season got off to the worst possible start for Mark Delaney as he was sent off in an Intertoto Cup tie with Czech side Dukla Pribram.

It went from bad to worse for the Welsh defender when ligament trouble caused him to miss the start of the Premiership campaign, but by the end of the season he had worked hard to get back into John Gregory's side and he will hope to be there at the start of the 2001–02 campaign.

After several appearances from the bench, it was not until New Year's Day that Delaney made his first Premiership start for 2000–01. The wing-back slowly worked his way back into the team, though, and he ended up being a regular starter in the final nine games of the campaign.

Delaney's crossing was poor for a player in his position, but defensively he did well, winning 76% of all his tackles and making a total of 69 clearances for Gregory's men. The Welshman also failed to get on the scoresheet or create a goal.

APPEARANCES	
Start (sub)	12(7)
Minutes on pitch	1344
GOAL ATTEMPTS	
Goals	0
PASSING & CROSSING	
Goal assists	0
Passing	573
Passing accuracy	72%
Crosses	33
Crossing accuracy	18%
DEFENDING	
Tackles	67
Tackles won %	76%
Blocks	9
Interceptions	10
Clearances	69
Shots cleared off line	0
DISCIPLINE	
Fouls	13
Yellow cards	1
Red cards	0
SEE PAGE 54 FOR FULL STATS	

Rory DELAP • 5
DERBY COUNTY • BORN: 6.7.76

APPEARANCES	
Start (sub)	32(1)
Minutes on pitch	2885
GOAL ATTEMPTS	
Goals	3
PASSING & CROSSING	
Goal assists	0
Passing	1027
Passing accuracy	60%
Crosses	61
Crossing accuracy	23%
DEFENDING	
Tackles	93
Tackles won%	71%
Blocks	22
Interceptions	10
Clearances	130
Shots cleared off line	1
DISCIPLINE	
Fouls	39
Yellow cards	3
Red cards	0
SEE PAGE 124 FOR FULL STATS	

Utility man Rory Delap played in almost every position for Derby in 2000–01 and was a vital ingredient in the Rams' quest to stay in the Premiership as they struggled near the foot of the table.

It was Delap who scored Derby's first winning goal of the season against Ipswich in December. He played that day as a striker, but midfield is the preferred position of the former Carlisle United man.

The Irishman notched three goals in total during 2001–02 – all while playing as a frontman – and made more than 1,000 passes in midfield for the Rams. But he is strong in all areas as befits his utility status. He attempted more than 100 dribbles and runs, won 71% of his tackles and contributed 130 clearances.

He also remained fairly fit, featuring in 33 out of 38 league games.

A club like Derby is unable to afford a large squad, so having a player like Delap on their books is a huge bonus and they would wish for many more like him.

CB

Marcel DESAILLY • 6
CHELSEA • BORN: 7.9.68

For a World Cup-winner like Marcel Desailly, a trophy-less season is quite a rarity, but he had only a UEFA Cup place to cheer at the end of a season of upheaval at Chelsea.

Desailly remained consistent despite many changes behind the scenes at Stamford Bridge. The Frenchman missed only three matches for the Blues in the Premiership during 2000–01 and was a good influence on the emerging talent of John Terry.

The former AC Milan man made a total of 125 tackles – the second-highest total from any Premiership defender – and 290 clearances in the Blues' backline. Suspect discipline let him down, though; he received a total of 10 yellows during the campaign.

On the positive side, though, he did get forward to net two goals.

Like many of Chelsea's stars, Desailly has voiced his concerns about the lack of success at the club, and if Chelsea fail to start putting together a serious trophy challenge in 2001–02 he could well be off to ensure his final few seasons are more successful.

APPEARANCES	
Start (sub)	34(0)
Minutes on pitch	3001
GOAL ATTEMPTS	
Goals	2
DEFENDING	
Blocks	54
Shots cleared off line	0
Headed clearances	176
Other clearances	114
Interceptions	18
Last man saving tackles	4
Tackles won	99
Tackles won %	79%
PASSING	
Passing accuracy own half	87%
Passing accuracy opp half	75%
DISCIPLINE	
Fouls	39
Fouls in danger area	11
Yellow cards	10
Red cards	0
SEE PAGE 96 FOR FULL STATS	

S

Paolo DI CANIO • 10
WEST HAM UNITED • BORN: 9.7.68

APPEARANCES	
Start (sub)	31(0)
Minutes on pitch	2784
GOAL ATTEMPTS	
Goals inside box	7
Goals outside box	2
Minutes per goal scored	309
Goals/shots ratio	18%
SHOOTING	
Shots on target inside box	17
Shots on target outside box	9
Shooting accuracy	53%
PASSING	
Goal assists	7
Key passes	75
Passing accuracy in opp half	66%
DISCIPLINE	
Fouls committed	26
Fouls won	62
Offside	33
Yellow cards	6
Red cards	0
SEE PAGE 306 FOR FULL STATS	

Paolo Di Canio had the opportunity to move to Chelsea early in the 2000–01 season, but he turned them down as he wanted to continue "having sex" at Upton Park – in a football sense, of course.

Di Canio's performance failed to measure up to the pleasures of the 1999–2000 campaign, when he romped home as Opta's player of the season, but he remained a key player for the Hammers with nine goals and seven assists during the campaign.

Highlight of the season for Di Canio was undoubtedly notching the late winner at Old Trafford which put Manchester United out of the FA Cup, but the club's eventual exit from that competition in the quarter-finals made his suicide threat if he failed to win a trophy look rather hasty.

A friend of the maverick Italian named his racehorse Di Canio and the four-legged version should stand a much better chance of trophy-winning while the original continues to enjoy his conjugal rights with the Hammers, albeit with a new boss at the helm.

0 Kaba Diawara has played for Arsenal, Blackburn and

M

Roberto DI MATTEO • 16
CHELSEA • BORN: 29.5.70

D

The 2000–01 campaign is one Roberto Di Matteo will all too quickly want to forget, as a career-threatening triple fracture of his left leg meant an abrupt end to the season as early as September for the Chelsea midfielder.

Di Matteo had been one of the Blues' better players in the opening weeks, but was struck down by the horrific injury in their UEFA Cup defeat at Swiss side St Gallen back in September. The Italian international, who was actually born in Switzerland, had to undergo four operations in a Zurich hospital before returning to London and described the following week as the worst time of his life.

It was always Di Matteo's aim to regain his fitness in time for the start of 2001–02, but he will have another battle on his hands to get back into the side. Chelsea will certainly be bolstering their squad in an attempt to make a Premiership challenge.

Di Matteo is one of many over-30s at the Bridge who may find themselves victims of Claudio Ranieri's pledge to lower the average age of the squad.

APPEARANCES	
Start (sub)	7(0)
Minutes on pitch	630
GOAL ATTEMPTS	
Goals	0
Shots on target	6
Shooting accuracy	46%
PASSING & CROSSING	
Goal assists	1
Passes in opp half	196
Passing accuracy in opp half	72%
Successful crosses	3
Cross completion	20%
DEFENDING	
Interceptions	0
Clearances	6
Tackles	22
Tackles won %	68%
DISCIPLINE	
Fouls	14
Yellow cards	0
Red cards	0
SEE PAGE 96 FOR FULL STATS	

 S

Kaba DIAWARA • 25
WEST HAM UNITED • BORN: 16.12.75

APPEARANCES	
Start (sub)	6(5)
Minutes on pitch	620
GOAL ATTEMPTS	
Goals inside box	0
Goals outside box	0
Minutes per goal scored	n/a
Goals/shots ratio	0%
SHOOTING	
Shots on target inside box	3
Shots on target outside box	1
Shooting accuracy	27%
PASSING	
Goal assists	0
Key passes	6
Passing accuracy in opp half	58%
DISCIPLINE	
Fouls committed	9
Fouls won	12
Offside	16
Yellow cards	0
Red cards	0
SEE PAGE 306 FOR FULL STATS	

Former Arsenal player Kaba Diawara made a less-than-successful return to the Premiership in 2000–01 in a loan period at West Ham.

Diawara left the Gunners in the summer of 1999 after being unable to tie down a first-team place and moved on to Marseille and then Paris St Germain.

He returned to England at the start of 2000–01 when Graeme Souness took him on loan to Blackburn and he scored in his first start for Rovers – a less-than-glamorous Worthington Cup tie against Rochdale.

The loan period ended in September and Harry Redknapp then snapped up Diawara on a temporary basis for West Ham. Once again he failed to feature regularly, making only six starts for the Hammers, managing just four shots on target and failing to score with any of them.

Not surprisingly, the move has not been made permanent and Diawara's seemingly never-ending search for a club continues. It is unlikely that we will see him in the Premiership again.

West Ham but is still without a league goal in England

Danièle DICHIO • 12
SUNDERLAND • BORN: 19.10.74

After another season as a bit-part player in the Sunderland set-up, and with Peter Reid being continually linked with strikers, Danny Dichio seemingly does not have a great role to play in the future for the Black Cats.

Former QPR man Dichio made just two starts in the league for Sunderland, scoring in one of these against Ipswich on New Year's Day. The rest of the time he had to make do with life on the bench, although he regularly took the place of fellow-lanky forward Niall Quinn, who was rested for a number of cup matches.

Dichio was sent off in one such game at Crystal Palace in the FA Cup, becoming another statistic in Sunderland's woeful disciplinary record.

And the former nightclub DJ, who had a spell at Sampdoria earlier on in his career, may well be shown the red card at Sunderland in the near future, following an unimpressive time with the north-east club.

Dichio has had a colourful career, involving spells at Sampdoria and Lecce in Serie "A", so is sure to have several suitors.

APPEARANCES	
Start (sub)	2(13)
Minutes on pitch	387
GOAL ATTEMPTS	
Goals inside box	1
Goals outside box	0
Minutes per goal scored	387
Goals/shots ratio	10%
SHOOTING	
Shots on target inside box	6
Shots on target outside box	0
Shooting accuracy	60%
PASSING	
Goal assists	1
Key passes	15
Passing accuracy in opp half	65%
DISCIPLINE	
Fouls committed	22
Fouls won	7
Offside	4
Yellow cards	2
Red cards	0
SEE PAGE 278 FOR FULL STATS	

Paul DICKOV • 9
MANCHESTER CITY • BORN: 1.11.72

APPEARANCES	
Start (sub)	15(6)
Minutes on pitch	1437
GOAL ATTEMPTS	
Goals inside box	4
Goals outside box	0
Minutes per goal scored	359
Goals/shots ratio	16%
SHOOTING	
Shots on target inside box	10
Shots on target outside box	2
Shooting accuracy	48%
PASSING	
Goal assists	2
Key passes	15
Passing accuracy in opp half	66%
DISCIPLINE	
Fouls committed	47
Fouls won	40
Offside	16
Yellow cards	7
Red cards	1
SEE PAGE 208 FOR FULL STATS	

Paul Dickov assured himself of a place in Manchester City folklore with the late play-off final goals which saw them climb out of Division Two.

And he did enough in the Premiership to warrant a call-up to the Scotland squad and win three international caps in the process.

With the arrival of George Weah and Paulo Wanchope at Maine Road in the close season, Dickov may have felt that his City days were numbered. But the former Gunner slowly forced his way back into the first-team picture and hit four goals during a good spell in the autumn.

These were Dickov's only Premiership goals, though, as he soon found himself back on the sidelines, only coming back into the first-team picture towards the end of the season. With City returning to Division One, Dickov will be looking to re-ignite his successful partnership with Shaun Goater, should new boss Kevin Keegan approve.

But the feisty forward will need to improve his disciplinary record.

Bernard DIOMEDE • 24
LIVERPOOL • BORN: 23.1.74

The only member of the Liverpool squad to have won a World Cup medal, Bernard Diomede was one of Gérard Houllier's seven summer signings.

Bought from Auxerre in June 2000 as cover for Patrik Berger on the left wing, the dreadlocked Frenchman's 2000–01 season was ravaged by injury.

His home debut against Sunderland saw him harshly denied a goal after a superb overhead kick was adjudged not to have bounced over the line. Following that game Diomede managed only one more appearance, as a substitute against Manchester City. Cautioned twice in two games, his disciplinary record may need to improve if he wants to compete in future Liverpool campaigns.

The 2001–02 season may see him struggle to gain a regular place and indeed speculation was rife that a swap deal with fellow-Frenchman Lauren Robert of Paris St Germain may be on the cards, as Houllier once again looks to strengthen his options on the left side of midfield.

APPEARANCES	
Start (sub)	1(1)
Minutes on pitch	108
GOAL ATTEMPTS	
Goals	0
Shots on target	1
Shooting accuracy	100%
Goals/shots ratio	0%
PASSING	
Goal assists	0
Passes in opp half	16
Passing accuracy in opp half	75%
Crosses	11
Crossing accuracy	36%
DRIBBLING	
Dribbles & runs	4
Dribble completion	50%
Corners forced	2
DISCIPLINE	
Fouls	6
Yellow cards	2
Red cards	0
SEE PAGE 194 FOR FULL STATS	

Lee DIXON • 2
ARSENAL • BORN: 17.3.64

APPEARANCES	
Start (sub)	26(3)
Minutes on pitch	2383
GOAL ATTEMPTS	
Goals	1
PASSING & CROSSING	
Goal assists	2
Passing	1381
Passing accuracy	77%
Crosses	67
Crossing accuracy	30%
DEFENDING	
Tackles	49
Tackles won %	71%
Blocks	16
Interceptions	6
Clearances	60
Shots cleared off line	1
DISCIPLINE	
Fouls	28
Yellow cards	2
Red cards	0
SEE PAGE 40 FOR FULL STATS	

When asked in a recent radio interview how long he thought he could carry on playing, Lee Dixon replied: "I just wish they'd find a replacement for me quick – I'm knackered."

Still first choice despite turning 37 in 2000–01, Dixon has benefited more than anyone from Arsène Wenger's dietary and fitness regimes. Not that the Manchester-born hard man would accept this as an explanation for the prolonging of his career – he simply seems too stubborn to allow anyone else to don his treasured number two shirt.

Dixon claims that he never wants to play for another club once his days with the Gunners are over: "I want to stay and finish my career at Arsenal. I'm a massive Manchester City fan, but I couldn't see myself playing anywhere else."

And why would he, with another crack at the Champions League in 2001–02?

While he may be tempted to consider any coaching roles that come his way, in the words of the man himself: "There's life in the old dog yet."

Bojan DJORDJIC • 32
MANCHESTER UNITED • BORN: 6.2.82

Yugoslav youngster Bojan Djordjic capped an impressive rise through the ranks at Manchester United by making his first-team debut against Tottenham on the final day of the 2000–01 season.

Midfielder Djordjic, son of former Red Star Belgrade player Branko Djordjic, joined United's Youth Academy in 1999. In his first season the club staff awarded him the Young Player of the Year award and he went on to become a regular in the reserves during 2000–01, scoring four goals.

The youngster came to the public's attention in a televised testimonial for Celtic's Tommy Boyd at Parkhead when he scored with a sublime chip over the 'keeper. Just four days later, he was making his Premiership bow, replacing Denis Irwin with 15 minutes to go at White Hart Lane.

Competiton for places at United is as tough as ever, but if Djordjic continues to impress then he may well feature more prominently.

SEE PAGE 222 FOR FULL STATS

Influence: Jason Dodd

 Jason DODD • 2
SOUTHAMPTON • BORN: 2.11.70

Dependable skipper Jason Dodd celebrated his testimonial year in the final ever season at The Dell, but he is bound to be around for the beginning of a new era at Saints' St Mary's ground.

Dodd joined the Saints for just £50,000 from Bath City in 1989 and has given the club excellent service. He appeared in all but seven of Saints' games in 2000–01 and would have been a steadying influence in the side following the departure of Glenn Hoddle to Tottenham Hotspur.

The full-back scored a rare goal in the 1–1 draw at Everton back in October, with one of only three shots that he managed during the season. His strength is at the back, though, and the experienced campaigner won 79% of all his challenges and made 142 defensive clearances.

Injury ended his campaign prematurely, but he still managed a 60-minute run-out in his testimonial against a side of former Southampton players – the penultimate game ever to be played at The Dell.

APPEARANCES	
Start (sub)	29(2)
Minutes on pitch	2588
GOAL ATTEMPTS	
Goals	1
PASSING & CROSSING	
Goal assists	1
Passing	1293
Passing accuracy	70%
Crosses	54
Crossing accuracy	28%
DEFENDING	
Tackles	75
Tackles won %	79%
Blocks	34
Interceptions	3
Clearances	142
Shots cleared off line	0
DISCIPLINE	
Fouls	26
Yellow cards	2
Red cards	0

SEE PAGE 264 FOR FULL STATS

7 Jason Dodd helped Southampton to seven consecutive clean

Gary DOHERTY • 12
TOTTENHAM HOTSPUR • BORN: 31.1.80

Flame-haired Irishman Gary Doherty was handed his chance to shine for Tottenham's first team in his first full Premiership campaign in the 2000–01 term.

Doherty was one of the clutch of lower-league stars which George Graham bought during his spell in charge at White Hart Lane and the £1 million signing from Luton has already shown more than a glimpse of his undoubted ability.

Used in defence and attack, Doherty showed his prowess at both ends of the pitch for Spurs. He scored three league goals and an additional three in the cups – including Spurs' semi-final consolation against Arsenal – and put in numerous strong performances in the rearguard. He won 75% of his tackles and weighed in with 124 clearances.

Gifted with both pace and aerial ability, the ex-Hatter looks set to continue in his preferred centre-back role at Tottenham and should feature strongly in Glenn Hoddle's plans to return the good times to the white half of north London.

APPEARANCES	
Start (sub)	18(4)
Minutes on pitch	1675
GOAL ATTEMPTS	
Goals	3
DEFENDING	
Blocks	13
Shots cleared off line	0
Headed clearances	75
Other clearances	49
Interceptions	4
Last man saving tackles	0
Tackles won	42
Tackles won %	75%
PASSING	
Passing accuracy own half	78%
Passing accuracy opp half	58%
DISCIPLINE	
Fouls	48
Fouls in danger area	3
Yellow cards	3
Red cards	0
SEE PAGE 292 FOR FULL STATS	

Didier DOMI • 4
NEWCASTLE UNITED • BORN: 2.5.78

APPEARANCES	
Start (sub)	11(3)
Minutes on pitch	1019
GOAL ATTEMPTS	
Goals	0
PASSING & CROSSING	
Goal assists	0
Passing	418
Passing accuracy	69%
Crosses	22
Crossing accuracy	14%
DEFENDING	
Tackles	36
Tackles won %	72%
Blocks	7
Interceptions	0
Clearances	29
Shots cleared off line	0
DISCIPLINE	
Fouls	10
Yellow cards	2
Red cards	0
SEE PAGE 250 FOR FULL STATS	

Didier Domi was part of Ruud Gullit's foreign legion at Newcastle, but despite starting the 2000–01 campaign for Bobby Robson's men he soon found himself going back to his roots with a £4 million move to Paris St Germain in January.

Domi began at PSG when he was just 13 and was there until December 1998, when Gullit paid £4 million to take the left-sided defender up to Tyneside. The French Under-21 player featured prominently in the Magpies' cup run of 1999, but he never really settled in the north east.

The left-back made 14 unspectacular appearances for the Magpies during 2000–01, attempting 36 tackles and 29 clearances. His last showing in the black-and-white stripes was a miserable experience, with a 5–0 defeat at Highbury in December. With the Toon not to his liking, it did not take him too long to accept a return to his former club once a fee was agreed with Newcastle.

A talented player, he will hope to prosper now that he is back home.

sheets between January and March, equalling the Premiership record

 **José DOMINGUEZ • 32**
TOTTENHAM HOTSPUR • BORN: 16.2.74

José Dominguez played a fleeting part for George Graham's men in 2000–01 before leaving these shores to try his hand at German side Kaiserslautern. The German experience will be a new one to him but, having played under Barry Fry at Birmingham, there can be no experience that will shock him.

The winger claimed: "I had a very difficult time with Graham at Spurs – he almost ruined my career. I didn't fit in with Graham's style of play and I'm over the moon to have left because I wasn't given a chance."

Graham retorted: "Basically he came to the club and realised he just wasn't a Premiership player – end of story."

The former Sporting Lisbon man is a pacy player with plenty of tricks, but with his lightweight frame he struggled to fit into the side George Graham was building at Spurs. His final appearance for the Lilywhites was a 3–1 Worthington Cup defeat against former side Birmingham.

SEE PAGE 292 FOR FULL STATS

 Mark DRAPER • 9
SOUTHAMPTON • BORN: 11.11.70

Unfulfilled: Mark Draper

Mark Draper returned to England following a loan spell at Spanish side Rayo Vallecano ready to rebuild his career under Glenn Hoddle at Southampton.

Regarded as a classy playmaker, the former Notts County and Leicester man was on the fringes of the England squad when Terry Venables was the national coach six years ago. Out of favour with John Gregory at Aston Villa, Draper's potential went unfulfilled and the move to Southampton was an opportunity to put things right.

All did not go to plan, though, and despite starting the first five games for the Saints, Draper drifted in and out of the side, unable to find any consistency. But his passing accuracy of 77% and tackle success of 85% shows he still has plenty to offer in the midfield engine-room.

With a new manager at Southampton for 2001–02, the curtains may soon be drawn on his Saints career, as it is believed he and his family would favour a move back to his native Midlands.

APPEARANCES	
Start (sub)	16(6)
Minutes on pitch	1559
GOAL ATTEMPTS	
Goals	1
Shots on target	4
Shooting accuracy	24%
PASSING & CROSSING	
Goal assists	1
Passes in opp half	432
Passing accuracy in opp half	71%
Successful crosses	13
Cross completion	30%
DEFENDING	
Interceptions	3
Clearances	37
Tackles	53
Tackles won %	85%
DISCIPLINE	
Fouls	26
Yellow cards	5
Red cards	0
SEE PAGE 264 FOR FULL STATS	

For more information visit our website:

Michael DUBERRY • 22
LEEDS UNITED • BORN: 14.10.75

The 2000–01 season was one to forget for Leeds man Michael Duberry, as injury restricted him to just five appearances in the Premiership and he missed the majority of his club's entertaining exploits against the big guns of Europe.

Duberry took up his place in the Leeds defence early on in the season and featured in their European glamour ties with Barcelona and AC Milan.

A ruptured Achilles tendon against Derby County in September left him on the sidelines for the remainder of the season and with Rio Ferdinand joining in a record deal, Duberry now has some stiff competition if he is to regain his place in the first team reckoning.

"Dubes" was back in the headlines later in the season, dramatically changing his testimony in the trial of Lee Bowyer and Jonathon Woodgate.

After being acquitted of attempting to pervert the course of justice and with the injury now healed, he will be looking to re-establish himself in the Premiership.

APPEARANCES
Start (sub)	5(0)
Minutes on pitch	405

GOAL ATTEMPTS
Goals	0

DEFENDING
Blocks	1
Shots cleared off line	0
Headed clearances	24
Other clearances	6
Interceptions	3
Last man saving tackles	0
Tackles won	6
Tackles won %	100%

PASSING
Passing accuracy own half	67%
Passing accuracy opp half	53%

DISCIPLINE
Fouls	12
Fouls in danger area	5
Yellow cards	0
Red cards	0

SEE PAGE 166 FOR FULL STATS

Dion DUBLIN • 9
ASTON VILLA • BORN: 22.4.69

APPEARANCES
Start (sub)	29(4)
Minutes on pitch	2641

GOAL ATTEMPTS
Goals inside box	8
Goals outside box	0
Minutes per goal scored	330
Goals/shots ratio	10%

SHOOTING
Shots on target inside box	29
Shots on target outside box	4
Shooting accuracy	41%

PASSING
Goal assists	4
Key passes	35
Passing accuracy in opp half	62%

DISCIPLINE
Fouls committed	90
Fouls won	58
Offside	34
Yellow cards	2
Red cards	0

SEE PAGE 54 FOR FULL STATS

Along with his Villa team-mates, Dion Dublin spent the summer of 2000 wearing an electronic tag likened to the kind of gadget a prisoner on parole would wear, so that coaching staff could monitor heart-rates to make sure that the players were keeping fit during their holidays.

The Villa stars agreed to wear the virtual ball and chain, but often played in 2000–01 as if they were weighed down by a real version.

Dublin took a lot of stick from fans, who were disappointed that he managed just eight league goals. This still made him Villa's top scorer and much of the criticism aimed at the wholehearted player seemed very harsh given the effort he always puts in.

Half his goals came when he escaped his marker to score with his head – only two Premiership players managed to beat that tally. The target man also weighed in with four assists, but he never had a settled strike partner up front and was often left in virtual solitary confinement in attack, so poor was his service.

Terry DUNFIELD • 37
MANCHESTER CITY • BORN: 20.2.82

The 2000–01 campaign may have been a massive disappointment for Manchester City, but youngster Terry Dunfield will remember it well after making his Premiership debut in the final game of the season against Chelsea at Maine Road.

The Canadian midfielder came on for the injured Jeff Whitley and his performance was anything but rocky. He made 39 passes and found a team-mate with 87% of them.

Dunfield made the breakthrough into the City first team after putting in some solid displays for the reserve side. He grabbed the attention by scoring against Manchester United in the final of the Manchester Senior Cup and the call-up to the first-team squad followed shortly afterwards.

City will now need to restructure for Division One and Dunfield will be hoping to make enough of an impression on new boss Kevin Keegan to be included in the plans for a return to the top flight.

SEE PAGE 208 FOR FULL STATS

Richard DUNNE • 22
MANCHESTER CITY • BORN: 21.9.79

Republic of Ireland international Richard Dunne linked up with former boss Joe Royle once again at City but, despite some solid displays at the back for the Citizens, he faces Nationwide League football in 2001–02 without his mentor Royle, who was sacked at the end of the season.

Dunne began the season at Everton, where he developed from the youth system. He made just three Premiership appearances for Walter Smith's side in 2000–01 before Royle paid £3 million for him to travel the short distance to Manchester City.

The defender gradually worked his way into the City first team and was an ever-present in the side for the second half of the season. He won 76% of his tackles and made 216 clearances in total as he forged a partnership with Steve Howey.

Dublin-born Dunne also managed to impress Republic of Ireland boss Mick McCarthy with his performances at international level and is now a regular starter in the Irish side after breaking into the team in April 2000.

Solid: Richard Dunne

APPEARANCES	
Start (sub)	27(1)
Minutes on pitch	2407
GOAL ATTEMPTS	
Goals	0
DEFENDING	
Blocks	42
Shots cleared off line	0
Headed clearances	130
Other clearances	86
Interceptions	9
Last man saving tackles	2
Tackles won	61
Tackles won %	76%
PASSING	
Passing accuracy own half	76%
Passing accuracy opp half	53%
DISCIPLINE	
Fouls	43
Fouls in danger area	11
Yellow cards	4
Red cards	0

SEE PAGES 138 & 208 FOR FULL STATS

81% Kieron Dyer's pass completion rate was better

Kieron DYER • 8
NEWCASTLE UNITED • BORN: 29.12.78

Kieron Dyer's off-the-field antics kept the tabloid readers regularly amused, but his displays on the pitch were equally worthy of attention. Certainly Manchester United and Leeds United kept close tabs on the England man, who is revelling in the Premiership spotlight.

Unfortunately for Dyer, injury trouble once again brought a premature end to his season and ruined his opportunity to impress Sven-Göran Eriksson. Dyer's strength, pace and skill are bound to catch the Swede's eye sooner or later, though, as is the former Ipswich player's adaptability.

A recognised midfielder, Dyer can play in defence too and also spent a period up front for the Magpies during 2000–01.

He scored five goals, created a further five and doubtless would have helped himself to more had his season not ended in February. Dyer showed fantastic awareness and passing ability, finding team-mates with 81% of his 1,023 passes and was also very strong in the tackle, winning 90% of all challenges.

APPEARANCES	
Start (sub)	25(1)
Minutes on pitch	2216
GOAL ATTEMPTS	
Goals	5
Shots on target	15
Shooting accuracy	43%
Goals/shots ratio	14%
PASSING	
Goal assists	5
Passes in opp half	722
Passing accuracy in opp half	78%
Crosses	65
Crossing accuracy	28%
DRIBBLING	
Dribbles & runs	149
Dribble completion	70%
Corners forced	29
DISCIPLINE	
Fouls	28
Yellow cards	0
Red cards	1
SEE PAGE 250 FOR FULL STATS	

High-flier: Kieron Dyer

than any player's outside of the top six clubs

AM Darren EADIE • 9
LEICESTER CITY • BORN: 10.6.75

Despite becoming Leicester's £3 million record signing back in December 1999, Darren Eadie has so far failed to live up to the wave of hype which greeted his arrival.

His first season was interrupted by injury and he has since struggled to stay fit for long enough to put a consistent run of form together.

Nevertheless, the 2000-01 season started brightly enough for the former England Under-21 star.

He notched the Foxes' first goal of the season in the 1–0 win at Upton Park, but did not strike again until the 3–0 victory over Middlesbrough in mid-November, when he ventured on as a substitute.

Eadie averaged a shot on target every two appearances and, with Leicester struggling to score during the latter stages of the campaign, he was always going to find it hard to maintain a place in the starting XI.

However, if he can put his injury problems behind him, Eadie is talented enough to be a success at Filbert Street.

APPEARANCES	
Start (sub)	16(8)
Minutes on pitch	1458
GOAL ATTEMPTS	
Goals	2
Shots on target	12
Shooting accuracy	57%
Goals/shots ratio	10%
PASSING	
Goal assists	1
Passes in opp half	253
Passing accuracy in opp half	69%
Crosses	46
Crossing accuracy	17%
DRIBBLING	
Dribbles & runs	76
Dribble completion	66%
Corners forced	12
DISCIPLINE	
Fouls	24
Yellow cards	4
Red cards	0

SEE PAGE 180 FOR FULL STATS

FB Richard EDGHILL • 3
MANCHESTER CITY • BORN: 23.9.74

APPEARANCES	
Start (sub)	6(0)
Minutes on pitch	495
GOAL ATTEMPTS	
Goals	0
PASSING & CROSSING	
Goal assists	0
Passing	222
Passing accuracy	67%
Crosses	13
Crossing accuracy	15%
DEFENDING	
Tackles	13
Tackles won %	85%
Blocks	3
Interceptions	1
Clearances	18
Shots cleared off line	0
DISCIPLINE	
Fouls	10
Yellow cards	1
Red cards	0

SEE PAGE 208 FOR FULL STATS

Within a week, the dream of playing in the Premiership had turned into a nightmare for Richard Edghill.

Having led the Citizens to promotion just months before, the demoralised defender was stripped of the captaincy and dropped indefinitely after scoring an own goal and being jeered by the City faithful in the 2–1 home defeat against Coventry.

A loan move to Birmingham ensued before the full-back burst back into the City first team, ironically at Highfield Road. He maintained his place for the following fixture, but a 4–0 drubbing by a rampant Leeds United saw Edghill return to the Maine Road wilderness.

He appeared one final time in the end-of-season clash with Chelsea and was again on the losing side.

The appointment of Kevin Keegan to the Maine Road hot-seat gives Edghill a chance to prove himself to a new manager, but it is still likely that his time at City is drawing to a close.

For more information visit our website:

EDU • 17
ARSENAL • BORN: 15.5.78

E

Arsène Wenger's persistent attempts to sign Edu finally paid off in January 2001. The Brazilian midfielder had been expected to finalise his move to Highbury in August 2000, but he was denied access to the country upon arrival at Heathrow airport after his passport was proved to be forged.

There were yet further problems ahead for Edu, though. He endured heartache on his Gunners debut when, after coming on as a second-half substitute against Leicester, he limped off after just 16 minutes. And in only Edu's second start for the club he put past his own 'keeper, helping Middlesbrough to an unlikely 3–0 win at Highbury.

In the few appearances Edu did make in 2000–01, he completed 79% of his passes, and showed glimpses of the quality which prompted Arsenal to sign him. But he will have to improve his efforts if he is to convince Wenger that he is the man to finally banish the ghost of Emmanuel Petit from Highbury's marble halls and prove a worthy successor to the Frenchman.

APPEARANCES	
Start (sub)	2(3)
Minutes on pitch	171
GOAL ATTEMPTS	
Goals	0
Shots on target	1
Shooting accuracy	33%
PASSING & CROSSING	
Goal assists	0
Passes in opp half	87
Passing accuracy in opp half	76%
Successful crosses	0
Cross completion	0%
DEFENDING	
Interceptions	1
Clearances	3
Tackles	14
Tackles won %	57%
DISCIPLINE	
Fouls	7
Yellow cards	0
Red cards	0
SEE PAGE 40 FOR FULL STATS	

 Marc EDWORTHY • 2
COVENTRY CITY • BORN: 24.12.72

APPEARANCES	
Start (sub)	18(6)
Minutes on pitch	1805
GOAL ATTEMPTS	
Goals	1
PASSING & CROSSING	
Goal assists	0
Passing	688
Passing accuracy	68%
Crosses	45
Crossing accuracy	11%
DEFENDING	
Tackles	44
Tackles won %	84%
Blocks	15
Interceptions	7
Clearances	66
Shots cleared off line	0
DISCIPLINE	
Fouls	27
Yellow cards	1
Red cards	0
SEE PAGE 110 FOR FULL STATS	

As part of a Coventry defence which shipped a staggering total of 63 goals in the 2000–01 campaign, Marc Edworthy is unlikely to look back on the season as one of his most enjoyable.

Edworthy contributed just 44 tackles as the Sky Blues slid towards relegation to the first division – fewer than any of Coventry's other regular defenders managed. The former Plymouth and Crystal Palace player also endured his share of fitness problems and was consequently forced to the fringes of the first team in the final months of 2000–01.

But he did gain some measure of personal satisfaction when scoring his first goal for the Sky Blues – a powerful effort from long range which helped clinch a 1–1 draw with Manchester City on New Year's Day.

Moreover, Edworthy's experience in winning promotion to the Premiership with Crystal Palace in 1997 could prove invaluable in 2001–02 as Gordon Strachan's side attempt to bounce back to the top flight at the first attempt.

Ugo EHIOGU • 17
MIDDLESBROUGH • BORN: 3.11.72

Ugo Ehiogu is known to enjoy wheeling and dealing in the financial markets. But even his head for numbers struggled to bring about the move away from Aston Villa he desired, after former club West Brom claimed that they would be owed a large slice of any transfer fee involved. However, after much wrangling from all parties concerned, Ehiogu finally got the move he desired in October 2000 when Middlesbrough snapped him up in an £8 million deal.

Although the powerful defender was then injured just five minutes into his Boro debut and kept out of action for a month, there can be no doubt that Ehiogu is far happier on Teesside.

Ehiogu finished the 2000–01 season as Middlesbrough's fourth-highest scorer with three goals – having netted with an excellent 27% of his shots – and was a pivotal figure in the club's successful fight against relegation. Ehiogu then took his goalscoring form to the international stage, heading a goal on his England comeback against Spain.

APPEARANCES	
Start (sub)	22(1)
Minutes on pitch	1953
GOAL ATTEMPTS	
Goals	3
DEFENDING	
Blocks	30
Shots cleared off line	0
Headed clearances	141
Other clearances	87
Interceptions	9
Last man saving tackles	1
Tackles won	41
Tackles won %	77%
PASSING	
Passing accuracy own half	82%
Passing accuracy opp half	56%
DISCIPLINE	
Fouls	27
Fouls in danger area	11
Yellow cards	2
Red cards	1

SEE PAGES 54 & 236 FOR FULL STATS

Tahar EL KHALEJ • 20
SOUTHAMPTON • BORN: 16.9.68

APPEARANCES	
Start (sub)	25(7)
Minutes on pitch	2329
GOAL ATTEMPTS	
Goals	1
Shots on target	12
Shooting accuracy	43%
PASSING & CROSSING	
Goal assists	0
Passes in opp half	322
Passing accuracy in opp half	63%
Successful crosses	5
Cross completion	15%
DEFENDING	
Interceptions	5
Clearances	163
Tackles	57
Tackles won %	75%
DISCIPLINE	
Fouls	58
Yellow cards	7
Red cards	0

SEE PAGE 264 FOR FULL STATS

Moroccan international Tahar El Khalej arrived at Southampton from Benfica with the reputation of being one of the most physical players in Portuguese football.

But since joining the Saints, El Khalej has been more noticeable for his sound distribution and tendency to venture forward from the back than his tenacity. Indeed, with team-mates Dean Richards and Claus Lundekvam the preferred centre-back pairing at the club, El Khalej has sometimes been deployed as a holding midfielder, a role to which he is clearly well-suited.

He was accurate with 70% of his passes in 2000–01 – better than any other defender at the club.

He also posed a threat at set-pieces, heading 14 efforts at goal – the third-highest total at Southampton – and scored with one to get the Saints back in the game in the thrilling 3–3 draw with Liverpool in August at The Dell.

El Khalej will hope that he has done enough to cement his future at Southampton.

2 Matt Elliott had his worst season in front of goal

CB — Matt ELLIOTT • 18
LEICESTER CITY • BORN: 1.11.68

Matt Elliott captained Leicester to their best-ever start to a top-flight season in 2000–01, as the Foxes stayed unbeaten in their opening eight league games. But after their promising start Elliott's and Leicester's performances began to fade rapidly. The club dropped swiftly into mid-table mediocrity and in December the media slammed Elliott after video evidence appeared to show him elbowing Coventry's Craig Bellamy.

It was the third such incident Elliott had been involved in over the past two years, after knocking over Michael Owen in 1999–2000 and being sent off for Scotland against the Faroe Islands in the same season.

Elliott did recover from that setback to block more shots and crosses than anyone bar Claus Lundekvam in 2000–01, and he also made the fourth-highest total of clearances in the Premiership.

A big Filbert Street favourite, Elliott has been linked with a move to Celtic, but Peter Taylor will fight hard to keep his star defender in Leicester.

APPEARANCES	
Start (sub)	34(0)
Minutes on pitch	2970
GOAL ATTEMPTS	
Goals	2
DEFENDING	
Blocks	54
Shots cleared off line	1
Headed clearances	255
Other clearances	111
Interceptions	9
Last man saving tackles	0
Tackles won	33
Tackles won %	63%
PASSING	
Passing accuracy own half	86%
Passing accuracy opp half	65%
DISCIPLINE	
Fouls	39
Fouls in danger area	16
Yellow cards	3
Red cards	0
SEE PAGE 180 FOR FULL STATS	

CB — Steve ELLIOTT • 19
DERBY COUNTY • BORN: 29.10.78

APPEARANCES	
Start (sub)	5(1)
Minutes on pitch	443
GOAL ATTEMPTS	
Goals	0
DEFENDING	
Blocks	7
Shots cleared off line	0
Headed clearances	30
Other clearances	17
Interceptions	1
Last man saving tackles	0
Tackles won	8
Tackles won %	73%
PASSING	
Passing accuracy own half	73%
Passing accuracy opp half	44%
DISCIPLINE	
Fouls	8
Fouls in danger area	1
Yellow cards	1
Red cards	0
SEE PAGES 124 FOR FULL STATS	

Steve Elliott was named Derby's Young Player of the Year for the 1999–2000 season. But the signing of several defensive players at Pride Park, as well as the emergence of fellow youth team graduate Chris Riggott, resulted in far fewer opportunities for the youngster in 2000–01.

Elliott featured in five of the Rams' opening six Premiership games, but with the side failing to win any of those matches, the young defender was relegated to the reserves and made just one further appearance.

Part of the reason why Elliott was passed over in the latter stages of the 2000–01 campaign was that his distribution lacked precision. He found a colleague with just 59% of his passes, which was the worst proportion of any of Derby's central defenders.

However, Elliott remains in manager Jim Smith's plans for the future and his defensive contribution of 47 clearances and seven blocks indicates that he could well have a more prominent role to play at Derby County in 2001–02.

since joining Leicester, scoring just two goals

S — Kevin ELLISON • 35
LEICESTER CITY • BORN: 23.2.79

Versatile forward Kevin Ellison became Peter Taylor's 11th signing at Leicester when he joined from Unibond Premier League club Altrincham in February 2001.

Ellison had scored 16 times for the non-league side in 1999–2000, despite spending much of his time out on the left wing. But his healthy goalscoring record was still not enough to prevent the club's relegation from the Nationwide Conference.

The young forward did not have the best of luck following his £50,000 move to Leicester either. Ellison made his debut in March 2001, coming on as a substitute in front of 67,000 at Old Trafford, with the Foxes holding Manchester United 0–0 and only six minutes remaining. However, the Red Devils scored two late goals and Ellison did not feature for Taylor's side again.

During those six minutes, Ellison failed to touch the ball, with his only contribution being a foul on Paul Scholes.

SEE PAGE 180 FOR FULL STATS

AM — Matthew ETHERINGTON • 28
TOTTENHAM HOTSPUR • BORN: 14.8.81

When David Ginola left Tottenham in the summer of 2000, few fans felt that the club had a ready-made replacement in Matthew Etherington, but the youngster could yet go on to surprise a few people.

Etherington had starred in Spurs' last away game of the 1999–2000 season at Old Trafford.

Surprisingly, though, the former Peterborough United player failed to start a single Premiership match before May, when he featured, ironically enough, against Manchester United on the last day of the 2000–01 campaign.

Tottenham ran out 3–1 winners in that match, with Etherington impressing in an attacking role. He whipped in six crosses – more than any other Spurs player – and was accurate with a healthy 70% of his passes.

Spurs' new manager Glenn Hoddle has already stated that he feels Etherington has a bright future, so the youngster seems sure to feature more in 2001–2002.

SEE PAGE 292 FOR FULL STATS

AM — Stefano ERANIO • 20
DERBY COUNTY • BORN: 29.12.66

Stefano Eranio was arguably Derby's most influential performer during the final months of the 2000–01 season, as the club successfully steered clear of relegation.

So it is somewhat perplexing that he is going back to Italy without a club to sign for!

Derby's loss came about because of their reluctance to renew Eranio's contract while relegation was still a possibility.

Consequently, the former Italian international made the decision to go back to his homeland in January, attempting to spare his family uncertainty over the future.

Pride Park will not be the same without Eranio. He set up a club-high total of six goals in 2000–01.

Moreover, his strike against Leicester in April was instrumental in ensuring the team's Premiership status.

Eranio was given a heart-warming send-off by the Derby fans.

And a similarly-grateful Jim Smith declared that a scouting role was his for the taking should he want to link up with the club in the future.

The affection that Eranio clearly holds for the club and the admiration they have for him may see him return in this capacity in the future.

APPEARANCES	
Start (sub)	25(3)
Minutes on pitch	1858
GOAL ATTEMPTS	
Goals	2
Shots on target	3
Shooting accuracy	33%
Goals/shots ratio	22%
PASSING	
Goal assists	6
Passes in opp half	585
Passing accuracy in opp half	74%
Crosses	50
Crossing accuracy	36%
DRIBBLING	
Dribbles & runs	84
Dribble completion	71%
Corners forced	10
DISCIPLINE	
Fouls	40
Yellow cards	7
Red cards	0

SEE PAGE 124 FOR FULL STATS

For more information visit our website:

M

John EUSTACE • 15
COVENTRY CITY • BORN: 3.11.79

When Gary McAllister moved from Coventry to Liverpool in the summer of 2000, Sky Blues boss Gordon Strachan challenged young midfielder John Eustace to assume the former Scotland international's mantle.

Eustace certainly took on much of the defensive responsibility at Highfield Road in 2000–01, going in for 94 tackles – more than any other player at the club. And he also started the 2000–01 campaign in good goalscoring form, netting in games against Middlesbrough and Tottenham.

But unfortunately Eustace was unable to provide the creative spark the Sky Blues needed in McAllister's absence. The young Scot was accurate with just 63% of his passes – well below the Premiership average - and the club's lack of invention in midfield played a large part in their slide towards relegation.

However, Eustace's drive and determination remain important to the Sky Blues' fortunes and he will surely be vital to the club in 2001–02, as they look to bounce back to the Premiership.

APPEARANCES	
Start (sub)	22(10)
Minutes on pitch	2108
GOAL ATTEMPTS	
Goals	2
Shots on target	13
Shooting accuracy	35%
PASSING & CROSSING	
Goal assists	1
Passes in opp half	405
Passing accuracy in opp half	53%
Successful crosses	5
Cross completion	22%
DEFENDING	
Interceptions	5
Clearances	27
Tackles	94
Tackles won %	72%
DISCIPLINE	
Fouls	56
Yellow cards	11
Red cards	0

SEE PAGE 110 FOR FULL STATS

 **AM**

Gareth EVANS • 31
LEEDS UNITED • BORN: 15.2.81

Leeds United's injury crisis at the start of the 2000–01 campaign prompted David O'Leary to promote Gareth Evans to the first-team squad. The youngster had come through the youth academy at Elland Road alongside Alan Smith, and was expected to make an impact on the left of midfield.

Evans made his debut in August, in front of 45,000 of 1860 Munich's famously-hostile fans at the Olympic Stadium. And he acquitted himself well, helping Leeds win the match 1–0 to seal the club's progress to the group stages of the Champions League.

The Rothwell-born midfielder made his Premiership bow the following month against Manchester City. Evans showed composure on the ball, but he failed to make another appearance during the rest of the 2000–01 season. And with Australian star Harry Kewell ahead of him in the pecking order, Evans may struggle to make a significant impression at Elland Road.

SEE PAGE 166 FOR FULL STATS

CB

Ian EVATT • 29
DERBY COUNTY • BORN: 19.11.81

With Derby's Premiership status already secured, manager Jim Smith took the opportunity to blood academy graduate Ian Evatt during the last game of the 2000–01 campaign against Ipswich.

Evatt had impressed for the Rams' youth team since joining the club as a trainee and was promoted to the first team squad ahead of the 1999–2000 season at the age of 17. By that stage, the club had already indicated how highly they rated him, letting him train with the first team and naming him as the Under-19s' captain.

When it came to the big day, Evatt showed no sign of nerves. Indeed, his composure in the 12 minutes he was afforded bodes extremely well for the future. Evatt was accurate with seven passes, which equated to an 88% passing accuracy.

Evatt showed plenty of tenacity and may be given further opportunities to impress in the near future.

SEE PAGE 124 FOR FULL STATS

Les FERDINAND • 9
TOTTENHAM HOTSPUR • BORN: 18.12.66

Despite his advancing years, Les Ferdinand was involved in the majority of Spurs' fixtures in the 2000–01 Premiership campaign.

The north London club finished in the bottom half of the table and suffered from inconsistent form, but Ferdinand was still able to convert 10 chances, which made him the club's top scorer, one ahead of strike partner Sergei Rebrov.

The highlight of Ferdinand's season came against Leicester at White Hart Lane, when he netted all of his side's goals in a 3–0 win over the Foxes.

Off the pitch, however, the former England striker's clean-cut reputation took a nosedive when he admitted to "helping a few people over the wall" during the notorious wrecking of the *Blue Peter* garden at BBC Television Centre in 1983.

It will be interesting to see if he can dig in and hold on to his first-team place during 2001–02 now that Teddy Sheringham has returned to the club following his four years at Manchester United.

APPEARANCES	
Start (sub)	25(3)
Minutes on pitch	2073
GOAL ATTEMPTS	
Goals inside box	8
Goals outside box	2
Minutes per goal scored	207
Goals/shots ratio	24%
SHOOTING	
Shots on target inside box	17
Shots on target outside box	4
Shooting accuracy	50%
PASSING	
Goal assists	1
Key passes	28
Passing accuracy in opp half	65%
DISCIPLINE	
Fouls committed	53
Fouls won	49
Offside	33
Yellow cards	4
Red cards	0
SEE PAGE 292 FOR FULL STATS	

Rio FERDINAND • 29
LEEDS UNITED • BORN: 7.11.78

APPEARANCES	
Start (sub)	35(0)
Minutes on pitch	3051
GOAL ATTEMPTS	
Goals	2
DEFENDING	
Blocks	30
Shots cleared off line	1
Headed clearances	233
Other clearances	132
Interceptions	22
Last man saving tackles	0
Tackles won	60
Tackles won %	74%
PASSING	
Passing accuracy own half	75%
Passing accuracy opp half	57%
DISCIPLINE	
Fouls	27
Fouls in danger area	7
Yellow cards	0
Red cards	0
SEE PAGES 166 & 306 FOR FULL STATS	

West Ham finally conceded defeat in their quest to hold on to Rio Ferdinand in November, when an £18 million fee – a world record for a defender – was agreed with Leeds for the England international's services.

Ferdinand did his best to justify the size of the deal by proving himself against Europe's élite in Leeds' Champions League run and held down a regular place at international level. Following Tony Adams's retirement from international football, Ferdinand became Sven-Göran Eriksson's first choice to play alongside Sol Campbell at the heart of the England defence.

In the Premiership, almost three-quarters of the 81 tackles Ferdinand attempted were successful and he was not booked during the 2000–01 campaign, a fantastic achievement considering he started 35 league matches.

Another indication as to just how highly Ferdinand is rated at Elland Road was when David O'Leary awarded the Peckham-born defender the Leeds captaincy in place of the injured Lucas Radebe.

0 Duncan Ferguson scored six goals,

Duncan FERGUSON • 24
EVERTON • BORN: 27.12.71

Everton striker Duncan Ferguson, no stranger to lengthy spells on the treatment table, was ruled out through injury for much of the 2000–01 season. But one ailment was acquired in heroic circumstances.

The Scotsman discovered burglars in his home following Everton's third-round win in the FA Cup at Watford. Ferguson fought the intruders off and was praised by the police for behaving "bravely and responsibly".

One of the offenders was hospitalised with head injuries, but Ferguson also had to go to casualty, having injured his hand in the fracas.

Ferguson rejoined the Toffees from Newcastle on the eve of the 2000–01 campaign and scored the first goals of his second spell on Merseyside in a 3–0 win over Charlton Athletic.

In nine Premiership starts and three substitute appearances, Ferguson packed a punch with a total of six goals, an impressive ratio considering the stop-start nature of his season — although surprisingly none of his strikes came from headers.

APPEARANCES	
Start (sub)	9(3)
Minutes on pitch	795
GOAL ATTEMPTS	
Goals inside box	6
Goals outside box	0
Minutes per goal scored	133
Goals/shots ratio	18%
SHOOTING	
Shots on target inside box	20
Shots on target outside box	2
Shooting accuracy	65%
PASSING	
Goal assists	2
Key passes	17
Passing accuracy in opp half	64%
DISCIPLINE	
Fouls committed	41
Fouls won	31
Offside	6
Yellow cards	2
Red cards	0
SEE PAGE 138 FOR FULL STATS	

Albert FERRER • 17
CHELSEA • BORN: 6.6.70

APPEARANCES	
Start (sub)	12(2)
Minutes on pitch	1007
GOAL ATTEMPTS	
Goals	0
PASSING & CROSSING	
Goal assists	0
Passing	475
Passing accuracy	74%
Crosses	26
Crossing accuracy	19%
DEFENDING	
Tackles	36
Tackles won %	78%
Blocks	6
Interceptions	4
Clearances	29
Shots cleared off line	0
DISCIPLINE	
Fouls	19
Yellow cards	2
Red cards	0
SEE PAGE 96 FOR FULL STATS	

Albert Ferrer will not remember the 2000–01 season with any great fondness. The Spanish international struggled to play a great deal of first-team football because of an ankle injury and the consistent form of Mario Melchiot.

When fit and selected Ferrer still showed touches of class, completing 74% of the 475 Premiership passes he attempted. Despite his injury problems, the former Barcelona full-back did not shirk his defensive responsibilities. Strong in the challenge, he won an above-average 78% of the 36 tackles he went in for.

His longest run in the side came between New Year's Day and mid-March. In this period he made seven starts and two substitute appearances.

Now that Dutchman Melchiot has made the right-back slot his own, Ferrer may not hold down a place in the 2001–02 season.

If that is the case, his reputation should ensure that there is no shortage of clubs, both in England and abroad, looking to sign him up.

but none were from headers

Gianluca FESTA • 5
MIDDLESBROUGH • BORN: 15.3.69

When Middlesbrough splashed out a club-record £8 million on Aston Villa defender Ugo Ehiogu, it appeared Gianluca Festa's days at The Riverside were numbered.

The Italian feared he would be unable to hold down a regular place in Bryan Robson's starting line-up and in November asked for a transfer, a request which was granted by his manager.

Festa's availability alerted a number of clubs, notably West Ham – who were looking to replace Rio Ferdinand – and Chelsea, whose French centre-back Frank Leboeuf had been linked with a move to Monaco.

The proposed switch to Stamford Bridge collapsed, however, so in the end Festa spent the whole of the 2000–01 season at The Riverside, where he won a superb 85% of his 65 challenges.

Once Terry Venables took over team affairs, the former Inter Milan stopper was used in all but two matches until a groin injury sustained against Sunderland in April put paid to his season.

APPEARANCES	
Start (sub)	21(4)
Minutes on pitch	1900
GOAL ATTEMPTS	
Goals	2
DEFENDING	
Blocks	17
Shots cleared off line	0
Headed clearances	111
Other clearances	60
Interceptions	11
Last man saving tackles	1
Tackles won	55
Tackles won %	85%
PASSING	
Passing accuracy own half	80%
Passing accuracy opp half	58%
DISCIPLINE	
Fouls	27
Fouls in danger area	11
Yellow cards	3
Red cards	0

SEE PAGE 236 FOR FULL STATS

Mark FISH • 36
CHARLTON ATHLETIC • BORN: 14.3.74

APPEARANCES	
Start (sub)	24(0)
Minutes on pitch	2030
GOAL ATTEMPTS	
Goals	1
DEFENDING	
Blocks	45
Shots cleared off line	2
Headed clearances	147
Other clearances	85
Interceptions	8
Last man saving tackles	2
Tackles won	58
Tackles won %	74%
PASSING	
Passing accuracy own half	82%
Passing accuracy opp half	63%
DISCIPLINE	
Fouls	21
Fouls in danger area	3
Yellow cards	0
Red cards	0

SEE PAGE 82 FOR FULL STATS

Widely regarded as one of the best defenders in Division One, Mark Fish was signed by Alan Curbishley in November 2000 to bolster the Addicks' back-line.

The South African international had been restless at Bolton and wanted to return to the Premiership, which is where Wanderers were when he joined them in 1998.

Once he had arrived at The Valley, Fish was a regular in Curbishley's successful Charlton side which finished the season in ninth place, way above where many pundits thought they would end up following their 1999–2000 promotion.

Fish showed his versatility by playing for some of the campaign at right-back, rather than his more familiar role in the centre of defence. He managed to clear the ball from danger on 232 occasions, a tally which of all the players in Curbishley's squad only Richard Rufus could better. In addition, the former Lazio man was not booked all term, a fine achievement considering the number of appearances he made.

For more information visit our website:

Curtis FLEMING • 2
MIDDLESBROUGH • BORN: 8.10.68

Middlesbrough have suffered many ups and downs in the past decade or so and one man who has been there throughout is Curtis Fleming.

The long-serving Irish international played a significant role for Boro during the 2000–01 season, starting 29 Premiership fixtures and coming on once as a substitute.

Fleming completed the majority of his passes and found a team-mate with 30% of his centres, a contribution which helped Boro become the Premiership's most accurate crossers of the ball over the course of the 2000–01 campaign.

Opposition wingers certainly had to be on top form to get the better of Fleming. He attempted more challenges than any other member of the Boro defence and picked up only four Premiership cautions – some achievement, considering the amount of pressure he found himself under in his side's fight to stay up.

Mick McCarthy was certainly impressed – he recalled Fleming to his Ireland squad for the country's World Cup qualifiers against Cyprus and Andorra in March.

APPEARANCES	
Start (sub)	29(1)
Minutes on pitch	2505
GOAL ATTEMPTS	
Goals	0
PASSING & CROSSING	
Goal assists	1
Passing	990
Passing accuracy	73%
Crosses	44
Crossing accuracy	30%
DEFENDING	
Tackles	84
Tackles won %	77%
Blocks	20
Interceptions	5
Clearances	75
Shots cleared off line	1
DISCIPLINE	
Fouls	32
Yellow cards	4
Red cards	0

SEE PAGE 236 FOR FULL STATS

F

 Tore Andre FLO • 19
CHELSEA • BORN: 15.6.73

APPEARANCES	
Start (sub)	5(9)
Minutes on pitch	705
GOAL ATTEMPTS	
Goals inside box	3
Goals outside box	0
Minutes per goal scored	235
Goals/shots ratio	15%
SHOOTING	
Shots on target inside box	10
Shots on target outside box	2
Shooting accuracy	60%
PASSING	
Goal assists	3
Key passes	2
Passing accuracy in opp half	69%
DISCIPLINE	
Fouls committed	24
Fouls won	16
Offside	3
Yellow cards	1
Red cards	0

SEE PAGE 96 FOR FULL STATS

Tore Andre Flo scored 10 times in the Premiership for Chelsea during the 1999–2000 season, but this was not enough to stop Gianluca Vialli from shattering the club's record transfer fee to bring in Jimmy Floyd Hasselbaink for a cool £15 million in the summer of 2000.

With Eidur Gudjohnsen also added to the ranks, it became clear to Flo that his opportunities at first-team level were going to be few and far between. Although the Norwegian played a part in all of Chelsea's opening 14 Premiership fixtures, nine of these appearances were from the bench.

Even after his brace in the enthralling 3–3 draw with Manchester United, he found himself among the subs for the next league match at home to Liverpool.

The frustration resulted in Flo securing a £12 million move north to Scottish giants Glasgow Rangers in November. He netted 11 SPL goals, including one on his debut in his new club's 5–1 demolition of Old Firm rivals Celtic.

Tim FLOWERS • 1
LEICESTER CITY • BORN: 3.2.67

Tim Flowers' performances for Leicester earned him a place in Opta's England Team of the Season with an average Index score of 983 points over the course of the campaign and plaudits from the pundits.

Flowers, who was named Carling Player of the Month for September, suffered greatly from injuries throughout the 2000–01 season.

First of all, a shoulder injury forced him off during the Foxes' 3–0 win over Middlesbrough in November.

He returned to action a month later, but then had to go off at half-time against Bradford at Filbert Street. A thigh problem was diagnosed, which then ruled him out for more than three months.

Fortunately, the injury improved in this period of time without the need for an operation and he played in four of Leicester's final six Premiership matches of the season.

Simon Royce proved to be a more than capable deputy, however, so Flowers may struggle to remain first choice if his injury problems continue in 2001–02.

APPEARANCES	
Start (sub)	22(0)
Minutes on pitch	1876
SHOT STOPPING	
Goals conceded (inside box)	21
Goals conceded (outside box)	5
Minutes per goal conceded	72
Clean sheets	6
Saves (shots inside box)	45
Saves (shots outside box)	49
Saves/shots	78%
DISTRIBUTION	
Long kick %	46%
Throws/short passes %	82%
CATCHING	
Crosses caught	39
Crosses punched	17
Crosses dropped	2
Catch success %	95%
DISCIPLINE	
Yellow cards	0
Red cards	0
SEE PAGE 180 FOR FULL STATS	

Craig FORREST • 22
WEST HAM UNITED • BORN: 20.9.67

APPEARANCES	
Start (sub)	3(1)
Minutes on pitch	315
SHOT STOPPING	
Goals conceded (inside box)	3
Goals conceded (outside box)	3
Minutes per goal conceded	53
Clean sheets	0
Saves (shots inside box)	11
Saves (shots outside box)	4
Saves/shots	71%
DISTRIBUTION	
Long kick %	55%
Throws/short passes %	86%
CATCHING	
Crosses caught	7
Crosses punched	2
Crosses dropped	1
Catch success %	88%
DISCIPLINE	
Yellow cards	0
Red cards	0
SEE PAGE 306 FOR FULL STATS	

Craig Forrest was required to play only a small part in the Hammers' 2000–01 Premiership season because of the excellent form of West Ham number one Shaka Hislop.

He made his first appearance as a half-time substitute for Hislop in the home match against Sunderland.

He then remained between the sticks for the Hammers' next Premiership match against Charlton before Hislop returned for the goalless draw with Spurs.

This comeback was a little premature, though and Forrest was recalled for two more matches before he himself was injured and had to sit out the match with bottom club Bradford City.

Considering the lack of opportunities he had, the Canadian international did well to come in and show that he was still sharp after so long out.

He made a total of 15 saves and dealt with all but one of the crosses he tried came for.

Season 2001–02 is unlikely to see more regular action for Forrest.

53% Robbie Fowler scored 53% of all

Quinton FORTUNE • 25
MANCHESTER UNITED • BORN: 21.5.77

While continuing to be little more than a squad member at Old Trafford, Quinton Fortune benefitted from Sir Alex Ferguson's rotation policy. He provided able cover for Ryan Giggs when needed, although only once could he persuade his boss to use him in two consecutive Premiership matches.

In keeping with the rest of the side, Fortune maintained an excellent 80% pass completion rate during 2000–01. He also provided a different option in attack and claimed two of United's goals in the 6–0 stuffing of Bradford in September.

Fortune may have been able to feature more heavily for his club were it not for his constant international commitments.

He featured in almost all of South Africa's fixtures during the campaign, which has necessitated a great deal of travelling and many United games missed.

Manchester United put Fortune on the transfer list at the end of the campaign and, at a price of £3 million, there should be plenty of interest.

APPEARANCES	
Start (sub)	6(1)
Minutes on pitch	538
GOAL ATTEMPTS	
Goals	2
Shots on target	5
Shooting accuracy	45%
Goals/shots ratio	18%
PASSING	
Goal assists	0
Passes in opp half	142
Passing accuracy in opp half	75%
Crosses	25
Crossing accuracy	28%
DRIBBLING	
Dribbles & runs	33
Dribble completion	61%
Corners forced	5
DISCIPLINE	
Fouls	6
Yellow cards	0
Red cards	0
SEE PAGE 222 FOR FULL STATS	

F

 Robbie FOWLER • 9
LIVERPOOL • BORN: 9.4.75

APPEARANCES	
Start (sub)	15(12)
Minutes on pitch	1563
GOAL ATTEMPTS	
Goals inside box	7
Goals outside box	1
Minutes per goal scored	195
Goals/shots ratio	16%
SHOOTING	
Shots on target inside box	19
Shots on target outside box	6
Shooting accuracy	49%
PASSING	
Goal assists	3
Key passes	14
Passing accuracy in opp half	60%
DISCIPLINE	
Fouls committed	16
Fouls won	27
Offside	22
Yellow cards	0
Red cards	0
SEE PAGE 194 FOR FULL STATS	

The media could not persuade the Liverpool faithful that Robbie Fowler was serious about wanting to leave Anfield.

Despite having to spend more time on the sidelines, Fowler has continued to prove his worth for the Merseyside club and was particularly effective in the Worthington Cup; he hit six goals on the way to winning the trophy, netting in Cardiff.

Fowler failed to feature in just five Premiership matches since returning from injury in September.

And despite warming the bench more frequently than he is used to, he still managed to net eight times in the Premiership, underlining his immense talent as a natural goalscorer. He also made a vital contribution to Liverpool's UEFA Cup campaign, scoring the Reds' fourth goal against Alaves.

As long as he can maintain a good level of fitness, he is also set for a good run in the England side and he will be hoping to keep the competition for places up front for Liverpool strong.

his goals in the cup competitions

CB — Hayden FOXE • 6
WEST HAM UNITED • BORN: 23.6.77

There must have been times when Hayden Foxe thought he might just as well pack his bags and clear off back to Oz.

His dream move to West Ham was derailed more than once by Home Office work permit regulations, and there were times when the Hammers seemed set to pull the plug on the whole deal.

But Harry Redknapp promised Foxe that the club would honour the deal and he duly made his debut at the end of March. It was not to be a happy occasion, however, as the Hammers went down 2–0 to Everton.

Despite appearing in Australia's thrashings of Oceanic minnows American Samoa and Tonga – "They really needed him, didn't they?" said Redknapp, with not a little sarcasm – Foxe went on to appear five times in all for his new club, demonstrating a reasonably solid defensive game.

He will be hoping to feature heavily in the plans of the new manager during 2001–02, but he will have to improve on his poor distribution.

APPEARANCES	
Start (sub)	3(2)
Minutes on pitch	327
GOAL ATTEMPTS	
Goals	0
DEFENDING	
Blocks	6
Shots cleared off line	1
Headed clearances	22
Other clearances	15
Interceptions	2
Last man saving tackles	0
Tackles won	4
Tackles won %	57%
PASSING	
Passing accuracy own half	82%
Passing accuracy opp half	63%
DISCIPLINE	
Fouls	10
Fouls in danger area	1
Yellow cards	2
Red cards	0

SEE PAGE 306 FOR FULL STATS

M — Steffen FREUND • 4
TOTTENHAM HOTSPUR • BORN: 19.1.70

APPEARANCES	
Start (sub)	19(2)
Minutes on pitch	1689
GOAL ATTEMPTS	
Goals	0
Shots on target	4
Shooting accuracy	19%
PASSING & CROSSING	
Goal assists	0
Passes in opp half	442
Passing accuracy in opp half	75%
Successful crosses	7
Cross completion	25%
DEFENDING	
Interceptions	5
Clearances	20
Tackles	61
Tackles won %	70%
DISCIPLINE	
Fouls	31
Yellow cards	4
Red cards	0

SEE PAGE 292 FOR FULL STATS

Steffen Freund, like so many others, saw his season disrupted by injuries. When fully-fit, Freund managed two separate stretches of eight and nine games in the starting line-up, but aside from these runs the midfield star could only notch up a further four Premiership appearances.

Freund's passing continued to be the major factor in his game. The 31-year-old maintained an excellent 76% pass completion rate, bettered only by Tim Sherwood in the entire Spurs side.

His tally of 61 tackles in the centre for the club also shows how committed Freund is in the midfield.

Although Glenn Hoddle has assured Freund that he has a future at the club, it remains to be seen how much the German will feature in the new boss's plans, with fresh signings likely to increase competition for places.

Kaiserslautern have allegedly inquired about his availability and the lure of his homeland may well prove too strong to resist for the combative German.

For more information visit our website:

Kevin GALLACHER • 32
S
NEWCASTLE UNITED • BORN: 23.11.66

Kevin Gallacher produced some committed displays leading the line for Newcastle after the Magpies suffered some horrendous injury problems to attacking players such as Alan Shearer, Carl Cort and Kieron Dyer.

Although the former Blackburn striker could only equal his goalscoring tally from 1999–2000, he did manage to improve his shooting accuracy by two percentage points to 48%.

Gallacher was Bobby Robson's first signing for the club and the former England boss once described him as "the Scarlet Pimpernel". Robson said: "Defences seek him here, they seek him there..."

But despite his energetic performances, his poor finishing saw him chalk up the lowest goals-to-shots ratio of any striker at St James' Park. Nevertheless he did net a priceless equaliser for Scotland in their vital World Cup qualifier in Croatia last October.

Out of contract at the end of the season, the veteran forward should have no problems getting himself fixed up with a new club.

APPEARANCES	
Start (sub)	12(7)
Minutes on pitch	1104
GOAL ATTEMPTS	
Goals inside box	2
Goals outside box	0
Minutes per goal scored	552
Goals/shots ratio	6%
SHOOTING	
Shots on target inside box	11
Shots on target outside box	4
Shooting accuracy	48%
PASSING	
Goal assists	0
Key passes	10
Passing accuracy in opp half	65%
DISCIPLINE	
Fouls committed	21
Fouls won	20
Offside	5
Yellow cards	0
Red cards	0

SEE PAGE 250 FOR FULL STATS

F
G

Anthony GARDNER • 30
CB
TOTTENHAM HOTSPUR • BORN: 18.8.81

APPEARANCES	
Start (sub)	5(3)
Minutes on pitch	544
GOAL ATTEMPTS	
Goals	0
DEFENDING	
Blocks	4
Shots cleared off line	0
Headed clearances	36
Other clearances	18
Interceptions	2
Last man saving tackles	0
Tackles won	19
Tackles won %	66%
PASSING	
Passing accuracy own half	82%
Passing accuracy opp half	55%
DISCIPLINE	
Fouls	12
Fouls in danger area	5
Yellow cards	0
Red cards	0

SEE PAGE 292 FOR FULL STATS

Anthony Gardner made his Premiership debut in the latter stages of the 2000–01 campaign and immediately impressed with a series of assured displays that suggests he has a very bright future at White Hart Lane.

The defender, who chose a career in football ahead of athletics, had to wait until the end of March 2001 to make his full debut, at Highbury in the north London derby.

But his confident and mature display saw him unfazed by tackling the likes of Thierry Henry, and his performances in subsequent matches against strikers such as Andy Cole and Michael Owen were extremely promising for all Spurs supporters.

Obvious comparisons have been made between Gardner and former Spurs captain Sol Campbell. Like the England stopper, Gardner was migrated into a defensive position from being a striker.

It may even be argued that Gardner is more adept at bringing the ball out of defence, as his 71% passing ratio was more impressive than Campbell's during the 2000–01 season.

Paul GASCOIGNE • 18
EVERTON • BORN: 27.5.67

A series of niggling injuries ruined Paul Gascoigne's inaugural campaign at Goodison Park after some highly encouraging displays in the opening matches of the 2000–01 Premiership season.

The former Middlesbrough midfielder's success rate of 81% in dribbles and runs was higher than that of Ryan Giggs, Robert Pires and Kieron Dyer, among others.

And when Everton took a point at the then-unbeaten leaders Leicester City, Gazza played a significant part with 15 challenges – the most by a single Toffees player in an individual game.

But after having to withdraw from the televised home defeat to Aston Villa in November, the Geordie made just a couple of substitute appearances after undergoing a number of operations on his groin and thigh.

Having admitted that his brains are in his feet, it would be disappointing if Gascoigne was unable to show Evertonians the truly intelligent ball skills that he possesses in 2001–02.

APPEARANCES	
Start (sub)	10(4)
Minutes on pitch	888
GOAL ATTEMPTS	
Goals	0
Shots on target	5
Shooting accuracy	56%
PASSING & CROSSING	
Goal assists	1
Passes in opp half	310
Passing accuracy in opp half	72%
Successful crosses	20
Cross completion	33%
DEFENDING	
Interceptions	3
Clearances	5
Tackles	47
Tackles won %	72%
DISCIPLINE	
Fouls	19
Yellow cards	2
Red cards	0

SEE PAGE 138 FOR FULL STATS

Diego GAVILAN • 21
NEWCASTLE UNITED • BORN: 1.3.80

South American wideman Diego Gavilan has failed to make an impact on Tyneside, despite the fact that Bobby Robson splashed out £2 million for him in January 2000.

The Paraguayan youngster only donned the famous black-and-white stripes for five minutes in the Premiership when he replaced Nolberto Solano in the closing stages of the goalless draw with Chelsea. Apart from this, a cameo role in the Worthington Cup tie against Leyton Orient was the only other time that the man nicknamed "Sparrowhawk" got the chance to stalk his prey.

Gavilan's unproductive time at St James' Park was made even worse when the home office and the FA began to investigate the authenticity of his passport.

But fortunately for the former Cerro Porteno schemer there was nothing wrong with his entry papers, which was a good thing, as he may be needing them again soon given his lack of involvement so far.

SEE PAGE 251 FOR FULL STATS

Encouraging: Paul Gascoigne

5 Diego Gavilan was one of five

Jason GAVIN • 29
MIDDLESBROUGH • BORN: 14.3.80

CB

Jason Gavin forced his way back into the Middlesbrough team during the latter stages of the season after being omitted from an earlier squad in the 2000–01 season. Bryan Robson dropped him for the Teessiders' trip to Macclesfield in the Worthington Cup, citing disciplinary reasons for the Irishman's absence, and it took him another three months before he appeared for the first team again, replacing suspended defender Ugo Ehiogu for the visit of Charlton. Gavin's 15 successful tackles and clearance off the line showed his commitment to Boro's cause.

When Ehiogu retuned to the side, Gavin was drafted into a right-back position and made a number of vital clearances to break up opponents' attacks. The Dublin-born defender was rewarded when Republic of Ireland manager Mick McCarthy called up the Boro man into the senior squad.

After such an encouraging end to the season, Gavin will be chomping at the bit to increase his profile with some more solid performances in 2001–02.

APPEARANCES	
Start (sub)	10(4)
Minutes on pitch	1035
GOAL ATTEMPTS	
Goals	0
DEFENDING	
Blocks	11
Shots cleared off line	1
Headed clearances	47
Other clearances	33
Interceptions	3
Last man saving tackles	0
Tackles won	15
Tackles won %	63%
PASSING	
Passing accuracy own half	81%
Passing accuracy opp half	57%
DISCIPLINE	
Fouls	16
Fouls in danger area	5
Yellow cards	4
Red cards	0

SEE PAGE 236 FOR FULL STATS

G

Scot GEMMILL • 17
EVERTON • BORN: 2.1.71

M

APPEARANCES	
Start (sub)	25(3)
Minutes on pitch	2286
GOAL ATTEMPTS	
Goals	2
Shots on target	7
Shooting accuracy	41%
PASSING & CROSSING	
Goal assists	1
Passes in opp half	717
Passing accuracy in opp half	71%
Successful crosses	5
Cross completion	15%
DEFENDING	
Interceptions	18
Clearances	31
Tackles	70
Tackles won %	61%
DISCIPLINE	
Fouls	46
Yellow cards	7
Red cards	0

SEE PAGE 138 FOR FULL STATS

Everton midfielder Scot Gemmill established himself in the Toffees' team during the 2000–01 season and in the process forced his way back into the Scotland reckoning.

The former Nottingham Forest schemer benefited from the absence of Paul Gascoigne through injury and became an automatic choice for manager Walter Smith. Providing a key link between defence and attack, Gemmill made 828 successful passes: only Thomas Gravesen completed more accurate passes for the Toffees during 2000–01.

Ranked as Opta's eighth-most effective player at Goodison Park, he ignored rumours of a switch to Birmingham City to weigh in with a couple of vital goals, including a crucial strike in the crunch relegation clash at Coventry.

Although he was labelled "Mavis" by the supporters of former club Nottingham Forest for a lack of tenacity, he hardened his ways on Merseyside, winning 43 challenges.

One area in which Gemmill needs to improve is his discipline. After amassing seven cautions in 2000–01 he served a suspension in February.

South Americans on Newcastle's books

Paul GERRARD • 1
EVERTON • BORN: 22.1.73

Paul Gerrard was the grateful recipient of arguably the best example of good sportsmanship in the Premiership.

In the closing stages of the home match against West Ham in December, Gerrard was lying flat-out on the edge of his box after an accidental collision.

With the score poised at 1–1, temperamental Italian Paolo Di Canio had a golden opportunity to win the match. But instead of heading into an empty goal, he simply picked the ball up and the referee awarded a drop ball.

Gerrard's luck was extended even further. After the subsequent six-game absence for his injury he won back his place in the team ahead of Norwegian international Thomas Myhre, although Gerrard's 66% saves-to-shots ratio was actually inferior to that of his rival.

Walter Smith's faith in Gerrard was rewarded when he saved a penalty from Bradford City's Robbie Blake which helped the Toffees to secure their Premiership status in their penultimate home match of 2000–01.

APPEARANCES	
Start (sub)	32(0)
Minutes on pitch	2879
SHOT STOPPING	
Goals conceded (inside box)	39
Goals conceded (outside box)	13
Minutes per goal conceded	55
Clean sheets	5
Saves (shots inside box)	55
Saves (shots outside box)	44
Saves/shots	66%
DISTRIBUTION	
Long kick %	49%
Throws/short passes %	81%
CATCHING	
Crosses caught	45
Crosses punched	24
Crosses dropped	5
Catch success %	90%
DISCIPLINE	
Yellow cards	2
Red cards	0
SEE PAGE 138 FOR FULL STATS	

Steven GERRARD • 17
LIVERPOOL • BORN: 30.4.80

APPEARANCES	
Start (sub)	29(4)
Minutes on pitch	2529
GOAL ATTEMPTS	
Goals	7
Shots on target	23
Shooting accuracy	46%
PASSING & CROSSING	
Goal assists	2
Passes in opp half	936
Passing accuracy in opp half	65%
Successful crosses	17
Cross completion	20%
DEFENDING	
Interceptions	18
Clearances	63
Tackles	128
Tackles won %	69%
DISCIPLINE	
Fouls	49
Yellow cards	4
Red cards	1
SEE PAGE 194 FOR FULL STATS	

PFA Young Player of the Year Steven Gerrard won further individual honours when player performance analysts Opta ranked him as the best English midfielder in the Premiership for his all-action displays.

A die-hard Liverpool fan, the Scouse terrier only had ambitions to play for the Reds and his passion and commitment shines through.

Gerrard won 88 tackles in the Premiership – the highest tally at Anfield – and only Reds midfielder Dietmar Hamann played more successful passes than Gerrard's 1,066.

Persistent back problems threatened to ruin his season, but a full analysis of his lifestyle was conducted, including his driving position and diet, in a bid to cure his ailment.

The treatment appeared to work, as he helped Liverpool to glory on three fronts and entry to the Champions League. Barcelona were so impressed by Gerrard's performances against them that they even considered a bid – although it is highly unlikely that the Reds would consider selling one of their most prized assets.

For more information visit our website:

Kevin GIBBENS • 28
SOUTHAMPTON • BORN: 4.11.79

Southampton-born Kevin Gibbens had to make do with limited action during the 2000–01 season when Glenn Hoddle drafted him into the team as cover for veteran right-back Jason Dodd. He performed admirably in the absence of the skipper and was cool enough not to be over-awed by the task. He conceded only one foul and confidently ventured forward on plenty of occasions.

The local lad was given a chance to demonstrate his versatility when he was used in a more advanced role in the draw at Coventry in December, but he had to wait two months for his next appearance in the disappointing FA Cup defeat at Tranmere Rovers.

Gibbens did not feature after that defeat and may have to look elsewhere for regular action in 2001–02.

While he will have to work hard, the statistics suggest that he could be a useful squad player – wherever he ends up.

SEE PAGE 264 FOR FULL STATS

Ryan GIGGS • 11
MANCHESTER UNITED • BORN: 29.11.73

Flamboyant: Ryan Giggs

It is said that Ryan Giggs has a tropical fish-tank which runs down the entire length of his staircase in his luxury Cheshire home.

Whether he is an avid collector of tetras, gouramies or dottybacks we shall probably never know, but this ostentatious piece of home décor is matched only by the Welshman's flamboyance on the pitch.

Giggs netted five times in 2000–01, including an outrageous looping header against Coventry on the day the title was won.

He skated down the left on more than 200 occasions and was successful in evading a tackle two-thirds of the time.

The speedy winger did not quite reach the heights of the previous campaign – much like his team – but he did hook in 165 crosses and set up eight goals for his avaricious team-mates.

Giggs seems very happy and will not be angling for a move, having just signed a new contract that should see him end his career at Old Trafford and add to his ever-growing collection of medals.

APPEARANCES	
Start (sub)	24(7)
Minutes on pitch	2219
GOAL ATTEMPTS	
Goals	5
Shots on target	25
Shooting accuracy	56%
Goals/shots ratio	11%
PASSING	
Goal assists	8
Passes in opp half	630
Passing accuracy in opp half	63%
Crosses	165
Crossing accuracy	27%
DRIBBLING	
Dribbles & runs	234
Dribble completion	66%
Corners forced	24
DISCIPLINE	
Fouls	20
Yellow cards	1
Red cards	0

SEE PAGE 222 FOR FULL STATS

CB Phil GILCHRIST • 15
LEICESTER CITY • BORN: 25.8.73

The name of Phil Gilchrist was unfamiliar to many until his move to West Bromwich Albion became the biggest transfer deal completed on deadline day in March 2001.

His £500,000 arrival at the Hawthorns was crucial, as the former Oxford United stopper helped the Baggies to reach the Division One Play-Offs.

During his time at Filbert Street in 2000–01, he made only six Premiership starts, covering for the absence of Northern Ireland international Gerry Taggart.

Gilchrist linked well with former Us team-mate Matt Elliott at the heart of the Foxes' defence making a total of 87 clearances and recorded a better tackle success rate than Elliott.

The Teessider's last appearance for Leicester came at Old Trafford when he helped the team to deny the champions until they struck with two goals in the last few minutes of the game. Following Gilchrist's departure, the team lost eight of their nine remaining fixtures in the Premiership as injuries hit the squad.

APPEARANCES	
Start (sub)	6(6)
Minutes on pitch	629
GOAL ATTEMPTS	
Goals	0
DEFENDING	
Blocks	18
Shots cleared off line	0
Headed clearances	58
Other clearances	29
Interceptions	3
Last man saving tackles	0
Tackles won	12
Tackles won %	67%
PASSING	
Passing accuracy own half	67%
Passing accuracy opp half	46%
DISCIPLINE	
Fouls	8
Fouls in danger area	2
Yellow cards	1
Red cards	0
SEE PAGE 180 FOR FULL STATS	

AM David GINOLA • 14
ASTON VILLA • BORN: 25.1.67

APPEARANCES	
Start (sub)	14(13)
Minutes on pitch	1329
GOAL ATTEMPTS	
Goals	3
Shots on target	12
Shooting accuracy	52%
Goals/shots ratio	13%
PASSING	
Goal assists	4
Passes in opp half	406
Passing accuracy in opp half	69%
Crosses	158
Crossing accuracy	21%
DRIBBLING	
Dribbles & runs	174
Dribble completion	63%
Corners forced	20
DISCIPLINE	
Fouls	25
Yellow cards	7
Red cards	0
SEE PAGE 54 FOR FULL STATS	

In Aston Villa's final match of the 2000–01 season at Newcastle, David Ginola was hauled off before the break as his team were struggling at 2–0 down.

Having received a torrent of abuse from the hordes of Magpies supporters for his abrupt departure in 1997, it was a game which reflected the Frenchman's disappointing campaign with Villa.

Forced out of Tottenham by George Graham, Ginola joined Villa for £3 million to act as a provider for Dion Dublin, but his crossing accuracy of 21% was 10 percentage points down on his previous ratio in 1999–2000 and well below the league average.

Ginola and John Gregory had disagreements over the player's weight problems, his best position on the pitch, his unwillingness to track back after losing possession and his failure to move closer to the Midlands.

In fact, Ginola managed to play the full 90 minutes in just five matches, a statistic which underlines how little faith Gregory had in the enigmatic Frenchman.

48% of David Ginola's appearances

Shay GIVEN • 1
NEWCASTLE UNITED • BORN: 24.4.76

Shay Given handed in a transfer request in January 2001 after failing to earn a recall to the side when he had recovered from a thigh injury.

But he got a chance to reclaim his place in the Newcastle side when Steve Harper was ruled out of the trip to Leeds.

After a convincing display in a 3–1 win for the Magpies, Given kept his position between the sticks for the remainder of the season and withdrew his transfer request. The former Blackburn custodian's 65 stops from shots struck inside the penalty box was the fourth-highest tally in the Premiership.

But his rival Harper did boast a more impressive catch success rate than Given's 95% and Given came within one game of setting an unwanted record. The club had conceded a goal in 29 consecutive matches, equalling a 42-year-old sequence.

Fortunately for Given he managed to keep a clean sheet against Leicester City, a match which the Magpies won with a last-minute strike from Carl Cort.

APPEARANCES	
Start (sub)	34(0)
Minutes on pitch	3015
SHOT STOPPING	
Goals conceded (inside box)	38
Goals conceded (outside box)	4
Minutes per goal conceded	72
Clean sheets	7
Saves (shots inside box)	65
Saves (shots outside box)	36
Saves/shots	71%
DISTRIBUTION	
Long kick %	60%
Throws/short passes %	96%
CATCHING	
Crosses caught	61
Crosses punched	23
Crosses dropped	3
Catch success %	95%
DISCIPLINE	
Yellow cards	I
Red cards	0
SEE PAGE 251 FOR FULL STATS	

G

Stephen GLASS • 19
NEWCASTLE UNITED • BORN: 23.4.76

APPEARANCES	
Start (sub)	5(9)
Minutes on pitch	563
GOAL ATTEMPTS	
Goals	3
Shots on target	3
Shooting accuracy	38%
Goals/shots ratio	38%
PASSING	
Goal assists	0
Passes in opp half	154
Passing accuracy in opp half	61%
Crosses	66
Crossing accuracy	39%
DRIBBLING	
Dribbles & runs	27
Dribble completion	59%
Corners forced	8
DISCIPLINE	
Fouls	II
Yellow cards	2
Red cards	0
SEE PAGE 251 FOR FULL STATS	

Stephen Glass was rarely more than a bit-part player for Newcastle during 2000–01 thanks to a combination of injury and competition for places.

With the likes of Nolberto Solano and Gary Speed ahead of him in the pecking order, Glass was forced to spend more time on the bench than he would have liked, and as a result made just five starts.

Glass seems likely to leave Newcastle during the summer as expected, he turns down the offer of a one-year contract with the Magpies.

If Glass does decide to bring the curtain down on his days at St James' Park, there should be no shortage of clubs interested in him, with Coventry City and Rangers already keen on the midfielder.

With three goals in his short time on pitch, Glass clearly has plenty to offer, and Newcastle may be wise to offer him his desired two-year deal, as the Scottish international midfielder certainly has the potential to become a big name in the Premiership.

for Aston Villa were as a substitute

S **Shaun GOATER • 10**
MANCHESTER CITY • BORN: 25.2.70

One of the best crowd chants the Premiership has heard in many a season came up with Manchester City for the start of the 2000−01 campaign. Unfortunately, injury meant that City fans had to wait until October for their first chance to sing: "Feed the Goat and he will score."

At one stage in the season the Bermudan netted four times in six games to give City hope of avoiding the drop − and his 19% goals-to-shots ratio throughout the season certainly showed the rest of the side how it should be done.

Indeed, it was only a lack of chances created by his team-mates that meant his tally was so low.

City fans will be expecting Goater to be spearheading their assault on the First Division title during 2001−02, and he will be odds-on favourite to finish as the club's top scorer at the end of the campaign. Some Division One defences who hoped they had seen the last of him may be shuddering at the thought of his return.

APPEARANCES	
Start (sub)	20(6)
Minutes on pitch	1752

GOAL ATTEMPTS	
Goals inside box	5
Goals outside box	1
Minutes per goal scored	292
Goals/shots ratio	19%

SHOOTING	
Shots on target inside box	10
Shots on target outside box	5
Shooting accuracy	47%

PASSING	
Goal assists	0
Key passes	13
Passing accuracy in opp half	65%

DISCIPLINE	
Fouls committed	45
Fouls won	17
Offside	19
Yellow cards	1
Red cards	0

SEE PAGE 208 FOR FULL STATS

CB **Alain GOMA • 5**
NEWCASTLE UNITED • BORN: 5.10.72

APPEARANCES	
Start (sub)	18(1)
Minutes on pitch	1567

GOAL ATTEMPTS	
Goals	1

DEFENDING	
Blocks	11
Shots cleared off line	0
Headed clearances	115
Other clearances	24
Interceptions	10
Last man saving tackles	1
Tackles won	42
Tackles won %	78%

PASSING	
Passing accuracy own half	75%
Passing accuracy opp half	59%

DISCIPLINE	
Fouls	32
Fouls in danger area	11
Yellow cards	4
Red cards	0

SEE PAGE 251 FOR FULL STATS

Alain Goma's second season at Newcastle was a little happier than his first. The Frenchman was a regular at the heart of the Magpies' defence until February, winning an excellent 78% of his attempted challenges.

He also managed to clear his lines more frequently than any other Newcastle player with the exception of Aaron Hughes. But he never managed to settle on Tyneside and it quickly became clear that he wanted a move away from St James' Park.

Fulham came in with an offer of £4 million for Goma and Bobby Robson duly accepted the bid, saying: "The sad thing is that he has never been happy here and he's been looking to get a move. I agreed a long time ago that, if the right offer came along, we would part amicably and that would be it."

It now remains to be seen whether Goma can settle in London, or if he may be tempted by a return to his homeland.

With Fulham gracing the top flight, Premiership attackers have not seen the last of this tough tackler just yet

For more information visit our website:

Andy GORAM • 14
G MANCHESTER UNITED • BORN: 13.4.64

In a tale that will go down as part of football folklore, Andy Goram's reaction to receiving a phone call from Sir Alex Ferguson, asking him to help Manchester United out in their time of need, was priceless.

Assuming it was his friend and tormentor Ally McCoist on the other end of the line, Goram accordingly told Sir Alex to leave him alone – although the language used was rather more colourful.

Thankfully the United boss was in forgiving mood and Goram duly completed his unlikely move to Old Trafford. Although the 'keeper crisis at the club was not as bad as first feared, Goram still went on to make two starts for the club, although he was substituted in each.

The former Glasgow Rangers legend had enjoyed great success in Scotland but could not resist the chance to try his luck at the mighty Manchester United.

Unfortunately, Goram made only two saves and conceded four goals in just 125 minutes on the pitch.

APPEARANCES	
Start (sub)	2(0)
Minutes on pitch	125
SHOT STOPPING	
Goals conceded (inside box)	4
Goals conceded (outside box)	0
Minutes per goal conceded	31
Clean sheets	0
Saves (shots inside box)	1
Saves (shots outside box)	1
Saves/shots	33%
DISTRIBUTION	
Long kick %	50%
Throws/short passes %	83%
CATCHING	
Crosses caught	0
Crosses punched	1
Crosses dropped	0
Catch success %	0%
DISCIPLINE	
Yellow cards	0
Red cards	0
SEE PAGE 222 FOR FULL STATS	

Dean GORDON • 3
FB MIDDLESBROUGH • BORN: 10.2.73

APPEARANCES	
Start (sub)	12(8)
Minutes on pitch	1268
GOAL ATTEMPTS	
Goals	1
PASSING & CROSSING	
Goal assists	2
Passing	469
Passing accuracy	59%
Crosses	65
Crossing accuracy	25%
DEFENDING	
Tackles	43
Tackles won %	74%
Blocks	20
Interceptions	4
Clearances	39
Shots cleared off line	0
DISCIPLINE	
Fouls	15
Yellow cards	2
Red cards	0
SEE PAGE 236 FOR FULL STATS	

Having had his previous campaign ruined by injury, Dean Gordon's main concern during 2000–01 was trying to hold down a regular first-team place in the face of some stiff competition.

When he was fit, Gordon vied for the left-back slot with Keith O'Neill throughout the season and as a result was limited to just 12 starts for Boro. His tackle success rate was more impressive than that of his main competitor for the position, with 74% of opponents dispossessed.

The experienced pro has demanded talks with the club over the possibility of extending his stay at The Riverside. His contract is due to expire at the end of the 2001–02 season and, although Gordon has stated that he would be "delighted to stay", his future currently seems less than clear.

If Gordon can maintain his fitness and his form throughout the 2001–02 campaign, Boro may well find it hard to continue to ignore his claims for a permanent place in the starting XI for the Teessiders.

CB | Richard GOUGH • 4
EVERTON • BORN: 5.4.62

Veteran defender Richard Gough had a stop-start 2000–01 during which, just like the majority of his colleagues, he spent a fair amount of time on the treatment table at Goodison Park.

Following September's draw with Derby County, injury forced the former Scottish international to sit out the following 20 league games before returning for the draw with Middlesbrough at the end of January.

With his fitness clearly causing problems, the well-travelled defender decided that it was time to bring his career to a close. However, as if any proof were needed of his professionalism, Gough waited until the Toffeemen were safe from the drop before announcing his decision.

Having spent time in the USA with both Kansas City Wizards and San José Clash, Gough has decided to return to the land of the free, although it is unlikely that British football has seen the back of him for good, as he has declared he is open to all management offers.

APPEARANCES	
Start (sub)	9(0)
Minutes on pitch	664
GOAL ATTEMPTS	
Goals	0
DEFENDING	
Blocks	9
Shots cleared off line	0
Headed clearances	51
Other clearances	17
Interceptions	4
Last man saving tackles	0
Tackles won	13
Tackles won %	87%
PASSING	
Passing accuracy own half	82%
Passing accuracy opp half	55%
DISCIPLINE	
Fouls	11
Fouls in danger area	3
Yellow cards	1
Red cards	0

SEE PAGE 138 FOR FULL STATS

 S | Gareth GRANT • 24
BRADFORD CITY • BORN: 6.9.80

Although yet to figure regularly in the Bantams' first team, Gareth Grant gained valuable experience of top-flight football during 2000–01. In all, the young striker came off the bench five times in the Premiership – and although he managed just one attempt on goal, he will be pleased to have struck it on target.

Having been farmed out on loan twice in the previous campaign, Lincoln City obtained his services in February.

He made four appearances for the Red Imps, scoring in the Worthington Cup and generally making a nuisance of himself in Division Three.

Although the Bantams have been relegated, it may turn out to be a blessing in disguise for Grant, who should be able to demonstrate his talents more easily in the lower division. Jim Jefferies' attempts to trim the wage bill may also work in Grant's favour as he looks to make a name for himself.

SEE PAGE 68 FOR FULL STATS

Transatlantic: Richard Gough

Tony GRANT • 28
MANCHESTER CITY • BORN: 14.11.74

Tony Grant's miserable time at Manchester City continued throughout 2000–01, as Joe Royle refused to allow him more than five Premiership starts, as well as denying him the opportunity of finding himself another club.

Grant's only respite from a wretched season came when he was loaned out to West Bromwich Albion in December. He made five appearances for the Baggies before returning to Maine Road.

Grant will be able to console himself with the fact that he began to feature more heavily in his manager's plans during the second half of the campaign – each of his appearances in the starting line-up came during the last 11 games of the season.

But with Kevin Keegan certain to introduce new faces, the former Everton midfielder may find himself back on the fringes, unless he can impress from the start. His pass completion rate of 72% will certainly go some way to showing just what he can do if given the opportunity, although he was far more wayward in opposition territory.

APPEARANCES	
Start (sub)	5(5)
Minutes on pitch	472
GOAL ATTEMPTS	
Goals	0
Shots on target	1
Shooting accuracy	25%
PASSING & CROSSING	
Goal assists	0
Passes in opp half	152
Passing accuracy in opp half	63%
Successful crosses	2
Cross completion	50%
DEFENDING	
Interceptions	4
Clearances	1
Tackles	18
Tackles won %	50%
DISCIPLINE	
Fouls	9
Yellow cards	1
Red cards	0
SEE PAGE 208 FOR FULL STATS	

FB **Danny GRANVILLE • 36**
MANCHESTER CITY • BORN: 19.1.75

APPEARANCES	
Start (sub)	16(3)
Minutes on pitch	1313
GOAL ATTEMPTS	
Goals	0
PASSING & CROSSING	
Goal assists	1
Passing	454
Passing accuracy	63%
Crosses	43
Crossing accuracy	19%
DEFENDING	
Tackles	35
Tackles won %	77%
Blocks	15
Interceptions	3
Clearances	88
Shots cleared off line	1
DISCIPLINE	
Fouls	19
Yellow cards	2
Red cards	0
SEE PAGE 208 FOR FULL STATS	

The way in which the mind of a football manager works can be as big a mystery as the meaning of life.

It is a fair bet that Danny Granville believes this to be true, as following one solitary substitute appearance back in September the London-born defender had to wait until the last game of 2000 before getting another look-in.

But having been brought on as a substitute against Charlton, Joe Royle employed Granville in every remaining game of the campaign, awarding him a start in each of the last 14 Premiership fixtures.

Earlier in the season, Granville had been sent out on loan to Norwich City, for whom he made six appearances before returning to Maine Road. His tough-tackling style was certainly a bonus for the Canaries and Royle ultimately decided that the former Chelsea and Leeds man was City's best option at left-back.

Granville will be hoping that a new left-back is not on Kevin Keegan's wanted list.

Thomas GRAVESEN • 16
EVERTON • BORN: 11.3.76

No one can say that Thomas Gravesen did not give his all during his first campaign in the Premiership. Unfortunately, on more than one occasion this meant referees needing to reach into their pockets.

With 69 fouls to his name during 2000–01, Gravesen committed more offences than any of his Everton colleagues and twice during the season he was suspended for his indiscretions, which included a ban for a red card in the Anfield leg of the Merseyside derby.

Not that it was a bad season for Gravesen. In fact, he provided one of Everton's few plus points during the campaign, with some excellent passing and a good work-rate in the midfield.

Having won more tackles than any of his team-mates, Gravesen has come to the attention of a number of clubs and the Toffeemen will be keen to ensure he remains at the club.

But he will need to improve his disciplinary record – Walter Smith is not known for his patience.

APPEARANCES	
Start (sub)	30(2)
Minutes on pitch	2661
GOAL ATTEMPTS	
Goals	2
Shots on target	16
Shooting accuracy	38%
PASSING & CROSSING	
Goal assists	2
Passes in opp half	827
Passing accuracy in opp half	62%
Successful crosses	42
Cross completion	28%
DEFENDING	
Interceptions	6
Clearances	38
Tackles	110
Tackles won %	75%
DISCIPLINE	
Fouls	69
Yellow cards	7
Red cards	1
SEE PAGE 138 FOR FULL STATS	

Michael GRAY • 3
SUNDERLAND • BORN: 3.8.74

APPEARANCES	
Start (sub)	36(0)
Minutes on pitch	3175
GOAL ATTEMPTS	
Goals	1
PASSING & CROSSING	
Goal assists	2
Passing	1611
Passing accuracy	67%
Crosses	206
Crossing accuracy	31%
DEFENDING	
Tackles	96
Tackles won %	70%
Blocks	19
Interceptions	22
Clearances	94
Shots cleared off line	0
DISCIPLINE	
Fouls	31
Yellow cards	5
Red cards	1
SEE PAGE 278 FOR FULL STATS	

Even though he continues to be overlooked by his country, 2000–01 was another excellent season for Michael Gray. Now the longest-serving player at Sunderland, Gray showed his enthusiasm for the game has not diminished with some splendid passing and crossing throughout the campaign.

Gray completed more passes than any of his colleagues as Sunderland chased that ultimately elusive UEFA Cup place. His distribution rate was a slightly-below-par 67%, but with so many passes attempted he can be forgiven for letting some go astray.

Gray also managed to send more than twice as many successful crosses over than any of his colleagues, and with Peter Reid employing a 4–4–2 formation it is also telling that his defensive duties were not forgotten, with an excellent 96 tackles made.

Having spent 10 years at the club, the Sunderland captain will be pleased that he has been granted a testimonial by the club – even if it may well make him feel like an old man.

Jonathan GREENING • 34
MANCHESTER UNITED • BORN: 2.1.79

Having been persuaded by Sir Alex Ferguson that his future lay at Old Trafford, following a small tantrum at his lack of first-team football, Jonathan Greening duly failed to break into the starting line-up during 2000–01.

He managed just seven appearances during the season and his performances were patchy, although his 85% pass completion rate showed that he was perfectly capable of filling in when called upon and highlighted just how much potential he has.

Ferguson seems unlikely to prevent the youngster from leaving should he decide to do so; Leicester and West Ham are rumoured to be among a considerable queue of clubs interested in securing the services of the England Under-21 star.

He will certainly hope to improve his luck wherever he goes, as his last outing was a painful one. Having scored the only goal of the game, Greening broke his ankle while playing for the England Under-21 side against Albania in March.

APPEARANCES	
Start (sub)	3(4)
Minutes on pitch	273
GOAL ATTEMPTS	
Goals	0
Shots on target	0
Shooting accuracy	0%
Goals/shots ratio	0%
PASSING	
Goal assists	1
Passes in opp half	113
Passing accuracy in opp half	85%
Crosses	16
Crossing accuracy	19%
DRIBBLING	
Dribbles & runs	21
Dribble completion	62%
Corners forced	4
DISCIPLINE	
Fouls	5
Yellow cards	1
Red cards	0
SEE PAGE 222 FOR FULL STATS	

 Andrew GRIFFIN • 12
NEWCASTLE UNITED • BORN: 17.3.79

APPEARANCES	
Start (sub)	14(5)
Minutes on pitch	1283
GOAL ATTEMPTS	
Goals	0
PASSING & CROSSING	
Goal assists	0
Passing	671
Passing accuracy	69%
Crosses	36
Crossing accuracy	22%
DEFENDING	
Tackles	46
Tackles won %	78%
Blocks	8
Interceptions	4
Clearances	50
Shots cleared off line	2
DISCIPLINE	
Fouls	13
Yellow cards	2
Red cards	0
SEE PAGE 251 FOR FULL STATS	

Injury-prone full-back Andy Griffin had yet another frustrating season for the Magpies. He spent as much time on the treatment table as off it and, although he will have been looking forward to the close season for a well-earned rest and time to recuperate, he would probably have preferred not to spend it on his back after a hernia operation!

As if unaware of how a jinx automatically follows such words, Griffin declared following the operation: "I just hope that I have put my injury problems behind me. I intend to work hard throughout the summer and I will be determined to stake a claim for a first-team place from the start of next season."

It was a position he managed to find himself in 14 times during 2000–01, but it was enough to remind Bobby Robson of his ability. His tackle success rate of 78% was impressively maintained, and he managed to clear his lines well when called upon.

A pass completion rate of 69% and a crossing accuracy of just 22% are areas to be worked on, though.

Gilles GRIMANDI • 18
ARSENAL • BORN: 11.11.70

The 2000–01 season was one of revelations from Gilles Grimandi, who used his personal website to regale all and sundry with his views and anecdotes.

How we commiserated with Grimandi's misery at turning 30. "This is a difficult birthday for any footballer," he said, before reassuring us by adding: "I'm not depressed about it, though."

Arsenal fans are likely to be more concerned with the midfielder's form during 2001–02, following his anonymity at the FA Cup final – and he is yet to convince that he is the ideal midfield partner for Patrick Vieira.

Going forward, the Frenchman managed only one league goal, against Everton in April and fired in just nine shots on target all season.

He weighed in with 81 tackles and 70 clearances in the Gunners' engine room, but was sent off in the goalless draw at Aston Villa in March.

Grimandi missed only eight league matches, but overall it was a frustrating campaign.

APPEARANCES	
Start (sub)	28(2)
Minutes on pitch	2394
GOAL ATTEMPTS	
Goals	1
Shots on target	9
Shooting accuracy	64%
PASSING & CROSSING	
Goal assists	2
Passes in opp half	632
Passing accuracy in opp half	77%
Successful crosses	4
Cross completion	19%
DEFENDING	
Interceptions	17
Clearances	70
Tackles	81
Tackles won %	77%
DISCIPLINE	
Fouls	45
Yellow cards	4
Red cards	1
SEE PAGE 40 FOR FULL STATS	

Jesper GRONKJAER • 30
CHELSEA • BORN: 12.8.77

APPEARANCES	
Start (sub)	6(8)
Minutes on pitch	657
GOAL ATTEMPTS	
Goals	1
Shots on target	8
Shooting accuracy	50%
Goals/shots ratio	6%
PASSING	
Goal assists	1
Passes in opp half	163
Passing accuracy in opp half	67%
Crosses	44
Crossing accuracy	25%
DRIBBLING	
Dribbles & runs	80
Dribble completion	69%
Corners forced	13
DISCIPLINE	
Fouls	10
Yellow cards	2
Red cards	0
SEE PAGE 96 FOR FULL STATS	

It was an unhappy start to life in England for Jesper Gronkjaer. Having signed for Chelsea from Ajax in December for £7.8 million, the Danish international made an excellent impression, making his debut against Arsenal in January.

But in his wisdom Claudio Ranieri decided to use the Dane sparingly and, much to his chagrin, Gronkjaer went on to make just six starts and a handful of substitute appearances during 2000–01.

Adding his name to a growing list of discontented Blues players, Gronkjaer grumbled: "Of course I realised that it would not be easy gaining a first-team place at Chelsea, but once I made an impression I was not expecting to spend so much time as a substitute."

A host of continental clubs would be interested should Gronkjaer wish to move. Nonetheless, the midfielder has time on his side and Ranieri is unlikely to be able to resist unleashing Gronkjaer on the top flight in a big way during 2001–02.

23% Eidur Gudjohnsen's goals-to-shots ratio

Eidur GUDJOHNSEN • 22
CHELSEA • BORN: 15.9.78

Although his longest run of starts for Chelsea during 2000–01 stretched to just nine games, Eidur Gudjohnsen is likely to view his first season at Stamford Bridge as a good one.

Currently third in the pecking order for the two striking positions available in the side, the Icelandic star will be pleased that he managed to make sufficient impression to push both Jimmy Floyd Hasselbaink and Gianfranco Zola hard for their first-team places.

Indeed, on occasions, he forced Zola to the bench or Claudio Ranieri to change the formation to 4–3–3.

Still in his early 20s, Gudjohnsen knew he may have to sit out most of Chelsea's games on the bench. Upon his arrival, he declared: "It's no shame on me if I don't play that much for the first three years. I still have a long time to prove myself."

It did not take as long as he envisaged. Gudjohnsen grabbed 10 goals during the campaign, and his superb shooting accuracy of 61% was well in excess of any of his front-line colleagues' averages.

APPEARANCES	
Start (sub)	17(13)
Minutes on pitch	1570
GOAL ATTEMPTS	
Goals inside box	8
Goals outside box	2
Minutes per goal scored	157
Goals/shots ratio	23%
SHOOTING	
Shots on target inside box	19
Shots on target outside box	8
Shooting accuracy	61%
PASSING	
Goal assists	6
Key passes	27
Passing accuracy in opp half	68%
DISCIPLINE	
Fouls committed	21
Fouls won	21
Offside	20
Yellow cards	0
Red cards	0
SEE PAGE 96 FOR FULL STATS	

G

Thordur GUDJONSSON • 14
DERBY COUNTY • BORN: 14.10.73

APPEARANCES	
Start (sub)	2(8)
Minutes on pitch	266
GOAL ATTEMPTS	
Goals	1
Shots on target	4
Shooting accuracy	50%
Goals/shots ratio	13%
PASSING	
Goal assists	0
Passes in opp half	64
Passing accuracy in opp half	67%
Crosses	8
Crossing accuracy	38%
DRIBBLING	
Dribbles & runs	16
Dribble completion	63%
Corners forced	2
DISCIPLINE	
Fouls	3
Yellow cards	1
Red cards	0
SEE PAGE 124 FOR FULL STATS	

Stoke City may well have been the expected destination for Thordur Gudjonsson when he decided to move to England from Las Palmas in March.

Instead he eschewed the lure of his father's club to join up with former Genk team-mate Branko Strupar at Derby County. Although Jim Smith used the Icelandic star primarily as a substitute, he featured in each of the Rams' last 10 league fixtures, netting in the 3–1 defeat at West Ham in April.

Gudjonsson was given the opportunity to show what he could do in the reserve side, where a series of fine performances was capped by a superb hat-trick against Nottingham Forest.

The Icelander's initial loan deal was due to expire at the end of the 2000–01 season, but it will be no surprise if we see Gudjonsson lining up for the Rams during 2001–02 as well. Derby fans will certainly be expecting Jim Smith to secure the exciting midfield player, whose 50% shooting accuracy showed great promise.

was higher than any other Chelsea player

Ivan GUERRERO • 19
COVENTRY CITY • BORN: 30.11.77

Along with compatriot Jairo Martinez, Honduran international Ivan Guerrero signed for Coventry in September 2000. But his first appearance for the Sky Blues had to be put on hold as the midfielder travelled to the other side of the world to compete in the Olympics that month.

Guerrero made three starts for Coventry upon his return, in a particularly unhappy spell for the side which saw each game end in defeat.

Clearly not used to the pace of the Premiership, he struggled to find his feet in the side with a lowly pass completion rate of just 60%. Although not entirely convincing with his praise, manager Gordon Strachan did say: "I thought he did very well in trying circumstances."

But following his three appearances Guerrero made no further outings in the side. With Strachan claiming that Coventry are going to look to increase the number of English players in the side, it seems unlikely that Guerrero will be sticking around.

APPEARANCES	
Start (sub)	3(0)
Minutes on pitch	226
GOAL ATTEMPTS	
Goals	0
PASSING & CROSSING	
Goal assists	0
Passing	70
Passing accuracy	60%
Crosses	5
Crossing accuracy	0%
DEFENDING	
Tackles	5
Tackles won %	80%
Blocks	1
Interceptions	0
Clearances	6
Shots cleared off line	0
DISCIPLINE	
Fouls	2
Yellow cards	0
Red cards	0
SEE PAGE 110 FOR FULL STATS	

Arnar GUNNLAUGSSON • 13
LEICESTER CITY • BORN: 6.3.73

APPEARANCES	
Start (sub)	3(14)
Minutes on pitch	569
GOAL ATTEMPTS	
Goals inside box	1
Goals outside box	2
Minutes per goal scored	190
Goals/shots ratio	19%
SHOOTING	
Shots on target inside box	4
Shots on target outside box	5
Shooting accuracy	56%
PASSING	
Goal assists	1
Key passes	4
Passing accuracy in opp half	72%
DISCIPLINE	
Fouls committed	7
Fouls won	17
Offside	0
Yellow cards	0
Red cards	0
SEE PAGE 180 FOR FULL STATS	

Along with Trevor Benjamin, Arnar Gunnlaugsson can lay claim to the dubious honour of most Premiership substitute appearances at Leicester during 2000–01. Each was introduced 14 times, but while Benjamin may be more content, Gunnlaugsson is likely to be less than happy with his current standing at the club.

The Icelandic forward was forced to wait until October's game with Derby for his first substitute outing. But he will have been more than pleased with his contribution, as he grabbed the Foxes' second goal in their fine 2–1 win.

Gunnlaugsson was not rewarded with a start in the next game, but a goal two matches later – once again having come off the bench – gave him fresh hope.

Yet he failed to feature in the following four games and, despite scoring again to make it three goals in four sub appearances, he never became a regular in the side. Perhaps Peter Taylor began to believe Gunnlaugsson's "supersub" moniker.

For more information visit our website:

Steve GUPPY • 11
AM LEICESTER CITY • BORN: 29.3.69

Just at the stage of his career when he needed regular football to try to get back into the picture for another England call-up, Steve Guppy found himself marginalised by Peter Taylor for much of the 2000–01 campaign. But he did end the season with five starts in the last six games.

Taylor's decision to leave Guppy on the bench for a large portion of the campaign is somewhat perplexing, as the midfielder's crossing eclipsed that of any of his club colleagues.

Guppy put over 64 successful crosses and corners during the season – more than twice the number delivered by any other Leicester City player.

Following his omission from Kevin Keegan's Euro 2000 party, Guppy would have been hoping for greater opportunities to shine for his country, but he has instead become England's forgotten left-sided player. It seems likely that his only hope for a recall lies in prolonged first-team action, be it with the Foxes or elsewhere.

G
H

APPEARANCES	
Start (sub)	17(11)
Minutes on pitch	1708
GOAL ATTEMPTS	
Goals	1
Shots on target	4
Shooting accuracy	29%
Goals/shots ratio	7%
PASSING	
Goal assists	3
Passes in opp half	445
Passing accuracy in opp half	65%
Crosses	225
Crossing accuracy	28%
DRIBBLING	
Dribbles & runs	73
Dribble completion	74%
Corners forced	22
DISCIPLINE	
Fouls	14
Yellow cards	1
Red cards	0
SEE PAGE 180 FOR FULL STATS	

 Alf Inge HAALAND • 15
M MANCHESTER CITY • BORN: 23.11.72

APPEARANCES	
Start (sub)	35(0)
Minutes on pitch	3043
GOAL ATTEMPTS	
Goals	3
Shots on target	13
Shooting accuracy	42%
PASSING & CROSSING	
Goal assists	1
Passes in opp half	688
Passing accuracy in opp half	58%
Successful crosses	7
Cross completion	17%
DEFENDING	
Interceptions	10
Clearances	76
Tackles	83
Tackles won %	72%
DISCIPLINE	
Fouls	57
Yellow cards	6
Red cards	0
SEE PAGE 208 FOR FULL STATS	

Norwegian Alf Inge Haaland began his Premiership career at Manchester City with a dismal 4–0 opening day defeat against Charlton at The Valley.

He was so embarrassed by this poor start to the campaign that he gave petrol money to disgruntled Manchester City fans on their way back up north!

But while the country suffered its own petrol crisis, Haaland never stopped running efficiently in City's engine room.

In fact, City may well have been relegated sooner were it not for Haaland, whose all-round contribution showed more than 1,000 passes attempted, as well as a 72% tackle success rate.

Fortunate to get away without serious injury after Roy Keane's lunge at his knee in the Manchester derby in April, Haaland will take relegation on the chin.

If the City captain remains with the Citizens, he will do more than most to make sure Kevin Keegan's side make an immediate return to the top flight.

Moustapha HADJI • 10
COVENTRY CITY • BORN: 16.11.71

The departure of Gary McAllister from Highfield Road enabled Moustapha Hadji to wear his beloved number 10 shirt, but this was not too popular with the many City fans who had his name and number 11 already printed on their replica shirts!

Already a fans' favourite, Hadji offered £18,000 to cover the cost of 400 such shirts, earning plenty of praise in Coventry for footing the bill.

The Moroccan international also gave everything to Coventry in their battle against the drop.

His six Premiership goals made him the club's joint top scorer with Welsh strike pair Craig Bellamy and John Hartson. And Hadji was often used as a striker himself.

The sight of Fezzes at Highfield Road may soon become a thing of the past, though. Hadji announced at the end of 2000–01 that chairman Bryan Richardson had told him the club might have to sell him, which would make an immediate return to the top flight for the Sky Blues even more difficult.

APPEARANCES	
Start (sub)	28(1)
Minutes on pitch	2516
GOAL ATTEMPTS	
Goals	6
Shots on target	26
Shooting accuracy	33%
Goals/shots ratio	8%
PASSING	
Goal assists	3
Passes in opp half	622
Passing accuracy in opp half	52%
Crosses	91
Crossing accuracy	24%
DRIBBLING	
Dribbles & runs	119
Dribble completion	54%
Corners forced	27
DISCIPLINE	
Fouls	39
Yellow cards	1
Red cards	1
SEE PAGE 111 FOR FULL STATS	

Marcus HALL • 24
COVENTRY CITY • BORN: 24.3.76

APPEARANCES	
Start (sub)	21(0)
Minutes on pitch	1871
GOAL ATTEMPTS	
Goals	0
PASSING & CROSSING	
Goal assists	0
Passing	551
Passing accuracy	58%
Crosses	65
Crossing accuracy	15%
DEFENDING	
Tackles	49
Tackles won %	82%
Blocks	17
Interceptions	4
Clearances	96
Shots cleared off line	0
DISCIPLINE	
Fouls	15
Yellow cards	2
Red cards	0
SEE PAGE 111 FOR FULL STATS	

After featuring sporadically for the Sky Blues in 1999–2000 due to injury, Marcus Hall cemented himself a first–team slot at left-back for much of the 2000–01 campaign at Highfield Road.

Despite aggravating a troublesome knee injury in October, the former England Under-21 international still managed to start 21 games in Coventry's disappointing season mainly due to the long-term injury and eventual retirement of Steve Froggatt.

Although willing to come forward when called upon, Hall was relatively ineffective as a creative force in the opposition half, completing only 15% of crosses and a lowly 58% of all passes attempted. He also failed to register an assist for Gordon Strachan's struggling side all season.

It will not be easy for the Sky Blues to get back in the Premiership in 2001–02, but if Hall maintains his progress, improves on his attacking play and stays injury free, he could play an important role in Coventry's promotion push.

53 Only two players had more shots

Gunnar HALLE • 18
FB
BRADFORD CITY • BORN: 11.8.65

After being a regular in Bradford's successful bid for survival in 1999–2000, veteran Norwegian defender Gunnar Halle endured a nightmare 2000–01. The first half of his season was hampered by injuries, notably a fractured fibula, and when he returned, the Bantams were relegation certainties.

Incoming Bantams manager Jim Jefferies played Halle at right-back after a defensive reshuffle following the departure of Andy O'Brien to Newcastle. The ex-Latic played solidly in his stint at the end of the season, winning 81% of his tackles and averaging more than eight clearances per start.

Halle has one year left on his current contract at Valley Parade and has already stated a desire to return to Scandinavia after seeing out the last 12 months.

If this is the case, the former Leeds man will have spent a decade in English football earning a reputation as a solid professional in the process. As it is, with Bradford's relegation, Halle has already said farewell to the Premiership.

APPEARANCES	
Start (sub)	10(3)
Minutes on pitch	1033
GOAL ATTEMPTS	
Goals	0
PASSING & CROSSING	
Goal assists	0
Passing	339
Passing accuracy	68%
Crosses	30
Crossing accuracy	13%
DEFENDING	
Tackles	37
Tackles won %	81%
Blocks	11
Interceptions	6
Clearances	88
Shots cleared off line	1
DISCIPLINE	
Fouls	24
Yellow cards	0
Red cards	0
SEE PAGE 68 FOR FULL STATS	

H

Dietmar HAMANN • 16
M
LIVERPOOL • BORN: 27.8.73

APPEARANCES	
Start (sub)	26(4)
Minutes on pitch	2333
GOAL ATTEMPTS	
Goals	2
Shots on target	10
Shooting accuracy	28%
PASSING & CROSSING	
Goal assists	3
Passes in opp half	774
Passing accuracy in opp half	74%
Successful crosses	4
Cross completion	14%
DEFENDING	
Interceptions	13
Clearances	37
Tackles	114
Tackles won %	76%
DISCIPLINE	
Fouls	49
Yellow cards	5
Red cards	1
SEE PAGE 194 FOR FULL STATS	

After scoring "that" goal for Germany against England at Wembley on 7 October, Dietmar Hamann returned to club football with Liverpool, playing an important part in the Reds' fantastic 2000–01 season.

The German was a regular for Liverpool and his partnership with Steven Gerrard in the centre of midfield was one of the main reasons behind the Reds' success.

Hamann improved his all-round game throughout the campaign. He set up and scored one more league goal than he did in 1999–2000 – the only blip on his record was the red card against Arsenal in the second game of the league campaign.

Perhaps he will be disappointed not to have scored a few more goals, as he has always prided himself on his ability to get forward, but overall he can be happy with his season.

After committing himself to Anfield, the German star will be looking forward to playing a leading role in the continued revival of Liverpool and adding to the three cup medals earned in 2000–01.

off target than Moustapha Hadji

FB Jon HARLEY • 34
CHELSEA • BORN: 26.9.79

Big things were expected of Jon Harley in 2000–01 with Gianluca Vialli declaring himself a big fan of the Kentish left-back. But the axe fell on the Italian manager and Harley struggled to make an impression on new boss, Claudio Ranieri.

His best spell of the season came when he was shipped out to Wimbledon on loan. He scored a brace on his debut for the Dons against Crewe. This won him many friends at the south London club and they were disappointed when he returned to Stamford Bridge in November.

With Graeme Le Saux and Celestine Babayaro ahead of him in the pecking order, Harley played little football in Chelsea's season. His last appearance of the campaign was in the Blues' victory against Gillingham in the fourth round of the FA Cup.

Despite his reluctance to pick Harley, Ranieri has said he admires the player, so Harley must hope for more chances in 2001–02 as the Italian continues his rebuilding job at Stamford Bridge.

APPEARANCES	
Start (sub)	6(4)
Minutes on pitch	525
GOAL ATTEMPTS	
Goals	0
PASSING & CROSSING	
Goal assists	0
Passing	187
Passing accuracy	66%
Crosses	15
Crossing accuracy	27%
DEFENDING	
Tackles	20
Tackles won %	85%
Blocks	5
Interceptions	0
Clearances	8
Shots cleared off line	0
DISCIPLINE	
Fouls	8
Yellow cards	1
Red cards	0

SEE PAGE 96 FOR FULL STATS

G Steve HARPER • 13
NEWCASTLE UNITED • BORN: 3.2.74

APPEARANCES	
Start (sub)	4(1)
Minutes on pitch	405
SHOT STOPPING	
Goals conceded (inside box)	6
Goals conceded (outside box)	2
Minutes per goal conceded	51
Clean sheets	0
Saves (shots inside box)	10
Saves (shots outside box)	6
Saves/shots	67%
DISTRIBUTION	
Long kick %	44%
Throws/short passes %	100%
CATCHING	
Crosses caught	2
Crosses punched	3
Crosses dropped	0
Catch success %	100%
DISCIPLINE	
Yellow cards	0
Red cards	0

SEE PAGE 251 FOR FULL STATS

Bobby Robson seemed unsure of his best goalkeeper and the 2000–01 season again saw Steve Harper and Shay Given battle it out for supremacy between the sticks.

Republic of Ireland star Given played the lion's share of the time but Harper did manage 405 minutes of football.

Unfortunately, he did not manage to keep a clean sheet in that time, but he was playing behind a defence which seemed to be in a trance for much of the winter and his saves-to-shots ratio suffered accordingly.

A talented shot-stopper who has been a loyal servant to Newcastle down the years, rumours emerged that Harper might be looking for a new club, such was his rage at not commanding a regular first-team spot.

But this theory was scuppered when the 'keeper signed a new four-year deal in May 2001. "Nothing quite beats playing in front of a full house at St James' Park," he said.

Season 2001–02 will see another battle between Harper and Given, but Robson is lucky to have two good 'keepers.

Ian HARTE • 3
LEEDS UNITED • BORN: 31.8.77

After a sticky start to the 2000–01 season which briefly saw him dropped from David O'Leary's starting line-up, Ian Harte recovered his form well, eventually taking his place at left-back in Opta's Premiership Team of the Season.

Harte is an accomplished defender, but it is his ability in the opposition half that really sets him apart from his peers.

Arguably the only player in the top flight as dangerous from dead-ball situations as David Beckham, Harte scored four goals direct from free-kicks, taking his tally to seven for the season – a figure which made him the Premiership's highest scoring defender.

He also set up six goals from his dangerous set-piece deliveries.

His performances on the European stage in Leeds' thrilling Champions League campaign proved that he is one of the top full-backs in European football at the moment. Still in his mid-20s, he is sure to be a fixture in both the Leeds and Republic of Ireland sides for many years to come.

APPEARANCES	
Start (sub)	29(0)
Minutes on pitch	2610
GOAL ATTEMPTS	
Goals	7
PASSING & CROSSING	
Goal assists	6
Passing	1305
Passing accuracy	65%
Crosses	186
Crossing accuracy	30%
DEFENDING	
Tackles	73
Tackles won %	78%
Blocks	23
Interceptions	4
Clearances	93
Shots cleared off line	1
DISCIPLINE	
Fouls	23
Yellow cards	1
Red cards	0

SEE PAGE 166 FOR FULL STATS

John HARTSON • 5
COVENTRY CITY • BORN: 5.4.75

APPEARANCES	
Start (sub)	12(0)
Minutes on pitch	1054
GOAL ATTEMPTS	
Goals inside box	6
Goals outside box	0
Minutes per goal scored	176
Goals/shots ratio	17%
SHOOTING	
Shots on target inside box	15
Shots on target outside box	1
Shooting accuracy	44%
PASSING	
Goal assists	0
Key passes	25
Passing accuracy in opp half	55%
DISCIPLINE	
Fouls committed	47
Fouls won	29
Offside	18
Yellow cards	4
Red cards	0

SEE PAGE 111 FOR FULL STATS

Gordon Strachan showed some bald ambition when he brought John Hartson to Coventry in February. The ginger striker had been hampered by injuries throughout 2000–01, setbacks which had seen transfers to Spurs and Glasgow Rangers fall through.

But a ground-breaking deal was arranged with Wimbledon, whereby Coventry paid the Dons every time Hartson appeared in a Sky Blue shirt.

And it was a transfer which very nearly worked to perfection as Hartson inspired City when he arrived at the club.

He bagged six goals and led the line impressively, but ultimately it was too late and his team slid into the dark confines of the Football League.

It remains to be seen whether Hartson will stay at Highfield Road or be moved on to another Premiership club struggling to stay up in 2001–02. He seems to be addicted to such battles, but after failure to beat the drop with both Wimbledon and Coventry, he will be wary of another relegation fight.

Jimmy Floyd HASSELBAINK • 9
CHELSEA • BORN: 27.3.72

S

After the disastrous performance of Chris Sutton in 1999–2000, Chelsea could have been forgiven for being wary of splashing big money on another striker, but they went ahead and paid £15 million to bring Jimmy Floyd Hasselbaink back to English football from Atletico Madrid.

And in a stark contrast to Sutton, Hasselbaink proved to be the striker of the 2000–01 Premiership season. He rifled 23 league goals for the Pensioners – making him the Premiership's leading goalscorer – and gave them a cutting edge up front which they had been missing for years. Some of his strikes will live in the memory for a long time, such was their power.

He was creative, too, ending the campaign with nine assists – only two players set up more goals – but he must have been disappointed his team-mates could not match him. He mused on this, saying: "Sometimes I think I am in the wrong place at the wrong time. I'm not very lucky with the teams I choose to play for."

APPEARANCES	
Start (sub)	35(0)
Minutes on pitch	2920
GOAL ATTEMPTS	
Goals inside box	17
Goals outside box	6
Minutes per goal scored	127
Goals/shots ratio	20%
SHOOTING	
Shots on target inside box	31
Shots on target outside box	24
Shooting accuracy	49%
PASSING	
Goal assists	9
Key passes	55
Passing accuracy in opp half	70%
DISCIPLINE	
Fouls committed	51
Fouls won	56
Offside	42
Yellow cards	6
Red cards	1

SEE PAGE 97 FOR FULL STATS

Danny HAY • 24
LEEDS UNITED • BORN: 15.5.75

CB

APPEARANCES	
Start (sub)	2(2)
Minutes on pitch	299
GOAL ATTEMPTS	
Goals	0
DEFENDING	
Blocks	6
Shots cleared off line	0
Headed clearances	23
Other clearances	16
Interceptions	1
Last man saving tackles	1
Tackles won	5
Tackles won %	71%
PASSING	
Passing accuracy own half	85%
Passing accuracy opp half	63%
DISCIPLINE	
Fouls	1
Fouls in danger area	1
Yellow cards	0
Red cards	0

SEE PAGE 166 FOR FULL STATS

Leeds' Antipodean raids have bolstered their squad in recent times and Danny Hay joined the club in summer 2000 from Perth Glory.

The New Zealand-born defender played only 299 minutes of Premiership action in 2000–01, but he will have been pleased to mark his card.

He will remember his trip to the Nou Camp, Barcelona in the Champions League when he sat on the bench as his team were mauled 4–0 – a harsh introduction to the rigours of European football for the Kiwi.

In the Premiership, Hay made just seven tackles but did prove a menace from set-pieces, ghosting into the box to fire in five shots, three of which hit the target. Such stats augur well for the youngster. At least he can be confident that he is at a club which is not afraid to plunge rookies into the spotlight when the need arises. His big chance could be just around the corner.

But, with the club looking to continue its development and compete with the best, Hay is up against it.

23 Jimmy Floyd Hasselbaink was the first Chelsea player

David HEALY • 35
S
MANCHESTER UNITED • BORN: 5.8.79

Big things were expected of young David Healy at Manchester United. The Northern Ireland international was tipped to make the breakthrough to the first team but, despite a 30-minute run-out against Ipswich in 2000–01, he was sold to Preston North End in January and enjoyed considerable success.

He did not manage to score in his short appearance for the Red Devils but looked sharp enough and completed 92% of his passes.

He really came to life when he moved down a division, though, scoring 10 times for North End as they surged to the Division One play-off final. His partnership with Jon Macken – another Manchester United graduate – prospered and, despite defeat to Bolton in the final, Healy can look back on some real progress in 2000–01.

He scored three times for Northern Ireland and looks to have a promising future at international level.

SEE PAGE 222 FOR FULL STATS

Magnus HEDMAN • 1
G
COVENTRY CITY • BORN: 19.3.73

Highly-rated goalkeeper Magnus Hedman was one of Sweden's best performers at Euro 2000 and so the disappointment of the subsequent 2000–01 campaign will have hurt the amiable shot-stopper.

Coventry manager Gordon Strachan was able to call on the services of talented youngster Chris Kirkland and, despite Hedman's experience, the rookie seems to have won the battle to be the Sky Blues' number one. Nevertheless, Hedman still only conceded 23 goals in the Premiership – fewer than his young rival.

Hedman kept nine clean sheets in 1999–2000, but this figure fell to just two in 2000–01, while his saves-to-shots ratio also declined. Despite playing for a team marooned in relegation trouble, Hedman continued to be linked with a number of clubs in England and Europe, including the likes of Barcelona and Arsenal.

He is unlikely to relish Division One football and, with the emergence of Kirkland as first choice 'keeper, the club are likely to cash in on one of their main assets.

H

Vegard HEGGEM • 14
FB
LIVERPOOL • BORN: 13.7.75

Vegard Heggem spent the majority of the 2000–01 season in the treatment room with a recurring hamstring problem which saw him miss out on all the Liverpool success at the campaign's conclusion.

Popular with the fans and with a lot of attacking ability, Heggem may struggle to regain his place in the Liverpool team in 2001–02 such was the quality of Markus Babbel's play.

Heggem was left to comment on the season on his website, where he revealed that he enjoyed himself among the Preston fans when North End played Watford at Vicarage Road. His other highlight came when the Liverpool squad were treated to an evening's entertainment from Reds fan Chris de Burgh.

As well as his own songs, he sang a medley of hits from such artists as The Beatles and Elvis Presley – to uproarious approval from Heggem and the other Liverpool players.

SEE PAGE 194 FOR FULL STATS

APPEARANCES	
Start (sub)	15(0)
Minutes on pitch	1350
SHOT STOPPING	
Goals conceded (inside box)	23
Goals conceded (outside box)	0
Minutes per goal conceded	59
Clean sheets	2
Saves (shots inside box)	37
Saves (shots outside box)	24
Saves/shots	73%
DISTRIBUTION	
Long kick %	47%
Throws/short passes %	54%
CATCHING	
Crosses caught	46
Crosses punched	9
Crosses dropped	2
Catch success %	96%
DISCIPLINE	
Yellow cards	0
Red cards	0

SEE PAGE 111 FOR FULL STATS

to win the Golden Boot since Kerry Dixon in 1985

CB **Stephane HENCHOZ • 2**
LIVERPOOL • BORN: 9.9.74

Swiss stopper Stephane Henchoz was quietly effective in 2000–01, his partnership with Sami Hyypia one of the strengths of the Liverpool team.

A pass completion of 80% is a testament to his calmness in possession.

He will be keen to see if Liverpool's treble triumphs are released on a DVD as he is a big fan of the format. Henchoz said on his *Icons* website: "Because my laptop also has a DVD I can watch films when I'm on an away trip, either with Liverpool or with the Swiss national team. DVD is fantastic."

He enthused further: "I like to visit places when I have the day off. I also like going to the cinema. But I don't mind staying indoors, either. I'm not bad around the house, and when I'm not doing the odd job I tend to watch a film on DVD or go on my computer." There is surely no doubt that Henchoz will have his three cup-winning performances transferred onto his favourite format.

Life certainly is a non-stop thrill for the former Blackburn defender!

APPEARANCES	
Start (sub)	32(0)
Minutes on pitch	2851
GOAL ATTEMPTS	
Goals	0
DEFENDING	
Blocks	41
Shots cleared off line	1
Headed clearances	147
Other clearances	128
Interceptions	13
Last man saving tackles	3
Tackles won	73
Tackles won %	80%
PASSING	
Passing accuracy own half	88%
Passing accuracy opp half	63%
DISCIPLINE	
Fouls	42
Fouls in danger area	14
Yellow cards	3
Red cards	0
SEE PAGE 194 FOR FULL STATS	

M **Lee HENDRIE • 17**
ASTON VILLA • BORN: 18.5.77

APPEARANCES	
Start (sub)	27(5)
Minutes on pitch	2443
GOAL ATTEMPTS	
Goals	6
Shots on target	23
Shooting accuracy	43%
PASSING & CROSSING	
Goal assists	5
Passes in opp half	842
Passing accuracy in opp half	77%
Successful crosses	8
Cross completion	32%
DEFENDING	
Interceptions	7
Clearances	25
Tackles	49
Tackles won %	69%
DISCIPLINE	
Fouls	28
Yellow cards	3
Red cards	2
SEE PAGE 55 FOR FULL STATS	

It seems an eternity since Lee Hendrie shone on his England debut, being touted as a future international star.

However, the Aston Villa midfielder impressed during 2000–01, making it into Opta's England Team of the Season on the left-hand side of midfield.

Hendrie lost his place in the Villa side to Paul Merson in 1999–2000, but the following season John Gregory accommodated them both, to good effect.

Hendrie matched Merson's total of six Premiership goals, and also chipped in with five assists, missing just six matches.

But for all his footballing ability the Villa playmaker remains a volatile and often petulant character.

Sendings-off against Arsenal and Manchester City made Hendrie just one of four players to see red twice in the season. Gregory will be keen for the Birmingham-born man to curb his disciplinary problems in the future, especially as England manager Sven-Göran Eriksson takes a very dim view of such misdemeanours.

Colin HENDRY • 5
COVENTRY CITY • BORN: 7.12.65

Colin Hendry took to the field at the start of the 2000–01 campaign eager to make up for a slightly disappointing previous season.

But after an opening day defeat to Middlesbrough, Hendry never started another game for the Sky Blues, only coming on after 82 minutes against Tottenham in October as a substitute.

Soon after that, Hendry was sent on loan to Bolton Wanderers, who eventually paid £250,000 to secure his services. He helped his new side to a third-placed finish in Division One which culminated with victory in the play-offs and promotion to the Premiership.

Ironically, his former club Coventry City were relegated from the top flight after 34 years, with what was originally a step down for Hendry proving to be an excellent move.

Still a regular for the Scottish national side, despite a FIFA ban for elbowing an opponent, Hendry will be hoping 2001–02 offers regular Premiership football, culminating in a trip to the 2002 World Cup Finals to be held in Japan and South Korea.

APPEARANCES	
Start (sub)	1(1)
Minutes on pitch	98
GOAL ATTEMPTS	
Goals	0
DEFENDING	
Blocks	1
Shots cleared off line	0
Headed clearances	6
Other clearances	1
Interceptions	2
Last man saving tackles	0
Tackles won	0
Tackles won %	0%
PASSING	
Passing accuracy own half	79%
Passing accuracy opp half	54%
DISCIPLINE	
Fouls	0
Fouls in danger area	0
Yellow cards	0
Red cards	0
SEE PAGE 111 FOR FULL STATS	

Thierry HENRY • 14
ARSENAL • BORN: 17.8.77

APPEARANCES	
Start (sub)	27(8)
Minutes on pitch	2589
GOAL ATTEMPTS	
Goals inside box	13
Goals outside box	4
Minutes per goal scored	152
Goals/shots ratio	14%
SHOOTING	
Shots on target inside box	39
Shots on target outside box	24
Shooting accuracy	51%
PASSING	
Goal assists	9
Key passes	41
Passing accuracy in opp half	57%
DISCIPLINE	
Fouls committed	56
Fouls won	39
Offside	75
Yellow cards	4
Red cards	0
SEE PAGE 40 FOR FULL STATS	

Arsenal fans must be wondering whether or not they want to kiss or dismiss Thierry Henry after a rollercoaster season.

The Frenchman remains one of the most exciting players in Europe to watch and his 17 Premiership goals highlight perfectly the immense talent he has.

But a glaring miss against Valencia in the Champions League quarter-finals proved costly, then a month later in the FA Cup final, a handful of clear-cut goalscoring opportunities were spurned as Liverpool snatched the cup from Arsenal's grasp with two late goals.

Yet this is the same striker who scored one of the goals of the season against Manchester United in October, flicking the ball up 30 yards out with his back to goal, before turning and sending a dipping volley over Fabien Barthez.

Few managers would choose not to have the swift Frenchman in their line-up. With Henry chasing Premiership, European and World Cups during 2001–02, plenty of goals are sure to follow.

Emile HESKEY • 8
LIVERPOOL • BORN: 11.1.78

There were many who questioned the £11 million Gérard Houllier paid Leicester City for the services of Emile Heskey, but he rewarded the French manager's faith in him by enjoying his best-ever goalscoring season and helping the Reds to their trophy treble.

"Bruno" retains the power and strength that shot him to fame at Leicester, but has added a far more clinical side to his game since moving to Anfield.

He hit 14 goals in the Premiership in 2000–01 including a stunning hat-trick at Derby. He also bagged vital goals in all three of Liverpool's cup runs and scored his second goal in England colours against Spain, during Sven-Göran Eriksson's first game in charge.

With competition for striking places at Liverpool intense, Heskey benefits from his adaptability in being able to fit in alongside any partner. On top of scoring goals, he had four assists and looks set to enjoy continued success at the Merseyside club, where it appears Michael Owen and Robbie Fowler are competing to partner him.

APPEARANCES	
Start (sub)	33(3)
Minutes on pitch	2694

GOAL ATTEMPTS	
Goals inside box	11
Goals outside box	3
Minutes per goal scored	192
Goals/shots ratio	17%

SHOOTING	
Shots on target inside box	31
Shots on target outside box	12
Shooting accuracy	52%

PASSING	
Goal assists	4
Key passes	41
Passing accuracy in opp half	65%

DISCIPLINE	
Fouls committed	76
Fouls won	54
Offside	44
Yellow cards	4
Red cards	0

SEE PAGE 195 FOR FULL STATS

Power: Emile Heskey

33 Emile Heskey started more Premiership games in 2000–01

M Tony HIBBERT • 32
EVERTON • BORN: 20.2.81

Tony Hibbert received the worst possible introduction to Premiership football when he was almost cut in half by a Stuart Pearce challenge at Upton Park. Thankfully the Liverpool-born player was able to pick himself up and continue in the biggest game of his fledgling career.

Hibbert came through the youth ranks at Goodison and was a member of Everton's FA Youth Cup winning side of 1998.

Initially a midfielder, the player converted to right-back and adapted well to his new defensive position.

He became a regular feature in Everton's reserve team in 2000–01 before deservedly getting a call-up to the first team for the game at West Ham at the end of March.

Hibbert went on to make two more appearances for the Toffees as a substitute against Arsenal and Bradford. And with many on Merseyside predicting a bright future for the tough-tackling youngster, he can be expected to make more appearances in the first XI in 2001–02.

H

APPEARANCES	
Start (sub)	1(2)
Minutes on pitch	143
GOAL ATTEMPTS	
Goals	0
Shots on target	0
Shooting accuracy	0%
PASSING & CROSSING	
Goal assists	0
Passes in opp half	26
Passing accuracy in opp half	50%
Successful crosses	2
Cross completion	25%
DEFENDING	
Interceptions	1
Clearances	7
Tackles	10
Tackles won %	100%
DISCIPLINE	
Fouls	1
Yellow cards	0
Red cards	0
SEE PAGE 138 FOR FULL STATS	

FB Danny HIGGINBOTHAM • 15
DERBY COUNTY • BORN: 29.12.78

APPEARANCES	
Start (sub)	23(3)
Minutes on pitch	2057
GOAL ATTEMPTS	
Goals	0
PASSING & CROSSING	
Goal assists	1
Passing	643
Passing accuracy	58%
Crosses	65
Crossing accuracy	29%
DEFENDING	
Tackles	50
Tackles won %	72%
Blocks	27
Interceptions	13
Clearances	158
Shots cleared off line	0
DISCIPLINE	
Fouls	21
Yellow cards	3
Red cards	0
SEE PAGE 125 FOR FULL STATS	

Manchester-born Danny Higginbotham made a tough decision in the summer of 2000, wrenching himself away from the club he supported as a boy, Manchester United, to join Derby County in order to gain regular first-team experience.

Jim Smith's £2 million signing made the right choice as he went straight into the Rams' starting line-up at the beginning of the season. Higginbotham had little time to settle, though, as sheepish defending saw Derby leak goals like a sieve and the new boy, along with the rest of the Rams backline, came in for plenty of stick.

The arrival of Colin Todd at Pride Park led to a re-organisation of the defence, though, and as the season went by, Higginbotham improved along with the rest of his colleagues.

The former Red Devil performed heroics on his return to Old Trafford in the game which secured Derby's Premiership survival – taking three points and keeping a clean sheet must have been a sweet feeling.

than any other Liverpool striker has since the 1997–98 season

Shaka HISLOP • 1
WEST HAM UNITED • BORN: 22.2.69

Trinidad and Tobago international Shaka Hislop battled back from injury in 1999–2000 to take his place between the West Ham sticks in 2000–01.

A broken leg suffered against Bradford in February 2000 kept the former Newcastle stopper out for the remainder of that campaign, but following an uncertain start, he soon regained his customary dominance in the Hammers' goal in 2000–01, keeping eight clean sheets throughout the disappointing league campaign.

Hislop patrolled his penalty box with confidence, dropping just two catches all season and making 109 saves – a total only five 'keepers topped in 2000–01.

But like the rest of his team-mates Hislop was affected by the end-of-season slump in form, conceding 18 of the 43 goals he shipped in total in his last 11 appearances.

With his contract due to expire in 2002, Hislop delayed talks until the summer of 2001 after rejecting the new deal he was offered midway through the season.

APPEARANCES	
Start (sub)	34(0)
Minutes on pitch	3015
SHOT STOPPING	
Goals conceded (inside box)	32
Goals conceded (outside box)	11
Minutes per goal conceded	70
Clean sheets	8
Saves (shots inside box)	52
Saves (shots outside box)	57
Saves/shots	72%
DISTRIBUTION	
Long kick %	46%
Throws/short passes %	84%
CATCHING	
Crosses caught	37
Crosses punched	12
Crosses dropped	2
Catch success %	95%
DISCIPLINE	
Yellow cards	1
Red cards	0

SEE PAGE 306 FOR FULL STATS

Thomas HITZLSPERGER • 21
ASTON VILLA • BORN: 5.4.82

While one young Bayern Munich player made several headlines in the English press for his performances in the latter stages of the European Cup, another slipped relatively quietly into the Premiership in 2000–01.

Owen Hargreaves came through the ranks at Bayern to secure a first-team spot, while German youngster Thomas Hitzlsperger was unable to make as big an impression as Hargreaves, instead joining Aston Villa on a free transfer in the summer of 2000.

It is not the first time Hitzlsperger has tasted disappointment in his fledgling career. Playing in the Under-17 World Cup in 1999 and with Germany leading 1–0 against Australia, he put through his own net. His side went on to lose 2–1 and crash out of the tournament.

His one Premiership substitute appearance came against Liverpool. Villa were trailing 3–0 when he took to the pitch, and Hitzlsperger could do nothing to change that.

SEE PAGE 55 FOR FULL STATS

Dominance: Shaka Hislop

Matt HOLLAND • 8
IPSWICH TOWN • BORN: 11.4.74

Midfield lynchpin Matt Holland was a vital cog in the Ipswich Town engine-room as the Tractor Boys ploughed through the 2000–01 Premiership to gain a UEFA Cup spot for 2001–02. Holland's input was as crucial as anyone's in George Burley's side, with the Republic of Ireland international forging an effective midfield partnership with Jim Magilton for Town.

Ipswich's influential captain maintained an outstanding 81% pass completion rate throughout the campaign, which was the best ratio of any Town player and one of the highest recorded by any top-flight midfielder.

Holland complemented his industry with plenty of guile. He supplied the assists for five Ipswich goals and netted three himself – most notably a wonderfully-crafted equaliser at home to Manchester City in their penultimate fixture of the season.

After failing to make the Premiership grade with West Ham earlier in his career, Holland proved emphatically in 2000–01 that he has what it takes to grace the English top flight.

APPEARANCES	
Start (sub)	38(0)
Minutes on pitch	3379
GOAL ATTEMPTS	
Goals	3
Shots on target	14
Shooting accuracy	34%
PASSING & CROSSING	
Goal assists	5
Passes in opp half	886
Passing accuracy in opp half	76%
Successful crosses	6
Cross completion	30%
DEFENDING	
Interceptions	15
Clearances	46
Tackles	111
Tackles won %	68%
DISCIPLINE	
Fouls	20
Yellow cards	0
Red cards	0
SEE PAGE 152 FOR FULL STATS	

H

 Darren HOLLOWAY • 14
SUNDERLAND • BORN: 3.10.77

APPEARANCES	
Start (sub)	5(0)
Minutes on pitch	400
GOAL ATTEMPTS	
Goals	0
PASSING & CROSSING	
Goal assists	0
Passing	123
Passing accuracy	76%
Crosses	4
Crossing accuracy	25%
DEFENDING	
Tackles	10
Tackles won %	40%
Blocks	1
Interceptions	4
Clearances	10
Shots cleared off line	0
DISCIPLINE	
Fouls	9
Yellow cards	4
Red cards	0
SEE PAGE 278 FOR FULL STATS	

After six years at the club, Darren Holloway finally decided to call it quits at Sunderland in September 2000.

He duly secured a £1.25 million move to Wimbledon, ending his spell at the Stadium of Light, where he had found it increasingly difficult to break into the first team.

Sunderland began the 2000–01 campaign with a shortage of fit midfielders and Holloway duly found himself in the starting line-up in an unfamiliar position for the opening five Premiership fixtures. His distribution was composed, with an excellent 74% of his attempted passes finding a red-and-white shirt – an average bettered by few in the side.

But he also managed to pick up four yellow cards and, although Peter Reid is known to like a player to get stuck in, this was likely to try even his patience.

When players began to return to fitness, Holloway saw his days in the first team numbered and snapped up the chance to move to the Dons.

David HOPKIN • 30
BRADFORD CITY • BORN: 21.8.70

With the Bantams having successfully survived their first season in the top flight, David Hopkin clearly felt a move to Leeds' neighbours Bradford would be good for his career. He had been overtaken by younger squad members at Elland Road and a new challenge seemed to be a good option at the time.

His opening six appearances suggested that the Bantams had made a fine investment.

Hopkin used his good passing skills and his desire to get forward to terrorise opposition defences and was particularly impressive in the Bantams' superb 2–0 win over Chelsea in August.

But he then picked up an ankle ligament injury which sidelined him for four months.

His return to the side in January was short-lived and in March he fell foul of Jim Jefferies' aim to cut costs.

He secured an emotional return to former club Crystal Palace, helping the Eagles survive relegation to Division Two with a goal at Tranmere Rovers.

APPEARANCES	
Start (sub)	8(3)
Minutes on pitch	754
GOAL ATTEMPTS	
Goals	0
Shots on target	3
Shooting accuracy	27%
PASSING & CROSSING	
Goal assists	0
Passes in opp half	131
Passing accuracy in opp half	60%
Successful crosses	0
Cross completion	0%
DEFENDING	
Interceptions	0
Clearances	7
Tackles	26
Tackles won %	73%
DISCIPLINE	
Fouls	7
Yellow cards	1
Red cards	0
SEE PAGE 68 FOR FULL STATS	

Kevin HORLOCK • 6
MANCHESTER CITY • BORN: 1.11.72

APPEARANCES	
Start (sub)	14(0)
Minutes on pitch	1025
GOAL ATTEMPTS	
Goals	2
Shots on target	8
Shooting accuracy	47%
PASSING & CROSSING	
Goal assists	1
Passes in opp half	271
Passing accuracy in opp half	62%
Successful crosses	23
Cross completion	28%
DEFENDING	
Interceptions	3
Clearances	26
Tackles	33
Tackles won %	76%
DISCIPLINE	
Fouls	19
Yellow cards	1
Red cards	0
SEE PAGE 208 FOR FULL STATS	

Manchester City midfielder Kevin Horlock had a miserable season for the club, even aside from the Citizens' relegation.

Blighted with the most obvious nickname known to footballers called Kevin, "Super Kev" also had to contend with a broken ankle which at one point threatened to put an end to his career.

The season began well for the Northern Ireland international. Horlock was named in the starting XI for the first eight league fixtures of the campaign and netted twice during the period – one from the penalty spot and the other a simple tap-in, unlike the long-range efforts he has been known for during his career.

Sadly, an injury forced him to sit out seven matches and although he returned in force for six more starts, his ankle gave way after 28 minutes of December's match with Charlton and his season was over.

Thankfully, his fears of having to retire were unfounded and he should be back in City's 2001–02 line-up.

CB — Steve HOWEY • 24
MANCHESTER CITY • BORN: 26.10.71

Joe Royle paid Newcastle United £2 million for former England international Steve Howey, a move which was applauded by the Manchester City fans, who knew that their defence needed strengthening.

But ultimately Howey did not add enough to the Citizens' defence to stop them from being relegated at the conclusion of a dismal 2000–01 season.

The big stopper was one of the side's better performers, though, making almost 100 tackles and scoring six times.

Such escapades endeared him to the fans and he will be hoping the arrival of Kevin Keegan at the club will inspire them to a swift return to top-flight football.

After City were relegated, Howey commented: "It's difficult to describe how I feel. It's not nice at all. But if we're half as good as our fans we'll come straight back up. We're very confident." It remains to be seen whether the team are that good, or whether they are destined for another spell in the wilderness.

APPEARANCES	
Start (sub)	36(0)
Minutes on pitch	3146
GOAL ATTEMPTS	
Goals	6
DEFENDING	
Blocks	42
Shots cleared off line	3
Headed clearances	241
Other clearances	92
Interceptions	14
Last man saving tackles	3
Tackles won	75
Tackles won %	77%
PASSING	
Passing accuracy own half	79%
Passing accuracy opp half	56%
DISCIPLINE	
Fouls	64
Fouls in danger area	20
Yellow cards	7
Red cards	0

SEE PAGE 209 FOR FULL STATS

H

FB — Hermann HREIDARSSON • 32
IPSWICH TOWN • BORN: 11.7.74

APPEARANCES	
Start (sub)	35(1)
Minutes on pitch	3107
GOAL ATTEMPTS	
Goals	1
PASSING & CROSSING	
Goal assists	4
Passing	1305
Passing accuracy	66%
Crosses	89
Crossing accuracy	25%
DEFENDING	
Tackles	89
Tackles won %	72%
Blocks	38
Interceptions	12
Clearances	214
Shots cleared off line	0
DISCIPLINE	
Fouls	63
Yellow cards	3
Red cards	0

SEE PAGE 152 FOR FULL STATS

Some people were surprised that Ipswich Town decided to pay Wimbledon £4 million for the services of Hermann Hreidarsson, but as with almost every decision at Portman Road in 2000–01, it turned out for the best.

The club record signing – who was famously discovered for Crystal Palace by disc jockey David "Kid" Jensen's wife – was pivotal in the success of Ipswich's return to the top flight, both at centre-back and, more surprisingly, left-back.

He and Titus Bramble loved to surge out of defence with the ball whenever possible. He ended the campaign with four assists to his name, plus a goal against Manchester City.

A keen fan of heavy metal, "The Hermannator" surprised his team-mates when he prepared for matches by banging his head against the dressing-room wall.

He raised more eyebrows with his declaration that his favourite food was puffin, a staple food in his native Iceland. Such antics have endeared him to the Suffolk fans – although not to the RSPB.

goals than any other defender

Darren HUCKERBY • 21
MANCHESTER CITY • BORN: 23.4.76

The promise shown by Darren Huckerby in the early part of his career seems to have given way to disappointment and inconsistency, as the Nottingham-born striker again failed to live up to the expectations which have followed him since his days with Coventry.

Huckerby was rarely given an opportunity at Leeds during 2000–01. He made only seven appearances for United – including just two starts – before finally ending his miserable spell by signing for Manchester City in December.

But although he scored on his debut for the Citizens, the strike was only from the penalty spot and in 12 further appearances he failed to score a single goal. Worse still, he registered just three shots on target.

Injuries also hampered his progress but, more importantly, the speedy enthusiasm of old had clearly given way to despondency at his situation.

Perhaps a season in the first division will do Huckerby good, provided City do not decide to cash in on their £3 million investment.

APPEARANCES	
Start (sub)	10(10)
Minutes on pitch	951
GOAL ATTEMPTS	
Goals inside box	1
Goals outside box	0
Minutes per goal scored	951
Goals/shots ratio	6%
SHOOTING	
Shots on target inside box	4
Shots on target outside box	2
Shooting accuracy	38%
PASSING	
Goal assists	1
Key passes	12
Passing accuracy in opp half	55%
DISCIPLINE	
Fouls committed	19
Fouls won	26
Offside	27
Yellow cards	2
Red cards	0

SEE PAGES 167 & 209 FOR FULL STATS

Mark HUDSON • 36
MIDDLESBROUGH • BORN: 24.10.80

A sure sign that a player has hit the big time is his appearance in the Merlin football sticker album and Mark Hudson of Middlesbrough can proudly boast that his mug-shot will be in the 2002 edition.

Hudson made three substitute appearances for Boro during 2000–01, having been catapulted into the reckoning thanks to some excellent outings in the reserve side.

A skilful midfielder, who has come through the ranks at The Riverside, Hudson impressed with his close control while in the side and found a colleague with 74% of his passes.

He can also double as a striker, although he did not attempt any shots during his Premiership appearances.

"Unassuming and level-headed" off the field, according to the club's website, Hudson will need to have his wits about him as he looks to establish himself at The Riverside.

Boro appear to rate him highly and he will be hopeful of making the grade.

SEE PAGE 236 FOR FULL STATS

Despondent: Darren Huckerby

For more information visit our website:

CB

Aaron HUGHES • 18
NEWCASTLE UNITED • BORN: 8.11.79

Since establishing himself in the first team 12 months ago, Aaron Hughes has become a permanent fixture in the Newcastle rearguard and enhanced his ever-growing reputation with a number of assured displays throughout 2000–01.

Bobby Robson's faith in the Irish defender was reflected by the fact that he started 31 games in succession and offered an element of stability amid changes in personnel.

Central defensive partner Alain Goma departed for Fulham and Andrew O'Brien joined from Bradford but, seemingly unphased, Hughes kept his mind on the job and was one of three Magpies to amass more than 1,000 passes.

The Northern Ireland international proved ideally-equipped for combating aerial attacks and nodded more than a century of balls away from the danger area. He also cleared a shot off the line in the Geordies' desperate bid to maintain a morale-boosting clean sheet. With a settled team around him, Hughes could ably provide part of the spine of a future successful Newcastle team.

APPEARANCES	
Start (sub)	34(1)
Minutes on pitch	2994
GOAL ATTEMPTS	
Goals	0
DEFENDING	
Blocks	29
Shots cleared off line	1
Headed clearances	125
Other clearances	91
Interceptions	6
Last man saving tackles	0
Tackles won	57
Tackles won %	76%
PASSING	
Passing accuracy own half	84%
Passing accuracy opp half	64%
DISCIPLINE	
Fouls	13
Fouls in danger area	4
Yellow cards	2
Red cards	0

SEE PAGE 251 FOR FULL STATS

 S

Mark HUGHES • 23
EVERTON • BORN: 1.11.63

APPEARANCES	
Start (sub)	6(3)
Minutes on pitch	453
GOAL ATTEMPTS	
Goals inside box	0
Goals outside box	0
Minutes per goal scored	n/a
Goals/shots ratio	0%
SHOOTING	
Shots on target inside box	5
Shots on target outside box	1
Shooting accuracy	86%
PASSING	
Goal assists	0
Key passes	0
Passing accuracy in opp half	68%
DISCIPLINE	
Fouls committed	18
Fouls won	17
Offside	16
Yellow cards	1
Red cards	0

SEE PAGE 139 FOR FULL STATS

The name Mark Hughes is becoming synonymous with the term "morale crusader" after his latest season of goodwill.

When Everton suffered an injury crisis in the final two months of the 1999–2000 campaign, Walter Smith lured the Welsh manager from The Dell to fill the breach at Goodison, and he did.

Then fellow-Scotsman Graeme Souness followed suit by signing Hughes on a free transfer in October to bolster Blackburn's promotion push, and they finished second in Division One.

He may not run around with the pace of old, but "Sparky" still possesses the enthusiasm of a trainee. There were no spectacular goals in his nine outings, but an 86% shooting accuracy is evidence enough that his boots are still full of venom. And the fact that he was fouled 17 times implied that defenders continued to view him as a threat.

With 12 months left on his current contract, Hughes may be afforded one final opportunity to wreak havoc at the top.

Stephen HUGHES • 10
EVERTON • BORN: 18.9.76

Stephen Hughes moved to Everton after bemoaning the lack of first-team opportunities available at Highbury.

Sadly, at Goodison Park he played the full 90 minutes only 10 times in the 2000–01 Premiership season.

Former team-mate Dennis Bergkamp said Hughes was right to move on, as Arsenal do not have a huge reputation for bringing through young players, but it is still not clicking for him on Merseyside.

Hughes failed to settle in the north and has not fulfilled his true potential.

His tackle success rate of 65% was below-average for a midfielder, as was his pass completion rate of 70%.

An extended run in the side would help his confidence although it is unlikely that manager Walter Smith will have too much room in his team to carry passengers as Everton face another tough season in 2001–02.

Hughes will probably move on if another club comes in with the right offer.

APPEARANCES	
Start (sub)	16(2)
Minutes on pitch	1352
GOAL ATTEMPTS	
Goals	0
Shots on target	4
Shooting accuracy	33%
PASSING & CROSSING	
Goal assists	1
Passes in opp half	390
Passing accuracy in opp half	66%
Successful crosses	9
Cross completion	21%
DEFENDING	
Interceptions	6
Clearances	22
Tackles	62
Tackles won %	65%
DISCIPLINE	
Fouls	30
Yellow cards	3
Red cards	0
SEE PAGE 139 FOR FULL STATS	

Andy HUNT • 9
CHARLTON ATHLETIC • BORN: 9.6.70

APPEARANCES	
Start (sub)	8(0)
Minutes on pitch	680
GOAL ATTEMPTS	
Goals inside box	4
Goals outside box	0
Minutes per goal scored	170
Goals/shots ratio	44%
SHOOTING	
Shots on target inside box	6
Shots on target outside box	0
Shooting accuracy	67%
PASSING	
Goal assists	1
Key passes	10
Passing accuracy in opp half	72%
DISCIPLINE	
Fouls committed	21
Fouls won	17
Offside	12
Yellow cards	0
Red cards	0
SEE PAGE 82 FOR FULL STATS	

Charlton striker Andy Hunt was forced to retire from football after failing to recover from post-viral fatigue syndrome.

Understandably, Hunt said he was "devastated" that he would not be able to play a part in Charlton's future success.

The Addick was the club's top goalscorer in their promotion season of 1999–2000 and scored four times in the first eight games of the 2000–01 campaign.

In what turned out to be his final professional match, he netted before his substitution – a fitting exit for a forward who helped the team into the élite.

Manager Alan Curbishley said it would cost the club something like £4 million or £5 million to sign a player of the same quality.

In the Premiership games he did play for Charlton, Hunt fired nine shots and hit the target with six of them, illustrating how potent a player he was for the south Londoners.

He will be sadly-missed by everyone at The Valley.

Don HUTCHISON • 4
SUNDERLAND • BORN: 9.5.71

Famed for his antics with a Budweiser beer label, Don "Wasssuup" Hutchison has been a revelation since his move to Sunderland.

Spending most of the season playing in right-midfield for Peter Reid did not prevent him from netting eight goals, including a vital strike in the win over rivals Newcastle. Only Kevin Phillips scored more for the team.

His shooting accuracy of 52% throughout the 2000–01 season showed why he was asked to fill in on a couple of occasions as a stand-in striker – a position which he also fills for Scotland.

The Black Cat also set up six goals for team-mates, making him the top creator at the Stadium of Light.

That assist tally comes as no surprise when you consider that no other Sunderland midfielder completed more successful passes than Hutchison.

With increasingly impressive performances for club and country, it appears that he has put the misdemeanours of the past behind him. True.

APPEARANCES	
Start (sub)	30(2)
Minutes on pitch	2671
GOAL ATTEMPTS	
Goals	8
Shots on target	24
Shooting accuracy	52%
Goals/shots ratio	17%
PASSING	
Goal assists	6
Passes in opp half	801
Passing accuracy in opp half	61%
Crosses	105
Crossing accuracy	30%
DRIBBLING	
Dribbles & runs	92
Dribble completion	58%
Corners forced	13
DISCIPLINE	
Fouls	80
Yellow cards	11
Red cards	1

SEE PAGE 278 FOR FULL STATS

H

Sami HYYPIA • 12
LIVERPOOL • BORN: 7.10.73

APPEARANCES	
Start (sub)	35(0)
Minutes on pitch	3150
GOAL ATTEMPTS	
Goals	3
DEFENDING	
Blocks	28
Shots cleared off line	0
Headed clearances	345
Other clearances	121
Interceptions	16
Last man saving tackles	3
Tackles won	64
Tackles won %	69%
PASSING	
Passing accuracy own half	85%
Passing accuracy opp half	59%
DISCIPLINE	
Fouls	29
Fouls in danger area	11
Yellow cards	0
Red cards	0

SEE PAGE 195 FOR FULL STATS

Giant Finn Sami Hyypia has become the symbolic totem of Liverpool's defensive solidity under Gérard Houllier.

It seemed for many years that Liverpool would never have a defender in the true Ron Yates or Larry Lloyd mould, but for a bargain £2.6 million the Reds have an old-fashioned stopper. It is appropriate that it was chief scout Yates himself who recommended him to Houllier.

Hyypia made more clearances than any other defender in the Premiership during the 2000–01 season, but it was his three goal-line clearances in the FA Cup final which epitomised his worth to the resurgent Reds.

In the UEFA Cup against Barcelona, the defender kept the likes of Rivaldo, Kluivert and Overmars in check and will be remembered at Anfield for a powerful tackle on the Brazilian.

Hyypia swiped the ball away just as Rivaldo was about to shoot, sending the Brazilian flying and prompting TV pundit Alan Hansen to shout: "That's the way to stop him, Sami!"

Premiership's most fouled player

Sasa ILIC • 13
G CHARLTON ATHLETIC • BORN: 18.7.72

Following his heroics in the 1998 Division One play-off final victory over Sunderland, Sasa Ilic inspired Charlton fan and poet Ted Smith-Orr to pen *Sasa Ilic Saves*, which includes the immortal words: "Red and white stripes converge like accelerated toothpaste down the exits. CHARLTON ARE PREMIER LEAGUE."

But wind forward three years and the Addicks' shot-stopper is relying on others' misfortune to get a game.

Injury to first-choice goalkeeper Dean Kiely provided Ilic with an opportunity to dust off his gloves and return to the Charlton goal in February 2001.

This was a welcome respite for a player who had spent the best part of two seasons idling on the substitutes' bench.

He kept the Tottenham and Newcastle frontrunners at bay to record consecutive shut-outs in his first two appearances and remained between the posts until the end of the campaign. But Ilic's spell ended on a sour note when Liverpool beat him four times on the final day.

APPEARANCES	
Start (sub)	13(0)
Minutes on pitch	1170
SHOT STOPPING	
Goals conceded (inside box)	15
Goals conceded (outside box)	4
Minutes per goal conceded	62
Clean sheets	5
Saves (shots inside box)	25
Saves (shots outside box)	22
Saves/shots	71%
DISTRIBUTION	
Long kick %	42%
Throws/short passes %	93%
CATCHING	
Crosses caught	32
Crosses punched	15
Crosses dropped	5
Catch success %	86%
DISCIPLINE	
Yellow cards	1
Red cards	0
SEE PAGE 82 FOR FULL STATS	

Andy IMPEY • 24
AM LEICESTER CITY • BORN: 13.9.71

APPEARANCES	
Start (sub)	29(4)
Minutes on pitch	2606
GOAL ATTEMPTS	
Goals	0
Shots on target	1
Shooting accuracy	13%
Goals/shots ratio	0%
PASSING	
Goal assists	1
Passes in opp half	419
Passing accuracy in opp half	72%
Crosses	106
Crossing accuracy	25%
DRIBBLING	
Dribbles & runs	101
Dribble completion	66%
Corners forced	16
DISCIPLINE	
Fouls	22
Yellow cards	2
Red cards	0
SEE PAGE 181 FOR FULL STATS	

Darren Eadie describes team-mate Andy Impey as a "typical Jamaican" for his laid-back approach to life but, fortunately for Leicester, Impey was as alert as ever when donning the blue shirt in 2000–01.

The energetic wing-back is renowned for his willingness to fly down the flanks and he attempted more dribbles and runs than any of his colleagues, beating his marker 66% of the time. Despite his effectiveness in the opposition half, Impey did not neglect his defensive duties and emerged triumphant from more than three-quarters of his tackles.

The Hammersmith-born livewire may have stuck close to his roots earlier in his career, turning out for Londoners QPR and West Ham respectively, but he now appears content in the Midlands.

Although originally a Martin O'Neill purchase, current Foxes boss Peter Taylor was keen to secure Impey's future at the club and he duly signed a two-year extension to his existing contract, which will keep him at Filbert Street until 2004.

For more information visit our website:

Paul INCE • 9
MIDDLESBROUGH • BORN: 21.10.67

Having helped Middlesbrough stave off the threat of relegation for nine months, captain Paul Ince would no doubt be looking forward to unwinding during a stress-free summer.

He may settle for a gentle swim in the pool rather than risk a visit to the physiotherapist, after mistakenly stripping off for a "masseuse" in an industrial unit and promptly being offered "a full set of sexual services".

But on the field of play he held his own. "The Guv'nor" bossed the midfield and won more tackles than any of his team-mates during the Teessiders' quest for safety.

He netted a crucial 89th-minute equaliser against fellow-strugglers Bradford and racked up more than 950 passes throughout 2000–01, proving there is still life in the ageing campaigner.

Ince maintained his "hardman" image by collecting eight bookings – the same total that he amassed during 1999–2000 – and he will doubtless be itching to throw his studs into the next chapter of Riverside history in season 2001–02.

APPEARANCES	
Start (sub)	30(0)
Minutes on pitch	2686
GOAL ATTEMPTS	
Goals	2
Shots on target	21
Shooting accuracy	62%
PASSING & CROSSING	
Goal assists	1
Passes in opp half	738
Passing accuracy in opp half	66%
Successful crosses	10
Cross completion	26%
DEFENDING	
Interceptions	12
Clearances	54
Tackles	108
Tackles won %	69%
DISCIPLINE	
Fouls	33
Yellow cards	8
Red cards	0

SEE PAGE 236 FOR FULL STATS

Denis IRWIN • 3
MANCHESTER UNITED • BORN: 31.10.65

APPEARANCES	
Start (sub)	20(1)
Minutes on pitch	1760
GOAL ATTEMPTS	
Goals	0
PASSING & CROSSING	
Goal assists	2
Passing	1080
Passing accuracy	81%
Crosses	77
Crossing accuracy	31%
DEFENDING	
Tackles	40
Tackles won %	78%
Blocks	14
Interceptions	3
Clearances	73
Shots cleared off line	0
DISCIPLINE	
Fouls	14
Yellow cards	2
Red cards	0

SEE PAGE 222 FOR FULL STATS

When Denis Irwin casts his eye over an illustrious career in future years, 2000–01 will surely stand out as one of his most memorable campaigns. On St Patrick's Day, the Irishman captained United to victory over Leicester and became only the sixth player in the club's history to have made 500 appearances in the famous red shirt.

In his testimonial season, Irwin once again lived up to his "Mr Dependable" tag and performed solidly in the back four. His tackle success rate was four percentage points above the Premiership average and he distributed the ball with the assured precision of a veteran.

The former Oldham defender cost the Red Devils a mere £625,000 in 1990 and represents one of the bargain buys of the last decade. But a combination of injuries, squad rotation and competition from younger players restricted Irwin to 20 starts and he may find first-team opportunities even more limited in 2001–02 should he remain at Old Trafford.

Steffen IVERSEN • 10
TOTTENHAM HOTSPUR • BORN: 10.11.76

S

Steffen Iversen's hotly-anticipated partnership with Sergei Rebrov was put on ice after just nine games of the 2000–01 season. The former Rosenborg striker underwent surgery to repair cartilage damage and, after requiring a second operation, he was sidelined for almost four months.

On his brief return, the Norwegian international rifled home two strikes in five games, netting against Coventry and Bradford. In total he fired 12 shots on target, but limited playing time meant his goals-to-shots ratio was not even half as prolific as the 15% he achieved in 1999–2000.

Iversen missed the remaining six games of the season after being knocked unconscious against the battling Bantams and had little time to impress new manager Glenn Hoddle.

Revelations of his off-field antics will not have helped his cause, after it emerged that he ended up drunk and naked in a caravan after scoring Norway's winner against Spain in Euro 2000 – a mentality that his spiritual boss will be keen to exorcise.

APPEARANCES	
Start (sub)	10(4)
Minutes on pitch	858
GOAL ATTEMPTS	
Goals inside box	2
Goals outside box	0
Minutes per goal scored	429
Goals/shots ratio	7%
SHOOTING	
Shots on target inside box	7
Shots on target outside box	5
Shooting accuracy	41%
PASSING	
Goal assists	1
Key passes	14
Passing accuracy in opp half	67%
DISCIPLINE	
Fouls committed	11
Fouls won	16
Offside	3
Yellow cards	2
Red cards	0
SEE PAGE 293 FOR FULL STATS	

Muzzy IZZET • 6
LEICESTER CITY • BORN: 31.10.74

AM

APPEARANCES	
Start (sub)	27(0)
Minutes on pitch	2242
GOAL ATTEMPTS	
Goals	7
Shots on target	17
Shooting accuracy	59%
Goals/shots ratio	24%
PASSING	
Goal assists	1
Passes in opp half	692
Passing accuracy in opp half	71%
Crosses	82
Crossing accuracy	23%
DRIBBLING	
Dribbles & runs	70
Dribble completion	56%
Corners forced	14
DISCIPLINE	
Fouls	25
Yellow cards	4
Red cards	0
SEE PAGE 181 FOR FULL STATS	

When Neil Lennon departed for Celtic in December, the onus fell on Muzzy Izzet to continue to provide Leicester with a level of midfield dynamism.

He responded in determined fashion by notching a further four goals to become the second-highest scorer at the club in 2000–01.

The Turkish international was always bustling with energy in the Foxes' engine room. In defensive mode he tracked back to win 64 challenges and, when in possession, found a blue shirt with 77% of his distribution.

But his season was cut short by a persistent calf injury and it is no coincidence that Leicester's season collapsed without their inspirational schemer.

Back at home Izzet could spend time with his baby daughter, whose birth had quite an impact on his game.

Two days after Ella was born, an emotionally-drained Izzet ventured out against Coventry, but later confessed: "My legs were just not there."

24% Muzzy Izzet's goals-to-shots ratio

CB **Richard JACKSON • 18**
DERBY COUNTY • BORN: 18.4.80

After signing a new three-year deal at Pride Park, young defender Richard Jackson led Derby's excellent reserve side to their second successive title in 2000–01, but was unable to emulate Chris Riggott's success at first-team level.

Signed from Scarborough for a fee of £30,000, Jackson played just twice for the senior side in 2000–01 – once against Everton and again on the last day of the season in the Rams' 1–1 draw with Ipswich.

Jackson was lucky to play any part in Derby's campaign at all, though. In January, he collided with Rams hardman Seth Johnson while training, breaking his cheekbone in four places.

That injury was expected to rule him out for the remainder of the season, but after a successful operation Jackson battled back well to stake his claim for a more regular spot in Jim Smith's plans. He is widely expected to feature more regularly in 2001–02.

SEE PAGE 125 FOR FULL STATS

Battling Bantam: Wayne Jacobs

  FB **Wayne JACOBS • 22**
BRADFORD CITY • BORN: 3.2.69

Wayne Jacobs has seen off the challenge of several players signed to replace him down the years and it seems that he will once again be Bradford City's first-choice left-back in 2001–02.

It could all have been so different, though. While playing for Hull City in 1993, Jacobs sustained a career-threatening knee injury and was released from the club.

Rotherham United picked him up, but the old injury flared up again and his career looked to be over.

Bradford took a chance on Jacobs, though and he has never looked back.

While he still suffers from niggling injuries, his form has been such that the likes of Andy Myers and Ian Nolan have been unable to force him out of the starting line-up when fit.

A wholehearted competitor, Jacobs recorded a 74% tackle success rate in 2000–01 and his battling displays prompted one Bantams fan to declare: "Some players would walk through a brick wall for the club. Wayne puts those showboaters to shame."

APPEARANCES	
Start (sub)	19(2)
Minutes on pitch	1679
GOAL ATTEMPTS	
Goals	2
PASSING & CROSSING	
Goal assists	0
Passing	665
Passing accuracy	66%
Crosses	63
Crossing accuracy	32%
DEFENDING	
Tackles	46
Tackles won %	74%
Blocks	16
Interceptions	13
Clearances	71
Shots cleared off line	0
DISCIPLINE	
Fouls	18
Yellow cards	2
Red cards	0
SEE PAGE 68 FOR FULL STATS	

was the highest at Leicester City

David JAMES • 1
ASTON VILLA • BORN: 1.8.70

David James signed a new contract at Aston Villa in 2001, something which had looked unlikely in December 2000 when the England star handed in a transfer request.

Like many of Villa's players, James had expressed his dissatisfaction at the club's apparent lack of ambition, but John Gregory moved to convince his 'keeper that his future lay in Birmingham and James eventually put pen to paper on a new deal.

The former Liverpool number one certainly provided Villa with value for money – and, despite dropping more crosses than any other goalkeeper in 2000–01, James earned himself a regular place in Sven-Göran Eriksson's England squad.

James's modelling career also went from strength to strength, although his days on the catwalk almost came to an end after he sustained a facial injury while playing against Everton.

Thankfully there was no lasting damage to James's face, ensuring that he remains free to model the finest in male *haute couture*.

APPEARANCES	
Start (sub)	38(0)
Minutes on pitch	3420
SHOT STOPPING	
Goals conceded (inside box)	39
Goals conceded (outside box)	4
Minutes per goal conceded	80
Clean sheets	9
Saves (shots inside box)	60
Saves (shots outside box)	53
Saves/shots	72%
DISTRIBUTION	
Long kick %	47%
Throws/short passes %	66%
CATCHING	
Crosses caught	102
Crosses punched	26
Crosses dropped	10
Catch success %	91%
DISCIPLINE	
Yellow cards	0
Red cards	0
SEE PAGE 55 FOR FULL STATS	

Francis JEFFERS • 14
EVERTON • BORN: 25.1.81

APPEARANCES	
Start (sub)	10(2)
Minutes on pitch	893
GOAL ATTEMPTS	
Goals inside box	6
Goals outside box	0
Minutes per goal scored	149
Goals/shots ratio	19%
SHOOTING	
Shots on target inside box	18
Shots on target outside box	3
Shooting accuracy	68%
PASSING	
Goal assists	1
Key passes	2
Passing accuracy in opp half	71%
DISCIPLINE	
Fouls committed	17
Fouls won	7
Offside	24
Yellow cards	3
Red cards	0
SEE PAGE 139 FOR FULL STATS	

Francis Jeffers turned down a new deal at the end of the 2000–01 season and, with just one year left on his contract, the Toffees decided to cash in on their young star before he was able to leave on a free transfer.

The youngster was placed on the transfer list in May 2001.

Jeffers started the 2000–01 season in blistering fashion, scoring five goals in Everton's first five games.

A lengthy lay-off after injury put paid to any hopes he might have had of taking the Golden Boot, but he was quickly back among the goals on his return five months later scoring after just eight minutes against Leicester.

A goals-to-shots ratio of 19% marks Jeffers out as a top talent and his departure will come as a bitter blow to Everton.

As a boyhood fan of the Toffees, Jeffers' desire to leave Goodison Park merely underlines how far Everton have fallen down the Premiership pecking order.

There will be no shortage of admirers keen to get his signature.

Claus JENSEN • 20
CHARLTON ATHLETIC • BORN: 29.4.77

Claus Jensen – signed from Bolton Wanderers for £4 million – played more than 3,000 minutes of football in 2000–01 for Charlton, yet he committed just 10 fouls and was not booked once.

This made him the cleanest player in the Premiership, something he is sure to cherish for a short while.

He also ended the campaign as London's most accurate corner-taker, as he capped a fine first season at The Valley. Ipswich and the Addicks battled it out for the Dane's services in the summer of 2000 and, luckily for Charlton, he chose Alan Curbishley's team.

Five goals and three assists capped an exciting term and Jensen seemed to have secured a regular spot in the Danish national side, too.

Along with players such as Chris Powell, Matthias Svensson and Shaun Bartlett, he has added an international flavour to the south London club, in keeping with the Premiership élite with whom they comfortably rubbed shoulders in 2000–01.

APPEARANCES	
Start (sub)	37(1)
Minutes on pitch	3174
GOAL ATTEMPTS	
Goals	5
Shots on target	31
Shooting accuracy	51%
PASSING & CROSSING	
Goal assists	3
Passes in opp half	990
Passing accuracy in opp half	77%
Successful crosses	90
Cross completion	34%
DEFENDING	
Interceptions	5
Clearances	16
Tackles	57
Tackles won %	77%
DISCIPLINE	
Fouls	10
Yellow cards	0
Red cards	0
SEE PAGE 82 FOR FULL STATS	

Eoin JESS • 29
BRADFORD CITY • BORN: 13.12.70

APPEARANCES	
Start (sub)	17(0)
Minutes on pitch	1504
GOAL ATTEMPTS	
Goals	3
Shots on target	14
Shooting accuracy	48%
Goals/shots ratio	10%
PASSING	
Goal assists	4
Passes in opp half	412
Passing accuracy in opp half	76%
Crosses	77
Crossing accuracy	26%
DRIBBLING	
Dribbles & runs	62
Dribble completion	76%
Corners forced	8
DISCIPLINE	
Fouls	10
Yellow cards	0
Red cards	0
SEE PAGE 68 FOR FULL STATS	

Bradford brought Eoin Jess back to the Premiership in December 2000 and the Scotsman certainly impressed at Valley Parade, scoring three goals and creating a further four.

His passing was above average for Bradford and unsurprisingly he became a favourite with the beleaguered fans.

Aberdeen supporters were sad to see him leave Pittodrie for a second time, as he certainly enjoyed his best spell there, but the chance to link up with Jim Jefferies was too tempting for Jess.

He made an immediate impact, scoring 25 minutes into his debut on New Year's Day at Leicester City.

The strike helped Bradford to their only away win of the season in the league. Despite the Yorkshire club's relegation to Nationwide Division One, Jess was more than happy to sign a three-year contract in May 2001.

He looks set to be at Valley Parade for some time and will hope to help Scotland qualify for the 2002 World Cup.

Phil JEVONS • 26
EVERTON • BORN: 1.8.79

Four substitute appearances – that was all Phil Jevons had to show for his toils at the end of the 2000–01 season.

In all, he managed to play just 105 minutes for the Toffeemen – 44 fewer than he racked up during the previous campaign.

Jevons could not even claim that bigger names in the Everton side kept him out, as Walter Smith had to juggle his pack more than any other manager in the Premiership due to the ongoing injury crisis and yet rarely turned to the young forward.

Jevons managed two shots during his time on the field – hardly enough for an indication of his talents – although, for the record, his accuracy sat at 50%.

With Tranmere Rovers among those interested in Jevons should he fail to secure a new contract at Goodison Park, a move away from Everton seems the best possible way for the former FA Youth Cup winner to resurrect his career.

But with Francis Jeffers set to leave perhaps 2001–02 will offer Jevons a chance.

APPEARANCES	
Start (sub)	0(4)
Minutes on pitch	105
GOAL ATTEMPTS	
Goals	0
Shots on target	1
Shooting accuracy	50%
Goals/shots ratio	0%
PASSING	
Goal assists	0
Passes in opp half	38
Passing accuracy in opp half	50%
Crosses	2
Crossing accuracy	50%
DRIBBLING	
Dribbles & runs	6
Dribble completion	67%
Corners forced	2
DISCIPLINE	
Fouls	4
Yellow cards	0
Red cards	0
SEE PAGE 139 FOR FULL STATS	

Julian JOACHIM • 12
ASTON VILLA • BORN: 20.9.74

APPEARANCES	
Start (sub)	11(9)
Minutes on pitch	1188
GOAL ATTEMPTS	
Goals inside box	6
Goals outside box	1
Minutes per goal scored	170
Goals/shots ratio	29%
SHOOTING	
Shots on target inside box	11
Shots on target outside box	6
Shooting accuracy	71%
PASSING	
Goal assists	1
Key passes	12
Passing accuracy in opp half	68%
DISCIPLINE	
Fouls committed	17
Fouls won	27
Offside	16
Yellow cards	0
Red cards	0
SEE PAGE 55 FOR FULL STATS	

Julian Joachim and John Gregory began a furious row in summer 2000 as the Aston Villa manager allegedly reneged on a deal to give his striker an improved contract.

This infuriated Joachim and the tiny striker announced that he would never play for Villa again, branding his boss "gutless".

Unfortunately for him, such stands are rarely popular with the fans and Gregory was able to use it to his benefit, announcing that the fans were right to boo players who wanted to leave the Midlands club.

Gregory selected Joachim to play throughout the season, though often as a substitute. The result was that the former Leicester man scored more goals in 2000–01 than he did in 1999–2000, despite playing for less than half the time.

In fact he was the league's top-scoring substitute, netting four times from the bench.

He did not win the fans over completely, though – and his future at the club was still uncertain going into the summer along with several other Villa players.

4 Julian Joachim scored more goals as a

Joseph-Desiré JOB • 16
MIDDLESBROUGH • BORN: 1.12.77

Bryan Robson seemingly had a mission to have the world's largest collection of strikers in 2000 and he signed the entertainingly named Joseph-Desiré Job from French club Lens.

He joined such players as Alun Armstrong, Brian Deane, Alen Boksic, Hamilton Ricard, Andy Campbell and others in the overpopulated Boro squad.

As a result, the Cameroonian did not see as much action as he would have hoped – playing just 679 minutes for the Teesside club.

The season started well enough, with a debut goal at Coventry, but just two more followed, one in September and one on the final day of the season.

He converted a reasonable 14% of his chances and 59% of all his efforts were on target, so he certainly has ability.

Job was frustrated about his lack of first-team opportunities but, with a fresh regime on the cards at The Riverside, he will have to do a lot of impressing if he is to get another chance.

APPEARANCES	
Start (sub)	8(4)
Minutes on pitch	679
GOAL ATTEMPTS	
Goals inside box	3
Goals outside box	0
Minutes per goal scored	226
Goals/shots ratio	14%
SHOOTING	
Shots on target inside box	11
Shots on target outside box	2
Shooting accuracy	59%
PASSING	
Goal assists	1
Key passes	8
Passing accuracy in opp half	64%
DISCIPLINE	
Fouls committed	8
Fouls won	10
Offside	11
Yellow cards	0
Red cards	0
SEE PAGE 237 FOR FULL STATS	

J

Jonatan JOHANSSON • 21
CHARLTON ATHLETIC • BORN: 16.8.75

APPEARANCES	
Start (sub)	27(4)
Minutes on pitch	2445
GOAL ATTEMPTS	
Goals inside box	11
Goals outside box	0
Minutes per goal scored	222
Goals/shots ratio	15%
SHOOTING	
Shots on target inside box	37
Shots on target outside box	5
Shooting accuracy	58%
PASSING	
Goal assists	3
Key passes	15
Passing accuracy in opp half	59%
DISCIPLINE	
Fouls committed	37
Fouls won	29
Offside	65
Yellow cards	2
Red cards	0
SEE PAGE 82 FOR FULL STATS	

Charlton spent wisely in summer 2000 and the £3.75 million they paid Glasgow Rangers for Finnish striker Jonatan Johansson was a bargain. The Justin Timberlake lookalike scored 11 times for the Addicks, helping them to a top-half finish.

The majority of his shots were on target and he linked up with the rest of his team-mates in style.

With his curly mop and cheeky smile, he became a Woolwich icon. He was capable when he pulled wide, too, creating three goals and whipping in 81 crosses.

A lot of clubs had thought about investing in the striker, but were slightly wary. Charlton showed no nerves and have profited from their astute gamble.

The one disappointment was the way in which his goals dried up towards the end of the season.

Johansson's goal against Coventry in February was his fourth in four games, but he was not to hit the back of the net again in 2000–01.

substitute than any other player

Ronny JOHNSEN • 5
MANCHESTER UNITED • BORN: 10.6.69

Ronny Johnsen is known as "Sicknote" among the United staff and his knees do seem to be as delicate as a balsa-wood construction.

He managed to play 893 minutes in 2000–01. But Alex Ferguson had to do without the Norwegian for long spells and Wes Brown and Jaap Stam became the gaffer's first-choice defensive partnership, leaving Johnsen's future at Old Trafford less secure than in previous seasons.

He did score a goal in 2000–01, a strike in the 2–0 win against Newcastle in August, but he rarely hit such heights again. He took no part in any of United's "big" games, and did not feature at all between November and the end of April.

Season 2001–02 is the final year of Johnsen's contract at Old Trafford and it is likely to be his last campaign unless he can regain full fitness.

Whatever happens, he has certainly got his money's worth in terms of medals since moving to the seven-times Premiership champions.

APPEARANCES	
Start (sub)	11(0)
Minutes on pitch	893
GOAL ATTEMPTS	
Goals	1
DEFENDING	
Blocks	4
Shots cleared off line	0
Headed clearances	42
Other clearances	16
Interceptions	3
Last man saving tackles	0
Tackles won	9
Tackles won %	69%
PASSING	
Passing accuracy own half	94%
Passing accuracy opp half	78%
DISCIPLINE	
Fouls	24
Fouls in danger area	5
Yellow cards	1
Red cards	0
SEE PAGE 222 FOR FULL STATS	

David JOHNSON • 9
IPSWICH TOWN • BORN: 15.8.76

APPEARANCES	
Start (sub)	6(8)
Minutes on pitch	608
GOAL ATTEMPTS	
Goals inside box	0
Goals outside box	0
Minutes per goal scored	n/a
Goals/shots ratio	0%
SHOOTING	
Shots on target inside box	3
Shots on target outside box	2
Shooting accuracy	24%
PASSING	
Goal assists	1
Key passes	5
Passing accuracy in opp half	67%
DISCIPLINE	
Fouls committed	22
Fouls won	7
Offside	17
Yellow cards	0
Red cards	0
SEE PAGE 152 FOR FULL STATS	

Having fired in 22 goals for Ipswich in their 1999–2000 promotion campaign, David Johnson would have hoped for a better season than the one he got in 2000–01.

He began the season as a first choice in the Ipswich line-up, but squandered a number of chances to open his Premiership account.

With injury problems developing and Marcus Stewart in impressive form, Johnson found it difficult to hold down a first-team place.

A popular figure at the club, Ipswich hoped to hold on to him as a squad player, but a £3.5 million bid from Nottingham Forest in January persuaded the Suffolk side to part with the former Manchester United trainee.

Johnson arrived in Nottingham harbouring hopes of another run to play-offs, but he struggled to find the goals that came so easily in 1999–2000.

Very much a confidence player, this lack of goals harmed his performances and now he will have to settle for another year at least in Nationwide Division One as Forest seek to get promoted.

For more information visit our website:

Seth JOHNSON • 7
DERBY COUNTY • BORN: 12.3.79

Seth Johnson's season was blighted by disciplinary problems, culminating in an horrific tackle on Stuart McCall in April that saw him sent off and forced to apologise to his team-mates.

It was particularly disappointing as he had been made captain for the game.

As well as that aberration, Johnson was shown 10 yellow cards and had to go before an FA disciplinary panel to explain his waywardness. Such events distracted from his undoubted ability.

The 2000–01 campaign did have its high points, though, as Peter Taylor selected him for the England squad which travelled to Italy in November.

Johnson was named as a sub and came on with 17 minutes to play. He almost scored with his first touch and it was a great experience for the former Crewe midfielder.

But any hopes of further appearances for the national side will have to be tempered if he cannot remain calmer on the pitch and avoid getting cautioned so often.

APPEARANCES	
Start (sub)	30(0)
Minutes on pitch	2657

GOAL ATTEMPTS	
Goals	1
Shots on target	6
Shooting accuracy	29%

PASSING & CROSSING	
Goal assists	5
Passes in opp half	689
Passing accuracy in opp half	61%
Successful crosses	23
Cross completion	31%

DEFENDING	
Interceptions	11
Clearances	68
Tackles	94
Tackles won %	70%

DISCIPLINE	
Fouls	38
Yellow cards	10
Red cards	1

SEE PAGE 125 FOR FULL STATS

Slavisa JOKANOVIC • 10
CHELSEA • BORN: 16.8.68

APPEARANCES	
Start (sub)	7(12)
Minutes on pitch	760

GOAL ATTEMPTS	
Goals	0
Shots on target	1
Shooting accuracy	20%

PASSING & CROSSING	
Goal assists	1
Passes in opp half	291
Passing accuracy in opp half	76%
Successful crosses	1
Cross completion	13%

DEFENDING	
Interceptions	2
Clearances	22
Tackles	50
Tackles won %	72%

DISCIPLINE	
Fouls	22
Yellow cards	5
Red cards	0

SEE PAGE 97 FOR FULL STATS

Slavisa Jokanovic was Claudio Ranieri's first signing as Chelsea manager, when he paid £1.7 million to Deportivo La Coruña for the Yugoslav midfielder.

The player did not settle in too well, playing just 760 minutes thanks to a combination of injury and tactical selections.

The Pensioners' midfield may have lost the excellent Roberto Di Matteo, but the improvement in Sam Dalla Bona meant that Jokanovic was often left on the bench.

After scoring during Euro 2000 for his country, Jokanovic would have been disappointed not to open his Chelsea account in 2000–01.

He almost got into trouble in March when he appeared to stamp on Don Hutchison's head in Chelsea's 4–2 home defeat to the Wearsiders, but the case was dropped, with Hutchison arguing: "I'm not sure he meant it, as he's not that type of player."

Jokanovic is unlikely to have a memorable career at Chelsea, as the club attempt to reduce the average age of their squad.

Matthew JONES • 7
LEICESTER CITY • BORN: 1.9.80

Peter Taylor was not averse to introducing new talent to the Leicester City squad in 2000–01 and he spent £3 million on bringing Matthew Jones to Filbert Street.

Jones came as a replacement for Neil Lennon, who had joined Celtic – and the former Leeds youngster made an impressive debut for the club in a 3–1 win for the Foxes against Charlton.

Ironically, his last game for Leeds was at Leicester in a 3–1 win for City. But little did the home fans know that the opposition player being substituted after 61 minutes would soon be bolstering their squad.

His low point of the season came when he was sent off in Leicester's home game with Arsenal in January.

He failed to score for either of his teams in 2000–01, but he is a solid player boasting international experience with Wales.

The 2001–02 campaign could be a tricky one for the Foxes and they will need Jones to impose himself and justify his fee if he is to emulate Lennon's success.

APPEARANCES	
Start (sub)	13(2)
Minutes on pitch	998
GOAL ATTEMPTS	
Goals	0
Shots on target	4
Shooting accuracy	44%
PASSING & CROSSING	
Goal assists	0
Passes in opp half	234
Passing accuracy in opp half	61%
Successful crosses	2
Cross completion	50%
DEFENDING	
Interceptions	1
Clearances	27
Tackles	22
Tackles won %	77%
DISCIPLINE	
Fouls	21
Yellow cards	0
Red cards	1
SEE PAGES 167 & 181 FOR FULL STATS	

Paul JONES • 1
SOUTHAMPTON • BORN: 18.4.67

APPEARANCES	
Start (sub)	35(0)
Minutes on pitch	3150
SHOT STOPPING	
Goals conceded (inside box)	35
Goals conceded (outside box)	8
Minutes per goal conceded	73
Clean sheets	14
Saves (shots inside box)	67
Saves (shots outside box)	50
Saves/shots	73%
DISTRIBUTION	
Long kick %	48%
Throws/short passes %	84%
CATCHING	
Crosses caught	64
Crosses punched	28
Crosses dropped	7
Catch success %	90%
DISCIPLINE	
Yellow cards	0
Red cards	0
SEE PAGE 264 FOR FULL STATS	

Paul Jones was often seen as a favourite of former Southampton manager and namesake Dave Jones, so when the latter left the club many Saints fans were hoping that reserve 'keeper Neil Moss would get his chance.

But Glenn Hoddle also favoured Jones and, in fairness, the former Stockport keeper had a good season.

He kept 14 clean sheets for the south coast side – a tally unsurpassed in the 2000–01 Premiership – as Saints enjoyed one of their best seasons for some time.

When things did go wrong, though, they were dramatic – like the 4–3 FA Cup defeat at Tranmere Rovers.

His saves-to-shots ratio of 73% was solid enough, but he did drop seven catches – and some critics claim that handling is his main weakness.

He also elected to punch almost a quarter of the crosses that came into his box and it remains to be seen whether a new regime at Southampton will be enamoured with the Welsh international.

7 consecutive clean sheets for Paul Jones

Hassan KACHLOUL • 30
SOUTHAMPTON • BORN: 19.2.73

Hassan Kachloul claims he was so desperate to get out of joining the French army that he starved himself and feigned madness.

The Saints' attacking midfielder was hungrier for success on the football fields than the killing fields – and the army's loss was Southampton's gain.

While only finding the back of the net four times, the Moroccan with dual nationality set up more goals than any other Saints player, despite being used in a variety of positions throughout the 2000–01 campaign.

Kachloul was nicknamed "Forrest Gump" by team-mates because of his ability to run up and down the pitch all day long.

Indeed, at times watching him play is "just like a box of chocolates" – you never know what you are going to get.

Linked with a move to Tottenham, interest from Spurs seemed to dwindle and Southampton were hopeful of getting the former St Etienne and Metz winger to sign a new improved contract offer and stay at the club.

APPEARANCES	
Start (sub)	26(6)
Minutes on pitch	2307
GOAL ATTEMPTS	
Goals	4
Shots on target	16
Shooting accuracy	36%
Goals/shots ratio	9%
PASSING	
Goal assists	7
Passes in opp half	563
Passing accuracy in opp half	58%
Crosses	272
Crossing accuracy	29%
DRIBBLING	
Dribbles & runs	109
Dribble completion	58%
Corners forced	34
DISCIPLINE	
Fouls	39
Yellow cards	5
Red cards	1
SEE PAGE 264 FOR FULL STATS	

J

K

Andrei KANCHELSKIS • 12
MANCHESTER CITY • BORN: 23.1.69

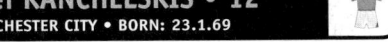

APPEARANCES	
Start (sub)	7(3)
Minutes on pitch	679
GOAL ATTEMPTS	
Goals	0
Shots on target	2
Shooting accuracy	18%
Goals/shots ratio	0%
PASSING	
Goal assists	1
Passes in opp half	173
Passing accuracy in opp half	69%
Crosses	43
Crossing accuracy	19%
DRIBBLING	
Dribbles & runs	52
Dribble completion	62%
Corners forced	6
DISCIPLINE	
Fouls	6
Yellow cards	0
Red cards	0
SEE PAGE 209 FOR FULL STATS	

Former Manchester United star Andrei Kanchelskis risked the wrath of City fans by joining from Rangers in October on a three-month loan.

It was the second time Joe Royle had signed the speedy winger, having previously laid out £5 million to take Kanchelskis from Manchester United to Everton.

But it was not to be quite such a successful spell for either, as Kanchelskis failed to score in 10 appearances for the Citizens and set up just one goal.

Despite having the likes of Paulo Wanchope and Shaun Goater to aim for in the middle, Kanchelskis found a team-mate with only 19% of his crosses into the penalty area, some way below the Premiership average for the 2000–01 season.

Sent to a school for gifted footballers at the age of just 15, Kanchelskis has clearly learnt about the pace of the Premiership, but it remains to be seen exactly where and with whom his footballing future lies in the 2001–02 campaign.

Frederic KANOUTE • 14
WEST HAM UNITED • BORN: 2.9.77

Former Hammers boss Harry Redknapp has always been known as a wheeler-dealer – and Frederic Kanouté will go down as one of his best signings.

The former Lyon striker impressed so much on loan at the end of the 1999–2000 season that a £3.75 million move was sealed soon afterwards.

He proved to be a great acquisition. With more tricks than Paul Daniels and the ability to outpace a greyhound Kanouté was a constant threat to Premiership defenders and he finished the campaign as West Ham's top scorer with 11 league goals.

The 2000–01 season was only half-way through when the Frenchman was linked with a move to the likes of Juventus and Manchester United but, despite all the upheaval at Upton Park, Kanouté stayed.

Having made more dribbles than any other player in the Premiership during the 2000–01 season, Hammers fans will no doubt be frothing at the mouth once again in 2001–02 at the sight of Kanouté's skills.

APPEARANCES	
Start (sub)	32(0)
Minutes on pitch	2662
GOAL ATTEMPTS	
Goals inside box	11
Goals outside box	0
Minutes per goal scored	242
Goals/shots ratio	14%
SHOOTING	
Shots on target inside box	32
Shots on target outside box	14
Shooting accuracy	58%
PASSING	
Goal assists	4
Key passes	50
Passing accuracy in opp half	60%
DISCIPLINE	
Fouls committed	63
Fouls won	84
Offside	65
Yellow cards	5
Red cards	0
SEE PAGE 306 FOR FULL STATS	

Nwankwo KANU • 25
ARSENAL • BORN: 1.8.76

APPEARANCES	
Start (sub)	13(14)
Minutes on pitch	1328
GOAL ATTEMPTS	
Goals inside box	3
Goals outside box	0
Minutes per goal scored	443
Goals/shots ratio	8%
SHOOTING	
Shots on target inside box	17
Shots on target outside box	5
Shooting accuracy	58%
PASSING	
Goal assists	5
Key passes	25
Passing accuracy in opp half	75%
DISCIPLINE	
Fouls committed	27
Fouls won	25
Offside	7
Yellow cards	1
Red cards	0
SEE PAGE 40 FOR FULL STATS	

The 2000–01 campaign was one of frustration for Nwankwo Kanu, who spent more time on the bench than on the pitch.

The Nigerian international remains a handful for defences and he still managed to set up five Premiership goals for his team-mates.

Kanu scored three himself, although the first did not come until December, in a 5–0 win over Newcastle.

His third and last goal of the campaign was more significant, however, coming in a vital 2–1 away win at Derby, a result which would prove vital in Arsenal finishing the season as runners-up.

Kanu's impressive pass completion rate in the opposition half shows that he has lost none of his ability, but it was consistency more than anything else which was missing from his game.

The former Ajax ace has been linked with a move back to another of his previous clubs, Inter Milan. But if he stays at Highbury, he will be hoping for more opportunities to impress in 2001–02.

For more information visit our website:

Christian KAREMBEU • 8
MIDDLESBROUGH • BORN: 3.12.70

Middlesbrough chairman Steve Gibson described Christian Karembeu and the Frenchman's stunning girlfriend Adriana Sklenarikova as a "down-to-earth"' couple and, on confirming the £2.1 million signing of Karembeu, stated that they would fit in perfectly in the town.

The Middlesbrough chairman's predictions seem to have come true and the couple have settled well. And there is no doubt that signing the former Real Madrid midfielder was a real coup for the club.

Karembeu featured in all but five of Boro's Premiership matches, scoring four times and setting up just as many.

Though it took him a while to adapt to the Premiership, he ended the season as one of the team's better performers.

He certainly endeared himself to the fans in the last two games of the season, scoring in both matches with goals which at the time were crucial in his side's battle against relegation. The supporters will hope for an even greater contribution in 2001–02.

APPEARANCES	
Start (sub)	31(2)
Minutes on pitch	2576
GOAL ATTEMPTS	
Goals	4
Shots on target	9
Shooting accuracy	53%
PASSING & CROSSING	
Goal assists	4
Passes in opp half	769
Passing accuracy in opp half	60%
Successful crosses	34
Cross completion	37%
DEFENDING	
Interceptions	3
Clearances	25
Tackles	83
Tackles won %	73%
DISCIPLINE	
Fouls	43
Yellow cards	3
Red cards	1

SEE PAGE 237 FOR FULL STATS

K

 Robbie KEANE • 7
LEEDS UNITED • BORN: 8.7.80

APPEARANCES	
Start (sub)	12(6)
Minutes on pitch	1037
GOAL ATTEMPTS	
Goals inside box	8
Goals outside box	1
Minutes per goal scored	115
Goals/shots ratio	33%
SHOOTING	
Shots on target inside box	17
Shots on target outside box	3
Shooting accuracy	74%
PASSING	
Goal assists	3
Key passes	9
Passing accuracy in opp half	62%
DISCIPLINE	
Fouls committed	13
Fouls won	22
Offside	24
Yellow cards	1
Red cards	0

SEE PAGE 167 FOR FULL STATS

Leeds brought to an end Robbie Keane's frustrating time at Inter Milan by signing the Republic of Ireland international in December, initially on loan, then later in the season in a permanent £12 million deal.

Ineligible to participate in Leeds' heroic Champions League run, Keane made a huge impact in the Premiership, despite just 12 appearances in the starting XI.

His nine goals from 27 shots made him the deadliest striker in the top flight. And with a 74% shooting accuracy, he was a constant thorn in the side of Premiership goalkeepers.

If these figures are even closely matched during 2001–02 it will not just be Keane turning cartwheels after each goal, with the youngster already looking like a bargain despite commanding such a big fee.

While Alan Smith and Mark Viduka grabbed most of the headlines during 2000–01, Keane was arguably the most impressive and consistent striker at the club, with hopefully more of the same to follow in 2001–02 from the Irishman.

Roy KEANE • 16
MANCHESTER UNITED • BORN: 10.8.71

Opta Player of the Season for 2000–01 was Manchester United captain Roy Keane, who once again used his leadership qualities to help guide his team to their seventh Premiership in just nine seasons.

Despite missing 10 league games, Keane still made more passes than any other player for the second season in succession, confirming him as the finest midfielder in the top flight. In front of goal, Keane scored just twice; the fact that only 32% of his efforts were on target suggests that he should leave shooting in 2001–02 to £19 million man Ruud Van Nistelrooy.

A season review on the Republic of Ireland captain would not be complete without a touch of controversy. In 2000–01 it came in the Manchester derby at Old Trafford, when Keane was sent off for a dreadful lunge at Alf Inge Haaland.

That aside, the feisty schemer stayed out of trouble, receiving just two additional cautions and committing less than a foul a game on average.

APPEARANCES	
Start (sub)	28(0)
Minutes on pitch	2386
GOAL ATTEMPTS	
Goals	2
Shots on target	15
Shooting accuracy	32%
PASSING & CROSSING	
Goal assists	7
Passes in opp half	1247
Passing accuracy in opp half	82%
Successful crosses	10
Cross completion	19%
DEFENDING	
Interceptions	8
Clearances	32
Tackles	77
Tackles won %	75%
DISCIPLINE	
Fouls	26
Yellow cards	2
Red cards	1

SEE PAGE 223 FOR FULL STATS

Leadership qualities: Roy Keane

2,184 Roy Keane made more

Gary KELLY • 2
LEEDS UNITED • BORN: 9.7.74

One of the more experienced players in the Leeds squad in 2000–01, Gary Kelly was a permanent fixture in the starting line-up at the beginning of the campaign, as well as featuring early on in Leeds' successful Champions League run.

While things continued to go swimmingly for O'Leary's side, Kelly picked up an injury halfway through the season and, despite making a speedy recovery, his replacement Danny Mills had been so impressive in Kelly's absence that the Republic of Ireland international was forced to spend much of the remainder of the campaign on the bench.

But Kelly's passing and crossing were more accurate than in 1999–2000 and he remains a vital member of the squad, particularly with Mills often having to plug gaps in the middle of defence.

Kelly rarely lets himself or his team-mates down when selected and has been a loyal servant to the club. The dependable full-back is sure to be utilised more as Leeds chase four trophies in 2001–02.

APPEARANCES	
Start (sub)	22(1)
Minutes on pitch	2025
GOAL ATTEMPTS	
Goals	0
PASSING & CROSSING	
Goal assists	3
Passing	891
Passing accuracy	68%
Crosses	77
Crossing accuracy	29%
DEFENDING	
Tackles	40
Tackles won %	68%
Blocks	12
Interceptions	8
Clearances	63
Shots cleared off line	0
DISCIPLINE	
Fouls	16
Yellow cards	1
Red cards	0
SEE PAGE 167 FOR FULL STATS	

K

Mark KENNEDY • 34
MANCHESTER CITY • BORN: 15.5.76

APPEARANCES	
Start (sub)	15(10)
Minutes on pitch	1479
GOAL ATTEMPTS	
Goals	0
Shots on target	6
Shooting accuracy	33%
Goals/shots ratio	0%
PASSING	
Goal assists	4
Passes in opp half	326
Passing accuracy in opp half	59%
Crosses	248
Crossing accuracy	27%
DRIBBLING	
Dribbles & runs	87
Dribble completion	77%
Corners forced	23
DISCIPLINE	
Fouls	11
Yellow cards	2
Red cards	0
SEE PAGE 209 FOR FULL STATS	

Manchester City winger Mark Kennedy featured more often than not for the Citizens, but was never a permanent fixture in the line-up.

Kennedy started the season as a regular and by mid-October was a more prolific and accurate crosser than David Beckham.

But after mid-December he was to start just five more Premiership matches and mostly watched from the sidelines as City's miserable season ended in relegation and the sacking of Joe Royle.

A pacy winger with a sweet left foot, no City player set up more goals than Kennedy, who must have wondered why he was not featuring more regularly in the side, having missed a total of just five games in the memorable 1999–2000 promotion campaign.

He had, after all, seemingly adapted well to the rigours of Premiership football.

With a new division and a new manager facing Manchester City in 2001–02, Kennedy's future would appear to be unclear. However, if it does not lie with City, there should be no shortage of clubs willing to offer him first-team football.

passes than any other player

CB — Martin KEOWN • 5
ARSENAL • BORN: 24.7.66

Martin Keown graced the Premiership for another season, but he must have been howling mad at Arsenal's failure to win a trophy.

Keown started 28 Premiership matches – more than any other Arsenal centre-back – and once again continued to hold his own against top-class opposition.

His tackling continued to be of a no-nonsense style, although occasionally his competitive streak spilled over into indiscipline and he ended the season with the threat of an FA inquiry hanging over his head.

With Sven-Göran Eriksson looking towards the future, Keown's international days could be nearing an end, but he continued to serve his country well when called upon.

He certainly remains a great servant to the Gunners and will be looking to end his Highbury career with one more Championship medal. While Arsène Wenger has made no secret of his search for new defenders, Keown is likely to play a significant role for Arsenal in 2001–02.

APPEARANCES	
Start (sub)	28(0)
Minutes on pitch	2520
GOAL ATTEMPTS	
Goals	0
DEFENDING	
Blocks	22
Shots cleared off line	1
Headed clearances	160
Other clearances	69
Interceptions	6
Last man saving tackles	1
Tackles won	40
Tackles won %	69%
PASSING	
Passing accuracy own half	86%
Passing accuracy opp half	66%
DISCIPLINE	
Fouls	38
Fouls in danger area	8
Yellow cards	3
Red cards	0

SEE PAGE 40 FOR FULL STATS

M — Brian KERR • 25
NEWCASTLE UNITED • BORN: 12.10.81

Young midfielder Brian Kerr had the choice of Glasgow Rangers or signing for Newcastle United as a youngster – and it looks as though he made the right choice.

Having already won schoolboy and youth caps with Scotland, Kerr made his Premiership debut at Coventry City in September, coming on as a last-minute substitute for Argentinean Daniel Cordone in a 2–0 win.

Kerr earned a three-year contract at the age of 17 and has since signed an extension on that deal, so the north-east giants clearly see him as a future first-team player.

Originally a striker, Kerr has adapted more to a midfield role, where he played as captain of the Newcastle United youth team.

With Bobby Robson more than willing to give youth a chance, Kerr will be hoping that further opportunities will arise in 2001–02 and that he can become more of a first-team regular, although competition for midfield places at Newcastle will be intense.

SEE PAGE 251 FOR FULL STATS

M — Scott KERR • 25
BRADFORD CITY • BORN: 11.12.81

With Bradford already relegated on the final day and making plans for the 2001–02 season in Division One, youngster Scott Kerr was brought on with seven minutes remaining and given his first taste of Premiership football.

The midfielder had played for the first team once before, in an Intertoto Cup match against FK Atlantas in July 2000 – the same month in which Kerr was awarded a two-year professional contract with the Bantams.

Prior to his Premiership debut, Kerr was named on the teamsheet in the home game against Southampton in September, but then-manager Chris Hutchings resisted the temptation to throw the youngster into the fray.

With Bradford dropping a division, and big names having now left the club, the likes of Kerr may be handed more first-team opportunities in the Nationwide League and City fans may see a lot more of the talented young midfield starlet.

SEE PAGE 68 FOR FULL STATS

For more information visit our website:

Harry KEWELL • 10
LEEDS UNITED • BORN: 22.9.78

Aussie jewel Harry Kewell was on the sidelines until 2001, recovering from an operation on his injured Achilles tendon.

While Leeds were progressing in Europe as well as chasing Premiership points, David O'Leary was adamant that he would not rush one of his prized assets back into first-team action too soon, no matter what the circumstances.

Kewell's comeback appearance came as a substitute in a 3–1 defeat at Leicester City, although this was overshadowed by the debut of £18 million signing Rio Ferdinand.

Two games later Kewell made his first start, but still was not looking back to his best and was subsequently rested for seven games.

That break seemed to do him good and he featured in Leeds' last 19 matches, including those in the Champions League, scoring twice.

With expectancy levels around Elland Road continuing to rise, players of the calibre of Kewell will need to perform at the very best of their ability if Leeds are to collect any silverware in 2002.

APPEARANCES	
Start (sub)	12(5)
Minutes on pitch	1165
GOAL ATTEMPTS	
Goals	2
Shots on target	10
Shooting accuracy	33%
Goals/shots ratio	7%
PASSING	
Goal assists	4
Passes in opp half	297
Passing accuracy in opp half	70%
Crosses	73
Crossing accuracy	25%
DRIBBLING	
Dribbles & runs	125
Dribble completion	57%
Corners forced	20
DISCIPLINE	
Fouls	18
Yellow cards	2
Red cards	0

SEE PAGE 167 FOR FULL STATS

K

Dean KIELY • 1
CHARLTON ATHLETIC • BORN: 10.10.70

APPEARANCES	
Start (sub)	25(0)
Minutes on pitch	2205
SHOT STOPPING	
Goals conceded (inside box)	30
Goals conceded (outside box)	8
Minutes per goal conceded	58
Clean sheets	9
Saves (shots inside box)	43
Saves (shots outside box)	41
Saves/shots	69%
DISTRIBUTION	
Long kick %	44%
Throws/short passes %	75%
CATCHING	
Crosses caught	45
Crosses punched	13
Crosses dropped	3
Catch success %	94%
DISCIPLINE	
Yellow cards	1
Red cards	0

SEE PAGE 82 FOR FULL STATS

Charlton's main aim for the 2000–01 season was consolidation and they achieved that early in the season, thanks in no small part to goalkeeper Dean Kiely.

While they were never going to win the title – Kiely should be so lucky – the Addicks almost sneaked a UEFA Cup spot and, while injury deprived him of an appearance from February onwards, Kiely could put his hand on his heart and say he gave his all.

The Charlton keeper often preferred to catch rather than punch, but as Kiely would say, "it's better the devil you know".

He dropped just three catches all season and was reliable whenever called upon, more steady and composed than spinning around his box.

Now pressing Shay Given for the Republic of Ireland goalkeeping spot, he will surely continue to grace the Premiership, as any decision to sell him would surely result in Kiely saying: "Je ne sais pas pourquoi." Certainly no amount of poor puns can disguise his contribution to the Charlton cause.

AM Kevin KILBANE • 11
SUNDERLAND • BORN: 1.2.77

Republic of Ireland international Kevin Kilbane was a regular feature in the Sunderland starting line-up in 2001–02.

The arrival of left-sided Argentinean midfielder Julio Arca may have had Kilbane slightly perturbed at the start of the campaign, but Peter Reid often employed Kilbane on the right wing.

But the Irishman's crossing accuracy of 16% was disappointing, not just as it was 11 percentage points down on the Premiership average for an attacking midfielder, but also as Kilbane had registered a 30% success rate the season before.

The Sunderland winger did chip in with four Premiership goals, as the Black Cats appeared to rely much less on Niall Quinn and Kevin Phillips as a source of firepower.

Kilbane doubled his 1999–2000 tally of assists, albeit with just two, but a red card against Chelsea in October suggests that the Irishman has a way to go in the coming seasons if he is to develop into a top-class Premiership player.

APPEARANCES	
Start (sub)	26(4)
Minutes on pitch	2351
GOAL ATTEMPTS	
Goals	4
Shots on target	19
Shooting accuracy	51%
Goals/shots ratio	11%
PASSING	
Goal assists	2
Passes in opp half	492
Passing accuracy in opp half	62%
Crosses	163
Crossing accuracy	16%
DRIBBLING	
Dribbles & runs	123
Dribble completion	55%
Corners forced	31
DISCIPLINE	
Fouls	33
Yellow cards	2
Red cards	1

SEE PAGE 278 FOR FULL STATS

CB Ledley KING • 26
TOTTENHAM HOTSPUR • BORN: 12.10.80

APPEARANCES	
Start (sub)	18(0)
Minutes on pitch	1526
GOAL ATTEMPTS	
Goals	1
DEFENDING	
Blocks	14
Shots cleared off line	0
Headed clearances	30
Other clearances	22
Interceptions	0
Last man saving tackles	0
Tackles won	43
Tackles won %	83%
PASSING	
Passing accuracy own half	78%
Passing accuracy opp half	70%
DISCIPLINE	
Fouls	9
Fouls in danger area	1
Yellow cards	0
Red cards	0

SEE PAGE 293 FOR FULL STATS

It was not all bad news at White Hart Lane during 2000–01, with many youngsters coming through to perform excellently in the first team: not least Ledley King, who made the transition from centre-back to central midfield look easy with a string of composed performances for the club.

King crowned a good campaign by writing his name into the record books with the fastest goal in Premiership history when he scored after just 10 seconds in a 3–3 draw with Bradford City in December.

Along with the likes of Simon Davies, Matthew Etherington, Gary Doherty and Alton Thelwell, King completes an impressive set of Spurs youngsters being given first-team opportunities.

A regular for the England Under-21 side, King may well also become a permanent fixture in the Spurs line-up in 2001–02. While it is still perhaps a little early to talk about full international honours, King seems well-placed to capitalise on the departure of the inspirational Sol Campbell.

83% Ledley King had the best

Georgi KINKLADZE • 10
DERBY COUNTY • BORN: 6.11.73

With Derby County desperately struggling near the foot of the table, manager Jim Smith saw the need for his side to grind out results with dogged displays.

Consequently, the imaginative Georgi Kinkladze spent most of the middle part of the 2000–01 season on the bench.

From the start of December to mid-April the Georgian started just one Premiership match, although once the Rams started to edge away from the danger of relegation he was brought into the fray more often.

Kinky's only goal of the campaign came in the home match against Leeds in September, although he did show his creative streak with three assists.

Always a joy to watch, Kinkladze's passing accuracy in the opposition half of 82% perhaps negates the fact that he was seen as a liability when Derby were struggling.

The craft and guile of the talented midfielder, together with an ability to pass accurately at the most important of times, remain very much intact.

APPEARANCES	
Start (sub)	13(11)
Minutes on pitch	1366
GOAL ATTEMPTS	
Goals	1
Shots on target	3
Shooting accuracy	30%
Goals/shots ratio	10%
PASSING	
Goal assists	3
Passes in opp half	470
Passing accuracy in opp half	82%
Crosses	49
Crossing accuracy	51%
DRIBBLING	
Dribbles & runs	103
Dribble completion	82%
Corners forced	6
DISCIPLINE	
Fouls	18
Yellow cards	2
Red cards	0

SEE PAGE 125 FOR FULL STATS

K

 ## Mark KINSELLA • 8
CHARLTON ATHLETIC • BORN: 12.8.72

APPEARANCES	
Start (sub)	27(5)
Minutes on pitch	2492
GOAL ATTEMPTS	
Goals	2
Shots on target	20
Shooting accuracy	59%
PASSING & CROSSING	
Goal assists	2
Passes in opp half	870
Passing accuracy in opp half	71%
Successful crosses	9
Cross completion	31%
DEFENDING	
Interceptions	17
Clearances	48
Tackles	103
Tackles won %	79%
DISCIPLINE	
Fouls	26
Yellow cards	4
Red cards	0

SEE PAGE 82 FOR FULL STATS

Club captain Mark Kinsella can be immensely proud of his achievements and those of Charlton Athletic throughout the club's successful 2000–01 season.

The Addicks surpassed all expectations by finishing in the top half of the table. "If you look back over the entire campaign, you can find no better highlight than that one fact," beamed Kinsella.

After a goal on the opening day of the season, Kinsella went on to score his first goal for the Republic of Ireland, against Estonia.

He was then named his country's Player of the Year and in November captained his national side for the first time.

But not everything went wonderfully. He was forced to sit out half a dozen matches to undergo a knee operation, having decided along with Alan Curbishley to do something about the pain he was experiencing.

That aside, Kinsella can look back on a fantastic campaign and hope that 2001–02 culminates in a trip to the World Cup finals in Japan and Korea.

tackle success rate at Tottenham

Chris KIRKLAND • 13
COVENTRY CITY • BORN: 2.5.81

When you are just 19 years old and understudy to a goalkeeper whom your manager describes as one of the best in the world, your chances of regular first-team action would appear to be rather slim.

But such was the impact made by Chris Kirkland at Coventry that the impressive youngster kept Magnus Hedman on the bench for most of the season.

After his debut against Tottenham, Kirkland had an eventful next appearance in London at Stamford Bridge.

The Sky Blues' keeper was sent off after just 22 minutes in a game which Coventry lost 6–1 to Chelsea, although his red card was later rescinded on appeal.

Kirkland kept goal in a 4–1 defeat at Anfield, but made saves from a further seven shots on target, impressing not just his own boss but Liverpool chief Gérard Houllier too.

While Strachan may sometimes be seen as a bit of a comedian, he has been proved right with Kirkland, who seems destined for a big-money move very soon.

APPEARANCES	
Start (sub)	23(0)
Minutes on pitch	2002

SHOT STOPPING	
Goals conceded (inside box)	27
Goals conceded (outside box)	7
Minutes per goal conceded	59
Clean sheets	4
Saves (shots inside box)	44
Saves (shots outside box)	44
Saves/shots	72%

DISTRIBUTION	
Long kick %	44%
Throws/short passes %	61%

CATCHING	
Crosses caught	33
Crosses punched	10
Crosses dropped	4
Catch success %	89%

DISCIPLINE	
Yellow cards	1
Red cards	1

SEE PAGE 110 FOR FULL STATS

Radostin KISHISHEV • 2
CHARLTON ATHLETIC • BORN: 30.7.74

APPEARANCES	
Start (sub)	25(2)
Minutes on pitch	2107

GOAL ATTEMPTS	
Goals	0

PASSING & CROSSING	
Goal assists	3
Passing	928
Passing accuracy	64%
Crosses	43
Crossing accuracy	28%

DEFENDING	
Tackles	81
Tackles won %	83%
Blocks	9
Interceptions	12
Clearances	73
Shots cleared off line	0

DISCIPLINE	
Fouls	38
Yellow cards	4
Red cards	0

SEE PAGE 82 FOR FULL STATS

Alan Curbishley rarely makes a bad signing – and Radostin Kishishev is testament to that.

The Bulgarian international put pen to paper in August 2000 for an initial £300,000, which could rise to a total of £1.8 million depending on appearances.

A veteran of Euro 96 and France 98, Kishishev started his Charlton career as a right-back, but was rested after some indifferent performances.

However, Curbishley moved Kishishev into midfield and the Bulgarian seemed to relish his new attacking role.

The former Liteks Lovech player set up three goals and his crossing accuracy of 28% often caused problems in the opponents' box.

While failing to feature in 11 Premiership matches for Charlton throughout the 2000–01 season, Kishishev was a vital member of the squad and the fact that he settled so well on the right-hand side of midfield could cause welcome selection problems for Curbishley.

Whatever the Charlton boss decides to do, it seems certain that Kishishev will be very much a part of his plans in the future.

Paul KITSON • 12
WEST HAM UNITED • BORN: 9.1.71

Paul Kitson suffered another frustrating season at West Ham, making just two substitute appearances at the start of the 2000–01 campaign.

Soon afterwards he went to Crystal Palace on loan but, after four games without a goal for the Eagles, he was sent back to east London.

Kitson never played again and when, on the last day of the season, Jermain Defoe was brought on, the former Newcastle United striker must have realised that his days at Upton Park were over.

Having started just four Premiership matches for the Hammers in 1999–2000, Kitson must feel continually disheartened at his lack of first-team opportunities and his tremendous partnership with John Hartson in 1996–97 must seem light years away.

The sacking of Harry Redknapp and possible sale of Frederic Kanouté may give Kitson hope, but it would appear that his footballing future lies elsewhere.

SEE PAGE 306 FOR FULL STATS

Paul KONCHESKY • 18
CHARLTON ATHLETIC • BORN: 15.5.81

Promising Charlton youngster Paul Konchesky had to play second fiddle to England defender Chris Powell for most of the 2000–01 season, but was offered sporadic spells to impress at The Valley. And the Barking-born full-back did not disappoint his manager.

Konchesky demonstrated a combination of tough tackling at the back and a willingness to stride forward and support the frontrunners when possible.

His crosses from the left flank often caused panic in the opposition box and his delivery rate was nine percentage points better than the Premiership average for a defender. It is therefore no surprise that he weighed in with two goal assists for his colleagues.

If Konchesky can improve his overall distribution slightly, Curbishley has a definite prospect on his hands whom he will not want to let out of his sight.

England Under-21 boss Howard Wilkinson struggled to track the Addick down on holiday, after selecting him to play in a European Championship match in Greece!

Elusive full-back: Paul Konchesky

APPEARANCES	
Start (sub)	11(12)
Minutes on pitch	1078
GOAL ATTEMPTS	
Goals	0
PASSING & CROSSING	
Goal assists	2
Passing	473
Passing accuracy	64%
Crosses	20
Crossing accuracy	35%
DEFENDING	
Tackles	27
Tackles won %	89%
Blocks	15
Interceptions	5
Clearances	65
Shots cleared off line	0
DISCIPLINE	
Fouls	14
Yellow cards	3
Red cards	0

SEE PAGE 82 FOR FULL STATS

Muhamed KONJIC • 26
COVENTRY CITY • BORN: 14.5.70

The 2000–01 season held little respite for Coventry defender Muhamed Konjic, who has experienced a torrid time since arriving on English soil from Monaco in January 1999.

Sidelined through injury at the start of the campaign, he did not make his first appearance until November.

Konjic then enjoyed a run of seven starts in the first team – his longest spell since joining the Sky Blues – but was later substituted after just 27 minutes of the home defeat against Everton and failed to appear again.

With the Coventry defence under constant pressure to perform, Konjic did not get a realistic chance to forge an understanding with his team-mates.

However, he won a determined 83% of his challenges and completed more than a century of clearances for the Coventry cause.

It remains to be seen whether the former soldier will gain an opportunity to shine in Nationwide Division One, where he may be able to get to grips with the pace of English football.

APPEARANCES	
Start (sub)	8(0)
Minutes on pitch	580
GOAL ATTEMPTS	
Goals	0
DEFENDING	
Blocks	4
Shots cleared off line	0
Headed clearances	81
Other clearances	20
Interceptions	1
Last man saving tackles	0
Tackles won	15
Tackles won %	83%
PASSING	
Passing accuracy own half	66%
Passing accuracy opp half	41%
DISCIPLINE	
Fouls	7
Fouls in danger area	2
Yellow cards	0
Red cards	0
SEE PAGE 111 FOR FULL STATS	

Willem KORSTEN • 15
TOTTENHAM HOTSPUR • BORN: 21.1.75

APPEARANCES	
Start (sub)	8(6)
Minutes on pitch	697
GOAL ATTEMPTS	
Goals inside box	1
Goals outside box	2
Minutes per goal scored	232
Goals/shots ratio	21%
SHOOTING	
Shots on target inside box	2
Shots on target outside box	9
Shooting accuracy	79%
PASSING	
Goal assists	0
Key passes	4
Passing accuracy in opp half	56%
DISCIPLINE	
Fouls committed	14
Fouls won	13
Offside	5
Yellow cards	0
Red cards	1
SEE PAGE 293 FOR FULL STATS	

Willem Korsten will testify that good things come to those who wait.

His first season at White Hart Lane was ravaged by injury and, even after regaining his fitness early in the 2000–01 season, the Dutchman was forced to bide his time in the reserves after failing to impress during his brief forays in the first team.

Recognising Korsten's obvious talent, new manager Glenn Hoddle lamented: "There is a player in there waiting to come out" – and within weeks the striker had notched his first goal for the Lilywhites against Liverpool.

And his scoring spree did not end at Anfield. On the final day of the season, the former Vitesse Arnhem star netted a brace against champions Manchester United, including a stunning goal-of-the-season contender from long range.

Hoddle will be hoping that opportunities breed confidence within Korsten, whose dribble success rate and crossing accuracy were both well below the Premiership average for a player in his position.

Kevin KYLE • 34
SUNDERLAND • BORN: 7.6.81

When Niall Quinn finally hangs up his boots at the Stadium of Light, Peter Reid has a ready-made replacement in Kevin Kyle, although at 6'3" the youngster can hardly be described as living in the popular Irishman's shadow!

Kyle was spotted playing for his hometown club Ayr Boswell and, after trials with Chelsea, Blackpool and Oldham, eventually journeyed to Wearside.

He featured prominently for the Black Cats' reserves in 2000–01 and also enjoyed loan spells at Darlington and Rochdale in order to gain Football League experience.

The Scottish Under-21 international made his Premiership bow in the final 15 minutes at The Dell in April and made two further substitute appearances against Charlton and Everton respectively, replacing the ageing Quinn.

Kyle may have played less than an hour of top-flight football, but he made a lasting impression by feeding Kevin Phillips for his second goal at Goodison Park.

SEE PAGE 278 FOR FULL STATS

Bernard LAMBOURDE • 21
CHELSEA • BORN: 11.5.71

Bernard Lambourde is unlikely to look back on the 2000–01 season with any great fondness.

The French defender failed to convince Claudio Ranieri that he was first-team material and was farmed out to Portsmouth on loan in September.

Having made six appearances for the south coast side – where he was often seen to attempt Premiership-quality passes to first division team-mates – he was sent back to Stamford Bridge in October and returned to his place in the Blues' reserves.

One substitute appearance for the Blues followed, against Manchester United in February, but with the likes of Albert Ferrer and Mario Melchiot ahead of Lambourde in the pecking order, it seemed likely that his days with the club were numbered.

A rumoured reunion with former boss Gianluca Vialli at Watford seemed an attractive proposition, although his Pompey experience may have caused the 30-year-old to think twice about dropping down a division.

SEE PAGE 97 FOR FULL STATS

K

L

Frank LAMPARD • 18
WEST HAM UNITED • BORN: 20.6.78

APPEARANCES	
Start (sub)	30(0)
Minutes on pitch	2646
GOAL ATTEMPTS	
Goals	7
Shots on target	26
Shooting accuracy	43%
PASSING & CROSSING	
Goal assists	3
Passes in opp half	684
Passing accuracy in opp half	67%
Successful crosses	16
Cross completion	41%
DEFENDING	
Interceptions	5
Clearances	28
Tackles	104
Tackles won %	76%
DISCIPLINE	
Fouls	26
Yellow cards	3
Red cards	0
SEE PAGE 306 FOR FULL STATS	

The 2000–01 season was a bitter-sweet period in the life of West Ham and England midfielder Frank Lampard.

He was a regular in the national squad; earned a second international cap against Spain in February, helped with the development of young midfield allies Joe Cole and Michael Carrick, scored seven Premiership goals and set up three others.

But those positive aspects were soured at the end of the campaign, when Frank Snr – Lampard's father and the Hammers' assistant manager – was forced to leave the club along with boss Harry Redknapp.

Those departures, coupled with that of his best friend Rio Ferdinand to Leeds, have left a frustrated Lampard apparently claiming that he will never play for the Upton Park club again.

Lampard has seemingly been around for years, yet is still in his early 20s, and in Aston Villa, Leeds, Tottenham and Chelsea there were no shortage of takers, despite West Ham's reported demands for a £11 million transfer fee.

penalties than any other teams

LAUREN • 12
ARSENAL • BORN: 19.1.77

Cameroon midfielder Lauren was voted Player of the Tournament when his country won the African Nations Cup and completed a £7.2 million move to Arsenal in May 2000.

His Gunners career actually got under way in the far from glamorous surroundings of Borehamwood, though, in a pre-season friendly.

Having been brought in to fill the void left by the departure of Emmanuel Petit to Barcelona, there was a great deal of pressure on Lauren to perform. And he got off to a flying start with a goal seven minutes into his home debut against Liverpool.

But Arsenal lost his services when he went to the Olympics with Cameroon – where he won a gold medal – and then he missed several more games through injury.

As the season progressed his performances grew stronger and, when selected, he showed a good understanding with Patrick Vieira.

Equally comfortable at right-back or in midfield, Lauren was successful with a better-than-average 79% of his passes.

APPEARANCES	
Start (sub)	15(3)
Minutes on pitch	1228

GOAL ATTEMPTS	
Goals	2
Shots on target	4
Shooting accuracy	40%
Goals/shots ratio	20%

PASSING	
Goal assists	0
Passes in opp half	375
Passing accuracy in opp half	74%
Crosses	27
Crossing accuracy	19%

DRIBBLING	
Dribbles & runs	34
Dribble completion	68%
Corners forced	8

DISCIPLINE	
Fouls	30
Yellow cards	3
Red cards	0

SEE PAGE 40 FOR FULL STATS

Jamie LAWRENCE • 7
BRADFORD CITY • BORN: 8.3.70

APPEARANCES	
Start (sub)	15(2)
Minutes on pitch	1383

GOAL ATTEMPTS	
Goals	0
Shots on target	2
Shooting accuracy	22%
Goals/shots ratio	0%

PASSING	
Goal assists	1
Passes in opp half	218
Passing accuracy in opp half	62%
Crosses	23
Crossing accuracy	13%

DRIBBLING	
Dribbles & runs	66
Dribble completion	55%
Corners forced	8

DISCIPLINE	
Fouls	28
Yellow cards	4
Red cards	0

SEE PAGE 68 FOR FULL STATS

Jamie Lawrence certainly let the side down in 2000–01. In the face of stiff opposition from the likes of Fredrik Ljungberg and Taribo West, Lawrence struggled to make any impact in the Opta "most ludicrous barnet" Index, despite his superb showing during the Bantams' first Premiership season.

It was a mixed campaign for Lawrence: he made fewer Premiership starts for the Bantams than during the 1999–2000 season and could not repeat his feat of helping to secure Bradford's top-flight future.

However, his international career continued to blossom and with competitions such as the Copa Caribe to play in for his adopted homeland of Jamaica, the grim reality of an English winter struggling to beat the drop seemed vastly unattractive in comparison.

His Bradford future looks far from certain: he has informed manager Jim Jefferies that he would prefer to move to the south of England than stay in Yorkshire.

Perhaps he thinks it will be a little bit warmer closer to the equator.

For more information visit our website:

FB Graeme LE SAUX • 14
CHELSEA • BORN: 17.10.68

Having spent the majority of the 1999–2000 campaign on the treatment table, 2000–01 treated Graeme Le Saux a little more kindly. He began the season on the bench, still not fully fit, but eventually broke back into the first team in Chelsea's 2–2 draw with Arsenal in September.

However, two bookable offences at Sunderland saw the Jersey-born full-back ordered off in mid-October and an ankle injury picked up in training, combined with the subsequent suspension, meant Le Saux's next appearance was not until the end of January.

Having eventually overcome his troublesome injury, Le Saux became a first-team regular once more, featuring in each of Chelsea's last 12 league matches. More frequently employed as a winger by Claudio Ranieri, the Channel Islander enjoyed his attacking role, looking more than comfortable bringing the ball forward.

But his England career appears to be on hold, unless he can convince the Swede-in-chief otherwise with some sterling club performances during 2001–02.

APPEARANCES	
Start (sub)	18(2)
Minutes on pitch	1540
GOAL ATTEMPTS	
Goals	0
PASSING & CROSSING	
Goal assists	2
Passing	697
Passing accuracy	73%
Crosses	70
Crossing accuracy	26%
DEFENDING	
Tackles	72
Tackles won %	71%
Blocks	9
Interceptions	2
Clearances	59
Shots cleared off line	1
DISCIPLINE	
Fouls	29
Yellow cards	2
Red cards	1
SEE PAGE 97 FOR FULL STATS	

L

AM Matthew LE TISSIER • 7
SOUTHAMPTON • BORN: 14.10.68

APPEARANCES	
Start (sub)	2(6)
Minutes on pitch	232
GOAL ATTEMPTS	
Goals	1
Shots on target	3
Shooting accuracy	75%
Goals/shots ratio	25%
PASSING	
Goal assists	0
Passes in opp half	60
Passing accuracy in opp half	73%
Crosses	36
Crossing accuracy	39%
DRIBBLING	
Dribbles & runs	4
Dribble completion	75%
Corners forced	3
DISCIPLINE	
Fouls	4
Yellow cards	1
Red cards	0
SEE PAGE 264 FOR FULL STATS	

Looking through the eyes of a rational man, Matthew Le Tissier had a poor season for the second campaign running.

He managed just two starts for Southampton and completed a full 90 minutes just once.

Of course, that hardly matters for a player as idolised by supporters as "Le God" – and especially not when you consider the importance of the goal Le Tissier scored on 19 May 2001.

After the match with Arsenal, he said: "Stuart [Gray] said very little. He told me to go and get warmed up and when I came back he told me I was going on and asked me to get him a goal."

Le Tissier was happy to oblige – a superb half-volley, typical of the man, to secure a 3–2 win over the Gunners, which sent the home fans into a state of delirium.

It was the last ever competitive goal to be scored at The Dell, from which the Saints are now moving.

How fitting that their hero should score it after such a barren campaign.

Frank LEBOEUF • 5
CHELSEA • BORN: 22.1.68

CB

Frank Leboeuf's fifth season at Stamford Bridge saw mixed fortunes for the French defender. His overall form was good during the first half of the campaign, but the distraction of a proposed move to Monaco, plus the emergence of young defensive upstart John Terry, meant that Leboeuf ended the campaign on the bench.

The Monaco transfer was on and off for nearly a month before the French side eventually pulled the plug on the deal. At the time, Leboeuf declared that he was more than happy to stay at Chelsea, but the seeds of doubt had been sown.

His relationship with the Chelsea faithful had taken a turn for the worse and managing director Colin Hutchinson stated: "It's no secret that Frank Leboeuf has said he'd like to finish his career in France, given the opportunity, and now we have defensive cover that could be a possibility."

With compatriot William Gallas added to the Chelsea roster, Leboeuf's Stamford Bridge days seemed numbered.

APPEARANCES	
Start (sub)	23(2)
Minutes on pitch	1996
GOAL ATTEMPTS	
Goals	0
DEFENDING	
Blocks	21
Shots cleared off line	0
Headed clearances	95
Other clearances	89
Interceptions	22
Last man saving tackles	2
Tackles won	63
Tackles won %	78%
PASSING	
Passing accuracy own half	85%
Passing accuracy opp half	61%
DISCIPLINE	
Fouls	30
Fouls in danger area	7
Yellow cards	6
Red cards	0

SEE PAGE 97 FOR FULL STATS

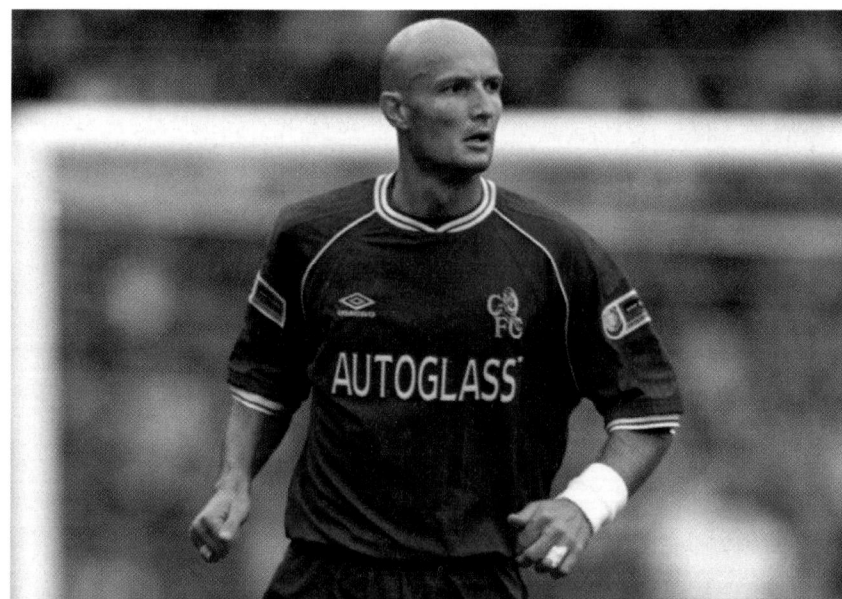

Seeds of doubt: Frank Leboeuf

Robert LEE • 7
NEWCASTLE UNITED • BORN: 1.2.66

Considered to be one of the greatest bargains Newcastle United have ever found, Rob Lee would have been a regular in the Magpies' starting line-up but for a number of niggling injuries.

Lee began his Newcastle career as far back as 1992, following his £700,000 move from Charlton, and was captain of the side until close friend Alan Shearer took over the responsibility in 1998.

Now in his mid-30s, age is beginning to creep up on the London-born midfielder, but his commitment to the Magpies' cause never seemed likely to waver in 2000–01.

Lee managed 21 starts for Newcastle and, having attempted the second-highest tally of tackles of any Newcastle player, his hunger for possession was clearly as strong as ever.

Of course he cannot go on indefinitely and, in Christian Bassedas, the club have a ready-made replacement. But few would bet against Lee beating off the pretender to his crown and retaining his first-team place for yet another season.

APPEARANCES	
Start (sub)	21(1)
Minutes on pitch	1749
GOAL ATTEMPTS	
Goals	0
Shots on target	4
Shooting accuracy	31%
PASSING & CROSSING	
Goal assists	0
Passes in opp half	616
Passing accuracy in opp half	75%
Successful crosses	7
Cross completion	37%
DEFENDING	
Interceptions	7
Clearances	45
Tackles	84
Tackles won %	68%
DISCIPLINE	
Fouls	47
Yellow cards	3
Red cards	0

SEE PAGE 251 FOR FULL STATS

L

Neil LENNON • 7
LEICESTER CITY • BORN: 25.6.71

APPEARANCES	
Start (sub)	15(0)
Minutes on pitch	1304
GOAL ATTEMPTS	
Goals	0
Shots on target	1
Shooting accuracy	100%
PASSING & CROSSING	
Goal assists	3
Passes in opp half	438
Passing accuracy in opp half	77%
Successful crosses	12
Cross completion	38%
DEFENDING	
Interceptions	3
Clearances	17
Tackles	35
Tackles won %	69%
DISCIPLINE	
Fouls	13
Yellow cards	4
Red cards	0

SEE PAGE 181 FOR FULL STATS

Following Martin O'Neill's departure from Leicester to Celtic, it seemed inevitable that he would take some of his most successful acquisitions with him. Seeing as Celtic were Neil Lennon's boyhood idols, it was no surprise that he was keen to join up with his mentor once again.

After much negotiation, the Bhoys had to part with £5.75 million to persuade Leicester to let go of their man, who was again playing a pivotal role in the Foxes midfield. Lennon created three goals and made 836 passes as he helped Peter Taylor stay with the front-runners during the early part of the campaign.

Leicester's subsequent slump shows how sorely Lennon was missed, but the Northern Ireland international was nothing short of sensational in the Scottish Premier League, helping Celtic dominate the season and claim the treble.

The only downside came on the international front, where sectarian abuse from the terraces left Lennon contemplating his international future.

the top five of Leicester City's most prolific passers

AM · Oyvind LEONHARDSEN · 17
TOTTENHAM HOTSPUR • BORN: 17.8.70

Norwegian international Oyvind Leonhardsen suffered a frustrating season through injury – something which is becoming all too familiar in the career of the former Wimbledon man.

After missing out on Euro 2000 because of an Achilles injury, 'Leo' worked hard through the summer to be fit in time for Tottenham's 2000–01 campaign.

His season looked to be going well, especially after he hit a brace against Derby County, but then the injury curse struck again.

A pulled hamstring followed by a chipped bone in his leg saw him miss large parts of the season, although he returned to full fitness for the final part of the campaign under new boss Glenn Hoddle.

There's no doubting how effective a fully-fit Leonhardsen can be, with three goals and four assists to show from his small contribution to the 2000–01 season.

If he can remain clear of the treatment table he can look forward to a good run, not only for Tottenham, but also for his international side as well.

APPEARANCES	
Start (sub)	23(2)
Minutes on pitch	1903
GOAL ATTEMPTS	
Goals	3
Shots on target	11
Shooting accuracy	44%
Goals/shots ratio	12%
PASSING	
Goal assists	4
Passes in opp half	434
Passing accuracy in opp half	70%
Crosses	37
Crossing accuracy	30%
DRIBBLING	
Dribbles & runs	32
Dribble completion	72%
Corners forced	13
DISCIPLINE	
Fouls	37
Yellow cards	0
Red cards	0

SEE PAGE 293 FOR FULL STATS

M · Junior LEWIS · 25
LEICESTER CITY • BORN: 9.10.73

APPEARANCES	
Start (sub)	15(0)
Minutes on pitch	1350
GOAL ATTEMPTS	
Goals	0
Shots on target	2
Shooting accuracy	22%
PASSING & CROSSING	
Goal assists	0
Passes in opp half	360
Passing accuracy in opp half	68%
Successful crosses	1
Cross completion	10%
DEFENDING	
Interceptions	4
Clearances	51
Tackles	45
Tackles won %	67%
DISCIPLINE	
Fouls	14
Yellow cards	1
Red cards	0

SEE PAGE 181 FOR FULL STATS

Junior Lewis was resigned to spending the season in and out of the Gillingham first team until former boss Peter Taylor suddenly thrust him into the Premiership limelight with Leicester City.

Taylor obviously knew Lewis well, having managed him at both the Gills and Dover Athletic, and so had no qualms about taking him to Filbert Street – initially on loan – to provide cover for the Foxes midfield.

Lewis, known as "Flip-Flop" to his team-mates, did enough in his loan spell to earn a permanent move and never missed a game after making his debut at Southampton at the end of January.

The Wembley-born player was a striker during his non-league days, but has now converted to midfield and played in a holding role during his time at Leicester.

His performances were reasonably solid if unspectacular, but Taylor was clearly happy with the job done by the player, who cost just £150,000 when he made his move permanent before deadline day.

For more information visit our website:

Kevin LISBIE • 29
CHARLTON ATHLETIC • BORN: 17.10.78

Kevin Lisbie was a surprise starter in Charlton's latest Premiership quest as the Addicks found themselves short of fit strikers at the beginning of 2000–01.

Former youth team player Lisbie stepped into the breach though and could have had a hat-trick on the opening day against Manchester City, but poor finishing let him down.

Lisbie was the top scorer for Charlton's reserves during 1999–2000 with 14 goals in 18 games. He previously spent loan spells at Reading and Gillingham, but has never really made an impact on the Addicks' first team.

He can play as a striker or wide on the right where the pace and skill of the former England Under-18 international can cause a great deal of problems.

Despite starting the season in the side, Lisbie lost his place when Charlton strengthened their squad and some of the more experienced strikers returned from injury, leaving the youngster to spend the majority of the season on the bench.

APPEARANCES	
Start (sub)	5(13)
Minutes on pitch	544
GOAL ATTEMPTS	
Goals inside box	0
Goals outside box	0
Minutes per goal scored	n/a
Goals/shots ratio	0%
SHOOTING	
Shots on target inside box	3
Shots on target outside box	1
Shooting accuracy	40%
PASSING	
Goal assists	2
Key passes	3
Passing accuracy in opp half	59%
DISCIPLINE	
Fouls committed	13
Fouls won	12
Offside	17
Yellow cards	0
Red cards	0
SEE PAGE 82 FOR FULL STATS	

L

 Jari LITMANEN • 37
LIVERPOOL • BORN: 20.2.71

APPEARANCES	
Start (sub)	4(1)
Minutes on pitch	334
GOAL ATTEMPTS	
Goals inside box	1
Goals outside box	0
Minutes per goal scored	334
Goals/shots ratio	14%
SHOOTING	
Shots on target inside box	3
Shots on target outside box	2
Shooting accuracy	71%
PASSING	
Goal assists	0
Key passes	8
Passing accuracy in opp half	70%
DISCIPLINE	
Fouls committed	3
Fouls won	3
Offside	3
Yellow cards	1
Red cards	0
SEE PAGE 195 FOR FULL STATS	

Jari Litmanen was described by Gérard Houllier as "one of Liverpool FC's most exciting signings" when the Finnish legend ended a nightmare time at Barcelona by moving to Anfield on a free transfer in January 2001.

Litmanen could have become a professional ice-hockey player, but he chose to follow in his father's footsteps and play football.

He clearly made the right choice and, with spells at Ajax and Barcelona under his belt, he is regarded as being the most famous Finnish footballer of all time.

An injury playing for Finland against England cut short his season, but in his few appearances for Liverpool he showed enough of the excellent technique and vision to suggest he can be a major player in 2001–02.

He hit just one Premiership goal – against Sunderland – but his outstanding display in the Worthington Cup semi-final second leg win over Crystal Palace helped to underline the strength of the strikeforce Houllier has now built up at Anfield.

Fredrik LJUNGBERG • 8
ARSENAL • BORN: 16.4.77

Fredrik Ljungberg claims that he will not have sex the night before a match, as it makes his feet feel like concrete.

Maybe this is the reason he was seen hiding in a cupboard to avoid the attentions of amorous Swedish actress Lina Perned early on in the season.

If his theory was being put to the test, though, it must have been cocoa and late-night videos all round towards the end of the campaign, as Ljungberg finished in blistering form for Arsenal.

After a solid season, Ljungberg signed off in style, hitting five goals in the last seven league games.

Fiorentina were said to be making a move for the Swede, but having performed so well in 2000–01 the Gunners were unlikely to let him go without a fight.

The summer break should see Ljungberg's sex life pick up, but after his prolific tail-end to the season he will need to be extremely careful not to return with concrete feet in the 2001–02 season.

APPEARANCES	
Start (sub)	25(5)
Minutes on pitch	2203
GOAL ATTEMPTS	
Goals	6
Shots on target	32
Shooting accuracy	55%
Goals/shots ratio	10%
PASSING	
Goal assists	3
Passes in opp half	614
Passing accuracy in opp half	70%
Crosses	57
Crossing accuracy	19%
DRIBBLING	
Dribbles & runs	127
Dribble completion	72%
Corners forced	18
DISCIPLINE	
Fouls	31
Yellow cards	3
Red cards	0
SEE PAGE 41 FOR FULL STATS	

Gary LOCKE • 19
BRADFORD CITY • BORN: 16.6.75

APPEARANCES	
Start (sub)	6(1)
Minutes on pitch	461
GOAL ATTEMPTS	
Goals	0
PASSING & CROSSING	
Goal assists	0
Passing	155
Passing accuracy	70%
Crosses	17
Crossing accuracy	41%
DEFENDING	
Tackles	6
Tackles won %	67%
Blocks	2
Interceptions	0
Clearances	11
Shots cleared off line	0
DISCIPLINE	
Fouls	8
Yellow cards	2
Red cards	0
SEE PAGE 68 FOR FULL STATS	

Scottish full-back Gary Locke began the season playing under Jim Jefferies for Hearts in the UEFA Cup and ended the campaign playing under the same manager but for relegated Bradford.

Jefferies called on Locke as he was trying to bolster the Bradford squad with battlers who could try and fight their way out of the drop zone.

Locke joined a distinctly Scottish-looking squad, with the likes of Eoin Jess, Billy McKinlay and Stuart McCall already at the club. But he could contribute little to arrest Bradford's inevitable slide back to Division One.

The lifelong Hearts fan made his Bantams debut at Southampton in February, but featured in just seven games overall for Bradford. He proved to be an accurate crosser of the ball, finding a team mate with 41% of his centres.

He was unable to shine elsewhere, though, and he may find the drop to Division One more suitable for a player of his ability.

l Fredrik Ljungberg is the only Swedish player

Steve LOMAS • 11
WEST HAM UNITED • BORN: 18.1.74

Club captain Steve Lomas demonstrated his loyalty to the Hammers by staying on at Upton Park despite having the chance to move back to his former club Manchester City.

Harry Redknapp had accepted bids from both City and Everton for the midfield star, but Lomas insisted on staying on at the club he has played for since 1997.

The experienced veteran Lomas is by no means the oldest player in an ageing West Ham squad, but his know-how has been vital, particularly to the younger players in the squad – and his versatility to be able to play in both defence and his more familiar midfield role has been a huge benefit.

Lomas's season was cruelly cut short by a serious knee injury in January which required several operations.

The Northern Ireland captain bagged one goal – against Manchester City – and made a total of 770 passes before his injury struck, having performed in defence, midfield and at wing-back in his 20 appearances in the 2000–01 season.

APPEARANCES	
Start (sub)	20(0)
Minutes on pitch	1800
GOAL ATTEMPTS	
Goals	1
Shots on target	4
Shooting accuracy	36%
PASSING & CROSSING	
Goal assists	0
Passes in opp half	473
Passing accuracy in opp half	66%
Successful crosses	9
Cross completion	21%
DEFENDING	
Interceptions	2
Clearances	54
Tackles	51
Tackles won %	71%
DISCIPLINE	
Fouls	27
Yellow cards	4
Red cards	0
SEE PAGE 306 FOR FULL STATS	

Lomana Tresor LUA LUA • 20
NEWCASTLE UNITED • BORN: 28.12.80

APPEARANCES	
Start (sub)	3(18)
Minutes on pitch	582
GOAL ATTEMPTS	
Goals inside box	0
Goals outside box	0
Minutes per goal scored	n/a
Goals/shots ratio	0%
SHOOTING	
Shots on target inside box	2
Shots on target outside box	8
Shooting accuracy	50%
PASSING	
Goal assists	2
Key passes	8
Passing accuracy in opp half	64%
DISCIPLINE	
Fouls committed	10
Fouls won	15
Offside	7
Yellow cards	2
Red cards	0
SEE PAGE 251 FOR FULL STATS	

Newcastle paid £2.25 million in December for a player who came to England in order to improve his skills as a gymnast.

However, having being spotted playing football at an east London college by Colchester United, Lomana Tresor Lua Lua became one of the most sought-after players in the lower leagues and sparked off a fierce bidding war between several of the Premiership's big guns.

Bobby Robson won the race to sign the talented youngster – but only at a price.

His name translates as "Unique Treasure" and that is certainly something former manager Steve Whitton would agree with, saying: "He's worth the admission fee alone: you could sit and watch him all night."

Lua Lua hit six goals for the Us in 2000–01 before his big money move to the north-east.

The African-born starlet had little chance to impress at Newcastle, making just three starts and mainly appearing as a substitute, but he still created two goals and attempted 20 shots.

ever to have scored in an FA Cup final

John LUKIC • 24
ARSENAL • BORN: 11.12.60

If popular trivia buffs were to be believed, John Lukic is supposed to have survived the 1958 Munich Air disaster, with his pregnant mother allegedly being a stewardess on the doomed plane.

This is patently not true, as the Arsenal 'keeper was not born until 1960, but at least the story keeps the anoraks entertained during those long winter months.

Being born in 1960, though, did make Lukic the Premiership's oldest player in 2000–01 after he received a surprise first-team call-up for Arsenal.

Injuries to David Seaman and Alex Manninger left the Gunners short of goalkeeping cover and Lukic returned to the limelight at the club for which he first played back in 1983.

Lukic's call-up came in the Olympic Stadium in Rome for the Champions League tie with Lazio, where he helped Arsenal to a 1–1 draw.

He then made three appearances in the Premiership, letting no-one down by keeping a clean sheet on each occasion.

APPEARANCES	
Start (sub)	3(0)
Minutes on pitch	270
SHOT STOPPING	
Goals conceded (inside box)	0
Goals conceded (outside box)	0
Minutes per goal conceded	n/a
Clean sheets	3
Saves (shots inside box)	0
Saves (shots outside box)	3
Saves/shots	100%
DISTRIBUTION	
Long kick %	66%
Throws/short passes %	100%
CATCHING	
Crosses caught	0
Crosses punched	2
Crosses dropped	0
Catch success %	0%
DISCIPLINE	
Yellow cards	0
Red cards	0
SEE PAGE 40 FOR FULL STATS	

Claus LUNDEKVAM • 5
SOUTHAMPTON • BORN: 22.3.73

APPEARANCES	
Start (sub)	38(0)
Minutes on pitch	3351
GOAL ATTEMPTS	
Goals	0
DEFENDING	
Blocks	65
Shots cleared off line	0
Headed clearances	272
Other clearances	121
Interceptions	17
Last man saving tackles	0
Tackles won	41
Tackles won %	69%
PASSING	
Passing accuracy own half	79%
Passing accuracy opp half	49%
DISCIPLINE	
Fouls	23
Fouls in danger area	8
Yellow cards	3
Red cards	0
SEE PAGE 265 FOR FULL STATS	

Cynical Saints fans used to nickname Norwegian defender Claus Lundekvam "Santa Claus" due to the number of gifts he often presented to opposition strikers.

Lundekvam has gradually improved, though, and produced some exceptional performances in the Premiership, although he is known to be occasionally accident-prone.

At times in 2000-01 Claus was a colossus at the back for the Saints, though, and formed an excellent partnership alongside Dean Richards at the heart of the defence.

Lundekvam made a total of 393 clearances – the second-highest total for any player – and also made more blocks than anyone else.

Described by team-mate Hassan Kachloul as being a very slow person ("He walks slow, he trains slow"), Lundekvam at least showed an improvement in the application and mental attitude which many fans believed were the causes of some of the more calamitous errors which gave birth to his nickname.

Now all that the towering stopper has to work on is his speed.

For more information visit our website:

Oleg LUZHNY • 22
ARSENAL • BORN: 5.8.68

There has been some debate among Arsenal fans about the genuine nickname for Ukrainian defender Oleg Luzhny.

The official club line is that he was nicknamed "The Horse" when at Dynamo Kiev, due to his trademark gallops up the flanks.

However, a translation from Ukrainian reveals that he was actually called "The Moose", although whether this means he has a penchant for hanging around on Canadian mountain-sides is anybody's guess.

Despite being transfer-listed at the end of 1999–2000, Luzhny reappeared for the Gunners and featured frequently during the opening weeks of the season.

He has the ability to play anywhere in the back four, which makes him a useful squad player and he was soon taken off the transfer list.

Luzhny lost his place in the starting line-up, though, and made only four appearances after the turn of the year. He managed a total of 83 clearances at the back, while he had an impressive passing accuracy of 82%.

APPEARANCES	
Start (sub)	16(3)
Minutes on pitch	1394
GOAL ATTEMPTS	
Goals	0
PASSING & CROSSING	
Goal assists	2
Passing	742
Passing accuracy	82%
Crosses	29
Crossing accuracy	24%
DEFENDING	
Tackles	47
Tackles won %	68%
Blocks	1
Interceptions	9
Clearances	83
Shots cleared off line	0
DISCIPLINE	
Fouls	8
Yellow cards	1
Red cards	0
SEE PAGE 41 FOR FULL STATS	

L
M

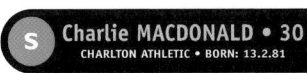
Charlie MACDONALD • 30
CHARLTON ATHLETIC • BORN: 13.2.81

Young forward Charlie MacDonald made three substitute appearances for Charlton during 2000–01 totalling just 88 minutes. He was the club's Young Player of the Year in 1999–2000 after scoring nine goals in 18 full reserve games and the fact that he appeared in the first team at all during Charlton's return to the top flight is testament to the belief that the club obviously have in him.

The London-born player only found time to fire in two efforts in his sojourn in the 2000–01 Premiership, but manager Alan Curbishley will no doubt feel that a slower introduction to the demands of top-flight football is the sensible approach.

MacDonald was farmed out on loan to Division Three side Cheltenham, but never quite looked at the races, scoring twice in eight appearances for the Whaddon Road club before returning to The Valley.

The first-team experience, however, will have served him well for the future.

SEE PAGE 83 FOR FULL STATS

Gallops: Oleg Luzhny

Jurgen MACHO • 30
G SUNDERLAND • BORN: 24.8.77

Austrian 'keeper Jurgen Macho made his Sunderland debut in the opening game of the season when he replaced the injured Dane Thomas Sorensen.

Macho kept his place for the next four Premiership games and manager Peter Reid was impressed enough to say he believed that the goalkeeper had the ability to push for a first-team place.

But just as vampire children have to be taught early on not to run with wooden stakes, so 'keepers have been taught to be sure when coming for crosses.

Of the 12 Macho ventured off his line for, he caught only three of them, dropped one and punched eight, stats which gave the Sunderland fans a few nervy moments. And when you consider that he managed to save just 69% of the shots which were fired at him, it was little surprise when fit-again Sorensen reclaimed his place for the rest of the season.

Macho might struggle to displace the Dane in 2001–02, but he is certainly adequate cover for the Black Cats' number one position.

APPEARANCES

Start (sub)	4(1)
Minutes on pitch	405

SHOT STOPPING

Goals conceded (inside box)	8
Goals conceded (outside box)	1
Minutes per goal conceded	45
Clean sheets	0
Saves (shots inside box)	11
Saves (shots outside box)	9
Saves/shots	69%

DISTRIBUTION

Long kick %	53%
Throws/short passes %	75%

CATCHING

Crosses caught	3
Crosses punched	8
Crosses dropped	1
Catch success %	75%

DISCIPLINE

Yellow cards	0
Red cards	0

SEE PAGE 278 FOR FULL STATS

Jim MAGILTON • 7
M IPSWICH TOWN • BORN: 6.5.69

APPEARANCES

Start (sub)	32(1)
Minutes on pitch	2828

GOAL ATTEMPTS

Goals	1
Shots on target	7
Shooting accuracy	25%

PASSING & CROSSING

Goal assists	5
Passes in opp half	1309
Passing accuracy in opp half	73%
Successful crosses	38
Cross completion	37%

DEFENDING

Interceptions	3
Clearances	27
Tackles	65
Tackles won %	72%

DISCIPLINE

Fouls	28
Yellow cards	1
Red cards	0

SEE PAGE 153 FOR FULL STATS

Jim Magilton was arguably the key player in Ipswich's pass-and-move success story of the 2000–01 season.

The Irishman made more than 2,000 passes during the season – only Manchester United skipper Roy Keane could boast more – and when you consider that Magilton found a team-mate with 80% of his distribution, then it is clear why he became the fulcrum of George Burley's midfield.

His passion was never in doubt; in fact it got him into trouble in January when he was banned and fined for swearing at referee Andy D'Urso. Of the non-verbal challenges, Magilton attempted 65 tackles and won a healthy 72% of them as he exerted his immense presence on the Ipswich midfield.

But do not dare call his team the Tractor Boys. "It drives us doolally," he said. "It conjures up imagines of carrot-crunching yokels coming out of the tunnel with straw stuck between their teeth." One glance at his excellent Opta stats should be enough to ease those frustrations.

2,122 passes for Jim Magilton: only

Chris MAKIN • 36
IPSWICH TOWN • BORN: 8.5.73

Ipswich Town paid Sunderland £1.25 million in March for the services of Chris Makin. Quite why he was allowed to go so cheaply is a mystery to some and a source of conspiracy theories to others in the north east.

The former Marseille defender won a stunning 88% of his tackles after joining George Burley's Suffolk side and added steel to the defence which critics predicted would let Ipswich down upon their return to the top flight of English football.

Burley's men continued to play the same brand of attractive football which won them promotion, and to pass the ball well. In that respect, Makin also fitted in. His pass completion rate of 74% following his move was also above-average for a defender and his forays into the opposition's half produced a total of 23 crosses.

Makin's new manager appears to be as astute in the transfer market as he is with his team selection and the talented full-back will be looking forward to another exciting season as Ipswich bid for UEFA Cup success.

APPEARANCES	
Start (sub)	31(2)
Minutes on pitch	2793
GOAL ATTEMPTS	
Goals	0
PASSING & CROSSING	
Goal assists	3
Passing	1287
Passing accuracy	73%
Crosses	59
Crossing accuracy	34%
DEFENDING	
Tackles	110
Tackles won %	75%
Blocks	12
Interceptions	10
Clearances	87
Shots cleared off line	1
DISCIPLINE	
Fouls	39
Yellow cards	2
Red cards	0

SEE PAGES 153 & 278 FOR FULL STATS

M

Stefan MALZ • 19
ARSENAL • BORN: 15.6.72

After signing Stefan Malz from 1860 Munich, Gunners manager Arsène Wenger simply said of his new man: "He is another sound acquisition for us and further strengthens our squad."

Despite the departure of Emmanuel Petit, there were still few opportunities for the German and during 2000–01 he only made one fleeting 16-minute appearance, in the 1–0 defeat at Charlton. Malz also came off the bench a couple of times in Arsenal's FA Cup run, but had you blinked you might well have missed him.

Having scored for Arsenal in their final game of 1999–2000, Malz would have hoped for more opportunities at the north London club. He was sorely disappointed, though, and with some fantastic talent emerging from the youth ranks and plenty of money in the bank at Highbury it seems Malz has a fight on his hands even to gain a place on the bench. A move away from Highbury may well be on the cards for the German schemer.

SEE PAGE 41 FOR FULL STATS

Steely: Chris Makin

Roy Keane attempted more

Roberto MANCINI • 10
LEICESTER CITY • BORN: 27.11.64

One of the most unlikely transfers of the season saw Italian legend Roberto Mancini end his playing career in the rather inauspicious surroundings of Filbert Street.

Mancini had been Sven-Göran Eriksson's assistant at Lazio, but headed for Blighty at the same time as his boss. The Italian claimed: "Playing in England is an experience that I have always wanted to have. I feel it will be important for me to learn more that I can take into my coaching."

Another reason that he left Serie 'A' may have been that under Italian rules he was unable to go straight into another playing or coaching job in Italy. Mancini continued work on his coaching badges and, after four appearances in the Premiership, headed back to Italy to coach Serie 'A' side Fiorentina.

Foxes fans will have enjoyed seeing a world superstar don the blue shirt, but in truth he offered little to Leicester's cause. He managed only three shots at goal in his brief East Midlands career, two of them testing opposition goalkeepers.

APPEARANCES	
Start (sub)	3(1)
Minutes on pitch	243
GOAL ATTEMPTS	
Goals inside box	0
Goals outside box	0
Minutes per goal scored	n/a
Goals/shots ratio	0%
SHOOTING	
Shots on target inside box	2
Shots on target outside box	0
Shooting accuracy	67%
PASSING	
Goal assists	0
Key passes	3
Passing accuracy in opp half	62%
DISCIPLINE	
Fouls committed	6
Fouls won	2
Offside	2
Yellow cards	0
Red cards	0
SEE PAGE 181 FOR FULL STATS	

Alex MANNINGER • 13
ARSENAL • BORN: 4.6.77

APPEARANCES	
Start (sub)	11(0)
Minutes on pitch	990
SHOT STOPPING	
Goals conceded (inside box)	12
Goals conceded (outside box)	3
Minutes per goal conceded	66
Clean sheets	3
Saves (shots inside box)	15
Saves (shots outside box)	11
Saves/shots	63%
DISTRIBUTION	
Long kick %	44%
Throws/short passes %	98%
CATCHING	
Crosses caught	15
Crosses punched	8
Crosses dropped	0
Catch success %	100%
DISCIPLINE	
Yellow cards	0
Red cards	0
SEE PAGE 40 FOR FULL STATS	

When Austrian Alex Manninger is out and about in public, he likes to tell people that he is a professional skier. Having seen his performances in 2000-01, Arsenal fans would probably agree that his form has certainly been hurtling downhill.

Since he has been in England, Manninger has had to make do with being the second-choice 'keeper behind David Seaman. And despite the assertion from his national coach that he needs regular first-team football, he decided to stick with the Gunners.

When opportunity knocked for him in 2000-01, though, he did nothing to suggest that he could make the number one shirt his own. He conceded a total of 15 goals in the Premiership and his saves-to-shots ratio of 63% was way below average.

His total of just three clean sheets from 11 starts was extremely disappointing.

Arsenal made no secret of the fact they were looking at other 'keepers during the season and Manninger may be left with plenty of time to concentrate on his ski-ing.

CB Elena MARCELINO • 3
NEWCASTLE UNITED • BORN: 26.9.71

Spanish defender Elena Marcelino did not enjoy the best of seasons at Newcastle in 1999–2000 and, following another miserable campaign at St James' Park in 2000–01, he must be wondering why he swapped the holiday island of Majorca for the colder climbs of the north east.

The Spaniard came with the reputation of being arguably the best defender in his country and physically he looks the part. He is not only big and strong but also comfortable on the ball. However, he has often lacked confidence when he has turned out for the Magpies.

Marcelino played in the opening-day defeat at Manchester United, but went on to make just four more starts in the Premiership and Newcastle failed to keep a clean sheet when the big man appeared in defence.

Clubs on the continent have made enquiries about the defender and a return to a warmer climate in the not-too-distant future should not be ruled out as Marcelino managed only 451 minutes on pitch in 2000–01.

APPEARANCES

Start (sub)	5(1)
Minutes on pitch	451

GOAL ATTEMPTS

Goals	0

DEFENDING

Blocks	5
Shots cleared off line	0
Headed clearances	32
Other clearances	11
Interceptions	1
Last man saving tackles	0
Tackles won	14
Tackles won %	70%

PASSING

Passing accuracy own half	75%
Passing accuracy opp half	59%

DISCIPLINE

Fouls	8
Fouls in danger area	2
Yellow cards	1
Red cards	0

SEE PAGE 251 FOR FULL STATS

M

CB Javier MARGAS • 30
WEST HAM UNITED • BORN: 14.1.68

APPEARANCES

Start (sub)	3(0)
Minutes on pitch	238

GOAL ATTEMPTS

Goals	0

DEFENDING

Blocks	2
Shots cleared off line	0
Headed clearances	14
Other clearances	2
Interceptions	3
Last man saving tackles	0
Tackles won	6
Tackles won %	75%

PASSING

Passing accuracy own half	76%
Passing accuracy opp half	61%

DISCIPLINE

Fouls	3
Fouls in danger area	1
Yellow cards	1
Red cards	0

SEE PAGE 307 FOR FULL STATS

A recurring knee injury forced Chilean defender Javier Margas to retire from the game just three matches in to the 2000–01 Premiership season.

But the popular stopper left with a tremendous parting gesture for all Hammers supporters. "I own 15 hotels," he said, "some in Santiago and some on the beach, and West Ham fans coming over can stay for free."

This was the second time he has made grand gestures to prove his love for the club after dying his hair claret and blue during the 1999–2000 season.

Margas famously went AWOL just days after joining West Ham, but after settling to English ways he managed to force himself into first-team reckoning.

He started the Hammers' first three games in 2000–01, but once again found himself struggling with the knee injury which has dogged much of his career. He duly called it a day and can now spend his days with his feet up by the pool at a resort in Chile, surrounded by holidaying Hammers supporters.

Carlos Arturo MARINELLI • 23
MIDDLESBROUGH • BORN: 28.8.80

Being a talented youngster from Argentina, it was inevitable that Carlos Marinelli would have been given the tag of "the new Maradona" at some point.

No pressure, then, on the player whom Middlesbrough signed ahead of Manchester United back in October 1999.

A tall, lanky, awkward-looking midfielder, Marinelli's looks belie his ability. With some of the flashes of skill he has shown, he has already reminded Middlesbrough fans of Juninho, although team-mates have likened him to West Ham and England starlet Joe Cole.

Marinelli mainly appeared as a substitute for Boro during 2000–01, making just two Premiership starts. He was sent off in the first one against Bradford and did not manage to start another game until the final day of the season.

He was a regular on the bench, though, and if he continues to develop the potential he has shown, the former Boca Juniors man could become a permanent fixture in the first team in the 2001–02 season.

APPEARANCES	
Start (sub)	2(11)
Minutes on pitch	305
GOAL ATTEMPTS	
Goals	0
Shots on target	3
Shooting accuracy	60%
Goals/shots ratio	0%
PASSING	
Goal assists	0
Passes in opp half	133
Passing accuracy in opp half	77%
Crosses	34
Crossing accuracy	32%
DRIBBLING	
Dribbles & runs	31
Dribble completion	52%
Corners forced	3
DISCIPLINE	
Fouls	8
Yellow cards	1
Red cards	1
SEE PAGE 237 FOR FULL STATS	

Chris MARSDEN • 4
SOUTHAMPTON • BORN: 3.1.69

APPEARANCES	
Start (sub)	19(4)
Minutes on pitch	1606
GOAL ATTEMPTS	
Goals	0
Shots on target	2
Shooting accuracy	14%
PASSING & CROSSING	
Goal assists	1
Passes in opp half	444
Passing accuracy in opp half	70%
Successful crosses	10
Cross completion	34%
DEFENDING	
Interceptions	7
Clearances	28
Tackles	82
Tackles won %	67%
DISCIPLINE	
Fouls	44
Yellow cards	4
Red cards	0
SEE PAGE 265 FOR FULL STATS	

Chris Marsden battled hard to earn his place in Southampton's starting line-up with some solid, workmanlike performances, but injuries and infrequent selection frustrated the former Birmingham man.

Never known as being one of the most skilful players around, Marsden is more of a battler and midfield grafter – qualities recognised by Lou Macari, who made a bid to take Marsden to Huddersfield just before deadline day. The move never materialised, though, and the midfielder – known as "Bod" – saw out the remainder of the season at Southampton.

Marsden finished the campaign as a regular in the Saints' side, showing that he loves to be in the thick of the action by making 82 tackles. His success in the challenge is below average, though, which a player in his mould would not be happy about.

His passing and crossing stats were better, but with just one assist during the season he was not always finding his own players when it mattered.

Lee MARSHALL • 26
LEICESTER CITY • BORN: 21.1.79

Lee Marshall exchanged one City for another when he moved from Norwich to Leicester just before deadline day to once again link up with Peter Taylor – the man who selected him to play for the England Under-21 side.

Shortly after signing him, Taylor said: "He is a hungry player who wants to get better. I have my eye on him for next season."

But Marshall quickly found himself in the Leicester side for the remainder of the 2000–01 campaign. His versatility – he can play at the back, in midfield or up front – meant that he was perfect cover for the Foxes during an injury crisis.

With bags of ability, his main problem while at Norwich was one of inconsistency. Since his move to the Premiership that has remained the case, as Marshall produced a handful of good performances and a couple of bad ones. For example, he endured a difficult time on the final day of the season against Leeds.

But he was playing in a weakened Leicester side lacking in confidence and with more solid support, he should improve in 2001–02.

APPEARANCES	
Start (sub)	7(2)
Minutes on pitch	689
GOAL ATTEMPTS	
Goals	0
Shots on target	0
Shooting accuracy	0%
PASSING & CROSSING	
Goal assists	I
Passes in opp half	159
Passing accuracy in opp half	66%
Successful crosses	4
Cross completion	15%
DEFENDING	
Interceptions	5
Clearances	21
Tackles	23
Tackles won %	65%
DISCIPLINE	
Fouls	4
Yellow cards	0
Red cards	0
SEE PAGE 181 FOR FULL STATS	

Lilian MARTIN • 16
DERBY COUNTY • BORN: 28.5.71

APPEARANCES	
Start (sub)	7(2)
Minutes on pitch	550
GOAL ATTEMPTS	
Goals	0
PASSING & CROSSING	
Goal assists	I
Passing	204
Passing accuracy	64%
Crosses	24
Crossing accuracy	42%
DEFENDING	
Tackles	14
Tackles won %	93%
Blocks	3
Interceptions	2
Clearances	13
Shots cleared off line	0
DISCIPLINE	
Fouls	7
Yellow cards	3
Red cards	0
SEE PAGE 125 FOR FULL STATS	

Derby County's attempts to bolster their woeful defence in the early part of the 2000–01 season took them to the south of France, where they picked up full-back Lilian Martin on a free transfer from Olympique Marseille in October.

Martin made his debut for the Rams in a home game with West Ham and that was the first clean sheet Jim Smith's men kept in 2000–01.

He went on to start the following six games and during this period helped to shore up the leaky back line at Pride Park. Discipline was letting him down, though, and he picked up three yellow cards in his first four games as he found it difficult to come to terms with the pace of the Premiership.

After his initial promise, Martin began to struggle and he made his final appearance in a Rams shirt in the FA Cup tie with Blackburn. His contract was eventually cancelled by Derby at the beginning of May.

It is extremely doubtful that we will see the Gallic defender in the Premiership again.

G **Nigel MARTYN • 1**
LEEDS UNITED • BORN: 11.8.66

Leeds 'keeper Nigel Martyn was pleased to finish the campaign in goal for the Whites after suffering a frustrating period out of the side through injury in the middle of the season.

Martyn is not a player who is struck down with injury very often, but the serious groin strain he suffered kept him out for 15 Premiership games during the season.

He said: "It was quite lonely just thinking of all the big games that I was going to miss – Manchester United, Barcelona, other Champions League games, other big Premiership games and England World Cup qualifiers. It was sickening, really."

Fortunately he recovered and, once back in the side, showed the form which had Leeds' followers hailing him as "England's number one". He saved on average an excellent 78% of the shots he faced in the Premiership.

When he did don the 'keeper's jersey for England he also came up trumps, keeping out a penalty in a friendly against Spain, a great moment for the popular Cornishman.

APPEARANCES	
Start (sub)	23(0)
Minutes on pitch	2051
SHOT STOPPING	
Goals conceded (inside box)	18
Goals conceded (outside box)	2
Minutes per goal conceded	103
Clean sheets	8
Saves (shots inside box)	34
Saves (shots outside box)	35
Saves/shots	78%
DISTRIBUTION	
Long kick %	56%
Throws/short passes %	81%
CATCHING	
Crosses caught	35
Crosses punched	16
Crosses dropped	2
Catch success %	95%
DISCIPLINE	
Yellow cards	0
Red cards	0
SEE PAGE 166 FOR FULL STATS	

Lonely: Nigel Martyn

For more information visit our website:

Dominic MATTEO • 21
LEEDS UNITED • BORN: 24.4.74

The £4.25 million transfer of Dominic Matteo from Liverpool to Leeds at the start of 2000–01 almost fell through when the Scottish-born player failed his medical.

A few eyebrows were raised when Leeds insisted on progressing with the deal despite Matteo's knee injury, but they will be glad that they did, as he repaid their faith in an impressive season for David O'Leary's men.

The versatile player began on the left of midfield but later moved on to play in defence. Surplus to requirements at Liverpool, he suddenly found himself playing in the Champions League and even scoring a crucial goal for Leeds against AC Milan at the San Siro.

Matteo also chose 2000–01 to pledge his international future to the country of his birth, rather than his mother's native England. Despite having represented the England Under-21 side and overtures from Sven-Göran Eriksson, he earned his first international cap for Scotland in the 2–0 defeat against Australia.

APPEARANCES	
Start (sub)	30(0)
Minutes on pitch	2597
GOAL ATTEMPTS	
Goals	0
Shots on target	4
Shooting accuracy	67%
PASSING & CROSSING	
Goal assists	1
Passes in opp half	640
Passing accuracy in opp half	65%
Successful crosses	5
Cross completion	16%
DEFENDING	
Interceptions	11
Clearances	118
Tackles	86
Tackles won %	77%
DISCIPLINE	
Fouls	34
Yellow cards	1
Red cards	0
SEE PAGE 167 FOR FULL STATS	

M

Youl MAWENE • 17
DERBY COUNTY • BORN: 16.7.79

APPEARANCES	
Start (sub)	7(1)
Minutes on pitch	578
GOAL ATTEMPTS	
Goals	0
DEFENDING	
Blocks	12
Shots cleared off line	1
Headed clearances	27
Other clearances	20
Interceptions	2
Last man saving tackles	0
Tackles won	23
Tackles won %	66%
PASSING	
Passing accuracy own half	76%
Passing accuracy opp half	60%
DISCIPLINE	
Fouls	12
Fouls in danger area	5
Yellow cards	2
Red cards	0
SEE PAGE 125 FOR FULL STATS	

In the summer of 2000, Lens defender Youl Mawene came over to England to spend a fortnight training with Derby County. Clearly the famous attractions of the East Midlands city, such as the Wyvern Business Park and Toyota car plant, had a lasting effect on the industrious young man and he soon signed a four-year deal with the Rams.

Mawene is a product of the Lens Youth Academy and made seven appearances for the French side towards the end of the 1999–2000 season, including the UEFA Cup tie against Arsenal. He was signed by Jim Smith as a "future star". Smith said: "We expect him to be featuring in the first team at the start of next season (2001–02)."

The French defender has already broken through, though, making his Premiership debut at Southampton at the end of December. He made seven more league appearances for the Rams, including an impressive performance against champions Manchester United as Derby ensured their Premiership survival.

CB David MAY • 4
MANCHESTER UNITED • BORN: 24.6.70

Oldham-born defender David May was a Manchester City fan as a child, so 2000–01 would have been a massive disappointment for him. Not only did boyhood heroes City go down, but he also had the agony of another injury-ridden campaign.

A ruptured Achilles at the end of the 1999–2000 season left many doubting May's future in football, but he slowly managed to recover. He became a regular in the reserve side and began to make appearances on the bench for United.

He came on in United's penultimate league game against Southampton and made his only Premiership start of the season against Tottenham on the final day.

With the last three campaigns having been ruined by injury, May could be forgiven for thinking he has been jinxed – although given the team he supported as a child, many United fans would say he has been cursed from a very early age.

SEE PAGE 223 FOR FULL STATS

M Gary McALLISTER • 21
LIVERPOOL • BORN: 25.12.64

Cult hero: Gary McAllister

Brian Clough once stormed out of transfer negotiations with Gary McAllister when he discovered the Scotsman was wearing a pair of cowboy boots. Whether the midfielder's dress sense has improved with age is debatable, but his footballing ability appears to getting better all the time.

McAllister was initially targeted by Liverpool during Kenny Dalglish's reign, but there were a few eyebrows raised when the Merseysiders finally got their man on a free transfer from Coventry in the summer of 2000. With his intelligent passing and vital goals, he turned into one of the signings of the season and is fully deserving of the one-year extension to his contract he was handed.

The former Scottish international scored five goals and made a further five in the Premiership season.

But he earned cult hero status among Liverpool fans when he notched vital winners against local rivals Everton and then Barcelona in the UEFA Cup during a crucial four-day period in April.

APPEARANCES	
Start (sub)	21(9)
Minutes on pitch	1926
GOAL ATTEMPTS	
Goals	5
Shots on target	13
Shooting accuracy	54%
PASSING & CROSSING	
Goal assists	5
Passes in opp half	648
Passing accuracy in opp half	71%
Successful crosses	70
Cross completion	38%
DEFENDING	
Interceptions	5
Clearances	34
Tackles	48
Tackles won %	75%
DISCIPLINE	
Fouls	25
Yellow cards	1
Red cards	1
SEE PAGE 195 FOR FULL STATS	

4 Gary McAllister scored in four consecutive league games

Stuart McCALL • 4
BRADFORD CITY • BORN: 10.6.64

Bradford legend Stuart McCall could not prevent the club's slide back into the Nationwide League, but equally he could not have done more to try, holding a number of positions at the club during the course of the 2000–01 season.

As well as being club captain, McCall took on the mantle of assistant manager when Chris Hutchings became boss in the summer of 2000. McCall was dismissed at Charlton for two bookable offences – not the right example to set – but he was soon promoted to caretaker manager following Hutchings' departure.

McCall ruled himself out of the running to take on the manager's role full-time and when Jim Jefferies took charge, the former Rangers and Everton man was installed as first team coach.

None of this affected McCall's ability on the pitch, though, with the Scottish international attempting 148 tackles – the second-highest total in the Premiership – and completing 70% of his attempted passes in Bradford's doomed season.

APPEARANCES	
Start (sub)	36(1)
Minutes on pitch	3241
GOAL ATTEMPTS	
Goals	1
Shots on target	2
Shooting accuracy	20%
PASSING & CROSSING	
Goal assists	0
Passes in opp half	983
Passing accuracy in opp half	64%
Successful crosses	4
Cross completion	13%
DEFENDING	
Interceptions	14
Clearances	93
Tackles	148
Tackles won %	61%
DISCIPLINE	
Fouls	47
Yellow cards	4
Red cards	1
SEE PAGE 69 FOR FULL STATS	

M

Gavin McCANN • 8
SUNDERLAND • BORN: 10.1.78

APPEARANCES	
Start (sub)	22(0)
Minutes on pitch	1932
GOAL ATTEMPTS	
Goals	3
Shots on target	9
Shooting accuracy	43%
PASSING & CROSSING	
Goal assists	3
Passes in opp half	600
Passing accuracy in opp half	65%
Successful crosses	20
Cross completion	30%
DEFENDING	
Interceptions	7
Clearances	23
Tackles	105
Tackles won %	65%
DISCIPLINE	
Fouls	59
Yellow cards	4
Red cards	0
SEE PAGE 279 FOR FULL STATS	

Gavin McCann was the proud "winner" of a penalty shoot-out to decide who had to wear Niall Quinn's leopard-skin thong on the beach during the team's end-of-season sunshine break.

Stringfellow-esque garments aside, McCann does like to keep it tight in the tackle department and no player attempted more challenges for the team than the former Evertonian, who got stuck in 105 times in the 2000–01 season.

But McCann's passing was not so foxy. With just 65% of his distribution finding a team-mate, there was a need for improvement. He did, however, set up three goals for colleagues as well as netting three vital efforts himself in the Premiership.

Manager Peter Reid called him "an outstanding player" and McCann vindicated those words playing in midfield for England. His debut against Spain will surely not be his last international appearance. although his outrageous underwear alone is unlikely to impress England boss Sven-Göran Erikkson.

Grant McCANN • 38
WEST HAM UNITED • BORN: 14.4.80

Hammers youngster Grant McCann experienced English league football for the first time in 2000–01 having spent time on loan at Notts County and Cheltenham Town before making his Premiership bow for West Ham in their final game of the season.

McCann, a Northern Ireland Under-21 international, spent the first month of the season at Meadow Lane, making three appearances for the Nottingham club.

He was then farmed out to Cheltenham, where the midfielder made a big impression on Robins boss Steve Cotterill, who persuaded Harry Redknapp to extend the loan until the end of the season.

The on-loan Hammer was a regular feature on the left-hand side for Cheltenham and scored three goals during his time at Whaddon Road. He returned to West Ham at the end of the Nationwide season and, at Middlesbrough on the final day of the campaign, he was a last-minute substitute for Scott Minto.

SEE PAGE 307 FOR FULL STATS

 George McCARTNEY • 24
SUNDERLAND • BORN: 29.4.81

Northern Ireland Under-21 international George McCartney finally made the breakthrough into the Black Cats' first team during 2000–01 but he has tough competition to claim a regular place.

McCartney's first appearance in the red-and-white stripes came in the Worthington Cup tie with Luton and in February he made his Premiership debut in the 2–0 defeat at Leicester. The tall left-back will struggle to oust Stadium of Light favourites Michael Gray and Julio Arca from the side, but after a series of good performances in the youth team and at reserve level he would hope eventually to be chosen on merit.

Ulsterman McCartney was an integral member of the "Fab Four" who made up the Sunderland reserve team defence, with the side just missing out on the title. The youngster will be looking to get more than just two Premiership appearances under his belt in 2001–02.

SEE PAGE 279 FOR FULL STATS

 Dave McEWEN • 27
TOTTENHAM HOTSPUR • BORN: 2.11.77

Dave McEwen's Premiership dream came to an end when Glenn Hoddle released him at the end of the 2000–01 season. The local lad, who was plucked from the obscurity of Dulwich Hamlet in January 2000, made three substitute appearances at the start of 2001 when the club suffered from a lack of available first-choice strikers.

His biggest opportunity came when Les Ferdinand had to withdraw from the match against Southampton with just 20 minutes of the game gone, but McEwen found it difficult to break down a mean Saints defence which was in the middle of a consecutive run of seven clean sheets.

Hoddle, then in charge of the south coast side, could not have been too impressed by the youngster, who failed to fire a single effort at goal. Having graduated from university with a business studies degree, McEwen has other fields available to him should he need to seek an alternative career.

SEE PAGE 293 FOR FULL STATS

 John McGRATH • 24
ASTON VILLA • BORN: 27.3.80

Aston Villa prodigy John McGrath found his first-team opportunities rather limited in 2000–01, as Villans boss John Gregory preferred the more experienced options of Alan Wright or Steve Staunton down the left-hand flank.

The Republic of Ireland Under-21 international is highly-rated by other senior figures at the club. Assistant boss Steve Harrison is a fan of his fantastic left foot and described McGrath as a "springer" for the way his game has developed in a short space of time.

Goalkeeper David James urged the Villa hierarchy to give McGrath a chance at the end of the season, but the midfielder had to make do with a couple of brief substitute appearances.

McGrath played at Bradford and Chelsea and got his first run-out on home soil when he played the second half of the 3–0 defeat at the hands of Liverpool. The Irishman will be hoping for better luck in 2001–02.

SEE PAGE 55 FOR FULL STATS

For more information visit our website:

John McGREAL • 4
IPSWICH TOWN • BORN: 2.6.72

Former Tranmere defender John McGreal started the 2000–01 campaign on the bench at Ipswich. But he quickly forced his way into the first team, becoming an integral member of the side as Town surprised everyone in their first season back in the top flight.

Like most of the Ipswich side, McGreal is comfortable on the ball and found a colleague with a steady 84% of the passes that he played in his own half.

He even grabbed the first goal of his Town career on his first return to Merseyside in the Premiership, as Ipswich trounced Everton 3–0 at Goodison Park.

While that goal was undoubtedly sweet for the lifelong Liverpool fan, going to Anfield to defeat the Reds 1–0 in December was "simply unbelievable". McGreal did let himself down by getting sent off for dissent in the clash with Chelsea in January, but came back strongly to help steer Ipswich to UEFA Cup qualification.

Still aged under 30, McGreal will hope to feature strongly in Town's European adventure in the 2001–02 season.

APPEARANCES	
Start (sub)	25(3)
Minutes on pitch	2257

GOAL ATTEMPTS	
Goals	1

DEFENDING	
Blocks	18
Shots cleared off line	1
Headed clearances	122
Other clearances	76
Interceptions	11
Last man saving tackles	1
Tackles won	47
Tackles won %	70%

PASSING	
Passing accuracy own half	84%
Passing accuracy opp half	59%

DISCIPLINE	
Fouls	24
Fouls in danger area	4
Yellow cards	1
Red cards	1

SEE PAGE 153 FOR FULL STATS

Billy McKINLAY • 27
BRADFORD CITY • BORN: 22.4.69

APPEARANCES	
Start (sub)	10(1)
Minutes on pitch	909

GOAL ATTEMPTS	
Goals	0
Shots on target	1
Shooting accuracy	20%

PASSING & CROSSING	
Goal assists	0
Passes in opp half	241
Passing accuracy in opp half	62%
Successful crosses	3
Cross completion	25%

DEFENDING	
Interceptions	0
Clearances	10
Tackles	39
Tackles won %	62%

DISCIPLINE	
Fouls	28
Yellow cards	3
Red cards	0

SEE PAGE 69 FOR FULL STATS

Billy McKinlay started the 2000–01 season with Blackburn Rovers, but then joined Leicester City on loan.

He made just one appearance for the Foxes, a 3–0 hammering at home to Crystal Palace in the Worthington Cup which saw the then-holders crash spectacularly out of the competition.

Three weeks later, Bradford City signed McKinlay on a free from Graeme Souness's Blackburn. The former Scotland international went on to make 11 appearances for the Bantams, as the Yorkshire side tried in vain to escape relegation from the Premiership.

McKinlay failed to score or set up a goal, managing just a solitary shot on target.

His distribution was not much better, with only 62% of his passes in the opposition half reaching a fellow-Bantam, although playing in a team bottom of the Premiership would be hard for any player.

However, an experienced schemer of his stature could prove very handy as Bradford aim to bounce straight back into the Premiership.

M Kevin McLEOD • 29
EVERTON • BORN: 12.9.80

One of many graduates of the Youth Academy at Goodison Park, Kevin McLeod was rewarded for some fine performances in the reserves with his first-team debut in the home game against Ipswich in September.

McLeod is a left-sided midfielder who is just as happy playing as an out-and-out winger and made a total of five brief appearances as a substitute throughout the season.

Manager Walter Smith is clearly willing to give youth a chance at the club and this bodes well for players like McLeod.

With budgets tight at Goodison and a number of players due to be sold to balance the books, McLeod may well get plenty more opportunities to impress the folk of Merseyside in the 2001–02 season.

Everton will be hoping that if he does fulfil his promise, McLeod will prove more loyal to the Everton cause than some of his former youth team-mates, who have indicated a desire to leave the club.

SEE PAGE 139 FOR FULL STATS

S Erik MEIJER • 18
LIVERPOOL • BORN: 2.8.69

With Michael Owen, Robbie Fowler and Emile Heskey all at Gérard Houllier's disposal, it was no surprise that Erik Meijer left the Reds for Hamburg on a free transfer midway through the 2000–01 campaign.

Meijer made three substitute appearances for Liverpool at the start of the season, but was quickly shipped off to Preston North End on loan, playing nine times for David Moyes's Division One high-fliers.

However, the Dutchman failed to score in all 12 appearances in the 2000–01 season and with competition for places up front at Liverpool so hot Meijer was always unlikely to become a first-team regular.

Meijer made a total of 23 appearances in his Liverpool career, mostly as a substitute, but failed to hit the back of the net once.

He fared better at Hamburg, however, scoring three goals in the Bundesliga – and is clearly happy to be playing regular first-team football at last.

SEE PAGE 195 FOR FULL STATS

M Stephen McPHAIL • 14
LEEDS UNITED • BORN: 9.12.79

It must have been an extremely frustrating 2000–01 season for Stephen McPhail.

Having burst on to the Premiership scene in 1999–2000, the London-born Irishman was forced to watch from the sidelines as his team-mates marched to the semi-finals of the Champions League and finished fourth in the Premiership.

After making five appearances before the end of October, McPhail underwent an operation on his Achilles tendon and did not return until May, when he made two substitute appearances.

Those in the know have been raving about McPhail for years and the left-footed midfielder has already been capped by the Republic of Ireland.

Competition for places in the Peacocks' midfield is sure to be intense, but McPhail has proved he has what it takes to force his way into contention.

Winner of Leeds' Young Player of the Year title in 1997, McPhail is without doubt a star of the future for both club and country and having him fully fit for the 2001–02 season will be a major bonus for David O'Leary, as he seeks to put some long-overdue silverware in the Elland Road trophy cabinet.

APPEARANCES	
Start (sub)	3(4)
Minutes on pitch	356
GOAL ATTEMPTS	
Goals	0
Shots on target	0
Shooting accuracy	0%
PASSING & CROSSING	
Goal assists	0
Passes in opp half	115
Passing accuracy in opp half	77%
Successful crosses	1
Cross completion	20%
DEFENDING	
Interceptions	2
Clearances	3
Tackles	10
Tackles won %	90%
DISCIPLINE	
Fouls	1
Yellow cards	0
Red cards	0

SEE PAGE 167 FOR FULL STATS

5 Paul Merson hit the woodwork

Mario MELCHIOT • 15
CHELSEA • BORN: 4.11.76

While at Ajax, Mario Melchiot made a record with team-mates Benni McCarthy and Dean Gorre called *Midas Touch*.

That is certainly what Melchiot appeared to have during the 2000–01 season, missing just seven Premiership matches for Chelsea compared to the season before when he made only five appearances.

He performed excellently as well, playing at both right-back and centre-back under Claudio Ranieri – and scored a wonderful individual goal in the Charity Shield against Manchester United.

Melchiot's most upsetting moment of the season came when British R&B singer Craig David failed to win an award at the 2001 Brit Awards, despite being nominated in so many categories.

"I couldn't believe that", he raged on his website. "It's like fancying too many women in one club and ending up with none of them."

Melchiot and his Chelsea team-mates will be hoping for more awards than David, as another season without any silverware for the Kings Road outfit would be deemed a big failure.

APPEARANCES	
Start (sub)	27(4)
Minutes on pitch	2431
GOAL ATTEMPTS	
Goals	0
PASSING & CROSSING	
Goal assists	4
Passing	1184
Passing accuracy	80%
Crosses	47
Crossing accuracy	23%
DEFENDING	
Tackles	75
Tackles won %	77%
Blocks	13
Interceptions	7
Clearances	92
Shots cleared off line	0
DISCIPLINE	
Fouls	35
Yellow cards	2
Red cards	0
SEE PAGE 97 FOR FULL STATS	

M

Paul MERSON • 10
ASTON VILLA • BORN: 20.3.68

APPEARANCES	
Start (sub)	38(0)
Minutes on pitch	3359
GOAL ATTEMPTS	
Goals	6
Shots on target	18
Shooting accuracy	29%
Goals/shots ratio	10%
PASSING	
Goal assists	6
Passes in opp half	1519
Passing accuracy in opp half	68%
Crosses	279
Crossing accuracy	32%
DRIBBLING	
Dribbles & runs	200
Dribble completion	73%
Corners forced	37
DISCIPLINE	
Fouls	13
Yellow cards	2
Red cards	0
SEE PAGE 55 FOR FULL STATS	

Not many players are keen to fall foul of the squad rotation system, but Paul Merson virtually called for its introduction after starting every game of the 2000–01 campaign. The disgruntled midfielder conceded: "It would be a sign of all-round improvement for Villa if I found it more difficult to get into the side."

The former England international was voted the Villans' Player of the Year for his evergreen displays in the claret-and-blue shirt.

A sublime chip in the dying seconds at Goodison Park earned the visitors maximum points in November, while Merson's awareness of his team-mates was also a telling factor throughout the season. He completed more than 1,500 passes and created six goals with his vision.

Although keen to stay at Villa, the former Gunner applied to be player-manager at Crystal Palace at the end of the season. He was flatly refused by the Eagles and his future at Villa Park was far from certain after his summer pay demands.

more often than any other player

G — Alan MILLER • 34
COVENTRY CITY • BORN: 29.3.70

Journeyman goalkeeper Alan Miller received quite a lot of newspaper coverage during 2000–01: not for anything he did on a football pitch, but because his ex-girlfriend Claire Sweeney (Lindsey in *Brookside*) took part in *Celebrity Big Brother* as part of Comic Relief.

Unfortunately, Sweeney just missed out to Jack Dee on winning the gameshow, although she did at least make the last two.

Sadly, a glance at the league table shows that Coventry did too. And it was City for whom Miller made his one Premiership appearance of the season: at Chelsea, when the on-loan Blackburn 'keeper replaced red-carded Chris Kirkland. It was hardly a confidence-booster for the former Baggie; Miller saw six goals fly past him, four from the boot of Jimmy Floyd Hasselbaink, although he did make eight saves to stop the score being even more embarrassing.

If Miller is to secure regular football, it is likely to be away from Ewood Park.

SEE PAGE 110 FOR FULL STATS

FB — Scott MINTO • 20
WEST HAM UNITED • BORN: 6.8.71

Scott Minto has been ravaged by knee injuries in recent seasons and 2000–01 saw him play just one game for the Hammers: the last match of the season at Middlesbrough.

But the upbeat former Chelsea and England prospect is determined to make an impact in 2001–02. Speaking in February, he said: "I'm pretty sure it's a case of 'Scott who?' for a lot of people. They've probably forgotten about me or wondered whether I'm still at West Ham. But there's nothing I can do about that – I've got to have nothing but positive thoughts that everything's going to be all right.

"I've never been out this long before in my career – it's unbelievable."

Minto is a popular figure among Hammers supporters and still has much to offer at the highest level of English football.

West Ham will hope that he can avoid mishap in 2001–02 and establish himself in the team. It will be like buying a new player – and a good one at that.

SEE PAGE 307 FOR FULL STATS

FB — Danny MILLS • 18
LEEDS UNITED • BORN: 18.5.77

Danny Mills spent much of his first season at Leeds on the bench. But he excelled in 2000–01, playing a prominent role during the club's successes at home and abroad.

Mills played most of the 2000–01 campaign at right-back, but he also filled in at centre-half during Leeds' frequent injury crises and became a hugely popular figure among the club's fans thanks to his wholehearted displays. Mills won an excellent 83% of his tackles – the best proportion at Elland Road – to oust Gary Kelly and even earn his first England cap in the friendly against Mexico.

Team-mates claim that the former Charlton defender considers himself to be the "hardman" of the team, which has become a bit of a in-joke at Elland Road where the players have dubbed him "Bulldog".

Indeed, for Mills's sake, one can only hope that he asked for permission from David Batty and Lee Bowyer before attempting to assume their roles at the club.

Some observers were surprised when Leeds splashed out on the former Addick, but he has proved to be a sound investment by David O'Leary and chairman Peter Ridsdale.

APPEARANCES	
Start (sub)	20(3)
Minutes on pitch	1860
GOAL ATTEMPTS	
Goals	0
PASSING & CROSSING	
Goal assists	1
Passing	780
Passing accuracy	62%
Crosses	44
Crossing accuracy	27%
DEFENDING	
Tackles	54
Tackles won %	83%
Blocks	21
Interceptions	7
Clearances	113
Shots cleared off line	1
DISCIPLINE	
Fouls	30
Yellow cards	8
Red cards	0

SEE PAGE 167 FOR FULL STATS

For more information visit our website:

Robert MOLENAAR • 12
BRADFORD CITY • BORN: 27.2.69

Burly defender Robert Molenaar caught the bus from Leeds to Bradford in December 2000 and joined the happy campers at Valley Parade for a fee of £500,000.

He was greeted by his new manager Jim Jeffries, who told the world: "He's perfect for us." Considering the Bantams were rooted to the foot of the Premiership, Molenaar might well have taken this the wrong way – but he settled in well and became a popular figure at the club.

Nicknamed "The Terminator" at Leeds, Molenaar careered into a series of tackles and clearances in an attempt to shore up the Bantams' defence. He even managed a rare goal, scoring in his third appearance for the club away at Newcastle.

However, his passing left much room for improvement, particularly upfield and he was unable to stop the club from sliding into the Nationwide League, but his former career as an electrician should at least ensure floodlight problems are a thing of the past at any ground where he is playing.

APPEARANCES	
Start (sub)	21(0)
Minutes on pitch	1820

GOAL ATTEMPTS	
Goals	1

DEFENDING	
Blocks	31
Shots cleared off line	0
Headed clearances	178
Other clearances	51
Interceptions	6
Last man saving tackles	1
Tackles won	38
Tackles won %	64%

PASSING	
Passing accuracy own half	71%
Passing accuracy opp half	43%

DISCIPLINE	
Fouls	33
Fouls in danger area	11
Yellow cards	4
Red cards	0

SEE PAGE 69 FOR FULL STATS

M

John MONCUR • 16
WEST HAM UNITED • BORN: 22.9.66

APPEARANCES	
Start (sub)	6(10)
Minutes on pitch	609

GOAL ATTEMPTS	
Goals	0
Shots on target	3
Shooting accuracy	60%

PASSING & CROSSING	
Goal assists	0
Passes in opp half	163
Passing accuracy in opp half	71%
Successful crosses	2
Cross completion	33%

DEFENDING	
Interceptions	1
Clearances	8
Tackles	22
Tackles won %	59%

DISCIPLINE	
Fouls	25
Yellow cards	6
Red cards	0

SEE PAGE 307 FOR FULL STATS

With his untucked shirt and upturned collar, John Moncur blazed a path for fancy players and their whims.

The former Swindon man has been one of the craftiest midfielders of the past decade and still showed glimpses of his ability for West Ham in 2000–01.

He did not score, but his trickery on the ball persuaded the club to give him a new one-year contract. Moncur said: "I had offers from other clubs even this year and some have offered me a couple of years. I'd rather play for West Ham for a year than go somewhere else and earn a bit more money and go on a bit longer. It means more to me to play for West Ham than money or anything else."

And while he is unlikely to play a significant part in the Hammers' 2001–02 campaign, he is a wise head alongside the youthful exuberance of Michael Carrick and Joe Cole. Those talented young upstarts are sure to benefit from Moncur's wealth of Premiership experience. Maybe he will even learn something from them!

Garry MONK • 25
SOUTHAMPTON • BORN: 6.3.79

Fresh-faced defender Garry Monk loves the sea, having moved from Torquay United to Southampton in his short career. He has found it hard to make waves in the Saints' first XI, though, and only played 159 minutes of Premiership football in 2000–01.

On the one occasion his manager did call Monk to the office, it was to tell him that Division Two strugglers Oxford United wanted to take him on loan.

The defender duly went to the Manor Ground but could not slow the Us' relegation charge, finishing on the defeated side in four out of five games.

His tackling, when he did make the Southampton team, was crisp and he won every challenge he went in for. He was also comfortable bringing the ball forward. His best chance for first-team action at the Saints' new stadium is if some of the more senior defenders decide to follow Glenn Hoddle's example and leave for pastures new.

SEE PAGE 265 FOR FULL STATS

Joe-Max MOORE • 19
EVERTON • BORN: 23.2.71

Zero: Joe-Max Moore

Ships used to take people from Liverpool to the United States for a better life and many players at struggling Everton must wish they still ran. Yankee hitman Joe-Max Moore has travelled in the other direction, but may be making a return journey soon.

He failed to build on his impressive introduction to English football in 1999–2000, when he scored six goals, by bagging a grand total of zero in 2000–01. He figured in 21 league games, but was just a substitute in 13 of them, firing only eight shots on target.

One commentator noted that he "would score loads in the first division but can't quite do it in the top flight."

Whether this is true or not, in February Moore was linked with a return to America, with Major League Soccer outfit Miami Fusion the club interested in him.

His pass completion rate of 74% was not too bad, but as he heads into his 30s it seems likely that he will follow the likes of fellow-US imports Cobi Jones and Roy Wegerle into vague memory, football trivia and pub quizzes.

APPEARANCES	
Start (sub)	8(13)
Minutes on pitch	853
GOAL ATTEMPTS	
Goals inside box	0
Goals outside box	0
Minutes per goal scored	n/a
Goals/shots ratio	0%
SHOOTING	
Shots on target inside box	5
Shots on target outside box	3
Shooting accuracy	62%
PASSING	
Goal assists	1
Key passes	7
Passing accuracy in opp half	69%
DISCIPLINE	
Fouls committed	15
Fouls won	14
Offside	6
Yellow cards	2
Red cards	0

SEE PAGE 139 FOR FULL STATS

2 Garry Monk's only two appearances for Southampton

Jody MORRIS • 20
CHELSEA • BORN: 22.12.78

Fiery midfielder Jody Morris may have enjoyed life under the management of Gianluca Vialli, but was used far more sparingly under new Chelsea boss Claudio Ranieri.

After a relative spree of three goals in the 1999–2000 season, the cupboard was bare in 2000–01 as Morris struggled to find his form and to find a place in the team.

With Ranieri importing players such as Slavisa Jokanovic, Morris became frustrated and the midfielder was linked with a number of clubs – most notably Leicester City – throughout the season.

His passing remained as slick as ever, with 80% of his balls reaching a team-mate, but there is no doubt that he stagnated in the 2000–01 campaign.

Whether he needs to leave Chelsea to progress remains to be seen, but Morris was once touted as an ideal replacement for Dennis Wise, both as a player and a captain. Such a career path remains open to the former England Under-21 star but he will need to play more football in 2001–02.

APPEARANCES	
Start (sub)	13(8)
Minutes on pitch	1330
GOAL ATTEMPTS	
Goals	0
Shots on target	3
Shooting accuracy	30%
PASSING & CROSSING	
Goal assists	0
Passes in opp half	379
Passing accuracy in opp half	77%
Successful crosses	3
Cross completion	27%
DEFENDING	
Interceptions	6
Clearances	13
Tackles	38
Tackles won %	55%
DISCIPLINE	
Fouls	33
Yellow cards	5
Red cards	0
SEE PAGE 97 FOR FULL STATS	

M

Lee MORRIS • 11
DERBY COUNTY • BORN: 30.4.80

APPEARANCES	
Start (sub)	4(16)
Minutes on pitch	592
GOAL ATTEMPTS	
Goals	0
Shots on target	0
Shooting accuracy	0%
Goals/shots ratio	0%
PASSING	
Goal assists	0
Passes in opp half	88
Passing accuracy in opp half	51%
Crosses	10
Crossing accuracy	20%
DRIBBLING	
Dribbles & runs	30
Dribble completion	60%
Corners forced	2
DISCIPLINE	
Fouls	9
Yellow cards	3
Red cards	0
SEE PAGE 125 FOR FULL STATS	

Once described by Derby County manager Jim Smith as "the fastest thing on two legs", Lee Morris is in danger of being dubbed "the most expensive thing in the reserve team" as he struggled to make any progress in 2000–01.

The former Sheffield United striker, brought to Pride Park for £3 million, failed to score for the Rams and in fact did not even manage a shot on target. 16 of his 20 league appearances were from the bench, a statistic which highlights the youngster's failure to impress the coaching team.

He did manage one goal in a brief loan spell at Huddersfield in March, but he should have been producing more.

It did not seem to affect the England Under-21 selectors, though, and Morris was called up to the squad on a number of occasions.

He certainly has the potential, but cannot live on that for too long. There is a long list of players who were tipped for great things but achieved nothing. Morris needs to head the engravers off at the pass and make 2001–02 a triumphant return to form.

came in wins over Arsenal and Manchester United

Andy MORRISON • 5
MANCHESTER CITY • BORN: 30.7.70

CB

Man-mountain Andy Morrison was hoping to make a big impression on the Premiership, but played just 216 minutes in total – and spent the majority of the season being shipped to lower-league clubs on loan.

City gaffer Joe Royle was keen to strengthen his defence when the Citizens made the leap to the top flight and Morrison must have known that his chances of pounding the turf were decreasing.

He went on loan to Blackpool and Crystal Palace in the autumn, before a brief recall by a desperate City in January saw him appear at the highest level. Sadly, his side conceded six goals in three games and Morrison's heroic dream was over.

He ended the 2000–01 campaign loaned out to Sheffield United. Morrison is unlikely ever to enter the Premier League Hall Of Fame, but he has been a solid performer at England's top table. It is doubtful that new City manager Kevin Keegan will see Morrison as part of his long-term plans, so the player's future was in doubt at the end of the 2000–01 season.

APPEARANCES	
Start (sub)	3(0)
Minutes on pitch	216
GOAL ATTEMPTS	
Goals	0
DEFENDING	
Blocks	2
Shots cleared off line	0
Headed clearances	18
Other clearances	9
Interceptions	1
Last man saving tackles	0
Tackles won	5
Tackles won %	71%
PASSING	
Passing accuracy own half	71%
Passing accuracy opp half	57%
DISCIPLINE	
Fouls	4
Fouls in danger area	1
Yellow cards	1
Red cards	0

SEE PAGE 209 FOR FULL STATS

Neil MOSS • 13
SOUTHAMPTON • BORN: 10.5.75

G

APPEARANCES	
Start (sub)	3(0)
Minutes on pitch	270
SHOT STOPPING	
Goals conceded (inside box)	5
Goals conceded (outside box)	0
Minutes per goal conceded	54
Clean sheets	0
Saves (shots inside box)	4
Saves (shots outside box)	4
Saves/shots	62%
DISTRIBUTION	
Long kick %	56%
Throws/short passes %	82%
CATCHING	
Crosses caught	3
Crosses punched	3
Crosses dropped	0
Catch success %	100%
DISCIPLINE	
Yellow cards	0
Red cards	0

SEE PAGE 265 FOR FULL STATS

Neil Moss must have hoped that his first-team chances would increase with the departure of manager Dave Jones from Southampton. Many fans felt that Jones's long association with first-choice 'keeper Paul Jones was the only reason the latter kept his place.

But Glenn Hoddle seemed in no hurry to change the status quo and Moss featured in only three Premiership games for the Saints. He did not do too well either, letting in five goals and making just eight saves.

Paul Jones was prowling the touchline waiting for a chance to return and when he did, he kept the green jersey for the rest of the season.

Moss made his name in the lower leagues with AFC Bournemouth. He was a popular figure at Dean Court under Mel Machin and he may have to make a return to that level if he is to kick-start his footballing career. He is unlikely to get many chances in the 2001–02 season at Southampton, unless Jones suffers another injury. But a return to the Nationwide League might give him the chance to shine.

For more information visit our website:

Danny MURPHY • 13
LIVERPOOL • BORN: 18.3.77

Danny Murphy enjoyed his best season at Anfield in 2000–01, finally getting recognition from the fans in the form of a song about him.

Such honours are unsurprising when you consider that his curling free-kick was the reason Liverpool won 1–0 at Old Trafford on their way to a league double over the champions. Sadly, Murphy was sent off in the return game at Anfield. The youngster also powered home a terrific volley in the Worthington Cup against Crystal Palace.

Murphy's skill with a dead ball was used on more than one occasion and he ended the campaign with four goals and four assists. More importantly, he ended the season with three medals and clamour for a call-up to the England squad.

Gérard Houllier admitted that when he took over as manager he was not intending to keep Murphy at the club. But the former Crewe schemer worked so hard on his game that he made it impossible to ignore him and he should play a vital part in Liverpool's rebirth.

APPEARANCES	
Start (sub)	13(14)
Minutes on pitch	1378
GOAL ATTEMPTS	
Goals	4
Shots on target	10
Shooting accuracy	43%
Goals/shots ratio	17%
PASSING	
Goal assists	4
Passes in opp half	442
Passing accuracy in opp half	66%
Crosses	45
Crossing accuracy	33%
DRIBBLING	
Dribbles & runs	46
Dribble completion	63%
Corners forced	10
DISCIPLINE	
Fouls	16
Yellow cards	1
Red cards	1
SEE PAGE 195 FOR FULL STATS	

Adam MURRAY • 30
DERBY COUNTY • BORN: 30.9.81

APPEARANCES	
Start (sub)	4(10)
Minutes on pitch	506
GOAL ATTEMPTS	
Goals	0
Shots on target	0
Shooting accuracy	0%
PASSING & CROSSING	
Goal assists	0
Passes in opp half	121
Passing accuracy in opp half	57%
Successful crosses	2
Cross completion	50%
DEFENDING	
Interceptions	2
Clearances	10
Tackles	29
Tackles won %	72%
DISCIPLINE	
Fouls	12
Yellow cards	1
Red cards	0
SEE PAGE 125 FOR FULL STATS	

More and more players in the Premiership were born in the 1980s, giving them little chance of remembering the popularity of American football in Britain at one stage. Indeed, traditionalists were concerned that gridiron would overtake Association Football, with teams such as the Miami Dolphins providing entertainment.

Derby scout Les Dolphin spotted Adam Murray and this youngster continued to make significant progress in 2000–01.

He played 506 minutes of football for the Rams and, while he did not score, he demonstrated the attributes which saw him on the fringes of the England Under-21 squad in the 1999–2000 season.

He went one step better in 2000–01 and made the Under-21 team, along with Rams team-mates Malcolm Christie and Lee Morris: all evidence that youth is given its chance at Pride Park and the good judgement of Les Dolphin. Murray may not want to watch the Superbowl in 2002, but he might want to score a super goal for the Rams.

Robbie MUSTOE • 7
MIDDLESBROUGH • BORN: 28.8.68

Middlesbrough midfielder Robbie Mustoe was involved in another relegation battle with the Teesside outfit; something which was not expected at the start of the 2000–01 season, as the club had again strengthened the squad.

The former Oxford player has been at Boro for more than 10 years now and, despite competition for places, he still managed 1,340 minutes of Premiership football. In fact, his appearance in the game with Manchester City in February was his 400th for the club.

His passing was reasonable and he created one goal, but it was not a campaign he is likely to look back on with fondness.

Indeed, in May he lamented that the season had been a case of "one step forward and two steps back". Mustoe enjoyed plenty of opportunity in the Bryan Robson years, but with changes afoot at the club, 2001–02 could be the start of the twilight years for the veteran midfielder.

He may well look elsewhere for regular first-team football should he struggle to get in the starting line-up.

APPEARANCES	
Start (sub)	13(12)
Minutes on pitch	1340
GOAL ATTEMPTS	
Goals	0
Shots on target	2
Shooting accuracy	33%
PASSING & CROSSING	
Goal assists	1
Passes in opp half	284
Passing accuracy in opp half	70%
Successful crosses	1
Cross completion	14%
DEFENDING	
Interceptions	5
Clearances	17
Tackles	52
Tackles won %	77%
DISCIPLINE	
Fouls	24
Yellow cards	2
Red cards	0
SEE PAGE 237 FOR FULL STATS	

Andy MYERS • 3
BRADFORD CITY • BORN: 3.11.73

APPEARANCES	
Start (sub)	15(5)
Minutes on pitch	1421
GOAL ATTEMPTS	
Goals	1
PASSING & CROSSING	
Goal assists	0
Passing	428
Passing accuracy	64%
Crosses	3
Crossing accuracy	0%
DEFENDING	
Tackles	57
Tackles won %	81%
Blocks	19
Interceptions	10
Clearances	122
Shots cleared off line	1
DISCIPLINE	
Fouls	16
Yellow cards	2
Red cards	0
SEE PAGE 69 FOR FULL STATS	

Former Chelsea defender Andy Myers fought his way back into the first-team picture at Bradford in 2000–01. In fact, fighting was the theme to his season, as he scrapped with team-mate Stuart McCall at Leeds in May.

Bradford were trailing 5–1 before half-time when tempers flared and the two players started skirmishing. Amazingly, they both remained on the field in the second half and apologised after the game.

The Bantams' supporters were not too enraged, though, as it demonstrated that the players at least cared about being thrashed by local rivals, even in a game that had no bearing on league position.

Myers managed to get on the scoresheet once in 2000–01, bagging a goal in Bradford's defeat at Everton. His defending was sturdy, as he won more than 80% of his challenges while collecting just two bookings in 20 Premiership games.

He should be one of the better defenders in Division One next season, assuming he does not turn his hand to boxing.

74% Carlo Nash's saves-to-shots ratio was

Thomas MYHRE • 35
EVERTON • BORN: 16.10.73

Norwegian goalkeeper Thomas Myhre played only a bit-part in Everton's 2000–01 season, appearing for the Toffees only in December and January. Before that he had been loaned out to Tranmere Rovers, where he played four games.

Ironically, one of his rare matches in the New Year for Everton was against Tranmere in the FA Cup and the Division One team embarrassed their neighbours with a 3–0 win which was one of the performances of the season. In the league he could only manage a saves-to-shots ratio of 68%.

Myhre is popular with the Everton fans and it must have been frustrating for a respected international goalkeeper to be sat on the sidelines so often. Luckily, his position in the Norwegian team has not been affected by his club's form.

Nevertheless, the 2000–01 campaign ended with Myhre on loan at Danish side FC Copenhagen. It is likely that the goalkeeper will leave Everton as he seems unable to dislodge Paul Gerrard from between the posts.

APPEARANCES	
Start (sub)	6(0)
Minutes on pitch	540
SHOT STOPPING	
Goals conceded (inside box)	7
Goals conceded (outside box)	0
Minutes per goal conceded	77
Clean sheets	1
Saves (shots inside box)	6
Saves (shots outside box)	9
Saves/shots	68%
DISTRIBUTION	
Long kick %	46%
Throws/short passes %	25%
CATCHING	
Crosses caught	12
Crosses punched	7
Crosses dropped	0
Catch success %	100%
DISCIPLINE	
Yellow cards	0
Red cards	0
SEE PAGE 139 FOR FULL STATS	

M
N

Carlo NASH • 20
MANCHESTER CITY • BORN: 13.9.73

APPEARANCES	
Start (sub)	6(0)
Minutes on pitch	540
SHOT STOPPING	
Goals conceded (inside box)	9
Goals conceded (outside box)	1
Minutes per goal conceded	54
Clean sheets	1
Saves (shots inside box)	16
Saves (shots outside box)	13
Saves/shots	74%
DISTRIBUTION	
Long kick %	38%
Throws/short passes %	100%
CATCHING	
Crosses caught	10
Crosses punched	5
Crosses dropped	0
Catch success %	100%
DISCIPLINE	
Yellow cards	0
Red cards	0
SEE PAGE 208 FOR FULL STATS	

It has been a bizarre journey to the Manchester City first team for goalkeeper Carlo Nash. Having decided to quit football at the age of 14 following a car accident, Nash only returned to the game via the far-flung reaches of the Burnley and District Saturday Morning League.

Nash was snapped up by Crystal Palace following an appearance in the 1996 FA Trophy final. He stayed at Selhurst Park for more than two years before signing for Stockport County.

Having lost out to Lee Jones for the County number one shirt, Nash spent a period on loan at Wolves before Joe Royle decided he needed more cover for Nicky Weaver and brought him to Manchester City.

Nash ultimately dislodged Weaver from the first team, although he will want to forget his debut – a 4–0 defeat to Arsenal.

He may also regret telling his City colleagues about his former modelling career, considering the stick he is reported to have received in the dressing-room.

13 percentage points higher than that of Nicky Weaver

Richard NAYLOR • 12
IPSWICH TOWN • BORN: 28.2.77

Being part of the most unexpectedly-impressive side in the Premiership is surely a pleasure in itself, but there can be little doubt that striker Richard Naylor would have liked to play a bigger part in Ipswich Town's remarkable success in 2000–01.

Naylor has been at the Suffolk club since first signing professional forms in 1995. His finest hour came in 1999–2000, when the Leeds-born hitman struck home Town's second goal in their 4–2 play-off win over Barnsley at Wembley.

Naylor has been forced to warm the bench more often than he would have hoped in the Premiership, sitting behind the likes of Marcus Stewart, James Scowcroft and Alun Armstrong in the pecking order.

But he did force Horacio Carbonari into heading Ipswich's equalising goal into his own net in the final game of the season against Derby. At the time he cheekily claimed that goal himself, but he will be hoping to net some more strikes of his own during the 2001–02 season.

APPEARANCES	
Start (sub)	5(8)
Minutes on pitch	543
GOAL ATTEMPTS	
Goals inside box	0
Goals outside box	1
Minutes per goal scored	543
Goals/shots ratio	9%
SHOOTING	
Shots on target inside box	3
Shots on target outside box	2
Shooting accuracy	45%
PASSING	
Goal assists	2
Key passes	8
Passing accuracy in opp half	66%
DISCIPLINE	
Fouls committed	16
Fouls won	19
Offside	2
Yellow cards	0
Red cards	0
SEE PAGE 153 FOR FULL STATS	

Gary NAYSMITH • 15
EVERTON • BORN: 16.11.78

APPEARANCES	
Start (sub)	17(3)
Minutes on pitch	1553
GOAL ATTEMPTS	
Goals	2
PASSING & CROSSING	
Goal assists	1
Passing	665
Passing accuracy	68%
Crosses	34
Crossing accuracy	29%
DEFENDING	
Tackles	60
Tackles won %	77%
Blocks	13
Interceptions	8
Clearances	58
Shots cleared off line	2
DISCIPLINE	
Fouls	21
Yellow cards	3
Red cards	0
SEE PAGE 139 FOR FULL STATS	

Despite having all but agreed a move to Coventry back in October, it was compatriot Walter Smith who eventually secured the signature of Gary Naysmith for Everton. The Scottish youngster had developed into an excellent prospect during his time at Hearts and Smith had no qualms about coughing up the £1.75 million asking price.

The tough-tackling left-back made his Everton debut as a substitute in the Toffeemen's 1–0 win over Newcastle. Once Walter Smith had awarded Naysmith his first start two games later, he set about making the position his own.

But a troublesome knee injury restricted him to just 17 starts during 2000–01 and in March it was feared his season was over, although he did feature in the final two matches of the campaign.

If Naysmith can maintain his fitness in the seemingly accident-prone Everton squad, many more starts seem likely during 2001–02 and he is certain to add to his haul of caps as Scotland seek to qualify for the World Cup.

For more information visit our website:

Gary NEVILLE • 2
MANCHESTER UNITED • BORN: 18.2.75

Forget the fight for the Premiership, Champions League and FA Cup: the only battle of any note in England this season was, of course, for the title of Most Impressive Neville Brother.

Gary has been one of United's most consistent players this season, failing to make the line-up on just six occasions and beating his brother by no fewer than eight starts.

Gary's England career has continued to blossom although a troublesome knee injury, which ruled him out of the final four league games of the season, also saw him miss out on the squad for England's games with Mexico and Greece.

He will be hoping that injury does not prevent him from playing a part in his country's remaining World Cup qualifying matches.

The only other downside in a season that saw him add yet another winner's medal to his creaking trophy cabinet was an FA charge and ban for dissent following Paolo Di Canio's FA Cup-winning goal at Old Trafford against West Ham in January.

APPEARANCES	
Start (sub)	32(0)
Minutes on pitch	2849
GOAL ATTEMPTS	
Goals	1
PASSING & CROSSING	
Goal assists	1
Passing	1691
Passing accuracy	81%
Crosses	43
Crossing accuracy	35%
DEFENDING	
Tackles	50
Tackles won %	68%
Blocks	17
Interceptions	15
Clearances	194
Shots cleared off line	0
DISCIPLINE	
Fouls	23
Yellow cards	4
Red cards	0

SEE PAGE 223 FOR FULL STATS

N

Mr Consistency: Gary Neville

FB Philip NEVILLE • 12
MANCHESTER UNITED • BORN: 21.1.77

Despite losing out to his brother in terms of the amount of football each played, Phil Neville can certainly argue that the overall quality of his game overshadowed that of his elder sibling.

As usual, United made use of his renowned versatility, which means he covered equally adeptly in midfield, on the wings or in either full-back slot rather than making any position his own and guaranteeing a role in the starting line-up.

He cracked in a scorching goal versus Middlesbrough and with a superb tackle success rate – the best of any United defender – there can be little doubt he made life harder for opposing players than most.

Neville is yet to cement his place in the England line-up, too, despite featuring in the majority of his country's recent squads. His versatility continues to work against him as does the legacy of his ill-judged challenge on Viorel Moldovan which saw him concede the penalty which famously ended England's Euro 2000 hopes.

APPEARANCES	
Start (sub)	24(5)
Minutes on pitch	2188
GOAL ATTEMPTS	
Goals	1
PASSING & CROSSING	
Goal assists	0
Passing	1365
Passing accuracy	80%
Crosses	85
Crossing accuracy	28%
DEFENDING	
Tackles	57
Tackles won %	79%
Blocks	18
Interceptions	3
Clearances	63
Shots cleared off line	0
DISCIPLINE	
Fouls	26
Yellow cards	4
Red cards	0

SEE PAGE 223 FOR FULL STATS

AM Shaun NEWTON • 7
CHARLTON ATHLETIC • BORN: 20.8.75

APPEARANCES	
Start (sub)	1(9)
Minutes on pitch	220
GOAL ATTEMPTS	
Goals	0
Shots on target	0
Shooting accuracy	0%
Goals/shots ratio	0%
PASSING	
Goal assists	1
Passes in opp half	61
Passing accuracy in opp half	66%
Crosses	6
Crossing accuracy	33%
DRIBBLING	
Dribbles & runs	10
Dribble completion	50%
Corners forced	3
DISCIPLINE	
Fouls	1
Yellow cards	0
Red cards	0

SEE PAGE 83 FOR FULL STATS

A frustrating season for Shaun Newton was highlighted when the Addicks midfielder handed in a transfer request in February. Having made just six appearances as a substitute for the club by that time, it is easy to see why the Camberwell-born player would see his future elsewhere.

Newton, who won three caps for the England Under-21s, has been in and out of the Charlton side over the past two seasons. His progress has been hampered by a series of injuries, but he has still managed to notch up more than 200 appearances for the Addicks in his eight years, having made his debut as a 17-year-old back in 1993.

He is powerfully built for a winger and at 5'8" is adept at rounding a giant centre-back with ease. At the beginning of the summer, Wimbledon and Barnsley were rumoured to be interested in signing Newton, although Charlton remained confident of keeping him at the club.

He will hope for more opportunities in the first team in 2001–02.

25% Luc Nilis's goals-to-shots ratio

Luc NILIS • 20
ASTON VILLA • BORN: 25.5.67

Luc Nilis was no doubt grateful to compatriot Jean-Marc Bosman for helping to pave the way for his free transfer from PSV Eindhoven to Aston Villa in July 2000. But he is very probably cursing the litigious Belgian now.

Nilis made an excellent start to his Villa career. Ten minutes into his debut for the club against Chelsea, the veteran striker demonstrated his immense talent by turning Alan Wright's mediocre cross into a spectacular goal – thumping in a thunderous left-foot shot past the helpless Blues goalkeeper.

Sadly, just two appearances for the Villans later, disaster struck. Eight minutes into Villa's match with Ipswich at Portman Road the Belgian chased a Dion Dublin flick, but collided with goalkeeper Richard Wright and crumpled to the floor in obvious agony with a broken leg.

With that one challenge, Nilis, nicknamed "Lucky Luc", saw his career come to a painful end – and football said goodbye to one of Europe's most consistent marksmen.

APPEARANCES	
Start (sub)	3(0)
Minutes on pitch	168
GOAL ATTEMPTS	
Goals inside box	1
Goals outside box	0
Minutes per goal scored	168
Goals/shots ratio	25%
SHOOTING	
Shots on target inside box	2
Shots on target outside box	1
Shooting accuracy	75%
PASSING	
Goal assists	0
Key passes	2
Passing accuracy in opp half	70%
DISCIPLINE	
Fouls committed	1
Fouls won	2
Offside	4
Yellow cards	0
Red cards	0
SEE PAGE 55 FOR FULL STATS	

N

Ian NOLAN • 2
BRADFORD CITY • BORN: 9.7.70

APPEARANCES	
Start (sub)	17(4)
Minutes on pitch	1596
GOAL ATTEMPTS	
Goals	0
PASSING & CROSSING	
Goal assists	0
Passing	638
Passing accuracy	66%
Crosses	40
Crossing accuracy	20%
DEFENDING	
Tackles	41
Tackles won %	83%
Blocks	13
Interceptions	4
Clearances	52
Shots cleared off line	4
DISCIPLINE	
Fouls	14
Yellow cards	0
Red cards	0
SEE PAGE 69 FOR FULL STATS	

Following Sheffield Wednesday's relegation, Ian Nolan opted for a move across Yorkshire to Bradford for the 2000–01 campaign, as the Bantams looked to strengthen to avoid a second successive relegation battle.

Nolan began the season as Bradford's first-choice left-back, starting 15 of their first 18 games. However, injury forced the Northern Ireland international out of the reckoning for three months and he only broke back into the first XI for the final two games of the season.

Nonetheless, Nolan was told by Jim Jefferies that he was wanted at the club for 2001–02, before learning from a report on Teletext that he had been placed on the transfer list. Believing he had been lied to, Nolan was furious, before discovering that the report had been an unfortunate clerical error.

The fact that the report had been a mistake failed to appease the angry full-back, though.

"In the circumstances I think it is only right that the club should now issue a statement or apology to say why this has happened," he grumbled.

before retiring through injury

Alex NYARKO • 8
EVERTON • BORN: 15.10.73

Ghanaian midfielder Alex Nyarko signed for Everton from French club Lens in July 2000.

His reasons for joining the Toffeemen were made clear when he stated: "It has never been a particular ambition of mine to come to England. What attracted me first of all was the contract Everton were offering me."

His excellent 78% pass completion rate often put his team-mates to shame, but injuries meant Nyarko managed to make just 19 starts during 2000–01.

One of those appearances will be long remembered after an Everton fan ran on to the field to offer Nyarko his shirt and some multi-purpose abuse during a 4–1 defeat at Highbury.

Nyarko left the field in a rage, never to play for the club again.

But the disgruntled fan in question should be counting his lucky stars.

Nyarko said: "Some years back I would have finished that guy. But I have come to find God and the scripture of God says, 'Turn the other cheek.'"

APPEARANCES	
Start (sub)	19(3)
Minutes on pitch	1647
GOAL ATTEMPTS	
Goals	1
Shots on target	8
Shooting accuracy	42%
PASSING & CROSSING	
Goal assists	0
Passes in opp half	404
Passing accuracy in opp half	75%
Successful crosses	0
Cross completion	0%
DEFENDING	
Interceptions	6
Clearances	25
Tackles	49
Tackles won %	63%
DISCIPLINE	
Fouls	29
Yellow cards	6
Red cards	1

SEE PAGE 139 FOR FULL STATS

Andy OAKES • 24
DERBY COUNTY • BORN: 11.1.77

APPEARANCES	
Start (sub)	6(0)
Minutes on pitch	460
SHOT STOPPING	
Goals conceded (inside box)	2
Goals conceded (outside box)	0
Minutes per goal conceded	230
Clean sheets	3
Saves (shots inside box)	11
Saves (shots outside box)	9
Saves/shots	91%
DISTRIBUTION	
Long kick %	35%
Throws/short passes %	100%
CATCHING	
Crosses caught	18
Crosses punched	5
Crosses dropped	2
Catch success %	90%
DISCIPLINE	
Yellow cards	0
Red cards	0

SEE PAGE 124 FOR FULL STATS

Having spent 1999–2000 waiting in the wings as Derby's third-choice goalkeeper, 2000–01 was the season when Andy Oakes was finally given the chance to show what he could do.

Oakes signed from Hull City, but was forced to bide his time in the reserves until an injury to Mart Poom saw the young stopper fill the resulting vacancy between the sticks for six league matches.

Unfortunately, an injury in the 10th minute of the Rams' game at Coventry allowed Poom back in, but it was a testament to Oakes's talent that Jim Smith had been willing to allow his Estonian number one more time to rest, with the Englishman deputising so ably.

Having conceded just two goals in his first five matches for the club, Oakes proved himself to be an extremely capable shot-stopper, and as a result he may not be willing to play second fiddle to Poom at Pride Park for much longer.

Other clubs will be watching his progress with a keen interest.

For more information visit our website:

Stefan OAKES • 17
LEICESTER CITY • BORN: 6.9.78

During his time at Filbert Street, former boss Martin O'Neill rated young midfielder Stefan Oakes as one of the most promising players at Leicester.

So when Oakes's main rival for a place in the Foxes' midfield, Neil Lennon, left for Celtic in December, he must have felt confident of taking his place in the first team.

The left-footed midfielder did start the first match after Lennon's departure, a 1–0 defeat by Coventry, but the subsequent signings of Matthew Jones and Junior Lewis meant that Oakes was again forced to play a bit-part role for most of 2000–01.

Oakes's passing accuracy throughout the 2000–01 season was a disappointing 64%, although he did manage to set up two goals.

Unfortunately, his longest run in the first team coincided with the Foxes' most disappointing spell since Peter Taylor took over in the summer of 2000. Indeed, the club lost each of the last seven games in which Oakes appeared, a dismal statistic which does not do justice to the player's talents.

APPEARANCES	
Start (sub)	5(8)
Minutes on pitch	631
GOAL ATTEMPTS	
Goals	0
Shots on target	0
Shooting accuracy	0%
PASSING & CROSSING	
Goal assists	2
Passes in opp half	178
Passing accuracy in opp half	52%
Successful crosses	11
Cross completion	26%
DEFENDING	
Interceptions	5
Clearances	8
Tackles	21
Tackles won %	71%
DISCIPLINE	
Fouls	5
Yellow cards	0
Red cards	0

SEE PAGE 181 FOR FULL STATS

Matt OAKLEY • 8
SOUTHAMPTON • BORN: 17.8.77

APPEARANCES	
Start (sub)	35(0)
Minutes on pitch	2965
GOAL ATTEMPTS	
Goals	1
Shots on target	11
Shooting accuracy	39%
PASSING & CROSSING	
Goal assists	0
Passes in opp half	940
Passing accuracy in opp half	70%
Successful crosses	15
Cross completion	35%
DEFENDING	
Interceptions	19
Clearances	42
Tackles	110
Tackles won %	75%
DISCIPLINE	
Fouls	43
Yellow cards	1
Red cards	0

SEE PAGE 265 FOR FULL STATS

American psychologists would have us believe the car a person drives is directly linked to their personality.

So what can we infer from the fact that Matthew Oakley drives James Bond's favourite vehicle, the Aston Martin DB7?

If the young midfielder is attempting to create an alter-ego to match his screen hero, the England Under-21 player clearly has some way still to go.

Oakley is hardly a crack shot, having hit the target with only 39% of his shots. Just four per cent of his efforts resulted in a goal for the Saints.

Moreover, Oakley's approach play often lacked the flair that is 007's trademark, failing to set up a single goal throughout the 2000–01 Premiership campaign.

And if reports from his Saints colleagues are to be believed, Oakley was not exactly the most sophisticated dresser at the Southampton Christmas party.

One can only wonder how he would react in a room full of scantily-clad Russian agents.

CB Andrew O'BRIEN • 5
NEWCASTLE UNITED • BORN: 29.6.79

One of the few Bradford players to emerge with his reputation enhanced by his performances in 2000–01, Andy O'Brien jumped ship before the Bantams sank into the Nationwide League.

The Irish Under-21 international moved to Newcastle in March in a £2 million sale which Bradford chairman Geoffrey Richmond described as the "most difficult to sanction" of his career.

It is easy to see why O'Brien was so highly-regarded, as he made 150 clearances, blocks and interceptions at Bradford as well as two last-ditch challenges to prevent goals.

O'Brien was quick to make an impression at St James' Park, scoring his first goal of 2000–01 in the local derby with Sunderland and improving his passing accuracy from the 58% he recorded at Bradford to 77%.

He helped the Magpies keep three clean sheets in their last five games, which was some achievement considering they had previously gone 25 games without a shut-out – a Premiership record.

APPEARANCES	
Start (sub)	26(1)
Minutes on pitch	2310
GOAL ATTEMPTS	
Goals	1
DEFENDING	
Blocks	33
Shots cleared off line	0
Headed clearances	105
Other clearances	75
Interceptions	11
Last man saving tackles	3
Tackles won	55
Tackles won %	72%
PASSING	
Passing accuracy own half	75%
Passing accuracy opp half	51%
DISCIPLINE	
Fouls	14
Fouls in danger area	2
Yellow cards	1
Red cards	0

SEE PAGES 69 & 251 FOR FULL STATS

M Paul OKON • 14
MIDDLESBROUGH • BORN: 5.4.72

APPEARANCES	
Start (sub)	23(1)
Minutes on pitch	1972
GOAL ATTEMPTS	
Goals	0
Shots on target	1
Shooting accuracy	17%
PASSING & CROSSING	
Goal assists	1
Passes in opp half	626
Passing accuracy in opp half	74%
Successful crosses	5
Cross completion	31%
DEFENDING	
Interceptions	5
Clearances	49
Tackles	56
Tackles won %	68%
DISCIPLINE	
Fouls	26
Yellow cards	6
Red cards	0

SEE PAGE 237 FOR FULL STATS

When he signed for Middlesbrough in the summer of 2000, Paul Okon declared that he was coming to Teesside to win trophies.

After a decade of success across the continent with Club Brugge in Belgium and Fiorentina and Lazio in Italy, Okon had become accustomed to winning wherever he played.

But with Boro languishing near the foot of the table for much of 2000–01, Okon was forced to rethink his ambitions with the club, knuckle down and help the side avoid relegation from the Premiership.

Okon's measured distribution in midfield was crucial as the club moved slowly up the table in the second half of 2000–01.

He found a team-mate with an excellent 80% of his passes, making him the most accurate passer at Middlesbrough.

The Australian international also achieved some measure of success with the Socceroos when he captained his country to a morale-boosting 2–0 win over Scotland at Hampden Park in November.

0 The number of clean sheets for Middlesbrough

Brian O'NEIL • 3
M — DERBY COUNTY • BORN: 6.9.72

The tactical skills of Wolfsburg coach Wolfgang Wolf helped convert Brian O'Neil into one of the most respected man-markers in the Bundesliga, after the Scot had moved to Germany in 1998.

O'Neil, however, decided he wanted his daughter to be educated in Britain and secured a move to Derby in a swap deal involving Stefan Schnoor in November 2000.

The former Aberdeen defender instantly complained at the number of domestic games played in England, claiming the German system of 34 league games and just one cup competition was far more sensible.

O'Neil need not have worried, as injuries restricted him to just 180 minutes of Premiership football.

He picked up a calf strain during his first Scotland international of the 2000–01 season and then got clattered by Roy Keane just a minute into his Derby debut, sustaining an injury which kept him out for most of 2000-01.

Welcome to the Premiership!

APPEARANCES
Start (sub)	3(1)
Minutes on pitch	180

GOAL ATTEMPTS
Goals	0
Shots on target	0
Shooting accuracy	0%

PASSING & CROSSING
Goal assists	0
Passes in opp half	53
Passing accuracy in opp half	53%
Successful crosses	0
Cross completion	0%

DEFENDING
Interceptions	1
Clearances	6
Tackles	7
Tackles won %	100%

DISCIPLINE
Fouls	3
Yellow cards	1
Red cards	0

SEE PAGE 125 FOR FULL STATS

Keith O'NEILL • 12
AM — MIDDLESBROUGH • BORN: 16.2.76

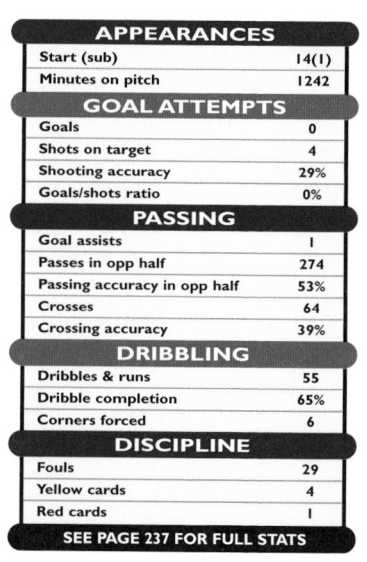

APPEARANCES
Start (sub)	14(1)
Minutes on pitch	1242

GOAL ATTEMPTS
Goals	0
Shots on target	4
Shooting accuracy	29%
Goals/shots ratio	0%

PASSING
Goal assists	1
Passes in opp half	274
Passing accuracy in opp half	53%
Crosses	64
Crossing accuracy	39%

DRIBBLING
Dribbles & runs	55
Dribble completion	65%
Corners forced	6

DISCIPLINE
Fouls	29
Yellow cards	4
Red cards	1

SEE PAGE 237 FOR FULL STATS

Ladies' man Keith O'Neill is said to have set his home up as a typical "bachelor pad" according to Boro fans – and given his record for injuries and suspensions, the former Norwich man will have plenty of time to make ample use of it.

A left-sided player who can play just about anywhere on the pitch, O'Neill loves to tackle, but has a suspect temperament and has often found himself getting needlessly booked or injured.

The Irishman managed just 14 starts for Boro during the 2000–01 campaign, but still picked up four yellow cards and was dismissed against Manchester City for a crunching challenge on Gerard Wiekens.

O'Neill had a disappointing season overall on the pitch. The quality of his crossing was one of the strengths of his game and he showed this with a 39% accuracy, but he only managed one assist all season.

Eventually, injury cut short his campaign once again to leave him time to concentrate on his ladies.

before the arrival of Terry Venables

Egil OSTENSTAD • 27
MANCHESTER CITY • BORN: 2.1.72

After failing to make an impression at Blackburn Rovers at the start of the 2000–01 campaign, Egil Ostenstad moved on loan to Manchester City to try and re-establish himself in the Premiership.

Fellow-Norwegian international and City captain Alf-Inge Haaland enthused upon Ostenstad's arrival that his new club-mate was "a goalscorer and a good finisher".

But the former Southampton striker was given few opportunities to show off his goalscoring skills. He started just one match during his time at Maine Road and failed to fire a single goal, reeling off just four shots.

His brief spell was typical of Joe Royle's less-than-successful sorties into the transfer market.

Ostenstad was sent back to Ewood Park, where his future looks far from secure. At least the Norwegian was able to feed his heavy metal addiction while at Maine Road, having rocked at a Marilyn Manson concert with Haaland. Who says Norwegians are only into Europop?

APPEARANCES	
Start (sub)	1(3)
Minutes on pitch	175
GOAL ATTEMPTS	
Goals inside box	0
Goals outside box	0
Minutes per goal scored	n/a
Goals/shots ratio	0%
SHOOTING	
Shots on target inside box	0
Shots on target outside box	2
Shooting accuracy	50%
PASSING	
Goal assists	0
Key passes	5
Passing accuracy in opp half	73%
DISCIPLINE	
Fouls committed	7
Fouls won	3
Offside	6
Yellow cards	0
Red cards	0
SEE PAGE 209 FOR FULL STATS	

John OSTER • 28
SUNDERLAND • BORN: 8.12.78

APPEARANCES	
Start (sub)	2(6)
Minutes on pitch	228
GOAL ATTEMPTS	
Goals	0
Shots on target	2
Shooting accuracy	67%
Goals/shots ratio	0%
PASSING	
Goal assists	0
Passes in opp half	63
Passing accuracy in opp half	54%
Crosses	19
Crossing accuracy	16%
DRIBBLING	
Dribbles & runs	13
Dribble completion	77%
Corners forced	4
DISCIPLINE	
Fouls	7
Yellow cards	0
Red cards	1
SEE PAGE 279 FOR FULL STATS	

Welsh winger John Oster struggled to make the starting XI at the Stadium of Light in 2000–01 after Sunderland signed Argentinean Under-21 starlet Julio Arca, who became first choice in his favoured left-wing role.

During his fleeting appearances in the Premiership, Oster failed to realise his vast potential. He was accurate with a disappointing 62% of his passes, which did not endear him to team-mates Niall Quinn and Kevin Phillips, who rely upon quality service from midfield.

Oster was desperate to make a mark during his first start of the 2000–01 season against Leicester in February while Arca was away on international duty.

But he only harmed his chances of regular first-team football by getting sent off for two bookable offences awarded for fouls on Muzzy Izzet and Robbie Savage.

Unsurprisingly, the former Everton man featured in just one more game during the rest of the season, but will be keen to get his career back on track as soon as possible.

For more information visit our website:

Michael OWEN • 10
LIVERPOOL • BORN: 14.12.79

With three England internationals vying for just two attacking roles at Liverpool, even a player of Michael Owen's calibre will struggle to make the first team from time to time.

But there can be no doubt that Owen finished the 2000–01 season as first choice, both for club and country.

He was Liverpool's top scorer with 16 league goals, having converted a club-high 23% of his Premiership shots. The pacy forward also fired a memorable late two-goal blitz to steal the FA Cup from Arsenal's clutches and has already been earmarked for a regular spot in the England side under new national coach Sven-Göran Eriksson.

The nation's schoolchildren also chose Owen as their number one. The majority of the 1,000 five- to 10-year-olds who were questioned in a poll said if they could be any person in the world, they would be the Liverpool striker.

Indeed, it seems that British kids would rather be Owen than be crowned King, such is the little frontman's popularity.

APPEARANCES	
Start (sub)	20(8)
Minutes on pitch	1787

GOAL ATTEMPTS	
Goals inside box	15
Goals outside box	1
Minutes per goal scored	112
Goals/shots ratio	23%

SHOOTING	
Shots on target inside box	38
Shots on target outside box	4
Shooting accuracy	60%

PASSING	
Goal assists	3
Key passes	18
Passing accuracy in opp half	70%

DISCIPLINE	
Fouls committed	21
Fouls won	33
Offside	34
Yellow cards	0
Red cards	0

SEE PAGE 195 FOR FULL STATS

Kop King: Michael Owen

Marian PAHARS • 17
SOUTHAMPTON • BORN: 5.8.76

The 2000–01 season started in sensational style for Saints striker Marian Pahars as he racked up six goals for the south coast side by the end of September.

The pacy forward had shown signs of flourishing under the stewardship of Glenn Hoddle towards the end of the 1999–2000 campaign and this continued, with several clubs rumoured to be monitoring the progress of the little Latvian.

Hoddle saw Pahars as more than just an out-and-out striker and he was frequently utilised out wide, where his pace caused trouble for opposing defenders.

The goals dried up for Pahars until well into the New Year, but the busy player created six for his team-mates and completed an impressive 30% of the 169 crosses he whipped in.

The season ended with Pahars finding his goalscoring touch once again. In 2001–02, Pahars will not only have a new manager but also a new stadium in which to display his undoubted talent.

APPEARANCES	
Start (sub)	26(5)
Minutes on pitch	2340
GOAL ATTEMPTS	
Goals inside box	9
Goals outside box	0
Minutes per goal scored	260
Goals/shots ratio	16%
SHOOTING	
Shots on target inside box	16
Shots on target outside box	8
Shooting accuracy	42%
PASSING	
Goal assists	6
Key passes	34
Passing accuracy in opp half	68%
DISCIPLINE	
Fouls committed	19
Fouls won	32
Offside	21
Yellow cards	1
Red cards	0

SEE PAGE 265 FOR FULL STATS

Flourishing: Marian Pahars

0 Southampton were the only

CB **Gary PALLISTER • 6**
MIDDLESBROUGH • BORN: 30.6.65

Boro's veteran defender Gary Pallister, known to Boro fans as "Glass Back" because of his recurring back problem, once again had an injury-hit season and made only eight appearances in the Premiership for the Teesside club.

Throughout his career he has been plagued by injury trouble, which is partly the reason why the talented defender picked up just 22 international caps when a player with his talent and ability would normally warrant many more.

The former Manchester United stalwart started Boro's first four games before injury struck, and despite an attempted comeback, his last appearance was against his former side back in November.

Now in his twilight years, it is doubtful Pallister can keep on going much longer; and with competition for places likely to increase in 2001–02, retirement may soon be imminent. This will allow him plenty of time to explore his own home, which is reportedly one of the biggest on Teesside.

APPEARANCES	
Start (sub)	8(0)
Minutes on pitch	678

GOAL ATTEMPTS	
Goals	0

DEFENDING	
Blocks	7
Shots cleared off line	0
Headed clearances	53
Other clearances	23
Interceptions	8
Last man saving tackles	0
Tackles won	17
Tackles won %	63%

PASSING	
Passing accuracy own half	85%
Passing accuracy opp half	64%

DISCIPLINE	
Fouls	6
Fouls in danger area	2
Yellow cards	0
Red cards	0

SEE PAGE 237 FOR FULL STATS

M **Carlton PALMER • 14**
COVENTRY CITY • BORN: 5.12.65

P

APPEARANCES	
Start (sub)	12(3)
Minutes on pitch	1153

GOAL ATTEMPTS	
Goals	0
Shots on target	2
Shooting accuracy	40%

PASSING & CROSSING	
Goal assists	0
Passes in opp half	291
Passing accuracy in opp half	63%
Successful crosses	3
Cross completion	25%

DEFENDING	
Interceptions	2
Clearances	16
Tackles	43
Tackles won %	74%

DISCIPLINE	
Fouls	9
Yellow cards	4
Red cards	1

SEE PAGE 111 FOR FULL STATS

Carlton Palmer has featured for a plethora of clubs recently, as the gangly midfielder enters the swansong of his playing years.

All appeared well after a successful period at Coventry in 1999–2000, but the player, who joined the Sky Blues after a bust-up at Nottingham Forest, was soon to be courting controversy again.

Palmer had been a regular in the starting line-up, but received his marching orders against Tottenham for a wild kick on Chris Perry. This caused relations with manager Gordon Strachan to deteriorate and the former England international headed off to Watford on loan in December.

Having made one substitute appearance on his return to the Sky Blues, Palmer was quickly shown the door again following criticism of the manager to a group of match sponsors. The controversial midfielder finally ended up in Division One at former club Sheffield Wednesday, where he helped them avoid a second successive relegation. He now seems keen to start a career in management.

Premiership side not to win a penalty

Christian PANUCCI • 2
CHELSEA • BORN: 12.4.73

Inter Milan's highly-experienced right-back Christian Panucci arrived on loan at Stamford Bridge just before the start of the season with high hopes of making a name for himself in the English game.

It all turned sour, though, and the former Italian international departed amid reports of rows with his manager and team-mates.

Gianluca Vialli put Panucci straight into the first team at the start of the season at the expense of Albert Ferrer.

Initially Panucci impressed, and his tackle success rate of 85% clearly shows he had a lot to offer. But when rumours of dressing-room disruption grew, the finger was pointed firmly in his direction.

Following Vialli's departure, Panucci was involved in a heated on-the-field bust-up with team-mate Jimmy Floyd Hasselbaink, and new boss Claudio Ranieri soon dropped him from the first team.

Panucci's loan period finally ended in January when he headed off to Monaco for the remainder of the season.

APPEARANCES	
Start (sub)	7(1)
Minutes on pitch	656
GOAL ATTEMPTS	
Goals	0
PASSING & CROSSING	
Goal assists	0
Passing	298
Passing accuracy	66%
Crosses	34
Crossing accuracy	12%
DEFENDING	
Tackles	20
Tackles won %	85%
Blocks	2
Interceptions	3
Clearances	44
Shots cleared off line	0
DISCIPLINE	
Fouls	10
Yellow cards	4
Red cards	0

SEE PAGE 97 FOR FULL STATS

Scott PARKER • 17
CHARLTON ATHLETIC • BORN: 13.10.80

APPEARANCES	
Start (sub)	15(5)
Minutes on pitch	1266
GOAL ATTEMPTS	
Goals	1
Shots on target	11
Shooting accuracy	48%
PASSING & CROSSING	
Goal assists	0
Passes in opp half	389
Passing accuracy in opp half	59%
Successful crosses	3
Cross completion	33%
DEFENDING	
Interceptions	3
Clearances	12
Tackles	96
Tackles won %	79%
DISCIPLINE	
Fouls	26
Yellow cards	5
Red cards	0

SEE PAGE 83 FOR FULL STATS

Scott Parker will forever have the unfortunate tag of being "the McDonalds kid", but his performances for Charlton this season have proved that he is no clown in the Premiership.

The youngster made his debut for the Addicks in the 1997–98 season, but it was not until the latter part of the 2000–01 campaign that he really looked the part in the centre of Charlton's midfield.

Famed for his silky skills in the TV ad, Parker is an altogether different proposition in real life, as a tough-tackling, ball-winning midfielder.

The Lambeth-born youngster started 15 games for Alan Curbishley's side in 2000–01, winning a total of 76 tackles – the second-highest amount for any Charlton player.

If there is one area of his game that needs more attention it is discipline, as his aggression sometimes got the better of him, leaving him with five yellow cards despite featuring in just over half of Charlton's league games.

Ray PARLOUR • 15
AM ARSENAL • BORN: 7.3.73

It was an indifferent season for Ray Parlour, who celebrated his second hat-trick in Arsenal colours, but fell down the England pecking order and had to end the season once again without a trophy.

The energetic Parlour featured in all but five of Arsenal's Premiership matches during 2000–01 and his undoubted highlight came when he smashed home a treble in the 5–0 drubbing of Newcastle.

A former Arsenal trainee, Parlour is always willing to give his all to the cause and attempted 99 tackles in the middle of the park.

Creatively, though, he disappointed, with only one goal assist and a cross completion rate of just 19% – rather a poor ratio for a recognised wide-man.

Out of favour with the new England regime, Parlour will clearly have to improve his game if he is to win his international place back and he will also need to keep his form good if he is to guarantee himself first-team football at Highbury in 2001–02.

APPEARANCES	
Start (sub)	28(5)
Minutes on pitch	2484
GOAL ATTEMPTS	
Goals	4
Shots on target	14
Shooting accuracy	41%
Goals/shots ratio	12%
PASSING	
Goal assists	1
Passes in opp half	810
Passing accuracy in opp half	74%
Crosses	77
Crossing accuracy	19%
DRIBBLING	
Dribbles & runs	114
Dribble completion	72%
Corners forced	22
DISCIPLINE	
Fouls	45
Yellow cards	4
Red cards	0
SEE PAGE 41 FOR FULL STATS	

Ian PEARCE • 19
CB WEST HAM UNITED • BORN: 7.5.74

P

APPEARANCES	
Start (sub)	13(2)
Minutes on pitch	1149
GOAL ATTEMPTS	
Goals	1
DEFENDING	
Blocks	12
Shots cleared off line	0
Headed clearances	79
Other clearances	61
Interceptions	2
Last man saving tackles	0
Tackles won	10
Tackles won %	71%
PASSING	
Passing accuracy own half	74%
Passing accuracy opp half	52%
DISCIPLINE	
Fouls	19
Fouls in danger area	3
Yellow cards	0
Red cards	0
SEE PAGE 307 FOR FULL STATS	

Ian Pearce is clearly having no luck with injuries after making a long-awaited comeback in 2000–01.

The former Blackburn man was crocked at the start of the 1999–2000 campaign and did not play again until the Hammers' home game with Newcastle.

His season once again finished prematurely when he suffered concussion and memory loss following a collision with team-mate Rigobert Song.

The big defender made 13 starts for the Hammers in 2000–01 in what was an experienced back line. He scored in only his third game back from injury, the 4–1 win over Manchester City, but it was in the return game with the Citizens that his injury jinx struck once again.

Pearce helped to add some stability at the back for the Hammers, who struggled early on in the season, and his return coincided with some of their best form. He will be hoping luck is on his side and he can steer clear of the treatment table in 2001–02.

CB Stuart PEARCE • 3
WEST HAM UNITED • BORN: 24.4.62

Former England skipper Stuart Pearce began the season promoting his autobiography *Psycho*, but after a campaign in which he was named as West Ham supporters' Player of the Year, he may have to make room for a few more chapters.

Age was no barrier for the terrace hero who acquitted himself in his usual inspirational style on the pitch and as ever took no prisoners. He made a total of 105 tackles and 345 clearances – more than any other Hammer managed.

Pearce, of course, also played a key role in West Ham's famous FA Cup run and helped put Manchester United out of the competition at Old Trafford for the second time in his career.

With Pearce now approaching 40, he has made no secret of his desire to move back into management and spent much of the 2000–01 season studying for his FA coaching badges. There are few players in the Premiership who would dare argue with a gaffer like "Psycho".

APPEARANCES	
Start (sub)	34(0)
Minutes on pitch	2929
GOAL ATTEMPTS	
Goals	2
DEFENDING	
Blocks	42
Shots cleared off line	1
Headed clearances	199
Other clearances	146
Interceptions	17
Last man saving tackles	2
Tackles won	76
Tackles won %	72%
PASSING	
Passing accuracy own half	74%
Passing accuracy opp half	53%
DISCIPLINE	
Fouls	47
Fouls in danger area	14
Yellow cards	9
Red cards	1
SEE PAGE 307 FOR FULL STATS	

M Mark PEMBRIDGE • 11
EVERTON • BORN: 29.11.70

APPEARANCES	
Start (sub)	20(1)
Minutes on pitch	1706
GOAL ATTEMPTS	
Goals	0
Shots on target	8
Shooting accuracy	30%
PASSING & CROSSING	
Goal assists	0
Passes in opp half	523
Passing accuracy in opp half	66%
Successful crosses	10
Cross completion	24%
DEFENDING	
Interceptions	6
Clearances	20
Tackles	84
Tackles won %	74%
DISCIPLINE	
Fouls	29
Yellow cards	3
Red cards	0
SEE PAGE 139 FOR FULL STATS	

Like so many of Everton's squad during 2000–01, Mark Pembridge fell foul of an injury curse which severely limited his time on pitch. A thigh injury kept him out at the start of the campaign and a similar problem had him treading gingerly as the crucial run-in approached.

But Pembridge bounced back to help his team secure Premiership football for another season and earn a call-up to the Wales squad for the World Cup qualifiers in June.

Despite his lack of appearances, the former Derby midfielder won an impressive 62 tackles and only three fellow-Toffees could better that tally.

The Welshman was tidy if not overly creative when picking out colleagues, with 70% of his passes finding their intended target but none directly setting up a goal.

Pembridge can usually be relied upon to grab a few goals, but he failed to find the net during 2000–01 – not particularly surprising, however, with a very modest 30% shooting accuracy to his name.

CB — Chris PERRY • 6
TOTTENHAM HOTSPUR • BORN: 26.4.73

With Sol Campbell injured for a large chunk of the season and Ramon Vega joining Celtic on loan midway through the campaign, Chris Perry was an important fixture in the Tottenham defence in 2000–01.

The former Don took the responsibility in his stride, making nearly 300 clearances and winning 89 tackles – the sixth-highest total in the Premiership.

Unlike centre-back colleagues Campbell and Gary Doherty, Perry concentrated almost solely on his defensive duties, although a rare sortie forward culminated in him grabbing his only goal of the season in the 4–3 defeat by Leeds.

While he has been a reliable figure at the heart of the Tottenham defence, Perry will be disappointed that, two years since leaving Selhurst Park for White Hart Lane, he does not appear any closer to an England call-up.

While this may be irritating for him, "The Rash" will be itching to make big progress under former national coach Glenn Hoddle in the 2001–02 season.

APPEARANCES	
Start (sub)	30(2)
Minutes on pitch	2633

GOAL ATTEMPTS	
Goals	1

DEFENDING	
Blocks	30
Shots cleared off line	1
Headed clearances	184
Other clearances	112
Interceptions	12
Last man saving tackles	2
Tackles won	89
Tackles won %	72%

PASSING	
Passing accuracy own half	78%
Passing accuracy opp half	59%

DISCIPLINE	
Fouls	35
Fouls in danger area	12
Yellow cards	3
Red cards	0

SEE PAGE 293 FOR FULL STATS

AM — Dan PETRESCU • 24
SOUTHAMPTON • BORN: 22.12.67

APPEARANCES	
Start (sub)	24(2)
Minutes on pitch	1977

GOAL ATTEMPTS	
Goals	3
Shots on target	12
Shooting accuracy	71%
Goals/shots ratio	18%

PASSING	
Goal assists	2
Passes in opp half	492
Passing accuracy in opp half	67%
Crosses	65
Crossing accuracy	29%

DRIBBLING	
Dribbles & runs	31
Dribble completion	61%
Corners forced	12

DISCIPLINE	
Fouls	21
Yellow cards	1
Red cards	0

SEE PAGES 69 & 265 FOR FULL STATS

Dan Petrescu will not look back on the 2000–01 season with great joy as he was caught up in a chaotic chain of events.

Not long after Petrescu had signed for Bradford from Chelsea, Chris Hutchings was sacked and Stuart McCall took over as caretaker-manager until the arrival of Jim Jefferies in November.

Petrescu had arguably been one of Bradford's better players, but Jefferies was forced to reduce City's wage bill and sold the Romanian to Southampton, where he linked up with former mentor Glenn Hoddle in January 2001.

But two months later, Hoddle had left for Tottenham and Petrescu's fifth manager of the campaign, Stuart Gray, took charge. To top it all off, Petrescu's season ended when he injured his groin in April – ironically against old club Chelsea.

In between, Petrescu managed three goals from an excellent shooting accuracy of 71% and laid a further two on for team-mates. He will be glad to see the back of 2000–01.

to score in the 2000–01 Premiership

Kevin PHILLIPS • 10
SUNDERLAND • BORN: 25.7.73

After a blistering debut season in the Premiership, Kevin Phillips must have relished the chance to carry on where he had left off in 1999–2000 and impress incoming England manager Sven-Göran Eriksson in the process.

But the pint-sized predator struggled to recapture the sensational form of the previous campaign and finished 2000–01 with a disappointing tally of 14 league goals.

It did not help that Phillips' partnership with Niall Quinn did not reach the heights it had done the previous year, but a goals-to-shots ratio of 13% – 12 percentage points down on his debut top-flight season – indicates that the former Hornet clearly lost his sting in 2000–01.

Phillips' tally of 60 shots off-target was the joint-highest in the Premiership. A pass completion rate of 71% in the opposition half and four assists shows that there was nothing wrong with the striker's link-up play, but the call from Eriksson failed to materialise during the season.

APPEARANCES	
Start (sub)	34(0)
Minutes on pitch	3057
GOAL ATTEMPTS	
Goals inside box	12
Goals outside box	2
Minutes per goal scored	218
Goals/shots ratio	13%
SHOOTING	
Shots on target inside box	33
Shots on target outside box	19
Shooting accuracy	46%
PASSING	
Goal assists	4
Key passes	32
Passing accuracy in opp half	71%
DISCIPLINE	
Fouls committed	46
Fouls won	57
Offside	27
Yellow cards	10
Red cards	0
SEE PAGE 279 FOR FULL STATS	

 John PIERCY • 37
TOTTENHAM HOTSPUR • BORN: 18.9.79

John Piercy is one of a number of young players at White Hart Lane who will be looking to make a big impression on Glenn Hoddle during 2001-02.

While Ledley King, Stephen Clemence and Simon Davies all enjoyed substantial Premiership exposure in 2000–01, Piercy's was a more reserved role, with the youngster making just five substitute appearances towards the end of the campaign. But the experience will be good for him, with his fleeting appearances coming against Arsenal, Liverpool, Chelsea, Sunderland and the 3–1 victory at home to Manchester United.

Under Theo Foley's tutelage, the young striker has made good progress in Tottenham's second string and featured prominently in one of the highlights of their season – a 1–0 win over arch-rivals Arsenal. With age on his side, Piercy will be keen for more first-team football in 2001–02, but may find it tough to break into the big time.

SEE PAGE 293 FOR FULL STATS

Pint-sized predator: Kevin Phillips

For more information visit our website:

AM — Robert PIRES • 7
ARSENAL • BORN: 29.1.73

Who would be a mother?

Madame Pires takes maternal devotion to the extreme when it comes to her son Robert.

Just days after joining Arsenal it was revealed the French international apparently pops a pair of pants into the post to *Maman*, for her to pass to the local priest to bless.

Once sanctified, the briefs are despatched back to Pires, who slips them on for match day and does not change them until the team loses – which, when you are playing for Arsenal, can be a considerable period of time.

Like his underwear, his football was divine and at times silky during 2000–01. The Frenchman put the skids under the opposition with 168 successful dribbles – the Premiership's highest total – as he went on to score four times and create seven goals for his Highbury team-mates.

But following unfortunate FA Cup and Champions League disappointments in 2000–01, Pires may consider changing his priest along with his pants in 2001–02.

APPEARANCES	
Start (sub)	29(4)
Minutes on pitch	2491
GOAL ATTEMPTS	
Goals	4
Shots on target	23
Shooting accuracy	59%
Goals/shots ratio	10%
PASSING	
Goal assists	7
Passes in opp half	1000
Passing accuracy in opp half	78%
Crosses	209
Crossing accuracy	25%
DRIBBLING	
Dribbles & runs	224
Dribble completion	75%
Corners forced	35
DISCIPLINE	
Fouls	17
Yellow cards	1
Red cards	0

SEE PAGE 41 FOR FULL STATS

FB — Alessandro PISTONE • 3
EVERTON • BORN: 27.7.75

APPEARANCES	
Start (sub)	5(2)
Minutes on pitch	437
GOAL ATTEMPTS	
Goals	0
PASSING & CROSSING	
Goal assists	0
Passing	186
Passing accuracy	75%
Crosses	14
Crossing accuracy	36%
DEFENDING	
Tackles	15
Tackles won %	67%
Blocks	4
Interceptions	1
Clearances	30
Shots cleared off line	0
DISCIPLINE	
Fouls	4
Yellow cards	2
Red cards	1

SEE PAGE 139 FOR FULL STATS

One of a band of players who can operate at either left-back or in the centre of defence at Goodison Park, Alessandro Pistone joined up with Walter Smith's men in June 2000 for a fee of £3 million from Newcastle.

Also in common with a sizeable proportion of the Everton squad, Pistone spent more time in the treatment room than he did on the pitch during 2000–01, having damaged his cruciate ligaments just a couple of weeks into the season.

Then, on his first start in more than seven months, in Everton's crucial 3–1 victory over Manchester City, the Italian was dismissed when he reacted to a hefty challenge by Paul Dickov, who also saw red.

A subsequent three-match ban meant that as the season drew to a close he found himself back where he had started the campaign – on the sidelines and unable to make an impact.

In his short time on the pitch, however, he showed willing, making 30 clearances and 15 tackles.

Mart POOM • 1
DERBY COUNTY • BORN: 3.2.72

A bizarre injury in a charity match against rockers Iron Maiden in the summer of 2000 threatened to keep Estonian heart-throb Mart Poom on the sidelines at the start of what was a fantastic 2000–01 for him.

The metal legends recently penned *When Two Worlds Collide* for their *Virtual XI* album and Poom, playing up front for former club Talinn FC Flora, should have heeded this spookily-coded warning.

Instead, he careered into the opposition goalkeeper when heading a goal, suffering a knock to the cheek and reportedly injuring his "groin area" in the process.

Another Maiden favourite, *Can I Play With Madness*, seems particularly apt, although Poom might have wished he had added an "instead" to that – and was undoubtedly hoping he would not be *Wasting Love* in the future as a result of the clash.

Thankfully he recovered sufficiently to pull off some remarkable saves during 2000–01 – 140 in all, which was more than any other goalkeeper barring Neil Sullivan.

APPEARANCES	
Start (sub)	32(1)
Minutes on pitch	2960
SHOT STOPPING	
Goals conceded (inside box)	45
Goals conceded (outside box)	12
Minutes per goal conceded	52
Clean sheets	10
Saves (shots inside box)	76
Saves (shots outside box)	64
Saves/shots	71%
DISTRIBUTION	
Long kick %	42%
Throws/short passes %	83%
CATCHING	
Crosses caught	105
Crosses punched	26
Crosses dropped	7
Catch success %	94%
DISCIPLINE	
Yellow cards	0
Red cards	0
SEE PAGE 124 FOR FULL STATS	

Steve POTTS • 4
WEST HAM UNITED • BORN: 7.5.67

APPEARANCES	
Start (sub)	2(6)
Minutes on pitch	281
GOAL ATTEMPTS	
Goals	0
PASSING & CROSSING	
Goal assists	0
Passing	79
Passing accuracy	68%
Crosses	2
Crossing accuracy	50%
DEFENDING	
Tackles	8
Tackles won %	50%
Blocks	1
Interceptions	0
Clearances	14
Shots cleared off line	0
DISCIPLINE	
Fouls	4
Yellow cards	0
Red cards	0
SEE PAGE 307 FOR FULL STATS	

Hammers veteran defender Steve Potts has seen it all since joining the club in 1984.

But Harry Redknapp's departure was a move even George Orwell might not have seen coming – and Potts will have been as rocked as any by his manager's exit.

Potts is one of a handful of West Ham players to have been at the club during all of Redknapp's seven-year tenure at Upton Park and the two-time Hammer of the Year has always given loyal service to his beloved club, despite his first-team chances becoming increasingly limited as the years wear on.

Indeed, during 2000–01 he started just two games for the east Londoners – at home to Aston Villa and Chelsea – and was largely consigned to reserve-team football.

With less than five hours of league football under his belt Potts had little to add in 2000–01 to his prolonged career, but he did pass the milestone of 500 competitive appearances for the side during a turbulent season at the Boleyn Ground.

Chris POWELL • 3
CHARLTON ATHLETIC • BORN: 8.9.69

Chris Powell was as shocked as the rest of the country when he found out that, at the age of 31, he had been called up to Sven-Göran Eriksson's first England squad to face Spain.

The Addicks' left-back admitted he would not even have picked himself, but Powell certainly held his own on the international stage, shining on his debut and playing an important part in the 2–1 victory over Finland at Anfield in the 2002 World Cup qualifier.

Indeed, in many ways his success story in 2000–01 reflects that of his club. His performances in the Premiership were steady, if unspectacular.

He won a decent 77% of his challenges and made nearly 100 clearances in defence, while proving an efficient foil when breaking forward down the left flank.

Powell's solid delivery was a regular feature of Charlton's attacking play.

He made a connection with a healthy 28% of crosses – one of the best ratios at the club – and set up two goals.

APPEARANCES

Start (sub)	31(2)
Minutes on pitch	2769

GOAL ATTEMPTS

Goals	0

PASSING & CROSSING

Goal assists	2
Passing	1112
Passing accuracy	65%
Crosses	76
Crossing accuracy	28%

DEFENDING

Tackles	71
Tackles won %	77%
Blocks	33
Interceptions	8
Clearances	94
Shots cleared off line	1

DISCIPLINE

Fouls	16
Yellow cards	1
Red cards	0

SEE PAGE 83 FOR FULL STATS

Darryl POWELL • 4
DERBY COUNTY • BORN: 15.11.71

P

APPEARANCES

Start (sub)	27(0)
Minutes on pitch	2236

GOAL ATTEMPTS

Goals	1
Shots on target	11
Shooting accuracy	48%

PASSING & CROSSING

Goal assists	0
Passes in opp half	494
Passing accuracy in opp half	68%
Successful crosses	3
Cross completion	14%

DEFENDING

Interceptions	8
Clearances	39
Tackles	71
Tackles won %	69%

DISCIPLINE

Fouls	46
Yellow cards	3
Red cards	0

SEE PAGE 125 FOR FULL STATS

Darryl Powell revealed his one superstition in 2000–01 – namely that if he sees a solitary magpie, he always salutes the bird.

Given that he rarely played at full fitness throughout the campaign, hobbling off against Leicester in April 2000–01 to end what was a disappointing season from his point of view, he must have forgotten to salute one of his feathered friends somewhere along the way.

Certainly his output in the final third of the pitch is something he will look to improve on in 2001–02. Powell managed just one goal all season – against Manchester City – and failed to assist any directly for a fellow-Ram.

Nevertheless, the Jamaican international was a rare exception to the squad as he completed more than 70% of his passes, while despite the knee problems which held him back, he still contested 71 tackles, with a 69% success rate. Powell's contribution helped Derby stave off relegation, and the midfielder will be hoping that in 2001–02 the Rams can ease up the table.

Gustavo POYET • 8
CHELSEA • BORN: 15.11.67

Chelsea's Uruguayan midfielder Gustavo Poyet had another highly-influential season for the Blues, but then saddened fans by announcing his intention to leave at the end of 2000–01.

Poyet had become increasingly frustrated at the lack of first-team chances with Claudio Ranieri's outfit – and looking at his stats for the season, he can certainly feel justified.

In spite of his limited time on pitch, his tally of 11 Premiership goals was the best for any midfielder in the 2000–01 campaign, while he also created a further seven strikes for team-mates. Since August 1998 Poyet has scored 32 league goals and set up 15, clearly making him one of Chelsea's most effective players over the three seasons and cementing his place in the hearts of Blues followers.

Only three Chelsea players completed more passes in opposition territory during 2000–01 and his effervescent displays in advanced positions will be sorely missed at Stamford Bridge.

APPEARANCES	
Start (sub)	22(8)
Minutes on pitch	2019
GOAL ATTEMPTS	
Goals	11
Shots on target	26
Shooting accuracy	43%
Goals/shots ratio	18%
PASSING	
Goal assists	7
Passes in opp half	699
Passing accuracy in opp half	70%
Crosses	31
Crossing accuracy	23%
DRIBBLING	
Dribbles & runs	39
Dribble completion	72%
Corners forced	12
DISCIPLINE	
Fouls	32
Yellow cards	3
Red cards	0

SEE PAGE 97 FOR FULL STATS

Martin PRINGLE • 14
CHARLTON ATHLETIC • BORN: 18.11.70

APPEARANCES	
Start (sub)	1(7)
Minutes on pitch	208
GOAL ATTEMPTS	
Goals inside box	1
Goals outside box	0
Minutes per goal scored	208
Goals/shots ratio	25%
SHOOTING	
Shots on target inside box	2
Shots on target outside box	0
Shooting accuracy	50%
PASSING	
Goal assists	0
Key passes	3
Passing accuracy in opp half	65%
DISCIPLINE	
Fouls committed	4
Fouls won	10
Offside	2
Yellow cards	0
Red cards	0

SEE PAGE 83 FOR FULL STATS

The highlight of Martin Pringle's injury-hampered 2000–01 season was undoubtedly his late clincher in Charlton's 2-0 win at home to Chelsea.

In his first appearance of the campaign, Pringle came off the bench to head home the Addicks' second goal in the last minute of normal time. But that moment aside, the Swedish striker saw little action in the Premiership and he will be spending the summer recuperating from the shin splints problem that blighted his season.

In his brief cameo he proved a handful for opposition defences and won 10 fouls, but with seven of his eight appearances coming from the bench he had little chance to affect Charlton's encouraging performances.

The former Benfica attacker was a revelation when he first arrived in 1998–99 on loan from the Portuguese side, but unfortunately has not been able to recapture that sort of form. The signing of Shaun Bartlett will make it even harder for him to get back in the side.

For more information visit our website:

Spencer PRIOR • 7
MANCHESTER CITY • BORN: 22.4.71

After playing an integral part in ensuring Manchester City's promotion to the 2000–01 Premiership, Spencer Prior would have been looking forward to an instant return to the top flight, having left Derby to join the Citizens.

Prior grabbed three goals in nine games for Joe Royle's men in 1999–2000, as he filled the void left by the injured Andy Morrison, but despite some committed performances the former Ram did not enjoy nearly as much success in 2000–01.

A permanent fixture in City's opening 16 Premiership matches, Prior started just twice after the 2–1 defeat at Chelsea, with Richard Dunne joining from Everton and slotting in well beside Steve Howey in central defence.

Prior showed his aerial strength with nearly 150 headed clearances and again when heading home Mark Kennedy's corner against West Ham for his solitary strike of the campaign. But a miserable season was rounded off when Royle placed Prior on the transfer list.

APPEARANCES	
Start (sub)	18(3)
Minutes on pitch	1673
GOAL ATTEMPTS	
Goals	1
DEFENDING	
Blocks	13
Shots cleared off line	0
Headed clearances	149
Other clearances	42
Interceptions	7
Last man saving tackles	1
Tackles won	28
Tackles won %	67%
PASSING	
Passing accuracy own half	80%
Passing accuracy opp half	64%
DISCIPLINE	
Fouls	22
Fouls in danger area	5
Yellow cards	3
Red cards	0
SEE PAGE 209 FOR FULL STATS	

Barry QUINN • 22
COVENTRY CITY • BORN: 9.5.79

APPEARANCES	
Start (sub)	25(0)
Minutes on pitch	2123
GOAL ATTEMPTS	
Goals	0
PASSING & CROSSING	
Goal assists	1
Passing	804
Passing accuracy	59%
Crosses	66
Crossing accuracy	24%
DEFENDING	
Tackles	62
Tackles won %	76%
Blocks	22
Interceptions	9
Clearances	116
Shots cleared off line	1
DISCIPLINE	
Fouls	16
Yellow cards	4
Red cards	0
SEE PAGE 111 FOR FULL STATS	

Gordon Strachan will be comforted to know he has a potential reserve goalkeeper in Barry Quinn should a crisis ever occur. Although his favoured position is midfield, the Irishman was usually utilised as a full-back during the latter half of the campaign and confessed: "I'd even play in goal if he [Strachan] asked me."

Quinn was on the periphery of the first team during 1999–2000 and made just 11 appearances for the Sky Blues – half a dozen as a substitute.

But it was his versatility which created more playing opportunities in 2000–01, and he enjoyed a run of 23 starts from December until the end of the season.

The Republic of Ireland Under-21 captain completed more than a century of clearances in his predominantly defensive role, which also led to a yellow card for every four fouls conceded on average.

But it was this sort of commitment which earned Quinn a new four-year contract at Highfield Road.

Niall QUINN • 9
SUNDERLAND • BORN: 15.8.66

S

Wherever he plies his trade, Niall Quinn has no trouble earning cult status among the fans. At Manchester City it was for wearing his now-legendary "disco pants" when out celebrating a Barry McGuigan boxing victory, while at Sunderland it is for his goalscoring exploits alongside Kevin Phillips. And the lanky hitman reaffirmed his standing during 2000–01 with a couple of notable strikes.

He netted the only goal of the game against his former club Arsenal on the opening day of the season, but more memorably in the north-east Quinn scored against arch-rivals Newcastle to help earn the club a second successive league victory at St James' Park. And he continued to remain a menace in the danger area by landing more than half of his shots on target throughout the campaign.

His appetite for the game is still ripe and, for the second year running, Quinn was the third-most-fouled player in the Premiership.

It will come as no surprise, given his ability in the air, that Quinn made more headed flick-ons than any player.

APPEARANCES	
Start (sub)	32(2)
Minutes on pitch	2595
GOAL ATTEMPTS	
Goals inside box	7
Goals outside box	0
Minutes per goal scored	371
Goals/shots ratio	11%
SHOOTING	
Shots on target inside box	27
Shots on target outside box	7
Shooting accuracy	56%
PASSING	
Goal assists	2
Key passes	34
Passing accuracy in opp half	55%
DISCIPLINE	
Fouls committed	84
Fouls won	86
Offside	48
Yellow cards	5
Red cards	0

SEE PAGE 279 FOR FULL STATS

Wayne QUINN • 14
NEWCASTLE UNITED • BORN: 19.11.76

FB

APPEARANCES	
Start (sub)	14(1)
Minutes on pitch	1273
GOAL ATTEMPTS	
Goals	0
PASSING & CROSSING	
Goal assists	1
Passing	621
Passing accuracy	64%
Crosses	86
Crossing accuracy	23%
DEFENDING	
Tackles	17
Tackles won %	82%
Blocks	15
Interceptions	4
Clearances	39
Shots cleared off line	0
DISCIPLINE	
Fouls	15
Yellow cards	0
Red cards	0

SEE PAGE 251 FOR FULL STATS

Wayne Quinn spent the first half of the 2000–01 season trying to take Sheffield United into the play-offs and give them hopes of Premiership football. He beat them to it, though, moving initially on loan to Newcastle before signing for Bobby Robson's men full-time in February.

The left-sided player is equally at home in defence or midfield and missed only one game for the north-east side following his £800,000 move from the Blades. He made his debut in the 3–1 home win over Coventry back in January and went on to make 14 more appearances in the black-and-white stripes.

Quinn is strong in the tackle, winning 82% of all his challenges, but he also proved to be a fair player, committing just 15 fouls and not picking up a single caution during his time with the Magpies.

However, his distribution still has room for improvement. Having established himself as a first team regular, Quinn will be hoping to be among the honours in the 2001–02 season with the Magpies.

292 Niall Quinn attempted more

G Paul RACHUBKA • 33
MANCHESTER UNITED • BORN: 21.5.81

Starting the season as very much the third-choice 'keeper at Old Trafford, California-born Paul Rachubka was only dreaming of getting a first-team opportunity for Manchester United in 2000–01.

But the youngster was handed a surprise chance to make his Premiership debut in March, when Fabien Barthez was ruled out of the game against Leicester with a recurrence of a thigh strain injury in the warm-up.

Rachubka, whose only previous appearances had come as a substitute in the World Club Championships and Worthington Cup, kept a clean sheet in the 2–0 win, although the shot-shy Foxes did not force him into a single save.

The return to fitness of Barthez and number two Raimond van der Gouw, coupled with the loan signing of Andy Goram, forced Rachubka back into reserve-team football for the closing stages of the campaign, during which time he played in the Manchester Senior Cup final.

SEE PAGE 222 FOR FULL STATS

CB Lucas RADEBE • 5
LEEDS UNITED • BORN: 12.4.69

Having played such a key role in Leeds' success in 2000–01, Lucas Radebe was heartbroken to be ruled out of action in March with medial ligament damage, just as things were getting to boiling point in the Premiership and Champions League.

He sustained the knee injury against Real Madrid in the Bernabeu and then aggravated it at Sunderland, missing 11 games as a result. Although record signing Rio Ferdinand and Dominic Matteo filled the gap in central defence admirably, boss David O'Leary was gutted to lose his skipper, of whom he once said: "Lucas should be concreted in stone and never allowed to leave this club."

One of only four players in the Elland Road squad aged over 30, Radebe's experience and calming influence are still valuable assets to United, as were his contributions of 101 tackles and 142 clearances.

"The Chief" will expect to be recalled to first-team action as soon as his recuperation is complete. He is hugely popular among Leeds supporters and players alike.

The Chief: Lucas Radebe

Q
R

APPEARANCES	
Start (sub)	19(1)
Minutes on pitch	1641
GOAL ATTEMPTS	
Goals	0
DEFENDING	
Blocks	15
Shots cleared off line	1
Headed clearances	100
Other clearances	42
Interceptions	21
Last man saving tackles	2
Tackles won	72
Tackles won %	71%
PASSING	
Passing accuracy own half	83%
Passing accuracy opp half	68%
DISCIPLINE	
Fouls	26
Fouls in danger area	7
Yellow cards	7
Red cards	1
SEE PAGE 167 FOR FULL STATS	

Alex RAE • 16
SUNDERLAND • BORN: 30.9.69

Alex Rae's preparations for 2000–01 were hardly ideal. He suffered an ankle ligament injury in pre-season training which, combined with a four-match ban for a dismissal at the tail end of 1999–2000, kept him out of action until October.

But Rae did enjoy a significant role in the middle part of the Black Cats' campaign, despite revelations that he was attending the Priory Clinic.

The steely Scot started 18 games in a row between October and February, scoring in consecutive fixtures against Charlton and Everton and setting up three goals. Following on from eight yellow and two red cards in 1999–2000, Rae's disciplinary record was also vastly improved, as he was booked just twice in the Premiership.

However, the red mist descended against Manchester United when he was sent off for clashing with Andy Cole. The subsequent ban and another injury meant the season ended for Rae the same way it had begun: on the sidelines.

APPEARANCES	
Start (sub)	18(0)
Minutes on pitch	1571
GOAL ATTEMPTS	
Goals	2
Shots on target	9
Shooting accuracy	38%
PASSING & CROSSING	
Goal assists	3
Passes in opp half	506
Passing accuracy in opp half	68%
Successful crosses	24
Cross completion	25%
DEFENDING	
Interceptions	3
Clearances	23
Tackles	75
Tackles won %	63%
DISCIPLINE	
Fouls	31
Yellow cards	2
Red cards	1

SEE PAGE 279 FOR FULL STATS

Isaiah RANKIN • 19
BRADFORD CITY • BORN: 22.5.78

The prospects of Isaiah Rankin getting a run in the Bradford first team were severely hampered in the summer of 2000 following the arrivals of Benito Carbone and Ashley Ward and the departure of the manager who had signed him, Paul Jewell.

After playing in a couple of Intertoto Cup ties, Rankin was loaned out to Bolton for the start of 2000–01, where he played 16 games in a three-month loan spell.

On his return to Yorkshire, the former Arsenal youngster was handed his only Premiership action of the season in the New Year's Day victory at Leicester – the Bantams' only away-day success of the season.

Coming on for Dean Saunders for the final three minutes of the game, Rankin touched the ball just once.

Later in January, Rankin was sold to Barnsley for £350,000, where he scored one goal in six starts as the Tykes secured a mid-table finish in Division One.

SEE PAGE 69 FOR FULL STATS

Red Mist: Alex Rae

Sergei REBROV • 11
TOTTENHAM HOTSPUR • BORN: 3.6.74

When he was not in the thick of the Premiership action or practising his ball skills on Tottenham's Chigwell training ground, pint-sized striker Sergei Rebrov enjoyed nothing more than an afternoon fiddle with his equipment – his radio equipment, that is.

The wireless enthusiast shipped his gadgets from Ukraine to London when he joined Spurs and passed any spare time by broadcasting over the amateur airwaves – not for Rebrov the traditional footballer's hobbies of snooker and golf.

He was pretty tuned in on the pitch, too, scoring nine league goals for the club, 12 in all competitions, including a 'smashy' and a 'nicey' in the FA Cup quarter-final win over West Ham.

The £11 million man was also on the same frequency as his team-mates, as he showed by creating four goals and making 662 successful passes. But according to reports, Rebrov was unhappy at the departure of skipper Sol Campbell and is reconsidering his future at White Hart Lane.

APPEARANCES	
Start (sub)	28(1)
Minutes on pitch	2429
GOAL ATTEMPTS	
Goals inside box	8
Goals outside box	1
Minutes per goal scored	270
Goals/shots ratio	16%
SHOOTING	
Shots on target inside box	16
Shots on target outside box	12
Shooting accuracy	49%
PASSING	
Goal assists	4
Key passes	31
Passing accuracy in opp half	65%
DISCIPLINE	
Fouls committed	33
Fouls won	45
Offside	26
Yellow cards	1
Red cards	0
SEE PAGE 293 FOR FULL STATS	

Michael REDDY • 27
SUNDERLAND • BORN: 24.3.80

By scoring a Premiership goal against Middlesbrough and unsettling several defences with his pace, Irish striker Michael Reddy made a fairly noticeable impact during 1999–2000 – his debut season as a professional with Sunderland.

But in 2000–01, chances were at a premium for the up-and-coming 21-year-old, who was used just twice in league matches by Black Cats boss Peter Reid, both times as a substitute in the first week of the campaign.

He was handed a starting berth for the Worthington Cup clashes against Luton – when he scored in a 2–1 win – and Bristol Rovers, before dropping back into the reserves.

In January, Reddy was loaned out to second division Swindon where he made an excellent impression, scoring four goals in 18 appearances. Two of those strikes were at Cambridge and Colchester, earning the Robins a vital six points in their successful fight against relegation.

SEE PAGE 279 FOR FULL STATS

Tuned-in: Sergei Rebrov

Martijn REUSER • 30
IPSWICH TOWN • BORN: 1.2.75

After he helped Ipswich Town gain promotion to the Premiership with four goals in the run-in to 1999–2000, the loan signing of Dutch midfielder Martijn Reuser was made permanent in the summer for a fee of £1 million.

But the former Vitesse Arnhem and Ajax player struggled to adapt to the English top flight for the first two-thirds of the 2000–01 campaign.

He was used sporadically, mainly as a substitute during this period, by Town boss George Burley who said: "He's always had the ability but I've told him I want more from him in games."

And with a third of the season left, Reuser finally started to deliver the goods as he found some drastically-improved form to help the Portman Road side gain an unlikely UEFA Cup place.

The Dutchman scored six goals in the final 10 matches and created two others. He also contributed 174 crosses to Ipswich's team total of 1,110 – the highest tally in the Premiership.

APPEARANCES	
Start (sub)	13(13)
Minutes on pitch	1275
GOAL ATTEMPTS	
Goals	6
Shots on target	25
Shooting accuracy	66%
Goals/shots ratio	16%
PASSING	
Goal assists	2
Passes in opp half	387
Passing accuracy in opp half	64%
Crosses	174
Crossing accuracy	34%
DRIBBLING	
Dribbles & runs	50
Dribble completion	60%
Corners forced	19
DISCIPLINE	
Fouls	19
Yellow cards	1
Red cards	0

SEE PAGE 153 FOR FULL STATS

Hamilton RICARD • 19
MIDDLESBROUGH • BORN: 12.1.74

APPEARANCES	
Start (sub)	22(5)
Minutes on pitch	1782
GOAL ATTEMPTS	
Goals inside box	4
Goals outside box	0
Minutes per goal scored	446
Goals/shots ratio	10%
SHOOTING	
Shots on target inside box	14
Shots on target outside box	6
Shooting accuracy	49%
PASSING	
Goal assists	3
Key passes	24
Passing accuracy in opp half	55%
DISCIPLINE	
Fouls committed	75
Fouls won	54
Offside	19
Yellow cards	5
Red cards	0

SEE PAGE 237 FOR FULL STATS

The 2000–01 season is not one Middlesbrough striker Hamilton Ricard will look back upon with great fondness.

The Colombian's goal tally decreased for the third campaign running, even though he was given a fair crack of the whip in attack alongside former Lazio man Alen Boksic.

Ricard netted just four times in the Premiership, compared to 12 in 1999–2000 and 15 in 1998–1999. Although his total was improved by five strikes in cup competitions, three of those came against Macclesfield in a Worthington Cup tie.

On a brighter note, the hard-working frontman curled in a Goal of the Season contender in the FA Cup victory at Bradford and he found the net in vital 3–0 away wins against Arsenal and Leicester City late on in the term.

A confidence player who thrives when things are going well but is not so hot when the chips are down, Ricard will be hoping the managerial reshuffles on Teesside will indicate an upturn in his own fortunes.

5 Dean Richards made more goal line

Dean RICHARDS • 6
SOUTHAMPTON • BORN: 9.6.74

Fans of Southampton were understandably thrilled when key defender Dean Richards signed a two-year extension to his contract in March, tying him to the club until 2005.

A Bosman-free signing at the beginning of 1999–2000, Richards excelled once more in 2000–01, proving himself to be a highly-effective player at Premiership level. He made 315 clearances, 69 tackles and helped the Saints keep a club-record seven consecutive clean sheets between January and March.

Shortly before Glenn Hoddle's departure from The Dell to take over as Tottenham manager, Richards was hotly-tipped to move to White Hart Lane in a £10 million move. But the former Wolves defender ended speculation by putting pen to paper on a new deal to cap another excellent season on the south coast.

As overjoyed Southampton chairman Rupert Lowe said: "He is a terrific player who, I believe, stands on the threshold of international recognition and everyone at the club is delighted he has signed."

APPEARANCES	
Start (sub)	28(0)
Minutes on pitch	2494

GOAL ATTEMPTS	
Goals	1

DEFENDING	
Blocks	30
Shots cleared off line	5
Headed clearances	232
Other clearances	83
Interceptions	32
Last man saving tackles	1
Tackles won	52
Tackles won %	75%

PASSING	
Passing accuracy own half	75%
Passing accuracy opp half	52%

DISCIPLINE	
Fouls	32
Fouls in danger area	10
Yellow cards	1
Red cards	0

SEE PAGE 265 FOR FULL STATS

Effective: Dean Richards

clearances than any other player

CB | **Chris RIGGOTT • 21**
DERBY COUNTY • BORN: 1.9.80

A virtual unknown before 2000–01, Derby defender Chris Riggott had a fairytale first full season of professional football.

The England Under-21 star was called up for his first-ever Premiership start in September 2000 and did not look back, playing all but two of the Rams' final 31 fixtures and scoring three goals along the way from his only three shots on target.

He deservedly scooped the fans' Player of the Year award in May with 42% of all the votes cast.

Get those tissues ready; here comes Riggott's acceptance speech: "I have so many people to thank for this – from the manager for making me a first-team regular to the likes of Billy McEwan and Steve Round, who have helped with my development over the years. The senior players have also been great, welcoming me into the side and making it very easy for me to settle in. Most importantly, as a Rams fan myself, I'd like to thank the supporters who voted for me. It's been an unbelievable year."

APPEARANCES	
Start (sub)	29(2)
Minutes on pitch	2536
GOAL ATTEMPTS	
Goals	3
DEFENDING	
Blocks	36
Shots cleared off line	0
Headed clearances	208
Other clearances	103
Interceptions	13
Last man saving tackles	0
Tackles won	62
Tackles won %	69%
PASSING	
Passing accuracy own half	75%
Passing accuracy opp half	46%
DISCIPLINE	
Fouls	37
Fouls in danger area	10
Yellow cards	6
Red cards	0
SEE PAGE 125 FOR FULL STATS	

 AM | **Stuart RIPLEY • 14**
SOUTHAMPTON • BORN: 20.11.67

APPEARANCES	
Start (sub)	1(2)
Minutes on pitch	106
GOAL ATTEMPTS	
Goals	0
Shots on target	0
Shooting accuracy	0%
Goals/shots ratio	0%
PASSING	
Goal assists	0
Passes in opp half	42
Passing accuracy in opp half	38%
Crosses	15
Crossing accuracy	40%
DRIBBLING	
Dribbles & runs	9
Dribble completion	67%
Corners forced	1
DISCIPLINE	
Fouls	2
Yellow cards	0
Red cards	0
SEE PAGE 265 FOR FULL STATS	

During his time as coach of England, Glenn Hoddle rated veteran winger Stuart Ripley highly enough to hand him an international cap. But when the pair met up again at Southampton, they rarely saw eye to eye.

Ripley was selected for just three Premiership games in 2000–01, coming on as a substitute in games against Newcastle United and his former club Middlesbrough and starting the fixture versus Manchester City posting a mere 106 minutes of first-team football.

It became clearer still that Ripley was not in the Saints' long-term plans when he was loaned to Barnsley and Sheffield Wednesday, moves he was keen to make permanent.

"I am looking for the opportunity to join a northern club – my children live up north and it would be nice to be within driving distance of them. But in a footballing sense, I just want to be playing again," he said.

With 11 northern teams competing in Division One in 2001–02, Ripley may well get his wish.

For more information visit our website:

Paul RITCHIE • 16
MANCHESTER CITY • BORN: 21.8.75

Several English clubs were keen to snap up Scotland international Paul Ritchie when he announced he would be leaving Hearts as a free agent at the end of the 1999–2000 season.

But the resolute stopper chose to stay north of the border and joined defending Scottish Premier League champions Rangers.

However, as early as August 2000 Ritchie had decided Ibrox was not the place for him and he jumped at the chance to head south to Manchester City in a £500,000 deal.

Soon after coming to Maine Road, the Kirkcaldy-born player helped City keep three clean sheets in quick succession and bolstered a defence which had been worryingly leaky before his arrival.

But Ritchie's season fell apart in November, when he sustained a pelvis injury in the match at West Ham.

It limited his contribution from that point on to just two games and in May he went to France for specialist treatment in the hope of regaining fitness for 2001–02.

APPEARANCES	
Start (sub)	11(1)
Minutes on pitch	939

GOAL ATTEMPTS	
Goals	0

DEFENDING	
Blocks	11
Shots cleared off line	0
Headed clearances	44
Other clearances	26
Interceptions	2
Last man saving tackles	1
Tackles won	35
Tackles won %	83%

PASSING	
Passing accuracy own half	72%
Passing accuracy opp half	57%

DISCIPLINE	
Fouls	17
Fouls in danger area	8
Yellow cards	1
Red cards	0

SEE PAGE 209 FOR FULL STATS

John ROBINSON • 11
CHARLTON ATHLETIC • BORN: 29.8.71

APPEARANCES	
Start (sub)	21(8)
Minutes on pitch	1811

GOAL ATTEMPTS	
Goals	2
Shots on target	18
Shooting accuracy	60%
Goals/shots ratio	7%

PASSING	
Goal assists	2
Passes in opp half	488
Passing accuracy in opp half	66%
Crosses	85
Crossing accuracy	27%

DRIBBLING	
Dribbles & runs	71
Dribble completion	56%
Corners forced	17

DISCIPLINE	
Fouls	26
Yellow cards	4
Red cards	0

SEE PAGE 83 FOR FULL STATS

Following the £4 million signing of Claus Jensen and the emergence of Scott Parker at The Valley, competition for places in Charlton's midfield in 2000–01 was fierce.

But to John Robinson's credit, he remained an integral part of Alan Curbishley's squad, featuring in 29 Premiership games, despite a change of system to 3–5–2 which resulted in limited opportunities for wide players.

The ex-Brighton man scored a memorable late equaliser against Manchester United in December and created two other goals during the season, while his total of 56 tackles is testament to an impressively high work-rate.

Having won the Wales Player of the Year award ahead of illustrious compatriots Gary Speed and Ryan Giggs, you could forgive Robinson for thinking he deserved a more significant role at club level.

But he confessed: "I'm part of a successful Premiership club and I couldn't be happier. There's three years to go on my contract and I'm glad to have a long-term deal with Charlton."

Paul ROBINSON • 13
LEEDS UNITED • BORN: 15.10.79

Paul Robinson came of age in the 2000–01 season, filling in admirably for injured Leeds number one Nigel Martyn and earning international recognition along the way.

Robinson got his first chance at Premiership level for 17 months in October when Martyn limped out of the action against West Ham. The Beverley-born star played the next 22 games in league and cup, producing some stunning saves against the likes of AC Milan, Lazio and Real Madrid.

He deservedly got a call-up to the senior England squad for a friendly against Italy in November and is widely regarded as Sven-Göran Eriksson's choice to become the country's number one goalkeeper before too long.

The 6'5" 'keeper still has plenty to learn, though; not least the art of minding your choice of phrase in question-and-answer sessions. When asked if he had any superstitions, Robinson replied: "I always dress to the left on match days." Not sure we really needed to know that, Paul.

APPEARANCES	
Start (sub)	15(1)
Minutes on pitch	1369
SHOT STOPPING	
Goals conceded (inside box)	19
Goals conceded (outside box)	4
Minutes per goal conceded	60
Clean sheets	3
Saves (shots inside box)	23
Saves (shots outside box)	23
Saves/shots	67%
DISTRIBUTION	
Long kick %	53%
Throws/short passes %	74%
CATCHING	
Crosses caught	19
Crosses punched	9
Crosses dropped	2
Catch success %	90%
DISCIPLINE	
Yellow cards	0
Red cards	0
SEE PAGE 166 FOR FULL STATS	

Uwe ROSLER • 11
SOUTHAMPTON • BORN: 15.11.68

APPEARANCES	
Start (sub)	6(14)
Minutes on pitch	661
GOAL ATTEMPTS	
Goals inside box	0
Goals outside box	0
Minutes per goal scored	n/a
Goals/shots ratio	0%
SHOOTING	
Shots on target inside box	8
Shots on target outside box	1
Shooting accuracy	39%
PASSING	
Goal assists	0
Key passes	3
Passing accuracy in opp half	66%
DISCIPLINE	
Fouls committed	27
Fouls won	14
Offside	12
Yellow cards	3
Red cards	0
SEE PAGE 265 FOR FULL STATS	

Veteran German striker Uwe Rosler became a free agent in the summer of 2000 when his club – the splendidly-named Tennis Borussia Berlin – were liquidated by a federal court for financial irregularities.

He decided to come back to England, where he had played for Manchester City for four seasons in the mid '90s, scoring 50 goals. He had been so popular in his spell at Maine Road that various fans made unsubstantiated claims through T-shirts and chants that: "Uwe's grandad bombed my house."

But Rosler's form at his new club, Southampton, was not quite so explosive.

He failed to score a single Premiership goal in 2000–01, despite banging in 23 shots in total. In fact, his only strike of the season came in a second-leg Worthington Cup match against Mansfield when the Saints were already 2–0 up from the first tie.

From September onwards, Rosler made just 12 appearances as a substitute and will probably have a bit-part role again in the 2001–02 campaign.

Cedric ROUSSEL • 9
COVENTRY CITY • BORN: 6.1.78

Cedric Roussel and John Hartson have never been team-mates: it is possible that they had never even met.

But in 2000–01 they were to play key roles in each other's career paths – and the future of Coventry City.

Belgian striker Roussel was having a steady, if unspectacular, season in Coventry's attack when in January the club agreed to release him to Wimbledon as a makeweight in the deal to sign Hartson.

But having just fathered his first child Roussel refused to move to London, leaving the big Welshman stuck at Selhurst Park and the Sky Blues struggling for goals in their relegation fight.

Eventually Roussel agreed to move on, bringing in funds and freeing up space on the wage bill in preparation for Hartson's arrival.

The 6'3" target man joined Wolves for a fee of £1.53 million, which could rise to £2 million depending on appearances, and played eight games for the Molineux men in the run-in to the end of 2000–01.

APPEARANCES	
Start (sub)	10(7)
Minutes on pitch	964

GOAL ATTEMPTS	
Goals inside box	2
Goals outside box	0
Minutes per goal scored	482
Goals/shots ratio	10%

SHOOTING	
Shots on target inside box	8
Shots on target outside box	3
Shooting accuracy	55%

PASSING	
Goal assists	0
Key passes	6
Passing accuracy in opp half	63%

DISCIPLINE	
Fouls committed	8
Fouls won	11
Offside	27
Yellow cards	0
Red cards	0

SEE PAGE 111 FOR FULL STATS

Gary ROWETT • 2
LEICESTER CITY • BORN: 6.3.74

APPEARANCES	
Start (sub)	38(0)
Minutes on pitch	3406

GOAL ATTEMPTS	
Goals	2

DEFENDING	
Blocks	32
Shots cleared off line	1
Headed clearances	152
Other clearances	134
Interceptions	21
Last man saving tackles	4
Tackles won	69
Tackles won %	75%

PASSING	
Passing accuracy own half	83%
Passing accuracy opp half	54%

DISCIPLINE	
Fouls	28
Fouls in danger area	13
Yellow cards	4
Red cards	0

SEE PAGE 181 FOR FULL STATS

Peter Taylor took a fair amount of stick in 2000–01 for his activities in the transfer market with not every buy being a major success.

One clear exception to this was Gary Rowett, who enjoyed an excellent season for the Foxes following his £3 million switch from Birmingham. He made 286 clearances and won 75% of the tackles he made.

In fact, Rowett settled in so quickly that he had plenty of time to indulge in some of his hobbies, which include childminding and playing the guitar. The former Derby man also had a hand in devising nicknames for new arrivals at Filbert Street.

"We christened Junior Lewis 'Flip-Flop' but I'm not sure why," said Rowett, "and we tried to call Dean Sturridge 'Tic Tac' because he looks like that tiny bloke on the advert – but he wasn't too happy about that.

"But I haven't really got one, to be honest. Matt Elliott tried to call me 'Scarecrow' when I first joined, which I thought was rich coming from him."

R

of home goals in the Premiership season

M Eric ROY • 19
SUNDERLAND • BORN: 26.9.67

Eric Roy's 17-month love affair with north-east football came to an end in January 2001 when he was released by Peter Reid from Sunderland to join French first division club Troyes.

After a successful first campaign in 1999–2000, Roy was only a peripheral member of Peter Reid's squad in 2000–01, making just three Premiership appearances as Gavin McCann, Stefan Schwarz and Alex Rae established themselves in the Black Cats' central midfield positions.

The Frenchman's luck failed to improve on his return to his homeland, as he was dismissed for two bookings on his Troyes debut and sustained a calf injury in a game against Metz soon after.

On his official website, Roy mused that perhaps things were not so bad at Sunderland after all, saying "I really liked playing in England; I really enjoyed the atmosphere there. I've already spoken to two or three English sides who'd like to sign me again. Who knows what will happen?"

APPEARANCES	
Start (sub)	1(2)
Minutes on pitch	149
GOAL ATTEMPTS	
Goals	0
Shots on target	0
Shooting accuracy	0%
PASSING & CROSSING	
Goal assists	0
Passes in opp half	28
Passing accuracy in opp half	50%
Successful crosses	1
Cross completion	100%
DEFENDING	
Interceptions	0
Clearances	0
Tackles	4
Tackles won %	75%
DISCIPLINE	
Fouls	4
Yellow cards	0
Red cards	0

SEE PAGE 279 FOR FULL STATS

G Simon ROYCE • 12
LEICESTER CITY • BORN: 9.9.71

APPEARANCES	
Start (sub)	16(3)
Minutes on pitch	1544
SHOT STOPPING	
Goals conceded (inside box)	21
Goals conceded (outside box)	4
Minutes per goal conceded	62
Clean sheets	3
Saves (shots inside box)	36
Saves (shots outside box)	27
Saves/shots	72%
DISTRIBUTION	
Long kick %	50%
Throws/short passes %	88%
CATCHING	
Crosses caught	26
Crosses punched	19
Crosses dropped	5
Catch success %	84%
DISCIPLINE	
Yellow cards	0
Red cards	0

SEE PAGE 180 FOR FULL STATS

Leicester boss Peter Taylor moved quickly to snap up out-of-contract Simon Royce just before the 2000–01 season, soon after Pegguy Arphexad had moved to Liverpool on a free transfer.

Royce, who had been Southend's goalkeeper during Taylor's time in charge at Roots Hall, probably expected to be sat on the bench for the majority of the season as cover for Foxes first choice Tim Flowers. But persistent injuries to the former England and Blackburn man gave Royce the opportunity to play a run of Premiership games and he responded superbly to the challenge.

In 1,544 minutes of action, he pulled off 63 saves and kept three clean sheets in a struggling Leicester side.

So pleased were Leicester's management team with Royce's displays, they rewarded him with an improved contract in March. "Simon has been excellent for us," said Taylor. "His form has meant we haven't had to rush Tim back into action quickly – it was appropriate that we looked after him."

For more information visit our website:

Richard RUFUS • 5
CHARLTON ATHLETIC • BORN: 12.1.75

One of the longest-serving players in the Premiership despite still being in his mid-20s, Richard Rufus had a typically solid season in the heart of the Charlton defence.

He made a total of 296 clearances – more than anyone else at the club – and won 69% of his tackles. He also chipped in with crucial goals in the draw against Coventry and the impressive win over Ipswich.

Although he was suspended for the final two games of 2000–01 after a dismissal against Aston Villa, the season has to be judged a success for Rufus as the club established their top-flight credentials.

In March, the Lewisham-born stopper was strongly linked in the media with a move to Tottenham as a replacement for Sol Campbell. But Charlton are likely to do everything in their power to hold on to a player as consistent as Rufus.

Described by the club's official website as having "recovery powers to rival those of the AA", to Charlton fans Rufus is the first emergency service.

APPEARANCES	
Start (sub)	32(0)
Minutes on pitch	2827
GOAL ATTEMPTS	
Goals	2
DEFENDING	
Blocks	27
Shots cleared off line	0
Headed clearances	175
Other clearances	121
Interceptions	18
Last man saving tackles	2
Tackles won	59
Tackles won %	69%
PASSING	
Passing accuracy own half	73%
Passing accuracy opp half	53%
DISCIPLINE	
Fouls	57
Fouls in danger area	15
Yellow cards	7
Red cards	1
SEE PAGE 83 FOR FULL STATS	

 John SALAKO • 28
CHARLTON ATHLETIC • BORN: 11.2.69

R
S

APPEARANCES	
Start (sub)	4(13)
Minutes on pitch	467
GOAL ATTEMPTS	
Goals	0
Shots on target	1
Shooting accuracy	33%
Goals/shots ratio	0%
PASSING	
Goal assists	1
Passes in opp half	123
Passing accuracy in opp half	70%
Crosses	44
Crossing accuracy	11%
DRIBBLING	
Dribbles & runs	24
Dribble completion	71%
Corners forced	3
DISCIPLINE	
Fouls	3
Yellow cards	1
Red cards	0
SEE PAGE 83 FOR FULL STATS	

Despite remaining a fringe player at The Valley, in March John Salako signed a new one-year deal to stay at Charlton until the end of the 2001–02 season.

He seems to be suited to the club although it is likely he would like more of a role in the first team.

All in all, the former Coventry and Crystal Palace winger played just 467 minutes of football in 2000–01, largely as a substitute. His experience and crossing ability are useful to have on the bench, but his best days seem to be behind him now.

His finest hour in 2000–01 came when he saved the south London club from a humiliating FA Cup exit at the hands of Nationwide Conference team Dagenham and Redbridge. The minnows were winning at The Valley until a cruelly-deflected effort from Salako earned the Addicks a replay.

That goal was Salako's only strike of the season. He only managed one shot on target in the Premiership from a paltry three attempts.

CB — Jlloyd SAMUEL • 31
ASTON VILLA • BORN: 29.3.81

Aston Villa youngster Jlloyd Samuel is tipped as one of the best prospects at the club, and hopes are high that he could establish himself in the first XI in the near future.

In 2000–01 he played 102 minutes of football for the Villans, making a couple of tackles and finding a team-mate with 76% of his passes.

Villa coach Steve Harrison said of Samuel: "He's got pace in abundance and he's really worked hard on not getting caught out by giving the ball away."

With Gareth Southgate still looking to leave the club, there could be an opportunity to play a lot more first-team football in 2001–02, and it seems as if Samuel is ready. But he is 22 now and needs to make a breakthrough soon or he will start to stagnate. John Gregory may give him his chance but he may need to look elsewhere.

The alternative, of course, is that he could find himself farmed out on loan to gain the necessary first-team experience outside of the Premiership pressure-cooker.

APPEARANCES	
Start (sub)	1(2)
Minutes on pitch	102

GOAL ATTEMPTS	
Goals	0

DEFENDING	
Blocks	0
Shots cleared off line	0
Headed clearances	0
Other clearances	1
Interceptions	0
Last man saving tackles	0
Tackles won	1
Tackles won %	50%

PASSING	
Passing accuracy own half	93%
Passing accuracy opp half	60%

DISCIPLINE	
Fouls	2
Fouls in danger area	0
Yellow cards	0
Red cards	0

SEE PAGE 55 FOR FULL STATS

S — Dean SAUNDERS • 21
BRADFORD CITY • BORN: 21.6.64

APPEARANCES	
Start (sub)	4(6)
Minutes on pitch	399

GOAL ATTEMPTS	
Goals inside box	0
Goals outside box	0
Minutes per goal scored	n/a
Goals/shots ratio	0%

SHOOTING	
Shots on target inside box	1
Shots on target outside box	0
Shooting accuracy	14%

PASSING	
Goal assists	0
Key passes	2
Passing accuracy in opp half	69%

DISCIPLINE	
Fouls committed	3
Fouls won	4
Offside	6
Yellow cards	0
Red cards	0

SEE PAGE 69 FOR FULL STATS

Like an ageing greyhound, time finally seemed to catch up with Bradford City's Dean Saunders in 2000–01 and the veteran striker did not manage to score a single goal for the Premiership's whipping-boys.

In fact, in 399 minutes of top-flight action, Saunders fired only one shot on target, something that will have frustrated the former Welsh international. It surprised few people when manager Jim Jefferies decided to release the ex-Liverpool hitman at the conclusion of the 2000–01 season.

Saunders' wife is a keen fan of competitions in magazines and claims to have won many prizes in her time. Perhaps she could interest her husband in the hobby in the coming months, although Saunders is sure to want to find another club.

He could probably still play at a lower level, but with the amount of experience he possesses, he may look to move into management in the near future.

Realising he is near the end of his career, he retired from international football.

Robbie SAVAGE • 8
LEICESTER CITY • BORN: 18.10.74
M

Robbie Savage diced with danger in 2000–01 when he had to rescue his dog Naz from an electric fence.

The Welsh midfielder was unaware of the current and was electrocuted. Fans and players up and down the country might have been eager to see that, but had to make do with Savage's typical all-action displays in Premiership games.

The Foxes star seemed to grow in stature when Neil Lennon departed for Celtic and he was one of the best performers in a season which went rapidly downhill after Christmas. Four goals will be the personal highlight for Savage, but he will be disappointed that Leicester fell away in the style they did towards the end of the season.

Unusually for Savage, he was outbattled by Wycombe midfielder Steve Brown in the FA Cup quarter-finals and the Foxes crashed out in one of the shocks of the season. Even his Ferrari started to rust and the bustling schemer must have been pleased to leave for his summer holidays.

APPEARANCES	
Start (sub)	33(0)
Minutes on pitch	2942
GOAL ATTEMPTS	
Goals	4
Shots on target	8
Shooting accuracy	33%
PASSING & CROSSING	
Goal assists	0
Passes in opp half	724
Passing accuracy in opp half	64%
Successful crosses	16
Cross completion	21%
DEFENDING	
Interceptions	10
Clearances	71
Tackles	125
Tackles won %	66%
DISCIPLINE	
Fouls	45
Yellow cards	7
Red cards	0

SEE PAGE 181 FOR FULL STATS

Electric: Robbie Savage (right)

S

more matches than any other team

John SCALES • 15
CB IPSWICH TOWN • BORN: 4.7.66

After being released by Tottenham Hotspur at the conclusion of the 1999–2000 season, John Scales managed to secure a one-year deal with Ipswich Town.

But once again the unfortunate centre-back's miserable season was racked with injuries and he appeared in an Ipswich shirt for only 180 minutes.

It was no surprise when he decided to retire at the end of the 2000–01 season and devote himself full-time to the sports marketing company he has set up.

He commented: "I've suffered enough disappointment to know that football is a very harsh, very competitive environment. Yes, the rewards are great, but only for very few. Many players who get released aren't strong enough to cope with that and are unprepared for life without football."

He can look back on a distinguished career which saw him play for clubs such as Spurs and Liverpool, but he will also regret that he suffered so many serious injuries and missed so much football.

APPEARANCES	
Start (sub)	2(0)
Minutes on pitch	180
GOAL ATTEMPTS	
Goals	0
DEFENDING	
Blocks	3
Shots cleared off line	0
Headed clearances	13
Other clearances	4
Interceptions	1
Last man saving tackles	0
Tackles won	2
Tackles won %	50%
PASSING	
Passing accuracy own half	79%
Passing accuracy opp half	65%
DISCIPLINE	
Fouls	0
Fouls in danger area	0
Yellow cards	1
Red cards	0

SEE PAGE 153 FOR FULL STATS

Sebastien SCHEMMEL • 30
FB WEST HAM UNITED • BORN: 2.6.75

APPEARANCES	
Start (sub)	10(2)
Minutes on pitch	809
GOAL ATTEMPTS	
Goals	0
PASSING & CROSSING	
Goal assists	0
Passing	391
Passing accuracy	72%
Crosses	41
Crossing accuracy	29%
DEFENDING	
Tackles	38
Tackles won %	68%
Blocks	2
Interceptions	5
Clearances	4
Shots cleared off line	0
DISCIPLINE	
Fouls	13
Yellow cards	0
Red cards	0

SEE PAGE 307 FOR FULL STATS

Having seen Trevor Sinclair and Steve Lomas struck down by long-term injuries, West Ham boss Harry Redknapp was in desperate need of right-sided cover for the second half of 2000–01. Wing-back Sebastien Schemmel answered the call, joining on loan until the end of the season from Metz.

The Frenchman's availability only came about, though, after he had landed himself in hot water for confronting two journalists who had questioned his commitment. But that did not put off the Hammers, who had been impressed with Schemmel after his performances against them in the 1999–2000 Intertoto Cup final.

He became a first-choice player in east London, playing key roles in the FA Cup wins over Manchester United and Sunderland and contributing 41 crosses in the Premiership.

Schemmel was keen to make the move permanent, saying: "I hope to be transferred full time so I never go back to Metz. They destroyed me in front of other French clubs. They did everything to break me."

For more information visit our website:

Stefan SCHNOOR • 3
DERBY COUNTY • BORN: 24.4.71

Experienced and versatile, German defender Stefan Schnoor had been a useful member of Jim Smith's Derby squad for two seasons, having joined the club in the summer of 1998.

But with several new defensive arrivals at Pride Park, Schnoor's opportunities in 2000–01 were limited and it seemed to be in the best interests of both club and player for him to move on.

He did so in November, when Bundesliga side Wolfsburg snapped up the veteran in an exchange deal for Scottish international defender Brian O'Neil.

It was a move that suited all parties, as Rams chief executive Keith Loring admitted: "With Stefan's contract coming to an end this season, he was keen for a return to Germany. The opportunity for a swap deal with O'Neil arose and it seemed to be the ideal solution."

In the 564 minutes of action he played in 2000–01 Schnoor made 21 tackles, 38 clearances and signed off with a goal assist for Dean Sturridge against Everton.

APPEARANCES	
Start (sub)	6(2)
Minutes on pitch	564
GOAL ATTEMPTS	
Goals	0
DEFENDING	
Blocks	9
Shots cleared off line	0
Headed clearances	23
Other clearances	15
Interceptions	2
Last man saving tackles	0
Tackles won	16
Tackles won %	76%
PASSING	
Passing accuracy own half	82%
Passing accuracy opp half	52%
DISCIPLINE	
Fouls	6
Fouls in danger area	1
Yellow cards	2
Red cards	0
SEE PAGE 125 FOR FULL STATS	

Paul SCHOLES • 18
MANCHESTER UNITED • BORN: 16.11.74

APPEARANCES	
Start (sub)	28(4)
Minutes on pitch	2451
GOAL ATTEMPTS	
Goals	6
Shots on target	21
Shooting accuracy	38%
Goals/shots ratio	11%
PASSING	
Goal assists	5
Passes in opp half	914
Passing accuracy in opp half	79%
Crosses	24
Crossing accuracy	21%
DRIBBLING	
Dribbles & runs	44
Dribble completion	89%
Corners forced	14
DISCIPLINE	
Fouls	53
Yellow cards	3
Red cards	0
SEE PAGE 223 FOR FULL STATS	

Another season, another successful chapter in the annals of Manchester United midfielder Paul Scholes.

A virtual ever-present in the fifth title-winning campaign of his career, Scholes was not as prolific in the Premiership compared to some previous seasons, scoring just six goals. But he more than made up for it by netting half-a-dozen more in the Champions League, including a fantastic strike against Panathinaikos which was the culmination of an excellent 32-pass move.

Seventy-eight tackles and an 83% passing accuracy record illustrate the sublime ability Scholes possesses away from sticking the ball in the net and that all-round game has already marked him out as one of England coach Sven-Göran Eriksson's favourite players.

A quiet man on and off the pitch, Scholes seems more than happy with his lot and celebrated the birth of his second child by signing a contract extension at Old Trafford at the end of 2000–01.

S

Stefan SCHWARZ • 20
SUNDERLAND • BORN: 18.4.69

An Achilles tendon rupture towards the end of the 1999–2000 season ruled Sunderland midfielder Stefan Schwarz out of the European Championships and presented him with the prospect of a long, hard summer of rehabilitation.

But as he has displayed on the pitch throughout his lengthy career with club and country, Schwarz is not afraid of a challenge and fought his way back into first-team contention sooner than expected.

By December he was a regular again in Sunderland's line-up, showing that injury had not diminished his competitiveness as he slid into 58 tackles, picking up five cautions along the way. He also scored one goal and created three others, with his classy left foot providing balance in midfield and a useful weapon at set-pieces.

Having made a comeback at international level in March, the former Arsenal playmaker has the qualification matches for the 2002 World Cup and a full season of action for Sunderland to look forward to in 2001–02.

APPEARANCES
Start (sub)	17(3)
Minutes on pitch	1468

GOAL ATTEMPTS
Goals	1
Shots on target	8
Shooting accuracy	40%

PASSING & CROSSING
Goal assists	3
Passes in opp half	319
Passing accuracy in opp half	64%
Successful crosses	10
Cross completion	29%

DEFENDING
Interceptions	7
Clearances	16
Tackles	58
Tackles won %	64%

DISCIPLINE
Fouls	27
Yellow cards	5
Red cards	0

SEE PAGE 279 FOR FULL STATS

Competitive: Stefan Schwarz

Mark SCHWARZER • 1
MIDDLESBROUGH • BORN: 6.10.72

Despite spending 2000–01 as goalkeeper for a struggling team, there were only positive things to be said about Mark Schwarzer at the end of the season.

The 6'4" star produced some excellent performances in the Premiership, making 117 saves and keeping nine clean sheets in 31 appearances. He also re-established himself in international football with Australia and can now be hopeful of featuring in the 2002 World Cup if his country qualifies for the finals.

Not surprisingly, several admiring glances were cast Schwarzer's way and press reports suggested that both Arsenal and Manchester United were lining up bids for the custodian towards the end of the term.

But then Boro boss Bryan Robson was adamant that he was going nowhere: "There is absolutely no chance at all of Mark leaving this club. He still has four years of his contract to run and our policy is to hang on to our best players. He is just not for sale and that's the end of the matter."

APPEARANCES	
Start (sub)	31(0)
Minutes on pitch	2790
SHOT STOPPING	
Goals conceded (inside box)	26
Goals conceded (outside box)	8
Minutes per goal conceded	82
Clean sheets	9
Saves (shots inside box)	59
Saves (shots outside box)	58
Saves/shots	77%
DISTRIBUTION	
Long kick %	48%
Throws/short passes %	77%
CATCHING	
Crosses caught	82
Crosses punched	20
Crosses dropped	5
Catch success %	94%
DISCIPLINE	
Yellow cards	1
Red cards	0
SEE PAGE 236 FOR FULL STATS	

James SCOWCROFT • 10
IPSWICH TOWN • BORN: 15.11.75

APPEARANCES	
Start (sub)	22(12)
Minutes on pitch	2196
GOAL ATTEMPTS	
Goals inside box	4
Goals outside box	0
Minutes per goal scored	549
Goals/shots ratio	10%
SHOOTING	
Shots on target inside box	10
Shots on target outside box	3
Shooting accuracy	33%
PASSING	
Goal assists	3
Key passes	28
Passing accuracy in opp half	64%
DISCIPLINE	
Fouls committed	56
Fouls won	60
Offside	7
Yellow cards	1
Red cards	0
SEE PAGE 153 FOR FULL STATS	

Ipswich's Player of the Year in the promotion season of 1999–2000, James Scowcroft failed to recreate that form quite so spectacularly in the Premiership, although his case was not helped by a spate of persistent injuries.

The former England Under-21 star still managed to feature in 34 Premiership games, but apart from a 13-match spell in the middle of 2000–01 he was in and out of the side and was often switched between midfield and attack.

Able to play wide or centrally in midfield, as a target man or just behind the strikers, Scowcroft was a very useful player for boss George Burley to have around and the stats show he is comfortable with the ball in several areas.

First and foremost, he tucked away four league goals, with three of them coming in wins over Southampton, Leeds and Leicester. He also set up three, a result of his 67% passing accuracy and the 31 crosses he delivered into the box.

S

G David SEAMAN • 1
ARSENAL • BORN: 19.9.63

Aside from the England captain, David Seaman is arguably the Premiership's most talked-about player. The majority of the talk is about his age and suitability at international level but, to be fair to the veteran shot-stopper, people also occasionally mention his hair.

There can be little doubt that "Spunky" remains one of the top 'keepers in the Premiership. He made 49 saves during the 2000–01 campaign and was certainly missed between the sticks when injury got the better of him for a lengthy spell in the run-up to the New Year.

He also continued to perform well for his country and, although blamed for poor positioning for Dietmar Hamann's winner for Germany over England, few can deny that he also saved two points against Finland with a remarkable last-minute stop from Liverpool striker Jari Litmanen.

The pony-tailed shot-stopper is sure to fill plenty more column inches in the tabloids once again in 2001–02.

APPEARANCES	
Start (sub)	24(0)
Minutes on pitch	2160
SHOT STOPPING	
Goals conceded (inside box)	17
Goals conceded (outside box)	6
Minutes per goal conceded	94
Clean sheets	11
Saves (shots inside box)	30
Saves (shots outside box)	19
Saves/shots	68%
DISTRIBUTION	
Long kick %	55%
Throws/short passes %	97%
CATCHING	
Crosses caught	31
Crosses punched	8
Crosses dropped	0
Catch success %	100%
DISCIPLINE	
Yellow cards	0
Red cards	0
SEE PAGE 40 FOR FULL STATS	

AM Lee SHARPE • 16
BRADFORD CITY • BORN: 27.5.71

APPEARANCES	
Start (sub)	6(5)
Minutes on pitch	470
GOAL ATTEMPTS	
Goals	0
Shots on target	0
Shooting accuracy	0%
Goals/shots ratio	0%
PASSING	
Goal assists	1
Passes in opp half	118
Passing accuracy in opp half	58%
Crosses	41
Crossing accuracy	32%
DRIBBLING	
Dribbles & runs	8
Dribble completion	75%
Corners forced	1
DISCIPLINE	
Fouls	3
Yellow cards	0
Red cards	0
SEE PAGE 69 FOR FULL STATS	

Former England winger Lee Sharpe started 2000–01 fighting a relegation battle in the Premiership and ended up in another nail-biting scrap at the bottom of Division One.

Although he had to drop out of the top flight to gain some first-team action, Sharpe at least had the consolation that his new team Portsmouth survived while Bradford, the club he left, ended up bottom of the pile in the Premiership.

The ex-Manchester United star had started the 2000–01 campaign as the Bantams' first-choice player on the left flank, making 41 crosses and setting up a goal.

But a change of management saw Sharpe drop out of favour at Valley Parade and in February he was loaned to Portsmouth for three months. He found a new vocation in central midfield on the south coast and, without scoring a goal, quietly impressed the Fratton Park faithful.

The transfer is likely to become a permanent one before the beginning of the 2001–02 season.

CB Richard SHAW • 6
COVENTRY CITY • BORN: 11.9.68

Although the adage "If it ain't broke, don't fix it" hardly applies to the Coventry defence, Gordon Strachan clearly felt something had to be done when, in November, Richard Shaw lost his place in the Sky Blues line-up.

Strachan instead employed Paul Williams and Gary Breen, and Shaw was banished to the reserves.

Eleven matches later, Strachan had seen his side record just one clean sheet without Shaw in the side and the Brentford-born defender was duly recalled, missing just two games for the rest of the campaign.

Although his two chief rivals for the centre-back role were more successful with their tackling, Shaw still made a considerable contribution at the back and also maintained a reasonable pass completion rate as his side looked for a way out of their predicament.

It was in vain, of course and Shaw must now decide whether first division football is for him with just one year left on his contract.

The former Crystal Palace defender may decide the time is right to move on.

APPEARANCES	
Start (sub)	23(1)
Minutes on pitch	2115

GOAL ATTEMPTS	
Goals	0

DEFENDING	
Blocks	28
Shots cleared off line	0
Headed clearances	121
Other clearances	71
Interceptions	10
Last man saving tackles	1
Tackles won	35
Tackles won %	70%

PASSING	
Passing accuracy own half	76%
Passing accuracy opp half	51%

DISCIPLINE	
Fouls	29
Fouls in danger area	15
Yellow cards	1
Red cards	0

SEE PAGE 111 FOR FULL STATS

S Alan SHEARER • 9
NEWCASTLE UNITED • BORN: 13.8.70

APPEARANCES	
Start (sub)	19(0)
Minutes on pitch	1710

GOAL ATTEMPTS	
Goals inside box	5
Goals outside box	0
Minutes per goal scored	342
Goals/shots ratio	12%

SHOOTING	
Shots on target inside box	22
Shots on target outside box	4
Shooting accuracy	63%

PASSING	
Goal assists	2
Key passes	17
Passing accuracy in opp half	61%

DISCIPLINE	
Fouls committed	51
Fouls won	57
Offside	25
Yellow cards	1
Red cards	0

SEE PAGE 251 FOR FULL STATS

Having confirmed his decision to quit international football after Euro 2000, Alan Shearer once again got ready to set the Premiership alight with no other distractions. Sadly, his dodgy knees had other ideas.

Shearer played the full 90 minutes in the first 15 Premiership games of the season, scoring five goals. However, his recurring tendonitis problem soon began to flare up. After missing two games he came back for two more, but his subsequent spell on the sidelines ruled him out of seven league fixtures.

Following two final appearances against Manchester City and Everton, it became obvious that he required extensive treatment and Shearer's season was over. He summed up his problems well by saying: "At least my knee problem gives me some breathing space as far as my back and hamstring injuries are concerned."

It may soon be time to hang up his boots if problems persist, but Shearer fans should rest easy – we have many years of his thrilling insights as a pundit ahead of us.

Teddy SHERINGHAM • 10
MANCHESTER UNITED • BORN: 2.4.66

Teddy Sheringham's 2000–01 campaign was packed with incident from the first kick to the last – and beyond.

The classy veteran set off in August content with being one of the four rotated strikers at Manchester United.

But his early-season form was excellent as he romped to the top of the Premiership's goal chart, made it virtually impossible for Sir Alex Ferguson to leave him out of the team and earned his first England cap in more than a year against Finland.

By mid-season, Sheringham was a vital player in the Red Devils' assault on domestic and European honours and come May, he had another title medal, 15 goals and the two high-profile Player of the Year awards under his belt.

Finally, he scored a splendid free-kick for England in a 4–0 win over Mexico and a day later rejoined his former club Tottenham Hotspur on a two-year contract after turning down the one-year deal on offer at Old Trafford. He is sure to get a fine reception from his adoring Spurs supporters.

APPEARANCES	
Start (sub)	23(6)
Minutes on pitch	2006

GOAL ATTEMPTS	
Goals inside box	15
Goals outside box	0
Minutes per goal scored	134
Goals/shots ratio	27%

SHOOTING	
Shots on target inside box	21
Shots on target outside box	7
Shooting accuracy	50%

PASSING	
Goal assists	5
Key passes	31
Passing accuracy in opp half	70%

DISCIPLINE	
Fouls committed	15
Fouls won	20
Offside	16
Yellow cards	1
Red cards	0

SEE PAGE 223 FOR FULL STATS

Romp: Teddy Sheringham

10 Teddy Sheringham scored three goals in a 10-minute

Tim SHERWOOD • 8
TOTTENHAM HOTSPUR • BORN: 2.2.69

First mate Tim Sherwood led Spurs' charge towards mid-table obscurity a number of times during 2000–01, in the absence of regular skipper Sol Campbell. Following a solid season in the centre for Spurs, Sherwood may well fancy himself for the captain's armband on a permanent basis upon Campbell's departure.

No Spurs player distributed the ball more impressively than Sherwood during the course of the season. The former Blackburn man found a colleague with no fewer than 1,321 passes – a tally bettered by only a handful of other Premiership players.

His overall completion rate of 77% was also excellent, as Sherwood demonstrated to the younger players exactly how it should be done. However, at the same time he displayed the other side of his game, committing more fouls than any of his colleagues.

Should Glenn Hoddle decide to go for youth over experience, a return to former club Watford could be on the cards for the St Albans-born midfielder.

APPEARANCES	
Start (sub)	31(2)
Minutes on pitch	2821
GOAL ATTEMPTS	
Goals	2
Shots on target	10
Shooting accuracy	28%
PASSING & CROSSING	
Goal assists	3
Passes in opp half	1080
Passing accuracy in opp half	73%
Successful crosses	18
Cross completion	31%
DEFENDING	
Interceptions	7
Clearances	71
Tackles	77
Tackles won %	62%
DISCIPLINE	
Fouls	61
Yellow cards	4
Red cards	0
SEE PAGE 293 FOR FULL STATS	

 Greg SHIELDS • 16
CHARLTON ATHLETIC • BORN: 21.8.76

APPEARANCES	
Start (sub)	2(2)
Minutes on pitch	205
GOAL ATTEMPTS	
Goals	0
PASSING & CROSSING	
Goal assists	0
Passing	74
Passing accuracy	66%
Crosses	4
Crossing accuracy	0%
DEFENDING	
Tackles	4
Tackles won %	75%
Blocks	1
Interceptions	0
Clearances	5
Shots cleared off line	0
DISCIPLINE	
Fouls	1
Yellow cards	0
Red cards	0
SEE PAGE 83 FOR FULL STATS	

Greg Shields was originally brought into the Charlton squad as a replacement for Danny Mills and he established himself as a competent attacking full-back.

With his surging runs down the flank and stubborn defending, the young defender played a major role in the side which won promotion to the Premiership.

But during the 2000–01 season the Scottish Under-21 international was hit by injury and the subsequent signing of Radostin Kishishev also saw his first-team chances limited.

Shields made only two starts and two substitute appearances during 2000–01 and was eventually placed on the transfer list in the spring of 2001.

Charlton subsequently slapped a £500,000 price tag on the defender.

He won three out of the four tackles he attempted and completed 66% of his passes, but it is clear that the former Glasgow Rangers player is going to have to secure a move out of south London if he is to further his career at both domestic and international level.

S

Mikael SILVESTRE • 27
MANCHESTER UNITED • BORN: 9.8.77

FB

Mikael Silvestre made a shaky start to his career at Old Trafford and the Frenchman's positional sense was a cause for concern. But during 2000–01 it appeared that those problems had been largely ironed out with his excellent showings for the champions.

The former Inter player once said of the training methods at United: "The players go on to the training pitch clutching cups of coffee. Afterwards they are given bacon sandwiches with all kinds of colourful sauces. That would be unthinkable in France."

Perhaps the docker's breakfasts helped build him up a little bit, as he won an excellent 86% of the 83 tackles he attempted in the 2000–01 Premiership.

Silvestre also loves to use his pace and get forward down the wing.

In fact the statistics show that only Ryan Giggs made more dribbles and runs than the 123 the Frenchman did.

Perhaps he benefited from all the caffeine in those cups of coffee down at the United training ground.

APPEARANCES	
Start (sub)	25(5)
Minutes on pitch	2251
GOAL ATTEMPTS	
Goals	1
PASSING & CROSSING	
Goal assists	2
Passing	1290
Passing accuracy	73%
Crosses	73
Crossing accuracy	19%
DEFENDING	
Tackles	83
Tackles won %	86%
Blocks	13
Interceptions	10
Clearances	118
Shots cleared off line	0
DISCIPLINE	
Fouls	27
Yellow cards	2
Red cards	0
SEE PAGE 223 FOR FULL STATS	

Getting forward: Mikael Silvestre

For more information visit our website:

SILVINHO • 16
ARSENAL • BORN: 12.4.74

When Arsène Wenger asked Silvinho what he has learned most from coming to England he replied: "How to defend." How reassuring for the manager.

During 2000–01 the Brazilian was the first-choice left-back until he picked up an injury and Ashley Cole moved in. The young Englishman impressed so much it became hard for the former Corinthians player to regain his place in the side.

Silvinho's tackle success rate of 72% was just below average and his Brazilian dribbling skills appear to have deserted him, as he only retained the ball with 32% of his dribbles. But then he has stated he has little interest in samba and is a member of the evangelical church Athletes For Christ, so there will not be a lack of faith on his behalf.

His love of crosses has seen him put in 72 centres for the Gunners and, although only 11 of those reached a team-mate, Silvinho is still a bright star worth following. A dearth of effective Arsenal target men was undoubtedly a factor in that poor crossing accuracy.

APPEARANCES	
Start (sub)	23(1)
Minutes on pitch	2012
GOAL ATTEMPTS	
Goals	2
PASSING & CROSSING	
Goal assists	2
Passing	908
Passing accuracy	76%
Crosses	136
Crossing accuracy	15%
DEFENDING	
Tackles	78
Tackles won %	72%
Blocks	10
Interceptions	9
Clearances	60
Shots cleared off line	1
DISCIPLINE	
Fouls	32
Yellow cards	3
Red cards	0

SEE PAGE 41 FOR FULL STATS

Steve SIMONSEN • 13
EVERTON • BORN: 3.4.79

Steve Simonsen did not bother turning up for training at Tranmere Rovers one morning because he thought – wrongly – that his transfer to Everton had been sorted out. Rovers boss John Aldridge was not impressed.

The move did eventually go through, but during the 2000–01 season the young goalkeeper was one of the season's one-minute wonders, appearing for just 60 seconds in a game against West Ham.

During that time he did not even touch the ball and he spent the season in the shadow of Paul Gerrard.

Simonsen once kept seven consecutive clean sheets in his Prenton Park days and as an England Under-21 international he had a glittering career ahead of him. But since joining Everton for £3.3 million he has been languishing in the reserves. If this young 'keeper intends to resurrect his international ambitions, then some more first-team football is not only recommended but essential.

SEE PAGE 138 FOR FULL STATS

Faith: Silvinho

FB — Frank SINCLAIR • 3
LEICESTER CITY • BORN: 3.12.71

Frank Sinclair was in and out of the Leicester side throughout the 2000–01 season due to a run of injuries, but when he was playing for the Foxes it was clear that he knew what he was doing.

The big stopper won 50 of the 58 tackles he went in for and that no-nonsense style helped to make him a favourite with the fans at Filbert Street.

His pass completion rate of 62% was not so impressive for his position, but the Foxes' more direct style of football would have contributed to that.

The injury frustration was summed up by Sinclair after picking up another knock in a tackle with Steven Gerrard: "I've done my medial ligaments – I'm falling to bits! This has been a nightmare season for me. I've had a hernia problem, hamstring injury, calf injury and now this."

If he can stay fit, then he will be a valuable addition to Peter Taylor's squad. Unfortunately he managed to play less than half a season for Leicester in 2000–01 and he will be anxious to improve on that in 2001–02.

APPEARANCES	
Start (sub)	14(3)
Minutes on pitch	1199
GOAL ATTEMPTS	
Goals	0
PASSING & CROSSING	
Goal assists	2
Passing	476
Passing accuracy	62%
Crosses	32
Crossing accuracy	25%
DEFENDING	
Tackles	58
Tackles won %	86%
Blocks	11
Interceptions	7
Clearances	71
Shots cleared off line	1
DISCIPLINE	
Fouls	12
Yellow cards	4
Red cards	0
SEE PAGE 181 FOR FULL STATS	

AM — Trevor SINCLAIR • 8
WEST HAM UNITED • BORN: 2.3.73

APPEARANCES	
Start (sub)	19(0)
Minutes on pitch	1688
GOAL ATTEMPTS	
Goals	3
Shots on target	7
Shooting accuracy	44%
Goals/shots ratio	19%
PASSING	
Goal assists	3
Passes in opp half	392
Passing accuracy in opp half	66%
Crosses	54
Crossing accuracy	30%
DRIBBLING	
Dribbles & runs	63
Dribble completion	51%
Corners forced	14
DISCIPLINE	
Fouls	9
Yellow cards	1
Red cards	0
SEE PAGE 307 FOR FULL STATS	

Team-mate Frederic Kanouté described Trevor Sinclair as "the most physical player in the team" which may come as a surprise to Hammers defender Stuart Pearce.

The former QPR winger mostly played in the wing-back role in 2000–01, but used his strength to get stuck into 33 tackles, although his 67% success rate was actually below average.

As a wing-back Sinclair got forward to make 63 dribbles and runs during the 2000–01 season and kept possession 51% of the time. A pass completion rate of 63% in the final third illustrated his attacking potential for the London club, although he was forced to miss much of the 2000–01 Premiership campaign with injury.

That forward thinking allowed him to get forward and swing in 54 crosses. His three assists and three goals are tallies that he will want to improve on if he is to re-establish himself in the England squad and as the Hammers continue their Premiership fight without the leadership of Harry Redknapp.

9 Vladimir Smicer set up nine goals –

Vladimir SMICER • 7
LIVERPOOL • BORN: 24.5.73

Vladimir Smicer appeared in 27 of Liverpool's Premiership games in 2000–01 as well as playing vital parts in their triple cup success, and the Czech star appears to have overcome the earlier injury problems that ruined his 1999–2000 season.

Smicer once scored 11 goals in a game as his youth team ran out 13–0 winners and that tempted Slavia Prague to pay a full £800 for his services.

But at Liverpool most of his good work is done in midfield. He set up nine goals for team-mates during the 2000–01 Premiership – the most at the club – which included creating all three of the Reds' goals in the 3–3 draw with Southampton.

The season almost turned sour, though, when he thought he had lost his UEFA Cup winners' medal.

He later said: "I was convinced I'd put it in my suit, but I looked through the pockets in my jacket and I couldn't find it." It turned up in his trouser pocket. Always the last place you look.

APPEARANCES	
Start (sub)	16(11)
Minutes on pitch	1503
GOAL ATTEMPTS	
Goals	2
Shots on target	11
Shooting accuracy	34%
Goals/shots ratio	6%
PASSING	
Goal assists	9
Passes in opp half	471
Passing accuracy in opp half	65%
Crosses	102
Crossing accuracy	27%
DRIBBLING	
Dribbles & runs	101
Dribble completion	68%
Corners forced	23
DISCIPLINE	
Fouls	29
Yellow cards	2
Red cards	0
SEE PAGE 195 FOR FULL STATS	

Alan SMITH • 17
LEEDS UNITED • BORN: 28.10.80

APPEARANCES	
Start (sub)	26(7)
Minutes on pitch	2411
GOAL ATTEMPTS	
Goals inside box	11
Goals outside box	0
Minutes per goal scored	219
Goals/shots ratio	19%
SHOOTING	
Shots on target inside box	22
Shots on target outside box	6
Shooting accuracy	47%
PASSING	
Goal assists	6
Key passes	20
Passing accuracy in opp half	65%
DISCIPLINE	
Fouls committed	90
Fouls won	80
Offside	42
Yellow cards	7
Red cards	1
SEE PAGE 167 FOR FULL STATS	

Despite having to share the two striking positions at Leeds with Mark Viduka and Robbie Keane, Alan Smith continued his meteoric rise to fame with the Yorkshire club. The young striker was even singled out by Sven-Göran Eriksson as one of the most promising forwards in Europe and duly won his first England cap.

Having started the first 19 league fixtures for the club, the Wakefield-born marksman found himself employed more as a substitute for Premiership games following Keane's arrival, while being used to the full during Leeds' European campaign.

Nonetheless, he managed to notch up 11 league goals to finish as the club's second-highest scorer behind Viduka; and his 19% goals-to-shots ratio was an example to strikers everywhere, even if his indiscipline frequently landed him in hot water.

However, he does also have to put up with enormous expectancy from Smiths everywhere, as the only player with that name in the entire top flight.

S

Nolberto SOLANO • 15
NEWCASTLE UNITED • BORN: 12.12.74

Nolberto Solano is not normally one to blow his own trumpet. In fact he plays a cornet, and apparently calls up manager Bobby Robson at night and serenades his boss with soothing horn music.

Robson should have been wary, though – Solano's favourite song to play is *Spanish Eyes* and the winger has reportedly had an eye on a move to Real Madrid. Toon fans would be distraught to see the popular wide man leave

With 10 assists to his name in 2000–01, he had a huge influence on the side. The Peruvian Magpie also chipped in with six goals, which surprisingly made him the joint-top scorer at St James' Park.

If you need further proof that Solano is a key figure in the Newcastle team, then note that he swung in 110 successful crosses – more than any other player in the Premiership beating even England skipper David Beckham.

If Robson convinces Solano that his future lies in Newcastle then maybe he should ask him to learn some local songs – *Fog On The Tyne*, perhaps.

APPEARANCES	
Start (sub)	31(2)
Minutes on pitch	2632

GOAL ATTEMPTS	
Goals	6
Shots on target	18
Shooting accuracy	46%
Goals/shots ratio	15%

PASSING	
Goal assists	10
Passes in opp half	1099
Passing accuracy in opp half	67%
Crosses	327
Crossing accuracy	34%

DRIBBLING	
Dribbles & runs	87
Dribble completion	69%
Corners forced	23

DISCIPLINE	
Fouls	42
Yellow cards	3
Red cards	2

SEE PAGE 251 FOR FULL STATS

Soothing: Nolberto Solano

For more information visit our website:

Ole Gunnar SOLSKJAER • 20
MANCHESTER UNITED • BORN: 26.2.73

Although he professes not to mind, 2000–01 was another season of spending very nearly as much time on the bench than off it for Ole Gunnar Solskjaer.

His longest run of games in the side was still only eight matches, following Andy Cole's Achilles operation.

Of course, one of the most frightening sights a Premiership defender can witness is that of Solskjaer warming up to come on and the Norwegian did little to reverse his tag of "supersub". He continued to create havoc when introduced to the game late, scoring two of his 10 Premiership goals when coming off the substitutes' bench.

The 1999 Champions League winner was sad to see the back of colleague Teddy Sheringham, saying, "I've really learned a lot from him and I wish he was still here", especially since it meant no less competition for places up front: with Cole, Dwight Yorke and now Ruud van Nistelrooy to worry about, Solskjaer will still struggle for a regular starting berth.

APPEARANCES	
Start (sub)	19(12)
Minutes on pitch	1754
GOAL ATTEMPTS	
Goals inside box	10
Goals outside box	0
Minutes per goal scored	175
Goals/shots ratio	14%
SHOOTING	
Shots on target inside box	34
Shots on target outside box	8
Shooting accuracy	61%
PASSING	
Goal assists	4
Key passes	16
Passing accuracy in opp half	73%
DISCIPLINE	
Fouls committed	25
Fouls won	24
Offside	21
Yellow cards	1
Red cards	0

SEE PAGE 223 FOR FULL STATS

Trond Egil SOLTVEDT • 32
SOUTHAMPTON • BORN: 15.2.67

APPEARANCES	
Start (sub)	3(3)
Minutes on pitch	367
GOAL ATTEMPTS	
Goals	1
Shots on target	1
Shooting accuracy	33%
PASSING & CROSSING	
Goal assists	0
Passes in opp half	77
Passing accuracy in opp half	61%
Successful crosses	0
Cross completion	0%
DEFENDING	
Interceptions	0
Clearances	8
Tackles	11
Tackles won %	64%
DISCIPLINE	
Fouls	2
Yellow cards	0
Red cards	0

SEE PAGE 265 FOR FULL STATS

Norwegian midfielder Trond Egil Soltvedt's second season with the Saints proved little better than the first.

He made just three starts for the south coast outfit before finally ending his unhappy spell by securing a move to Sheffield Wednesday in March following a month on loan with the Owls.

Glenn Hoddle chose to tell the Scandinavian that it was guts and determination to win matches which he lacked, which was why he refused to pick him. This surprised Soltvedt, who said on his official website: "That has always been my trademark and I think that's still the case".

Of course, his time on the sidelines gave him ample opportunity to enjoy a traditional Norwegian Christmas. Soltvedt's best-ever present was a black cat – with a red bow – which he got when he was six or seven years old. As if that is not enough, his favourite hymn is Silent Night in Norwegian.

Christmas sounds like a raucous time of year in his household.

S

CB   Ragnvald SOMA • 36
WEST HAM UNITED • BORN: 10.11.79

One of Harry Redknapp's many lesser-known signings, Ragnvald Soma signed for the London club in January 2001. He joined from Norwegian club Bryne for £800,000, as cover for the likes of Igor Stimac and Rigobert Song in the defence.

Sadly for Soma, the West Ham defence proved more resilient than he would have hoped and he managed to record just two starts and two substitute appearances during the season. He did, however, rack up 15 challenges during his time on the field, with a fine 80% success rate which bodes well for the future.

His previous club have struggled since Soma left, and they were looking to take the 6'2" defender back to Norway for the summer. The club were hoping that he would help them in their quest to avoid relegation from the Tippeliga, before returning him to West Ham for the start of the season.

It could be a good deal for all parties concerned – and underlines the youngster's appetite for the game.

APPEARANCES	
Start (sub)	2(2)
Minutes on pitch	189
GOAL ATTEMPTS	
Goals	0
DEFENDING	
Blocks	1
Shots cleared off line	0
Headed clearances	2
Other clearances	3
Interceptions	3
Last man saving tackles	0
Tackles won	12
Tackles won %	80%
PASSING	
Passing accuracy own half	84%
Passing accuracy opp half	61%
DISCIPLINE	
Fouls	0
Fouls in danger area	0
Yellow cards	0
Red cards	0
SEE PAGE 307 FOR FULL STATS	

FB   Rigobert SONG • 15
WEST HAM UNITED • BORN: 1.7.76

APPEARANCES	
Start (sub)	21(1)
Minutes on pitch	1925
GOAL ATTEMPTS	
Goals	0
PASSING & CROSSING	
Goal assists	0
Passing	613
Passing accuracy	59%
Crosses	27
Crossing accuracy	30%
DEFENDING	
Tackles	85
Tackles won %	72%
Blocks	16
Interceptions	15
Clearances	180
Shots cleared off line	1
DISCIPLINE	
Fouls	41
Yellow cards	4
Red cards	0
SEE PAGES 195 & 307 FOR FULL STATS	

Rigobert Song has been a regular for Cameroon since he was 17. He has played in two World Cups, scored the penalty which won his country the African Nations Cup in 2000, helped the side to Olympic gold in Sydney and experienced life in French and Italian football.

Indeed, Song's Cameroonian team-mates rate him so highly that they call him "German", a reference to his ruthless efficiency.

But despite Song's impeccable credentials at international level, he failed to make the positive impact expected of him during his spell at Liverpool and was bought by West Ham United in November 2000 to replace Rio Ferdinand.

Although Song was a regular fixture at Upton Park, making 72 tackles and 14 interceptions, he did not show his "German" characteristics too often.

In fact, the former Metz star's arrival coincided with a slump in the Hammers' form which saw the club drop from 11th to 15th in the Premiership as they kept only three clean sheets in 19 matches.

1 Thomas Sorensen was the first goalkeeper

Thomas SORENSEN • 1
SUNDERLAND • BORN: 12.6.76

Sunderland shot-stopper Thomas Sorensen enjoyed another solid season in the Premiership in 2000–01. He kept 12 clean sheets – the fourth-highest total in the top flight – and blocked an impressive 75% of the shots he faced.

As far as Black Cats fans are concerned, the most important save Sorensen made in the 2000–01 campaign was undoubtedly from Alan Shearer's late penalty for Newcastle back in November, which secured Sunderland's 2–1 win over their fierce local rivals.

However, Sorensen himself might feel that the most significant moment of his season came in a game in which he did not even play. At 7:35pm on 25 April, Danish legend Peter Schmeichel retired from international football, giving a chance to the nation's younger generation of goalkeepers.

Sorensen has been named as the Sporting Lisbon 'keeper's successor and may at last be given a run in the Denmark team after spending so many frustrating years as Schmeichel's understudy.

APPEARANCES	
Start (sub)	34(0)
Minutes on pitch	3015
SHOT STOPPING	
Goals conceded (inside box)	29
Goals conceded (outside box)	3
Minutes per goal conceded	94
Clean sheets	12
Saves (shots inside box)	59
Saves (shots outside box)	36
Saves/shots	75%
DISTRIBUTION	
Long kick %	54%
Throws/short passes %	86%
CATCHING	
Crosses caught	68
Crosses punched	17
Crosses dropped	7
Catch success %	91%
DISCIPLINE	
Yellow cards	0
Red cards	0

SEE PAGE 278 FOR FULL STATS

Solid Season: Thomas Sorensen

to save a penalty in 2000–01

Gareth SOUTHGATE • 4
CB
ASTON VILLA • BORN: 3.9.70

Gareth Southgate was one of several first-team players at Aston Villa to declare that he wanted to leave the club at the end of the 1999–2000 campaign. However, a projected move to Chelsea fell through when the two clubs failed to agree on a fee and the England defender reluctantly remained at Villa Park, as captain, throughout 2000–01.

Southgate showed his value to the team by blocking a club-high total of 41 shots and crosses, and he also made four last-ditch challenges to prevent goals – the second-highest total in the Premiership.

But by the end of the 2000–01 season, Southgate finally looked set to leave Villa after he officially relinquished the captain's armband, sparking renewed interest from across the country.

Despite the uncertainty over Southgate's future at club level, he remained an important figure for England. The former Crystal Palace star featured in the matches against France and Italy – and even skippered the side in the second half of the friendly with Mexico.

APPEARANCES	
Start (sub)	31(0)
Minutes on pitch	2663
GOAL ATTEMPTS	
Goals	2
DEFENDING	
Blocks	41
Shots cleared off line	2
Headed clearances	176
Other clearances	113
Interceptions	15
Last man saving tackles	4
Tackles won	61
Tackles won %	73%
PASSING	
Passing accuracy own half	84%
Passing accuracy opp half	58%
DISCIPLINE	
Fouls	23
Fouls in danger area	9
Yellow cards	6
Red cards	0

SEE PAGE 55 FOR FULL STATS

Gary SPEED • 11
M
NEWCASTLE UNITED • BORN: 8.9.69

APPEARANCES	
Start (sub)	35(0)
Minutes on pitch	3144
GOAL ATTEMPTS	
Goals	5
Shots on target	20
Shooting accuracy	27%
PASSING & CROSSING	
Goal assists	3
Passes in opp half	1162
Passing accuracy in opp half	67%
Successful crosses	6
Cross completion	23%
DEFENDING	
Interceptions	10
Clearances	51
Tackles	113
Tackles won %	68%
DISCIPLINE	
Fouls	74
Yellow cards	8
Red cards	1

SEE PAGE 251 FOR FULL STATS

Although 2000–01 was an unspectacular campaign for Newcastle, there were some moments that midfielder Gary Speed will look back on with pride. He broke the record for Premiership appearances in the match against Leicester in April and finished the campaign with a total of 322 games.

The Welsh international captain showed why he has been an automatic selection wherever he has played, by making more passes and more tackles than any other player at Newcastle in the 2000–01 season.

Speed also produced some inspirational performances for his country, scoring against Belarus and leading the side to impressive draws with Norway, Ukraine and Poland.

However, he had a few words to say to FIFA after the 0–0 draw in Poland. The skipper blasted their global ranking system as "rubbish" and one can see why he feels so incensed, as at the end of the 2000–01 campaign Speed's men were ranked 110th in the World, some 80 places below Poland and behind Barbados, Haiti and Thailand.

For more information visit our website:

CB

Jaap STAM • 6
MANCHESTER UNITED • BORN: 17.7.72

Fitness problems kept Jaap Stam out of the Manchester United first team for much of the 2000–01 season.

The £10.75 million Dutch defender sustained an Achilles injury against Sunderland in September which kept him out of action until the following January, by which time United had built up a sizeable lead in the Premiership.

Stam returned to help the Red Devils cruise to the title and displayed great anticipation by making 18 interceptions – more than any other United player. Indeed, a sign of Stam's value to the team is that Sir Alex Ferguson's side did not lose a single league game in which he featured over the course of the 2000–01 campaign.

However, on a trip to the cinema with his wife, the man whom Johan Cruyff once described as "a one-man defence" showed a weakness that Premiership forwards do not often get to see, as sweet-toothed Stam and his partner chomped their way through a staggering total of 936 sweets during the movie *Gladiator*.

APPEARANCES	
Start (sub)	15(0)
Minutes on pitch	1235
GOAL ATTEMPTS	
Goals	0
DEFENDING	
Blocks	9
Shots cleared off line	1
Headed clearances	44
Other clearances	27
Interceptions	18
Last man saving tackles	1
Tackles won	28
Tackles won %	74%
PASSING	
Passing accuracy own half	93%
Passing accuracy opp half	78%
DISCIPLINE	
Fouls	10
Fouls in danger area	4
Yellow cards	1
Red cards	0

SEE PAGE 223 FOR FULL STATS

S

Sweet-toothed: Jaap Stam

Phil STAMP • 24
MIDDLESBROUGH • BORN: 12.12.75

Phil Stamp has never been more than a squad player at Middlesbrough, but his chances in the first team became even more limited after Terry Venables joined the club as head coach in December 2000.

Venables started Stamp in just two of his games in charge and substituted the midfielder on both occasions, clearly preferring to use the talents of Christian Karembeu and former Liverpool favourite Paul Ince in central midfield.

Despite developing a reputation as one of the hardest-working players at Boro, Stamp's performances in the 2000–01 campaign were not up to the standards he had set in previous seasons. The former England youth international won the ball in only 49% of the challenges he made, which is an extremely disappointing proportion for a player who prides himself on his fighting spirit.

Stamp's attacking abilities were similarly inadequate as he hit the target with just 31% of his shots, vindicating Venables' decision to drop him.

APPEARANCES	
Start (sub)	11(8)
Minutes on pitch	998
GOAL ATTEMPTS	
Goals	1
Shots on target	4
Shooting accuracy	31%
PASSING & CROSSING	
Goal assists	1
Passes in opp half	203
Passing accuracy in opp half	62%
Successful crosses	4
Cross completion	13%
DEFENDING	
Interceptions	3
Clearances	11
Tackles	35
Tackles won %	49%
DISCIPLINE	
Fouls	15
Yellow cards	4
Red cards	1

SEE PAGE 237 FOR FULL STATS

Mario STANIC • 12
CHELSEA • BORN: 10.4.72

APPEARANCES	
Start (sub)	8(4)
Minutes on pitch	563
GOAL ATTEMPTS	
Goals	2
Shots on target	5
Shooting accuracy	42%
Goals/shots ratio	17%
PASSING	
Goal assists	0
Passes in opp half	157
Passing accuracy in opp half	62%
Crosses	23
Crossing accuracy	9%
DRIBBLING	
Dribbles & runs	26
Dribble completion	77%
Corners forced	6
DISCIPLINE	
Fouls	20
Yellow cards	1
Red cards	0

SEE PAGE 97 FOR FULL STATS

Few players in the world can claim to have made as impressive a debut as Mario Stanic did at Chelsea. The Croatian international had stated upon his arrival at Stamford Bridge: "I have won the Super Cup, UEFA Cup and the Italian Cup but I think I will win more at Chelsea."

The omens certainly looked good for Stanic after he scored twice on his league bow against West Ham United, including an incredible, screaming 35-yard volley which followed an audacious bout of flick-ups on the half-way line.

But the former Parma star sustained a serious knee injury in his next match for the Blues at Aston Villa, which kept him out of action until January – a big disappointment for everyone at the west London club.

Although Stanic was unable to add to his goals tally when he returned to full fitness at the end of 2000–01, he did play an integral part in Chelsea's late push for a UEFA Cup place, finishing the season with more than 200 passes to his name.

6 Phil Stamp was one of the six

CB | **Steve STAUNTON • 11**
ASTON VILLA • BORN: 19.1.69

During his second spell at Liverpool, Steve Staunton became great friends with fellow-left-back Dominic Matteo and even drove his team-mate to training on a daily basis after the Scottish international had been banned from driving for six months.

But neither player was guaranteed a regular place at Anfield and when Matteo left for Leeds, Staunton went on loan to Crystal Palace, where some solid individual performances and an amazing goal from the halfway line against Tranmere Rovers convinced his former club Aston Villa to re-sign him in December.

While at Villa, Staunton proved that he could still perform at the highest level and featured strongly as the club surged up the table in the second half of 2000–01.

The Republic of Ireland international's ability to bring the ball out of defence proved a valuable weapon. He whipped in 65 crosses to set up two goals and even got on the scoresheet for his country with a powerful effort against Finland in November.

APPEARANCES	
Start (sub)	13(2)
Minutes on pitch	1116

GOAL ATTEMPTS	
Goals	0

DEFENDING	
Blocks	10
Shots cleared off line	0
Headed clearances	27
Other clearances	25
Interceptions	6
Last man saving tackles	0
Tackles won	21
Tackles won %	60%

PASSING	
Passing accuracy own half	78%
Passing accuracy opp half	57%

DISCIPLINE	
Fouls	7
Fouls in danger area	1
Yellow cards	0
Red cards	0

SEE PAGES 55 & 195 FOR FULL STATS

 CB | **Igors STEPANOVS • 3**
ARSENAL • BORN: 21.1.76

APPEARANCES	
Start (sub)	9(0)
Minutes on pitch	810

GOAL ATTEMPTS	
Goals	0

DEFENDING	
Blocks	8
Shots cleared off line	1
Headed clearances	64
Other clearances	22
Interceptions	1
Last man saving tackles	1
Tackles won	13
Tackles won %	72%

PASSING	
Passing accuracy own half	84%
Passing accuracy opp half	72%

DISCIPLINE	
Fouls	9
Fouls in danger area	1
Yellow cards	0
Red cards	0

SEE PAGE 41 FOR FULL STATS

After failing to land Brazilian defender Edmilson, Arsène Wenger signed Latvian international Igors Stepanovs for a cut-price fee of £1 million.

Unlike many foreign imports in the Premiership, Stepanovs was honest enough to confess that he was having trouble communicating with people at the club during his first few months at Highbury, admitting, "Nobody tells me anything yet" when asked if he would be picked for the clash with Manchester United. Stepanovs was named in the Gunners' starting XI for the top-of-the-table fixture, but his confusion seemed to transfer itself directly to his performance and he was largely culpable for their demoralising 6–1 defeat by the champions.

However, Stepanovs was able to show the skills which had prompted Wenger's interest in other games. He was accurate with an excellent 80% of his passes over the course of the 2000–01 season and showed great aerial strength to score a header in the Worthington Cup against Ipswich on his debut.

S

Middlesbrough players sent off in 2000–01

Marcus STEWART • 11
IPSWICH TOWN • BORN: 8.11.72

Marcus Stewart was beginning to develop a reputation as a journeyman footballer after spending the entirety of his career in the lower leagues with Bristol Rovers, Huddersfield and Ipswich.

Indeed, there were many who felt that Stewart, like the rest of the Ipswich team, would struggle to adapt to the pace of the Premiership. How wrong they were!

Stewart started the 2000–01 season in brilliant form and led the top scorers' list for much of his first campaign in top-flight football. Indeed, the Bristol-born forward's outstanding performances even led to speculation that he could be in line for a call-up to the England team.

Opta statistics certainly showed that Stewart would not look out of place on the international scene. He finished the 2000–01 campaign with a total of 19 goals, having hit the target with 59% of his shots and scored with 23% of his efforts – both the third-best proportions of all English strikers in the Premiership.

APPEARANCES	
Start (sub)	33(1)
Minutes on pitch	2713

GOAL ATTEMPTS	
Goals inside box	19
Goals outside box	0
Minutes per goal scored	143
Goals/shots ratio	23%

SHOOTING	
Shots on target inside box	38
Shots on target outside box	10
Shooting accuracy	59%

PASSING	
Goal assists	4
Key passes	27
Passing accuracy in opp half	74%

DISCIPLINE	
Fouls committed	42
Fouls won	47
Offside	36
Yellow cards	2
Red cards	1

SEE PAGE 153 FOR FULL STATS

Outstanding: Marcus Stewart

Michael STEWART • 28
MANCHESTER UNITED • BORN: 26.2.81

Since signing for Manchester United as a 15-year-old, talented midfield starlet Michael Stewart has made a steady progression through the club ranks.

The Scot excelled in the youth team until he forced his way into United's reserves in 1999–2000, where he was a regular before joining feeder club Royal Antwerp in Belgium.

Stewart returned to England to make his full United debut in the Worthington Cup win over Watford in October and had a run in the first team at the end of the 2000–01 Premiership season, after the title had been clinched.

Stewart says that he bases his game on captain Roy Keane, which shows in his committed style of play. Stewart went in for a challenge every 18 minutes on average in 2000–01, which is more frequently than any other player at the club – Keane included – and has been rewarded for his progress with further call-ups to the Scotland Under-21 squad.

His final – and most difficult – challenge will be breaking into the fist team on a more regular basis.

APPEARANCES	
Start (sub)	3(0)
Minutes on pitch	239
GOAL ATTEMPTS	
Goals	0
Shots on target	1
Shooting accuracy	25%
PASSING & CROSSING	
Goal assists	0
Passes in opp half	90
Passing accuracy in opp half	69%
Successful crosses	0
Cross completion	0%
DEFENDING	
Interceptions	2
Clearances	0
Tackles	13
Tackles won %	69%
DISCIPLINE	
Fouls	8
Yellow cards	1
Red cards	0

SEE PAGE 223 FOR FULL STATS

Igor STIMAC • 5
WEST HAM UNITED • BORN: 6.9.67

APPEARANCES	
Start (sub)	19(0)
Minutes on pitch	1566
GOAL ATTEMPTS	
Goals	0
DEFENDING	
Blocks	13
Shots cleared off line	0
Headed clearances	115
Other clearances	56
Interceptions	17
Last man saving tackles	0
Tackles won	41
Tackles won %	67%
PASSING	
Passing accuracy own half	82%
Passing accuracy opp half	56%
DISCIPLINE	
Fouls	27
Fouls in danger area	10
Yellow cards	3
Red cards	1

SEE PAGE 307 FOR FULL STATS

Croatian defender Igor Stimac made just 19 starts for West Ham during the 2000–01 campaign. Worryingly for the big centre-back, the longest spell he managed in the side was just seven games before his fitness again deteriorated, raising concerns over his future in the Premiership.

He did not help himself by shoulder-barging Leicester's Robbie Savage in the second league match of the campaign and receiving his second booking of the game, although the Hammers faithful hardly helped Stimac by cheering him on while he did so.

Stimac racked up the second-highest tally of clearances of any Hammer during the season. West Ham will need to do all they can to hang on to the Croatian, who has already voiced concerns over his future.

The former Derby County hero continues to express his love for the Rams, stating: "I don't think my mission with Derby is done yet. I want to return there and I also want to be a manager when I finish playing, so why not Derby?"

S

Steve STONE • 18
ASTON VILLA • BORN: 20.8.71

Diminutive Aston Villa midfielder Steve Stone's season was trundling along nicely when John Gregory decided to shift to a 4–4–2 formation towards the end of the campaign, meaning that one of the midfield needed to be sacrificed.

It was the unfortunate Stone whose head ended up on the block.

He has vowed to force his way back into the side during 2001–02, having been forced to warm the bench for the final four league matches of the campaign. In Stone's own words: "Someone had to come out of the midfield and it was me. I did not enjoy it, but I accepted that it had to be done for the benefit of the team."

However, following his poor 1999–2000 campaign, Stone was probably thrilled to have featured in so many of Villa's matches during the following season.

Furthermore, even though his England days now seem to be behind him, his 75% pass completion rate shows that he has lost none of his talent.

APPEARANCES	
Start (sub)	33(1)
Minutes on pitch	2777
GOAL ATTEMPTS	
Goals	2
PASSING & CROSSING	
Goal assists	2
Passing	1376
Passing accuracy	75%
Crosses	107
Crossing accuracy	28%
DEFENDING	
Tackles	86
Tackles won %	76%
Blocks	12
Interceptions	9
Clearances	64
Shots cleared off line	1
DISCIPLINE	
Fouls	57
Yellow cards	8
Red cards	0

SEE PAGE 55 FOR FULL STATS

Gavin STRACHAN • 21
COVENTRY CITY • BORN: 23.12.78

Like father, like son: Gavin Strachan had a miserable 2000–01. He managed to convince Strachan Senior to allow him into the first team just twice, although he did start each of the matches he featured in.

Somewhat surprisingly, he was never used as a substitute, despite being named on the bench on a number of occasions. His injury woes seemed to have subsided a little following a disastrous previous two seasons with the Sky Blues, but this appeared to have had little effect on the manager's team selection.

Neither did he manage to convince his father that a loan move might be the answer to gain some first-team experience elsewhere, following a successful spell at Dundee during 1999–2000.

The future hardly seems bright for Strachan, although the drop to Division One may assist him in his quest for action, should his short-tempered dad decide to offload some of his midfield stars.

SEE PAGE 111 FOR FULL STATS

Diminutive: Steve Stone

Branko STRUPAR • 25
DERBY COUNTY • BORN: 9.2.70

Belgian striker Branko Strupar rarely had the opportunity to harass Premiership defenders during 2000–01, due to his seemingly never-ending injury problems.

But the glimpses Derby supporters were offered of their mercurial forward did show precisely why the Rams seem so content to persevere with him.

Strupar had time to strike just 14 efforts goalwards during the campaign, and yet six of these managed to find the back of the net. His shooting accuracy of 64% showed that the time spent on his back did little to affect his eye for goal.

Sadly for the former Croatian, who counts snooker and tennis among his numerous hobbies and is a particular fan of pasta, he looks likely to sit out much of 2001–02, following another operation on his troublesome groin.

If nothing else, Strupar at least knows he has made it. Not every player gets a website entirely dedicated to them by two "crazy" Belgian girls called Stephanie and Jolijn.

APPEARANCES	
Start (sub)	7(2)
Minutes on pitch	648
GOAL ATTEMPTS	
Goals inside box	4
Goals outside box	2
Minutes per goal scored	108
Goals/shots ratio	43%
SHOOTING	
Shots on target inside box	4
Shots on target outside box	5
Shooting accuracy	64%
PASSING	
Goal assists	0
Key passes	4
Passing accuracy in opp half	54%
DISCIPLINE	
Fouls committed	15
Fouls won	9
Offside	6
Yellow cards	1
Red cards	0
SEE PAGE 125 FOR FULL STATS	

Graham STUART • 4
CHARLTON ATHLETIC • BORN: 24.10.70

APPEARANCES	
Start (sub)	33(2)
Minutes on pitch	2939
GOAL ATTEMPTS	
Goals	5
Shots on target	14
Shooting accuracy	38%
Goals/shots ratio	14%
PASSING	
Goal assists	9
Passes in opp half	907
Passing accuracy in opp half	66%
Crosses	47
Crossing accuracy	21%
DRIBBLING	
Dribbles & runs	103
Dribble completion	74%
Corners forced	16
DISCIPLINE	
Fouls	30
Yellow cards	7
Red cards	0
SEE PAGE 83 FOR FULL STATS	

Ever-reliable Graham Stuart failed to feature in just three league matches during Charlton Athletic's immensely successful return to the Premiership.

His performances throughout the season were superb and with one breath Charlton fans were declaring him as a candidate for Player of the Season, before hailing "Stuart for England" with the next.

That may be a little far-fetched at the moment, but there can be little doubt that Stuart was in prime form during the 2000–01 season.

In almost all areas of the game he was up there with the best in the Charlton side, most notably in terms of his passing – only two of his colleagues managed to find a red shirt more frequently with their distribution.

His discipline left something to be desired, however, with the joint-highest tally of yellow cards in the squad. Stuart was booked seven times during the season and was fortunate that his fifth came after the automatic suspensions deadline.

Branko Strupar's goals – the best rate in the league

Dean STURRIDGE • 21
LEICESTER CITY • BORN: 27.7.73

Dean Sturridge's potential has been there for all to see for more than five years. An excellent run in the Derby County side saw the native Brummie linked with a move to the biggest clubs in the country, but a disappointing 1999–2000 season saw hopes of a bright future fade.

His 2000–01 campaign began poorly as Sturridge managed just one goal in 14 appearances for the Rams, although he was mainly used as a substitute.

At the time he was Derby's longest-serving player, but it became clear that his spell at the club was coming to an end and, following a failed attempt by Birmingham City to take Sturridge back to the place of his birth, he was snapped up by Leicester City manager Peter Taylor in January.

Although hardly prolific, his form for the Foxes was sound and he netted three times in 12 starts to help ease Leicester's striking woes. He will need to find his form quickly in 2001–02, however, to justify his £350,000 price tag.

APPEARANCES	
Start (sub)	15(12)
Minutes on pitch	1371
GOAL ATTEMPTS	
Goals inside box	4
Goals outside box	0
Minutes per goal scored	343
Goals/shots ratio	13%
SHOOTING	
Shots on target inside box	8
Shots on target outside box	4
Shooting accuracy	39%
PASSING	
Goal assists	4
Key passes	6
Passing accuracy in opp half	58%
DISCIPLINE	
Fouls committed	58
Fouls won	28
Offside	15
Yellow cards	6
Red cards	0
SEE PAGES 125 & 181 FOR FULL STATS	

Davor SUKER • 9
WEST HAM UNITED • BORN: 1.1.68

APPEARANCES	
Start (sub)	7(4)
Minutes on pitch	589
GOAL ATTEMPTS	
Goals inside box	2
Goals outside box	0
Minutes per goal scored	295
Goals/shots ratio	17%
SHOOTING	
Shots on target inside box	6
Shots on target outside box	0
Shooting accuracy	50%
PASSING	
Goal assists	0
Key passes	6
Passing accuracy in opp half	61%
DISCIPLINE	
Fouls committed	13
Fouls won	8
Offside	10
Yellow cards	5
Red cards	0
SEE PAGE 307 FOR FULL STATS	

Legendary Croatian striker Davor Suker spent just one season at Arsenal and, despite missing a penalty during the Gunners' shoot-out defeat in the 2000 UEFA Cup final, he left the club as something of a fans' favourite.

He was hoping for the same at West Ham, the club to which he moved during the summer of 2000.

Two goals in his first four games for the club suggested he would be a great success at Upton Park, but ultimately 'Sukerman' rarely demonstrated the kind of form he has shown for his country throughout his career.

Suker seems certain to leave the club, having earlier in the season stated: "If I play once more [for West Ham], my contract would be automatically renewed and I don't want that."

More worrying for the enigmatic Croat, he faces a possible jail sentence in his homeland for alleged avoidance of compulsory military service.

Perhaps that is why a possible move to Mexico has been mooted.

For more information visit our website:

Neil SULLIVAN • 13
TOTTENHAM HOTSPUR • BORN: 24.2.70

One of Spurs' few successes in a turbulent season, goalkeeper Neil Sullivan deservedly picked up his club's Player of the Season award at the end of the campaign.

Opta's statistics show that the award was certainly justified. Sullivan kept his side in the game on any number of occasions and, were it not for the Scottish international's agility, the club would surely have struggled to pick up results.

Sullivan made an extraordinary 142 saves during the course of the season, preventing the ball from crossing his line more often than any other top-flight 'keeper.

And now with Sol Campbell on his way, Sullivan's saves will be more vital than ever during 2001–02.

He will, however, be hoping to avoid a repeat of his performance against Newcastle in January when, having already had to pick the ball out of his net once, he brought down Kieron Dyer in the box to concede a penalty and earn himself an early shower in the progress.

APPEARANCES	
Start (sub)	35(0)
Minutes on pitch	3108
SHOT STOPPING	
Goals conceded (inside box)	46
Goals conceded (outside box)	5
Minutes per goal conceded	61
Clean sheets	9
Saves (shots inside box)	84
Saves (shots outside box)	58
Saves/shots	74%
DISTRIBUTION	
Long kick %	51%
Throws/short passes %	89%
CATCHING	
Crosses caught	84
Crosses punched	5
Crosses dropped	2
Catch success %	98%
DISCIPLINE	
Yellow cards	1
Red cards	1

SEE PAGE 292 FOR FULL STATS

Mark SUMMERBELL • 22
MIDDLESBROUGH • BORN: 30.10.76

APPEARANCES	
Start (sub)	5(2)
Minutes on pitch	483
GOAL ATTEMPTS	
Goals	1
Shots on target	3
Shooting accuracy	100%
PASSING & CROSSING	
Goal assists	0
Passes in opp half	65
Passing accuracy in opp half	60%
Successful crosses	0
Cross completion	0%
DEFENDING	
Interceptions	3
Clearances	7
Tackles	31
Tackles won %	71%
DISCIPLINE	
Fouls	11
Yellow cards	4
Red cards	0

SEE PAGE 237 FOR FULL STATS

The 2000–01 season was due to be the one which saw Mark Summerbell finally establish himself as a first-team regular at Middlesbrough. Although the previous campaign had seen him make eight starts for Boro, he had failed to show his worth fully, but was determined to ensure his place was made secure in the side.

Sadly, events conspired against the Durham-born midfielder. Having sat out the first game of the season, Summerbell had a good match against Spurs at The Riverside, scoring Boro's goal in the 1–1 draw.

Despite his performance he was dropped to the bench for the following four games and, failing to convince upon his return to the side, he duly found himself back in the reserves, having made a total of just five starts in all.

Worse still, any hopes of forcing his way back into the reckoning were dashed by a shoulder injury picked up in December, which ultimately ruled Summerbell out for the rest of the campaign.

Matthias SVENSSON • 26
CHARLTON ATHLETIC • BORN: 24.9.74

Having flown the nest of Charlton's neighbours Crystal Palace for a bargain £600,000 in January 2000, Matthias Svensson's first full season at Charlton was, on balance, a success. Despite often having to play second fiddle to the likes of Jonatan Johansson and Shaun Bartlett, Svensson managed to notch up 18 starts for the club during the campaign.

To say that Svensson was confident about his first top-flight season would be something of an understatement. The cocky Swede declared: "I have to say the Premiership does not look difficult from the touchline. There are more opportunities for strikers than in the first division because you are given more time on the ball."

He certainly took his chances. His 19% goals-to-shots ratio clearly demonstrated his ample talents and with five Premiership goals – including twice scoring to win the game 1–0 for the Addicks – Svensson looks likely to continue to be a handful for Premiership defenders in 2001–02.

APPEARANCES	
Start (sub)	18(4)
Minutes on pitch	1420
GOAL ATTEMPTS	
Goals inside box	5
Goals outside box	0
Minutes per goal scored	284
Goals/shots ratio	19%
SHOOTING	
Shots on target inside box	11
Shots on target outside box	2
Shooting accuracy	48%
PASSING	
Goal assists	0
Key passes	16
Passing accuracy in opp half	59%
DISCIPLINE	
Fouls committed	51
Fouls won	36
Offside	9
Yellow cards	3
Red cards	0
SEE PAGE 83 FOR FULL STATS	

Gerry TAGGART • 4
LEICESTER CITY • BORN: 18.10.70

APPEARANCES	
Start (sub)	24(0)
Minutes on pitch	2020
GOAL ATTEMPTS	
Goals	2
DEFENDING	
Blocks	24
Shots cleared off line	1
Headed clearances	147
Other clearances	68
Interceptions	11
Last man saving tackles	0
Tackles won	43
Tackles won %	80%
PASSING	
Passing accuracy own half	82%
Passing accuracy opp half	52%
DISCIPLINE	
Fouls	26
Fouls in danger area	10
Yellow cards	10
Red cards	1
SEE PAGE 181 FOR FULL STATS	

Gerry Taggart is a keen amateur chef and is rightly proud of his private library of cookbooks. At the moment the Ulsterman's collection runs to just 24 well-thumbed volumes, but he is apparently adding new recipes all the time.

Italian food is Gerry's favourite dish, so he was understandably delighted when Roberto Mancini arrived at Filbert Street. The Italian legend did not hang around long enough to give Gerry any tips, though, leaving Leicester before Taggart had had a chance to invite him round to dinner.

In Mancini's absence Robbie Savage might have expected an invitation to dine at Taggart Towers, but dinner seems to be off the menu after the two men had a very public falling-out during Leicester's 0–0 draw with Arsenal in 2001, a dispute which ended when Gerry served Robbie up with a slap.

Taggart assured everyone that the two have since made up, which is a good thing as both men are important ingredients in Peter Taylor's recipe for success.

10 Leicester kept 10 of their 11 clean sheets when

Idan TAL • 33
EVERTON • BORN: 13.9.75

Independent Everton website Toffeeweb was moved to hail Israeli international Idan Tal as "Pat Nevin reincarnate" after the man from Petah-Tikvah made an impressive start to his career at Goodison Park.

Sadly, that assessment of the tricky Tal proved to be a little wide of the mark, as he struggled for form all too often.

Tal struck just two goals for Walter Smith's strugglers, but of more concern for a man whom Opta classify as an attacking midfielder was the diminutive winger's failure to set up a single goal for his team-mates.

His pass completion rate, crossing accuracy and dribble success rates were also well below the Premiership average for a player of his position, suggesting that he may not have the necessary qualities needed to prosper at the top level in England.

Having said that, Walter Smith is hardly spoilt for attacking options given Everton's tight budgets, so we can expect to see Tal given another chance to impress in the 2001–02 season.

APPEARANCES	
Start (sub)	12(10)
Minutes on pitch	1120
GOAL ATTEMPTS	
Goals	2
Shots on target	9
Shooting accuracy	36%
Goals/shots ratio	8%
PASSING	
Goal assists	0
Passes in opp half	292
Passing accuracy in opp half	58%
Crosses	72
Crossing accuracy	21%
DRIBBLING	
Dribbles & runs	57
Dribble completion	61%
Corners forced	12
DISCIPLINE	
Fouls	35
Yellow cards	4
Red cards	0

SEE PAGE 139 FOR FULL STATS

Mauricio TARICCO • 3
TOTTENHAM HOTSPUR • BORN: 10.3.73

APPEARANCES	
Start (sub)	2(3)
Minutes on pitch	235
GOAL ATTEMPTS	
Goals	0
PASSING & CROSSING	
Goal assists	0
Passing	115
Passing accuracy	73%
Crosses	7
Crossing accuracy	43%
DEFENDING	
Tackles	9
Tackles won %	78%
Blocks	0
Interceptions	2
Clearances	9
Shots cleared off line	0
DISCIPLINE	
Fouls	1
Yellow cards	1
Red cards	0

SEE PAGE 293 FOR FULL STATS

Tottenham's Argentinean legends Ossie Ardiles and Ricky Villa set high standards at White Hart Lane. And while Mauricio Taricco struggled gamely to emulate the feats of his countrymen, living up to the Legends of the Lane has not been easy.

A combination of poor form and injury limited Taricco to just five early-season appearances for Tottenham in 2000–01 and, with the appointment of a new manager in Glenn Hoddle, his future would seem to be in doubt ahead of 2001–02.

His failure to make the grade at Tottenham is sad, particularly as he was regarded as a bright talent when George Graham brought him to White Hart Lane from Ipswich.

A move away from Spurs would probably be the best thing for Taricco now. He still has many qualities which would make him an asset to a club in the top two divisions of English football, and would also fare well on the continent.

But his Opta stats suggest he was low on confidence in north London.

S

T

Gerry Taggart played the full 90 minutes

Ian TAYLOR • 7
ASTON VILLA • BORN: 4.6.68

Holte End hero Ian Taylor has come a long way since his days as a non-league player at Moor Green. Back then Taylor drove a forklift truck for a living and, at 22, must have given up hope of ever making the grade in professional football.

In 1993, though, Port Vale manager John Rudge took a gamble on the hard-working midfielder, paying Moor Green £15,000 for his services and Taylor has never looked back.

In two years at Vale Park Taylor scored 35 goals from midfield, paving the way for a £1 million move to Sheffield Wednesday. He stayed at Hillsborough for just one season before Brian Little offered him the chance to fulfil a boyhood dream by signing for Villa.

Taylor has been a regular in the Villa team for six seasons now and, while 2000–01 was not one of his most productive campaigns, he remains a big favourite with the Villa fans.

But he blotted his copybook on the last day of the season at Newcastle, when he was sent off for fighting with Gary Speed, although the red was reduced to a yellow on appeal.

APPEARANCES	
Start (sub)	25(4)
Minutes on pitch	2197

GOAL ATTEMPTS	
Goals	4
Shots on target	8
Shooting accuracy	42%

PASSING & CROSSING	
Goal assists	2
Passes in opp half	462
Passing accuracy in opp half	68%
Successful crosses	1
Cross completion	13%

DEFENDING	
Interceptions	10
Clearances	32
Tackles	87
Tackles won %	74%

DISCIPLINE	
Fouls	38
Yellow cards	3
Red cards	1

SEE PAGE 55 FOR FULL STATS

Paul TELFER • 12
COVENTRY CITY • BORN: 21.10.71

APPEARANCES	
Start (sub)	27(4)
Minutes on pitch	2362

GOAL ATTEMPTS	
Goals	0
Shots on target	5
Shooting accuracy	29%

PASSING & CROSSING	
Goal assists	6
Passes in opp half	617
Passing accuracy in opp half	57%
Successful crosses	33
Cross completion	27%

DEFENDING	
Interceptions	4
Clearances	48
Tackles	50
Tackles won %	64%

DISCIPLINE	
Fouls	18
Yellow cards	1
Red cards	0

SEE PAGE 111 FOR FULL STATS

Fitness fanatic Paul Telfer lists cross-country running as his biggest hobby outside of football. The Scottish international likes nothing better after a gruelling game of football than unwinding with a gentle jog through the picturesque Coventry countryside.

All that running has certainly helped improve Telfer's impressive stamina levels and he remains the Sky Blues' most energetic player, bombing forward from midfield at every available opportunity to lay on chances for his struggling team-mates.

Telfer racked up six goal assists in 2000–01 – the highest number at Highfield Road – and was as disappointed as anyone that Coventry failed to last the course in the race for Premiership survival.

Nationwide football is not the reward that the hard-working Scotsman deserves for his efforts, but as a runner he is used to uphill struggles and will do his best to help Coventry reach the winning post as they embark on a marathon tour of the Nationwide League in 2001–02.

For more information visit our website:

John TERRY • 26
CHELSEA • BORN: 7.12.80

It might not be as unsettling as the infamous public school "biscuit game", but John Terry and his chums at Chelsea shocked manager Claudio Ranieri with their post-training warm-down routine in 2000–01.

Terry, who is widely-tipped as a future England international, revealed that he and young pals including Jon Harley and Robert Wolleaston often play "strip penalties".

Terry revealed: "There's no-one about when we do this. It ends up with someone having to stand around naked while everyone else takes a penalty...it's a good laugh."

It is not known whether the likes of little Gianfranco Zola joined in with the fun, or whether Ranieri is planning to integrate the game into his rigorous training routine.

One thing is for sure, though: the Chelsea boss will not be coming down too hard on the young centre-back.

The former youth team starlet was one of the finds of the 2000–01 season, often outshining World Cup-winner Marcel Desailly at the back for the Blues.

APPEARANCES	
Start (sub)	19(3)
Minutes on pitch	1764
GOAL ATTEMPTS	
Goals	1
DEFENDING	
Blocks	29
Shots cleared off line	2
Headed clearances	114
Other clearances	91
Interceptions	11
Last man saving tackles	0
Tackles won	38
Tackles won %	73%
PASSING	
Passing accuracy own half	87%
Passing accuracy opp half	64%
DISCIPLINE	
Fouls	24
Fouls in danger area	5
Yellow cards	3
Red cards	0
SEE PAGE 97 FOR FULL STATS	

Jo TESSEM • 21
SOUTHAMPTON • BORN: 28.2.72

APPEARANCES	
Start (sub)	27(6)
Minutes on pitch	2462
GOAL ATTEMPTS	
Goals	4
Shots on target	21
Shooting accuracy	48%
Goals/shots ratio	9%
PASSING	
Goal assists	2
Passes in opp half	524
Passing accuracy in opp half	64%
Crosses	101
Crossing accuracy	22%
DRIBBLING	
Dribbles & runs	81
Dribble completion	65%
Corners forced	35
DISCIPLINE	
Fouls	48
Yellow cards	1
Red cards	0
SEE PAGE 265 FOR FULL STATS	

Former policeman Jo Tessem patrolled the right side of Southampton's midfield to great effect in 2000–01. The Norwegian international gave several arresting performances for the Saints, scoring four goals and setting up two for his team-mates.

A bargain £600,000 signing from Norwegian club Molde, Tessem has become a big favourite with the fans since his introduction to the first team in November 1999. And whoever takes over in the Southampton hot-seat long-term will be keen to hang on to his services.

While his team-mates also rate Tessem highly, the Scandinavian's fashion sense has not gone down well at The Dell. Former Saints player John Beresford was recently moved to remark: "Tessem's brown jacket should be burnt."

While he may not be the most sartorially-elegant of players, Tessem remains a key member of Saints' line-up. His form for the club has seen him emerge on the Norwegian international scene and he can be delighted with his progress during 2000–01.

Ben THATCHER • 18
TOTTENHAM HOTSPUR • BORN: 30.11.75

Ben Thatcher's move to Tottenham had many people tipping the volatile full-back as a future England international. But things have not gone to plan for the former Wimbledon star and he described 2000–01 as "the worst season of my career."

Thatcher was an automatic first choice for the first couple of months of the season, but was hit by groin and hip injuries which ruled him out for the majority of the campaign.

When he did start Thatcher hardly impressed, although in his defence the player himself claimed that he had often played when not fully fit. His tackle success rate and passing accuracy were very disappointing for a player of his calibre and reputation.

Thatcher came close to a first-team return on a number of occasions; yet after just a handful of reserve games the old injury problems flared up again.

He has now had an operation he hopes will put an end to his injury problems and allow him to fulfil the promise which prompted Tottenham to sign him in the first place.

APPEARANCES	
Start (sub)	10(2)
Minutes on pitch	901
GOAL ATTEMPTS	
Goals	0
PASSING & CROSSING	
Goal assists	0
Passing	291
Passing accuracy	57%
Crosses	27
Crossing accuracy	30%
DEFENDING	
Tackles	36
Tackles won %	61%
Blocks	2
Interceptions	1
Clearances	40
Shots cleared off line	0
DISCIPLINE	
Fouls	21
Yellow cards	2
Red cards	1

SEE PAGE 293 FOR FULL STATS

Alton THELWELL • 31
TOTTENHAM HOTSPUR • BORN: 5.9.80

APPEARANCES	
Start (sub)	13(3)
Minutes on pitch	1200
GOAL ATTEMPTS	
Goals	0
DEFENDING	
Blocks	17
Shots cleared off line	0
Headed clearances	54
Other clearances	39
Interceptions	6
Last man saving tackles	0
Tackles won	31
Tackles won %	67%
PASSING	
Passing accuracy own half	75%
Passing accuracy opp half	54%
DISCIPLINE	
Fouls	16
Fouls in danger area	9
Yellow cards	0
Red cards	0

SEE PAGE 293 FOR FULL STATS

One of Spurs' first experiments with younger players during the campaign, Alton Thelwell made his debut at the heart of the defence against Liverpool at White Hart Lane in November. Considering the Lilywhites won the game 2–1, it seemed very much like a worthwhile try-out.

Team-mate Stephen Carr enthused about Thelwell's performance: "Alton was unbelievable in the centre of defence. Considering he was up against Owen and Fowler, he hardly put a foot wrong all day."

Thelwell duly kept his place in the side for the following seven matches and returned to the fray for a number of games towards the end of the season when injuries began to take their toll on the squad.

Nonetheless, he may face a tough task getting into the first team in 2001–02. Thelwell was recently voted the sixth-most-improved young player in the squad on a Spurs website, though he may have preferred there to have been more than six players in the poll.

3 Alton Thelwell conceded more

Paul THIRLWELL • 21
SUNDERLAND • BORN: 13.2.79

Sunderland midfielder Paul Thirlwell spent the majority of the 2000–01 campaign alternating between the reserves and the substitutes' bench.

He became something of a forgotten man at the Stadium of Light and one may be forgiven for thinking that Peter Reid simply liked to have the Newcastle-born player nearby at all times.

Having started the first three games of the campaign – demonstrating an excellent 82% pass completion rate – he found himself relegated to the sidelines.

He duly spent 19 further games on the bench during the season, but remarkably was introduced just twice.

So close to football he could almost taste it for 17 games, Thirlwell became understandably frustrated – and tales in the news of deep-vein thrombosis were unlikely to have improved his mood. Nonetheless, he seems willing to bide his time and wait for action before resorting to anything as rash as a transfer request.

APPEARANCES	
Start (sub)	3(2)
Minutes on pitch	226
GOAL ATTEMPTS	
Goals	0
Shots on target	0
Shooting accuracy	0%
PASSING & CROSSING	
Goal assists	0
Passes in opp half	44
Passing accuracy in opp half	77%
Successful crosses	2
Cross completion	50%
DEFENDING	
Interceptions	0
Clearances	4
Tackles	7
Tackles won %	29%
DISCIPLINE	
Fouls	3
Yellow cards	1
Red cards	0

SEE PAGE 279 FOR FULL STATS

 Emerson THOME • 36
SUNDERLAND • BORN: 30.3.72

APPEARANCES	
Start (sub)	31(1)
Minutes on pitch	2796
GOAL ATTEMPTS	
Goals	1
DEFENDING	
Blocks	31
Shots cleared off line	0
Headed clearances	205
Other clearances	105
Interceptions	10
Last man saving tackles	0
Tackles won	77
Tackles won %	79%
PASSING	
Passing accuracy own half	78%
Passing accuracy opp half	49%
DISCIPLINE	
Fouls	71
Fouls in danger area	15
Yellow cards	6
Red cards	0

SEE PAGES 97 & 279 FOR FULL STATS

When Emerson Thome lined up for Chelsea for their second game of the season, it seemed unlikely that it would be his last game for the club. But two weeks later he was wearing the red and white of Sunderland, as Peter Reid had snapped up the Brazilian defender for a club record £4.5 million.

Thome went on to become one of the most important members of the side, with an excellent 79% tackle success rate and the second-highest number of clearances of any of the Black Cats.

Nicknamed "The Wall", Thome has one regret about signing for the Mackems. Despite some sterling performances – which have brought him to the attention of Italian giants Juventus – he is yet to play for his country, although he does know why.

"I don't think the Brazilian Federation has a man in the north-east of England", he groaned. Unless anyone at the federation wishes to swap the golden beaches and palm trees of Brazil for "The Bridges" shopping centre in Sunderland, that is unlikely to change.

T

penalties than any other player

David THOMPSON • 7
COVENTRY CITY • BORN: 12.9.77

One thing is for sure about David Thompson – he certainly gets stuck in. Unfortunately for the former Liverpool midfielder, referees were not always willing to let his challenges go unpunished in 2000–01.

It was not the greatest start to his Sky Blues career – he was sent off 71 minutes into his debut against Middlesbrough at Highfield Road for two bookable offences. He duly had to wait until November for anything like a consistent run in the side.

On occasions Thompson – who was once rated in the same bracket as Steven Gerrard - provided flashes of the form which had marked him out as an exciting prospect at Liverpool, but like so many of his Highfield Road team-mates he was unable to put a run of decent good form together.

He finished the 2000–01 season with three goals and three assists but, having accrued an unhealthy total of nine bookings and one red card, he was often suspended when the struggling Sky Blues needed him most in their vain battle for survival.

APPEARANCES	
Start (sub)	22(3)
Minutes on pitch	1866
GOAL ATTEMPTS	
Goals	3
Shots on target	11
Shooting accuracy	24%
Goals/shots ratio	7%
PASSING	
Goal assists	3
Passes in opp half	452
Passing accuracy in opp half	57%
Crosses	212
Crossing accuracy	27%
DRIBBLING	
Dribbles & runs	100
Dribble completion	53%
Corners forced	23
DISCIPLINE	
Fouls	47
Yellow cards	9
Red cards	1
SEE PAGE 111 FOR FULL STATS	

Danny TIATTO • 19
MANCHESTER CITY • BORN: 22.5.73

APPEARANCES	
Start (sub)	31(2)
Minutes on pitch	2734
GOAL ATTEMPTS	
Goals	2
Shots on target	11
Shooting accuracy	37%
PASSING & CROSSING	
Goal assists	3
Passes in opp half	826
Passing accuracy in opp half	57%
Successful crosses	35
Cross completion	25%
DEFENDING	
Interceptions	15
Clearances	61
Tackles	111
Tackles won %	70%
DISCIPLINE	
Fouls	53
Yellow cards	9
Red cards	2
SEE PAGE 209 FOR FULL STATS	

"Tiatto is not a dirty player. Like most Aussies, he's very competitive." Such was the informed opinion on the combatative midfielder Danny Tiatto from his experienced club captain, Alf Inge Haaland.

The statistics, unfortunately, seem to suggest otherwise. During the course of the 2000–01 campaign, only Paulo Wanchope could match Tiatto's tally of nine yellow cards for City.

And it was clear that referee Rob Styles was no fan of the little Australian. Against both Arsenal and Aston Villa, Styles felt that Tiatto had done enough to deserve a red card and he duly became one of only four Premiership players to receive two early showers during the season.

But Tiatto has become a hero at Maine Road as, despite his indiscipline, he won more tackles than any of his colleagues. City fans will be hoping that a season in Division One appeals to the Aussie star, although with Aston Villa, among others, on his trail it seems like a tall order.

For more information visit our website:

Hannu TIHINEN • 28
WEST HAM UNITED • BORN: 1.7.76

With a nickname like "Iron Mountain", Hannu Tihinen appeared to be made for West Ham and certainly did his utmost to convince Harry Redknapp to sign him after an impressive three-month loan spell.

The Viking Stavanger defender is Sami Hyypia's central defensive partner for the Finnish national side and showed similar steel to the Liverpool man during his Upton Park sojourn. Tihinen was particularly impressive in the early stages of his loan spell, helping the happy Hammers dump Manchester United out of the FA Cup in only his third start for the east Londoners.

In the league he made 34 clearing headers and launched himself into 16 tackles, one of which was an excellent last-ditch effort to prevent Oyvind Leonhardsen from pouncing on a rebound in the goalless draw at Upton Park.

While Harry Redknapp was keen to sign the Finn, he could not agree a price for him with Viking before transfer deadline day 2001 and the unhappy centre-back left the Boleyn Ground to the chagrin of the fans.

APPEARANCES	
Start (sub)	5(3)
Minutes on pitch	490
GOAL ATTEMPTS	
Goals	0
DEFENDING	
Blocks	6
Shots cleared off line	1
Headed clearances	34
Other clearances	11
Interceptions	2
Last man saving tackles	1
Tackles won	11
Tackles won %	69%
PASSING	
Passing accuracy own half	75%
Passing accuracy opp half	53%
DISCIPLINE	
Fouls	6
Fouls in danger area	0
Yellow cards	1
Red cards	0

SEE PAGE 307 FOR FULL STATS

Carl TILER • 6
CHARLTON ATHLETIC • BORN: 11.2.70

APPEARANCES	
Start (sub)	7(0)
Minutes on pitch	572
GOAL ATTEMPTS	
Goals	0
DEFENDING	
Blocks	12
Shots cleared off line	0
Headed clearances	50
Other clearances	17
Interceptions	1
Last man saving tackles	0
Tackles won	8
Tackles won %	80%
PASSING	
Passing accuracy own half	76%
Passing accuracy opp half	57%
DISCIPLINE	
Fouls	12
Fouls in danger area	4
Yellow cards	0
Red cards	1

SEE PAGE 83 FOR FULL STATS

Carl Tiler finished the 1999–2000 season in a Charlton side running away with a comfortable Division One title, but ended 2000–01 in the same division, embroiled in a relegation battle with struggling Portsmouth.

The former Nottingham Forest defender has plenty of top-flight experience and might have expected to feature more regularly for Alan Curbishley's men in 2000–01.

When he did play for the Addicks he used his aerial presence to good effect, nodding away the danger on 50 occasions.

But the signing of South African international Mark Fish in November meant that Tiler was destined for only a bit-part role at the south London club. After a short spell on loan at Birmingham, the lanky centre-back became Graham Rix's first signing for Pompey.

He helped the south coast club stutter to safety, following a last-day victory over the team with which he started his career – Barnsley – and will be one of the more experienced performers under Rix in 2001–02.

T

CB | Andy TODD • 19
CHARLTON ATHLETIC • BORN: 21.9.74

The son of Colin, Andy Todd, was bought from Bolton for £1 million, but had already made his reputation as a man not to be messed with. Todd was allegedly involved in an incident which left Phil Brown – the Trotters' assistant manager – requiring medical treatment.

On the pitch for Charlton he went in for 48 tackles and won a respectable 71% of them throughout the 2000–01 season for the newly-promoted side.

Despite his reputation as a hot-headed player, Todd was only booked twice throughout the whole of the 2000–01 season and in a defensive role at The Valley he proved he can comfortably compete with the rest of the top flight.

Although he missed most of the first half of the season, he came on strong after Boxing Day and netted his first Premiership goal for the club in the 2–0 win over Leicester City in April.

Better things are likely to follow as Todd develops his obvious talent.

APPEARANCES	
Start (sub)	19(4)
Minutes on pitch	1748
GOAL ATTEMPTS	
Goals	1
DEFENDING	
Blocks	19
Shots cleared off line	1
Headed clearances	88
Other clearances	39
Interceptions	7
Last man saving tackles	1
Tackles won	34
Tackles won %	71%
PASSING	
Passing accuracy own half	78%
Passing accuracy opp half	68%
DISCIPLINE	
Fouls	22
Fouls in danger area	11
Yellow cards	2
Red cards	0
SEE PAGE 83 FOR FULL STATS	

S | Svetoslav TODOROV • 37
WEST HAM UNITED • BORN: 30.8.78

APPEARANCES	
Start (sub)	2(6)
Minutes on pitch	412
GOAL ATTEMPTS	
Goals inside box	1
Goals outside box	0
Minutes per goal scored	412
Goals/shots ratio	8%
SHOOTING	
Shots on target inside box	7
Shots on target outside box	1
Shooting accuracy	62%
PASSING	
Goal assists	1
Key passes	8
Passing accuracy in opp half	60%
DISCIPLINE	
Fouls committed	14
Fouls won	8
Offside	4
Yellow cards	1
Red cards	0
SEE PAGE 307 FOR FULL STATS	

Bulgarian international Svetoslav Todorov signed for West Ham in January 2001 from Liteks Lovech for £500,000.

Another of Harry Redknapp's bargain buys, Todorov's main role was as support for the club's two chief strikers.

But for the last two games of the campaign Todorov earned his place in the starting line-up and responded with his first league goal for the club against Middlesbrough.

However, this was not before he had succeeded in tapping, bobbling and rolling seven of his attempted efforts at a succession of goalkeepers, including an extraordinary miss when faced with an open goal against Manchester City. To make matters worse, his side were 1–0 down and the miss was in stoppage time.

Nonetheless, Todorov will be hoping to feature strongly in the new manager's plans at Upton Park.

He may want to lose the odd-looking hair band, of course – it seems unlikely to win him any new fans in the East End.

3 David Unsworth scored more

FB Djimi TRAORE • 30
LIVERPOOL • BORN: 1.3.80

Djimi Traore was a target for AC Milan and Lazio before Liverpool swooped to pick him up from French second division side Laval. A French Under-21 international, he is a big talent and played as the Reds' left-back for the first six games of the season.

Although Traore always appeared to be totally committed to the cause, he was prone to occasional lapses and Jamie Carragher eventually took over in that position.

Traore won 67% of his tackles and made 50 clearances, blocks and interceptions, but it appeared he might need a bit longer in the reserves.

In his spare time Traore fancies himself as the next Trevor Nelson. The young R&B fan just loves to hit the decks with his funk platters. "I've got all the equipment I need in my apartment to do a bit of DJ-ing," he revealed. "I've got the records, the turntables, the microphones, the lot."

It seems, sadly, as though we may well be exposed to another *Anfield Rap* in the near future.

APPEARANCES	
Start (sub)	8(0)
Minutes on pitch	695
GOAL ATTEMPTS	
Goals	0
PASSING & CROSSING	
Goal assists	0
Passing	256
Passing accuracy	63%
Crosses	9
Crossing accuracy	11%
DEFENDING	
Tackles	27
Tackles won %	67%
Blocks	7
Interceptions	3
Clearances	40
Shots cleared off line	0
DISCIPLINE	
Fouls	9
Yellow cards	1
Red cards	0
SEE PAGE 195 FOR FULL STATS	

FB David UNSWORTH • 6
EVERTON • BORN: 16.10.73

APPEARANCES	
Start (sub)	17(12)
Minutes on pitch	1775
GOAL ATTEMPTS	
Goals	5
PASSING & CROSSING	
Goal assists	3
Passing	766
Passing accuracy	63%
Crosses	82
Crossing accuracy	29%
DEFENDING	
Tackles	68
Tackles won %	76%
Blocks	6
Interceptions	5
Clearances	150
Shots cleared off line	0
DISCIPLINE	
Fouls	50
Yellow cards	7
Red cards	0
SEE PAGE 139 FOR FULL STATS	

After previously deciding that the Midlands was not for him, David Unsworth went on to forge a defensive partnership with David Weir in 1999–2000. But after the arrival of Gary Naysmith from Hearts the powerful, tough-tackling defender saw his 2000–01 season reduced to bit-part appearances.

Michael Ball took on Unsworth's role in the centre of defence and the former Hammer was shifted to left-back, where he jockeyed with Naysmith for a starting berth.

With numerous injuries to the squad, Unsworth challenged as the club's top scorer in 2000–01 with a total of five goals, three hammered home from the spot. But after missing from 12 yards in the last game of the season against Sunderland, he again had to watch as Ball took over his role, this time as penalty-taker, to restore Everton's lead.

Unsworth, who also made 150 clearances and won 76% of his tackles, was reported to be seeking a regular first-team place elsewhere after missing chunks of the 2000–01 campaign.

penalties than any other defender

Matthew UPSON • 20
ARSENAL • BORN: 18.4.79

If there is one thing that Matthew Upson has learned since signing for Arsenal in 1997, it is to be patient.

Upson has bided his time in the reserves, gaining only occasional first-team experience, while in December 1999 the former Luton centre-back suffered a cruciate ligament injury which kept him out of the game for nearly a year.

He made a welcome comeback to the Premiership in November 2000, coming on as a substitute away to Everton, but was then sent on loan to Nottingham Forest.

The unfortunate youngster jarred his back on his first appearance and was forced to cut short his spell, not playing again in the league until March 2001, when he was loaned to Division One strugglers Crystal Palace.

A second taste of action in the 3–2 defeat to Southampton summed up a frustrating season for Upson, but he will be happy to have at least featured after his injury.

SEE PAGE 41 FOR FULL STATS

Simo VALAKARI • 28
DERBY COUNTY • BORN: 28.4.73

Midfielder Simo Valakari struggled somewhat in his first Premiership season following his free transfer from Motherwell.

Indeed, Derby failed to win a single Premiership match when Valakari played, coming closest when he scored the second to go 2–0 up at home to Charlton, only for the Londoners to come back and earn a 2–2 draw.

Having attempted 444 passes with a completion rate of 77%, Valakari can look back on a reasonable campaign. But the transition from the Scottish to the English Premiership proved tricky on occasions.

Following a poor performance in the Rams' 4–0 capitulation against Liverpool at Pride Park in November, the Finn featured in only a further four Premiership matches.

Valakari did not have to cope with such selection woes at international level and managed three starts for Finland, including an appearance in the 0–0 draw with England in Helsinki alongside fellow-Premiership players Sami Hyypia, Jari Litmanen and Jonatan Johansson.

Struggle: Simo Valakari

APPEARANCES	
Start (sub)	9(2)
Minutes on pitch	851
GOAL ATTEMPTS	
Goals	1
Shots on target	2
Shooting accuracy	40%
PASSING & CROSSING	
Goal assists	1
Passes in opp half	248
Passing accuracy in opp half	74%
Successful crosses	1
Cross completion	14%
DEFENDING	
Interceptions	1
Clearances	10
Tackles	30
Tackles won%	77%
DISCIPLINE	
Fouls	21
Yellow cards	3
Red cards	0
SEE PAGE 125 FOR FULL STATS	

For more information visit our website:

Raimond VAN DER GOUW • 17
MANCHESTER UNITED • BORN: 24.3.63

Dutch goalkeeper Raimond van der Gouw made only 10 appearances for Manchester United in the 2000–01 season, playing second fiddle to the enigmatic Frenchman Fabien Barthez.

With Barthez in dominant form, van der Gouw seemed reasonably happy earning his wage warming the Red Devils' bench. Quite how many more seasons he has left in him at the top level remains to be seen, but the 2001–02 season will probably be his last at Old Trafford.

He made 19 catches and ended the campaign with a 100% cross claimed rate, but he conceded 10 goals in 10 games, keeping only one clean sheet in the process. He also committed an embarrassing howler against Chelsea at Old Trafford.

But the man they call 'The Model' at Old Trafford, thanks to his rugged good looks, remains a popular figure in the United dressing-room and, although his days may be numbered at the Theatre of Dreams, he is always likely to be made welcome at the club.

APPEARANCES	
Start (sub)	5(5)
Minutes on pitch	529
SHOT STOPPING	
Goals conceded (inside box)	6
Goals conceded (outside box)	4
Minutes per goal conceded	53
Clean sheets	1
Saves (shots inside box)	5
Saves (shots outside box)	8
Saves/shots	57%
DISTRIBUTION	
Long kick %	60%
Throws/short passes %	91%
CATCHING	
Crosses caught	19
Crosses punched	5
Crosses dropped	0
Catch success %	100%
DISCIPLINE	
Yellow cards	0
Red cards	0

SEE PAGE 222 FOR FULL STATS

Stanislav VARGA • 32
SUNDERLAND • BORN: 8.10.72

APPEARANCES	
Start (sub)	9(3)
Minutes on pitch	767
GOAL ATTEMPTS	
Goals	1
DEFENDING	
Blocks	9
Shots cleared off line	0
Headed clearances	53
Other clearances	20
Interceptions	7
Last man saving tackles	2
Tackles won	36
Tackles won %	86%
PASSING	
Passing accuracy own half	83%
Passing accuracy opp half	55%
DISCIPLINE	
Fouls	20
Fouls in danger area	8
Yellow cards	2
Red cards	1

SEE PAGE 279 FOR FULL STATS

When Stanislav Varga arrived at the Stadium of Light in the summer of 2000, it was hardly the big-name signing Sunderland supporters were dreaming of.

But the shaggy-haired defender impressed Black Cats supporters with a phenomenal debut performance against Arsenal when he almost single-handedly kept the Gunners at bay in a 1–0 victory.

However, events went drastically wrong in just the second game of 2000–01 when Varga sustained a potentially career-threatening calf injury at Manchester City. From that point on he only featured sporadically, managing just 767 minutes of action.

In the games he did play the Slovakian captain was a useful member of Peter Reid's team, using his height and aerial ability to make 53 headed clearances in double-quick time.

With a goal at West Ham, Varga also earned himself the honour of being the first player to score in front of Sven-Göran Eriksson after he took the England job.

U
V

Darius VASSELL • 22
ASTON VILLA • BORN: 13.6.80

Youngster Darius Vassell enjoyed a breakthrough season during 2000–01. But this came after a disappointing start to the campaign, when the pacy starlet failed to convince in early substitute appearances and seldom looked like scoring.

However, a resurgent second half of the campaign saw Vassell showing the sort of form manager John Gregory always believed he was capable of.

Starting up front for Villa in place of the disappointing Juan Pablo Angel, Vassell was the most-used substitute in the Premiership – alongside Newcastle's Lomana Tresor Lua Lua – and scored four times in the league.

He rose from the bench to put Villa into the lead in their 3–3 draw at Charlton, netted a brace at Valley Parade and started the Villa revival in their 3–2 win against local rivals Coventry City.

Now a bright England Under-21 prospect, Vassell ended the 2000–01 campaign with a goals-to-shots ratio of 20%, his four goals coming from just 20 efforts.

APPEARANCES	
Start (sub)	5(18)
Minutes on pitch	793
GOAL ATTEMPTS	
Goals inside box	4
Goals outside box	0
Minutes per goal scored	198
Goals/shots ratio	20%
SHOOTING	
Shots on target inside box	8
Shots on target outside box	0
Shooting accuracy	40%
PASSING	
Goal assists	1
Key passes	7
Passing accuracy in opp half	62%
DISCIPLINE	
Fouls committed	31
Fouls won	17
Offside	15
Yellow cards	2
Red cards	0
SEE PAGE 55 FOR FULL STATS	

Ramon VEGA • 34
TOTTENHAM HOTSPUR • BORN: 14.6.71

APPEARANCES	
Start (sub)	8(2)
Minutes on pitch	761
GOAL ATTEMPTS	
Goals	0
DEFENDING	
Blocks	9
Shots cleared off line	0
Headed clearances	67
Other clearances	20
Interceptions	7
Last man saving tackles	0
Tackles won	18
Tackles won %	78%
PASSING	
Passing accuracy own half	80%
Passing accuracy opp half	52%
DISCIPLINE	
Fouls	27
Fouls in danger area	5
Yellow cards	3
Red cards	0
SEE PAGE 293 FOR FULL STATS	

Ramon Vega experienced the full spectrum of emotions in an eventful 2000–01 season. He failed to get a first-team place ahead of Sol Campbell and Chris Perry, enjoying his longest spell in the side when the England defender was out injured in September and October.

The lowest point came during a Worthington Cup tie with Birmingham at White Hart Lane. The home fans booed Vega during the 3–1 defeat, a gesture which was arguably the deciding factor in his quitting Spurs for a loan move to Celtic in mid-December.

Vega made an immediate impact on his Celtic debut, scoring twice in the Bhoys' 6–0 win over Aberdeen. Martin O'Neill's side went on to concede only eight league goals in Vega's 18 matches.

The Swiss international finished the season with winners' medals in the SPL, Tennents Scottish Cup and CIS Cup.

Strangely, given his treatment by the Spurs fans, Vega has expressed a desire to return to White Hart Lane, even though Celtic have offered him the chance of a permanent move.

I Paolo Vernazza fired in just one

CB

Mark VENUS • 6
IPSWICH TOWN • BORN: 6.4.67

Mark Venus netted the Premiership's first goal of the 2000–01 campaign, nine minutes into Ipswich's 3–1 defeat at Spurs.

All three of the former Wolves man's goals came from his left foot, but Venus also caught the eye with his excellent defensive performances in George Burley's back four, an experienced head alongside Titus Bramble.

Venus completed 73% of the 1,064 passes he laid off, while his expertise at dead-ball situations meant that he was Ipswich's key man at set-pieces; hence the high number of crosses he swung into the penalty area.

More than 100 of the 181 clearances he made were with his head and he attempted 53 challenges, although his tackle success rate of 60% was 14 percentage points below the Premiership average for a defender.

Venus joined Ipswich in the summer of 1997 and is a fine example of George Burley's ability to spot talented players and help them realise their potential while saving the club a small fortune in the transfer market.

APPEARANCES	
Start (sub)	23(2)
Minutes on pitch	2060

GOAL ATTEMPTS	
Goals	3

DEFENDING	
Blocks	16
Shots cleared off line	0
Headed clearances	109
Other clearances	72
Interceptions	6
Last man saving tackles	1
Tackles won	32
Tackles won %	60%

PASSING	
Passing accuracy own half	85%
Passing accuracy opp half	63%

DISCIPLINE	
Fouls	30
Fouls in danger area	8
Yellow cards	4
Red cards	0

SEE PAGE 153 FOR FULL STATS

 M

Paolo VERNAZZA • 30
ARSENAL • BORN: 1.11.79

The fact that Paolo Vernazza scored with his only shot of the 2000–01 Premiership season was not enough to persuade Arsenal boss Arsène Wenger to keep him at Highbury.

The exotically-named midfielder from Islington was sold to Watford for a fee of £300,000 in December, ending an association with the Gunners formed as a schoolboy.

He went on to play 20 games in Division One, three more as substitute, scoring against Sheffield Wednesday and Gillingham along the way. His sole Premiership strike came in September, when he stepped off the bench to net against Coventry.

Apart from that match, Vernazza came on as substitute at Ipswich, started a Worthington Cup match against the same team and made a fleeting appearance in the Champions League clash with Shakhtar Donetsk.

As an Arsenal fan, leaving the Gunners must have been hard for Vernazza. Everyone at Highbury will wish him well at Watford.

SEE PAGE 41 FOR FULL STATS

V

Experienced: Mark Venus

shot in the Premiership and scored

CB — Steve VICKERS • 4
MIDDLESBROUGH • BORN: 13.10.67

Veteran Steve Vickers, Middlesbrough's "Mr Dependable", is not ready to end his playing days just yet and, after making a commendable 246 clearances and winning 42 of the 55 tackles he attempted, who can argue with the no-nonsense central defender?

Although playing in Boro's defence, Vickers recorded one of the club's highest passing accuracy rates of 77%, bettered only by midfielder Paul Okon.

The never-say-die attitude of the Teessiders' longest-serving player makes him a valuable man to have around when the chips are down, highlighted by the 292 clearances, blocks and interceptions he made throughout the 2000–01 season.

The grizzled stopper set an excellent example to the younger players in Terry Venables' squad by posting an admirable record of just two yellow cards all season.

It remains to be seen whether a new regime at The Riverside will allow him further chances at the highest level, but he has served Middlesbrough well down the years.

APPEARANCES	
Start (sub)	29(1)
Minutes on pitch	2513

GOAL ATTEMPTS	
Goals	0

DEFENDING	
Blocks	34
Shots cleared off line	0
Headed clearances	161
Other clearances	85
Interceptions	12
Last man saving tackles	0
Tackles won	42
Tackles won %	76%

PASSING	
Passing accuracy own half	85%
Passing accuracy opp half	57%

DISCIPLINE	
Fouls	38
Fouls in danger area	15
Yellow cards	2
Red cards	0

SEE PAGE 237 FOR FULL STATS

S — Mark VIDUKA • 9
LEEDS UNITED • BORN: 9.10.75

APPEARANCES	
Start (sub)	34(0)
Minutes on pitch	3014

GOAL ATTEMPTS	
Goals inside box	16
Goals outside box	1
Minutes per goal scored	177
Goals/shots ratio	27%

SHOOTING	
Shots on target inside box	29
Shots on target outside box	2
Shooting accuracy	48%

PASSING	
Goal assists	4
Key passes	50
Passing accuracy in opp half	61%

DISCIPLINE	
Fouls committed	65
Fouls won	68
Offside	58
Yellow cards	5
Red cards	0

SEE PAGE 167 FOR FULL STATS

Stocky Aussie Mark Viduka started his Premiership career in stunning style after the move south from the more "comfortable" challenges of the Scottish Premier League.

Proving that he takes his chances in front of goal, Viduka bagged four goals from just four shots on target in the compelling 4–3 thriller at home to Liverpool.

The "V-Bomber" scored six headed goals, more than any other Premiership player in the 2000–01 season – a statistic which underlines his much-admired aerial prowess.

His poaching skills, massive power and surprisingly delicate touch have alerted the likes of AC Milan and Real Madrid and, although the Leeds chairman Peter Ridsdale has declared that his top players are not for sale, Viduka himself was quoted as saying: "All players want to progress, and to go to the best team in the world would be good for me."

David O'Leary would not be happy at losing his star striker to anyone, though – and Viduka is likely to start the 2001–02 season at Elland Road.

Patrick VIEIRA • 4
ARSENAL • BORN: 23.6.76

Booked nine times and sent off once in the 1999–2000 Premiership campaign, Patrick Vieira endured a turbulent start to the 2000–01 season. Sent off on the opening day, Vieira was dismissed for the second time just two days later during Arsenal's 2–0 victory over Liverpool.

Those dismissals prompted the Frenchman to declare that he had had enough of English football and sparked interest from the likes of Barcelona and Juventus.

But to his credit Vieira recovered, improving his behaviour and inspiring Arsenal on many occasions with his surging runs from midfield and tough tackling. His fine form was not enough to impress the PFA, but did win him the Carling Player of the Year award.

After their elimination from the Champions League, Vieira was moved to criticise Arsenal for selling Emmanuel Petit and Marc Overmars and was once again linked with a move. Not surprisingly, that speculation led to talk of season ticket-holders threatening to burn their tickets if Arsenal were ever to sell him.

APPEARANCES	
Start (sub)	28(2)
Minutes on pitch	2542

GOAL ATTEMPTS	
Goals	5
Shots on target	11
Shooting accuracy	41%

PASSING & CROSSING	
Goal assists	4
Passes in opp half	1084
Passing accuracy in opp half	79%
Successful crosses	3
Cross completion	27%

DEFENDING	
Interceptions	9
Clearances	68
Tackles	122
Tackles won %	62%

DISCIPLINE	
Fouls	67
Yellow cards	5
Red cards	2

SEE PAGE 41 FOR FULL STATS

Speculation: Patrick Vieira

Gregory VIGNAL • 27
LIVERPOOL • BORN: 19.7.81

Promising young defender Gregory Vignal was snapped up from Montpellier by Gérard Houllier for just £500,000 in September 2000.

A key member of France's all-conquering Under-18 squad, Vignal was expected to take time to settle but is ahead of schedule.

Making his Reds debut at 19, the stylish French full-back did not manage to secure a regular first-team place in Liverpool's remarkable 2000–01 season, thanks largely to the excellent form of Jamie Carragher on the left side of defence; but although he played only four full league games in the 2000–01 Premiership season, Vignal still notched up a commendable 76% tackle success rate.

His workrate when called upon was excellent and he impressed the Liverpool management team so much that Vignal now seems to have moved above Christian Ziege in the Anfield pecking-order.

Big things are expected of Vignal and, while Carragher remains first choice, the ever-improving Frenchman will provide a stiff challenge for his place in 2001-02.

APPEARANCES	
Start (sub)	4(2)
Minutes on pitch	392

GOAL ATTEMPTS	
Goals	0

PASSING & CROSSING	
Goal assists	0
Passing	178
Passing accuracy	62%
Crosses	8
Crossing accuracy	0%

DEFENDING	
Tackles	21
Tackles won %	76%
Blocks	1
Interceptions	6
Clearances	23
Shots cleared off line	0

DISCIPLINE	
Fouls	10
Yellow cards	2
Red cards	0

SEE PAGE 195 FOR FULL STATS

Nelson VIVAS • 23
ARSENAL • BORN: 18.10.69

APPEARANCES	
Start (sub)	3(9)
Minutes on pitch	418

GOAL ATTEMPTS	
Goals	0
Shots on target	1
Shooting accuracy	50%

PASSING & CROSSING	
Goal assists	1
Passes in opp half	124
Passing accuracy in opp half	73%
Successful crosses	7
Cross completion	33%

DEFENDING	
Interceptions	4
Clearances	8
Tackles	15
Tackles won %	80%

DISCIPLINE	
Fouls	5
Yellow cards	0
Red cards	0

SEE PAGE 41 FOR FULL STATS

After the little Argentinean's tough 1999–2000 season, Opta predicted that it would not be any easier for him to break into the Arsenal side in the 2000–01 Premiership campaign; and, despite spending almost twice as much time on the pitch, Nelson Vivas managed only three starts.

Deputising where necessary, sometimes on the right side of defence but often in midfield, he was on the losing side only twice. But he had a great chance to avert one of these defeats against Charlton from the penalty spot; he missed and his team lost the game.

Making more successful passes in the opposition half than his own, Vivas found his target with 80% of his distribution. But having to compete with the sublime skills of Patrick Vieira and the tenacious tackling of Gilles Grimandi, this statistic will not hold much weight going into season 2001-02.

Vivas could once again be making himself comfortable on the bench, although Paris Saint Germain are rumoured to be ready to rescue him from the reserves.

82% Ian Walker's saves-to-shots

Ian WALKER • 1
TOTTENHAM HOTSPUR • BORN: 31.10.71

Ian Walker found himself playing second fiddle to Neil Sullivan for the majority of the 2000–01 season, so it was a frustrating nine months for the Watford-born goalkeeper. Despite not missing a single second of Premiership action in 1999–2000, Walker's misery began when Kevin Keegan overlooked him for England's Euro 2000 squad.

The trained martial arts expert did not take the chop too well and upon his return for pre-season, the club's longest-serving player found himself frozen out of the first-team picture. His only three starts came when Sullivan was unavailable for selection.

Nevertheless, Walker could boast a saves-to-shots ratio eight percentage points better than his rival.

He once posed as a centrefold for a women's magazine and said: "It was just a laugh, but then people start seeing you in that light and suddenly it's all a bit serious."

Walker may soon have to make serious decisions about his footballing future if he is unable to regain his place.

APPEARANCES	
Start (sub)	3(1)
Minutes on pitch	312
SHOT STOPPING	
Goals conceded (inside box)	2
Goals conceded (outside box)	1
Minutes per goal conceded	104
Clean sheets	2
Saves (shots inside box)	10
Saves (shots outside box)	4
Saves/shots	82%
DISTRIBUTION	
Long kick %	51%
Throws/short passes %	75%
CATCHING	
Crosses caught	10
Crosses punched	1
Crosses dropped	0
Catch success %	100%
DISCIPLINE	
Yellow cards	0
Red cards	0

SEE PAGE 292 FOR FULL STATS

Ronnie WALLWORK • 22
MANCHESTER UNITED • BORN: 10.9.77

APPEARANCES	
Start (sub)	4(8)
Minutes on pitch	557
GOAL ATTEMPTS	
Goals	0
Shots on target	0
Shooting accuracy	0%
PASSING & CROSSING	
Goal assists	0
Passes in opp half	112
Passing accuracy in opp half	71%
Successful crosses	0
Cross completion	0%
DEFENDING	
Interceptions	2
Clearances	25
Tackles	15
Tackles won %	73%
DISCIPLINE	
Fouls	1
Yellow cards	0
Red cards	0

SEE PAGE 223 FOR FULL STATS

Former Old Trafford trainee Ronnie Wallwork collected his first Premiership winner's medal after making more than 10 appearances for the champions during 2000–01.

And this represents a precious piece of silverware for a player who is fortunate to be plying his trade in football at all after a lifetime playing ban was rescinded following an incident in Belgium while he was on loan at Royal Antwerp.

Back in Manchester, he was often pitched into a midfield role rather than his familiar central defensive berth. But Wallwork proved versatile enough to win many plaudits for his efforts and completed 90% of his penetrative dribbles and runs and found a fellow-Red Devil with 82% of his distribution.

A self-confessed United fan, he will be hoping to gain further opportunities to prove his potential in 2001–02 and become a first-team regular rather than look on from the fringes. But this may prove a tall order with the likes of Roy Keane and Paul Scholes ruling the middle of the park and equally tough competition at the back.

V

W

ratio was higher than Neil Sullivan's

G — Gary WALSH • 1
BRADFORD CITY • BORN: 21.3.68

After a brief loan spell with Middlesbrough, Gary Walsh returned to Bradford to take over as the Bantams' number one after Matt Clarke had a bust-up with City boss Jim Jefferies in December.

Many questioned Jefferies' decision to reinstate Walsh and the doubters' fears seemed to be confirmed after an amazing howler against former club Manchester United.

The former Red Devils star completely missed a routine clearance, leaving Teddy Sheringham to fire into an empty net and break the deadlock after 72 minutes. But this incident was a rare mistake by the veteran goalkeeper, who made a number of impressive displays despite the Bantams' relegation.

Walsh was constantly under pressure and made just under a century of saves. But after having to deal with 138 shots during the course of the campaign, he was never going to be short of things to do.

With Matt Clarke unlikely to return to the first team, Walsh will hope to retain the number one jersey in 2001–02.

APPEARANCES	
Start (sub)	22(0)
Minutes on pitch	1972

SHOT STOPPING	
Goals conceded (inside box)	33
Goals conceded (outside box)	6
Minutes per goal conceded	51
Clean sheets	3
Saves (shots inside box)	67
Saves (shots outside box)	32
Saves/shots	72%

DISTRIBUTION	
Long kick %	43%
Throws/short passes %	73%

CATCHING	
Crosses caught	35
Crosses punched	9
Crosses dropped	3
Catch success %	92%

DISCIPLINE	
Yellow cards	2
Red cards	0

SEE PAGES 68 & 236 FOR FULL STATS

CB — Steve WALSH • 5
LEICESTER CITY • BORN: 3.11.64

Leicester's first game of the campaign against Aston Villa was also veteran defender Steve Walsh's last for the Foxes. Walsh managed just a single clearance as a substitute before departing the club he had served for 14 years.

The move followed Peter Taylor's decision that Walsh would be considered for first-team action only when injuries hit the club – and clearly hurt by this, Walsh launched a stinging attack on his former boss as the season drew to a close.

The Leicester hero declared that Taylor had "systematically destroyed" the side put together by Martin O'Neill: comments that angered the Foxes chief. "I was disappointed and hurt at what Steve said," said Taylor, before adding, somewhat ominously: "I will find him and then have my say on matters to his face."

Despite the Taylor rumpus, Walsh remains a legend at Filbert Street. Should he decide to move into coaching or management, a post at Leicester would be most attractive.

SEE PAGE 181 FOR FULL STATS

Howler: Gary Walsh

Paulo WANCHOPE • 23
MANCHESTER CITY • BORN: 31.7.76

When he scored a stunning hat-trick on his Manchester City home debut against Sunderland, Paulo Wanchope looked worth every penny of the £3.65 million transfer fee that had taken him to Maine Road from West Ham.

But after that excellent start, Wanchope's 2000–01 season deteriorated into a series of frustrating and controversial events, with the only respite coming from the occasional goal or glimpse of magic.

Matters came to a head in January when the lanky Costa Rican was substituted in the FA Cup clash against Coventry. His visible anger at being replaced did not go down well with boss Joe Royle, who sentenced him to a stay of almost three months on the sidelines.

On his return, Wanchope lent some much-needed flair to City's front line – scoring a typically stylish goal in a 2–1 win at Leicester – but it was not nearly enough to save the club from relegation.

Whether Wanchope fits into the plans of new manager Kevin Keegan remains to be seen.

APPEARANCES	
Start (sub)	25(2)
Minutes on pitch	2204
GOAL ATTEMPTS	
Goals inside box	8
Goals outside box	1
Minutes per goal scored	245
Goals/shots ratio	14%
SHOOTING	
Shots on target inside box	26
Shots on target outside box	9
Shooting accuracy	55%
PASSING	
Goal assists	3
Key passes	18
Passing accuracy in opp half	61%
DISCIPLINE	
Fouls committed	85
Fouls won	56
Offside	43
Yellow cards	9
Red cards	0

SEE PAGE 209 FOR FULL STATS

 ## Ashley WARD • 9
BRADFORD CITY • BORN: 24.11.70

APPEARANCES	
Start (sub)	24(9)
Minutes on pitch	2274
GOAL ATTEMPTS	
Goals inside box	4
Goals outside box	0
Minutes per goal scored	569
Goals/shots ratio	7%
SHOOTING	
Shots on target inside box	20
Shots on target outside box	10
Shooting accuracy	54%
PASSING	
Goal assists	4
Key passes	28
Passing accuracy in opp half	64%
DISCIPLINE	
Fouls committed	95
Fouls won	98
Offside	30
Yellow cards	9
Red cards	0

SEE PAGE 69 FOR FULL STATS

Valley Parade holds bad memories for Ashley Ward, as it is the ground where he broke his leg during his one and only appearance for first club Manchester City.

Ten years on, Ward was back in West Yorkshire after Bantams boss Chris Hutchings spent £1.5 million on the journeyman striker in the hope he could provide the firepower to help Bradford survive.

But there were more unhappy times to come for Ward. He struggled to find a place in the first team initially and then had to suffer relegation for the fourth time in his career.

Despite featuring in 33 of Bradford's Premiership games, it was not until March that he managed to hit his first goal, against former side Manchester City. Three more followed but it was all much too little, too late for the Bantams.

The Mancunian forward's robust style also proved too much for most Premiership referees. He committed 95 fouls and earned nine cautions during the course of the 2000–01 campaign.

W

Steve WATSON • 2
EVERTON • BORN: 1.4.74

Having struggled to hold down a first-team place at Aston Villa in 1999–2000, Steve Watson enjoyed a more satisfactory season in 2000–01 after moving to Everton for a fee of £2.5 million.

Only Scotsman David Weir accumulated more minutes of Premiership action than Watson, whose contributions were significant in helping the Toffees avoid the drop.

A tally of 157 clearances was the third-highest at the club, while he was equally effective on his forays upfield from the right wing-back position. The former Newcastle apprentice chalked up 107 successful dribbles – the fifth-highest total by an Englishman in the Premiership.

Along with fellow-Geordie Paul Gascoigne, Watson was reported to have gatecrashed a picturesque wedding in a Cheshire hotel during the autumn. Evertonians will be hoping that Watson remains married to the club long after his honeymoon period is over. A divorce would leave Walter Smith with a major void to fill in the Goodison Park defence.

APPEARANCES	
Start (sub)	34(0)
Minutes on pitch	3004

GOAL ATTEMPTS	
Goals	0

PASSING & CROSSING	
Goal assists	3
Passing	1192
Passing accuracy	66%
Crosses	97
Crossing accuracy	25%

DEFENDING	
Tackles	78
Tackles won %	71%
Blocks	38
Interceptions	5
Clearances	157
Shots cleared off line	1

DISCIPLINE	
Fouls	50
Yellow cards	5
Red cards	0

SEE PAGE 139 FOR FULL STATS

George WEAH • 22
MANCHESTER CITY • BORN: 1.10.66

APPEARANCES	
Start (sub)	5(2)
Minutes on pitch	474

GOAL ATTEMPTS	
Goals inside box	1
Goals outside box	0
Minutes per goal scored	474
Goals/shots ratio	9%

SHOOTING	
Shots on target inside box	7
Shots on target outside box	0
Shooting accuracy	64%

PASSING	
Goal assists	1
Key passes	5
Passing accuracy in opp half	66%

DISCIPLINE	
Fouls committed	9
Fouls won	3
Offside	5
Yellow cards	0
Red cards	0

SEE PAGE 209 FOR FULL STATS

Manchester City fans thought they had seen everything over the last few years. But when the club signed former World Player of the Year George Weah in the summer of 2000, few could resist a sharp bout of eyebrow-raising.

By snapping up the ex-AC Milan man from Chelsea, City seemed to be indicating that they were finally prepared to fulfil their potential in the top flight of English football, but things did not go to plan.

Weah played a paltry 474 minutes of football in the Premiership, scoring just one goal against Liverpool in a 3–2 defeat. He left the club as quickly as he had arrived, claiming that Joe Royle had treated him with little respect and that he had not been given a fair chance to impress. Weah's fleeting spell at Manchester City epitomised the club's dismal return to the top flight following two successive promotion campaigns.

At least the Liberian now knows which colour the Maine Road men play in, after he was rumoured to have said on his arrival in Manchester, "I thought you wore red!"

64% Nicky Weaver's saves-to-shots ratio was

Nicky WEAVER • 1
MANCHESTER CITY • BORN: 2.3.79

Nicky Weaver faced a real baptism of fire during 2000–01 – his debut season in the Premiership – and will probably want to forget the bulk of the campaign.

The former Mansfield goalkeeper made a total of 96 saves – the fourth-highest tally of any English custodian in the Premiership, but despite some good displays, he was all too often found wanting at the highest level.

The England Under-21 international committed a series of high-profile blunders which eventually saw him dropped from the starting line-up by Joe Royle.

Weaver's replacement Carlo Nash went on to put in some excellent performance, casting doubts over Weaver's long-term future at the club.

However, Weaver is still considered an excellent prospect. If he shows the strength of character to come back from the disappointments of the 2000–01 season, he could yet realise his dream of playing for the national team – although that prospect looks a long way off at the moment.

APPEARANCES	
Start (sub)	31(0)
Minutes on pitch	2790
SHOT STOPPING	
Goals conceded (inside box)	43
Goals conceded (outside box)	11
Minutes per goal conceded	52
Clean sheets	6
Saves (shots inside box)	53
Saves (shots outside box)	43
Saves/shots	64%
DISTRIBUTION	
Long kick %	49%
Throws/short passes %	80%
CATCHING	
Crosses caught	34
Crosses punched	21
Crosses dropped	4
Catch success %	89%
DISCIPLINE	
Yellow cards	2
Red cards	0
SEE PAGE 208 FOR FULL STATS	

Baptism of fire: Nicky Weaver

W

lower than any other regular goalkeeper

CB — David WEIR • 5
EVERTON • BORN: 10.5.70

Scottish defender David Weir was one of the few players to feature regularly for Everton in the 2000–01 season because of the crippling injury problems at Goodison Park.

Luckily, the former Hearts man was in solid form throughout the campaign, making a highly-impressive total of 363 defensive clearances – the third-highest by a British defender in the Premiership.

Arguably one of Walter Smith's shrewdest-ever signings at just £250,000, Weir also turned in some steady performances at international level to further enhance his standing north of the border. And he is likely to remain a key figure in his country's quest to reach the 2002 World Cup Finals in Japan and South Korea.

After starting his career in the USA on a soccer scholarship and moving to England after spending six seasons in the SPL, Weir clearly relishes a challenge.

That is probably just as well, with Everton still struggling to recapture their glory years of the mid-'80s.

APPEARANCES	
Start (sub)	37(0)
Minutes on pitch	3250
GOAL ATTEMPTS	
Goals	1
DEFENDING	
Blocks	36
Shots cleared off line	1
Headed clearances	243
Other clearances	120
Interceptions	9
Last man saving tackles	2
Tackles won	63
Tackles won %	73%
PASSING	
Passing accuracy own half	75%
Passing accuracy opp half	57%
DISCIPLINE	
Fouls	36
Fouls in danger area	10
Yellow cards	4
Red cards	0
SEE PAGE 139 FOR FULL STATS	

CB — Taribo WEST • 34
DERBY COUNTY • BORN: 26.3.74

APPEARANCES	
Start (sub)	18(0)
Minutes on pitch	1620
GOAL ATTEMPTS	
Goals	0
DEFENDING	
Blocks	34
Shots cleared off line	1
Headed clearances	70
Other clearances	61
Interceptions	19
Last man saving tackles	0
Tackles won	45
Tackles won %	74%
PASSING	
Passing accuracy own half	73%
Passing accuracy opp half	56%
DISCIPLINE	
Fouls	28
Fouls in danger area	8
Yellow cards	3
Red cards	0
SEE PAGE 125 FOR FULL STATS	

Derby's successful fight for Premiership survival was achieved in no small part thanks to the excellent contribution made by Taribo West in his spell at the club.

The Nigerian international arrived at Pride Park claiming to have come on a mission from God to save the Rams' top-flight status.

There certainly seemed to be some kind of divine intervention going on when the former Inter Milan star helped Jim Smith's side keep nine clean sheets in his first 13 games at the club. A total of 19 interceptions – the highest at the club – illustrated the kind of shrewd defending West bought to a previously shaky back-line.

But his regular sojourns to represent his country upset boss Smith, who felt the situation disrupted valuable training time with the rest of the Derby defence.

That was a major reason behind Smith's decision to release West at the end of 2000–01, but the former Auxerre star should have had no problems getting fixed up with a new club.

For more information visit our website:

G Sander WESTERVELD • 1
LIVERPOOL • BORN: 23.10.74

Dutchman Sander Westerveld enjoyed a highly-successful 2000–01 campaign, recovering from a slightly erratic start to help cement a Champions League slot for Liverpool.

Occasionally shaky when dealing with crosses, Westerveld suffered from an early-season howler against Chelsea when he palmed a Dennis Wise corner into his own net under no pressure.

But he bounced back and at the end of the season was able to boast figures which included a 96% catch success rate and a clean sheet at the Nou Camp stadium. And, of course, he had three cup-winners medals on his mantelpiece by May.

Impressive tallies of 14 Premiership clean sheets – equalled by only Paul Jones and Fabien Barthez – and 122 saves also make good reading for the £4 million former Vitesse Arnhem man.

Now one of the Premiership's most established 'keepers, all that is left for Westerveld is to earn some more international caps to go with the six he has picked up so far.

APPEARANCES	
Start (sub)	38(0)
Minutes on pitch	3420
SHOT STOPPING	
Goals conceded (inside box)	35
Goals conceded (outside box)	4
Minutes per goal conceded	88
Clean sheets	14
Saves (shots inside box)	55
Saves (shots outside box)	67
Saves/shots	76%
DISTRIBUTION	
Long kick %	56%
Throws/short passes %	84%
CATCHING	
Crosses caught	71
Crosses punched	29
Crosses dropped	3
Catch success %	96%
DISCIPLINE	
Yellow cards	1
Red cards	0
SEE PAGE 194 FOR FULL STATS	

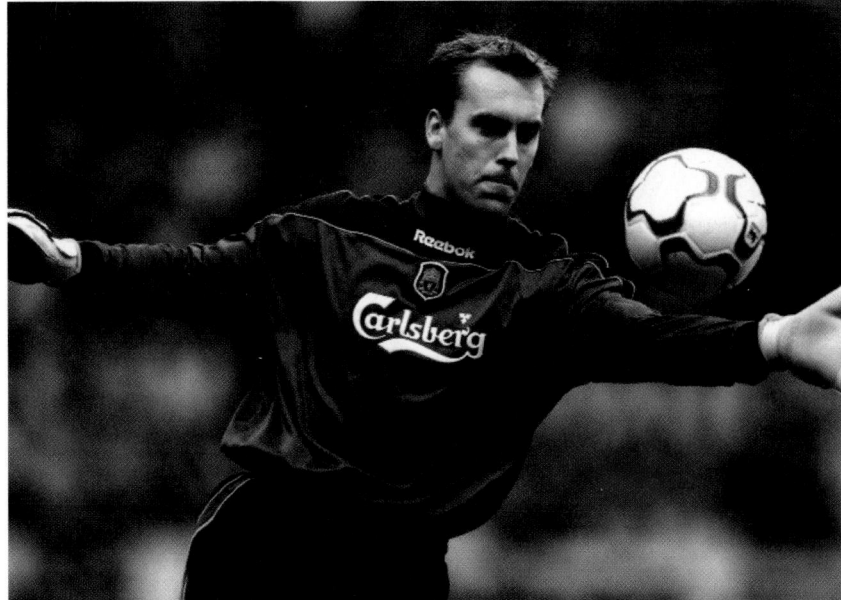

Established: Sander Westerveld

W

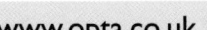

CB · David WETHERALL • 5
BRADFORD CITY • BORN: 14.3.71

Former Sheffield Wednesday trainee David Wetherall was joined in Bradford's defence by former Leeds team-mates Gunnar Halle and Robert Molenaar for the 2000–01 season.

A City defence which began as it finished – leaking goals – paired Wetherall with the Newcastle-bound Andy O'Brien and ended with the partnership of the aforementioned former Elland Road duo Halle and Molenaar.

Making 179 clearances and 42 tackles, with a success rate of 74%, Wetherall was one of the better-performing defenders in Bradford's squad and, had he managed to remain fit more often, could have had a major say in City's quest for Premiership survival.

As it was, there was to be no repeat of 1999–2000's Houdini act when Wetherall scored the goal against Liverpool that kept the Bantams up on the last day of the season against the odds.

And the 2001–02 season will see the vastly-experienced Wetherall involved in the battle to win back Bradford's treasured place in the Premiership.

APPEARANCES	
Start (sub)	18(0)
Minutes on pitch	1569
GOAL ATTEMPTS	
Goals	1
DEFENDING	
Blocks	22
Shots cleared off line	0
Headed clearances	143
Other clearances	36
Interceptions	8
Last man saving tackles	2
Tackles won	31
Tackles won %	74%
PASSING	
Passing accuracy own half	74%
Passing accuracy opp half	45%
DISCIPLINE	
Fouls	31
Fouls in danger area	11
Yellow cards	3
Red cards	0

SEE PAGE 69 FOR FULL STATS

M · Gareth WHALLEY • 6
BRADFORD CITY • BORN: 19.12.73

APPEARANCES	
Start (sub)	17(2)
Minutes on pitch	1439
GOAL ATTEMPTS	
Goals	0
Shots on target	3
Shooting accuracy	38%
PASSING & CROSSING	
Goal assists	1
Passes in opp half	449
Passing accuracy in opp half	73%
Successful crosses	10
Cross completion	29%
DEFENDING	
Interceptions	7
Clearances	14
Tackles	37
Tackles won %	68%
DISCIPLINE	
Fouls	8
Yellow cards	0
Red cards	0

SEE PAGE 69 FOR FULL STATS

Another product of Dario Gradi's famous youth system at Crewe, defensive midfielder Gareth Whalley endured a difficult campaign, struggling to find form in a Bradford side suffering from a lack of quality in most areas of the pitch.

Mancunian Whalley attempted 37 tackles, with a success rate of 68%, and his commitment to the Bantams' cause was never in question.

However, at times he found himself out of his depth at the heart of a Premiership midfield.

Jim Jefferies has made no secret of the fact that he does not rate Whalley and has told the combative midfielder he can move on if another club comes in with the right offer. Despite much speculation, that club is unlikely to be Crewe, however.

The Railwaymen were linked with an £800,000 swoop for their former player but Whalley said: "I have a number of options and at the moment I don't think going back to Crewe is the best one."

9 Bradford cleared more shots

Noel WHELAN • 26
MIDDLESBROUGH • BORN: 30.12.74

Noel Whelan's £2.2 million move from Coventry in the summer of 2000 was seen by many on Teesside as a move by Bryan Robson to bring a much-needed attacking edge to a Middlesbrough side that struggled for goals in 1999–2000.

However, the former Leeds star endured an inconsistent campaign. With only one Premiership goal to his name, Whelan often disappointed in front of goal.

And his miserable season was summed up when he sliced a cross into his own net against old club Coventry at The Riverside – much to the delight of the travelling Sky Blues fans.

Having attempted 573 passes with a completion rate of 69%, Whelan occasionally shone going forward, but Boro will surely look elsewhere to find other quality attacking options in the future.

Whelan has plenty of talent, though, and if he can get his career back on track could still go on to fulfil the rich promise he showed in his early days at Elland Road.

APPEARANCES	
Start (sub)	13(14)
Minutes on pitch	1338
GOAL ATTEMPTS	
Goals inside box	1
Goals outside box	0
Minutes per goal scored	1338
Goals/shots ratio	6%
SHOOTING	
Shots on target inside box	6
Shots on target outside box	2
Shooting accuracy	44%
PASSING	
Goal assists	1
Key passes	13
Passing accuracy in opp half	63%
DISCIPLINE	
Fouls committed	22
Fouls won	18
Offside	9
Yellow cards	3
Red cards	0

SEE PAGE 237 FOR FULL STATS

Jeff WHITLEY • 18
MANCHESTER CITY • BORN: 28.1.79

APPEARANCES	
Start (sub)	28(3)
Minutes on pitch	2477
GOAL ATTEMPTS	
Goals	1
Shots on target	10
Shooting accuracy	37%
PASSING & CROSSING	
Goal assists	4
Passes in opp half	677
Passing accuracy in opp half	69%
Successful crosses	4
Cross completion	18%
DEFENDING	
Interceptions	7
Clearances	37
Tackles	96
Tackles won %	79%
DISCIPLINE	
Fouls	46
Yellow cards	7
Red cards	0

SEE PAGE 209 FOR FULL STATS

Jeff Whitley was born in Zambia, but has chosen to play his international football for Northern Ireland and has now made almost 10 international appearances, scoring once.

While Northern Ireland have enjoyed limited success, appearing at international level must have provided welcome respite for the former City youth team star in 2000–01.

Playing at full-back, central midfield and out wide for the Citizens during the 2000–01 season Whitley tried, mostly in vain, to inject some much-needed craft and steel into an unimaginative Manchester City midfield.

With a tackle success rate of 79% and a 72% pass completion rate, Whitley was certainly one of City's more consistent performers, but even though he set up four goals for his team-mates he was unable to inspire them to victory often enough to avoid the drop.

A regular under Joe Royle in 2000–01, Whitley has worked hard to establish himself in the first-team picture, but it remains to be seen what part he will play under Kevin Keegan.

W

M — Gerard WIEKENS • 4
MANCHESTER CITY • BORN: 25.2.73

Versatile Dutchman Gerard Wiekens was Manchester City's best passer during their brief sojourn in the Premiership, according to Opta's statistics.

The former SC Veendam player completed 74% of his distribution; no mean feat in a team which had an average pass completion rate of 67%.

Wiekens, whose preferred position is in defence, was asked to play in a more advanced central midfield berth by Joe Royle and he relished his new role in the centre of the park, winning 62 tackles during the course of the 2000–01 campaign.

He was rewarded for his consistent form with a new four-year contract.

Primarily employed as a holding midfielder, Wiekens' fantastic strike at Elland Road in September, which set the team up for their the best result of the season, provided a brief glimpse of his prowess in front of goal.

But overall he was quiet in and around the penalty area, scoring just twice from 13 shots all season.

APPEARANCES	
Start (sub)	29(5)
Minutes on pitch	2534
GOAL ATTEMPTS	
Goals	2
Shots on target	8
Shooting accuracy	62%
PASSING & CROSSING	
Goal assists	0
Passes in opp half	670
Passing accuracy in opp half	69%
Successful crosses	2
Cross completion	13%
DEFENDING	
Interceptions	3
Clearances	80
Tackles	80
Tackles won %	78%
DISCIPLINE	
Fouls	39
Yellow cards	2
Red cards	0

SEE PAGE 209 FOR FULL STATS

AM — Jason WILCOX • 16
LEEDS UNITED • BORN: 15.7.71

APPEARANCES	
Start (sub)	7(10)
Minutes on pitch	796
GOAL ATTEMPTS	
Goals	0
Shots on target	4
Shooting accuracy	57%
Goals/shots ratio	0%
PASSING	
Goal assists	1
Passes in opp half	220
Passing accuracy in opp half	66%
Crosses	73
Crossing accuracy	21%
DRIBBLING	
Dribbles & runs	36
Dribble completion	83%
Corners forced	4
DISCIPLINE	
Fouls	8
Yellow cards	0
Red cards	0

SEE PAGE 167 FOR FULL STATS

Despite his Lancashire roots, former Blackburn Rovers star Jason Wilcox has become a popular figure at Elland Road.

The left-sided England international was brought to Leeds to provide Harry Kewell with competition for his place. But, unfortunately for David O'Leary, injury ruled both players out of contention in the early part of the 2000–01 season.

But when Wilcox overcame his knee and ankle injuries, he gave Leeds some much-needed width down the left flank. Nevertheless Wilcox's crossing accuracy of 21% was 13 percentage points down on his efforts in 1999–2000 and he registered only one assist in the Premiership.

With Kewell now recovered from the persistent injury problems which have dogged him, Wilcox has been linked with a move away from Elland Road. O'Leary seems keen to keep his experienced winger, though, and there is no doubt that, when fit, Wilcox gives his manager a useful option on the left side of midfield.

For more information visit our website:

Darren WILLIAMS • 18
SUNDERLAND • BORN: 28.4.77

Darren Williams was pondering a career in the armed forces before he made his mark in professional football; and the former York City man was a valuable member of Peter Reid's army in 2000–01 as Sunderland just missed out on a European place.

Filling in as a right-back or central midfielder, Williams was exactly the sort of foot soldier the Black Cats needed in the trenches. His distribution rate of 69% was eight percentage points more accurate than he managed in 1999–2000, but the versatile player failed to make an impact on the team in the second half of the season and voiced his discontent at being left out of some of Sunderland's major battles of the campaign.

However, the man who once earned notoriety for nutmegging Danish legend Michael Laudrup in a friendly match was given a five-year contract as recognition for his loyal service. Now all Williams needs are some winners medals to go along with all the commendations he has received from his superiors.

APPEARANCES	
Start (sub)	21(7)
Minutes on pitch	2028
GOAL ATTEMPTS	
Goals	0
PASSING & CROSSING	
Goal assists	0
Passing	764
Passing accuracy	69%
Crosses	30
Crossing accuracy	17%
DEFENDING	
Tackles	78
Tackles won %	73%
Blocks	20
Interceptions	7
Clearances	61
Shots cleared off line	0
DISCIPLINE	
Fouls	33
Yellow cards	7
Red cards	0
SEE PAGE 279 FOR FULL STATS	

Paul WILLIAMS • 4
COVENTRY CITY • BORN: 26.3.71

APPEARANCES	
Start (sub)	27(3)
Minutes on pitch	2401
GOAL ATTEMPTS	
Goals	0
DEFENDING	
Blocks	43
Shots cleared off line	0
Headed clearances	158
Other clearances	99
Interceptions	16
Last man saving tackles	2
Tackles won	59
Tackles won %	76%
PASSING	
Passing accuracy own half	74%
Passing accuracy opp half	41%
DISCIPLINE	
Fouls	35
Fouls in danger area	15
Yellow cards	7
Red cards	0
SEE PAGE 111 FOR FULL STATS	

Paul Williams suffered one of his most frustrating seasons as a professional as the Sky Blues' 34-year reign in the top flight came to an end.

The former Derby County defender was also offered the opportunity to represent Jamaica in their bid for qualification for the 2002 World Cup finals, but was forced to turn that chance down after playing for the England Under-21s several times earlier in his career.

Only Gary Breen bettered his 257 clearances during the season, but then the Irishman did play more games than Williams as the powerful defender lost his place to Richard Shaw in the latter part of the 2000–01 season.

Evidence of Williams' frustration was clear when he kicked the fourth official's electronic board after being sent off in a Worthington Cup tie at Preston in September.

Sky Blues boss Gordon Strachan will hope that his former captain will set a better example as the team aim to bounce straight back into the top flight.

W

Fabian WILNIS • 2
IPSWICH TOWN • BORN: 23.8.70

Fabian Wilnis's first campaign in the top flight ended on a sour note as the affable Dutchman found his position taken by Ipswich's £1.5 million recruit from Sunderland, Chris Makin.

Previously, Wilnis had played an integral part in helping George Burley's team establish themselves in the Premiership, making his mark with a cracking drive past Manchester United's Fabien Barthez for the team's first goal at Portman Road in 2000–01.

That strike earned a well-deserved point against the champions and gave Town confidence, which they used as a launchpad for the rest of the campaign.

Although Wilnis netted a smart last-gasp header which gave Ipswich all three points at Coventry in November, his main asset was his commitment. Only Titus Bramble and skipper Matt Holland bettered his 72 successful tackles.

Wilnis will hope he can win his right-sided slot back during 2001–02 and help the club achieve European glory just like his compatriots Arnold Muhren and Frans Thijssen did in 1981.

APPEARANCES	
Start (sub)	27(2)
Minutes on pitch	2274
GOAL ATTEMPTS	
Goals	2
PASSING & CROSSING	
Goal assists	3
Passing	1116
Passing accuracy	70%
Crosses	98
Crossing accuracy	28%
DEFENDING	
Tackles	85
Tackles won %	85%
Blocks	16
Interceptions	10
Clearances	57
Shots cleared off line	0
DISCIPLINE	
Fouls	28
Yellow cards	7
Red cards	0
SEE PAGE 153 FOR FULL STATS	

Sylvain WILTORD • 11
ARSENAL • BORN: 10.5.74

APPEARANCES	
Start (sub)	20(7)
Minutes on pitch	1758
GOAL ATTEMPTS	
Goals inside box	8
Goals outside box	0
Minutes per goal scored	220
Goals/shots ratio	15%
SHOOTING	
Shots on target inside box	22
Shots on target outside box	8
Shooting accuracy	57%
PASSING	
Goal assists	5
Key passes	23
Passing accuracy in opp half	69%
DISCIPLINE	
Fouls committed	11
Fouls won	25
Offside	49
Yellow cards	0
Red cards	0
SEE PAGE 41 FOR FULL STATS	

Sylvain Wiltord arrived in England with a great reputation after scoring the equaliser which forced extra-time and denied Italy the Euro 2000 championship. But his inconsistent displays for Arsenal have left some supporters questioning whether Arsène Wenger was right to make him the club's record signing at £13 million in August 2000.

His ineffectual performances in crucial matches such as the FA Cup final and Champions League quarter-final with Valencia did not go down well with the Highbury faithful.

But, in his defence, out of the four main Arsenal strikers in 2000–01, Wiltord possessed the best goals-to-shots ratio and he finished the season as the joint-top scorer in the FA Cup with six goals.

Wiltord, who is a big fan of singer Vanessa Paradis, was rumoured to be considering leaving Highbury at the end of the season, but Wenger has stated that he has no plans to sell the former Bordeaux star, stating that he believes Wiltord can become the "new Ian Wright".

6 Sylvain Wilford was the joint-top

Dean WINDASS • 20
MIDDLESBROUGH • BORN: 1.4.69

Dean Windass's decision to join Middlesbrough last March proved to be a good one, as the tigerish former Bradford City player will now have the chance to extend his stay in the Premiership.

His Riverside career got off to the most freakish of starts, though when he sustained a back injury while retrieving his kit bag from the boot of his car at training. But when he recovered he soon became a popular figure among Boro supporters after netting at Chelsea on his debut.

Overall, Windass's shooting accuracy dropped from 47% in 1999–2000 as he failed to match the 10-goal tally he managed for the Bantams in their successful relegation fight under Paul Jewell's stewardship.

As a player capable of playing either up front or in midfield, the burly Windass has proved to be a useful addition to the Middlesbrough squad.

And after two consecutive seasons fighting the drop, the Yorkshireman will hope to be challenging at the right end of the table in the 2001–02 campaign.

APPEARANCES	
Start (sub)	30(2)
Minutes on pitch	2677

GOAL ATTEMPTS	
Goals	5
Shots on target	23
Shooting accuracy	34%
Goals/shots ratio	22%

PASSING	
Goal assists	2
Passes in opp half	643
Passing accuracy in opp half	60%
Crosses	34
Crossing accuracy	32%

DRIBBLING	
Dribbles & runs	48
Dribble completion	69%
Corners forced	16

DISCIPLINE	
Fouls	56
Yellow cards	12
Red cards	0

SEE PAGES 69 & 237 FOR FULL STATS

Tigerish: Dean Windass

scorer in the 2000–01 FA Cup

Nigel WINTERBURN • 17
WEST HAM UNITED • BORN: 11.12.63

After 13 seasons at Highbury, Nigel Winterburn left to link up with London rivals, West Ham, in the summer. After joining the Hammers he was a regular on the left side of defence, bringing the same level of performance and commitment that was apparent throughout his time at Arsenal.

Winterburn was often deployed as a wing-back for the Hammers, but while he seemed to revel in his new responsibilities it was once again in defence that he did most of his best work. Only three other Premiership players made more tackles in 2000–01 and few of Winterburn's peers could match his tally of 90 successful challenges.

With Stuart Pearce also enjoying a renaissance at Upton Park, West Ham can lay claim to having the two most consistent left-backs of their generation on their books.

If some of the Hammers' other stars showed just half the desire that Pearce and Winterburn clearly still possess, West Ham would have finished a lot higher up the 2000–01 Premiership table.

APPEARANCES	
Start (sub)	33(0)
Minutes on pitch	2862
GOAL ATTEMPTS	
Goals	1
PASSING & CROSSING	
Goal assists	1
Passing	1122
Passing accuracy	76%
Crosses	45
Crossing accuracy	29%
DEFENDING	
Tackles	131
Tackles won %	69%
Blocks	19
Interceptions	13
Clearances	58
Shots cleared off line	1
DISCIPLINE	
Fouls	41
Yellow cards	7
Red cards	0

SEE PAGE 307 FOR FULL STATS

Dennis WISE • 11
CHELSEA • BORN: 16.12.66

APPEARANCES	
Start (sub)	35(1)
Minutes on pitch	3151
GOAL ATTEMPTS	
Goals	3
Shots on target	16
Shooting accuracy	67%
PASSING & CROSSING	
Goal assists	3
Passes in opp half	1100
Passing accuracy in opp half	73%
Successful crosses	62
Cross completion	34%
DEFENDING	
Interceptions	11
Clearances	25
Tackles	77
Tackles won %	65%
DISCIPLINE	
Fouls	54
Yellow cards	9
Red cards	0

SEE PAGE 97 FOR FULL STATS

Dennis Wise's 2000–01 season began in successful fashion, with Chelsea's Charity Shield victory over Manchester United securing some more silverware for the Stamford Bridge club three months after their FA Cup win over Aston Villa.

But, despite that successful start, it was to be an uncertain season for the most successful skipper in Chelsea's history.

Wise was clearly unhappy with the decision to sack Gianluca Vialli, expressing his concern at Claudio Ranieri's methods of management.

In fact, Wise was so disenchanted with life at the Bridge that he asked for a transfer, something that would have been unthinkable under Vialli's stewardship. But after appeals from supporters and team-mates, he withdrew his request and ended the season in fine style, skippering his side to a UEFA Cup spot.

As the summer approached, he was once again linked with a move. Whether he stays or goes, Wise will no doubt be back with the usual mix of tough tackling and tidy passing which has always been his trademark.

For more information visit our website:

CB Jonathon WOODGATE • 6
LEEDS UNITED • BORN: 22.1.80

The 2000–01 season was an unhappy one for Jonathon Woodgate. In Leeds' second Premiership fixture against Middlesbrough, he left the field injured halfway through the first period and then limped out again in the thrilling clash with Liverpool in November suffering from a thigh strain.

In total, Woodgate started 14 league matches, making his last appearance in late January. In that time he still managed to dominate the Leeds back-line, making 124 clearances and 65 tackles.

But by then, the England international had more serious matters on his mind. Unlike Lee Bowyer, who played throughout the court case they were involved in, Woodgate was reported to be suffering from a heel injury to explain his absence from the team. It transpired that Woodgate could not handle the pressure as well as Bowyer and was therefore relieved of his playing responsibilities by the club.

Following the collapse of the trial, the process was scheduled to begin all over again in October 2001.

APPEARANCES	
Start (sub)	14(0)
Minutes on pitch	1067
GOAL ATTEMPTS	
Goals	1
DEFENDING	
Blocks	17
Shots cleared off line	0
Headed clearances	92
Other clearances	32
Interceptions	8
Last man saving tackles	6
Tackles won	47
Tackles won %	72%
PASSING	
Passing accuracy own half	81%
Passing accuracy opp half	54%
DISCIPLINE	
Fouls	20
Fouls in danger area	10
Yellow cards	4
Red cards	0
SEE PAGE 167 FOR FULL STATS	

FB Alan WRIGHT • 3
ASTON VILLA • BORN: 28.9.71

APPEARANCES	
Start (sub)	35(1)
Minutes on pitch	3111
GOAL ATTEMPTS	
Goals	1
PASSING & CROSSING	
Goal assists	4
Passing	1578
Passing accuracy	74%
Crosses	92
Crossing accuracy	35%
DEFENDING	
Tackles	71
Tackles won %	70%
Blocks	23
Interceptions	14
Clearances	99
Shots cleared off line	0
DISCIPLINE	
Fouls	17
Yellow cards	3
Red cards	0
SEE PAGE 55 FOR FULL STATS	

He may not attract the same publicity as his higher-profile team mates, but Alan Wright's effective performances on the left for Aston Villa were a major plus for the Midlands club in their 2000–01 campaign.

Wright's ability going forward was evident to all observers. He provided four assists – a total bettered at Villa Park only by Paul Merson and Lee Hendrie – and 35% of his crosses were met by team-mates.

Against Derby he showed off his finishing skills, too, netting a well-struck effort from the edge of the box in Villa's 4–1 demolition of the Rams – his only goal of the season.

Despite the frequency of his forays forward, Wright still made valuable contributions in defence, especially once John Gregory abandoned his wing-backs formation in favour of 4–4–2.

Wright made 71 tackles, but conceded few fouls and was booked on just three occasions – a fine achievement considering that he featured in all but two of Villa's Premiership matches.

W

Jermaine WRIGHT • 14
IPSWICH TOWN • BORN: 21.10.75

One of the reasons for Ipswich's success during the 2000–01 campaign was that some of their younger players, with no previous experience of Premiership football, had few problems adjusting to life in the top flight.

Jermaine Wright was one member of manager George Burley's cultured squad who fell into that category.

Playing in a key role on the right of midfield for much of the season, Wright supported the attack effectively, scoring twice and getting a further 12 efforts on target.

He laid the ball off accurately 74% of the time and saw three of the chances he created finished off by team-mates, but still broke up play when necessary, winning 75% of the 67 challenges he attempted.

Wright still has the majority of his career ahead of him and with UEFA Cup football on the horizon for Town, the 2001–02 season should provide the former Crewe man with the chance to conquer another challenge – this time among Europe's élite.

APPEARANCES	
Start (sub)	35(2)
Minutes on pitch	2876
GOAL ATTEMPTS	
Goals	2
Shots on target	14
Shooting accuracy	41%
PASSING & CROSSING	
Goal assists	3
Passes in opp half	1095
Passing accuracy in opp half	71%
Successful crosses	26
Cross completion	35%
DEFENDING	
Interceptions	3
Clearances	22
Tackles	67
Tackles won %	75%
DISCIPLINE	
Fouls	22
Yellow cards	1
Red cards	0
SEE PAGE 153 FOR FULL STATS	

Richard WRIGHT • 1
IPSWICH TOWN • BORN: 5.11.77

APPEARANCES	
Start (sub)	36(0)
Minutes on pitch	3240
SHOT STOPPING	
Goals conceded (inside box)	34
Goals conceded (outside box)	7
Minutes per goal conceded	79
Clean sheets	12
Saves (shots inside box)	62
Saves (shots outside box)	41
Saves/shots	72%
DISTRIBUTION	
Long kick %	51%
Throws/short passes %	86%
CATCHING	
Crosses caught	76
Crosses punched	20
Crosses dropped	7
Catch success %	92%
DISCIPLINE	
Yellow cards	0
Red cards	0
SEE PAGE 152 FOR FULL STATS	

Following his eventful England debut against Malta before Euro 2000, questions were asked as to whether Richard Wright had the temperament to cope in big matches.

Ipswich's promotion to the Premiership gave Wright the opportunity to play in a whole season of high-profile games – and, thankfully for him, he did enough to restore his reputation as the potential long-term successor to David Seaman.

With Seaman, David James and Nigel Martyn chosen by Sven-Göran Eriksson on a regular basis, it would appear that Wright has his work cut out for the time being.

His target may well be to establish himself as the top young 'keeper around, so that when the likes of Seaman retire the Ipswich-born stopper is selected ahead of Chris Kirkland and Paul Robinson.

Wright made more than 100 saves and kept a total of 12 clean sheets in Ipswich's successful 2000–01 Premiership campaign. He played in all but two of Town's 38 League fixtures.

28 The number of shots attempted by Jermaine Wright

Stephen WRIGHT • 29
LIVERPOOL • BORN: 8.2.80

Stephen Wright watched most of Liverpool's record-breaking 2000–01 season from the dugout, but he was given the chance to come off the bench in two Premiership fixtures.

His league debut was against West Ham at Anfield, in which he came on for 56 minutes in place of Markus Babbel. The youngster completed 69% of his passes and capped an impressive outing by providing an assist for one of Liverpool's three goals in their win over the Hammers.

A week later, at Sunderland's Stadium of Light, Wright made a brief appearance for the final three minutes of the match, replacing Igor Biscan.

In cup competitions, Wright made his Liverpool debut in their 8–0 Worthington Cup drubbing of Stoke, while his first start came in the sixth-round FA Cup tie with Tranmere.

He finished the season with a UEFA Cup-winner's medal, as he was an unused sub in Liverpool's win over Alaves.

SEE PAGE 195 FOR FULL STATS

 Tommy WRIGHT • 13
MANCHESTER CITY • BORN: 29.8.63

Owing to the early-season form of Nicky Weaver, Tommy Wright had just one opportunity to play in Manchester City's 2000–01 Premiership campaign.

With Weaver out injured, Wright was selected for the game against Newcastle United, where he spent a number of years in the late 80s and early 90s and a short loan spell during 1999–2000.

Wright rolled back the years with a superb performance, pulling off a total of seven saves, three of which came from Gary Speed efforts. Unfortunately, despite his heroics, he could not stop Alan Shearer from scoring the only goal of the game.

In January, Wright moved on loan to Bolton to provide goalkeeping cover following Jussi Jaaskelainen's knee ligament injury.

Having been refused permission by City to play in Bolton's FA Cup fifth-round tie with Blackburn, Wright joined Wanderers on a full-time basis in March.

SEE PAGE 208 FOR FULL STATS

 Shaun WRIGHT-PHILLIPS • 29
MANCHESTER CITY • BORN: 25.10.81

APPEARANCES	
Start (sub)	9(6)
Minutes on pitch	906
GOAL ATTEMPTS	
Goals	0
Shots on target	4
Shooting accuracy	20%
Goals/shots ratio	0%
PASSING	
Goal assists	0
Passes in opp half	218
Passing accuracy in opp half	59%
Crosses	33
Crossing accuracy	21%
DRIBBLING	
Dribbles & runs	68
Dribble completion	65%
Corners forced	7
DISCIPLINE	
Fouls	10
Yellow cards	0
Red cards	0

SEE PAGE 209 FOR FULL STATS

After being released from Nottingham Forest, for not being "big enough or strong enough", Shaun Wright-Phillips's signing for Manchester City was hardly seen as a massive coup. However, behind the youngster's diminutive stature is a highly competitive team player not unlike his adopted father Ian Wright.

After two early-season appearances as a substitute, Wright-Phillips made his first Premiership start at Upton Park and then went on to make nine consecutive starts, impressing with his speed and dribbling skills.

His season ended early, after Joe Royle decided to rest him from the rigours of first-team football, before he picked up an injury that might curtail a promising start to his fledgling career.

If he continues to progress and shows some added composure in front of goal, where he only hit the target four times from 20 shots, Wright-Phillips could be a leading light in the Manchester club's push for a Premiership return next season.

from outside the box – the most by any Ipswich player

CB Abel XAVIER • 28
EVERTON • BORN: 30.11.72

With a preposterous bleached-blond hairstyle and the only top-flight surname that begins with the letter 'X', Abel Xavier already has two advantages in his attempts to stand out in the Premiership crowd.

But his performances in 2000-01 often left him in the shade, as he has failed to convince observers that he is truly committed to the Everton cause.

Xavier's second term in England saw just 10 starts for the Mozambique-born defender – eight fewer than he managed to notch up during the previous campaign. Injuries plagued the Portuguese international's season, forcing him back down the pecking order, although he is able to slot into the midfield as easily as he can into his more common defensive role.

Xavier was forced to sit out the final three games of the campaign with a shin injury picked up while playing for his country although, thanks to his red card against Arsenal, he was suspended for one of those matches anyway.

APPEARANCES	
Start (sub)	10(1)
Minutes on pitch	875

GOAL ATTEMPTS	
Goals	0

DEFENDING	
Blocks	6
Shots cleared off line	0
Headed clearances	37
Other clearances	21
Interceptions	2
Last man saving tackles	0
Tackles won	19
Tackles won %	76%

PASSING	
Passing accuracy own half	86%
Passing accuracy opp half	58%

DISCIPLINE	
Fouls	12
Fouls in danger area	3
Yellow cards	2
Red cards	1

SEE PAGE 139 FOR FULL STATS

In the shade: Abel Xavier

For more information visit our website:

Dwight YORKE • 19
MANCHESTER UNITED • BORN: 3.11.71

By his own high standards, Dwight Yorke did not have his most productive campaign for Manchester United. Despite the club lifting its seventh title in the last nine seasons, Yorke often generated more column inches in the tabloids for his extra-curricular activities than for his goalscoring exploits.

The striker hit the back of the net 11 times fewer than he did in the previous campaign and, with just two headed goals, could not match his Premiership high of eight in 1999–2000.

Yorke's most impressive 90 minutes came in the 6–1 routing of Arsenal which emphasised the gap between the champions and the rest of the league. The former Aston Villa striker netted a quick-fire hat-trick inside the first quarter of the game and helped skipper Roy Keane notch the fourth.

Sadly, this type of performance was all-too-rare from the Premiership's biggest *Only Fools And Horses* fan, and this time next year he could find himself eclipsed by multi-million-pound signing Ruud van Nistelrooy.

APPEARANCES	
Start (sub)	15(7)
Minutes on pitch	1474
GOAL ATTEMPTS	
Goals inside box	8
Goals outside box	1
Minutes per goal scored	164
Goals/shots ratio	17%
SHOOTING	
Shots on target inside box	21
Shots on target outside box	8
Shooting accuracy	55%
PASSING	
Goal assists	4
Key passes	24
Passing accuracy in opp half	78%
DISCIPLINE	
Fouls committed	20
Fouls won	13
Offside	35
Yellow cards	2
Red cards	0
SEE PAGE 223 FOR FULL STATS	

Luke YOUNG • 21
TOTTENHAM HOTSPUR • BORN: 19.7.79

APPEARANCES	
Start (sub)	19(4)
Minutes on pitch	1704
GOAL ATTEMPTS	
Goals	0
PASSING & CROSSING	
Goal assists	0
Passing	629
Passing accuracy	64%
Crosses	32
Crossing accuracy	13%
DEFENDING	
Tackles	56
Tackles won %	82%
Blocks	19
Interceptions	8
Clearances	103
Shots cleared off line	1
DISCIPLINE	
Fouls	10
Yellow cards	2
Red cards	0
SEE PAGE 293 FOR FULL STATS	

Luke Young established himself as a regular in the Tottenham defence in 2001 after injuries had hampered his progress in the opening months of the campaign.

The England Under-21 international spent two months on the sidelines after suffering a broken foot in November's victory against Liverpool.

That day he managed to shackle Michael Owen by winning all his challenges and making a total of 17 clearances, more than Liverpool's Sami Hyypia – no mean feat, as the Finn made more clearances than any other player over the course of the 2000–01 Premiership season.

Young is comfortable on the ball with either foot and capable of playing anywhere in defence. He demonstrated his versatility by covering for centre-back Sol Campbell or dropping into the left-back role, where he became a regular in the side.

One of the unsung heroes at the club, Young is sure to play a key role in Glenn Hoddle's revolution at White Hart Lane.

Christian ZIEGE • 3
LIVERPOOL • BORN: 1.2.72

FB

Christian Ziege had to go through the courts to secure his release from Middlesbrough.

The Teesside club were reluctant to part with him, but Liverpool had allegedly been tipped off about a release clause in the German's contract.

The move to Merseyside was not a qualified success for Ziege, who found himself watching from the sidelines as Jamie Carragher admirably filled the left-back role in Liverpool's fantastic climax to 2000–01. But Ziege can feel a little hard done-by, as he boasted a better tackle success rate than Carragher. He also made the same number of interceptions as Markus Babbel, despite playing far fewer minutes than his compatriot.

Ziege has been tipped to leave Anfield, but Gérard Houllier's squad could do with his experience of Champions League football, garnered during spells at AC Milan and Bayern Munich.

The most disappointing aspect is that Ziege is apparently the highest-paid player at the club and a better return would have been expected.

APPEARANCES	
Start (sub)	11(5)
Minutes on pitch	985

GOAL ATTEMPTS	
Goals	1
Shots on target	4
Shooting accuracy	25%
Goals/shots ratio	6%

PASSING	
Goal assists	2
Passes in opp half	233
Passing accuracy in opp half	58%
Crosses	64
Crossing accuracy	20%

DRIBBLING	
Dribbles & runs	31
Dribble completion	68%
Corners forced	3

DISCIPLINE	
Fouls	16
Yellow cards	3
Red cards	0

SEE PAGE 195 FOR FULL STATS

On the sidelines: Christian Ziege

16 Gianfranco Zola scored two headed goals, boosting

Gianfranco ZOLA • 25
CHELSEA • BORN: 5.7.66

Gianfranco Zola delighted Chelsea supporters when he agreed a new two-year contract which will keep him at Stamford Bridge until the end of the 2002–03 campaign.

A firm favourite at the club, there was speculation that the Sardinian would return to his native homeland and end his playing days with Cagliari.

But his new deal includes an option on joining the coaching staff, and Zola has always stated his desire to go into management when he hangs up his boots.

Under current Chelsea boss Claudio Ranieri, Zola was ranked seventh-best striker in the Premiership under the Opta system of analysis in the 2000–01 campaign, as his nine goals and four assists helped the Blues secure a UEFA Cup place.

Surprisingly, he also weighed in with two headed goals as Chelsea's 16 nodded strikes proved a higher tally than any other team managed in the Premiership. On his day, Zola can be head and shoulders above most of his peers in English football.

APPEARANCES	
Start (sub)	31(5)
Minutes on pitch	2603
GOAL ATTEMPTS	
Goals inside box	6
Goals outside box	3
Minutes per goal scored	289
Goals/shots ratio	17%
SHOOTING	
Shots on target inside box	13
Shots on target outside box	11
Shooting accuracy	45%
PASSING	
Goal assists	4
Key passes	62
Passing accuracy in opp half	73%
DISCIPLINE	
Fouls committed	20
Fouls won	37
Offside	19
Yellow cards	1
Red cards	0

SEE PAGE 97 FOR FULL STATS

Ysrael ZUNIGA • 11
COVENTRY CITY • BORN: 27.8.76

APPEARANCES	
Start (sub)	7(8)
Minutes on pitch	673
GOAL ATTEMPTS	
Goals inside box	1
Goals outside box	0
Minutes per goal scored	673
Goals/shots ratio	6%
SHOOTING	
Shots on target inside box	5
Shots on target outside box	3
Shooting accuracy	47%
PASSING	
Goal assists	0
Key passes	9
Passing accuracy in opp half	67%
DISCIPLINE	
Fouls committed	17
Fouls won	18
Offside	11
Yellow cards	2
Red cards	0

SEE PAGE 111 FOR FULL STATS

Peruvian striker Ysrael Zuniga failed to establish himself in the Coventry City side as the club ended its 34-year reign in the top flight, with a lack of punch up front one of their main failings.

Former South American Golden Boot-winner Zuniga could add only one goal to his Sky Blues account – a glancing header against Premiership champions Manchester United. And his goals-to-shots ratio was poor considering half of his shots hit the back of the net in 1999–2000.

His 47% shooting accuracy was also a disappointing return for a player who failed to live up to all the pre-season expectations of him.

Despite rumours of a move back to his homeland, Zuniga – or "Cachete" as he is known – will be determined to prove his worth to City supporters.

He will hope to assist the Sky Blues in making an instant return to the Premiership, by tormenting defences in Nationwide Division One in 2001–02.

Z

Chelsea's total to 16, the most in the Premiership

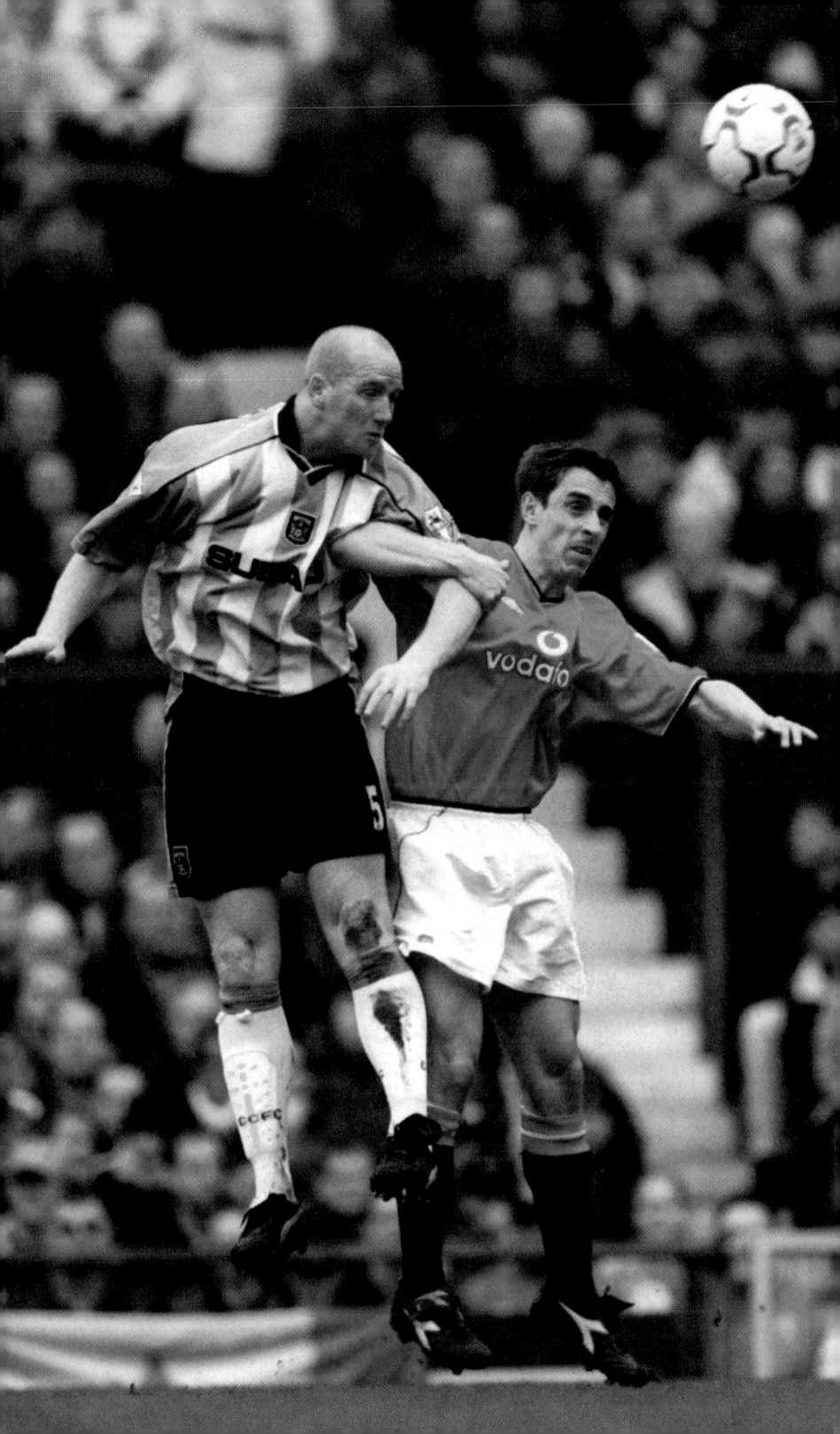

COMPARATIVE TABLES

Debates will inevitably rage about which team is the best, which players are better than others and which referee is the strictest in the league.

Now you can settle all those arguments with the definitive guide to the 2000–01 Premiership season. Our comparative tables show how teams fared in relation to each other, how the top 20 players ranked in certain categories and who were the top players of the season.

This section is divided up to analyse key aspects of the game.

THE TEAMS

All the Premiership teams are compared and contrasted over a number of categories. Find out which team were the best and worst passers, tacklers and defenders, plus which sides had the best and worst disciplinary records.

THE PLAYERS

The top 20 players in each category are compared and contrasted to highlight the best goalscorers, passers, tacklers and goalkeepers, as well as the players with the best and worst disciplinary records.

THE INDEX

Who was the best player in each position and who was the most influential player of the season? The Opta Index takes an objective view.

TEAMS OF THE SEASON

Everybody's favourite pastime – with a twist. Opta select their teams of the season based on actual performance in key areas.

REFEREES

An in-depth look at the disciplinary record of the 2000–01 season in terms of the fouls and penalties awarded and yellow and red cards issued by referees.

THE TEAMS

How did your team rate against the other Premiership sides in key categories? You will find the answer in this section. All 20 teams are featured in each table and are ranked according to a key category, which is explained beneath each chart.

The tables will show you the main areas of strength and weakness within each team and will go some way to explaining why certain teams were successful and why others struggled over the course of the 2000–01 season.

For example, on page 618 you will see that Bradford managed a goals-to-shots ratio of just 7.7% compared with Manchester United's 14.0%. This shows how the Bantams had to attempt nearly twice as many shots to score a goal as the Premiership champions, which is clearly a key factor in the relative success of each team.

You can discover which team scored the most headed goals, which won the most tackles, which earned the most disciplinary points and which side suffered most at the hands of their opponents.

There is an explanation beneath each of the charts showing how the ranking is calculated and how to access the information.

The most important table of all, of course, is the Premiership league table. Opposite you will see how all 20 teams finished in the 2000–01 Premiership

season, their home and away records and what they achieved.

Manchester United won the title by 10 points from Arsenal, who finished second and qualified for the Champions League. Third-placed Liverpool also qualified for the 2001–02 Champions League, but they will enter the competition only if they progress past a qualifying round. If they are eliminated at that stage, they will enter the UEFA Cup.

Leeds United's fourth position secured them a spot in the UEFA Cup alongside fifth-placed Ipswich Town and sixth-placed Chelsea. Those two clubs earned their berths due to the fact that Liverpool won both the Worthington Cup and the FA Cup, which meant the European places reverted to league positioning. Aston Villa entered the Intertoto Cup in a bid to reach the UEFA Cup.

Bradford City were the first side to be relegated when they lost to Everton on 28 April. They were joined by Coventry City and Manchester City in those clubs' penultimate fixtures, ending a 34-year and a single-season sojourn respectively in the top flight.

FA PREMIERSHIP
SEASON 2000–2001

	PLD	HOME W	D	L	F	A	AWAY W	D	L	F	A	PTS	GD
Man Utd	38	15	2	2	49	12	9	6	4	30	19	80	48
Arsenal	38	15	3	1	45	13	5	7	7	18	25	70	25
Liverpool	38	13	4	2	40	14	7	5	7	31	25	69	32
Leeds Utd	38	11	3	5	36	21	9	5	5	28	22	68	21
Ipswich	38	11	5	3	31	15	9	1	9	26	27	66	15
Chelsea	38	13	3	3	44	20	4	7	8	24	25	61	23
Sunderland	38	9	7	3	24	16	6	5	8	22	25	57	5
Aston Villa	38	8	8	3	27	20	5	7	7	19	23	54	3
Charlton	38	11	5	3	31	19	3	5	11	19	38	52	-7
Southampton	38	11	2	6	27	22	3	8	8	13	26	52	-8
Newcastle	38	10	4	5	26	17	4	5	10	18	33	51	-6
Tottenham	38	11	6	2	31	16	2	4	13	16	38	49	-7
Leicester	38	10	4	5	28	23	4	2	13	11	28	48	-12
Middlesbro	38	4	7	8	18	23	5	8	6	26	21	42	0
West Ham	38	6	6	7	24	20	4	6	9	21	30	42	-5
Everton	38	6	8	5	29	27	5	1	13	16	32	42	-14
Derby Co	38	8	7	4	23	24	2	5	12	14	35	42	-22
Man City	38	4	3	12	20	31	4	7	8	21	34	34	-24
Coventry	38	4	7	8	14	23	4	3	12	22	40	34	-27
Bradford	38	4	7	8	20	29	1	4	14	10	41	26	-40

the lowest tally in Premiership history

GOALSCORING

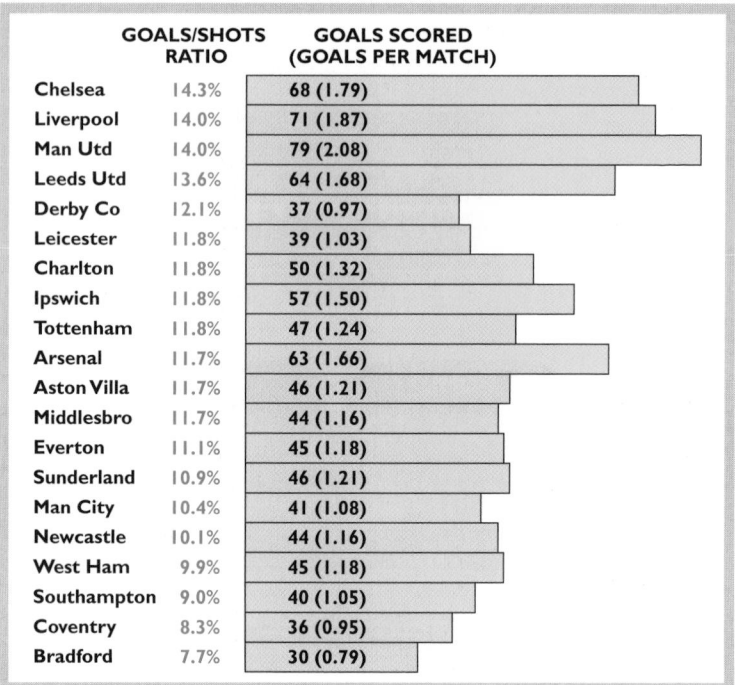

	GOALS/SHOTS RATIO	GOALS SCORED (GOALS PER MATCH)
Chelsea	14.3%	68 (1.79)
Liverpool	14.0%	71 (1.87)
Man Utd	14.0%	79 (2.08)
Leeds Utd	13.6%	64 (1.68)
Derby Co	12.1%	37 (0.97)
Leicester	11.8%	39 (1.03)
Charlton	11.8%	50 (1.32)
Ipswich	11.8%	57 (1.50)
Tottenham	11.8%	47 (1.24)
Arsenal	11.7%	63 (1.66)
Aston Villa	11.7%	46 (1.21)
Middlesbro	11.7%	44 (1.16)
Everton	11.1%	45 (1.18)
Sunderland	10.9%	46 (1.21)
Man City	10.4%	41 (1.08)
Newcastle	10.1%	44 (1.16)
West Ham	9.9%	45 (1.18)
Southampton	9.0%	40 (1.05)
Coventry	8.3%	36 (0.95)
Bradford	7.7%	30 (0.79)

After a bountiful 1999–2000 campaign, there was a significant decline in goalscoring during 2000–01. From a record haul of 1,060 strikes, the total fell to 992 as some teams struggled to find the net as freely as before. There were some teams who improved their tally, though – none more so than Chelsea.

The Pensioners saw their goals-to-shots ratio increase by almost four percentage points and they finished the season as the deadliest team in the Premiership. The signing of Jimmy Floyd Hasselbaink was the key, but he was ably supported by his team-mates.

Manchester United again finished as the league's top scorers, but scored 18 fewer goals than in 1999–2000. Nevertheless, they were still the only team to average more than two goals a game.

United were also the most clinical side up until the point when they won the league. With players rested and little pressure to perform, their goals-to-shots ratio consequently dipped in the last five games.

The season's other goalscoring heroes were Liverpool, who were the only other team to score more than 70 goals – and did so with a better conversion rate than their north-west rivals.

Arsenal's problems in front of goal were well-documented and the Gunners' goals-to-shots ratio dropped to 11.7%. It was particularly poor away from home, where just 10 goals were accrued in the first 15 games on the road.

Manchester United recorded the biggest win, defeating Bradford 6–0, while there were four games which ended in a 6–1 scoreline.

The Bantams were – unsurprisingly – the least-lethal team in the top flight, scoring with just 7.7% of their shots, while Coventry, Southampton and West Ham also saw fewer than one in 10 shots find the back of the net.

SHOOTING

SHOOTING ACCURACY

Team	Accuracy	Shots on target	Shots off target
Arsenal	51.2%	267	254
Charlton	50.5%	201	197
Leicester	47.4%	152	169
Leeds Utd	46.1%	214	250
Chelsea	45.9%	215	253
Sunderland	45.9%	194	229
Liverpool	45.8%	229	271
West Ham	45.4%	202	243
Man Utd	45.2%	246	298
Everton	45.2%	184	223
Ipswich	44.8%	205	253
Middlesbro	44.6%	153	190
Newcastle	43.8%	182	234
Tottenham	42.7%	167	224
Man City	42.6%	156	210
Derby Co	42.3%	130	177
Bradford	41.9%	158	219
Southampton	40.0%	168	252
Coventry	38.8%	154	243
Aston Villa	38.7%	152	241

KEY ■ Shots on target □ Shots off target

Only two teams in the 2000–01 Premiership fired more than half their shots on target – London neighbours Arsenal and Charlton Athletic.

The Gunners could not find the net easily, but they certainly made the opposition goalkeepers work. They had more shots on target than any other team for the third year running.

As for the Addicks, they coped with top-flight football admirably and their diligence in the penalty box paid off.

Nevertheless, an overall Premiership accuracy of 44.45% was lower than in 1998–99 and 1999–2000 and this reflected a lack of composure throughout the division.

Aston Villa and Coventry City both ended the season with a shooting accuracy of less than 40%. Such profligacy contributed to the Sky Blues surrendering their top-flight status.

Southampton were the most accurate team in 1999–2000 but slipped to 18th place in 2000–01.

But that decline did not affect them too much as they enjoyed one of their better seasons, particularly while under the management of Glenn Hoddle.

Sir Alex Ferguson will not have been pleased to see the shooting accuracy of the champions fall from 51.4% in 1999–2000 to a measly 45.2%.

The Red Devils hit 298 of their shots off target, more than any other team in the Premiership. The arrival of Ruud Van Nistelrooy at Old Trafford should help reverse this trend.

Derby County hit the target on fewer occasions than any other side, with just 130 accurate shots – the lowest figure in three years for any Premiership team.

It was also the third successive season in which their marksmanship declined, something which the club will be keen to arrest in 2001–02.

PASSING

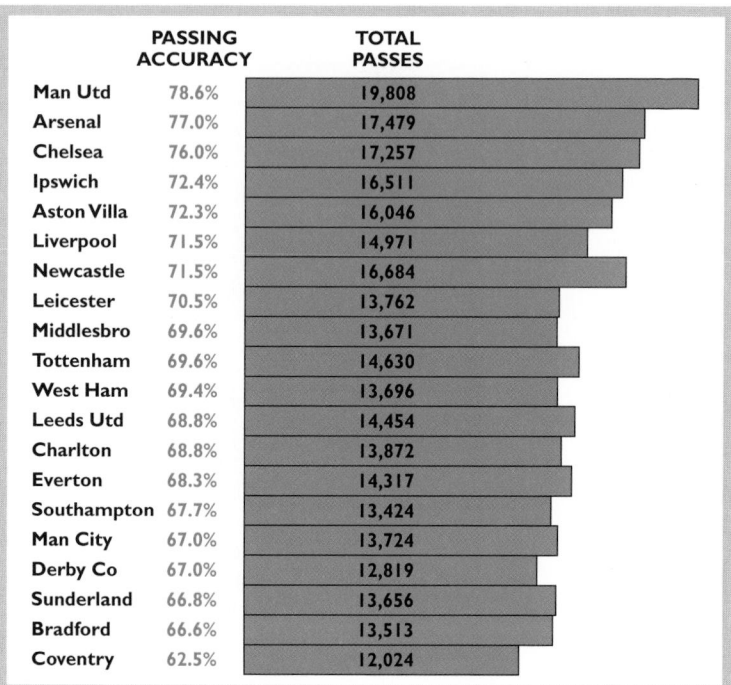

	PASSING ACCURACY	TOTAL PASSES
Man Utd	78.6%	19,808
Arsenal	77.0%	17,479
Chelsea	76.0%	17,257
Ipswich	72.4%	16,511
Aston Villa	72.3%	16,046
Liverpool	71.5%	14,971
Newcastle	71.5%	16,684
Leicester	70.5%	13,762
Middlesbro	69.6%	13,671
Tottenham	69.6%	14,630
West Ham	69.4%	13,696
Leeds Utd	68.8%	14,454
Charlton	68.8%	13,872
Everton	68.3%	14,317
Southampton	67.7%	13,424
Man City	67.0%	13,724
Derby Co	67.0%	12,819
Sunderland	66.8%	13,656
Bradford	66.6%	13,513
Coventry	62.5%	12,024

Manchester United were the best passers in the Premiership for the third season in succession, increasing their overall accuracy from 77.7% in 1999–2000 to an impressive 78.6% in 2000–01.

They also came within 192 passes of reaching a total of 20,000 – a marvellous achievement.

United's total of 19,808 is 7,784 passes more than Coventry City made, a clear indication of the gap between the top and the bottom of the league.

Chelsea, Arsenal and Newcastle have made up the top four with United in the previous two seasons, but 2000–01 saw Ipswich Town replace the Magpies. Bobby Robson's team slipped down to seventh place, while George Burley's attractive side outpassed even Liverpool by almost one percentage point.

As usual, the sides with good passing reputations are at the top of the table, although the fact that Leicester featured in eighth place belied their reputation as a long-ball team. The Foxes showed greater accuracy in 2000–01 despite the departure of midfielder Neil Lennon mid-way through the campaign.

Sunderland were the lowest-placed of the leading teams, largely the result of a consistent reliance on the aerial strength of Niall Quinn.

The Black Cats were the eighth-best passing team in 1999–2000, but fell away dramatically in 2000–01. After missing out on a European spot for the second season running, perhaps the club will have to re-think their tactics.

Aston Villa's passing returned to form after a disastrous 1999–2000 season and the Midlands club ended the year as the fifth-most accurate team in the Premiership. The lack of a consistent goalscorer meant that John Gregory's side were less likely to hit long balls to the frontline.

PASSING IN OPPOSITION HALF

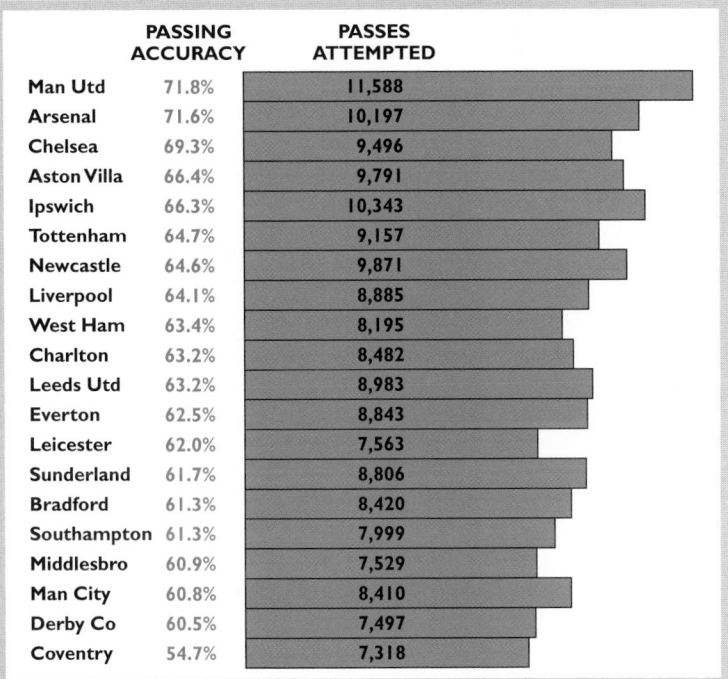

	PASSING ACCURACY	PASSES ATTEMPTED
Man Utd	71.8%	11,588
Arsenal	71.6%	10,197
Chelsea	69.3%	9,496
Aston Villa	66.4%	9,791
Ipswich	66.3%	10,343
Tottenham	64.7%	9,157
Newcastle	64.6%	9,871
Liverpool	64.1%	8,885
West Ham	63.4%	8,195
Charlton	63.2%	8,482
Leeds Utd	63.2%	8,983
Everton	62.5%	8,843
Leicester	62.0%	7,563
Sunderland	61.7%	8,806
Bradford	61.3%	8,420
Southampton	61.3%	7,999
Middlesbro	60.9%	7,529
Man City	60.8%	8,410
Derby Co	60.5%	7,497
Coventry	54.7%	7,318

Taking the game to the opposition and being able to play slickly in their half of the pitch is the hallmark of all the best sides – and yet again Manchester United were the Premiership's best passers in the attacking half.

Their pass completion figure of 71.8% was slightly down on 1999–2000, but it still identified United as the most dangerous attacking force in the top flight. Arsenal, however, closed the gap to just 0.2%, a marked improvement for the swashbuckling Gunners.

The Premiership's top two both recorded more than 10,000 passes in the opposition half. The only other team to manage this was Ipswich Town.

The Tractor Boys were not as accurate with their distribution as Chelsea or Aston Villa in that area, but it demonstrated the confidence they had throughout the campaign.

Coventry propped up yet another table with figures way adrift of any other team in the top flight.

Gordon Strachan's claim that all his side needed was someone to score goals looks less convincing when you consider the Sky Blues were almost six percentage points less accurate than any other team from the top division.

Derby's passing also suffered when they ventured further forward.

Tottenham improved from seventh to sixth, belying some of their league performances, while David O'Leary's Leeds fell from 10th in 1999–2000 to 11th in 2000–01: surprising when they could call on the services of the skilful Mark Viduka up front.

Bradford may have been the second-worst passers overall, but they were slightly stronger in the opposition half, though that may be a reflection of the standard of their defending rather than the quality of their attacking.

more than 100 passes in a single game

SHORT PASSING

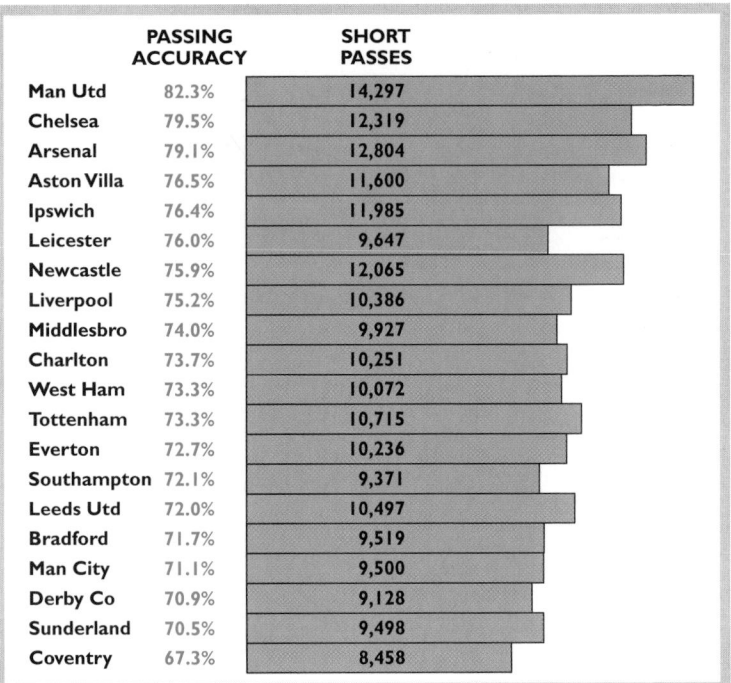

	PASSING ACCURACY	SHORT PASSES
Man Utd	82.3%	14,297
Chelsea	79.5%	12,319
Arsenal	79.1%	12,804
Aston Villa	76.5%	11,600
Ipswich	76.4%	11,985
Leicester	76.0%	9,647
Newcastle	75.9%	12,065
Liverpool	75.2%	10,386
Middlesbro	74.0%	9,927
Charlton	73.7%	10,251
West Ham	73.3%	10,072
Tottenham	73.3%	10,715
Everton	72.7%	10,236
Southampton	72.1%	9,371
Leeds Utd	72.0%	10,497
Bradford	71.7%	9,519
Man City	71.1%	9,500
Derby Co	70.9%	9,128
Sunderland	70.5%	9,498
Coventry	67.3%	8,458

For the second season running, Manchester United were the only team in the Premiership to complete more than 80% of their short passes – passes under 25 yards in distance – as they glided seemingly with little effort to their third league championship title in a row.

Their total of 14,297 short passes represented 72% of their total distribution throughout 2000–01 and 82.3% of it found a team-mate.

There is little excuse for not finding a player from the same side over such a short distance, but once again Coventry City found themselves at the foot of a passing table.

The Sky Blues were the only side to have a short passing accuracy of less than 70%, an extremely wayward average. This was an improvement on 1999–2000, however, when four clubs were beneath that mark.

Southampton made considerable progress in 2000–01, rising from 18th to 14th, largely because of the football philosophy of Glenn Hoddle. The other team to fare better were Aston Villa, who seem to have made strides in their game if not their league position.

Chelsea and Arsenal almost matched Manchester United's short passing, but they could not break the 80% barrier. The Stamford Bridge club are capable of highly-entertaining football on their day and this was the third year in which they occupied second slot. The Gunners made more short passes than the Blues, but with slightly less accuracy.

Treble-winners Liverpool were down in eighth place and it seems likely that they will have to improve their short passing if they are to mount a concerted challenge for the Premiership title in 2001–02.

Aston Villa and Ipswich Town were very tidy on the ball, while only three top-flight sides attempted more short passes than Newcastle United.

82% Roy Keane was the most accurate

LONG PASSING

	PASSING ACCURACY	LONG PASSES
Arsenal	71.3%	4,675
Man Utd	69.2%	5,511
Chelsea	67.2%	4,938
Liverpool	63.1%	4,585
Ipswich	61.6%	4,526
Aston Villa	61.2%	4,446
Leeds Utd	60.3%	3,957
Newcastle	60.0%	4,619
Tottenham	59.5%	3,915
West Ham	58.4%	3,624
Sunderland	58.3%	4,158
Middlesbro	58.0%	3,744
Man City	58.0%	4,224
Leicester	57.7%	4,115
Southampton	57.5%	4,053
Derby Co	57.2%	3,691
Everton	57.2%	4,081
Charlton	54.8%	3,621
Bradford	54.4%	3,994
Coventry	51.0%	3,566

Claims that the signing of Emile Heskey would not encourage Liverpool to use the long ball are challenged by the statistics, as 31% of the Reds' balls were long passes. The only other sides to hit such a large percentage of lengthy balls were Manchester City, Southampton and Sunderland.

But Liverpool were far more accurate than the other three clubs, largely thanks to the midfield skills of Steven Gerrard and Gary McAllister. However, they still lagged behind Chelsea, Manchester United and Arsenal at this discipline, with the Gunners topping the charts for the third year running.

Arsène Wenger's team were the only side to find a team-mate with more than 70% of long passes, a tremendous achievement and a clear improvement on 1999–2000. The pace of Thierry Henry gives the team a profitable outlet in any game.

Nevertheless, only 27% of the Gunners' passes were long balls, one of the lowest proportions in the Premiership.

The other clubs to spurn the longer delivery as much were Tottenham, West Ham and Charlton, suggesting that the London air is not conducive to such play!

Once again, Coventry City were at the foot of a passing table. Nearly half of their long balls went awry, although the arrival of John Hartson helped them a little.

Many of the less-accurate teams employed a target man, Everton, Sunderland and Leicester among them. Charlton and Bradford are not noted for "Route One" tactics, but both fielded big men up front at times.

Conversely, the accurate teams often used long passes more constructively, switching play with a sweeping ball from one flank to the other.

The moral of the tale seems to be that hopeful passes to the front do not pay dividends in the Premiership.

CROSSING

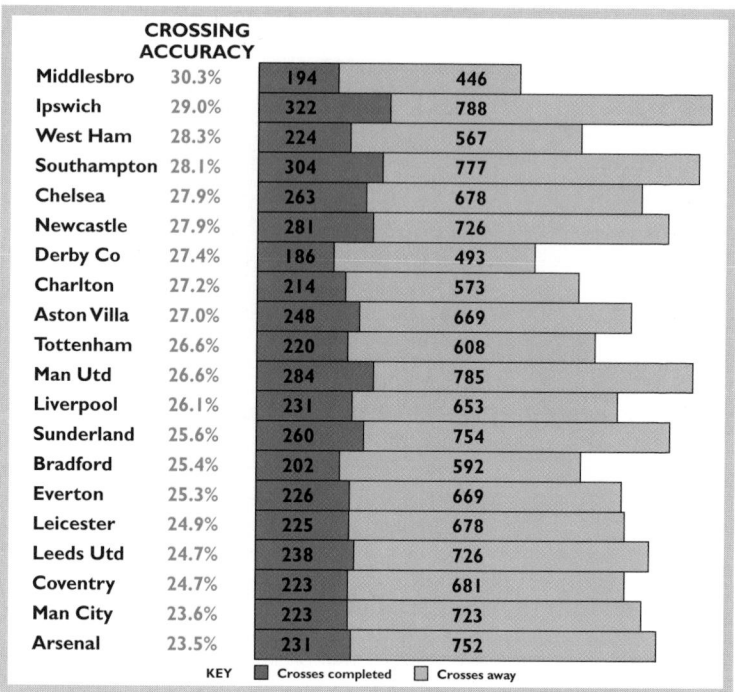

	CROSSING ACCURACY			
Middlesbro	30.3%	194	446	
Ipswich	29.0%	322	788	
West Ham	28.3%	224	567	
Southampton	28.1%	304	777	
Chelsea	27.9%	263	678	
Newcastle	27.9%	281	726	
Derby Co	27.4%	186	493	
Charlton	27.2%	214	573	
Aston Villa	27.0%	248	669	
Tottenham	26.6%	220	608	
Man Utd	26.6%	284	785	
Liverpool	26.1%	231	653	
Sunderland	25.6%	260	754	
Bradford	25.4%	202	592	
Everton	25.3%	226	669	
Leicester	24.9%	225	678	
Leeds Utd	24.7%	238	726	
Coventry	24.7%	223	681	
Man City	23.6%	223	723	
Arsenal	23.5%	231	752	

KEY ■ Crosses completed ■ Crosses away

Being able to call on a seemingly-endless supply of big strikers, Middlesbrough ended the 2000–01 campaign with the best cross completion rate in the Premiership. The Teesside team were the only side to have a rate of more than 30%, a considerable decline from 1999–2000 when nine teams achieved this feat. But Boro also made the fewest crosses – just 640 – so failed to take advantage of this element in their armoury.

Newcomers Ipswich Town, on the other hand, were the second-best crossers and also made the highest total: 1,110. The sharpness of Marcus Stewart was an obvious benefit to the Suffolk team. Southampton also delivered a lot of centres, buoyed by the presence of an in-form James Beattie. In fact, Ipswich and the Saints were the only teams to complete more than 300 crosses.

Chelsea slipped from fourth in 1999–2000 to fifth in 2000–01, but still remained one of the better teams from wide in the top flight. The signing of lightning-quick winger Jesper Gronkjaer only added to the Pensioners' flank play.

Newcastle fell from first to sixth, missing the presence of their main strikers for much of the season, but still being able to utilise the skills of Nolberto Solano.

Manchester United hit the second-highest number of incomplete crosses, perhaps surprising when they can call on the services of Ryan Giggs and David Beckham. But the former often cuts inside, while the champions have increasingly used the latter in a central role.

For the second time in three years, Arsenal were the Premiership's least-accurate crossers. The Gunners do not have a recognised target man up front and many of their attacks come through the middle. Robert Pires is capable of supplying the ammunition, but the team needs someone to finish the job.

23.5% Arsenal's crossing accuracy was the

TACKLING

	TACKLES WON %	Tackles won	Tackles lost
Coventry	75.9%	675	214
Charlton	75.2%	723	239
Man Utd	75.0%	642	214
Southampton	74.7%	721	244
Leeds Utd	73.9%	819	290
Man City	73.8%	690	245
Liverpool	73.6%	788	283
Ipswich	73.3%	682	249
Arsenal	72.8%	735	275
Chelsea	72.6%	700	264
Everton	72.2%	791	305
Newcastle	72.1%	689	266
Leicester	71.7%	674	266
Bradford	71.5%	704	280
Tottenham	71.5%	700	279
Aston Villa	71.2%	665	269
Middlesbro	71.1%	654	266
Sunderland	70.9%	709	291
Derby Co	70.6%	722	301
West Ham	69.4%	752	332

KEY ■ Tackles won □ Tackles lost

Goalscoring, passing and crossing may not have been Coventry's forté in 2000–01, but the West Midlands club topped the charts when it came to tackling. They certainly did not go down without a fight.

The Sky Blues won more than three-quarters of their challenges, one of only three clubs to do so. The other two were Charlton Athletic and Manchester United, both clubs able to call on the services of a Republic of Ireland midfielder, in the form of Mark Kinsella and Roy Keane respectively. But the Red Devils made the fewest tackles in the Premiership, a clear benefit of dominating games in the manner they do – they rarely need to win back possession.

Their rivals Leeds United made the most tackles, though, with David Batty, Olivier Dacourt and Lee Bowyer forming a stern midfield which augmented their uncompromising defence. The biggest change from the 1999–2000 season was the rise of Southampton from 19th place to fourth. Defensive reorganisation under Glenn Hoddle certainly paid off for the south coast club.

There was not a great difference between the 20 clubs, but West Ham were the only team to win fewer than 70% of their tackles and the Hammers' defensive frailties did threaten to drag them into the relegation battle at one stage. Even so, only two other teams attempted more tackles than the east London side. With Stuart Pearce and Nigel Winterburn at the club this was no surprise, but it was Michael Carrick who was their most prolific ball-winner.

Like Coventry, Manchester City were good at winning back possession but, as ever, it is what a team does with the ball once they have possession that decides their fate. In those cases, the stark answer is: not enough.

CLEARANCES

	TOTAL CLEARANCES	Headed clearances	Other clearances
Leicester	1,538	893	645
Liverpool	1,556	891	665
Southampton	1,453	889	564
Coventry	1,500	873	627
Man City	1,452	869	583
Tottenham	1,482	850	632
Derby Co	1,563	841	722
West Ham	1,478	841	637
Middlesbro	1,372	808	564
Everton	1,342	800	542
Charlton	1,374	794	580
Bradford	1,347	776	571
Sunderland	1,310	759	551
Aston Villa	1,303	716	587
Leeds Utd	1,189	680	509
Newcastle	1,186	675	511
Ipswich	1,184	674	510
Chelsea	1,245	665	580
Arsenal	1,093	639	454
Man Utd	1,049	588	461

KEY ▨ Headed clearances ▢ Other clearances

Those who extol the benefits of the Premiership insist that the league is exciting and stylish. And while there are examples of these trends most weeks, the big clearance from a burly centre-back is still an integral part of the game. Indeed, the phrase "no-one has ever scored from row Z" is as apt as ever and there were more than 27,000 clearances in the 2000–01 season.

Leicester City led the way in terms of headed clearances, making 893 in total. This is unsurprising considering the bulky presence of Matt Elliott and Gerry Taggart. The Foxes were a defensive unit under the leadership of Peter Taylor and the statistics reflect this.

They were closely followed by treble heroes Liverpool. The Reds may have been banging in the goals, but their strength was founded on the impressive figure of Sami Hyypia.

The difference between headed clearances and those with the trusty boot is pronounced. Six teams made more headed clearances overall than Derby, but the Rams were the only side to clear the ball with feet more than 700 times.

Teams who filled the upper echelons of the Premiership table in 2000–01 dominate the other end of the table. Manchester United made just 1,049 clearances and were the only side who made fewer than 600 with the head.

Clubs do attack the Red Devils quite rarely and their forays were repelled with apparent ease.

Arsenal were also called upon to clear the ball on fewer occasions than most. The likes of Tony Adams and Martin Keown may be dominant in the air, but they are allowed the time to build slowly from the back.

Similarly patient teams like Chelsea, Ipswich, Newcastle and Leeds are just ahead of the Gunners.

CHANCES ALLOWED

	SHOTS ALLOWED	Goals conceded	Saves made
Man Utd	125	31	94
Arsenal	116	38	78
Liverpool	161	39	122
Sunderland	156	41	115
Ipswich	149	42	107
Aston Villa	156	43	113
Leeds Utd	158	43	115
Middlesbro	198	44	154
Chelsea	139	45	94
Southampton	173	48	125
Newcastle	167	50	117
West Ham	180	50	130
Leicester	208	51	157
Tottenham	210	54	156
Charlton	189	57	132
Everton	173	59	114
Derby Co	219	59	160
Coventry	220	63	157
Man City	197	65	132
Bradford	240	70	170

KEY ▢ Goals conceded ▢ Saves made

"Close him down!" is a familiar shout heard on touchlines everywhere, from the Premiership to park football. It is a mantra that is hammered into the minds of defenders until they can remember to do nothing else. But which teams were the masters of this art in 2000–01 and which sides relied on the brilliance of their goalkeeper to keep the ball out of the net?

Manchester United ended the season with the best defence, conceding just 31 goals, but the Champions allowed nine more shots at their goal than Arsenal. Indeed, the Gunners saw just 116 shots on target against them in 2000–01, yet they conceded seven more goals than United.

Inferences can be drawn from this, namely that the Red Devils relied on the eccentric but highly effective Fabien Barthez to keep the score down, while Arsenal protected the often-criticised David Seaman with some stout defensive work. In total, 33% of shots on target against the Gunners found their way into the net.

But football is never as simple as that. This is illustrated by the fact that Liverpool – a team regarded as having a strong defence but an occasionally fallible 'keeper – allowed more shots to be fired at their goal than seven other Premiership teams.

Cross-city rivals Everton were even leakier. They were the worst side, seeing 34% of shots on target against them result in goals.

In contrast, Middlesbrough – aided by the excellent Mark Schwarzer – were beaten by just 44 out of 198 shots on target, a miserly 22%.

Even teams like Bradford and Derby, which leaked goals all season, saw better performances from their goalkeepers than Arsenal, Everton and Chelsea.

DISCIPLINE – FOULS CONCEDED

DISCIPLINARY POINTS		Foul committed	Yellow card	Red card
Sunderland	926	662	76	6
Everton	916	658	78	4
Leeds Utd	869	641	70	3
Man City	868	643	69	3
Derby Co	854	593	81	3
Coventry	813	561	76	4
Chelsea	811	571	76	2
Middlesbro	810	552	74	6
Aston Villa	779	572	63	3
Newcastle	748	568	50	5
Bradford	737	560	57	1
Tottenham	733	571	48	3
West Ham	728	509	69	2
Liverpool	719	542	49	5
Southampton	706	553	49	1
Arsenal	703	547	46	3
Leicester	680	497	57	2
Charlton	636	483	45	3
Man Utd	611	461	44	3
Ipswich	573	462	33	2

KEY   Foul committed = 1pt   Yellow card = 3pts   Red card = 6pts

The issue of discipline is never very far from the back pages and season 2000–01 was no different. After several high-profile incidents of indiscipline during the 1999–2000 campaign, the FA announced a "get tough" policy ahead of the 2000–01 season whereby any team with more than five men carded in a match would be subject to an automatic fine.

A special video advisory panel was also introduced to deal with incidents not spotted by referees.

While Arsenal, Aston Villa, Derby, Everton, Middlesbrough and Manchester City all picked up fines under the new rules and several high-profile players fell foul of the new panel, statistically speaking the FA's changes had little effect.

Teams conceded an average of 29 fouls a game in 2000–01, compared to 28 a match the previous season. Bookings were down slightly from an average of 3.34 a match in 1999–2000 to 3.18 in 2000–01 and there were six fewer red cards than in 1999–2000.

Sunderland, who topped the indiscipline charts in 1999–2000, were once again the Premiership's worst offenders in 2000–01, racking up 926 Opta disciplinary points.

Along with Middlesbrough, Sunderland saw red more than any other team in 2000–01 – and they also committed the most fouls.

Derby were the Premiership's most-booked side, picking up a total of 81 yellow cards.

And at the other end of the table, Ipswich displaced Manchester United as the Premiership's cleanest team.

Strangely, Newcastle – who received 50 yellow cards and five reds – were entered into the draw for a UEFA Cup place based on their performance in UEFA's Fair Play League, although there were several teams which received fewer cautions than the Magpies.

DISCIPLINE – FOULS WON

DISCIPLINARY POINTS

Team	Points	Foul committed	Yellow card	Red card
Leeds Utd	998	647	109	4
Sunderland	939	675	76	6
Arsenal	835	574	73	7
Middlesbro	800	611	61	1
Everton	788	572	60	6
Aston Villa	780	561	65	4
Leicester	776	566	62	4
Chelsea	760	586	50	4
Coventry	748	547	65	1
Newcastle	740	551	57	3
Man City	730	520	62	4
Ipswich	726	543	57	2
West Ham	724	559	51	2
Liverpool	719	506	65	3
Charlton	716	536	58	1
Derby Co	708	543	51	2
Man Utd	697	529	50	3
Tottenham	684	516	48	4
Bradford	684	552	40	2
Southampton	668	512	50	1

KEY: ■ Foul committed = 1pt ■ Yellow card = 3pts ■ Red card = 6pts

Arsène Wenger made headlines during 2000–01 when he claimed that teams were afraid to tackle Manchester United and that the champions enjoyed a respect not given to other sides.

At the time, the statistics supported his notion and even at the end of the season United were 17th in the 'fouls against' table, compared with third for Arsenal. The Gunners saw more opposition players sent-off than any other team, with seven players seeing red.

Conversely, Southampton, Coventry, Charlton and Middlesbrough – teams with no 'big club' reputation – each saw just one opposing man ordered from the field of play.

Sunderland were the most-fouled team, with midfielder Don Hutchison suffering more illegal challenges than any other player in the Premiership.

Other players to be frequently fouled included Olivier Dacourt, Alan Smith and Patrick Vieira, illustrating the fact that so-called 'hardmen' have to put up with a lot of physical attention too.

A team was most likely to see a yellow card when playing Leeds, with more than 100 being flashed by referees. And considering that David O'Leary's team finished third in the 'sinners' table, the sound of a whistle blowing was a common one when United were in town.

Liverpool won the fewest fouls, but the officials were more likely to book or send players off against Liverpool than they were with lots of teams.

Bradford drew the fewest yellow cards in the Premiership, while the most-sinned-against team of 1999–2000 – Tottenham – fell to 18th, a dramatic slide indeed.

There were 64 red cards shown in 2000–01 and 36% of them were shown to the opponents of the teams which eventually made up the top six in the Premiership.

GOALS CONCEDED

	GOALS CONCEDED	CLEAN SHEETS
Man Utd	31	17
Arsenal	38	17
Liverpool	39	14
Sunderland	41	13
Ipswich	42	13
Leeds Utd	43	11
Aston Villa	43	9
Middlesbro	44	9
Chelsea	45	10
Southampton	48	14
West Ham	50	8
Newcastle	50	7
Leicester	51	11
Tottenham	54	11
Charlton	57	14
Derby Co	59	13
Everton	59	6
Coventry	63	6
Man City	65	7
Bradford	70	6

Bang goes the 0–0 draw – or so the manufacturers of the new ball introduced at the start of the 2000–01 Premiership season claimed. Nike's new lightweight ball was meant to increase the number of goals scored and make life harder for goalkeepers.

But while there were plenty of good goals scored, the overall tally of goals was down on 1999–2000. So were defences on top in 2000–01?

There were 10 more clean sheets than there had been the previous season and 68 fewer goals. But of the 17 sides which played in the Premiership in 1999–2000 and 2000–01, eight conceded more goals in 2000–01 than they had the previous season, while eight conceded fewer. Only Leeds finished with exactly the same number of goals against in both seasons.

Sunderland's defence showed the biggest improvement, conceding 15 fewer goals than they had in 1999–2000,

although Manchester United and Southampton were not far behind, conceding 14 fewer goals in 2000–01 than they had in 1999–2000.

United's achievement was made even more impressive by the fact that they also kept 17 clean sheets, the joint-highest total along with Arsenal.

As in 1999–2000, the three teams to concede the most goals were relegated from the Premiership, although Bradford's final tally of goals conceded was up by just two on the previous season.

Coventry's defence declined badly, conceding nine more goals than in 1999–2000 and keeping just six clean sheets. But, surprisingly, the Sky Blues backline did not show the biggest decline, relatively speaking.

That award went to Chelsea, who conceded 11 more goals and kept seven fewer clean sheets than they had in 1999–2000.

28 There were 28 0–0 draws

TEAM RECORDS
SHOTS, PASSES, OFFSIDES & FOULS

There is nothing more enraging for the fans than to see their side dominate a game, yet fail to secure the win, or to be seemingly persecuted by the men in black. Here, Opta show the matches in which one team were keeping either the officials or the opposing defence very busy indeed.

MOST SHOTS IN ONE GAME

MATCH	SHOTS (ON TARGET)	RESULT
NEWCASTLE v Leicester	28 (7)	1–1
ARSENAL v Leicester	26 (15)	6–1
IPSWICH v Charlton	26 (9)	2–0
CHELSEA v Coventry	25 (17)	6–1
LEEDS UTD v Leicester	23 (11)	3–0

Five different teams – and no Manchester United for once – featured in the top five for most shots in one game, illustrating how vibrant and entertaining the Premiership can be. Newcastle hammered 28 shots in their home game with Leicester, but only seven of them hit the target, the main reason the Foxes escaped with a 1–1 draw.

But Arsenal found their shooting boots when Peter Taylor's team came to Highbury and smashed six goals past them, despite Tim Flowers making nine saves.

MOST PASSES IN ONE GAME

In a repeat of 1999–2000, Manchester United occupied four of the five spots for the teams making the most passes in a game, but once again it was Chelsea who led the way with their utter dominance of Coventry City at Stamford Bridge.

The Blues made 588 successful passes as they pummelled the Sky Blues 6–1. Sir Alex Ferguson can console himself with the fact that his side completed more than 500 passes in four games as they flexed their championship muscle again.

TEAM	OPPONENTS	PASSES COMPLETED
CHELSEA	v Coventry (h)	588
MAN UTD	v Leicester (h)	576
MAN UTD	v West Ham (h)	523
MAN UTD	v Liverpool (h)	522
MAN UTD	v Derby Co (a)	517

MOST OFFSIDES IN ONE GAME

TEAM	OPPONENTS	OFFSIDES
TOTTENHAM	v Bradford (a)	17
EVERTON	v Man Utd (h)	16
DERBY CO	v Sunderland (h)	16
CHARLTON	v Newcastle (a)	14
LEEDS UTD	v Man Utd (h)	14

Tottenham fans might look back on their 3–3 draw at Bradford as one of the more entertaining games of George Graham's reign, but do they remember that Spurs were caught offside an incredible 17 times? The chief offender was striker Chris Armstrong, who was flagged on eight occasions.

Everton and Derby County pushed them close with 16 offsides in games with Manchester United and Sunderland respectively. It puts the highest figure of 13 in 1999–2000 into perspective.

MOST FOULS IN ONE GAME

Sunderland featured in three of the five matches containing the most fouls, although they were the victims in two of those games: their meeting with bitter rivals Newcastle saw them foul the Magpies 29 times. The main culprits were Alex Rae, Emerson Thome and Don Hutchison, with five fouls apiece.

Leeds v Chelsea fixtures are always fiery and the clash at Stamford Bridge saw 28 United offences, while Derby County committed 26 fouls in two separate games.

TEAM	OPPONENTS	FOULS
SUNDERLAND	v Newcastle (a)	29
LEEDS UTD	v Chelsea (a)	28
LIVERPOOL	v Sunderland (a)	27
DERBY CO	v Sunderland (a)	26
DERBY CO	v Leicester (a)	26

COMEBACKS

LOST AFTER LEADING		WON AFTER BEING BEHIND	
	MATCHES		MATCHES
Ipswich	5	Ipswich	5
Man City	4	Tottenham	5
Coventry	3	Aston Villa	4
Leeds Utd	3	Everton	4
Middlesbro	3	Leeds Utd	4
Newcastle	3	Chelsea	3
Bradford	2	Leicester	3
Charlton	2	Newcastle	3
Chelsea	2	Sunderland	3
Everton	2	Man Utd	2
Liverpool	2	West Ham	2
Southampton	2	Arsenal	1
Tottenham	2	Bradford	1
Arsenal	1	Southampton	1
Aston Villa	1	Charlton	none
Derby Co	1	Coventry	none
Leicester	1	Derby Co	none
Sunderland	1	Liverpool	none
West Ham	1	Man City	none
Man Utd	none	Middlesbro	none

If you like exciting comebacks and unpredictable matches, Ipswich were the team to watch in 2000–01.

George Burley's men lost more matches after leading than any other team, but the Suffolk side were also the Premiership's comeback kings, winning five games after trailing. That record was matched by Tottenham, who launched four comebacks at White Hart Lane, but won just once – against Sunderland – after trailing away from home.

Manchester United went behind a few times in 2000–01, but the champions did not lose a single game after getting their noses in front – the only side in the Premiership to hold that record.

Manchester City and Coventry, who let leads slip four and three times respectively, will have the most regrets about their inability to hold on to an advantage.

Both teams were relegated at the end of the season, but might have retained their Premiership status had they remained a bit tighter at the back.

Joe Royle and Gordon Strachan's teams both dropped out of the top flight after losing games in which they had taken the lead at some stage.

Coventry were the first to go, losing 3–2 against Aston Villa after going 2–0 up: and just two days later Manchester City succumbed to the dreaded drop, losing 2–1 against Ipswich after Shaun Goater had given them a precious lead.

Bradford were the only one of the three relegated teams to win any match in which they went behind – ironically against Coventry in a 2–1 victory at Valley Parade.

Liverpool, who earned a famous late victory against Arsenal in the FA Cup final after going 1–0 down, never recovered after going behind in the Premiership and did so on only one other occasion in their 25 cup ties – against Slovan Liberec.

0 Manchester United were the only team

FOUR OR MORE GOALS

SCORED IN A MATCH		CONCEDED IN A MATCH	
	MATCHES		MATCHES
Arsenal	6	Man City	6
Chelsea	5	Derby Co	5
Leeds Utd	4	Bradford	3
Liverpool	4	Charlton	3
Man Utd	4	Coventry	3
Sunderland	3	Arsenal	2
Charlton	2	Everton	2
Man City	2	Ipswich	2
West Ham	2	Newcastle	2
Aston Villa	1	Tottenham	2
Leicester	1	Chelsea	1
Middlesbro	1	Leicester	1
Tottenham	1	Liverpool	1
Bradford	none	Southampton	1
Coventry	none	Sunderland	1
Derby Co	none	West Ham	1
Everton	none	Aston Villa	none
Ipswich	none	Leeds Utd	none
Newcastle	none	Man Utd	none
Southampton	none	Middlesbro	none

The Premiership now boasts some of the world's top attacking talent, so it comes as no surprise that the top flight witnessed its fair share of heavy drubbings in 2000–01.

Arsenal led the way, hammering in four or more goals on six occasions. The Gunners were made to pay more than once for their penalty-box profligacy, but when Arsène Wenger's team did get their act together up front, the goals rained in.

Two of Arsenal's biggest victories came against Manchester City. But the Londoners were not the only side to dish out a heavy beating to Joe Royle's relegated side. City fell to a total of six defeats by four or more goals and embarrassingly three of these defeats came at Maine Road.

Derby came in for some heavy punishment as well, conceding four goals on five occasions.

One of those defeats came at Pride Park against Chelsea, who knocked in four or more goals on five occasions, a total which puts them just ahead of Leeds United, Liverpool and Manchester United. In fact the Blues bagged four home and away against Derby.

Lovers of high-scoring draws were to be disappointed in 2000–01. Although there were six 3–3 draws, no team conceding four or more goals managed to salvage a point.

There were some close shaves, though, most notably at Elland Road, where Leeds beat both Tottenham and Liverpool by the odd goal in seven.

But as exciting as both of those games were, neither saw enough goals to earn the title of the 2000–01 season's highest-scoring match.

That honour went to the game between Arsenal and Charlton at Highbury, in which the Gunners ran out 5–3 winners in an eight-goal thriller despite being behind for much of the game.

NARROW MARGINS

WON BY A SINGLE GOAL		LOST BY A SINGLE GOAL	
	MATCHES		MATCHES
Arsenal	10	Man City	12
Ipswich	10	Middlesbro	11
Leeds Utd	10	Everton	10
Southampton	10	Coventry	9
Sunderland	10	Ipswich	8
Aston Villa	8	Leicester	8
Charlton	8	West Ham	8
Newcastle	8	Bradford	7
Derby Co	7	Leeds Utd	7
Leicester	7	Newcastle	7
Man Utd	7	Southampton	7
Tottenham	7	Chelsea	6
Chelsea	6	Derby Co	6
Coventry	6	Liverpool	6
Everton	6	Sunderland	6
Liverpool	6	Aston Villa	5
West Ham	5	Charlton	5
Man City	4	Tottenham	5
Middlesbro	4	Arsenal	4
Bradford	2	Man Utd	4

Manchester City took their fair share of drubbings in 2000-01, but the Citizens also fell to more narrow defeats than any other side, losing a total of 12 games by a margin of just one goal.

Joe Royle was heard to complain about his team's lack of luck on more than one occasion, but as galling as losing by such a narrow margin must be, it seems that the best teams have all mastered the knack of eking out results when need be.

The next three teams in the list also struggled at the foot of the table. Middlesbrough, Everton and Coventry all dropped valuable points thanks to defeats by the odd goal.

Arsenal, Ipswich, Leeds, Sunderland and, more surprisingly, Southampton all won 10 games by a margin of just one goal in 2000-01, while City finished with just four victories by the odd goal. Only wooden spoon-winners Bradford had a worse record than that.

Manchester United usually had enough firepower to blow the opposition away, but when needs dictated the Red Devils were as adept as anyone at stealing the points: Sir Alex Ferguson's team won seven games by one clear goal.

The champions were the hardest team to beat in the Premiership. Sir Alex Ferguson's men were left pointless just six times in the league and only Liverpool and Tottenham Hotspur managed to beat them by more than one clear goal.

Arsenal were not far behind. Like United, the Gunners also lost just four games by a one-goal margin, but Arsène Wenger's men took a few uncharacteristic heavy beatings as well, losing 6-1 at Old Trafford and 4-0 at Anfield.

Southampton and Sunderland were the masters of the 1-0 victory, winning seven games by that scoreline, while Bradford were the only team not to win a game 1-0 all season.

4 Manchester United lost on each of

SHUT–OUTS

FAILING TO SCORE			KEEPING A CLEAN SHEET	
	MATCHES			MATCHES
Bradford	18		Arsenal	17
Tottenham	16		Man Utd	17
Leicester	15		Charlton	14
Aston Villa	13		Liverpool	14
Coventry	13		Southampton	14
Newcastle	13		Derby Co	13
Man City	12		Ipswich	13
Southampton	12		Sunderland	13
Sunderland	12		Leeds Utd	11
West Ham	12		Leicester	11
Derby Co	11		Tottenham	11
Everton	11		Chelsea	10
Middlesbro	11		Aston Villa	9
Arsenal	10		Middlesbro	9
Charlton	10		West Ham	8
Chelsea	9		Man City	7
Liverpool	6		Newcastle	7
Leeds Utd	5		Bradford	6
Man Utd	4		Coventry	6
Ipswich	3		Everton	6

Very few pundits expected Bradford to survive a second season in the Premiership and the Yorkshiremen duly struggled throughout the campaign.

The Bantams failed to score in 18 of their league games, a figure which helps illuminate the problems they faced.

The next three teams in the table, however, were all sides that finished in the comfort of mid-table. Tottenham, Leicester and Aston Villa all suffered spells when they could not find the back of the net, with Spurs particularly labouring in January and February, when they drew 0–0 four games in a row – equalling a Premiership record.

Ipswich were the team which had least trouble opening their account in any given game. There were just three occasions when George Burley's side failed to make an impression on the scoresheet. Champions and Premiership top scorers Manchester United were almost as consistent, finishing with a blank sheet just four times, losing on each occasion.

Their defence may be creaking more heavily than ever, but Arsenal – along with Manchester United – led the way in keeping clean sheets.

Both sides achieved a shut-out on 17 occasions, with the Gunners racking up eight clean sheets in nine games at one point. Unfortunately, the game in which they did concede was the 6–1 thrashing at Old Trafford, which ended any faint hopes of regaining the title.

Charlton managed 14 clean sheets: only three more than they managed in 1998–99, but it helped them finish in the top half of the table with relative ease.

At the bottom, Everton, Bradford and Coventry managed just six clean sheets each, the latter two sides suffering relegation, while Newcastle United endured a spell of 25 games without a defensive shut-out.

WHERE GOALS SCORED

GOALS FROM OUTSIDE BOX

Team	%	Outside box (set-pieces)	Inside box (penalties)
Everton	6.7%	3(0)	42(5)
Man City	7.3%	3(0)	38(2)
Charlton	8.0%	4(0)	46(3)
Middlesbro	9.1%	4(1)	40(3)
Newcastle	9.1%	4(1)	40(5)
Arsenal	14.3%	9(0)	54(1)
Southampton	15.0%	6(1)	34(0)
Leicester	15.4%	6(1)	33(3)
Derby Co	16.2%	6(3)	31(2)
Coventry	16.7%	6(3)	30(3)
West Ham	17.8%	8(1)	37(4)
Chelsea	19.1%	13(1)	55(4)
Tottenham	19.1%	9(1)	38(3)
Leeds Utd	20.3%	13(6)	51(3)
Ipswich	21.1%	12(4)	45(3)
Aston Villa	21.7%	10(1)	36(1)
Sunderland	21.7%	10(3)	36(2)
Man Utd	22.8%	18(5)	61(2)
Liverpool	23.9%	17(4)	54(3)
Bradford	26.7%	8(1)	22(2)

KEY ■ Outside box (set-pieces) ■ Inside box (penalties)

The number of goals in the 2000–01 season was down on the previous year – and the shooting accuracy inside the penalty area declined too. Nevertheless, 80% of Premiership goals came from within 18 yards of the goal.

Everton were the most likely team to score inside the box, purely because of their poor performance from long range. The Toffees scored just three goals from distance, a figure matched by fellow-strugglers Manchester City.

At the opposite end of the scale, Bradford City scored the highest proportion of their goals from long range, but that was more to do with their failures from close in – they only scored 22 times from inside the box – than anything else.

Still, all but one of their eight long-distance efforts came from open play, testament to the shooting prowess of such talented players as Benito Carbone and Robbie Blake.

Southampton were hampered by the fact they were not awarded a single penalty all season, while Newcastle and Everton scored five spot-kicks apiece. Both teams also contrived to miss two.

Leeds United bagged the highest number of goals direct from set-pieces with six. Chief architect was Irish star Ian Harte, who scored four times with his lethal left foot.

This figure was eclipsed by David Beckham, however, with the England captain scoring all five of Manchester United's set-piece strikes.

Chelsea scored the lowest proportion of long-range goals in 1999–2000, but improved considerably in 2000–01.

The acquisition of Jimmy Floyd Hasselbaink helped, the Dutchman scoring six times from open play from outside the box – more than any other player and double the total of the entire team in the previous year.

0 Southampton were the only team not

WHERE GOALS CONCEDED

Team	GOALS FROM OUTSIDE BOX	Outside box (set-pieces)	Inside box (penalties)
Aston Villa	9.3%	4(0)	39(3)
Sunderland	9.8%	4(0)	37(2)
Liverpool	10.3%	4(0)	35(3)
Coventry	11.1%	7(2)	56(2)
Tottenham	11.1%	6(0)	48(6)
Newcastle	12.0%	6(4)	44(6)
Chelsea	13.3%	6(1)	39(1)
Leeds Utd	14.0%	6(3)	37(1)
Ipswich	16.7%	7(2)	35(3)
Southampton	16.7%	8(2)	40(3)
Leicester	17.6%	9(3)	42(1)
Man City	18.5%	12(2)	53(4)
Bradford	18.6%	13(4)	57(2)
Derby Co	20.3%	12(1)	47(3)
Charlton	21.1%	12(1)	45(3)
Everton	22.0%	13(2)	46(3)
Man Utd	22.6%	7(1)	24(1)
Middlesbro	22.7%	10(0)	34(3)
Arsenal	23.7%	9(4)	29(1)
West Ham	28.0%	14(5)	36(3)

KEY: ■ Outside box (set-pieces) ■ Inside box (penalties)

The top three teams for conceding goals inside the penalty area in 2000–01 were all sides that finished in the top half of the table.

This was a clear change from 1999–2000 when two of the relegated teams – Sheffield Wednesday and Wimbledon – were laxest in their own box.

Aston Villa and Sunderland both conceded more than 90% of their goals inside the penalty area, while Liverpool were not far behind.

All three teams have goalkeepers who – while renowned for their shot-stopping – have sometimes attracted questions about their dominance of the box.

Coventry City also conceded the vast majority of their goals from close range, despite the best efforts of both Magnus Hedman and Chris Kirkland.

Newcastle and Spurs both conceded six goals from penalties each, something that sees them relatively high in this table.

There were five sides which only saw a single spot-kick slip into their net, including Manchester United, perhaps unsurprisingly.

Arsenal avoided finishing as the team which conceded the highest ratio of long-range goals for the third year in a row, but only by one place. West Ham, who conceded more than a quarter of their goals from distance, took their place.

The Hammers also conceded five direct set-pieces in 2000–01, the highest number of any team and the new boss will clearly have to work on his players' ability to set up a wall in free-kick situations.

Middlesbrough, on the other hand, did not concede a single direct free-kick, but were beaten from range on 10 occasions.

Manchester United matched Liverpool's 1999–2000 total of conceding just 24 goals from shots inside the box, but seven teams were more defensively sound from long range than the champions.

HOW GOALS WERE SCORED

Team	Headed Goals %	Headers	Own goals	Other	Left foot	Right foot
Coventry	36.1%	13		3	7	13
Southampton	30.0%	12		2	9	17
Middlesbro	27.3%	12	4	1	11	16
Derby Co	27.0%	10			6	21
Bradford	26.7%	8	1		5	16
Leicester	25.6%	10	1	1	11	16
Tottenham	25.5%	12	1		10	24
Ipswich	24.6%	14	3	2	17	21
Charlton	24.0%	12	3		14	21
Chelsea	23.5%	16			11	40
Leeds Utd	23.4%	15	1		19	29
Aston Villa	21.7%	10			10	26
Liverpool	21.1%	15	1		20	35
Sunderland	19.6%	9			11	26
Newcastle	18.2%	8	2		12	22
West Ham	17.8%	8	1		10	26
Man City	17.1%	7	3		11	20
Man Utd	11.4%	9	3	2	15	50
Everton	11.1%	5			17	23
Arsenal	9.5%	6	2		20	35

KEY: Headers / Own goals / Other / Left foot / Right foot

It was no surprise to see that 50% of all goals in the 2000–01 Premiership were scored with the right foot. Nor did it come as a shock to see that champions Manchester United notched up the most goals in this category.

But the Premiership also saw plenty of left-footed and headed goals.

Chelsea scored the most headers – 16 in total – while, surprisingly for a club which included both Duncan Ferguson and Kevin Campbell in its squad, it was Everton who scored the fewest headed goals. Campbell notched up two of Everton's headers – but Ferguson, who scored six goals in total, amazingly failed to bag a single headed goal in 2000–01.

The signing of John Hartson saw Coventry end the season as the team most reliant on headed goals, though. The Sky Blues scored 36% of all their goals from headers, the highest proportion in the Premiership.

Arsenal's lack of aerial presence in the penalty area once again made them the Premiership's least threatening team in the air, with just 9.5% of all the Gunners' goals coming via headers – the third season in succession that Arsène Wenger's men have finished bottom of the headed goals table.

Arsenal and Liverpool finished with the joint-highest number of left-footed goals, although Ipswich's Marcus Stewart scored more goals with his left foot than any other player – 11 in total.

Just three per cent of all the Premiership's goals came via own goals. Middlesbrough were the biggest beneficiaries of opposition blunders, seeing four goals scored for them by the opposition. Aston Villa, Sunderland, Derby and Everton were the only teams not to benefit from a single own goal.

Ipswich and Manchester United scored two each in the category "Other", meaning other parts of the anatomy.

9.5% Arsenal scored the lowest proportion of

HOW GOALS WERE CONCEDED

Team	HEADED GOALS %	Headers	Own goals	Other	Left foot	Right foot
Leeds Utd	30.2%	13	2		6	22
Man Utd	29.0%	9	1		5	16
Middlesbro	27.3%	12	2		11	19
Everton	27.1%	16	4	1	11	27
Chelsea	26.7%	12			14	19
Leicester	25.5%	13		1	14	23
Aston Villa	23.3%	10	4	1	9	19
Southampton	22.9%	11	2		12	23
Coventry	22.2%	14			14	35
Newcastle	22.0%	11			9	30
West Ham	22.0%	11	4		10	25
Sunderland	22.0%	9			11	21
Tottenham	20.4%	11		1	14	28
Man City	18.5%	12	1	1	15	36
Arsenal	18.4%	7	2	1	10	18
Bradford	17.1%	12	2		24	32
Ipswich	16.7%	7	1	1	10	23
Liverpool	15.4%	6		1	10	22
Derby Co	15.3%	9	3		17	30
Charlton	10.5%	6	2		20	29

KEY ▢ Headers ▢ Own goals ▢ Other ▢ Left foot ▢ Right foot

Gérard Houllier has spent a lot of time and money tightening up Liverpool's defence and the Reds are now reaping the benefits.

Once famed for their fragility in the air, Liverpool's defence are now one of the hardest teams in the Premiership to score a headed goal against.

Along with Charlton Athletic, Liverpool conceded the fewest headed goals in the 2000–01 Premiership – just six in total. Charlton were the least likely to be undone by a headed strike, as just 10.5% of all goals conceded by the Addicks came from headers.

The Reds' Merseyside rivals, Everton, were the Premiership team most susceptible to headed goals. Walter Smith's side, which also scored fewer headers than any other club, conceded 16 goals from headers.

Leeds were also undone by their fair share of headed goals. The Yorkshiremen conceded fewer headers than Everton, but overall 30.2% of all the goals they conceded came from headers – the highest proportion in the Premiership.

Manchester United conceded nine headers, accounting for 29% of all goals conceded, perhaps illustrating a weakness that other teams failed to exploit.

Unsurprisingly, the situation at Maine Road was rather different. Manchester City's porous defence leaked 36 right-footed goals – the most in the Premiership.

Aston Villa, Everton and West Ham scored the most own goals, shipping four bloopers apiece. One of the Hammers' own goals came from Rio Ferdinand, who also put through his own net after signing for Leeds, making him the only player to register an own goal for two different clubs in 2000–01.

Chelsea, Leicester, Newcastle, Coventry and Sunderland were the only clubs not to concede an own goal.

headed goals for the third season in a row

WHEN GOALS WERE SCORED

	FIRST HALF GOALS %	0–15 mins	16–30 mins	31–45 mins	46–60 mins	61–75 mins	76–90 mins	SECOND HALF GOALS %
Sunderland	32.6%	4	8	3	12	11	8	67.4%
Ipswich	35.1%	8	7	5	14	7	16	64.9%
Aston Villa	39.1%	6	5	7	8	9	11	60.9%
Liverpool	39.4%	13	8	7	14	12	17	60.6%
Southampton	40.0%	6	6	4	9	5	10	60.0%
West Ham	40.0%	5	3	10	6	11	10	60.0%
Middlesbro	40.9%	4	5	9	11	6	9	59.1%
Everton	42.2%	5	6	8	8	6	12	57.8%
Leeds Utd	43.8%	10	8	10	11	9	16	56.3%
Man City	43.9%	4	7	7	4	10	9	56.1%
Arsenal	44.4%	9	14	5	7	11	17	55.6%
Newcastle	45.5%	9	6	5	9	8	7	54.5%
Leicester	46.2%	5	7	6	7	5	9	53.8%
Man Utd	46.8%	10	12	15	10	15	17	53.2%
Tottenham	51.1%	2	8	14	7	9	7	48.9%
Chelsea	51.5%	8	9	18	8	14	11	48.5%
Coventry	52.8%	4	7	8	3	7	7	47.2%
Bradford	53.3%	8	6	2	2	5	7	46.7%
Charlton	54.0%	10	6	11	6	5	12	46.0%
Derby Co	54.1%	5	3	12	5	5	7	45.9%

KEY: ▪ 0–15 mins ▪ 16–30 mins ▪ 31–45 mins ▪ 46–60 mins ▪ 61–75 mins ▪ 76–90 mins

Missing the first few minutes of a Sunderland game was not too disastrous in 2000–01, as they kept their fans waiting for goals the longest. The Black Cats scored just 32.6% of their goals in the first half, while Ipswich – success notwithstanding – also kept their fans hanging on until the bitter end before disturbing the scoreboard attendant.

The strength of Liverpool's attack was illustrated by the fact that, although they scored fewer than 40% of their goals in the first half, they still scored more times in the opening 15 minutes than any other team in the top flight.

Bradford City bagged more than a quarter of their goals in the opening 15 minutes of their games, but must have been loath to leave the dressing-room a second time, as they scored just two goals in the period directly after the half-time interval.

For the second season in a row, Tottenham Hotspur scored 30% of their goals in the 15 minutes before the break, yet they were the side least likely to score a goal late in the second half. The biggest percentage was claimed by Derby County, who notched 32% of their efforts at the end of the first half.

Liverpool and Ipswich were the teams which did best immediately after the break, scoring 14 goals apiece in that period. That total accounted for a quarter of Town's goals in 2000–01, but just a fifth of Liverpool's.

The strength of the top teams seemed to tell in the final 15 minutes of matches, with the top three Premiership sides all hitting 17 goals in that period.

Leeds and Ipswich, the sides in fourth and fifth, were just behind with 16 apiece.

Overall, 55% of goals were scored in the second half and 22% of all strikes came in the final 15 minutes, as teams tired and strikers took full advantage.

2 Tottenham scored the fewest goals in the opening

WHEN GOALS WERE CONCEDED

	FIRST HALF GOALS %	0–15 mins	16–30 mins	31–45 mins	46–60 mins	61–75 mins	76–90 mins	SECOND HALF GOALS %
Coventry	36.5%	8	9	6	16	7	17	63.5%
Charlton	36.8%	6	4	11	7	12	17	63.2%
Southampton	37.5%	3	6	9	9	11	10	62.5%
Bradford	38.6%	6	15	6	12	17	14	61.4%
Leicester	39.2%	6	7	7	6	10	15	60.8%
Man City	40.0%	7	7	12	12	12	15	60.0%
Arsenal	42.1%	3	5	8	12	5	5	57.9%
Chelsea	42.2%	7	5	7	6	7	13	57.8%
Derby Co	42.4%	9	5	11	14	9	11	57.6%
Newcastle	44.0%	8	7	7	2	11	15	56.0%
Everton	44.1%	9	9	8	10	9	14	55.9%
Middlesbro	45.5%	7	4	9	10	7	7	54.5%
Liverpool	46.2%	8	4	6	5	7	9	53.8%
Ipswich	47.6%	4	9	7	7	11	4	52.4%
Sunderland	48.8%	8	5	7	5	4	12	51.2%
Aston Villa	51.2%	7	10	5	4	6	11	48.8%
Tottenham	51.9%	10	7	11	9	7	10	48.1%
Man Utd	54.8%	6	5	6	1	6	7	45.2%
West Ham	56.0%	9	8	11	9	7	6	44.0%
Leeds Utd	60.5%	4	10	12	5	5	7	39.5%

KEY: 0–15 mins, 16–30 mins, 31–45 mins, 46–60 mins, 61–75 mins, 76–90 mins

Commentators love referring to teams getting caught by the "sucker punch" and Coventry and Charlton were the teams to watch to see such an effect in action during the 2000–01 season.

Both the Sky Blues and the Addicks conceded a league high of 17 goals in the final 15 minutes of games.

Conversely, the side caught cold most often was Tottenham, who conceded 10 goals in the opening quarter hour of games. As a ratio, though, Liverpool and Sunderland suffered more, letting in 21% and 20% of their season's goals in the opening section.

Leeds were the team which suffered throughout the first half of games, with 60% of goals against the Peacocks coming in that period. They tightened up after the half-time break, however, letting in just 17 second-half strikes.

The sternest defence after half-time belonged to Manchester United, who saw just 14 goals slip through all season.

United were also the only team not to concede more than seven goals in any given 15-minute period.

Only five teams let in more goals in the first half than in the second period, suggesting that tiredness does weaken defences considerably.

Ipswich were the strongest side in the closing stages, letting in just four goals in that period, a mere 10% of their total. That was still one more than Arsenal managed in 1999–2000, when the Gunners saw just 7% of their tally go against them in that final period.

That ratio almost doubled to 13% in 2000–01, but Arsène Wenger's side were weakest in the 15 minutes after half-time, when they conceded almost a third of all goals against them. This was the highest ratio in the entire Premiership, with the Gunners clearly being too relaxed by their half-time oranges.

WHO SCORED THE "GOALS FOR"

	% GOALS BY ATTACKERS	Attack	Midfield	Defence	Own goals
Chelsea	66.2%	45	19	3	
Bradford	60.0%	18	6	5	
Leeds Utd	57.8%	37	16	10	
Tottenham	57.4%	27	10	9	
Ipswich	56.1%	32	12	10	3
Charlton	56.0%	28	15	4	3
Everton	55.6%	25	9	11	
Man Utd	54.4%	43	29	4	3
Derby Co	54.1%	20	12	5	
Liverpool	53.5%	38	25	7	
Southampton	52.5%	21	14	3	2
Man City	51.2%	21	8	9	3
West Ham	51.1%	23	17	4	
Coventry	50.0%	18	13	2	3
Arsenal	49.2%	31	22	8	2
Sunderland	47.8%	22	20	4	
Middlesbro	47.7%	21	11	8	4
Aston Villa	45.7%	21	22	3	
Leicester	43.6%	17	14	7	
Newcastle	34.1%	15	25	2	2

KEY ■ Attack ■ Midfield □ Defence ■ Own goals

Manchester United are strong in every area of the pitch, but it is their midfield which really sets them apart from the rest of the Premiership.

The 2000–01 season saw United notch up more goals from midfield than any other side – 29 in total.

Of course the Red Devils' strikers were also lethal, scoring 43 goals between them, but this was not the best return in the Premiership. That honour went to Chelsea who, thanks largely to Golden Boot-winner Jimmy Floyd Hasselbaink, notched up 45 goals via their strikers.

It could be argued the Blues were too reliant on their frontmen, though. Just 27.9% of all their goals came from midfield, a figure some way behind the likes of Manchester United. In fact, Gustavo Poyet was responsible for 11 of the 19 strikes from the Blues' engine room. And only 4.4% of their goals came from defenders, the lowest percentage in the Premiership.

At the other end of the scale were Newcastle. The Magpies suffered badly in the absence of Alan Shearer and Carl Cort through injury, scoring just 15 goals through their strikers, the lowest number in the Premiership.

Luckily for Bobby Robson, his midfielders chipped in with plenty of goals (25) which equated to 56.8% of Newcastle's total, the highest ratio for midfield goals in the Premiership.

Aston Villa, who also experienced their fair share of problems up front, joined Newcastle as the only sides to score more goals through their midfielders than their strikers.

Everton's penalty-takers Michael Ball and David Unsworth helped the Toffees earn the title of the team with the most free-scoring defenders. They were closely followed by Ipswich and Leeds with 10 goals apiece from the back.

11 Gustavo Poyet scored more goals

WHO SCORED THE "GOALS AGAINST"

	% GOALS BY ATTACKERS	Attack	Midfield	Defence	Own goals
Man Utd	67.7%	21	6	3	1
Chelsea	66.7%	30	10	5	
Ipswich	64.3%	27	10	4	1
Newcastle	62.0%	31	13	6	
Charlton	61.4%	35	17	3	2
Leicester	60.8%	31	12	8	
Coventry	58.7%	37	22	4	
Middlesbro	56.8%	25	11	6	2
Liverpool	56.4%	22	12	4	1
Arsenal	55.3%	21	12	3	2
Southampton	54.2%	26	12	8	2
Sunderland	51.2%	21	12	8	
Everton	50.8%	30	16	9	4
Tottenham	50.0%	27	21	5	1
Derby Co	49.2%	29	22	5	3
Man City	47.7%	31	25	8	1
Bradford	42.9%	30	30	8	2
Aston Villa	37.2%	16	15	8	4
West Ham	36.0%	18	23	5	4
Leeds Utd	34.9%	15	18	8	2

KEY ■ Attack ■ Midfield □ Defence ■ Own goals

While Manchester United's midfield were busy laying waste to the opposition, it seems that their rivals' men in the middle were too busy trying to contain the champions' star-studded foursome to make much of an impact in United's penalty area.

United did such a good job containing opposition playmakers that they conceded just six goals to opposition midfielders all season, comfortably the lowest figure in the Premiership and some 24 goals fewer than Bradford, who conceded 30 goals to midfielders – the most in the Premiership during 2000–01.

Bradford also conceded plenty of goals to strikers. But although the Bantams were the Premiership's poorest defenders, they were not punished by the top flight's frontmen as often as relegation rivals Coventry City.

The Sky Blues allowed opposition strikers to score 37 goals against them in 2000–01, more than any other side. Gordon Strachan's team were also heavily punished by midfielders, although West Ham too suffered at the hands of the men in the middle, with 46% of the 50 goals they let in conceded to midfielders.

Leeds' defenders proved to be the most effective at containing opposing strikers. David O'Leary's side conceded just 15 goals to strikers all season, a fantastic record which only Aston Villa and West Ham came close to matching.

Everton, who scored more goals through their defenders than any other team, were also the victims of more goals from defenders than any other top-flight side – nine in total.

In all, 19% of goals scored in Premiership matches involving Everton were scored by defenders, a figure seven percentage points higher than the Premiership average and one unlikely to be repeated in the 2001–02 season.

than any other Premiership midfielder

THE PLAYERS

The top scorer is easy enough for anyone to monitor — but who was the top tackler, the most prolific passer, the best crosser or the best shot-stopper? And which players had the best and worst disciplinary records in the league?

The answers to these and many more questions are contained in this section — and only Opta can provide this information, because of the unique way in which they monitor every single touch of the ball.

But it is not just quantity that counts — it is quality, too. So although many of the categories are sorted on total number of successful outcomes, you can also see percentage completion rates to judge for yourself how good players really are.

The bar charts show several pieces of information. For example, in the chart showing which player had the most shots in total on page 652, you will also be able to see the player who had the most shots on target; in addition, the figure shown alongside the bars indicates how accurate their shooting was.

There is an explanation beneath each of the charts showing how the ranking is calculated and what it means.

The Golden Boot was won by Jimmy Floyd Hasselbaink, who finished the season with 23 Premiership goals — the third season in a row in which the Dutchman has topped the scoring charts in the league in which he was playing. He was the only player to net more than 20 goals in 2000–01, though special mention should go to Marcus Stewart who bagged 19 strikes in his first Premiership season and ran Hasselbaink closest for the title of top scorer.

Thierry Henry bagged 17 goals, despite firing in more shots than any other player, while 1999–2000's Golden Boot winner, Kevin Phillips, scored just 14 Premiership goals in 2000–01.

PLAYER RECORDS
SHOTS, PASSES, FOULS & SAVES

As soon as a player crosses the white line on to the pitch the responsibility is theirs to produce the goods. There is no hiding place in the Premiership and players can leave the fans lauding their name or baying for blood. Here are the most prolific individual performances of the 2000–01 season.

MOST SHOTS IN ONE GAME

PLAYER	MATCH	SHOTS ATTEMPTED (ON TARGET)	GOALS
T Henry	v Leicester (h)	9 (8)	3
J F Hasselbaink	v Coventry (h)	9 (7)	4
K Phillips	v Bradford (a)	8 (5)	3
J Johansson	v Coventry (h)	8 (5)	1
K Phillips	v Everton (h)	8 (5)	1

Arsenal's Thierry Henry is a man who is never shy in front of goal and against Leicester on Boxing Day he was in fine fettle, with nine shots on goal – eight on target – and the match ball for his efforts.

Premiership top scorer Jimmy Floyd Hasselbaink also managed nine shots in Chelsea's rout of Coventry, four of which found their way into the back of the net, while those managing eight efforts in a game were Kevin Phillips (twice) and Jonatan Johansson.

MOST PASSES IN ONE GAME

Manchester United skipper Roy Keane once again proved that he is the Premiership's pass master, racking up the two highest totals for individual passes in a game. The Boxing Day trip to Aston Villa saw Keane notch up a century of passes, while he fell one short of the 100 at home to Leicester. Chelsea captain Dennis Wise helped tear Coventry apart with 96 passes while United featured twice more in the top five thanks to David Beckham and Denis Irwin.

PLAYER	MATCH	PASSES COMPLETED
Roy Keane	v Aston Villa (a)	102
Roy Keane	v Leicester (h)	99
Dennis Wise	v Coventry (h)	96
David Beckham	v West Ham (h)	94
Denis Irwin	v Leicester (h)	93

MOST FOULS IN ONE GAME

PLAYER	MATCH	FOULS CONCEDED	CARDS
D Burton	v Everton (a)	11	Y
D Bergkamp	v Liverpool (h)	8	0
H Ricard	v Charlton (a)	8	0
J Lawrence	v Derby (a)	8	0
A Smith	v Arsenal (a)	8	0
F Kanouté	v Middlesbrough (h)	8	0

Reggae Boy Deon Burton let out all the frustrations of Derby's disappointing season during their trip to Goodison by committing a total of 11 fouls in just that one game, resulting in a yellow card for Jim Smith's feisty forward.

A further five players all committed eight offences during a single game, including not only the tempestuous Alan Smith and Hamilton Ricard but also the usually more timid figures of Frederic Kanouté and Dennis Bergkamp.

MOST SAVES IN ONE GAME

Five of the Premiership's top stoppers were forced into action a total of 10 times in a game during the 2000–01 season, meaning they have to share the season's best performance. Tim Flowers and Chris Kirkland were both able to walk away with clean sheets after their heroics against West Ham and Chelsea respectively.

David James earned Villa a point at the Stadium of Light, while Shaka Hislop and Neil Sullivan saved their sides further embarrassment at Newcastle and Arsenal.

PLAYER	MATCH	SAVES MADE	CONCEDED
T Flowers	v West Ham (a)	10	0
C Kirkland	v Chelsea (h)	10	0
D James	v Sunderland (a)	10	1
S Hislop	v Newcastle (a)	10	1
N Sullivan	v Arsenal (a)	10	2

GOALS – FREE KICKS, PENALTIES, HEADERS, GOALS FROM OUTSIDE THE BOX

With ever-increasing riches awaiting the most successful Premiership teams, it is no wonder that clubs are willing to invest fortunes in those players who possess the natural ability to score goals. Here are 2000–01's supreme exponents in the art of headed goals, set-piece successes, long-range strikes and penalty executions.

PENALTIES

Sixty-eight penalties were awarded in the 2000–01 Premiership campaign, with 54 being comfortably slotted home. But nine were saved and five were missed, resulting in a success rate of 79%.

Jimmy Floyd Hasselbaink proved to be the hottest shot from the spot, bagging four penalties. Paolo Di Canio and David Unsworth notched three each – the latter seeing one saved on the season's final day – while a further 12 players netted twice from the spot.

PLAYER	PENALTY GOALS
Jimmy Floyd Hasselbaink	4
Paolo Di Canio	3
David Unsworth	3
12 players on	2

SET-PIECES

PLAYER	SET-PIECE GOALS
David Beckham	5
Ian Harte	4
Gary McAllister	3
5 players on	2

Free-kick techniques seem to be improving in the Premiership, with 37 goals coming directly from set-pieces in 2000–01, compared to just 23 during the previous campaign. The trusty right boot of England skipper David Beckham was once again a potent weapon and the Manchester United star punished sides with five goals from costly free-kicks. Irish full-back Ian Harte enjoyed four free-kick successes for Leeds, while treble winner Gary McAllister had a set-piece trio of his own to celebrate.

HEADED GOALS

Nearly a quarter of all the Premiership goals scored in 2000–01 came courtesy of headers. Players were clearly using their heads more as, although fewer goals were scored overall, a greater number came via the head. The Leeds strike duo of Mark Viduka and Alan Smith were obviously ahead of the rest when it came to using their loaf, with Viduka leading the race with six while his younger colleague was only just behind with five.

PLAYER	HEADED GOALS
Mark Viduka	6
Alan Smith	5
11 players on	4

GOALS FROM OUTSIDE THE BOX

PLAYER	LONG-RANGE GOALS
David Beckham	7
Jimmy Floyd Hasselbaink	6
Ian Harte	5
Benito Carbone	4
Steven Gerrard	4
Thierry Henry	4

There is nothing like a spectacular long-range goal to get a crowd buzzing and in the 2000–01 campaign a total of 169 goals came via strikes outside the area.

David Beckham was the most dangerous from distance with seven goals, while Golden Boot winner Jimmy Floyd Hasselbaink proved that he was not just a poacher by following close behind with six. Ian Harte produced five goals from outside the box, with Benito Carbone, Steven Gerrard and Thierry Henry all managing four.

GOALSCORERS

It is one thing knowing who the most potent goalscorers are, but it helps to know the situation they thrive in. Some prefer the glory of scoring in front of their own fans, while others prefer to be away. Some will get a match off to a flying start, while others can be relied on late in the game. Opta show here who were better home and away, who were frequently first goalscorers and who were strong in the final 15 minutes.

HOME

PLAYER	HOME GOALS
Jimmy Floyd Hasselbaink	15
Thierry Henry	14
Michael Owen	12
Mark Viduka	12
Teddy Sheringham	11

There was no place like home for Jimmy Floyd Hasselbaink, whose form mirrored that of his team, being far stronger at Stamford Bridge than on the road. He scored 15 of his 23 goals on home ground – benefiting from greater confidence around him when playing in front of the home crowd. Most of the Premiership's other hotshots preferred their own turf, with Thierry Henry, Michael Owen, Mark Viduka and Teddy Sheringham all having a significantly better record when at home.

AWAY

Marcus Stewart was the striker who most liked to play away from home and he was the only Premiership player to have reached double figures on his travels. He hit 11 of his 19 goals away from Portman Road in his debut Premiership season. Alen Boksic and Kevin Phillips both preferred to be playing away from their home crowd, Hasselbaink showed that he also had the ability on the road and Emile Heskey hit seven away from Anfield.

PLAYER	AWAY GOALS
Marcus Stewart	11
Alen Boksic	9
Kevin Phillips	9
Jimmy Floyd Hasselbaink	8
Emile Heskey	7

FIRST GOALSCORERS

PLAYER	FIRST GOALS
Marcus Stewart	11
Jimmy Floyd Hasselbaink	8
James Beattie	7
Emile Heskey	7
3 players on	6

If you are ever laying a bet on the first goalscorer in a game, then you could do a lot worse than to back Ipswich striker Marcus Stewart. He was the quickest off the mark on 11 occasions in 2000–01, giving Town the initiative to take enough points to claim a place in Europe. Hasselbaink bagged the first goal on eight occasions, while there were seven each for Southampton striker James Beattie and Liverpool's Emile Heskey.

LATE GOALSCORERS

Surprisingly, Premiership top scorer Hasselbaink failed to appear as one of the most frequent scorers of late goals, despite bagging a total of 23 in 2000–01. It was Arsenal's Thierry Henry who finished games stronger than any other striker, with seven of his season's tally coming in the final 15 minutes of matches. Mark Viduka also finished strongly with six late goals, while Marcus Stewart claimed five of his tally in the final quarter of an hour.

PLAYER	LATE GOALS
Thierry Henry	7
Mark Viduka	6
Marcus Stewart	5
6 players on	4

205 The opening goal of a game was scored in

FASTEST / LATEST GOALS
IN 2000–01 PREMIERSHIP

		PLAYER	MATCH	TIME MINS SECS	
FASTEST	1	Ledley King	Bradford City v TOTTENHAM	0	10
	2	Mark Viduka	Charlton v LEEDS UTD	0	12
	3	Craig Bellamy	Leicester v COVENTRY	0	45
	4	Dion Dublin	ASTON VILLA v Everton	1	11
	5	David Beckham	Man City v MAN UTD	1	36
LATEST	1	Hamilton Ricard	MIDDLESBRO v Derby Co	94	52
	2	Frederic Kanouté	WEST HAM v Southampton	94	43
	3	Gary McAllister	Everton v LIVERPOOL	93	44
	4	Lee Hendrie	Charlton v ASTON VILLA	93	31
	5	Carl Cort	NEWCASTLE v Leicester	93	08

As Brian Clough once said: "It only takes a second to score a goal" – and players took full advantage of the fact in 2000–01 by making the most of the entire 90 minutes plus stoppage time to get themselves on to the scoresheet.

Early goals during the campaign had people checking their stopwatches and reaching for the record books as a new Premiership record was set. Rookie Tottenham midfielder Ledley King scored the fastest-ever Premiership goal against Bradford at Valley Parade in December. Just 10 seconds after kick-off the ball was in the Bantams' net, thanks to King's deflected long-range drive. Indeed, this meant Bradford conceded the quickest goal for the second season in a row.

All watches were being double-checked at The Valley in March, though, as Mark Viduka put visitors Leeds one up almost immediately after kick-off. The big Aussie took just two seconds longer than King to

find the net, so the Tottenham man's record still stands.

Craig Bellamy was another player to score with less than a minute on the clock, while Villa's Dion Dublin and David Beckham in the Manchester derby also wasted little time in getting the scoring started.

The amount of stoppage time the referee adds on can also give a side extra incentive in the chase for goals, with strikes frequently coming after the standard 90 minutes.

Hamilton Ricard scored the latest of the season, almost five minutes into stoppage time against Derby at The Riverside, although Frederic Kanouté was almost as late firing home for West Ham against Southampton.

Gary McAllister's Merseyside derby winner was the third-latest, while Lee Hendrie and Carl Cort also proved it pays to play until the final whistle.

GOALSCORING

GOALS/SHOTS RATIO		Headers	Shots
Jimmy Hasselbaink	20.4%	3	20
Marcus Stewart	23.5%	4	15
Mark Viduka	26.6%	6	11
Thierry Henry	13.8%		17
Michael Owen	22.9%	2	14
Teddy Sheringham	26.8%	2	13
Emile Heskey	17.1%	4	10
Kevin Phillips	12.5%		14
Alen Boksic	18.2%	2	10
Alan Smith	18.6%	5	6
Gustavo Poyet	18.3%	4	7
Jonatan Johansson	15.1%	1	10
James Beattie	14.5%	4	7
Frederic Kanouté	13.8%	4	7
Les Ferdinand	23.8%	4	6
Eidur Gudjohnsen	22.7%		10
Ole Solskjaer	14.5%	1	9
Robbie Keane	33.3%		9
Andy Cole	20.9%	1	8
Kevin Campbell	19.6%	2	7

KEY ☐ Headers ☐ Shots

Jimmy Floyd Hasselbaink arrived at Stamford Bridge billed as the final piece of the Chelsea jigsaw – a striker who would score 20 goals in a season and deliver the title.

The club had a disappointing season, finishing only sixth, but Jimmy did what he set out to do, his 23 Premiership goals making him the top scorer in the league in which he was playing for the third successive season.

He was joint top scorer in the 1998–99 Premiership and in 1999–2000 he topped the scoring charts in La Liga in Spain, despite his side being relegated.

Behind the Dutchman came Marcus Stewart, who helped Ipswich to finish fifth in the Premiership and gain entry to the 2001–02 UEFA Cup. Of Stewart's 19 goals, 11 were left-footed strikes, which was more than any other player.

The former Huddersfield frontman was also a friend to the punters, scoring the first goal in 11 separate matches, again more than any other player.

The Golden Boot winner of 1999–2000, Kevin Phillips, again featured, this time in eighth place.

New signings who proved their worth included Alen Boksic of Middlesbrough and Mark Viduka of Leeds United, while the Australian's team-mate Robbie Keane was the deadliest striker on the list.

Keane was initially signed on loan from Inter Milan and scored his nine goals with 33% of his shots. It was no surprise when Leeds made the move permanent.

The only non-striker on the list is Gustavo Poyet, who enjoyed yet another successful campaign with Chelsea, scoring 11 goals, which made the Uruguayan the Premiership's top-scoring midfielder and attracted Glenn Hoddle's eye at Spurs.

Half the list features Englishmen, proving that big-money signings from abroad are not always necessary.

MINUTES PER GOAL

	MINUTES PER GOAL	Headers	Shots
Branko Strupar	108.0	1	5
Michael Owen	111.7	2	14
Robbie Keane	115.2		9
Jimmy Hasselbaink	127.0	3	20
Duncan Ferguson	132.5		6
Teddy Sheringham	133.7	2	13
Marcus Stewart	142.8	4	15
Andy Cole	146.2	1	8
Francis Jeffers	148.8		6
Thierry Henry	152.3		17
Eidur Gudjohnsen	157.0		10
Dwight Yorke	163.8	2	7
Julian Joachim	169.7		7
Andy Hunt	170.0	2	2
Ole Solskjaer	175.4	1	9
John Hartson	175.7	4	2
Mark Viduka	177.3	6	11
Danny Cadamarteri	180.5	1	3
Alen Boksic	181.6	2	10
Carl Cort	183.0	3	3

KEY ▢ Headers ▢ Shots

Every good striker needs consistency, as their team will always rely on them putting the ball in the net at crucial times. Jimmy Floyd Hasselbaink may well have been the Premiership's top scorer, but it is perhaps surprising that Derby's Branko Strupar was the striker who scored with the most frequency.

The Rams spent the season struggling at the foot of the table, but if the Belgian international had not been plagued by injury problems they could have found themselves better off. Certainly if Strupar had maintained his record of scoring once every 108 minutes the situation would have been brighter at Pride Park.

Opta's top-ranked striker Michael Owen came second to Strupar with regards to frequency, netting every 111.7 minutes. The England starlet finished the season in prolific style, which boosted his average, and he can always be relied upon to come up with the goods on the big occasion.

Loan signing Robbie Keane endeared himself to Leeds by scoring every 115.2 minutes, putting his brief spell in Italy behind him.

He proved to be a valuable asset in David O'Leary's armoury in the absence of one of 1999–2000's most frequent scorers, Michael Bridges.

Hasselbaink's 23 goals for the season came at an average of one every 127 minutes, while Duncan Ferguson's return to Goodison Park saw him net on average every 132.5 minutes.

Not surprisingly, the league's top scorers Manchester United are well-represented in the top 20, with all four of their main strikers putting in an appearance.

Teddy Sheringham netted more than his rivals and also did so more often – every 133.7 minutes or so.

Big-money buys such as Carl Cort, Alen Boksic and Mark Viduka also showed their worth by hitting the net frequently.

SHOOTING

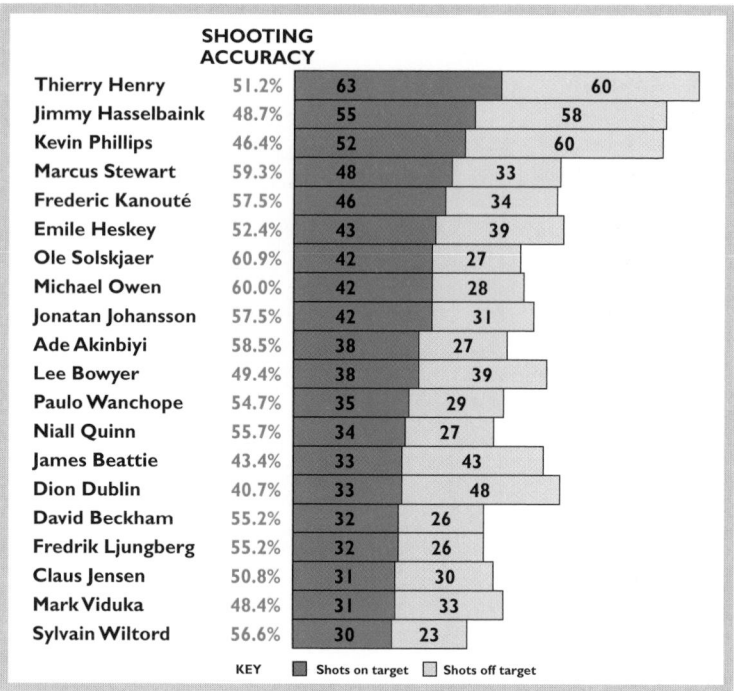

	SHOOTING ACCURACY		
Thierry Henry	51.2%	63	60
Jimmy Hasselbaink	48.7%	55	58
Kevin Phillips	46.4%	52	60
Marcus Stewart	59.3%	48	33
Frederic Kanouté	57.5%	46	34
Emile Heskey	52.4%	43	39
Ole Solskjaer	60.9%	42	27
Michael Owen	60.0%	42	28
Jonatan Johansson	57.5%	42	31
Ade Akinbiyi	58.5%	38	27
Lee Bowyer	49.4%	38	39
Paulo Wanchope	54.7%	35	29
Niall Quinn	55.7%	34	27
James Beattie	43.4%	33	43
Dion Dublin	40.7%	33	48
David Beckham	55.2%	32	26
Fredrik Ljungberg	55.2%	32	26
Claus Jensen	50.8%	31	30
Mark Viduka	48.4%	31	33
Sylvain Wiltord	56.6%	30	23

KEY ■ Shots on target □ Shots off target

Probably the biggest nightmare for Premiership goalkeepers in 2000–01 was the sight of Thierry Henry bearing down on goal.

For the second season in succession, Arsenal had more shots on target than any other side and the lightning-quick Frenchman was anything but shot-shy, letting fly more times than any other player in the Premiership.

The former Juventus man was second in the list in the 1999–2000 season, but he went one better in 2000–01, firing 123 shots in all.

Henry was closely followed by Jimmy Floyd Hasselbaink, the top scorer in the Premiership, while Kevin Phillips was the only other player to register more than 100 attempts on goal.

The most accurate shooter of the top 20 was Ole Gunnar Solskjaer. The Norwegian had not featured in the list for the previous two seasons, as he rarely got enough time on the Old Trafford pitch!

In 2000–01, however, he had more shots than any other Manchester United player, proving once again what a vital part of the squad he is.

Four midfielders also feature in the list. Lee Bowyer and David Beckham scored nine goals apiece, while Fredrik Ljungberg and Claus Jensen also helped out their team's strikers by joining in frequently with attacks.

Of the relegated teams, only Paulo Wanchope featured. He was actually more accurate than Henry, but a return of nine goals was not enough to prevent Manchester City from returning to the Nationwide League.

Least accurate player on the list was Dion Dublin, who was top of this category in 1998–99, but even then only hit the target with 40.2% of his shots, probably explaining why he took some criticism from Aston Villa fans.

GOAL ASSISTS

Player	From open play	From set-pieces
David Beckham	11	1
Nolberto Solano	8	2
Jimmy Hasselbaink	9	
Graham Stuart	9	
Thierry Henry	9	
Vladimir Smicer	7	2
Ryan Giggs	7	1
Gustavo Poyet	7	
Roy Keane	6	1
Hassan Kachloul	6	1
Stephen Clemence	5	2
Paolo Di Canio	5	2
Robert Pires	4	3
Stefano Eranio	6	
Marian Pahars	6	
Eidur Gudjohnsen	6	
Alan Smith	6	
Don Hutchison	6	
Ian Harte	4	2
Paul Telfer	3	3

KEY ☐ From open play ☐ From set-pieces

Just as in the 1999–2000 season, the two players who created the most goals in the Premiership in 2000–01 were wing wizards David Beckham and Nolberto Solano.

Whereas previously they tied with the highest number of assists in 2000–01, it was Beckham who achieved the honour outright, by setting up 12 goals for his Manchester United team-mates. Only one of these assists came from a set-piece, with Beckham proving that his silver-clad right boot can be equally effective from open play as from dead-ball situations.

Peruvian Solano has often been linked with a move away from the Premiership but he has consistently proved to be one of the best goal providers around. "Nobby" set up a total of 10 goals and if only Newcastle could put together a regular strike pairing, they would be sure to enjoy the supply line provided by the South American.

Jimmy Floyd Hasselbaink and Thierry Henry both showed that there was more to their game than goalscoring by setting up nine goals apiece, a total which was also achieved by Graham Stuart and Vladimir Smicer.

The latter was surprisingly the only player from third-placed Liverpool to appear in the top 20.

David Beckham's midfield partners from United, Ryan Giggs and Roy Keane, also feature in the top 20, demonstrating what a formidable midfield Sir Alex Ferguson has developed at Old Trafford.

Leeds full-back Ian Harte is the only defender to appear after creating six goals this season for the Yorkshire side.

His ability with his left foot from set-pieces is well-known, but four of these assists were actually from open play.

Gary McAllister actually recorded the highest number of assists from set-pieces with four of the five he created coming from dead-ball delivery.

PASSING

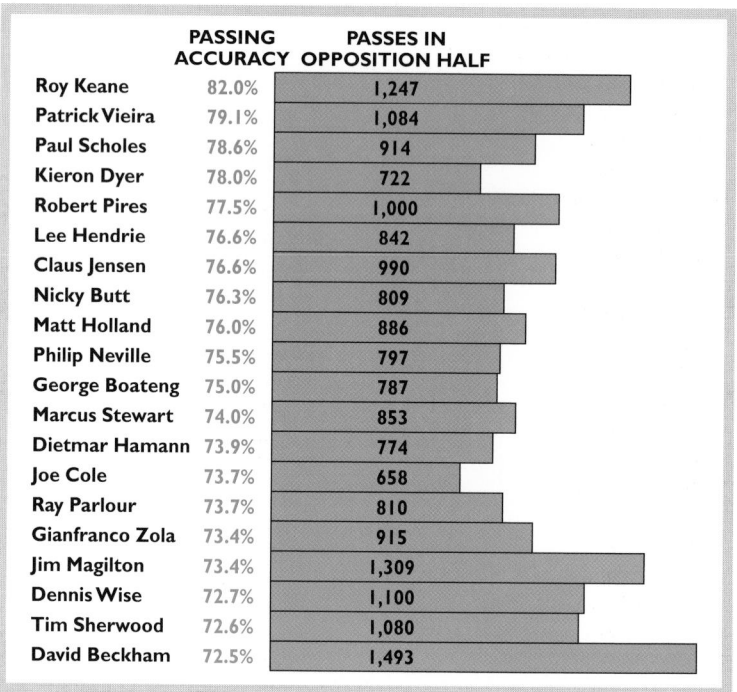

	PASSING ACCURACY	PASSES IN OPPOSITION HALF
Roy Keane	82.0%	1,247
Patrick Vieira	79.1%	1,084
Paul Scholes	78.6%	914
Kieron Dyer	78.0%	722
Robert Pires	77.5%	1,000
Lee Hendrie	76.6%	842
Claus Jensen	76.6%	990
Nicky Butt	76.3%	809
Matt Holland	76.0%	886
Philip Neville	75.5%	797
George Boateng	75.0%	787
Marcus Stewart	74.0%	853
Dietmar Hamann	73.9%	774
Joe Cole	73.7%	658
Ray Parlour	73.7%	810
Gianfranco Zola	73.4%	915
Jim Magilton	73.4%	1,309
Dennis Wise	72.7%	1,100
Tim Sherwood	72.6%	1,080
David Beckham	72.5%	1,493

It is no great surprise to see Roy Keane and Patrick Vieira at the top of the passers' table.

Both men were once again pivotal to their teams in 2000–01, acting as the fulcrums of their respective sides throughout the campaign.

Keane ended the season as the most accurate passer in the Premiership, going two better than in 1999–2000, as he guided Manchester United to their seventh title in nine years.

Vieira was only 10th in the list in 1999–2000, but improved his pass completion rate in the opposition half by five percentage points to be second in the 2000–01 table.

Completing the top three is Paul Scholes, who leaps two places into third with a 78.6% pass completion rate in the opposition half.

Manchester United have five representatives in the top 20, with Phil Neville the most surprising inclusion.

Neville played on the left-hand side of midfield at times during the 2000–01 campaign and even as a full-back he frequently joined United attacks, not least at home where the Premiership champions love to attack from all areas.

Arsenal and Ipswich are represented by three players each, while third-placed Liverpool only have Dietmar Hamann in the list, due to Gérard Houllier often rotating his midfield.

David Beckham just made the list, although he did attempt more passes in the opposition half than any other player and also set up 12 goals. Beckham's total of assists was unsurpassed for the third season in succession.

Marcus Stewart and Gianfranco Zola are the only strikers to appear, although the talented Zola has now featured in the list for three consecutive seasons, proving what a skilful player he is on the ball.

23.5% Arsenal posted the worst crossing

CROSSING

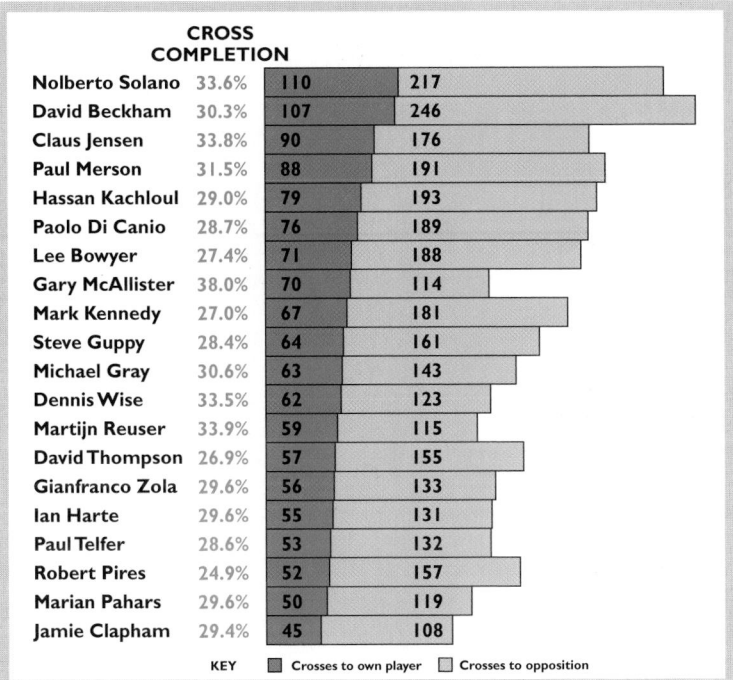

CROSS
COMPLETION

Player	%	Crosses to own player	Crosses to opposition
Nolberto Solano	33.6%	110	217
David Beckham	30.3%	107	246
Claus Jensen	33.8%	90	176
Paul Merson	31.5%	88	191
Hassan Kachloul	29.0%	79	193
Paolo Di Canio	28.7%	76	189
Lee Bowyer	27.4%	71	188
Gary McAllister	38.0%	70	114
Mark Kennedy	27.0%	67	181
Steve Guppy	28.4%	64	161
Michael Gray	30.6%	63	143
Dennis Wise	33.5%	62	123
Martijn Reuser	33.9%	59	115
David Thompson	26.9%	57	155
Gianfranco Zola	29.6%	56	133
Ian Harte	29.6%	55	131
Paul Telfer	28.6%	53	132
Robert Pires	24.9%	52	157
Marian Pahars	29.6%	50	119
Jamie Clapham	29.4%	45	108

KEY ■ Crosses to own player □ Crosses to opposition

With an increase in the number of headed goals in the Premiership, the delivery of the ball into the box has taken on extra significance. With that in mind Newcastle's Nolberto Solano should be particularly satisfied with his season's work after supplying more accurate crosses than any other player.

A total of 110 centres left the boot of Solano and found a fellow-Magpie during the 2000–01 season, leaving "Nobby" with an impressive crossing accuracy of 33.6%. Solano provided the third-highest number of crosses during the 1999–2000 campaign and is turning out to be one of Kenny Dalglish's better buys for the club.

You would expect to see David Beckham feature high up in a crossing table – and sure enough he comes just behind Solano with just three fewer successful crosses, although the Manchester United man attempted more centres overall.

Experience appears to play a key part in the ability to cross the ball well, as several of the Premiership's old-timers are included here.

Paul Merson, Paolo Di Canio, Gary McAllister, Steve Guppy, Dennis Wise and Gianfranco Zola are all aged over 30, yet they clearly proved that what they lack in youthfulness they make up for in technical ability.

McAllister, in particular, was able to boast an accuracy of 38%, better than any other player in the top 20, even though he is not naturally a wide man.

The dearth of left-sided players in the English game is highlighted by the majority of the top 20 crossers being right-footed. Of the left-sided players only three are English: Steve Guppy, Michael Gray and Jamie Clapham.

One interesting point to note is that 19 of the top 20 posted an accuracy higher than the league average, the exception being Robert Pires of Arsenal.

accuracy in the top flight

DRIBBLING

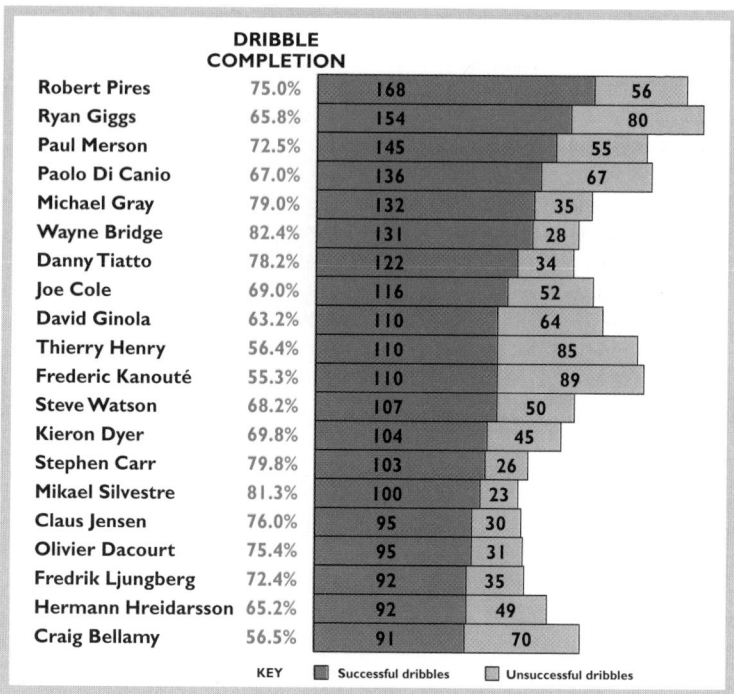

DRIBBLE COMPLETION

Player	Completion	Successful dribbles	Unsuccessful dribbles
Robert Pires	75.0%	168	56
Ryan Giggs	65.8%	154	80
Paul Merson	72.5%	145	55
Paolo Di Canio	67.0%	136	67
Michael Gray	79.0%	132	35
Wayne Bridge	82.4%	131	28
Danny Tiatto	78.2%	122	34
Joe Cole	69.0%	116	52
David Ginola	63.2%	110	64
Thierry Henry	56.4%	110	85
Frederic Kanouté	55.3%	110	89
Steve Watson	68.2%	107	50
Kieron Dyer	69.8%	104	45
Stephen Carr	79.8%	103	26
Mikael Silvestre	81.3%	100	23
Claus Jensen	76.0%	95	30
Olivier Dacourt	75.4%	95	31
Fredrik Ljungberg	72.4%	92	35
Hermann Hreidarsson	65.2%	92	49
Craig Bellamy	56.5%	91	70

KEY ▪ Successful dribbles ▫ Unsuccessful dribbles

Arsenal's £6 million investment in Robert Pires appeared sound during 2000–01. Arsenal fans will forever remember him for scoring the winning goal in the FA Cup semi-final against Tottenham, but throughout the campaign he looked good on the ball.

Pires completed more successful dribbles than any other Premiership player, ending the 2000–01 season with a 75% dribble completion rate.

His ability to cut in also saw him score some memorable goals, such as against Chelsea at Highbury.

His team-mate Fredrik Ljungberg also appeared in the list but, despite impressive dribbling, Arsenal still lacked the ability to send good crosses into the box.

Ryan Giggs was runner-up, with the only other Manchester United player to feature being Mikael Silvestre.

Silvestre was not the only full-back who enjoyed haring down the flanks. The likes of Michael Gray, Wayne Bridge, Danny Tiatto and Stephen Carr all showed their ability to join attacks and take players on.

West Ham were criticised earlier in the 2000–01 season for having too much flair and not enough grit in their side.

The flair is certainly highlighted by the presence of Paolo Di Canio, Joe Cole and Frederic Kanouté in the top 20 dribblers.

All three can be mesmerising on their day, yet it is unlikely that all three will be found on the same pitch at the same time quite so often in 2001–02.

Only six Englishmen featured in the table, with just Joe Cole and Kieron Dyer establishing themselves as England squad members. The dribbler with the highest completion rate was Wayne Bridge. He developed well at Southampton under the guidance of Glenn Hoddle, who believed the young left-sided player could become an England international.

TACKLES

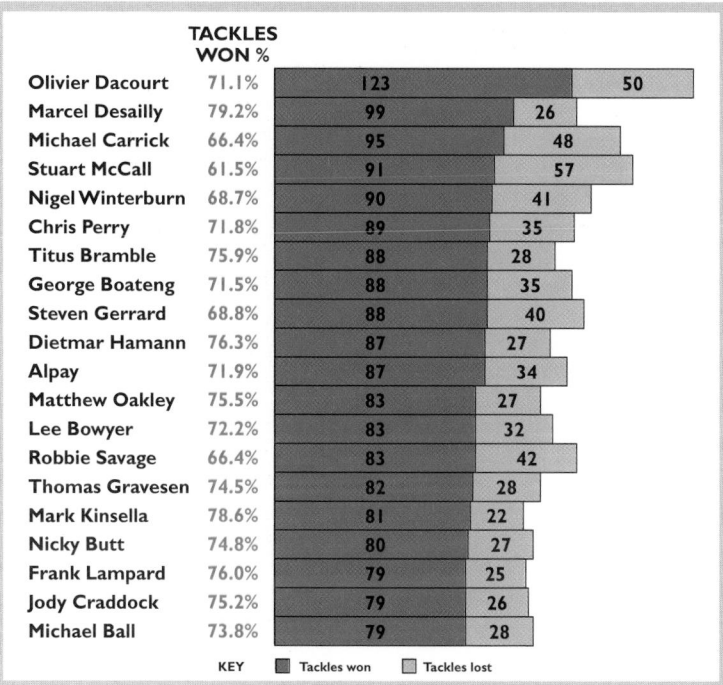

	TACKLES WON %	Tackles won	Tackles lost
Olivier Dacourt	71.1%	123	50
Marcel Desailly	79.2%	99	26
Michael Carrick	66.4%	95	48
Stuart McCall	61.5%	91	57
Nigel Winterburn	68.7%	90	41
Chris Perry	71.8%	89	35
Titus Bramble	75.9%	88	28
George Boateng	71.5%	88	35
Steven Gerrard	68.8%	88	40
Dietmar Hamann	76.3%	87	27
Alpay	71.9%	87	34
Matthew Oakley	75.5%	83	27
Lee Bowyer	72.2%	83	32
Robbie Savage	66.4%	83	42
Thomas Gravesen	74.5%	82	28
Mark Kinsella	78.6%	81	22
Nicky Butt	74.8%	80	27
Frank Lampard	76.0%	79	25
Jody Craddock	75.2%	79	26
Michael Ball	73.8%	79	28

KEY ■ Tackles won ■ Tackles lost

After clocking up more tackles than any other player during his last visit to the Premiership with Everton, Olivier Dacourt has proved that lightning can strike twice, by putting himself about more than anyone else in 2000–01.

Leeds' expensive summer signing was the only player to win more than 100 challenges during the season and he was an important part of the engine room which fired David O'Leary's men towards UEFA Cup qualification. Dacourt made 173 tackles in total and will be happy with his success rate of 71.1%.

Fellow Frenchman Marcel Desailly came second behind Dacourt, but he was unable to make anything like as many challenges as the Leeds man.

West Ham's blend of youth and experience is reflected at the top of the tackling table with teenager Michael Carrick and veteran Nigel Winterburn both holding down places in the top five. In between them another veteran, Stuart McCall, clearly gave his all in a vain attempt to try to keep Bradford City in the Premiership, as he attempted the second-highest number of tackles by any player, coming out on top in 91 of them.

Carrick was not the only English youngster to have impressed with his determined ball-winning skills. It was also encouraging to see the likes of Steven Gerrard, Matthew Oakley, Lee Bowyer, Frank Lampard and Michael Ball all taking their place in the top 20.

Nicky Butt was the only representative of Premiership Champions Manchester United in the list of the top tacklers, but with United dominating possession in most matches they played, there were far fewer ball-winning opportunities.

No striker made the top 20, but the appearance of 13 midfielders shows that most ball-winning is done in the middle of the park.

THE DIRTIEST

DISCIPLINARY POINTS

Player	Points	Foul committed = 1pt	Yellow card = 3pts	Red card = 6pts
Olivier Dacourt	133	94	13	
Ashley Ward	122	95	9	
Don Hutchison	119	80	11	1
Alan Smith	117	90	7	1
Paulo Wanchope	112	85	9	
Deon Burton	106	88	4	1
Gary Speed	104	74	8	1
George Boateng	101	74	9	
Niall Quinn	99	84	5	
Thomas Gravesen	96	69	7	1
Dion Dublin	96	90	2	
Patrick Vieira	94	67	5	2
Danny Tiatto	92	53	9	2
Dean Windass	92	56	12	
Alpay	91	55	12	
James Beattie	90	75	5	
Hamilton Ricard	90	75	5	
John Eustace	89	56	11	
Emerson Thome	89	71	6	
Emile Heskey	88	76	4	

KEY ☐ Foul committed = 1pt ☐ Yellow card = 3pts ■ Red card = 6pts

Leeds United won many friends off the pitch after a superb 2000–01, but very few on it, with Olivier Dacourt ending the campaign as the most ill-disciplined player in the Premiership.

The French midfielder was booked 13 times – more than any other player – and earned the highest number of Opta disciplinary points in the top flight.

Dacourt's team-mate Alan Smith was not far behind. The young hothead was booked seven times and also sent off, as he was too in the Champions League.

Smith ended the 2000–01 season with a call-up to the England squad, but Sven-Göran Eriksson's assistant Tord Grip made it clear that Smith would have to curb, or at least better control his aggression if he was to become a world-class striker.

The Opta stats certainly prove Grip's point, with only three players committing more fouls than Smith.

Somewhat surprisingly, the player who committed the most fouls was Bradford City striker Ashley Ward. The former Blackburn player was also booked nine times and as a result is second in the table behind Dacourt.

Patrick Vieira and Danny Tiatto featured largely because they were both sent off twice, with the Frenchman's dismissals coming in the first two matches of the season.

Aston Villa's Lee Hendrie and Newcastle United's Nolberto Solano also received their marching orders on two separate occasions, but were not persistent enough offenders to make it into the table.

Exactly half the players in the list are strikers, highlighting their often-illegal attempts to win the ball in the air and the frustration which often results.

Don Hutchison was third in the list, but was also the most-fouled player in the Premiership, with the Sunderland midfielder always giving as good as he got.

81 Derby picked up more yellow cards than any

THE CLEANEST

Name	Minutes/ Disciplinary Point	Foul committed = 1pt	Yellow card = 3pts
Claus Jensen	317.4	10	
Gareth Whalley	179.9	8	
Paul Merson	176.8	13	2
Ledley King	169.6	9	
Matt Holland	169.0	20	
Sylvain Wiltord	159.8	11	
Aaron Hughes	157.6	13	2
Eoin Jess	150.4	10	
Chris Powell	145.7	16	1
Trevor Sinclair	140.7	9	1
Andrew O'Brien	135.9	14	1
Jamie Clapham	135.2	13	2
Oleg Luzhny	126.7	8	1
Robert Pires	124.6	17	1
Laurent Charvet	122.9	13	1
Wayne Bridge	122.1	25	1
Alan Wright	119.7	17	3
Jermaine Wright	115.0	22	1
Ian Nolan	114.0	14	
Gianfranco Zola	113.2	20	1

KEY: Foul committed = 1pt; Yellow card = 3pts

It seems that everyone loves a villain, with pundits and supporters all having their opinion on who are the bad boys of the Premiership – and cult status is often afforded to each club's "hardmen".

Little mention is given to those who steer clear of trouble and stay out of the referees' notebooks, though, so here Opta give credit to the Premiership's good guys in a table calculated on their average minutes per disciplinary point.

The biggest halo and angel's wings should go to Charlton's Claus Jensen, who went through the entire season without receiving a single caution and was pulled up for committing just 10 fouls. Jensen was streets ahead at the top of Opta's 'cleanest' table, picking up a disciplinary point on average every 317.4 minutes.

Behind Jensen was Bradford's Gareth Whalley, who did not let the disappointment of relegation boil over into his play and only caused the referee to blow up on eight occasions, none of which was deemed worthy of a caution.

Whalley was just ahead of Paul Merson, whose "bad boy" reputation off the pitch was certainly not matched on it.

Ipswich's ever-present Matt Holland made the list, having committed just 20 fouls in his 38 appearances in 2000–01.

He was one of three players from the Suffolk side to have made the clean list, along with Jamie Clapham and Jermaine Wright.

Another side with three of the cleanest players was Arsenal, with Sylvain Wiltord, Oleg Luzhny and Robert Pires all warranting little action from the officials. Wiltord was also the cleanest striker in the Premiership, having committed just 11 fouls in 2000–01 and not picking up a caution for any of them.

The list, of course, only includes outfield players who played a significant amount of football in 2000–01.

SAVES

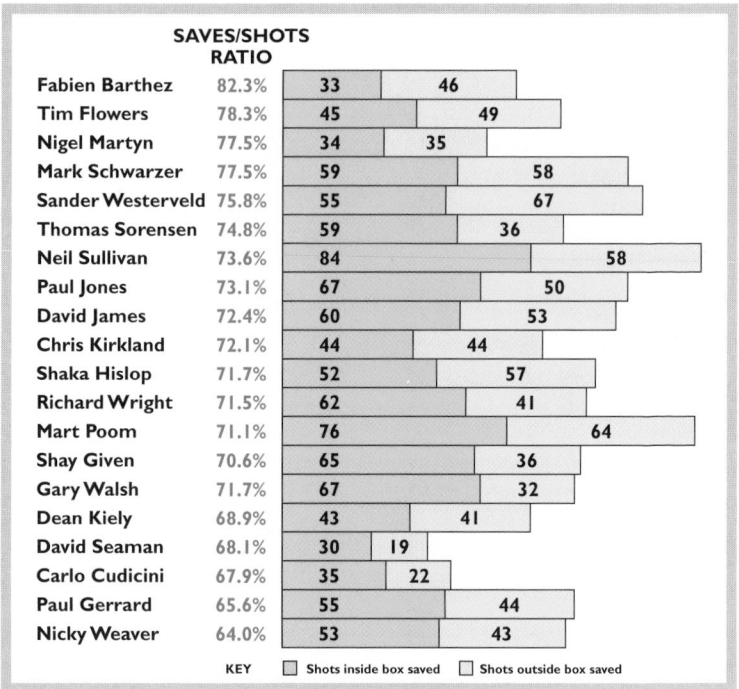

SAVES/SHOTS RATIO

	Ratio	Shots inside box saved	Shots outside box saved
Fabien Barthez	82.3%	33	46
Tim Flowers	78.3%	45	49
Nigel Martyn	77.5%	34	35
Mark Schwarzer	77.5%	59	58
Sander Westerveld	75.8%	55	67
Thomas Sorensen	74.8%	59	36
Neil Sullivan	73.6%	84	58
Paul Jones	73.1%	67	50
David James	72.4%	60	53
Chris Kirkland	72.1%	44	44
Shaka Hislop	71.7%	52	57
Richard Wright	71.5%	62	41
Mart Poom	71.1%	76	64
Shay Given	70.6%	65	36
Gary Walsh	71.7%	67	32
Dean Kiely	68.9%	43	41
David Seaman	68.1%	30	19
Carlo Cudicini	67.9%	35	22
Paul Gerrard	65.6%	55	44
Nicky Weaver	64.0%	53	43

KEY: ▢ Shots inside box saved ▢ Shots outside box saved

Manchester United finally found the replacement they wanted for Peter Schmeichel with the £7.8 million signing of Fabien Barthez in the summer and the French number one did not let them down, proving to be the Premiership's top shot-stopper.

Barthez tends to get as much recognition for his flamboyant antics outside the area as for what he does between the sticks, but his supreme goalkeeping ability should not be underestimated.

The 5'11" stopper had far and away the best saves-to-shots ratio in the Premiership, keeping out an average of 82.3% of all the shots he faced. This enabled United to keep the best defensive record in the Premiership and Barthez was beaten on only 17 occasions during the league campaign.

A Frenchman may have led the field, but there were two English international

'keepers following him. Tim Flowers' international career may be over but he has plenty to offer Leicester, as his 78.3% saves-to-shots ratio showed. With the Foxes hardly prolific at the other end of the field, Flowers played a key role in their fine early-season form before he was affected by injury. Behind him was Nigel Martyn, who fought off competition from youngster Paul Robinson to retain his place as Leeds' number one, saving 77.5% of the shots he faced.

One England 'keeper who will not be happy is the current international number one David Seaman. His saves-to-shots ratio of 68.1% was an improvement on 1999–2000's disappointing campaign, but still a poor return for an international player. Only Carlo Cudicini, Paul Gerrard and Nicky Weaver had a worse average among first-choice 'keepers and a player of Seaman's stature would want to be producing something better.

82.3% Fabien Barthez saved the highest

SAVES INSIDE

	SAVES/SHOTS RATIO	SHOTS INSIDE BOX SAVED
Fabien Barthez	70.2%	33
Mark Schwarzer	69.4%	59
Tim Flowers	68.2%	45
Thomas Sorensen	67.0%	59
Gary Walsh	67.0%	67
Paul Jones	65.7%	67
Nigel Martyn	65.4%	34
Neil Sullivan	64.6%	84
Richard Wright	64.6%	62
David Seaman	63.8%	30

When it came to pulling off saves from shots struck inside the area, Fabien Barthez was the Premiership's number one in his first season in English football. The follically-challenged French goalkeeper denied opponents 33 times in his area, stopping a ratio of 70.2% of the shots he faced.

Boro's Aussie shot-stopper Mark Schwarzer followed close behind, while the best English 'keeper from close range was Leicester's former international Tim Flowers.

SAVES OUTSIDE

	SAVES/SHOTS RATIO	SHOTS OUTSIDE BOX SAVED
Nigel Martyn	94.6%	35
Sander Westerveld	94.4%	67
Fabien Barthez	93.9%	46
David James	93.0%	53
Thomas Sorensen	92.3%	36
Neil Sullivan	92.1%	58
Tim Flowers	90.7%	49
Shay Given	90.0%	36
Carlo Cudicini	88.0%	22
Mark Schwarzer	87.9%	58

For the second season running, England 'keeper Nigel Martyn proved to be the hardest man to beat from distance as he saved 35 shots from outside the area, stopping on average 94.6% of the long-range efforts he faced.

Liverpool's Sander Westerveld saved more long-range shots than any other 'keeper, while Martyn's fellow-Englishmen David James and Tim Flowers also proved tricky to beat from outside the box throughout the season.

percentage of shots on target

GOALS CONCEDED

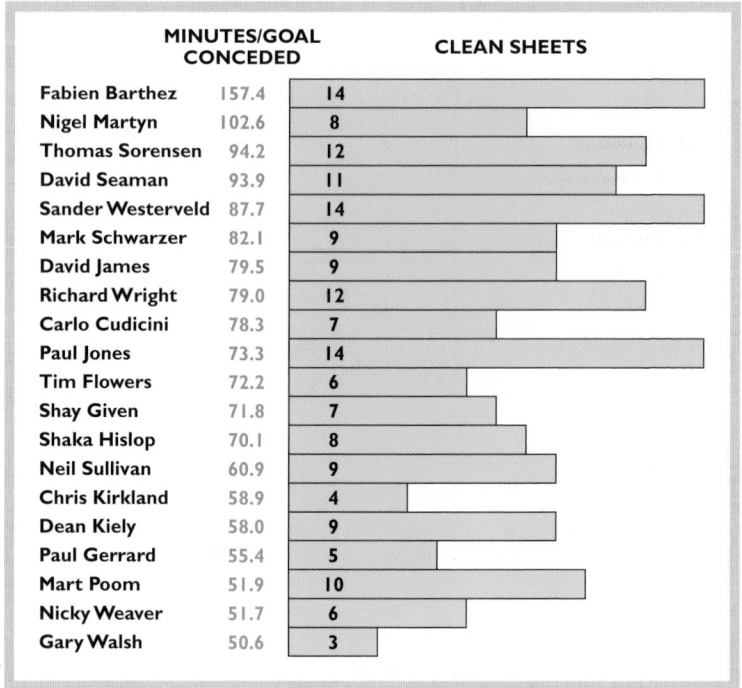

	MINUTES/GOAL CONCEDED	CLEAN SHEETS
Fabien Barthez	157.4	14
Nigel Martyn	102.6	8
Thomas Sorensen	94.2	12
David Seaman	93.9	11
Sander Westerveld	87.7	14
Mark Schwarzer	82.1	9
David James	79.5	9
Richard Wright	79.0	12
Carlo Cudicini	78.3	7
Paul Jones	73.3	14
Tim Flowers	72.2	6
Shay Given	71.8	7
Shaka Hislop	70.1	8
Neil Sullivan	60.9	9
Chris Kirkland	58.9	4
Dean Kiely	58.0	9
Paul Gerrard	55.4	5
Mart Poom	51.9	10
Nicky Weaver	51.7	6
Gary Walsh	50.6	3

Fabien Barthez's season at Manchester United failed to get off to the best of starts when he drove to Liverpool's training ground by mistake – but his fortunes on the pitch were in stark contrast to that slip-up.

On average Barthez enjoyed longer breaks between trips to pick the ball out of the net than any other 'keeper, with the Frenchman conceding a goal every 157.4 minutes.

The World Cup winner also managed a total of 14 clean sheets during the 2000–01 Premiership campaign, a tally which only Sander Westerveld at Liverpool and Southampton's Paul Jones were able to equal.

Across the Pennines another United 'keeper was also enjoying a good season between the sticks. Despite missing the middle part of the campaign through injury, Nigel Martyn of Leeds United maintained the high standards which have

kept him in the national squad. The Cornish-born 'keeper went 102.6 minutes on average between conceding goals, although he was only able to keep eight clean sheets during the course of an injury-hit season.

Sunderland's Thomas Sorensen continued to enhance his ever-growing reputation, while David Seaman, despite a poor saves-to-shots ratio, benefited from the strong defence in front of him, conceding every 93.9 minutes on average.

At the other end of the scale, there was little to smile about for the 'keepers of the Premiership's weaker sides.

Gary Walsh took over in the Bradford goal midway through the season and was kept busy – mainly picking the ball out of the net.

But Mart Poom of Derby was still able to keep a total of 10 clean sheets, despite conceding a goal on average every 51.9 minutes.

CATCHING

	CATCH SUCCESS	Balls caught	Balls punched
David Seaman	100%	31	8
Neil Sullivan	98%	84	5
Carlo Cudicini	98%	42	11
Sander Westerveld	96%	71	29
Shay Given	95%	61	23
Tim Flowers	95%	39	17
Shaka Hislop	95%	37	12
Nigel Martyn	95%	35	16
Mark Schwarzer	94%	82	20
Mart Poom	94%	105	26

KEY ☐ Balls caught ☐ Balls punched

There were quite rightly many question marks over David Seaman's hairstyle in 2000–01, but no-one could question the England number one's handling skills. The veteran 'keeper had an unblemished record as far as catching was concerned, although a meagre total of 31 crosses claimed suggests a reluctance to come off his line.

He was followed by Neil Sullivan and Italian Carlo Cudicini, while Mart Poom's tally of 105 catches was the highest of any 'keeper.

DISTRIBUTION

	ACCURACY	Throws/short kicks	Long kicks
Shay Given	65%	115	608
Fabien Barthez	65%	116	479
David Seaman	62%	74	356
Sander Westerveld	59%	74	601
Simon Royce	59%	85	313
Nigel Martyn	58%	42	407
Carlo Cudicini	58%	62	373
Thomas Sorensen	57%	57	597
Richard Wright	55%	91	691
Neil Sullivan	53%	55	746

KEY ☐ Throws/short kicks ☐ Long kicks

There was little cheer for Newcastle on the pitch during 2000–01, but at least 'keeper Shay Given restored a modicum of Geordie pride by providing the best distribution of any Premiership stopper, along with Fabien Barthez.

The top four 'keepers, distribution-wise, have all represented their home nations in internationals, but in fifth place was rookie Leicester stopper Simon Royce, who managed to find his own players with 59% of his clearances.

goals than any other team

OPTA PLAYER OF THE SEASON

Indomitable: Roy Keane

Who is the best player in the Premiership? Who is the best player in his particular position? Who makes the biggest contribution match-by-match? This section details Opta's answers.

Teddy Sheringham was voted by the players as the PFA Player of the Year and by the media as the Football Writers' Footballer of the Year. The PFA Young Player of the Year was Liverpool's Steven Gerrard.

But do these choices match up to the facts and figures? The Opta Index monitors each touch of the ball made by every player and offers a more objective viewpoint on the contribution that all players make on the pitch.

You may find the results surprising. The Index is only a guide to player performance and deals with the data in as objective a way as possible. Opta do not make subjective judgements on the quality of goals, the importance of winning strikes or the fact that successful dribbles by David Ginola are usually more pleasing on the eye than those by Tony Adams.

Players earn points for everything they contribute on the pitch, not just the eye-catching skills, goalscoring feats or spectacular saves. There is a subjective element, though, as the points allocated for actions are calculated on the basis of the judgement of Don Howe and Opta analysts' opinions as to the value of those actions.

For an in-depth explanation of the Index, see page 12.

Opta's player of the 2000–01 season was Roy Keane of Manchester United. The champions may have felt they had a below-par season by the very high standards which they have set over the last decade, but their skipper was again at the heart of all United's success.

No player made more passes during the season and this was despite Keane missing six matches through suspension and several more through injury or being rested.

The Irish midfield dynamo also recorded the best pass completion rate of any player in the top flight who made a significant number of passes.

He scored two goals and set up a further seven as United racked up 79 goals – the highest tally in the top flight yet again.

Keane also contested 77 tackles and his indomitable attitude helped secure the Premiership title in record time, but his unwillingness to accept second-best saw him hit out several times at supporters, team-mates and opponents.

Season 2000–01 will always be remembered for his quotes about prawn sandwiches, but the fiery Keane also labelled some of his team-mates complacent and claimed that United were an average side for whom defeat by Bayern Munich could be "the end of the road".

Despite being linked with a move to Celtic, the 1999–2000 double Player of the Year and 2000–01 Opta star man should be spearheading Manchester United's hunt for silverware in 2001–02 as they seek to end Sir Alex Ferguson's reign in winning style.

GOALKEEPERS

PLAYER NAME	TEAM	OPTA POINTS
Fabien Barthez	Man Utd	990
Tim Flowers	Leicester	983
Neil Sullivan	Tottenham	974
Mark Schwarzer	Middlesbro	892
Mart Poom	Derby Co	890
Shay Given	Newcastle	836
Thomas Sorensen	Sunderland	836
Nigel Martyn	Leeds Utd	811
Paul Jones	Southampton	808
Sander Westerveld	Liverpool	803
Richard Wright	Ipswich	753
David James	Aston Villa	731
Gary Walsh	Bradford	724
Simon Royce	Leicester	717
Chris Kirkland	Coventry	689
Dean Kiely	Charlton	686
David Seaman	Arsenal	630
Shaka Hislop	West Ham	620
Carlo Cudicini	Chelsea	607
Nicky Weaver	Man City	514

After the goal-fest that was 1999–2000, with a 20-team Premiership record of 1,060 strikes registered, the pressure was squarely on the league's shot-stoppers in 2000–01.

And as it turned out, the season saw fewer goals than the previous campaign, with some excellent performances from the 'keepers a large factor in this.

Leading the way was the outstanding Fabien Barthez. He saved a league-best 82% of all shots levelled on his goal and maintained 14 clean sheets, going 157 minutes on average between conceding.

The £7.8 million record fee for a Premiership goalkeeper looked fully-justified after Barthez's contributions – especially considering Arsenal's David Seaman saved a lowly 68% of shots. He ended up languishing in 17th place after propping up the 1999–2000 rankings.

Former England 'keeper Tim Flowers had a memorable season for Leicester. He was instrumental in helping Peter Taylor's side maintain a top three position for the first half of the campaign, helping City to eight clean sheets in their opening 14 matches and saving 78% of shots.

Tottenham's Neil Sullivan ranked third with Opta, firmly establishing himself as number one at Spurs and recording an unrivalled tally of 142 saves – 19 of these coming in the two matches with north London rivals Arsenal.

Mark Schwarzer's heroics did much to keep Middlesbrough afloat, likewise Mart Poom for Derby. Behind Barthez, Schwarzer was the second-best stopper of efforts struck inside the area, while Poom's 140 saves meant only Sullivan was busier than the Estonian.

Rookie Chris Kirkland's low score reflects those of his team-mates, while Nicky Weaver saved a woeful 64% of shots on his goal and was dropped by Joe Royle, but at least he made the top 20.

DEFENDERS

PLAYER NAME	TEAM	OPTA POINTS
Sami Hyypia	Liverpool	1,086
Ian Harte	Leeds Utd	1,046
Tony Adams	Arsenal	1,046
Marcel Desailly	Chelsea	1,039
John Terry	Chelsea	1,037
Denis Irwin	Man Utd	968
Gary Neville	Man Utd	948
Mark Venus	Ipswich	941
Mikael Silvestre	Man Utd	938
Gareth Southgate	Aston Villa	905
Philip Neville	Man Utd	904
Gerry Taggart	Leicester	903
Mark Fish	Charlton	901
Dean Richards	Southampton	898
Silvinho	Arsenal	881
Matt Elliott	Leicester	874
Ugo Ehiogu	Middlesbro	870
Stuart Pearce	West Ham	870
Rio Ferdinand	Leeds Utd	869
Sol Campbell	Tottenham	866

For the second season in succession, Finnish colossus Sami Hyypia was the Premiership's most effective defender according to Opta.

Hyypia has enjoyed two campaigns of aerial dominance of the English game. His total of 345 clearing headers in 2000–01 was comfortably more than the next man and he also scored three thumping headers in the league. In fact, only four players had more headed efforts on target than Hyypia, while his stoic resistance paved the way for Red glory.

Despite a lack of silverware, Leeds also had an encouraging campaign. Ian Harte at one stage battled with Dominic Matteo for a first-team place, but by the season's end he had scored seven Premiership goals and created a further six – both best figures for a defender – to end up second behind Hyypia.

Tony Adams showed age has not withered his ability, having quit international football to concentrate on his club career. The Gunners' captain led the side to the last eight of the European Cup and second spot in the Premiership and will be looking for his side to go one better in the 2001–02 title race.

The burgeoning talents of youngster John Terry came to the fore alongside World Cup winner Marcel Desailly in Chelsea's defence and the two made an appearance in the top five having buoyed the Blues' late charge.

Unsurprisingly, seeing as they boasted the best defensive record in 2000–01, four Manchester United stars – all full-backs by trade – made the top 11 of the defenders Index for their part in United's success.

Honorary mentions should go to Mark Venus and Mark Fish who helped their newly-promoted sides to flourish where others before have failed, while Ugo Ehiogu and Rio Ferdinand coped well with high-profile transfers during 2000–01.

For more information visit our website:

MIDFIELDERS

PLAYER NAME	TEAM	OPTA POINTS
Roy Keane	Man Utd	1,377
Patrick Vieira	Arsenal	1,088
Steven Gerrard	Liverpool	1,034
Mark Kinsella	Charlton	999
Nicky Butt	Man Utd	980
Gary McAllister	Liverpool	960
Jim Magilton	Ipswich	931
Dietmar Hamann	Liverpool	912
Claus Jensen	Charlton	912
Frank Lampard	West Ham	870
Paul Ince	Middlesbro	850
Olivier Dacourt	Leeds Utd	847
Alex Rae	Sunderland	824
Gilles Grimandi	Arsenal	819
Matt Holland	Ipswich	814
Michael Carrick	West Ham	809
Eoin Jess	Bradford	801
Dennis Wise	Chelsea	798
Gary Speed	Newcastle	778
Tim Sherwood	Tottenham	774

The one man who has consistently stood out among his peers for the last few seasons is Manchester United's powerhouse midfielder Roy Keane.

Arguably the Premiership's most effective player in recent campaigns, United's skipper topped Opta's midfielders Index for 2000–01 after driving his troops to another emphatic title success.

Keane completed more passes than any other top-flight player for the third year running, setting up seven goals, while his ferocious approach to the game saw him emerge triumphant in 58 of his 77 challenges.

Arsenal enforcer Patrick Vieira suffered an inauspicious start to the season, having received his marching orders in the Gunners' first two league matches, but showed true character and self-discipline to avert the crisis that threatened to engulf his campaign.

Vieira went more than 23 hours before picking up his next card in the Premiership, while the Frenchman's five goals, four assists and 122 tackles went a long way to securing Champions League football in 2001–02 for the Gunners.

Meanwhile Steven Gerrard built on a good display against Germany in Euro 2000 to establish himself as an England regular during 2000–01 and inspire Liverpool to cup treble glory.

A bundle of energy with vision, skill, tenacity and an eye for goal, he impressed all who saw him play and reached double figures in all competitions with 10 strikes.

Mark Kinsella made the top five in 1998–99 and did so again in 2000–01 with a terrific all-round contribution which was fundamental to Charlton's achievement.

West Ham youngster Michael Carrick came to prominence, along with colleague Frank Lampard, while Nicky Butt's fifth-placed ranking illustrated Manchester United's strength in depth.

ATTACKING MIDFIELDERS

PLAYER NAME	TEAM	OPTA POINTS
David Beckham	Man Utd	1,347
Paul Scholes	Man Utd	1,088
Robert Pires	Arsenal	1,060
Fredrik Ljungberg	Arsenal	1,056
Gustavo Poyet	Chelsea	1,052
Muzzy Izzet	Leicester	974
Ryan Giggs	Man Utd	939
Lee Hendrie	Aston Villa	893
Joe Cole	West Ham	881
Lee Bowyer	Leeds Utd	876
Nolberto Solano	Newcastle	851
Paul Merson	Aston Villa	817
Don Hutchison	Sunderland	800
Darren Anderton	Tottenham	787
Graham Stuart	Charlton	779
Dan Petrescu	Southampton	775
Jamie Clapham	Ipswich	765
Ray Parlour	Arsenal	763
Hassan Kachloul	Southampton	741
Steve Stone	Aston Villa	740

Manchester United led the way as Arsenal followed in the 2000–01 Premiership – and the same is true of the Opta Index for the season.

In David Beckham and Paul Scholes United boasted the top two attacking midfielders according to the Premiership's official player performance statisticians, with Robert Pires and Fredrik Ljungberg third and fourth.

In fact Beckham and Scholes swapped places after 1999–2000, with United's wing king overtaking his colleague on the back of 12 assists during 2000–01.

And while some argued that Beckham was not quite reaching his usual excellent standards – certainly after the turn of the year – there was still no-one to rival him on Opta's system, with his nine goals demonstrating an increasingly clinical finishing streak developing in his game.

Team-mate Scholes was as tenacious and industrious as ever in the middle of the park and he did not neglect his attacking duties either, notching six league goals and setting up a further five.

While Scholes was a dynamo down the centre, Gunners duo Pires and Ljungberg scampered busily down the flanks.

Pires used his sleight of foot to embark on 168 successful dribbles and runs – the most in the league.

Ljungberg's frequent bursts towards the penalty area reaped six Premiership goals for the Swede, along with the strike which seemed to have won the FA Cup for Arsenal.

And with Ryan Giggs and Ray Parlour also in the top 20, the two sides enjoyed a near-monopoly of 2000–01's most dangerous midfield playmakers.

Uruguayan star Gustavo Poyet secured a third consecutive top five place, scoring 11 goals and creating seven for the Blues. Fellow-South American Nolberto Solano's 10 assists saw him well-placed along with the rejuvenated Don Hutchison.

ATTACKERS

PLAYER NAME	TEAM	OPTA POINTS
Michael Owen	Liverpool	1,083
Teddy Sheringham	Man Utd	1,057
Thierry Henry	Arsenal	1,025
Marcus Stewart	Ipswich	1,001
Jimmy F Hasselbaink	Chelsea	984
Emile Heskey	Liverpool	919
Gianfranco Zola	Chelsea	891
Paolo Di Canio	West Ham	883
Kevin Phillips	Sunderland	788
Frederic Kanouté	West Ham	746
Alan Shearer	Newcastle	740
Benito Carbone	Bradford	733
Marian Pahars	Southampton	731
Mark Viduka	Leeds Utd	719
Alan Smith	Leeds Utd	712
Les Ferdinand	Tottenham	712
Sergei Rebrov	Tottenham	685
Jonatan Johansson	Charlton	680
James Beattie	Southampton	679
Ashley Ward	Bradford	675

Following a string of league goals at the start and finish of the 2000–01 Premiership, Michael Owen edged out Football Writers' and PFA Player of the Year Teddy Sheringham to head Opta's attackers Index for the season.

Owen finished the campaign with 16 strikes, after losing his way in front of goal midway through 2000–01. Indeed, he grabbed 12 of those in the opening and closing two weeks of the season combined, and overall he scored once every 112 minutes on average – more frequently than any regular Premiership striker.

While Owen's late peak of form helped secure cup success and Liverpool's place in cup history, Sheringham's early-season heroics gave Manchester United a lead they never lost in their stroll to the title.

Little was expected of Sheringham after a quiet 1999–2000 but his 15 goals – representing an outstanding goals-to-shots ratio of 27% – earned him his personal double and an England recall.

Thierry Henry matched the veteran striker stride-for-stride before the end of 2000, but his finishing powers waned drastically as the gruelling campaign took its toll.

Leading the line for Ipswich, Marcus Stewart was perhaps an even bigger revelation than Sheringham in 2000–01. Having nurtured his game through the lower climes of English football, Stewart employed his hard-earned nous to net 19 times in the top flight for Ipswich.

And while he may have finished below Jimmy Floyd Hasselbaink in the shoot-out for the Golden Boot, Stewart outdid the free-scoring Dutchman in Opta's acclaimed scoring system.

Hasselbaink's ability to finish is unquestioned but Stewart's stronger link-up play and willingness to drop further back and help out meant that he accrued more points.

TEAMS OF THE SEASON

OPTA XIs

Every week in most newspapers, there is a team of the week picked by the journalists, or their suggestion to the England manager about which players should feature in the latest squad.

And in every pub, school and office, a favourite pastime is picking a personal England team, an all-star team or a World XI.

This section is a definitive guide to the teams of the 2000-01 season. There are the top scorers, the most accurate marksmen, the best passers and the best and worst-behaved players.

There is also an England XI, an overseas team and an Under-21 side, all based on the Opta Index.

Each team is laid out in a 4-4-2 formation graphic like the one shown below. Each player was selected based on being the best (or worst) in his particular position and will be shown as indicated.

For example, Ian Harte will always feature as a left-back, Roy Keane as a central midfield player and Michael Owen as a striker.

However, there are occasions where a versatile player such as Steven Gerrard may feature in different positions for different teams in this section.

82% Fabien Barthez saved a higher proportion of

TEAM OF THE SEASON

Opta's team of the season for 2000–01 is a mixture of youth and experience, Brits and imports, flair and guile. But not one player from outside the Premiership's top four clubs makes the line-up, an indication perhaps of how strong the division is becoming at the highest echelon.

Not surprisingly, Manchester United were the side with the biggest representation of players in the team – five in total, including the man of the year according to the stats, Roy Keane.

The fiery captain was a significant driving force behind the Old Trafford club's seventh Premiership title in nine years, making good with 87% of his passes and crunching into 77 tackles.

While he provided the steel, David Beckham had an exceptional season on the creative front, particularly before the turn of the year. The England skipper created a total of 12 goals – more than anyone else in the top flight – and scored nine himself.

Teddy Sheringham, the PFA and Football Writers' Player of the Year, also made the Opta XI after banging in 15 goals from just 56 shots.

The other members of Sir Alex Ferguson's team to make it were defender Gary Neville and 'keeper Fabien Barthez, both of whom had excellent campaigns in preserving United's Premiership-best "goals against" record.

Second-placed Arsenal had three players in the side, most notably Patrick Vieira, who produced a string of imperious displays after a poor start to 2000–01. The Frenchman is joined by his skipper Tony Adams and compatriot Robert Pires.

The best Opta points average of any defender was enjoyed by Finn Sami Hyypia, the Liverpool stopper who has made the team of the season in each of his two terms in England.

His Anfield ally Michael Owen joined Sheringham in attack after a late burst of form in the league, which saw him rattle in seven goals in four games.

Ian Harte was the only player from a club outside of the top three places in the table to make the team. The Leeds United defender had a slow start to the season, but finished the 2000–01 campaign as one of the Premiership's most consistent full-backs.

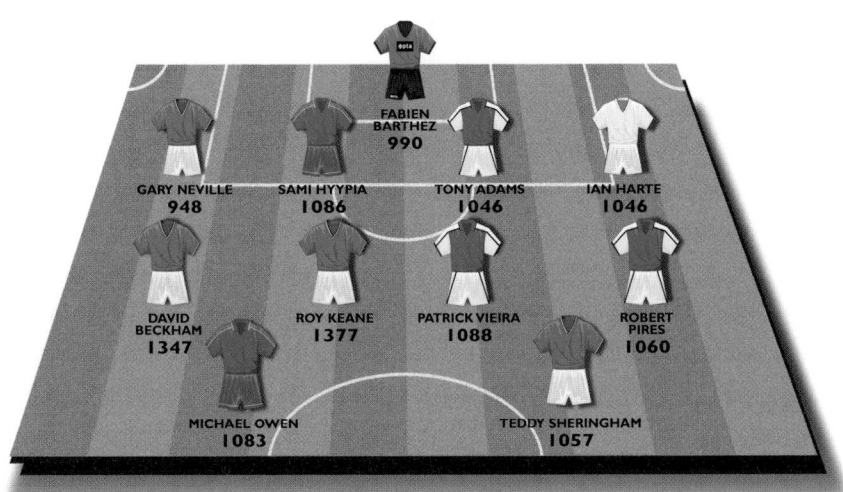

FABIEN BARTHEZ 990

GARY NEVILLE 948 SAMI HYYPIA 1086 TONY ADAMS 1046 IAN HARTE 1046

DAVID BECKHAM 1347 ROY KEANE 1377 PATRICK VIEIRA 1088 ROBERT PIRES 1060

MICHAEL OWEN 1083 TEDDY SHERINGHAM 1057

opposition shots than any top-flight 'keeper

GOALSCORERS

Jimmy Floyd Hasselbaink is from that rare and precious breed of strikers who almost guarantee their team 20 goals a season wherever they go.

Chelsea splashed out a club record £15 million on that premise and he did not let them down, scoring 23 times in the league from 113 shots. A four-goal blast against Coventry aside, the Surinam-born forward usually scored no more than once per game, which meant the race for the Golden Boot went almost to the wire.

But by notching braces in consecutive matches against Everton and Liverpool, Hasselbaink took the award from Ipswich's Marcus Stewart, who ended up with a superb total of 19 strikes in his first-ever season in the top flight.

Chelsea also boasted the Premiership's leading midfield goalscorer in Gus Poyet. Despite starting just 22 games, the Uruguayan slammed in 11 goals, two more than each of his nearest midfield challengers – Manchester United's David Beckham and Leeds man Lee Bowyer – and three more than Sunderland's Don Hutchison, who finished on eight.

Bowyer might not have been able to match Poyet's feats in the Premiership, but the Leeds midfielder did notch up six goals in the Champions League to take his overall tally to 15 for the season – more than any other midfielder in the English top flight.

Leeds left-back Ian Harte's net-busting exploits distinguished him in two categories. Firstly, his total of seven strikes was the highest of any Premiership defender, while every one of his goals came from dead-ball situations – four from free-kicks and three from penalties – which was a tally no-one could better.

Penalty-taking Everton man David Unsworth hit the back of the net five times and Spurs right-back Stephen Carr rattled in three. Manchester City's Steve Howey, meanwhile, did remarkably well to score half a dozen goals in a struggling team when he had only notched six times in almost 200 games for his previous club Newcastle.

Manchester United 'keeper Fabien Barthez was the man responsible for conceding the fewest goals – the Frenchman let in just 17 in his 30 appearances for the champions.

FABIEN BARTHEZ
17

STEPHEN CARR 3   STEVE HOWEY 6   DAVID UNSWORTH 5   IAN HARTE 7

DAVID BECKHAM 9   LEE BOWYER 9   DON HUTCHISON 8   GUSTAVO POYET 11

JIMMY FLOYD HASSELBAINK 23   MARCUS STEWART 19

5 David Beckham scored more goals direct from

PERFORMANCES

As well as being the Premiership's top goalscorer, Jimmy Floyd Hasselbaink also turned in one of the best individual performances of 2000–01 when he ran riot in Chelsea's 6–1 victory over Coventry at Stamford Bridge in October.

The Holland international smashed four goals past the Sky Blues' substitute 'keeper Alan Miller. He had replaced the unlucky Chris Kirkland, who was dismissed for a professional foul leading to the penalty for the first goal. Hasselbaink could easily have had five – a feat no Premiership player achieved in 2000–01 – but saw three shots saved and hit two efforts wide.

Across London, though, Arsenal's Thierry Henry squeezed the Chelsea man into second place in the list of best displays. The pacy frontrunner scored a hat-trick in the 6–1 thrashing of Leicester on Boxing Day but, as he admitted afterwards, took as much satisfaction from setting up two of the other goals for Patrick Vieira and Tony Adams.

Two other Arsenal players made the team of the best performances. Fredrik Ljungberg helped the Gunners to a 4–1 win over Everton in April by scoring the

opening goal, but that feat was put in the shade by Ray Parlour, who became the only midfield player to score a hat-trick in 2000–01 when he struck three past Newcastle in December.

The highlight of Muzzy Izzet's season came in a 2–1 win over Derby in October when he scored one goal and created the other, while Ipswich's Martijn Reuser netted two when his side beat Bradford. Defenders Marcel Desailly, Gareth Southgate and Ian Harte all scored in their season-best displays. In addition to their goals, Chelsea defender Desailly also completed 86% of his passes away against Aston Villa, England centre-back Southgate made seven tackles against Leeds United and Irish full-back Harte fired in six shots in the match against Derby County. And while Denis Irwin did not manage to score, he completed 89% of his passes when Manchester United overcame Leicester at Old Trafford.

Kirkland is between the sticks after he made 10 saves in a 0–0 draw with Chelsea, prompting opposing players to describe the performance of the Coventry 'keeper as "the game of his life".

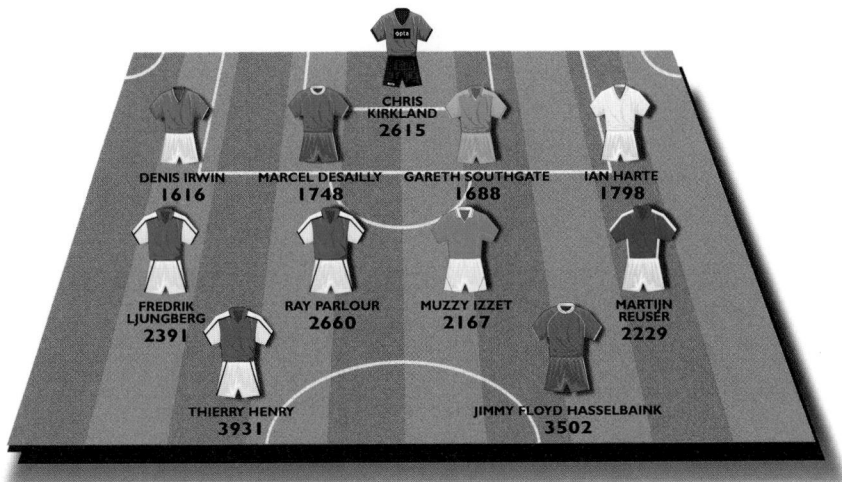

CHRIS KIRKLAND 2615

DENIS IRWIN 1616   MARCEL DESAILLY 1748   GARETH SOUTHGATE 1688   IAN HARTE 1798

FREDRIK LJUNGBERG 2391   RAY PARLOUR 2660   MUZZY IZZET 2167   MARTIJN REUSER 2229

THIERRY HENRY 3931   JIMMY FLOYD HASSELBAINK 3502

set-pieces than any other Premiership player

PASSING

Few teams regularly win football matches without dominating possession and using it effectively. In 2000–01, no team did that better than Manchester United; they reaped the benefits of wearing opponents down by retaining the ball.

The fulcrum of many United passing movements was Opta's Player of the Year Roy Keane. The Old Trafford skipper completed an amazing 87% of his passes and while many of those were admittedly in his own half, he still managed to make 451 successful deliveries in the final third of the pitch – a total only three players could better.

Four of his United team-mates join Keane in the slickest-passing team of the season: defenders Gary Neville, Denis Irwin and Wes Brown and midfielder Paul Scholes. The success rate of Scholes was particularly impressive, as he plays most of his football high up the pitch where players are put under more pressure, but he still managed to create five goals and complete 83% of his passes.

Surprisingly, another team to have more than one player in the passing XI is

Newcastle, whose goalkeeper Shay Given joins Kieron Dyer in the line up. Like Scholes, the accuracy of Dyer is notable as he plays at great pace in and around the penalty box. Given's high ratio is more understandable, as he has nearly always had a target man like Alan Shearer, Carl Cort or Shola Ameobi at whom to aim his kicks upfield.

Chelsea also boast two members of the side in Marcel Desailly and Gianfranco Zola, the latter of whom is jointly the country's most accurate-passing striker along with Ipswich man Marcus Stewart, whose 76% completion rate proves he can do more than just score goals.

The former Bristol Rovers and Huddersfield man is becoming more and more adept at dropping out of the frontline to link up play with his midfield. His Portman Road team-mates benefited as Stewart created four goals having made a staggering total of 853 passes in the opposition half.

Making up the side is Aston Villa's Lee Hendrie, who made good with 80% of his distribution in what was an underrated season for the midfielder.

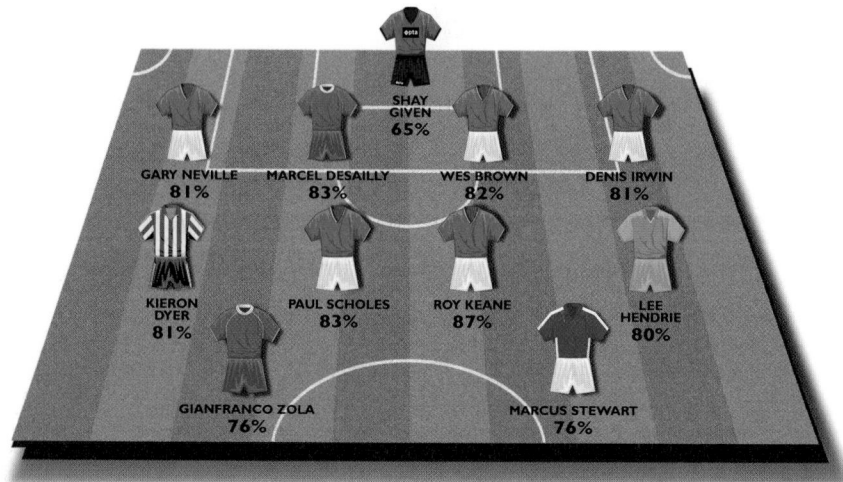

SHAY GIVEN 65%

GARY NEVILLE 81%   MARCEL DESAILLY 83%   WES BROWN 82%   DENIS IRWIN 81%

KIERON DYER 81%   PAUL SCHOLES 83%   ROY KEANE 87%   LEE HENDRIE 80%

GIANFRANCO ZOLA 76%   MARCUS STEWART 76%

1,893 Roy Keane completed the highest

TACKLING

West Ham gained a reputation in 2000–01 for playing some of the most attractive football in the Premiership.

But the stylish stuff turned out by Paolo Di Canio, Joe Cole, Frederic Kanouté, Trevor Sinclair and Co was matched in equal measure by the hard graft put in by the likes of Nigel Winterburn, Michael Carrick and, perhaps surprisingly, Di Canio again.

England squad member Carrick was the Hammers' most prolific tackler, winning 95 of the 143 challenges he attempted. Veteran left-back Winterburn was not far behind his young team-mate, retaining possession with 90 of the tackles he attempted, while Di Canio won the ball on 42 occasions – more often than any other top-flight striker.

But none of them come close to matching Leeds man Olivier Dacourt who, with 123 successful challenges, was far and away the top tackler in the division. However, as with his previous spell in England with Everton in 1998–99, Dacourt's competitiveness did not always go down well with referees, who showed the Frenchman 13 yellow cards in Premiership games.

Conversely, Tottenham defender Chris Perry picked up just three yellow cards in the process of winning 89 challenges, an impressive tally only improved upon by Chelsea's Marcel Desailly among all the central defenders in the league.

Despite all those tackles by Perry, Spurs goalkeeper Neil Sullivan was still required to come off his goal line and make smothering saves more often than any other custodian. The Scotland international was called into action 15 times, pouncing to snatch the ball from the feet of a number of advancing strikers.

Ipswich man Fabian Wilnis epitomised his team's spirit by crunching into 85 challenges, 72 of which resulted in possession won for the Tractor Boys.

Liverpool duo Steven Gerrard and Emile Heskey complete the team, having won 88 and 41 tackles respectively.

The hunger that the Reds duo showed was epitomised in the FA Cup semi-final against Wycombe when they both came off the bench to turn the tie in their side's favour and both were prominent in Liverpool's superb season.

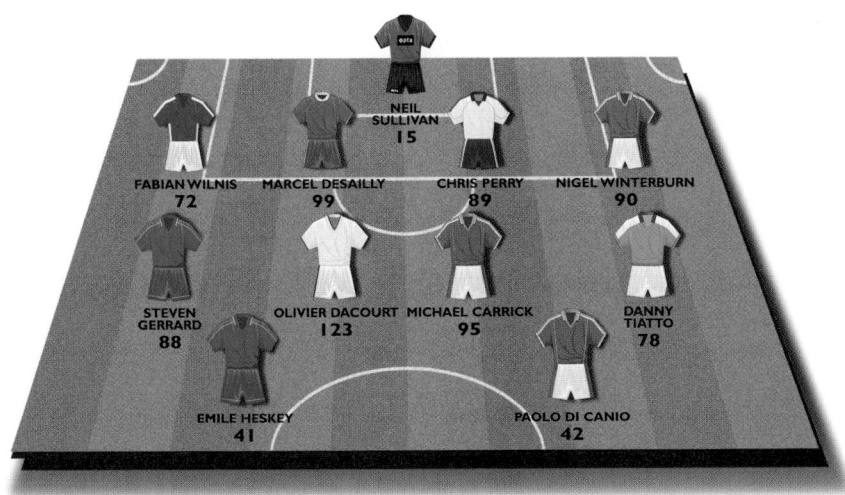

NEIL SULLIVAN
15

FABIAN WILNIS
72

MARCEL DESAILLY
99

CHRIS PERRY
89

NIGEL WINTERBURN
90

STEVEN GERRARD
88

OLIVIER DACOURT
123

MICHAEL CARRICK
95

DANNY TIATTO
78

EMILE HESKEY
41

PAOLO DI CANIO
42

tally of successful passes in 2000-01

ENGLISH XI

The 2000–01 season saw, for the first time ever, the arrival of a foreign manager to take charge of the England national side. As Sven-Göran Eriksson will have worked out by now, having travelled thousands of miles to watch dozens of games, there is plenty of talent at his disposal, including some players earmarked by the stats who may not necessarily have come into the Swede's thinking.

Aston Villa's Lee Hendrie, for example, who won his one and only cap back in 1998 under Glenn Hoddle, enjoyed an excellent campaign at club level and could be an alternative to the likes of Nick Barmby and Steve McManaman in the troublesome left-midfield role. Hendrie scored six goals and created five others for the Midlanders, although he was also dismissed twice.

The one as-yet-uncapped player in the team is England Under-21 captain John Terry, who has shone in the heart of Chelsea's defence since establishing himself in the side under new manager Claudio Ranieri.

Current England regulars Michael Owen, Steven Gerrard, Paul Scholes and skipper David Beckham all make the team, as does PFA Player of the Year Teddy Sheringham, who has earned an international reprieve since the departure of Kevin Keegan as boss in October.

The Neville brothers, favourites of all England managers over the last five years, have both done well to average Index scores over 900 in 2000–01 and have been two of the most accurate passers out of defence in the whole of the top flight, but Ashley Cole would have featured if he had accrued more Premiership football.

Leicester's Tim Flowers fills the number one jersey after making 94 saves in the Foxes' patchy season.

The former Blackburn number one may well have found himself back in the international set-up had injury not disrupted his season and he may have to admit that his England days are up after 11 caps.

One player who, according to the stats, should be in the England side but definitely will not be is Tony Adams, who hung up his international boots in 2000–01 after winning 66 caps for his country.

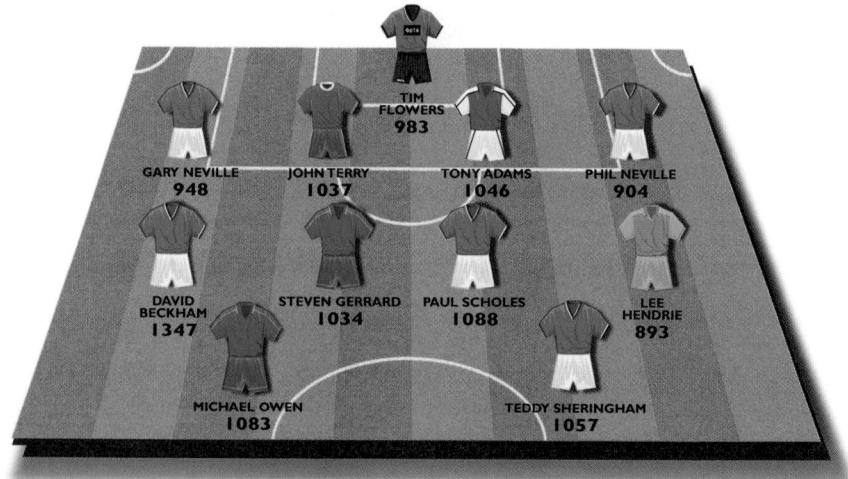

TIM FLOWERS
983

GARY NEVILLE
948

JOHN TERRY
1037

TONY ADAMS
1046

PHIL NEVILLE
904

DAVID BECKHAM
1347

STEVEN GERRARD
1034

PAUL SCHOLES
1088

LEE HENDRIE
893

MICHAEL OWEN
1083

TEDDY SHERINGHAM
1057

BRITISH ISLES XI

There was a time when you could barely move in top-flight English football without bumping into a Scot, a Welshman or an Irishman; in fact, the team which clinched the double for Liverpool in 1986 contained just two players from foreign shores, but not a single Englishman.

The influx of overseas talent has significantly reduced the number of non-English "Brits" featuring in today's Premiership to 86, just 16% of the 543 players to figure in 2000–01.

Despite the drop in numbers, some of the division's most significant players hail from the British Isles, not least Roy Keane, Opta's Player of the Season.

Including the Manchester United skipper, five of this line-up are taken from Mick McCarthy's Republic of Ireland squad, including both of the full-backs. Tottenham's Stephen Carr had an injury-ravaged campaign, but was impressive when he did play, scoring three goals and embarking on 129 dribbles. On the opposite flank, Leeds man Ian Harte enjoyed an even better season after a tricky start, rattling in seven goals – 13 in all competitions for club and country.

Charlton skipper Mark Kinsella had an equally satisfying time, leading his side away from the Premiership relegation scrap and into the top half of the table. The midfielder was directly involved in four goals and made more than 100 tackles.

Veteran Niall Quinn proved that he was still a handful on the biggest stage, even though his appearances were limited through injury. He still managed to net seven times and made more aerial flick-ons than any other top-flight striker.

His Stadium of Light team-mate Don Hutchison is one of four Scots in the team along with Leicester captain Matt Elliott, Spurs goalkeeper Neil Sullivan and Liverpool's evergreen midfield man Gary McAllister.

Wales' Ryan Giggs and Gerry Taggart of Northern Ireland complete the side.

Giggs was superb at club level, scoring five goals and creating eight others. His form was not so good on the international stage. He missed golden opportunities in World Cup games against Poland and Ukraine as his side slipped out of the qualification race.

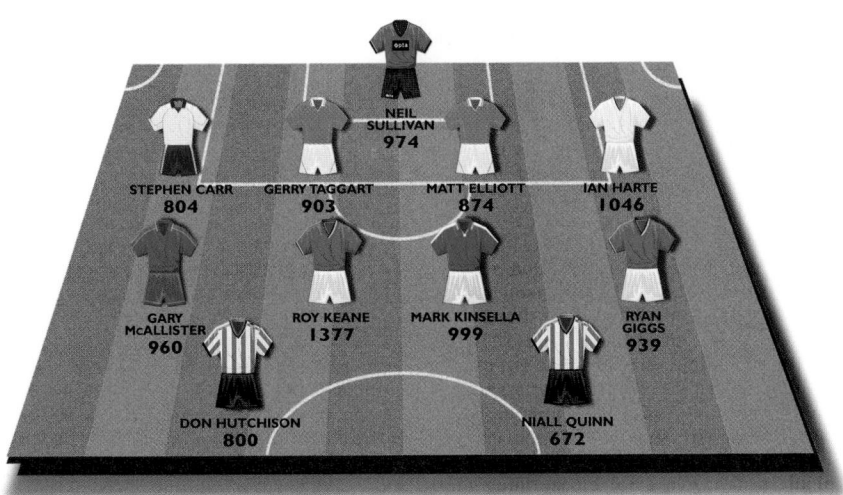

NEIL SULLIVAN 974

STEPHEN CARR 804 GERRY TAGGART 903 MATT ELLIOTT 874 IAN HARTE 1046

GARY McALLISTER 960 ROY KEANE 1377 MARK KINSELLA 999 RYAN GIGGS 939

DON HUTCHISON 800 NIALL QUINN 672

OVERSEAS XI

Of the 543 players to appear in the 2000–01 Premiership season, 38% were born outside the British Isles and between them they represented a total of 52 different countries, underlining how cosmopolitan the English top flight has become.

The highest proportion of those foreigners came from France; 27 in total, six of whom make the Opta overseas team of the season.

Not surprisingly, each of those Frenchmen is an international and all, apart from Manchester United's Mikael Silvestre, have World Cup and European Championship medals on their sideboards at home.

Arsenal's Patrick Vieira, who also makes the overall Opta team of the season, boasts the most impressive stats from 2000–01. However, Robert Pires with seven assists and 17-goal striker Thierry Henry also made significant contributions to Arsenal's term and both are in the line-up.

Henry fired in some wonderful strikes including an amazing Goal of the Season contender against Manchester United.

The other Frenchmen in the side are Manchester United's goalkeeper Fabien Barthez, who enjoyed an excellent campaign between the sticks following his £7.8 million move from Monaco and left-back Silvestre who laid on two goals for team-mates and contributed 83 tackles to the Red Devils' cause.

The only other nation to have more than one player in the XI is Germany, which supplies Liverpool duo Dietmar Hamann and Markus Babbel, both of whom played key roles in the Reds' astonishing season. Hamann made 114 tackles and scored two goals, while Babbel completed 218 clearances and got forward to strike home three shots.

Holland, Sweden and Finland complete the overseas selection with one representative apiece.

Dashing Dutchman Jimmy Floyd Hasselbaink scored 23 goals and set up nine others; Arsenal's super Swede Fredrik Ljungberg netted six times in the league as well as an impressive FA Cup final strike; and Liverpool's fantastic Finn Sami Hyypia made more clearances than any other Premiership defender.

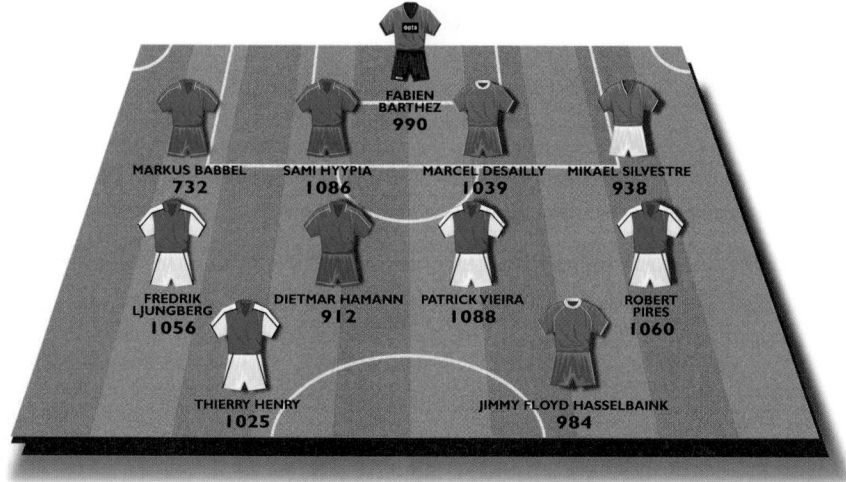

FABIEN BARTHEZ
990

MARKUS BABBEL
732

SAMI HYYPIA
1086

MARCEL DESAILLY
1039

MIKAEL SILVESTRE
938

FREDRIK LJUNGBERG
1056

DIETMAR HAMANN
912

PATRICK VIEIRA
1088

ROBERT PIRES
1060

THIERRY HENRY
1025

JIMMY FLOYD HASSELBAINK
984

466 Sami Hyypia made more defensive

UNDER-21

The optimism which swept through English football in 2000–01 was at an unrivalled high and on the evidence of the Opta Under-21 team of the season it is not hard to understand why.

The side is of an incredibly high standard with the majority of its players already full internationals and the rest looking almost certain to follow in the coming year or two. If the 11 members of the line-up were to be sold by their clubs tomorrow, they would probably fetch well over £100 million in the transfer market.

Liverpool's Michael Owen would be responsible for a fair chunk of that money. The 21-year-old had an excellent 2000–01 season, scoring in three more internationals, netting twice in the FA Cup final and accruing a grand total of 27 strikes in all competitions, despite the fact that he missed a sizeable amount of action through injury.

But his Index points average was still lower than that of Arsenal left-back Ashley Cole, who has progressed rapidly to become one of the likely left-backs for his country, if not indeed the first choice.

Titus Bramble of Ipswich also made big strides both physically and metaphorically in 2000–01, earning himself many comparisons to a young Sol Campbell and a handful of Under-21 call-ups. His partner in central defence is Chelsea's John Terry, with current England star Wes Brown filling the right-back position.

West Ham pair Joe Cole – the Premiership's second-best dribbler after Ryan Giggs – and Michael Carrick are in midfield, with 11-goal Leeds man Alan Smith in attack.

All three fledgling superstars made their full England debuts in the friendly against Mexico at the tail end of the 2000–01 campaign. Coming off the substitutes' bench, none of the trio looked out of their depth and are likely to add more caps to their collections in the not-too-distant future.

Despite playing for a relegated club, Coventry's Chris Kirkland is the team's 'keeper with 88 saves to his name in 2000–01, while Sunderland's Julio Arca is the only non-English player in the side, testimony to the high standard of current homegrown talent and good news for England boss Sven-Göran Eriksson.

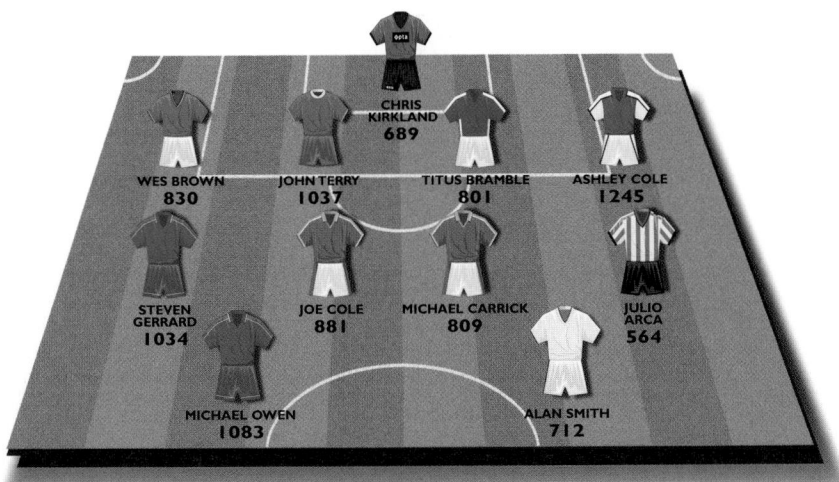

CHRIS KIRKLAND
689

WES BROWN
830

JOHN TERRY
1037

TITUS BRAMBLE
801

ASHLEY COLE
1245

STEVEN GERRARD
1034

JOE COLE
881

MICHAEL CARRICK
809

JULIO ARCA
564

MICHAEL OWEN
1083

ALAN SMITH
712

AGED 21 OR UNDER ON 19/8/00

DIRTY DOZEN

Opta's Dirty Dozen team is based on the average number of minutes it took a player to accumulate disciplinary points, with one point per foul conceded, three per yellow card and six per dismissal.

Despite being an affable kind of chap with an interest in architecture and a colourful history to talk of, Bradford striker Ashley Ward accrued more Opta disciplinary points on average than anyone else in the 2000–01 Premiership.

The former Barnsley and Derby hitman committed a sin around every 19 minutes, conceding a total of 95 fouls and picking up nine yellow cards. He took a fair amount of stick in return, though; in fact, only Don Hutchison was fouled on more occasions than Ward.

Manchester City's Paulo Wanchope made the team for the second season running after committing 85 misdemeanours, slightly more than Sunderland's Hutchison. The Scot's team were rated the dirtiest side overall according to Opta.

With 13 to his name, Olivier Dacourt of Leeds picked up the highest-number of yellow cards in the top flight, while David Thompson was sent off once and booked nine times in just 1,866 minutes of action for Coventry.

Those figures capped a disappointing season for the young Sky Blue. He had featured in the Liverpool side in 1999–2000 and was as highly rated as Steven Gerrard, but the move to Highfield Road did not work in his favour.

In Steve Stone and the seven-times-booked David Ginola, Aston Villa had two players in the line-up and their former player David Unsworth was in for Everton having accumulated seven cautions, the most by any player at Goodison Park.

Spurs youngster Gary Doherty notched up 48 fouls, while Southampton's Tahar El Khalej managed to receive seven cards despite neither player being a first-team regular. Similarly, Bradford's Matt Clarke was booked three times in just 17 run-outs in 2000–01.

Leeds' Alan Smith – who, as well as being cautioned seven times and dismissed once in the Premiership, was red-carded in an England Under-21 match and the Champions League – just missed out on the starting XI, but makes the Opta bad boys' subs' bench.

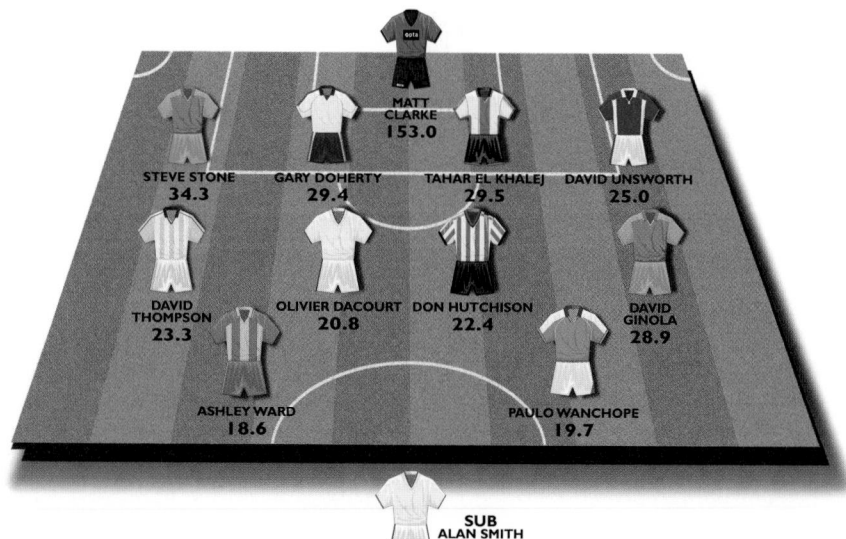

MATT CLARKE 153.0

STEVE STONE 34.3

GARY DOHERTY 29.4

TAHAR EL KHALEJ 29.5

DAVID UNSWORTH 25.0

DAVID THOMPSON 23.3

OLIVIER DACOURT 20.8

DON HUTCHISON 22.4

DAVID GINOLA 28.9

ASHLEY WARD 18.6

PAULO WANCHOPE 19.7

SUB
ALAN SMITH
20.6

95 Ashley Ward committed the most fouls

CLEAN XI

Opta's clean team is based on the average number of minutes it took a player to accumulate disciplinary points, with one point per foul conceded, three per yellow card and six per dismissal.

Mild-mannered Charlton midfielder Claus Jensen kept an incredibly high level of discipline in 2000–01, conceding a free-kick less than once in every three games on average.

And the Danish schemer also managed to go the whole campaign without picking up a single booking – a great achievement considering the competitiveness of the Premiership and the unpredictable nature of some referees.

He was joined in the clean team by his Addicks team-mate Chris Powell, who gave away just 16 free-kicks in a season which saw him become an England international.

The other two teams with a couple of players in the line-up were Arsenal and Aston Villa.

Gunners right-back Oleg Luzhny was not a regular choice throughout 2000–01, but when he was called upon, the Ukrainian skipper never let the side down, giving up just eight free-kicks. It was a similar story

with Sylvain Wiltord, who had to spend much of the term on the substitutes' bench but showed no signs of frustration when he was selected, committing a total of just 11 fouls and avoiding any cards during the Premiership season.

At Villa Park, England internationals Paul Merson and David James were both on their best behaviour, the latter notably so, as he was the only top-flight regular not to concede a single foul in the campaign.

Newcastle's Aaron Hughes and Chelsea's Gianfranco Zola both made the side for the second season running, while Spurs youngster Ledley King and Bradford midfielder Gareth Whalley each enjoyed booking-free terms.

West Ham's only representative was wide man Trevor Sinclair, who averaged a disciplinary point just once in around a game and a half.

Unfortunately for the talented ex-QPR winger, his season was cut drastically short by a series of injuries. He will be hoping to come back strong in 2001–02 and finally earn the England cap that has seemingly been on the cards on many occasions during his career.

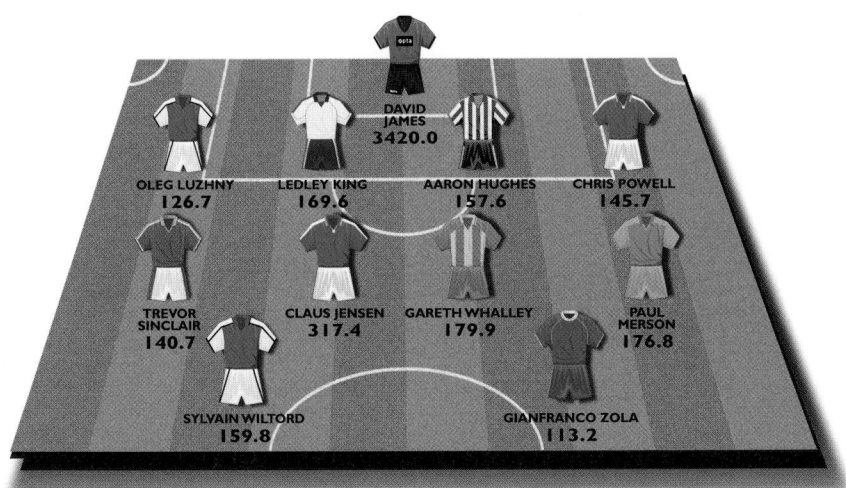

DAVID JAMES 3420.0

OLEG LUZHNY 126.7 LEDLEY KING 169.6 AARON HUGHES 157.6 CHRIS POWELL 145.7

TREVOR SINCLAIR 140.7 CLAUS JENSEN 317.4 GARETH WHALLEY 179.9 PAUL MERSON 176.8

SYLVAIN WILTORD 159.8 GIANFRANCO ZOLA 113.2

by an individual in the Premiership

Season 2000–01 was the year the FA got tough with offenders. Chief executive Adam Crozier's new "zero tolerance" policy was designed to deter serial offenders, clamp down on dissent and clarify the disciplinary process for all involved.

New rules which were implemented included: fines for clubs or docked points if players intimidated match officials or became embroiled in a mass confrontation with the opposition; fines for clubs which collected six or more bookings in a single match; and a video advisory panel to review incidents missed by officials during a game.

The panel could not overturn referees' decisions, except in cases of mistaken identity or wrongful dismissal for a red card offence carrying a three-match ban.

Unfortunately, the tough new measures actually caused some controversy. A good example was when Arsène Wenger was charged with pushing fourth official Paul Taylor in the players' tunnel at the Stadium of Light and was initially banned for 12 matches. But on appeal the Arsenal boss was cleared.

And Matt Elliott, Hassan Kachloul and Patrick Vieira were charged on video evidence, but received less than the mandatory three-match ban.

The powers of the video advisory panel were also questioned after Arsenal played Liverpool in the opening week. The panel, which comprised former professionals, referees and managers, recommended that Gary McAllister's red card should be wiped out, but Graham Poll refused to change his decision, instead recommending that Dietmar Hamann's second yellow card be removed from the records.

With the game's coverage expanding at a huge rate, there were the usual discussions over professional referees, "third eye" technology and the breakdown of relationships between officials and the playing side.

With microphones being thrust under managers' noses immediately after games, there were the usual gripes and groans about decisions, or claims that the incident was not seen.

The President of the Referees' Association, Peter Willis, called for more respect. He said: "We don't need these emotional outbursts. There is a proper agreed procedure with the League Managers' Association for complaints. You don't hear referees bad-mouthing managers and players after a game."

Many supporters were disheartened by the fact that the new clampdown did not address the real issues such as foul play, lack of sportsmanship or dissent and only penalised petty offences. Lee Hendrie was charged after celebrating too enthusiastically with the crowd and referee Stephen Lodge was criticised for failing to book Patrick Vieira and Silvinho when they took their shirts off to celebrate goals against Charlton.

As for the debate about professionalism, that still rumbles on. Referee Paul Durkin felt it was only a matter of time before officials would be full-time and that it would help raise standards. He said: "There has always been the misconception by players that we are amateurs; the feeling, in effect, that we are part-timers, that we don't care. People don't understand the work, effort and commitment a referee puts in."

Referees' officer Philip Don backed his colleague, saying: "The accusation in this

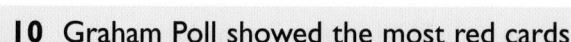

10 Graham Poll showed the most red cards

OVERALL RECORD

REFEREE NAME	MATCHES	FOULS	PENALTIES	YELLOW CARDS	RED CARDS	AVERAGE POINTS
G Barber	18	635	6	86	2	51.28
M Riley	19	627	1	83	1	46.58
P Jones	15.33	503	1	61	2	45.73
R Harris	11	359	2	41	2	45.45
M Messias	3	106	0	10	0	45.33
G Poll	22.5	737	3	69	10	45.02
B Knight	15	471	2	56	5	45.00
P Taylor	12.5	414	3	36	1	42.96
A D'Urso	20	607	3	66	7	42.80
D Elleray	21	638	7	67	4	42.10
R Styles	17.67	493	5	62	4	40.63
D Gallagher	20	570	2	64	4	39.60
C Wilkes	9	257	2	31	0	39.56
M Halsey	16	459	0	48	2	38.44
S Dunn	19	543	1	50	2	37.26
A Wiley	23	638	7	61	2	37.13
N Barry	18	509	0	47	3	37.11
J Winter	23	596	5	70	3	36.48
P Durkin	22	649	7	40	2	36.45
S Bennett	18.25	460	6	50	6	36.38
P Richards	0.75	24	0	1	0	36.00
S Lodge	18	475	2	53	1	35.89
M Dean	18	436	3	58	1	34.72
Totals	**380**	**11,206**	**68**	**1,210**	**64**	**40.59**

country is that referees are the only amateurs in a professional game. Maybe they are amateurs in how much money they get, but in terms of preparation they couldn't be more professional."

In fact, Don suggested that referees went professional in 1998, but was voted down by the Premiership club chairmen by 18 votes to two.

The key thing that both sides agree upon is the need to improve the level of communication.

Derby are one of the first clubs to experiment in this area. To help improve their appalling disciplinary record, they brought in ex-referee Kevin Lynch. Among his suggestions was that the Derby players should not shave their heads. He said: "One of the things we discussed was the question of shaved heads and what that suggests to a referee. It may lead to him pre-judging a player as being aggressive."

This may seem silly on the face of it but, looking at Opta's top 12 offenders, nine had shaved heads in 2000–01.

Lynch has also advised the players to communicate with officials in a positive manner. He said: "I've also advised the players to try to establish a dialogue with referees by using their first names and showing some understanding of the difficulties of their job."

Opta's referees tables offer a detailed assessment of the disciplinary measures meted out by officials. Every foul, penalty or card has been logged.

In Opta's unique comparative table, each foul is awarded one point, each penalty or yellow card three points and each red card six points. The final total of disciplinary points for each referee is then divided by the number of games officiated to give a snapshot of who the strictest or the most lenient referees were during 2000–01.

It is interesting to note that the number of yellow cards dropped by 59 from 1999–2000 and the number of dismissals went down by six.

Perhaps the disciplinary measures introduced by Adam Crozier are starting to have the desired effect.

in the 2000–01 Premiership season

HOME TEAMS

REFEREE NAME	GAMES	FOULS	PENALTIES	YELLOW CARDS	RED CARDS	POINTS	POINTS/ GAME
G Barber	18	303	3	37	1	429	23.83
M Messias	3	53	0	5	0	68	22.67
M Riley	19	304	1	39	1	430	22.63
P Jones	15.33	250	0	23	2	331	21.59
G Poll	22.5	346	1	30	5	469	20.84
B Knight	15	211	0	23	4	304	20.27
P Taylor	12.5	191	2	15	1	248	19.84
R Harris	11	173	0	15	0	218	19.82
A D'Urso	20	276	2	29	4	393	19.65
D Elleray	21	314	0	23	3	401	19.10
P Richards	0.75	14	0	0	0	14	18.67
A Wiley	23	311	4	31	2	428	18.61
R Styles	17.67	237	2	24	2	327	18.51
C Wilkes	9	123	1	13	0	165	18.33
D Gallagher	20	275	1	24	2	362	18.10
S Dunn	19	268	0	25	0	343	18.05
S Bennett	18.25	245	2	24	1	329	18.03
M Halsey	16	216	0	19	2	285	17.81
N Barry	18	249	0	19	0	306	17.00
M Dean	18	215	1	29	1	305	16.94
P Durkin	22	303	4	17	1	372	16.91
J Winter	23	288	2	27	1	381	16.57
S Lodge	18	211	0	21	0	274	15.22
Total	380	5,376	26	512	32	7,182	18.90

AWAY TEAMS

REFEREE NAME	GAMES	FOULS	PENALTIES	YELLOW CARDS	RED CARDS	POINTS	POINTS/ GAME
G Barber	18	332	3	49	1	494	27.44
R Harris	11	186	2	26	2	282	25.64
B Knight	15	260	2	33	1	371	24.73
G Poll	22.5	391	2	39	5	544	24.18
P Jones	15.33	253	1	38	0	370	24.14
M Riley	19	323	0	44	0	455	23.95
A D'Urso	20	331	1	37	3	463	23.15
P Taylor	12.5	223	1	21	0	289	23.12
D Elleray	21	324	7	44	1	483	23.00
M Messias	3	53	0	5	0	68	22.67
R Styles	17.67	256	3	38	2	391	22.13
D Gallagher	20	295	1	40	2	430	21.50
C Wilkes	9	134	1	18	0	191	21.22
S Lodge	18	264	2	32	1	372	20.67
M Halsey	16	243	0	29	0	330	20.63
N Barry	18	260	0	28	3	362	20.11
J Winter	23	308	3	43	2	458	19.91
P Durkin	22	346	3	23	1	430	19.55
S Dunn	19	275	1	25	2	365	19.21
A Wiley	23	327	3	30	0	426	18.52
S Bennett	18.25	215	4	26	5	335	18.36
M Dean	18	221	2	29	1	320	17.78
P Richards	0.75	10	0	1	0	13	17.33
Total	380	5,830	42	698	32	8,242	21.69

5 Graham Barber issued the highest average

HOME AND AWAY

REFEREES

anagers are always calling for consistency from referees. But when referees apply the letter of the law, everyone laments that the men in black are unable to use their common sense.

The officials have been fairly consistent in certain aspects over the past three seasons, according to Opta's unique stats.

Against away side	1998–99	1999–00	2000–01
Fouls	52%	52%	52%
Yellows	57%	57%	58%
Penalties	64%	65%	62%
Reds	61%	69%	50%

In each of the three campaigns, 52% of all fouls have been awarded against the away teams. While this may be construed by some as a bias toward home teams, it is more likely that more fouls are committed by visiting sides, as they have more defensive work to do.

With the onus on home teams to attack, the desperate lunge or persistent offender is probably a more frequent occurrence, too. And this may go some way to explaining why 58% of all yellow cards were meted out to away teams, a very small increase on the previous two campaigns, once again showing an interesting level of uniformity in the Premiership.

There was a slight decline in the proportion of penalties awarded against away sides, but the most marked change is apparent with dismissals. While there was an increase between 1998–99 and 1999–2000, there was a significant levelling effect in 2000–01, which saw exactly half of the red cards awarded to home teams and half to their visitors.

Steve Bennett was the only official to award more fouls against home teams than away sides, with Stephen Lodge at the other end of the table whistling for 55% of all offences in favour of the host club.

But of all referees, David Elleray's stats show a marked propensity to punish the visitors more harshly. The man who in February officiated at his first Manchester United game for more than 18 months, after enraging the Red Devils with his handling of a game with Liverpool in May 1999, awarded 23 yellow cards to home sides while booking 44 from visiting teams. Elleray also awarded seven spot-kicks – all in the home side's favour.

He was not alone, though, with seven referees awarding more than 60% of all cards they showed to members of the away teams.

As far as cautions were concerned, the only referee who booked more home players than visitors was Alan Wiley.

REFEREES – CARDS PER GAME

REFEREE	CARDS PER GAME
G Barber	5.00
M Riley	4.47
B Knight	4.40
P Jones	4.24
R Harris	4.09
A D'Urso	4.00
R Styles	3.96
G Poll	3.96
D Gallagher	3.60
D Elleray	3.57
C Wilkes	3.44
S Bennett	3.40
M Dean	3.33
M Messias	3.33
J Winter	3.30
M Halsey	3.25
S Lodge	3.06
P Taylor	3.04
N Barry	2.94
S Dunn	2.84
A Wiley	2.83
P Durkin	2.00
P Richards	1.33

For the second season in a row, there was a reduction in the number of cards shown – this despite the number of fouls actually increasing.

Cautions were down by 59 over the course of the season and there were six fewer dismissals than in 1999–2000.

One referee who did not follow the trend, though, was Graham Barber. He averaged five cards per match – higher than any referee in either of the previous two seasons. This rate of bookings was also far higher than the 3.80 cautions per match he averaged in 1999–2000.

The most lenient referees of 1999–2000 were once again the most reluctant officials to show cards. Alan Wiley lowered his average from 3.17 per game to 2.83, but the most marked reduction saw Paul Durkin show just 2.00 cards per match compared to his 1999–2000 average of 3.17.

Part of the reason for the overall reduction was that 1999–2000's strictest official Mike Reed and colleague Alan Wilkie, who averaged 4.00 cautions per match, reached the mandatory retirement age to be replaced by several more lenient men in black, such as Paul Taylor, Mike Dean, Rob Styles and Clive Wilkes.

REFEREES – FOULS PER CARD

With the number of fouls committed increasing and the number of cards issued decreasing, it follows that the average number of fouls penalised before an official lost patience rose from season 1999–2000.

The two strictest men from the previous campaign had both ended their careers so there was clearly going to be a new name heading this particular table.

It turned out to be newcomer Rob Styles, who was the least patient of all referees, but his average of 7.04 fouls per card shown was still higher than five officials from the 1999–2000 campaign. Not far behind him was Graham Barber who handed out more yellows than any other referee over the season, posting a massive tally of 86 yellow cards and two reds.

At the other end of the scale, Paul Durkin was the most lenient of the regular Premiership officials, waiting for an average of 14.75 offences before reaching for his pocket.

Newcomers Paul Taylor and Matt Messias were the next most-lenient, while FA Cup final referee Steve Dunn also waited for fouls to get into double figures before resorting to flourishing a card.

REFEREE	FOULS PER CARD
R Styles	7.04
G Barber	7.06
B Knight	7.14
M Dean	7.27
M Riley	7.38
S Bennett	7.42
A D'Urso	7.59
P Jones	7.74
J Winter	7.84
D Gallagher	7.92
R Harris	7.98
G Poll	8.28
C Wilkes	8.29
D Elleray	8.51
S Lodge	8.64
M Halsey	8.83
N Barry	9.60
A Wiley	9.82
S Dunn	10.06
M Messias	10.60
P Taylor	10.89
P Durkin	14.75
P Richards	24.00

7 David Elleray awarded the highest number of penalties